P9-AFA-137

Psychology

FIRST CANADIAN EDITION

Douglas A. Bernstein
University of South Florida
University of Southampton

Louis Penner
Wayne State University

Alison Clarke-Stewart
University of California–Irvine

Edward J. Roy
University of Illinois at Urbana–Champaign

Kenneth M. Cramer
University of Windsor

Kimberley D. Fenwick
St. Thomas University

Ian Fraser
St. Thomas University

Houghton Mifflin Company Boston New York

To the researchers, past and present,
whose work embodies psychology today,
and to the students who will follow in their footsteps
to shape the psychology of tomorrow.

Executive Publisher: George Hoffman
Project Manager: Timothy Cullen
Sponsoring Editor: Jane Potter
Development Editor: Glen Herbert
Senior Project Editor: Margaret Park Bridges
New Title Project Manager: James Lonergan
Senior Marketing Manager: David Tonen

Cover image: *Binoculars Pointing to Falls.* Courtesy of Chris Thomaidis, Getty Images

CREDITS
Credits begin after the References, on page C-1.

Printed in the U.S.A.

Library of Congress Control Number: 2006937980

ISBN-10: 0-618-78368-7
ISBN-13: 978-0-618-78368-7

Instructor's Edition and Student Study supplements are available online. Please contact us for details at Canada@hmco.com

1 2 3 4 5 6 7 8 9 VH 11 10 09 08 07

Brief Contents

Contents

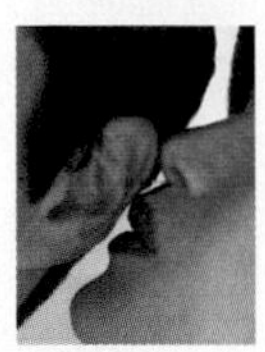

4 Sensation 104

5 Perception 150

6 Learning 190

17 Social Behaviour 635

Features

Linkages

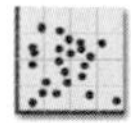

Focus on Reseach Methods

Thinking Critically

Preface

It has been the goal of this edition to:

- explore the full range of psychology, from cell to society, in an eclectic manner as free as possible of theoretical bias;
- balance our need to explain the content of psychology with an emphasis on the doing of psychology, through a blend of conceptual discussion and description of research studies;
- foster scientific attitudes and to help students learn to think critically by examining the ways that psychologists have solved, or failed to solve, fascinating puzzles of behaviour and mental processes;
- produce a text that, without oversimplifying psychology, is clear, accessible, and enjoyable to read; and
- demonstrate that, in spite of its breadth and diversity, psychology is an integrated discipline in which each subfield is linked to other subfields by common interests and overarching research questions. The productive cross-fertilization among social, clinical, and biological psychologists in researching health and illness is just one example of how different types of psychologists benefit from and build on one another's work.

In preparing the Canadian Edition, we sought to respond to the needs of instructors who wanted us to reduce or expand coverage of various topics, and to create a sound text that spoke to the specific needs and interests of a Canadian readership. We also sought to strike an ideal balance between classic and current research. The important historic findings of psychological research are here, but so is coverage of much recent work.

Throughout the Canadian Edition, we highlighted research conducted at universities nationwide by citing not just the researchers but also their university affiliation and the location of the university. We also used Canadian statistics and relevant examples from Canadian news stories, and sports and cultural events to illustrate various psychological phenomena. Where applicable, we also used famous Canadians or well-known Canadian icons to enhance the sense of cultural relevance for our students.

Special Features

Psychology contains a number of special features designed to promote efficient learning and students' mastery of the material.

Linkages

In our experience, most students enter the introductory course thinking that psychology concerns itself mainly with personality, psychological testing, mental disorders, psychotherapy, and other aspects of clinical psychology. They have little or no idea of how broad and multifaceted psychology is. Many students are surprised, therefore, when we ask them to read about neuroanatomy, neural communication, the endocrine system, sensory and perceptual processes and principles, prenatal risk factors, and many other topics that they tend to associate with disciplines other than psychology.

We have found that students are better able to appreciate the scope of psychology when they see it not as a laundry list of separate topics but as an interrelated set of subfields, each of which contributes to and benefits from the work going on in all of the others. To help students see these relationships, we have built into the book an integrating tool called "Linkages."

The Linkages elements combine with the text narrative to highlight the network of relationships among psychology's subfields. This Linkages program is designed to help students see the "big picture" that is psychology—no matter how many chapters their instructor assigns, or in what sequence.

Thinking Critically

Throughout the book, research on psychological phenomena is described in a way that reveals the logic of the scientific enterprise, that identifies possible flaws in design or interpretation, and that leaves room for more questions and further research. In other words, we try to display critical thinking processes. The "Thinking Critically" sections in each chapter are designed to make these processes more explicit and accessible by providing a framework for analyzing evidence before drawing conclusions. The framework is built around five questions that the reader should find useful in analyzing not only studies in psychology but also other forms of communication. These questions are first introduced when we discuss the importance of critical thinking in Chapter 2.

1. What am I being asked to believe or accept?
2. What evidence is available to support the assertion?
3. Are there alternative ways of interpreting the evidence?
4. What additional evidence would help to evaluate the alternatives?
5. What conclusions are most reasonable?

Focus on Research Methods

This feature, appearing in Chapters 3 through 17, examines the ways in which the research methods described in Chapter 2, Research in Psychology, have been applied to help advance our understanding of some aspect of behaviour and mental processes. To make this feature more accessible, it is organized around five questions.

1. What was the researcher's question?
2. How did the researcher answer the question?
3. What did the researcher find?
4. What do the results mean?
5. What do we still need to know?

Examples of these Focus on Research Methods sections include the use of experiments to study attention (Chapter 5, Perception), learned helplessness (Chapter 6, Learning), the use of neuroimaging technology to locate areas of the brain involved in analogical thinking (Chapter 8, Cognition and Language), the development of physical knowledge (Chapter 12, Human Development), and self-esteem (Chapter 17, Social Behaviour). Other sections illustrate the use of survey, longitudinal, and laboratory analogue designs.

An Emphasis on Active Learning

To help students become active learners, not just passive readers, we have developed new "PsychAssist" animations available online and on CD-ROM, referenced by a new icon in select In Review charts. These tutorials walk students through some of the most difficult concepts encountered in their text. Topics such as reinforcement, opponent-process theory, drive-reduction theory, and priming—among others—are brought to life in an interactive format with an opportunity for self-testing to confirm understanding.

Behavioural Genetics Appendix

This feature is designed to amplify the coverage of behavioural genetics methodology that is introduced in Chapter 2, Research in Psychology. The appendix has been revised to include a discussion of the impact of the Human Genome Project, and includes a section on the basic principles of genetics and heredity, a brief history of genetic research in psychology, a discussion of what it means to say that genes influence behaviour, and an analysis of what behavioural genetics research can—and cannot—tell us about the origins of such human attributes as intelligence, personality, and mental disorders.

In Review Charts

In Review charts summarize information in a convenient tabular format. We have placed two or three In Review charts strategically in each chapter to help students synthesize and assimilate large chunks of information—for example, on drug effects, key elements of personality theories, and stress responses and mediators. As previously mentioned, our new PsychAssist animations are correlated to appropriate In Review charts.

Key Terms

Key terms and their definitions appear in the margin of the text where the terms are first used and in the glossary at the end of the book.

Integrated Teaching and Learning Support Package

Many useful materials have been developed to support *Psychology*, emphasizing its role as an integrated teaching and learning experience for instructors, teaching assistants, and students alike. These materials are well integrated with the text and include some of the latest technologies.

Instructor Supplements

Electronic Instructor's Resource Manual and Media Integration Guide • by *Douglas Bernstein*, available on the Instructor Web site or on HM ClassPrep CD-ROM, includes for each chapter learning objectives, chapter outlines, suggested readings, and numerous teaching aids. This manual also contains sections on implementing active-learning and critical-thinking techniques and materials to support teachers of large introductory courses, such as a section on classroom management and administration of large multi-section courses. The Instructor's Media Integration Guide outlines all of the multimedia resources offered with this text and strategies on how to use them most effectively.

HM ClassPrep • HM ClassPrep contains a multitude of text-specific resources for instructors to use to enhance the classroom experience, including PowerPoint® lecture outlines, art from the textbook, and many materials from the complete Instructors Resource Manual.

Canadian Edition Electronic Test Bank • by *Douglas Bernstein*, is the market-leading test bank for introductory psychology. It contains more than 3000 multiple-choice items plus three essay questions for each chapter of the text. More than 2,100 questions have been class-tested. *HM Testing* computerized database brings instructors the power and flexibility to create multiple testing, use various types of questions within a test, preview an entire test, and export the test into a course management system such as Blackboard™ or WebCT. The test bank is also available in MS Word® or print format upon request.

Canadian Edition PowerPoint® Slides • A complete set of PowerPoint® slides to accompany this Canadian Edition are available on the Instructor Web site.

Classroom Response System PowerPoint® Slides

Instructor Web Site • Additional instructor resources can be found on www.hmco.ca/bernstein—these include the Electronic Instructor's Resource Manual, Media Integration Guide, the PowerPoint® presentation files, Classroom Response System (CRS) PowerPoint® Slides, Overhead Transparencies, *Psych in Film* Teching Tips, a Video Guide, the *Lecture Starter* Video Guide, textbook art files, chapter outlines, the *In Review* charts, *Linkages* diagrams, and the *Behavioural Genetics* appendix with additional chapter activities and handouts to accompany it.

HM ClassPresent™ CD-ROM • An easy-to-navigate CD-ROM containing 25 newly developed PsychAssist animations and select art from the text that can be inserted into PowerPoint® slides or projected from the CD to enhance classroom lectures.

Eduspace™ Course Management System • A customizable, powerful, and interactive platform that provides instructors with text-specific online courses and content. Eduspace enables instructors to create all or part of their courses online using the widely recognized tools of Blackboard™ and resources for *Psychology* including PsychAssist animations, *Psych in Film* video clips with pedagogy, and automatically graded quizzes.

Course Content Cartridges for delivery via Blackboard™ or WebCT™

Films for the Humanities and Sciences • Select videos from the Films for the Humanities and Sciences collection (www.films.com) are available (Quantity based on number of copies adopted).

Lecture Starter Video DVD/VHS and Guide • The Lecture Starter Video contains a series of high-interest, concise segments that instructors can use to begin a class or change to a new topic.

The Psychology Show • Contains 19 motion segments plus nearly 100 still images. The Psychology Show is designed to expand on text coverage and to stimulate class discussion.

Psych in Film • ***Exclusive to Houghton Mifflin!*** Bring psychology to life in the classroom by showing short clips from popular films! Clips from ***A Beautiful Mind***, ***Schindler's List***, ***Snow Falling on Cedars***, and many others are combined with commentary and discussion questions to show students how psychology works in the real world. A complete description of all the clips on this DVD or VHS is available upon request.

Student Supplements

Canadian Study Guide • by *Douglas Bernstein and Wendy Bourque*, employs numerous techniques to help students learn. Each chapter—including the optional *Industrial/Organizational Psychology* chapter—contains a detailed outline, a key-terms section that presents fresh examples and learning aids, plus a fill-in-the-blank test, learning objectives, a concepts and exercises section that shows students how to apply their knowledge of psychology to everyday issues and concerns, a critical-thinking exercise, and personal learning activities. In addition, each chapter concludes with a two-part self-quiz consisting of 40 multiple-choice questions. An answer key tells the student not only which response is correct but also why each of the other choices is wrong, and quiz analysis tables enable students to track patterns to their wrong answers, either by topic or by type of question—definition, comprehension, or application.

Student CD-ROM • Contains interactive PsychAssist animations correlated to the text's In Review charts. These tutorials walk you through some of the more difficult concepts in the text by bringing them to life through creative game scenarios or simulated research and gives you several opportunities to test your understanding through a range of pre- and post-tests.

Student Web Site • Includes additional study aids, *ACE* Online Practice Quizzes, electronic flashcards, *PsychAssist* animations, web tutorials, net-labs, evaluating research web exercises, critical thinking exercises, and an interative sample research report. • www.hmco.ca/bernstein

Psychology in Context: Voices and Perspectives, Second Edition by David N. Sattler and Virginia Shabatay • ISBN: 0-395-95962-4

Acknowledgments

Many people provided us with help, criticism, and encouragement throughout the development of the Canadian Edition.

We also owe an enormous debt to them for their prerevision evaluations of the manuscript or reviewing it as it was being developed:

Glen Bodner, *University of Calgary*

James Duffy, *Memorial University*

Mindi Foster, *Wilfrid Laurier University*

Lynne Jackson, *University of Western Ontario*

Melike Schalomon, *Grant MacEwan College*

Sandra Wright, *Memorial University*

Jeff Webster, *Langara College*

Shirley Louth, *Langara College*

Christine Tsang, *Huron University College at Western*

We'd like to thank Patricia Tutunjian of Houghton Mifflin International for her foresight and dedication to the creation of a Canadian edition, as well as her colleagues in Boston and in Canada who provided guidance on Canadian market needs and trends. Glen Herbert attended to the development of the edition and we are grateful for his guidance and support throughout the project. Thanks to Merrill Peterson and his staff who handled the production phase of the project. Many thanks to Louise Bond-Fraser for her helpful suggestions and her editorial assistance.

Ken Cramer, University of Windsor

Kim Fenwick, St. Thomas University

Ian Fraser, St. Thomas University

Psychology

An Integrated Pedagogical System

THINKING CRITICALLY
Does Acupuncture Relieve Pain?

Acupuncture is an ancient and widely used treatment in Asian medicine that is alleged to relieve pain (Ulett, 2003). The method is based on the idea that body energy flows along lines called *channels* (Vincent & Richardson, 1986). It is said that there are fourteen main channels and that a person's health supposedly depends on the balance of energy flowing in them. Inserting thin needles into the skin and twirling them is meant to stimulate these channels and restore a balanced flow of energy. The needles produce an aching and tingling sensation called *Teh-ch'i* at the site of stimulation, but they relieve pain at distant, seemingly unrelated parts of the body.

- **What am I being asked to believe or accept?**

Acupuncturists assert that twirling a needle in the skin can relieve pain caused by everything from tooth extraction to cancer.

- **What evidence is available to support the assertion?**

There is no scientific evidence for the existence of the energy channels proposed in the theory behind acupuncture. However, as described in the chapter on biological aspects of psychology, some acupuncture stimulation sites are near peripheral nerves, and evidence from MRI scans suggests that stimulating these sites changes

THINKING CRITICALLY
Can Subliminal Stimuli Influence Your Behaviour?

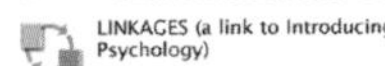
LINKAGES (a link to Introducing Psychology)

In 1957, an adman named James Vicary claimed that a New Jersey theatre flashed messages such as "buy popcorn" and "drink Coke" on a movie screen, too briefly to be noticed, while customers watched the movie *Picnic*. He said that these subliminal messages caused a 15 percent rise in sales of Coca Cola and a 58 percent increase in popcorn sales. Can such "mind control" really work? Many people seem to think so: They spend millions of dollars each year on audiotapes and videos that promise subliminal help to lose weight, raise self-esteem, quit smoking, make more money, or achieve other goals.

- **What am I being asked to believe or accept?**

Two types of claims have been made about subliminal stimuli. The more general claim is that subliminal stimuli can influence our behaviour. The second, more specific assertion is that subliminal stimuli provide an effective means of changing people's buying habits, political opinions, self-confidence, and other complex attitudes and behaviours, with or without their awareness or consent.

- **What evidence is available to support the assertion?**

Most evidence for the first claim—that subliminal stimuli can influence behaviour in a general way—comes from research on visual perception. For example, using a method called *subliminal priming*, participants are shown clearly visible (supraliminal) stimuli, such as pictures of people, and then asked to make some sort of

THINKING CRITICALLY
Does Watching Violence on Television Make People More Violent?

If observational learning is important, then surely television, and televised violence, must teach children a great deal. It is estimated that the average Canadian child spends approximately 15.5 hours a week watching television (Statistics Canada, 2001). Forty-five percent of the time Canadians are watching foreign programming (Statistics Canada, 2003). Canada is one of the largest importers of programming from the United States (Media Awareness Network, 2006). Prime time entertainment programs from the United States present an average of five acts of simulated violence per hour. Some American Saturday-morning cartoons include more than twenty per hour (American Psychological Association, 1993; Gerbner, Morgan, & Signorielli, 1994). Comparable Canadian programming produces 23.4% fewer violent acts than its American counterpart (Gosselin et al., 1997). It has been estimated, however, that a typical Canadian child will have witnessed approximately 12,000 violent deaths on television before his or her twelfth birthday (Chidley, 1996).

Psychologists have speculated that watching so much violence might be emotionally arousing, making the viewers more likely to react violently to frustration (Huston & Wright, 1989). Televised violence might also provide models that viewers imitate, particularly if the violence is carried out by attractive, impressive models—the "good guys," for example (Huesmann et al., 2003). Finally, prolonged viewing of violent TV programs might "desensitize" viewers, making them less distressed when they see others suffer and less disturbed about inflicting pain on others (Aronson, 1999; Donnerstein, Shabby, & Eron, 1995). Concern over the influence of violence on television led to the development of the violence-blocking V-Chip for new television sets in Canada (Canadian Intellectual Property Office, 2004).

- **What am I being asked to believe or accept?**

Many have argued that, through one or more of the mechanisms just listed, watching violence on television causes violent behaviour in viewers (Anderson et al., 2003; Anderson & Bushman, 2002b; Bushman & Huesmann, 2000; Eron et al., 1996; Husemann, 1998). A review of past research, conducted for the Canadian Paediatric Society, has demonstrated that over 1,000 studies have linked violent television to increased aggressive behaviour, and that this link is particularly prevalent in boys (Psychosocial Paediatrics Committee, 2003).

THINKING CRITICALLY

A dedicated section in every chapter models the critical-thinking process and through the use of ***five questions*** encourages readers to analyze research studies before drawing conclusions:

1. What am I being asked to believe or accept?
2. Is there evidence available to support the claim?
3. Can that evidence be interpreted another way?
4. What evidence would help to evaluate the alternatives?
5. What conclusions are most reasonable?

FOCUS ON RESEARCH METHODS

In these sections, focused attention on a particular study through the use of ***five focus questions*** helps readers understand the value of empirical research, the creativity with which it is conducted, and how it furthers understanding of behaviour and mental processes:

1. What was the researcher's question?
2. How did the researcher answer the question?
3. What did the researcher find?
4. What do the results mean?
5. What do we still need to know?

FOCUS ON RESEARCH METHODS
Manipulating Genes in Animal Models of Human Disease

Alzheimer's disease is named for Alois Alzheimer, a German neurologist. Almost a century ago, Alzheimer examined the brain of a woman who had died after years of progressive mental deterioration and dementia. In looking for the cause of her disorder, he found that cells in her cerebral cortex and hippocampus were bunched up like a rope tied in knots and that cellular debris had collected around the affected nerves. These features came to be known as tangles and plaques. *Tangles* are twisted fibres within neurons; their main protein component is called *tau*. *Plaques* are deposits of protein and parts of dead cells found between neurons. The major component of plaques was found to be a small protein called *beta-amyloid*, which is made from a larger protein called *amyloid precursor protein*. Accumulation of beta-amyloid plaques can now be visualized in living people through the use of PET scans (Klunk et al., 2004; see Figure 3.16).

• What was the researchers' question?

Ever since Alzheimer described plaques and tangles, researchers have been trying to learn about the role they play. One specific question that researchers have addressed is whether the proteins found in plaques and tangles actually *cause* Alzheimer's disease. They are certainly correlated with Alzheimer's, but as emphasized in the chapter on research in psychology, we can't confirm a causal relationship from a correlation alone. To discover if beta-amyloid and tau cause the death of neurons seen in Alzheimer's disease, researchers knew that controlled experiments would be necessary. This means manipulating an independent variable and measuring its effect on a dependent variable. In the case of Alzheimer's, the experiment would involve creating plaques and tangles (the independent variable) and looking for their effects on memory (the dependent variable). Such experiments

FOCUS ON RESEARCH METHODS
Measuring Explicit Versus Implicit Memory

Endel Tulving and his colleagues undertook a series of experiments to map the differences between explicit and implicit memory (Tulving, Schacter, & Stark, 1982).

• What was the researcher's question?

Tulving knew he could measure explicit memory by giving a recognition test. On such a test, participants are given a set of words and asked to say whether they remember seeing each of the words on a previous list. The question was, How would it be possible to measure implicit memory?

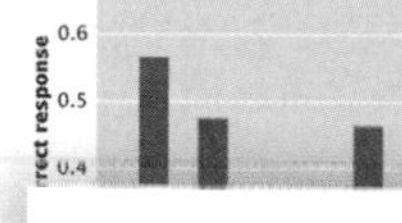

• How did the researcher answer the question?

First, Tulving asked the participants in his experiment to study a long list of words—the "study list." An hour later, they took a recognition test involving explicit memory—saying which words on a new list had been on the original study list. Then, to test their implicit memory, Tulving asked them to perform a "fragment completion" task (Warrington & Weiskrantz, 1970). In this task, participants were shown a "test list" of word fragments, such as *d_li_u_*, and asked to complete the word (in this case, *delirium*). On the basis of priming studies such as those described in the chapter on consciousness, Tulving assumed that mem-

FOCUS ON RESEARCH METHODS
Tracking Cognitive Abilities over the Life Span

As described in the chapter on human development, significant changes in cognitive abilities occur from infancy through adolescence, but development does not stop there. Roger Dixon at the University of Alberta and his colleagues are conducting a major study on the changes in cognitive ability during adulthood. This study, known as the Victoria Longitudinal Study, has yielded interesting findings regarding the cognitive skills of older adults (Dixon & de Frais, 2004).

• What was the researchers' question?

The researchers began by asking what appears to be a relatively simple question: How do adults' cognitive abilities change over time?

• How did the researchers answer the question?

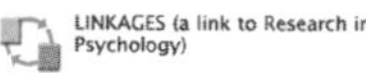
LINKAGES (a link to Research in Psychology)

Answering this question is extremely difficult because findings about age-related changes in cognitive abilities depend to some extent on the methods that are used to observe those changes. None of the methods includes true experiments, because psychologists cannot randomly assign people to be a certain age and then give them mental tests. So changes in cognitive abilities must be explored through a number of other research designs.

One of these, the *cross-sectional study*, compares data collected at the same point in time from people of different ages. However, cross-sectional studies contain a major confounding variable: Because people are born at different times, they may have had very different educational, cultural, nutritional, and medical experiences. This confounding variable is referred to as a *cohort effect*. Suppose two cohorts, or age groups, are tested on their ability to imagine the rotation of an object in space. The cohort born around 1940 might not do as well as the one born around 1980, but does the difference reflect declining spatial ability in the older people? It might, but it might also be due in part to the younger group's greater experience with video games and other spatial tasks. In other words, differences in experience, and not just age, could account for differences in ability between older and younger people in a cross-sectional study.

Changes associated with age can also be examined through *longitudinal studies*, in which a group of people is repeatedly tested as its members grow older. But longitudinal designs, too, have some built-in problems. For one thing, fewer and fewer members of an age cohort can be tested over time as death, physical disability, relocation, and lack of interest reduce the sample size. Researchers call this problem the *mortality effect*. Further, the remaining members are likely to be the healthiest in the group and may also have retained better mental powers than the dropouts (Botwinick, 1977). As a result, longitudinal studies may underestimate the degree to which abilities decline with age. Another confounding factor can come from the *history effect*. Here, some event—such as a reduction in health care benefits for senior citizens—might have an effect on cognitive ability scores that is mistakenly attributed to age. Finally, longitudinal studies may be confounded by *testing effects*, meaning that participants may improve over time because of what they learn during repeated testing procedures. People who become "test wise" in this way might even remember answers from one testing session to the next.

One method used to combat the problems associated with the cross-sectional and longitudinal designs, used in the Victoria Longitudinal Study and others like it, is to combine cross-sectional with longitudinal methods in what is called a *cross-sequential with resampling design*. In a cross-sequential design, people from two or more age groups are compared initially (i.e., the cross-sectional component) and then the groups are compared again after a period of time has passed (i.e., the longitudinal component). This method allows the researcher to take advantage of the benefits of both the cross-sectional and longitudinal methods.

LINKAGES

Linkages help students understand psychology as a whole, linking the content in each chapter and showing how the subfields contribute to and benefit from one another.

Selecting Research Participants Imagine that as a social psychologist, you want to study people's willingness to help each other. You have developed a method for testing helpfulness, but now you want a random sample of people to test. Take a minute to think about the steps necessary to select a truly random sample; then ask yourself how you might obtain a representative sample, instead. Remember that although the names are similar, *random sampling* is not the same as

other people in that group. This point is important, because psychologists often study behaviour or mental processes that are affected by age, gender, ethnicity, cultural background, socio economic status, sexual orientation, disability, or other participant characteristics. The more of these characteristics that are represented in a research sample, the broader can be the conclusions from research results.

In theory, psychologists could draw representative samples of people in general, of Canadians, of university students from British Columbia, or of any other group by choosing them at random from the entire population of interest. To do this, though, they would first have to enter hundreds of thousands, perhaps millions, of names into a computer, then run a program to randomly select participants from this vast population, then track them down and invite them to take part in the research. This method would result in a truly **random sample**, because every member of the population to be studied would have an equal chance of being chosen. Any selection procedure that does not offer this equal chance is said to result in a **biased sample**.

Unfortunately, not even a truly random sample will create a perfectly representative sample of Canadians, British Columbia university students, or the like. For one thing, the people who happen to be selected may be slightly different from the people who are not selected. In other words, the luck of the draw creates what psychologists call *sampling error*. Further, not everyone who is randomly selected for a research project will agree to participate, creating a problem called *nonresponse error*. These two kinds of errors help explain why the results of random surveys are not always accurate. Still, a group of individuals selected at random from a larger population will usually provide a reasonably representative sample of that population. The big problem, though, is that random sampling is often too expensive and time-consuming to be practical.

So in the real world of research, psychologists sometimes draw their participants from the populations that are conveniently available. The populations from which these *convenience samples* are drawn depend to some extent on the size of the researcher's budget. They might include, for example, the students enrolled in a particular course, students enrolled on a local campus, the students who are willing to sign up for a study, or visitors to Web sites or chat rooms (e.g., Nosek, Banaji, & Greenwald, 2002; Stone & Pennebaker, 2002). Ideally, this selection process will yield a sample that fairly represents the population from which it was drawn, but the researcher will check this by noting the age, gender, ethnicity, and other characteristics of the participants. In all cases, scientific researchers are obliged to limit the conclusions they draw in light of the samples they draw (Kraut et al., 2004). Because of this obligation, psychologists often conduct additional studies to determine the extent to which their initial conclusions will apply to people who differ in important ways from their original sample (Case & Smith, 2000; Gray-Little & Hafdahl, 2000).

Every chapter explores one linkage in depth.

LINKAGES Psychological Resea

LINKAGES (a link to Biological Aspects of Psychology)

Wherever a linkage is discussed in the text, a marginal callout directs students to further discussion.

random sample A group of research participants selected from a population whose members all had an equal chance of being chosen.

biased sample A group of research participants selected from a population each of whose members did not have an equal chance of being chosen.

n psychology is to find ways in which people's th environmental events to shape their behaviour l twins who were both are for them. John grew loved. Mark went from his natural father's second wife. In other words, these genetically identical people had encountered quite different environments. When they met for the first time at the age of twenty-four, they discovered similarities that went beyond physical appearance. They used the

itoring animal research—first determine that the discomfort is justified by the expected benefits to human welfare.

The responsibility for conducting research in the most humane fashion is just one aspect outlined in the *Canadian Code of Ethics for Psychologists* developed by the Canadian Psychological Association. This document not only emphasizes the importance of ethical behaviour but also describes specific ways in which psychologists can protect and promote the welfare of society and the particular people with whom they work in any capacity. So as teachers, psychologists should give students complete, accurate, and up-to-date coverage of each topic, not a narrow, biased point of view. Psychologists should perform only those services and use only those techniques for which they are adequately trained; a psychologist untrained in clinical methods, for example, should not try to offer psychotherapy. Except in the most unusual circumstances (discussed in the chapter on treatment of psychological disorders), psychologists should not reveal information obtained from clients or students. They should also avoid situations in which a conflict of interest might impair their judgment or harm someone else. They should not, for example, have sexual relations with their clients, their students, or their employees.

LINKAGES

As noted in the chapter on introducing psychology, all of psychology's subfields are related to one another. Our discussion of behavioural genetics illustrates just one way in which the topic of this chapter, research in psychology, is linked to the subfield of biological psychology (see the chapter on biological aspects of psychology). The Linkages diagram shows ties to two other subfields as well, and there are many more ties throughout the book. Looking for linkages among subfields will help you see how they all fit together and help you better appreciate the big picture that is psychology.

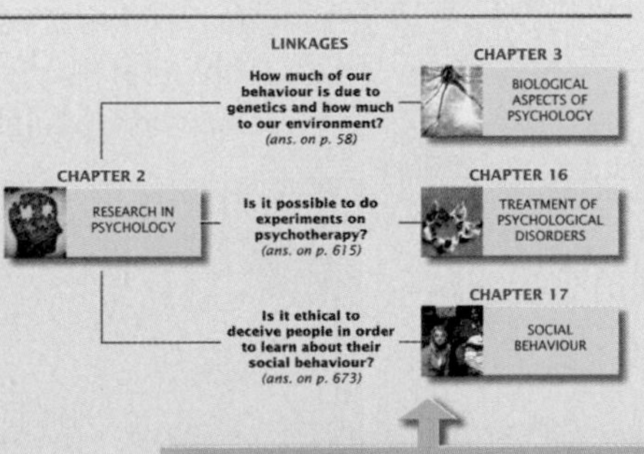

LINKAGES
CHAPTER 2
RESEARCH IN PSYCHOLOGY
How much of our behaviour is due to genetics and how much to our environment? (ans. on p. 58)
CHAPTER 3
BIOLOGICAL ASPECTS OF PSYCHOLOGY
Is it possible to do experiments on psychotherapy? (ans. on p. 615)
CHAPTER 16
TREATMENT OF PSYCHOLOGICAL DISORDERS
Is it ethical to deceive people in order to learn about their social behaviour? (ans. on p. 673)
CHAPTER 17
SOCIAL BEHAVIOUR

Within the active review, a diagram plots out the relationship among the linkages in that chapter.

Highlights of Available Media Resources

For Students

Tutorials

Interactive tutorials correlated to the text's In Review charts bring difficult concepts to life through simulated research or creative game scenarios.

in review Seeing

Aspect of Sensory System	Elements	Key Characteristics
Energy	Light—electromagnetic radiation from about 400 nm to about 750 nm	The intensity and wavelength of light waves determine the brightness and colour of visual sensations
Accessory structures	Eye—cornea, pupil, iris, lens	Light rays are bent to focus on the retina
Transduction mechanism	Photoreceptors (rods and cones) in the retina	Rods are more sensitive to light than cones, but cones discriminate among colours. Sensations of colour depend first on the cones, which respond differently to different light wavelengths. Interactions among cells of the retina exaggerate differences in the light stimuli reaching the photoreceptors, enhancing the sensation of contrast.
Pathways and representations	Optic nerve to optic chiasm to LGN of thalamus to primary visual cortex	Neighbouring points in the visual world are represented at neighbouring points in the LGN and primary visual cortex. Neurons there respond to particular aspects of the visual stimulus—such as colour, movement, distance, or form.

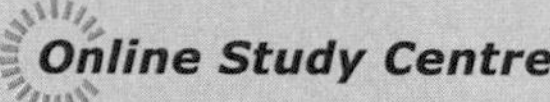

Ace Quizzes, Evaluating Research, Thinking Critically, and Flashcards

Interactive learning tools available on the student Web site help to consolidate concepts learned and improve grades.

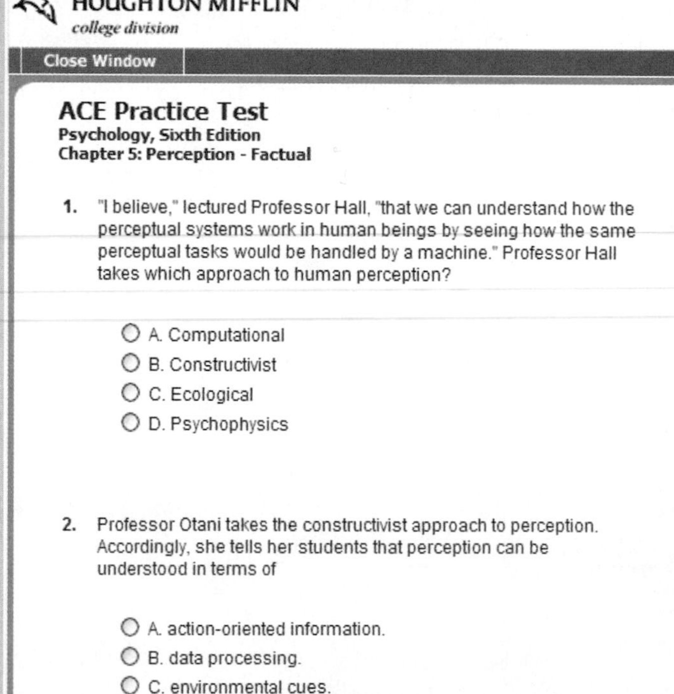

HOUGHTON MIFFLIN
college division
Close Window
ACE Practice Test
Psychology, Sixth Edition
Chapter 5: Perception - Factual
1. "I believe," lectured Professor Hall, "that we can understand how the perceptual systems work in human beings by seeing how the same perceptual tasks would be handled by a machine." Professor Hall takes which approach to human perception?
A. Computational
B. Constructivist
C. Ecological
D. Psychophysics
2. Professor Otani takes the constructivist approach to perception. Accordingly, she tells her students that perception can be understood in terms of
A. action-oriented information.
B. data processing.
C. environmental cues.
D. experientially-based inferences.

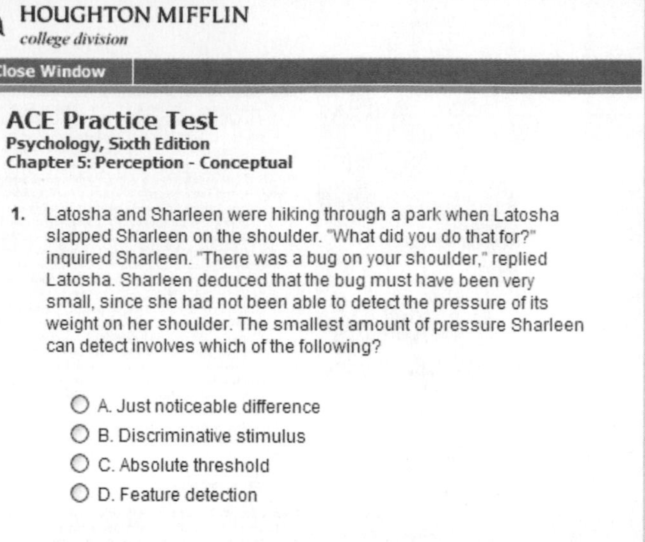

HOUGHTON MIFFLIN
college division
Close Window
ACE Practice Test
Psychology, Sixth Edition
Chapter 5: Perception - Conceptual
1. Latosha and Sharleen were hiking through a park when Latosha slapped Sharleen on the shoulder. "What did you do that for?" inquired Sharleen. "There was a bug on your shoulder," replied Latosha. Sharleen deduced that the bug must have been very small, since she had not been able to detect the pressure of its weight on her shoulder. The smallest amount of pressure Sharleen can detect involves which of the following?
A. Just noticeable difference
B. Discriminative stimulus
C. Absolute threshold
D. Feature detection

For Instructors

HMClass Present®

Includes 65 newly developed PsychAssist animations that project effectively in a lecture hall. Easy to navigate and searchable by thumbnail images organized by topic.

Eduspace®

A powerful course management system powered by Blackboard® that makes preparing, presenting, and managing courses and tracking student grades easier.

Includes suggested lesson plans, Tutorials, quizzing (including HMTesting), video clips, and other presentation tools such as PowerPoints and art from the textbook.

Psych in Film®

Houghton Mifflin's Psych in Film® contains 35 clips from Universal Studios films illustrating key concepts in psychology. Available on DVD and VHS.

HOUGHTON MIFFLIN
PSYCHOLOGY IN FILM
VERSION 2
TOPIC MENU
DVD-ROM: Teaching Tips
How to Use This Disc
Credits
Film clips courtesy of Universal Studios Licensing

1 Introducing Psychology

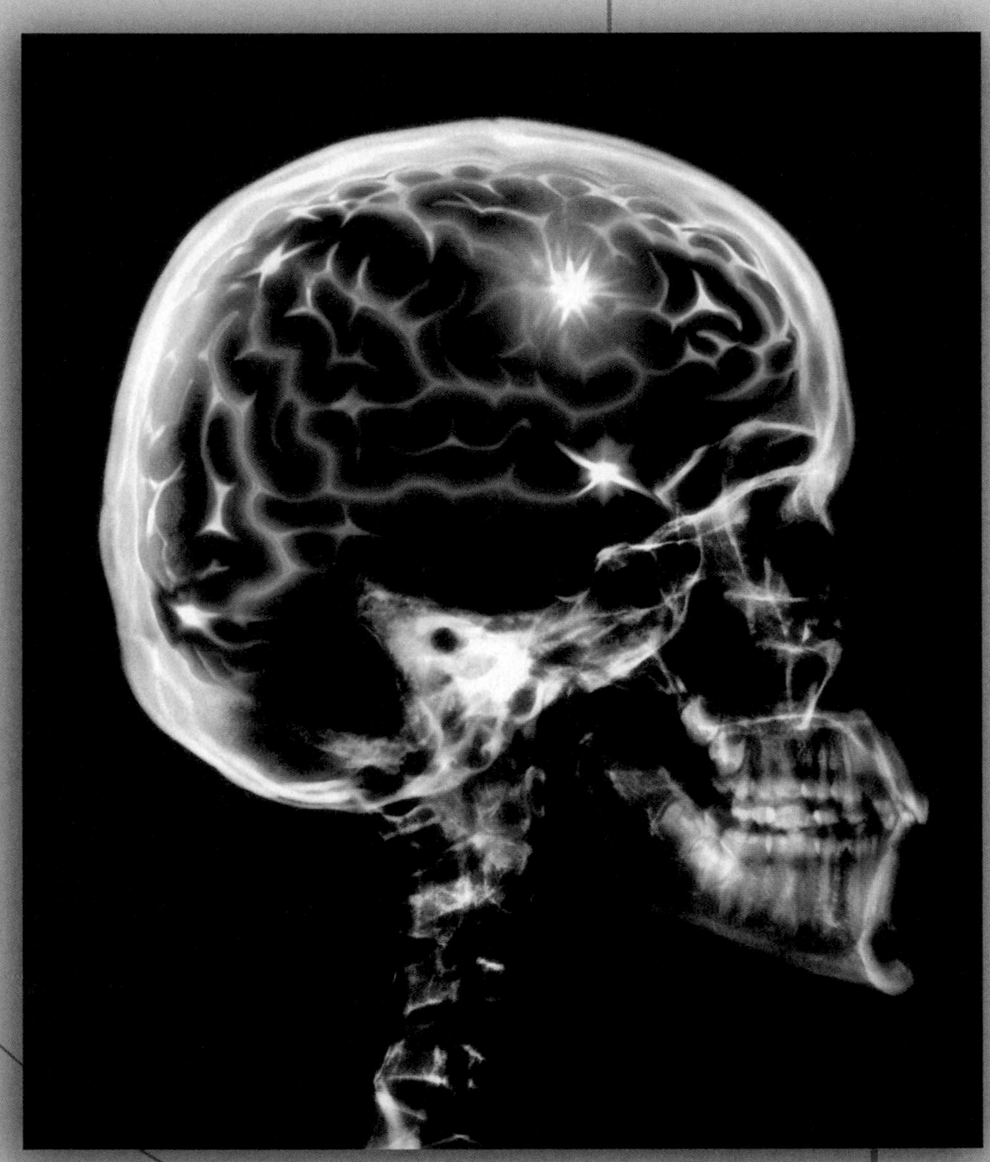

Our goal in this opening chapter is to give you an overview of psychology and its subfields and to show how psychology's subfields are linked to one another and to other subjects, such as economics and medicine. We then tell the story of how psychology came to be and the various ways in which psychologists approach their work. We have organized the chapter as follows:

The World of Psychology: An Overview

Let's go out on a limb and consider that, as you read this chapter, you're relaxing alone with your legs stretched out on a couch or bed. You're highlighting carefully (with your left hand—curious, both mom and dad are also left-handed) what you read so you'll remember that information better when you return for a final round of studying. You chose to study alone (and with the TV off) because you won't be as distracted and your concentration will be better. You wish you'd made yourself something to eat because now you're getting hungry; even the mention of food (maybe a piping hot, pepperoni-and-cheese pizza) makes your mouth water. But you promised yourself that you would get through this chapter; it makes you nervous that you've put it off for so long—not that you're a procrastinator. Admittedly, you feel a lot of pressure because of school and work and friends. Many people are counting on you to get good grades—your family and friends. Face it, even your own personal expectations are high. After all, your career goals are quite competitive. That grad school takes only the most talented and brightest people who apply, like your brother who got into the same specialized program last year. You look at the clock—it's getting so late (maybe you're getting sleepy, you're more of a morning person anyway), and your eyes just don't focus well at this hour. Maybe a brighter lightbulb would help. You feel a headache coming on (hope you're not getting sick). You could take some headache pills but those might be addictive. You once heard that if you take a fake pill (called a placebo) but think it's legitimate, it can have the same effect as the real thing.

This single moment, captured while you read your chapter, provides a terrific backdrop to so much about what this book will uncover: we will talk about the usefulness of highlighters in learning and retaining information (see Chapters 6 & 7 on learning and memory, and Chapter 8 on thinking and reasoning), about the choice to be with others or be alone (see Chapter 17 on social psychology), about our place in the family constellation (see Chapter 12 on developmental psychology). We will challenge the idea about what is "brightness" (see Chapter 10 on intelligence). We will talk about coping with pressures (see Chapter 13 on health and stress), about feeling hungry and tired and how we reach our goals (see Chapter 11 on motivation), about attention spans and our sleeping schedule (see Chapter 9 on consciousness), about what *type* of people we are—procrastinating, nervous, or competitive (see Chapter 15 on personality), about when stress and anxiety are manageable (see Chapters 11 & 13 on emotion and coping), and when they're not, so much so that they may then require special attention (see Chapter 16 on treatment of mental disorders). We will look deep into your eyes (see Chapter 4 on sensation) and how we appreciate the features and changes in our environment (see Chapter 5 on perception). We will consider the role of genetics and what it means to be left-handed (see Chapter 3 on brain and behaviour), and we will consider whether there is any truth to the *placebo effect*—where merely believing something (such as, a sugar pill is headache medicine) can make it so (see Chapter 2 on research methods).

These topics and others fall under the umbrella of **psychology,** the science that seeks to understand *behaviour* and *mental processes* and to apply that understanding in the service of human welfare. We will discuss why we talk about psychology as a *science* in detail in the next chapter, but suffice it is based not on the topic (behaviour and mental processes), but on the tools (scientific tools rather than common sense and intuition) used to investigate those topics. Frankly, it is of little wonder that this book's table of contents includes so many topics, including some—such as vision and biology—that you might not have expected to see in a book about psychology. Indeed, the topics have to be diverse in order to capture the full range of

psychology The science of behaviour and mental processes.

behaviours and mental processes that make you who you are and that come together in other ways in people of every culture around the world.

Subfields of Psychology

When psychologists choose to focus their attention on certain aspects of behaviour and mental processes, they enter one of psychology's subfields. Let's take a quick look at the typical interests and activities of psychologists in each subfield. We will describe their work in more detail in later chapters.

Biological Psychology **Biological psychologists,** also called *physiological psychologists,* use high-tech scanning devices and other methods to study how biological processes in the brain and other organs affect, and are affected by, behaviour and mental processes (see Figure 1.1). Biological psychologists have found, for example, that when mental patients "hear voices" or "see things" that are not really there, activity appears in regions of the brain that help process information about real sounds and sights. In the chapter on biological aspects of psychology, we describe biological psychologists' research on many other topics, such as how your brain controls your movements and speech and what organs help you to cope with stress and fight disease. Psychologists work with computer scientists and engineers on artificial-intelligence machines that rival humans in their ability to recognize voices and images, to reason, and to make decisions. Psychologists also collaborate with specialists in neuroanatomy, neurophysiology, neurochemistry, genetics, and other disciplines in a new field known as *neuroscience.* The goal of this multidisciplinary research is to examine the structure and function of the nervous system in animals and humans at levels ranging from the individual cell to overt behaviour. Someday, biological psychologists, like the colleagues with whom they work, may simply be known as **"neuroscientists."**

During his lifetime, Donald Olding Hebb (1904–1985) was an enormously influential figure, not only in Canadian psychology circles but also around the world. He envisioned psychology as a biological (neurological) science, he challenged the widely accepted principles of radical behaviourism (that we are nothing more than what we learn), and offered a very simple explanation of how neurons (acting together in assemblies) could yield perception, learning, and thinking—all of which helped to pave the way for the cognitive revolution to follow.

figure 1.1

Visualizing Brain Activity

Magnetic resonance imaging (MRI) allows biological psychologists to study the brain activity accompanying various mental processes (Poldrack & Wagner, 2004). This study found that males (left) and females (right) show different patterns of brain activity (indicated by the brightly coloured areas) while reading (Shaywitz et al., 1995).

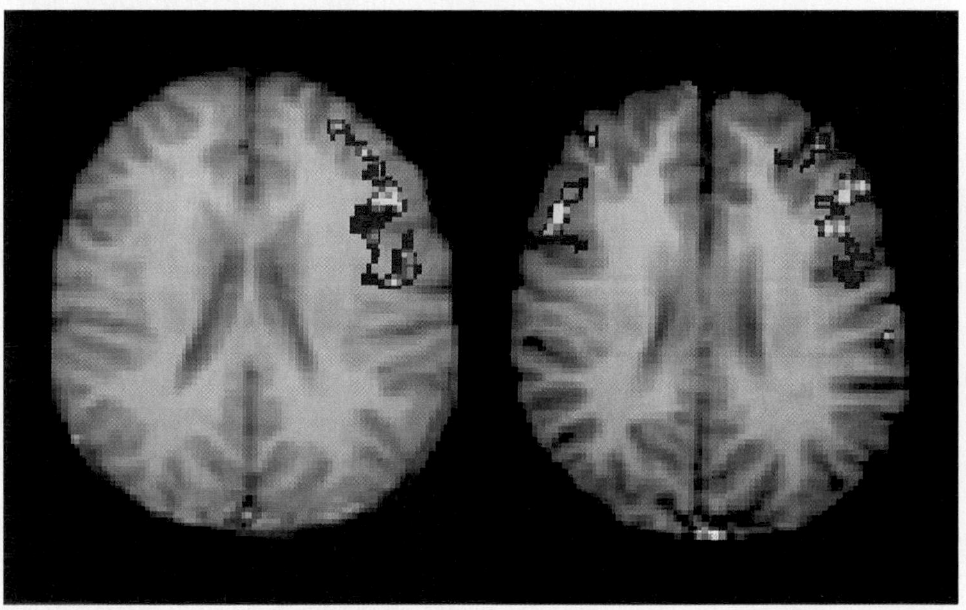

biological psychologists Psychologists who analyze the biological factors influencing behaviour and mental processes.

neuroscientists Psychologists who examine the role of the brain and neural networks in behaviour and mental processes.

figure 1.2

Where Would You Put a Third Eye?

In a study of how thinking processes develop, children were asked to show where they would place a third eye, if they could have one. Nine-year-old children, who were still in an early stage of mental development, drew the extra eye between their existing eyes, "as a spare." Having developed more advanced thinking abilities, eleven-year-olds drew the third eye in more creative places, such as the palm of the hand "so I can see around corners" (Shaffer, 1973).

Source: Shaffer (1973), Box 4-2.

Drawing by a nine-year-old　　Drawing by an eleven-year-old

In the course of his research, Hebb explored the impact of brain injury and surgery on human behaviour and intelligence. At Queen's University, Hebb developed animal and human intelligence tests and designed the Hebb-Williams Maze, still used extensively to investigate the intelligence of many species. For instance, Hebb's studies on intelligence led him to conclude that experience played a greater role in determining intelligence than we originally believed. Moreover, Hebb explained that *all* behaviour is determined jointly by environment and heredity. His book *The Organization of Behavior: A Neuropsychological Theory* attracted many scientists to psychology, put McGill on the map as a North American hotbed for brain mechanism research, and steered contemporary psychology onto its fruitful present path.

Since his death in 1985, Hebb's seminal ideas continue to exert a growing influence on those interested in mind (cognitive science), brain (neuroscience), and how brains implement mind (cognitive neuroscience). In the psychological literature, references to Hebb and cell-assembly increase each year. These ideas are now applied in engineering, robotics, and computer science.

Developmental Psychology **Developmental psychologists** describe the changes in behaviour and mental processes that occur from birth through old age and try to understand the causes and effects of those changes (see Figure 1.2). Their research on the development of memory and other mental abilities, for example, is used by judges and attorneys in deciding how old a child has to be in order to serve as a reliable witness in court or to be responsible for choosing which parent to live with after a divorce. The chapter on human development describes other research by developmental psychologists and how it is being applied in areas such as parenting, evaluating day care, and preserving mental capacity in elderly people.

Cognitive Psychology Stop reading for a moment and look left and right. Your ability to follow this suggestion, to recognize whatever you saw, and to understand the words you are reading right now are the result of mental, or *cognitive,* abilities. Those abilities allow you to receive information from the outside world, understand it, and act on it. **Cognitive psychologists** (some of whom prefer to be called *experimental psychologists*) study mental abilities such as sensation and perception, learning and memory, thinking, consciousness, intelligence, and creativity. Cognitive psychologists have found, for example, that we don't just receive incoming information—we manipulate it mentally. For example, the drawing in Figure 1.3 stays physically the same, but two different versions emerge, depending on which of its features *you* emphasize.

developmental psychologists Psychologists who seek to understand, describe, and explore how behaviour and mental processes change over the course of a lifetime.

cognitive psychologists Psychologists who study the mental processes underlying judgment, decision making, problem solving, imagining, and other aspects of human thought or cognition.

figure 1.3

Husband and Father-in-Law

This figure is called "Husband and Father-in-Law" (Botwinick, 1961) because you can see an old man or a young man, depending upon how you mentally organize its features. The elderly father-in-law faces to your right and is turned slightly toward you. He has a large nose, and the dark areas represent his coat pulled up to his protruding chin. However, the tip of his nose can also be seen as the tip of a younger man's chin; the younger man is in profile, also looking to your right, but away from you. The old man's mouth is the young man's neck band. Both men are wearing a broad-brimmed hat.

Applications of cognitive psychologists' research are all around you. Research by those whose special interest is **engineering psychology**—also known as *human factors*—has helped designers create computer keyboards, Web sites, aircraft instrument panels, nuclear power plant controls, and even TV remotes that are more logical, easier to use, and less likely to cause errors. You will read more about human factors research and many other aspects of cognitive psychology in several chapters of this book.

Personality Psychology **Personality psychologists** study similarities and differences among people. Some of them use tests, interviews, and other measures to compare individuals on characteristics such as openness to experience, emotionality, reliability, agreeableness, and sociability. Personality psychologists also study the characteristics of people who are prejudiced against others, who tend to be pessimistic or depressed, or even who claim to have been abducted by space aliens. Researchers interested in *positive psychology* are working to pinpoint the personality characteristics that allow some people to remain optimistic even in the face of stress or tragedy and to find happiness in life (Lucas, Diener, & Larson, 2003). As described in the personality chapter, research by personality psychologists has been applied in the diagnosis of mental disorders, in the identification of people who are most likely to develop stress-related health problems, and in many other ways.

Clinical, Counselling, Community, and Health Psychology **Clinical psychologists** and **counselling psychologists** conduct research on the causes of mental disorders and offer services to help troubled people overcome those disorders. They have found, for example, that many irrational fears, called *phobias,* are learned through the bad experiences people have with dogs or public speaking, for example, and that fearful people literally can be taught to overcome their fears. Research by other clinical psychologists has resulted in a listing of treatment methods that are most effective with particular kinds of disorders.

A Bad Design Consultation by human factors psychologists would probably have changed the design of this self-service gasoline pump. The pump will not operate until you press the red spot (see right) under the yellow "push to start" label, which is difficult to locate among all the other signs and stickers. Such user-unfriendly designs are all too common these days (e.g., Cooper, 2004; visit www.baddesigns.com for some amazing examples).

Photograph courtesy of www.baddesigns.com.

engineering psychology A field in which psychologists study human factors in the use of equipment and help designers create better versions of that equipment.

personality psychologists Psychologists who study the characteristics that make individuals similar to, or different from, one another.

clinical and counselling psychologists Psychologists who seek to assess, understand, and change abnormal behaviour.

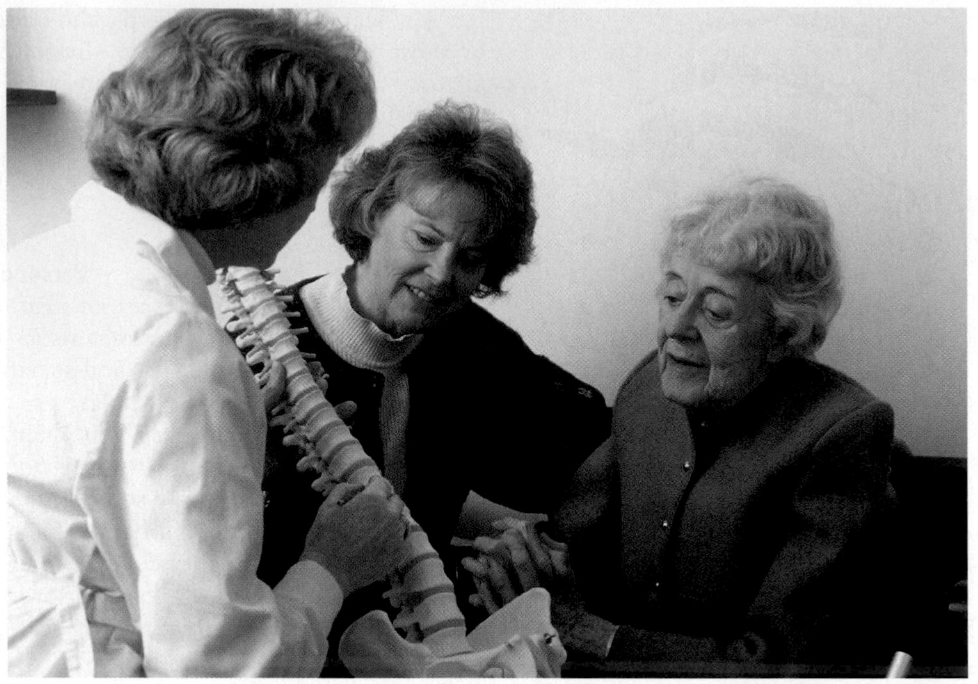

Getting Ready for Surgery Health psychologists have learned that when patients are mentally prepared for a surgical procedure, they are less stressed by it and recover more rapidly. Their research is now routinely applied in hospitals through programs in which children and adults are given more information about what to expect before, during, and after their operation (e.g., Block et al., 2003; Mahler & Kulik, 2002; O'Conner-Von, 2000).

Community psychologists work to ensure that psychological services reach the homeless and others who need help but tend not to seek it. They also try to *prevent* psychological disorders by working for changes in schools and neighbourhood organizations in the hope of reducing the poverty and other stressful conditions that so often lead to disorders. **Health psychologists** study the effects of behaviour on health, as well as the effect that illness has on people's behaviour and emotions. Their research is applied in programs that help people reduce the risk of cancer, heart disease, and stroke by giving up smoking, eating a healthy diet, and exercising more. You can read more about the work of clinical, counselling, community, and health psychologists in the chapters on health, stress, and coping; psychological disorders; and treatment of psychological disorders.

Educational and School Psychology **Educational psychologists** conduct research and develop theories about teaching and learning. The results of their work are applied in programs designed to improve teacher training, refine school curricula, reduce dropout rates, and help students learn more efficiently. For example, they have supported the use of the "jigsaw" technique, a type of classroom activity, described in the social cognition chapter, in which children from various ethnic groups must work together to complete a task or solve a problem. These cooperative experiences appear to promote learning, generate mutual respect, and reduce intergroup prejudice.

School psychologists traditionally specialized in IQ testing, diagnosing learning disabilities and other academic problems, and setting up programs to improve students' achievement and satisfaction in school. Today, however, they are also involved in activities such as early detection of students' mental health problems and crisis intervention following school violence (Benjamin & Baker, 2004).

Social Psychology **Social psychologists** study the ways that people think about themselves and others and how people influence one another. Their research on social persuasion has been applied to public health campaigns aimed at preventing the spread of AIDS and promoting the use of seat belts, not to mention the creation of compelling advertisements. Social psychologists also explore how peer pressure affects us, what determines whom we like (or even love), and why and how

community psychologists Psychologists who work to obtain psychological services for people in need of help and to prevent psychological disorders by working for changes in social systems.

health psychologists Psychologists who study the effects of behaviour and mental processes on health and illness, and vice versa.

educational psychologists Psychologists who study methods by which instructors teach and students learn and who apply their results to improving such methods.

school psychologists Psychologists who test IQs, diagnose students' academic problems, and set up programs to improve students' achievement.

social psychologists Psychologists who study how people influence one another's behaviour and mental processes, individually and in groups.

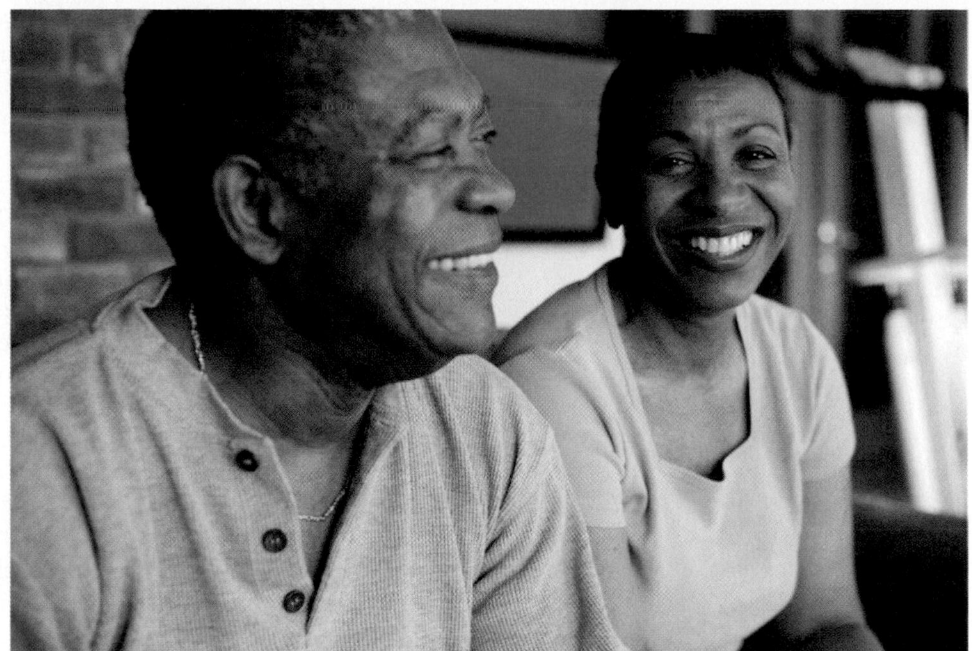

Canadian couple who meet online Many commercial dating and matchmaking services apply social psychologists' research findings on interpersonal attraction in an effort to pair up people who are most likely to be compatible.

prejudice forms. They have found that although we may pride ourselves on not being prejudiced, we may actually hold unconscious negative beliefs about certain groups that affect the way we relate to people from those groups. The chapters on social cognition and social influence describe these and many other examples of research in social psychology.

Industrial/Organizational Psychology **Industrial/organizational psychologists** study leadership, stress, competition, pay scales, and other factors that affect the efficiency, productivity, and satisfaction of workers and the organizations that employ them. They conduct research on topics such as increasing the motivation of current employees and helping companies select the best new workers. They also explore the ways in which businesses and industrial organizations work—or fail to work—and they make recommendations for helping them to work better

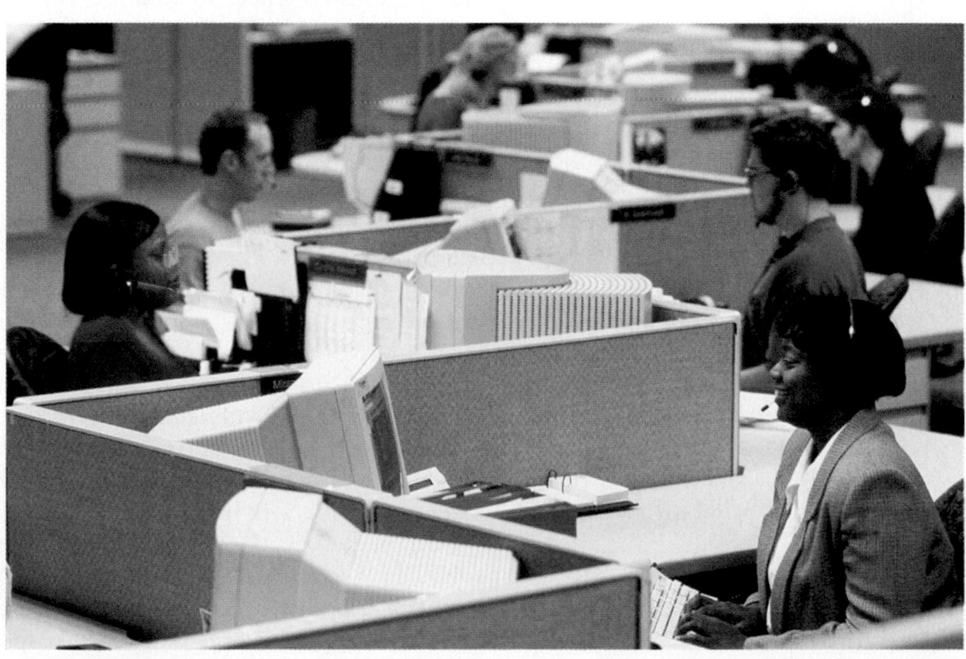

Working Underground Before moving its data processing centre to the basement of a new office building, executives of a large corporation consulted an environmental psychologist. They wanted to know how employees' performance and morale might be affected by working in a windowless space. The psychologist described the possible negative effects and, to combat those effects, recommended that architects create shafts that let in natural light. He also suggested that the area include plants and artwork depicting nature's beauty (Sommer, 1999).

industrial/organizational psychologists Psychologists who study ways to improve efficiency, productivity, and satisfaction among workers and the organizations that employ them.

(Spector, 2003). Companies all around the world are applying the research finding of industrial/organizational psychologists in the development of effective employee training programs, ambitious but realistic goal-setting procedures, fair and reasonable evaluation tools, and incentive systems that motivate and reward outstanding performance.

Quantitative Psychology According to University of Manitoba's Harvey Kesselman and colleagues (2004), **quantitative psychologists** develop and use statistical tools to analyze vast amounts of data collected by their colleagues in many other subfields. These tools help to evaluate the reliability and validity of psychological tests, to trace the relationships between childhood experiences and adult behaviours, and even to estimate the relative contributions of heredity and environment in determining intelligence. To what extent are people born smart—or not so smart—and to what extent are their mental abilities created by their environment? This is one of the hottest topics in psychology today, and quantitative psychologists are right in the middle of it.

Other Subfields Our list of psychology's subfields is still not complete. There are **sport psychologists,** who use visualization and relaxation training programs, for example, to help athletes reduce excessive anxiety, focus attention, and make other changes that let them perform at their best. **Forensic psychologists** assist in jury selection, evaluate defendants' mental competence to stand trial, and deal with other issues involving psychology and the law. And **environmental psychologists** study the effects of the environment on people's behaviour and mental processes. The results of their research are applied by architects and interior designers as they plan or remodel residence halls, shopping malls, auditoriums, hospitals, prisons, offices, and other spaces to make them more comfortable and functional for the people who will occupy them. There are also military psychologists, consumer psychologists, rehabilitation psychologists, and more.

Further information about the subfields we have mentioned and some that we haven't is available in books (e.g., Stec & Bernstein, 1999; Super & Super, 2001), as well as on the Web sites of the Canadian Psychological Association (http://www.cpa.ca) and the American Psychological Association (http://www.apa.org/about/division.html).

Where do the psychologists in all these subfields work? Table 1.1 contains the latest figures on where some of Canada's psychologists find employment.

Linkages Within Psychology and Beyond

We have listed psychology's subfields as though they were separate, but they often overlap, and so do the activities of the psychologists working in them. When developmental psychologists study the changes in children's thinking skills, for example, their research is linked to the research of cognitive psychologists. Similarly, biological psychologists have one foot in clinical psychology when they look at how chemicals in the brain affect the symptoms of depression. And when social psychologists apply their research on cooperation to promote group learning activities in the classroom, they are linking up with educational psychology. Even when psychologists work mainly in one subfield, they are still likely to draw on, and contribute to, knowledge in other subfields.

So if you want to understand psychology as a whole, you have to understand the linkages among its subfields. To help you recognize these linkages, we highlight three of them in a Linkages diagram at the end of each chapter—similar to the one shown on the next page. Each linkage is represented by a question that connects two subfields, and the page numbers in parentheses tell you where you can read more about each question. You will find that we pay particular attention to one question in each diagram by discussing it in a special Linkages section. If you look at the

quantitative psychologists Psychologists who develop and use statistical tools to analyze research data.

sport psychologists Psychologists who explore the relationships between athletic performance and such psychological variables as motivation and emotion.

forensic psychologists Psychologists who assist in jury selection, evaluate defendants' mental competence to stand trial, and deal with other issues involving psychology and the law.

environmental psychologists Psychologists who study the effects of the physical environment on behaviour and mental processes.

table 1.1

Typical Activities and Work Settings for Psychologists

The fact that psychologists can work in such a wide variety of settings and do so many interesting—and often well-paying—jobs helps account for the popularity of psychology as an undergraduate major. Psychology courses also provide excellent background for students planning to enter medicine, law, business, and many other fields.

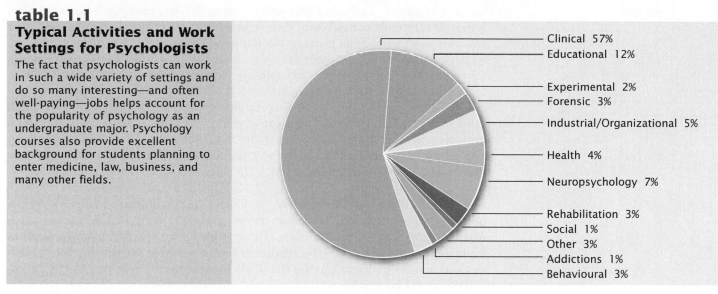

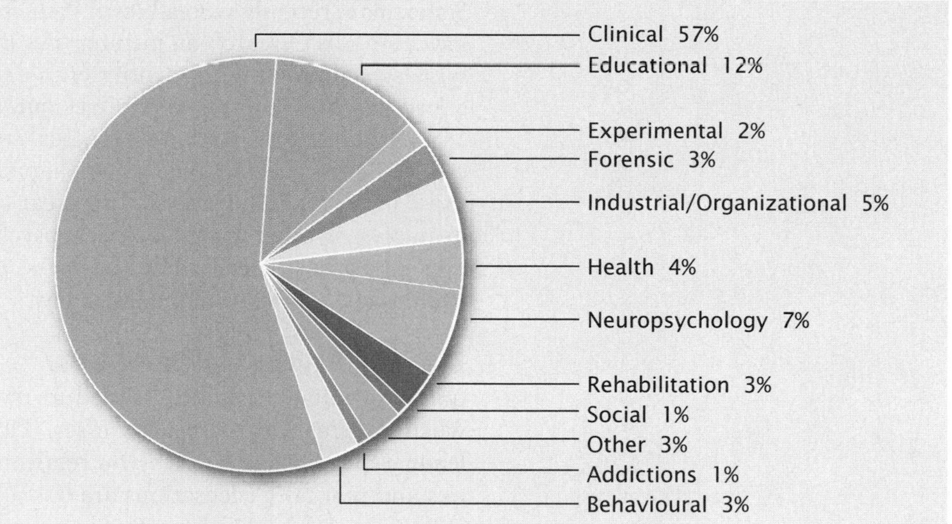

Source: Adapted from *Speciality Areas of Licensed Psychologists in Ontario*, 2004.

Linkages diagrams and follow the links where they lead, the relationships among psychology's many subfields will become much clearer. We hope you find this kind of detective work to be interesting and that it will lead you to look for the many other linkages that we did not mention. Tracing linkages might even improve your grade in the course, because it is often easier to remember material in one chapter by relating it to linked material in other chapters.

LINKAGES

By staying alert to the many linkages among psychology's subfields as you read this book, you will come away not only with threads of knowledge about each subfield but also with an appreciation of the fabric of psychology as a whole. We discuss one linkage in detail in each chapter in a special Linkages section.

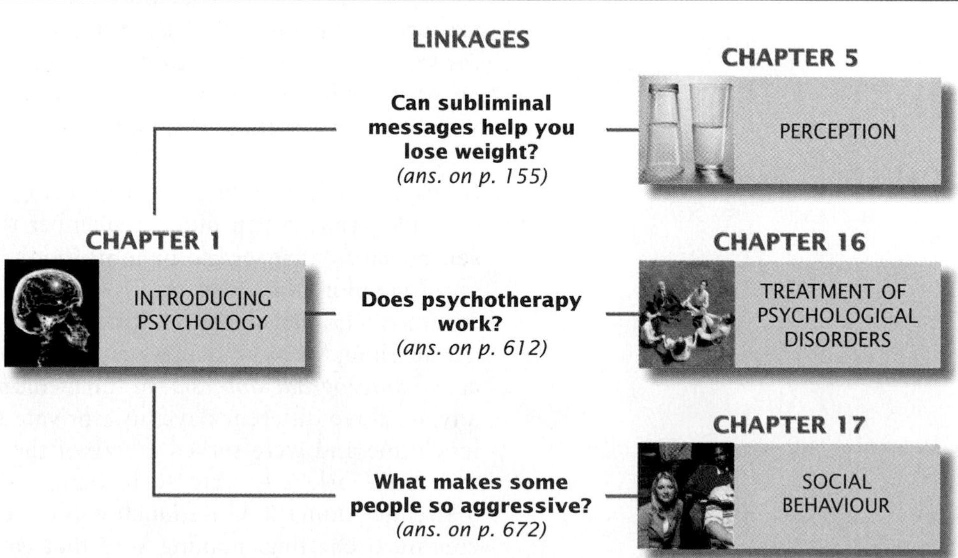

Links to Other Fields Much as psychology's subfields are linked to one another, psychology itself is linked to many other fields. Some of these linkages are based on interests that are shared by psychologists and researchers from other disciplines. Economists use the results of research by psychologists to better understand the thought processes that influence people's (good and not-so-good) decisions about investments and other financial matters. In fact, one psychologist, Daniel Kahneman, recently won a Nobel Prize in economics for his work in this area. Other psychologists' research on memory has influenced how lineups are displayed to eyewitnesses attempting to identify criminals, how attorneys question eyewitnesses in court, and how lawyers and judges question witnesses and instruct juries (Memon, Vrij, & Bull, 2004). And psychological studies of the effect of brain disorders on elderly patients' mental abilities is shaping doctors' recommendations about when those patients should stop driving a car (Reger et al., 2004). This book is filled with examples of other ways in which psychological theories and research have been applied to health care, law, business, engineering, architecture, aviation, public health, and sports, to name just a few.

Linking Psychology and Law Cognitive psychologists' research on the quirks of human memory has led to revised guidelines for police and prosecutors when dealing with crime witnesses. These guidelines warn that asking witnesses leading questions (e.g., "Do you remember seeing a gun?") can distort their memories and that false accusations are less likely if witnesses are told that the real criminal might not be in a lineup or in a group of photos.

Research: The Foundation of Psychology

The knowledge that psychologists share across subfields and with other disciplines stems from the research they conduct on many aspects of behaviour and mental processes. So instead of just speculating about why, for example, people eat as much or as little as they do, psychologists look for answers by using the methods of science. This means that they perform experiments and other scientific procedures to systematically gather and analyze information about behaviour and mental processes and then base their conclusions—and their next questions—on the results of those procedures.

To take just one example related to eating, let's consider a fascinating study conducted by Paul Rozin and his associates (Rozin et al., 1998) on what causes people to begin and end a meal. Suppose you have just finished a big lunch at your favourite restaurant when a server gets mixed up and brings you another plate of the same food that was meant for someone else. You would almost certainly send it away, but why? Decisions to start eating or stop eating are affected by many biological factors, including signals from your blood that tell your brain how much "fuel" you have available. Rozin was interested in how these decisions are affected by psychological factors, such as being aware that you have already eaten. For example, what if you didn't remember that you just had lunch? Would you have started eating that second plate of food?

To explore this question, Rozin conducted a series of tests with R.H. and B.R., two men who had suffered a kind of brain damage that left them unable to remember anything for more than a few minutes. (You can read more about this condition, called *anterograde amnesia,* in the memory chapter.) The men were tested individually, on three different days, in a private room where they sat with a researcher at lunchtime and were served a tray of their favourite food. Before and after eating, they were asked to rate their hunger on a scale from 1 (extremely full) to 9 (extremely hungry). Once lunch was over, the tray was removed, and the researcher continued chatting, making sure that each man drank enough water to clear his mouth of food residue. After ten to thirty minutes, a hospital attendant entered with a meal tray carrying the identical food as before and announced "Here's lunch." These men had no memory of having eaten lunch already, but would signals from their stomachs or their blood be enough to keep them from eating another one?

Apparently not. Table 1.2 shows that, in every test session, R.H. and B.R. ate all or part of the second meal and, in all but one session, ate at least part of a third lunch that was offered to them ten to thirty minutes after the second one. Rozin conducted

table 1.2

The Role of Memory in Deciding When to Eat

Here are the results of a study in which brain-damaged people were offered a meal shortly after having eaten an identical meal. Their hunger ratings (1–9, where 9 = extremely hungry) before and after eating are shown in parentheses. B.R. and R.H. had a kind of brain damage that left them unable to remember recent events (anterograde amnesia); J.C. and T.A. had normal memory. These results suggest that the decision to start eating is determined partly by knowing when we last ate. Notice that hunger ratings, too, were more consistently affected by eating for the people who remembered having eaten.

Session	B.R. (Amnesia)	R.H. (Amnesia)	J.C.	T.A.
One				
Meal 1	Finished (7/8)	Partially eaten (7/6)	Finished (5/2)	Finished (5/4)
Meal 2	Finished (2/5)	Partially eaten (7/7)	Rejected (0)	Rejected (3)
Meal 3	Rejected (3)	Partially eaten (7/7)	—	—
Two				
Meal 1	Finished (6/5)	Partially eaten (7/6)	Finished (7/2)	Finished (7/3)
Meal 2	Finished (5/3)	Partially eaten (7/6)	Rejected (1)	Rejected (3)
Meal 3	Partially eaten (5)[a]	Partially eaten (7/6)	—	—
Three				
Meal 1	Finished (7/3)	Partially eaten (7/6)	—	—
Meal 2	Finished (2/3)	Partially eaten (7/6.5)	—	—
Meal 3	Partially eaten (5/3)	Partially eaten (7.5)	—	—

[a]B.R. began eating his third meal but was stopped by the researcher, presumably to avoid illness.

Source: Adapted from Rozin et al. (1998).

similar tests with J.C. and T.A., a woman and a man who had also suffered brain damage but who still had normal memory for recent events. In each of two test sessions, these people finished their lunch but refused the opportunity to eat a second one. These results suggest that the memory of when we last ate can indeed be a factor in guiding decisions about when to eat again. They also support a conclusion described in the motivation and emotion chapter, namely that eating is controlled by a complex combination of biological, social, cultural, and psychological factors. As a result, we may eat when we *think* it is time to eat, regardless of what our bodies tell us about our physical need to eat.

Rozin's study illustrates the fact that although psychologists often begin with speculation about behaviour and mental processes, they take additional steps toward understanding those processes. Using scientific methods to test their ideas, they reach informed conclusions and generate new questions. Even psychologists who don't conduct research benefit from it. They are constantly applying the results of their colleagues' studies to improve the quality, accuracy, and effectiveness of their teaching, writing, or service to clients and organizations.

The rules and methods of science that guide psychologists in their research are summarized in the chapter on research in psychology. We have placed that chapter early in the book to highlight the fact that without scientific research methods and the foundation of evidence they provide, psychologists' statements and recommendations about behaviour and mental processes would carry no more weight than those of astrologers, psychics, or tabloid journalists. Accordingly, we will rely on the results of psychologists' scientific research when we tell you what they have discovered so far about behaviour and mental processes and also when we evaluate their efforts to apply that knowledge to improve the quality of human life.

Plato and Aristotle Ancient Greek philosophers sharply disagreed on the origins of human knowledge. Whereas Aristotle's school of *empiricism* believed that knowledge was gained by using our five senses to understand the world around us, Plato's school of *rationalism* argued that the senses could be easily fooled (by magic or illusions) and instead believed reasoning would pave the way to the truth.

A Brief History of Psychology

Psychologists have been conducting research on behaviour and mental processes for more than 125 years. The birth date of modern psychology is usually given as 1879, the year that Wilhelm Wundt (pronounced "voont") established the first formal psychology research laboratory at the University of Leipzig, Germany (Benjamin, 2000). However, the roots of psychology can be traced back through centuries of history in philosophy and science. Since at least the time of Socrates, Plato, and Aristotle in ancient Greece, there has been debate about where human knowledge comes from, the nature of the mind and soul, the relationship of the mind to the body, and whether it is possible to study such things scientifically (Wertheimer, 1987).

As a rationalist, Plato (Socrates' pupil) was convinced that the senses could be deceived by illusions, drugs, even dreams. The only thing one could be sure of was what could be derived by careful thought (for example, it has always been true and remains true to this day and forever since that 2 + 3 = 5. You don't even need a basket of apples to prove it's true. And where did these basic truths come from? From within—because knowledge was essentially self-understood; you merely needed to look inside and find it, and it could be found in each of us.

Alternatively, Plato's student Aristotle admitted that, on the one hand, although our senses can be fooled (for example, a pencil appears to bend in water), the more we use our senses and experiment with the ways of the world (for example, move the pencil in and out of the water), we will eventually uncover the nature of light and water. We call this principle of using our senses to reveal the world's truths *empiricism*.

In the seventeenth century, René Descartes would further challenge the idea of inborn knowledge by stripping away everything he had learned in the course of his life. Descartes doubted everything he previously knew: his learning, his memories, his perceptions. Could he even be certain he was alive, that his whole life wasn't merely a dream? He doubted everything. But there was one thing he couldn't doubt: he couldn't doubt that he was doubting and, because doubting requires a doubter, he was certain that he was alive, which conclusion led to his famous quote: "Cogito ergo sum"—I think [doubt], therefore I am [I exist].

Empiricism would also see some transformations in these pivotal years. In the seventeenth century, proponents—such as British philosophers John Locke, George Berkeley, and David Hume—challenged Plato's view that some knowledge is innate. Empiricists claimed that what we know about the world comes to us through experience and observation, not through imagination or intuition. This view suggests that, at birth, our minds are like a blank slate (in Latin, *tabula rasa*) upon which our experiences write a lifelong story.

René Descartes Seventeenth-century French philosopher René Descartes doubted the existence of everything around him—his name, his surroundings, his relationships. How could he be sure it wasn't a dream? But the one thing he couldn't doubt was that he was doubting—and that meant that he himself must exist because doubting requires a doubter.

Wundt and the Structuralism of Titchener By the nineteenth century, a number of German physiologists, including Hermann von Helmholtz and Gustav Fechner (pronounced "FECK-ner"), were conducting scientific studies of the structure and function of vision, hearing, and the other sensory systems and perceptual processes that empiricism had identified as the channels through which human knowledge flows. Fechner's work was especially valuable because he realized that one could study these mental processes by observing people's reactions to changes in sensory stimuli. By exploring, for example, how much brighter a light must become before we see it as twice as bright, Fechner discovered complex, but predictable, relationships between changes in the *physical* characteristics of stimuli and changes in our *psychological experience* of them. Fechner's approach, which he called *psychophysics,* paved the way for much of the research described in the chapter on perception.

As a physiologist, Wundt, too, used the methods of laboratory science to study sensory-perceptual systems, but the focus of his work was *consciousness,* the mental experiences created by these systems. Wundt wanted to describe the basic elements of consciousness, how they are organized, and how they relate to one another

Wilhelm Wundt (1832–1920) In an early experiment on the speed of mental processes, Wundt (third from left) first measured how quickly people could respond to a light by releasing a button they had been holding down. He then measured how much longer the response took when they held down one button with each hand and had to decide—based on the colour of the light—which one to release. Wundt reasoned that the additional response time reflected how long it took to perceive the colour and decide which hand to move. As noted in the chapter on cognition and language, the logic behind this experiment remains a part of research on cognitive processes today.

(Schultz & Schultz, 2002). For example, he developed ingenious laboratory methods to study the speed of decision making and other mental events. And in an attempt to observe conscious experience, Wundt used the technique of *introspection,* which means "looking inward." After training research participants in this method, he repeatedly showed a light or made a sound and asked them to describe the sensations and feelings these stimuli created. Wundt concluded that "quality" (for example, cold or blue) and "intensity" (for example, brightness or loudness) are the two essential elements of any sensation and that feelings can be described in terms of pleasure, displeasure, tension-relaxation, and excitement-depression (Schultz & Schultz, 2002). In conducting this kind of research, Wundt began psychology's transformation from the *philosophy* of mental processes to the *science* of mental processes.

Edward Titchener, an Englishman who had been one of Wundt's students, used introspection in his own laboratory at Cornell University. He studied Wundt's basic elements of consciousness, as well as images and other aspects of conscious experience that are harder to quantify (see Figure 1.4). One result was that Titchener added "clearness" as an element of sensation (Schultz & Schultz, 2002). Titchener called his approach *structuralism* because he was trying to define the structure of consciousness.

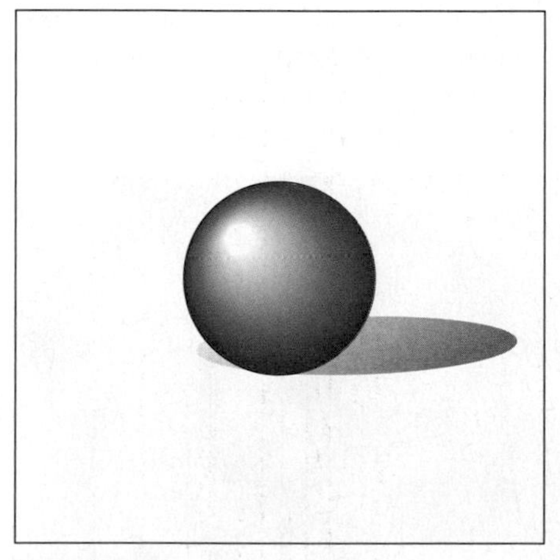

figure 1.4

A Stimulus for Introspection

Look at this object and try to ignore what it is. Instead, try to describe only your conscious experience, such as redness, brightness, and roundness, and how intense and clear the sensations and images are. If you can do this, you would have been an excellent research assistant in Titchener's laboratory.

Wundt was not alone in the scientific study of mental processes, nor was his work universally accepted. Some of his fellow German scientists, such as Hermann Ebbinghaus, saw the use of introspection to analyze consciousness as less important than exploring the capacities and limitations of mental processes such as learning and memory. Ebbinghaus's own laboratory experiments—in which he served as the only participant—formed the basis for some of what we know about memory today. Other German colleagues, including Max Wertheimer, Kurt Koffka, and Wolfgang Köhler, argued against Wundt's efforts to break down human experience or consciousness into its component parts. They were called Gestalt psychologists because they pointed out that the whole (*Gestalt,* in German) of conscious experience is not the same as the sum of its parts. Wertheimer noted, for example, that if a pair of lights go on and off in just the right sequence, we experience not two flashing lights but a single light "jumping" back and forth. You have probably seen this *phi phenomenon* in action on advertising signs that create the impression of a series of lights racing around a display. Movies provide another example. Imagine how boring it would be to browse slowly through the thousands of still images that are printed on a reel of film. Yet when those same images are projected onto a screen at a particular rate, they combine to create a rich, emotional experience.

Freud and Psychoanalysis While Wundt and his colleagues in Leipzig were conducting scientific research on consciousness, Sigmund Freud (1856–1939) was in Vienna, Austria, beginning to explore the unconscious. As a physician, Freud had presumed that all behaviour and mental processes have *physical* causes somewhere in the nervous system. He began to question that assumption in the late 1800s, however, after encountering several patients who displayed a variety of physical ailments that had no apparent physical cause. After interviewing these patients using hypnosis and other methods, Freud became convinced that the causes of these people's physical problems were not physical. The real causes, he said, were deep-seated problems that the patients had pushed out of consciousness (Breuer & Freud, 1895; Friedman & Schustack, 2003). He eventually came to believe that all behaviour—from everyday slips of the tongue to severe forms of mental disorder—is motivated by *psychological* processes, especially by mental conflicts that occur without our awareness, at an unconscious level. For the next forty years, Freud developed his ideas into a body of work known as *psychoanalysis,* which included a theory of personality and mental disorder, as well as a set of treatment methods. Partly because they were based on a small number of medical cases, not a series of laboratory experiments, Freud's ideas have long been the subject of controversy. Still, they have had an undeniable influence on the thinking of many psychologists around the world.

William James and Functionalism Scientific research in psychology began in North America not long after Wundt started his work in Germany. William James founded a psychology laboratory at Harvard University in the late 1870s, though it was used mainly to conduct demonstrations for his students (Schultz & Schultz, 2002). It was not until 1883 that G. Stanley Hall at Johns Hopkins University established the first psychology research laboratory in the United States. The first Canadian psychology research laboratory was established in 1889 at the University of Toronto by James Mark Baldwin, Canada's first modern psychologist and a pioneer in research on child development.

Like the Gestalt psychologists, William James rejected both Wundt's approach and Titchener's structuralism. He saw no point in breaking consciousness into component parts that never operate on their own. Instead, in accordance with Charles Darwin's theory of evolution, James wanted to understand how images, sensations, memories, and the other mental events that make up our flowing "stream of

William James's Lab William James (1842–1910) established this psychology demonstration laboratory at Harvard University in the late 1870s. Like the Gestalt psychologists, James saw the approach used by Wundt and Titchener as a scientific dead end. He said that trying to understand consciousness by studying its components is like trying to understand a house by looking at individual bricks (James, 1884). He preferred instead to study the ways in which consciousness functions to help people adapt to their environments.

consciousness" function to help us adapt to our environment (James, 1890, 1892). This idea was consistent with an approach to psychology called *functionalism,* which focused on the role of consciousness in guiding people's ability to make decisions, solve problems, and the like.

James's emphasis on the functions of mental processes encouraged North American psychologists to look not only at how those processes work to our advantage but also at how they differ from person to person. Some of these psychologists began to measure individual differences in learning, memory, and other mental processes associated with intelligence, made recommendations for improving educational practices in the schools, and even worked with teachers on programs tailored to children in need of special help (Nietzel et al., 2003).

John B. Watson and Behaviourism Besides fuelling James's interest in the functions of consciousness, Darwin's theory of evolution led other psychologists—especially those in North America after 1900—to study animals as well as humans. They suggested that if all species evolved in similar ways, perhaps the behaviour and mental processes of all species followed similar laws. If so, we could learn something about people by studying animals. Psychologists could not expect cats or rats or pigeons to introspect, so they watched what animals did when confronted with laboratory tasks such as finding the correct path through a maze. From these observations, they made *inferences* about the animals' conscious experiences and about the general laws of learning, memory, problem solving, and other mental processes that might apply to people as well as animals.

John B. Watson, a psychology professor at Johns Hopkins University, believed that the observable behaviour of animals and humans is the most important source of scientific information for psychology. However, Watson thought it utterly unscientific to use behaviour as the basis for making inferences about consciousness, as structuralists and functionalists did—let alone about the unconscious, as Freudians did. In 1913, Watson published an article titled "Psychology as the Behaviourist Views It." In it, he argued that psychologists should ignore mental events and base psychology only on what they can actually see in overt behaviour and in responses to various stimuli (Watson, 1913, 1919).

Watson's view, called *behaviourism,* recognized the existence of consciousness but did not consider it worth studying because it would always be private and therefore not observable by scientific methods. In fact, said Watson, preoccupation with consciousness would prevent psychology from ever being a true science. Watson believed that the most important determinant of behaviour is *learning* and that it is through learning that animals and humans are able to adapt to their environments. He was famous for claiming that with enough control over the environment, he could create learning experiences that would turn any infant into a doctor, a lawyer, or even a criminal.

American psychologist B. F. Skinner was another early champion of behaviourism. From the 1930s until his death in 1990, Skinner worked on mapping out the details of how rewards and punishments shape, maintain, and change behaviour through what he termed "operant conditioning." He also used a *functional analysis* of behaviour to explain, for example, that children's tantrums are sometimes accidentally made more likely by the attention they attract from parents and teachers, and how a virtual addiction to gambling can result from the occasional and unpredictable rewards it brings.

Many psychologists were drawn to Watson's and Skinner's vision of psychology as the learning-based science of observable behaviour. Behaviourism dominated psychological research from the 1920s through the 1960s, while the study of consciousness received less attention, especially in North America. ("In Review: The Development of Psychology" summarizes behaviourism and the other schools of thought that influenced psychologists in the past century.)

in review The Development of Psychology

School of Thought	Early Advocates	Goals	Methods
Structuralism	Edward Titchener, trained by Wilhelm Wundt	To study conscious experience and its structure	Experiments, introspection
Gestalt psychology	Max Wertheimer	To describe organization of mental processes: "The whole is greater than the sum of its parts."	Observation of sensory/ perceptual phenomena
Psychoanalysis	Sigmund Freud	To explain personality and behaviour; to develop techniques for treating mental disorders	Study of individual cases
Functionalism	William James	To study how the mind works in allowing an organism to adapt to the environment	Naturalistic observation of animal and human behaviour
Behaviourism	John B. Watson, B. F. Skinner	To study only observable behaviour and explain behaviour via learning principles	Observation of the relationship between environmental stimuli and behavioural responses

PsychAssist: Psychology Schools of Thought Timeline

Psychology Today Psychologists continue to study all kinds of overt behaviour in humans and in animals. By the end of the 1960s, however, many had become dissatisfied with the limitations imposed by behaviourism (some, especially in Europe, had never accepted it in the first place). They grew uncomfortable ignoring mental processes that might be important in more fully understanding behaviour (e.g., Ericsson & Simon, 1994). The dawn of the computer age influenced these psychologists to think about mental activity in a new way—as information processing. Computers and rapid progress in computer-based biotechnology began to offer psychologists exciting new ways to study mental processes and the biological activity that underlies them. As shown in Figure 1.1, for example, it is now possible to literally see what is going on in the brain when, for example, a person thinks or makes decisions.

Armed with ever more sophisticated research tools, psychologists today are striving to do what Watson thought was impossible: to study mental processes with precision and scientific objectivity. In fact, there are probably now as many psychologists who study cognitive and biological processes as there are who study observable behaviours. So mainstream psychology has come full circle, once again accepting consciousness—in the form of cognitive processes—as a legitimate topic for scientific research and justifying the definition of psychology as the science of behaviour and mental processes (Kimble, 2000).

Unity and Diversity in Psychology

Psychologists today are unified by their commitment to empiricism and scientific research, by their linked interests in behaviour and mental processes, and by the debt they owe to predecessors whose work has shaped psychology over its 125-year history. In other ways, however, psychologists are an amazingly diverse group. This diversity is reflected not only in the many subfields they choose but also in who they are and how they approach their work.

Mary Whiton Calkins (1863–1930) Mary Whiton Calkins studied psychology at Harvard University, where William James described her as "brilliant." Because she was a woman, Harvard refused to grant her a doctoral degree unless she received it through Radcliffe, which was then an affiliated school for women. She refused, but went on to do research on memory and, in 1905, became the first woman president of the American Psychological Association.

As in other academic disciplines in the early twentieth century, most psychologists were white, middle-class men (Walker, 1991). Almost from the beginning, however, women and people of colour were also part of the field (Schultz & Schultz, 2002). Throughout this book you will find the work of their modern counterparts, whose contributions to research, service, and teaching have all increased in tandem with their growing representation in psychology. This shift reflects continuing efforts by psychological organizations and governmental bodies, especially in North America, to promote the recruitment, graduation, and employment of women and members of ethnic minorities in psychology.

Approaches to Psychology

Diversity among psychologists can also be seen in the different ways in which they think about, study, and try to change behaviour and mental processes. Suppose that you are a psychologist, and you want to know why some people stop to help a sick or injured stranger and others just keep walking. Where would you start? You could look for answers in people's brain cells and hormones; in their genetic background; in their personality traits; and in what they have learned from family, friends, and cultural traditions, to name just a few possibilities. With so many research directions available, you'd have to decide which sources of information were most likely to explain helping behaviour.

Psychologists have to make the same kinds of decisions, not only about where to focus their research but also about what kind of treatment methods to use, or what services to provide to schools, businesses, government agencies, or other clients. Their decisions are guided mainly by their overall *approach* to psychology—that is, by the assumptions, questions, and methods they believe will be most helpful in their work. The approaches we described earlier as structuralism and functionalism are gone now, but the psychodynamic and behavioural approaches remain, along with others known as biological, evolutionary, cognitive, and humanistic approaches. Some psychologists adopt just one of these approaches, but most psychologists are *eclectic.* This means that they blend assumptions and methods from two or more approaches in an effort to more fully understand behaviour and mental processes (e.g., Cacioppo et al., 2000). Today, some approaches to psychology are more influential than others, but we should review the main features of all of them to help you understand how they differ and how they have affected psychologists' work over the years.

The Biological Approach As its name implies, the **biological approach** to psychology assumes that behaviour and mental processes are largely shaped by biological processes. Psychologists who take this approach study the psychological effects of hormones, genes, and the activity of the nervous system, especially the brain. So if they are studying memory, they might try to identify the changes taking place in the brain as information is stored there (Figure 7.19, in the chapter on memory, shows an example of these changes). Or if they are studying thinking, they might look for patterns of brain activity associated with, say, making quick decisions or reading a foreign language.

Research discussed in nearly every chapter of this book reflects the enormous influence of the biological approach on psychology today. To help you better understand the terms and concepts used in that research, we have included an appendix on the principles of genetics and a chapter on biological aspects of psychology.

biological approach An approach to psychology in which behaviour and behaviour disorders are seen as the result of physical processes, especially those relating to the brain and to hormones and other chemicals.

The Evolutionary Approach Biological processes also figure prominently in an approach to psychology based on Charles Darwin's book *The Origin of Species.* Darwin argued that the forms of life we see today are the result of *evolution*—of changes in life forms that occur over many generations. He said that evolution occurs through *natural selection,* which promotes the survival of the fittest individuals. Most evolutionists now see natural selection operating at the level of genes, but at either level, the process is the same. Genes that result in characteristics and behaviours that are adaptive and useful in a certain environment will enable the creatures that inherited them to survive and reproduce, thereby passing those genes on to the next generation. Genes that result in characteristics that are not adaptive in that environment are not passed on to subsequent generations, because the creatures possessing them don't survive to reproduce. So evolutionary theory says that many (but not all) of the genes we possess today are the result of natural selection.

The **evolutionary approach** to psychology assumes that the *behaviour* of animals and humans today is also the result of evolution through natural selection. Psychologists who take this approach see aggression, for example, as a form of territory protection and they see gender differences in mate-selection preferences as reflecting different ways of helping one's genes to survive in future generations. The evolutionary approach has generated a growing body of research (Buss, 2004; Cosmides & Tooby, 2004). In later chapters, you will see how it is applied in relation to topics such as helping and altruism, mental disorders, temperament, and interpersonal attraction.

The Psychodynamic Approach The **psychodynamic approach** to psychology offers a different slant on the role of inherited instincts and other biological forces in human behaviour. Rooted in Freud's psychoanalysis, this approach assumes that our behaviour and mental processes reflect constant, and mostly unconscious, psychological struggles raging within each person (see Figure 1.5). Usually, these struggles involve conflict between the impulse to satisfy instincts (such as aggression or for food or sex) and the need to follow the rules of civilized society. Psychologists taking the psychodynamic approach would see aggression, for example, as a case of primitive urges overcoming a person's defenses against expressing those urges. They would see anxiety, depression, or other disorders as overt signs of inner turmoil.

A Father's Love Mothers are solely responsible for the care and protection of their offspring in almost all species of mammals. These species survive without male involvement in parenting, so why are some human fathers so involved in child rearing? Do evolutionary forces make fathering more adaptive for humans? Is it a matter of learning to care? Is it a combination of both? Psychologists who take an evolutionary approach study these questions and others relating to the origins of human social behaviour (Buss, 2004).

evolutionary approach An approach to psychology that emphasizes the inherited, adaptive aspects of behaviour and mental processes.

psychodynamic approach A view developed by Freud that emphasizes the interplay of unconscious mental processes in determining human thought, feelings, and behaviour.

figure 1.5

What Do You See?
Take a moment to jot down what you see in these clouds. According to the psychodynamic approach to psychology, what we see in cloud formations and other vague patterns reflects unconscious wishes, impulses, fears, and other mental processes. In the personality chapter, we discuss the value of personality tests based on this assumption.

Freud's original theories are not as influential today as they once were, but you will encounter modern versions of the psychodynamic approach in other chapters when we discuss theories of personality, psychological disorders, and psychotherapy.

The Behavioural Approach The assumptions of the **behavioural approach** to psychology contrast sharply with those of the psychodynamic, biological, and evolutionary approaches. As founded by John Watson, behaviourism characterizes behaviour as primarily the result of *learning*. From a strict behaviourist point of view, biological, genetic, and evolutionary factors simply provide "raw material" that is then shaped by learning experiences into what we see in each individual's actions. So, strict behaviourists seek to understand all behaviour—whether it is aggression or drug abuse, shyness or sociability, confidence or anxiety—by looking at the individual's learning history, especially the patterns of reward and punishment the person has experienced. They also believe that people can change problematic behaviours, from overeating to criminality, by unlearning old habits and developing new ones.

Many of today's behaviourists have broadened their approach to include attention to people's thoughts, or cognitions, as well as their overt behaviour. Those who take this *cognitive-behavioural,* or *social-cognitive,* approach explore how learning affects the development of thoughts, attitudes, and beliefs and, in turn, how these learned cognitive patterns affect overt behaviour.

The Cognitive Approach The growth of the cognitive-behavioural perspective reflects the influence of a broader cognitive approach to psychology. The **cognitive approach** focuses on how we take in, mentally represent, and store information; how we perceive and process that information; and how cognitive processes are related to our behaviour. In other words, psychologists who take the cognitive approach study the rapid series of hidden mental events—including those taking place outside of awareness—that accompany the behaviour they can see. Here is how a psychologist might use the cognitive approach to describe the information processing that occurs during an aggressive incident outside a movie theatre: The aggressive person (1) *perceives* that someone has butt into the ticket line, (2) *recalls* information stored in memory about appropriate social behaviour, (3) *decides* that the other person's action was inappropriate, (4) *labels* the person as rude and

behavioural approach An approach to psychology that emphasizes that human behaviour is determined mainly by what a person has learned, especially from rewards and punishments.

cognitive approach A way of looking at human behaviour that emphasizes research on how the brain takes in information, creates perceptions, forms and retrieves memories, processes information, and generates integrated patterns of action.

Why Is He So Aggressive?
Psychologists who take the cognitive-behavioural approach suggest that children's aggressiveness is largely learned. They say this learning occurs partly through seeing family and friends acting aggressively, but also through hearing people talk about aggression as the only way to deal with disagreements (e.g., Pettit & Dodge, 2003).

inconsiderate, (5) *considers* possible responses and their likely consequences, (6) *decides* that shoving the person is the best response, and (7) *executes* that response.

Psychologists who take a cognitive approach focus on these and other mental processes to understand many kinds of individual and social behaviours, from decision making and problem solving to interpersonal attraction and intelligence, to name but a few. In the situation we just described, for example, the person's aggression would be seen as the result of poor problem solving, because there were probably several better ways to deal with the problem of butting into a line. Cognitive psychologists are working with researchers from computer science, the biological sciences, engineering, linguistics, philosophy, and other disciplines in a multidisciplinary field called *cognitive science*. Together, they are trying to discover the building

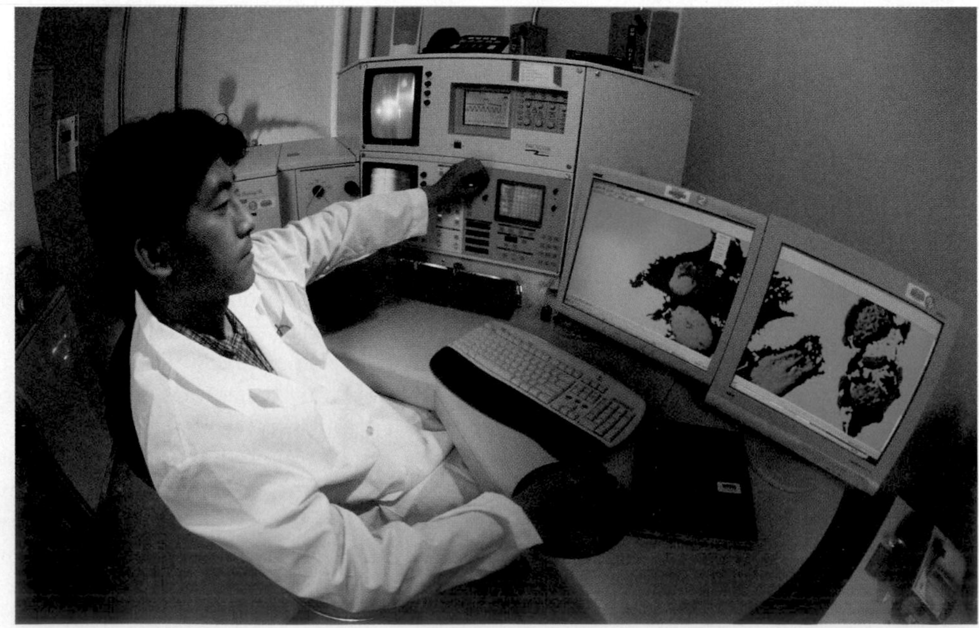

Cognitive Science at Work
Psychologists and other cognitive scientists are working on a "computational theory of the mind" in which they create computer programs that simulate how humans process information. In the chapter on cognition and language, we discuss their progress in creating "artificial intelligence" in computers that can help make medical diagnoses and perform other complex cognitive tasks.

blocks of cognition and to determine how these components produce complex behaviours such as remembering a fact, naming an object, writing a word, or making a decision.

The Humanistic Approach Mental events play a different role in the **humanistic approach** to psychology (also known as the *phenomenological approach*). Psychologists who favour the humanistic perspective see behaviour as determined primarily by each person's capacity to choose how to think and act. They don't see these choices as driven by instincts, biological processes, or rewards and punishments, but by each individual's unique perceptions of the world. So if you see the world as a friendly place, you are likely to be optimistic and secure. If you perceive it as full of hostile, threatening people, you will probably be defensive and fearful.

Like their cognitively oriented colleagues, psychologists who choose the humanistic approach would see aggression in a theatre queue as stemming from a perception that aggression is justified. But where the cognitive approach leads psychologists to search for laws governing *all* people's thoughts and actions, humanistic psychologists try to understand how each individual's unique experiences guide *that* person's thoughts and actions. In fact, many proponents of the humanistic approach say that behaviour and mental processes can be fully understood only by understanding the perceptions and feelings of individuals. Humanistic psychologists also believe that people are essentially good, that they are in control of themselves, and that they have an innate tendency to grow toward their highest potential.

The humanistic approach began to attract attention in North America in the 1940s through the writings of Carl Rogers (1902–1987), a psychologist who had been trained in, but later rejected, the psychodynamic approach. We describe his views on personality and his psychotherapy methods in the chapters on personality and the treatment of psychological disorders. Abraham Maslow (1908–1970) also shaped and promoted the humanistic approach through his famous hierarchy-of-needs theory of motivation, which we describe in the chapters on motivation and emotion and personality. Today, however, the impact of the humanistic approach to psychology is limited, mainly because many psychologists find humanistic concepts and predictions too vague to be expressed and tested scientifically. (For a summary of the approaches we have discussed, see "In Review: Approaches to Psychology.")

in review Approaches to Psychology

Approach	Characteristics
Biological	Emphasizes activity of the nervous system, especially of the brain; the action of hormones and other chemicals; and genetics.
Evolutionary	Emphasizes the ways in which behaviour and mental processes are adaptive for survival.
Psychodynamic	Emphasizes internal conflicts, mostly unconscious, that usually pit sexual or aggressive instincts against environmental obstacles to their expression.
Behavioural	Emphasizes learning, especially each person's experience with rewards and punishments.
Cognitive	Emphasizes mechanisms through which people receive, store, retrieve, and otherwise process information.
Humanistic	Emphasizes individual potential for growth and the role of unique perceptions in guiding behaviour and mental processes.

humanistic approach An approach to psychology that views behaviour as controlled by the decisions that people make about their lives based on their perceptions of the world.

Human Diversity and Psychology

A final aspect of diversity in psychology lies in the wide range of people psychologists study and serve. This was not always the case, because most psychologists once assumed that all people are very much alike and that whatever principles emerged from research or treatment efforts with one group would apply to everyone, everywhere. They were partly right, because people around the world *are* alike in many ways. They tend to live in groups; have religious beliefs; and create rules, music, dances, and games. The principles of nerve cell activity or reactions to heat or a sour taste are the same in men and women everywhere, as is their recognition of a smile. But are all people's moral values, achievement motivation, or communication styles the same, too? Would the results of research on white male college students in Ontario apply to Aboriginal women or to people in Greece, Korea, Argentina, or Egypt? Not always. These and many other aspects of behaviour and mental processes are affected by *sociocultural factors,* including people's gender, ethnicity, social class, and the culture in which they grow up (Miller, 2002). These variables create many significant differences in behaviour and mental processes, especially from one culture to another (e.g., Kitayama & Uchida, 2003; Shiraev & Levy, 2004).

Culture has been defined as the accumulation of values, rules of behaviour, forms of expression, religious beliefs, occupational choices, and the like for a group of people who share a common language and environment (Fiske et al., 1998). Culture is an organizing and stabilizing influence. It encourages or discourages particular behaviours and thoughts; it also allows people to understand and know what to expect from others in that culture. It is a kind of group adaptation, passed along by tradition and example rather than by genes from one generation to the next (Castro & Toro, 2004). Culture determines, for example, whether children's education will focus on skill at hunting or reading, how close people stand during a conversation, and whether or not they form lines in public places.

Psychologists and anthropologists have found that cultures can differ in many ways (Abi-Hashem, 2000; Triandis, 1998). They may have strict or loose rules governing social behaviour. They might place great value on achievement or on self-awareness. Some seek dominance over nature; others seek harmony with it. Time is of great importance in some cultures, but not in others. Psychologists have tended to focus on the differences between cultures that can best be described as individualist or collectivist (Triandis & Trafimow, 2001). As shown in Table 1.3, many people in *individualist* cultures, such as those typical of North America and Western Europe, tend to value personal rather than group goals and achievement. Competitiveness to distinguish oneself from others is common in these cultures, as is a sense of isolation. By contrast, many people in *collectivist* cultures, such as Japan, tend to think of themselves mainly as part of family or work groups. Cooperative effort aimed at advancing the welfare of such groups is highly valued and, although loneliness is seldom a problem, fear of rejection by the group is common.

A culture is often associated with a particular country, but most countries are actually *multicultural.* In other words, they host many *subcultures* within their borders. Often, these subcultures are formed by people of various ethnic origins. The population of Canada, for instance, includes both First Nations peoples and those of African or Asian descent, as well as people of European background whose families came from Italy, Germany, Britain, Poland, Ireland, and many other places (see Figure 1.6). In each of these groups, the individuals who identify with their cultural heritage tend to share behaviours, values, and beliefs based on their culture of origin, thus forming a subculture.

Like fish unaware of the water in which they are immersed, people often fail to notice how their culture or subculture has shaped their patterns of thinking and behaviour until they come in contact with people whose culture or subculture

culture The accumulation of values, rules of behaviour, forms of expression, religious beliefs, occupational choices, and the like for a group of people who share a common language and environment.

table 1.3

Some Characteristics of Behaviour and Mental Processes Typical of Individualist Versus Collectivist Cultures

Variable	Individualist	Collectivist
Personal identity	Separate from others	Connected to others
Major goals	Self-defined, be unique, realize your personal potential, compete with others	Defined by others, belong, occupy your proper place, meet your obligations to others, be like others
Criteria for self-esteem	Ability to express unique aspects of the self, ability to be self-assured	Ability to restrain the self and be part of a social unit, ability to be modest
Sources of success and failure	Success comes from personal effort; failure, from external factors	Success is due to help from others, failure is due to personal faults
Major frame of reference	Personal attitudes, traits, and goals	Family, work group

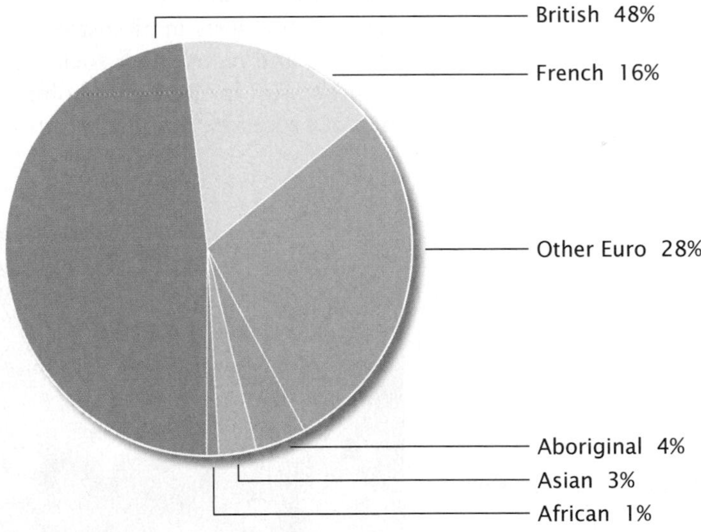

figure 1.6

Cultural Diversity in Canada

The people of Canada represent a wide array of cultural backgrounds, adding both richness and challenge to our national character. Since before Confederation in 1867, the English-French language issue has remained a contentious issue. Talk of "distinct societies" and provincial separation can spur either resentment and mistrust or nationalism and unity. You might recall television hockey announcer Don Cherry's slander of Francophone hockey players choosing to wear protective visors, a controversial comment that prompted many Canadians to consider whether it was time for the commentator to step down.

Whereas many other countries are also multicultural, this fact becomes obvious to outsiders only when conflicts flare among a country's subcultures, as they have in Iraq, Afghanistan, Rwanda, Yemen, Bosnia, India, Pakistan, and Indonesia, to name a few.[1] Closer to home, we have seen conflicts and protests concerning Native rights regarding fishing in New Brunswick, land titles in Ontario and British Columbia, and law enforcement in Quebec and Saskatchewan.

[1] *Source:* Statistics Canada (2005)

has shaped different patterns. For example, a Canadian teaching in Korea discovered that some people there believe it is in poor taste to write a student's name in red ink (Stevens, 1999). He was told that doing so conveys a prediction or wish that the person will die, because red ink was traditionally used to record names in official death registers. Similarly, the "thumbs-up" sign means that "everything is OK" to people in North America and Europe, but it is considered a rude gesture in Australia. Even some of the misunderstandings that occur between men and women in the same culture can be traced to slight culturally influenced differences in their communication styles (Tannen, 1994). Here in Canada, for example, many women's efforts to connect with others by talking are perceived by some men as "pointless" unless the discussion is aimed at solving a specific problem. As a result, women may feel frustrated and misunderstood by men who offer well-intentioned but unwanted advice instead of conversation.

Psychologists and anthropologists have noticed that cultures can create certain general tendencies in behaviour and mental processes among the people living in them (Bhagat et al., 2002). As shown here, individualist cultures tend to support the idea of placing one's personal goals before the goals of the extended family or work group, whereas collectivist cultures tend to encourage putting the goals of those groups ahead of personal goals. Remember, however, that these labels represent very rough categories. Cultures cannot be pigeonholed as being either entirely individualist or entirely collectivist, and not everyone raised in a particular culture always thinks or acts in exactly the same way (Oyserman, Coon, & Kemmelmeier, 2002).

For decades, the impact of culture on behaviour and mental processes was mainly of concern to a relatively small group of researchers working in *cross-cultural psychology* (Miller, 2002). In the chapters to come, however, you will see that psychologists in almost every subfield are now looking at how ethnicity, gender, age, and many other sociocultural variables can influence behaviour and mental processes. In short, psychology is striving to be the science of *all* behaviour and mental processes, not just of those in the cultures where it began.

The Impact of Culture Culture helps shape almost every aspect of our behaviour and mental processes, from how we dress to how we think to what we believe is important. Because we grow up immersed in our culture, we may be unaware of its influence on our own thoughts and actions until—like these young women who immigrated from Africa to Denmark—they encounter people whose culture has shaped them in different ways (Nisbett & Masuda, 2003).

SUMMARY

Psychology is the science that seeks to understand behaviour and mental processes and to apply that understanding in the service of human welfare.

The World of Psychology: An Overview

The concept of "behaviour and mental processes" is a broad one, encompassing virtually all aspects of what it means to be a human being.

Subfields of Psychology

Because the subject matter of psychology is so diverse, most psychologists work in particular subfields within the discipline. For example, *biological psychologists,* also called physiological psychologists, study topics such as the role played by the brain in regulating normal and disordered behaviour. *Developmental psychologists* specialize in trying to understand the development of behaviour and mental processes over a lifetime. *Cognitive psychologists,* some of whom prefer to be called *experimental psychologists,* focus on basic psychological processes such as learning, memory, and perception; they also study judgment, decision making, and problem solving. *Engineering psychology,* the study of human factors in the use of equipment, helps designers create better versions of that equipment. *Personality psychologists* focus on characteristics that set people apart from one another. *Clinical psychologists* and *counselling psychologists* provide direct service to troubled people and conduct research on abnormal behaviour. *Community psychologists* work to prevent mental disorders and to extend mental health services to those who need them. *Health psychologists* study the relationship between behaviour and health and help promote healthy lifestyles. *Educational psychologists* conduct and apply research on teaching and learning, whereas *school psychologists* specialize in assessing and alleviating children's academic problems. *Social psychologists* examine questions regarding how people influence one another. *Industrial/organizational psychologists* study ways to increase efficiency and productivity in the workplace. *Quantitative psychologists* develop ways to analyze research data from all subfields. *Sport psychologists, forensic psychologists,* and *environmental psychologists* exemplify some of psychology's many other subfields.

Linkages Within Psychology and Beyond

Psychologists often work in more than one subfield and usually share knowledge with colleagues in many subfields. Psychologists also draw on, and contribute to, knowledge in other disciplines, such as computer science, economics, and law.

Research: The Foundation of Psychology

Psychologists use the methods of science to conduct research. This means that they perform experiments and use other scientific procedures to systematically gather and analyze information about psychological phenomena.

A Brief History of Psychology

Rationalists like Plato and Descartes helped to call on the utility of reason and logic to solve problems and derive hypotheses. This form of *knowledge* appeared to be inborn. Empiricists like Aristotle and Locke used experimentation and observation to test those hypotheses. The founding of modern psychology is usually marked as 1879, when Wilhelm Wundt established the first psychology research laboratory. Wundt studied consciousness in a manner that was expanded by Edward Titchener into an approach he called structuralism. It was in the late 1800s, too, that Freud, in Vienna, began his study of the unconscious, while in the United States, William James took the functionalist approach, suggesting that psychologists should study how consciousness helps us adapt to our environments. In 1913, John B. Watson founded behaviourism, arguing that to be scientific, psychologists should study only the behaviour they can see, not private mental events. Behaviourism dominated psychology for decades, but psychologists are once again studying consciousness in the form of cognitive processes.

Unity and Diversity in Psychology

Psychologists are unified by their commitment to empirical research and scientific methods, by their linked interests, and by the legacy of psychology's founders, but they are diverse in their backgrounds, in their activities, and in the approaches they take to their work. Most of the prominent figures in psychology's early history were white males, but women and members of minority groups made important contributions from the start and continue to do so.

Approaches to Psychology

Psychologists differ in their approaches to psychology—that is, in their assumptions, questions, and research methods. Some adopt just one approach; many others combine features of two or more approaches. Those adopting a *biological approach* focus on how physiological processes shape behaviour and mental processes. Psychologists who prefer the *evolutionary approach* emphasize the inherited, adaptive aspects of behaviour and mental processes. In the *psychodynamic approach,* behaviour and mental processes are seen as reflecting struggles to resolve conflicts between raw impulses and the rules of society that limit the expression of those impulses. Psychologists who take the *behavioural approach* view behaviour as determined primarily by learning based on experiences with rewards and punishments. The *cognitive approach* assumes that behaviour can be understood through analysis of the basic mental processes that underlie it. To those adopting the *humanistic approach,* behaviour is controlled by the decisions that people make about their lives based on their perceptions of the world.

Human Diversity and Psychology

Psychologists are increasingly taking into account the influence of culture and other sociocultural variables such as gender and ethnicity in shaping human behaviour and mental processes.

2 Research in Psychology

Our goal in this chapter is to describe the research methods psychologists use to help answer their questions about behaviour and mental processes. We will also describe the critical thinking processes that help psychologists to form those questions and to make sense of research results. We have organized our presentation as follows:

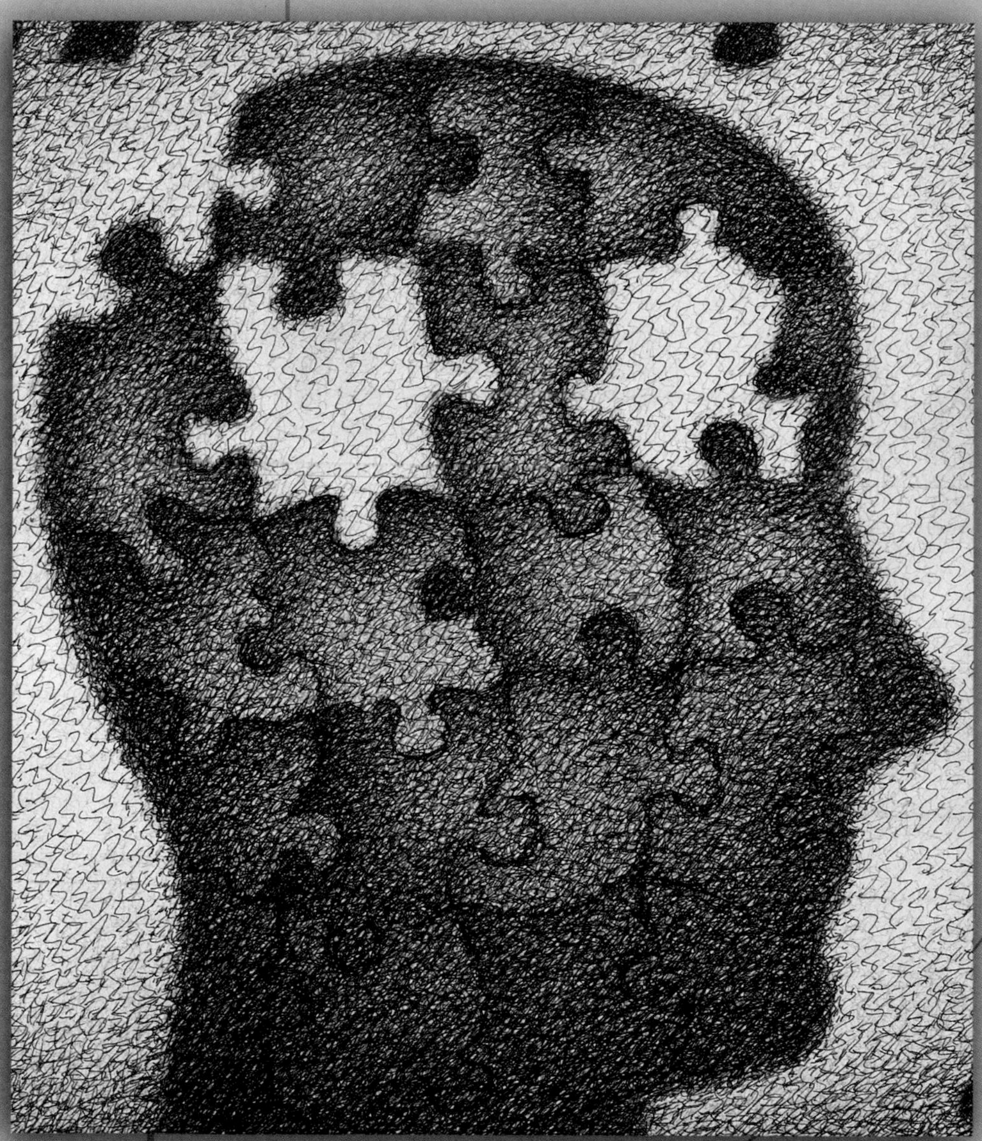

Francine Shapiro, a clinical psychologist in northern California, had an odd experience while taking a walk one day in 1987. She had been thinking about some distressing events when she noticed that her emotional reaction to them was fading away (Shapiro, 1989a). In trying to figure out why this should be, she recalled that she had been moving her eyes from side to side. Could these eye movements have caused the change in her emotions? To test this possibility, she made more deliberate eye movements and found that the emotion-reducing effect was even stronger. Was this a fluke, or would the same thing happen to others? Curious, she first tested the effects of side-to-side eye movements with friends and colleagues, and then with clients who had suffered traumatic experiences such as sexual abuse, military combat, or rape. She asked these people to think about unpleasant experiences in their lives while keeping their eyes on her finger as she moved it rapidly back and forth in front of them. Like her, they found that during and after these eye movement sessions, their reactions to unpleasant thoughts faded away. Most notably, her clients reported that their emotional flashbacks, nightmares, fears, and other trauma-related problems had decreased dramatically (Shapiro, 1989a).

Based on the success of these cases, Shapiro developed a treatment method she calls *eye movement desensitization and reprocessing,* or EMDR (Shapiro, 1991, 2001, 2002). She and her associates at EMDR Institute, Inc., have now trained more than 30,000 therapists in 52 countries to use EMDR in the treatment of an ever-widening range of anxiety-related problems in adults and children, from phobias and post-traumatic stress disorder to marital conflicts and skin rashes (Beaulieu, 2003; Gupta & Gupta, 2002; Maxwell, 2003; Shapiro & Maxfield, 2002; Sikes & Sikes, 2003).

Suppose you had an anxiety-related problem. Would the increased use of EMDR be enough to convince you to spend your own money on it? If not, what would you want to know about EMDR before deciding? As a cautious person, you would probably ask some of the same questions that have occurred to many scientists in psychology: Are the effects of EMDR caused by the treatment itself, or by the faith that clients might have in any new and impressive treatment? And are EMDR's effects faster, stronger, and longer lasting than those of other treatments?

Raising tough questions about cause and effect, quality, and value is part of the process of *critical thinking*. Whether you are choosing a therapy method or an Internet service, a college or a stereo, a political candidate or a mobile phone plan, critical thinking can guide you to ask the kinds of questions that lead to informed decisions. But asking good questions is not enough; you also have to try answering them. Critical thinking helps here, too, by prompting you to do some research on each of your options. For most people, this means asking the advice of friends or relatives, reading *Consumer Reports* or the *Canadian Consumer Handbook,* surfing the Internet, studying a candidate's background, or the like. For psychologists, research means using scientific methods to gather information about behaviour and mental processes.

In this chapter, we summarize five questions that emerge when thinking critically about behaviour and mental processes. Then we describe the scientific methods psychologists use in their research and show how some of those methods have been applied in evaluating EMDR.

Thinking Critically About Psychology (or Anything Else)

Ask several friends and relatives if mental patients become more agitated when the moon is full, if psychics help the police solve crimes, and if people have suddenly burst into flames for no reason. They will probably agree with at least one of these statements, even though not one of them is true (see Table 2.1). Perhaps you already knew that, but don't feel too smug. At one time or another, we all accept things we are told simply because the information seems to come from a reliable source or because "everyone knows" it is true (Losh et al., 2003). If this were not the case,

table 2.1
Some Popular Myths

Many people believe in the statements listed here, but critical thinkers who take the time to investigate them will discover that they are not true.

Myth	Fact
Many children are injured each year when razor blades, needles, or poison is put in Halloween candy.	Reported cases are rare, most turn out to be hoaxes, and, in the only documented case of a child dying from poisoned candy, the culprit was the child's own parent (Brunvald, 1989). Jeffrey Derevensky of McGill University says that the distribution of candy that has been tampered with "is a relatively rare occurrence but, still, as parents you want to try [to] protect your children as much as possible." (Moore, 2005)
If your roommate commits suicide during the school term, you automatically get A's in all your classes for that term.	No college or university anywhere has ever had such a rule.
People have been known to burst into flames and die from fire erupting within their own bodies.	In rare cases, humans have been consumed by fires that caused little or no damage to the surrounding area. However, this phenomenon has not been duplicated in a laboratory, and each alleged case of "spontaneous human combustion" has been traced to an external source of ignition (Benecke, 1999; Nienhuys, 2001).
Most big-city police departments rely on the advice of psychics to help them solve murders, kidnappings, and missing persons cases.	"It's not an investigative practice for the police service to use psychics." (Constable Murray Cowan of Estevan, Saskatchewan) (*Court TV*, 2005) Very few police departments ever seek psychics' advice, and the advice is seldom more helpful than other means of investigation (Nickell, 1997; Wiseman, West, & Stemman, 1996).
Murders, suicides, animal bites, and episodes of mental disorder are more likely to occur when the moon is full.	Records of crimes, dog bites, and mental hospital admissions do not support this common belief (Bickis, Kelly, & Byrnes, 1995; Chapman & Morrell, 2000; Rotton & Kelly, 1985).
You can't fool a lie detector.	John Furedy of the University of Toronto believes that "Polygraph testing is no better than the reading of entrails" (McMillian, 2005). Michael Bradley of the University of New Brunswick has been attempting to improve the accuracy of lie detectors. The basic problem appears to be that the physiological responses measured by the polygraph are not unique to deception. (Sones & Sones, 2003; Bradley et al., 2004). (see the chapter on motivation and emotion).
Viewers never see David Letterman walking to his desk after the opening monologue because his contract prohibits him from showing his backside on TV.	When questioned about this story on the air, Letterman denied it and, to prove his point, lifted his jacket and turned a full circle in front of the cameras and studio audience (Brunvald, 1989).
Psychics have special abilities to see into the future.	Even the most famous psychics are almost always wrong, as in these predictions for the year 2004: "Osama bin Laden will die of kidney disease"; "Saddam Hussein will be shot to death"; "Fidel Castro will die"; "A live dinosaur thousands of years old will be captured." Not only were these psychics wrong—they often miss major events. "Although the psychics were always predicting things for Princess Diana, they completely missed her death." (Emery, 2004). Other predictions for 2004 included: "A gold rush north of Alberta; an attack on Niagara Falls; a quasi missile will hit North America; Mike Myers will build a movie studio in Toronto." (Nikki, 2004).
If you are stopped for drunken driving, sucking on a penny will cause a police Breathalyzer test to show you are sober.	"Drunk drivers kill an average of 4.5 people and injure 125 Canadians every 24 hours, each day, every day of the week." The Breathalyzer is one of many tools used by law enforcement agencies in the fight against drunk driving. Sucking on a penny cannot fool the Breathalyzer, nor can you fool it by gargling with mouth wash or chewing on candy. (*Be a Zero Hero: A Presenter's Guide to Ending Impaired Driving*, 2005). Unfortunately people will resort to extreme measures in order to foil a Breathalyzer. An Ontario man, for example, stuffed his mouth with his own feces. Needless to say, the trick didn't work. The machine still registered a level twice the legal limit (Robertson, 2005).

Uncritically accepting claims for the value of astrologers' predictions, "get-rich-quick" investment schemes, new therapies, or proposed government policies can be embarrassing, expensive, and dangerous. Critical thinkers carefully evaluate evidence for *and* against such claims before drawing a final conclusion.

DOONESBURY

advertisers, politicians, salespeople, social activists, and others who seek our money, our votes, or our loyalty would not be as successful as they are. These people want you to believe their promises or claims without careful thought. In other words, they don't want you to think critically.

Often, they get their wish. Millions of people waste billions of dollars every year on worthless predictions made by on-line and telephone "psychics"; on bogus cures for cancer, heart disease, and arthritis; on phony degrees offered by nonexistent Internet universities; and on "miracle" defrosting trays, eat-all-you-want weight-loss pills, "effortless" exercise gadgets, and other consumer products that simply don't work. Millions more are lost in investment scams and fraudulent charity appeals (Cassel & Bernstein, 2001).

Critical thinking is the process of assessing claims and making judgments on the basis of well-supported evidence (Wade, 1988). One way to apply critical thinking to EMDR—or to any other topic—is by asking the following five questions:

1. ***What am I being asked to believe or accept?*** In this case, the assertion to be examined is that EMDR reduces or eliminates anxiety-related problems.

2. ***What evidence is available to support the assertion?*** Shapiro experienced a reduction in her own emotional distress following certain kinds of eye movements. Later, she found the same effect in others.

3. ***Are there alternative ways of interpreting the evidence?*** The dramatic effects reported by Shapiro might not have been due to EMDR but to people's desire to overcome their problems or perhaps their desire to prove her right. And who knows? They might have eventually improved on their own, without any treatment. Even the most remarkable evidence can't automatically be accepted as proof of an assertion until other plausible alternatives such as these have been ruled out. The ruling-out process leads to the next step in critical thinking: conducting scientific research.

4. ***What additional evidence would help to evaluate the alternatives?*** The ideal method for collecting further evidence about the value of EMDR would be to identify three groups of people with anxiety-related problems who were alike in every way except for the anxiety treatment they received. One group would receive EMDR. A second group would get an equally motivating but useless treatment, and a third group would get no treatment at all. Now suppose the people in the EMDR group improved much more than those who got no treatment or the motivating, but useless, treatment. Results such as these would make it harder to explain away the improvements following EMDR as due to client motivation or the mere passage of time.

5. ***What conclusions are most reasonable?*** The research evidence collected so far has not yet ruled out alternative explanations for the effects of EMDR (for example, Goldstein et al., 2000; Lohr et al., 2003). And although those effects are often greater than the effects of no treatment at all, they appear to be no stronger than those of several other kinds of treatment (Davidson & Parker,

critical thinking The process of assessing claims and making judgments on the basis of well-supported evidence.

Taking Your Life in Your Hands? Does exposure to microwave radiation from mobile phone antennas cause brain tumors? Do the dangers of hormone replacement therapy (HRT) for postmenopausal women outweigh its benefits? And what about the value of herbal remedies, dietary supplements, and other controversial treatments for cancer, AIDS, and depression (Specter, 2004)? These questions generate intense speculation, strong opinions, and a lot of wishful thinking, but the answers ultimately depend on scientific research based on critical thinking. So, even though there is no conclusive evidence that mobile phones cause tumours, some scientists suggest there may be danger in long-term exposure (Lonn et al., 2004). Evidence that HRT may be related to breast cancer and heart disease led to the cancellation of a large clinical trial in the United States (Kolata, 2003), and scientists are calling for new research on the safety of the testosterone replacement therapy that about 50,000 Canadian men receive each year (Harmen et al., 2001 and Stats Canada, 1991).

2001; Ironson et al., 2002; Taylor et al., 2003). So the only reasonable conclusions to be drawn at this point are that (1) EMDR remains a controversial treatment, (2) it seems to have an impact on some clients, and (3) further research is needed in order to understand it.

Does that sound wishy-washy? True, critical thinking sometimes does seem to be indecisive thinking. Like everyone else, scientists in psychology would love to find quick, clear, and final answers to their questions, but the conclusions they reach have to be supported by evidence. So if the evidence about EMDR is limited in some way, conclusions about whether and why the treatment works have to be limited, too. In the long run, though, critical thinking opens the way to understanding. To help you sharpen your own critical thinking skills, we include in each chapter to come a section called "Thinking Critically," in which we examine an issue by asking the same five questions we raised here about EMDR.

Critical Thinking and Scientific Research

Scientific research often begins with questions born of curiosity, such as "Can eye movements reduce anxiety?" Like many seemingly simple questions, this one is more complex than it first appears. Are we talking about horizontal, vertical, or diagonal eye movements? How long do they continue in each session, and how many sessions should there be? What kind of anxiety is to be treated, and how will we measure improvement? In other words, scientists have to ask *specific* questions in order to get meaningful answers.

hypothesis In scientific research, a prediction stated as a specific, testable proposition about a phenomenon.

Psychologists and other scientists clarify their questions about behaviour and mental processes by phrasing them in terms of a **hypothesis**—a specific, testable

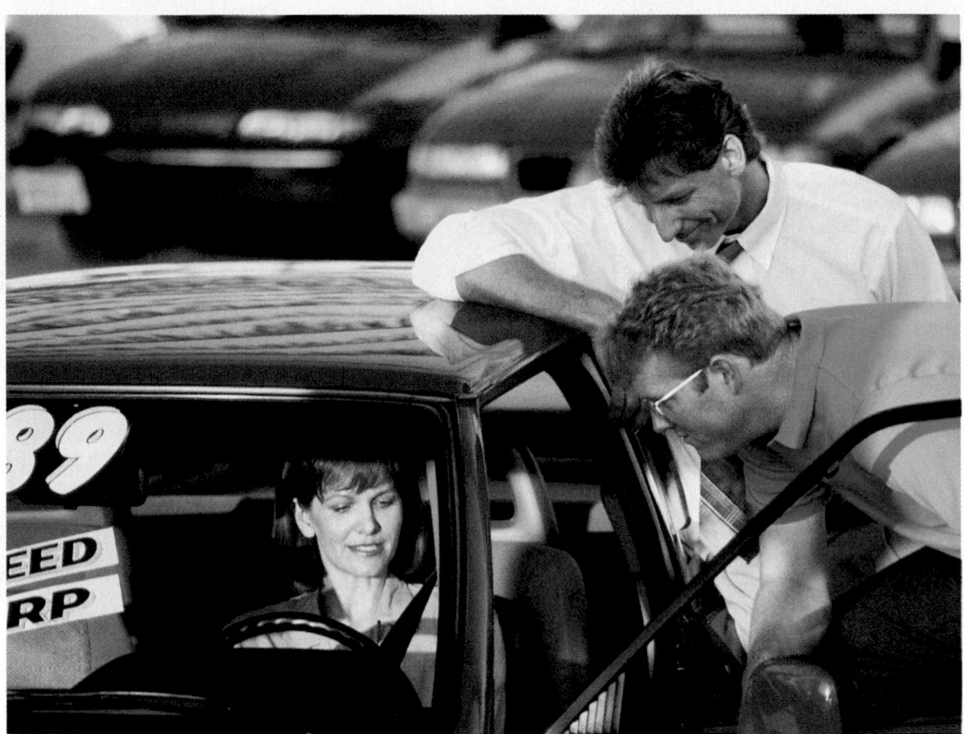

I Love It! When we want something—or someone—to be perfect, we may ignore all evidence to the contrary. This is one reason people end up in faulty used cars—or in bad relationships. Psychologists and other scientists use special procedures, such as the "double-blind" methods described in this chapter, to help keep confirmation bias from distorting the conclusions they draw from research evidence.

proposition about something they want to study. Hypotheses state in clear, precise words what researchers think may be true and how they will know if it is not. A hypothesis about EMDR might be: *EMDR treatment causes significant reduction in anxiety.* To make it easier to understand and evaluate their hypotheses, scientists employ **operational definitions**—descriptions of the exact operations or methods they will use in their research. In relation to our EMDR hypothesis, for example, "EMDR treatment" might be operationally defined as creating a certain number of side-to-side eye movements per second for a particular period of time. And "significant reduction in anxiety" might be operationally defined as a decline of 10 points or more on a test that measures clients' anxiety. The kind of treatment a client is given (say, EMDR versus no treatment) and the results of that treatment (the amount of anxiety reduction observed) are examples of research **variables,** the specific factors or characteristics that are manipulated and measured in research.

To determine whether a study's results provide support for a hypothesis, researchers look at the numbers or scores that represent client improvement or whatever other variables are of interest. This kind of evidence is called **data** (the plural of *datum*), or a *data set.* The data themselves are objective, and scientists try to be objective when interpreting them. But like all other human beings, scientists may sometimes pay a little more attention to numbers or scores that confirm their hypotheses, especially if they expect or hope that those hypotheses are true. This *confirmation bias* is described in the chapter on cognition and language. Scientists have a special responsibility to combat confirmation bias by looking for evidence that contradicts their hypotheses, not just for evidence that supports them.

Scientists must also consider the value of the evidence they collect. They usually do this by evaluating its reliability and validity. *Reliability* is the degree to which the data are stable and consistent. The *validity* of data is the degree to which they accurately represent the topic being studied. For example, the first evidence for EMDR was based on Shapiro's own experience with eye movements. If she had not been able to consistently repeat, or *replicate,* those initial effects in other people, she would have had to question the reliability of her data. And if her clients' reports of reduced anxiety were not supported by, say, their overt behaviour or the reports of their close relatives, she would have had to doubt the validity of her data.

operational definition A statement that defines the exact operations or methods used in research.

variable A factor or characteristic that is manipulated or measured in research.

data Facts and statistics/results that represent research findings and provide the basis for research conclusions.

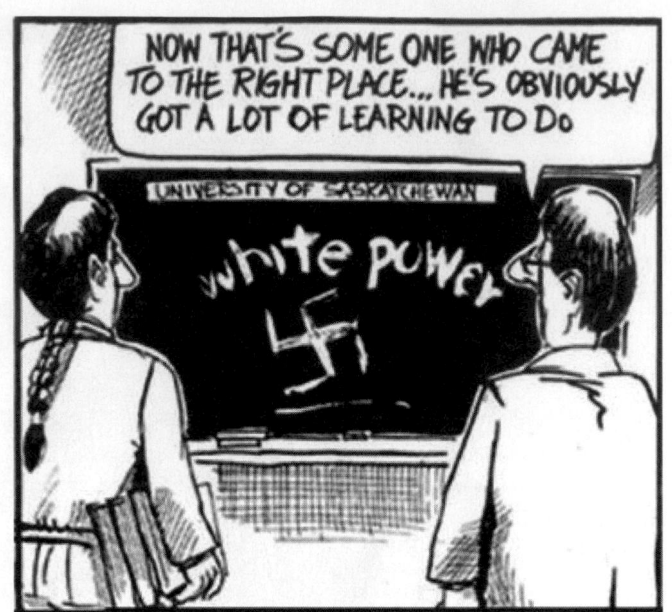

Where Does Prejudice Come From? It is all too easy these days to spot evidence of prejudice against almost any identifiable group, including Aboriginals, Muslims, Jews, Protestants, Catholics, Blacks, Hispanics, Asians, gays and lesbians, and even teenagers and the elderly. Researchers have proposed several theories about the causes of prejudice—and how to prevent it (see Chapter 17 on Social Behaviour). The testing of these theories by other researchers is an example of how theory and research go hand in hand. Without research results, there would be nothing to explain; without explanatory theories, the results might never be organized in a useful way. The knowledge generated by psychologists over the past 125 years has been based on this constant interaction of theory and research.

The Role of Theories

After examining research evidence, scientists may begin to favour certain explanations of why these results occurred. Sometimes they organize their explanations into a **theory,** which is a set of statements designed to account for, predict, and even suggest ways of controlling certain phenomena. For example, Shapiro's theory about the effects of EMDR suggests that eye movements activate parts of the brain in which information about trauma or other unpleasant experiences has been stored but never fully processed. EMDR, she says, promotes the "adaptive information processing" required for the elimination of certain anxiety-related emotional and behavioural problems (Shapiro, 1995, 2001, 2002). In the chapter on introducing psychology, we reviewed broader and more famous examples of explanatory theories, including Sigmund Freud's theory of psychoanalysis.

Theories are tentative explanations that must be subjected to scientific examination based on critical thinking. For example, Shapiro's theory about EMDR has been criticized as being vague, as lacking empirical support, and as being less plausible than other, simpler explanations (e.g., Herbert et al., 2000; Lohr et al., 2003). In other words, theories are based on research results, but they also generate hypotheses to be tested in further research. The predictions of one psychologist's theory will be evaluated by many other psychologists. If research does not support a theory, the theory will be revised or abandoned.

The process of creating, evaluating, and revising psychological theories does not always lead to a single "winner." You will discover in later chapters that there are several competing explanations for colour vision, memory, sleep, aggression, prejudice, and many other behaviours and mental processes. As research on these topics continues, explanations become more complete, and, sometimes, they change. So the conclusions we offer are always based on what is known so far, and we always cite the need for additional research. We do this because research often raises at least as many questions as it answers. The results of one study might not apply in every situation or to all people. A treatment might be effective for mild depression in women, for example, but it would have to be tested in more severe cases, and in both sexes, before drawing final conclusions about its value. Keep this point in mind the next time you hear a talk-show guest confidently offering simple solutions to complex problems such as obesity or anxiety, or presenting easy formulas for a happy marriage and perfect children. These self-proclaimed experts—called "pop" (for *popular*) psychologists by the scientific community—tend to oversimplify issues, to cite evidence for their views without con-

theory An integrated set of propositions that can be used to account for, predict, and even suggest ways of controlling certain phenomena.

cern for its reliability or validity, and to ignore good evidence that contradicts the pet theories that they live on.

Psychological scientists are much more cautious. They don't offer conclusions and recommendations, especially about complex behaviours and mental processes, until they have enough high-quality data to support what they say. And those data have allowed them to say a lot. Research in psychology has created an enormous body of knowledge that is being put to good use in many ways (Zimbardo, 2004). Psychologists in all subfields use current knowledge as the foundation for the research that will increase tomorrow's understanding of behaviour and mental processes. In the rest of this chapter, we describe their research methods and some of the pitfalls that lie in the path of progress toward their goals.

Research Methods in Psychology

Like other scientists, psychologists strive to achieve four main goals in their research: to *describe* behaviour and mental processes, to make accurate *predictions* about them, to demonstrate some *control* over them, and ultimately to *explain* how and why behaviour and mental processes occur. Consider depression, for example. Researchers in clinical psychology and other subfields have been involved in *describing* the nature, intensity, and duration of depressive symptoms, as well as the various kinds of depressive disorders that commonly appear in various cultures around the world. They are also studying the genetic characteristics, personality traits, life situations, and other factors that allow better *predictions* about those who are at the greatest risk for developing depressive disorders. In addition, clinical researchers have developed and tested a whole range of treatments designed to *control* depressive symptoms and even to prevent them from appearing in the first place. Finally, they have proposed a number of theories to *explain* depression, including why and how it occurs, why it is more common in women than in men, and why particular treatment methods are (or are not) likely to be effective.

Certain research methods are especially useful for reaching certain of these goals. For example, psychologists tend to use *naturalistic observation*, *case studies*, *surveys*, and *correlational studies* to describe and predict behaviour and mental processes. They use *experiments* to control and explain behaviour and mental processes. For example, Shapiro initially used naturalistic observation to describe the effects of eye movements on her emotional state. She then conducted case studies to test her prediction that, if the change in her emotions had something to do with eye movements, other people should have the same result. Later we discuss an experiment in which she tried to more systematically control people's emotional reactions and to evaluate various explanations for EMDR's apparent effects.

Let's take a closer look at how psychologists use these and other scientific research methods as they seek to describe, predict, control, and explain many kinds of behaviour and mental processes.

Naturalistic Observation: Watching Behaviour

Sometimes, the best way to describe behaviour is through **naturalistic observation,** which is the process of watching without interfering as behaviour occurs in the natural environment (Hoyle, Harris, & Judd, 2002). This method is especially valuable when more intrusive methods might alter the behaviour you want to study or create false impressions about it. If you ask people to keep track of how often they visit their local gym, they might begin to work out more than usual, thus providing an inaccurate picture of their typical behaviour. Similarly, if you ask people whether they wash their hands after using toilet facilities, 95 percent of them say they do; but naturalistic observations of 7836 people in public restrooms across the United States showed the true figure to be about 67 percent (American Society for Microbiology, 2000).

naturalistic observation The process of watching without interfering as a phenomenon occurs in the natural environment.

Little Reminders If you asked this person what he needs to use various computer programs efficiently, he might not think to mention the notes on his monitor that list all his log-in names and passwords. Accordingly, researchers in human factors and industrial/organizational psychology usually arrange to watch employees at work rather than just ask them what they do, how they do it, and how they interact with machines and fellow employees.

With proper permission, psychologists can observe people in many kinds of situations. For example, much of what we know about gender differences in how children play and communicate with each other has come from observations in classrooms and playgrounds. Jeff Small, of the University of British Columbia, has used observation in his study of Alzheimer's patients. He audio-taped caregivers as they engaged in conversations with people suffering from Alzheimer's disease in an attempt to ascertain the most effective form of communication. He has noticed that communication appears to be more effective when caregivers use yes/no rather than open-ended questions (Small and Perry, 2005). Observation can also be useful in the workplace. To understand the problems people encounter in doing their jobs, human-factors psychologists often find it helpful to observe employees as they work.

Although naturalistic observation can provide large amounts of useful research evidence, it is not problem free (Nietzel et al., 2003). For one thing, if people know they are being observed (and ethics usually requires that they do know), they tend to act differently than they otherwise would. Researchers usually combat this problem by observing long enough for participants to get used to the situation and begin behaving more naturally. Observational data can also be distorted if the observers expect to see certain behaviours. Suppose you were hired to watch videotapes of people who had just participated in a study of EMDR. Your job is to rate how anxious they appear to be, but if you knew which participants had received EMDR and which had not, you might tend to see the treated participants as less anxious, no matter how they actually behave. To get the most out of naturalistic observation, psychologists have to counteract problems such as these. So when conducting observational evaluations of treatment, for example, they don't tell the observers which participants have received treatment.

Case Studies: Taking a Closer Look

Observations are often an important part of **case studies,** which are intensive examinations of behaviour or mental processes in a particular individual, group, or situation. Case studies can also include tests; interviews; and the analysis of letters, school transcripts, or other written records. Case studies are especially useful when studying something that is new, complex, or relatively rare (Sacks, 2002). Shapiro's EMDR treatment, for example, first attracted psychologists' attention through case studies of its remarkable effects on her clients (Shapiro, 1989a).

Translating Naturalistic Observation into Data It is easy to observe people in natural situations, but it is not so easy to translate the observations into meaningful data. To make this translation process easier and more consistent, psychologists create coding systems that tell observers how to categorize the various kinds of behaviour that might occur during a live or videotaped observation session. Imagine that you are studying these children at play. Try creating your own coding system by making a list of the exact behaviours that you would count as "aggressive," "shy," "fearful," "cooperative," and "competitive."

case study A research method involving the intensive examination of some phenomenon in a particular individual, group, or situation.

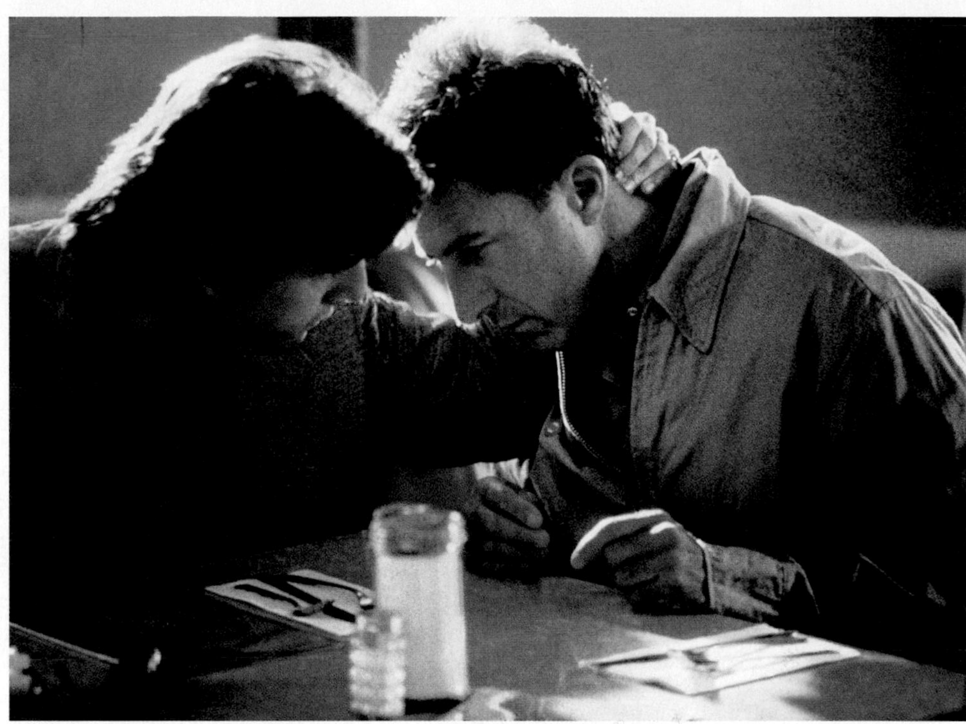

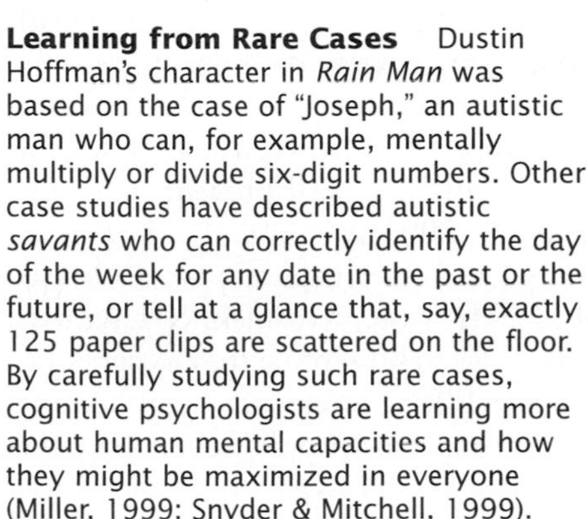

Learning from Rare Cases Dustin Hoffman's character in *Rain Man* was based on the case of "Joseph," an autistic man who can, for example, mentally multiply or divide six-digit numbers. Other case studies have described autistic *savants* who can correctly identify the day of the week for any date in the past or the future, or tell at a glance that, say, exactly 125 paper clips are scattered on the floor. By carefully studying such rare cases, cognitive psychologists are learning more about human mental capacities and how they might be maximized in everyone (Miller, 1999; Snyder & Mitchell, 1999).

In fact, case studies have a long tradition in clinical work. Freud's theory of psychoanalysis was largely developed from case studies of people whose paralysis or other physical symptoms disappeared when they were hypnotized or asleep. Case studies have also played a special role in *neuropsychology,* the study of the relationships among brain activity, thinking, and behaviour. Consider the case of HM, a patient described by Brenda Milner of the Montreal Neurological Institute. HM was suffering from severe epilepsy, a neurological condition that is caused by the abnormal firing of brain cells. In order to reduce his epileptic seizures, HM had undergone an operation in which parts of the temporal lobe on both sides of his brain were removed. After surgery, it became apparent that HM had difficulty remembering subsequent events. He couldn't, for example, ever remember meeting Dr. Milner even though he was part of her case study. Dr. Milner noticed, however, that HM's memories for events before the surgery appeared unaffected. The findings from this study were early evidence of the existence of multiple memory systems (Milner & Penfield, 1955).

Using case studies such as this one, pioneers in neuropsychology have found a common link between cases like HM's. It appears that most of these individuals have damage to an area of the brain known as the hippocampus. The hippocampus is often referred to as the "gateway to memory" and is believed to be involved in the formation of new memories (Milner, 2005). (For more information on the hippocampus see the chapter on the biological aspects of psychology.)

Case studies are even used by industrial/organizational psychologists. For example, an I/O psychologist might review documents, make observations, and conduct interviews with an employee team in order to understand how its members handled a production problem, an interpersonal conflict, or a change in company policy. Case studies would then help guide the psychologist's recommendations for how company executives might increase productivity, reduce stress, or improve communication with employees.

Case studies do have their limitations, however. They may contain only the evidence that a particular researcher considered important (Loftus & Guyer, 2002), and, of course, they are unlikely to be representative of people in general. Nonetheless, case studies can provide valuable raw material for further research. They can also be vital sources of information about particular people, and they serve as the testing ground for new treatments, training programs, and other applications of research (Tavris, 2004).

Surveys: Looking at the Big Picture

In contrast to the individual close-ups provided by case studies, surveys provide wide-angle views of large groups. In **surveys**, researchers use interviews or questionnaires to ask people about their behaviour, attitudes, beliefs, opinions, or intentions. Just as politicians and advertisers rely on opinion polls to test the popularity of policies or products, psychologists use surveys—conducted in person, through the mail, or even online—to gather descriptive data on just about anything related to behaviour and mental processes, from parenting practices to sexual behaviour. For example, a survey was conducted at St. Thomas University, in New Brunswick, in an attempt to assess the attitudes of military personnel toward other personnel suffering from post-traumatic stress disorder (PTSD)—an anxiety disorder that occurs when a person witnesses or is involved in a severely traumatic event. The results of the survey demonstrated that there was a negative attitude toward personnel suffering from PTSD (Fish, 2005). This negative attitude may well prevent personnel suffering from PTSD from seeking help (Hoge et al., 2004).

However, the validity of survey data depends partly on how questions are phrased and whether the wording is clear (Bhopal et al., 2004; Visser, Krosnick, & Lavrakas, 2000). In one survey at a health clinic, patients were asked how often they experienced headaches, stomach aches, and other symptoms of illness (Schwarz & Scheuring, 1992). If the question was worded so as to suggest that most people frequently experience such symptoms, the patients said that they frequently experienced them, too. But if the wording suggested that most people rarely have these symptoms, the patients said that they had them infrequently. For example, 75 percent of the patients said that the weather affected their health when the wording suggested that this was a common phenomenon, but only 21 percent said so when the wording suggested that this was an uncommon phenomenon. Were the people in the first group actually sicker than the people in the second? Probably not. It is more likely that they reported more symptoms because of the way the question was worded.

A survey's validity also depends on who is included in it. If the particular people surveyed do not represent the views of the population you are interested in, it is easy to be misled by survey results (Gosling et al., 2004; Kraut et al., 2004). If you were interested in Canadians' views on the prevalence of racial and ethnic prejudice, you would come to the wrong conclusion if you surveyed only people of colour or Canadians of northern European background. To get a complete picture, you would have to survey people of many ethnic backgounds so that each group's opinions could be fairly represented.

Designing Survey Research How do people feel about whether gay men and lesbians should have the right to legally marry? To appreciate the difficulties of survey research, try writing a question about this issue that you think is clear enough and neutral enough to generate valid data. Then ask some friends whether or not they agree it would be a good survey question and why.

survey A research method that involves giving people questionnaires or special interviews designed to obtain descriptions of their attitudes, beliefs, opinions, and intentions.

Other limitations of the survey method are more difficult to avoid. The results of surveys that ask people to say whether they cheat on exams, use illegal drugs, drive while drunk, or engage in other forms of socially disapproved or dangerous behaviour will probably underestimate the frequency of these behaviours. Even if they can't be personally identified, people may be reluctant to admit undesirable or embarrassing things about themselves. Or they might say what they think they *should* say about an issue. Further, suppose you send everyone in the phone book a questionnaire about raising local taxes. If those who are opposed to the tax increase are more likely to return their questionnaire, you will probably get an inaccurate view of public opinion (Visser et al., 2000). So survey results—and the conclusions drawn from them—can be distorted to the extent that these response tendencies and data collection problems occur (Hoyle et al., 2002). Still, surveys provide an efficient way to gather large amounts of data about people's attitudes, beliefs, or other characteristics.

Correlational Studies: Looking for Relationships

The data collected from naturalistic observations, case studies, and surveys provide valuable descriptions of behaviour and mental processes, but they can do more than that. These data can also be examined to see what they reveal about the relationships, or correlations, between one research variable and another. For example, surveys done for the Applied Research Branch of Human Resources Canada have shown that child hunger in Canada is directly related to a number of factors, one of which is family dysfunction. Specifically, increases in child hunger are more likely to occur in households where there is a dramatic and immediate decline in household income, usually associated with loss of a job (McIntyre et al., 2001). **Correlational studies** examine relationships between variables in order to describe research data more fully, to test predictions, to evaluate theories, and to suggest new hypotheses about why people think and act as they do.

Consider the question of how aggression develops. One theory suggests that people learn to be aggressive by seeing aggressiveness in others. Psychologists have tested this theory through correlational studies that focus on the relationship between children's aggressiveness and the amount of aggression they see on television. Just as the theory predicts, those who watch a lot of televised violence do tend to be more aggressive than other children. Another theory asserts that sexual aggressiveness in adults can be triggered by viewing pornography. And, in fact, correlational analyses of case studies and surveys show that sex criminals often view pornographic material just prior to committing their offenses. And correlational studies of observational data indicate that children in daycare for more than thirty hours a week are more aggressive than those who stay home with their mothers.

Do violent television, pornography, and separation from parents actually *cause* the various forms of aggressiveness with which they have been associated? They might, but psychologists must be careful about jumping to such conclusions. The most obvious explanation for the relationship found in a correlational study may not always be the correct one (see Table 2.2). Perhaps the correlation between aggression and violent television appears because children who were the most aggressive in the first place are also the ones who choose to watch the most violent television. Perhaps sex offenders exaggerate the role of pornography in their crimes because they hope to avoid taking responsibility for those crimes. And perhaps the aggressiveness seen among some children in daycare might have something to do with the children themselves or with what happens to them in daycare, not just with separation from their parents.

One way psychologists evaluate hypotheses such as these is to conduct further correlational studies in which they look for trends in observational, case study, and survey data that support or conflict with those hypotheses. Further analysis of daycare research, for example, shows that the aggressiveness seen in preschoolers who spend a lot of time in daycare is the exception, not the rule. Most children don't exhibit any behaviour problems, no matter how much time they have spent in daycare. This more

correlational study A research method that examines relationships between variables in order to analyze trends in data, to test predictions, to evaluate theories, and to suggest new hypotheses.

table 2.2
Correlation and Causation

Look at the correlations described in the left-hand column, then ask yourself why the two variables in each case are related. Could one variable be causing an effect on the other? If so, which variable is the cause, and how might it exert its effect? Could the relationship between the two variables be caused by a third one? If so, what might that third variable be? We suggest some possible explanations in the right-hand column. Can you think of still others?

Correlation	Possible Explanations
The number of reported cases of drownings varies during the year as does the amount of ice cream sold each month.	This relationship probably reflects a third variable—time of year—that affects both ice-cream consumption and the likelihood of swimming and boating (Brenner et al., 2001).
In Canada, the rate of criminal violence increases with the number of reported cases of parricide (the murder of a close relative) (cf. Marleau and Webanck, 1997).	This may suggest that some of the factors that influence violent crime also influence parricide. In the United States, however, the reverse is true. Increases in criminal violence are related to a decrease in parricides (cf. Young, 1993).
A recent study found that the more antibiotics a woman has taken, and the longer she has taken them, the greater is her risk of developing breast cancer (Velicer et al., 2004).	Long-term antibiotic use might have impaired the women's immune systems, but the cancer risk might also have been increased by the diseases that were being treated with antibiotic drugs, not the drugs themselves. Obviously, much more research would be required before condemning the use of antibiotics.
Past studies have revealed a relationship between socio-economic status and health. It appears that the lower the socio-economic status, the greater the number of health-related problems reported.	Louise Lemyre of Ottawa University is seeking to understand the relationship between socio-economic status and health. She has conducted a study which suggests that a third variable, psychosocial stress, may also be a factor. Stress is known to have a negative impact on one's overall health, and psychosocial stressors are more frequently reported by people in lower socio-economic groups (cf. Orpana & Lemyre, 2004).

general trend suggests that whatever effect separation has, it may be different for different children in different settings, causing some to express aggressiveness, others to display fear, and still others to find enjoyment (see the chapter on human development). To explore this possibility, psychologists will have to conduct further studies to examine correlations between children's personality traits, qualities of different daycare programs, and reactions to daycare (NICHD Early Child Care Research Network, 2003). Throughout this book you will see many more examples of how correlational studies help to shed light on a wide range of topics in psychology.

Experiments: Exploring Cause and Effect

Still, the surest way to test hypotheses and confirm cause-effect relationships between variables is to exert some control over those variables. This kind of research usually takes the form of an experiment. **Experiments** are situations in which the researcher manipulates one variable and then observes the effect of that manipulation on another variable, while holding all other variables constant.

Consider the experiment Shapiro conducted in an attempt to better understand the effects of EMDR. As illustrated in Figure 2.1, she first identified twenty-two people who were suffering the ill effects of traumas such as rape or military combat. These were her research participants. She then assigned each of the participants to one of two groups. The first group received a single fifty-minute session of EMDR treatment; the second group focused on their unpleasant memories for eight minutes, but without moving their eyes back and forth (Shapiro, 1989b).

The group that receives an experimental treatment such as EMDR is called, naturally enough, the **experimental group**. The group that receives no treatment or some other treatment is called the **control group**. Control groups provide baselines

experiment A situation in which the researcher manipulates one variable and then observes the effect of that manipulation on another variable, while holding all other variables constant.

experimental group In an experiment, the group that receives the experimental treatment.

control group In an experiment, the group that receives no treatment or provides some other baseline against which to compare the performance or response of the experimental group.

independent variable The variable manipulated by the researcher in an experiment.

dependent variable In an experiment, the factor affected by the independent variable.

confounding variable In an experiment, any factor that affects the dependent variable, along with or instead of the independent variable.

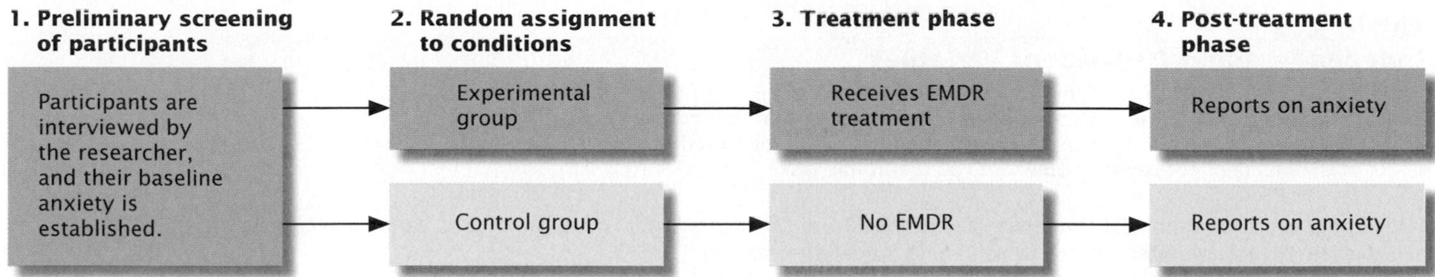

figure 2.1

A Simple Two-Group Experiment

Ideally, the only difference between the experimental and control groups in experiments such as this one is whether the participants receive the treatment the experimenter wishes to evaluate. Under such ideal circumstances, any difference in the two groups' reported levels of anxiety at the end of the experiment would be due only to whether or not they received treatment.

against which to compare the performance of other groups. In Shapiro's experiment, having a control group allowed her to measure how much change in anxiety could be expected from exposure to bad memories without EMDR treatment. If everything about the two groups was exactly the same before the experiment, then any difference in anxiety between the groups afterward should have been due to the treatment given. At the same time, hypotheses about alternative causes of improvement, such as the mere passage of time, became less plausible.

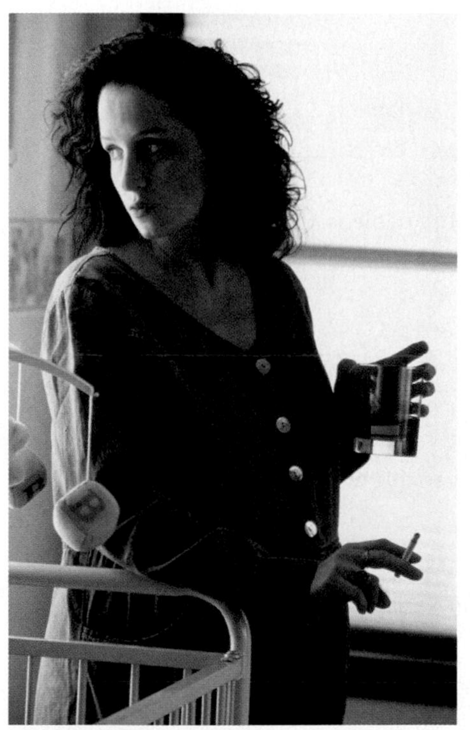

Looking for Correlations It would be possible to draw firm conclusions about the impact of drug use during pregnancy by keeping one group of pregnant women drug free while giving others varying amounts of alcohol. One could then observe how much alcohol it takes to cause birth defects. But such procedures would be utterly unethical. To explore these kinds of research questions, psychologists employ correlational studies, which have great value in describing the outcomes associated with drug use, dropping out of school, and the like. Correlational studies can also be mined for clues about why those outcomes occurred.

Notice that Shapiro controlled one variable in her experiment, namely which kind of treatment her participants received. In an experiment, the variable controlled by the experimenter is called the **independent variable.** It is called *independent* because the experimenter is free to adjust it at will, offering one, two, or three kinds of treatment, for example, or perhaps setting the length of treatment at one, five, or ten sessions. Notice, too, that Shapiro looked for the effects of treatment by measuring a different variable, namely her clients' anxiety level. This second variable is called the **dependent variable** because it is affected by, or depends on, the independent variable. So in Shapiro's experiment, the presence or absence of treatment was the independent variable, because she manipulated it. Her participants' anxiety level was the dependent variable, because she measured it to see how it was affected by treatment. (Table 2.3 describes the independent and dependent variables in other experiments.)

The results of Shapiro's (1989b) experiment showed that participants who received EMDR treatment experienced a complete and nearly immediate reduction in anxiety related to their traumatic memories, whereas those in the control group showed no change. This difference suggests that EMDR caused the improvement. But look again at the structure, or design, of the experiment. The EMDR group's session lasted about fifty minutes, but the control group focused on their memories for only eight minutes. Would the people in the control group have improved, too, if they had spent fifty minutes focusing on their memories? We don't know, because the experiment did not compare methods of equal duration.

Anyone who conducts or relies on research must be on guard for such flaws in experimental design. So before drawing conclusions from research, experimenters must consider factors that might confound, or confuse, the interpretation of results. Any factor, such as differences in treatment length, that might have affected the dependent variable along with or instead of the independent variable can become a **confounding variable.** When confounding variables are present, the experimenter cannot know whether the independent variable or the confounding variable produced the results. Let's examine three sources of confounding: random variables, participants' expectations, and experimenter bias.

table 2.3

Independent and Dependent Variables

Fill in the names of the independent and dependent variables in each of these experiments (the answers are listed at the bottom of page 41). Remember that the independent variable is manipulated by the experimenter. The dependent variable is measured to determine the effect of the independent variable. How did you do on this task?

1. Virgina Grant of Memorial University has demonstrated that rats that are given unlimited access to a running wheel after eating are more likely to elicit symptoms of activity anorexia than are rats that are placed in a cage without access to a running wheel (cf. Sparkes, Grant & Lett, 2003).	The independent variable is ____________. The dependent variable is ____________.
2. Thomy Nilsson of the University of Prince Edward Island has been investigating the ease with which a person can read words printed in different colours on various coloured backgrounds (cf. Nilsson, 2005).	The independent variable is ____________. The dependent variable is ____________.
3. Christine Chambers of Dalhousie University is attempting to find a face-scale rating that best measures children's post-operative pain (children point at the face that best represents how they feel). In her most recent study, Dr. Chambers compared a scale that began with a neutral face with one that began with a happy face to see which scale most accurately measured the child's post-operative pain (cf. Chambers, Hardial, Craig, Court, & Montgomery, 2005).	The independent variable is ____________. The dependent variable is ____________.
4. Michael Houlihan and Ian Fraser of St. Thomas University are studying the effects that alterations of facial features have on eyewitness accuracy (cf. Houlihan, Fraser & Welling, 2005).	The independent variable is ____________. The dependent variable is ____________.
5. Frances Aboud of McGill University is interested in the development of prejudicial attitudes in children. She has conducted a study to assess whether or not in-group favouritism (looking favourably on the group to which you belong) is related to the development of out-group prejudice (the negative attitudes you hold toward people not within the group) (cf. Aboud, 2003).	The independent variable is ____________. The dependent variable is ____________.
6. Madhulika Gupta of the University of Western Ontario and Aditya Gupta of the University of Toronto have conducted research that suggests that Eye-Movement Desensitization and Reprocessing (EDMR) may be helpful in the treatment of certain skin disorders (cf. Gupta & Gupta, 2002).	The independent variable is ____________. The dependent variable is ____________.
7. Wendy Josephson of the University of Winnipeg and Jocelyn Proulx, a research associate at The Manitoba Research Centre, have been assessing whether a new school curriculum called "Healthy Relationships" can help to reduce violence against women (cf. Josephson & Proulx, 2000).	The independent variable is ____________. The dependent variable is ____________.
8. Margaret McKim of the University of Saskatchewan is interested in determining whether or not a mother's attitude toward placing her child into daycare has any bearing on the stability of the care the child experiences (cf. McKim, Cramer, Stuart, & O'Connor, 1999).	The independent variable is ____________. The dependent variable is ____________.
9. Darren Hansen of the University of Lethbridge is interested in the phenomenon known as *kindling*. It appears that repeated electrical stimulation of parts of the brain will induce seizures (the abnormal firing of brain cells) (cf. Hannesonn, 2002).	The independent variable is ____________. The dependent variable is ____________.
10. Sherry Beaumont of University of Northern British Columbia is interested in men's self-identity and its effects on their feelings of self-worth (cf. Beaumont & Zukanovic, 2005).	The independent variable is ____________. The dependent variable is ____________.

Random Variables In an ideal research world, everything about the experimental and control groups would be the same except for their exposure to the independent variable (such as whether or not they received treatment). In reality, however, there are always other differences between the groups that reflect random variables. **Random variables** are uncontrolled, sometimes uncontrollable, factors, such as the time of year when research takes place and differences in the participants' backgrounds, personalities, life experiences, and vulnerability to stress, for example.

In fact, there are so many ways in which participants might differ from each other that it is usually impossible to form groups that are matched on all points. Instead, experimenters simply flip a coin or use some other random process to assign each research participant to experimental or control groups. These procedures—called **random assignment**—are presumed to distribute the impact of uncontrolled variables randomly (and probably about equally) across groups, thus minimizing the chance that these variables will distort the results of the experiment (Shadish, Cook, & Campbell, 2002).

Participants' Expectations After eight minutes of focusing on unpleasant memories, participants in the control group in Shapiro's (1989b) experiment were instructed to begin moving their eyes. At that point they, too, said they began to experience a reduction in anxiety. Was this improvement caused by the eye movements themselves, or could it be that the instructions made the participants feel more confident that they were now getting "real" treatment? This question illustrates a second source of confounding: differences in what people *think* about the experimental situation. If participants who receive an impressive treatment expect that it will help them, they may try harder to improve than those in a control group who receive no treatment or a less impressive treatment. When improvement is created by a participant's knowledge and expectations, it is called the *placebo effect*. A **placebo** (pronounced "pla-SEE-boe") is a treatment that contains nothing known to be helpful but that nevertheless produces benefits because a person believes it will be beneficial.

How can researchers measure the extent to which a result is caused by the independent variable or by a placebo effect? Usually, they include a special control group that receives *only* a placebo treatment. Then they compare results for the experimental group, the placebo group, and a group that receives no treatment. For example, in one study to help people quit smoking, participants in a placebo group took sugar pills described by the experimenter as "fast-acting tranquilizers" that would help them learn to endure the stress of giving up cigarettes (Bernstein, 1970). These people did far better at quitting than those who got no treatment; in

random variable In an experiment, a confounding variable in which uncontrolled or uncontrollable factors affect the dependent variable, along with or instead of the independent variable.

random assignment The procedure by which random variables are evenly distributed in an experiment by putting participants into various groups through a random process.

placebo A physical or psychological treatment that contains no active ingredient but produces an effect because the person receiving it believes it will.

Answer key to Table 2.3:
a. Running wheel – independent; Activity Anorexia – dependent
b. Coloured Fonts and Coloured Backgrounds – both independents; Ease of reading – dependent
c. Type of scale – independent; Accuracy of post-operative pain – dependent
d. Facial features – independent; Eyewitness accuracy – dependent
e. Out group prejudice – independent; In group favouritism – dependent
f. EDMR – independent; Skin disorders – dependent
g. New curriculum – independent; Violence against females – dependent
h. Mothers attitudes – independent; Child's experience – dependent
i. Repeated stimulation – independent; Seizures – dependent
j. Identity – independent; Self-worth – dependent

The independent variable (IDV) in experiment 1 is the type of reading class; the dependent variable (DV) is reading skill. In experiment 2, the IDV is the quality of sleep; the DV is the score on a memory test. In experiment 3, the IDV is amount of exercise; the DV is lung capacity. In experiment 4, the IDV is using or not using a cell phone; the DV is performance on a simulated driving task.

They Are All the Same Scientists have succeeded in cloning mice, thus creating a population of genetically identical animals. These animals can be assigned to various experimental and control groups with no worries about the confounding effects that individual differences might have on the dependent variable. Laws and research ethics rule out creating a pool of cloned people, so the process of random assignment will remain a vital component of psychological research with human beings.

fact, they did as well as participants in the experimental group, who received extensive treatment. These results suggested that the success of the experimental group may have been due largely to the participants' expectations, not to the treatment-methods. Placebo effects may not be as strong as experimenters once assumed (Hrobjartsson & Gotzsche, 2001), but some people do improve after receiving medical or psychological treatment, not because of the treatment itself but because they believe that it will help them (e.g., Stewart-Williams & Podd, 2004; Wager et al., 2004).

Research on EMDR treatment suggests that the eye movements themselves may not be responsible for improvement, inasmuch as staring, finger tapping, or listening to rapid clicks or tones while focusing on traumatic memories has also produced benefits (e.g., Carrigan & Levis, 1999; Cusack & Spates, 1999; Rosen, 1999). In fact, although EMDR appears to have some positive effects on some clients, it often fails to outperform impressive placebo treatments or other established anxiety treatment methods (e.g., Taylor, 2003). These results have led many researchers to conclude that EMDR should not be a first-choice treatment for anxiety-related disorders (Davison & Parker, 2001; Lohr et al., 2003; Taylor et al., 2003).

Experimenter Bias

Another potential confounding variable comes from **experimenter bias**, the unintentional effect that experimenters can exert on their results. Robert Rosenthal (1966) was one of the first to demonstrate one kind of experimenter bias, called *experimenter expectancies*. His research participants were laboratory assistants whose job was to place rats in a maze. Rosenthal told some of the assistants that their rats were particularly "maze-bright"; he told others that their rats were "maze-dull." In fact, both groups of rats were randomly drawn from the same population and had about equal maze-learning capabilities. But the "maze-bright" animals learned the maze significantly faster than the "maze-dull" rats. Why? Rosenthal concluded that the result had nothing to do with the rats and everything to do with the experimenters. He suggested that the assistants' expectations about their rats' supposedly superior (or inferior) capabilities caused them to slightly alter their training and handling techniques. These slight differences may have speeded (or slowed) the animals' learning. Similarly,

Ever Since I Started Wearing These Magnets . . . Placebo-controlled experiments are vital for establishing cause-effect relationships between treatment and outcome with human participants. For example, many people swear that magnets held against their joints relieve the pain of sports injuries and even arthritis. But experiments show that magnets are no more effective than placebo treatment with an identical, but nonmagnetic, metal object (e.g., Collacott et al., 2000; Winemiller et al., 2003). Something other than magnets—wishful thinking, perhaps—appears to be causing the reported benefits.

experimenter bias A confounding variable that occurs when an experimenter unintentionally encourages participants to respond in a way that supports the hypothesis.

Keeping Experimenters "Blind" Suppose you are a sport psychologist conducting an experiment to evaluate two methods for reducing performance anxiety: standard coaching versus a new relaxation-based technique. How could you create a double-blind design in this experiment? If you could not, how would you at least try to keep coaches in the dark about which method is expected to produce the best results?

when experimenters give different kinds of anxiety treatments to different groups of people, they might do a slightly better job with the treatment they believe to be the best. This slight, unintentional difference could improve the effects of that treatment compared with the others.

To prevent experimenter bias from confounding results, experimenters often use a **double-blind design.** In this arrangement, both the research participants and those giving the treatments are unaware of, or "blind" to, who is receiving a placebo, and they do not know what results are expected from various treatments. Only researchers who have no direct contact with participants have this information, and they do not reveal it until the experiment is over. The fact that double-blind studies of EMDR have not yet been conducted is another reason for caution in drawing conclusions about this treatment.

In short, experiments are vital tools for examining cause-effect relationships between variables, but, like the other methods we have described (see "In Review: Methods of Psychological Research"), they are vulnerable to error. To maximize the value of their experiments, psychologists try to eliminate as many confounding

THE WIZARD OF ID Brant parker and Johnny hart

To best control for participant expectancies and experimenter bias, neither experimenters nor participants should know who is getting the experimental treatment and who is getting placebo treatment. In practice, though, it is often difficult to establish and maintain experimenter "blindness" (Fergusson et al., 2004).

double-blind design A research design in which neither the experimenter nor the participants know who is in the experimental group and who is in the control group.

in review Methods of Psychological Research

Method	Features	Strengths	Pitfalls
Naturalistic observation	Observation of human or animal behaviour in the environment in which it typically occurs	Provides descriptive data about behaviour presumably uncontaminated by outside influences	Observer bias and participant self-consciousness can distort results
Case studies	Intensive examination of the behaviour and mental processes associated with a specific person or situation	Provide detailed descriptive analyses of new, complex, or rare phenomena	May not provide representative picture of phenomena
Surveys	Standard sets of questions asked of a large number of participants	Gather large amounts of descriptive data relatively quickly and inexpensively	Sampling errors, poorly phrased questions, and response biases can distort results
Correlational studies	Examine relationships between research variables	Can test predictions, evaluate theories, and suggest new hypotheses	Cannot confirm causal relationships between variables
Experiments	Manipulation of an independent variable and measurement of its effects on a dependent variable	Can establish a cause-effect relationship between independent and dependent variables	Confounding variables may prevent valid conclusions

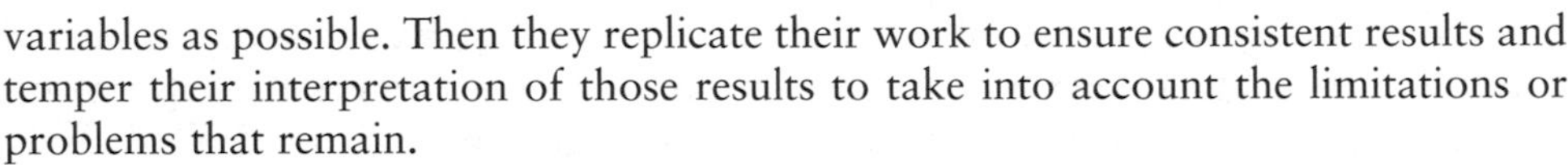

variables as possible. Then they replicate their work to ensure consistent results and temper their interpretation of those results to take into account the limitations or problems that remain.

Selecting Human Participants for Research

Visitors from outer space would be wildly mistaken if they tried to describe the typical Canadian after meeting only, say, William Shatner, Wayne Gretzky, Pamela Anderson, and a beaver. Likewise, the conclusions that psychologists draw from their observations, case studies, surveys, correlational studies, and experiments will be distorted if the participants they study are not typical of the people or animals they are interested in. Accordingly, the process of selecting participants for research, called **sampling,** is an extremely important step.

Suppose, for example, that you are conducting a survey of television viewing habits. Your research budget is small, so you restrict your survey to the residents of your apartment building, all of whom, by some strange coincidence, turn out to be male concert violinists of Asian background. The responses you get from these people might be perfectly accurate, but their favorite shows might differ significantly from those of the general population. So sampling procedures can not only affect research results but also limit their meaning. In this case, your results would probably apply, or *generalize,* mainly to other male musicians of Asian background. If that were the only group you want to draw conclusions about, then your limited sample might not be too problematic—assuming the men in your building were typical of other Asian American musicians. If they were all also ex-convicts, your results would be even more limited!

sampling The process of selecting participants who are members of the population that the researcher wishes to study.

representative sample A group of research participants whose characteristics fairly reflect the characteristics of the population from which they were selected.

The main point is that if psychologists want to make scientific statements about the behaviour and mental processes of any large group, they must select a **representative sample** of participants whose characteristics fairly reflect the characteristics of

Selecting Research Participants
Imagine that as a social psychologist, you want to study people's willingness to help each other. You have developed a method for testing helpfulness, but now you want a random sample of people to test. Take a minute to think about the steps necessary to select a truly random sample; then ask yourself how you might obtain a representative sample, instead. Remember that although the names are similar, *random sampling* is not the same as *random assignment*. Random sampling is used in many kinds of research to ensure that the people studied are representative of some larger group. Random assignment is used in experiments to create equivalence among various groups.

other people in that group. This point is important, because psychologists often study behaviour or mental processes that are affected by age, gender, ethnicity, cultural background, socio economic status, sexual orientation, disability, or other participant characteristics. The more of these characteristics that are represented in a research sample, the broader can be the conclusions from research results.

In theory, psychologists could draw representative samples of people in general, of Canadians, of university students from British Columbia, or of any other group by choosing them at random from the entire population of interest. To do this, though, they would first have to enter hundreds of thousands, perhaps millions, of names into a computer, then run a program to randomly select participants from this vast population, then track them down and invite them to take part in the research. This method would result in a truly **random sample,** because every member of the population to be studied would have an equal chance of being chosen. Any selection procedure that does not offer this equal chance is said to result in a **biased sample.**

Unfortunately, not even a truly random sample will create a perfectly representative sample of Canadians, British Columbia university students, or the like. For one thing, the people who happen to be selected may be slightly different from the people who are not selected. In other words, the luck of the draw creates what psychologists call *sampling error*. Further, not everyone who is randomly selected for a research project will agree to participate, creating a problem called *nonresponse error*. These two kinds of errors help explain why the results of random surveys are not always accurate. Still, a group of individuals selected at random from a larger population will usually provide a reasonably representative sample of that population. The big problem, though, is that random sampling is often too expensive and time-consuming to be practical.

So in the real world of research, psychologists sometimes draw their participants from the populations that are conveniently available. The populations from which these *convenience samples* are drawn depend to some extent on the size of the researcher's budget. They might include, for example, the students enrolled in a particular course, students enrolled on a local campus, the students who are willing to sign up for a study, or visitors to Web sites or chat rooms (e.g., Nosek, Banaji, & Greenwald, 2002; Stone & Pennebaker, 2002). Ideally, this selection process will yield a sample that fairly represents the population from which it was drawn, but the researcher will check this by noting the age, gender, ethnicity, and other characteristics of the participants. In all cases, scientific researchers are obliged to limit the conclusions they draw in light of the samples they draw (Kraut et al., 2004). Because of this obligation, psychologists often conduct additional studies to determine the extent to which their initial conclusions will apply to people who differ in important ways from their original sample (Case & Smith, 2000; Gray-Little & Hafdahl, 2000).

LINKAGES

Psychological Research Methods and Behavioural Genetics

LINKAGES (a link to Biological Aspects of Psychology)

random sample A group of research participants selected from a population whose members all had an equal chance of being chosen.

biased sample A group of research participants selected from a population each of whose members did not have an equal chance of being chosen.

One of the most fascinating and difficult challenges in psychology is to find research methods that can help us understand the ways in which people's genetic inheritance (their biological *nature*) intertwines with environmental events and conditions before and after birth (often called *nurture*) to shape their behaviour and mental processes. Consider Mark and John, identical twins who were both adopted at birth because their parents were too poor to care for them. John grew up with a married couple who made him feel secure and loved. Mark went from orphanage to foster home to hospital and, finally, back to his natural father's second wife. In other words, these genetically identical people had encountered quite different environments. When they met for the first time at the age of 24, they discovered similarities that went beyond physical appearance. They used the same aftershave lotion, smoked the same brand of cigarettes, used the same imported brand of toothpaste, liked the same sports, and their IQ scores were nearly identical. How had genetic influences operated in two different environments to shape such similarities?

Exploring questions such as these has taken psychologists into the field of **behavioural genetics,** the study of how genes and environments work together to shape behaviour. They have discovered that most behavioural tendencies are likely to be influenced by interactions between the environment and many different genes. Accordingly, research in behavioural genetics is designed to explore the relative roles of genetic and environmental factors in creating differences among people in personality, mental ability, mental disorders, and other phenomena. It also seeks to identify specific genes that contribute to hereditary influences.

Some behavioural genetics research takes the form of experiments, mainly on the selective breeding of animals. For example, Stephen Suomi (1999) identified monkeys whose genes predisposed them to show strong or weak reactions to stress. He then mated strong reactors with other strong reactors and mated weak reactors with other weak reactors. Within a few generations, descendants of the strong-reactor pairs reacted much more strongly to stressors than did the descendants of the weak-reactor pairs. Selective-breeding experiments must be interpreted with caution, though, because animals do not inherit specific behaviours. What they inherit instead are differing sets of physical structures and capacities that make certain behaviours more likely or less likely. But these behavioural tendencies can be altered by the environment (Grigorenko, 2002). For example, when Suomi (1999) placed young, highly stress-reactive monkeys with unrelated "foster mothers," he discovered that the foster mothers' own stress reactivity amplified or dampened the youngsters' genetically influenced behavioural tendencies. If stress-reactive monkeys were placed with stress-reactive foster mothers, they tended to be fearful of exploring their environments and had strong reactions to stressors. But if equally stress-reactive young monkeys had calm, supportive foster mothers, they appeared eager to explore their environments and were much less upset by stressors than their peers with stress-reactive foster mothers.

Research on behavioural genetics in humans must be interpreted with even greater care. Legal, moral, and ethical considerations obviously prohibit experiments on the selective breeding of people, so research in human behavioural genetics depends on correlational studies. These usually take the form of family studies, twin studies, and adoption studies (Plomin, de Fries, et al., 2001; Rutter et al., 2001). Let's consider the logic of these behavioural genetics research methods. (For more on the basic principles of genetics and heredity that underlie these methods, see the appendix on behavioural genetics.)

In *family studies,* researchers look at whether close relatives are more likely than distant ones to show similar behaviour and mental processes. If increasing similarity is associated with closer family ties, the similarities might be inherited. For example, family studies suggest a genetic basis for schizophrenia because this severe mental disorder appears much more often in the closest relatives of schizophrenics than in other people (see Figure 2.2). But remember that a correlation between variables does not guarantee that one is causing the other. The appearance of similar disorders in close relatives might be due to environmental factors instead of, or in addition to, genetic ones. After all, close relatives tend to share environments, as well as genes. So family studies alone cannot establish the role of genetic factors in mental disorders or other characteristics.

Twin studies explore the heredity-environment mix by comparing the similarities seen in identical twins with those of fraternal pairs. Twins usually share the same family environment as they grow up, and they may also be treated very much the same by parents and others. So if identical twins (whose genes are exactly

behavioural genetics The study of how genes and environments affect behaviour.

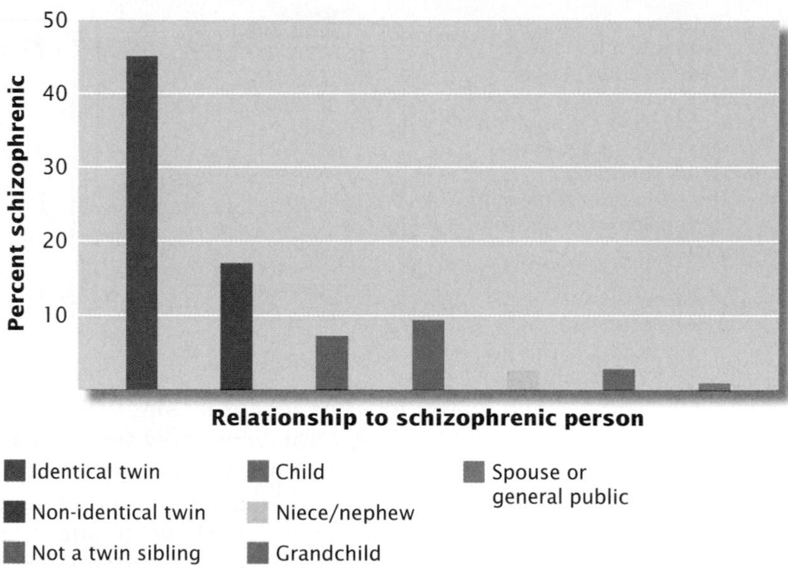

figure 2.2

Family and Twin Studies of Schizophrenia

The risk of developing schizophrenia, a severe mental disorder, is highest for the siblings and children of schizophrenia patients and lowest for those who are not genetically related to anyone with schizophrenia. Does this mean that schizophrenia is inherited? These results are consistent with that interpretation, but the question cannot be answered through family studies alone. Environmental factors, such as stressors that close relatives share, could also play an important role. Studies comparing identical and fraternal twins also suggest genetic influence, but even twin studies do not eliminate the role of environmental influences.

the same) are more alike on some characteristic than fraternal twins (whose genes are no more similar than those of other siblings), that characteristic may have a significant genetic component. As we will see in later chapters, this pattern of results holds for a number of characteristics, including some measures of intelligence and some mental disorders. As shown in Figure 2.2, for example, if one member of an identical twin pair develops schizophrenia, the chances are about 45 percent that the other twin will, too. Those chances drop to about 17 percent if the twins are fraternal.

Adoption studies take scientific advantage of cases in which babies are adopted very early in life. The logic of these studies is that if adopted children's characteristics are more like those of their biological parents than of their adoptive parents, genetics probably plays a clear role in those characteristics. In fact, as described in the chapter on personality, the traits of young adults who were adopted at birth tend to be more like those of their biological parents than those of their adoptive parents. Adoption studies can be especially valuable when they

Research in Behavioural Genetics
Like identical twins, each of the identical Dionne quintuplets has genes identical to the others. Twin studies and adoption studies help to reveal the interaction of genetic and environmental influences in human behaviour and mental processes. Cases in which identical twins who have been separated at birth are found to have similar interests, personality traits, and mental abilities suggest that these characteristics have a significant genetic component.

Descriptive statistics are valuable for summarizing research results, but we must evaluate them carefully before drawing conclusions about what they mean. Given this executive's reputation for uncritical thinking, you can bet that Dogbert's impressive-sounding restatement of the definition of median will win him an extension of his pricey consulting contract.

focus on identical twins who, like Mark and John, were separated at or near birth. If identical twins show similar characteristics after years of living in very different environments, the role of heredity in those characteristics is highlighted. Adoption studies of intelligence tend to support the role of genetics in variations in mental ability, but they show the impact of environmental influences, too.

Family, twin, and adoption studies have played an important role in behavioural genetics research, but when you read in other chapters about the role of genes in personality, intelligence, mental disorders, and other characteristics, remember this important point: Research on human behavioural genetics can tell us about the relative roles of heredity and environment in creating differences *among* individuals, but it cannot determine the degree to which a *particular* person's behaviour is due to heredity or environment. The two factors are too closely entwined in an individual to be separated that way. In the future, though, behavioural genetics will also be shaped by research methods made possible by the Human Genome Project, which has now unlocked the genetic code contained in the DNA that makes each human being unique (International Human Genome Sequencing Consortium, 2001; Venter et al., 2001; see the appendix on behavioural genetics).

This achievement has allowed behavioural geneticists and other scientists to begin pinpointing some of the many genes that contribute to individual differences in disorders such as autism, learning disabilities, hyperactivity, and Alzheimer's disease, as well as to the normal variations in personality and mental abilities that we see all around us (Plomin et al., 2002). Finding the DNA differences responsible for certain personal attributes and behaviours will eventually make it possible to understand exactly how heredity interacts with the environment as development unfolds.

Statistical Analysis of Research Results

The data gathered through naturalistic observations, case studies, surveys, correlational studies, and experiments usually take the form of numbers that represent research findings and provide the basis for conclusions about them. Like other scientists, psychologists use descriptive and inferential *statistics* to summarize and analyze their data and interpret what they mean. As their name suggests, **descriptive statistics** describe data. **Inferential statistics** are mathematical procedures that help psychologists make inferences about what the data mean. Here, we describe a few statistical terms that you will encounter in later chapters; you can find more information about these terms in the appendix on statistics.

descriptive statistics Numbers that describe and summarize a set of research data.

inferential statistics A set of mathematical procedures that help researchers infer what their data might mean.

Descriptive Statistics

The three most important descriptive statistics are *measures of central tendency,* which describe the typical score (or value) in a set of data; *measures of variability,*

table 2.4

Here are scores representing people's self-ratings, on a 1–100 scale, of their fear of the dark.

A Set of Pretreatment Anxiety Ratings

Data from 11 Participants		Data from 12 Participants	
Participant Number	**Anxiety Rating**	**Participant Number**	**Anxiety Rating**
1	20	1	20
2	22	2	22
3	28	3	28
4	35	4	35
5	40	5	40
6	45 (Median)	6	45 (Median = 46*)
7	47	7	47
8	49	8	49
9	50	9	50
10	50	10	50
11	50	11	50
		12	100

Data from 11 Participants	Data from 12 Participants
Measures of central tendency	**Measures of central tendency**
Mode = 50	Mode = 50
Median = 45	Median = 46
Mean = 436/11 = 39.6	Mean = 536/12 = 44.7
Measures of variability	**Measures of variability**
Range = 30	Range = 80
Standard deviation = 11.064	Standard deviation = 19.763

*When there is an even number of scores, the exact middle of the list lies between two numbers. The median is the value halfway between those numbers.

which describe the spread, or dispersion, among the scores in a set of data; and *correlation coefficients,* which describe relationships between variables.

Measures of Central Tendency Suppose you wanted to test the effects of EMDR treatment on fear of the dark. Looking for participants, you collect the eleven self-ratings of anxiety listed on the left side of Table 2.4. What is the typical score, the central tendency, that best represents the anxiety level of this group of people? There are three measures designed to capture this typical score: the mode, the median, and the mean.

The **mode** is the value or score that occurs most frequently in a data set. You can find it by simply counting how many times each score appears. On the left side of Table 2.4, the mode is 50, because the score of 50 occurs more often than any other.

Notice, however, that in this data set the mode is actually an extreme score. Sometimes, the mode acts like a microphone for a small but vocal minority that, though speaking loudest or most frequently, does not represent the views of the majority.

Unlike the mode, the median takes all of the scores into account. The **median** is the halfway point in a set of data. When scores are arranged from lowest to highest, half the scores fall above the median, and half fall below it. For the scores on the left side of Table 2.4, the halfway point—the median—is 45.

The third measure of central tendency is the **mean,** which is the *arithmetic average* of a set of scores. When people talk about the "average" in everyday conversation,

mode A measure of central tendency that is the value or score that occurs most frequently in a data set.

median A measure of central tendency that is the halfway point in a set of data.

mean A measure of central tendency that is the arithmetic average of the scores in a set of data.

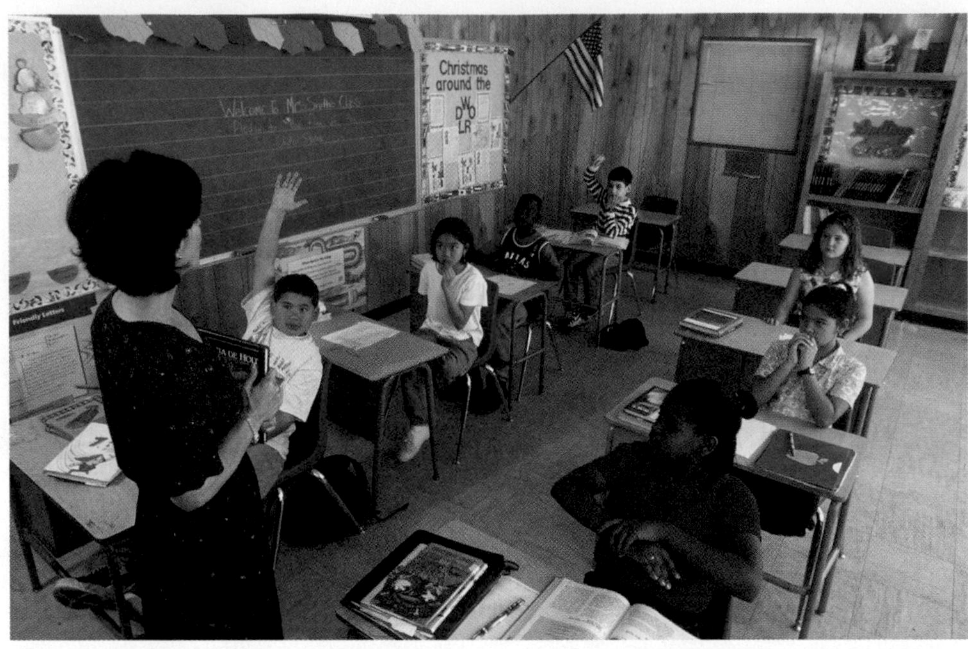

The Effect of Variability Suppose that on your first day as a substitute teacher at a new school, you are offered either of two classes. The mean IQ score in both classes is 100, but the standard deviation (SD) of scores is 16 in one class and 32 in the other. Before you read the next sentence, ask yourself which class you would choose if you wanted an easy day's work or if you wanted a tough challenge. (Higher standard deviation means more variability, so students in the class with the SD of 32 will vary more in ability, thus creating a greater challenge for the teacher.)

they are usually referring to the mean. To find the mean, add the scores and divide by the number of scores. For the data on the left side of Table 2.4, the mean is 436/11 or 39.6.

Like the median (and unlike the mode), the mean reflects all the data to some degree, not just the most frequent data. Notice, however, that the mean reflects the actual values of all the scores, whereas the median gives each score equal weight, whatever its value. This distinction can have a big effect on how well the mean and median represent the scores in a particular set of data. Suppose, for example, that you add to your sample a twelfth participant, whose anxiety rating is 100. When you reanalyze the anxiety data (see the right side of Table 2.4), the median hardly changes, because the new participant counts as just one more score. However, when you compute the new mean, the actual *amount* of the new participant's rating is added to everyone else's ratings; as a result, the mean jumps five points. As this example shows, the median is sometimes a better measure of central tendency than the mean because the median is less sensitive to extreme scores. But because the mean is more representative of the values of all the data, it is often the preferred measure of central tendency.

Measures of Variability The variability (also known as *spread* or *dispersion*) in a set of data is described by statistics known as the *range* and the *standard deviation*. The **range** is simply the difference between the highest and the lowest scores in a data set. In contrast, the **standard deviation**, or **SD**, measures the average difference between each score and the mean of the data set. So the standard deviation tells us how much the scores in a data set vary, or differ, from one another. The more variable the data are, the higher the standard deviation will be. In the appendix on statistics, we show how to calculate the standard deviation.

range A measure of variability that is the difference between the highest and the lowest values in a data set.

standard deviation (SD) A measure of variability that is the average difference between each score and the mean of the data set.

correlation In research, the degree to which one variable is related to another.

Correlation and Correlation Coefficients When we described correlational studies on the relationship between media violence and aggression, we left out one important question: How do psychologists describe the correlation between these variables or between any other pair of variables?

Correlation means just what it says, "co-relation," and it refers both to how strongly one variable is related to another and to the direction of the relationship. A *positive correlation* means that two variables increase together or decrease together.

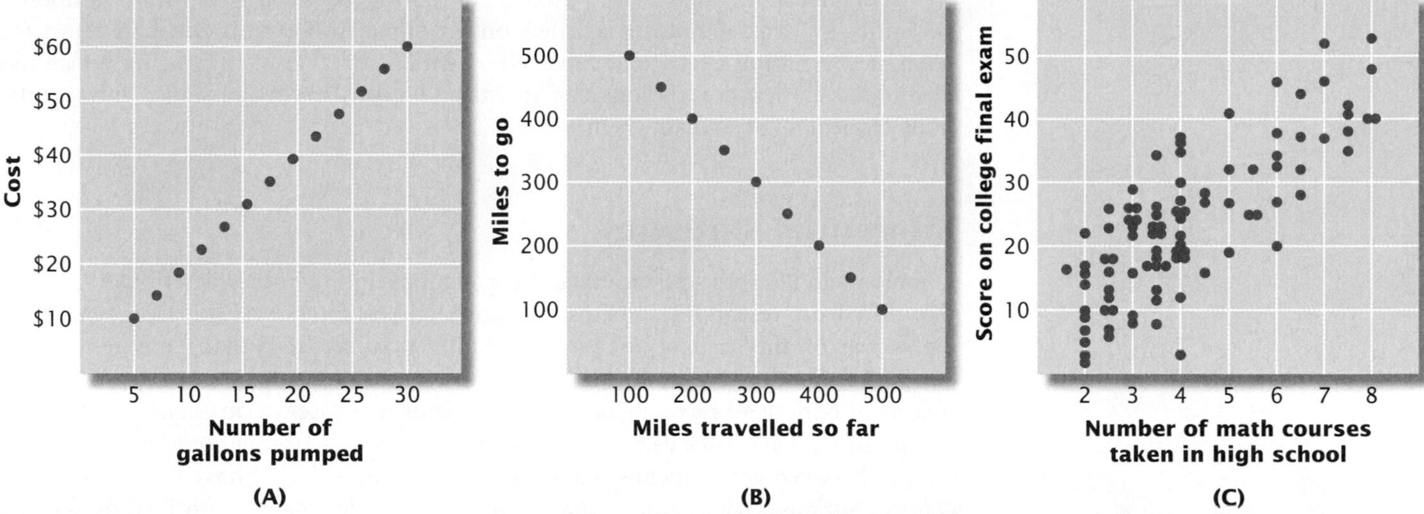

figure 2.3

Three Correlations

The strength and direction of the correlation between variables can be seen in a graph called a *scatterplot*. Here are three examples. In Part A, we have plotted the cost of a gasoline purchase against the number of litres pumped. The number of litres is positively and perfectly correlated with their cost, so the scatterplot appears as a straight line, and you can predict the value of either variable from a knowledge of the other. Part B shows a perfect negative correlation between the number of kilometres you have travelled toward a destination and the distance remaining. Again, one variable can be exactly predicted from the other. Part C illustrates a correlation of +.81 between the number of math courses students had in high school and their scores on a university math exam; each dot represents one student (Hays, 1981). As correlations decrease, they are represented by less and less organization in the pattern of dots. A correlation of 0.00 would appear as a shapeless cloud.

A *negative correlation* means that the variables move in opposite directions: When one increases, the other decreases. For example, James Schaefer observed 4,500 customers in 65 bars and found that the tempo of jukebox music was negatively correlated with the rate at which the customers drank alcohol; the slower the tempo, the faster the drinking (Schaefer et al., 1988).

Does this mean that Schaefer could have worn a blindfold and predicted exactly how fast people were drinking by timing the music? Or could he have plugged his ears and determined the musical tempo by watching how fast people drink? No and no, because the accuracy of predictions about one variable from knowledge of another depends on the strength of the correlation. Only a perfect correlation between two variables would allow you to predict the exact value of one from a knowledge of the other. The weaker the correlation, the less one variable can tell you about the other.

Psychologists describe correlations using a statistic called the **correlation coefficient** (the appendix on statistics shows how to calculate it). The correlation coefficient is given the symbol *r*, and it can vary from +1.00 to −1.00. The actual size of the correlation, such as .20 or .80, tells us how strong the correlation is. The higher the number, the stronger the correlation. The plus or minus sign tells us the direction of the correlation. A plus sign says the correlation is positive. A minus sign says the correlation is negative.

So an *r* of +.80 between people's height and weight would tell us that the correlation between these two variables is strong and positive: The taller people are, the more they tend to weigh. A correlation of +.01 between their shoe size and the age of their cars would indicate that there is almost no relationship between these two variables. An *r* of −1.00 describes a perfectly predictable, but negative, relationship between two variables (see part B of Figure 2.3). The variables that psychologists study are seldom perfectly correlated. Most of the correlational studies described in this book yield correlation coefficients in the .20 to .50 range, though some are as high as .90.

correlation coefficient A statistic, *r*, that summarizes the strength and direction of a relationship between two variables.

Remember, too, that even a strong correlation between two variables doesn't guarantee that one is *causing* an effect on the other. And even if one *does* affect the other, a correlation coefficient can't tell us which variable is influencing which. As mentioned earlier, correlations can reveal and describe relationships, but correlations alone cannot explain them.

Inferential Statistics

To help them interpret the meaning of correlations and the other descriptive statistics that flow from research results, psychologists rely on *inferential statistics.* For example, it was on the basis of analyses using inferential statistics that many researchers concluded that the benefits of EMDR are not great enough when compared with other treatment options to recommend it as a first choice in cases of anxiety.

Inferential statistics use certain rules to evaluate whether a correlation or a difference between group means is a significant finding or might have occurred just by chance. Suppose, for example, that a group of people treated with EMDR showed a mean decrease of 10 points on a post-treatment anxiety test, whereas the scores of a control group that received no treatment decreased by a mean of 7 points. Does this 3-point difference between the groups' means reflect the impact of EMDR, or could it have been caused by random factors that made EMDR appear more powerful than it actually is? Traditionally, psychologists have answered questions such as this by using tests of statistical significance to estimate how likely it is that an observed difference was due to chance alone (Krueger, 2001). When those tests show that a correlation coefficient or the difference between two means is larger than would be expected by chance alone, that correlation or difference is said to be **statistically significant.** In the appendix on statistics, we describe some of these tests and discuss the factors that affect their results.

Positive outcomes on tests of statistical significance are important, but they do not necessarily prove that a difference is "real" or that a particular treatment is effective or ineffective. Accordingly, quantitative psychologists recommend that research findings be evaluated using other statistical analysis methods (e.g., Kline, 2004; Krueger, 2001). Whatever the methods, though, psychological scientists are more confident in, and pay the most attention to, correlations or other research findings that statistical analyses suggest are robust and not flukes. (For a review of the statistical measures discussed in this section, see "In Review: Descriptive and Inferential Statistics.")

Statistics and Research Methods as Tools in Critical Thinking

As you think critically about evidence for or against any hypothesis, remember that part of the process is to ask some tough questions. Does the evidence come from a study whose design is free of major confounds and other flaws? Have the results been subjected to careful statistical analysis? Have the results been replicated? Using your critical thinking skills to evaluate research designs and statistical methods becomes especially important when you encounter results that are dramatic or unexpected.

This point was well illustrated when Douglas Biklen (1990) began promoting a procedure called "facilitated communication (FC)" to help people with severe autistic disorder use language for the first time (autistic disorder is described in the chapter on psychological disorders). Biklen claimed that these people have language skills and coherent thoughts but no way to express them. He reported case studies in which autistic people were apparently able to answer questions and speak intelligently using a special keyboard, but only when assisted by a "facilitator" who physically supported their unsteady hands. Controlled experiments showed this claim to be groundless, however (Jacobson, Mulick, & Schwartz,

statistically significant A term used to describe research results when the outcome of a statistical test indicates that the probability of those results occurring by chance is small.

in review Descriptive and Inferential Statistics

Statistic	Characteristics Information	Provided
Mode	Describes the central tendencies of a set of scores	The score that occurs most frequently in a data set
Median	Describes the central tendencies of a set of scores	The halfway point in a data set; half the scores fall above this score, half below
Mean	Describes the central tendencies of a set of scores	The arithmetic average of the scores in a data set
Range	Describes the variability of a set of scores	The difference between the highest and lowest scores in a data set
Standard deviation	Describes the variability of a set of scores	The average difference between each score and the mean of a data set
Correlation coefficient	Describes the relationship between two variables	How strongly the two variables are related and whether the relationship is positive (variables move in same direction) or negative (variables move in opposite directions)
Tests of significance	Help make inferences about the relationships between descriptive statistics	How likely it is that the difference between measures of central tendencies or the size of a correlation coefficient is due to chance alone

1995; Mostert, 2001; Wegner, Fuller, & Sparrow, 2003). The alleged communication abilities of these autistic people disappeared under conditions in which the facilitator (1) did not know the question being asked of the participant or (2) could not see the keyboard (Delmolino & Romanczyk, 1995). The discovery that facilitators were—perhaps inadvertently (Spitz, 1997)—guiding participants' hand movements has allowed those who work with autistic people to see FC in a different light.

The Social Impact of Research The impact of research in psychology depends partly on the quality of the results and partly on how people feel about those results. Despite negative results of controlled experiments on facilitated communication, the Facilitated Communication Institute's Web site continues to announce training for the many professionals and relatives of autistic people who still believe in its value. The fact that some people ignore, or even attack, research results that challenge cherished beliefs reminds us that scientific research has always affected, and been affected by, the social and political values of the society in which it takes place (Bjork, 2000; Hagen, 2001; Lynn et al., 2003; Oellerich, 2000; Tavris, 2002).

The role of experiments and other scientific research methods in understanding behaviour and mental processes is so important that in each chapter to come we include a special feature called "Focus on Research Methods." These features describe in detail the specific procedures used in one particularly interesting research project. Our hope is that by reading these sections, you will see how the research methods discussed in this chapter are applied in every subfield of psychology.

Ethical Guidelines for Psychologists

The obligation to analyze and report research fairly and accurately is one of the many ethical requirements that guide psychologists in their work. Preserving the welfare and dignity of research participants, both animal and human, is another. So although researchers *could* measure severe anxiety by putting a loaded gun to people's heads, or study marital conflicts by telling one partner that the other has been unfaithful, those methods might cause harm and are therefore unethical. Whatever their research topic, psychologists' first priority is to investigate it in accordance with the highest ethical standards. They must find ways to protect their participants from harm while still gathering data that will have potential benefits for everyone. So to measure anxiety a researcher might ask people to enter a situation that is anxiety provoking but not traumatic (for example, approaching an animal they fear, or sitting in a dark room). And research on marital conflict usually involves videotaping couples as they discuss problems in their relationship.

Caring for Animals in Research
Psychologists are careful to protect the welfare of animal participants in research. They do not wish to see animals suffer and, besides, undue stress on animals can create reactions that can act as confounding variables. For example, in a study of how learning is affected by food rewards, the researcher could starve animals to make them hungry enough to want rewards. But this would introduce discomfort that would make it impossible to separate the effects of the rewards from the effects of starvation.

Psychologists take very seriously the obligation to minimize any immediate discomfort or risk for research participants, as well as the need to protect those participants from long-term harm. They are careful to inform prospective participants about every aspect of the study that might influence the decision to participate, and they ensure that each person's involvement is voluntary. But what if the purpose of the study is to measure people's emotional reactions to being insulted? Participants might not react normally if they know ahead of time that an "insult" will be part of the experiment. When deception is necessary to create certain experimental conditions, ethical standards require the researcher to "debrief" participants as soon as the study is over by revealing all relevant information about the research and correcting any misconceptions it created.

Government regulations in Canada, and many other countries, require that any research involving human participants must be approved by an institutional research ethics board (REB) whose members have no connection to the research. If a proposed study is likely to create risks or discomfort for participants, the REB members weigh its potential benefits in terms of knowledge and human welfare against its potential for harm. The REB follows the standards set out in the Tri-Council Policy Statement entitled: *Ethical Conduct in Research Involving Humans*. The Tri-Council is comprised of the three main Canadian Government research funding agencies: The National Science and Engineering Research Council of Canada (NSERC), The Social Sciences and Humanties Research Council of Canada (SSHRC), and The Canadian Institute of Health Research (CIHR).

The obligation to protect participants' welfare also extends to animals, which are used in a small percentage of psychological research studies (Plous, 1996). Psychologists study animals partly because their behaviour is interesting and partly because research with animals can provide information that would be impossible or unethical to collect from humans. For example, researchers can randomly assign animals to live alone or with others and then look at how these conditions affect later social interactions. The same thing could not ethically be done with people, but animal studies such as this can provide clues about how social isolation might affect humans (see the chapter on motivation and emotion).

Contrary to the claims of some animal-rights activists, animals used in psychological research are not routinely subjected to extreme pain, starvation, or other inhumane conditions. Even in the small proportion of studies that require the use of electric shock, the discomfort created is mild, brief, and not harmful. High standards for the care and treatment of animal participants are outlined in the Canadian Council on Animal Care (CCAC) document entitled *Guide to the Care and Use of Experimental Animals*. In those relatively rare studies that require animals to undergo short-lived pain or other forms of moderate stress, legal and ethical standards require that funding agencies—as well as local committees charged with monitoring animal research—first determine that the discomfort is justified by the expected benefits to human welfare.

The responsibility for conducting research in the most humane fashion is just one aspect outlined in the *Canadian Code of Ethics for Psychologists* developed by the Canadian Psychological Association. This document not only emphasizes the importance of ethical behaviour but also describes specific ways in which psychologists can protect and promote the welfare of society and the particular people with whom they work in any capacity. So as teachers, psychologists should give students complete, accurate, and up-to-date coverage of each topic, not a narrow, biased point of view. Psychologists should perform only those services and use only those techniques for which they are adequately trained; a psychologist untrained in clinical methods, for example, should not try to offer psychotherapy. Except in the most unusual circumstances (discussed in the chapter on treatment of psychological disorders), psychologists should not reveal information obtained from clients or students. They should also avoid situations in which a conflict of interest might impair their judgment or harm someone else. They should not, for example, have sexual relations with their clients, their students, or their employees.

LINKAGES

As noted in the chapter on introducing psychology, all of psychology's subfields are related to one another. Our discussion of behavioural genetics illustrates just one way in which the topic of this chapter, research in psychology, is linked to the subfield of biological psychology (see the chapter on biological aspects of psychology). The Linkages diagram shows ties to two other subfields as well, and there are many more ties throughout the book. Looking for linkages among subfields will help you see how they all fit together and help you better appreciate the big picture that is psychology.

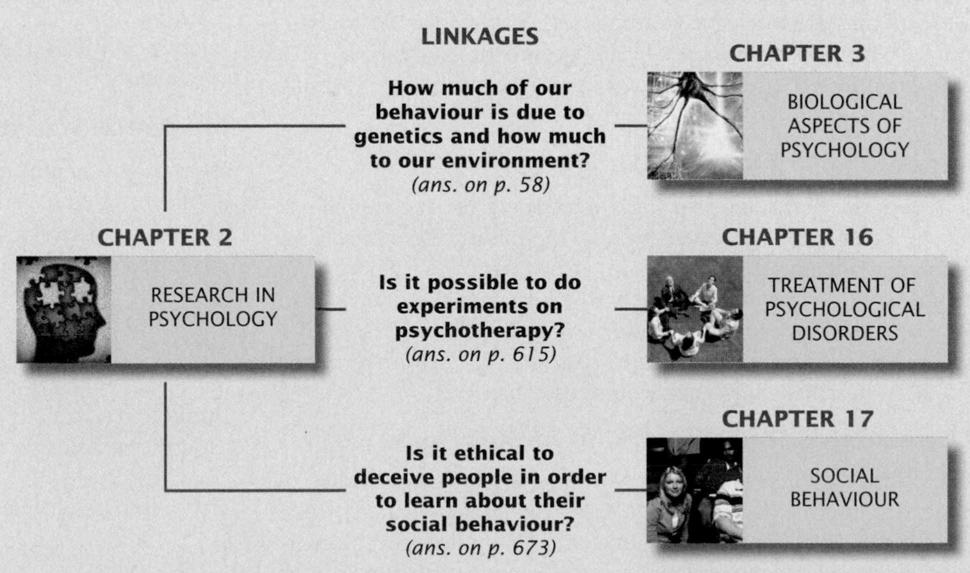
LINKAGES
CHAPTER 2
RESEARCH IN PSYCHOLOGY
How much of our behaviour is due to genetics and how much to our environment?
(ans. on p. 58)
CHAPTER 3
BIOLOGICAL ASPECTS OF PSYCHOLOGY
Is it possible to do experiments on psychotherapy?
(ans. on p. 615)
CHAPTER 16
TREATMENT OF PSYCHOLOGICAL DISORDERS
Is it ethical to deceive people in order to learn about their social behaviour?
(ans. on p. 673)
CHAPTER 17
SOCIAL BEHAVIOUR

SUMMARY

Thinking Critically About Psychology (or Anything Else)

Critical thinking is the process of assessing claims and making judgments on the basis of well-supported evidence.

Critical Thinking and Scientific Research

Often, questions about behaviour and mental processes are phrased in terms of *hypotheses* about *variables* that have been specified by *operational definitions.* Tests of hypotheses are based on objective, quantifiable evidence, or *data,* representing the variables of interest. If data are to be useful, they must be evaluated for reliability and validity.

The Role of Theories

Explanations of phenomena often take the form of a *theory,* which is a set of statements that can be used to account for, predict, and even suggest ways of controlling certain phenomena. Theories must be subjected to careful evaluation.

Research Methods in Psychology

Research in psychology, as in other sciences, focuses on four main goals: description, prediction, control, and explanation.

Naturalistic Observation: Watching Behaviour

Naturalistic observation entails watching without interfering as behaviour occurs in the natural environment. This method can be revealing, but care must be taken to ensure that observers are unbiased and do not alter the behaviour being observed.

Case Studies: Taking a Closer Look

Case studies are intensive examinations of a particular individual, group, or situation. They are useful for studying new or rare phenomena and for evaluating new treatments or training programs.

Surveys: Looking at the Big Picture

Surveys ask questions, through interviews or questionnaires, about behaviour, attitudes, beliefs, opinions, and intentions. They provide an efficient way to gather large amounts of data from many people at a relatively low cost, but their results can be distorted if questions are poorly phrased, if answers are not given honestly, or if respondents are not representative of the population whose views are of interest.

Correlational Studies: Looking for Relationships

Correlational studies examine relationships between variables in order to describe research data, test predictions, evaluate theories, and suggest hypotheses. Correlational studies are an important part of psychological research. However, the reasons behind the relationships they reveal cannot be established by correlational studies alone.

Experiments: Exploring Cause and Effect

In *experiments,* researchers manipulate an *independent variable* and observe the effect of that manipulation on a *dependent variable.* Participants receiving experimental treatment are called the *experimental group*; those in comparison conditions are called *control groups.* Experiments can reveal cause-effect relationships between variables, but only if researchers use *random assignment, placebo* conditions, *double-blind designs,* and other strategies to avoid being misled by *random variables,* participants' expectations, *experimenter bias,* and other *confounding variables.*

Selecting Human Participants for Research

Psychologists' research can be limited if their *sampling* procedures do not give them a fair cross-section of the population they want to study and about which they want to draw conclusions. Anything other than a *random sample* is said to be a *biased sample* of participants. In most cases, psychologists try to select *representative samples* of the populations that are available to them.

Statistical Analysis of Research Results

Psychologists use *descriptive statistics* and *inferential statistics* to summarize and analyze data.

Descriptive Statistics

Descriptive statistics include measures of central tendency (such as the *mode, median,* and *mean*), measures of variability (such as the *range* and *standard deviation,* or SD), and *correlation coefficients.* Although valuable for describing relationships, *correlations* alone cannot establish that two variables are causally related, nor can they determine which variable might affect which, or why.

Inferential Statistics

Psychologists employ inferential statistics to guide conclusions about data and, especially, to determine if correlations or differences between means are *statistically significant*—that is, larger than would be expected by chance alone.

Statistics and Research Methods as Tools in Critical Thinking

Scientific evaluation of research requires the use of critical thinking to carefully assess the design and statistical analysis of even the most dramatic or desirable results.

Ethical Guidelines for Psychologists

Ethical guidelines promote the protection of humans and animals in psychological research. They also set the highest standards for behaviour in all other aspects of psychologists' scientific and professional lives.

Biological Aspects of Psychology

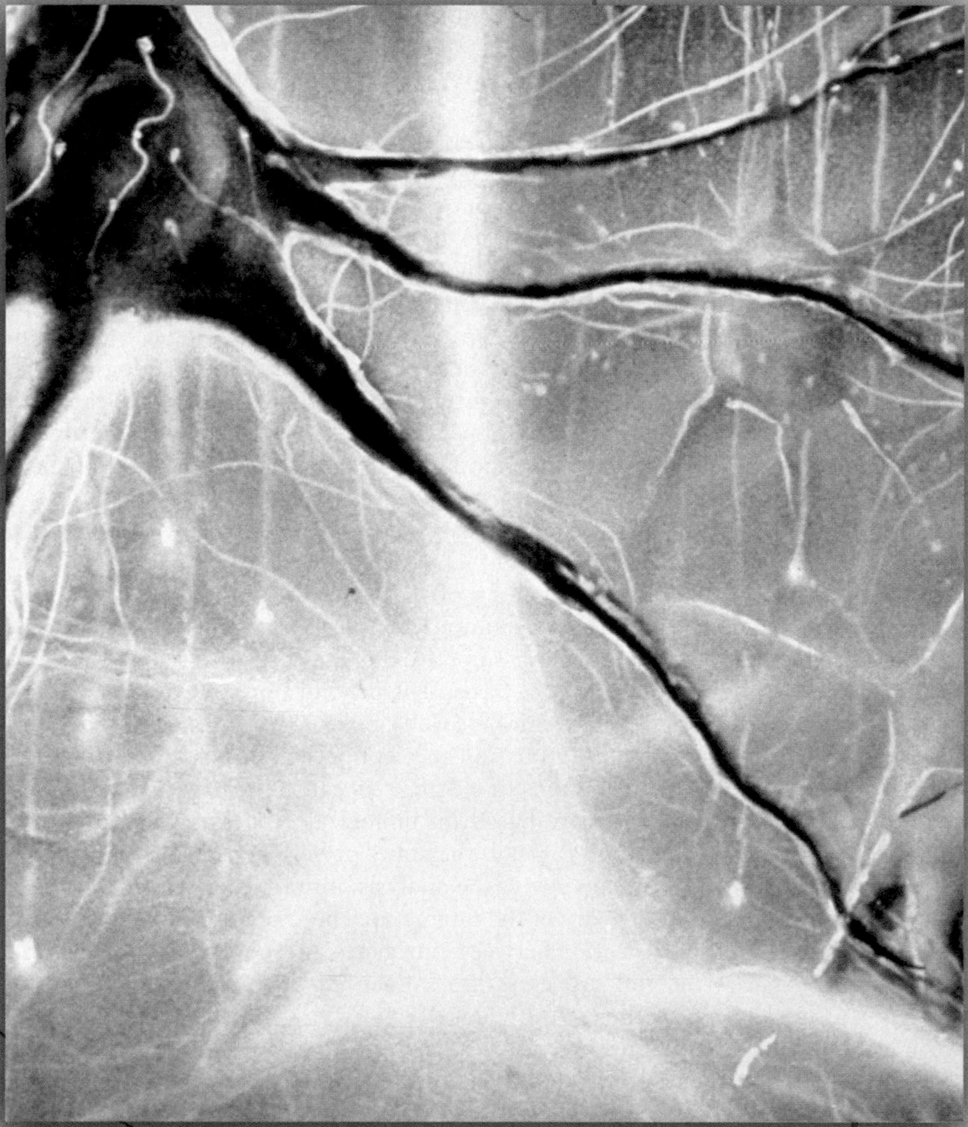

Everything you do—including how you feel and think—is based on some kind of biological activity in your body, especially in your brain. This chapter tells the story of that activity, beginning with the neuron, one of the body's most basic biological units. We describe how neurons form systems capable of receiving and processing information and translate it into behaviour, thoughts, and biochemical changes. We have organized our presentation as follows:

Do you drink coffee? Do you like beer or wine? Are you still unable to quit smoking? If so, you know that caffeine, alcohol, and nicotine can change the way you feel. The effects of these substances are based largely on their ability to change the chemistry of your brain. There are many other examples of how our mental experiences, and our identity as individuals, are rooted in biological processes. Each year, millions of people who suffer anxiety, depression, and other psychological disorders take prescription drugs that alter brain chemistry in ways that relieve their distress. And severe brain disorders such as Alzheimer's disease cause their victims to "lose themselves" as they become progressively less able to think clearly, to express themselves, to remember events, or even to recognize their families.

These examples of biological influences on behaviour and mental processes reflect the biological approach to psychology discussed in the chapter on introducing psychology. The importance and impact of that approach stems from the fact that brain cells, hormones, genes, and other biological factors are related to everything you think and feel and do, from the fleeting memory you had a minute ago to the anxiety or excitement or fatigue you felt last night to the movements of your eyes as you read right now. In this chapter, we describe these biological factors in more detail. Reading it will take you into the realm of **biological psychology,** which is the study of the cells and organs of the body and the physical and chemical changes involved in behaviour and mental processes. It is here that we begin to consider the relationship between your body and your mind, your brain and your behaviour.

It is a complex relationship. Scientific psychologists are no doubt correct when they say that every thought, every feeling, and every action are represented somehow in the nervous system and that none of these events could occur without it. However, we must be careful not to oversimplify or overemphasize biological explanations in psychology. Many people assume, for example, that if a behaviour or mental process has a strong biological basis, it is beyond our control—that "biology is destiny." Accordingly, many smokers don't even try to quit, simply because they are sure that their biological addiction to nicotine will doom them to failure. This is not necessarily true, as millions of ex-smokers can confirm. The fact that all behaviour and mental processes are based on biological processes does not mean that they can be fully understood through the study of biological processes alone.

In fact, reducing all of psychology to the analysis of brain chemicals would seriously underestimate the complexity of the interactions between our biological selves and our psychological experiences, between our genes and our environments. Just as all behaviours and mental processes are influenced by biology, all biological processes are influenced by the environment. We will see later that the experiences we have can change our brain chemistry and even our brain anatomy—often by affecting whether certain aspects of our genetic makeup are expressed. For example, consider height. Your height is strongly influenced by genetics, but how tall you actually become depends heavily on nutrition and other environmental factors (Tanner, 1992). Hereditary and environmental influences also combine to determine intelligence, personality, mental disorders, and all our other characteristics.

In short, understanding behaviour and mental processes requires that we combine information from many sources, ranging from the activity of cells and organ systems to the activity of individuals and groups in social contexts. This chapter focuses on the biological level, not because it reveals the whole story of psychology but because it tells an important part of that story.

We begin by considering the **nervous system**: the billions of cells that make up your brain, your spinal cord, and other nerve fibres. The combined activity of these cells tells you what is going on inside and outside your body and allows you

biological psychology The psychological specialty that researches the physical and chemical changes that cause, and occur in response to, behaviour and mental processes.

nervous system A complex combination of cells whose primary function is to allow an organism to gain information about what is going on inside and outside the body and to respond appropriately.

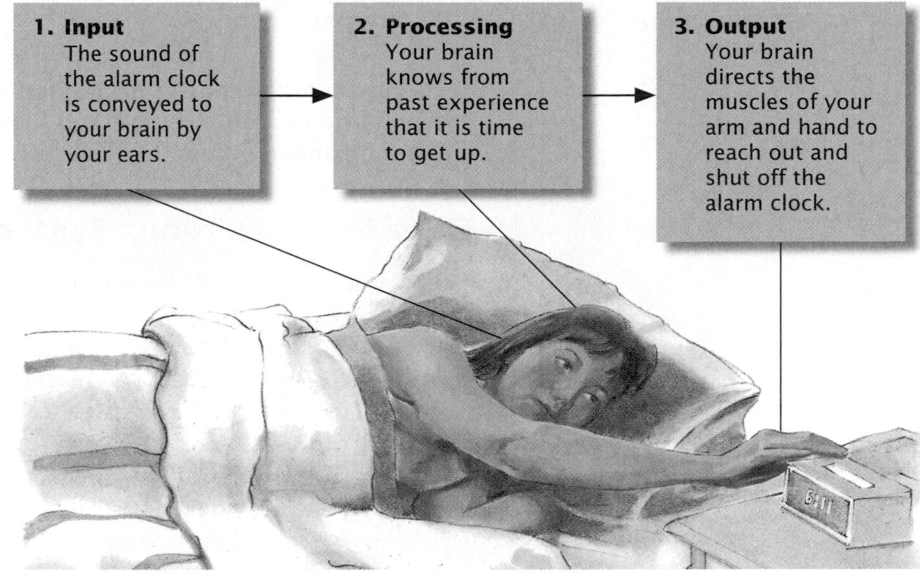

1. Input
The sound of the alarm clock is conveyed to your brain by your ears.
2. Processing
Your brain knows from past experience that it is time to get up.
3. Output
Your brain directs the muscles of your arm and hand to reach out and shut off the alarm clock.

figure 3.1

Three Functions of the Nervous System

The nervous system's three main functions are to receive information (input), integrate that information with past experiences (processing), and guide actions (output). When the alarm clock goes off, this person's nervous system, like yours, gets the message, recognizes what it means, decides what to do, and then creates action—to get out of bed or perhaps hit the snooze button.

to make appropriate responses. For example, if you are jabbed with a pin, your nervous system gets the message and immediately causes you to flinch. But your nervous system can do far more than detect information and execute responses. When information about the world reaches the brain, that information is *processed*—meaning that it is combined with information about past experiences and current wants and needs to make a decision about how to respond. The chosen action is then taken (see Figure 3.1). In other words, your nervous system displays the characteristics of an information-processing system: It has input, processing, and output capabilities.

The processing capabilities of the nervous system are especially important, not only because the brain interprets information, makes decisions, and guides action but also because the brain can actually adjust the impact of incoming information. This phenomenon helps explain why you can't tickle yourself. In one study, simply telling ticklish people that they were about to be touched on the bottom of their feet caused advance activation in the brain region that receives sensory information from the foot (Carlsson et al., 2000). The anticipation of being touched made these people all the more sensitive to that touch. However, when they were asked to touch the bottoms of their own feet, there was far less advance activation of this brain region, and they did not overreact to their touch. Why? The explanation is that when the brain plans a movement, it also predicts which of its own touch-detecting regions will be affected by that movement. So predictable, self-controlled touches, even in a normally "ticklish" spot, reduce activation of the sensory regions associated with that spot (Blakemore, Wolpert, & Frith, 2000).

The nervous system is able to do what it does partly because it is made up of cells that communicate with each other. Like all cells in the body—indeed, like all living cells—those in the nervous system can respond to various kinds of signals. Many of the signals that cells respond to come in the form of chemicals released by other cells. So even as various cells specialize during prenatal development to become skin, bone, hair, and other tissues, they still "stay in touch" through chemical signals. Bone cells, for example, add or lose calcium in response to hormones secreted in another part of the body. Cells in the bloodstream respond to viruses and other invaders by destroying them.

We'll focus first on the cells of the nervous system, because their ability to communicate is the most efficient and complex.

The Nervous System

We begin our exploration of the nervous system at the "bottom," with a description of the individual cells and molecules that compose it. Then we consider how these cells are organized to form the structures of the human nervous system.

Cells of the Nervous System

Two major types of cells—neurons and glial cells—allow the nervous system to carry out its complex signaling tasks so efficiently. **Neurons** are cells that are specialized to rapidly respond to signals and quickly send signals of their own. Most of our discussion of brain cells will be about neurons, but glial cells are important as well. *Glial* means "glue," and scientists had long believed that glial cells did no more than hold neurons together. Recent research shows, however, that **glial cells** also help neurons communicate by directing their growth, keeping their chemical environment stable, providing energy, secreting chemicals to help restore damage, and even responding to signals from neurons (Auld & Robitaille, 2003; Parish et al., 2002). Without glial cells, neurons could not function.

Common Features of Neurons Figure 3.2 shows three features that neurons share with almost every other kind of cell in the body. First, neurons have an *outer membrane* that acts like a fine screen, letting some substances pass in and out while blocking others. Second, nervous system cells have a *cell body*, that contains a *nucleus* (only red blood cells have no nucleus). The nucleus carries the genetic information that determines how a cell will function. Third, nervous system cells contain *mitochondria* (pronounced "my-toh-CON-dree-ah"), which are structures that turn oxygen and glucose into energy. This process is especially vital to brain cells. Although the brain accounts for only 2 percent of the body's weight, it consumes more than 20 percent of the body's oxygen (Sokoloff, 1981). All of this energy is required because brain cells transmit signals among themselves to an even greater extent than do cells in the rest of the body.

Besides being similar to other cells in the body, neurons are also amazingly similar to the cells in all living organisms, from bacteria to plants to humans. For example, bacteria, plant cells, and brain cells all synthesize similar proteins when they are subjected to reduced oxygen or elevated temperatures. Because of this similarity, we can learn something about human brain cells by studying cells in much simpler organisms. For example, research on the cells in worms and flies have recently provided clues to the causes of Alzheimer's disease (Driscoll & Gerstbrein, 2003).

Special Features of Neurons However, neurons have three special features that enable them to communicate signals efficiently. The first is their structure. Although neurons come in many shapes and sizes, they all have long, thin fibres that extend outward from the cell body (see Part A of Figure 3.2). When these fibres get close to other neurons, communication between the cells can occur. The intertwining of all these fibres with fibres from other neurons allows each neuron to be close to thousands or even hundreds of thousands of other neurons.

The fibres extending from a neuron's cell body are called axons and dendrites. **Axons** are the fibres that carry signals away from the cell body, out to where communication occurs with other neurons. Each neuron generally has only one axon leaving the cell body, but that one axon can have many branches. Axons can be very short or several feet long, like the axon that sends signals from your spinal cord all the way down to your big toe. **Dendrites** are the fibres that receive signals from the axons of other neurons and carry those signals to the cell body. A neuron can have many dendrites. Dendrites, too, usually have many branches. Remember that axons carry signals away from the cell body, whereas dendrites detect signals from other cells.

neuron Fundamental unit of the nervous system.

glial cell Cell in the nervous system that holds neurons together and helps them communicate with one another.

axon A neuron fibre that carries signals from the body of a neuron out to where communication occurs with other neurons.

dendrite A neuron fibre that receives signals from the axons of other neurons and carries those signals to the cell body.

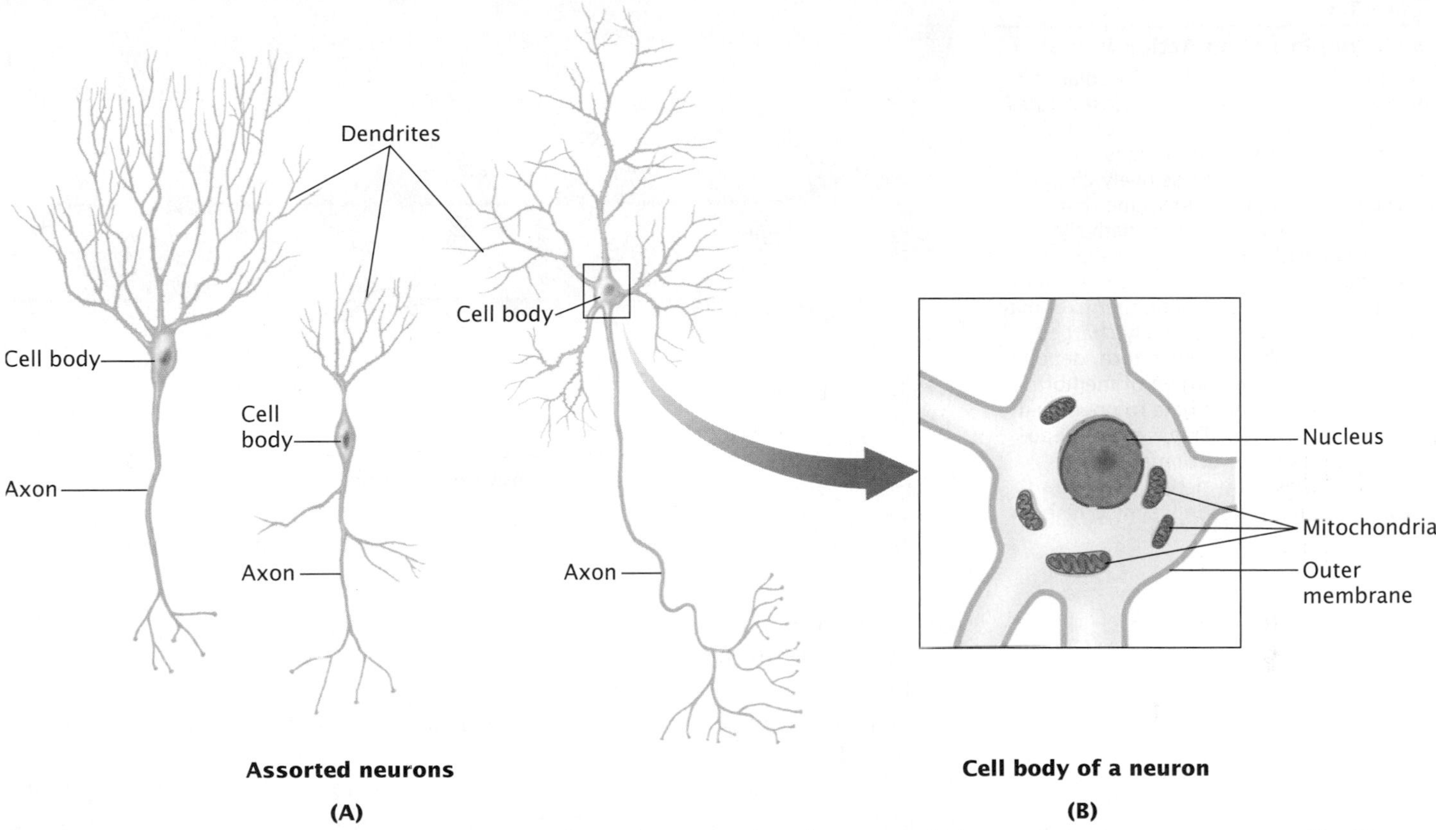

figure 3.2

The Neuron

Part A shows three examples of neurons, which are cells in the nervous system. The fibres extending outward from the cell body—the axons and dendrites—are among the features that make neurons unique. Part B is a drawing of the cell body of a neuron. The cell body of every neuron has typical cell elements, including an outer membrane, a nucleus, and mitochondria.

The neuron's ability to communicate efficiently also depends on two other features: the "excitable" surface membrane of some of its fibres and the tiny gap between neurons, called a **synapse.** Let's consider how these features allow a signal to be sent rapidly from one end of a neuron to the other and from one neuron to another.

Action Potentials

To understand how signals are sent in the nervous system, you first need to know something about nerve cell membranes and the chemicals within and outside these cells. The neuron's cell membrane is a *semipermeable* barrier, meaning that, as already mentioned, it lets some chemical molecules pass through but blocks others. Many of these molecules carry a positive or negative electrical charge. Normally, the cell pumps positively charged molecules out through its membrane, making the inside of the cell slightly more negative than the outside. In this state, the cell membrane is said to be *polarized.* Molecules with a positive charge are attracted to those with a negative charge. This attraction creates a force called an *electrochemical potential*, which drives the positively charged molecules toward the inside of the cell.

The cell membrane keeps out many of these positively charged molecules, but some are able to enter by passing through special openings, or *channels*, in the membrane. These channels are distributed along the axon and dendrites and act as gates that can be opened or closed (see Figure 3.3). Normally the channels along the axon are closed, but changes in the environment around the cell can *depolarize* part of its membrane, causing the gates in that area to swing open and allowing positively charged molecules to rush in. When this happens, the next area of the axon becomes depolarized, causing the neighbouring gate to open. This

synapse The tiny gap between neurons across which they communicate.

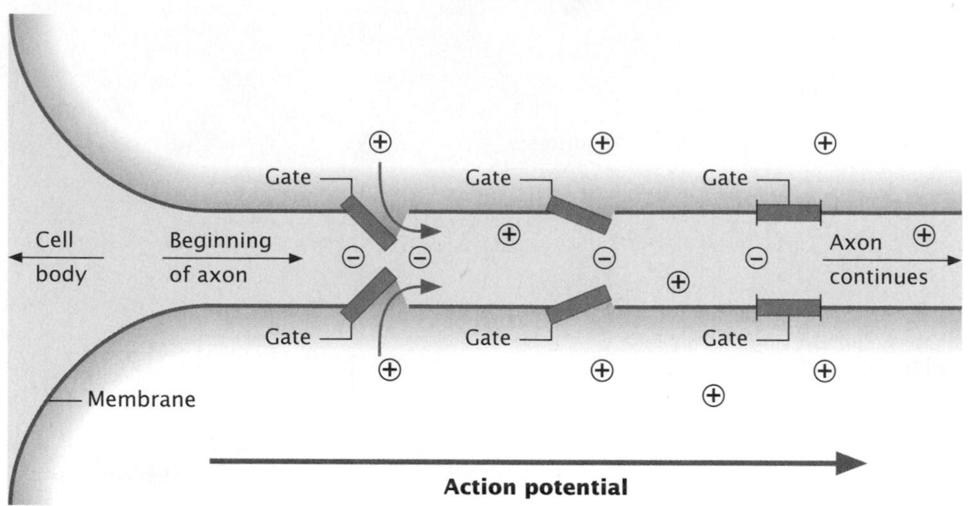

figure 3.3

The Beginning of an Action Potential

This greatly simplified view of a polarized nerve cell shows the normally closed gates in the cell membrane. The electrochemical potential across the membrane is created because there are more positively charged molecules outside the membrane than inside. There are also more negatively charged molecules on the inside than on the outside. If stimulation causes depolarization near a particular gate, that gate may swing open, allowing positively charged molecules to rush in. This, in turn, depolarizes the neighbouring region of membrane and stimulates the next gate to open, and so on down the axon. This wave of depolarization is called an *action potential.* Membrane gates allow action potentials to spread along dendrites in a similar fashion.

sequence continues, creating a wave of changes in electrochemical potential that spreads rapidly all the way down the axon.

This abrupt wave of electrochemical changes in the axon is called an **action potential.** When an action potential shoots down an axon, the neuron is said to have "fired." This term is appropriate because action potentials in axons are like gunshots: The cell either fires at full strength or it does not fire at all. For many years, scientists believed that only axons were capable of generating action potentials. However, research has now revealed that action potentials also occur in dendrites (Magee & Johnston, 1997). In many neurons, action potentials beginning in the axon go in both directions—down the axon and also "backward" through the cell body and into the dendrites. Action potentials that spread into the dendrites from the cell body appear to reach some dendritic branches and not others, leading scientists to conclude that these messages may be important in strengthening particular connections between neurons that are important to learning and memory (Golding, Staff, & Spruston, 2002; Stuart & Hausser, 2001).

The speed of the action potential as it moves down an axon is constant for a particular cell, but in different cells that speed can range from 0.2 metres per second to 120 metres per second. The speed depends on the diameter of the axon—larger ones are faster—and on whether myelin is present. **Myelin** (pronounced "MY-a-lin") is a fatty substance that wraps around some axons and speeds action potentials. Larger, myelinated cells are usually found in parts of the nervous system that carry the most urgently needed information. For example, the neurons that receive information from the environment about oncoming cars, hot irons, and other dangers are fast-acting, myelinated cells. Multiple sclerosis (MS), a severe brain disorder that destroys myelin, may occur because some viruses are very similar to components of myelin (Martin, Gran, et al., 2001). When the immune system of the person with MS attacks those viruses, it destroys vital myelin as well, resulting in disruption of vision, speech, balance, and other important functions.

Neurons can fire over and over again because their membrane gates open only briefly and then close. Between firings there is a very short rest, called a **refractory period,** during which the neuron cannot fire. As the positively charged molecules are pumped back outside the membrane, the cell returns to its original polarized state. When this *repolarization* process is complete, the neuron can fire again. The rate of firing can vary from just a few action potentials per second to as many as 1000 per second. The pattern of neurons' firing activity amounts to a coded message that, for example, tells us about the intensity of light or sound. We describe some of the codes used by the nervous system in the chapter on sensation.

action potential An abrupt wave of electrochemical changes travelling down an axon when a neuron becomes depolarized.

myelin A fatty substance that wraps around some axons and increases the speed of action potentials.

refractory period A short rest period between action potentials.

figure 3.4

A Synapse

This photograph taken with an electron microscope shows part of a neural synapse magnified 50 000 times. The ending of the presynaptic cell's axon is shaded green; the green ovals are mitochondria. The red spots are neurotransmitter-containing vesicles. The synapse itself appears as the narrow gap between the presynaptic cell's axon and the dendrite of the postsynaptic cell, which is shaded blue.

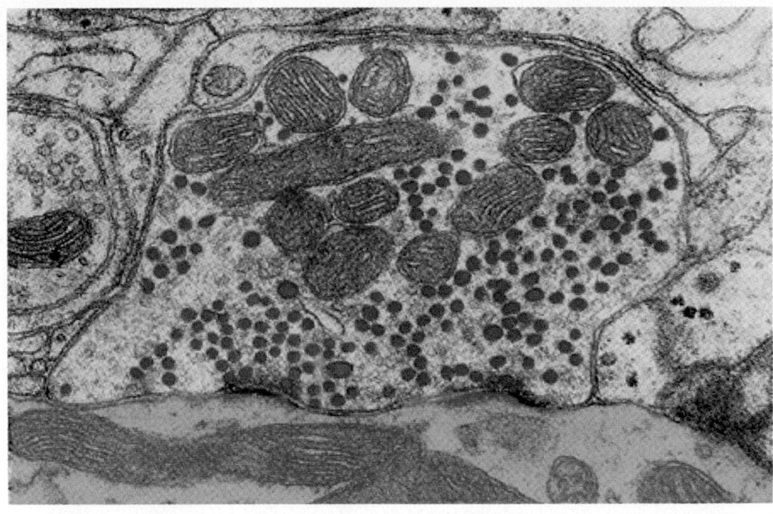

Synapses and Communication Between Neurons

How does an action potential fired by one neuron affect the activity of other neurons? For communication to occur between cells, a signal must be transmitted across the synapse, or gap, between neurons. Usually, the axon of one cell delivers its signals across a synapse to the dendrites of a second cell. Those dendrites, in turn, transmit the signal to their cell body, which may relay the signal down its axon to a third cell, and so on. But there can be other communication patterns, too. Axons can signal to other axons or even directly to the cell body of another neuron. And dendrites of one cell can send signals to the dendrites of other cells (Didier et al., 2001). These varied communication patterns allow the brain to conduct extremely complex information-processing tasks.

Neurotransmitters Communication between neurons across the synapse relies first on chemical messengers called **neurotransmitters.** These chemicals are stored in numerous little "bags," called *vesicles*, at the tips of axons (see Figure 3.4). When an action potential reaches the end of an axon, a neurotransmitter is released into the synapse, where it spreads to reach the next, or *postsynaptic*, cell (see Figure 3.5). (In the less common case of dendrite-to-dendrite communication, neurotransmitters are released by unknown mechanisms; Pape, Munsch, & Budde, 2004.)

When they reach the membrane of the postsynaptic cell, neurotransmitters attach to proteins called **receptors.** Like a puzzle piece fitting into its proper place, a neurotransmitter snugly fits, or "binds" to, its own receptors but not to receptors for other neurotransmitters (see Figure 3.6). Although each receptor "recognizes" only one type of neurotransmitter, each neurotransmitter type can bind to several different receptor types. As a result, the same neurotransmitter can have different effects depending on the type of receptor to which it binds.

When a neurotransmitter binds to a receptor, it stimulates channels in the membrane of the postsynaptic cell to open, allowing charged molecules to flow in or out. The flow of these charged molecules into and out of the postsynaptic cell produces a change in its membrane potential. So the *chemical* signal that crosses the synapse creates an *electrochemical* signal in the postsynaptic cell.

Excitatory and Inhibitory Signals The change that takes place in the membrane potential of the postsynaptic cell is called the **postsynaptic potential.** The change can make the cell either more likely or less likely to fire. For example, if the neurotransmitter depolarizes the membrane of the neighbouring cell (making it more likely to fire), the transmitter has created an **excitatory postsynaptic potential** or **EPSP.** However, if the neurostransmitter hyperpolarizes the neighbouring cell (making the cell less likely to fire), it has created an **inhibitory postsynaptic potential** or **IPSP.**

neurotransmitter Chemical that assists in the transfer of signals from one neuron to another.

receptor Site on the surface of a cell that allows only one type of neurotransmitter to fit into it, triggering a chemical response that may lead to an action potential.

postsynaptic potential The change in the membrane potential of a neuron that has received stimulation from another neuron.

excitatory postsynaptic potential A postsynaptic potential that depolarizes the neuronal membrane, making the cell more likely to fire an action potential.

inhibitory postsynaptic potential A postsynaptic potential that hyperpolarizes the neuronal membrane, making a cell less likely to fire an action potential.

figure 3.5

Communication Between Neurons

When a neuron fires, an action potential shoots to the end of its axon, triggering the release of a neurotransmitter into the synapse. This process stimulates neighbouring neurons and may cause them to fire their own action potentials.

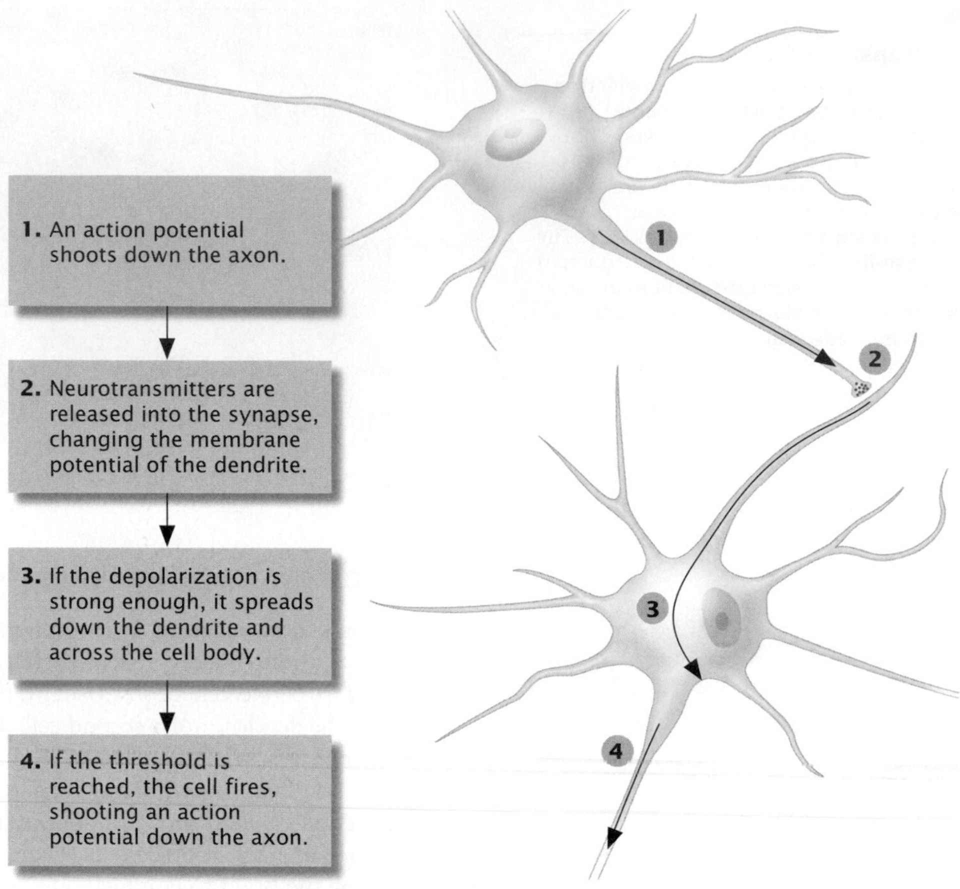

1. An action potential shoots down the axon.
2. Neurotransmitters are released into the synapse, changing the membrane potential of the dendrite.
3. If the depolarization is strong enough, it spreads down the dendrite and across the cell body.
4. If the threshold is reached, the cell fires, shooting an action potential down the axon.
1
2
3
4

The postsynaptic potential spreads along the membrane of the postsynaptic cell. But unlike the action potential in an axon, which remains at a constant strength, the postsynaptic potential fades as it goes along. Usually, it is not strong enough to pass all the way along the dendrite and through the cell body to the axon, so a single EPSP will not cause a neuron to fire. However, each neuron is constantly receiving EPSPs and

figure 3.6

The Relationship Between Neurotransmitters and Receptors

Neurotransmitters influence postsynaptic cells by stimulating special receptors on the surface of those cells' membranes. Each type of receptor receives only one type of neurotransmitter; the two fit together like puzzle pieces or like a lock and its key. As shown here, when stimulated by its neurotransmitter, a cell's receptors can help generate a wave of depolarization in that cell's dendrites, making it more likely to fire. A cell's receptors can also receive signals that have the opposite effect, making the cell less likely to fire.

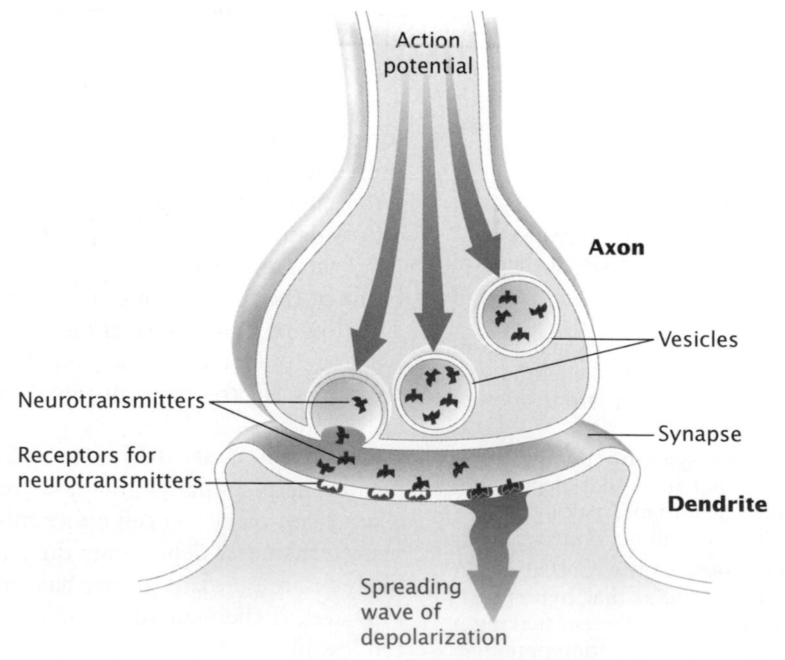

figure 3.7

Integration of Neural Signals

Most of the signals that a neuron receives arrive at its dendrites or at its cell body. These signals typically come from many neighbouring cells and can contain conflicting messages. Excitatory signals make the cell more likely to fire. Inhibitory signals make the cell less likely to fire. Whether or not the cell actually fires at any given moment depends on whether excitatory or inhibitory messages predominate at the junction of the cell body and the axon.

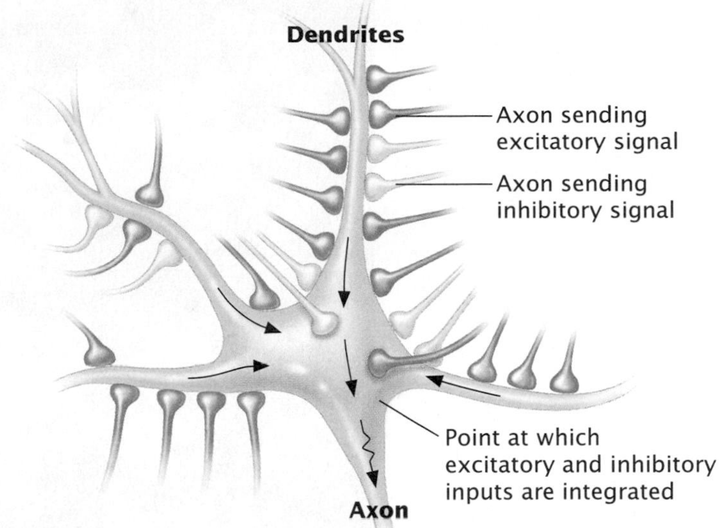

IPSPs. The combined effect of rapidly repeated potentials—or of potentials coming from many locations—can create a signal strong enough to reach the junction of the axon and cell body, a specialized region in which new action potentials are generated.

Whether or not the postsynaptic cell fires and how rapidly it fires depend on whether, at a given moment, there are more excitatory ("fire") or more inhibitory ("don't fire") signals from other neurons at this junction (see Figure 3.7). So, as neurotransmitters transfer information across many neurons, each neuron constantly integrates or processes this information.

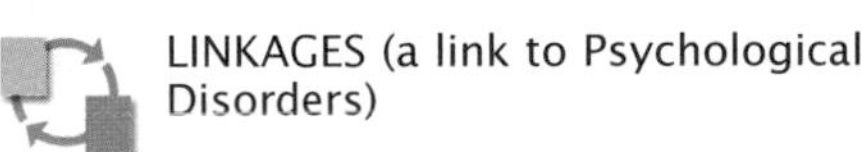
LINKAGES (a link to Psychological Disorders)

Neurotransmitters are involved in every aspect of behaviour and mental processes, as you will see later in this chapter and in other chapters, too. In the chapter on sensation, for example, we describe some of the neurotransmitters used in pathways that convey pain messages throughout the brain and spinal cord. In the consciousness chapter, we describe how neurotransmitters are affected by alcohol and illegal drugs. In the chapter on psychological disorders, we discuss the role

in review Neurons, Neurotransmitters, and Receptors

Part	Function	Type of Signal Carried
Axon	Carries signals away from the cell body	The action potential, an all-or-nothing electrochemical signal that shoots down the axon to vesicles at the tip of the axon, releasing neurotransmitters
Dendrite	Detects and carries signals to the cell body	The postsynaptic potential, an electrochemical signal moving toward the cell body
Synapse	Provides an area for the transfer of signals between neurons, usually between the axon of one cell and the dendrite of another	Chemicals that cross the synapse and reach receptors on another cell
Neurotransmitter	A chemical released by one cell that binds to the receptors on another cell	A chemical message telling the next cell to fire or not to fire its own action potential
Receptor	Protein on the cell membrane that receives chemical signals	Recognizes certain neurotransmitters, thus allowing it to begin a postsynaptic potential in the dendrite

PsychAssist: Action Potential
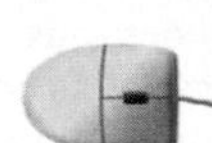

A Damaged Nervous System If axons, dendrites, or other components of the nervous system are damaged or disordered, serious problems can result. The spinal cord injury that Rick Hansen suffered cut the neural communication lines that had allowed him to feel and move the lower part of his body.

that neurotransmitters play in schizophrenia and depression; in the chapter on the treatment of psychological disorders, we consider how prescription drugs act on neurotransmitters to alleviate the symptoms of those disorders. Neurotransmitters are affected by many other chemicals, too, from the nerve agents used in biological weapons to the Botox used in anti-wrinkle treatments.

Organization and Functions of the Nervous System

Impressive as individual neurons are (see "In Review: Neurons, Neurotransmitters, and Receptors"), we can best understand their functions by looking at how they operate in groups. In the brain and spinal cord, neurons are organized into groups called **neural networks.** Many neurons in a network are closely connected, sending axons to the dendrites of many other neurons in the network. Signals from one network also go to other networks, and small networks are organized into bigger collections. By studying these networks, neuroscientists have begun to see that the nervous system conveys information not so much by the activity of single neurons sending single messages with a particular meaning but by the activity of groups of neurons firing together in varying combinations. So the same neurons may be involved in producing different patterns of behaviour, depending on which combinations of them are active.

The groups of neurons in the nervous system that provide information about the environment are known as the senses, or **sensory systems.** These systems—including hearing, vision, taste, smell, and touch—are described in the chapter on sensation. Integration and processing of information occur mainly in the brain. Output flows through **motor systems,** which are the parts of the nervous system that influence muscles and other organs to respond to the environment.

The nervous system has two major divisions that work together: the peripheral nervous system and the central nervous system (see Figure 3.8). The **peripheral nervous system (PNS),** which includes all of the nervous system that is not housed in bone, carries out sensory and motor functions. The **central nervous system (CNS)** is the part encased in bone. It includes the brain, which is inside the skull, and the spinal cord, which is inside the spinal column (backbone). The CNS is often called the "central executive" of the body because information is usually sent to the CNS to be processed and acted on. Let's take a closer look at these divisions of the nervous system.

neural network Neurons that operate together to perform complex functions.

sensory systems The parts of the nervous system that provide information about the environment.

motor systems The parts of the nervous system that influence muscles and other organs to respond to the environment in some way.

peripheral nervous system The parts of the nervous system not housed in bone.

central nervous system The parts of the nervous system encased in bone, including the brain and the spinal cord.

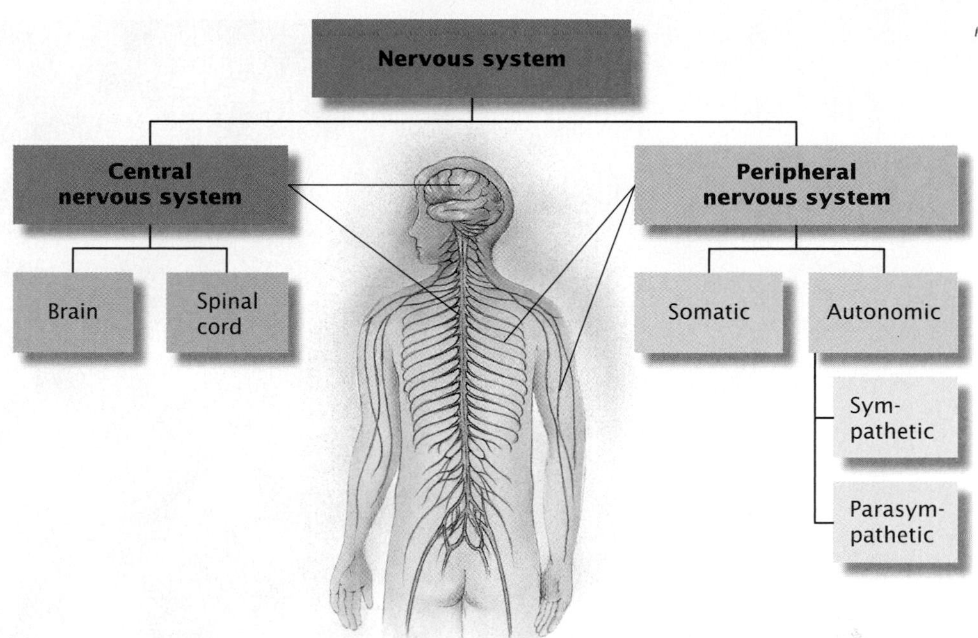

figure 3.8

Organization of the Nervous System

The brain and spinal cord make up the bone-encased central nervous system (CNS), the body's central information processor, decision maker, and director of actions. The peripheral nervous system, which is not housed in bone, functions mainly to carry messages. The somatic subsystem of the peripheral nervous system transmits information to the CNS from the outside world and conveys instructions from the CNS to the muscles. The autonomic subsystem conveys messages from the CNS that alter the activity of organs and glands, and it sends information about that activity back to the brain.

The Peripheral Nervous System: Keeping in Touch with the World

As shown in Figure 3.8, the peripheral nervous system has two components, each of which performs both sensory and motor functions.

The Somatic Nervous System

The first of these components is the **somatic nervous system**, which transmits information from the senses to the CNS and carries signals from the CNS to the muscles that move the skeleton. For example, when you lie in the sun at the beach, the somatic nervous system sends signals from the skin to the brain that become sensations of warmth. The somatic nervous system is also involved in every move you make. Neurons extend from the spinal cord to the muscles, where the release of a neurotransmitter onto them causes the muscles to contract. In fact, much of what we know about neurotransmitters was discovered in laboratory studies of this "neuromuscular junction," especially in the hind legs of frogs. At the neuromuscular junction, the action of a neurotransmitter allows a quick response that can mean the difference between life and death for a frog or any other animal, including humans.

The Autonomic Nervous System

The second component of the peripheral nervous system, the **autonomic nervous system,** carries messages back and forth between the CNS and the heart, lungs, and other organs and glands (Berthoud & Neuhuber, 2000). These messages increase or decrease the activity of the organs and glands to meet varying demands placed on the body. As you lie on the beach, it is your autonomic nervous system that makes your heart beat a little faster when an attractive person walks by and smiles at you.

The name *autonomic* means "autonomous" and suggests independent operation. This term is appropriate because, although the autonomic nervous system is influenced by the brain, it controls activities that are normally outside of conscious control, such as digestion and perspiration (sweating). The autonomic nervous system exercises this control through its two divisions: the sympathetic and parasympathetic branches. Generally, the *sympathetic system* mobilizes the body for action

somatic nervous system The subsystem of the peripheral nervous system that transmits information from the senses to the central nervous system and carries signals from the central nervous system to the muscles.

autonomic nervous system The subsystem of the peripheral nervous system that carries messages between the central nervous system and the heart, lungs, and other organs and glands.

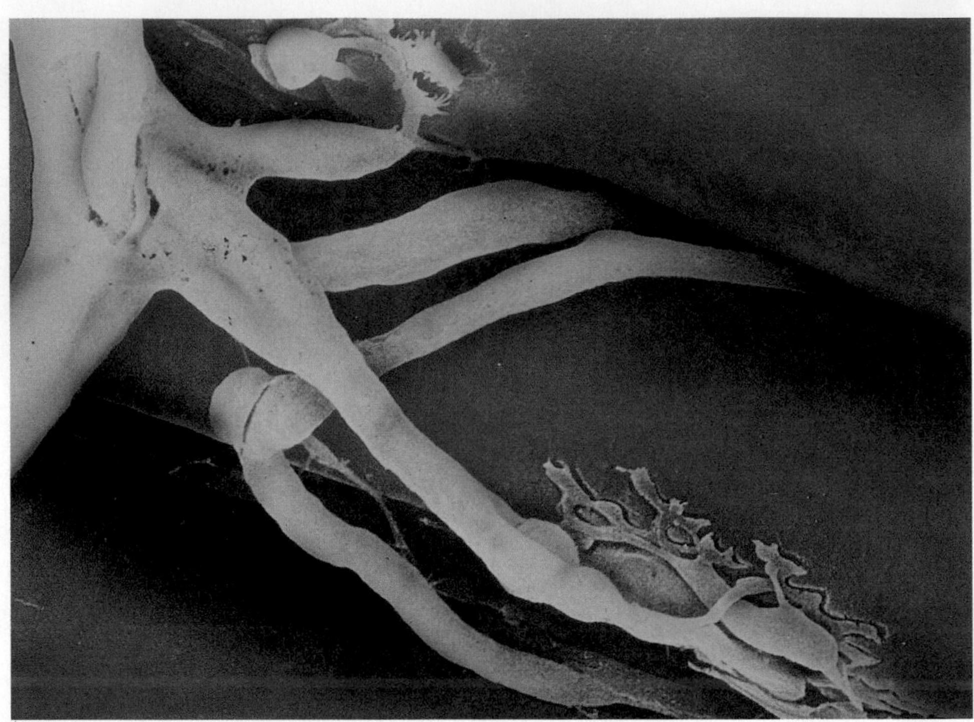

The Neuromuscular Junction When nerve cells (shown here as green fibres) release neurotransmitters onto muscle tissue, the muscle contracts.

in the face of stress. The responses that result are collectively referred to as the *fight-or-flight syndrome*. The *parasympathetic system* regulates the body's energy-conserving functions. These two branches often create opposite effects. For example, the sympathetic nervous system can make your heart beat faster, whereas the parasympathetic nervous system can slow it down.

The functions of the autonomic nervous system may not get star billing, but you would miss them if they were gone. Just as a race-car driver is nothing without a good pit crew, the somatic nervous system depends on the autonomic nervous system to get its job done. For example, when you want to move your muscles, you create a demand for energy. The autonomic nervous system fills the bill by increasing sugar (fuel) in the bloodstream. If you decide to stand up, you need increased blood pressure so that your blood does not flow out of your brain and settle in your legs. Again, the autonomic nervous system makes the adjustment. Disorders of the autonomic nervous system can make people sweat uncontrollably or faint whenever they stand up; they can also lead to other problems, such as an inability to have sex. We examine the autonomic nervous system in more detail in the chapter on motivation and emotion.

The Central Nervous System: Making Sense of the World

The amazing speed and efficiency of the neural networks that make up the central nervous system—the brain and spinal cord—have prompted many people to compare it to the central processor in a computer. In fact, to better understand how human and other brains work and how they relate to sensory and motor systems, *computational neuroscientists* have created neural network models on computers (Koch & Davis, 1994). Figure 3.9 shows an example of how the three components of the nervous system (input, processing, and output) might be represented in a neural network model. Notice that input simultaneously activates several paths in the network, so information is processed in various places at the same time. Accordingly, the activity of these models is described as *parallel distributed processing*. In the chapters on sensation, perception, learning, and memory, we describe how parallel distributed processing often characterizes the activity of the brain.

Donald Olding Hebb (1904–1985)
Dr. Donald Hebb, born in Chester, Nova Scotia, and educated at Dalhousie, McGill, and Harvard Universities, played a key role in the emergence of the subfield of biopsychology. He was also instrumental in the development of the concept of Neural Networks. In *The Organization of Behaviour* published in 1949, Dr. Hebb postulated that certain neural pathways are strengthened or become more efficient the more often they are used. This concept known as the Hebb Rule is still used today by cognitive scientists when developing artificial intelligence systems (Klein, 1999; Pinel, J., 2000).

Neural network models are neatly laid out like computer circuits or the carefully planned streets of a new suburb, but the flesh-and-blood central nervous system is more difficult to follow. In fact, the CNS looks more like Toronto or Halifax, with distinct neighbourhoods, winding back streets, and multi-lane highways. Its "neighbourhoods" are collections of neuronal cell bodies called **nuclei.** The "highways" of the central nervous system are made up of axons that travel together in bundles called **fibre tracts** or pathways. Like a highway ramp, the axon from a given cell may merge with and leave fibre tracts, and it may send branches into other tracts. The pathways travel from one nucleus to other nuclei, and scientists have learned much about how the brain works by tracing the connections among nuclei. To begin our description of some of these nuclei and anatomical connections, let's consider a practical example of nervous system functioning.

At 6 A.M., your alarm goes off. The day begins innocently enough with what appears to be a simple case of information processing. Input in the form of sound from the alarm clock is received by your ears, which convert the sound into neural signals that reach your brain. Your brain compares these signals with previous experiences stored in memory and correctly associates the sound with "alarm clock." However, your output is somewhat impaired because your brain's activity has not yet reached the waking state. It directs your muscles poorly: You get out of bed and shuffle into the kitchen, where, in your drowsy condition, you touch a hot burner as you reach for the coffeepot. Now things get more lively. Heat energy activates sensory neurons in your fingers, and action potentials flash along fibre tracts going into the spinal cord.

The Spinal Cord

The **spinal cord** receives signals from the senses, including pain and touch from the fingertips, and relays those signals to the brain through fibres within the cord. Neurons in the spinal cord also carry signals downward, from the brain to the muscles. In addition, cells of the spinal cord can direct some simple behaviours without instructions from the brain. These behaviours are called **reflexes** because the response to an incoming signal is directly "reflected" back out (see Figure 3.10).

For example, when you touched that hot burner, impulses from sensory neurons in your fingers reflexively activated motor neurons, which caused muscles in your

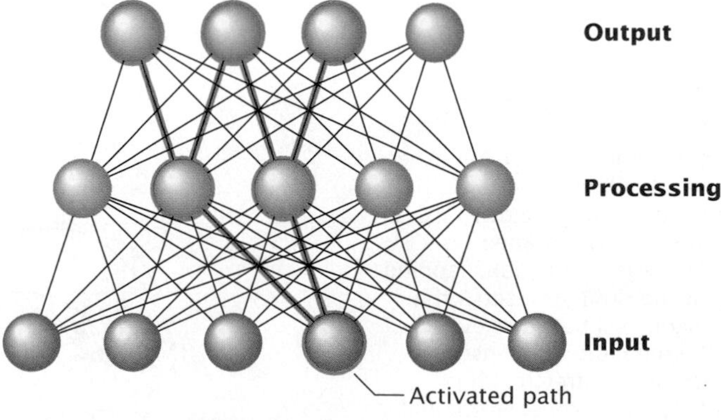

figure 3.9

A Neural Network Model

This simple computer-based neural network model includes an input layer, a processing layer, and an output layer. Notice that each element in each layer is connected to every other element in each of the other layers. As in the brain itself, these connections can be either excitatory or inhibitory, and the strength of the connections between elements can be modified (the Hebb Rule), depending on how often they are used and the results of the output; in other words, a computerized neural network model has the capacity to learn. We discuss examples of such "artificial intelligence" systems in the chapter on cognition and language.

nuclei Collections of nerve cell bodies in the central nervous system.

fibre tracts Axons in the central nervous system that travel together in bundles.

spinal cord The part of the central nervous system within the spinal column that relays signals from peripheral senses to the brain and conveys messages from the brain to the rest of the body.

reflex Involuntary, unlearned reaction in the form of swift, automatic, and finely coordinated movements in response to external stimuli.

arm to contract and quickly withdraw your hand. Because spinal reflexes like this one include few time-consuming synaptic links, they are very fast. And because spinal reflexes occur without instructions from the brain, they are considered involuntary. Still, they do send action potentials along fibre tracts going to the brain. So you officially "know" you have been burned a fraction of a second after your reflex got you out of further trouble.

The story does not end there, however. When a simple reflex set off by touching something hot causes one set of arm muscles to contract, an opposing set of muscles relaxes. If this did not happen, the arm would go rigid. Furthermore, muscles have receptors that send impulses to the spinal cord to let it know how extended they are, so that a reflex pathway can adjust the muscle contraction to allow smooth movement. This is an example of a *feedback system*, a series of processes in which information about the consequences of an action goes back to the source of the action so that adjustments can be made.

In the spinal cord, sensory neurons are called *afferent* neurons and motor neurons are termed *efferent* neurons, because *afferent* means "coming toward" and *efferent* means "going away." To remember these terms, notice that *afferent* and *approach* both begin with *a*; *efferent* and *exit* both begin with *e*.

LINKAGES (a link to Sensation)

The Brain

When pain messages from that hot burner reach your brain, you not only become aware of being burned. You might also realize that you have burned yourself twice before in the past week and get annoyed at your own carelessness. The brain is the most complex element in the central nervous system, and it is your brain's astonishing capacity for information processing that allows you to have these thoughts and feelings. A variety of new brain-scanning techniques, combined with some older techniques, have allowed neuroscientists to learn more than ever before about the workings of the human brain (Miller, 2003; see Table 3.1).

Each technique can indirectly measure the activity of neurons firing, and each has different advantages and disadvantages. One of the earliest of these techniques, called the *electroencephalograph (EEG)*, measures general electrical activity of the brain. Electrodes are pasted onto the scalp to detect the electrical fields resulting from the activity of billions of neurons. This tool can associate rapidly changing electrical activity with changes in the activity of the brain, but it cannot tell us exactly where the active cells are. EEG recordings have been used in a wide variety

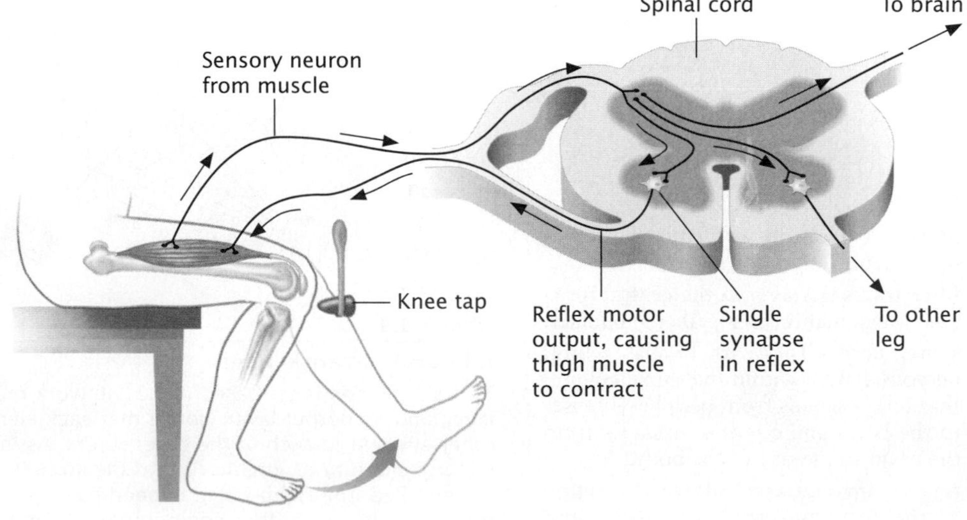

figure 3.10

A Reflex Pathway

Sit on a chair, cross one leg over the other, and then use the handle of a butter knife or some other solid object to gently tap your top knee, just below the kneecap, until you get a "knee jerk" reaction. Tapping your knee at just the right spot sets off an almost instantaneous sequence of events that begins with stimulation of sensory neurons that respond to stretch. When those neurons fire, their axons, which end within the spinal cord, cause spinal neurons to fire. This, in turn, stimulates the firing of motor neurons with axons ending in your thigh muscles. The result is a contraction of those muscles and a kicking of the lower leg and foot. Information about the knee tap and about what the leg has done also goes to your cerebral cortex, but the reflex is completed without waiting for guidance from the brain.

Dr. Wilder Graves Penfield (1891–1976) No discussion of the workings of the human brain would be complete without mentioning the Montreal Neurological Institute and the work of its founder, Dr. Penfield. During the mid- to late 1930s, Dr. Penfield and his team perfected a surgical treatment of severe epilepsy. During the surgical procedures, which were performed under a local anesthetic, Dr. Penfield mapped out the human brain using electrical stimulation while observing the effects it had on his patient. The technique, still used today, is referred to as the Montreal Procedure (Leitch, 1978, and Canadian Heirloom Series).

of applications, from the study of face recognition, to lie detection. For example, Dr. James Tanaka of the University of Victoria, British Columbia, has been using EEG recordings to study the neurological processes involved in object recognition. Dr. Tanaka has compared experts at object recognition, such as experienced bird watchers, to non-experts. He has found that expert bird watchers demonstrated a different brain wave pattern in the area of the visual cortex when categorizing birds (Tanaka and Curran, 2001).

A newer technique, called the *PET* scan can locate cell activity by recording where radioactive substances become concentrated when injected into the bloodstream. *PET* stands for *positron emission tomography*. It records images from the brain that indicate the location of the radioactivity as the brain performs various tasks. For instance, PET studies have revealed that specific brain regions are activated when we look at fearful facial expressions or engage in certain kinds of thoughts (Morris, Ohman, & Dolan, 1998; Wharton et al., 2000). PET scans can tell us a lot about where changes in brain activity occur, but they can't reveal details of the brain's physical structure. Endel Tulving of the University of Toronto has been using PET scans in the study of human memory. He and his colleagues ask people to memorize and later recall information while they are in the scanner to see which parts of the brain appear to be most active (Kapur et al., 1996).

LINKAGES (a link to Memory)

A detailed structural picture of the brain can be seen, however, using *magnetic resonance imaging*, or *MRI*. MRI exposes the brain to a magnetic field and measures the resulting radio frequency waves to get amazingly clear pictures of the brain's anatomical details (see Figure 3.11). *Functional MRI*, or *fMRI* (Figure 3.12), combines the advantages of PET and MRI and is capable of detecting changes in blood flow that reflect ongoing changes in the activity of neurons—providing a sort of "moving picture" of the brain (e.g., Shu et al., 2002). The newest techniques offer even better insight into brain activity, structure, and functioning. These techniques include a variant on fMRI called *diffusion tensor imaging (DTI)*, which traces activity of axon pathways, as well as a procedure called *transcranial magnetic stimulation (TMS)*, which temporarily disrupts the function of a particular part of the brain. This technique may also have potential in the treatment of certain psychological disorders (George, 2003; Rohan et al., 2004).

These tools have opened new frontiers for biological psychology, neuroscience, and medicine. Much of our growing understanding of how and why behaviour occurs comes from research with these techniques (e.g., Goldstein & Volkow, 2002; Hyman, 2003; Miller, 2003). Let's now explore some of the structures highlighted by these techniques, starting with the brain's three major subdivisions: the hind brain, the midbrain, and the forebrain.

The Hindbrain Incoming signals first reach the **hindbrain,** which is actually a continuation of the spinal cord. As you can see in Figure 3.13, the hindbrain lies just inside the skull. Blood pressure, heart rate, breathing, and many other vital autonomic functions are controlled by nuclei in the hindbrain, particularly in an area called the **medulla.** Reflexes and feedback systems are important to the functioning of the hindbrain, just as they are in the spinal cord. If you stand up very quickly, your blood pressure can drop so suddenly that it produces lightheadedness until the hindbrain reflex "catches up." If the hindbrain does not activate autonomic nervous system mechanisms to increase blood pressure, you will faint.

Threading throughout the hindbrain and into the midbrain is a collection of cells that are not arranged in any well-defined nucleus. Because the collection resembles a net, it is called the **reticular formation** (*reticular* means "net-like"). This network is very important in altering the activity of the rest of the brain. It is involved, for example, in arousal (the state of heightened awareness and alertness caused by a strong external stimulus such as danger or sexual interest) and attention. If the fibres from the reticular system are disconnected from the rest of the brain, a permanent coma results. Some of the fibres carrying pain signals from the spinal cord

hindbrain An extension of the spinal cord contained inside the skull where nuclei control blood pressure, heart rate, breathing, and other vital functions.

medulla An area in the hindbrain that controls blood pressure, heart rate, breathing, and other vital functions.

reticular formation A network of cells and fibres threaded throughout the hindbrain and midbrain that alters the activity of the rest of the brain.

table 3.1
Techniques for Studying Human Brain Function and Structure

Technique	What It Shows	Advantages (+) and Disadvantages (−)
EEG (electroencephalograph): Multiple electrodes are pasted to the outside of the head	Lines that chart the summated electrical fields resulting from the activity of billions of neurons	+ Detects very rapid changes in electrical activity, allowing analysis of stages of cognitive processing − Provides poor spatial resolution of the source of electrical activity; EEG is sometimes combined with magnetoencephalography (MEG), which localizes electrical activity by measuring magnetic fields associated with it
PET (positron emission tomography) and SPECT (single-photon emission computed tomography): Positrons and photons are emissions from radioactive substances	An image of the amount and localization of any molecule that can be injected in radioactive form, such as neurotransmitters, drugs, or tracers for blood flow or glucose use (which indicates specific changes in neuronal activity)	+ Allows functional and biochemical studies + Provides visual image corresponding to anatomy − Requires exposure to low levels of radioactivity − Provides spatial resolution better than that of EEG but poorer than that of MRI − Cannot follow rapid changes (faster than 30 seconds)
MRI (magnetic resonance imaging): Exposes the brain to a magnetic field and measures radio frequency waves	Traditional MRI provides high-resolution image of brain anatomy. Functional MRI (fMRI) provides images of changes in blood flow (which indicate specific changes in neural activity). A new variant, diffusion tensor imaging (DTI), shows water flow in neural fibers, thus revealing the "wiring diagram" of neural connections in the brain.	+ Requires no exposure to radioactivity + Provides high spatial resolution of anatomical details (< 1 mm) + Provides high temporal resolution ($< \frac{1}{10}$ second)
TMS (transcranial magnetic stimulation): Temporarily disrupts electrical activity of a small region of brain by exposing it to an intense magnetic field	Normal function of a particular brain region can be studied by observing changes after TMS is applied to a specific location	+ Shows which brain regions are necessary for given tasks − Long-term safety not well established

figure 3.11

Combining a PET Scan and Magnetic Resonance Imaging

Researchers have superimposed images from PET scans and MRI to construct a three-dimensional view of the living brain. Here you can see the brain of a young epileptic girl. The picture of the outer surface of the brain is from the MRI. The pink area is from the PET scan and shows the source of epileptic activity. The images at the right are the MRI and PET images at one plane, or "slice," through the brain (indicated by the line on the brain at the left).

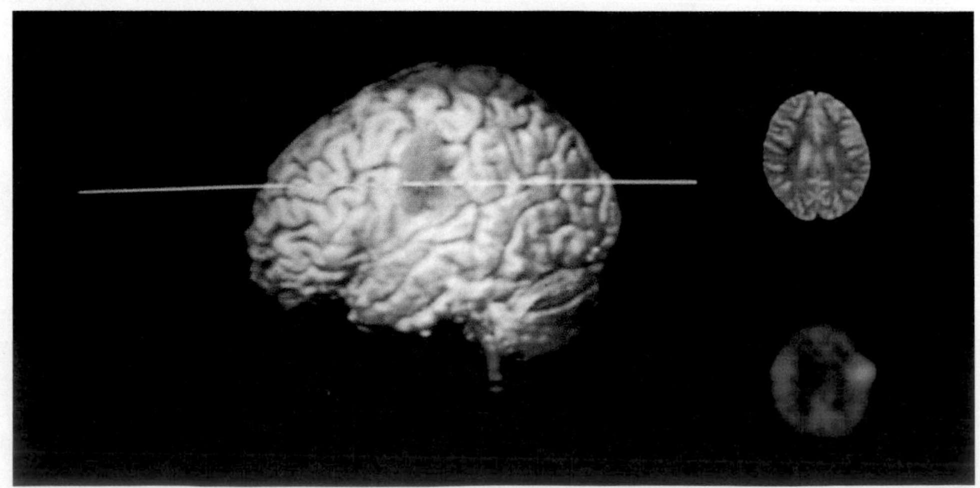

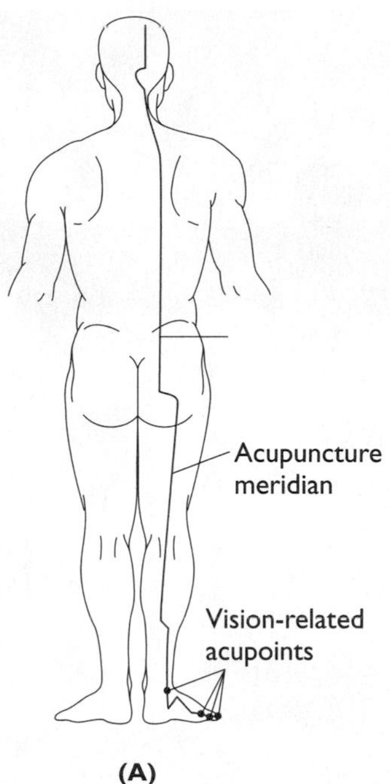

(A)

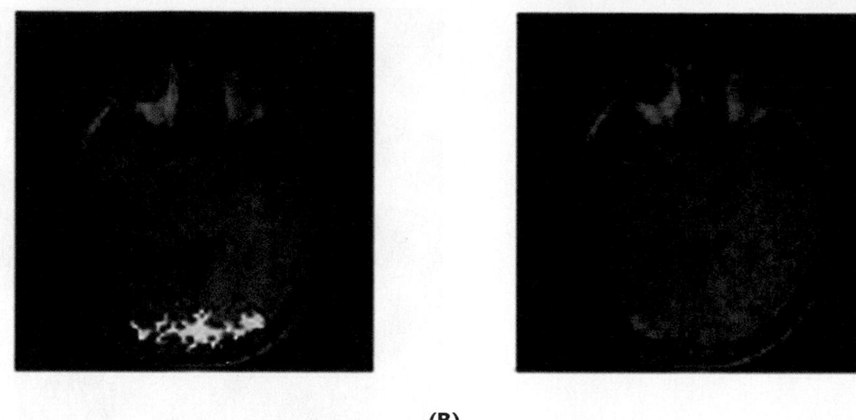

(B)

Acupuncture is an ancient Asian medical practice in which physical disorders are treated by stimulating specific locations in the skin with needles. Most acupuncture points are far from the organ being treated. For example, vision problems are treated by inserting needles at "acupoints" in the foot (Part A). In Part B, similar areas of the brain are activated by direct sensory stimulation and the related acupoints on the foot. The MRI images on the left are produced by visual stimuli. On the right is an MRI image showing activation of the same brain areas in response to acupuncture at a vision-related spot in the foot. These acupoints are located near nerves, but the pathways to specific parts of the brain have not been charted.

figure 3.12

Linking Eastern Medicine and Western Neuroscience Through Functional MRI

figure 3.13

Major Structures of the Brain (with Hindbrain Highlighted)

This side view of a section cut down the middle of the human brain reveals the forebrain, midbrain, hindbrain, and spinal cord. Many of these subdivisions do not have clear-cut borders, because they are all interconnected by fibre tracts. The anatomy of the mammalian brain reflects its evolution over millions of years. Newer structures (such as the cerebral cortex, which is the outer surface of the forebrain) that handle higher mental functions were built on older ones (such as the medulla) that coordinate heart rate, breathing, and other more basic functions.

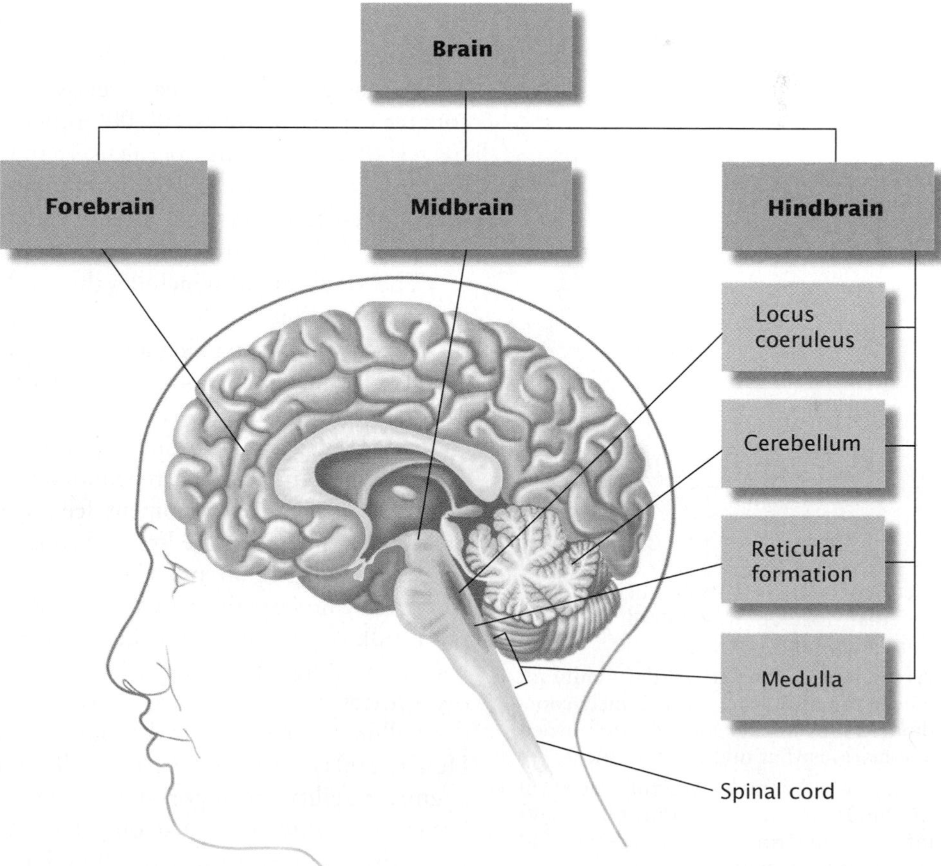

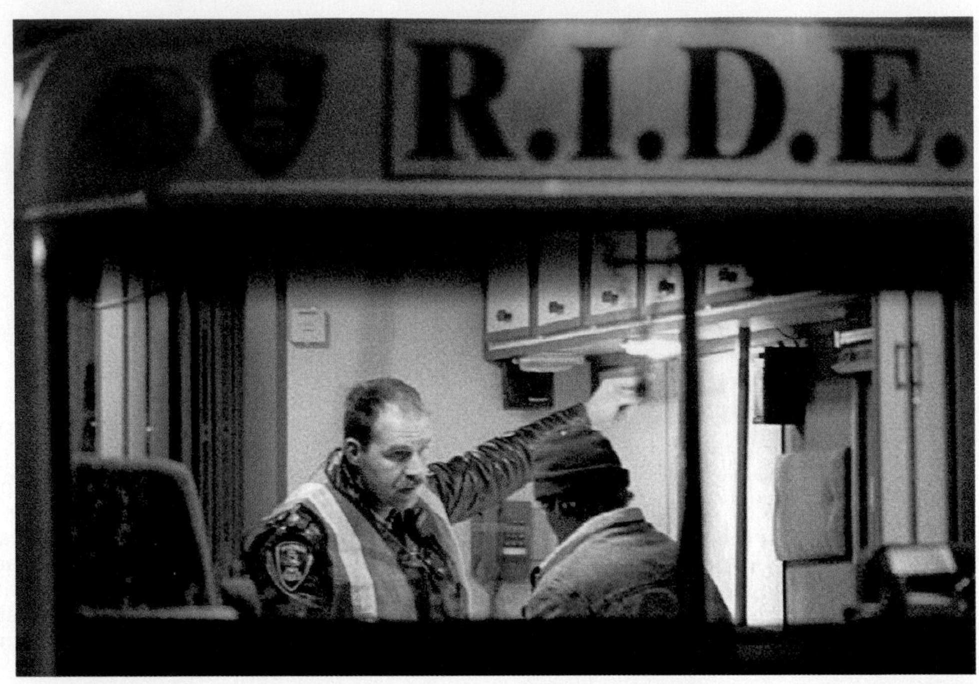

The Effects of Alcohol on the Cerebellum The cerebellum is involved in coordination, which is required for a number of activities including driving. When the cerebellum's activity is impaired by alcohol, these skills are severely disrupted.

make connections in the reticular formation, which immediately arouses the rest of the brain from sleep. Within seconds, the hindbrain causes your heart rate and blood pressure to increase.

Activity of the reticular formation also leads to activity in a small nucleus within it called the **locus coeruleus** (pronounced "LO-kus seh-ROO-lee-us"), which means "blue spot" (see Figure 3.13). There are relatively few cells in the locus coeruleus—only about 30 000 of the 100 billion or so in the human brain (Foote, Bloom, & Aston-Jones, 1983)—but each sends out an axon that branches extensively, making contact with as many as 100 000 other cells. Studies of rats, monkeys, and humans suggest that the locus coeruleus is involved in directing attention (Aston-Jones, Chiang, & Alexinsky, 1991). In humans, abnormalities in the locus coeruleus have been linked to depression, attention deficit hyperactivity disorder, sleep disorders, and post-traumatic stress disorder (Berridge & Waterhouse, 2003).

The hindbrain also includes the **cerebellum** (pronounced "sair-a-BELL-um"). Its primary function was long thought to be the coordination of movements, such as those involved in threading a needle. However, fMRI and other brain imaging studies have led neuroscientists to believe that the cerebellum is involved in many activities that are not directly related to physical movement, such as memory, impulse control, language, and other higher-order cognitive processes (Bower & Parsons, 2003). For example, the cerebellum appears to play a vital role in normal speech by integrating moment-to-moment feedback about vocal sounds with a sequence of precise movements of the lips and tongue (Leiner, Leiner, & Dow, 1993). When this process of integration and sequencing is disrupted, stuttering can result. Even non-stutterers who hear their own speech with a slight delay begin to stutter. (This is why radio talk-show hosts ask callers to turn off their radios. A momentary gap occurs before the shows are actually broadcast, and listening to the delayed sound of their own voices on the radio can cause callers to stutter.) PET studies indicate that the cerebellum is one of several brain regions involved in stuttering (De Nil, Kroll, & Houle, 2001). In short, the cerebellum seems to be involved in both physical and cognitive agility. Its importance is suggested by the fact that it is the brain's second largest structure, exceeded only by the cerebral cortex. Further, compared with other species, the human cerebellum has grown more than any other brain structure, tripling in size during the last million years of human history.

locus coeruleus A small nucleus in the reticular formation involved in attention, sleep, and mood.

cerebellum The part of the hindbrain whose function is to control finely coordinated movements and to store learned associations that involve movement.

midbrain A small structure between the hindbrain and forebrain that relays information from the eyes, ears, and skin and that controls certain types of automatic behaviours.

figure 3.14

Major Structures of the Forebrain

The structures of the forebrain are covered by an outer "bark" known as the *cerebral cortex.* This diagram shows some of the structures that lie within the forebrain. The amygdala, the hippocampus, the hypothalamus, the septum, and portions of the cerebral cortex are all part of the limbic system.

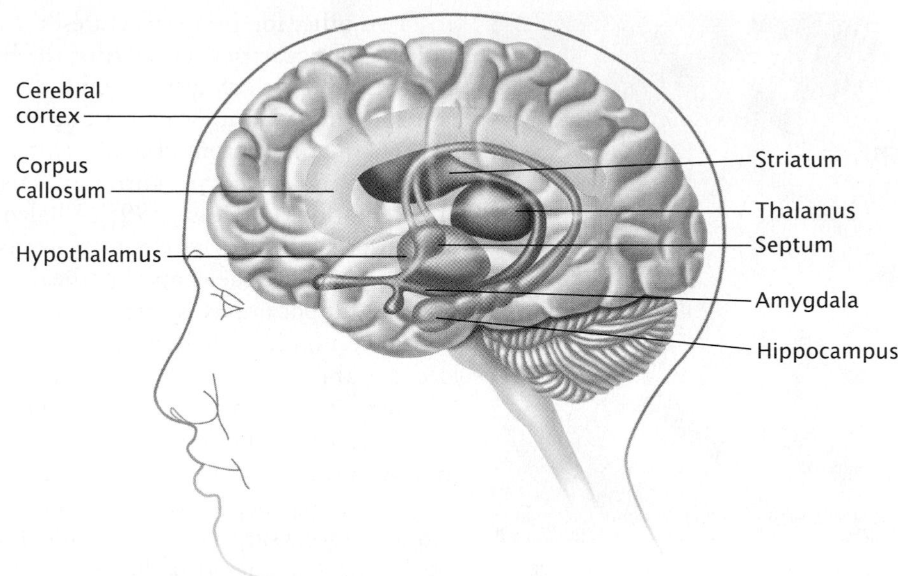

The Midbrain Above the hindbrain is the **midbrain.** In humans it is a small structure, but it serves some important functions. Certain types of automatic behaviours that integrate simple movements with sensory input are controlled there. For example, when you move your head, midbrain circuits allow you to move your eyes smoothly in the opposite direction, so that you can keep your eyes focused on an object despite moving your head. And when a loud noise causes you to turn your head reflexively and look in the direction of the sound, your midbrain circuits are at work.

One particularly important nucleus in the midbrain is the **substantia nigra,** meaning "black substance." This small area and its connections to the **striatum** (named for its "striped" appearance) in the forebrain are necessary in order to smoothly begin movements. Without them, you would find it difficult, if not impossible, to get up out of a chair, lift your hand to swat a fly, move your mouth to form words, or reach for that coffeepot at 6:00 A.M.

LINKAGES (a link to Motivation and Emotion)

The Forebrain Like the cerebellum, the human **forebrain** has grown out of proportion to the rest of the brain, so much so that it folds back over and completely covers the other parts. It is responsible for the most complex aspects of behaviour and mental life. As Figure 3.14 shows, the forebrain includes a variety of structures.

Two of these structures lie deep within the brain. The first is the **thalamus,** which relays pain signals from the spinal cord, as well as signals from the eyes and most other sense organs, to upper levels in the brain. It also plays an important role in processing and making sense out of this information. The other is the **hypothalamus,** which lies under the thalamus (*hypo* means "under") and is involved in regulating hunger, thirst, and sex drives. It has many connections to and from the autonomic nervous system, as well as to other parts of the brain. Destruction of one section of the hypothalamus results in an overwhelming urge to eat (see the chapter on motivation and emotion). Damage to another area of a male's hypothalamus causes his sex organs to degenerate and his sex drive to decrease drastically. There is also a fascinating part of the hypothalamus that contains the brain's own timepiece: the **suprachiasmatic nuclei** or **SCN.** The suprachiasmatic (pronounced "soo-pra-kye-as-MAT-ik") nuclei keep an approximately twenty-four-hour clock that establishes your biological rhythms. Dr. Michael Antle of the University of Calgary is attempting to find the relationship between neurons in the SCN in order to help to understand its overall function as a biological clock (Antle, 2005). We discuss these rhythms in the chapter on consciousness.

substantia nigra An area of the midbrain involved in the smooth initiation of movement.

striatum A structure within the forebrain that is involved in the smooth initiation of movement.

forebrain The most highly developed part of the brain; it is responsible for the most complex aspects of behaviour and mental life.

thalamus A forebrain structure that relays signals from most sense organs to higher levels in the brain and plays an important role in processing and making sense out of this information.

hypothalamus A structure in the forebrain that regulates hunger, thirst, and sex drives.

suprachiasmatic nuclei Nuclei in the hypothalamus that generate biological rhythms.

Brenda Milner In the early 1950s Dr. Brenda Milner arrived at McGill University to study with Dr. Donald Hebb. She later moved to the Montreal Neurological Institute to work with Dr. Wilder Penfield. Dr. Milner's study, of the now-famous patient HM, who suffered bilateral medial-temporal damage resulting in memory deficits, helped to demonstrate the existence of multi-memory systems (McGill, 2005).

Two other forebrain structures, the **amygdala** (pronounced "ah-MIG-duh-luh") and the **hippocampus,** are part of the **limbic system.** The interconnected structures of this system, which also includes the hypothalamus and the septum, play important roles in regulating memory and emotion. For example, the amygdala associates features of stimuli from two different senses, as when we link the shape and feel of objects in our memory (Murray & Mishkin, 1985). It is also involved in fear and other emotions (LeDoux, 1995; Whalen, 1998). Amygdala activity is altered in people suffering from post-traumatic stress disorder, for instance (Pitman, Shin, & Rauch, 2001; see the chapter on health, stress, and coping).

The hippocampus is important in the formation of memories, as becomes evident in certain cases of brain damage. People with damage to the hippocampus may lose the ability to remember new events, a condition called *anterograde amnesia.* You may have seen the film *Memento*, in which the character of Leonard Shelby developed this condition as the result of head injury. In the 1950s Dr. Brenda Milner (photo, left) joined Dr. Wilder Penfield at the Montreal Institute. Together they observed two epileptic patients—one an engineer, the other a glove cutter. Both men had undergone surgery by Dr. Penfield to remove the left medial-temporal region of the brain. This included the left hippocampus. The surgeries were performed in order to reduce and control their epileptic seizures. After surgery, both men demonstrated memory problems, in that they had difficulty encoding new memories. Although the engineer, for example, had no problem going back to work and producing excellent blueprints, if he happened to look away from his work for a brief period, he forgot what he was doing. Like the character, Leonard Shelby, in *Memento*, in order to overcome his handicap, the engineer took copious notes to substitute for his lack of short-term memory. Dr. Milner and Dr. Penfield concluded that both men must have had previous damage to their right hippocampus because patients who had previously undergone this procedure had not exhibited post-surgical memory problems. Later autopsies of both patients confirmed this conclusion (Penfield & Mathieson, 1974). Other cases, such as HM's and RB's, further added evidence in support of the importance of the hippocampus in the processing of new memories (Milner, 2005; Squire, 1986).

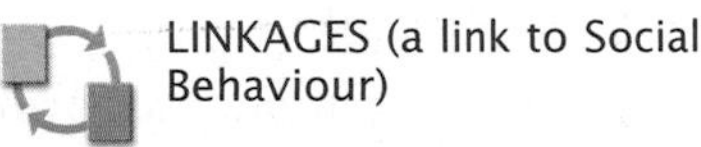

LINKAGES (a link to Social Behaviour)

The role of the hippocampus in memory is further supported by MRI studies of normal elderly people. These studies have found that memory ability is correlated with the size of the hippocampus (Golomb et al., 1996). In fact, a small hippocampus predicts severe memory problems even before they become evident (Kaye et al., 1997). Other studies suggest that some people's inborn response to stress includes a loss of neurons in the hippocampus (Caspi, Sugden, et al., 2003; Frodl et al., 2004; Gilbertson et al., 2002). The smaller size of the hippocampus in people who have suffered depression or post-traumatic stress disorder might help explain some of the memory problems some of these individuals experience (Bremner et al., 2003, 2004).

Although the hippocampus is vital in the creation of new memories, it doesn't keep them for long. Animal studies have shown that damage to the hippocampus within a day of a mildly painful experience erases memories of the experience but that removal of the hippocampus several days after the experience has no effect on the memory. So the memories must have been transferred elsewhere. Dr. Endel Tulving of the University of Toronto and his colleagues appear to have found the locations where episodic memories are encoded and retrieved. Using the PET scan technique, they have demonstrated a high activity level in the right prefrontal cortex during the encoding of episodic memories and a high activity level in the left prefrontal cortex during retrieval (Nyberg et al., 2000).

As described in the chapter on memory, maintaining your storehouse of memories—and having the ability to recall them—depends on the coordinated activities of many parts of the brain.

One of the greatest threats to the brain's memory capacities comes from Alzheimer's disease. Alzheimer's is a major cause of *dementia*, the deterioration of cognitive capabilities often associated with aging. The symptoms of Alzheimer's

amygdala A structure in the forebrain that, among other things, associates features of stimuli from two sensory modalities.

hippocampus A structure in the forebrain associated with the formation of new memories.

limbic system A set of brain structures that play important roles in regulating emotion and memory.

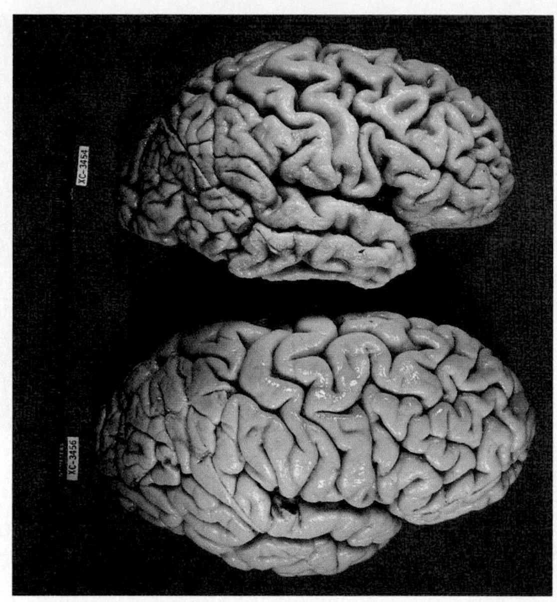

figure 3.15

Alzheimer's Disease and the Brain

These human brains, photographed after death, show that, compared to a normal brain (bottom), the brain of a person with Alzheimer's disease shows considerable degeneration in the cerebral cortex. The limbic system deteriorates, too (Callen et al., 2001). For example, the hippocampus of Alzheimer's patients is about 40 percent smaller than normal. In fact, a smaller than average hippocampus in the elderly predicts the onset of the disease (Jack et al., 1999).

disease stem from severe degeneration of neurons in specific regions of the hippocampus and other limbic system structures (Small et al., 2002; see Figure 3.15). About 5.1 percent of all Canadians over the age of sixty-five (approximately 161,000 people) suffer from the disorder (Canadian Medical Association, 1994). The financial cost of Alzheimer's may be high, but the cost in human suffering is incalculable. It is no wonder, then, that the search for its causes and cures has a high priority among researchers who study the brain.

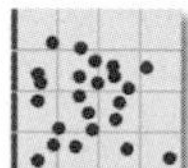

FOCUS ON RESEARCH METHODS

Manipulating Genes in Animal Models of Human Disease

Alzheimer's disease is named for Alois Alzheimer, a German neurologist. Almost a century ago, Alzheimer examined the brain of a woman who had died after years of progressive mental deterioration and dementia. In looking for the cause of her disorder, he found that cells in her cerebral cortex and hippocampus were bunched up like a rope tied in knots and that cellular debris had collected around the affected nerves. These features came to be known as tangles and plaques. *Tangles* are twisted fibres within neurons; their main protein component is called *tau. Plaques* are deposits of protein and parts of dead cells found between neurons. The major component of plaques was found to be a small protein called *beta-amyloid*, which is made from a larger protein called *amyloid precursor protein.* Accumulation of beta-amyloid plaques can now be visualized in living people through the use of PET scans (Klunk et al., 2004; see Figure 3.16).

• What was the researchers' question?

Ever since Alzheimer described plaques and tangles, researchers have been trying to learn about the role they play. One specific question that researchers have addressed is whether the proteins found in plaques and tangles actually *cause* Alzheimer's disease. They are certainly correlated with Alzheimer's, but as emphasized in the chapter on research in psychology, we can't confirm a causal relationship from a correlation alone. To discover if beta-amyloid and tau cause the death of neurons seen in Alzheimer's disease, researchers knew that controlled experiments would be necessary. This means manipulating an independent variable and measuring its effect on a dependent variable. In the case of Alzheimer's, the experiment would involve creating plaques and tangles (the independent variable) and looking for their effects on memory (the dependent variable). Such experiments

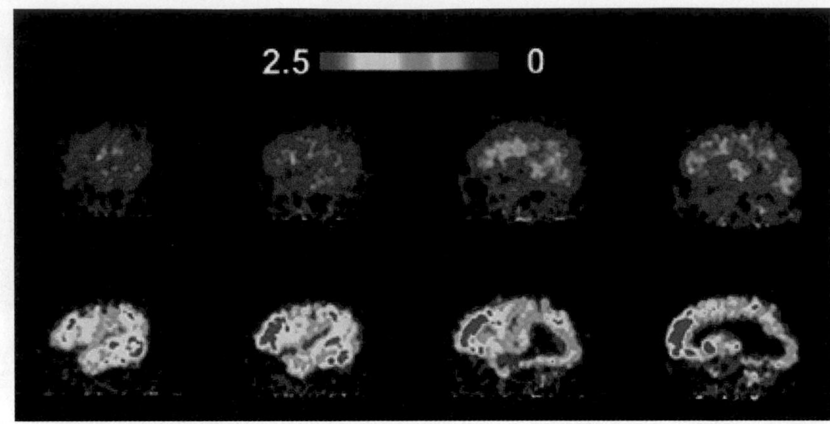

figure 3.16

Diagnosing Alzheimer's Disease

A research team has recently developed a molecule that binds with beta-amyloid plaques and can be seen on a PET scan. As shown in the brightly coloured areas of these scans, when the molecule was injected into Alzheimer's patients (bottom row), it became concentrated in the hippocampus and other regions where amyloid usually accumulates in people with Alzheimer's disease (Klunk et al., 2004). As shown by the darker colours in the upper row, the molecule does not build up in the brains of older people who do not have the disease. This procedure holds great promise as a tool for diagnosing Alzheimer's disease long before its symptoms appear, allowing treatment efforts to begin as early as possible (see also Hampel et al., 2004).

cannot ethically be conducted on humans, so scientists began looking for Alzheimer's-like conditions in another species. Progress in finding the causes of Alzheimer's disease depended on their finding an "animal model" of the disease.

● How did the researchers answer the question?

Previous studies of the genes of people with Alzheimer's disease had revealed that it is associated with a mutation, or error, in the beta-amyloid precursor protein. However, the mutations seen in many Alzheimer's patients appeared not in this protein but in other ones. Researchers called these other proteins *presenilins* because they are associated with senility. To determine whether these mutated proteins could actually cause the brain damage and memory impairment associated with Alzheimer's disease, they had to find a way to insert the proteins into the cells of animals. New genetic engineering tools allowed them to do just that. Genes can now be modified, eliminated, or added to cells, and if those cells give rise to sperm or eggs, the animals that result will have these altered genes in all their cells. Such animals are called "transgenic."

In their first attempts to create an animal model of Alzheimer's disease, researchers inserted into one group of mice a gene for a mutant form of beta-amyloid precursor protein. If Alzheimer's disease is, indeed, caused by faulty beta-amyloid precursor protein, inserting the gene for this faulty protein should cause deposits of beta-amyloid and the loss of neurons in the same brain structures that are affected in human Alzheimer's victims. No such changes should be observed in a control group of untreated animals.

● What did the researchers find?

For more than a decade, scientists have been creating transgenic mice with differing abnormalites in the proteins associated with tangles and plaques. As a result of this work, most researchers believe that amyloid is somehow involved as a cause of Alzheimer's disease. When multiple abnormalities in amyloid are introduced into mice, the animals show memory impairments, and they develop plaques in the brain. However, they do not develop tangles. Memory problems, plaques, *and* tangles do appear, though, in transgenic mice with faulty tau, the protein component of tangles (Götz et al., 2004). But faulty tau can't be the main cause of Alzheimer's, because mutations in tau protein do not appear in human Alzheimer's patients. Recently, researchers using other genetic engineering techniques have created mice that exhibit memory impairments as they age and that show neurodegeneration and abnormal tau but that do not develop amyloid deposits (Saura et al., 2004). In other words, scientists are getting ever closer to a good animal model of Alzheimer's disease, but they still have a way to go.

Nevertheless, transgenic mice have paved the way for an exciting new possibility in the treatment of Alzheimer's disease: a vaccine against beta-amyloid. Mice given this vaccine have shown not only improved memory but also a reversal of beta-amyloid deposits in their brains (Morgan et al., 2000; Younkin, 2001). Early clinical trials of beta-amyloid vaccines in humans showed encouraging results, but a small percentage of patients developed fatal reactions, so the trials have been stopped until these rare reactions can be understood and prevented (Broytman & Malter, 2004).

What do the results mean?

Regardless of whether this particular vaccine works, scientists will continue to use transgenic mice to evaluate the roles of mutations in beta-amyloid precursor protein, presenilins, tau, and other proteins in causing Alzheimer's disease. This research is important not only because it might eventually solve the mystery of this terrible disorder but also because it illustrates the power of experimental modification of animal genes for testing all kinds of hypotheses about biological factors influencing behaviour.

Besides inserting new or modified genes into brain cells, scientists also can manipulate an independent variable by "knocking out" specific genes, then looking at the effect on dependent variables (Feng et al., 2004). One research team has shown, for example, that knocking out a gene for a particular type of neurotransmitter receptor causes mice to become obese and to overeat even when given appetite-suppressant drugs (Tecott et al., 1995). And genetic elimination of proteins that modify neurotransmitter activity in mice cancelled out the stimulating effects of cocaine (Sora et al., 2001).

What do we still need to know?

The scarcity of animal models of obesity, drug addiction, and other problems has slowed progress in finding biological treatments for them. As animal models for these conditions become more available through genetic engineering techniques, they will open the door to new types of animal studies that are directly relevant to human problems. The next challenge will be to use these animal models to develop and test treatments that can be applied effectively in humans.

The Cerebral Cortex

So far, we have described some key structures *within* the forebrain; now we turn to a discussion of the structures on its surface. The outermost part of the brain appears rather round and has right and left halves that are similar in appearance. These halves are called the **cerebral hemispheres.** The outer part of the cerebral hemispheres, the **cerebral cortex**, has a surface area of one to two square feet—an area that is larger than it looks because of the folds that allow the cortex to fit inside the skull. The cerebral cortex is much larger in humans than in most other animals (dolphins are an exception). Like a computer's central processing unit, the cerebral cortex is our primary processing area. It is associated with the analysis of information from all the senses, control of voluntary movements, higher-order thought, and other complex aspects of our behaviour and mental processes.

The left side of Figure 3.17 shows the *anatomical* or physical features of the cerebral cortex. The folds of the cortex give the surface of the human brain its wrinkled appearance—its ridges and valleys. The ridges are called *gyri* (pronounced "ji-rye"), and the valleys are called *sulci* (pronounced "sulk-eye") or *fissures*. As you can see in the figure, several deep sulci divide the cortex into four areas: the *frontal*, *parietal*, *occipital*, and *temporal* lobes. The right side of Figure 3.17 depicts the areas of the cerebral cortex in which various *functions* or activities occur. The functional areas do not exactly match the anatomical areas, because some functions occur in more than one area. Let's consider three of these functional areas—the sensory cortex, the motor cortex, and the association cortex.

Sensory Cortex The **sensory cortex** lies in the parietal, occipital, and temporal lobes and is the part of the cerebral cortex that receives information from our

cerebral hemispheres The left and right halves of the rounded, outermost part of the brain.

cerebral cortex The outer surface of the brain.

sensory cortex The parts of the cerebral cortex that receive stimulus information from the senses.

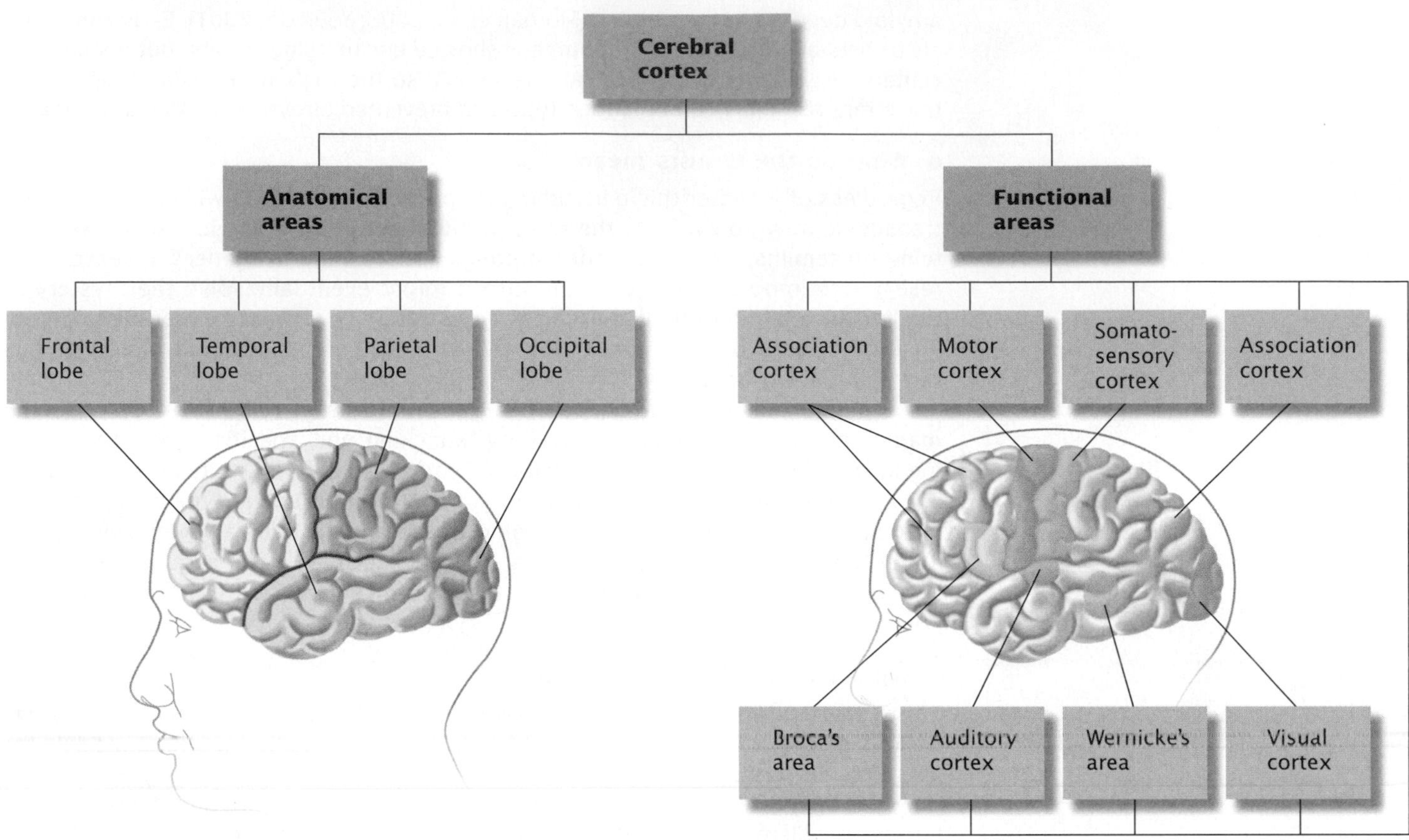

figure 3.17

The Cerebral Cortex (viewed from the left side)

The brain's ridges (gyri) and valleys (sulci) are landmarks that divide the cortex into four lobes: the frontal, parietal, occipital, and temporal. These terms describe where the regions are (the lobes are named for the skull bones that cover them), but the cortex is also divided in terms of function. These functional areas include the motor cortex (which controls movement), sensory cortex (including somatosensory, auditory, and visual areas that receive information from the senses), and association cortex (which integrates information). Also labelled are Wernicke's area and Broca's area, two regions that are found only on the left side of the cortex and that are vital to the interpretation and production of speech.

senses. Different regions of the sensory cortex receive information from different senses. Visual information is received by the *visual cortex*, made up of cells in the occipital lobe; auditory information is received by the *auditory cortex*, made up of cells in the temporal lobe; and information from the skin about touch, pain, and temperature is received in the *somatosensory cortex*, made up of cells in the parietal lobe (*soma* is Greek for "body").

Information about skin sensations from neighbouring parts of the body comes to neighbouring parts of the somatosensory cortex. As Figure 3.18 illustrates, the places on the cortex where information from each area of skin arrives can be represented by the figure of a tiny person, stretched out along the cortex. This figure is called the sensory *homunculus*, which is Latin for "little man." The links between skin locations and locations in somatosensory cortex have been demonstrated during brain surgery. If a surgeon stimulates a particular spot on the somatosensory cortex, the patient experiences a touch sensation at the place on the skin that normally sends information to that spot of cortex. It was long assumed that the organization of the homunculus remains the same throughout life, but recent research has shown that the amount of sensory cortex that responds to particular sensory inputs can be changed by experience (Candia et al., 2003). For example, if a person loses a limb, the areas of somatosensory cortex that had been stimulated by that limb will eventually be stimulated by other regions of skin. Even practicing the violin can

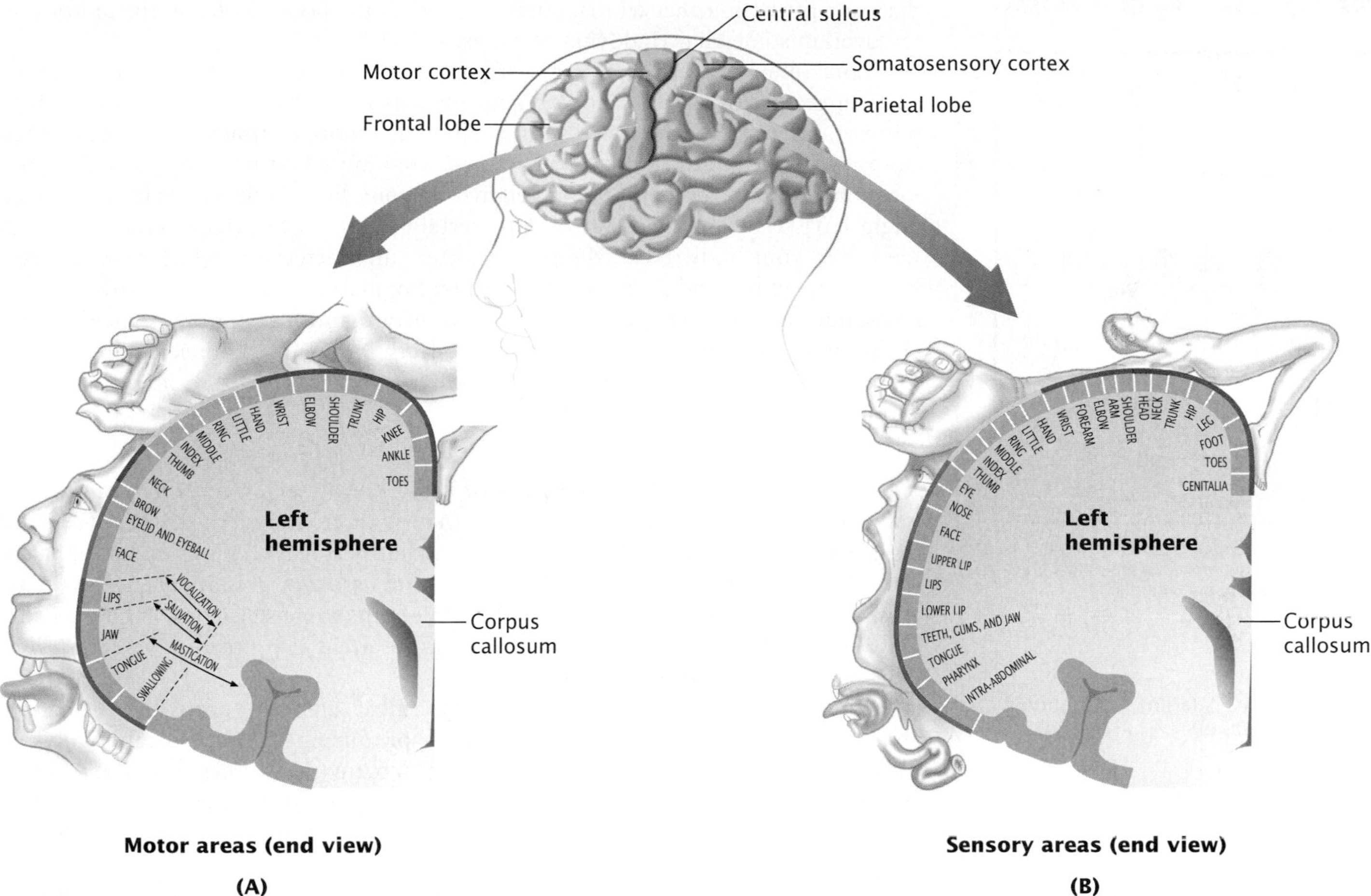

figure 3.18

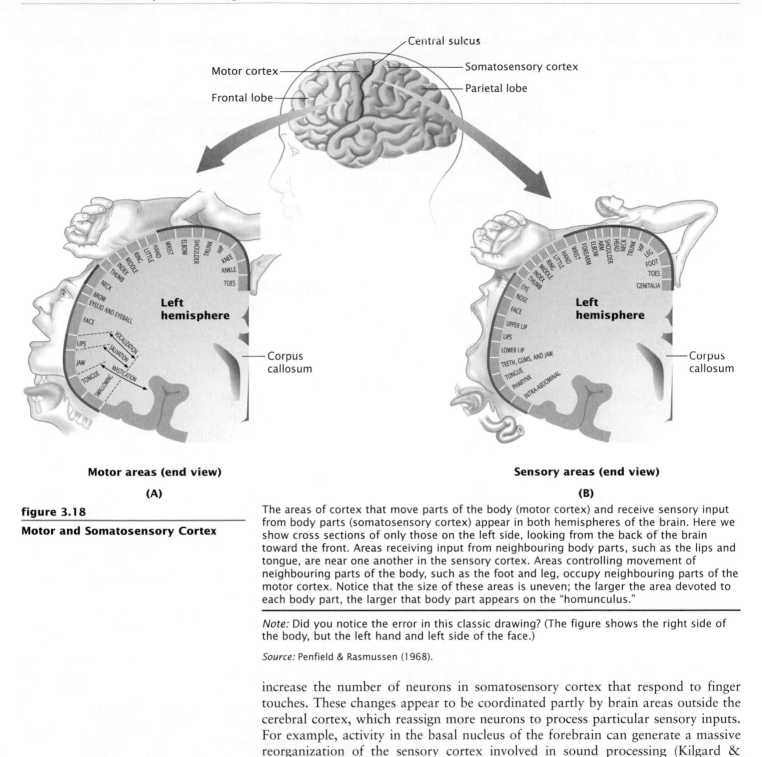

Motor and Somatosensory Cortex

The areas of cortex that move parts of the body (motor cortex) and receive sensory input from body parts (somatosensory cortex) appear in both hemispheres of the brain. Here we show cross sections of only those on the left side, looking from the back of the brain toward the front. Areas receiving input from neighbouring body parts, such as the lips and tongue, are near one another in the sensory cortex. Areas controlling movement of neighbouring parts of the body, such as the foot and leg, occupy neighbouring parts of the motor cortex. Notice that the size of these areas is uneven; the larger the area devoted to each body part, the larger that body part appears on the "homunculus."

Note: Did you notice the error in this classic drawing? (The figure shows the right side of the body, but the left hand and left side of the face.)

Source: Penfield & Rasmussen (1968).

increase the number of neurons in somatosensory cortex that respond to finger touches. These changes appear to be coordinated partly by brain areas outside the cerebral cortex, which reassign more neurons to process particular sensory inputs. For example, activity in the basal nucleus of the forebrain can generate a massive reorganization of the sensory cortex involved in sound processing (Kilgard & Merzenich, 1998).

Motor Cortex Neurons in specific areas of the **motor cortex,** which is in the frontal lobe, create voluntary movements in specific parts of the body. Some control movement of the hand; others stimulate movement of the foot, the knee, the head, and so on. As you can see in Figure 3.18, the motor homunculus mirrors the somatosensory homunculus. That is, the parts of the motor cortex that control the hands, for instance, are near parts of the somatosensory cortex that receive sensory information from the hands. The specific muscles activated by these regions are linked not to specific neurons but, as mentioned earlier, to the patterned activity of many neurons. For example, some of the same neurons are active in moving more

motor cortex The part of the cerebral cortex whose neurons control voluntary movements in specific parts of the body.

THE FAR SIDE By GARY LARSON

"Whoa! *That* was a good one! Try it, Hobbs—just poke his brain right where my finger is."

than one finger. In other words, different parts of the homunculus in the motor cortex overlap somewhat (Indovina & Sanes, 2001).

Controlling the movement of your body seems simple: You have a map of body parts in the motor cortex, and you activate cells in the hand region if you want to move your hand. But the process is actually much more complex. Recall again your sleepy reach for the coffeepot. The motor cortex must first translate the coffeepot's location in space into a location relative to your body. For example, your hand might have to be moved forward and a certain number of degrees to the right or to the left of your body. Next, the motor cortex must determine which muscles must be contracted to produce those movements. Populations of neurons work together to produce just the right combinations of direction and force in the particular muscle groups necessary to create the desired effects. Many interconnected areas of the motor cortex are involved in making these determinations (Graziano, Taylor, & Moore, 2002; Krauzlis, 2002).

Association Cortex The parts of the cerebral cortex not directly involved with either receiving specific sensory information or creating movement are referred to as **association cortex.** These are the areas that perform complex cognitive tasks, such as associating words with images. The term *association* is appropriate because these areas either receive information from more than one sense or combine sensory and motor information. Damage to association areas can create severe losses, or deficits, in all kinds of mental abilities.

LINKAGES (a link to Cognition and Language)

One of the most devastating deficits, called *aphasia* (pronounced "a-FAY-zhuh"), creates difficulty in understanding or producing speech and can involve all the functions of the cerebral cortex. Language information comes from the auditory cortex (for spoken language) or from the visual cortex (for written language). Areas of the motor cortex produce speech (Geschwind, 1979). But language also involves activity in the association cortex.

Scientists have long known that two areas of association cortex are involved in different aspects of language. In 1860, Paul Broca described the difficulties that result from damage to the association cortex in the frontal lobe near motor areas that control facial muscles, an area now called *Broca's area* (see Figure 3.17). When Broca's area is damaged, the mental organization of speech suffers, a condition called *Broca's aphasia*. Victims have great difficulty speaking, and what they say is often grammatically incorrect. Each word comes slowly.

A different set of language problems result from damage to a portion of the association cortex first described in the 1870s by Carl Wernicke (pronounced "VER-nick-ee") and thus called *Wernicke's area*. As Figure 3.17 shows, it is located in the temporal lobe, near an area of the cortex that receives information from the ears and eyes. Wernicke's area is involved in the interpretation of both speech and written words. Damage to this area can leave a person able to speak, but it disrupts the ability to understand the meaning of words or to speak understandably.

Case studies illustrate the differing effects of damage to Broca's area versus Wernicke's area (Lapointe, 1990). In response to the request "Tell me what you do with a cigarette," a person with Broca's aphasia replied, "Uh . . . uh . . . cigarette (pause) smoke it." Though halting and ungrammatical, this speech was meaningful. In response to the same request, a person with Wernicke's aphasia replied, "This is a segment of a pegment. Soap a cigarette." Here, the speech is fluent, but without meaning. A fascinating aspect of Broca's aphasia is that when a person with the disorder sings, the words come fluently and correctly. Presumably, words set to music are handled by a different part of the brain than spoken words (Besson et al., 1998). Capitalizing on this observation, "melodic intonation therapy" helps Broca's aphasia patients gain fluency in speaking by teaching them to speak in a "singsong" manner (Lapointe, 1990).

It appears that differing areas of association cortex are activated, depending on whether language is spoken or written and whether particular grammatical and

association cortex Those parts of the cerebral cortex that receive information from more than one sense or that combine sensory and motor information to perform complex cognitive tasks.

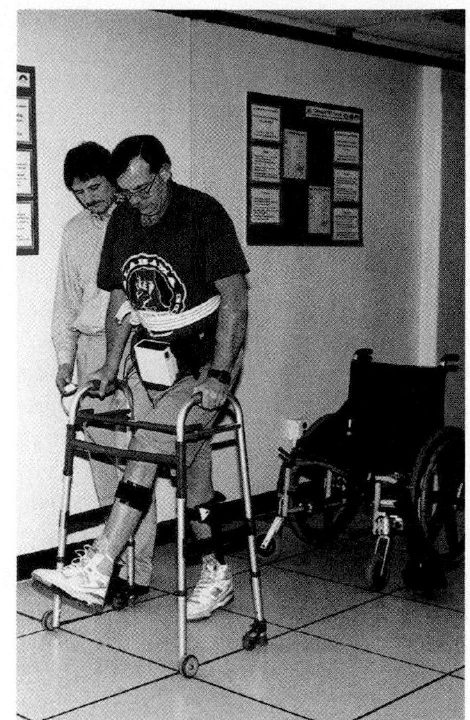

Movement and the Brain Scientists are still trying to understand exactly how smooth movements are coordinated by neural activity in both the brain and the spinal cord (Graziano, Taylor, & Moore, 2002; Krauzlis, 2002). The complexity of the processes involved presents a challenge to researchers working on devices to restore movement in paralyzed individuals. Delivering computer-controlled electrical stimulation to the leg muscles allows walking movements to occur, but they are jerkier than those the brain normally produces.

conceptual categories are involved. For example, consider the cases of two women who had strokes that damaged different language-related parts of their association cortex (Caramazza & Hillis, 1991). Neither woman had difficulty speaking or writing nouns, but both had difficulty with verbs. One woman could write verbs but could not speak them: She had difficulty pronouncing *watch* when it was used as a verb in the sentence "I watch TV," but she spoke the same word easily when it appeared as a noun in "My watch is slow." The other woman could speak verbs but had difficulty writing them. Another odd language abnormality following brain damage, known as "foreign accent syndrome," was illustrated by a thirty-two-year-old stroke victim whose native language was English. His speech was slurred immediately after the stroke, but as it improved, he began to speak with a Scandinavian accent, adding syllables to some words ("How are you today-ah?") and pronouncing *hill* as "heel." His normal accent did not fully return for four months (Takayama et al., 1993). Case studies of "foreign accent syndrome" suggest that specific regions of the brain are involved in the sound of language, whereas others are involved in various aspects of its meaning.

Regions of association cortex long assumed to be involved mainly with spoken or written language also appear to be involved in processing the "language" of music. For example, brain scan studies have found that Broca's area is activated when people hear a chord in a progression that disobeys musical "rules of grammar" (Maess et al., 2001).

The Divided Brain in a Unified Self

A striking idea emerged from observations of people with damage to the language areas of the brain. Researchers noticed that when damage was limited to areas of the left hemisphere, there were impairments in the ability to use or understand language. Damage to corresponding parts of the right hemisphere usually did not have these effects. Perhaps, they reasoned, the right and left halves of the brain serve different functions.

This concept was not entirely new. It had long been understood, for example, that most sensory and motor pathways cross over as they enter or leave the brain. As a result, the left hemisphere receives information from, and controls movements

Language Areas of the Brain Have you ever tried to write notes while you were talking to someone? Like this teacher, you can probably write and talk at the same time, because each of these language functions uses different areas of association cortex. However, stop reading for a moment, and try writing one word with your left hand and a different word with your right hand. If you had trouble, it is partly because you asked the same language area of your brain to do two things at once.

of, the right side of the body, whereas the right hemisphere receives input from, and controls movements of, the left side of the body. However, both sides of the brain perform these functions. The fact that language centres, such as Broca's area and Wernicke's area, are found almost exclusively on the left side of the brain suggested that each hemisphere might be specialized to perform some functions almost independently of the other hemisphere (Stephan et al., 2003).

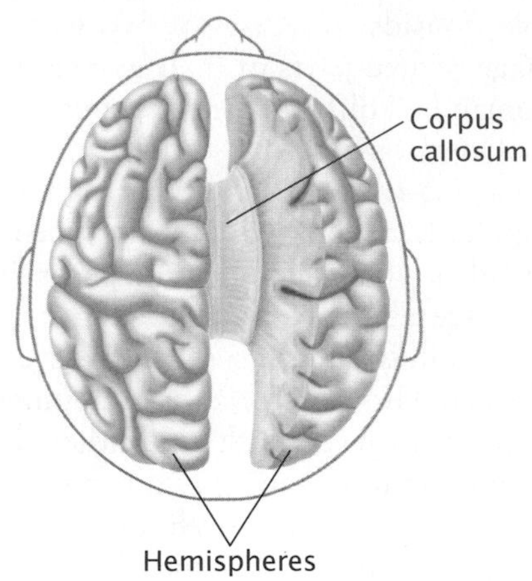

figure 3.19

The Brain's Left and Right Hemispheres

The brain's two hemispheres are joined by a core bundle of nerve fibres known as the *corpus callosum*. In this figure the hemispheres are separated to reveal the corpus callosum. The two cerebral hemispheres look nearly the same but perform somewhat different tasks. For one thing, the left hemisphere receives sensory input from, and controls movement on, the right side of the body. The right hemisphere senses and controls the left side of the body.

Split-Brain Studies As far back as the late 1800s, scientists had wanted to test the hypothesis that the cerebral hemispheres might be specialized, but they had no techniques for doing so. Then, during the 1960s, Roger Sperry, Michael Gazzaniga, and their colleagues began to study *split-brain* patients—people who had undergone a surgical procedure in an attempt to control severe epilepsy. Before the surgery, their seizures began in one hemisphere and then spread to engulf the whole brain. As a last resort, surgeons isolated the two hemispheres from each other by severing the **corpus callosum,** a massive bundle of more than a million fibres that connects the two hemispheres (see Figure 3.19).

After the surgery, researchers used a special apparatus to present visual images to only one side of these patients' split brains (see Figure 3.20). They found that severing the tie between the hemispheres had dramatically affected the way these people thought about and dealt with the world. For example, when the image of a spoon was presented to the left, language-oriented side of one patient's split brain, she could say what the spoon was; but when the spoon was presented to the right side of her brain, she could not describe the spoon in words. She still *knew* what it was, however. Using her left hand (controlled by the right hemisphere), she could pick out the spoon from a group of other objects by its shape. But when asked what she had just grasped, she replied, "A pencil." The right hemisphere recognized the object, but the patient could not describe it because the left (language) half of her brain did not see or feel it (Sperry, 1968).

Although the right hemisphere has no control over spoken language in split-brain patients, it does have important capabilities, including some related to nonspoken language. For example, a split-brain patient's right hemisphere can guide the left hand in spelling out words with Scrabble tiles (Gazzaniga & LeDoux, 1978). Thanks to this ability, researchers discovered that the right hemisphere of split-brain

figure 3.20

Apparatus for Studying Split-Brain Patients

When the person stares at the dot on the screen, images briefly presented on one side of the dot go to only one side of the brain. For example, a picture of a spoon presented on the left side of the screen goes to the right side of the brain. The right side of the brain can find the spoon and direct the left hand to touch it. However, because the language areas on the left side of the brain did not see the spoon, the person is unable to say what it is.

corpus callosum A massive bundle of fibres that connects the right and left cerebral hemispheres and allows them to communicate with each other.

figure 3.21

Lateralization of the Cerebral Hemispheres

These PET scans show overhead views of a section of a person's brain while the person was receiving different kinds of stimulation. At the upper left, the person was resting, with eyes open and ears plugged. Note that the greatest brain activity (as indicated by the red area) was in the visual cortex, which was receiving input from the eyes. As shown at the lower left, when the person listened to spoken language, the auditory cortex in the left temporal lobe became more active, but the right temporal lobe did not. When the person listened to music (lower right), there was intense activity in the right temporal lobe but little in the left. When the person heard both words and music, the temporal cortex on both sides of the brain became activated. Here is visual evidence of the involvement of each side of the brain in processing different kinds of information (Phelps & Mazziotta, 1985).

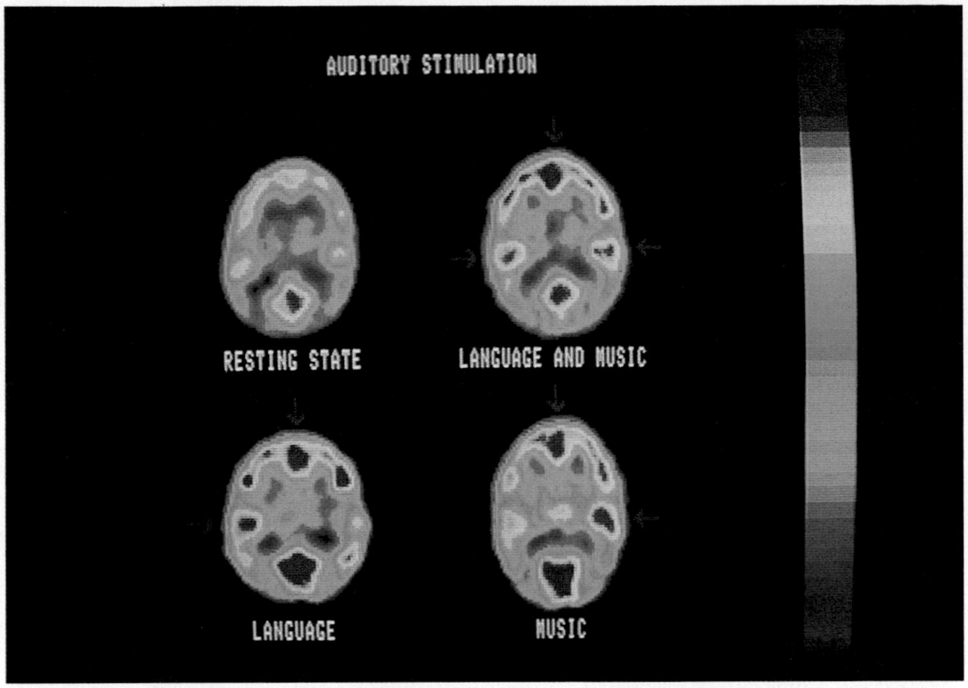

patients has self-awareness and normal learning abilities. In addition, it is superior to the left hemisphere on tasks dealing with spatial relations (especially drawing three-dimensional shapes) and at recognizing human faces.

Lateralization of Normal Brains Sperry (1974, p. 7) concluded from his studies that each hemisphere in the split-brain patient has its own "private sensations, perceptions, thoughts, and ideas all of which are cut off from the corresponding experiences in the opposite hemisphere. . . . In many respects each disconnected hemisphere appears to have a separate 'mind of its own.'" But what about people whose hemispheres are connected normally? Are certain of their functions, such as mathematical reasoning or language skills, lateralized? A **lateralized** task is one that is performed more efficiently by one hemisphere than the other.

To find out, researchers presented images to just one hemisphere of people with normal brains and then measured how fast they could analyze information. If information is presented to one side of the brain, and if that side is specialized to analyze that type of information, a person's responses will be faster than if the information must first be transferred to the other hemisphere for analysis. These studies have confirmed that the left hemisphere has better logical and language abilities than the right, whereas the right hemisphere has better spatial, artistic, and musical abilities (Springer & Deutsch, 1989). Positron emission tomography (PET) scans of normal people receiving varying kinds of auditory stimulation also demonstrate these differences (see Figure 3.21). We know that the language abilities of the left hemisphere are not specifically related to auditory information, though, because people who are deaf also use the left hemisphere more than the right for sign language (Hickok, Bellugi, & Klima, 1996).

The precise nature and degree of lateralization vary quite a bit among individuals. Functional MRI studies show, for example, that one in ten people show activation of both hemispheres during language tasks, and the brains of another 10 percent appear to coordinate language in the right hemisphere (Fitzgerald, Brown, & Daskalakis, 2002). Both of these patterns are seen mostly in left-handed people (Knecht et al., 2002). Evidence of sex differences in brain laterality comes from studies of the cognitive abilities of normal men and women, of the effects of brain damage on cognitive function, and of anatomical differences between the sexes. Among

lateralized Referring to the tendency for one cerebral hemisphere to excel more at a particular function or skill than the other hemisphere.

normal individuals, there are sex differences in the ability to perform tasks that are known to be lateralized in the brain. For example, Dr. Doreen Kimura of Simon Fraser University points out that men are better at mental rotation, throwing objects, and mathematical reasoning, whereas women are better at verbal memory and recalling the location of objects (Kimura, 2004).

Damage to just one side of the brain is more disabling to men than to women. In particular, men show more damage to language ability than women when the left side is damaged (McGlone, 1980). This difference may reflect a wider distribution of language abilities in the brains of women compared with those of men. When participants in one study performed language tasks, such as thinking about whether particular words rhyme, MRI scans showed increased activity on the left side of the brain for men but on both sides for women (Shaywitz et al., 1995; see Figure 1.1 in the chapter on introducing psychology). Women appear to have proportionately more of their association cortex devoted to language tasks (Harasty et al., 1997). However, although humans and animals show definite sex differences in brain anatomy (Allen, Hines, et al., 1989; Gur et al., 1995; Juraska, 1998), no particular anatomical feature has been identified as underlying sex differences in lateralization. One study reported that the corpus callosum is larger in women than in men (de Lacoste-Utamsing & Holloway, 1982), but more than 50 attempts to replicate this finding have all failed to do so (Olivares, Michalland, & Aboitz, 2000). Despite the overwhelming evidence against it, the original report of a sex difference in the corpus callosum continues to be cited, suggesting that scientists are sometimes not entirely unbiased.

Having two somewhat specialized hemispheres allows the brain to more efficiently perform some tasks, particularly difficult ones, but the differences between the hemispheres should not be exaggerated. The corpus callosum usually integrates the functions of the "two brains," a role that is particularly important in tasks that require sustained attention (Rueckert et al., 1999). As a result, the hemispheres work so closely together, and each makes up so well for whatever lack of ability the other may have, that people are normally unaware that their brains are made up of two partially independent, somewhat specialized halves (Banich & Heller, 1998; Staudt et al., 2001).

Plasticity in the Central Nervous System

We mentioned earlier that the amount of somatosensory cortex devoted to finger touch changes as people practise a musical instrument. Such changes are possible because of **plasticity.** Christopher Shaw and Jill McEachren of the University of British Columbia describe neuroplasticity as the ability of the nervous system to change over time as a "function of age and/or experiences" (Shaw and McEachren, 2001). The nervous system achieves neuroplasticity by strengthening existing connections, as well as establishing new ones (Cohen-Corey, 2002; Kolb, Gibb, & Robinson, 2001).

Plasticity depends partly on neurons and partly on glial cells (Ullian et al., 2001), and it provides the basis for the learning and memory processes described in other chapters. It occurs throughout the central nervous system. Even the simplest reflex in the spinal cord can be modified by experience (Feng-Chen & Wolpaw, 1996).

Brain scanning technology now allows researchers to directly observe the effects of plasticity. They have seen that, as blind people learn to read Braille, the amount of sensory cortex devoted to the "reading" fingertip increases dramatically (Pascual-Leone & Torres, 1993). They have seen, too, that as blind people read Braille, there is activity in the occipital lobe, a brain area that normally receives visual information (Chen, Cohen, & Hallett, 2002). MRI studies of individuals who were learning to juggle found an increase in the density of cortical regions associated with processing

plasticity The ability to create new synapses and to change the strength of synapses.

visual information about moving objects (Draganski et al., 2004). Motor cortex is "plastic," too. Musicians have a larger portion of cortex devoted to the movements of their hands than non-musicians. And the amount of cortex devoted to this task of non-musicians who practise making rhythmic finger movements increases as they become better at it (Munte, Altenmuller, & Jancke, 2002). Even more amazing is the finding that merely *imagining* practicing these movements causes changes in the motor cortex (Pascual-Leone, 2001). Athletes have long engaged in exercises in which they visualize skilled sports movements; brain imaging research reveals that this "mental practice" can change the brain.

Repairing Brain Damage Unfortunately, the power of plasticity is limited, especially when it comes to repairing damage to the brain and spinal cord. Unlike the skin or the liver, the adult central nervous system does not automatically replace damaged cells. Still, the central nervous system does display a certain amount of self-healing. Undamaged neurons may take over for damaged ones, partly by changing their own function and partly by sprouting axons whose connections help neighbouring regions take on new functions (Bareyre et al., 2004; Cao et al., 1994). These changes rarely result in restoration of lost functions, though, so most victims of severe stroke, Alzheimer's disease, spinal cord injury, or other central nervous system disorders are permanently disabled in some way.

Scientists are searching for ways to help a damaged central nervous system heal some of its own wounds. One approach has been to transplant, or graft, tissue from a still-developing fetal brain into the brain of an adult animal. If the receiving animal does not reject it, the graft sends axons out into the brain and makes some functional connections. This treatment has reversed animals' learning difficulties, movement disorders, and other results of brain damage (Noble, 2000). The technique has also been used to treat a small number of people with *Parkinson's disease*—a disorder characterized by tremors, rigidity of the arms and legs, difficulty in initiating movements, and poor balance (Lindvall & Hagell, 2001). The initial results were encouraging, but improvement faded after a year, and some patients suffered side effects involving uncontrollable movements (Freed et al., 2001).

The brain-tissue transplant procedure is promising, but because its use with humans requires tissue from aborted fetuses, it has generated considerable controversy. As an alternative, some scientists have tried transplanting neural tissue from another species into humans. For example, Russian physicians transplanted tissue from fruit flies into the brains of Parkinson's patients. The results were beneficial, and there were no immediate side effects (Saveliev et al., 1997), but the fruit fly neurons were eventually rejected by the patients' bodies (Korochkin, 2000).

The most promising source for new neurons now appears to be an individual's own brain. This is a revolutionary idea, because it was long believed that once humans reached adulthood, the cells of the central nervous system stopped dividing, leaving each of us with a fixed set of neurons (Rakic, 2002). However, research has shown that cell division *does* take place in the adult central nervous systems of humans, non-human primates, and other animals (Altman & Das, 1965; Eriksson et al., 1998; Gould et al., 1999; Steindler & Pincus, 2002). These new cells have been found in areas such as the hippocampus, which is critical to the formation of new memories and is vulnerable to degeneration through Alzheimer's disease. The factors that influence how much cell division occurs in the brain are being investigated in rats and mice, with surprising findings. For example, exercise increases the rate of neuronal cell division in mice (van Praag et al., 1999), as does exposure to a complex environment, even in old mice (Kempermann, Gast, & Gage, 2002). Some stress hormones and antidepressant drugs also increase the rate of neuronal cell division (Cameron, Tanapat, & Gould, 1998; Malberg et al., 2000).

Finding newly divided neurons in the brain led to the discovery that there are *neural stem cells* in the adult brain. These are special glial cells that are capable of dividing to form new tissue, including new neurons (Sanai et al., 2004). This discovery has created a great deal of excitement and controversy. There is excitement because stem cells raise hope that damaged tissue may someday be replaced by cells created from a person's own body, but there is controversy because stem cells are linked in many people's minds with the cloning of whole individuals. Beyond the ethical storm raging around stem cell research, there is also some disagreement within the ranks of stem cell researchers. Some say that stem cells can be harvested from bone marrow and made to grow into brain cells (Koshizuka et al., 2004). Others deny this claim (Stewart & Przyborski, 2002). The outcome of the controversy is important, because if brain cells can indeed be grown from cells in bone marrow or other relatively accessible sites, the benefits in treating brain disorders would be substantial. Patients suffering from spinal cord injuries, as well as Parkinson's disease and Alzheimer's disease, might someday be cured by treatments that replace damaged or dying neurons with new ones grown from the patients' own stem cells (Horner & Gage, 2002; Mezey et al., 2003; Sanchez-Ramos et al., 2000; Teng et al., 2002; Zhao et al., 2003).

Generating new neurons is only half the battle, however. The new cells, axons and dendrites would still have to reestablish all the synaptic connections that had been lost to damage or disease. In the peripheral nervous system, glial cells form "tunnels" that guide the regrowth of axons. But in the central nervous system, reestablishing communication links is much more difficult, because glial cells actively suppress connections between newly sprouted axons and other neurons (Olson, 1997). Scientists have also found several related proteins that prevent newly sprouted axons from making connections with other neurons in the central nervous system. The first one they discovered was aptly named *Nogo*.

Despite these challenges, researchers are reporting exciting results in their efforts to promote healing in damaged brains and spinal cords. They have found, for example, that blocking the receptor for the Nogo proteins in rats allowed surviving neurons to make new axonal connections and actually repair spinal cord damage (Schwab, 2004). Other research with animals has shown that both spontaneous recovery and the effectiveness of brain-tissue transplants can be greatly enhanced by adding naturally occurring proteins called *growth factors*, or *neurotrophic factors*, which promote the survival of neurons (Hoglinger et al., 2001). One of these proteins is called *nerve growth factor*. Another, called *glial cell line-derived neurotrophic factor*, or *GDNF*, actually causes neurons to produce the neurotransmitter needed to reverse the effects of Parkinson's disease (Kordower et al., 2000; Theofilopoulos et al., 2001). The best way to deliver these growth factors is still being determined. In one case, nerve growth factor was infused directly into the brain of a person with Alzheimer's disease (Seiger et al., 1993). The early results seemed encouraging, but the continuous delivery of the protein into the brain caused unacceptable side effects (Nabeshima & Yamada, 2000). Another way to deliver the growth factors is to use gene therapy, in which a gene for the desired growth factor is inserted into a patient's neurons. Clinical trials of this approach are now underway (Tuszynski & Blesch, 2004).

While scientists continue to try to make such therapies a reality, there are things that patients themselves can do to promote the neural plasticity needed to restore lost central nervous system functions. Special mental and physical exercise programs appear useful in "rewiring" the brains of stroke victims and spinal cord injury patients, thus reversing some forms of paralysis and improving some sensory and cognitive abilities (Blakeslee, 2001; Liepert et al., 2000; Robertson & Murre, 1999). Christopher Reeve, the actor who portrayed Superman, was an inspiring case in point. After his spinal cord injury in 1995, Reeve was told he would never again be able to move or feel his body. He refused to accept this gloomy prediction, and in the years before his death in 2004, an exercise-oriented rehabilitation program allowed him to regain some movement and to feel sensations from much of his body (Blakslee, 2002). Physicians and physical therapists continue to work on the best ways to design such therapy programs (for example, Molteni et al., 2004).

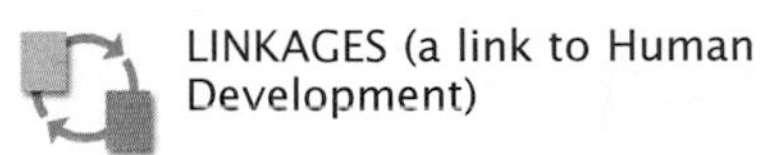

LINKAGES
Human Development and the Changing Brain

LINKAGES (a link to Human Development)

Fortunately, most of the changes that take place in the brain throughout life are not the kind that produce degenerative diseases. What are these changes, and what are their effects? How are they related to the developments in sensory and motor capabilities, mental abilities, and other characteristics described in the chapter on human development?

By conducting anatomical studies and, more recently, PET scans and functional MRIs, researchers are beginning to answer these questions. They have uncovered some interesting correlations between changes in neural activity and the behaviour of human newborns and young infants. Among newborns, activity is relatively high in the thalamus but low in the striatum. This pattern may be related to the way newborns move: They make non-purposeful, sweeping movements of the arms and legs, much like adults who have a hyperactive thalamus and a degenerated striatum (Chugani & Phelps, 1986). During the second and third months after birth, activity increases in many regions of the cortex, a change that is correlated with the loss of reflexes such as the grasping reflex. When infants are around eight or nine months old, activity in the frontal cortex increases, a development that correlates well with the apparent beginnings of cognitive activity in infants (Chugani & Phelps, 1986). The brain continues to mature even through adolescence, showing evidence of ever more efficient neural communication in its major fibre tracts (Gogtay et al., 2004; Paus et al., 1999; Thompson et al., 2000).

These changes mainly reflect brain plasticity—changes in neural connections—not the appearance of new cells. After birth, the number of dendrites and synapses increases. In one area of the cortex, the number of synapses increases tenfold from birth to twelve months of age (Huttenlocher, 1990). By the time children are six or seven years old, their brains have more dendrites and use twice as much metabolic fuel as those of adults (Chugani & Phelps, 1986). Then, in early adolescence, the number of dendrites and neural connections begins to drop, so that the adult level is reached by about the age of fourteen (see Figure 3.22). MRI scans show an actual loss of grey-matter volume in the cortex throughout the adolescent years as adult cognitive abilities develop (Sowell et al., 2003). In other words, as we reach adulthood, we develop more brainpower with less brain.

Throughout our lifespan, the brain retains its plasticity, rewiring itself to form new connections and to eliminate connections, too (Hua & Smith, 2004). Our genes apparently determine the basic pattern of growth and the major lines of connections—the "highways" of the brain and its general architecture. (For a summary of this architecture, see "In Review: Organization of the Brain.") But the details of the connections depend on experience, including the amount of complexity and stimulation in the environment. For example, researchers have compared the brains of rats raised alone with only a boring view of the side of their cages to the brains of rats raised with interesting toys and stimulating playmates. The cerebral cortex of those from the enriched environment had more and longer dendrites, as well as more synapses and neurotrophic factors, than the cortex of animals from barren, individual housing (Klintsova & Greenough, 1999; Torasdotter et al., 1998). Furthermore, the number of cortical synapses increased when isolated animals were moved to an enriched environment. To the extent that these ideas and research findings apply to humans, they hold obvious implications for how people raise children and treat the elderly.

figure 3.22

Developmental Changes in the Cerebral Cortex

During childhood, the brain overproduces neural connections, establishes the usefulness of certain connections, and then "prunes" the extra connections. Overproduction of synapses, especially in the frontal cortex, may be essential for children to develop certain intellectual abilities. Scientists believe that connections that are used survive, whereas others die.

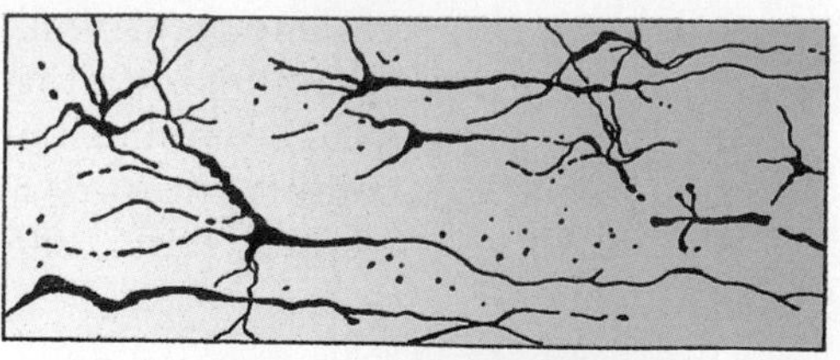

At birth

(A)

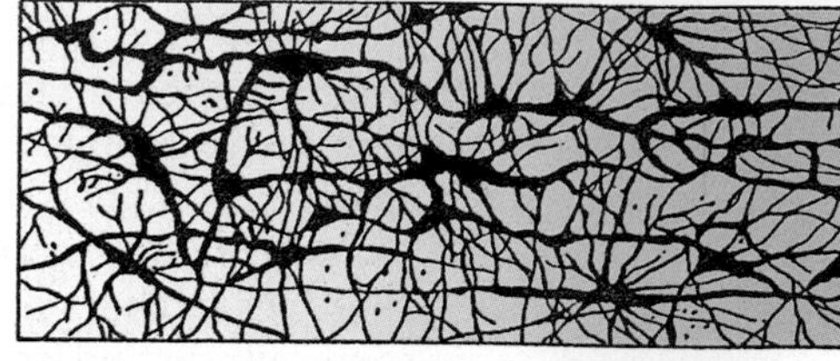

Six years old

(B)

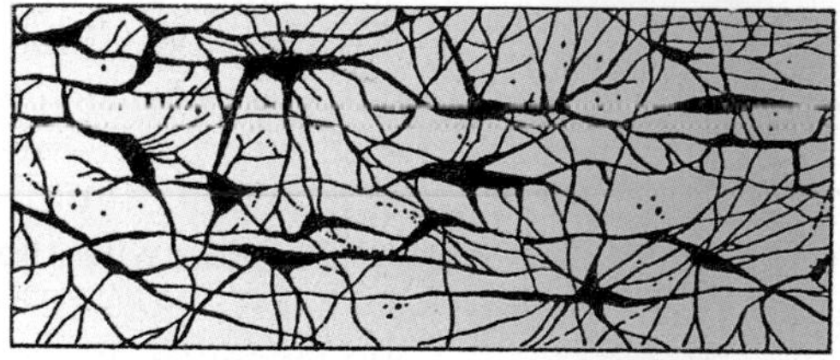

Fourteen years old

(C)

In any event, this line of research highlights the interaction of environmental and genetic factors. Some overproduced synapses may reflect genetically directed preparation for certain types of experiences. Generation of these synapses is an "experience-expectant" process, and it accounts for sensitive periods during development when certain things can be most easily learned. But overproduction of synapses also occurs in response to totally new experiences; this process is "experience dependent" (Greenough, Black, & Wallace, 1987). Within constraints set by genetics, interactions with the world mould the brain itself (e.g., Chang & Merzenich, 2003).

The Chemistry of Psychology

We have now described how the cells of the nervous system communicate by releasing neurotransmitters at their synapses, and we have outlined some of the basic structures of the nervous system and their functions. Let's now pull these topics together by considering which neurotransmitters occur in which structures, and how neurotransmitters affect behaviour. As we mentioned earlier, different sets of neurons use different neurotransmitters; a group of neurons that communicates using the same neurotransmitter is called a **neurotransmitter system.** Certain neurotransmitter systems play a dominant role in particular functions, such as emotion or memory, and in particular problems, such as Alzheimer's disease.

neurotransmitter system A group of neurons that communicates by using the same neurotransmitter.

in review Organization of the Brain

Major Division	Some Important Structures	Some Major Functions
Hindbrain	Medulla	Regulation of breathing, heart rate, and blood pressure
	Reticular formation (also extends into midbrain)	Regulation of arousal and attention
	Cerebellum	Control of fine movements and coordination of certain cognitive processes
Midbrain	Various nuclei	Relay of sensory signals to forebrain, creation of automatic responses to certain stimuli
	Substantia nigra	Smooth initiation of movement
Forebrain	Hypothalamus	Regulation of hunger, thirst, and sex drives
	Thalamus	Interpretation and relaying of sensory information
	Hippocampus	Formation of new memories
	Amygdala	Connection of sensations and emotions
	Cerebral cortex	Analysis of sensory information; control over voluntary movements, abstract thinking, and other complex cognitive activity
	Corpus callosum	Transfer of information between the two cerebral hemispheres

PsychAssist: Relationships among the nervous, endocrine, and immune systems

Chemical neurotransmission was first demonstrated, in frogs, by Otto Loewi (pronounced "LOW-ee") in 1921. Since then, more than a hundred different neurotransmitters have been identified. Some of the chemicals that act on receptors at synapses have been called *neuromodulators*, because they act slowly and often modify or "modulate" a cell's response to other neurotransmitters. The distinction between neurotransmitter and neuromodulator is not always clear, however. Depending on the type of receptor it acts on at a given synapse, the same substance can function as either a neuromodulator or a neurotransmitter.

Three Classes of Neurotransmitters

The neurotransmitters used in the nervous system fall into three main categories, based on their chemical structure: *small molecules*, *peptides*, and *gases*. Let's consider some examples in each category.

Small Molecules The *small-molecule* neurotransmitters were discovered first, partly because they occur in both the central nervous system and the peripheral nervous system. For example, **acetylcholine** (pronounced "a-see-tull-KO-leen")

acetylcholine A neurotransmitter used by neurons in the peripheral and central nervous systems in the control of functions ranging from muscle contraction and heart rate to digestion and memory.

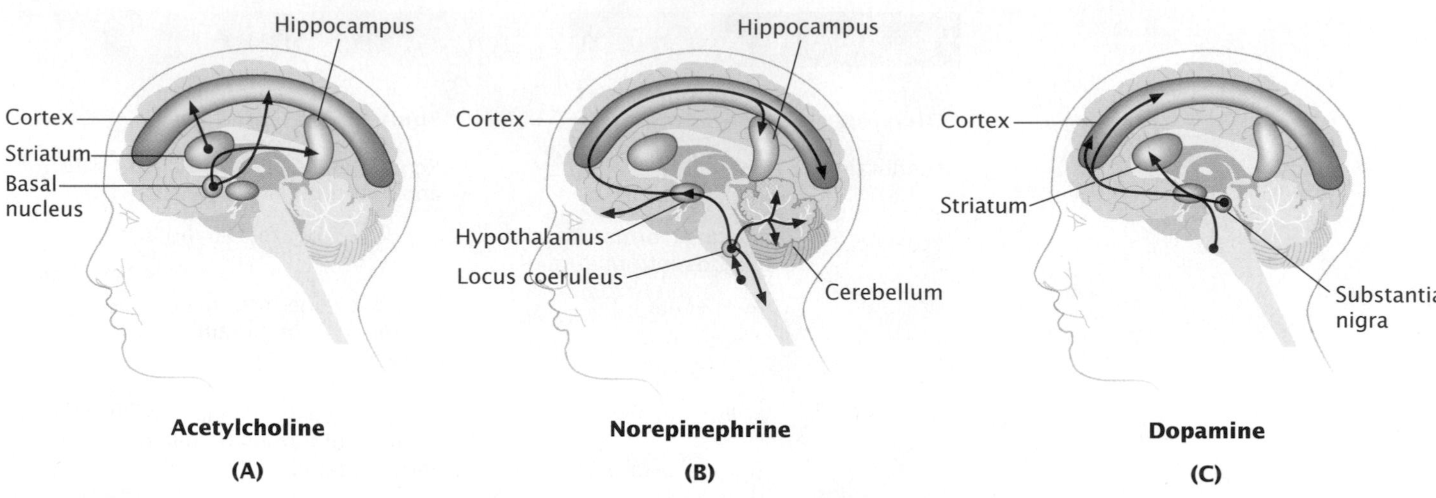

figure 3.23

Some Neurotransmitter Pathways

Neurons that use a certain neurotransmitter may be concentrated in one particular region (indicated by dots) and send fibres into other regions with which they communicate (see arrows). Here are examples for three major neurotransmitters. Psychoactive drugs affect behaviour and mental processes by altering these systems. In the chapter on consciousness, we discuss how drugs of abuse, such as cocaine, affect neurotransmitters. The neurotransmitter effects of therapeutic drugs are described in the chapter on the treatment of psychological disorders.

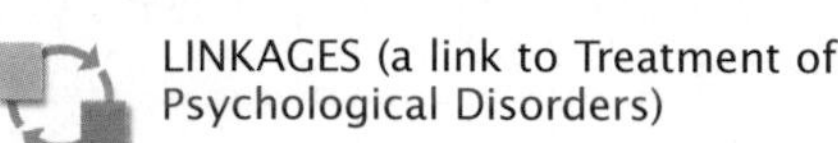
LINKAGES (a link to Treatment of Psychological Disorders)

is used by neurons of the parasympathetic nervous system to slow the heartbeat and activate the digestive system and by neurons that make muscles contract. In the brain, neurons that use acetylcholine (called *cholinergic* neurons) are especially plentiful in the midbrain and striatum, where they occur in circuits that are important for movement (see Figure 3.23). Axons of cholinergic neurons also make up major pathways in the limbic system, including the hippocampus, and in other areas of the forebrain that are involved in memory. Drugs that interfere with acetylcholine prevent the formation of new memories. In Alzheimer's disease, there is a nearly complete loss of cholinergic neurons in a nucleus in the forebrain that sends fibres to the cerebral cortex and hippocampus—a nucleus that normally enhances plasticity in these regions (Kilgard & Merzenich, 1998).

Three other small-molecule neurotransmitters are known as *catecholamines* (pronounced "cat-ah-KO-lah-meens"). They include *norepinephrine*, *serotonin*, and *dopamine*. **Norepinephrine** (pronounced "nor-eppa-NEF-rin"), also called *noradrenaline*, occurs in both the central and peripheral nervous systems. In both places, it contributes to arousal. Norepinephrine (and its close relative, epinephrine, or adrenaline) are the neurotransmitters used by the sympathetic nervous system to activate you and prepare you for action. Approximately half of the norepinephrine in the entire brain is contained in cells of the *locus coeruleus*, which is near the reticular formation in the hindbrain (see Figure 3.23). Because norepinephrine systems cover a lot of territory, it is logical that norepinephrine would affect several broad categories of behaviour. Indeed, norepinephrine is involved in the appearance of wakefulness and sleep, in learning, and in the regulation of mood.

Serotonin is similar to norepinephrine in several ways. First, most of the cells that use it as a neurotransmitter occur in an area along the midline of the hindbrain. Second, axons from neurons that use serotonin send branches throughout the forebrain, including the hypothalamus, the hippocampus, and the cerebral cortex. Third, serotonin affects sleep and mood. Serotonin differs from norepinephrine, however, in that the brain can get one of the substances from which it is made, *tryptophan*, directly from food. So what you eat can affect the amount of serotonin in your brain. Carbohydrates increase the amount of tryptophan reaching the brain and therefore affect how much serotonin is made. A meal high in carbohydrates

norepinephrine A neurotransmitter involved in arousal, as well as in learning and mood regulation.

serotonin A neurotransmitter used by cells in parts of the brain involved in the regulation of sleep, mood, and eating.

produces increased levels of serotonin, which normally causes a reduction in the desire for carbohydrates. Some researchers suspect that malfunctions in the serotonin feedback system are responsible for the disturbances of mood and appetite seen in certain types of obesity, premenstrual tension, and depression (Lira et al., 2003; Wurtman & Wurtman, 1995). Serotonin has also been implicated in aggression and impulse control. One of the most consistently observed relationships between a particular neurotransmitter system and a particular behaviour is the low level of serotonin metabolites in the brains of suicide victims, who tend to show a combination of depressed mood, self-directed aggression, and impulsivity (Oquendo & Mann, 2000).

Dopamine is the neurotransmitter used in the substantia nigra and striatum, which are important for movement. Malfunctioning of the dopamine-using (or *dopaminergic*) system in these regions contributes to movement disorders, including Parkinson's disease. As dopamine cells in the substantia nigra degenerate, Parkinson's disease victims experience severe shakiness and difficulty in beginning movements. Parkinson's disease is most common in elderly people, and it may result in part from sensitivity to environmental toxins. These toxins have not yet been identified, but there is evidence from animal studies that chemicals in some common garden pesticides damage dopaminergic neurons (Jenner, 2001). Parkinson's disease has been treated, with partial success, using drugs that enable neurons to make more dopamine (Chase, 1998). Malfunctioning of dopaminergic neurons whose axons go to the cerebral cortex may be partly responsible for schizophrenia, a severe disorder in which perception, emotional expression, and thought are severely distorted (Marenco & Weinberger, 2000).

Other dopaminergic systems that send axons from the midbrain to the forebrain are important in the experience of reward or pleasure (Wise & Rompre, 1989). Animals will work hard in order to receive a direct infusion of dopamine into the forebrain. These dopamine systems play a role in the rewarding properties of many drugs, including cocaine.

Two other small-molecule neurotransmitters—*GABA* and *glutamate*—are amino acids. Neurons in widespread regions of the brain use **GABA,** or gamma-amino butyric acid. GABA reduces the likelihood that postsynaptic neurons will fire an action potential. In fact, it is the major inhibitory neurotransmitter in the central nervous system. When you fall asleep, neurons that use GABA deserve part of the credit.

Malfunctioning of GABA systems has been implicated in a variety of disorders, including severe anxiety and *Huntington's disease*, an inherited and incurable disorder in which the victim is plagued by uncontrollable jerky movement of the arms and legs, along with dementia. Huntington's disease results in the loss of many GABA-containing neurons in the striatum. Normally these GABA systems inhibit dopamine systems; so when they are lost through Huntington's disease, the dopamine systems may run wild, impairing many motor and cognitive functions. Because drugs that block GABA receptors produce intense repetitive electrical discharges, known as *seizures*, researchers suspect that malfunctioning GABA systems probably contribute to *epilepsy*, a brain disorder associated with seizures and convulsive movements. Repeated or sustained seizures can result in permanent brain damage. Drug treatments can reduce their frequency and severity, but completely effective drugs are not yet available.

Glutamate is the major excitatory neurotransmitter in the central nervous system. It is used by more neurons than any other neurotransmitter, and its synapses are especially plentiful in the cerebral cortex and the hippocampus. Glutamate is particularly important because it plays a major role in the ability of the brain to "strengthen" its synaptic connections—that is, to allow messages to cross the synapse more efficiently. This process is necessary for normal development and may be at the root of learning and memory (Bredt & Nicoll, 2003). At the same time, overactivity of glutamate synapses can cause neurons to die. In fact, this overactivity is the main cause of the brain damage that occurs when oxygen is cut off from

dopamine A neurotransmitter used in the parts of the brain involved in regulating movement and experiencing pleasure.

GABA A neurotransmitter that inhibits the firing of neurons.

glutamate An excitatory neurotransmitter that helps strengthen synaptic connections between neurons.

neurons during a stroke. Glutamate can "excite neurons to death," so blocking glutamate receptors immediately after a brain trauma can prevent permanent brain damage (Colak et al., 2003). Recent studies have revealed that glutamate helps neurons and glial cells communicate with one another (Newman, 2003).

Peptides Hundreds of chemicals called *peptides* have been found to act as neurotransmitters. The first of these were discovered in the 1970s, when scientists were investigating *opiates*, such as heroin and morphine. Opiates can relieve pain, produce feelings of elation, and, in high doses, bring on sleep. After marking morphine with a radioactive substance, researchers traced where it became concentrated in the brain. They found that opiates bind to receptors that were not associated with any known neurotransmitter. Because it was unlikely that the brain had developed opiate receptors just in case a person might want to use morphine or heroin, researchers reasoned that the body must already contain a substance similar to opiates. This hypothesis led to the search for a naturally occurring, or endogenous, morphine, which was called *endorphin* (short for endogenous morphine). As it turned out, there are many natural opiate-like compounds. So the term **endorphin** refers to any neurotransmitter that can bind to the same receptors stimulated by opiates. Neurons in several parts of the brain use endorphin, including neuronal pathways that modify pain signals to the brain.

Gases The concept of what neurotransmitters can be was radically altered following the recent discovery that *nitric oxide* and *carbon monoxide*—two toxic gases that contribute to air pollution—can act as neurotransmitters (Boehning & Snyder, 2003). When nitric oxide or carbon monoxide is released by a neuron, it spreads to nearby neurons, sending a signal that affects chemical reactions inside those neurons rather than binding to receptors on their surface. Nitric oxide is not stored in vesicles, as most other neurotransmitters are; it can be released from any part of the neuron. Nitric oxide appears to be one of the neurotransmitters responsible for such diverse functions as penile erection and the formation of memories—not at the same site, obviously. (For a summary of the main neurotransmitters and the consequences of malfunctioning neurotransmitter systems, see "In Review: Classes of Neurotransmitters.")

in review Classes of Neurotransmitters

Neurotransmitter Class	Normal Function	Disorder Associated with Malfunction
Small Molecules		
Acetylcholine	Memory, movement	Alzheimer's disease
Norepinephrine	Mood, sleep, learning	Depression
Serotonin	Mood, appetite, impulsivity	Depression
Dopamine	Movement, reward	Parkinson's disease, schizophrenia
GABA	Sleep, movement	Anxiety, Huntington's disease, epilepsy
Glutamate	Memory	Damage after stroke
Peptides		
Endorphins	Pain control	No established disorder
Gases		
Nitric oxide	Memory	No established disorder

endorphin One of a class of neurotransmitters that bind to opiate receptors and moderate pain.

THINKING CRITICALLY

Are There Drugs That Can Make You Smarter?

Advertisements and articles in health magazines and on the Internet describe a number of dietary supplements that are said to improve memory and other cognitive skills. And people do use them, even though scientific evidence for their effectiveness is mixed. For example, one well-controlled experiment on the herbal supplement *Gingko biloba* found it to be no more effective than a placebo at improving memory (Solomon et al., 2002). Evidence from some other experiments suggests that dietary supplements can, in fact, enhance memory (Gold, Cahill, & Wenk, 2003; McDaniel, Maier, & Einstein, 2002). Scientists are sufficiently intrigued by some of the less extreme claims about these supplements to investigate them further. For example, the US National Institute of Health has funded a $15 million multi-centre trial to determine the effect of ginkgo in normal and mildly impaired elderly. The results will be available in 2006.

Other scientists are looking for "smart drugs," also known as cognitive enhancers or *nootropics* (pronounced "know-oh-TROW-pics"). Some of these drugs are already being prescribed for Alzheimer's disease and attention deficit disorders (Courtney et al., 2004; Farah et al., 2004). Others are still in development (Hall, 2003; Marshall, 2004). One popular magazine article described them as "Viagra for the Brain" (Langreth, 2002).

- **What am I being asked to believe or accept?**

Some researchers believe that it will someday be possible for people without brain disorders to take "smart pills" that will enhance their memory skills enough to help them to do better than they otherwise would on academic exams, in business presentations, and at other cognitive tasks.

- **What evidence is available to support the assertion?**

As described in the chapter on memory, the ability to store and retrieve information depends on several cognitive processes, including perception, attention, and arousal. There are already prescription drugs available that affect these processes. For example, methylphenidate (Ritalin) and modafinil (Provigil) alter arousal by affecting dopamine and norepinephrine systems and reduce the symptoms of attention deficit hyperactivity disorder (ADHD) and a sleep disorder called narcolepsy (see the chapter on consciousness). Research on people without these disorders shows that taking Ritalin and Provigil improves memory on a variety of tasks (Mehta, Goodyer, & Sahakian, 2004; Turner et al., 2003). Many students have come to believe that Ritalin can help them study and do better on exams; its illicit use on high school and college campuses is becoming widespread (Babcock & Byrne, 2000).

Some of the drugs that doctors prescribe for Alzheimer's have also been shown to benefit performance in normal individuals on some memory tasks. These drugs work by enhancing the availability and action of acetylcholine. In one study, pilots who had received training on a flight simulator took either Aricept (donepezil) or a placebo for thirty days. At the end of this period, they were all retested on the simulator. The Aricept group did better than the placebo group, especially in setting up their landing approach and in handling simulated emergencies (Yesavage et al., 2002). Other completely new types of drugs with names such as MEM 1414, MEM 1003, C105, and CX516 have produced beneficial effects on memory in animals. These drugs, which act by amplifying neurons' responses to various neurotransmitters, are now being developed for testing in humans.

- **Are there alternative ways of interpreting the evidence?**

These drugs might indeed be creating genuine improvements in memory and other aspects of intelligence, but their effects might also reflect just a temporary improvement of people's alertness and attentiveness. One critic put it this way: "It

(Ritalin) increases your vigilance when things are boring and hard, but it doesn't make you any smarter, more creative, or more organized" (Dulcan, 2004, cited in Deardorff, 2004, p. Q1). So are these drugs any better than the caffeine and other stimulant study aids that have been used by students for decades? Possibly not. One controlled study of Provigil in sleep-deprived participants showed that it significantly improved cognitive performance, but its effect was matched in participants who were given caffeine (Wesensten et al., 2002).

- **What additional evidence would help to evaluate the alternatives?**

Although certain drug-related risks may be acceptable in some circumstances, such as when treating disorders such as Alzheimer's and perhaps ADHD, those risks may not be justified simply to improve students' exam scores or to help an aging car salesperson remember the features and options on every model in the showroom. So we have to have more information about the effects, and the side effects, of nootropic drugs. For example, sleep disruption is often associated with stimulants. Excessive use of drugs such as Ritalin and Provigil might actually impair rather than enhance a sleepless student's exam performance. The big questions associated with drugs, such as MEM 1414, are whether the cognitive enhancements they produce in rats will appear as cognitive benefits in humans, and what side effects there might be.

In short, even more than in the case of dietary supplements, it is crucial to have long-term experimental trials to establish the safety and effectiveness of nootropic drugs. The outcome of such trials is far from certain. If the drugs are found to be effective in people with memory impairments, and if the side effects are not too serious, they will certainly be approved for use in helping such people. If their impact on cognitive ability is found to stem mainly from their effects on attention and arousal, their value will be seen as more limited. In any case, it will be several years before clinical trials of these prescription drugs are completed, and many more years before over-the-counter versions might be available for purchase in your local pharmacy.

- **What conclusions are most reasonable?**

Given the evidence available, the most reasonable conclusion about the effectiveness of nootropic drugs is one of cautious optimism. The more that scientists learn about the neurochemical changes that underlie learning and memory, the more likely it is that they will succeed at creating drugs capable of enhancing at least some aspects of these cognitive functions. The drugs may not be available for another ten years or so, but they are coming. They will probably first be approved for the treatment of Alzheimer's disease and other specific disorders. Once that happens, they will probably be prescribed for other disorders and eventually used—with or without a legitimate prescription—by people who just want to be "smarter." As the use of nootropics becomes more widespread, society will have to confront ethical and other issues about how much chemical enhancement of cognitive function is acceptable. The debate will probably be similar to that currently raging in the sports world with respect to the use of performance-enhancing drugs. Some observers believe that the ethical debate will eventually subside and that people will someday take nootropic drugs much as they drink coffee today.

The Endocrine System: Coordinating the Internal World

endocrine system Cells that form organs called *glands* and that communicate with one another by secreting chemicals called *hormones*.

gland An organ that secretes hormones into the bloodstream.

As we mentioned earlier, neurons are not the only cells that can use chemicals to communicate with one another in ways that affect behaviour and mental processes. Another class of cells with this ability resides in the **endocrine system** (pronounced "EN-doh-krinn"), which regulates functions ranging from stress responses to physical growth. The cells of endocrine organs, or **glands,** communicate by secreting chemicals, much as neurons do. In the case of endocrine organs, the chemicals are

figure 3.24

Some Major Glands of the Endocrine System

Each of the glands shown releases its hormones into the bloodstream. Even the hypothalamus, a part of the brain, regulates the nearby pituitary gland by secreting hormones.

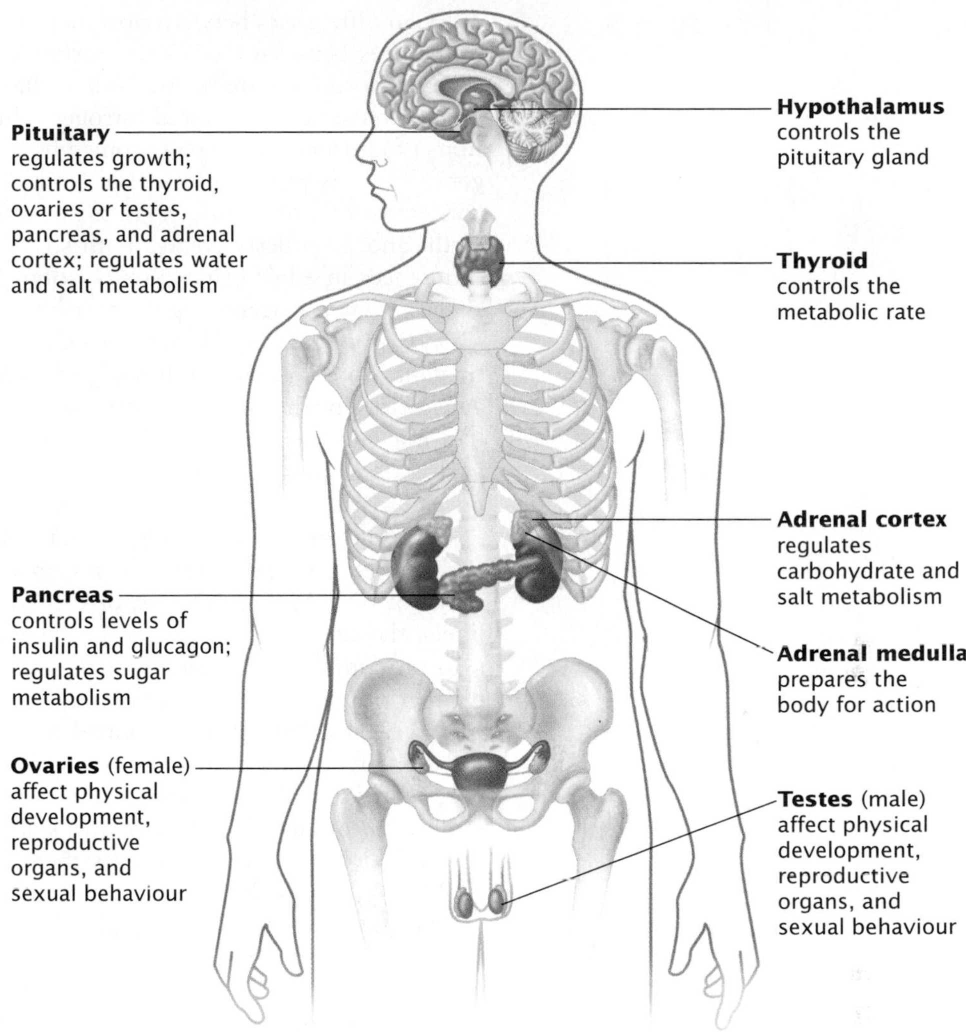
Pituitary
regulates growth; controls the thyroid, ovaries or testes, pancreas, and adrenal cortex; regulates water and salt metabolism
Hypothalamus
controls the pituitary gland
Thyroid
controls the metabolic rate
Adrenal cortex
regulates carbohydrate and salt metabolism
Pancreas
controls levels of insulin and glucagon; regulates sugar metabolism
Adrenal medulla
prepares the body for action
Ovaries (female)
affect physical development, reproductive organs, and sexual behaviour
Testes (male)
affect physical development, reproductive organs, and sexual behaviour

called **hormones.** Figure 3.24 shows the location and functions of some of the major endocrine glands.

Hormones secreted from the endocrine organs are similar to neurotransmitters. In fact, many of these chemicals, including norepinephrine and the endorphins, act both as hormones and as neurotransmitters. However, whereas neurons release neurotransmitters into synapses, endocrine organs put their chemicals into the bloodstream, which carries them throughout the body. In this way, endocrine glands can stimulate cells with which they have no direct connection. But not all cells receive the hormonal message. Hormones, like neurotransmitters, can influence only those cells with receptors capable of receiving them. Organs whose cells have receptors for a hormone are called *target organs*.

Each hormone acts on many target organs, producing coordinated effects throughout the body. For example, when the sex hormone *estrogen* is secreted by a woman's ovaries, it activates her reproductive system. It causes the uterus to grow in preparation for nurturing an embryo; it enlarges the breasts to prepare them for nursing; it stimulates the brain to enhance interest in sexual activity; and it stimulates the pituitary gland to release another hormone that causes a mature egg to be released by the ovary for fertilization. Male sex organs, called the *testes*, secrete *androgens*, which are sex hormones such as *testosterone*. Androgens stimulate the maturation of sperm, increase a male's motivation for sexual activity, increase his aggressiveness, and affect his responses to social stimuli (Romeo, Richardson, & Sisk, 2002).

hormone Chemical secreted by a gland into the bloodstream, which carries it throughout the body.

Can differences between hormones in men and women account for some of the differences between the sexes? During development and in adulthood, sex differences in hormones are relative rather than absolute. In other words, both men and women have androgens and estrogens, but men have relatively higher concentrations of androgens, whereas women have relatively higher concentrations of estrogens. There is plenty of evidence from animal studies that the presence of higher concentrations of androgens in males during development, at around the time of birth, and at puberty creates both structural sex differences in the brain and sex differences in adult behaviours (Gooren & Kruijver, 2002). Other animal studies suggest that estrogens might contribute to the development of the female brain (Bakker et al., 2003). Humans, too, may be affected by hormones early in development. For example, studies of girls who were exposed to high levels of androgens before birth found that they were later more aggressive than their sisters who had not had such exposure (Berenbaum & Resnick, 1997). Even the artwork of such girls is affected by exposure to androgens; they are more likely than nonexposed girls to draw pictures of cars, boats, and airplanes, for example (Iijima et al., 2001). And as shown in Figure 1.1, MRI studies have revealed specific brain regions that function differently in men and women. However, such sex differences may not be simple, inevitable, or caused by the actions of hormones alone. Most likely, the sex differences we see in behaviour depend not only on hormones but also on complex interactions of biological and social forces, as described in the chapter on motivation and emotion.

The brain has ultimate control over the secretion of hormones. Through the hypothalamus, it controls the pituitary gland, which in turn controls endocrine organs in the body. The brain is also one of the target organs for most endocrine secretions. In fact, the brain creates some of the same hormones that are secreted in the endocrine system and uses them for neural communication (Compagnone & Mellon, 2000). In summary, the endocrine system typically involves four elements: the brain, the pituitary gland, an endocrine organ, and the target organs, which include the brain. Each element in the system uses hormones to signal to the next element, and the secretion of each hormone is stimulated or suppressed by other hormones.

Hormones at Work The appearance of a threat activates a pattern of hormonal secretions and other physiological responses that prepare animals and humans to confront, or flee, the danger. This pattern is known as the "fight-or-flight syndrome."

For example, in stress-hormone systems, the brain controls the pituitary gland by signaling the hypothalamus to release hormones that stimulate receptors of the pituitary gland, which secretes another hormone, which stimulates another endocrine gland to secrete its hormones. More specifically, when the brain interprets a situation as threatening, the pituitary releases *adrenocorticotropic hormone (ACTH)*, which causes the adrenal glands to release the hormone *cortisol* into the bloodstream. These hormones, in turn, act on cells throughout the body, including the brain. One effect of cortisol, for example, is to activate the emotion-related limbic system, making it more likely that you will remember stressful or traumatic events (Cahill & McGaugh, 1998). The combined effects of the adrenal hormones and the activation of the sympathetic nervous system result in a set of responses called the **fight-or-flight syndrome,** which, as mentioned earlier, prepares the animal or person for action in response to danger or other stress. The heart beats faster, the liver releases glucose into the bloodstream, fuels are mobilized from fat stores, and the organism usually enters a state of high arousal.

The hormones provide feedback to the brain, as well as to the pituitary gland. Just as a thermostat and furnace regulate heat, this feedback system regulates hormone secretion so as to keep it within a certain range. If a hormone rises above a certain level, feedback about this situation signals the brain and pituitary to stop stimulating that hormone's secretion. So after the immediate threat is over, feedback about cortisol's action in the brain and in the pituitary terminates the secretion of ACTH and, in turn, cortisol. Because the feedback suppresses further action, this arrangement is called a *negative feedback system.*

The Immune System: Defending the Body

LINKAGES (a link to Health, Stress, and Coping)

Like the nervous system and endocrine system, the **immune system** serves as both a sensory system and a security system. It monitors the internal state of the body and detects invading cells and toxic substances that may have invaded. It recognizes and remembers foreign substances, and it engulfs and destroys foreign cells, as well as cancer cells. Individuals whose immune system is impaired—AIDS patients, for example—face death from invading bacteria or malignant tumours. However, if the system becomes overactive, the results can be just as devastating: Many diseases, including arthritis, diabetes, and multiple sclerosis, are now recognized as **autoimmune disorders,** in which cells of the immune system attack normal cells of the body, including brain cells (Marrack, Kappler, & Kotzin, 2001).

The immune system is as complex as the nervous system, and it contains as many cells as the brain. Some of these cells are in organs such as the thymus and spleen, whereas others circulate in the bloodstream and enter tissues throughout the body (see Figure 3.25). In the chapter on health, stress, and coping, we describe a few of the immune system's many cell types and how they work.

The nervous system and the immune system were once thought of as separate (Ader, Felten, & Cohen, 1990). However, five lines of evidence suggest important interactions between the two. First, stress can alter the outcome of disease in animals, and as discussed in the chapter on health, stress, and coping, there is clear evidence that psychological stressors also affect disease processes in humans (Sternberg, 2001). Second, immune responses can be "taught" using some of the principles outlined in the chapter on learning. In one study with humans, for example, exposure to the taste of sherbet was repeatedly associated with an injection of epinephrine, which increases immune system activity. Later, an increase in immune system activity could be prompted by the taste of sherbet alone (Exton et al., 2000). Third, animal studies have shown that stimulating or damaging specific parts of the hypothalamus, the cortex, or the brainstem that control the autonomic nervous system can enhance or impair immune functions (Felten et al., 1998). Fourth, activation of the immune system can produce changes in the electrical activity of the brain, in neurotransmitter

fight-or-flight syndrome Physical reactions initiated by the sympathetic nervous system that prepare the body to fight or to run from a threatening situation.

immune system The body's system of defense against invading substances and microorganisms.

autoimmune disorders Physical problems caused when cells of the body's immune system attack normal body cells as if they were foreign invaders.

figure 3.25

The Nervous System, Endocrine System, and Immune System

All three systems interact and influence one another. The nervous system affects the endocrine system by controlling secretion of hormones via the pituitary gland. It also affects the immune system through the autonomic nervous system's action on the thymus gland. The thymus, spleen, and bone marrow are sites of generation and development of immune cells. Hormones of the pituitary gland and adrenal gland modulate immune cells. Immune cells secrete cytokines and antibodies to fight foreign invaders. Cytokines are blood-borne messengers that regulate the development of immune cells and also influence the central nervous system.

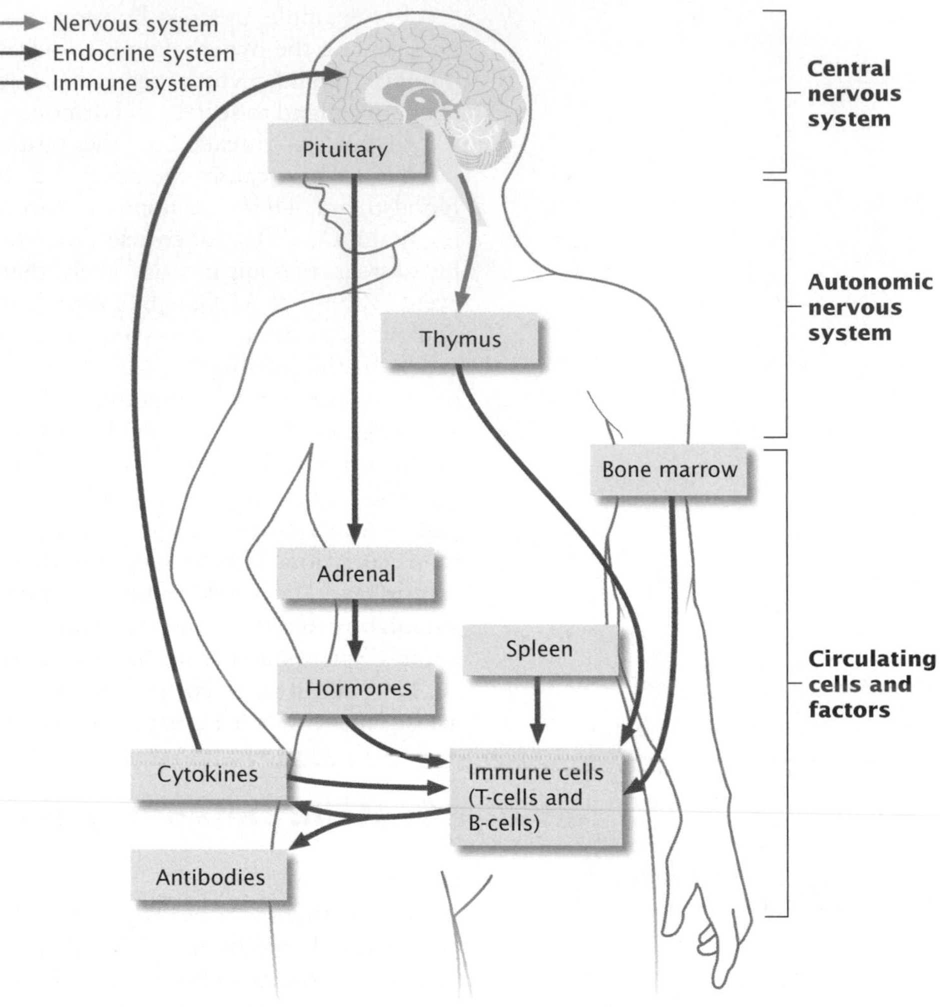

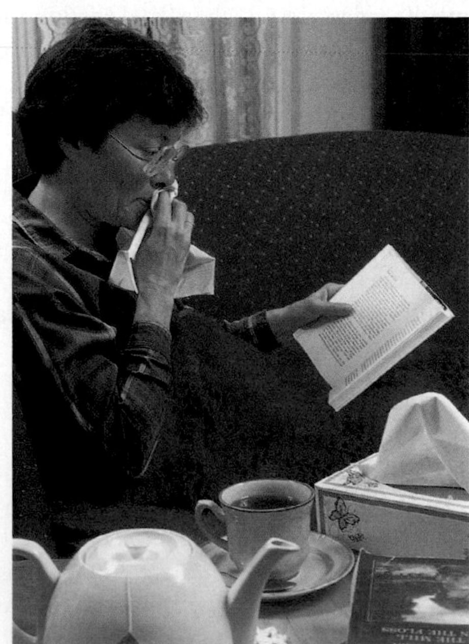

The Common Cold The interaction of the immune system and the nervous system can be seen in some of the symptoms associated with routine "sickness." Sleepiness, nausea, and fever are actually a result of chemicals released by immune cells called *cytokines*, which act directly on the brain through specific receptors (Pousset, 1994).

activity, in hormonal secretion, and in behaviour—including symptoms of illness (Kronfol & Remick, 2000). Finally, some of the same chemical messengers are found in both the brain and the immune system. For example, one way in which glial cells help to repair damaged neurons is by secreting "immune messengers" called *interleukins* (Parish et al., 2002).

These converging lines of evidence point to important relationships that illustrate the intertwining of biological and psychological functions, the interaction of body and mind. They highlight the ways in which the immune system, nervous system, and endocrine system—all systems of communication between and among cells—are integrated to form the biological basis for a smoothly functioning self that is filled with interacting thoughts, emotions, and memories and is capable of responding to life's challenges and opportunities with purposeful and adaptive behaviour.

LINKAGES

As noted in the chapter on introducing psychology, all of psychology's subfields are related to one another. Our discussion of developmental changes in the brain illustrates just one way in which the topic of this chapter, the biological aspects of psychology, is linked to the subfield of developmental psychology, which is described in the chapter on human development. The Linkages diagram shows ties to two other subfields as well, and there are many more ties throughout the book. Looking for linkages among subfields will help you see how they all fit together and help you better appreciate the big picture that is psychology.

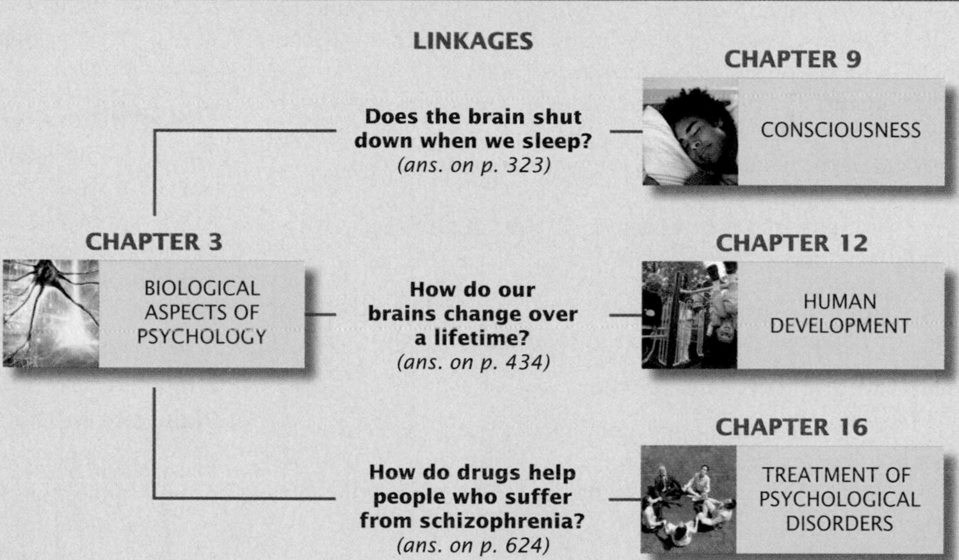
LINKAGES
CHAPTER 3
BIOLOGICAL ASPECTS OF PSYCHOLOGY
Does the brain shut down when we sleep?
(ans. on p. 323)
CHAPTER 9
CONSCIOUSNESS
How do our brains change over a lifetime?
(ans. on p. 434)
CHAPTER 12
HUMAN DEVELOPMENT
How do drugs help people who suffer from schizophrenia?
(ans. on p. 624)
CHAPTER 16
TREATMENT OF PSYCHOLOGICAL DISORDERS

SUMMARY

Biological psychology focuses on the biological aspects of our being, including the nervous system, that provide the physical basis for behaviour and mental processes. The *nervous system* is a system of cells that allows an organism to gain information about what is going on inside and outside the body and to respond appropriately.

The Nervous System

Much of our understanding of the biological aspects of psychology has stemmed from research on animal and human nervous systems at levels ranging from single cells to complex organizations of cells.

Cells of the Nervous System

The main units of the nervous system are cells called *neurons* and *glial cells*. Neurons are especially good at receiving signals from, and transmitting signals to, other neurons. Neurons have cell bodies and two types of fibres, called *axons* and *dendrites*. Axons usually carry signals away from the cell body, whereas dendrites usually carry signals to the cell body. Neurons can transmit signals because of the structure of these fibres, the excitable surface of some of the fibres, and the synapses, or gaps, between cells.

Action Potentials

The membranes of neurons normally keep the distribution of electrically charged molecules uneven between the inside of cells and the outside, creating an electrochemical force, or potential. The membrane surface of the axon can transmit a disturbance in this potential, called an *action potential*, from one end of the axon to the other. The speed of the action potential is fastest in neurons sheathed in *myelin*. Between firings there is a very brief rest, called a *refractory period*.

Synapses and Communication Between Neurons

When an action potential reaches the end of an axon, the axon releases a chemical called a *neurotransmitter*. This chemical crosses the synapse and interacts with the postsynaptic cell at special sites called *receptors*. This interaction creates a postsynaptic potential—either an *excitatory postsynaptic potential (EPSP)* or an *inhibitory postsynaptic potential (IPSP)*—that makes the postsynaptic cell more likely or less likely to fire an action potential. So whereas communication within a neuron is electrochemical, communication between neurons is chemical. Because the fibres of neurons have many branches, each neuron can interact with thousands of other neurons. Each neuron constantly integrates signals received at its many synapses; the result of this integration determines how often the neuron fires an action potential.

Organization and Functions of the Nervous System

Neurons are organized in *neural networks* of closely connected cells. *Sensory systems* receive information from the environment, and *motor systems* influence the actions of muscles and other organs. The two major divisions of the nervous system are the *peripheral nervous system (PNS)* and the *central nervous system (CNS)*, which includes the brain and spinal cord.

The Peripheral Nervous System: Keeping in Touch with the World

The peripheral nervous system has two components: the somatic nervous system and the autonomic nervous system.

The Somatic Nervous System

The first component of the peripheral nervous system is the *somatic nervous system*, which transmits information from the senses to the CNS and carries signals from the CNS to the muscles that move the skeleton.

The Autonomic Nervous System

The second component of the peripheral nervous system is the *autonomic nervous system*. It carries messages back and forth between the CNS and the heart, lungs, and other organs and glands.

The Central Nervous System: Making Sense of the World

The CNS is laid out in interconnected groups of neuronal cell bodies, called *nuclei*, whose collections of axons travel together in *fibre tracts*, or *pathways*.

The Spinal Cord

The *spinal cord* receives information from the peripheral senses and sends it to the brain; it also relays messages from the brain to the rest of the body. In addition, cells of the spinal cord can direct simple behaviours, called *reflexes*, without instructions from the brain.

The Brain

The brain's major subdivisions are the *hindbrain*, *midbrain*, and *forebrain*. The hindbrain includes the *medulla*, the *cerebellum*, and the *locus coeruleus*. The midbrain includes the *substantia nigra*. The *reticular formation* is found in both the hindbrain and the midbrain. The forebrain is the largest and most highly developed part of the brain; it includes many structures, including the *hypothalamus* and *thalamus*. A part of the hypothalamus called the *suprachiasmatic nuclei* maintains a clock that determines biological rhythms. Other forebrain structures include the *striatum*, *hippocampus*, and *amygdala*. Several of these structures form the *limbic system*, which plays an important role in regulating emotion and memory.

The Cerebral Cortex

The outer surface of the *cerebral hemispheres* is called the *cerebral cortex*; it is responsible for many of the higher functions of the brain, including speech and reasoning. The functional areas of the cortex include the *sensory cortex*, *motor cortex*, and *association cortex*.

The Divided Brain in a Unified Self

The right and left hemispheres of the cerebral cortex are specialized to some degree in their functions. In most people, the left hemisphere is more active in language and logical tasks and the right hemisphere, in spatial, musical, and artistic tasks. A task that is performed more efficiently by one hemisphere than the other is said to be *lateralized*. The hemispheres are connected through the *corpus callosum*, allowing them to operate in a coordinated fashion.

Plasticity in the Central Nervous System

Plasticity in the central nervous system, the ability to strengthen neural connections at its synapses as well as to establish new synapses, forms the basis for learning and memory. Scientists are searching for ways to increase plasticity following brain damage.

The Chemistry of Psychology

Neurons that use the same neurotransmitter form a *neurotransmitter system*.

Three Classes of Neurotransmitters

There are three classes of neurotransmitters: small molecules, peptides, and gases. *Acetylcholine* systems in the brain influence memory processes and movement. *Norepinephrine* is released by neurons whose axons spread widely throughout the brain; it is involved in arousal, mood, and learning. *Serotonin*, another widespread neurotransmitter, is active in systems regulating mood and appetite. *Dopamine* systems are involved in movement, motivation, and higher cognitive activities. Both Parkinson's disease and schizophrenia involve a disturbance of dopamine systems. *GABA* is an inhibitory neurotransmitter involved in anxiety and epilepsy. *Glutamate* is the most common excitatory neurotransmitter. It is involved in learning and memory and, in excess, may cause neuronal death. *Endorphins* are peptide neurotransmitters that affect pain pathways. Nitric oxide and carbon monoxide are gases that function as neurotransmitters.

The Endocrine System: Coordinating the Internal World

Like nervous system cells, those of the *endocrine system* communicate by releasing a chemical that signals to other cells. However, the chemicals released by endocrine organs, or *glands*, are called *hormones* and are carried by the bloodstream to remote target organs. The target organs often produce a coordinated response to hormonal stimulation. One of these responses is the *fight-or-flight syndrome*, which is triggered by adrenal hormones that prepare for action in times of stress. Hormones also affect brain development, contributing to sex differences in the brain and behaviour. Negative feedback systems are involved in the control of most endocrine functions. The brain is the main controller. Through the hypothalamus, it controls the pituitary gland, which in turn controls endocrine organs in the body. The brain is also a target organ for most endocrine secretions.

The Immune System: Defending the Body

The *immune system* serves both as a sensory system that monitors the internal state of the body and as a protective system for detecting and destroying invading cells and toxic substances. *Autoimmune disorders* result when cells of the immune system attack normal cells of the body. There are important interactions among the immune system, nervous system, and endocrine system.

4 Sensation

How do you know where you are right now? Your brain tells you, of course, but it must get its information from your eyes and ears and other senses. In this chapter, we draw your attention to the amazing processes through which your senses work and some of the problems that occur when they don't. We have organized our tour of the senses as follows:

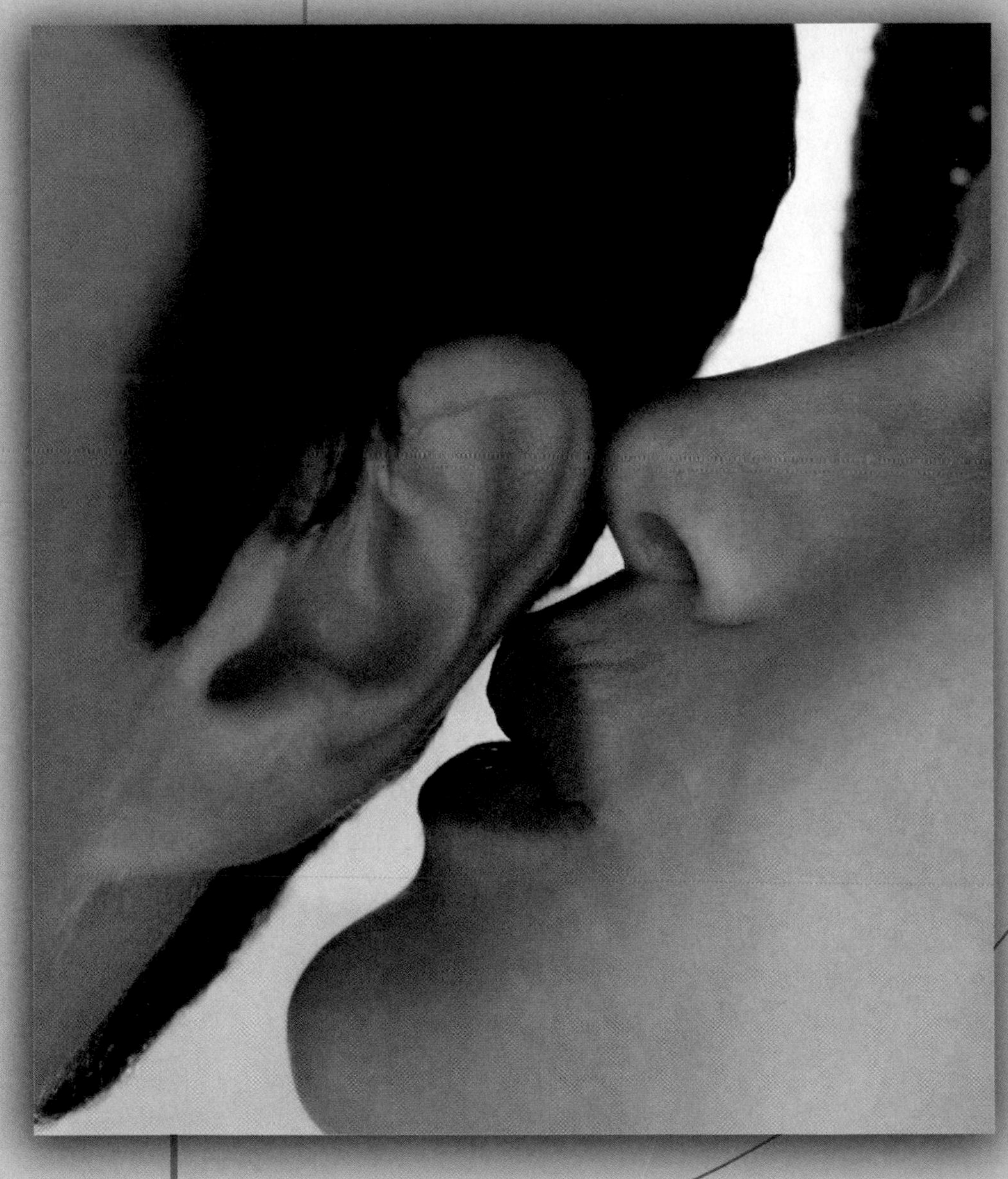

Years ago, Fred Aryee lost his right arm below the elbow in a boating accident, yet he still "feels" his missing arm and hand (Shreeve, 1993). Like Fred, many people who have lost an arm or a leg continue to experience itching and other sensations from a "phantom limb." When asked to "move" it, they can feel it move, and some people feel intense pain when their missing hand suddenly seems to tighten into a fist, digging nonexistent fingernails into a phantom palm. Worse, they may be unable to "open" their hand to relieve the pain. In an effort to help these people, scientists seated them at a table in front of a mirror, then angled the mirror to create the illusion that their amputated arm and hand had been restored. When these patients moved their real hands while looking in the mirror, they not only "felt" movement occurring in their phantom hands, but they could also "unclench" their phantom fists and stop their intense pain (Ramachandran & Rogers-Ramachandran, 2000). This clever strategy arose from research on how vision interacts with the sense of touch. To experience this interaction yourself, sit across a table from someone and ask that person to stroke the tabletop while stroking your knee under the table in exactly the same way, in exactly the same direction. If you watch the person's hand stroking the table, you will soon experience the touch sensations coming from the table, not your knee! If the person's two hands do not move in synch, however, the illusion will not occur.

LINKAGES (a link to Perception)

This illusion illustrates several points about our senses. It shows, first, that the streams of information coming from different senses can interact. Second, it reveals that experience can change the sensations we receive. Third, and most important, the illusion suggests that "reality" differs from person to person. This last point sounds silly if you assume that there is an "objective reality" that is the same for everyone. After all, the seat you sit on and the book you are reading are solid objects. You can see and feel them with your senses, so they must look and feel the same to you as they would to anyone else. But sensory psychologists tell us that reality is not that simple—that the senses do not reflect an objective reality. Just as people can feel a hand that is not objectively "there," the senses of each individual actively shape information about the outside world to create a *personal reality*. The sensory experiences of different species—and individual humans—vary. You do not see the same world a fly sees, people from British Columbia may not hear music quite the same way as do people from Singapore, and different people experience colour differently.

To understand how sensory systems create reality, consider some basic information about the senses. A **sense** is a system that translates information from outside the nervous system into neural activity. For example, vision is the system through which the eyes convert light into neural activity. This neural activity tells the brain something about the source of the light (e.g., that it is bright) or about objects from which the light is reflected (e.g., that there is a round, red object out there). These messages from the senses are called **sensations.** Because they provide the link between the self and the world outside the brain, sensations help shape many of the behaviours and mental processes studied by psychologists.

Traditionally, psychologists have distinguished between *sensation*—the initial message from the senses—and *perception*, the process through which messages from the senses are given meaning. They point out, for example, that you do not actually sense a cat lying on the sofa; you sense shapes and colours—visual sensations. You use your knowledge of the world to interpret, or perceive, these sensations as a cat. However, it is impossible to draw a clear line between sensation and perception. The reason is partly that the process of interpreting sensations begins in the sense organs themselves. For example, a frog's eye immediately interprets any small black object as "fly!"—thus enabling the frog to attack the fly with its tongue without waiting for its brain to process the sensory information (Lettvin et al., 1959).

sense A system that translates information from outside the nervous system into neural activity.

sensations Messages from the senses that make up the raw information that affects many kinds of behaviour and mental processes.

This chapter covers the first steps of the sensation-perception process; the chapter on perception deals with the later steps. Together, these chapters illustrate how we human beings, with our sense organs and brains, create our own realities. In this chapter we explore how sensations are produced, received, and acted upon. First, we consider what sensations are and how they inform us about the world. Then we examine the physical and psychological mechanisms involved in the auditory, visual, and chemical senses. And finally, we turn to a discussion of the somatic senses, which enable us to feel things, to experience temperature and pain, and to know where our body parts are in relation to one another. Together, these senses play a critical role in our ability as humans to adapt to and survive in our environment.

Sensory Systems

The senses gather information about the world by detecting various forms of energy, such as sound, light, heat, and physical pressure. The eyes detect light energy, the ears detect the energy of sound, and the skin detects the energy of heat and pressure. Humans depend primarily on vision, hearing, and the skin senses to gain information about the world; they depend less than other animals on smell and taste. To your brain, "the world" also includes the rest of your body, and there are sensory systems that provide information about the location and position of your body parts.

All of these senses must detect stimuli, encode them into neural activity, and transfer this coded information to the brain. Figure 4.1 illustrates these basic steps in sensation. At each step, sensory information is "processed" in some way: The information that arrives at one point in the system is not the same as the information that goes to the next step.

In some sensory systems, the first step in sensation involves **accessory structures,** which modify the energy created by something in the environment—such as a person talking or a flashing sign (Step 1 in Figure 4.1). The outer part of the ear is an accessory structure that collects sound; the lens of the eye is an accessory structure that changes incoming light by focusing it.

The second step in sensation is **transduction,** which is the process of converting incoming energy into neural activity (Step 2 in Figure 4.1). Just as a cell phone receives energy and transduces it into sounds, the ears receive sound energy and transduce it into neural activity that people recognize as voices, music, and other auditory experiences. Transduction takes place at structures called **sensory receptors,** specialized cells that detect certain forms of energy. Sensory receptors are somewhat like the neurons that we describe in the chapter on biological aspects of psychology; they respond to incoming energy by firing an action potential and releasing neurotransmitters that send a signal to neighbouring cells. (However, some

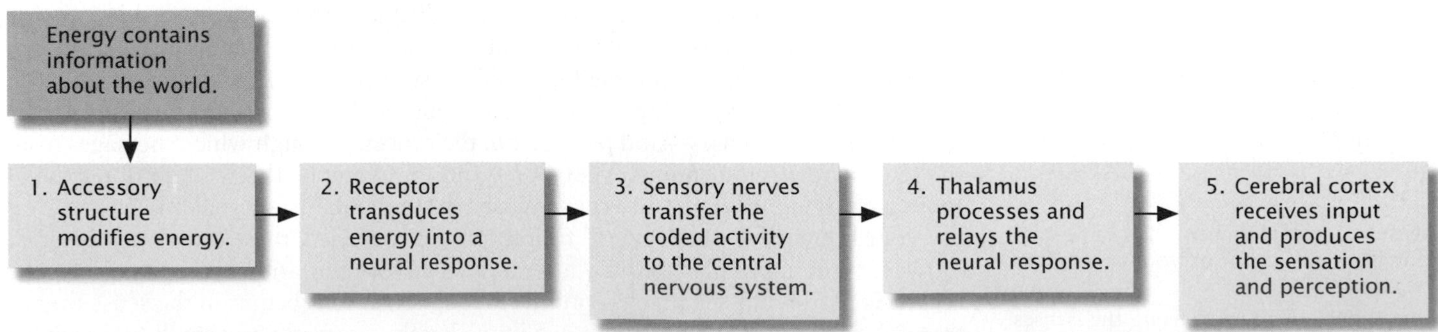

figure 4.1

Elements of a Sensory System

Objects in the world generate energy that is focused by accessory structures and detected by sensory receptors, which convert the energy into neural signals. The signals are then relayed through parts of the brain, which processes them into perceptual experiences.

sensory receptors do not have axons and dendrites, as neurons do.) Sensory receptors respond best to changes in energy (Graziano et al., 2002). A constant level of stimulation usually produces **adaptation**, a process through which responsiveness to an unchanging stimulus decreases over time. This is why the touch sensations you get from your glasses or wristwatch disappear shortly after you have put them on.

Next, sensory nerves carry the output from receptors to the central nervous system, which includes the spinal cord and the brain (Step 3 in Figure 4.1). For all the senses except smell, sensory information entering the brain goes first to the thalamus (Step 4). The thalamus does a preliminary analysis of the information, then relays it to sensory areas of the cerebral cortex (Step 5). It is in the sensory cortex that the most complex processing occurs.

The Problem of Coding

As sensory receptors transduce energy into patterns of nerve cell activity, they create a coded message that tells the brain about the physical properties of whatever stimulus has reached the receptors. The brain unscrambles this coded neural activity, allowing you to make sense of the stimulus—to determine, for example, whether you are looking at a cat, a dog, or a person. For each psychological dimension of a sensation, such as the brightness or colour of light, there must be a corresponding physical dimension coded by sensory receptors.

To better appreciate the problem of coding physical stimuli into neural activity, imagine that for your birthday you receive a Pet Brain. You are told that your Pet Brain is alive, but it does not respond when you open the box and talk to it. You remove it from the box and show it a hot-fudge sundae—no response. You show it pictures of other attractive brains—still no response. You are about to deposit your Pet Brain in the trash when you suddenly realize that the two of you are not talking the same language. As described in the chapter on biological aspects of psychology, the brain usually receives information from sensory neurons and responds by activating motor neurons. So if you want to communicate with your Pet Brain, you will have to send it messages by stimulating its sensory nerves. To read its responses you will have to record signals from its motor nerves.

After having this brilliant insight and setting up an electric stimulator and recording device, you are faced with an awesome problem. How do you describe a hot-fudge sundae to sensory nerves so that they will pass on the correct information to the brain? This is the problem of **coding**, the translation of the physical properties of a stimulus into a pattern of neural activity that specifically identifies those properties.

If you want the brain to see the sundae, you should stimulate the optic nerve (the nerve from the eye to the brain) rather than the auditory nerve (the nerve from the ear to the brain). This idea is based on the **doctrine of specific nerve energies**: Stimulation of a particular sensory nerve provides codes for that one sense, no matter how the stimulation takes place. For example, if you apply gentle pressure to your eyeball, you will produce activity in the optic nerve and sense little spots of light.

Having chosen the optic nerve to send visual information, you must next develop a code for the specific attributes of the sundae: the soft white curves of the vanilla ice cream, the dark richness of the chocolate, the bright red roundness of the cherry on top. These dimensions must be coded in the language of neural activity—that is, in the firing of action potentials.

Some attributes of a stimulus are coded relatively simply. For example, certain neurons in the visual system fire faster in response to a bright light than to a dim light. This is called a **temporal code**, because it involves changes in the *timing* pattern of nerve firing. Other temporal codes can be more complex. For example, a burst of firing followed by a slower firing rate means something different than does a steady rate of firing. Information about a stimulus can also take the form of a **spatial code**, which involves the *location* of neurons that are firing and those that are

accessory structures Structures, such as the lens of the eye, that modify a stimulus.

transduction The process of converting incoming energy into neural activity through receptors.

sensory receptors Specialized cells that detect certain forms of energy.

adaptation The process through which responsiveness to an unchanging stimulus decreases over time.

coding Translating the physical properties of a stimulus into a pattern of neural activity that specifically identifies those properties.

doctrine of specific nerve energies The discovery that stimulation of a particular sensory nerve provides codes for that sense, no matter how the stimulation takes place.

temporal codes Coding attributes of a stimulus in terms of changes in the timing of neural firing.

spatial codes Coding attributes of a stimulus in terms of the location of firing neurons relative to their neighbours.

What Is It? In the split second before you recognized this stimulus as parliament in Ottawa, sensory neurons in your visual system detected the light reflected off this page and transduced it into a neural code that your brain could interpret. The coding and decoding process occurs so quickly and efficiently in all our senses that we are seldom aware of it. Later in this chapter, we describe how this remarkable feat is accomplished.

not. For example, different sensory neurons will fire depending on whether someone touches your hand or your foot. Sensory information can also be recoded at several relay points as it makes its way to, and through, the brain.

In summary, the problem of coding is solved by means of sensory systems, which allow the brain to receive detailed, accurate, and useful information about stimuli in its environment. If you succeed in creating the right coding system, your Pet Brain will finally know what a hot-fudge sundae looks like.

LINKAGES
Sensation and Biological Aspects of Psychology

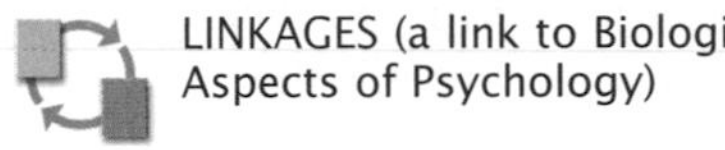

LINKAGES (a link to Biological Aspects of Psychology)

As sensory systems transfer information to the brain, they also organize that information. This organized information is called a *representation*. If you have read the chapter on biological aspects of psychology, you are already familiar with some characteristics of sensory representations. In humans, representations of vision, hearing, and the skin senses in the cerebral cortex share the following features:

1. The information from each of these senses reaches the cortex through the thalamus. (Figure 3.14 shows where these areas of the brain are.)
2. Each side of the cerebral cortex builds a sensory representation of the opposite, or *contralateral*, side of the world. For example, the left side of the visual cortex "sees" the right side of the world, whereas the right side of that cortex "sees" the left side of the world. This contralateral representation occurs because most sensory nerve fibres from each side of the body cross over to the opposite side of the thalamus and go from there to the opposite side of the cortex.
3. The cortex contains maps, or *topographical representations*, of each sense. Accordingly, features that are next to each other in the world eventually stimulate neurons that are next to each other in the brain. For example, two notes that are similar in pitch activate neighbouring neurons in the auditory cortex, and the neurons that respond to sensations in the elbow and in the forearm are relatively close to one another in the somatosensory

cortex. There are multiple maps representing each sense, but the area that receives information directly from the thalamus is called the *primary cortex* for that sense.

4. The density of nerve fibres in a sense organ determines how well it is represented in the cortex. The skin on your fingertip, for example, has more touch receptors per square inch than the skin on your back does. So the area of cortex that represents your fingertip is larger than the area that represents your back.

5. Each region of primary sensory cortex is divided into columns of cells, each of which has a somewhat specialized role in sensory processing. For example, some columns of cells in the visual cortex respond most strongly to diagonal lines, whereas other columns respond most strongly to horizontal lines.

6. For each of the senses, regions of cortex other than the primary areas do additional processing of sensory information. As described in the chapter on biological aspects of psychology, these areas of *association cortex* may contain representations of more than one sense, thus setting the stage for the combining of sensory information that we described at the beginning of this chapter.

In summary, sensory systems convert various forms of physical energy into neural activity. (As described in Figure 4.1, the energy may first be modified by accessory structures.) The resulting pattern of neural activity encodes the physical properties of the energy. The codes are modified as the information is transferred to the brain and processed further. In the remainder of this chapter we describe how these processes take place in hearing, vision, and other sensory systems.

Hearing

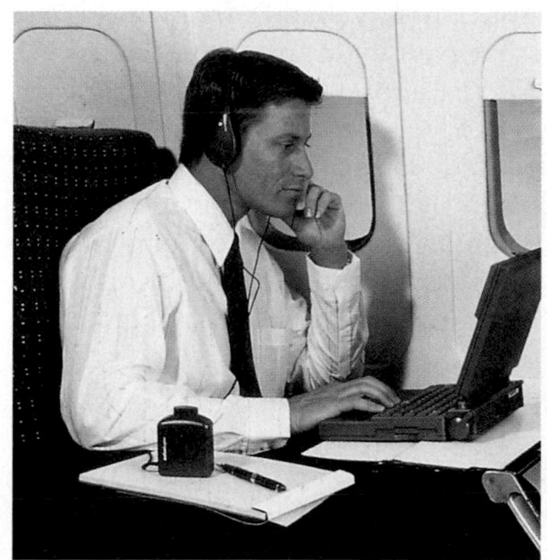

Noise Eliminators Complex sound, including noise, can be analyzed into its component, simple sine waves by means of a mathematical process called *Fourier analysis.* Noise-eliminating headphones perform this waveform analysis, then use a sound synthesizer to produce exactly opposite waveforms. The opposing waves cancel each other out, and the amazing result is silence. Similar devices are being developed to treat chronic tinnitus, or "ringing in the ear."

sound A repetitive fluctuation in the pressure of a medium, such as air.

In 1969, when Neil Armstrong became the first human to step onto the moon, millions of people back on earth heard his radio transmission: "That's one small step for a man, one giant leap for mankind." But if Armstrong had taken off his space helmet and shouted, "Whoo-ee! I can moonwalk!" another astronaut, a foot away, would not have heard him. Why? Because Armstrong would have been speaking into airless, empty space. **Sound** is a repeated fluctuation, a rising and falling, in the pressure of air, water, or some other substance called a *medium.* On the moon, which has almost no atmospheric medium, sound cannot exist.

Sound

Vibrations of an object produce the fluctuations in pressure that create sound. Each time the object moves outward, it increases the pressure in the medium around it. As the object moves back, the pressure drops. When you speak, for example, your vocal cords vibrate, producing fluctuations in air pressure that spread as waves. A *wave* is a repeated variation in pressure that spreads out in three dimensions. The wave can move great distances, but the air itself barely moves. Imagine a jam-packed line of people waiting to get into a movie. If someone at the rear of the line shoves the next person, a wave of people jostling against people might spread all the way to the front of the line, but the person who shoved first is still no closer to getting into the theatre.

Physical Characteristics of Sound Sound is represented graphically by waveforms like those in Figure 4.2. A *waveform* represents a wave in two dimensions, but remember that waves actually move through the air in all directions. This is the reason that, when people talk to each other in a movie theatre or a lecture, others all around them are distracted by the conversation.

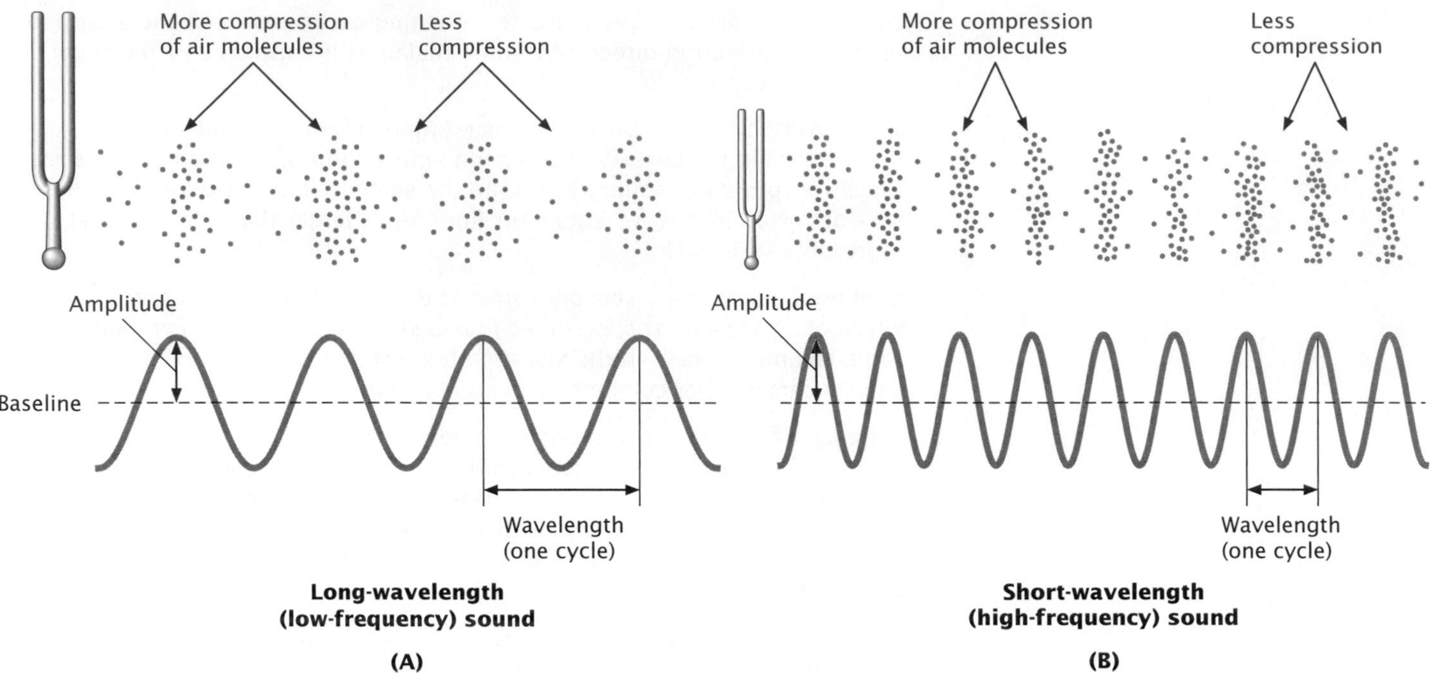

figure 4.2

Sound Waves and Waveforms

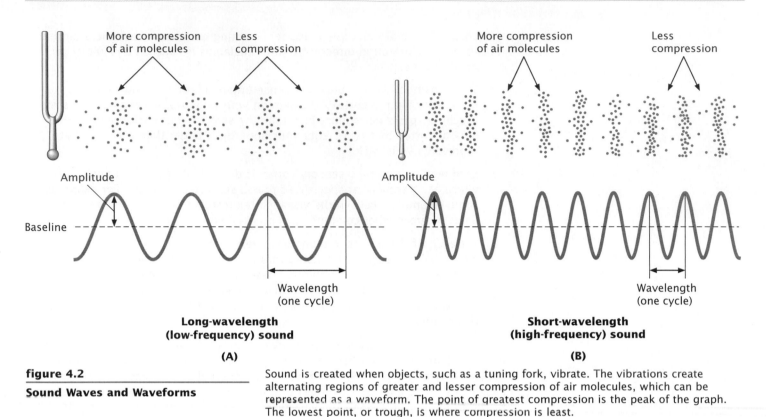

Sound is created when objects, such as a tuning fork, vibrate. The vibrations create alternating regions of greater and lesser compression of air molecules, which can be represented as a waveform. The point of greatest compression is the peak of the graph. The lowest point, or trough, is where compression is least.

Three characteristics of the waveform are important in understanding sounds. First, the difference in air pressure from the baseline to the peak of the wave is the **amplitude** of the sound, or its intensity. Second, the distance from one wave peak to the next is called the **wavelength.** Third, a sound's **frequency** is the number of complete waveforms, or cycles, that pass by a given point each second. Frequency is described in a unit called *hertz*, abbreviated *Hz* (for Heinrich Hertz, a nineteenth-century physicist). One cycle per second is 1 hertz. Because the speed of sound is constant in a given medium, wavelength and frequency are related: The longer the wavelength, the lower the frequency; the shorter the wavelength, the higher the frequency. Most sounds are mixtures of many different frequencies and amplitudes. In contrast, a pure tone is made up of only one frequency and can be represented by what is known as a *sine wave* (Figure 4.2 shows such sine waves).

Psychological Dimensions of Sound The amplitude and frequency of sound waves determine the sounds that you hear. These physical characteristics of the waves produce the psychological dimensions of sound known as *loudness*, *pitch*, and *timbre*.

Loudness is determined by the amplitude of the sound wave; waves with greater amplitude produce sensations of louder sounds. Loudness is described in units called *decibels*, abbreviated *dB*. By definition, zero decibels is the minimal detectable sound for normal hearing. Table 4.1 gives examples of the loudness of some common sounds.

Pitch, or how high or low a tone sounds, depends on the frequency of sound waves. High-frequency waves are sensed as sounds of high pitch. The highest note on a piano has a frequency of about 4000 hertz; the lowest note has a frequency of about 50 hertz. Humans can hear sounds ranging from about 20 hertz to about 20 000 hertz. Almost everyone experiences relative pitch; that is, they can tell whether one note is higher than, lower than, or equal to another note. However, some people have *perfect pitch*, which means they can identify specific frequencies

amplitude The difference between the peak and the baseline of a waveform.

wavelength The distance from one peak to the next in a waveform.

frequency The number of complete waveforms, or cycles, that pass by a given point in space every second.

loudness A psychological dimension of sound determined by the amplitude of a sound wave.

pitch How high or low a tone sounds.

table 4.1

Sound intensity varies across an extremely wide range. A barely audible sound is, by definition, 0 decibels (dB). Every increase of 20 dB reflects a tenfold increase in the amplitude of sound waves. So the 40-dB sounds of an office are actually 10 times as intense as a 20-dB whisper, and traffic noise of 100 dB is 10 000 times as intense as that whisper.

Intensity of Sound Sources

Sound	Source Level (dB)
Spacecraft launch (from 45 m)	180
Loudest rock band on record	160
Pain threshold (approximate)	140
Large jet motor (at 22 m)	120
Loudest human shout on record	111
Heavy auto traffic	100
Conversation (at about 1 m)	60
Quiet office	40
Soft whisper	20
Threshold of hearing	0

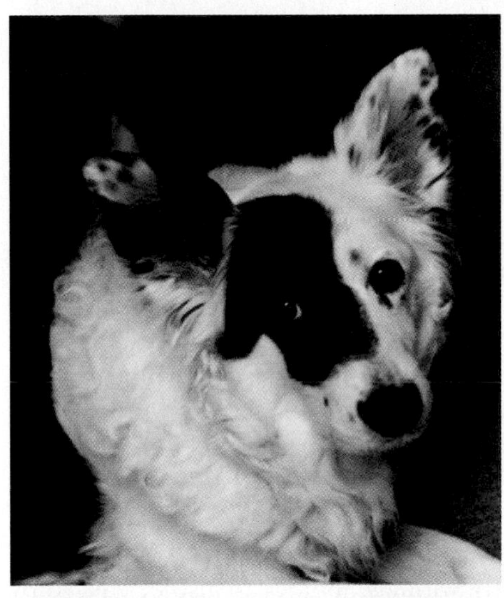

An Accessory Structure Some animals, like Annie here, have a large pinna that can be rotated to help detect sounds and locate their source.

and the notes they represent. They can say, for example, that a 262-hertz tone is middle C. Perfect pitch appears to be an inborn trait (Bella & Peretz, 2003; Stewart & Walsh, 2002; Zatorre, 2003a), but some children can improve their skill at pitch identification if given special training before about the age of six (Takeuchi & Hulse, 1993). About 4 percent of the population appear to be "tone deaf," which means they are not good at discriminating among musical tones, even though they can discriminate the pitches of non-musical sounds (Hyde & Peretz, 2004).

Timbre (pronounced "tamber") is the quality of sound. It is determined by complex wave patterns that are added onto the lowest, or *fundamental*, frequency of a sound. The extra waves allow you to tell, for example, the difference between a note played on a flute and the same note played on a clarinet.

The Ear

The human ear converts sound energy into neural activity through a series of accessory structures and transduction mechanisms.

Auditory Accessory Structures

Sound waves are collected in the outer ear, beginning with the *pinna*, the crumpled part of the ear visible on the side of the head. The pinna funnels sound down through the ear canal (see Figure 4.3). (A person straining to hear a faint sound might cup a hand to an ear and bend the pinna forward, which enlarges the sound-collection area. Try this yourself, and you will notice a clear difference in how sounds sound.) At the end of the ear canal, the sound waves reach the middle ear, where they strike a tightly stretched membrane known as the *eardrum*, or **tympanic membrane**. The sound waves set up matching vibrations in the tympanic membrane.

Next, the vibrations of the tympanic membrane are passed on by a chain of three tiny bones: the *malleus*, or *hammer*; the *incus*, or *anvil*; and the *stapes* (pronounced "STAY-peez"), or *stirrup* (see Figure 4.3). These bones amplify the changes in pressure produced by the original sound waves, by focusing the vibrations of the tympanic membrane onto a smaller membrane, the *oval window*.

Auditory Transduction

When sound vibrations pass through the oval window, they enter the inner ear, reaching the **cochlea** (pronounced "COCK-lee-ah"),

timbre The mixture of frequencies and amplitudes that make up the quality of sound.

tympanic membrane A membrane in the middle ear that generates vibrations that match the sound waves striking it.

cochlea A fluid-filled spiral structure in the ear in which auditory transdution occurs.

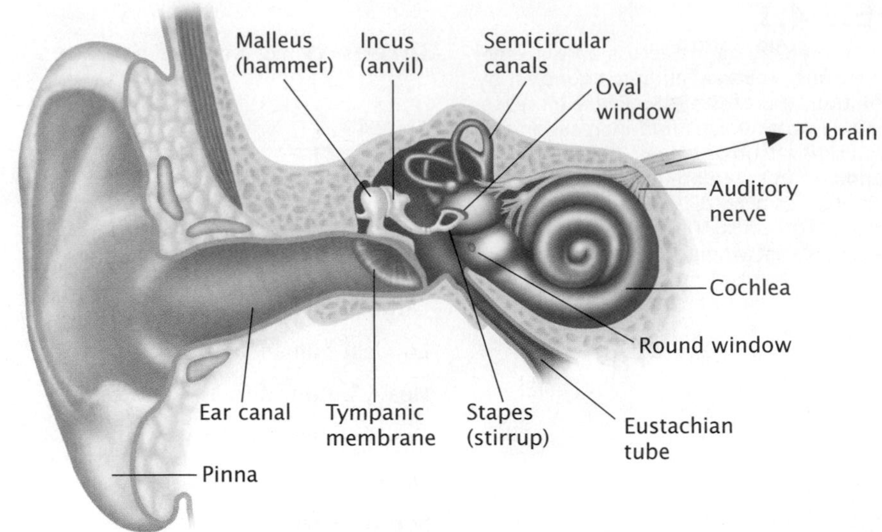

figure 4.3

Structures of the Ear

The outer ear (pinna and ear canal) channels sounds into the middle ear, where the vibrations of the tympanic membrane are amplified by the delicate bones that stimulate the cochlea. In the cochlea in the inner ear, the vibrations are transduced into changes in neural activity, which are sent along the auditory nerve to the brain.

the structure in which transduction occurs. The cochlea is wrapped into a coiled spiral. (*Cochlea* is derived from the Greek word for "snail.") If you unwrapped the spiral, you would see that a fluid-filled tube runs down its length. The **basilar membrane** forms the floor of this long tube (see Figure 4.4). Whenever a sound wave passes through the fluid in the tube, it moves the basilar membrane, and this movement bends *hair cells* of the *organ of Corti*, a group of cells that rests on the membrane. These hair cells connect with fibres from the **auditory nerve,** a bundle of axons that goes into the brain. When the hair cells bend, they stimulate neurons in the auditory nerve to fire in a pattern that sends the brain a coded message about the amplitude and frequency of the incoming sound waves. You sense this information as loudness and pitch.

Deafness *Conduction deafness* is caused when the three tiny bones of the middle ear fuse together, preventing accurate reproduction of vibrations. Conduction deafness can be treated by surgery to break the bones apart or to replace the natural bones with plastic ones (Ayache et al., 2003). Hearing aids that amplify incoming sounds can also help.

Nerve deafness results when the auditory nerve or, more commonly, the hair cells are damaged. Hair cell damage occurs gradually with age, but it can also be caused by extended exposure to the noise of jet engines, industrial equipment, gunfire, intense rock music, and the like (Goldstein, 1999; see Figure 4.5). For example, Stephen Stills, Pete Townshend, and other 1970s rock musicians have become partially deaf after

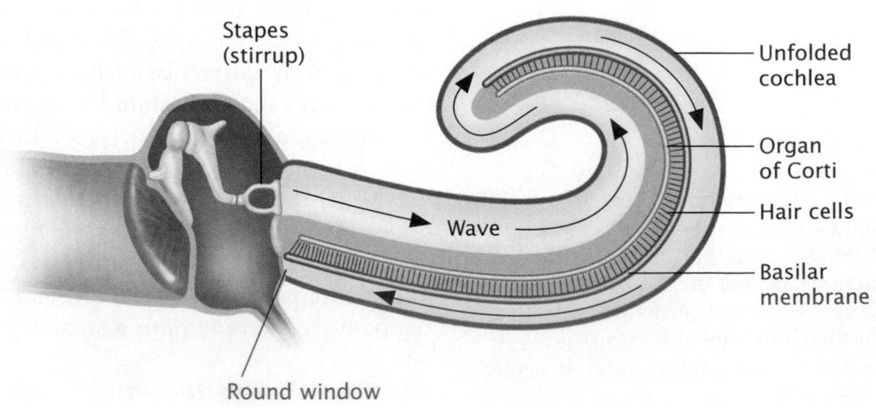

figure 4.4

The Cochlea

This drawing shows how vibrations of the stapes, or stirrup, set up vibrations in the fluid inside the cochlea. The coils of the cochlea are unfolded in this illustration to show the path of the fluid waves along the basilar membrane. Movements of the basilar membrane stimulate the hair cells of the organ of Corti, which transduce the vibrations into changes in neural firing patterns.

figure 4.5

Effects of Loud Sounds

High-intensity sounds can actually tear off the hair cells of the inner ear. Part (A) shows the organ of Corti of a normal guinea pig. Part (B) shows the damage caused by exposure to twenty-four hours of 2000 Hz sound at 120 decibels. Generally, any sound loud enough to produce tinnitus (ringing in the ears) causes some damage. In humans, small amounts of damage can accumulate over time to produce a significant hearing loss by middle age—as many middle-aged rock musicians can affirm.

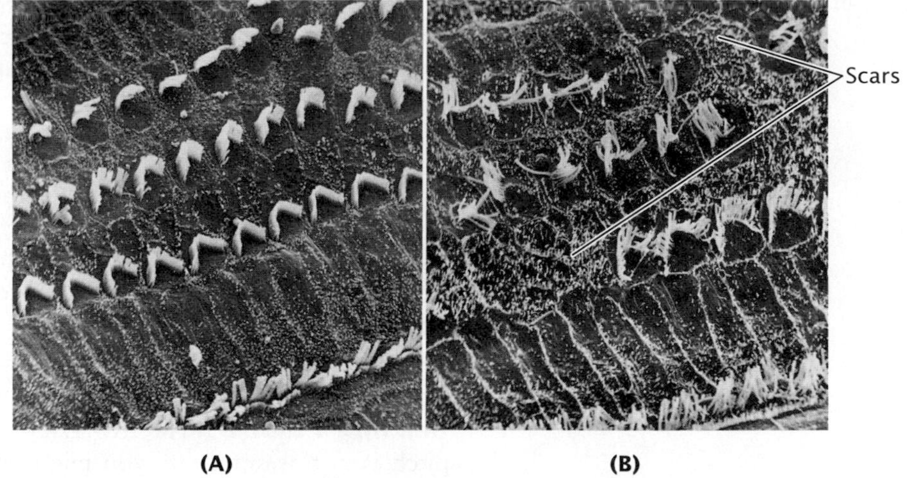

many years of performing extremely loud music (Ackerman, 1995). In the United States and other industrialized countries, people born after World War II are experiencing hearing loss at a younger age than did their forebears, possibly because noise pollution has increased during the past sixty years (Levine, 1999).

Although hair cells can regrow in chickens (who seldom listen to rock music), such regrowth was long believed impossible in mammals (Salvi et al., 1998). However, recent evidence that mammals can regenerate a related kind of inner-ear hair cell has fuelled optimism about finding a way to stimulate regeneration of human auditory hair cells (Malgrange et al., 1999). This feat might be accomplished by treating damaged areas with growth factors similar to those used to repair damaged brain cells (Shinohara et al., 2002; see the chapter on the biological aspects of psychology). Hair cell regeneration could revolutionize the treatment of nerve deafness, which cannot be overcome by conventional hearing aids. Meanwhile, scientists have developed an artificial cochlea for use as *cochlear implants* that can stimulate the auditory nerve (Francis & Niparko, 2003; Gates & Miyamoto, 2003; Rauschecker & Shannon, 2002; Tyler et al., 2003).

Auditory Pathways, Representations, and Experiences

Before sounds can be heard, the information coded in the activity of auditory nerve fibres must be sent to the brain and processed further. The auditory nerve, the bundle of axons that conveys this information, connects to structures in the brainstem, and from there to the thalamus. After preliminary processing in the thalamus, the sound information is relayed to the **primary auditory cortex** (He, 2003). As described in the chapter on the biological aspects of psychology, this area lies in the brain's temporal lobe, close to the areas involved in language perception and production (see Figure 3.17). It is in the primary auditory cortex, and in these nearby areas, that information about sound is subjected to the most intense and complex analysis (Semple & Scott, 2003).

Various aspects of sound are processed by different regions of the brain's auditory system. For example, information about the source of a sound and information about its frequency are processed in separate regions of the auditory cortex (Rauschecker, 1997). Further, cells in the cortex have similar *preferred frequencies*, meaning that they respond most vigorously to sounds of a particular frequency. The cells are arranged so as to create a frequency "map" in which cells with similar preferred frequencies are closer to each other than those with very different preferred frequencies. There are at least three such maps of sound frequencies in various areas of the brain (Kaas & Hackett, 2000). Each neuron in the auditory

basilar membrane The floor of the fluid-filled duct that runs through the cochlea.

auditory nerve The bundle of axons that carries stimuli from the hair cells of the cochlea to the brain.

primary auditory cortex The area in the brain's temporal lobe that is first to receive information about sounds from the thalamus.

nerve, too, is most responsive to a certain frequency, although each also responds to some extent to a range of frequencies. The auditory cortex must examine the pattern of activity of a number of neurons in order to determine the frequency of a sound.

Certain parts of the auditory cortex process certain types of sounds. One part, for example, specializes in responding to information coming from human voices (Belin, Zatorre, & Ahad, 2002); others are particularly responsive to musical sounds (Zatorre, 2003b). The primary auditory cortex receives information from other senses as well. It is activated, for example, when you watch someone say words (but not when the person makes other facial movements). This is the biological basis for the lip reading that helps you to hear what people say (Calvert et al., 1997).

Sensing Pitch The frequency of a sound determines its pitch, but sensing pitch is not as simple as you might expect. The reason is that most sounds are made up of mixtures of frequencies. The mixtures in musical chords and voices, for example, can produce sounds whose pitch is ambiguous, or open to interpretation. As a result, different people may experience the "same" sound as different pitches (Patel & Balaban, 2001). In fact, a sequence of chords can sound like a rising scale to one person and a falling scale to another. As mentioned earlier, pitch-recognition abilities are influenced by genetics (Drayna et al., 2001), but cultural factors are partly responsible for the way in which pitch is sensed (Cross, 2003). For instance, people in the United States tend to hear ambiguous musical scales as progressing in a direction that is opposite to the way they are heard by people from Canada and England (Dawe, Platt, & Welsh, 1998). This cross-cultural difference appears to be a reliable one, though researchers do not yet know exactly why it occurs.

Sound Localization Jack Kelly of Carleton University in Ottawa has been studying sound localization in rats and ferrets for over thirty years. He is particularly interested in the brain stuctures involved in the localization process and how these structures interact (cf. Kelly and Caspary, 2005). The ability to locate a sound

Shaping the Brain The primary auditory cortex is larger in trained musicians than in people whose jobs are less focused on fine gradations of sound. How much larger this area becomes is correlated with how long the musicians have studied their art. This finding reminds us that, as described in the chapter on biological aspects of psychology, the brain can literally be shaped by experience and other environmental factors.

Processing Language As this student and teacher communicate using American Sign Language, the visual information they receive from each other's hand movements is processed by the same areas of their brains that allow hearing people to understand spoken language (Neville et al., 1998).

is based partly on the very slight difference in the time at which a sound arrives at each of your ears (it reaches the closer ear slightly earlier). The brain also uses information about the difference in sound intensity at each ear (sounds that are closer to one ear are slightly louder in that ear). As a result, you can be reasonably sure where a voice or other sound is coming from even when you can't see its source. To perform this feat, the brain must analyze the activities of groups of neurons that, individually, signal only a rough approximation of the location (Fitzpatrick, Olsen, & Suga, 1998). It is the combined firing frequencies of these many neurons in the auditory cortex that creates a sort of "Morse code" that describes where a sound is coming from (Middlebrooks et al., 1994; Wright & Fitzgerald, 2001). Other codes tell the brain about the intensity and frequency of sounds. Let's consider those coding systems next.

Coding Intensity and Frequency

People can hear an incredibly wide range of sound intensities. The faintest sound that can be heard moves the inner ear's hair cells less than the diameter of a single hydrogen atom (Hudspeth, 1997). Sounds more than a trillion times more intense can also be heard. Between these extremes, the auditory system codes intensity in a

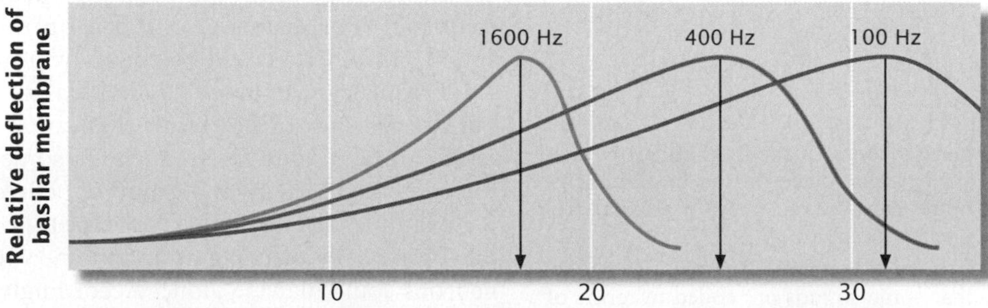

figure 4.6

Movements of the Basilar Membrane

As waves of fluid in the cochlea spread along the basilar membrane, the membrane is bent and then recovers. As shown in these three examples, the point at which the bending of the basilar membrane reaches a maximum is different for each sound frequency. According to place theory, these are the locations at which the hair cells receive the greatest stimulation.

straightforward way: The more intense the sound, the more rapid the firing of a given neuron.

The range of sound frequencies that humans can hear is not as wide as the range that dogs and some other animals can detect. People are much better than most other mammals, though, at hearing slight differences between frequencies (Shera, Guinan, & Oxenham, 2002). How do people discriminate these differences? Frequency appears to be coded in two ways that are described by place theory and frequency-matching theory.

Place Theory Georg von Bekesy's pioneering experiments in the 1930s and 1940s built on Hermann von Helmholtz's earlier research on how frequency is coded (von Bekesy, 1960; Evans, 2003). Studying human cadavers, von Bekesy created an opening in the cochlea in order to see the basilar membrane within. He then presented sounds of differing frequencies by vibrating a rubber membrane that was installed in place of the oval window. Using special optical instruments, von Bekesy observed ripples of waves moving down the basilar membrane. He noticed that the outline of the waves, called the *envelope*, grows and reaches a peak; then it quickly tapers off, much like an ocean wave that crests and then dissolves.

As shown in Figure 4.6, the critical feature of this wave is that the place on the basilar membrane where the envelope peaks depends on the frequency of the sound. High-frequency sounds produce a wave that peaks soon after it starts down the basilar membrane. Lower frequency sounds produce a wave that peaks farther along the basilar membrane, farther from the oval window.

How does the location of the peak affect the coding of frequency? Georg von Bekesy's expanation, which came to be known as **place theory,** also called *travelling wave theory*, suggested that the greatest response by hair cells occurs at the peak of the wave. Because the location of the peak varies with the frequency of the sound, it follows that hair cells at a particular place on the basilar membrane respond most to a particular frequency of sound, called a *characteristic frequency*. In other words, place theory describes a spatial, or place-related, code for frequency. When hair cells at a particular place respond to a sound, we sense a sound of those cells' characteristic frequency. One important result of this arrangement is that extended exposure to a very loud sound of a particular frequency can destroy hair cells at one spot on the basilar membrane, making it impossible to hear sounds of that frequency.

Frequency-Matching Theory Place theory accounts for a great deal of data on hearing, but it cannot explain the coding of very low frequencies, such as that of a deep bass note. We know this because, although no auditory nerve fibres respond to very low characteristic frequencies, humans can still hear frequencies as low as 20 hertz. These low frequencies must be coded in some other way. The answer is provided by **frequency-matching theory,** which is based on the fact that the firing rate of a neuron in the auditory nerve can match the frequency of a sound wave. Frequency matching provides a *temporal*, or timing-related, code for frequency. For example, one neuron might fire at every peak of a wave. So a sound of 20 hertz could be coded by a neuron that fires 20 times per second.

Frequency matching by individual neurons could apply up to about 1000 hertz, but no neuron can fire faster than 1000 times per second. A frequency-matching code can be created for frequencies somewhat above 1000 hertz, though, through the combined activity of a group of neurons. Some neurons in the group might fire, for example, at every other wave peak, others at every fifth peak, and so on, producing a *volley* of firing at a combined frequency that is higher than any of these neurons could manage alone. Accordingly, frequency-matching theory is sometimes called the *volley theory* of frequency coding.

place theory A theory that hair cells at a particular place on the basilar membrane respond most to a particular frequency of sound.

frequency-matching theory The view that some sounds are coded in terms of the frequency of neural firing.

in review Hearing

Aspect of Sensory System	Elements	Key Characteristics
Energy	Sound—pressure fluctuations of air produced by vibrations	The amplitude, frequency, and complexity of sound waves determine the loudness, pitch, and timbre of sounds
Accessory structures	Ear—pinna, tympanic membrane, malleus, incus, stapes, oval window, basilar membrane	Changes in pressure produced by the original wave are amplified
Transduction mechanism	Hair cells of the organ of Corti	Frequencies are coded by the location of the hair cells receiving the greatest stimulation (place theory) and by the firing rate of neurons (frequency-matching theory)
Pathways and representations	Auditory nerve to thalamus to primary auditory cortex	Neighbouring cells in the auditory cortex have similar preferred frequencies, thus providing a map of sound frequencies

PsychAssist: The Ear and Sound Waves

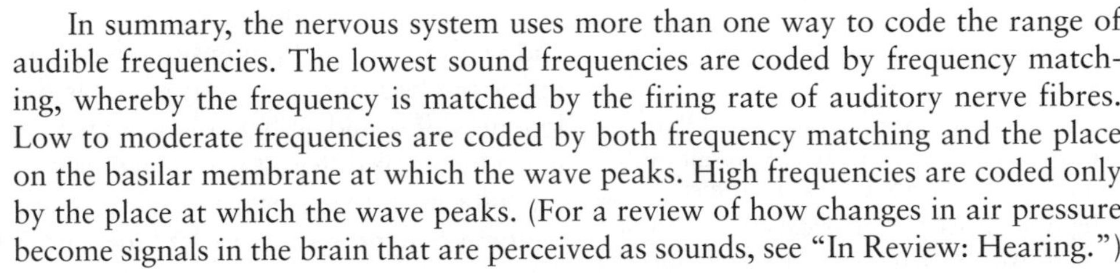

In summary, the nervous system uses more than one way to code the range of audible frequencies. The lowest sound frequencies are coded by frequency matching, whereby the frequency is matched by the firing rate of auditory nerve fibres. Low to moderate frequencies are coded by both frequency matching and the place on the basilar membrane at which the wave peaks. High frequencies are coded only by the place at which the wave peaks. (For a review of how changes in air pressure become signals in the brain that are perceived as sounds, see "In Review: Hearing.")

Vision

Soaring eagles have the incredible ability to see a mouse move in the grass from a mile away. Cats have special "reflectors" at the back of their eyes that help them to see even in very dim light. Through natural selection, over eons of time, each species has developed a visual system uniquely adapted to its way of life. The human visual system is also adapted to do many things well: It combines great sensitivity and great sharpness, enabling us to see objects near and far, during the day and at night. Our night vision is not as acute as that of some animals, but our colour vision is excellent. This is not a bad tradeoff; being able to appreciate a sunset's splendour seems worth an occasional stumble in the dark. In this section, we consider the human visual sense and how it responds to light.

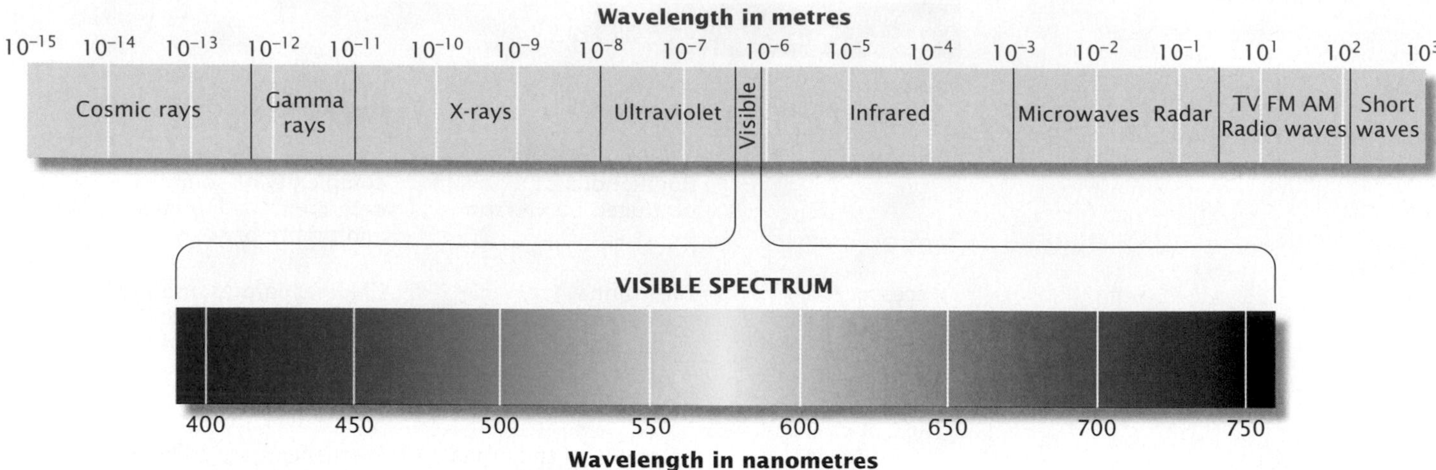

figure 4.7

The Spectrum of Electromagnetic Energy

The range of wavelengths that the human eye can see as visible light is limited to a band of only about 370 nanometres within the much wider spectrum of electromagnetic energy. To detect energy outside this range, we must rely on electronic instruments such as radios, TV sets, radar, and infrared night-vision scopes that can "see" this energy, just as the eye sees visible light.

Light

Light is a form of energy known as *electromagnetic radiation.* Most electromagnetic radiation—including x-rays, radio waves, television signals, and radar—passes through space undetected by the human eye. **Visible light** is electromagnetic radiation that has a wavelength from just under 400 nanometres to about 750 nanometres (a *nanometre* is one-billionth of a metre; see Figure 4.7). Unlike sound, light does not need a medium to pass through. So, even on the airless moon, astronauts can see one another, even if they can't hear one another without radios. Light waves are like particles that pass through space, but they vibrate with a certain wavelength. In other words, light has some properties of waves and some properties of particles, and it is correct to refer to light as either *light waves* or *light rays.*

Sensations of light depend on two physical dimensions of light waves: intensity and wavelength. **Light intensity** refers to how much energy the light contains; it determines the brightness of light, much as the amplitude of sound waves determines the loudness of sound. What colour you sense depends mainly on **light wavelength.** At a given intensity, different wavelengths produce sensations of different colours, much as different sound frequencies produce sensations of different pitch. For instance, 440-nanometre light appears violet blue, and 700-nanometre light appears orangish red.

Focusing Light

Just as sound energy is converted to nerve cell activity in the ear, light energy is transduced into neural activity in the eye. The first step in this process occurs as accessory structures in the human eye modify incoming light rays. The light rays enter the eye by passing through the curved, transparent, protective layer called the **cornea** (see Figure 4.8). Then the light passes through the **pupil,** the opening just behind the cornea. The **iris,** which gives the eye its colour, adjusts the amount of light allowed into the eye by constricting to reduce the size of the pupil or relaxing to enlarge it. Directly behind the pupil is the **lens.** The cornea and the lens of the human eye are both curved so that, like the lens of a camera, they bend light rays. The light rays are focused into an image on the surface at the back of the eye; this surface is called the **retina.** Light rays from the top of an object are focused at the bottom of the image on the retinal surface. Light rays from the right side of the object end up on the left side of the retinal image (see Figure 4.9). The brain rearranges this upside-down and reversed image so that we can see the object as it is.

visible light Electromagnetic radiation that has a wavelength of about 400 nanometres to about 750 nanometres.

light intensity A physical dimension of light waves that refers to how much energy the light contains; it determines the brightness of light.

light wavelength The distance between peaks in light waves.

cornea The curved, transparent, protective layer through which light rays enter the eye.

pupil An opening in the eye, just behind the cornea, through which light passes.

iris The colourful part of the eye that constricts or relaxes to adjust the amount of light entering the eye.

lens The part of the eye behind the pupil that bends light rays, focusing them on the retina.

retina The surface at the back of the eye onto which the lens focuses light rays.

figure 4.8

Major Structures of the Eye

As shown in this top view of the eye, light rays bent by the combined actions of the cornea and the lens are focused on the retina, where the light energy is transduced into neural activity. Nerve fibres known collectively as the *optic nerve* pass out of the back of the eye and continue to the brain.

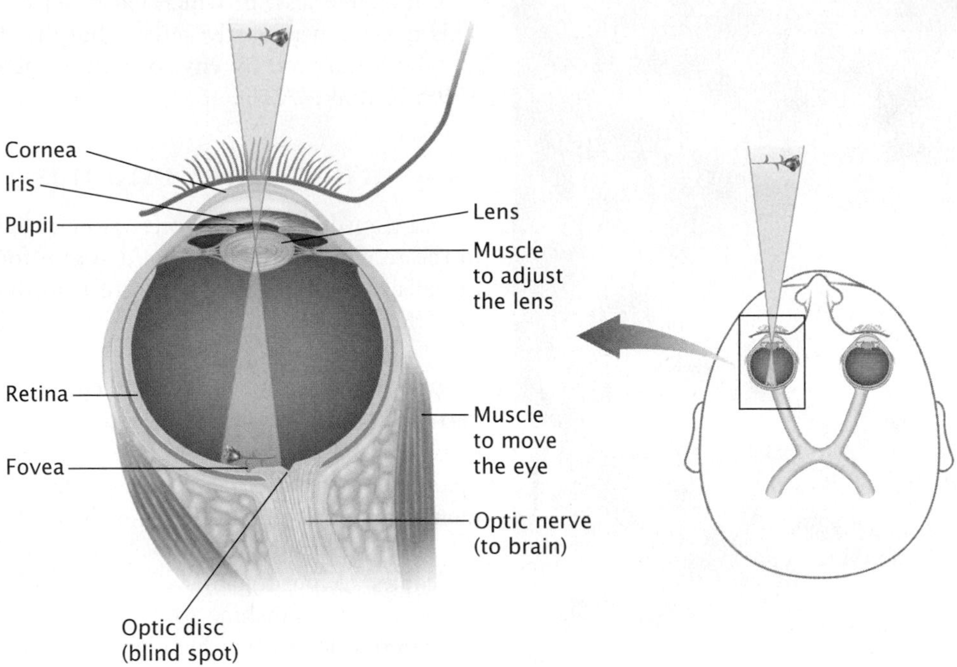

The lens of the human eye bends light rays entering the eye from various angles so that they meet on the retina (see Figure 4.9). If the rays meet either in front of the retina or behind it, the image will be out of focus. The muscles that hold the lens adjust its shape so that images of either near or far objects can be focused on the retina. If you peer at something that is very close, for example, your muscles must tighten the lens, making it more curved, to obtain a focused image. This ability to change the shape of the lens to bend light rays is called **accommodation.** Over time, the lens loses some of its flexibility, making accommodation more difficult. This is why most older people become "farsighted," seeing distant objects clearly but needing glasses for reading or close work. A more common problem in younger people

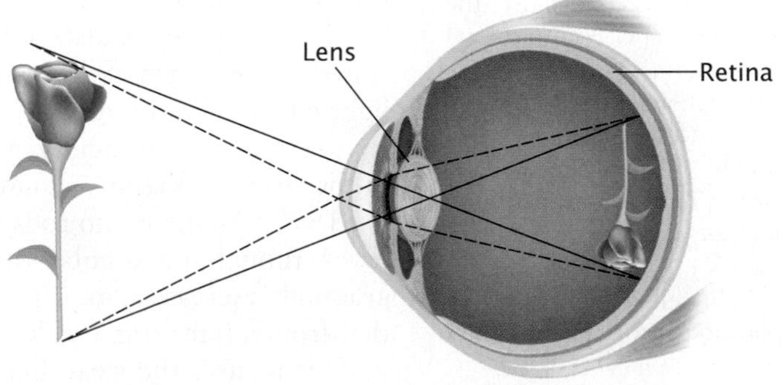

figure 4.9

The Lens and the Retinal Image

To see objects as they are, your brain must re-arrange the upside-down and reversed images that the lens focuses on the retina. If light rays are out of focus when they reach the retina, glasses can usually correct the problem. In some older people, vision is impaired by cataracts, a condition in which a "cloudy" lens severely reduces incoming light. Cataracts can be cleared up by laser surgery or by replacing the natural lens with an artificial one (Snellingen et al., 2002).

accommodation The ability of the lens to change its shape and bend light rays so that objects are in focus.

Reading and Nearsightedness Visual experience can modify the eye. When chicks are raised with diffusing goggles that allow only unpatterned light through, their eyeballs become elongated, and they become nearsighted (Wallman et al.,1987). Humans may be vulnerable to the same elongation because reading presents areas around the fovea with a constant, relatively unpatterned image.

is nearsightedness, in which close objects are in focus but distant ones are blurry. This condition is partly genetic but, as shown in the accompanying photo, it can also be influenced by environmental factors such as reading habits (Quinn et al., 1999; Zadnik, 2001).

Converting Light into Images

Visual transduction, the conversion of light energy into neural activity, takes place in the retina. The word *retina* is Latin for "net"; the retina is an intricate network of cells (Masland, 2001). Before transduction can occur, light rays must actually pass through several layers in this network to reach photoreceptor cells.

Photoreceptors **Photoreceptors** are specialized cells in the retina that convert light energy into neural activity. They contain **photopigments,** chemicals that respond to light. When light strikes a photopigment, the photopigment breaks apart, changing the membrane potential of the photoreceptor cell. This change in membrane potential generates a signal that can be transferred to the brain.

After a photopigment has broken down in response to light, new photopigment molecules are put together. This takes a little time, however. So when you first come in from bright sunshine to, say, a dark theatre, you cannot see because your photoreceptors do not yet have enough photopigment. In the dark, as your photoreceptors build up more photopigments, your ability to see gradually increases. In fact, you become about 10,000 times more sensitive to light after about half an hour in a darkened room. This increasing ability to see in the dark as time passes is called **dark adaptation.**

The retina has two main types of photoreceptors: **rods** and **cones.** As their names suggest, these cells differ in shape. They also differ in their makeup and their response to light. The photopigment in rods includes a substance called *rhodopsin* (pronounced "row-DOP-sin"), whereas the photopigment in cones includes one of three varieties of *iodopsin.* These three forms of iodopsin provide the basis for colour vision, as we explain later. Because rods have only one pigment, they are unable to discriminate colours. However, the rods are more sensitive to light than cones. So rods allow you to see even when there is very little light, as on a moonlit night. In dim light, you are seeing with your rods, which cannot discriminate-colours. Your colour-sensitive cones become most active only at higher light intensities. As a result, you may put on what you thought was a matched pair of socks in a darkened bedroom, only to go outside and discover that one is dark blue and the other is dark green.

Rods and cones also differ in their distribution in the eye. Cones are concentrated in the centre of the retina, a region called the **fovea,** where the eye focuses the light coming from objects you look at. This concentration of cones makes the ability to see details, or **acuity,** greatest in the fovea. Variations in the density of cones in the fovea probably account for individual differences in visual acuity (Curcio et al., 1987). There are no rods in the human fovea. With increasing distance from the fovea, though, the number of cones gradually decreases, and the proportion of rods gradually increases. So, if you are trying to detect a small amount of light, such as that from a faint star, it is better to look slightly away from where you expect to see it. This focuses the weak light on the rods outside the fovea, which are very sensitive to light. Because cones do not work well in low light, looking directly at the star will make it seem to disappear.

Interactions in the Retina If the eye simply transferred to the brain the stimuli that are focused on the retina, we would experience images that are somewhat like a blurred TV picture. Instead, interactions among the cells of the retina allow the eye to actually sharpen visual images. As illustrated in Figure 4.10, the

photoreceptors Nerve cells in the retina that code light energy into neural activity.

photopigments Chemicals in photoreceptors that respond to light and assist in converting light into neural activity.

dark adaptation The increasing ability to see in the dark as time in the dark increases.

rods Highly light-sensitive, but colour-insensitive, photoreceptors in the retina that allow vision even in dim light.

cones Photoreceptors in the retina that help us to distinguish colours.

fovea A region in the centre of the retina where cones are highly concentrated.

acuity Visual clarity, which is greatest in the fovea because of its large concentration of cones.

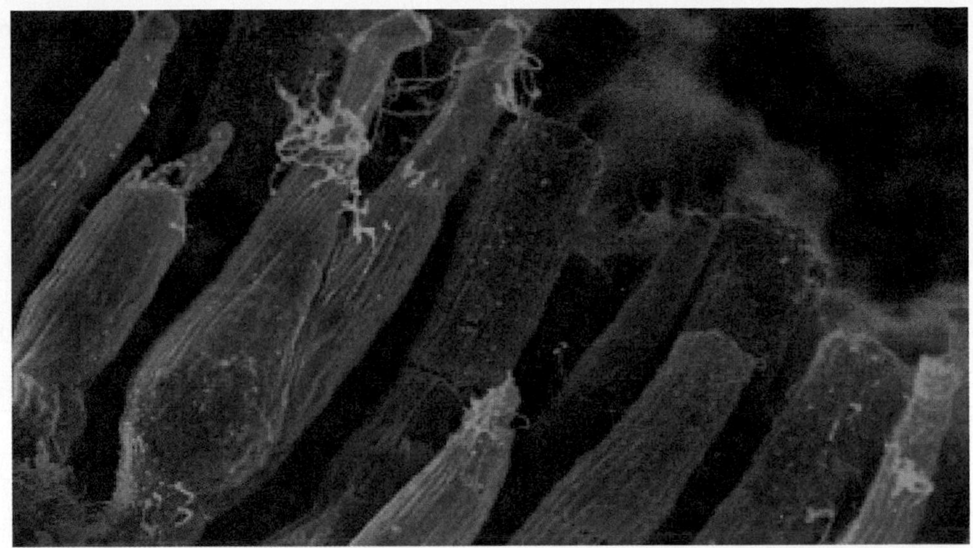

Rods and Cones This electron microscope view of rods (blue) and cones (aqua) shows what your light receptors look like. Rods are more light sensitive, but they do not detect colour. Cones can detect colour, but they require more light in order to be activated. To experience the difference in how these cells work, look at an unfamiliar colour photograph in a room where there is barely enough light to see. Even this dim light will activate your rods and allow you to make out images in the picture. But because there is not enough light to activate your cones, you will not be able to see colours in the photo.

most direct connections from the photoreceptor cells to the brain go first to *bipolar cells* and then to *ganglion cells*. The axons of the ganglion cells extend out of the eye and into the brain.

However, this direct pathway is modified by interactions with other cells that change the information reaching the brain. These interactions enhance the sensation of contrast between areas of light and dark. Here's how it works: Most of the time, the amount of light reaching any two photoreceptors will differ slightly, because the edges and other specific features of objects create differing patterns of incoming light. When this happens, the receptor that is receiving more light inhibits, or reduces, the activity of the nearby photoreceptor that is receiving less light. As a result, the brain gets the impression that there is even less light at that nearby cell's location than there really is. How can one photoreceptor suppress the output of its neighbour? The process is called **lateral inhibition,** and it is made possible by interneurons, which are cells that make sideways, or lateral, connections between photoreceptors (see Figure 4.10). In other words, the brain is always receiving comparisons of the light that is hitting neighbouring photoreceptors. Because of lateral inhibition, any difference in the amount of light reaching these photoreceptors will be exaggerated. This exaggeration helps us to see more clearly. The image of the buttons on your cell phone, for example, consists of lighter areas next to darker ones. Lateral inhibition in the retina amplifies these differences, creating greater contrast that sharpens the edges of the buttons and makes them more noticeable.

Ganglion Cells and Their Receptive Fields

Photoreceptors (rods and cones) and bipolar cells communicate by releasing neurotransmitters. But, as discussed in the chapter on the biological aspects of psychology, neurotransmitters cause only small, graded changes in the membrane potential of the next cell, which cannot travel the distance from the eye to the brain. It is the **ganglion cells** in the retina that generate action potentials that are capable of travelling that distance along axons that extend out of the retina and into the brain.

As illustrated in Figure 4.10, ganglion cells each receive information from a certain group of photoreceptors. Accordingly, each ganglion cell can tell the brain about what is going on only in its own particular **receptive field,** which is the part of the retina and the corresponding part of the visual world to which the cell responds (Sekuler & Blake, 1994). So, depending on their location in the retina, some ganglion cells respond to light in, say, the upper right-hand side of the visual field, whereas others respond to light in the lower left-hand side, and so on. The

lateral inhibition A process in which lateral connections allow one photoreceptor to inhibit the responsiveness of its neighbour, thus enhancing the sensation of visual contrast.

ganglion cells Cells in the retina that generate action potentials.

receptive field The portion of the retina, and the visual world, that affects a given ganglion cell.

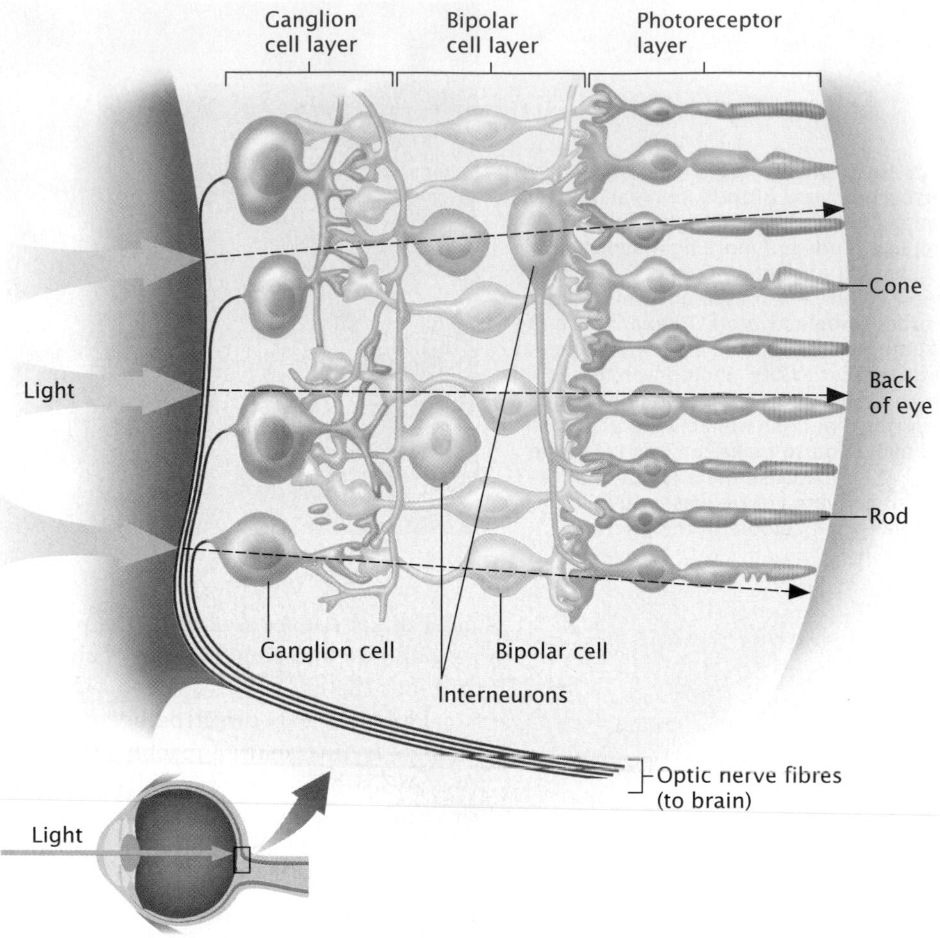

figure 4.10

Cells in the Retina

Light rays actually pass through several layers of cells before striking photoreceptors, which are called rods and cones. Signals generated by the rods and cones then go back toward the surface of the retina, passing through bipolar cells and ganglion cells and on to the brain. Interconnections among interneurons, bipolar cells, and ganglion cells allow the eye to begin analyzing visual information and sharpening images even before the information leaves the retina.

receptive fields of most ganglion cells are shaped a bit like a doughnut, with a centre and a surround. These *centre-surround receptive fields* allow ganglion cells to compare the amount of light stimulating photoreceptors in the centre of their receptive fields with the amount of light stimulating photoreceptors in the area around the centre. Some ganglion cells are called *centre-on cells* because they are activated by light in the centre of their receptive fields and inhibited by light in the regions around the centre (see Figure 4.11). *Centre-off* ganglion cells work in just the opposite way. They are inhibited by light in the centre of their receptive fields and activated by light in the surrounding areas.

The centre-surround receptive fields of ganglion cells make it easier for you to see edges and, as illustrated in Figure 4.12, also create a sharper contrast between darker and lighter areas than actually exists. By enhancing the sensation of important features, the retina gives your brain an "improved" version of the visual world. As described next, the brain performs even more elaborate processing of visual information than does the retina.

optic nerve A bundle of fibres composed of axons of ganglion cells that carries visual information to the brain.

blind spot The light-insensitive point at which axons from all of the ganglion cells converge and exit the eyeball.

optic chiasm Part of the bottom surface of the brain where half of each optic nerve's fibres cross over to the opposite side of the brain.

Visual Pathways

We have seen that visual information reaches the brain through the axons of ganglion cells that leave the eye as a bundle of fibres called the **optic nerve** (see Figure 4.10). There are no photoreceptors at the point where the optic nerve exits the eyeball, so you have a **blind spot** at that point, as Figure 4.13 shows.

After leaving the retina, about half the fibres of the optic nerve cross over to the opposite side of the brain at a structure called the **optic chiasm.** (*Chiasm* means "cross" and is pronounced "KYE-az-um.") Fibres from the inside half of

figure 4.11

Centre-Surround Receptive Fields of Ganglion Cells

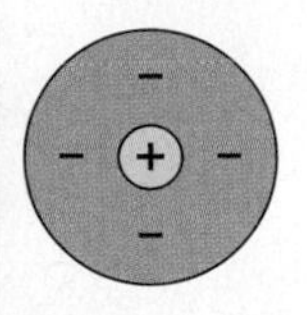

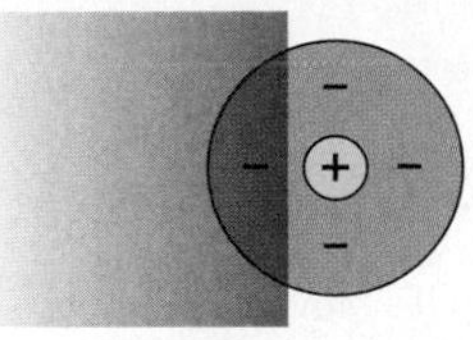

Baseline activity (light on centre and surround)

Higher activity (light on centre; dark on surround)

Low activity (dark on both centre and surround)

Having centre-surround receptive fields allows ganglion cells to act as edge detectors. As shown at the left, if an edge is outside the receptive field of a centre-on ganglion cell, there will be a uniform amount of light on both the excitatory centre and the inhibitory surround, creating some baseline level of activity. If, as shown in the middle drawing, the dark side of an edge covers part of the inhibitory surround but leaves light on the excitatory centre, the output of the cell will increase, signaling an edge in its receptive field. If, as shown at right, a dark area covers both the centre and the surround, the cell's activity will decrease, because neither segment of its receptive field is receiving much stimulation.

each eye, nearest to the nose, cross over; fibres from the outside half of each eye do not (see Figure 4.14). As a result of this arrangement, information from the right half of your visual field goes to the left hemisphere of your brain and information from the left half of your visual field goes to the right hemisphere (Roth, Lora, & Heilman, 2002).

The optic chiasm lies on the bottom surface of the brain. Beyond the chiasm, optic nerve fibres ascend into the brain itself. As shown in Figure 4.14, the axons from most of the retina's ganglion cells send their messages to a region of the thalamus called the **lateral geniculate nucleus (LGN).** Neurons in the LGN then send the visual input to the **primary visual cortex,** which lies in the occipital lobe at the back of the brain. Visual information is also sent from the primary visual cortex for processing in many other areas of cortex. Studies of monkeys have identified thirty-two separate visual areas interconnected by more than three hundred pathways (Van Essen, Anderson, & Felleman, 1992).

figure 4.12

The Hermann Grid

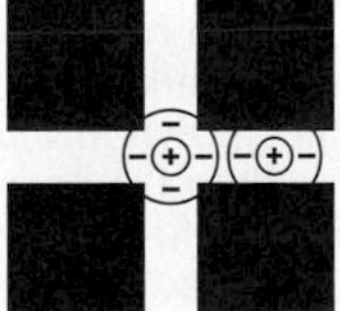

Shadows appear at the intersections of this *Hermann grid,* until you look directly at them. To understand why, look at the smaller grid at right. The circles on that grid represent the receptive fields of two centre-on ganglion cells in your retina. The cell whose receptive field includes the space at the intersection has more whiteness shining on its inhibitory surround than the cell whose receptive field is just to the right of the intersection. So the output of the "intersection" cell will be lower than that of the one on the right, creating the impression of darkness at the intersection. Looking directly at an intersection projects its image onto your fovea, the area of the retina where ganglion cells have the smallest receptive fields. Now the whiteness of the intersection is stimulating the excitatory centres of several ganglion cells, creating a greater sensation of whiteness and making the shadow disappear.

lateral geniculate nucleus (LGN) A region of the thalamus in which axons from most of the ganglion cells in the retina end and form synapses.

primary visual cortex An area at the back of the brain to which neurons in the lateral geniculate nucleus relay visual input.

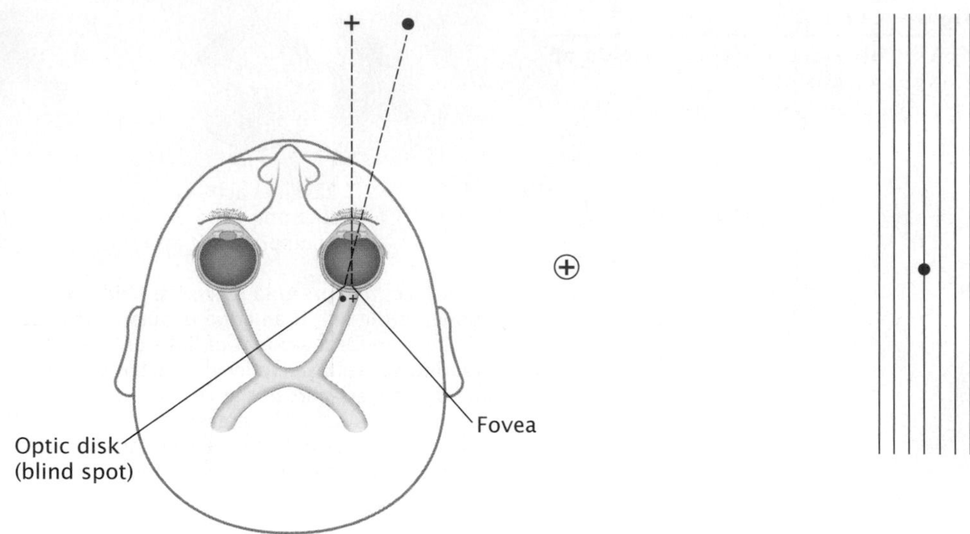

figure 4.13

Finding Your Blind Spot
There is a blind spot where axons from the ganglion cells leave the eye. To "see" your blind spot, cover your left eye and stare at the cross inside the circle. Move the page closer and then farther away, and at some point the dot to the right should disappear. However, the vertical lines around the dot will probably look continuous, because the brain tends to fill in visual information at the blind spot. We are normally unaware of this "hole" in our vision because the blind spot of one eye is in the normal visual field of the other eye.

The retina is organized to create a map of the visual world, such that neighbouring points on the retina receive information from neighbouring points in the visual world. A "copy" of this map is maintained in the LGN, in the primary visual cortex, and in each of the many other visual areas of the brain. Through this spatial coding system, neighbouring points in the retina are represented in neighbouring cells in the brain. Larger areas of cortex are devoted to the areas of the retina that have larger numbers of photoreceptors. For example, the fovea, which is densely packed with photoreceptors, is represented in an especially large segment of cortex.

Visual Representations

So the apparently effortless experience of sight is based on a very complex system, in which visual information is transmitted from the retina through the thalamus and on to various cortical regions. We can appreciate the complexities of this system by considering just two of its more remarkable characteristics: *parallel processing of visual properties* and *hierarchical processing of visual information.*

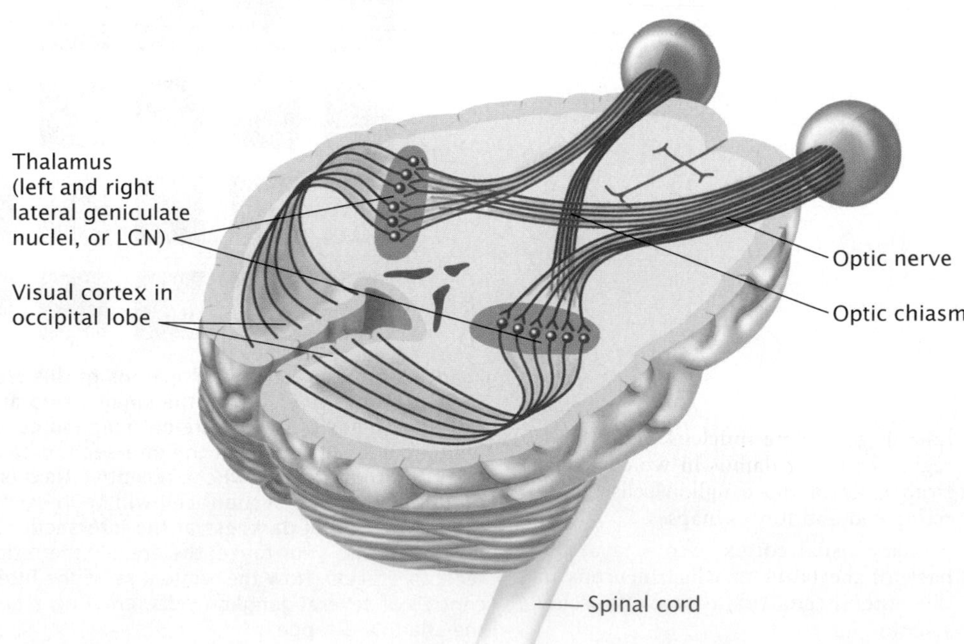

figure 4.14

Pathways from the Ganglion Cells into the Brain
Light rays from the right side of the visual field (the right side of what you are looking at) end up on the left half of each retina (shown in red). Light rays from the left visual field end up on the right half of each retina (shown in blue). From the right eye, axons from the nasal side of the retina (the side nearer the nose, which receives information from the right visual field) cross over the midline and travel to the left side of the brain with those fibres from the left eye that also receive input from the right side of the visual world. A similar arrangement unites left visual-field information from both eyes in the right side of the brain.

David H. Hubel Dr. David Hubel was born in Windsor Ontario and was educated at McGill College and McGill Medical School. While still at medical school, he spent his summers at the Montreal Neurological Institute where he became fascinated by the nervous system. In 1958 Hubel and his colleague, Torsten Wiesel, successfully recorded the firing of a single cell in a cat's visual cortex. After nine hours of trying to stimulate the cell to fire by presenting it with numerous and varied stimuli, they were finally successful when they happened to move the edge of an object in a particular orientation across a specific area of the retina. They continued using this procedure to map the striated cortex proving it was sensitive to stimulus orientation (Hubel, 1988; The Nobel Prize, 1981).

Parallel Processing of Visual Properties Like ganglion cells, neurons of the LGN in the thalamus have centre-surround receptive fields. However, the LGN is organized in several layers, and each layer contains a complete map of the retina. Further, neurons in different layers respond to particular aspects of visual stimuli. For example, the *form* of an object and its *colour* are handled by one set of neurons (called the "what" system), whereas the *movement* of an object and *cues to its distance* are handled by another set (called the "where" system; Creem & Proffitt, 2001). These are called *parallel processing systems* because they allow the brain to conduct separate kinds of analysis on the same information at the same time (Livingstone & Hubel, 1987).

These parallel streams of visual information are sent to the cerebral cortex, but the question of how they are assembled into a unified conscious experience is still being debated (Shafritz, Gore, & Marois, 2002; Derrington & Webb, 2004). Some researchers argue that the separate streams of processing never actually converge in a single brain region (Engel et al., 1992). Instead, they say, cortical regions that process separate aspects of visual sensation are connected, allowing them to integrate their activity and create a distributed, but unified, experience of vision (Gilbert, 1992).

Melvyn Goodale of the University of Western Ontario, suggests that visual information may run along two separate but integrated pathways. The first, called the *ventral pathway* is the one that typically involves our ability to identify objects and attach meaning to them. The second, called the *dorsal pathway* appears to be involved in establishing the exact location of the object from "moment-to-moment" and its location relative to us. This pathway helps to monitor our interaction with the object that is essential, for example, in hand-eye motor-coordination (Goodale, and Milner, 2004).

Positron emission tomography (PET) scans have provided evidence for the existence of separate processing channels. They have shown, for example, that one area of visual cortex is activated when a person views a colourful painting; a different area is activated by viewing black-and-white moving images (Zeki, 1992). Cases of brain damage have also helped to reveal these separate channels (Heilman & Valenstein, 2003). Damage in one area can leave a person unable to see colours or even remember them but still able to see and recognize objects. Damage in another area can leave a person able to see only stationary objects; as soon as an object moves, it disappears. People with brain damage in still other regions can see only moving objects, not stationary ones (Zeki, 1992). The same kinds of separate processing channels apparently operate even when we just imagine visual information. Some patients with brain damage can recall parts of a visual image, but not their correct spatial relationship. For example, they may be able to "see" a mental image of a bull's horns and ears but be unable to assemble them mentally to form a bull's head (Kosslyn, 1988).

Hierarchical Processing of Visual Information Figure 4.15 shows that individual cells in the visual cortex receive input from several LGN neurons in the thalamus. The receptive fields of these cortical cells are more complex than the centre-surround receptive fields of LGN cells. For example, a cell in the cortex might respond only to vertical edges that appear in its receptive field. One class of cells responds only to moving objects; a third class responds only to objects with corners, and so on. Because cortical cells respond to specific features of objects in the visual field, they have been described as **feature detectors** (Hubel & Wiesel, 1979).

Complex feature detectors can be built up out of more and more complex connections among simpler feature detectors (Hubel & Wiesel, 1979). For example, several centre-surround cells might feed into one cortical cell to make a line detector, and several line detectors might feed into another cortical cell to make a cell that responds to a particular orientation in space, such as vertical. With further connections, a more complex "box detector" might be built from simpler line and corner detectors. Feature detectors illustrate that some of the cortical processing of visual information occurs in a *hierarchical*, or stepwise, fashion.

feature detectors Cells in the cortex that respond to a specific feature of an object.

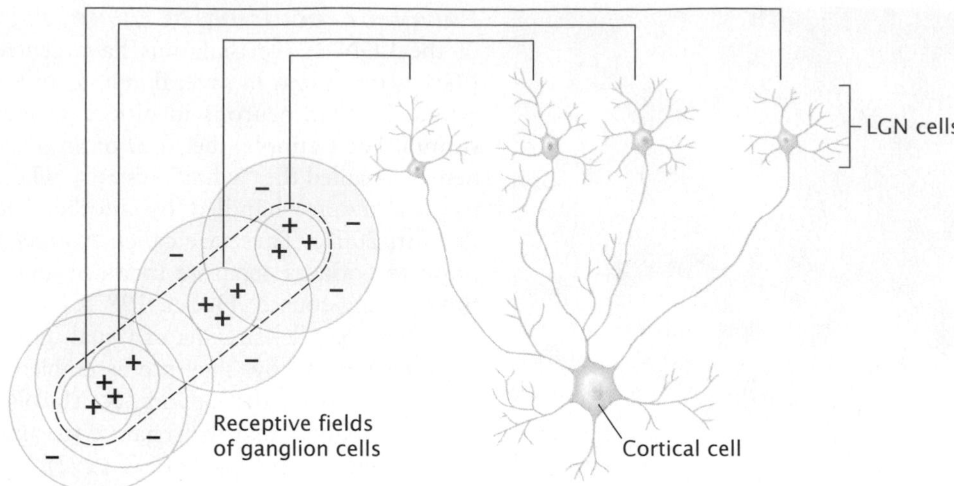

figure 4.15

Construction of a Feature Detector

This figure shows several centre-on ganglion cells connecting to several cells in the lateral geniculate nucleus (LGN) that connect to one cell in the visual cortex. This "wiring" means that the cortical cell will respond most vigorously when it receives stimulation from all the LGN cells that feed into it. That combined LGN cell stimulation will occur when light falls on the centre of the receptive fields of their ganglion cells. In this case, those receptive fields lie in an angled row, so it will take a bar-shaped feature at that same angle to stimulate all their centres. This cortical cell is called a feature detector because it responds best when a bar-shaped feature appears at a particular angle in its receptive field. If the bar were rotated to a different angle, this particular cortical cell would stop responding.

Cells that respond to similar kinds of stimulation are organized into columns in the cortex. These columns are arranged at right angles to the surface of the cortex. So if you locate a cell that responds to diagonal lines at a particular spot in the visual field, most of the cells above and below that cell will also respond to diagonal lines. Other properties, too, are represented by whole columns of cells. For example, there are columns in which all of the cells are most sensitive to a particular colour. Research has also revealed that individual neurons in the cortex perform several different tasks, allowing complex visual processing (Schiller, 1996). ("In Review: Seeing" summarizes how the nervous system gathers the information that allows people to see.)

Seeing Colour

Like beauty, colour is in the eye of the beholder. Many animals see only shades of grey, even when they look at a rainbow, but for humans colour is a major feature of vision. A marketer might tell you about the impact of colour on buying preferences, a poet might tell you about the emotional power of colour, but we will tell you about how you see colours—a process that is itself a thing of beauty and elegance.

Wavelengths and Colour Sensations We mentioned earlier that at a given intensity, each wavelength of light is sensed as a certain colour (look again at Figure 4.7). However, the eye is seldom, if ever, exposed to pure light of a single wavelength. Sunlight, for example, is a mixture of all wavelengths of light. When sunlight passes through a droplet of water, each wavelength of light within it bends to a different extent, separating into a colourful rainbow. The spectrum of colour found in the rainbow illustrates an important concept: The sensation produced by a mixture of different wavelengths of light is not the same as the sensations produced by separate wavelengths. So just as most sounds are a mixture of sound waves of different frequencies, most colours are a mixture of light of different wavelengths.

Three characteristics of this wavelength mixture determine the colour sensation: hue, saturation, and brightness. These are *psychological* dimensions that correspond roughly to the physical properties of light. **Hue** is the essential "colour," determined by the dominant wavelength in the mixture of the light striking the eye. For example, the wavelength of yellow is about 570 nanometres and that of red is about 700 nanometres. Black, white, and grey are not considered hues, because no wave length predominates in them. **Saturation** is related to the purity of a colour. A colour is more saturated and more pure if just one wavelength is relatively more intense—contains more energy—than other wavelengths. If many wavelengths are added to a pure hue, the colour is said to be *desaturated*. For example, pastels are colours that

hue The essential "colour," determined by the dominant wavelength of light.

saturation The purity of a colour.

brightness The sensation of the overall intensity of all of the wavelengths that make up light.

in review Seeing

Aspect of Sensory System	Elements	Key Characteristics
Energy	Light—electromagnetic radiation from about 400 nm to about 750 nm	The intensity and wavelength of light waves determine the brightness and colour of visual sensations
Accessory structures	Eye—cornea, pupil, iris, lens	Light rays are bent to focus on the retina
Transduction mechanism	Photoreceptors (rods and cones) in the retina	Rods are more sensitive to light than cones, but cones discriminate among colours. Sensations of colour depend first on the cones, which respond differently to different light wavelengths. Interactions among cells of the retina exaggerate differences in the light stimuli reaching the photoreceptors, enhancing the sensation of contrast.
Pathways and representations	Optic nerve to optic chiasm to LGN of thalamus to primary visual cortex	Neighbouring points in the visual world are represented at neighbouring points in the LGN and primary visual cortex. Neurons there respond to particular aspects of the visual stimulus—such as colour, movement, distance, or form.

PsychAssist: Opponent Processes; Synaesthesia

have been desaturated by the addition of whiteness. **Brightness** refers to the overall intensity of all of the wavelengths in the incoming light.

The colour circle shown in Figure 4.16 arranges hues according to their perceived similarities. If lights of two different wavelengths but of equal intensity are mixed, the colour you sense is at the midpoint of a line drawn between the two original colours on the colour circle. This process is known as *additive colour mixing*, because the effects of the wavelengths from each light are added together. If you

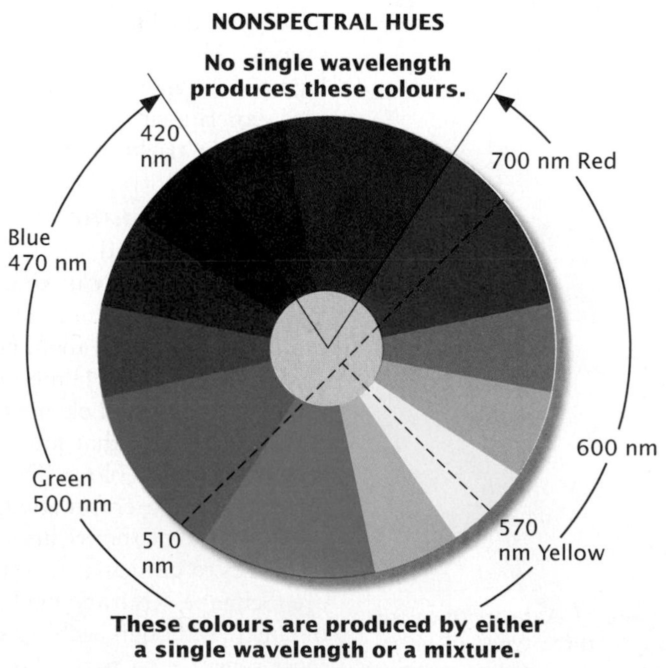

figure 4.16

The Colour Circle

Arranging colours according to their psychological similarities creates a colour circle that predicts the result of additive mixing of two coloured lights. The resulting colour will be on a line between the two starting colours, the exact location on the line depending on the relative proportions of the two colours. For example, mixing equal amounts of pure green and pure red light will produce yellow, the colour that lies at the midpoint of the line connecting red and green. (*Nm* stands for *nanometres*, the unit in which wavelengths are measured.)

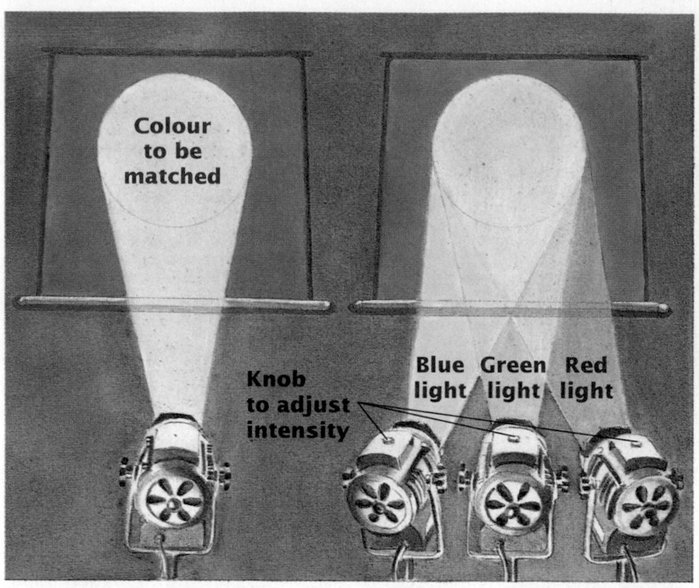

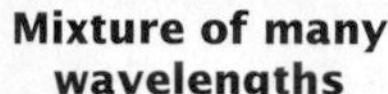

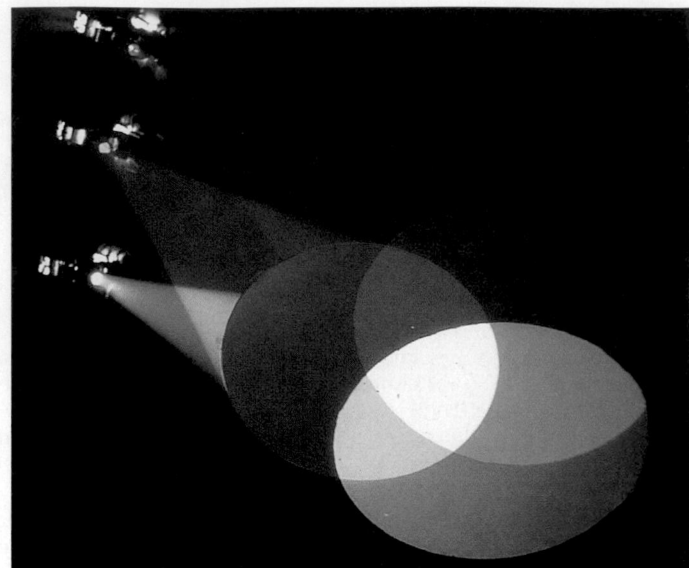

figure 4.17

Matching a Colour by Mixing Lights of Pure Wavelengths

In this experiment, coloured light is aimed at white paper, which reflects all wavelengths and therefore appears to be the colour of the light shining on it. A target colour is projected on the left-hand paper. The research participant's task is to adjust the intensity of different pure-wavelength lights until the resulting mixture looks exactly like the target colour. It turns out that a large number of colours can be matched by mixing two, pure-wavelength lights, but *any* colour can be matched by mixing three pure-wavelength lights. Experiments such as this provided information that led to the trichromatic theory of colour vision.

keep adding different coloured lights, you eventually get white (the combination of all wavelengths).

You are probably more familiar with a different form of colour mixing, called *subtractive colour mixing*, which occurs when paints are combined. Like other physical objects, paints reflect certain wavelengths and absorb all others. For example, grass is green because it absorbs all wavelengths except wavelengths that are sensed as green. White objects are white because they reflect all wavelengths. Light reflected from paints or other coloured objects is seldom a pure wavelength, so predicting the colour resulting from mixing paint is not as easy as combining pure wavelengths of light. But if you keep combining different coloured paints, all of the wavelengths will eventually be subtracted, resulting in black. (The discussion that follows refers to *additive colour mixing*, the mixing of light.)

By mixing lights of just a few wavelengths, we can produce different colour sensations. How many wavelengths are needed to create any possible colour? Figure 4.17 illustrates an experiment that addresses this question. The results of such experiments helped lead scientists to an important theory of how people sense colour—the trichromatic theory of colour vision.

The Trichromatic Theory of Colour Vision Early in the 1800s, Thomas Young and, later, Hermann von Helmholtz demonstrated that they could match any colour by mixing pure lights of only three wavelengths. For example, by mixing blue light (about 440 nanometres), green light (about 510 nanometres), and red light (about 700 nanometres) in different ratios, they could produce any other colour. Young and Helmholtz interpreted this evidence to mean that there must be three types of visual elements in the eye, each of which is most sensitive to different wavelengths, and that information from these three elements combines to produce the sensation of colour. This theory of colour vision is called the *Young-Helmholtz theory*, or the **trichromatic theory.**

Support for the trichromatic theory has come from research on photoreceptors' responses to particular wavelengths of light and on the activity of cones in the human eye (Schnapf, Kraft, & Baylor, 1987). This research reveals that there are three types of cones. Although each type responds to a broad range of wavelengths, each type is most sensitive to particular wavelengths. *Short-wavelength* cones respond most to light in the blue range. *Medium-wavelength* cones are most sensitive to light in the

trichromatic theory A theory of colour vision identifying three types of visual elements, each of which is most sensitive to different wavelengths of light.

figure 4.18

Relative Responses of Three Cone Types to Different Wavelengths of Light

Each type of cone responds to a range of light wavelengths but responds more to some wavelengths than to others. Any combination of wavelengths that creates a particular pattern of cone activity will create a particular colour sensation. For example, a pure light of 570 nanometres (see arrow A) stimulates long-wavelength cones at 1.0 relative units and medium-wavelength cones at about 0.7 relative units. This ratio of cone activity (1/0.7 = 1.4) gives the sensation of yellow. But any combination of wavelengths at the proper intensity that generates this same ratio of activity in these cone types will also produce the sensation of yellow.

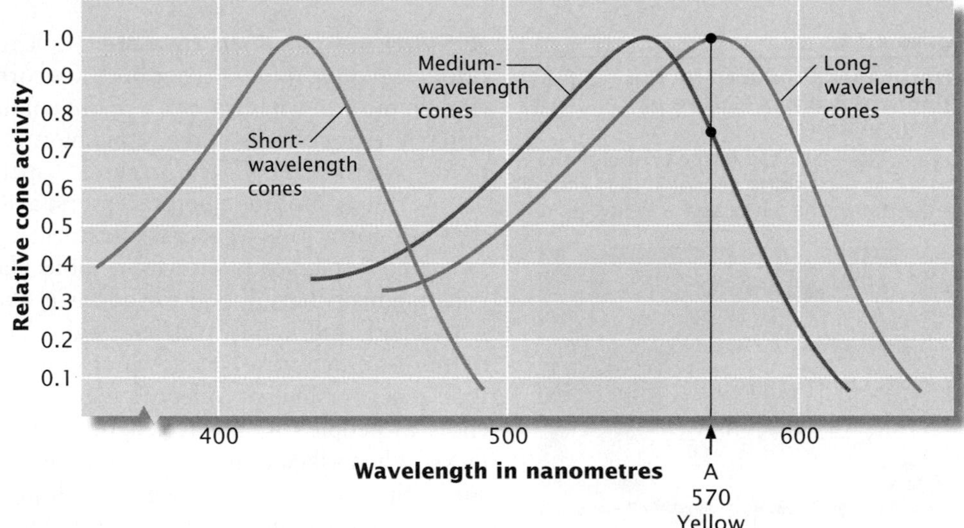

green range. *Long-wavelength* cones respond best to light in the reddish-yellow range (these have traditionally been called "red cones").

No single cone, by itself, can signal the colour of a light. It is the *ratio* of the activities of the three types of cones that indicates what colour will be sensed. In other words, colour vision is coded by the *pattern of activity* of the different cones. For example, a light is sensed as yellow if it has a pure wavelength of about 570 nanometres; this light stimulates both medium- and long-wavelength cones, as illustrated by arrow A in Figure 4.18. But yellow is also sensed whenever any mixture of other lights stimulates the same pattern of activity in these two types of cones. The trichromatic theory was applied in the creation of colour television screens, which contain microscopic elements of red, green, and blue. A television broadcast excites these elements to varying degrees, mixing their colours to produce many other colours. You see colour mixtures on the screen—not patterns of red, green, and blue dots—because the dots are too small and close together to be seen individually.

The Opponent-Process Theory of Colour Vision Brilliant as it is, the trichromatic theory cannot explain some aspects of colour vision. For example, it cannot account for the fact that if you stare at the flag in Figure 4.19 for thirty seconds and then look at the dot in the blank white space below it, you will see a colour afterimage. What was blue in the original image will be yellow in the afterimage, what was green before will appear red, and what was black will now appear white.

This type of phenomenon led Ewald Hering to offer an alternative to the trichromatic theory of colour vision, called the **opponent-process theory.** According to this theory, the colour-sensitive visual elements in the eye are grouped into three pairs, and the members of each pair oppose, or inhibit, each other. The three pairs are a *red-green element*, a *blue-yellow element*, and a *black-white element*. Each element signals one colour or the other—red or green, for example—but never both. This theory explains colour afterimages. When one part of an opponent pair is no longer stimulated, the other is activated. So, as in Figure 4.19, if the original image you look at is green, the afterimage will be red.

The opponent-process theory also explains the phenomenon of complementary colours. Two colours are *complementary* if a neutral colour, such as grey, appears when lights of the two colours are mixed. (The neutral colour can appear as anything from white to grey to black, depending on the intensity of the lights being mixed.) On the colour circle shown in Figure 4.16, complementary colours are roughly opposite each other. Red and green lights are complementary, as are yellow and blue. Notice that complementary colours are *opponent* colours in Hering's theory. According to opponent-process theory, complementary colours stimulate the same visual element (e.g., red-green) in opposite directions, cancelling each other out. This theory helps explain why mixing lights of complementary colours produces grey.

opponent-process theory A theory of colour vision stating that colour-sensitive visual elements are grouped into red-green, blue-yellow, and black-white elements.

figure 4.19

Afterimages Produced by the Opponent-Process Nature of Colour Vision

Stare at the black sail in the centre of the flag for at least thirty seconds, then fixate on the dot in the white space below it.

•

A Synthesis and an Update The trichromatic and opponent-process theories seem quite different, but both are correct to some extent, and together they can explain most of what is known about colour vision. Electrical recordings made from different types of cells in the retina have paved the way for a synthesis, or blending, of the two theories (Gegenfurtner & Kiper, 2003).

At the level of the photoreceptors, a slightly revised version of the trichromatic theory is correct. As a general rule, there *are* three types of cones that have three different photopigments. However, molecular biologists who isolated the genes for cone pigments have found variations in the genes for the cones sensitive to middle-wavelength and long-wavelength light. These variants have slightly different sensitivities to different wavelengths of light. So a person can have two, three, or even four genes for long-wavelength pigments (Neitz & Neitz, 1995). Individual differences in people's long-wavelength pigments become apparent in colour-matching tasks. When asked to mix a red light and a green light to match a yellow light, a person with one kind of long-wavelength pigment will choose a different red-to-green ratio than someone with a different long-wavelength pigment. Women are more likely than men to have four distinct photopigments, and the women who do have the four photopigments have a richer experience of colour. They can detect more shades of colour than people with the more common three photopigments, but their experience of colour pales in comparison to that of certain tropical shrimp. These shrimp live on colourful coral reefs and have twelve different photopigments that allow them to see colours even in the ultraviolet range that no human—male or female—can sense (Marshall & Oberwinkler, 1999).

Colour vision works a little differently at the level of ganglion cells. As we mentioned earlier, information about light from many photoreceptors feeds into each ganglion cell, and the output from each ganglion cell goes to the brain. We also said that the receptive fields of most ganglion cells are arranged in centre-surround patterns. It turns out that the centre and the surround are colour coded, as illustrated in Figure 4.20. The centre responds best to one colour, and the surround responds best to a different colour. This colour coding arises because varying proportions of the three cone types feed into the centre and the surround of the ganglion cell.

When either the centre or the surround of a ganglion cell's receptive field is stimulated, the other area is inhibited. In other words, the centre and the surround of a given ganglion cell's receptive field are most responsive to opponent colours. Recordings from many ganglion cells show that three very common pairs of opponent colours are the ones predicted by Hering's opponent-process theory: red-green, blue-yellow, and black-white. Stimulating both the centre and the surround of these cells' receptive fields cancels the effects of either light, producing grey. Black-white cells receive input from all types of cones, so it does not matter what colour stimulates

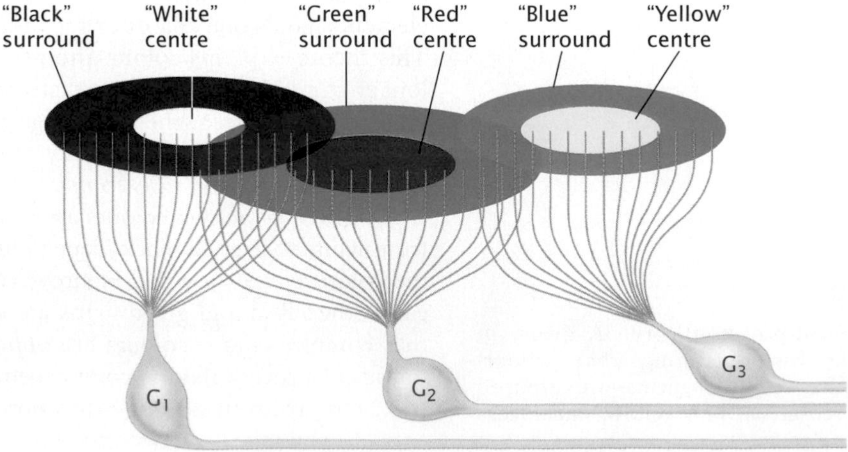

figure 4.20

Colour Coding and the Ganglion Cells

The centre-surround receptive fields of ganglion cells form the basis for opponent colours. Some ganglion cells, like G2, have a centre whose photoreceptors respond best to red wavelengths and a surround whose photoreceptors respond best to green wavelengths. Other ganglion cells pair blue and yellow, whereas still others receive input from all types of photoreceptors.

figure 4.21

Synaesthesia

In this experiment on synaesthesia, a triangular pattern of H's was embedded in a background of other letters, as shown at left. Most people find it difficult to detect the triangle, but "J.C.," a person with synaesthesia, picked it out immediately because, as simulated at right, he saw the H's as green, the F's as yellow, and the P's as red (Ramachandran & Hubbard, 2001).

Source: Figure 3 from Ramachandran & Hubbard (2001).

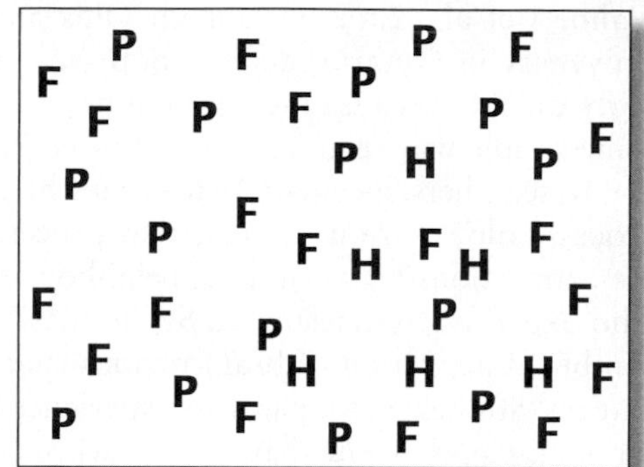

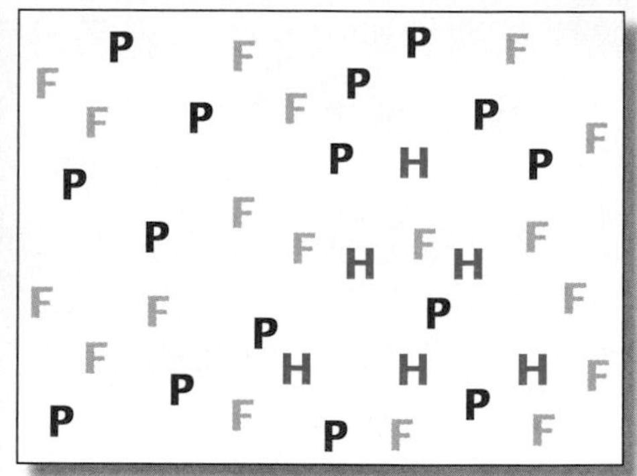

them. All this colour information is further analyzed in the brain, where cells in specific regions of the visual cortex also respond in opponent pairs that are sensitive to the red-green and blue-yellow input coming from ganglion cells in the retina (Engel, Zhang, & Wandell, 1997; Heywood & Kentridge, 2003).

In summary, colour vision is possible because three types of cones have different sensitivities to different wavelengths, as the trichromatic theory suggests. The sensation of different colours results from stimulating the three cone types in different ratios. Because there are three types of cones, any colour can be produced by mixing three different wavelengths of light. But the story does not end there. The output from cones is fed into ganglion cells whose receptive fields have centres and surrounds that respond to opponent colours and inhibit each other. This arrangement provides the basis for colour afterimages. So the trichromatic theory describes the properties of the photoreceptors, whereas the opponent-process theory describes the properties of the ganglion cells. Both theories are needed to account for the complexity of visual sensations of colour.

Interaction of the Senses: Synaesthesia

At the beginning of this chapter, we gave examples of the interaction of two senses: vision and touch (Blake, Sobel, & James, 2004). There are other sensory interactions, too. For example, hearing a brief sound just as lights are flashed can create the impression of more lights than there actually are (Shams, Kamitani, & Shimojo, 2000). Hearing a sound as objects collide can affect your perception of their motion (Watanabe & Shimojo, 2001). Sound can improve your ability to see an object at the sound's source, which can help you avoid or respond to danger (McDonald, Teder-Salejarvi, & Hillyard, 2000). Hearing sounds can also alter sensitivity to touch (Hötting & Röder, 2004). There is even evidence that smells are more readily detected when accompanied by images related to them (Gottfried & Dolan, 2003). Such interactions occur in everyone, but some people also report **synaesthesia** (pronounced "sin-ess-THEE-zhah"). Mike Dixon, Daniel Smilek, and Philip Merikle of the University of Waterloo, Ontario, describe synaesthesia as a "condition in which ordinary stimuli lead to extraordinary experiences" (Dixon et al., 2004). People may, for example, say that they "feel" colours or sounds as touches, or that they "taste" shapes; others claim that they sense certain colours, such as red, when they hear certain sounds, such as a trumpet. Some report experiencing certain tastes, numbers, or letters as vivid visual patterns or as particular colours (e.g., Laeng, Svartdal, & Oelmann, 2004).

Once dismissed as poetic delusions, some of these claims have now received scientific support from experiments such as the one illustrated in Figure 4.22 (Mattingly et al., 2001; Ramachandran & Hubbard, 2001). One man reported that he always sees numbers in distinct colours, even when they are printed in black ink. To him, he said, the 2s look orange and the 5s look green. And in fact, when he was asked to pick out a 2 that was embedded in an array of 5s, he could do so much more rapidly than other people. To him, the 2 seemed to "pop out" of the array

synaesthesia A blending of sensory experience that causes some people to "see" sounds or "taste" colours, for example.

(Palmeri et al., 2002). Elizabeth Olds and Ryan Punambolam of Wilfrid Laurier University in Ontario, define "pop out" as a type of search that can be executed fairly quickly because the target appears distinct as it differs from the distracters in some simple way (e.g., colour) (Olds & Punambolam, 2002).

Researchers speculate that synaesthesia occurs partly because brain areas that process colours are near areas that process letters and numbers and partly because the connections between these neighbouring areas may be more extensive in people who experience synaesthesia. Synaesthesia experiences also seem to result from the combined activation of brain regions that process different kinds of sensory information. Studies of people who experience colour sensations when they hear words, for example, do show that hearing words activates both auditory cortex in the temporal lobes and visual cortex in the occipital lobe (Aleman et al., 2001; Nunn et al., 2002). Similar, but less extensive, connections in nonsynaesthetic people may be partly responsible for their use of intersensory descriptions in which a shirt is "loud," a cheese is "sharp," or a wine is said to have "a light straw colour with greenish hues" (Martino & Marks, 2001).

The Chemical Senses: Smell and Taste

There are animals without vision, and there are animals without hearing, but there are no animals without some form of chemical sense. Chemical senses arise from the interaction of chemicals and receptors. **Olfaction** (our sense of smell) detects chemicals that are airborne, or volatile. **Gustation** (our sense of taste) detects chemicals in solution that come into contact with receptors inside the mouth.

Olfaction

As in other senses, accessory structures shape sensations in the olfactory system, too. In humans, these accessory structures include the nose, the mouth, and the upper part of the throat, all of which help funnel odour molecules to receptors. So just as bending the ear's pinna forward can help collect sound waves, taping nasal dilator strips over the bridge of the nose intensifies food odours (Raudenbush & Meyer,

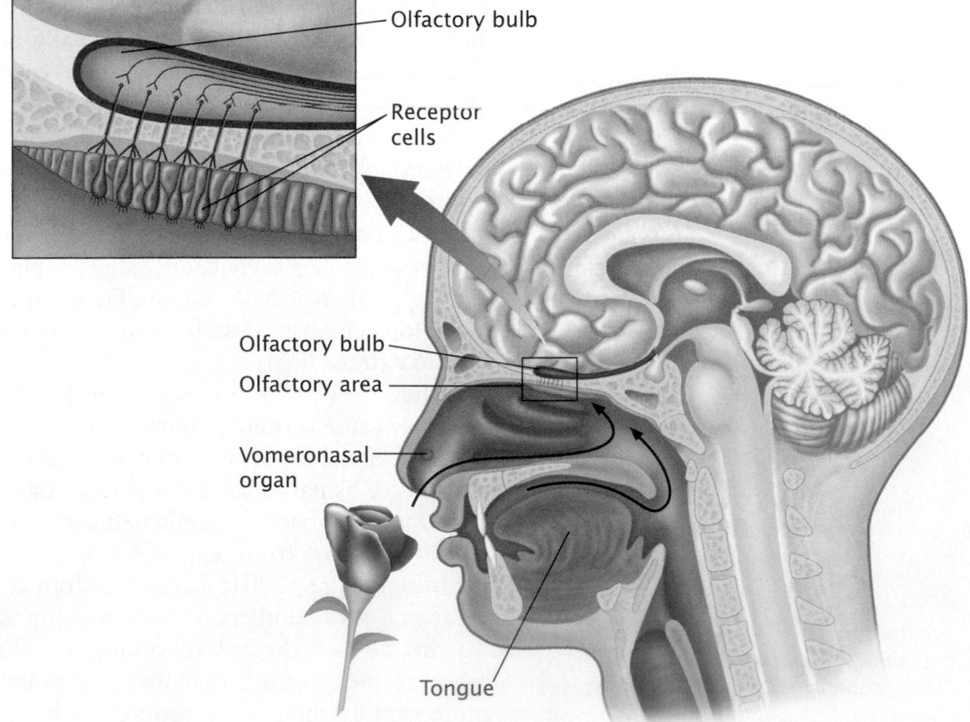

figure 4.22

The Olfactory System

Airborne chemicals from the rose reach the olfactory area through the nostrils and through the back of the mouth. Fibres pass directly from the olfactory area to the olfactory bulb in the brain, and from there signals pass to areas such as the hypothalamus and amygdala, which are involved in emotion.

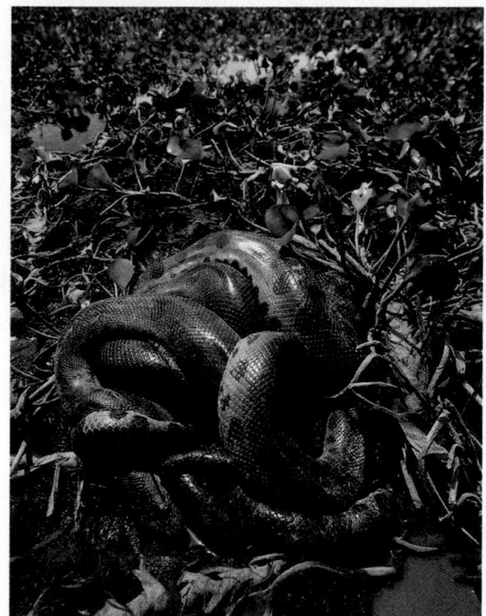

A "Mating Ball" Among snakes there is intense competition for females. Dozens of males will wrap themselves around a single female in a "mating ball." Snakes' forked tongues allow them to sample airborne chemicals at two different points and, hence, to follow an olfactory trail (Schwenk, 1994). Males with the best olfactory tracking abilities are the ones most likely to reach a female first, enabling them to pass on their genes to the next generation.

2002). Odour molecules can reach olfactory receptors in the nose either by entering the nostrils or by rising through an opening in the palate at the back of the mouth. This second route allows us to sample odours from food as we eat (see Figure 4.23). The olfactory receptors themselves are located on the dendrites of specialized neurons that extend into the moist lining of the nose, called the *mucous membrane*. Odour molecules bind to these receptors, causing depolarization of the dendrites' membrane, that in turn leads to changes in the firing rates of the neurons. A single molecule of an odorous substance can cause a change in the membrane potential of an olfactory neuron, but detection of the odour by a human normally requires about fifty such molecules (Menini, Picco, & Firestein, 1995; Reed, 2004). (A hot pizza generates lots more than that.) The number of molecules needed to trigger an olfactory sensation can vary, however. For example, women are more sensitive to odours during certain phases of their menstrual cycles (Navarrete-Palacios et al., 2003).

Olfactory neurons are continuously replaced with new ones, as each lives about only two months. Scientists are especially interested in this process because, as noted in the chapter on biological aspects of psychology, most neurons cannot divide to create new ones. An understanding of how new olfactory neurons are generated—and how they make appropriate connections in the brain—may someday be helpful in treating brain damage.

In contrast to vision, which uses only four basic receptor types (rods and three kinds of cones), the olfactory system employs about a thousand different types of receptors. In fact, up to 2 percent of the human genetic code is devoted to these olfactory receptors, perhaps because a good sense of smell helped humans to adapt and survive over thousands of years (Firestein, 2001). A given odour stimulates various olfactory receptors to varying degrees, and the combination of receptors stimulated creates codes for a particular odour sensation (Kajiya et al., 2001). The many combinations possible allow humans to discriminate tens of thousands of different odours. We know that substances with similar chemical structures tend to have similar odours, but exactly how olfactory receptors discriminate various smells and send coded messages about them to the brain is only now being determined (Keller & Vosshall, 2004; Reed, 2004). It has only recently been demonstrated, for example, that body position may have an effect on the coding of olfactory information. Johan Lundström, Julie Boyle, and Marilyn Jones-Gotman of the Montreal Neurological Institute, have conducted a study that suggests that people report a stronger sense of smell when sitting than when they are lying down (Lundström, et al., 2006).

The question of how smells are coded has been of special interest to the security industry. Researchers have been developing an "electronic nose" capable of detecting odourants associated with guns and explosives (Thaler, Kennedy, & Hanson, 2001). Versions of these devices are already in use at some airports. An "electronic nose" has also been developed that can detect the presence of diseases that might not be evident to an examining doctor, and other artificial olfactory devices are being used to examine the condition and composition of food products (Haugen, 2001; Saini, Barr, & Bessant, 2001).

Olfaction is the only sensory system that does not send its messages through the thalamus. Instead, axons from neurons in the nose extend through a bony plate and directly into the brain, where they have a synapse in a structure called the **olfactory bulb,** where processing of olfactory information continues (Urban, 2002). Pathways from the olfactory bulb send the information on for further processing in several brain regions, including the frontal lobe and the amygdala, which is involved in emotional experience (Kareken et al., 2003; Zou et al., 2001).

These features of the olfactory system may account for the strong relationship between olfaction and emotional memory (Stevenson & Boakes, 2003). For example, associations between a certain experience and a particular odour do not fade much with time or subsequent experiences (Lawless & Engen, 1977). So catching a whiff of the scent once worn by a lost loved one can reactivate intense feelings of

olfaction The sense of smell.
gustation The sense of taste.
olfactory bulb A brain structure that receives messages regarding olfaction.

love or sadness associated with that person. Odours can also bring back accurate memories of significant experiences linked with them, especially positive experiences (Engen, Gilmore, & Mair, 1991; Mohr et al., 2001).

The mechanisms of olfaction are remarkably similar in species ranging from humans to worms. Different species vary considerably, however, in their sensitivity to smell, and in the degree to which they depend on it for survival. For example, humans have about 9 million olfactory neurons, whereas there are about 225 million such neurons in dogs, a species that is far more dependent on smell to identify food, territory, and receptive mates. In addition, dogs and many other species depend on an accessory olfactory system that is able to detect pheromones. **Pheromones** (pronounced "FAIR-o-mones") are chemicals that are released by one animal and that, when detected by another, can shape the second animal's behaviour or physiology (Silvotti, Montanu, & Tirindelli, 2003). For example, when male snakes detect a chemical exuded on the skin of female snakes, they are stimulated to "court" the female.

In non-human mammals, pheromones can be nonvolatile chemicals that, when licked, are passed into a portion of the olfactory system called the **vomeronasal organ.** In female mice, for example, the vomeronasal organ detects chemicals in the male's urine. By this means, a male can cause a female to ovulate and become sexually receptive, and an unfamiliar male can cause a pregnant female to abort her pregnancy (Bruce, 1969).

The role of pheromones in humans is much less clear. At one extreme are perfume advertisers who want us to believe that their products contain sexual attractants that act as pheromones to subconsciously influence the behaviour of desirable partners. At the other extreme are those who argue that in humans, the vomeronasal organ is an utterly nonfunctional vestige, like the appendix. The best current scientific evidence supports a more measured set of conclusions. The human vomeronasal organ is, in fact, capable of responding to certain hormonal substances and can influence certain hormonal secretions (Berliner et al., 1996). Further, it is increasingly clear that humans do have some kind of pheromone-like system. For example, odourants that are not consciously detectable can nevertheless influence people's moods (Jacob & McClintock, 2000). Odourants can also alter activity in the cerebral cortex and other brain areas that are not directly involved in olfaction (Jacob et al., 2001). In one study, specific areas of the hypothalamus were activated in men and women when they were exposed to an odourless substance similar to the hormones—estrogen or testosterone—associated with the opposite sex (Savic et al., 2001). A possible human gene for pheromone receptors has been found (Rodriguez et al., 2000), and pheromones have been shown to cause reproduction-related physiological changes in humans. Specifically, pheromonal signals secreted in the perspiration of a woman can shorten or prolong the menstrual cycle of other women nearby (Stern & McClintock, 1998). In such cases, pheromones are responsible for *menstrual synchrony*—the tendency of women living together to menstruate at the same time.

Despite the perfume ads, though, there is still no solid evidence for a sexual attractant pheromone in humans, or even in non-human primates. Nevertheless, learned associations between certain odours and emotional experiences may enhance a person's readiness for sex. People also use olfactory information in other social situations. For example, after just a few hours of contact, mothers can usually identify their newborn babies by the infants' smell (Porter, Cernich, & McLaughlin, 1983). And if infants are breastfed, they can discriminate their own mothers' odour from that of other breastfeeding women, and they appear to be comforted by it (Porter, 1991). In fact, individual mammals, including humans, have a distinct "odourtype," that is determined by their immune cells and other inherited physiological factors (Beauchamp et al., 1995). During pregnancy, a woman's own odourtype combines with the odourtype of her fetus to form a third odourtype. Each of these three odours is distinguishable, suggesting that recognition of odourtypes may help establish the mother-infant bonds discussed in the chapter on human development.

pheromones Chemicals released by one animal and detected by another that shape the second animal's behaviour or physiology.

vomeronasal organ A portion of the mammalian olfactory system that is sensitive to pheromones.

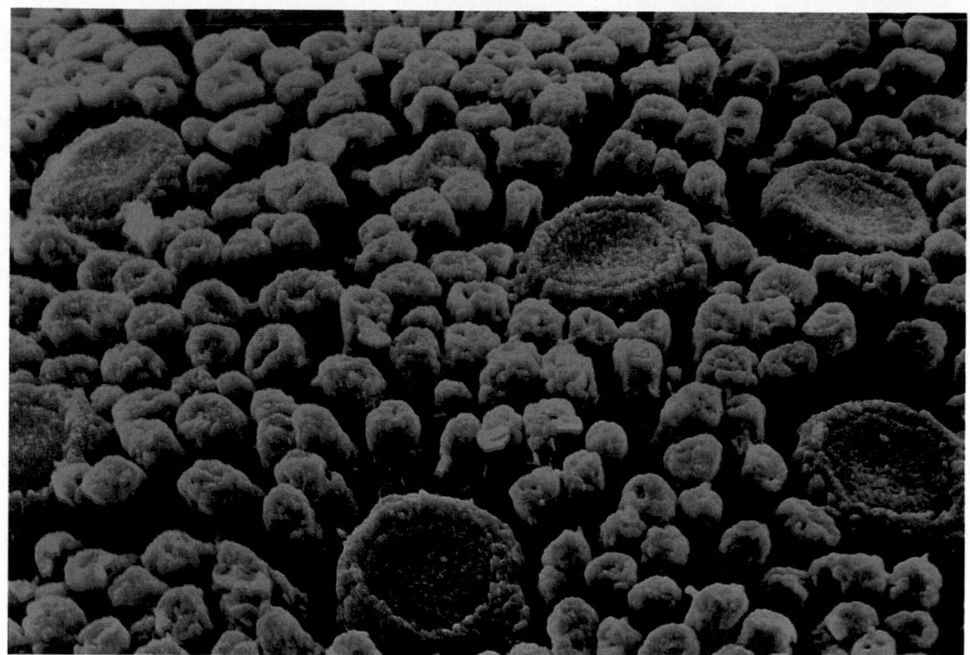

Taste Receptors Taste buds are grouped into structures called *papillae.* Two kinds of papillae are visible in this greatly enlarged photo of the surface of the human tongue.

Gustation

The chemical sense system in the mouth is gustation, or taste. The receptors for taste are in the taste buds, which are grouped together in structures called **papillae** (pronounced "pa-PILL-ee"). Normally, there are about 10 000 taste buds in a person's mouth, mostly on the tongue but also on the roof of the mouth and on the back of the throat.

In contrast to the olfactory system, which can discriminate thousands of different odours, the human taste system detects only a few elementary sensations. The most familiar of these are sweet, sour, bitter, and salty. Each taste bud responds best to one or two of these categories, but it also responds weakly to others (Zhang et al., 2003). The sensation of a particular substance appears to result from the responses of taste buds that are relatively sensitive to a specific category. Behavioural studies and electrical recordings from taste neurons have also established two additional taste sensations (Rolls, 1997). One, called *umami*, enhances other tastes and is produced by certain proteins, as well as by monosodium glutamate (MSG). The other, called *astringent*, is the taste produced by tannins, which are found in tea, for example.

Different tastes are transduced into neural activity by different types of taste receptors and in different ways (Small et al., 2003; Stewart, DeSimone, & Hill, 1997; Stillman, 2002). For example, sweet and bitter are signalled when chemicals fit into specific receptor sites (Montmayeur et al., 2001), whereas sour and salty act through more direct effects on the ion channels in membranes of taste cells. Understanding the chemistry of sweetness is allowing scientists to design new chemicals that fit into sweetness receptors and taste thousands of times sweeter than sugar. Many of these substances are now being tested for safety and may soon allow people to enjoy low-calorie hot-fudge sundaes.

A taste component in its own right, saltiness also enhances the taste of food by suppressing bitterness (Breslin & Beauchamp, 1997). In animals, taste responses to salt are determined during early development, before and after birth. Research with animals has shown that if mothers are put on a low-salt diet, their offspring are less likely to prefer salt (Hill & Przekop, 1988). In humans, experiences with salty foods over the first four years of life may alter the sensory systems that detect salt and contribute to enduring preferences for salty foods (Hill & Mistretta, 1990).

papillae Structures on the tongue containing groups of taste receptors, or taste buds.

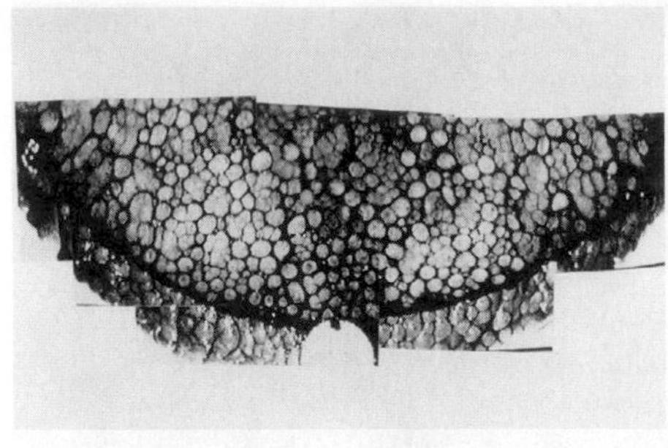

figure 4.23

Are You a Supertaster?

This photo shows the large number of papillae on the tongue of a "supertaster." If you don't mind a temporary stain on your mouth and teeth, you can look at your own papillae by painting the front of your tongue with a cotton swab soaked in blue food colouring. Distribute the dye by moving your tongue around and swallowing; then look into a magnifying mirror as you shine a flashlight on your tongue. The pink circles you see against the blue background are papillae, each of which has about six taste buds buried in its surface. Get several friends to do this test, and you will see that genes create wide individual differences in taste bud density.

There may be genetically determined differences in the ability to taste things. About 25 percent of the population are "supertasters"—individuals who have an especially large number of papillae on their tongues (Bartoshuk, 2000). Supertasters have thousands of taste buds, whereas "nontasters" have only hundreds of buds (see Figure 4.23). Most people fall between these extremes. Supertasters are more sensitive than other people to bitterness, as revealed in their reaction to foods such as broccoli, soy products, and grapefruit. Having different numbers of taste buds may help account for differences in people's food intake, as well as weight problems (Tepper & Ullrich, 2002). For example, Linda Bartoshuk has found that thin people have many more taste buds than overweight people (Duffy et al., 1999). Perhaps they do not have to eat as much to experience the good taste of various foods.

Smell, Taste, and Flavour

People with *anosmia* (pronounced "ay-NOSE-me-a") are unable to distinguish different smells. Some are born this way, but the condition can also result from brain damage (Leopold, 2002; Hawkes, 2003). Anosmic individuals also have trouble distinguishing different tastes, even though there is nothing wrong with their taste system. Why? For the same reason that, when you have a stuffy nose, everything tastes the same—usually like cardboard. Smell and taste act as two components of a single system, known as *flavour* (Rozin, 1982). Most of the properties that make food taste good are actually odours detected by the olfactory system, not activities of the taste system. The olfactory and gustatory pathways converge in the *orbitofrontal cortex* (de Araujo et al., 2003), where neurons also respond to the sight and texture of food. The responses of neurons in this "flavour cortex" are also influenced by conditions of hunger and satiety ("fullness").

Both tastes and odours prompt strong emotional responses. For tastes, the reaction to bitter flavours is inborn, but the associations of emotions with odours are all learned (Bartoshuk, 1991). Linda Parker of Wilfrid Laurier University in Waterloo, Ontario, has pointed out that many types of animals can easily learn taste aversion to particular foods when the taste is associated with nausea (Parker, 2003), but humans learn aversions to odours more readily than to tastes (Bartoshuk & Wolfe, 1990).

Variations in your nutritional state can affect the taste and flavour of food, as well as the motivation to eat particular foods. For example, being hungry or having a salt deficiency makes sweet or salty things taste better and more likely to be eaten. Influences on protein and fat intake are less direct. Protein and fat molecules have no particular taste or smell. So preferring or avoiding foods that contain these nutrients is based on associations between olfactory cues from other volatile substances in food and on the nutritional results of eating the foods (Bartoshuk, 1991; Schiffman et al., 1999). These findings have implications for dieting, which is discussed in the chapter on motivation and emotion.

Flavour includes other characteristics of food—how it feels in your mouth and, especially, its temperature. Temperature does not alter saltiness, but warm foods are experienced as sweeter. In fact, simply warming a person's taste receptors creates a sensation of sweetness (Cruz & Green, 2000). Aromas released from warm food rise from the mouth into the nose and create more flavour sensations. This is why some people find hot pizza delicious and cold pizza disgusting. Spicy "hot" foods actually stimulate pain fibres in the mouth because they contain a substance called *capsaicin* (pronounced "kap-SAY-uh-sin"), which opens ion channels in pain neurons that are also opened by heat. As a result, these foods are experienced as physiologically "hot" (Caterina et al., 1997). Why do people eat spicy foods even though they stimulate pain? The practice may have originated because many "hot" spices have antibacterial properties. In fact, researchers have found a strong correlation between frequent use of antibacterial spices and living in climates that promote bacterial contamination (Billing & Sherman, 1998). ("In Review: Smell and Taste" summarizes our discussion of these senses.)

in review Smell and Taste

Aspect of Sensory System	Elements	Key Characteristics
Energy	Smell: volatile chemicals Taste: chemicals in solution	The amount, intensity, and location of the chemicals determine taste and smell sensations
Structures of taste and smell	Smell: chemical receptors in the mucous membrane of the nose Taste: taste buds grouped in papillae in the mouth	Odour and taste molecules stimulate chemical receptors
Pathways to the brain	Olfactory bulb and taste buds	Axons from the nose bypass the thalamus and extend directly to the olfactory bulb

Somatic Senses and the Vestibular System

Some senses are not located in a specific organ, such as the eye or the ear. These are the somatic senses, also called *somatosensory systems*, which are spread throughout the body. The **somatic senses** include the skin senses of touch, temperature, and pain, as well as kinesthesia, the sense that tells the brain where the parts of the body are. Closely related to kinesthesia is the vestibular system, which tells the brain about the position and movements of the head. Although not strictly a somatosensory system, the vestibular system will also be considered in this section.

Touch and Temperature

Touch is crucial. People can function and prosper without vision, hearing, or smell, but a person without touch would have difficulty surviving. Without a sense of touch, you could not even swallow food, because you could not tell where it was in your mouth and throat.

Stimulus and Receptors for Touch The energy detected by the sense of touch is physical pressure on tissue, usually the skin, or hairs on the skin. The skin weighs approximately 9.09 kilos and covers approximately 1.67 square metres. The receptors that transduce pressure into neural activity are in, or just below, the skin.

Many nerve endings in the skin act as touch receptors. Some neurons come from the spinal cord, enter the skin, and simply end; these are called *free nerve endings*. Many other neurons end in a variety of elaborate, specialized structures. However, there is generally little relationship between the type of nerve ending and the type of sensory information carried by the neuron. Many types of nerve endings respond to mechanical stimuli, but the exact process through which they transduce mechanical energy is still unknown. These somatosensory neurons are unusual in that they have no dendrites. Their cell bodies are outside the spinal cord, and their axon splits and extends both to the skin and to the spinal cord. Action potentials travel from the nerve endings in the skin to the spinal cord, where they communicate across a synapse to dendrites of other neurons.

We do more than just passively respond to whatever happens to come in contact with our bodies. For humans, touch is also an active sense that is used to get specific information. In much the same way that you can look as well as just see,

somatic senses Senses of touch, temperature, pain, and kinesthesia.

you can also touch as well as feel. When people are involved in active sensing, they usually use the part of the sensory apparatus that has the greatest sensitivity. For vision, this is the eye's fovea; for touch, the fingertips. (The area of primary somatosensory cortex devoted to the fingertips is especially large.) Fingertip touch is the principal way people explore the textures of surfaces. It can be extremely sensitive, as evidenced by blind people who can read Braille as rapidly as 200 words per minute (Foulke, 1991) or by the ease with which sighted but blindfolded people can learn to recognize faces by touching them (Kilgour & Lederman, 2002).

Adaptation of Touch Receptors Constant input from all your touch neurons would provide a lot of unnecessary information. Once you get dressed, for example, you do not need to be constantly reminded that you are wearing clothes. Thanks in part to the process of adaptation mentioned earlier, you do not continue to feel your clothes against your skin.

The most important sensory information involves *changes* in touch—as when a broken lace suddenly makes your shoe feel loose. The touch sense emphasizes these changes and filters out the excess information. How? Typically, a touch neuron responds with a burst of firing when a stimulus is applied, then quickly returns to its baseline firing rate, even though the stimulus may still be in contact with the skin. If the touch pressure increases, the neuron again responds with an increase in firing rate, but then slows down. Some neurons in the somatosensory cortex also stop firing if a tactile stimulus remains constant for some time (Graziano et al., 2002). A few touch neurons adapt more slowly, continuing to fire at an elevated rate as long as pressure is applied to the skin. By attending to this input, you can sense a constant stimulus (try doing this by focusing on sensations from your glasses or shoes).

Coding and Representation of Touch Information The sense of touch codes information about two aspects of an object in contact with the skin: its weight and its location. The *intensity* of the stimulus—how heavy it is—is coded by both the firing rate of individual neurons and the number of neurons stimulated. A heavy object produces a higher rate of firing and stimulates more neurons than a light object. The *location* of touch is coded much as it is for vision—by the location of the neurons that are responding to the touch.

Touch information is organized such that signals from neighbouring points on the skin stay next to one another, even as they travel from the skin through the spinal cord to the thalamus and on to the somatosensory cortex. So just as there is a map of the visual field in the brain, the area of cortex that receives touch information resembles a map of the surface of the body (see Figure 3.18). As with the other senses, these representations are contralateral; that is, input from the left side of the body goes to the right side of the brain, and vice versa. In nonhuman primates, however, touch information from each hand is sent to both sides of the brain. This arrangement appears to amplify information from manual exploration of objects and to improve feedback from hand movements (Iwamura, Iriki, & Tanaka, 1994).

Temperature When you dig your toes into a sandy summer beach, the pleasant experience you get comes partly from the sensation of warmth. Touch and temperature seem to be separate senses and, to some extent, they are; but the difference between the two senses is not always clear.

Some of the skin's sensory neurons respond to a change in temperature, but not to simple contact. There are "warm fibres" that are nerve fibres that increase their firing rates when the temperature changes in the range of about 35° to 47°C. Temperatures above this range are painful and stimulate different fibres. Other nerve fibres are "cold fibres"; they respond to a broad range of cool temperatures. However, many of the fibres that respond to temperature also respond to touch, so sensations of touch and temperature sometimes interact. For example, warm and cold objects can feel up to 250 percent heavier than body-temperature objects (Stevens & Hooper, 1982). Also, if you touch an object made up of alternating warm and cool bars, you will have the sensation of intense heat (Thunberg, 1896, cited in Craig & Bushnell, 1994).

Stimulation of the touch sense can have psychological and physiological effects. For example, premature infants gain weight 47 percent faster when they are given massages. (They do not eat more but, rather, they process their food more efficiently.) Massage therapy is also associated with increased air flow in asthmatic children (Field et al., 1998) and with reduced pain and lowered stress hormones in arthritic children (Field et al., 1997). In adults, massage is associated with reduced anxiety, increased alertness, and improved performance on math tests (Field et al., 1996).

Pain

The skin senses can convey a great deal of pleasure, but if you increase the intensity of the same kind of stimulation, you have a much different sensation: pain. Pain provides you with information about the impact of the world on your body. It can tell you, for example, that "a hammer just crushed your left thumb." Pain also has a distinctly negative emotional component. Researchers have focused on the information-carrying aspects of pain, its emotional components, and the various ways that the brain can adjust the amount of pain that reaches consciousness.

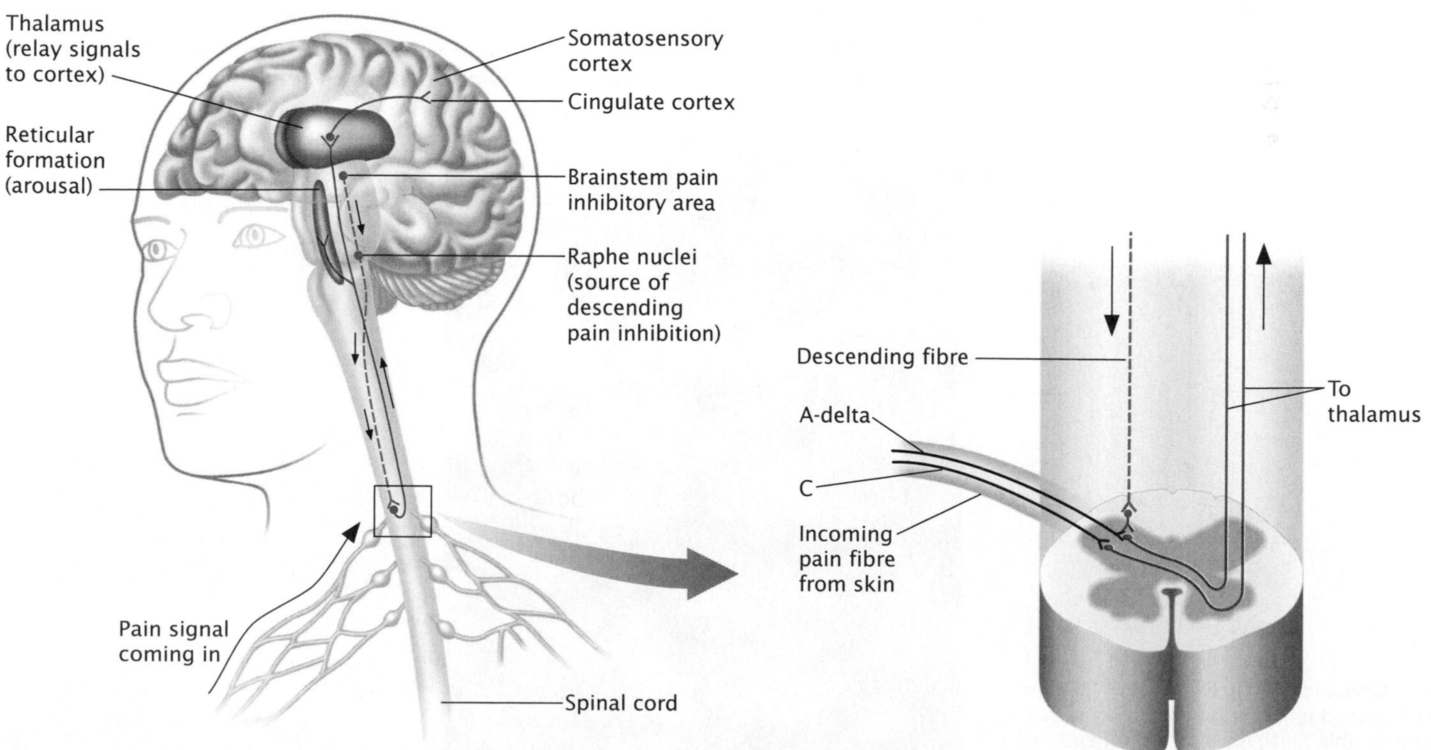

figure 4.24

Pain Pathways

Pain messages are carried to the brain by way of the spinal cord. Myelinated *A-delta fibres* carry information about sharp pain. Unmyelinated *C fibres* carry several types of pain, including chronic, dull aches. Pain fibres make synapses in the reticular formation, causing arousal. They also project to the thalamus and from there to the cortex. Pain sensations can be intensified when activity in pain-carrying neurons stimulates activity in glial cells in the spinal cord (Watkins & Maier, 2003; see the chapter on biological aspects of psychology).

Pain as an Information Sense The information-carrying aspect of pain is very similar to that of touch and temperature. The receptors for pain are free nerve endings. As mentioned earlier, for example, capsaicin, the active ingredient in chili peppers, creates pain in the mouth by stimulating these pain nerve endings. Painful stimuli cause the release of chemicals that fit into specialized receptors in pain neurons, causing them to fire. The axons of pain-sensing neurons release neurotransmitters not only near the spinal cord, sending information to the brain, but also near the skin, causing local inflammation.

Two types of nerve fibres carry pain signals from the skin to the spinal cord. *A-delta fibres* carry sharp, pricking pain sensations. Their axons are coated with myelin, which speeds the transmission of these sharp pain messages. *C fibres* carry long-lasting, dull aches and burning sensations. So when you stub your toe, the immediate wave of sharp, intense pain is signaled by messages from A-delta fibres. That slightly delayed wave of gnawing, dull pain is signalled by messages from C fibres.

Both kinds of pain come from the same place, but the sensations follow separate pain fibres all the way to the brain, where they activate different brain regions (Ploner et al., 2002). Pain fibres enter the spinal cord, where they form synapses with neurons that carry pain signals to the thalamus and other parts of the brain (see Figure 4.24). Different pain neurons are activated by different degrees of painful stimulation. Numerous types of neurotransmitters are used by different pain neurons, a phenomenon that has allowed the development of a variety of new drugs for pain management.

Scientists once thought that the cerebral cortex played little or no role in the experience of pain, but several lines of evidence have now reversed that conclusion. Functional magnetic resonance imaging (fMRI) studies of healthy volunteers have compared cortical activity during a pain experience with cortical activity during an attention-demanding task (Davis et al., 1997). These studies showed activation of the somatosensory cortex under both conditions and additional activity during pain in the *anterior cingulate cortex*, an evolutionarily primitive brain region thought to be important in emotions. Other studies have confirmed that the anterior cingulate

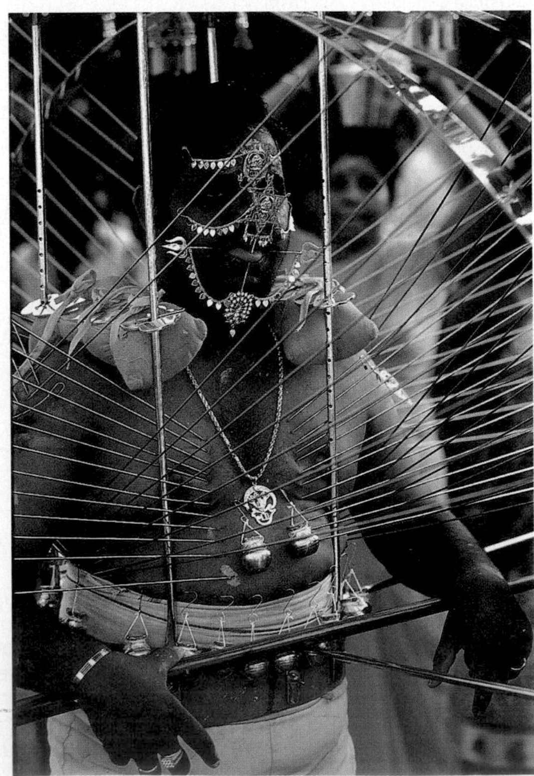

The Complex Nature of Pain If pain were based only on the nature of incoming stimuli, this participant in a purification ceremony in Singapore would be hurting. However, as described in the chapter on consciousness, the experience of pain is a complex phenomenon affected by psychological and biological variables that can make it more or, as in this case, less intense.

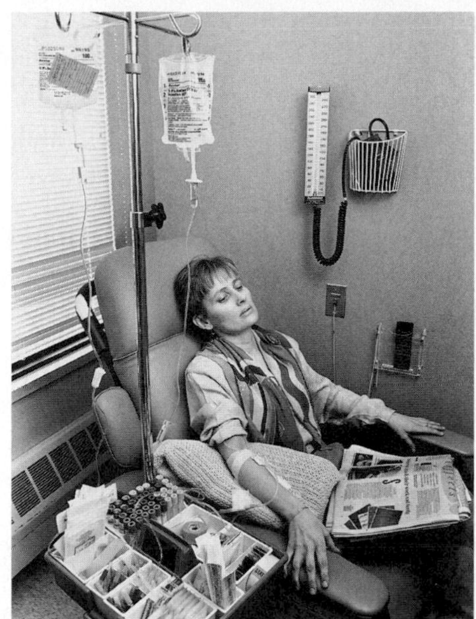

Easing Pain Candy containing capsaicin is sometimes given for the treatment of painful mouth sores associated with cancer chemotherapy (Berger et al., 1995). Capsaicin is what makes chili peppers "hot," but eating enough of it results in desensitization and a corresponding reduction in pain sensations (Bevan & Geppetti, 1994).

cortex and other cortical regions are activated during painful stimulation and that activation in these same regions is reduced when pain is relieved (Fulbright et al., 2001; Rainville, 2002; Wagner et al., 2004). Further, when hypnosis is used to increase or decrease the unpleasantness of pain, there are corresponding changes in the anterior cingulate cortex, but not in the somatosensory cortex (Rainville et al., 1997). Reductions in anterior cingulate cortex activity also occur in response to pain-reducing drugs and even to pain-reducing placebos (Petrovic et al., 2002). Finally, research suggests that pain can be experienced without any external stimulation of pain receptors. In such cases, the pain appears to originate in the activity of neurons within the thalamus and various regions of the cerebral cortex (Canavero et al., 1998; Gawande, 1998b; Helmchen et al., 2002).

Emotional Aspects of Pain All senses can have emotional components, most of which are learned responses. For example, the smell of baking cookies can make you feel good if it has been associated with happy childhood times. The emotional response to pain is more direct. Specific pathways carry an emotional component of the painful stimulus to areas of the hindbrain and reticular formation (see Figure 4.24), as well as to the cingulate cortex via the thalamus (Craig et al., 1994; Johansen, Fields, & Manning, 2001).

Nevertheless, the overall emotional response to pain depends greatly on cognitive factors, that is, on how we think about it (Flor, 2002; Keefe & France, 1999; Pincus & Morley, 2001). For example, experimenters compared responses to a painful stimulus in people who were informed about the nature of the stimulus and when to expect it with responses in people who were not given this information. Knowing about pain seemed to make it less objectionable, even though the sensation was reported to be just as noticeable (Mayer & Price, 1982). Another factor affecting emotional responses to pain sensations is the use of pain-reducing cognitive strategies, such as focusing on distracting thoughts. In one study, distraction created by a cognitively demanding task reduced both the unpleasantness of painful heat stimuli and activity in brain regions involved in processing pain sensations (Bantick et al., 2002).

Modulation of Pain: The Gate Control Theory Pain is extremely useful, because in the long run it protects you from harm. However, there are times when enough is enough. Fortunately, the nervous system has several mechanisms for controlling the experience of pain.

One explanation of how the nervous system controls the amount of pain that reaches the brain is the **gate control theory** (Melzack & Wall, 1965). It holds that there is a "gate" in the spinal cord that either lets pain impulses travel upward to the brain or blocks their progress. Many details of the original gate control theory turned out to be incorrect, but later work supported the idea that natural mechanisms can block pain sensations, so it remains the most comprehensive account of pain modulation (Stanton-Hicks & Salamon, 1997; Sufka & Price, 2002). According to gate control theory, input from other skin senses can come into the spinal cord at the same time the pain gets there and "take over" the pathways that the pain impulses would have used. This appears to be why rubbing the skin around a wound temporarily reduces pain from the wound, and why electrical stimulation of the skin around a painful spot relieves that pain. Gate control theory may also partially explain why scratching relieves itching, because itch sensations involve activity in fibres located close to pain fibres (Andrew & Craig, 2001).

The brain can also close the gate to pain impulses by sending signals down the spinal cord. The control of sensation by messages coming from the brain is a common aspect of sensory systems (Willis, 1988). In the case of pain, these messages from the brain block incoming pain signals at spinal cord synapses. The result is **analgesia**, the absence of the sensation of pain in the presence of a normally painful stimulus. For example, if part of a rat's hindbrain is electrically stimulated, pain signals generated in the skin never reach the brain (Reynolds, 1969). Permanently

gate control theory A theory suggesting that a functional "gate" in the spinal cord can either let pain impulses travel upward to the brain or block their progress.

analgesia The absence of pain sensations in the presence of a normally painful stimulus.

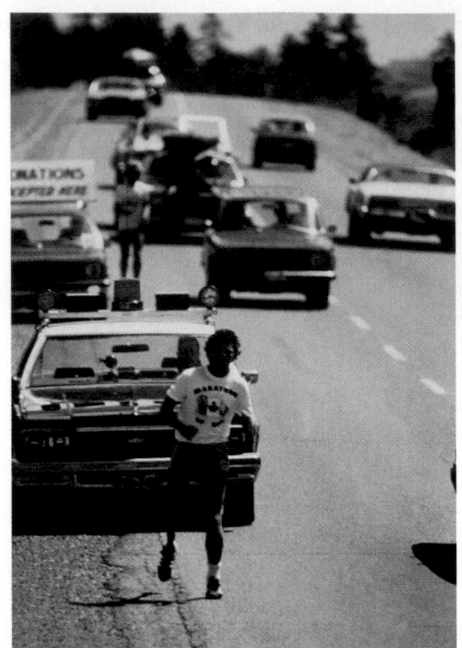

Natural Analgesia The stress of athletic exertion causes the release of endorphins, natural painkillers that may have helped Terry Fox cope with the pain as he ran his Marathon of Hope.

implanting electrodes that stimulate this same region of the human brain has reduced severe pain in some patients, but unfortunately it also produces a profound sense of impending doom (Hoffert, 1992).

Natural Analgesics At least two substances play a role in the brain's ability to block pain signals: (1) the neurotransmitter *serotonin* released by neurons descending from the brain, and (2) natural opiates called *endorphins*. As described in the chapter on biological aspects of psychology, endorphins are natural painkillers that act as neurotransmitters at many levels of the pain pathway, including the spinal cord, where they block the synapses of pain-carrying fibres. Endorphins may also relieve pain when secreted into the bloodstream as hormones by the adrenal and pituitary glands. The more endorphin receptors a person has inherited, the more pain tolerance that person has (Benjamin, Wilson, & Mogil, 1999; Uhl, Sora, & Wang, 1999).

Several conditions are known to cause the body to ease its own pain. For example, endorphins are released by immune cells that arrive at sites of inflammation (Cabot, 2001). And during the late stages of pregnancy, an endorphin system is activated that reduces the mother's labour pains (Dawson-Basoa & Gintzler, 1997). An endorphin system is also activated when people believe they are receiving a painkiller even though they are not (Benedetti & Amanzio, 1997). This phenomenon may be one of the mechanisms underlying the placebo effect, which is discussed in the chapter on research in psychology (Stewart-Williams, 2004). Remarkably, the resulting pain inhibition is experienced in the part of the body where relief was expected to occur, but not elsewhere (Benedetti, Arduino, & Amanzio, 1999). Physical or psychological stress, too, can activate natural analgesic systems. Stress-induced release of endorphins may account for cases in which injured soldiers or athletes continue to perform in the heat of battle or competition with no apparent pain.

There are also mechanisms for reactivating pain sensitivity once a crisis is past. Studies with animals show that they can learn that certain situations signal "safety" and that these safety signals trigger the release of a neurotransmitter that counteracts endorphins' analgesic effects (Wiertelak, Maier, & Watkins, 1992). Blocking these "safety signals" increases the painkilling effects brought on by a placebo (Benedetti & Amanzio, 1997).

THINKING CRITICALLY

Does Acupuncture Relieve Pain?

Acupuncture is an ancient and widely used treatment in Asian medicine that is alleged to relieve pain (Ulett, 2003). The method is based on the idea that body energy flows along lines called *channels* (Vincent & Richardson, 1986). It is said that there are fourteen main channels and that a person's health supposedly depends on the balance of energy flowing in them. Inserting thin needles into the skin and twirling them is meant to stimulate these channels and restore a balanced flow of energy. The needles produce an aching and tingling sensation called *Teh-ch'i* at the site of stimulation, but they relieve pain at distant, seemingly unrelated parts of the body.

- **What am I being asked to believe or accept?**

Acupuncturists assert that twirling a needle in the skin can relieve pain caused by everything from tooth extraction to cancer.

- **What evidence is available to support the assertion?**

There is no scientific evidence for the existence of the energy channels proposed in the theory behind acupuncture. However, as described in the chapter on biological aspects of psychology, some acupuncture stimulation sites are near peripheral nerves, and evidence from MRI scans suggests that stimulating these sites changes

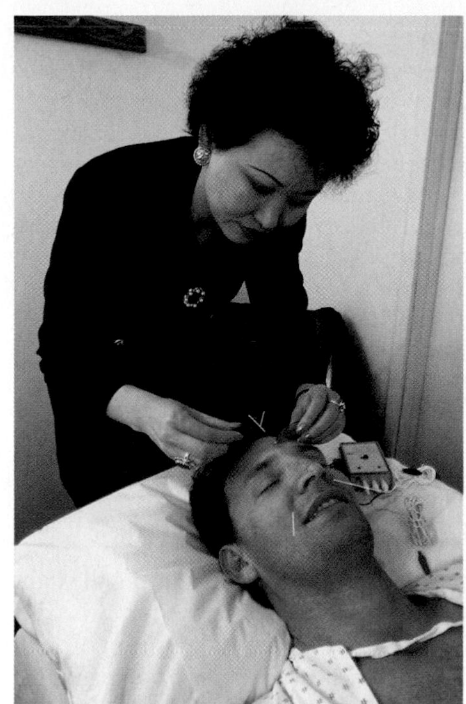

How Does Acupuncture Work? This acupuncturist is inserting fine needles in her patient's face in hopes of treating poor blood circulation in his hands and feet. Acupuncture treatments appear to alleviate a wide range of problems, including many kinds of pain, but the mechanisms through which it works are not yet determined.

activity in brain regions related to the targets of treatment (Cho et al., 1998; Cho, Wong, & Fallon, 2001).

What about the more specific assertions that acupuncture relieves pain and that it does so through direct physical mechanisms? Several studies have shown positive results in patients treated with acupuncture for various kinds of pain (Richardson & Vincent, 1986; Vickers et al., 2004). In one controlled study of headache pain, for example, 33 percent of the patients in a placebo group improved following mock electrical nerve stimulation (which is about the usual proportion of people who respond to a placebo), but 53 percent reported reduced pain following real acupuncture (Dowson, Lewith, & Machin, 1985). Another headache study found both acupuncture and drugs to be superior to a placebo. Each reduced the frequency of headaches, but the drugs were more effective than acupuncture at reducing the severity of headache pain (Hesse, Mogelvang, & Simonsen, 1994). Such well-controlled studies are rare, however, and their results are often contradictory (Ter Riet, Kleijnen, & Knipschild, 1990). Some studies of patients with back or neck pain, for example, have found acupuncture to be no better than a placebo or massage therapy (Cherkin et al., 2001; Irnich et al., 2001; Kerr, Walsh, & Baxter, 2003); others have found that acupuncture benefits certain patients (Kvorning et al., 2004; Meng et al., 2003).

There is evidence that acupuncture activates the endorphin system. It is associated with the release of endorphins in the brain, and drugs that slow the breakdown of opiates also prolong the analgesia produced by acupuncture (He, 1987). Furthermore, the pain-reducing effects of acupuncture during electrical stimulation of a tooth can be reversed by naloxone, a substance that blocks the painkilling effects of endorphins and other opiate drugs. This finding suggests that acupuncture somehow activates the body's natural painkilling system. If acupuncture does activate endorphins, is the activation brought about only through the placebo effect? Probably not entirely, because acupuncture produces naloxone-reversible analgesia in monkeys and rats, who could not have developed positive expectancies by reading about acupuncture (Ha et al., 1981; Kishioka et al., 1994).

● Are there alternative ways of interpreting the evidence?

Yes. Evidence about acupuncture might be interpreted as simply confirming that the body's painkilling system can be stimulated by external means. Acupuncture may merely provide one activating method; there may be other, even more efficient ways of doing so (Ulett, 2003). We already know, for example, that successful placebo treatments for human pain appear to operate by activating the endorphin system.

● What additional evidence would help to evaluate the alternatives?

More placebo-controlled studies of acupuncture are needed, but it is difficult to control for the placebo effect in acupuncture treatment, especially in double-blind fashion (e.g., Kaptchuk, 2001; White et al., 2003). (How could a therapist not know whether the treatment being given was acupuncture or not? And from the patient's perspective, what placebo treatment could look and feel like having a needle inserted and twirled in the skin?) Nevertheless, researchers have tried to separate the psychological and physical effects of acupuncture—for example, by using phony needles; by giving mock electrical nerve stimulation, in which electrodes are attached to the skin but no electricity is delivered; or by stimulating at pain-irrelevant locations (Park, White, & Ernst, 2001).

Researchers must also go beyond focusing on the effects of acupuncture to consider the general relationship between internal painkilling systems and external methods for stimulating them. Regarding acupuncture itself, scientists do not yet know what factors govern its ability to activate the endorphin system. Other important unknowns include the types of pain for which acupuncture is most effective, the types of patients who respond best, and the precise procedures that are most effective.

Balancing Act The smooth coordination of all physical movement, from scratching your nose to complex feats of balance, depends on proprioception, the senses that provide information about the position of the head and body, their movements, and where each body part is in relation to all the others.

- **What conclusions are most reasonable?**

There is little doubt that, although it is not a cure-all, acupuncture can, in some circumstances, relieve pain and reduce nausea (British Medical Association, 2000; National Institutes of Health Consensus Conference, 1998). One study, for example, found that preoperative acupuncture reduced postoperative pain and nausea, decreased the need for pain-relieving drugs, and reduced patients' stress responses (Kotani et al., 2001). Another found electrical-stimulation acupuncture to be more effective than either drugs or mock stimulation at reducing nausea following major breast surgery; the acupuncture group also reported the least postoperative pain (Gan et al., 2004). So although some critics argue that further expenditures for acupuncture research are not warranted, studies are likely to continue. The quality of the methodology and the nature of the results will determine whether acupuncture finds a prominent place in Western medicine.

Proprioception: Sensing Body Position

Most sensory systems receive information from the external world, such as the light reflected from a flower or the feeling of cool water. But, as far as the brain is concerned, the rest of the body is "out there," too. You know about the position of your body and what each of its parts is doing only because sensory systems provide this information to the brain. These sensory systems are called **proprioceptive senses** (*proprioceptive* means "received from one's own").

Vestibular Sense The **vestibular sense** tells the brain about the position of the head (and hence the body) in space and about its general movements. It is often thought of as the *sense of balance*. People usually become aware of the vestibular sense only when they overstimulate it and become dizzy.

The organs for the vestibular sense are two vestibular sacs and three semicircular canals that are part of the inner ear. (You can see the semicircular canals in Figure 4.3; the vestibular sacs connect these canals and the cochlea.) The **vestibular sacs** are filled with fluid and contain small crystals called **otoliths** ("ear stones") that rest on hair endings. The **semicircular canals** are fluid-filled, arc-shaped tubes; tiny hairs extend into the fluid in the canals. When your head moves, the otoliths shift in the vestibular sacs and the fluid moves in the semicircular canals, stimulating hair endings. This process activates neurons that travel with the auditory nerve, signalling the brain about the amount and direction of head movement.

The vestibular system has neural connections to the cerebellum, to the part of the autonomic nervous system (ANS) that affects the digestive system, and to the muscles of the eyes. The connections to the cerebellum help coordinate bodily movements. The connections to the ANS are partly responsible for the nausea that sometimes follows overstimulation of the vestibular system—on amusement park rides, for example. Finally, the connections to the eye muscles create *vestibular-ocular reflexes*. For instance, when your head moves in one direction, your eyes reflexively move in the opposite direction. This reflex allows your eyes to focus on a fixed point in space even if your head is moving—as when you track a ball in flight while running to catch it. You can experience this reflex by having a friend spin you around on a stool for a while. When you stop spinning, try to fix your gaze on one point in the room. You will be temporarily unable to do so, because the excitation of the vestibular system will cause your eyes to move repeatedly in the direction opposite to the spinning. Because vestibular reflexes adapt to the lack of gravity in outer space, astronauts returning to earth have postural and movement difficulties until their vestibular systems readjust to the effects of gravity (Paloski, 1998).

Kinesthesia The sense that tells you where the parts of your body are with respect to one another is **kinesthesia** (pronounced "kin-es-THEE-zha"). You proba-

proprioceptive senses The sensory systems that allow us to know about where we are and what each part of our body is doing.

vestibular sense The proprioceptive sense that provides information about the position of the head (and hence the body) in space and about its movements.

vestibular sacs Organs in the inner ear that connect the semicircular canals and the cochlea and contribute to the body's sense of balance.

otoliths Small crystals in the fluid-filled vestibular sacs of the inner ear that, when shifted by gravity, stimulate nerve cells that inform the brain of the position of the head.

semicircular canals Tubes in the inner ear whose fluid, when shifted by head movements, stimulates nerve cells that tell the brain about those movements.

kinesthesia The sense that tells you where the parts of your body are with respect to one another.

bly do not think much about kinesthetic information, but you definitely use it, and you can demonstrate it for yourself. Close your eyes, hold your arms out in front of you, and try to touch your two index fingertips together. You probably did this easily because your kinesthetic sense told you where each finger was with respect to your body. You also depend on kinesthetic information to guide all your movements. Otherwise, it would be impossible to develop or improve any motor skill, from basic walking to complex athletic movements. These movement patterns become simple and fluid because with practice, the brain uses kinesthetic information automatically.

Normally, kinesthetic information comes primarily from the joints, but it also comes from muscles. Receptors in muscle fibres send information to the brain about the stretching of muscles (McCloskey, 1978). When the position of the bones changes, receptors in the joints transduce this mechanical energy into neural activity, providing information about both the rate of change and the angle of the bones. This coded information goes to the spinal cord and is sent from there to the thalamus, along with sensory information from the skin. Eventually the information goes to the cerebellum and to the somatosensory cortex (see Figures 3.13 and 3.17), both of which are involved in the smooth coordination of movements.

Proprioception is a critical sense for success in physical therapy and rehabilitative medicine, especially for people who have to relearn how to move their muscles after strokes or other problems. Research in a branch of physics called *nonlinear dynamics* has been applied to problems in proprioception. For example, using the discovery that the right amount of random, background noise can improve the detection of signals, rehabilitation neurologists have added a small amount of vibration (or "noise") to muscle and joint sensations. This procedure dramatically increases patients' ability to detect joint movements and position (Glanz, 1997). (See "In Review: Body Senses" for a summary of our discussion of touch, temperature, pain, and kinesthesia.)

in review Body Senses

Sense	Energy	Conversion of Physical Energy to Nerve Activity	Pathways and Characteristics
Touch	Mechanical deformation of skin	Skin receptors (may be stimulated by hair on the skin)	Nerve endings respond to changes in weight (intensity) and location of touch
Temperature	Heat	Sensory neurons in the skin	Changes in temperature are detected by warm-sensing and cool-sensing fibres. Temperature interacts with touch
Pain	Increases with intensity of touch or temperature	Free nerve endings in or near the skin surface	Changes in intensity cause the release of chemicals detected by receptors in pain neurons. Some fibres convey sharp pain; others convey dull aches and burning sensations
Kinesthesia	Mechanical energy of joint and muscle movement	Receptors in muscle fibres	Information from muscle fibres is sent to the spinal cord, thalamus, cerebellum, and cortex

FOCUS ON RESEARCH METHODS

The Case of the Mysterious Spells

Early in this chapter we discussed the doctrine of specific nerve energies, which says that each sensory system can send information to the brain only about its own sense, regardless of how the stimulation occurs. So gently pressing on your closed eye will send touch sensations from the skin on your eyelid and visual sensations from your eye. The following case study suggests that this doctrine applies even when stimulation of sensory systems arises from within the brain itself.

- **What was the researcher's question?**

A thirty-one-year-old woman we'll call "Linda" reported that, for many years, she had been experiencing recurring "spells" that began with what seemed like sexual sensations (Janszky et al., 2002). These "orgasm-like euphoric erotic sensations" were followed by a staring, unresponsive state in which she lost consciousness. The spells, which occurred without warning and in response to no obvious trigger, interfered severely with her ability to function normally in everyday life. Linda was examined by József Janszky, a neurologist, who suspected that she might be suffering from epilepsy, a seizure disorder in which nerve cells in the brain suddenly start firing uncontrollably. The symptoms of an epileptic seizure depend on which brain areas are activated. Seizures that activate the motor area of the cerebral cortex will cause uncontrollable movements, seizures that activate visual cortex will create the sensation of images, and so on. Could there be a specific brain region that, when activated by a seizure, cause the sensations of orgasm that are normally caused by external stimulation?

- **How did the researcher answer the question?**

It is not easy to study the neurological basis of sexual sensations because most people are understandably reluctant to allow researchers to monitor their sexual activity. In the process of diagnosing Linda's problem, Janszky had a unique opportunity to learn something about the origin of orgasmic sensations without intruding on his patient's privacy. His approach exemplifies the *case study* method of research. As described in the chapter on research in psychology, case studies focus intensively on a particular individual, group, or situation. Sometimes they lead to important insights about clinical problems or other phenomena that occur so rarely that they cannot be studied through surveys or controlled experiments. In this case, Janszky decided to study Linda's brain activity while she was actually having a spell. He reasoned that if the spells were caused by seizures in a specific brain region, it might be possible to eliminate the problem through surgery.

- **What did the researcher find?**

Linda's brain activity was recorded during five of her spells, using electroencephalography (EEG), a method described in more detail in the chapter on biological aspects of psychology. During each spell, the EEG showed that she was having seizures in the right temporal lobe of her brain. A subsequent MRI of her brain revealed a small area of abnormal tissue in the same area of the right temporal lobe. The organization of nerve cells in abnormal brain tissue can make it easier for seizures to occur, so Linda was advised to have some tissue surgically removed from the problem area. After the surgery, her seizures stopped.

- **What do the results mean?**

Janszky concluded that Linda had been having "localization-related epilepsy," meaning that her spells were seizures coming from a specific brain location. This conclusion was supported by the fact that she had right temporal lobe seizures on the EEG each time she had a typical spell. Her MRI showed an abnormality in the same region that commonly gives rise to seizures, and her spells disappeared after the abnormality was removed. Linda's case also led Janszky to suggest that the right temporal lobe may play a special role in creating the sensory experience of orgasm.

- **What do we still need to know?**

Janszky's suggestion might indeed be correct, meaning that activation of the right temporal cortex may be sufficient for the sensory experience of orgasm. But at least one important question remains. How specific is the linkage between activity in this brain region and the sensory experiences of orgasm? Could seizures in other brain regions cause similar experiences, for example? Is right temporal cortex activity one of many ways to generate orgasm-like experiences, or is it necessary for these experiences? Answering this question would be easier if we knew whether Linda continued to experience orgasms during sexual activity. If she did, the implication would be that the area of right temporal lobe tissue that was removed was not necessary for the experience of orgasm. Unfortunately, Janszky's report is silent on this point, but future cases and further research will no doubt shed additional light on this fascinating sensory puzzle.

LINKAGES

As noted in the chapter on introducing psychology, all of psychology's many subfields are related to one another. Our discussion of the representation of the sensory system in the brain illustrates just one way in which the topic of this chapter, sensation, is linked to the subfield of biological psychology, which is the focus of the chapter on biological aspects of psychology. The Linkages diagram shows ties to two other subfields as well, and there are many more ties throughout the book. Looking for linkages among subfields will help you see how they all fit together and help you appreciate the big picture that is psychology.

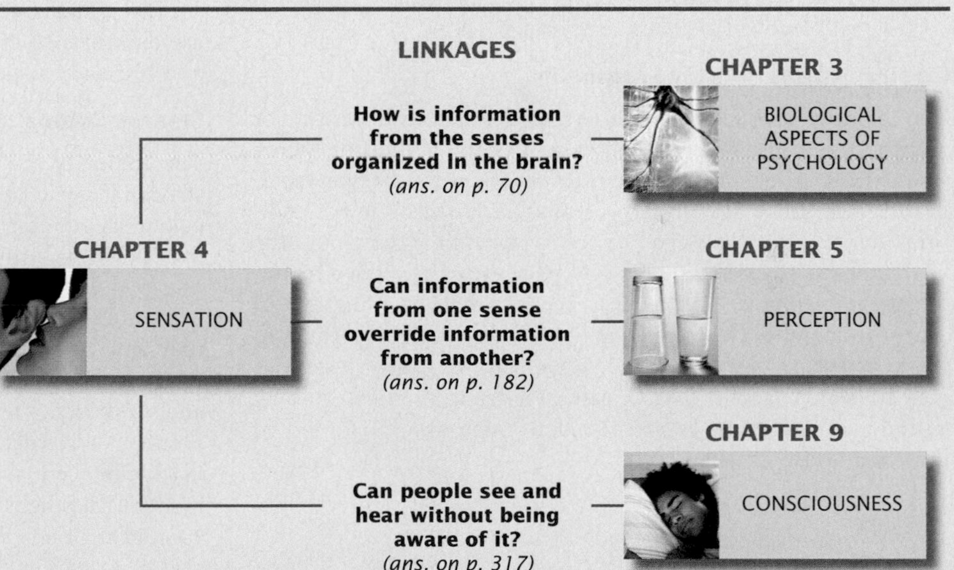
LINKAGES
CHAPTER 3
How is information from the senses organized in the brain?
(ans. on p. 70)
BIOLOGICAL ASPECTS OF PSYCHOLOGY
CHAPTER 4
SENSATION
CHAPTER 5
Can information from one sense override information from another?
(ans. on p. 182)
PERCEPTION
CHAPTER 9
Can people see and hear without being aware of it?
(ans. on p. 317)
CONSCIOUSNESS

SUMMARY

A *sense* is a system that translates information from outside the nervous system into neural activity. Messages from the senses are called *sensations*.

Sensory Systems

The first step in sensation involves *accessory structures*, which collect and modify sensory stimuli. The second step is *transduction*, the process of converting incoming energy into neural activity; it is accomplished by *sensory receptors*, cells specialized to detect energy of some type. *Adaptation* takes place when receptors receive unchanging stimulation. Neural activity is transferred through the thalamus (except in the case of olfaction) and on to the cortex.

The Problem of Coding

Coding is the translation of physical properties of a stimulus into a pattern of neural activity that specifically identifies those physical properties. It is the language the brain uses to describe sensations. Coding is characterized by the *doctrine of specific nerve energies*: Stimulation of a particular sensory nerve provides codes for that one sense, no matter how the stimulation takes place. There are two basic types of sensory codes: *temporal codes* and *spatial codes*.

Hearing

Sound is a repetitive fluctuation in the pressure of a medium such as air. It travels in waves.

Sound

The *frequency* (which is related to *wavelength*) and *amplitude* of sound waves approximately correspond to the psychological dimensions of *pitch* and *loudness*, respectively. *Timbre*, the quality of sound, depends on complex wave patterns added to the lowest frequency of the sound.

The Ear

The energy from sound waves is collected and transmitted to the *cochlea* through a series of accessory structures, including the *tympanic membrane*. Transduction occurs when sound energy stimulates hair cells of the organ of Corti on the *basilar membrane* of the cochlea that in turn stimulate the *auditory nerve*.

Auditory Pathways, Representations, and Experiences

Auditory information is relayed through the thalamus to the *primary auditory cortex* and to other areas of auditory cortex. Sounds of similar frequency activate neighbouring cells in the cortex, but loudness is coded temporally.

Coding Intensity and Frequency

The intensity of a sound stimulus is coded by the firing rate of auditory neurons. *Place theory* describes the coding of higher frequencies: They are coded by the place on the basilar membrane where the wave envelope peaks. Each neuron in the auditory nerve is most sensitive to a specific frequency (its characteristic frequency). Very low frequencies are coded by frequency matching, which refers to the fact that the firing rate of a neuron matches the frequency of a sound wave. According to *frequency-matching theory*, or volley theory, some frequencies may be matched by the firing rate of a group of neurons. Low to moderate frequencies are coded through a combination of these methods.

Vision

Light

Visible light is electromagnetic radiation with a wavelength of about 400 nanometres to about 750 nanometres. *Light intensity*, or the amount of energy in light, determines its brightness. Differing *light wavelengths* are sensed as different colours.

Focusing Light

Accessory structures of the eye include the *cornea*, *pupil*, *iris*, and *lens*. Through *accommodation* and other means, these structures focus light rays on the *retina*, the netlike structure of cells at the back of the eye.

Converting Light into Images

Photoreceptors in the retina—*rods* and *cones*—have *photopigments* and can transduce light into neural activity. Rods and cones differ in their shape, their sensitivity to light, their ability to discriminate colours, and their distribution across the retina. The *fovea*, the area of highest *acuity*, has only cones, which are colour sensitive. Rods are more sensitive to light but do not discriminate colours; they are distributed in areas around the fovea. Both types of photoreceptors contribute to *dark adaptation*. From the photoreceptors, energy transduced from light is transferred to bipolar cells and then to *ganglion cells*, aided by lateral connections between photoreceptors, bipolar cells, and ganglion cells. Through *lateral inhibition*, the retina enhances the contrast between dark and light areas. Most ganglion cells, in effect, compare the amount of light falling on the centre of their *receptive fields* with that falling on the surrounding area.

Visual Pathways

The ganglion cells send action potentials out of the eye, at a point where a *blind spot* is created. Axons of ganglion cells leave the eye as a bundle of fibres called the *optic nerve*; half of these fibres cross over at the *optic chiasm* and terminate in the *lateral geniculate nucleus* (LGN) of the thalamus. Neurons in the LGN send visual information on to the *primary visual cortex*.

Visual Representations

Visual form, colour, movement, and distance are processed by parallel systems. Complex *feature detectors* in the visual cortex are built in hierarchical fashion out of simpler units that detect and respond to features such as lines, edges, and orientations.

Seeing Colour

The colour of an object depends on which of the wavelengths striking it are absorbed and which are reflected. The sensation of colour has three psychological dimensions: *hue*, *saturation*, and *brightness*. According to the *trichromatic* (or Young-Helmholtz) *theory*, colour vision results from the fact that the eye has three types of cones, each of which is most sensitive to short, medium, or long wavelengths. Information from the three types combines to produce the sensation of colour. Individuals vary in the number and sensitivity of their cone pigments. According to the *opponent-process* (or Hering) *theory*, there are red-green, blue-yellow, and black-white visual elements in the eye. Members of each pair inhibit each other so that only one member of a pair may produce a signal at a time. This theory explains colour afterimages, as well as the fact that lights of complementary colours cancel each other out and produce grey when mixed together.

Interaction of the Senses: Synaesthesia

Various dimensions of vision interact, and vision can also interact with hearing and other senses in a process known as *synaesthesia*. For example, some people experience certain colours when stimulated by certain letters, numbers, or sounds.

The Chemical Senses: Smell and Taste

The chemical senses include olfaction (smell) and gustation (taste).

Olfaction

Olfaction detects volatile chemicals that come into contact with olfactory receptors in the nose. Olfactory signals are sent to the *olfactory bulb* in the brain without passing through the thalamus. *Pheromones* are odours from one animal that change the physiology or behaviour of another animal; in mammals, pheromones act through the *vomeronasal organ*.

Gustation

Gustation detects chemicals that come into contact with taste receptors in *papillae* on the tongue. Elementary taste sensations are limited to sweet, sour, bitter, salty, umami, and astringent. The combined responses of many taste buds determine a taste sensation.

Smell, Taste, and Flavour

The senses of smell and taste interact to produce flavour.

Somatic Senses and the Vestibular System

The *somatic senses*, or somatosensory systems, include skin senses and proprioceptive senses. The skin senses include touch, temperature, and pain.

Touch and Temperature

Nerve endings in the skin generate touch sensations when they are stimulated. Some nerve endings are sensitive to temperature, and some respond to both temperature and touch. Signals from neighbouring points on the skin stay next to one another all the way to the cortex.

Pain

Pain provides information about damaging stimuli. Sharp pain and dull, chronic pain are carried by different fibres—A-delta and C fibres, respectively. The emotional response to pain depends on how the painful stimulus is interpreted. According to the *gate control theory*, incoming pain signals can be blocked by a "gate" in the spinal cord. Messages sent down the spinal cord from the brain also can block pain signals, producing *analgesia*. Endorphins act at several levels of the pain systems to reduce sensations of pain.

Proprioception: Sensing Body Position

Proprioceptive senses provide information about the body. The *vestibular sense* provides information about the position of the head in space through the *otoliths* in *vestibular sacs* and the *semicircular canals*, and *kinesthesia* provides information about the positions of body parts with respect to one another.

5 Perception

You are using perception right now in order to understand this sentence. Perception allows you to translate the shapes and patterns of the letters you see here and turn them into meaningful words and sentences. Without perception, you could still see the letters, but they would make no more sense than if they were written in an unfamiliar alphabet. In this chapter, we tell you more about the amazing perceptual systems that allow you to understand what you see and hear. We have organized our presentation as follows:

At a traffic circle in Scotland, fourteen fatal accidents occurred in a single year, partly because drivers failed to slow down as they approached the circle. When warning signs failed to solve the problem, Gordon Denton, a British psychologist, proposed an ingenious solution. White lines were painted across the road leading to the circle, in a pattern that looked something like this:

/ / / / / / / / /////

If drivers crossed these progressively more closely spaced lines at a constant speed, they got the impression that they were going faster, and their automatic response was to slow down (Denton, 1980). During the fourteen months after Denton's idea was put to use, there were only two fatalities at the traffic circle. The same striping is now being used to slow drivers on roads approaching small towns in many countries, including Canada. Denton's solution to this problem relied heavily on his knowledge of the principles of human perception.

Perception is the process through which sensations are interpreted, using knowledge and understanding of the world, so that they become meaningful experiences. Perception is not a passive process of simply absorbing and decoding incoming sensations. If it were, our experience of the environment would be a constantly changing, utterly confusing mishmash of light and colour. Instead, our brains take sensations and create a coherent world, often by filling in missing information and using past experience to give meaning to what we see, hear, or touch. For example, the raw sensations coming to your eyes from Figure 5.1 convey only the information that there is a series of intersecting lines. But your perceptual system automatically interprets this image as a rectangle (or window frame) on its side.

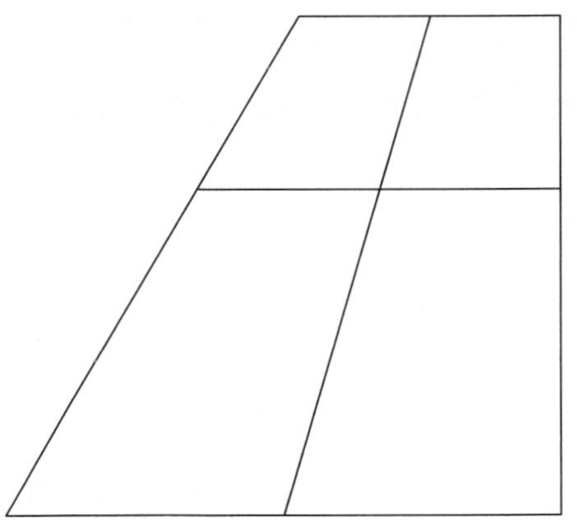

figure 5.1
What Do You See?

Let's first consider these perceptual processes and the various approaches that psychologists have taken in trying to understand them. We will then explore how people detect incoming sensory stimuli, organize these sensations into stable patterns, and recognize those patterns. We'll also examine the role of attention in guiding the perceptual system to analyze some parts of the world more closely than others. Finally, we provide examples of how research on perception has been applied to some practical problems.

The Perception Paradox

As in the case of drivers who find themselves slowing down in response to lines on the pavement, perception often takes place automatically, without conscious awareness. This quick and seemingly effortless aspect of perceptual processing suggests that perception is a rather simple affair. But perception contains a basic contradiction, or paradox: What is so easy for the perceiver to do has proven difficult for psychologists to understand and explain. The difficulty lies in the fact that to function so effectively and efficiently, our perceptual systems must be exceedingly complex.

To illustrate the workings of these complex systems, psychologists draw attention to *perceptual failures*, cases in which our perceptual experience of a stimulus differs from the actual characteristics of that stimulus. You can experience a perceptual failure for yourself by looking at Figure 5.2. Perceptual failures provide clues to the problems that our perception systems must solve and to the solutions they reach. Consider, for example, why the two lines in Figure 5.2 appear to differ in length. Part of the answer is that your visual system always tries to interpret stimuli as three-dimensional, even when they are not. A three-dimensional interpretation of the drawing would lead you to see the two lines as defining the edges of two parallel paths, one of which ends closer to you than the other. Because your eyes tell you that the two paths start at about the same point (the castle entrance), you solved the perceptual problem by assuming that the closer line must be the longer of the

perception The process through which people take raw sensations from the environment and interpret them, using knowledge, experience, and understanding of the world, so that the sensations become meaningful experiences.

figure 5.2

Misperceiving Reality

Which line is longer: Line A-C or Line A-B? They are exactly the same length, but you probably perceived A-C as longer. Understanding why our perceptual systems make this kind of error has helped psychologists understand the basic principles of perception.

two. You can remove the three-dimensional cues by tracing the two intersecting lines onto a sheet of clear plastic and placing it on a white surface. In this more clearly two-dimensional display, the impression of unequal length will disappear.

Three Approaches to Perception

Like Jim Parker, of the University of Calgary, Alberta, some researchers take the **computational approach** to try to determine the computations that a computer would have to perform to solve perceptual problems. Understanding these computations, they believe, will help explain how complex computations within the nervous systems of humans and animals might turn raw, sensory stimulation into representations of the world (Green, 1991; Heekeren, et al., 2004; Palmer, 1999; Parker, 2003). Computational theorists also hope that it might eventually be possible to build computer-based robots capable of near-human levels of perceptual skill at jobs such as bomb detection, product inspection, and the like (Zurada, 1995). The computational approach owes much to two earlier, but still influential, views of perception: the constructivist approach and the ecological approach.

Psychologists who take the **constructivist approach** argue that our perceptual systems construct a representation of reality from fragments of sensory information. They are particularly interested in situations in which the same stimulus creates different perceptions in different people. Stimuli such as those in Figure 5.2, for example, create optical illusions in some cultures but may not do so in those in which people have not had experience with the objects or perspectives shown (Leibowitz et al., 1969). Desmond Mulligan, Michael Dobson, and Janet McCracken of Simon Fraser University, British Columbia, suggest that the constructivist approach emphasizes the influence of past experiences and prior knowledge on the perceptual process (Mulligan et al., 2004). So, for example, if a desk prevents you from seeing the lower half of a person seated behind it, you still "see" the person as a complete human being. Experience tells you to expect that people remain intact even when parts of them are hidden.

Some researchers, such as Catherine Gustavino from the University of Toronto, Ontario, and her colleagues, are influenced by the ecological approach to perception (c.f. Gustavino et al., 2005). Researchers influenced by the **ecological approach**

computational approach An approach to perception that focuses on how computations by the nervous system translate raw sensory stimulation into an experience of reality.

constructivist approach A view of perception taken by those who argue that the perceptual system uses fragments of sensory information to construct an image of reality.

ecological approach An approach to perception maintaining that humans and other species are so well adapted to their natural environment that many aspects of the world are perceived without requiring higher-level analysis and inferences.

Is Anything Missing? Because you know what animals look like, you perceive a whole cat in this picture even though its midsection is hidden. The constructivist approach to perception emphasizes our ability to use knowledge and expectations to fill in the gaps in incomplete objects and to perceive them as unified wholes, not disjointed parts.

to perception claim that rather than depending on interpretations, inferences, and expectations, most of our perceptual experience comes directly from the wealth of information contained in the stimuli reaching us from the environment. This perspective has been summed up as follows: "Ask not what's inside your head, but what your head's inside of" (Mace, 1977). J. J. Gibson (1979), founder of the ecological approach, argued that the primary goal of perception is to support actions, such as walking, grasping, or driving, by "tuning in" to the part of the environmental stimulus array that is most important for performing those actions. So these researchers are less interested in our inferences about the person behind the desk than in how we would use visual information from that person, from the desk, and from other objects in the room to guide us as we walk toward a chair and sit down (Nakayama, 1994).

In summary: To explain perception, the *computational* approach focuses on the nervous system's manipulations of incoming signals, the *constructivist* approach emphasizes the inferences that people make about the environment, and the *ecological* approach emphasizes the information provided by the environment. Later, we discuss evidence in support of each of these approaches.

Psychophysics

How can psychologists measure perceptions when there is no way to get inside people's heads to experience what they are experiencing? One solution to this problem is to present people with lights, sounds, and other stimuli and ask them to report their perception of the stimuli, using special scales of measurement. This method of studying perception, called **psychophysics,** describes the relationship between *physical energy* in the environment and our *psychological experience* of that energy (e.g., Purves et al., 2004).

psychophysics An area of research focusing on the relationship between the physical characteristics of environmental stimuli and the psychological experiences those stimuli produce.

absolute threshold The minimum amount of stimulus energy that can be detected 50 percent of the time.

Absolute Thresholds: Is Something Out There?

How much stimulus energy is needed to trigger a conscious perceptual experience? The minimum amount of light, sound, pressure, or other physical energy we can detect is called the **absolute threshold** (see Table 5.1). Stimuli below this threshold—stimuli that are too weak or too brief for us to notice—are traditionally referred to

table 5.1

Absolute thresholds can be amazingly low. Here are examples of stimulus equivalents at the absolute threshold for the five primary senses in humans. Set up the conditions for testing the absolute threshold for sound, and see if you can detect this minimal amount of auditory stimulation. If you can't hear it, the signal-detection theory we discuss later in this chapter may help explain why.

Source: Galanter (1962).

Some Absolute Thresholds

Human Sense	Absolute Threshold Is Equivalent to:
Vision	A candle flame seen at 48.27 km on a clear night
Hearing	The tick of a watch under quiet conditions at 6.096 m
Taste	5 mL of sugar in 7.56 L of water
Smell	1 drop of perfume diffused into the entire volume of air in a 6-room apartment
Touch	The wing of a fly falling on your cheek from a distance of 1 cm

as **subliminal stimuli.** Stimuli above the absolute threshold—stimuli that are consistently perceived—are referred to as **supraliminal stimuli.**

If you were participating in a typical experiment to measure the absolute threshold for vision, you would sit in a darkened laboratory. After your eyes adapted to the darkness, you would be presented with a long series of brief flashes of light that varied in brightness. After each one, you would be asked if you saw a stimulus. If your absolute threshold were truly "absolute," your detection accuracy should jump from 0 to 100 percent at the exact level of brightness where your threshold is. This ideal absolute threshold is illustrated by the point at which the green line in Figure 5.3 suddenly rises. But research shows that the average of your responses over many trials would actually form a curve much like the purple line in that figure. In other words, the "absolute" threshold is not really an all-or-nothing phenomenon. Notice in Figure 5.3 that a flash whose brightness (intensity) is 3 is detected 20 percent of the time and missed 80 percent of the time. Is that stimulus *subliminal* or *supraliminal*? Psychologists have dealt with questions of this sort by redefining the absolute threshold as the minimum amount of stimulus energy that can be detected 50 percent of the time.

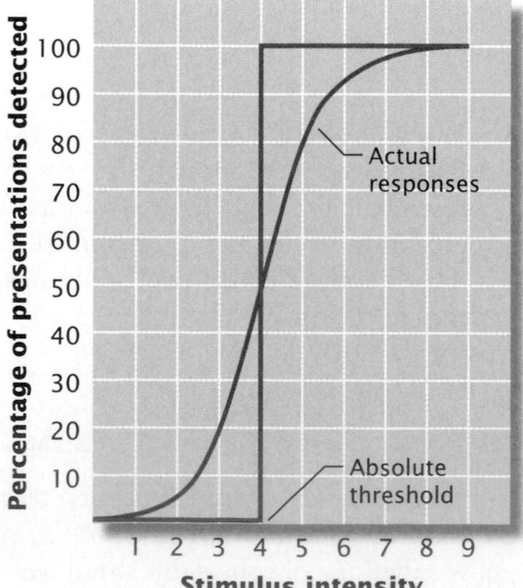

figure 5.3

The Absolute Threshold

The curve shows the relationship between the intensity of a signal and the likelihood that it will be detected. If the absolute threshold were truly absolute, signals at or above a particular intensity would always be detected, and signals below that intensity would never be detected (see green line). But this response pattern almost never occurs, so the "absolute" threshold is defined as the intensity at which the signal is detected with 50 percent accuracy.

subliminal stimuli Stimuli that are too weak or brief to be perceived.

supraliminal stimuli Stimuli that are strong enough to be consistently perceived.

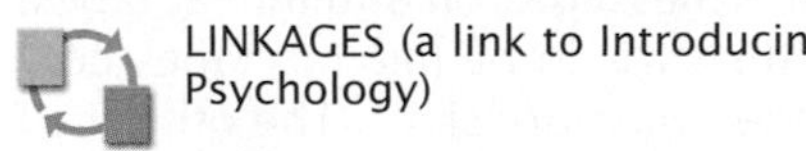

THINKING CRITICALLY

Can Subliminal Stimuli Influence Your Behaviour?

LINKAGES (a link to Introducing Psychology)

In 1957, an adman named James Vicary claimed that a New Jersey theatre flashed messages such as "buy popcorn" and "drink Coke" on a movie screen, too briefly to be noticed, while customers watched the movie *Picnic*. He said that these subliminal messages caused a 15 percent rise in sales of Coca Cola and a 58 percent increase in popcorn sales. Can such "mind control" really work? Many people seem to think so: They spend millions of dollars each year on audiotapes and videos that promise subliminal help to lose weight, raise self-esteem, quit smoking, make more money, or achieve other goals.

- **What am I being asked to believe or accept?**

Two types of claims have been made about subliminal stimuli. The more general claim is that subliminal stimuli can influence our behaviour. The second, more specific assertion is that subliminal stimuli provide an effective means of changing people's buying habits, political opinions, self-confidence, and other complex attitudes and behaviours, with or without their awareness or consent.

- **What evidence is available to support the assertion?**

Most evidence for the first claim—that subliminal stimuli can influence behaviour in a general way—comes from research on visual perception. For example, using a method called *subliminal priming*, participants are shown clearly visible (supraliminal) stimuli, such as pictures of people, and then asked to make some sort of judgment about them. Unbeknownst to the participants, however, each of the visible pictures is preceded by other pictures or words flashed so briefly that the participants are unaware of them. The critical question is whether the information in the subliminal stimuli influences participants' responses to the supraliminal stimuli that follow them.

In one subliminal priming study, visible pictures of individuals were preceded by subliminal pictures that were either "positive" (e.g., happy children) or "negative" (e.g., a monster). The participants in this study judged the people in the visible pictures as more likable, polite, friendly, successful, and reputable when their pictures had been preceded by a subliminal picture that was positive rather than negative (Krosnick et al., 1992). Researchers have also found that subliminally presented words can influence decisions about the meaning of words. For example, after being exposed to subliminal presentations of a man's name (e.g., "Tom"), participants were able to decide more rapidly whether a supraliminal stimulus (e.g., "John") was a man's or woman's name. However, the impact of the subliminally presented name lasted for only about one-tenth of a second (Greenwald, Draine, & Abrams, 1996).

Other research shows that subliminal stimuli can lead to a change in people's physiological responses. In one study, participants were exposed to subliminal photos of snakes, spiders, flowers, and mushrooms while researchers recorded their *galvanic skin resistance (GSR)*, a measure of physiological arousal. Although the slides were flashed too quickly to be perceived consciously, participants who were afraid of snakes or spiders showed increased GSR measurements (and reported fear) in response to snake and spider photos (Öhman & Soares, 1994).

The results of studies such as these support the claim that subliminal information can have at least a temporary impact on judgment and emotion, but they say little or nothing about the effects of subliminal advertising or the value of subliminal self-help tapes. In fact, there is no laboratory evidence to support the alleged effectiveness of such tapes. Their promoters offer only testimonials from satisfied customers.

- **Are there alternative ways of interpreting the evidence?**

Many claims for subliminal advertising—including those reported in the New Jersey theatre case we mentioned—have turned out to be publicity stunts using fabricated data (Haberstroh, 1995; Pratkanis, 1992). And testimonials from people who have purchased subliminal tapes may be biased by what these people want to believe about the product they bought. This interpretation is supported by experiments that manipulate the beliefs of participants regarding the messages on subliminal tapes. In one study, half the participants were told that they would be hearing tapes containing subliminal messages that would improve their memory skills. The other half were told that the subliminal messages would improve their self-esteem. However, half the participants who expected self-esteem tapes actually received memory-improvement tapes, and half the participants who expected memory-improvement tapes actually received self-esteem tapes. Regardless of which tapes they actually heard, participants who thought they had heard memory-enhancement messages reported improved memory; those who thought they had heard self-esteem messages said that their self-esteem had improved (Pratkanis, Eskenazi, & Greenwald, 1994). In other words, the effects of the tapes were determined by the listeners' expectations—not by the tapes' subliminal content.

- **What additional evidence would help to evaluate the alternatives?**

The effectiveness of self-help tapes and other subliminal products must be evaluated through further experiments—like the one just mentioned—that carefully control for expectations. Those who advocate subliminal influence methods are responsible for conducting those experiments, but as long as customers are willing to buy subliminal products on the basis of testimonials alone, any scientific evaluation efforts will probably come from those interested in consumer protection.

- **What conclusions are most reasonable?**

Available scientific evidence suggests that subliminal perception does occur but that it has no potential for "mind control" (Greenwald, Klinger, & Schuh, 1995). Subliminal effects are usually small and short-lived, and they mainly affect simple judgments and general measures of overall arousal. Most researchers agree that subliminal messages have no special power to create major changes in people's needs, goals, skills, or actions (Pratkanis, 1992). In fact, advertisements, political speeches, and other messages that people *can* perceive consciously have far stronger persuasive effects.

Signal-Detection Theory

Look again at Figure 5.3. It shows that stimuli just above and just below the absolute threshold are sometimes detected and sometimes missed. For example, a stimulus at intensity level 3 appears to be subliminal, even though you will perceive it 20 percent of the time; a stimulus at level 5 is above threshold, but it will be missed 20 percent of the time. Why should the "absolute" threshold vary this way? The two most important reasons have to do with sensitivity and our response criterion.

Sensitivity refers to our ability to pick out a particular stimulus, or *signal*. Sensitivity is influenced by the *intensity of the signal* (stronger ones are easier to detect), the *capacity of sensory systems* (good vision or hearing makes us more sensitive), and the *amount of background stimulation*, or *noise*, arriving at the same time. Some noise comes from outside the person, as when electrical equipment hums or overhead lights flicker. There is also noise coming from the spontaneous, random firing of cells of our own nervous system. Varying amounts of this *internal noise* is always occurring, whether or not we are stimulated by physical energy. You might think of it as a little like the "snow" on an unused television channel or the static between radio stations.

The second source of variation in absolute threshold comes from the **response criterion,** which reflects our willingness to respond to a stimulus. Motivation—wants and needs—as well as expectancies affect the response criterion. Suppose, for example, that you worked at an airport security checkpoint where you spent hours

sensitivity The ability to detect a stimulus.

response criterion The internal rule a person uses to decide whether or not to report a stimulus.

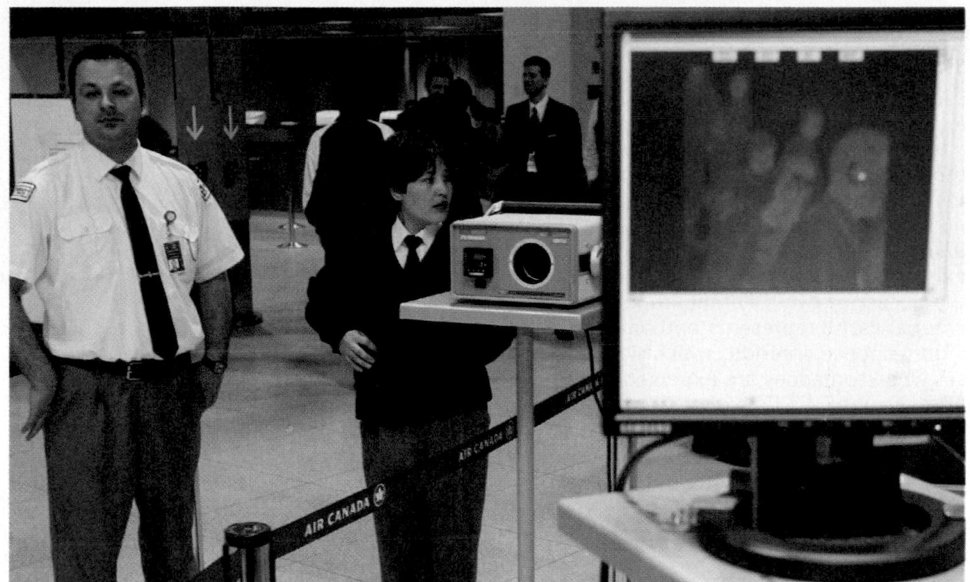

Detecting Vital Signals According to signal-detection theory, the likelihood that airport security screeners will detect the outline of a weapon in x-rays of a passenger's luggage depends partly on the sensitivity of their visual systems and partly on their response criterion. That criterion is affected by their expectations that weapons might appear and by how motivated they are to look carefully for them. To help keep inspectors' response criteria sufficiently low, airport security officials occasionally attempt to smuggle a simulated weapon through a checkpoint. This procedure serves to evaluate the inspectors, and it also helps keep them focused on their vital task (McCarley et al., 2004).

looking at x-ray images of people's handbags, briefcases, and luggage. The signal to be detected in this situation is a weapon, whereas the "noise" consists of harmless objects in a person's luggage, vague or distorted images on the viewing screen, and anything else that is not a weapon. If there were a terrorist attack, you would be put on special alert. Accordingly, your response criterion for saying some questionable object on the x-ray image might be a weapon would be much lower than it was before the attack. In other words, expecting a stimulus makes it more likely that you will detect it than if it is unexpected.

Once researchers understood that detecting a signal depends on a combination of each person's sensitivity and response criterion, they realized that the measurement of absolute thresholds could never be more precise than the 50 percent rule mentioned earlier. So they abandoned the notion of absolute thresholds and focused instead on **signal-detection theory,** a mathematical model of how each person's sensitivity and response criterion combine to determine decisions about whether or not a near-threshold stimulus has occurred (Green & Swets, 1966).

As in a threshold experiment, a psychologist using signal-detection theory would analyze your responses to a series of trials on which lights (or sounds) may or may not be presented. The lights would be so faint that you would find it hard to tell whether a signal occurred, or whether there was only background "noise." Your response on each trial would be placed into one of four categories: a false alarm, a miss, a hit, or a correct rejection. A *false alarm* is an error that occurs when external or internal noise is high enough to make you report a signal when no signal was presented. If a signal occurs but is so faint that it does not produce enough stimulation for you to detect it, you will have made an error known as a *miss.* A person with a more sensitive sensory system might have correctly detected that same stimulus when it occurred—which is called a *hit.* If no signal occurs and you don't report one, you will have made a *correct rejection.* By analyzing the pattern of hits, misses, false alarms, and correct rejections, research based on signal-detection theory allows precise measurement of people's sensitivity to stimuli of any kind. It also provides a way to understand and predict people's responses in a wide range of situations (Palmer, 1999; Swets, 1992, 1996).

Consider weather forecasting. Signal-detection theory can help us understand why, even with the latest Doppler radar systems, weather forecasters sometimes fail to warn of a tornado that local residents can clearly see (Stevens, 1995). The forecasters' task is not easy, because their sensitive radar systems respond not only to dangerous shifts in wind direction (wind shear) and a tornado's spinning funnel but also to trivial stimuli such as swirling dust and swarming insects. So even

signal-detection theory A mathematical model of what determines a person's report that a near-threshold stimulus has or has not occurred.

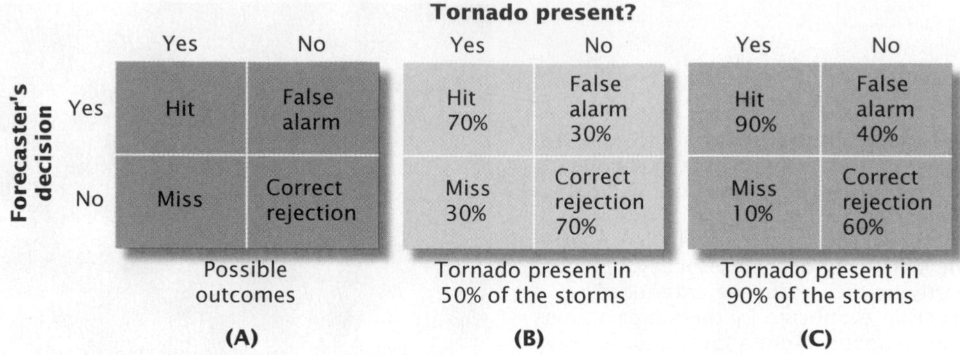

figure 5.4

Signal Detection

Part A shows the possible outcomes of examining a radar display for signs of a tornado: a *hit* (correctly detecting the tornado), a *miss* (failing to detect the tornado), a *correct rejection* (seeing no tornado when there is none), or a *false alarm* (reporting a tornado when none existed). The rest of the figure illustrates the impact of two different response criteria: Part B represents outcomes of a high response criterion, which would be set when tornadoes are expected only 50 percent of the time; Part C represents outcomes of a low response criterion, which would be set when tornadoes are expected 90 percent of the time.

the tell-tale radar "signature" of a tornado appears against a potentially confusing background of visual "noise." Whether or not that signature will be picked out and reported depends both on the forecaster's sensitivity to the signal and on the response criterion being used. In establishing the criterion for making a report, the forecaster must consider certain consequences. Setting the criterion too high might cause a tornado to go unnoticed. Such a miss could cost many lives if it left a populated area with no warning of danger. If the response criterion were set too low, however, the forecaster might deliver a false alarm that would unnecessarily disrupt people's lives, activate costly emergency plans, and reduce the credibility of future tornado warnings (see Figure 5.4A). In other words, there is a tradeoff. To minimize false alarms, the forecaster could set a very high response criterion, but doing so would also make misses more likely.

Let's examine how various kinds of expectations or assumptions can change the response criterion and how those changes might affect the accuracy of a forecaster's decisions. If a forecaster knows it's a time of year when tornadoes occur in only about 50 percent of the storm systems seen on radar, a rather high response criterion is likely to be used. That is, it will take relatively strong evidence to trigger a tornado warning. The hypothetical data in Figure 5.4B show that under these conditions, the forecaster correctly detected 70 percent of actual tornadoes but missed 30 percent of them. Also, 30 percent of the tornado reports were false alarms. Now suppose the forecaster learns that a different kind of storm system is on the way and that about 90 percent of such systems spawn tornadoes. This information is likely to increase the forecaster's expectation that a tornado signature will appear, thus lowering the response criterion. The forecaster will now require less visual evidence of a tornado before reporting one. Under these conditions, as shown in Figure 5.4C, the hit rate might rise from 70 percent to, say, 90 percent, but the false-alarm rate might also increase from 30 percent to 40 percent.

Sensitivity to tornado signals will also affect a forecaster's hit rate and false-alarm rate. Forecasters with greater sensitivity to these signals will have high hit rates and low false-alarm rates. Forecasters with less sensitivity are still likely to have high hit rates, but their false-alarm rates will be higher, too. As Figure 5.4 suggests, people do sometimes make mistakes at signal detection, whether it involves spotting tornadoes, inspecting luggage, diagnosing medical conditions, searching for oil, or looking for clues at a crime scene. Research on these and other perceptual abilities has led psychologists to suggest ways of improving people's performance on signal-detection tasks (Wickens, 1992). For example, psychologists recommend that manufacturers occasionally place flawed items among a batch of objects to be inspected. This strategy increases inspectors' expectations of seeing flaws, thus lowering their response criterion and raising their hit rate.

just-noticeable difference (JND) The smallest detectable difference in stimulus energy.

Weber's law A law stating that the smallest detectable difference in stimulus energy is a constant fraction of the intensity of the stimulus.

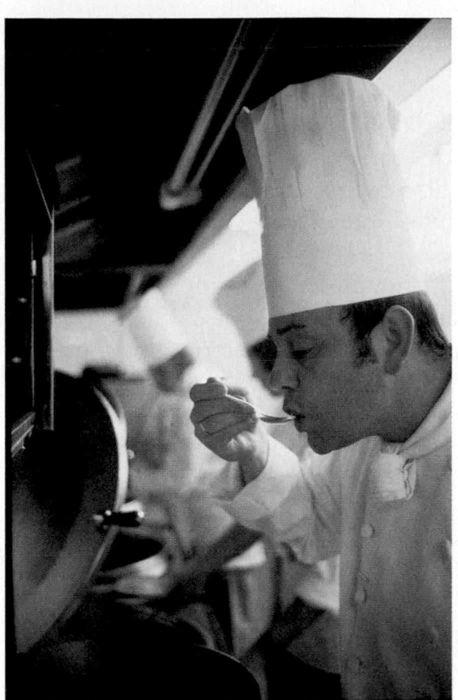

Perfect! This chef's ability to taste the difference in his culinary creation before and after he has adjusted the spices depends on psychophysical laws that also apply to judging differences in visual, auditory, and other sensory stimuli.

Judging Differences: Has Anything Changed?

Sometimes our perceptual task is not to detect a faint stimulus but rather to notice small differences as a stimulus changes or to judge whether there are differences between two stimuli. For example, when tuning up, musicians must focus on whether the notes played by two instruments are the same or different. When repainting part of a wall, you must judge whether the new colour matches the old. And you have to decide if your soup tastes any spicier after you have added some pepper.

The smallest difference between stimuli that we can detect is called the **difference threshold** or **just-noticeable difference (JND)**. How small is that difference? The size of a JND is determined by two factors. The first is how much of a stimulus there was to begin with. The weaker the stimuli are, the easier it is to detect small differences between them. For example, if you are comparing the weight of two envelopes, you will be able to detect a difference of as little as a fraction of an ounce. But if you are comparing two boxes weighing around 30 kilograms, you may not notice a difference unless it is a kilo or more. The second factor affecting people's ability to detect differences is which sense is being stimulated.

The relationship between these two factors is described by one of the oldest laws in psychology. Named after the nineteenth-century German physiologist Ernst Weber (pronounced "VAY-ber"), **Weber's law** states that the smallest detectable difference in stimulus energy is a constant fraction of the intensity of the stimulus. This fraction, often called *Weber's constant* or *Weber's fraction*, is given the symbol K. As shown in Table 5.2, K is different for each of the senses. The smaller K is, the more sensitive a sense is to stimulus differences.

Specifically, Weber's law says that $JND = KI$, where K is the Weber's constant for a particular sense and I is the amount, or intensity, of the stimulus. To compute the JND for a particular stimulus, we must know its intensity and what sense it is stimulating. For example, as shown in Table 5.2, the value of K for weight is .02. If an object weighs 10 kilos (I), the JND is only 225 gm. So while carrying a 10-k bag of groceries, you would have to add or remove 225gm before you would be able to detect a change in its weight. But candy snatchers beware: It takes a change of only 18.9 gm to determine that someone has been into a 1 kilogram box of chocolates!

Weber's constants vary somewhat among individuals, and as we get older we tend to become less sensitive to stimulus differences. There are exceptions to this rule, however. If you like candy, you will be happy to know that Weber's fraction for sweetness stays fairly constant throughout life (Gilmore & Murphy, 1989). Weber's law does not hold when stimuli are very intense or very weak, but it does apply to complex, as well as simple, stimuli. We all tend to have our own personal Weber's fractions that describe how much prices can increase before we notice or worry about the change. For example, if your Weber's fraction for cost is .10, then you would surely notice, and perhaps protest, a fifty-cent increase in a one-dollar bus fare. But the same fifty-cent increase in monthly rent would be less than a JND and thus unlikely to cause much notice or concern.

table 5.2
Weber's Fraction *(K)* for Different Stimuli

The value of Weber's fraction, *K*, differs from one sense to another. Differences in *K* demonstrate the adaptive nature of perception. Humans, who depend more heavily on vision than on taste for survival, are more sensitive to vision than to taste.

Stimulus	*K*
Pitch	.003
Brightness	.017
Weight	.02
Odour	.05
Loudness	.10
Pressure on skin	.14
Saltiness of taste	.20

Magnitude Estimation: How Intense Is That?

How much would you have to turn up the volume on your stereo to make it sound twice as loud as your neighbour's? How much would you have to turn it down to make it sound only half as loud as it was before your neighbour complained? These are questions about *magnitude estimation*—about how our perception of stimulus intensity is related to the actual strength of the stimulus. In 1860, Gustav Fechner (pronounced "FECK-ner") used Weber's law to study the relationship between the physical magnitude of a stimulus and its *perceived* magnitude. He reasoned that if just-noticeable differences get progressively larger as stimulus magnitude increases, then the amount of change in the stimulus required to double or triple its perceived intensity must get larger, too. He was right. For example, it takes only a small increase in volume to make a soft sound seem twice as loud, but imagine how much additional volume it would take to make a rock band seem twice as loud. To put it another way, constant increases in physical energy will produce progressively smaller increases in perceived magnitude. This observation, when expressed as a mathematical equation relating actual stimulus intensity to perceived intensity, became known as *Fechner's law*.

Fechner's law applies to most, but not all, stimuli. For example, it takes larger and larger increases in light or sound to create the same amount of change in perceived magnitude, but this is not the case for stimuli such as electric shock. It takes a relatively large increase in shock intensity to make a weak shock seem twice as intense, but if the shock is already painful, it takes only a small increase in intensity before you would perceive it as twice as strong. S. S. Stevens offered a formula (known as *Stevens's power law*) for magnitude estimation that works for a wider array of stimuli, including electric shock, temperature, and sound and light intensity. Stevens's law is still used today by psychologists who want to determine how much larger, louder, longer, or more intense a stimulus must be for people to perceive a specific difference or amount of change.

Overall, people do well at estimating differences between stimuli. For example, we are very good at estimating how much longer one line is than another. Yet as shown in Figure 5.2, this perceptual comparison process can be disrupted when the lines are embedded in more complex figures (Figure 5.5 offers some additional examples). The perceptual laws that we have discussed, and the exceptions to these laws, all emphasize a fundamental principle: Perception is a relative process. Our experience of one stimulus depends on its relationship to others. In the next section, on perceptual organization, we discuss what researchers have learned about the way in which our perceptual system relates one stimulus to another.

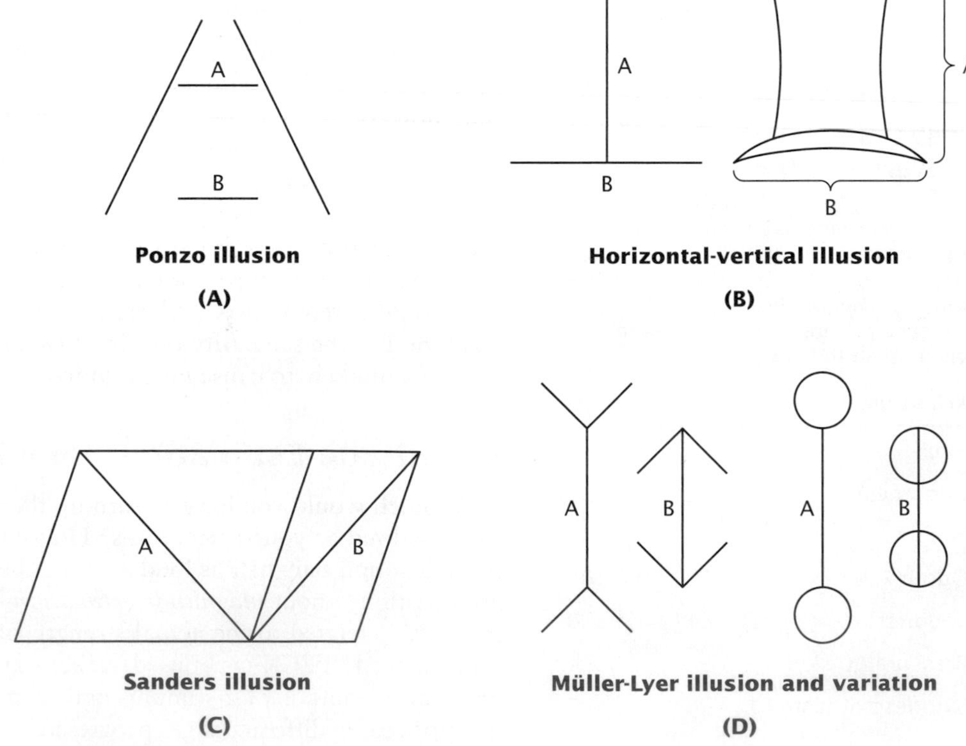

figure 5.5

Length Illusions

People can usually estimate line lengths very accurately, but this ability can be impaired under certain conditions. The pairs of lines marked A and B are the same length in each drawing, but most people report that line A appears longer than line B. These optical illusions, like the one in Figure 5.2, occur partly because of our tendency to see two-dimensional figures as three-dimensional. With the exception of the top hat, all or part of line A in each drawing can easily be interpreted as being farther away than line B. When two equal-size objects appear to be at different distances, the visual system tends to infer that the more distant object must be larger.

Organizing the Perceptual World

Suppose you are driving on a busy road while searching for Barney's Diner, an unfamiliar restaurant where you are supposed to meet a friend. The roadside is crammed with signs of all shapes and colours, some flashing and some rotating. If you are ever to recognize the sign that says "Barney's Diner," you must impose some sort of organization on this overwhelming array of visual information.

Perceptual organization is the task performed by the perceptual system to determine what edges and other stimuli go together to form an object (Peterson & Rhodes, 2003). In this case, the object would be the sign for Barney's Diner. It is perceptual organization, too, that makes it possible for you to separate the sign from its background of lights, colours, letters, and other competing stimuli. Figure 5.6 shows some of the ways in which your perceptual system can organize stimuli. The figure appears as a hollow cube, but notice that you can see it from two angles: either looking down at the top of the cube or looking up toward the bottom of the cube. Notice, too, that the "cube" is not really a cube at all but rather a series of unconnected arrows and Ys. Your perceptual system organizes these elements into a cube by creating imaginary connecting lines called *subjective contours*. That system can also change the apparent location of the cube. You probably first saw it as "floating" in front of a background of large black dots, but those dots can also become "holes" through which you see the cube against a solid black background "behind" the page. It may take a little time to see this second perceptual organization, but when you do, notice that the subjective contours you saw earlier are gone. They disappear because your perceptual system adjusts for the fact that when an object is partially obscured, we should not be able to see all of it.

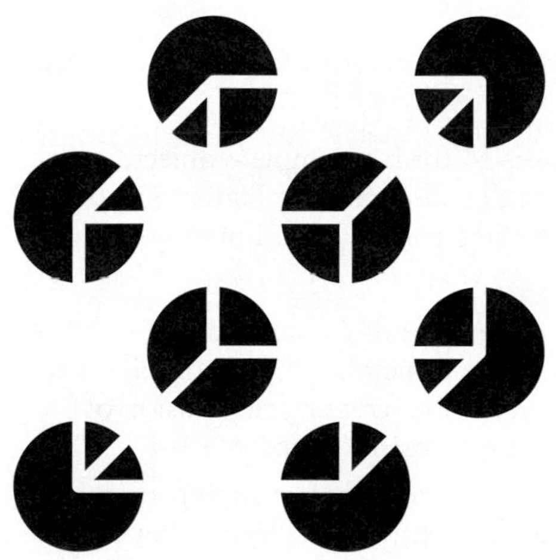

figure 5.6

Organize This!

Psychologists have employed the principles of figure-ground organization and grouping to help explain how your visual system allows you to perceive these disconnected lines as a cube, to see it from above or below, and to see it as being either on the page or "behind" it.

Basic Processes in Perceptual Organization

To explain phenomena such as these and to understand the way our perceptual systems organize more naturalistic scenes, psychologists have focused on two basic processes: *figure-ground organization* and *grouping*.

Figure-Ground Organization When you look at a complex scene or listen to a noisy environment, your perceptual apparatus automatically emphasizes certain features, objects, or sounds, and all other stimuli in that environment become the background. So as you drive toward an intersection, a stop sign stands out clearly against the background of trees, houses, and cars. This is an example of figure-ground organization. A *figure,* as the part of the visual field that has meaning, stands in front of the rest and always seems to include the contours or edges that separate it from the less relevant *ground,* or background (Rubin, 1915). As described in the chapter on sensation, edges are one of the most basic features detected by our visual system; they combine to form figures.

To experience how your perceptual system creates figure and ground, look at the drawings in Figure 5.7. These drawings are called *reversible images,* because you can repeatedly reverse your perceptual organization of what is figure and what is ground. Your ability to do this shows that perception is not only an active process but a categorical one as well. People usually organize sensory stimulation into one perceptual category or another, but rarely into both or into something in between. In Figure 5.7, for instance, you cannot easily see both faces and a vase, or the words *figure* and *ground,* at the same time.

Grouping To distinguish figure from ground, our perceptual system must first identify stimulus elements in the environment, such as the edges of a stop sign or billboard, that belong together as figures. We tend to group certain elements together more or less automatically. In the early 1900s, several German

perceptual organization The task of determining what edges and other stimuli go together to form an object.

(A)

(B)

figure 5.7

Reversible Images

Reversible images can be organized by your perceptual system in two ways. If you perceive Part A as the word *figure*, the space around the letters becomes meaningless background. Now emphasize the word *ground*, and what had stood out a moment ago now becomes background. In Part B, when you emphasize the white vase, the two black profiles become background; if you organize the faces as the figure, what had been a vase now becomes background.

psychologists began to study how this happens. They concluded that people perceive sights and sounds as organized wholes. These wholes, they said, are different from, and more than, just the sum of individual sensations, much as water is something more than just an assortment of hydrogen and oxygen atoms. Because the German word meaning (roughly) "whole figure" is *Gestalt* (pronounced "ge-SHTALT"), these researchers became known as *Gestalt psychologists*. They proposed a number of principles, or "Gestalt laws," that describe how perceptual systems group stimuli into a world of shapes and objects (Kimchi, 2003). Some of the most enduring of these principles are the following:

1. ***Proximity***. The closer objects or events are to one another, the more likely they are to be perceived as belonging together, as Figure 5.8(A) illustrates.
2. ***Similarity***. Similar elements are perceived to be part of a group, as in Figure 5.8(B).
3. ***Continuity***. Sensations that appear to create a continuous form are perceived as belonging together, as in Figure 5.8(C).
4. ***Closure***. We tend to fill in missing contours to form a complete object, as in Figure 5.8(D). The gaps are easy to see, but as illustrated in Figure 5.6, the tendency to fill in missing contours can be so strong that you may see faint connections that are not really there.
5. ***Common fate***. Objects that are moving in the same direction at the same speed are perceived together. Choreographers use the principle of common fate when they arrange for several dancers to move in unison, creating the illusion of waves of motion or of a single object moving across the stage.

Stephen Palmer (1999) has introduced three additional grouping principles, which may be even more important than many of the traditional laws. They include:

1. ***Synchrony***. Stimuli that occur at the same time are likely to be perceived as belonging together. For example, if you see a car ahead stop violently at the same instant you hear a crash, you will probably perceive these visual and auditory stimuli as part of the same event.
2. ***Common region***. Elements located within some boundary tend to be grouped together. The boundary can be created by an enclosing perimeter, as in Figure 5.8(E); a region of colour; or other factors.
3. ***Connectedness***. Elements that are connected by other elements tend to be grouped together. Figure 5.8(F) demonstrates how important this law is. The circles connected by dotted lines seem to go together even though they are farther apart than some pairs of unconnected circles. In this situation, the principle of connectedness appears more important than the principle of proximity.

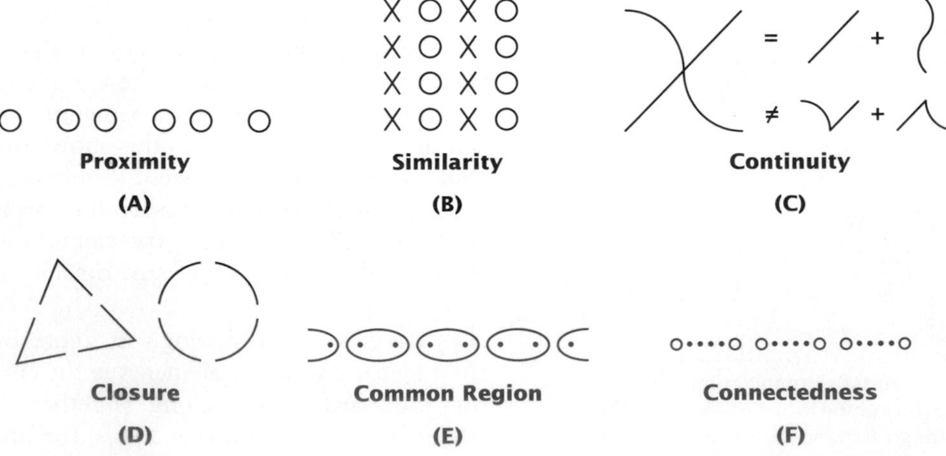

figure 5.8

Gestalt Principles of Perceptual Grouping

We tend to perceive Part A as two groups of two circles plus two single circles, rather than as, say, six single circles. In Part B, we see two columns of Xs and two columns of Os, not four rows of XOXO. We see the X in Part C as made out of two continuous lines, not a combination of the odd forms shown. We perceive the disconnected segments of Part D as a triangle and a circle. In Part E, we tend to pair up dots in the same oval even though they are far apart. Part F shows that connected objects are grouped together.

Why do we organize the world according to these grouping principles? One answer is that they reflect the way stimuli are likely to be organized in the natural world. Nearby elements are, in fact, more likely than separated elements to be part of the same object. Stimulus elements moving in the same direction at the same rate are also likely to be part of the same object. Your initial impression of the cube in Figure 5.6 reflects this *likelihood principle* in action. At first glance, you probably saw the cube as being below you rather than above you. This tendency makes adaptive sense, because boxes and other cube-shaped objects are more likely to be on the ground than hanging in midair.

The likelihood principle is consistent with both the ecological and constructivist approaches to perception. From the ecological perspective, the likelihood principle evolved because it worked, giving our ancestors reliable information about how the world is likely to be organized, and thus increasing their chances of survival. Constructivists point out, however, that our personal experiences in the world also help determine the likelihood of interpreting a stimulus array in one way over another. The likelihood principle operates automatically and accurately most of the time. As shown in Figure 5.9, however, when we try using it to organize very *unlikely* stimuli, it can lead to frustrating misperceptions.

Complementing the likelihood principle is the *simplicity principle*, which says that we organize stimulus elements in a way that gives us the simplest possible perception (Palmer, 1999; Pomerantz & Kubovy, 1986). Your visual system, for example, will group stimulus elements so as to reduce the amount of information that you must process. You can see the simplicity principle in action in Figure 5.6; it was simpler to see a single cube than an assortment of separate, unrelated arrows and Ys.

Perception of Location and Distance

One of the most important perceptual tasks we face is to determine where objects and sound sources are located. This task involves knowing both their two-dimensional position (left or right, up or down) and their distance from us.

Two-Dimensional Location Determining whether an object is to your right or your left appears to be simple. All the perceptual system has to do, it seems,

Common Fate When a set of objects, such as a flock of birds, move together, we see them as a group or even as a single large object in the sky. Marching band directors put this perceptual grouping process to good use. By arranging for musicians to move together, they make it appear as though huge letters and other large "objects" are in motion on the field during half-time shows at university football games.

figure 5.9

Impossible Objects

These objects can exist as two-dimensional drawings, but could they exist in three-dimensional space? When you try to use the likelihood principle to organize them as the three-dimensional objects you expect them to be, you'll discover that they are "impossible."

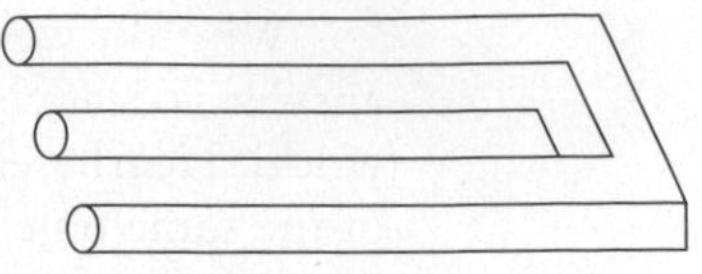

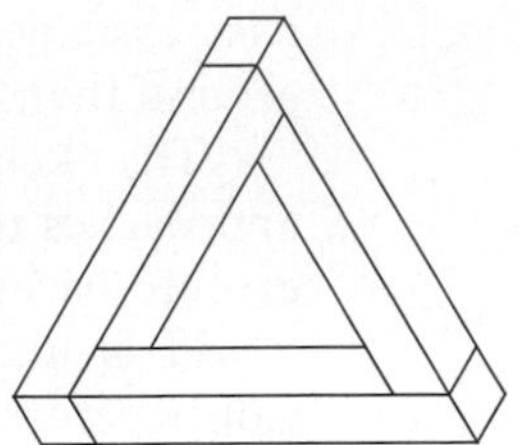

is determine where the object's image falls on the retina. If the image falls on the centre of the retina, then the object must be straight ahead. But when an object is, say, far to your right, and you focus its image on the centre of your retina by turning your head and eyes toward it, you do not assume it is straight ahead. According to the computational approach, your brain estimates the object's location by using an equation that takes information about where an image strikes the retina and adjusts it based on information about the movement of your eyes and head.

LINKAGES (a link to Sensation)

As mentioned in the chapter on sensation, localization of sounds depends on cues about differences in the information received by each of your ears. If a sound is continuous, sound waves coming toward the right side of your head will reach the right ear before reaching the left ear. Similarly, a sound coming toward the right side of your head will seem a little bit louder to the right ear than to the left ear, because your head blocks some of the sound to the left ear. The brain uses these slight differences in the timing and the intensity of a sound as cues to locate its source. Visual cues are often integrated with auditory cues to determine the exact identity and location of the sound source. Most often, information from the eyes and the ears converges on the same likely sound source. However, there are times when the two senses produce conflicting impressions; in such cases, we tend to believe our eyes rather than our ears. This bias toward using visual information is known as *visual dominance*. The phenomenon is illustrated by our impression that the sound of a television program is coming from the screen rather than the speaker. The next time someone is talking on your TV, close your eyes. If your television has a single speaker below or to the side of the screen, you will notice that the sound no longer seems to be coming from the screen but from the speaker itself. As soon as you open your eyes, the false impression resumes; words once again seem to come from the obvious visual source of the sound—the person on the screen.

Depth Perception One of the oldest puzzles in psychology relates to **depth perception,** our ability to perceive distance. How are we able to experience the world in three-dimensional depth even though the visual information we receive from it is projected onto two-dimensional retinas? The answer lies in the many *depth cues* provided by the environment and by certain properties of our visual system (Anderson, 2004).

To some extent, people perceive depth through the same cues that artists use to create the impression of depth and distance on a two-dimensional canvas. Figure 5.10 illustrates several of these cues:

- One of the most important depth cues is **interposition,** or *occlusion*: Closer objects block the view of things farther away. This cue is illustrated in Figure 5.10 by the person walking nearest to the car. Because his body blocks out part of the car, we perceive him as being closer than the car.

depth perception The ability to perceive distance.

interposition A depth cue whereby closer objects block one's view of things farther away.

figure 5.10

Stimulus Cues for Depth Perception

See if you can identify the cues of relative size, interposition, linear perspective, height in the visual field, textural gradient, and shadows that combine to create a sense of three-dimensional depth in this drawing.

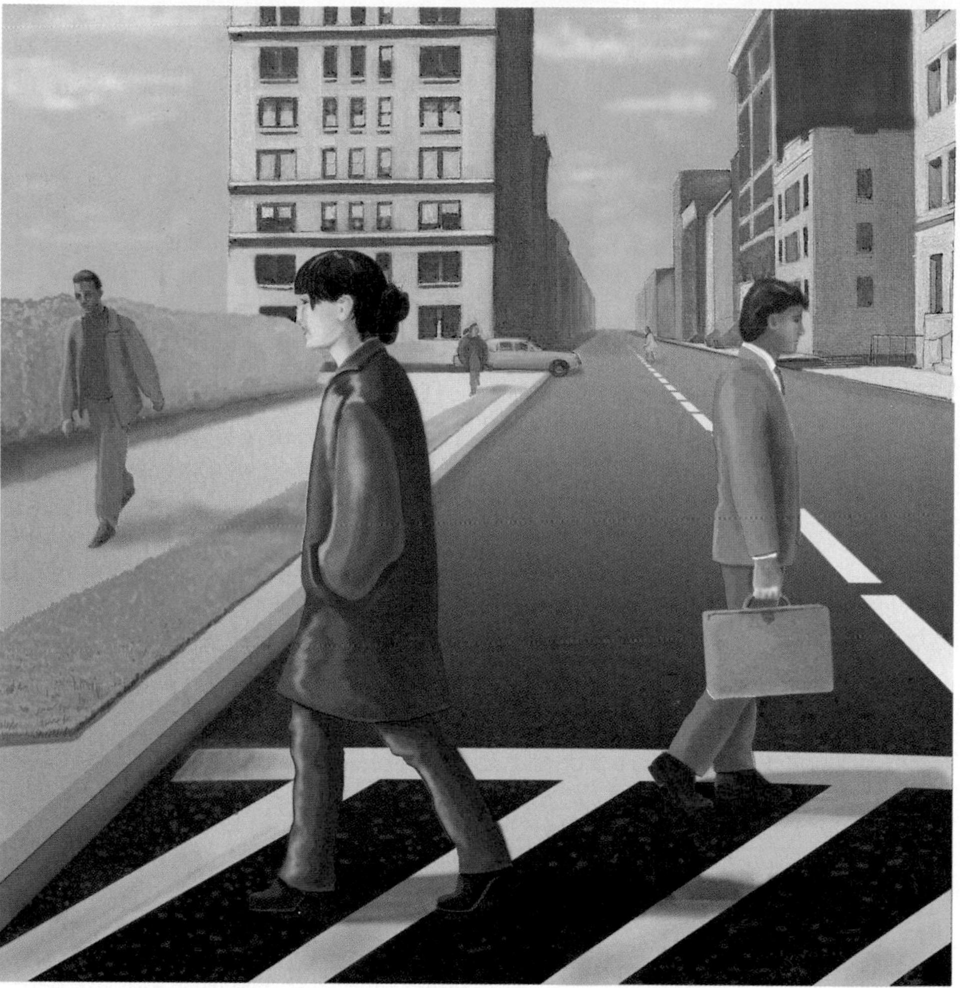

- The two people at the far left side of Figure 5.10 illustrate the cue of **relative size**: When two objects are assumed to be about equal in size, the one that casts the larger image on the retina is perceived to be closer.
- Another cue comes from **height in the visual field**: On the ground, more distant objects are usually higher in the visual field than those nearby. Because the buildings in Figure 5.10 are higher than the people in the foreground, the buildings appear to be farther away. This is one reason that objects higher in the visual field are more likely to be interpreted as the background for objects that are lower in a scene (Vecera, Vogel, & Woodman, 2002).
- A cue known as **texture gradient** involves a graduated change in the "grain" of the visual field. Texture appears less detailed as distance increases, so as the texture of a surface changes across the retinal image, we perceive a change in distance. In Figure 5.10, you can see a texture gradient as the grass, the sidewalk, and the street become less distinct toward the "back" of the drawing.
- The small figure crossing the centre line in Figure 5.10 is seen as very far away, partly because she is near the horizon line, which we know is quite distant. She appears far away also because she is near a point at which the road's edges, like all parallel lines that recede into the distance, appear to converge toward a single point. This apparent convergence provides a cue called **linear perspective.** Objects that are nearer the point of convergence are seen as farther away.

Still other depth cues depend on *clarity, colour,* and *shadows*. Distant objects often appear hazier and tend to take on a bluish tone. (Art students are taught

relative size A depth cue whereby larger objects are perceived as closer than smaller ones.

height in the visual field A depth cue whereby objects higher in the visual field are perceived as more distant.

texture gradient A graduated change in the texture, or grain, of the visual field, whereby objects with finer, less detailed textures are perceived as more distant.

linear perspective A depth cue whereby objects closer to the point at which two lines appear to converge are perceived as being at a greater distance.

A Case of Depth Misperception The runner in this photo is actually farther away than the man on the pitcher's mound. But because he is lower, not higher, in the visual field—and because it is easy to misperceive his leg as being in front of, not behind, the pitcher's leg—the runner appears smaller than normal rather than farther away.

to add a little blue when mixing paint for distant background features.) Light and shadow also contribute to the perception of depth (Kingdom, 2003; Ramachandran, 1988). The buildings in the background of Figure 5.10 are seen as three-dimensional, not flat, because of the shadows on their right faces. Figure 5.11 offers a more dramatic example of shadows' effect on depth perception.

An important visual depth cue that cannot be demonstrated in Figure 5.10, or in any other still image, comes from motion. You may have noticed, for example, that when you look out the side window of a moving car, objects nearer to you seem to speed across your visual field, whereas objects in the distance seem to move slowly, if at all. This difference in the apparent rate of movement is called **motion parallax,** and it provides cues to differences in the distance of various objects.

Several additional depth cues result from the way human eyes are built and positioned. As mentioned in the chapter on sensation, for example, the eye's lens changes shape, or *accommodates,* bending light rays and focusing images on the retina. To accomplish this task, muscles surrounding the lens either tighten, to make the lens more curved for focusing on close objects, or relax, to flatten the lens for focusing on more distant objects. Information about this muscle activity is relayed to the brain, providing an **accommodation** cue that helps create the perception of an object's distance.

The relative location of our two eyes produces two other depth cues. One is called **convergence.** Because the eyes are located a short distance apart, they must converge, or rotate inward, to project an object's image on each retina. The brain receives information about this movement from the eye muscles and uses it to help calculate an object's distance. The closer the object, the more the eyes must converge, which sends more intense stimulation to the brain. Focusing on more distant objects requires less convergence and creates less feedback from the eye muscles. To experience this effect, hold up a finger at arm's length and try to keep it in focus as you move it toward your nose.

Second, because of their differing locations, each eye receives a slightly different view of the world. The difference between the two retinal images of an object is called **binocular disparity.** For any particular object, this difference gets smaller as distance increases. The brain combines the two images, processes information about

motion parallax A depth cue whereby a difference in the apparent rate of movement of different objects provides information about the relative distance of those objects.

accommodation The ability of the lens of the eye to change its shape and bend light rays so that objects are in focus.

convergence A depth cue involving the rotation of the eyes to project the image of an object on each retina.

binocular disparity A depth cue based on the difference between two retinal images of the world.

looming A motion cue involving a rapid expansion in the size of an image so that it fills the available space on the retina.

Texture Gradient The details of a scene fade gradually as distance increases. This texture gradient helps us to perceive the people who appear in less detail in this photo as being farther away.

figure 5.11

Light, Shadow, and Depth Perception The shadows cast by these protruding rivets and deep dents make it easy to see them in three dimensions. But if you turn the book upside down, the rivets now look like dents and the dents look like bumps. This reversal in depth perception occurs partly because we normally assume that illumination comes from above and interpret the pattern of light and shadow accordingly. With the picture upside down, light coming from the top would produce the observed pattern of shadows only if the circles were dents, not rivets.

Binocular Disparity The disparity, or difference, between each eye's view of an object is smaller for distant objects and greater for closer ones. These binocular disparity cues help to create our perception of distance. To see how distance affects binocular disparity, hold a pencil vertically about six inches in front of your nose; then close one eye and notice where the pencil is in relation to the background. Now open that eye, close the other one, and notice how much the pencil "shifts." These are the two different views your eyes have of the pencil. Repeat the procedure while holding the pencil at arm's length. There is now less disparity or "shift," because there is less difference in the angles from which your two eyes see the pencil.

the amount of disparity, and generates the impression of a single object having depth as well as height and width. This impression of depth is created by 3-D movies and some virtual reality systems by displaying to each eye a separate image of a scene, each viewed from a slightly different angle.

The wealth of depth cues available to us is consistent with the ecological approach to perception. However, researchers taking the constructivist and computational approaches argue that even when temporarily deprived of these depth cues, we can still move about and locate objects in an environment. In one study, for example, participants viewed an object from a particular place in a room. Then, with their eyes closed, they were guided to a point well to the side of the object and asked to walk toward it from this new position. The participants were amazingly accurate at this task, leading the researchers to suggest that seeing an object at a particular point in space creates a spatial model in our minds—a model that remains intact even when immediate depth cues are removed.

Perception of Motion

Sometimes an object's most important property is not its size or shape or distance but its motion—how fast it is going and where it is heading. For example, a car in front of you may change speed or direction, requiring that you change your own speed or direction, often in a split second.

As with the detection of location and depth, your brain "tunes in" to a host of cues to perceive changes in motion. Many of these cues come from *optical flow,* or the changes in retinal images across the entire visual field. One particularly meaningful pattern of optical flow is known as **looming,** the rapid expansion in the size of an image so that it fills the retina. When an image looms, you tend to interpret it as an approaching stimulus. Your perceptual system quickly assesses whether the expansion on the retina is about equal in all directions or greater to one side than to the other. If it is greater to the right, for example, the approaching stimulus will miss you and pass to your right. If the retinal expansion is approximately equal in all directions, it means the object is coming straight for your eyes. In other words, you had better duck!

Two questions have been of particular interest to psychologists who study motion perception. First, how do we know whether the flow of images across the retina is due to the movement of objects in the environment or to our own movements? If changes in retinal images were the only factor contributing to motion perception, then moving your eyes would create the perception that everything in the visual field was moving. This is not the case, though, because, as noted earlier, the brain also receives and processes information about the motion of your eyes and head. If you look around the room right now, tables, chairs, and other stationary objects will not appear to move, because your brain determines that all the movement of images on your retinas is due to your eye and head movements. But now close one eye, and wiggle your open eyeball by gently pushing your lower eyelid. Because your brain receives no signals that your eye is being moved by its own muscles, everything in the room will appear to move.

A second question about motion perception relates to the fact that there is a delay of about one-twentieth of a second between the moment when an image is registered on the retina and the moment when information about that image reaches the brain. In theory, each moment's perception of, say, a dog running toward you is actually a perception of where the dog was about one-twentieth of a second earlier. How does the perceptual system deal with this time lag so as to accurately interpret information about an object's motion and location? Psychologists have found that when a stimulus is moving along a relatively constant path, the brain corrects for the image delay by predicting where the stimulus should be one-twentieth of a second in the future (Nijhawan, 1997).

Motion perception is of special interest to sport psychologists. They try to understand, for example, why some individuals are so good at perceiving motion. One team of British psychologists discovered a number of cues and computations apparently used by "expert catchers." In catching a ball, these individuals seem to be especially sensitive to the angle between their "straight ahead" gaze (i.e., a position with the chin parallel to the ground) and the gaze used when looking up at a moving ball. Their task is to move the body continuously, and often quickly, to make sure that this "gaze angle" never becomes too small (such that the ball falls in front of them) or too large (such that the ball sails overhead). In other words, these catchers appear to unconsciously use a specific mathematical rule: "Keep the tangent of the angle of gaze elevation to zero" (McLeod & Dienes, 1996; McLeod, Reed, & Dienes, 2003).

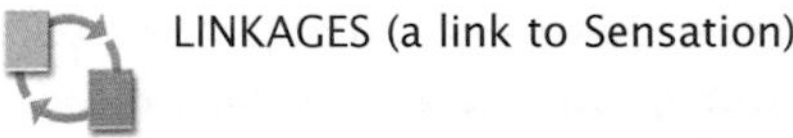

Sometimes, we perceive motion when there is none. Psychologists are interested in these motion illusions because they can tell us something about how the brain processes various kinds of movement-related information. When you accelerate in a car, for example, the experience of motion doesn't come just from the flow of visual information across your retinas. It also comes from touch information as you are pressed against the seat, and from vestibular information as your head tilts backward. If a visual flow suggests that you are moving but you don't receive appropriate sensations from other parts of your body, particularly the vestibular senses, you may experience a nauseating movement illusion. This form of motion sickness often occurs when people watch some 3-D movies; operate motion simulators; or play certain video games, especially those with virtual reality technology.

Other illusions of motion are much less unpleasant. The most important of these occurs when still images appear, one at a time, in rapid succession, as they do on films, videos, and DVDs. Because each image differs slightly from the preceding one, the brain sees the people and objects in each image appearing in one place for only a fraction of a second before they disappear and then quickly reappear in a slightly different location. The entertaining result is **stroboscopic motion,** an illusion of motion created when objects disappear and then quickly reappear nearby. The same illusion occurs when flashing lights on a theatre or casino sign appear to move around the sign. Stroboscopic motion is based on the organizing principles of likelihood and simplicity. Objects in the world do not usually disappear, only to be immediately replaced by a similar object nearby. Accordingly, your brain makes the simpler and more likely assumption that a disappearing and reappearing object has moved.

stroboscopic motion An illusion in which lights or images flashed in rapid succession are perceived as moving.

perceptual constancy The perception of objects as constant in size, shape, colour, and other properties despite changes in their retinal image.

Stroboscopic Motion If this series of still photographs of an athlete's handspring were presented to you, one at a time, in quick succession, an illusion called stroboscopic motion would cause you to perceive him to be moving.

Courtesy George Eastman House

Perceptual Constancy

Suppose that one sunny day you are watching someone walking toward you along a tree-lined sidewalk. The visual sensations produced by this person are actually rather strange. For one thing, the size of the image on your retinas keeps getting larger as the person gets closer. To see this for yourself, hold your hand out at arm's length and look at someone far away. The retinal image of that person will be so small that your hand can easily cover it. If you do the same when the person is a metre away, the retinal image will be much larger than your hand, but you will perceive the person as being closer now, not bigger. Similarly, if you watch people pass from bright sunshine through the shadows of trees, your retinas receive images that are darker, then lighter, then darker again. Still, you perceive individuals whose colouring remains the same.

These examples illustrate **perceptual constancy,** the perception of objects as constant in size, shape, colour, and other properties despite changes in their retinal image. Without perceptual constancy, the world would be an Alice-in-Wonderland kind of place in which objects continuously changed their properties.

figure 5.12

A Size Illusion

The monster that is higher in the drawing probably appears larger than the other one, but they are actually the same size. Why does this illusion occur? The converging lines of the tunnel provide strong depth cues telling us that the higher monster is farther away, but because that monster casts an image on our retinas that is just as big as the "nearer" one, we assume that the more distant monster must be bigger. (Look again at Figure 5.5 for other examples of this illusion.)

Size Constancy Why do objects appear to remain about the same size, no matter what changes occur in the size of their retinal image? One explanation emphasizes the computational aspects of perception. It suggests that as objects move closer or farther away, the brain perceives the change in distance and automatically adjusts the perception. This calculation can be expressed as a formula: The perceived size of an object is equal to the size of the retinal image multiplied by the perceived distance (Holway & Boring, 1941). As an object moves closer, its retinal image increases, but the perceived distance decreases at the same rate, so the perceived size remains constant. If, instead, a balloon is inflated in front of your eyes, perceived distance remains constant, and the perceived size (correctly) increases as the retinal image size increases.

The computational perspective is reasonably good at explaining most aspects of size constancy, but it cannot fully account for the fact that people are better at judging the true size (and distance) of familiar rather than unfamiliar objects. This phenomenon suggests that, in line with the constructivists' view, there is an additional, knowledge-based mechanism for size constancy: Our knowledge and experience tells us that most objects (aside from balloons) do not suddenly change size.

The perceptual system usually produces size constancy correctly and automatically, but it can sometimes fail, resulting in size illusions such as the one illustrated in Figure 5.12. Because this figure contains strong linear perspective cues (lines converging in the "distance"), and because objects nearer the point of convergence are interpreted as farther away, we perceive the monster near the top of the figure as the larger one, even though both are exactly the same size. Size illusions can have serious consequences when the objects involved are, say, moving automobiles. A small car produces a smaller retinal image than a large one at the same distance. As a result, the driver of a following vehicle can easily overestimate the distance to the small car (especially in dim light) and therefore fail to brake in time to avoid a collision. Size illusions may help explain why, in countries in which cars vary greatly in size, small cars have higher accident rates than large ones (Eberts & MacMillan, 1985). Size misjudgments illustrate the *inferential* nature of perception emphasized by constructivists: People make logical inferences or hypotheses about the world based on the available cues. Unfortunately, if the cues are misleading or the inferences are wrong, perceptual errors may occur.

Shape Constancy The principles behind shape constancy are closely related to those of size constancy. To see shape constancy at work, remember what page you are on, close this book, and tilt it toward and away from you several times.

A Failure of Shape Constancy When certain stimuli are viewed from an extreme angle, the brain's ability to maintain shape constancy can break down. British traffic engineers have taken this phenomenon into account in the design of road markings. The arrow in the top photo appears to be about the same height as the lettering below it, but it isn't. The arrow had to be greatly elongated, as shown in the side view, so that approaching drivers would see its shape clearly. If the arrow had been painted to match the height of the accompanying letters, it would appear "squashed" and only half as tall as the lettering.

figure 5.13

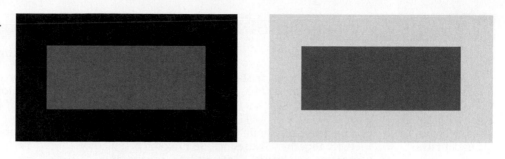

Brightness Contrast

At first glance, the inner rectangle on the left probably looks lighter than the inner rectangle on the right. But carefully examine the inner rectangles alone (covering their surroundings), and you will see that both are of equal intensity. The brighter surround in the right-hand figure leads you to perceive its inner rectangle as relatively darker.

The book will continue to look rectangular, even though the shape of its retinal image changes dramatically as you move it. The brain automatically integrates information about retinal images and distance as movement occurs. In this case, the distance information involves the difference in distance between the near and far edges of the book.

As with size constancy, much of the ability to judge shape constancy depends on automatic computational mechanisms in the nervous system, but expectations about the shape of objects also play a role. For example, in Western cultures, most corners are at right angles. Knowledge of this fact helps make "rectangle" the most likely interpretation of the retinal image shown in Figure 5.1. Sometimes, shape constancy mechanisms are so good at creating perceptions of a stable world that they can keep us from seeing changes when they occur. In one study, for example, participants looking at a computer display of a person's head failed to notice that, as the head turned, it morphed gradually into the head of a different person (Wallis & Bülthoff, 2001).

Brightness Constancy Even with dramatic changes in the amount of light striking an object, the object's perceived brightness remains relatively constant (MacEvoy & Paradiso, 2001). To see this for yourself, place a piece of charcoal in sunlight and a piece of white paper in nearby shade. The charcoal will look dark and the paper will look bright, even though a light meter would reveal much more light reflected from the sun-bathed coal than from the shaded paper. One reason the charcoal continues to look dark, no matter what the illumination, is that you *know* that charcoal is nearly black, illustrating once again the knowledge-based nature of perception. Another reason is that the charcoal is still the darkest object relative to its background in the sunlight, and the paper is the brightest object relative to its background in the shade. As shown in Figure 5.13, the brightness of an object is perceived in relation to its background.

For a summary of this discussion, see "In Review: Principles of Perceptual Organization and Constancy."

Recognizing the Perceptual World

In discussing how people organize the perceptual world, we have set the stage for addressing one of the most vital questions that perception researchers must answer: How do people recognize what objects are? If you are driving in search of Barney's Diner, exactly what happens when your eyes finally locate the pattern of light that spells out its name?

To know that you have finally found what you have been looking for, your brain must analyze incoming patterns of information and compare them with information stored in memory. If your brain finds a match, recognition takes place, and the stimulus is classified into a *perceptual category*. Once recognition occurs, your perception of a stimulus may never be the same again. Look at Figure 5.14. Do you see anything familiar? If not, look ahead to Figure 5.18, then look at Figure 5.14 again. You should now see it in an entirely new light. The difference between your "before" and "after" experiences of Figure 5.14 is the difference between the sensory world before and after a perceptual match occurs and recognition takes place.

in review Principles of Perceptual Organization and Constancy

Principle	Description	Example
Figure-ground organization	Certain objects or sounds are automatically identified as figures, whereas others become meaningless background.	You see a person standing against a building, not a building with a person-shaped hole in it.
Grouping (Gestalt laws)	Properties of stimuli lead us to automatically group them together. These include proximity, similarity, continuity, closure, common fate, synchrony, common region, and connectedness.	People who are sitting together, or who are dressed similarly, are perceived as a group.
Perception of location and depth	Knowing an object's two-dimensional position (left and right, up and down) and distance enables us to locate it. The image on the retina and the orientation of the head position provide information about the two-dimensional position of visual stimuli; auditory localization relies on differences in the information received by the ears. Depth or distance perception uses stimulus cues such as interposition, relative size, height in the visual field, texture gradients, linear perspective, clarity, colour, and shadow.	Large, clear objects appear closer than small, hazy objects.
Perceptual constancy	Objects are perceived as constant in size, shape, brightness, colour, and other properties, despite changes in their retinal images.	A train coming toward you is perceived as getting closer, not larger; a restaurant sign is perceived as rotating, not changing shape.

Exactly how does such matching occur? Some aspects of recognition begin at the "top," guided by knowledge, expectations, and other psychological factors. This phenomenon is called **top-down processing,** because it involves higher-level, knowledge-based information. Other aspects of recognition begin at the "bottom," relying on specific, detailed information elements from the sensory receptors that are integrated and assembled into a whole. This phenomenon is called **bottom-up processing,** because it begins with basic information units that serve as a foundation for recognition. Let's consider the contributions of bottom-up and top-down processing to recognition, as well as the use of neural network models to understand both.

LINKAGES (a link to Learning)

figure 5.14

Categorizing Perceptions

What do you see here? If you can't recognize this pattern of information as falling into any perceptual category, turn to Figure 5.18 for some help in doing so.

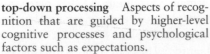

top-down processing Aspects of recognition that are guided by higher-level cognitive processes and psychological factors such as expectations.

bottom-up processing Aspects of recognition that depend first on the information about the stimulus that comes to the brain from the sensory receptors.

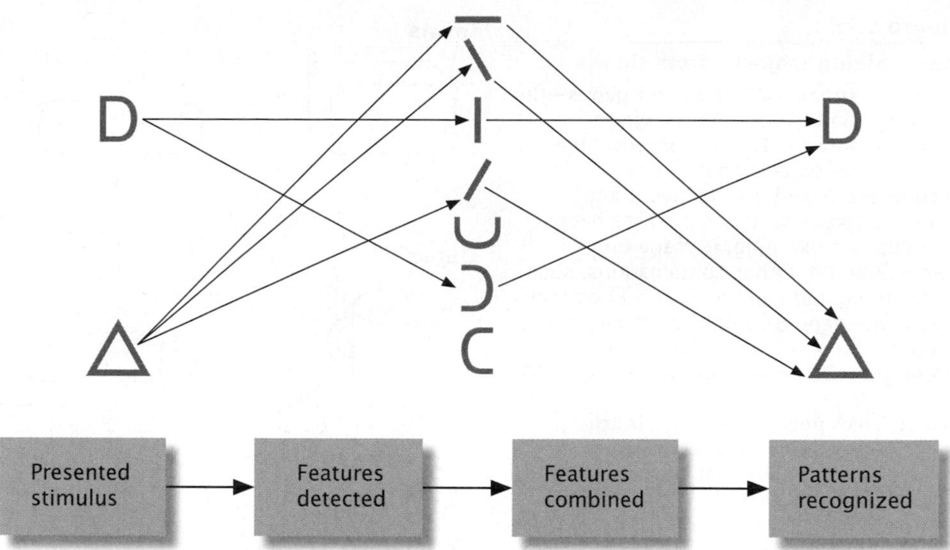

figure 5.15

Feature Analysis

Feature detectors operating at lower levels of the visual system detect features of incoming stimuli such as those shown in the centre of this figure. Later in the perceptual sequence, bottom-up processing might recombine these features to aid in pattern recognition, as in the examples on the right.

Bottom-Up Processing

Research on the visual system is providing a detailed picture of how bottom-up processing works. As described in the chapter on sensation, all along the path from the eye to the brain, certain cells respond to certain features of a stimulus. So the stimulus is first analyzed into basic features before those features are recombined to create a perceptual experience.

What are these features? As also noted in the sensation chapter, certain cells specialize in responding to stimuli that have certain orientations in space (Hubel & Wiesel, 1979). For example, one cell in the cerebral cortex might fire only in response to a diagonal line, so it acts as a feature detector for diagonal lines. Figure 5.15 illustrates how the analysis by such feature detectors, early in the information-processing sequence, may contribute to recognition of letters or judgments of shape. Colour, motion, and even corners are other sensory features that appear to be analyzed separately in different parts of the brain prior to full perceptual recognition (Beatty, 1995; Cowey, 1994; Treisman, 1999).

Features such as colour, motion, overall shape, and fine details can all contribute to our ability to recognize objects, but some carry more weight than others in various situations.

How do psychologists know that feature analysis is actually involved in pattern recognition? Recordings of brain activity indicate that the sensory features we have listed here cause particular sets of neurons to fire. In fact, scientists have recently shown that it may be possible to determine what category of object a person is looking at (e.g., a face vs. a house) based on the pattern of activity occurring in visual processing areas of the person's brain (Haxby et al., 2001). Further, as described in the chapter on sensation, people with certain kinds of brain damage show selective impairment in the ability to perceive certain sets of sensory features, such as an object's colour or movement (Banks & Krajicek, 1991; Treisman, 1999). Irving Biederman (1987) has proposed that people recognize three-dimensional objects by detecting and then combining simple forms, which he calls *geons*. Figure 5.16 shows some of these geons and how they can be combined to form a variety of recognizable objects. Evidence for Biederman's theory comes from experiments in which people must identify drawings in which some details have been removed. As shown in Figure 5.17, recognition becomes particularly difficult when removing details destroys geons.

Top-Down Processing

Bottom-up feature analysis can explain why you recognize the letters in a sign for Barney's Diner. But why is it that you can recognize the sign more easily if it appears

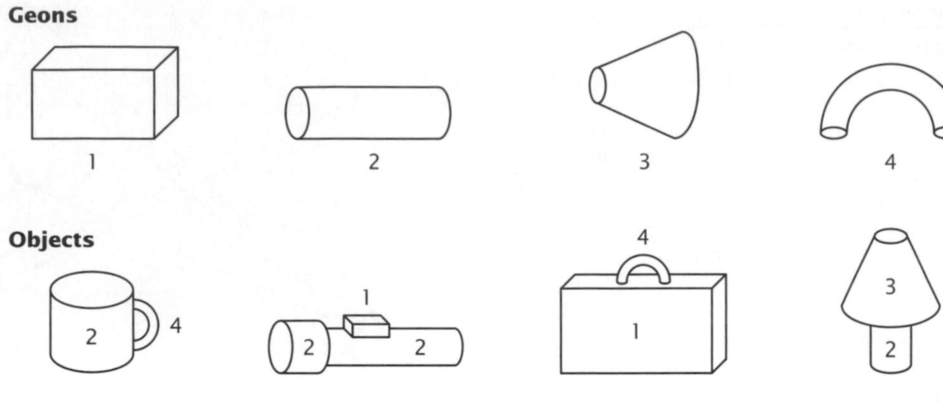

figure 5.16

Recognizing Objects from Geons

Research suggests that we use geons—the forms in the top row—to recognize complex objects. The bottom row shows examples of objects that can be recognized based on the layout and combination of only two or three geons. The cup, for example, is made up of geons 2 and 4. Other combinations, such as an elongated cylinder (geon 2) on top of a cone (geon 3), might produce a broom. Can you make a kettle out of these geons? The solution is on page 176.

Source: Taken from Biederman, I., Matching Image Edges to Object Memory, from the Proceedings of the IEEE First International Conference on Computer Vision, pp. 364–382, 1987, IEEE © 1997 IEEE.

where you were told to expect it rather than a block earlier? And why can you recognize it even if a few letters are missing from the sign? The answers are provided by top-down processing. Fo- ex-mp-e, y-u c-n r-ad -hi- se-te-ce -it- ev-ry -hi-d l-tt-r m-ss-ng. In top-down processing, people use their knowledge in making inferences or "educated guesses" to recognize objects, words, or melodies, especially when sensory information is vague or ambiguous (DeWitt & Samuel, 1990; Rock, 1983). Once you knew that there was a dog in Figure 5.14, it became much easier for you to perceive it. Similarly, police officers find it easy to recognize familiar people on blurry security camera videos, but it is much more difficult for them to recognize strangers (Burton et al., 1999).

Top-down processing is also involved in a phenomenon called *pareidolia* (pronounced "pare-eh-DOLE-ee-a"), the perception of some specific image in an ambiguous stimulus array. Expectancy plays a role, too. For example, look at Figure 5.19, which shows a fish stick that was burnt during cooking. The Ontario man who burnt the fish stick claims the resulting image resembles Jesus Christ. This interpretation requires some knowledge of paintings and other representations of Jesus Christ. Expectancy plays a role, too. People who have not heard of the image might not see Jesus Christ in this photo.

These examples illustrate that top-down processing can have a strong influence on pattern recognition. Our experiences create **schemas**, which are mental representations of what we know and have come to expect about the world. Schemas can bias our perception toward one recognition or another by creating a *perceptual set,* a

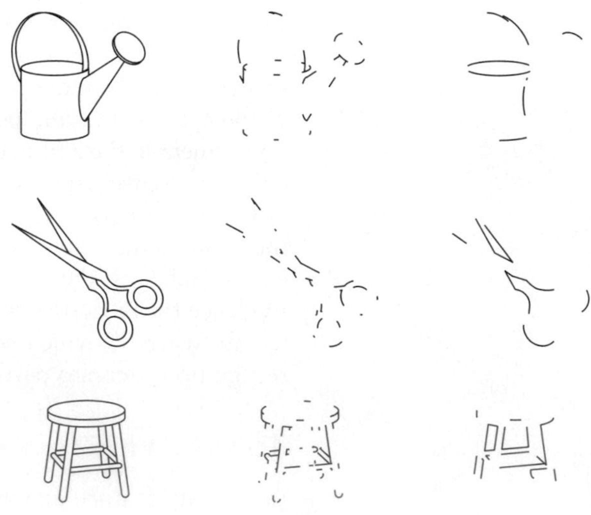

figure 5.17

Recognition of Objects With and Without All Their Geons

The drawings in columns 2 and 3 have had the same amount of ink removed, but in column 3 the deletions have destroyed many of the geons used in object recognition. The drawings in column 2 are far easier to recognize because their geons are still intact.

figure 5.18

Another Version of Figure 5.14

Now that you can identify a dog in this figure, it should be much easier to recognize when you look back at the original version.

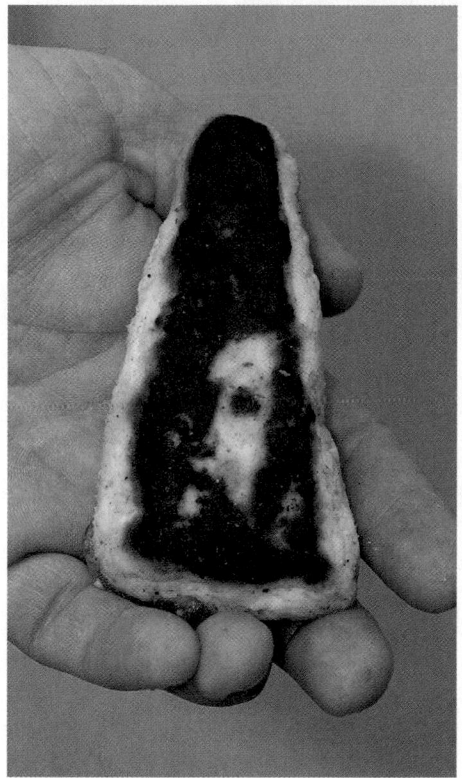

figure 5.19

What Does It Look Like to You?

Fred Whan of Ontario claimed that his fish stick, which burnt while he was cooking it, resembled Jesus Christ. This perceptual categorization results from a combination of bottom-up and top-down recognition processes. Feature-detectors automatically register the edges and colours of the images, whereas knowledge and beliefs give meaning to these features. A person who does not expect to see the face of Jesus—or whose cultural background does not include the concept of Jesus Christ—might not see the face until that interpretation is suggested. To check the possibility, show this photo to people from various religions and cultures who have not seen it before (don't tell them what to look for) and make a note of which individuals require prompting in order to identify the face of Jesus.

schemas Mental representations of what we know, and have come to expect, about the world.

readiness or predisposition to perceive a stimulus in a certain way. This predisposition can also be shaped by the immediate context in which a stimulus occurs. In one case we know of, a woman saw a masked man in the darkened hallway of a house she was visiting. Her first perception was that the man who lived there was playing a joke, but in fact she had confronted a burglar. Context has biasing effects for sounds, too. A gunshot heard in a parking lot, for example, is often perceived as a firecracker or a car backfiring. At a shooting range, it would immediately be interpreted as gunfire. So top-down processing allows us to identify objects and sounds even before examination of features is complete, or even when features are missing, distorted, or ambiguous.

Motivation is another aspect of top-down processing that can affect perception. If you are extremely hungry, you might misperceive a sign for "Burger's Body Shop" as indicating a place to eat. Similarly, if you have ever watched sports, you can probably remember a time when an obviously demented referee incorrectly called a penalty on your favorite team. You knew the call was wrong because you clearly saw the other team's player at fault. But suppose you had been cheering for that other team. The chances are good that you would have seen the referee's call as the right one.

Motivation and other aspects of top-down processing can even affect elements of the brain's bottom-up processing. For example, cells in the visual cortex that fire in response to specific features of an object show higher levels of activity if that object is of particular importance at the moment (Lamme, Zipser, & Spekreijse, 1998; Li, Piëch, & Gilbert, 2004). So corner-detecting cells will show more intense firing in response to the corners of the Barney's Diner sign you are looking for than to the corners of other signs.

Network Processing

Indeed, researchers taking a computational approach to perception have attempted to explain various aspects of object recognition in terms of both top-down and bottom-up processing. In one study, participants were asked to say whether a particular feature, like the dot and angled line at the left side of Figure 5.20, appeared within a pattern that was briefly flashed on a computer screen. The participants detected this feature faster when it was embedded in a pattern resembling a three-dimensional object than when it appeared within a random pattern of lines (Purcell

The Eye of the Beholder Top-down processing can affect our perception of people as well as objects. As noted in the chapter on social behaviour, for example, if you expect everyone in a certain ethnic or social group to behave in a certain way, you may perceive a particular group member's behaviour in line with this prejudice. On the other hand, have you ever come to perceive someone as physically more attractive or less attractive as you got to know the person better? This change in perception occurs largely because new information alters, in top-down fashion, your interpretation of the raw sensations you get from the person.

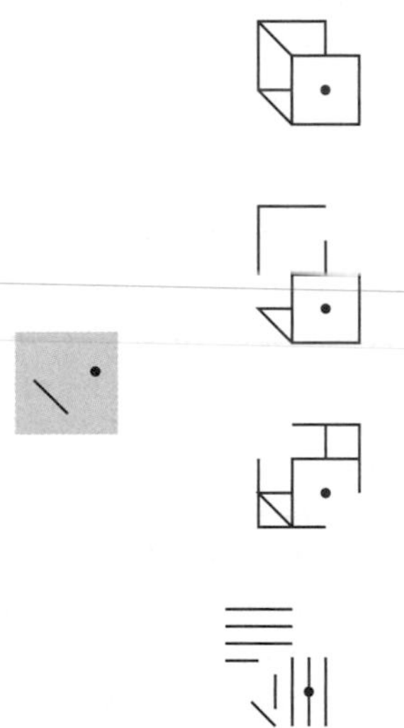

figure 5.20

The Object Superiority Effect

When people are asked to say whether the feature at left appears in patterns briefly flashed on a computer screen, the feature is more likely to be detected when it appears in patterns like those at the top right, which most resemble three-dimensional objects. This "object superiority effect" supports the importance of network processing in perception.

Source: Reprinted with permission from figures by Weisstein & Harris, *Science*, 1974, 186, 752–755. Copyright © 1974 by American Association of the Advancement of Science.

parallel distributed processing (PDP) models An approach to understanding object recognition in which various elements of the object are thought to be simultaneously analyzed by a number of widely distributed, but connected, neural units in the brain.

& Stewart, 1991). This result is called the *object superiority effect*. There is also a *word superiority effect*: When strings of letters are briefly flashed on a screen, people's ability to detect target letters is better if the string forms a word than if it is not a word (Prinzmetal, 1992).

Neural network models have been used to explain findings such as these. As described in the chapter on biological aspects of psychology, each element in these networks is connected to every other element, and each connection has a specific strength. Applying network processing models to pattern recognition involves focusing on the interactions among the various feature analyzers we have discussed (Rumelhart & Todd, 1992). More specifically, some researchers explain recognition using **parallel distributed processing (PDP) models** (Rumelhart & McClelland, 1986). According to PDP models, the units in a network operate in parallel—simultaneously. Connections between units either excite or inhibit other units. If the connection is excitatory, activating one unit spreads the activation to connected units. Using a connection may strengthen it.

How does this process apply to recognition? According to PDP models, recognition occurs as a result of the simultaneous operation of connected units. Units are activated when matched by features in a stimulus. To the extent that features, such as the letters in a word or the angles in a box, have occurred together in the past, the links between them will be stronger, and detection of any of them will be made more likely by the presence of all the others. This appears to be what happens in the word and object superiority effects, and the same phenomenon is illustrated in Figure 5.21. PDP models, sometimes called *connectionist models*, clearly represent the computational approach to perception. Researchers have achieved many advances in theories of pattern recognition by programming computers to carry out the kinds of complex computations that neural networks are assumed to perform in the human perceptual system. These computers have "learned" to read, recognize faces, and process colour in a manner that may turn out to be similar to the way humans learn and perform the same perceptual tasks (e.g. Behnke, 2003; Mel, 1997). (For a summary of our discussion of recognition processes, see "In Review: Mechanisms of Pattern Recognition.")

In Figure 5.16 you can create a kettle by adding a cone (geon 3) to a combination of geons 2 and 4 (the cup).

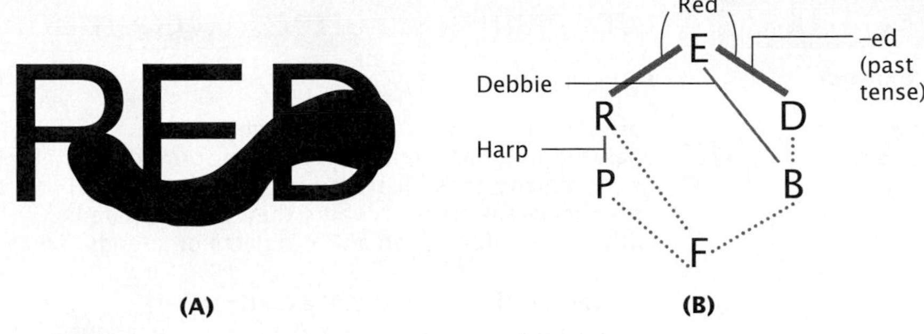

figure 5.21

Recognizing a Word

You probably recognized the pattern shown in Part A as the word *RED*, even though the first letter of the word shown could be *R* or *P*, the second *E* or *F*, and the third *D* or *B*. According to PDP models, your recognition occurred because, together, the letters excite each other's correct interpretation. This mutual excitation process is illustrated in Part B by a set of letter "nodes" (corresponding to activity sites in the brain) and some of the words they might activate. These nodes will be activated if the feature they detect appears in the stimulus array. They will also be activated if nodes to which they are linked become active. All six letters shown in Part B will initially be excited when the stimulus in Part A is presented, but mutual excitement along the strongest links leads to perception of the word "red" (Rumelhart & McClelland, 1986).

Source: Rumelhart & McClelland (1986).

Culture, Experience, and Perception

So far, we have talked as if all aspects of perception work or fail in the same way for everyone. Differing experiences, however, can affect people's perceptions by creating differing expectations and other knowledge-based, top-down processes (Kitayama et al., 2003). Janet Werker of the University of British Columbia and Richard Tees of the University of British Columbia have demonstrated that infants of English-speaking parents can discriminate the sounds (phonemes) used in different Inuit dialects more proficiently than English-speaking adults, but that, as the infants experience the sounds of their own language, they begin to lose the ability. The exposure of people in different cultures to substantially different visual environments also appears to affect their perceptual experiences. Researchers have compared responses to depth cues by people from cultures that do and do not use pictures and paintings to represent reality (Derogowski, 1989). This research suggests that people in cultures that provide little experience with pictorial representations, such as the Me'n or the Nuba in Africa, have a more difficult time judging distances shown in pictures (see Figure 5.22). These individuals also tend to have a harder time sorting pictures of three-dimensional objects into categories, even though they can easily sort the objects themselves (Derogowski, 1989).

figure 5.22

Culture and Depth Cues

Participants in various cultures were shown drawings like these and asked to judge which animal is closer to the hunter. People in cultures that provide lots of experience with pictured depth cues choose the antelope, which is at the same distance from the viewer as the hunter. Those in cultures less familiar with such cues may choose the elephant, which, though closer on the page, is more distant when depth cues are considered (Hudson, 1960).

Other research shows that the perception of optical illusions varies from culture to culture and is related to cultural differences in perceptual experiences. In one study, researchers enhanced the Ponzo illusion, shown in Figure 5.5(A), by superimposing its horizontal lines on a picture of railway tracks. This familiar image added depth cues for people in North America, but not for people in places where there were no railway tracks (Leibowitz et al., 1969). In short, although the structure and principles of human perceptual systems tend to create generally similar views of the world for all of us, our perception of reality is also shaped by experience, including the experience of living in a particular culture. As more and more cultures are "westernized," the visual stimulation they present to their children will become less distinctive. Eventually, it may become impossible to conduct research on the impact of differing experiences on perception.

in review Mechanisms of Pattern Recognition

Mechanism	Description	Example
Bottom-up processing	Raw sensations from the eye or the ear are analyzed into basic features, such as form, colour, or movement; these features are then recombined at higher brain centres, where they are compared with stored information about objects or sounds.	You recognize a dog as a dog because its features—four legs, barking, panting—match your perceptual category for "dog."
Top-down processing	Knowledge of the world and experience in perceiving allow people to make inferences about the identity of stimuli, even when the quality of raw sensory information is low.	On a dark night, what you see as a small, vague blob pulling on the end of a leash is recognized as a dog because the stimulus occurs at a location where you would expect a dog to be.
Network, or PDP, processing	Recognition depends on communication among feature-analysis systems operating simultaneously and enlightened by past experience.	A dog standing behind a picket fence will be recognized as a dog even though each disjointed "slice" of the stimulus may not look like a dog.

PsychAssist: Object Superiority Effect

LINKAGES
Perception and Human Development

LINKAGES (a link to Human Development)

Knowledge and experience play an important role in recognition, but are they also required for more basic aspects of perception? Which perceptual abilities are babies born with, and which do they develop by seeing, hearing, smelling, touching, and tasting things? How do their perceptions compare with those of adults? To learn about infants' perception, psychologists have studied two inborn patterns called *habituation* and *dishabituation*. For example, infants stop looking when they repeatedly see stimuli that are perceived to be the same. This is habituation. If a stimulus appears that is perceived to be different, infants resume looking. This is dishabituation. Researchers have used the habituation and dishabituation phenomena, along with measurements of electrical responses in the brain, to study colour perception in infants. They have found that newborns can perceive differences among stimuli showing different amounts of black-and-white contrast but that they are unable to distinguish among particular hues (Adams, Courage, & Mercer, 1994; Burr, Morrone, & Fiorentini, 1996). By three months of age, though, infants can discriminate among blue, green, yellow, and red (Adams, Courage, & Mercer, 1991). Other researchers have found that newborns can perceive differences in the angles of lines (Slater et al., 1991). These studies and others suggest that we are born with some, but not all, of the basic components of feature detection.

Face

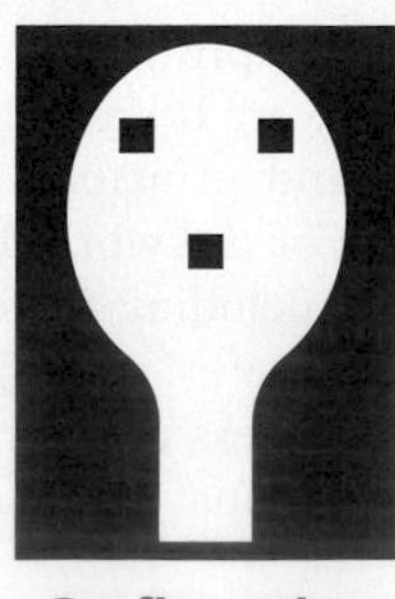
Configuration

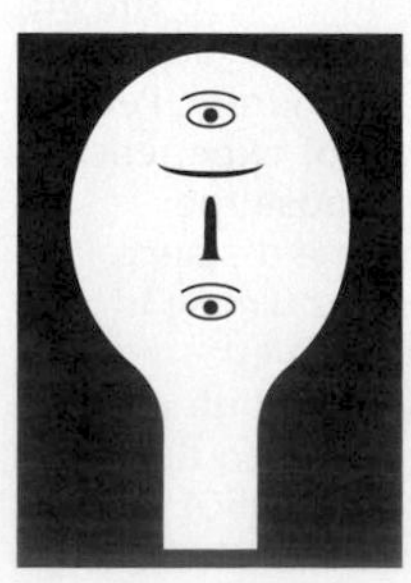
Linear

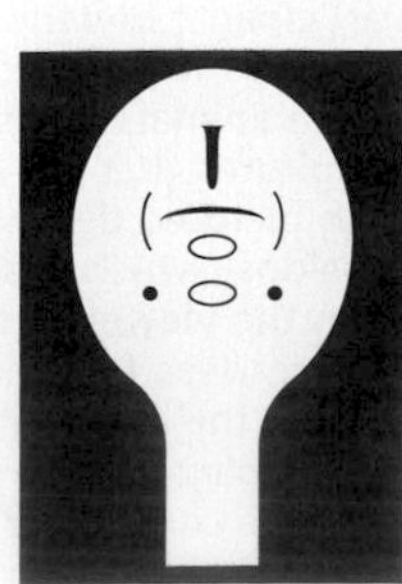
Scrambled

figure 5.23

Infants' Perceptions of Human Faces

Newborns show significantly greater interest in the face-like pattern at the far left than in any of the other patterns. Evidently, some aspects of face perception are innate.

Source: Johnson et al. (1991).

Are we also born with the ability to combine features into perceptions of whole objects? This question generates lively debate among specialists in infant perception. Some research indicates that at one month of age, infants concentrate their gaze on one part of an object, such as the corner of a triangle (Goldstein, 2001). By two months, though, the eyes systematically scan all the edges of the object, suggesting that only then has the infant begun to perceive the pattern of the object, or its shape, rather than just its component features. However, other researchers have found that once newborns have become habituated to specific combinations of features, they show dishabituation (that is, they pay attention) when those features are combined in a new way. The implication is that even newborns notice, and keep track of, the way some features are put together (Slater et al., 1991).

There is evidence that infants may be innately tuned to perceive at least one important complex pattern—the human face. In one study of newborns, some less than an hour old, patterns such as those in Figure 5.23 were moved slowly past the infants' faces (Johnson et al., 1991). The infants moved their heads and eyes to follow these patterns, but they tracked the face-like pattern shown on the left side of Figure 5.23 significantly farther than any of the non-faces. The difference in tracking indicates that the infants could discriminate between faces and non-faces and were more interested in the faces, or at least in face-like patterns (Simion et al., 2003; Valenza et al., 1996).

Infants also notice differences among faces. At first, this ability to discriminate applies to both human and non-human faces. So at the age of six months, infants are actually better than adults at discriminating among the faces of monkeys (Pascalis, de Haan, & Nelson, 2002). By about the age of nine months, however, face discrimination ability has become focused on human faces, the kind most babies see most often. Researchers who take an evolutionary approach suggest that interest in faces, especially human faces, is adaptive because it helps newborns focus on their only source of food and care.

Other research on perceptual development suggests that our ability to use certain distance cues develops more slowly than our recognition of object shapes (see Figure 5.24). For example, infants' ability to use binocular disparity and relative motion cues to judge depth appears to develop some time after about three months of age (Yonas, Arterberry, & Granrud, 1987). Infants do not use texture gradients

figure 5.24

The Visual Cliff

The *visual cliff* is a glass-topped table that creates the impression of a sudden drop-off. A ten-month-old placed at what looks like the edge will calmly crawl across the shallow side to reach a parent but will hesitate and cry rather than crawl over the "cliff" (Gibson & Walk, 1960). Changes in heart rate show that infants too young to crawl also perceive the depth but are not frightened by it. Here again, nature and nurture interact adaptively: Depth perception appears shortly after birth, but fear and avoidance of dangerous depth do not develop until an infant is old enough to crawl into trouble.

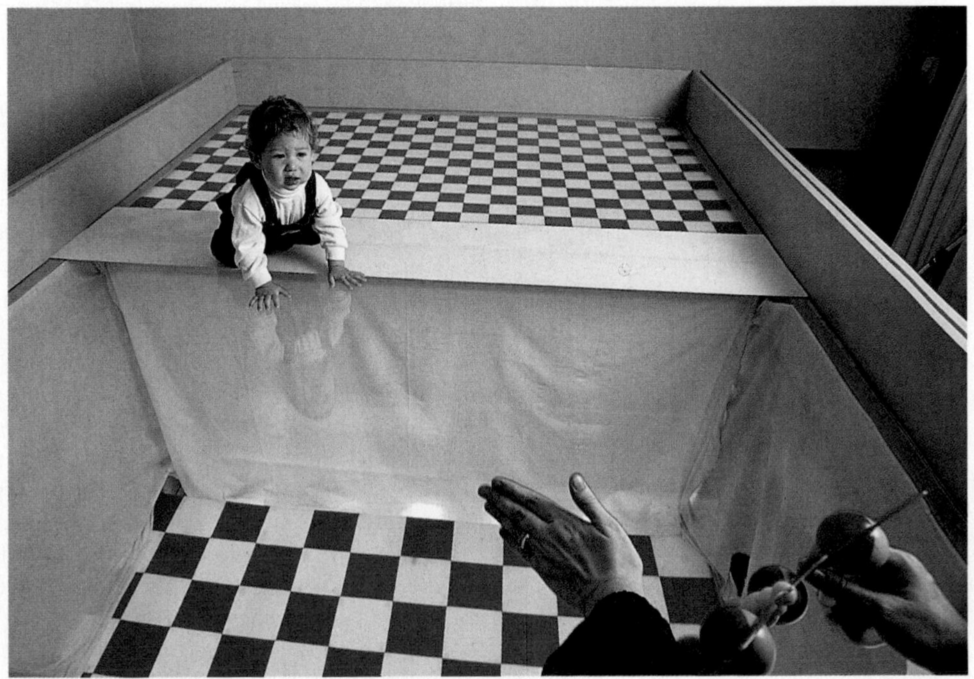

and linear perspective as cues about depth until they are three-to-seven months old (Arterberry, Yonas, & Bensen, 1989; Bhatt & Bertin, 2001).

In summary, there is little doubt that many of the basic building blocks of perception are present within the first few days after birth. The basics include organ-based cues to depth, such as accommodation and convergence. Maturation of the visual system adds to these basics as time goes by. For example, over the first few months after birth, the eye's fovea gradually develops the number of cone cells necessary for high visual acuity and perception of small differences in colour (Goldstein, 2001). However, visual experience may also be necessary if the infant is to recognize some patterns and objects in frequently encountered stimuli, to interpret depth and distance cues, and to use these cues in moving safely through the world. In other words, like so many aspects of human psychology, perception is the result of a blending of heredity and environment. From infancy onward, the perceptual system creates a personal reality based in part on the experience that shapes each individual's feature-analysis networks and knowledge-based expectancies (Johnson, 2004).

Attention

Believe it or not, you still haven't found Barney's Diner! By now, you understand *how* you will recognize the right sign when you perceive it, but how can you be sure you *will* perceive it? As you drive, the diner's sign will appear as just one small piece in a sensory puzzle that also includes road signs, traffic lights, sirens, talk radio, and dozens of other stimuli. You can't perceive all of them at once, so to find Barney's you are going to have to be sure that the information you select for perceptual processing includes the stimuli that will help you reach your goal. In other words, you are going to have to pay attention.

Attention is the process of directing and focusing certain psychological resources to enhance perception, performance, and mental experience. We use attention to *direct* our sensory and perceptual systems toward certain stimuli, to *select* specific information for further processing, to *ignore* or screen out unwanted stimuli, to *allocate* the mental energy required to process selected stimuli, and to *regulate* the flow of resources necessary for performing a task or coordinating several tasks at once (Wickens & Carswell, 1997). Todd Mondor of the University of Manitoba and Allen Finley of Dalhousie University in Nova Scotia realize the importance of selective attention for surgeons. While operating, the surgeon must be able to focus his or her attention on the task at hand yet, at the same time, monitor many pieces of equipment. Warning buzzers are often designed into the equipment to alert the surgeon to any problems. Todd Monder and Allen Finely have investigated the efficacy of different warning sounds (Mondor and Finely, 2003).

Psychologists have discovered three important characteristics of attention. First, it *improves mental processing*; you often have to concentrate attention on a task to do your best at it. If your attentional system temporarily malfunctions, you might drive right past Barney's Diner. Second, attention takes *effort*. Prolonged concentration of attention can leave you feeling drained (McNay, McCarty, & Gold, 2001). And when you are already tired, focusing attention on anything becomes more difficult. Third, attentional resources are *limited*. If your attention is focused on reading this book, for example, you'll have less attention left over to listen to a conversation in the next room.

To experience attention as a process, try "moving it around" a bit. When you finish reading this sentence, look at something behind you, then face forward and notice the next sound you hear, then visualize your best friend, and then focus on how your tongue feels. You just used attention to direct your perceptual systems toward different aspects of your external and internal environments. Sometimes, as when you looked behind you, shifting attention involves *overt orienting*—pointing sensory systems at a particular stimulus. But you were able to shift attention to an image of your

attention The process of directing and focusing psychological resources to enhance perception, performance, and mental experience.

friend's face without having to move a muscle. This is called *covert orienting*. (We've heard a rumour that students sometimes use covert orienting to shift their attention from their lecturer to thoughts that have nothing to do with the lecture.)

FOCUS ON RESEARCH METHODS

An Experiment in "Mind Reading"

Everyone knows what it is like to covertly shift attention, but how can we tell when someone else is doing it? The study of covert attention requires the sort of "mind reading" that has been made possible by innovative experimental research methods. These techniques are helping psychologists to measure where a person's attention is focused.

What was the researchers' question?

Michael Posner and his colleagues were interested in finding out what changes in perceptual processing occur when people covertly shift their attention to a specific location in space (Posner, Nissen, & Ogden, 1978). Specifically, the researchers addressed the question of whether these attentional shifts lead to more sensitive processing of stimuli in the location to which attention is focused.

How did the researchers answer the question?

Posner and his colleagues took advantage of an important property of mental events: They take time. Moreover, the time taken by mental events can vary considerably, thus providing important clues about internal processes such as covert attention.

The researchers designed a study in which participants were asked to focus their eyes on a fixation point that appeared at the centre of a computer screen. One second later, a tiny square appeared at either the right or left edge of the screen. The participants were then asked to indicate, by pressing a key as quickly as possible, when they detected the square. Because their vision was focused on the fixation point, they could detect the square only out of the "corners" of their eyes.

On any given trial, a participant could never be sure where the square would appear. However, the researchers provided a cue, or "hint," at the start of some of the trials, in the form of an arrow at the fixation point. Sometimes, the arrow pointed to the right edge of the screen (→). This cue gave correct information 80 percent of the time. On other trials, the arrow pointed to the left edge of the screen (←). This cue was also correct 80 percent of the time. On still other trials, participants saw a plus sign (+) at the fixation point, which indicated that the square was equally likely to appear on the left or the right.

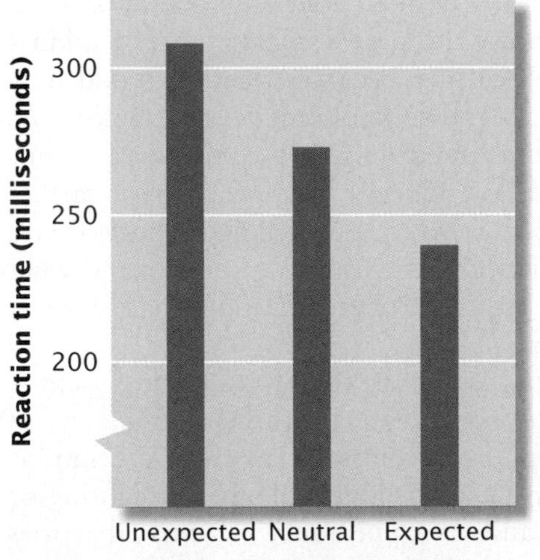

figure 5.25

It took people less time (measured in thousandths of a second) to detect a square appearing at an expected location than at an unexpected one. This result suggests that, even though their eyes did not move, these research participants covertly shifted their attention to the expected location before the stimulus was presented.

The researchers reasoned that when the plus sign appeared, the best strategy for quickly detecting the square would be to keep attention focused on the centre of the screen and to shift it only after the square appeared. When one of the arrow cues appeared, though, the best strategy would be to covertly shift attention in the direction indicated by the arrow before the square appeared. If the participants were covertly shifting their attention in this way, they should be able to detect the square fastest when the cue provided accurate information about where the square would appear—even though they were not actually moving their eyes.

The dependent variable in this study was the speed of target detection, measured in milliseconds. The independent variable was the type of cue given: correct, incorrect, or neutral. Correct cues were arrows that accurately predicted the target location; incorrect ones were arrows that pointed the wrong way. Neutral cues gave no guidance.

What did the researchers find?

As shown in Figure 5.25, the target square was detected significantly faster when the cue gave correct information about where the square would appear. Incorrect cues resulted in a distinct drop in target detection speed: When participants were led to covertly shift their attention in the wrong direction, it took them longer to detect the square.

● What do the results mean?

The data provide evidence that the participants used cues to shift their attention to the expected location. This shift readied their perceptual systems to detect information at that location. When a cue led them to shift their attention to the wrong location, they were less ready to detect information at the correct location, and their detection speed was slower. In short, attention can enhance the processing of information at one location, but it does so at the expense of processing information elsewhere.

● What do we still need to know?

More recent research on the costs and benefits associated with perceptual expectancies has been generally consistent with the findings of Posner's pioneering team (e.g., Ball & Sekuler, 1992; Carrasco & McElree, 2001). However, there are still many unanswered questions about how covert attention actually operates. How quickly can we shift attention from one location to another? Estimates range from about a quarter of a second all the way to a tenth of a second (Theeuwes, Godijn, & Pratt, 2004; Wolfe, 1998). And how quickly can we shift attention between sensory modalities—from watching to listening, for example? It will be difficult to find the methods necessary to address these questions, but they are fundamental to understanding our ability to deal with the potentially overwhelming load of stimuli that reaches our sensory receptors. Experiments designed to answer such questions not only expand our understanding of attention but also illustrate the possibility of measuring hidden mental events through observation of overt behaviour (Wolfe, Alvarez, & Horowitz, 2000).

LINKAGES (a link to Sensation)

Directing Attention

As shown in Posner's experiment on "mind reading," attending to some stimuli leaves us less able to attend to others. In other words, attention is *selective*; it is like a spotlight that can illuminate only a part of the external or internal environment at any particular moment. How do you control, or allocate, your attention?

Control over attention can be voluntary or involuntary (Yantis, 1993). *Voluntary*, or goal-directed, control occurs when you purposely focus your attention in order to perform a task, such as reading a book in a noisy room or watching for a friend in a crowd. Voluntary control reflects top-down processing, because attention is guided by intentions, beliefs, expectations, motivation, or other knowledge-based factors. As people learn certain skills, they voluntarily direct their attention to information they once ignored. For example, the experienced driver notices events taking place farther down the road than the first-time driver does. If you are watching a sports event, learning where to allocate your attention is important if you are to understand what is going on. And if you are competing in a sport, the proper allocation of attention is absolutely essential for success (Moran, 1996).

When, in spite of these top-down factors, some aspect of the environment—such as a loud noise—diverts your attention, control is said to be *involuntary*. In such cases, attentional control is a bottom-up, or stimulus-driven, process. Stimulus characteristics that tend to capture attention include sudden changes in lighting or colour (such as flashing signs), movement, and the appearance of unusual shapes (Folk, Remington, & Wright, 1994). Some psychologists use the results of attention research to help design advertisements, logos, and product packaging that "grab" potential customers' attention.

Ignoring Information

When the spotlight of your attention is voluntarily or involuntarily focused on one part of the environment, you may ignore, or be "blind" to, stimuli occurring in other parts. This phenomenon, called *inattentional blindness* (Mack & Rock, 1998;

Mack, 2003), can be helpful when it allows us to ignore construction noise while we are taking an exam. But it can also endanger us if we ignore information—such as a stop sign—that we should be noticing. Inattentional blindness can cause us to miss some rather dramatic changes in our environment (Most et al., 2001). In one study, a researcher asked a number of college students for directions to a campus building (Simons & Levin, 1997). During each conversation, two other researchers dressed as workmen passed between the first researcher and the student, carrying a large door. As the door hid the researcher from the student's view, one of the "workmen" took his place. This new person then resumed the conversation with the student as though nothing had happened. Amazing as it seems, only half of the students noticed that they were suddenly talking to a new person! The rest had apparently been paying so much attention to the researcher's question or to the map he was showing that they did not notice what he looked like. And half the participants in another study were so focused on their assigned task of counting the passes made during a videotaped basketball game that they did not notice that a woman in a gorilla suit walked in front of the camera, beat her chest, and walked away (Simons & Chabris, 1999). Magicians take advantage of inattentional blindness when they use sudden movements or other attention-grabbing stimuli to draw our attention away from the actions that lie behind their tricks. Ronald Rensink of the University of British Columbia has been studying a type of inattentional blindness known as "change blindness." This suggests that a person can miss a large change in a scene which would normally be fairly easy to notice (Simons and Rensink, 2005). To experience an example of change blindness, take a look at the photos in Figure 5.26.

Divided Attention

People can sometimes divide their attention in ways that allow them to do more than one thing at a time, a skill sometimes called *multitasking*. You can drive a car, listen to the radio, sing along, and keep a beat by drumming on the steering wheel, all at the same time. In fact, as the photo below illustrates, it is sometimes difficult to stop dividing our attention and to stay focused on just one thing. However, your attention can't be divided beyond a certain point without a loss in performance and mental processing ability. For example, it is virtually impossible to read and talk at the same time. The reason is that attention is a limited resource. If you try to spread it over too many targets, or between certain kinds of tasks, you "run out" of attention.

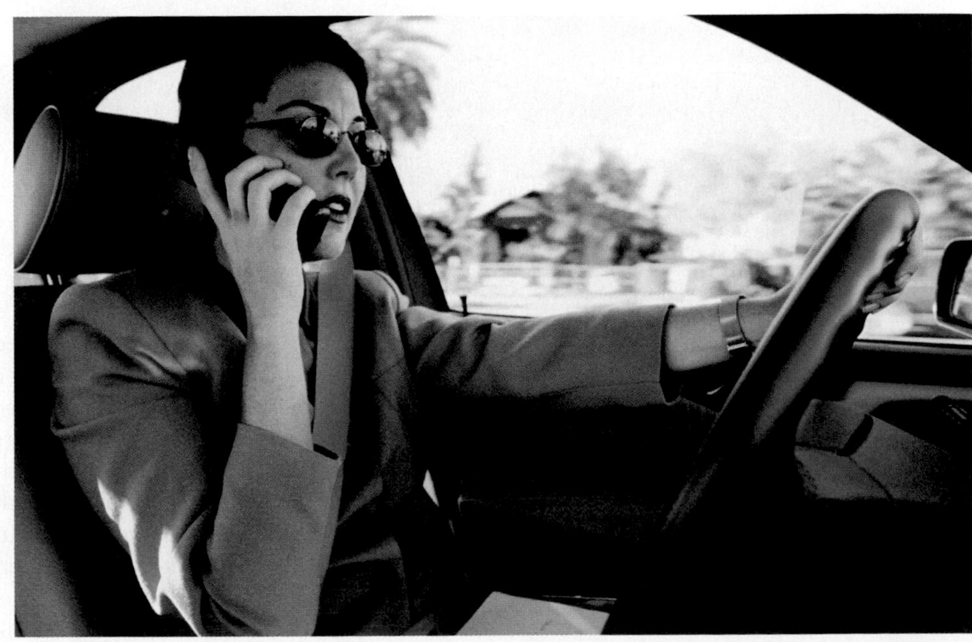

Driven to Distraction? About 65% of all Canadians would support a ban on the use of cell phones while driving and 64% consider the use of cell phones while driving an "extremely serious" problem (Transport Canada, 2003). Some cell phone manufacturers claim that hands-free models can eliminate any dangers associated with using a phone while driving, but a recent study by Joanne Harbluk and Ian Noy for Transport Canada suggests the use of any interactive on-board technology while driving, including hand free cell phones, is cause for serious concern, due to the distractions they can cause for the driver. (Harbluk & Noy, 2002).

figure 5.26

Change Blindness

These two photos are almost, but not exactly, the same. If you can't see the difference, or if it took you a while to see it, you may have been focusing your attention on the similarity of main features, resulting in blindness to one small, but obvious difference. (See page 186 for the answer.)

Why is it sometimes so easy and at other times so difficult to do two things at once? When one task is so *automatic* that it requires little or no attention, it is usually easy to do something else at the same time, even if the other task takes some attention (Schneider, 1985). When two tasks both require attention, it may still be possible to perform them simultaneously, as long as each taps into different kinds of attentional resources (Wickens, 2002). For example, some attentional resources are devoted to perceiving incoming stimuli, whereas others handle making responses. This specialization of attention allows a skilled pianist to read musical notes and press keys simultaneously, even when playing the piece for the first time. Apparently, the human brain has more than one type of attentional resource and more than one spotlight of attention (Wickens, 1989). This notion of different types of attention also helps explain why a driver can listen to the radio while steering safely and why voice control can be an effective way of performing a second task in an aircraft while the pilot's hands are

BLUE GREEN
GREEN ORANGE
PURPLE ORANGE
GREEN BLUE
RED RED
GREY GREY
RED BLUE
BLUE PURPLE

figure 5.27

The Stroop Task

Look at these words and, as rapidly as possible, call out the *colour of the ink* in which each word is printed. This Stroop task (Stroop, 1935) is not easy, because your brain automatically processes the *meaning* of each word, which then competes for attention with the response you are supposed to give. To do well, you must focus on the ink colour and not allow your attention to be divided between colour and meaning. Children just learning to read have less trouble with this task, because they do not yet process word meanings as automatically as experienced readers do. Derek Besner and Jennifer Stolz of the University of Waterloo, Ontario, have demonstrated that the process of word recognition may not be an automatic process as was first suggested. They have found that when you narrow spatial attention (cue the participant to look at only one letter in the word) the Stroop effect can be reduced (Besner and Stolz, 1999).

busy with the controls (Wickens, 1992). If two tasks require the same kind of attention, however, performance on both tasks will suffer (Just et al., 2001).

Attention and Automatic Processing

Your search for Barney's Diner will be aided by your ability to voluntarily allocate attention to a certain part of the environment, but it would be even easier if you knew that Barney's had the only bright red sign on that stretch of road (see "In Review: Attention"). Your search would not take much effort in this case because you could simply "set" your attention to filter out all signs except red ones. Actively ignoring certain information will help you find Barney's, but it will also continue to affect your perceptions for some time afterward. Suppose, for example, that while you are ignoring blue signs, you pass a billboard showing a giant blue palm tree. Jason Laboe of the University of Manitoba and Launa Leboe and Bruce Millikin of McMaster University in Ontario have found that your efforts to ignore certain stimuli may create negative priming (Laboe et al. 2003), making you slightly less able than before to identify palm trees of any colour for several minutes, hours, or days (DeSchepper & Treisman, 1996).

Psychologists use the words *parallel processing* to describe our ability to search for targets rapidly and automatically. It is as if you can examine all nearby locations at once (in parallel) and rapidly detect the target no matter where it appears. So if the sign you are looking for is bright red and twice as large as any other one on the road, you could conduct a parallel search, and it would quickly "pop out." The automatic, parallel processing that allows detection of colour or size suggests that these features are analyzed before the point at which attention is required. However, if the target you seek shares many features with others nearby, you must conduct a slower, serial search, examining each one in turn (Treisman, 1988).

Attention and the Brain

If directing attention to a task causes extra mental work to be done, there should be evidence of that work in brain activity. Such evidence has been provided by positron emission tomography (PET) and magnetic resonance imaging (MRI) scans, which reveal increased blood flow and greater neural activity in regions of the brain associated with the mental processing necessary for the task. In one study,

in review Attention

Characteristics	Functions	Mechanisms
Improves mental functioning	Directs sensory and perceptual systems toward stimuli	Overt orienting (e.g., cupping your ear to hear a whisper)
Requires effort	Selects specific information for further processing	Covert orienting (e.g., thinking about spring break while looking at the notes in front of you)
Has limits	Allows us to ignore some information	Voluntary control (e.g., purposefully looking for cars before crossing a street)
	Allocates mental energy to process information	Involuntary control (e.g., losing your train of thought when you're interrupted by a thunderclap)
	Regulates the flow of resources necessary for performing a task or coordinating multiple tasks	Automatic processing (e.g., no longer thinking about grammar rules as you become fluent in a foreign language)
		Divided attention (e.g., looking for an open teammate while you dribble a soccer ball down the field)

for example, people were asked either to focus attention on reporting only the colour of a stimulus or to divide attention in order to report its colour, speed of motion, and shape (Corbetta et al., 1991). When attention was focused on colour alone, increased blood flow appeared only in the part of the brain where that stimulus feature was analyzed; when attention was divided, the added supply of blood was shared between two locations. Similarly, increased neural activity occurs in two different areas of the brain when participants perform two different tasks, such as deciding whether sentences are true while also deciding whether two three-dimensional objects are the same or different (Just et al., 2001).

Because attention appears to be a linked set of resources that improve information processing at several levels and locations in the brain, it is not surprising that no single brain region has been identified as an "attention centre" (Posner & Peterson, 1990; Sasaki et al., 2001). However, scientists have found regions in the base of the brain and in the parietal lobe of the cerebral cortex that are involved in the *switching* of visual attention from one stimulus element or location to another (Posner & Raichle, 1994).

Applications of Research on Perception

Throughout this chapter we have mentioned ways in which perceptual systems shape people's ability to handle a variety of tasks, from recognizing restaurant signs to detecting tornadoes. We have also seen how research on perception explains the principles behind movies and videos and affects the design of advertisements. In this section we examine two other areas in which perception research has been applied: human-computer interaction and traffic safety.

Avoiding Perceptual Overload The pilot of a modern commercial jetliner is faced with a potentially overwhelming array of visual and auditory signals that must be correctly perceived and interpreted to ensure a safe flight. Psychologists such as Brian Tansley of the Human Computer Interaction Laboratory at Carleton University are helping to design instrument displays, warning systems, and communication links that make this task easier and errors less likely (cf. Tansley and Moggride, 2001).

Human-Computer Interaction

The Carleton University Human-Computer Interaction Laboratory in Ottawa is studying the interaction between humans and computers with the goal of making computers safer, more accessible and user-friendly. For example, in the world of computer displays, in line with the ecological approach to perception, many of the depth cues that help people to navigate in the physical world have been duplicated (Preece et al., 1994). The next time you use a word-processing or spreadsheet program, notice how shading cues make the "buttons" on the application toolbar at the top or bottom of the screen seem to protrude from their background, as real buttons would. Similarly, when you open several documents or spreadsheets, notice that interposition cues make them appear to be lying on top of one another.

The results of research on attention have even been applied to your cursor. It blinks to attract your attention, making it possible to do a quick, parallel search rather than a slow, serial search when you are looking for it amid all the other stimuli on the screen (Schneiderman, 1992). Perceptual principles have also guided creation of the pictorial images, or icons, that are used to represent objects, processes, and commands in your computer programs (Preece et al., 1994). These icons speed your use of the computer if their features are easy to detect, recognize, and interpret (McDougall, de Bruijn, & Curry, 2000; Niemela & Saarinen, 2000). This is the reason a little trash-can icon is used in some programs to show you where to click when you want to delete a file. A tiny eraser or paper shredder might have worked, too, but its features might be harder to recognize. These are just a few of the ways in which psychologists are applying perception research to make computers easier to use.

The difference between the two photos in Figure 5.26 is that the top picture includes a clump of trees just to the left of the statue's head.

Traffic Safety

Research on perception is being applied in many ways to enhance traffic safety. For example, psychologists are involved in the design of automotive night-vision displays that make it easier for drivers to see low-visibility targets, such as pedestrians dressed in dark clothing, or animals (Essock et al., 1999). Further, research on divided attention is informing the debate over the use of cell phones while driving. The demands of traffic safety groups and the examples set by many countries around the world have led the states of New York and New Jersey to outlaw drivers' use of hand-held cell phones. Most other U.S. states are considering similar laws; some of these laws would ban even hands-free phone conversations while driving. Cell phone manufacturers and network providers agree that using a phone while driving can be dangerous, but only because looking at the handset, pushing its buttons, and holding it in place during the call can distract the driver from steering and watching the road. They claim that hands-free phones and voice-controlled dialing eliminate any dangers associated with drivers' use of cell phones.

That argument is contradicted by research showing that driving performance is impaired while talking on *any* cell phone, even if it is a hands-free model (Spence & Read, 2003; Strayer & Johnston, 2001; Strayer, Drews, & Johnston, 2003). This research suggests that the dangers of driving while using a phone do not stem simply from listening to someone speak or even from talking. The driving performance of research participants was not impaired by listening to books on tape or by repeating words that they heard. Performance *did* decline, though, when participants were asked to do more elaborate processing of auditory information, such as rephrasing what they heard. (You may have experienced similar effects if you have ever missed a turn or had a near-accident while deeply engaged in conversation with a passenger.) One study of people' performance on a driving simulator found that the accident-avoidance skills of sober drivers talking on cell phones were impaired more than those of drivers who were legally drunk but not using phones (Strayer, Drews, & Crouch, 2003). These results suggest that using a cell phone while driving is dangerous not only because it can take your eyes off the road and a hand off the wheel but also because the phone conversation competes for the cognitive/attentional resources you need to drive safely. Perception researchers suggest that this competition and the dangers associated with it are unlikely to be reduced by hands-free phones (Just et al., 2001; Strayer, Drews, & Johnston, 2003; Strayer et al., 2004).

LINKAGES

As noted in the chapter on introducing psychology, all of psychology's subfields are related to one another. Our discussion of how perceptual processes develop in infants illustrates just one way in which the topic of this chapter, perception, is linked to the subfield of developmental psychology (which is the topic of the chapter on human development). The Linkages diagram shows ties to two other subfields as well, and there are many more ties throughout the book. Looking for linkages among subfields will help you see how they all fit together and better appreciate the big picture that is psychology.

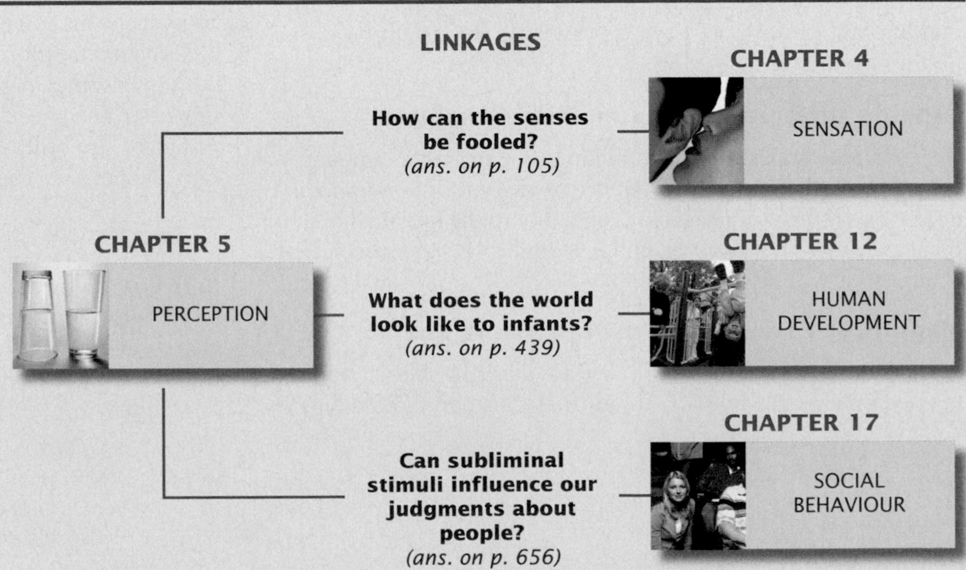
LINKAGES
CHAPTER 5
PERCEPTION
How can the senses be fooled?
(ans. on p. 105)
CHAPTER 4
SENSATION
What does the world look like to infants?
(ans. on p. 439)
CHAPTER 12
HUMAN DEVELOPMENT
Can subliminal stimuli influence our judgments about people?
(ans. on p. 656)
CHAPTER 17
SOCIAL BEHAVIOUR

SUMMARY

Perception is the process through which people actively use knowledge and understanding of the world to interpret sensations as meaningful experiences.

The Perception Paradox

Because perception often seems so rapid and effortless, it appears to be a rather simple operation; however, this is not the case. An enormous amount of processing is required to transform energy received by receptors into perceptual experience. The complexity of perception is revealed by various perceptual errors (for example, illusions).

Three Approaches to Perception

The *computational approach* to perception emphasizes the computations performed by the nervous system. The *constructivist approach* suggests that the perceptual system constructs the experience of reality, making inferences and applying knowledge in order to interpret sensations. The *ecological approach* holds that the environment itself provides the cues that people use to form perceptions.

Psychophysics

Psychophysics is the study of the relationship between stimulus energy and the psychological experience of that energy.

Absolute Thresholds: Is Something Out There?

Psychophysics has traditionally been concerned with matters such as determining absolute thresholds for the detection of stimuli. Research shows that this threshold is not, in fact, absolute. The *absolute threshold* has been redefined as the minimum amount of stimulus energy that can be detected 50 percent of the time. *Supraliminal stimuli* fall above this threshold; *subliminal stimuli* fall below it.

Signal-Detection Theory

Signal-detection theory describes how people respond to faint or ambiguous stimuli. Detection of a signal is affected by external and internal noise, *sensitivity*, and the *response criterion*. Signal-detection theory has been applied to understanding decision making and performance in areas such as the detection of tornadoes on radar.

Judging Differences: Has Anything Changed?

Weber's law states that the minimum detectable amount of change in a stimulus—the *difference threshold*, or *just-noticeable difference (JND)*—increases in proportion to the initial amount of the stimulus. The less the initial stimulation, the smaller the change that will be detected.

Magnitude Estimation: How Intense Is That?

Fechner's law and Stevens's power law describe the relationship between the magnitude of a stimulus and its perceived intensity.

Organizing the Perceptual World

Basic Processes in Perceptual Organization

Perceptual organization is the process whereby order is imposed on the information received by your senses. The perceptual system automatically distinguishes figure from ground, and it groups stimuli into patterns. Gestalt psychologists and others identified laws or principles that guide such grouping: proximity, similarity, continuity, closure, common fate, synchrony, common region, and connectedness. These laws appear to ensure that perceptual organization creates interpretations of incoming information that are simple and most likely to be correct. The process of mentally representing and interpreting sounds is called *auditory scene analysis*.

Perception of Location and Distance

Visual localization requires information about the position of the body and eyes, as well as information about where a stimulus falls on the retinas. Auditory localization depends on detecting differences in the information that reaches the two ears, including differences in timing and intensity. Perception of distance, or *depth perception*, depends partly on stimulus cues and partly on the physical structure of the visual system. Some of the stimulus cues for depth perception are interposition, relative size, height in the visual field, texture gradient, linear perspective, and motion parallax. Cues based on the structure of the visual system include *accommodation* (the change in the shape of the lenses as objects are brought into focus), *convergence* (the fact that the eyes must move to focus on the same object), and *binocular disparity* (the fact that the eyes are set slightly apart).

Perception of Motion

The perception of motion results, in part, from the movement of stimuli across the retinas. Expanding or *looming* stimulation is perceived as an approaching object. Movement of the retinal image is interpreted along with information about movement of the head, eyes, and other parts of the body so that one's own movement can be discriminated from the movement of external objects. *Stroboscopic motion* is an illusion that accounts for our ability to see smooth motion in films, videos, and DVDs.

Perceptual Constancy

Because of *perceptual constancy*, the brightness, size, and shape of objects are seen as constant even though the sensations received from those objects may change. Size constancy and shape constancy depend on the relationship between the retinal image of an object and the knowledge-based perception of its distance. Brightness constancy depends on the perceived relationship between the brightness of an object and its background.

Recognizing the Perceptual World

Both *bottom-up processing* and *top-down processing* contribute to recognition of the world. The ability to recognize objects is based on finding a match between the pattern of sensations organized by the perceptual system and a pattern that is stored in memory.

Bottom-Up Processing

Bottom-up processing seems to be accomplished by the analysis of stimulus features or combinations of features, such as form, colour, and motion.

Top-Down Processing

Top-down processing is influenced by expectancy and motivation. *Schemas* based on past experience can create a perceptual set, the readiness or predisposition to perceive stimuli in certain ways. Expectancies can also be created by the context in which a stimulus appears.

Network Processing

Research on pattern recognition has focused attention on network models, or *parallel distributed processing (PDP)* models, of perception. These emphasize the simultaneous activation and interaction of feature-analysis systems and the role of experience.

Culture, Experience, and Perception

To the extent that the visual environments of people in different cultures differ, their perceptual experiences—as evidenced by their responses to perceptual illusions—may differ as well.

Attention

Attention is the process of focusing psychological resources to enhance perception, performance, and mental experience. We can shift attention overtly—by moving the eyes, for example—or covertly, without any movement of sensory systems.

Directing Attention

Attention is selective; it is like a spotlight that illuminates different parts of the external environment or various mental processes. Control over attention can be voluntary and knowledge based or involuntary and driven by environmental stimuli.

Ignoring Information

Sometimes attention can be so focused that it results in inattentional blindness, a failure to detect or identify normally noticeable stimuli.

Divided Attention

Although there are limits to how well people can divide attention, they can sometimes attend to two tasks at once. For example, tasks that have become automatic can often be performed along with more demanding tasks, and tasks that require very different types of processing, such as gardening and talking, can be performed together because each task depends on a different supply of mental resources.

Attention and Automatic Processing

Some information can be processed automatically, in parallel, whereas other situations demand focused attention and a serial search.

Attention and the Brain

Although the brain plays a critical role in attention, no single brain region has been identified as the main attention centre.

Applications of Research on Perception

Research on human perception has numerous practical applications.

Human-Computer Interaction

Perceptual principles relating to recognition, depth cues, and attention are being applied by psychologists who work with designers of computers and computer programs.

Traffic Safety

Research on divided attention is being applied to help understand the potential dangers of driving while using various kinds of cell phones.

6 Learning

Live and learn. This simple phrase captures the idea that learning is a lifelong process that affects our behaviour every day. Understanding how learning takes place is an important part of understanding ourselves. In this chapter, we explore the learning process and the factors that affect it. We have organized our presentation as follows:

Can you recall how you felt on your first day of kindergarten? Like many young children, you may have been bewildered, even frightened, as the comforting familiarity of home or daycare suddenly was replaced by an environment filled with new names and faces, rules and events. But, like most youngsters, you probably adjusted to this new situation within a few days, much as you did again when you started high school, and college.

Your adjustment, or *adaptation,* to these new environments occurred in many ways. Ringing bells, lunch lines, midterm grades, and other once-strange new school events not only became part of your expectations about the world but also began to serve as signals. You soon realized that if a note was delivered to your teacher during class, someone would be called to the main office. If a substitute teacher appeared, it meant an easy lesson or a chance to act up. And if your teacher arrived with a box of papers, you'd know the tests had been graded. Adapting to school also meant developing new knowledge about what behaviours were appropriate and inappropriate in the new settings you encountered. Although your parents might have encouraged you to talk whenever you wanted to at home, perhaps you found that at school, you had to raise your hand first. And the messy finger painting that got you in trouble at home might have earned you praise in art class. You found, too, that there were things you could do—such as paying attention in class and getting to school on time—to reap rewards and avoid punishment. Finally, of course, you adapted to school by absorbing facts about the world and developing skills ranging from hockey to reading, writing, and debating.

The entire process of development, from birth to death, involves a biological adaptation to increasingly complex, ever-changing environments, using continuously updated knowledge gained through experience. Although perhaps most highly developed in humans, the ability to adapt to changing environments appears to varying degrees in members of all species. According to the evolutionary approach to psychology, it is individual variability in the capacity to adapt that shapes the evolution of appearance and behaviour in animals and humans. As Charles Darwin noted, individuals who don't adapt may not survive to reproduce.

Many forms of animal and human adaptation follow the principles of learning. **Learning** is the adaptive process through which experience modifies pre-existing behaviour and understanding. The pre-existing behaviour and understanding may have been present at birth, acquired through maturation, or learned earlier. Learning plays a central role in the development of most aspects of human behaviour. It allows us to build the motor skills we need to walk or tie a shoe, the language skills we use to communicate, and the object categories—such as "food," "vehicle," or "animal"—that help us organize our perceptions and think logically about the world. Sayings such as "Once burned, twice shy" and "Fool me once, shame on you; fool me twice, shame on me" reflect this vital learning process. If you want to know who you are and how you became the person you are today, examining what and how you have learned is a good place to start.

Humans and other animals learn primarily by experiencing events, observing relationships between those events, and noting the regularity in the world around them. When two events repeatedly take place together, people can predict the occurrence of one from knowledge of the other. They learn that a clear blue sky means dry weather, that too little sleep makes them irritable, that they can reach someone via e-mail by typing a certain address, and that screaming orders motivates some people and angers others. Some learning takes place consciously, as when we study for an exam, but, as mentioned later, we can also learn things without being aware we are doing so (Watanabe, Nanez, & Sasaki, 2001).

learning The modification through experience of pre-existing behaviour and understanding.

Psychological research on learning has been guided by three main questions: (1) Which events and relationships do people learn about? (2) What circumstances determine whether and how people learn? and (3) Is learning a slow process requiring lots of practice, or does it involve sudden flashes of insight? In this chapter we provide some of the answers to these questions.

We first consider the simplest forms of learning—learning about sights, sounds, and other individual stimuli. Then we examine the two major kinds of learning that involve *associations* between events—classical conditioning and operant conditioning. Next we consider some higher forms of learning and cognition, and we conclude by discussing how research on learning might help people learn better. As you read, notice that learning principles operate in education, in the workplace, in medical treatment, in psychotherapy, and in many other aspects of people's lives.

Learning about Stimuli

In a changing world, people are constantly bombarded by stimuli. If we tried to pay attention to every sight and sound, our information-processing systems would be overloaded, and we would be unable to concentrate on anything. People appear to be genetically tuned to attend to certain kinds of events, such as loud sounds, special tastes, or pain. *Novel* stimuli—stimuli we have not experienced before—also tend to attract our attention. Because of a process called *sensitization,* for example, people and animals show exaggerated responses to unexpected, potentially threatening sights or sounds, especially if they are emotionally aroused at the time. So while breathlessly exploring a dark, spooky house, you might scream, run, or violently throw something in response to the unexpected creaking of a door.

By contrast, our response to *unchanging* stimuli decreases over time. This aspect of adaptation is a simple form of learning called **habituation,** and it can occur in relation to sights, sounds, smells, tastes, or touches. Habituation is especially important for adapting to initially startling but harmless events such as the repeated popping of balloons, but it occurs in some degree to all kinds of stimuli and in all kinds of animals, from simple sea snails to humans (Gottfried, O'Doherty, & Dolan, 2003; Pinel, 1993). Through habituation, you eventually fail to notice that you are wearing glasses or a watch. And after having been in a room for a while, you no longer smell that musty or flowery odour or hear that loudly ticking clock. In fact, you may become aware of the clock again only when it stops because now something in your environment has changed. This reappearance of your original response when the stimulus changes is called *dishabituation.* In the perception chapter, we describe how habituation and dishabituation processes have helped psychologists determine what babies notice, and fail to notice, as perceptual skills develop.

Habituation and sensitization provide organisms with a useful way to adapt to their environments, but notice that this kind of learning results from the impact of one particular stimulus. It does not occur because a person or animal learned to associate one stimulus with another (Barker, 1997). For this reason, habituation and sensitization are examples of *nonassociative learning.*

Psychologists have been especially interested in how habituation occurs. According to Richard Solomon's (1980) *opponent-process theory,* new stimulus events—especially those that arouse strong positive or negative emotions—disrupt the individual's physiological state of equilibrium. But this disruption triggers an opposite, or opponent, process that counteracts the disruption and eventually restores equilibrium. If the arousing event occurs repeatedly, this opponent process gets stronger and occurs more rapidly. It eventually becomes so quick and strong that it actually suppresses the initial response to the stimulus, creating habituation.

As described in the motivation and emotion chapter, the opponent-process theory of habituation may help explain why some people skydive and engage in other highly arousing activities. It might also help explain some of the dangers associated with certain drugs. Consider, for example, what happens as someone continues to use a drug such as heroin. The pleasurable reaction (the high) obtained from a particular dose of

habituation The process of adapting to stimuli that do not change.

the drug begins to decrease with repeated doses. This habituation occurs, Solomon says, because the initial, pleasurable reaction to the drug is eventually followed by an unpleasant, opposing reaction that counteracts the drug's primary effects. As drug users become habituated, they must take progressively larger doses to get the same high. According to Solomon and other researchers, these opponent processes form the basis of drug tolerance and addiction (e.g., McDonald & Siegel, 2004).

Similar processes have been proposed as a possible cause of some accidental drug overdoses. Suppose the unpleasant reaction that counteracts a drug's initial effects becomes associated with a particular room, person, or other stimulus that is normally present when the drug is taken. This stimulus may eventually come to trigger the counteracting process, allowing the user to tolerate larger drug doses. Now suppose that a person takes this larger drug dose in an environment in which this stimulus is not present. The strength of the drug's primary effect will remain the same, but without the familiar environmental stimulus, the counteracting process may be weaker. The net result may be a stronger-than-usual drug reaction, possibly leading to an overdose (Melchior, 1990; Siegel et al., 1982; Turkkan, 1989).

Notice that opponent-process explanations of drug abuse and overdose are based not just on simple habituation and sensitization but also on a *learned association* between certain environmental stimuli and certain opponent responses. Indeed, the nonassociative processes of habituation and sensitization cannot, by themselves, explain many of the behaviours and mental processes that are the focus of psychology. To better understand how learning affects our thoughts and behaviours, we have to consider forms of learning that involve the building of associations between various stimuli, as well as between stimuli and responses. One major type of associative learning is called *classical conditioning*.

Classical Conditioning: Learning Signals and Associations

Learning to Live with It People who move to a big city may at first be distracted by the din of traffic, low-flying aircraft, and other urban sounds but, after a while, the process of habituation makes all this noise far less noticeable.

At the opening bars of the national anthem, a young hockey player's heart might start pounding; those sounds signal that the game is about to begin. A flashing light on a control panel might make an airplane pilot's adrenaline flow, because it means that something could be wrong. People are not born with these reactions. They learn them by observing relationships or *associations* between events in the world. The experimental study of this kind of learning was begun, almost by accident, by Ivan Petrovich Pavlov.

Pavlov's Discovery

Pavlov is one of the best-known figures in psychology, but he was not a psychologist. A Russian physiologist, Pavlov won a Nobel Prize in 1904 for his research on the digestive processes of dogs. In the course of this work, Pavlov noticed a strange phenomenon: The first stage of the digestive process—salivation, or drooling—sometimes occurred when no food was present. His dogs salivated, for example, when they saw the assistant who normally brought their food, even if the assistant was empty-handed.

Pavlov devised a simple experiment to determine why salivation occurred without an obvious physical cause. First he performed a simple operation to divert a dog's saliva into a container so that the amount of salivation could be measured precisely. He then placed the dog in an apparatus similar to the one shown in Figure 6.1. The experiment had three phases. In the first phase of the experiment, Pavlov and his associates (Anrep, 1920) confirmed that when meat powder was placed on the dog's tongue, the dog salivated, but that it did not salivate in response to a neutral stimulus—a musical tone, for example. Thus the researchers had established the two basic components for Pavlov's experiment: a natural reflex (salivation in response to meat powder) and a neutral stimulus (the sound of the tone). A *reflex*

figure 6.1

Apparatus for Measuring Conditioned Responses

In this more elaborate version of Pavlov's original apparatus, the amount of saliva flowing from a dog's cheek is measured, then recorded on a slowly revolving drum of paper.

is the swift, automatic response to a stimulus, such as shivering in the cold or flinching when you are jabbed with a needle. A *neutral stimulus* is a stimulus that initially does not trigger the reflex being studied, although it may cause other responses. For example, when the tone is first sounded, the dog will prick up its ears, turn toward the sound, and sniff around, but it will not salivate.

It was the second and third phases of the experiment that showed how one type of associative learning can occur. In the second phase, the tone sounded, and then a few seconds later meat powder was placed in the dog's mouth. The dog salivated. This *pairing*—the tone followed immediately by meat powder—was repeated several times. The tone predicted that the meat powder was coming, but the question remained: Would the animal learn that the tone signals the meat powder? The answer was yes. In the third phase of the experiment, the tone was sounded, and even though no meat powder was presented, the dog again salivated. In other words, the tone by itself now elicited salivation.

Pavlov's experiment was the first laboratory demonstration of a basic form of associative learning. Today, it is called **classical conditioning**—a procedure in which a neutral stimulus is repeatedly paired with a stimulus that already triggers a reflex-like response until the neutral stimulus alone comes to evoke a similar response. Figure 6.2 shows the basic elements of classical conditioning. The stimulus that elicits a response without conditioning, such as the meat powder in Pavlov's experiment, is called the **unconditioned stimulus (UCS).** The automatic reaction to this stimulus is called the **unconditioned response (UCR).** The new stimulus being paired with the unconditioned stimulus is called the **conditioned stimulus (CS)**, and the response it comes to elicit is the **conditioned response (CR).**

classical conditioning A procedure in which a neutral stimulus is repeatedly paired with a stimulus that elicits a reflex or other response until the neutral stimulus alone comes to elicit a similar response.

unconditioned stimulus (UCS) A stimulus that elicits a response without conditioning.

unconditioned response (UCR) The automatic or unlearned reaction to a stimulus.

conditioned stimulus (CS) The originally neutral stimulus that, through pairing with the unconditioned stimulus, comes to elicit a conditioned response.

conditioned response (CR) The response that the conditioned stimulus elicits.

extinction The gradual disappearance of a conditioned response when a conditioned stimulus no longer predicts the appearance of an unconditioned stimulus.

reconditioning The quick relearning of a conditioned response following extinction.

spontaneous recovery The reappearance of the conditioned response after extinction and without further pairings of the conditioned and unconditioned stimuli.

Conditioned Responses over Time: Extinction and Spontaneous Recovery

Continued pairings of a conditioned stimulus with an unconditioned stimulus strengthen conditioned responses. The curve on the left side of Figure 6.3 shows an example: Repeated associations of a tone (CS) with meat powder (UCS) caused Pavlov's dogs to increase their salivation (CR) to the tone alone.

What if the meat powder is no longer given? In general, if the conditioned stimulus continues to occur without being followed at least occasionally by the unconditioned stimulus, the conditioned response will gradually disappear. This fading

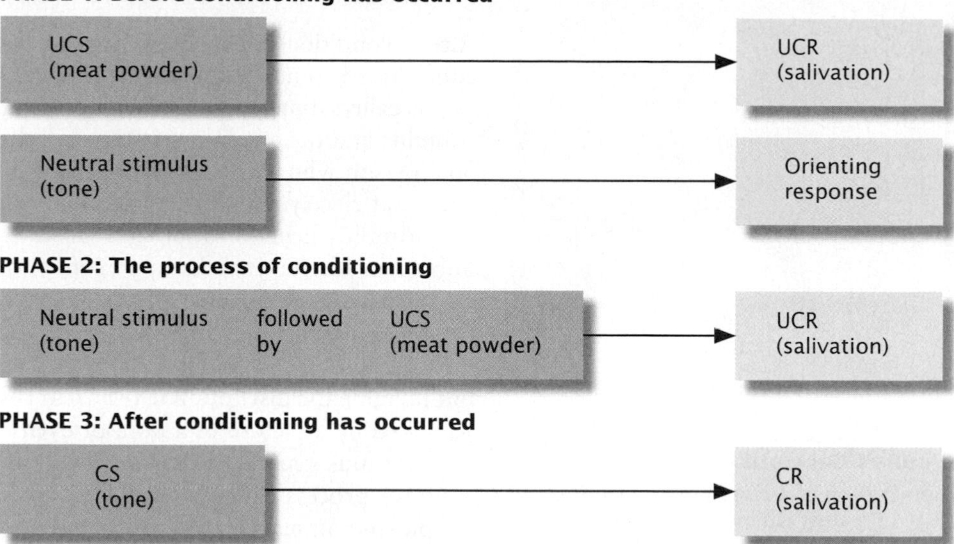

figure 6.2

Classical Conditioning

Before classical conditioning has occurred, meat powder on a dog's tongue produces salivation, but the sound of a tone—a neutral stimulus—does not. During the process of conditioning, the tone is repeatedly paired with the meat powder. After classical conditioning has taken place, the sound of the tone alone acts as a conditioned stimulus, producing salivation.

process is known as **extinction** (see the centre section of Figure 6.3). If the conditioned stimulus and the unconditioned stimulus are again paired after the conditioned response has been extinguished, the conditioned response returns to its original strength very quickly, often after only one or two trials. This quick relearning of a conditioned response after extinction is called **reconditioning.** Because reconditioning takes much less time than the original conditioning, extinction must not have erased the original learned association. Instead, the original learning had been suppressed by a newly learned tendency to not respond (Bouton, 2002).

Additional evidence for this conclusion is illustrated on the right side of Figure 6.3: An extinguished conditioned response will temporarily reappear if, after some time delay, the conditioned stimulus is presented again—even without the unconditioned stimulus. This reappearance of the conditioned response after extinction (and without further CS-UCS pairings) is called **spontaneous recovery.** In general, the longer the time between extinction and the re-presentation of the conditioned stimulus, the greater the recovered conditioned response. (However, unless the UCS is again paired with the CS, extinction rapidly occurs again.) In other words, even after they have been extinguished, associations may not be entirely forgotten. Spontaneous recovery may make them available even years later, as when a person hears a song or smells a scent associated with a long-lost lover and experiences a ripple of emotion—a conditioned response.

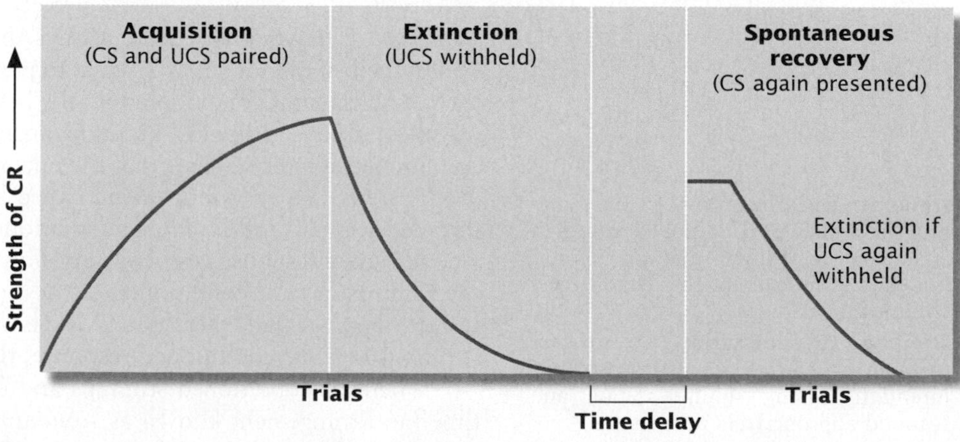

figure 6.3

Changes over Time in the Strength of a Conditioned Response (CR)

As the conditioned stimulus (CS) and the unconditioned stimulus (UCS) are repeatedly paired during initial conditioning, the strength of the conditioned response (CR) increases. If the CS is repeatedly presented without the UCS, the CR weakens—and eventually disappears—through a process called *extinction.* However, after a brief period, the CR reappears if the CS is again presented. This phenomenon is called *spontaneous recovery.*

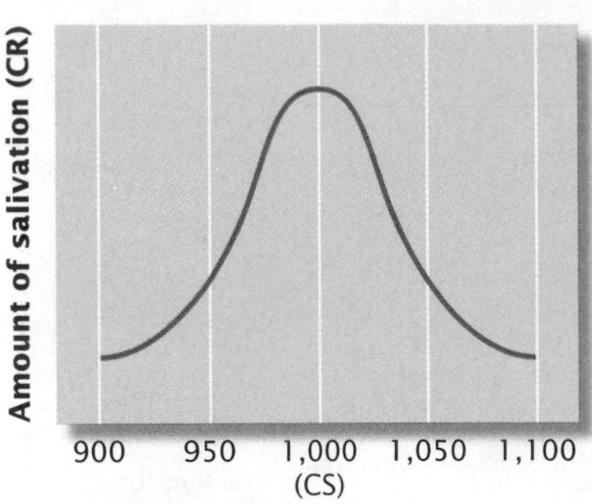

figure 6.4

Stimulus Generalization

The strength of a conditioned response (CR) is greatest when the original conditioned stimulus (CS) occurs, but the CR also appears following stimuli that closely resemble the CS. Here, the CS is the sound of a buzzer at 1,000 hertz, and the CR is salivation. Notice that the CR generalizes well to stimuli at 990 or 1010 hertz, but that it is weaker and weaker in response to stimuli that are less and less similar to the CS.

Stimulus Generalization and Discrimination

After a conditioned response is learned, stimuli that are similar but not identical to the conditioned stimulus also elicit the response—but to a lesser degree. This phenomenon is called **stimulus generalization.** Usually the greater the similarity between a new stimulus and the conditioned stimulus, the stronger the conditioned response will be. So a person who was bitten by a small, curly-haired dog is likely to be most afraid of dogs that closely resemble it. Figure 6.4 shows another example involving sounds.

Stimulus generalization has obvious adaptive advantages. For example, it is important for survival that a person who gets sick after drinking sour-smelling milk later avoids dairy products that give off an odour similar to the one associated with the illness. Generalization, however, would be a problem if it had no limits. Like most people, you would probably be frightened if you found a lion in your home, but imagine the disruption if your fear response generalized so widely that you were panicked by a picture of a lion, or even by reading the word *lion.*

Stimulus generalization does not run wild because it is balanced by a complementary process called **stimulus discrimination.** Through stimulus discrimination, people and animals learn to differentiate among similar stimuli. Many parents find that the sound of their own baby whimpering may become a conditioned stimulus that triggers a conditioned response that wakes them up. That conditioned response might not occur if a visiting friend's baby whimpers.

The Signalling of Significant Events

Is classical conditioning entirely automatic? Pavlov's research suggested that it is—that classical conditioning allows the substitution of one stimulus (the CS) for another (the UCS) in producing an automatic, reflexive response. This kind of learning helps animals and people prepare for events involving food, pain, or other unconditioned stimuli. For years, the study of classical conditioning focused mainly on its role in the control of such automatic, involuntary behaviour. However, psychologists now recognize the wider implications of classical conditioning (Hollis, 1997). Some argue that organisms acquire conditioned responses when one event reliably predicts, or *signals,* the appearance of another. These psychologists believe that instead of giving rise to simple robot-like reflexes, classical conditioning leads to responses based on the *information* provided by conditioned stimuli. As a result, animals and people develop *mental representations* of the relationships between important events in their environment and expectancies about when such events will occur (Rescorla, 1988). These representations and expectancies aid adaptation and survival.

What determines whether and how a conditioned response is learned? Important factors include the timing, predictability, and strength of signals; the amount of attention they receive; and how easily the signals can be associated with other stimuli.

Timing If your instructor always dismisses class at 9:59 and a bell rings at 10:00, the bell cannot act as a signal to prepare you for the dismissal. It is no wonder then, that classical conditioning works best when the conditioned stimulus precedes the unconditioned stimulus. In this arrangement, known as *forward conditioning,* the conditioned stimulus signals that the unconditioned stimulus is coming.

There is also an arrangement, called *backward conditioning,* in which the conditioned stimulus *follows* the unconditioned stimulus. When this happens, however, a conditioned response develops very slowly, if at all. (Part of the explanation is that the CS in backward conditioning comes too late to signal the approach of the UCS. In fact, the CS signals the *absence* of the UCS and eventually triggers a response that is opposite to the conditioned response, thus inhibiting its development.)

When the conditioned stimulus and unconditioned stimulus occur at the same time (an arrangement known as *simultaneous conditioning*), conditioning is much

stimulus generalization A phenomenon in which a conditioned response is elicited by stimuli that are similar but not identical to the conditioned stimulus.

stimulus discrimination A process through which individuals learn to differentiate among similar stimuli and respond appropriately to each one.

less likely to take place than it is in either forward or backward conditioning, and special techniques are required to detect its occurrence (Savastano & Miller, 1998).

Research shows that forward conditioning usually works best when there is an interval between the conditioned stimulus and the unconditioned stimulus. This interval can range from a fraction of a second to a few seconds to more than a minute, depending on the particular CS, UCS, and UCR involved (Longo, Klempay, & Bitterman, 1964; Ross & Ross, 1971). Classical conditioning will always be weaker if the interval between the CS and the UCS is longer than what is ideal for the stimuli and responses in a given situation. This makes adaptive sense. Normally, the appearance of food, predators, or other significant events is most reliably predicted by smells, growls, or other stimuli that occur at varying intervals before those events (Einhorn & Hogarth, 1982). So it is logical that organisms are "wired" to form associations most easily between things that occur in a relatively tight time sequence.

Predictability For classical conditioning to occur, though, it is not enough that the conditioned stimulus precede the unconditioned stimulus and that the two events are close together in time. Suppose you have two dogs, Moxie and Fang, each with different personalities. When Moxie growls, she sometimes bites, but sometimes she doesn't. Other times, she bites without growling first. Fang, however, growls *only* before biting. Your conditioned fear response to Moxie's growl will probably occur slowly, if at all, because her growl is a stimulus that does not reliably signal the danger of a bite. But you are likely to quickly develop a classically conditioned fear response to Fang's growl, because classical conditioning proceeds most rapidly when the conditioned stimulus *always* signals the unconditioned stimulus, and *only* the unconditioned stimulus. So even if both dogs provide the same number of pairings of the conditioned stimulus (growl) and the unconditioned stimulus (bite), it is only in Fang's case that the conditioned stimulus *reliably* predicts the unconditioned stimulus (Rescorla, 1968).

Signal Strength A conditioned response will be greater if the unconditioned stimulus is strong than if it is weak. So a predictive signal associated with a strong UCS, such as an intense shock, will come to evoke more fear than one associated with a weak shock. As with timing and predictability, the effect of signal strength on classical conditioning makes adaptive sense. It is more important to be prepared for major events than for events that have little impact.

How quickly a conditioned response is learned also depends on the strength of the conditioned stimulus. As described in the chapter on perception, louder tones, brighter lights, or other, more intense stimuli tend to get attention, so they are most rapidly associated with an unconditioned stimulus—as long as they remain reliable predictive signals.

Attention In the laboratory, a single neutral stimulus is presented, followed shortly by an unconditioned stimulus. In the natural environment, however, several stimuli might be present just before an unconditioned stimulus occurs. Suppose you are at the beach, sipping lemonade, reading a magazine, listening to a Beyoncé CD, and inhaling the scent of sunscreen, when you are suddenly stung by a wasp. Where your attention was focused at that moment can influence which potential conditioned stimulus—lemonade, magazine, Beyoncé, or sunscreen—becomes associated with that painful unconditioned stimulus. The stimulus you were attending to most closely—and thus most fully perceiving—is the one likely to be more strongly associated with pain than any of the others (Hall, 1991).

Second-Order Conditioning When a child suffers the pain of an injection (an unconditioned stimulus) at a doctor's office, noticeable stimuli—such as the doctor's white coat—that precede and predict the unconditioned stimulus can become conditioned stimuli for fear. Once the white coat can trigger a conditioned fear

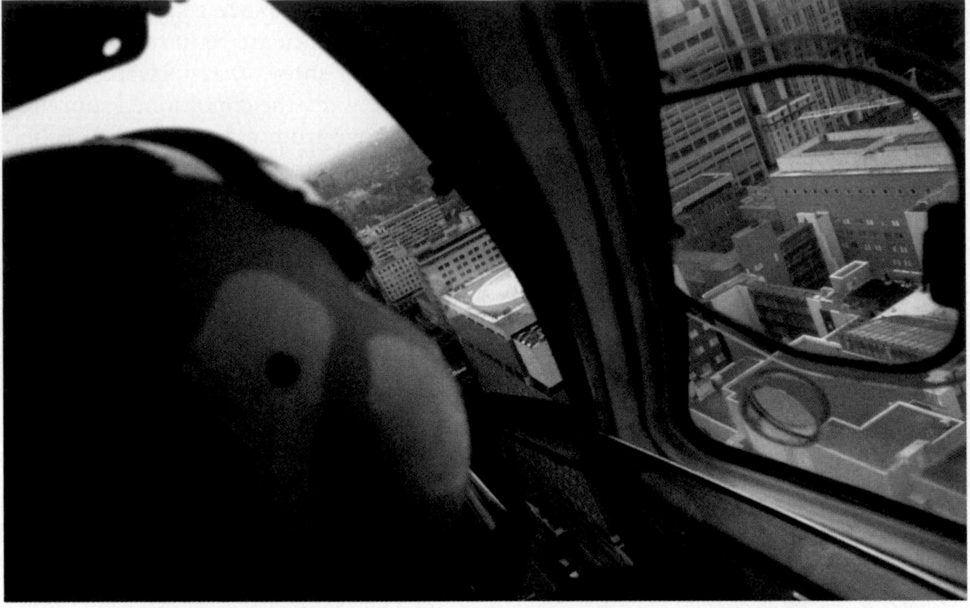

The Power of Second-Order Conditioning Cancer patients may feel queasy when they enter a chemotherapy room because they have *associated* the room with treatment that causes nausea. Through second-order conditioning, almost anything associated with that room can also become a conditioned stimulus for nausea. One cancer patient, flying out of town on a business trip, became nauseated just by seeing her hospital from the air.

response, it can take on some properties of an unconditioned stimulus. So at future visits, the once-neutral sight of the doctor's waiting room can become a conditioned stimulus for fear because it signals the appearance of the doctor's white coat, which in turn signals pain. When a conditioned stimulus acts like an unconditioned stimulus, creating conditioned stimuli out of events associated with it, the phenomenon is called **second-order conditioning.**

Conditioned fear, along with the second-order conditioning that can be based on it, illustrates one of the most important adaptive characteristics of classical conditioning: the ability to prepare a person or an animal for threatening events—unconditioned stimuli—that are reliably signalled by a conditioned stimulus. Unfortunately, second-order conditioning can also cause problems. For example, the high blood pressure seen in medical patients known as *white-coat hypertensives* (Myers et al., 1996) doesn't reflect a physical disorder. It occurs simply because the mere sight of a doctor or nurse has become a conditioned stimulus for fear.

Biopreparedness After Pavlov's initial experiments, many psychologists believed that the associations formed through classical conditioning were like Velcro. Just as Velcro pieces of any size or shape can be attached with equal ease, some believed that any conditioned stimulus has an equal potential for becoming associated with any unconditioned stimulus, as long as the two stimuli occur in the right time sequence. This view, called *equipotentiality,* was later challenged by experiments showing that certain signals or events are especially suited to form associations with other events (Logue, 1985). This apparent natural tendency for certain events to become linked suggests that humans and animals are "biologically prepared" or "genetically tuned" to develop certain conditioned associations.

The most dramatic example of this *biopreparedness* is seen in conditioned taste aversion. Consider the results of a study in which rats were either shocked or made nauseous in the combined presence of a bright light, a loud buzzer, and saccharin-flavoured water. Only certain conditioned associations were formed. Specifically, the animals that had been shocked developed a conditioned fear response to the light and the buzzer, but not to the flavoured water. Those animals that had been made nauseous developed a conditioned aversion to the flavoured water but showed no particular response to the light or buzzer (Garcia & Koelling, 1966). Notice that these associations are useful and adaptive: Nausea is more likely to be produced by

second-order conditioning A phenomenon in which a conditioned stimulus acts like an unconditioned stimulus, creating conditioned stimuli out of events associated with it.

in review Basic Phenomena in Classical Conditioning

Process	Description	Example
Acquisition	A neutral stimulus and an unconditioned stimulus (UCS) are paired. The neutral stimulus becomes a conditioned stimulus (CS), eliciting a conditioned response (CR).	A child learns to fear (conditioned response) the doctor's office (conditioned stimulus) by associating it with the reflexive emotional reaction (unconditioned response) to a painful injection (unconditioned stimulus).
Stimulus generalization	A conditioned response is elicited not only by the conditioned stimulus but also by stimuli similar to the conditioned stimulus.	A child fears most doctors' offices and places that smell like them.
Stimulus discrimination	Generalization is limited so that some stimuli similar to the conditioned stimulus do not elicit the conditioned response.	A child learns that his mother's doctor's office is not associated with the unconditioned stimulus.
Stimulus discrimination	The conditioned stimulus is presented alone, without the unconditioned stimulus. Eventually the conditioned stimulus no longer elicits the conditioned response.	A child visits the doctor's office several times for a checkup but does not receive an injection. Fear may eventually cease.

PsychAssist: Classical Conditioning—Pavlov's Study

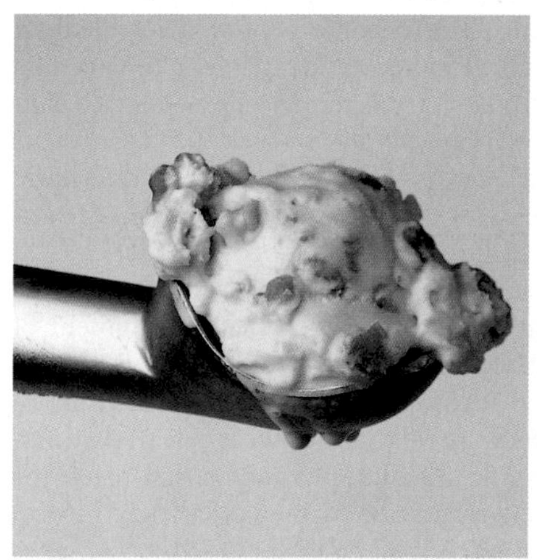

Taste Aversions Humans can develop classically conditioned taste aversions, even to preferred foods. Ilene Bernstein (1978) gave one group of cancer patients Mapletoff ice cream an hour before they received nausea-provoking chemotherapy. A second group ate the same kind of ice cream on a day they did not receive chemotherapy. A third group got no ice cream. Five months later, the patients were asked to taste several ice cream flavours. Those who had never tasted Mapletoff and those who had not eaten it in association with chemotherapy chose it as their favourite. Those who had eaten Mapletoff before receiving chemotherapy found it very distasteful.

food or drink than by a noise or some other external stimulus. Accordingly, nausea is more likely to become a conditioned response to an internal stimulus, such as a saccharine flavour, than to an external stimulus, such as a light or buzzer. In contrast, sudden pain is more likely to have been caused by an external stimulus, so it makes evolutionary sense that organisms should be "tuned" to associate pain with external stimuli such as sights or sounds.

Notice, too, that strong conditioned taste aversion can develop despite the fact that poisons or other nauseating substances do not usually produce their effects until minutes or hours after being ingested. These intervals are far longer than what is optimal for producing conditioning in most other situations, but once someone has experienced food poisoning, just the sight or smell of the type of food that caused it, can make the person so queasy that he or she will never eat that food again. Taste aversion makes sense in evolutionary terms, because organisms that are biologically prepared to link taste signals with illness, even if it occurs after a considerable delay, are more likely to survive than organisms not so prepared.

Evidence from several sources suggests other ways in which animals and people are innately prepared to learn aversions to certain stimuli. For example, people are much more likely to develop a conditioned fear of harmless dogs or snakes than of electrical outlets, knives, and other more dangerous objects (Öhman & Mineka, 2001, 2003). And experiments with animals suggest that they are prone to learn the types of associations that are most common in, or most relevant to, their environments (Wilcoxon, Dragoin, & Kral, 1971). For example, birds are strongly dependent upon their vision in searching for food and may develop taste aversions on the basis of visual stimuli. Coyotes and rats, more dependent on their sense of smell, tend to develop aversions related to odour.

Some Applications of Classical Conditioning

"In Review: Basic Phenomena in Classical Conditioning" summarizes the principles of classical conditioning. These principles have proven useful in overcoming fears, controlling predators, and predicting Alzheimer's disease, to name just a few examples.

Using Classical Conditioning to Save People and Bears A program has been suggested to the Alberta government to reduce the number of human and bear encounters in built-up areas. One of the recommendations is to place a foul-tasting chemical into the trash at dumpsites. When the animals attempt to eat the garbage, the foul taste (unconditioned stimulus) will be associated with the trash (conditioned stimulus), teaching them to avoid the dumpsite (Augustyn, 2001).

Phobias Classical conditioning can play a role in the development not only of mild fears (such as a child's fear of a doctor's white coat) but also of phobias (Bouton, Mineka, & Barlow, 2001). *Phobias* are extreme fears of objects or situations that either are not objectively dangerous—public speaking, for example—or are less dangerous than the phobic person's reaction suggests. In some instances, phobias can seriously disrupt a person's life. A child who is frightened by a large dog may learn a fear of that dog that is so intense that it generalizes to become a phobia of all dogs. Dangerous situations, too, can produce classical conditioning of very long-lasting fears. Decades after their war experiences, some military veterans still respond to simulated battle sounds with large changes in heart rate, blood pressure, and other signs of emotional arousal (Edwards & Acker, 1972). As described in the chapter on health, stress, and coping, these symptoms, combined with others such as distressing dreams about the troubling events, characterize post-traumatic stress disorder (PTSD).

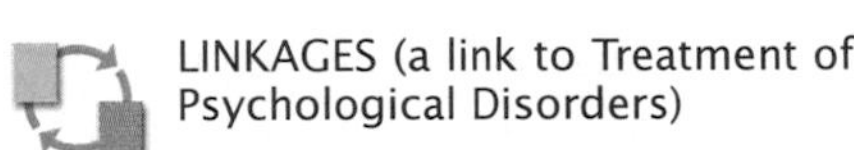

LINKAGES (a link to Treatment of Psychological Disorders)

Classical conditioning procedures can be employed to treat phobias, and even PTSD. Joseph Wolpe (1958; Wolpe & Plaud, 1997) pioneered the development of this methodology. Using techniques first developed with laboratory animals, Wolpe showed that irrational fears could be relieved through *systematic desensitization,* a procedure that associates a new response, such as relaxation, with a feared stimulus. To treat a thunderstorm phobia, for instance, a therapist might first teach the client to relax deeply and then associate that relaxation with increasingly intense sights and sounds of thunderstorms presented on videotape (Öst, 1978). Because, as Wolpe noted, a person cannot be relaxed and afraid at the same time, the new conditioned response (relaxation) to thunderstorms replaces the old one (fear). Desensitization is discussed in more detail in the chapter on the treatment of psychological disorders.

Predator Control Teresa Augustyn wrote a report for the Alberta Fisheries and Wildlife Management Division on the grizzly bear and its conflicts with humans. In the report she made a recommendation that the province, among other things, use the power of classically conditioned taste aversion to deter nuisance bears from rummaging through the trash close to human habitation. To alleviate this problem without killing the bear, an emetic or foul tasting chemical would be placed in the trash. The foul taste and/or nausea caused by the chemical would be associated with the garbage, therefore making it an undesirable meal (Augustyn, 2001).

Predicting Alzheimer's Disease A puff of air directed at your eye is an unconditioned stimulus that causes the reflexive unconditioned response we call an

figure 6.5

Thorndike's Puzzle Box

This drawing illustrates the kind of "puzzle box" used in Thorndike's research. His cats learned to open the door and reach food by stepping on the pedal, but the learning occurred gradually. Some cats actually took longer to get out of the box on one trial than on a previous trial.

eye blink (Hilgard & Marquis, 1936). If each air puff is preceded by a flash of light, the light will become a conditioned stimulus that can then cause an eye blink on its own. Research with animals has demonstrated that the hippocampus, a brain structure that is damaged in the early stages of Alzheimer's disease, is involved in the development of this type of conditioned response (Green & Woodruff-Pak, 2000). That research is now being applied to identify people who are at high risk for this devastating brain disorder. One study found that elderly people whose eye-blink conditioning was impaired were the ones most likely to develop Alzheimer's disease in the next two or three years (Downey-Lamb & Woodruff-Pak, 1999). Knowing who is at risk for Alzheimer's disease is important because it allows doctors to offer these people medication that can delay the emergence of the disease.

Instrumental and Operant Conditioning: Learning the Consequences of Behaviour

Classical conditioning is an important kind of learning, but it can't explain most of what people learn on a daily basis. In classical conditioning, neutral and unconditioned stimuli are predictably paired, and the result is an association between the two. The association is shown by the conditioned response that occurs when the conditioned stimulus appears. Notice that both stimuli occur *before* or *along with* the conditioned response. But people also learn associations between specific actions and the stimuli that *follow* them—in other words, between behaviour and its consequences (Colwill, 1994). A child learns to say "please" to get a piece of candy; a headache sufferer learns to take a pill to escape pain; a dog learns to "shake hands" to get a treat.

From the Puzzle Box to the Skinner Box

Edward L. Thorndike, an American psychologist did much of the groundwork for research on the consequences of behaviour. While Pavlov was exploring classical conditioning in animals, Thorndike was studying animals' intelligence and ability to solve problems. He would place an animal, usually a hungry cat, in a *puzzle box,* where it had to learn some response—say, stepping on a pedal—in order to unlock the door and get to some food (see Figure 6.5). The animal would solve the puzzle, but very slowly. It did not appear to understand, or suddenly gain insight into, the problem (Thorndike, 1898).

So what were Thorndike's cats learning? Thorndike argued that any response (such as pressing the pedal) that produces a satisfying effect (such as access to food) gradually becomes stronger, whereas any response (such as pacing or meowing) that does not produce a satisfying effect gradually becomes weaker. The cats' learning,

Edward L. Thorndike (1874–1949) and B. F. Skinner (1904–1990) Edward Thorndike (left) and B. F. Skinner (shown at right with a "Skinner box") studied instrumental and operant conditioning, respectively. Though similar in most respects, instrumental and operant conditioning differ in one way. In instrumental conditioning, the experimenter defines each opportunity for the organism to produce a response, and conditioning is usually measured by how long it takes for the response to appear. In operant conditioning, the organism can make responses at any time; conditioning is measured by the *rate* of responding. In this chapter, the term *operant conditioning* refers to both kinds of conditioning.

Edward Thorndike photo: Psychology Archives—The University of Akron.

said Thorndike, is governed by the **law of effect.** According to this law, if a response made in the presence of a particular stimulus is followed by satisfaction (such as a reward), that response is more likely to be made the next time the stimulus is encountered. Responses that produce discomfort are less likely to be performed again. Thorndike described this kind of learning as **instrumental conditioning,** because responses are strengthened when they are instrumental in producing rewards (Thorndike, 1905).

About forty years after Thorndike published his work, B. F. Skinner extended and formalized many of Thorndike's ideas. Skinner (1938) emphasized that during instrumental conditioning, an organism learns a response by *operating on* the environment, so he called the process of learning these responses **operant conditioning.** His primary aim was to analyze how behaviour is changed by its consequences. To study operant conditioning, Skinner devised a chamber that, despite his objections, became known as the *Skinner box*. This chamber differed from Thorndike's puzzle box in an important way: The puzzle box measured learning in terms of whether an animal successfully completed a trial (got out of the box) and how long it took to do so. The Skinner box measures learning in terms of how often an animal responds during a specified period of time (Barker, 1997).

law of effect A law stating that if a response made in the presence of a particular stimulus is followed by satisfaction, that response is more likely the next time the stimulus is encountered.

instrumental conditioning A process through which an organism learns to respond to the environment in a way that produces positive consequences and avoids negative ones.

operant conditioning A process through which an organism learns to respond to the environment in a way that produces positive consequences and avoids negative ones.

Basic Components of Operant Conditioning

The tools Skinner devised allowed him and other researchers to precisely arrange relationships between a response and its consequences and then to analyze how those consequences affected behaviour over time. They found that the basic phenomena seen in classical conditioning—such as stimulus generalization, stimulus discrimination, extinction, and spontaneous recovery—also occur in operant conditioning. However, operant conditioning involves additional concepts and processes as well. Let's consider these now.

Operants and Reinforcers Skinner introduced the term *operant* or *operant response* to distinguish the responses in operant conditioning from those in classical

figure 6.6

Positive and Negative Reinforcement

Remember that behaviour is strengthened through *positive reinforcement* when something pleasant or desirable occurs following the behaviour. Behaviour is strengthened through *negative reinforcement* when the behaviour results in the termination of something unpleasant. To see how these principles apply in your own life, list two examples of situations in which your behaviour was affected by positive reinforcement and two in which you were affected by negative reinforcement.

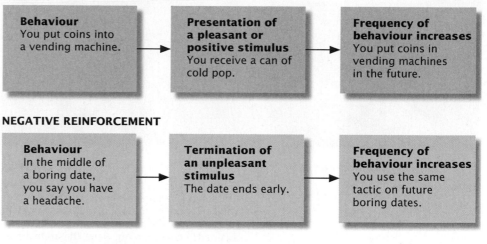

POSITIVE REINFORCEMENT

Behaviour You put coins into a vending machine.	→	**Presentation of a pleasant or positive stimulus** You receive a can of cold pop.	→	**Frequency of behaviour increases** You put coins in vending machines in the future.

NEGATIVE REINFORCEMENT

Behaviour In the middle of a boring date, you say you have a headache.	→	**Termination of an unpleasant stimulus** The date ends early.	→	**Frequency of behaviour increases** You use the same tactic on future boring dates.

conditioning. Recall that in classical conditioning, the conditioned response doesn't affect whether or when a stimulus occurs. Dogs salivated when a buzzer sounded, but the salivation had no effect on the buzzer or on whether food was presented. In contrast, an **operant** is a response that has some effect on the world; it is a response that *operates on* the environment. For example, when a child says, "Momma, I'm hungry," and is then fed, the child has made an operant response that influences when food will appear.

A **reinforcer** increases the probability that an operant behaviour will occur again. There are two main types of reinforcers: positive and negative. **Positive reinforcers** strengthen a response if they are experienced after that response occurs. They are roughly equivalent to rewards. The food given to a hungry pigeon after it pecks at a switch is a positive reinforcer; it increases the pigeon's switch pecking. For humans, positive reinforcers can include food, smiles, money, and other desirable outcomes. Presenting a positive reinforcer after a response is called *positive reinforcement.* **Negative reinforcers** are the *removal* of unpleasant stimuli such as pain, noise, threats, or a disapproving frown. For example, the disappearance of headache pain after you take a pain reliever acts as a negative reinforcer that makes you more likely to take that pain reliever in the future. When a response is strengthened by the removal of an unpleasant stimulus, the process is called *negative reinforcement.* So whether reinforcement takes the form of presenting something pleasant or removing something unpleasant, it always *increases* the strength of the behaviour that precedes it (see Figure 6.6).

Escape and Avoidance Conditioning The effects of negative reinforcement can be seen in escape conditioning and avoidance conditioning. **Escape conditioning** occurs as a person or animal learns responses that stop an aversive stimulus. The left-hand panel of Figure 6.7 shows a laboratory example in which dogs learn to jump over the barrier in a shuttle box to get away from a shock. In humans, escape conditioning appears not only when we learn to take pills to stop pain but also when parents learn to stop a child's annoying demands for a toy by agreeing to buy it. And television viewers learn to use the mute button to shut off obnoxious commercials.

When an animal or person responds to a signal in a way that avoids an aversive stimulus that has not yet arrived, **avoidance conditioning** has occurred. Look at the right-hand sections of Figure 6.7 and imagine that a buzzer sounds a few seconds before one side of the shuttle box is electrified. The animal will soon learn to jump over the barrier when the warning buzzer sounds, thus avoiding exposure to the shock. (In a similar way, some children learn that they can avoid getting in trouble for misbehaviour by apologizing as soon as they see their parent's frown.)

operant A response that has some effect on the world.

reinforcer A stimulus event that increases the probability that the response that immediately preceded it will occur again.

positive reinforcers Stimuli that strengthen a response if they follow that response.

negative reinforcers The removal of unpleasant stimuli, such as pain.

escape conditioning A type of learning in which an organism learns to make a particular response in order to terminate an aversive stimulus.

avoidance conditioning A type of learning in which an organism responds to a signal in a way that prevents exposure to an aversive stimulus.

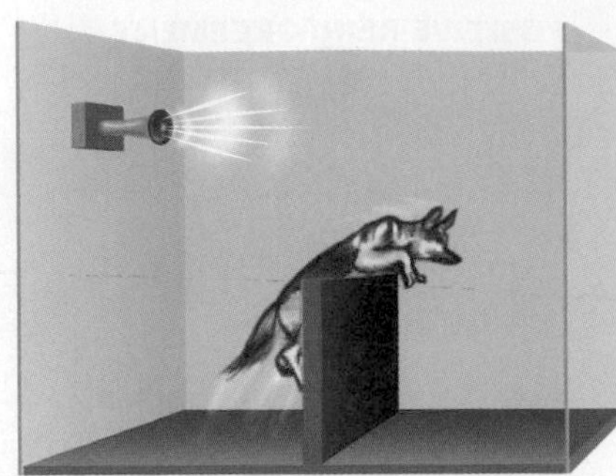

Escape conditioning **Avoidance conditioning**

figure 6.7

A Shuttle Box

A shuttle box has two sections, usually separated by a barrier, and its floor is an electric grid. Shock can be administered through the grid to either section. The left-hand panel shows escape conditioning, in which an animal learns to get away from a mild shock by jumping over the barrier when the electricity is turned on. The next two panels show avoidance conditioning. Here, the animal has learned to avoid shock altogether by jumping over the barrier when it hears a warning buzzer that sounds just before shock occurs.

Source: Adapted from Hintzman (1978).

Remember that in escape conditioning the learned response *stops* an aversive stimulus, whereas in avoidance conditioning the learned response *prevents* the aversive stimulus from occurring in the first place.

Notice that avoidance conditioning involves a marriage of classical and operant conditioning. In the shuttle box, for example, the buzzer signals that an unconditioned stimulus (shock) is about to occur. Through classical conditioning, this signal becomes a conditioned stimulus that triggers fear as a conditioned response. Like the shock itself, fear is unpleasant. Once the animal learns to jump over the barrier to avoid shock, this operant response is reinforced by its consequences—the reduction of fear. In short, avoidance conditioning takes place in two steps. The first step involves classical conditioning—a signal is repeatedly paired with shock. The second step involves operant conditioning—learning to make a response that reduces fear.

Along with positive reinforcement, avoidance conditioning is one of the most important influences on everyday behaviour. Most people go to work even when they would rather stay home, and they stop at red lights even when they are in a hurry. Each of these behaviours reflects avoidance conditioning, because each allows people to avoid a negative consequence, such as being fired or getting a traffic ticket or being hit by another car.

Once learned, avoidance is a difficult habit to break and contributes to the persistence of phobias. Why? Partly because avoidance responses continue to be reinforced by fear reduction even if the aversive stimulus never appears (Solomon, Kamin, & Wynne, 1953). In fact, avoidance responses prevent people from discovering that avoidance is no longer necessary. If you fear escalators and therefore avoid them, you'll never discover that they hold no real danger. Avoidance conditioning can also prevent people from learning new, more desirable behaviours. For example, fear of doing something embarrassing may cause people with limited social skills to shy away from social situations, thus depriving themselves of the chance to become more successful in those situations.

The study of avoidance conditioning has not only expanded our understanding of negative reinforcement but has also led some psychologists to consider more complex cognitive processes in learning. These psychologists suggest, for example, that in order for people to learn to avoid an unpleasant event (such as getting fired or paying a fine), they must have established an expectancy or other mental representation of that event. The role of such mental representations is emphasized in the cognitive theories of learning described later in this chapter.

"Oh, not bad. The light comes on, I press the bar, they write me a check. How about you?"

Although the artist may not have intended it, this cartoon nicely illustrates one way in which discriminative stimuli can affect behaviour.

Discriminative Stimuli and Stimulus Control One of the most important benefits of operant conditioning is that it enables quick adaptation to changes in the environment—an ability that has survival value in the real world. For example, even pigeons easily learn when they should respond and when they should not. If they are reinforced with food for pecking at a switch when a red light is on but are not reinforced for pecking when a green light is on, they will eventually peck only when they see a red light. Their behaviour demonstrates the effect of **discriminative stimuli,** which are stimuli that signal whether reinforcement is available if a certain response is made.

When an organism learns to make a particular response in the presence of one stimulus but not another, *stimulus discrimination* has occurred (see Figure 6.8).

figure 6.8

Stimulus Discrimination

In this experiment the rat could jump from a stand through any of three doors. However, it was reinforced only if it jumped through the door that differed from the other two. The rat learned to do this quite well. On this trial, it discriminated vertical from horizontal stripes.

discriminative stimuli Stimuli that signal whether reinforcement is available if a certain response is made.

Another way to say this is that the response is now under *stimulus control*. In general, stimulus discrimination allows people and animals to learn what is appropriate (reinforced) and inappropriate (not reinforced) in particular situations. Discrimination develops fastest when the discriminative stimulus signals that a behaviour is appropriate, and it develops slowest when the stimulus signals that a behaviour is inappropriate (Newman, Wolff, & Hearst, 1980). This selective sensitivity to different kinds of discriminative stimuli is an example of biopreparedness in operant learning (Dobrzecka, Szwejkowska, & Konorski, 1966).

Stimulus generalization also occurs in operant conditioning. That is, an animal or a person often performs a response in the presence of a stimulus that is similar, but not identical, to the one that previously signalled the availability of reinforcement. As in classical conditioning, the more similar the new stimulus is to the old, the more likely it is that the response will be performed. Suppose you ate a wonderful meal at a restaurant called "Captain Jack's," which was decorated to look like the inside of a sailing ship. You might later be attracted to other restaurants with nautical names or with interiors that look something like the one where you had that great meal.

As in classical conditioning, stimulus discrimination and stimulus generalization often complement each other in operant conditioning. In one study, for example, pigeons received food for pecking at a switch, but only when they saw certain works of art. When other paintings were shown, pecking was not reinforced (Watanabe, Sakamoto, & Wakita, 1995). As a result, these birds learned to discriminate the works of the impressionist painter Claude Monet from those of the cubist painter Pablo Picasso. Later, when the birds were shown new paintings by other impressionist and cubist artists, they were able to generalize from the original artists to other artists who painted in the same style. It was as if they had learned the conceptual categories of "impressionism" and "cubism." We humans learn to place people and things into even more finely detailed categories, such as "honest," "dangerous," or "tax deductible." We discriminate one stimulus from another and then, through generalization, respond similarly to all stimuli we perceive to be in a particular category. This ability to respond in a similar way to all members of a category can save us considerable time and effort, but it can also lead to the development of unwarranted prejudice against certain groups of people (see the chapter on social behaviour).

Forming and Strengthening Operant Behaviour

Daily life is full of examples of operant conditioning. People go to movies, parties, classes, and jobs primarily because doing so brings reinforcement. What is the effect of the type or timing of these reinforcers? How can new responses be established through operant conditioning?

Getting the Hang of It Learning to eat with a spoon is, as you can see, a hit-and-miss process at first. However, this child will learn to hit the target more and more often as the food reward gradually shapes a more efficient, and far less messy, pattern of behaviour.

Shaping Imagine that you want to train your dog, Henry, to sit and to "shake hands." The basic method using positive reinforcement is obvious: Every time Henry sits and shakes hands, you give him a treat. But the problem is also obvious: Smart as Henry is, he may never make the desired response on his own, so you will never be able to give the reinforcer. Instead of your teaching and Henry's learning, the two of you will just stare at each other (and he'll probably wag his tail).

The way around this problem is to *shape* Henry's behaviour. **Shaping** is accomplished by reinforcing *successive approximations*—that is, responses that come successively closer to the desired response. For example, you might first give Henry a treat whenever he sits down. Then you might reinforce him only when he sits and partially lifts a paw. Next, you might reinforce more complete paw lifting. Eventually, you would require that Henry perform the entire sit-lift-shake sequence before giving the treat. Shaping is an extremely powerful, widely used tool. Animal trainers use it to teach chimpanzees to roller-skate, dolphins to jump through hoops, and pigeons to play table tennis (Coren, 1999).

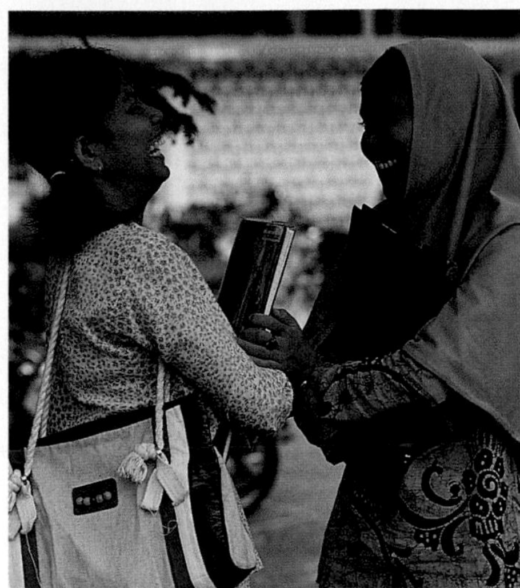

Secondary Reinforcers A touch or a smile, words of praise or thanks, and a loving or approving look are just a few of the social stimuli that can serve as secondary reinforcers for humans. Parents have used these reinforcers for generations to shape the behaviour of children in accordance with their cultural values.

Secondary Reinforcement Often, operant conditioning begins with the use of **primary reinforcers,** events or stimuli—such as food or water—that are innately rewarding. But Henry's training will be slowed if he must stop and eat every time he makes a correct response. Furthermore, once he is full, food will no longer act as an effective reinforcer. To avoid these problems, animal trainers and others in the teaching business rely on the principle of secondary reinforcement.

A **secondary reinforcer** is a previously neutral stimulus that, if paired with a stimulus that is already reinforcing, will take on reinforcing properties. In other words, secondary reinforcers are rewards that people or animals learn to like. For example, if you say, "Good boy!" a moment before you give Henry each food reward, these words will become associated with the food and can then be used alone to reinforce Henry's behaviour (as long as the words are again paired with food now and then). Does this remind you of classical conditioning? It should, because the primary reinforcer (food) is an unconditioned stimulus. If the sound of "Good boy!" predictably precedes, and thus signals, food, it becomes a conditioned stimulus. For this reason, secondary reinforcers are sometimes called *conditioned reinforcers.*

Secondary reinforcement greatly expands the power of operant conditioning (Schwartz & Reisberg, 1991). Money is the most obvious secondary reinforcer; some people will do anything for it (even though it tastes terrible!). Its reinforcing power lies in its association with the many rewards it can buy. Smiles and other forms of social approval (such as the words "Good job!") are also important secondary reinforcers for human beings. However, what becomes a secondary reinforcer can vary a great deal from person to person and culture to culture. For example, tickets to a rock concert are an effective secondary reinforcer for some people, but not everyone. A ceremony honouring outstanding job performance might be highly reinforcing to most employees in individualist cultures, but it might be embarrassing for some employees from cultures in which group cooperation is valued more than personal distinction (Miller, 2001). Still, when chosen carefully, secondary reinforcers can build or maintain behaviour even when primary reinforcement is absent for long periods.

Delay and Size of Reinforcement Much of our behaviour is learned and maintained because it is regularly reinforced. But many people overeat, smoke, drink too much, or procrastinate, even though they know these behaviours are bad for them. They want to change, but they seem to lack "self-control." If behaviour is controlled by its consequences, why do people do things that are ultimately self-defeating?

Part of the answer lies in the *timing* of reinforcers. In general, the effect of a reinforcer is stronger when it comes soon after a response occurs (Kalish, 1981). The good feelings (positive reinforcers) that follow, say, drinking too much are immediate. Hangovers and other negative consequences are usually delayed, so their effects on future drinking are weakened. Similarly, a dieter's efforts to eat less will eventually lead to weight loss, but because that positive reinforcer is delayed, it may have little impact today. Indeed, under some conditions, delaying a positive reinforcer for even a few seconds can decrease the effectiveness of positive reinforcement. (An advantage of praise or other secondary reinforcers is that they can easily be delivered immediately after a desired response occurs.)

The *size* of a reinforcer is also important. In general, operant conditioning generates more vigorous behaviour when the reinforcer is large than when it is small. For example, a strong electrical shock will elicit a faster avoidance or escape response than a weak one.

Schedules of Reinforcement We flip a light switch, and the light comes on. We put money in a vending machine, and we receive the item we want. When a reinforcer is delivered every time a particular response occurs, the arrangement is called a **continuous reinforcement schedule.** This schedule can be helpful when

shaping The process of reinforcing responses that come successively closer to the desired response.

primary reinforcers Reinforcers that meet an organism's basic needs, such as food and water.

secondary reinforcer A reward that people or animals learn to like.

continuous reinforcement schedule A pattern in which a reinforcer is delivered every time a particular response occurs.

Reinforcement Schedules on the Job Make a list of all the jobs you have ever held, along with the reinforcement schedule on which each employer paid you. Which of the four types of schedules (FR, FI, VR, VI) was most common, and which did you find most satisfying?

teaching someone a new skill, but it can be impractical in the long run. Imagine how inefficient it would be, for example, if an employer had to deliver praise or pay following every little task employees performed all day long. So quite often, reinforcement is administered only some of the time, on a **partial reinforcement schedule,** also called an *intermittent reinforcement schedule.*

Most partial reinforcement schedules can be described in terms of when and how reinforcers are given. "When" refers to the number of responses that have to occur, or the amount of time that must pass, before a reinforcer will occur. "How" refers to whether the reinforcer will be delivered in a predictable or unpredictable way. Accordingly, there are four basic types of intermittent reinforcement schedules:

1. ***Fixed-ratio (FR) schedules*** provide a reinforcer following a fixed number of responses. So rats might receive food after every tenth time they press the lever in a Skinner box (FR 10) or after every twentieth time (FR 20). Factory workers might be paid for every five computers they assemble (FR 5) or for every fifty (FR 50).

2. ***Variable-ratio (VR) schedules*** also provide a reinforcer after a given number of responses, but that number can vary. On these schedules, it is impossible to predict which particular response will bring reinforcement. A rat on a VR 30 schedule might sometimes be reinforced after ten lever presses, sometimes after fifty, and sometimes after five, but the *average* number of responses required to get a reinforcer would be thirty. Gambling offers humans a similar variable-ratio schedule. A slot machine, for example, pays off only after a frustratingly unpredictable number of lever pulls, averaging perhaps one in twenty. Problem gambling in Canada appears to be fairly stable and involves less than 5% of the population (Doiron and Nicki, 2001).

3. ***Fixed-interval (FI) schedules*** provide a reinforcer for the first response that occurs after some fixed time has passed since the last reward, regardless of how many responses have been made during that interval. For example, on an FI 60 schedule, the first response after sixty seconds have passed will be rewarded. Some radio stations create fixed-interval schedules by telling listeners who just won a prize that they are not eligible to win again for thirty days. Under these circumstances, there is no point in competing until that time has elapsed.

4. ***Variable-interval (VI) schedules*** reinforce the first response after some period of time, but the amount of time varies. On a VI 60 schedule, for example, the first response to occur after an *average* of 60 seconds is reinforced, but the actual time between reinforcements might vary from, say, 1 second to 120 seconds. Some teachers use VI schedules to help keep order in class by giving "points"—at unpredictably varying intervals—to children who are in their seats. A VI schedule has also been successfully used to encourage seat-belt use: During a ten-week test in Illinois, police stopped drivers at random times and awarded prizes to those who were buckled up (Mortimer et al., 1988).

Different schedules of reinforcement produce different patterns of responding, as Figure 6.9 shows (Skinner, 1961). The figure illustrates two important points. First, both fixed-ratio and variable-ratio schedules produce high rates of behaviour overall. The reason in both cases is that the frequency of the reward depends directly on the rate of responding. Industrial/organizational psychologists have applied this principle to help companies increase worker productivity and reduce absenteeism. Workers who are paid on the basis of the number of items they produce or the number of days they show up for work usually produce more items and miss fewer workdays (Muchinsky, 1993; Yukl, Latham, & Purcell, 1976). Similarly, gamblers reinforced on a variable-ratio schedule for pulling a slot machine handle, rolling dice, or playing other games of chance tend to maintain a high rate of responding—some people may become virtually unable to stop.

partial reinforcement schedule A pattern in which a reinforcer is administered only some of the time after a particular response occurs.

fixed-ratio (FR) schedule A partial reinforcement schedule that provides reinforcement following a fixed number of responses.

variable-ratio (VR) schedule A partial reinforcement schedule that provides reinforcement after a varying number of responses.

fixed-interval (FI) schedule A partial reinforcement schedule that provides reinforcement for the first response that occurs after some fixed time has passed since the last reward.

variable-interval (VI) schedule A partial reinforcement schedule that provides reinforcement for the first response after varying periods of time.

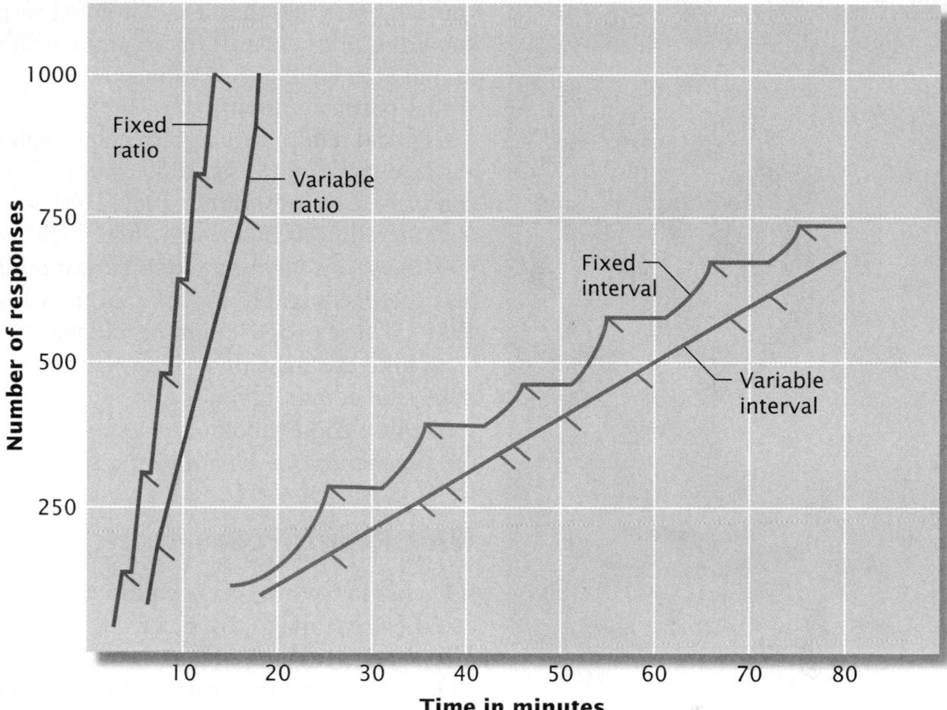

figure 6.9

Schedules of Reinforcement

These curves illustrate the patterns of behaviour typically seen under different reinforcement schedules. The steeper the curve, the faster the response rate. The thin diagonal lines crossing the curves show when reinforcement was given. In general, the rate of responding is higher under ratio schedules than under interval schedules.

Source: Adapted from Skinner (1961).

The second important aspect of Figure 6.9 relates to the curves, or "scallops," shown in the fixed-interval schedule. Under this schedule, it does not matter how many responses are made during the time between rewards. As a result, the rate of responding typically drops dramatically immediately after a reinforcer occurs and then increases as the time for another reward approaches. When teachers schedule all their quizzes in advance, for example, some students study just before each quiz and then virtually stop studying in that course until just before the next quiz. Behaviour rewarded on variable-interval schedules looks quite different. The unpredictable timing of rewards typically generates slow, steady responding. So if you know that your teacher might give a pop quiz at any class session, you might be more inclined to study more steadily from day to day (Kouyoumdjian, 2004; Ruscio, 2001).

Schedules and Extinction Just as breaking the predictive link between a conditioned and an unconditioned stimulus weakens a classically conditioned response, ending the relationship between an operant response and its reinforcers weakens that response. In other words, failure to reinforce a response *extinguishes* that response. The response occurs less often and eventually may disappear. If lever pressing no longer brings food, a rat stops pressing; if repeated text messages to a friend are not answered, you eventually stop sending them. As in classical conditioning, **extinction** in operant conditioning does not totally erase learned relationships. If a signalling stimulus reappears at some time after an operant response has been extinguished, that response may recur (spontaneously recover), and if it is again reinforced, it will be quickly relearned.

In general, behaviours learned under a partial reinforcement schedule are far more difficult to extinguish than those learned on a continuous reinforcement schedule. This phenomenon—called the **partial reinforcement extinction effect**—is easy to understand if you imagine yourself in a gambling casino, standing near a broken slot machine and a broken candy machine. You might put money in the broken candy machine once, but this behaviour will probably stop (extinguish) very quickly. The candy machine should deliver its goodies on a continuous reinforcement schedule, so

extinction The gradual disappearance of operant behaviour due to elimination of rewards for that behaviour.

partial reinforcement extinction effect A phenomenon in which behaviours learned under a partial reinforcement schedule are more difficult to extinguish than behaviours learned on a continuous reinforcement schedule.

Superstition and Partial Reinforcement Partial reinforcement helps to sustain superstitious athletic rituals—such as a fixed sequence of actions prior to hitting a golf ball or shooting a free throw in a basketball game. If the ritual has preceded success often enough, failure to execute it may upset the player and disrupt performance. Wayne Gretzky for example, would always get dressed the same way before every game. "He put on his left shin pad, left outer pad, then right, same order, left sock, hockey sock, shin pad, then pants, then left skate, right skate, shoulder pads, then left elbow pad, right elbow pad, sweater, tuck the right side in, go out on the ice for warm-ups and then miss the first shot wide right" (Lee, 1981).

you can easily tell that it is not going to provide a reinforcer. But slot machines are known to offer rewards on an unpredictable intermittent schedule. So you might put in coin after coin, unsure of whether the machine is broken or is simply not paying off at that particular moment.

Partial reinforcement also helps explain why superstitious behaviour is so resistant to extinction (Vyse, 2000). Suppose you take a shower just before hearing that you passed an important exam. The shower did nothing to cause this outcome; the reward followed it through sheer luck. Still, for some people, this *accidental reinforcement* can function like a partial reinforcement schedule, strengthening actions that preceded, and thus appeared to "cause," good news or other rewards (Chance, 1988). Those people might decide that it is "lucky" to shower after taking an exam, or to take exams with a "lucky pen," or to wear a certain "lucky shirt" (Hendrick, 2003). Of course, if you wear that shirt often enough, the laws of chance dictate that something good is bound to follow every now and then, thus further strengthening the superstitious behaviour on a sparse partial schedule (Vyse, 2000).

Why Reinforcers Work

What makes reinforcers reinforcing? For primary reinforcers, at least, the reason could be that they satisfy hunger, thirst, and other needs that are basic to survival. This explanation is incomplete, however, because substances such as saccharin, which have no nutritional value, can have as much reinforcing power as sugar, which is nutritious. Further, addictive drugs are powerful reinforcers even though they pose a long-term threat to the health of people who use them. So psychologists have sought other explanations for the mechanisms of reinforcement.

Some psychologists have argued that reinforcement is based not on a stimulus itself but on the opportunity to engage in an activity that involves the stimulus. According to David Premack (1965), for example, at any moment each person maintains a list of behavioural preferences, ranked from most desirable to least desirable, like a kind of psychological "Top Ten." The higher on the list an activity is, the greater is its power as a reinforcer. This means that a preferred activity can serve as a reinforcer for any other activity that is less preferred at the moment. For example, when parents allow their teenage daughter to use the car in return for mowing the lawn, they are using something high on her preference list (driving) to reinforce an activity that is lower on the list (lawn mowing). This idea is known as the *Premack principle*.

Taking the Premack principle a step further, some psychologists have suggested that virtually any activity can become a reinforcer if a person or animal has not been allowed to perform that activity for a while (Timberlake, 1980; Timberlake & Farmer-Dougan, 1991). To understand how this *disequilibrium hypothesis* works, suppose that you would rather study than work out at the gym. Now suppose that the gym has been closed for several weeks, and you have been unable to have a workout. According to the disequilibrium hypothesis, because your opportunity to exercise has been held below its normal level, its value as a reinforcer has been raised. In fact, it might have become so preferred that it could be used to reinforce studying! In short, under certain circumstances, even activities that are normally not strongly preferred can become reinforcers for normally more preferred activities. The disequilibrium hypothesis helps explain why money is such a powerful secondary reinforcer: It can be exchanged for whatever a person finds reinforcing at the moment. In fact, some researchers believe that the disequilibrium hypothesis may provide a better overall explanation of why reinforcers work than the Premack principle does (Hergenhahn & Olson, 1997).

Research by biological psychologists suggest that the stimuli and activities we know as reinforcers may work by exerting particular effects within the brain. This possibility was raised decades ago when James Olds and Peter Milner (1954) discovered that mild electrical stimulation of certain areas of the hypothalamus can be

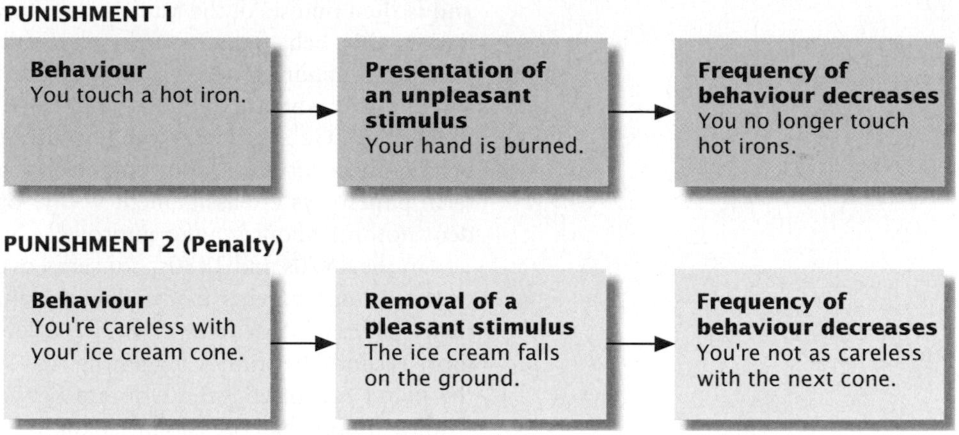

figure 6.10

Two Kinds of Punishment

In one form of punishment, a behaviour is followed by an aversive or unpleasant stimulus. In a second form of punishment, sometimes called *penalty*, a pleasant stimulus is removed following a behaviour. In either case, punishment decreases the chances that the behaviour will occur in the future. When a toddler reaches toward an electric outlet and her father says "NO!" and gently taps her hand, is that punishment or negative reinforcement? (If you said "punishment," you are right, because it will *reduce* the likelihood of touching outlets in the future.)

PUNISHMENT 1

Behaviour You touch a hot iron.	→	**Presentation of an unpleasant stimulus** Your hand is burned.	→	**Frequency of behaviour decreases** You no longer touch hot irons.

PUNISHMENT 2 (Penalty)

Behaviour You're careless with your ice cream cone.	→	**Removal of a pleasant stimulus** The ice cream falls on the ground.	→	**Frequency of behaviour decreases** You're not as careless with the next cone.

such a powerful reinforcer that a hungry rat will ignore food in a Skinner box, preferring to spend hours pressing a lever that stimulates these "pleasure centres" in its brain (Olds, 1973). It is not yet clear whether physiological mechanisms underlie the power of all reinforcers, but evidence available so far suggests that these mechanisms are important components of the process (Waelti, Dickinson, & Schultz, 2001). For example, as mentioned in the chapter on biological aspects of psychology, activation of dopamine systems is associated with the pleasure of many stimuli, including food, music, sex, the uncertainty involved in gambling, and some addictive drugs, such as cocaine (Berns et al., 2001; Blood & Zatorre, 2001; Breiter et al., 2001; Cardinal et al., 2001; Ciccocioppo, Sanna, & Weiss, 2001).

Punishment

So far, we have discussed positive and negative reinforcement, both of which *increase* the frequency of a response, either by presenting something pleasurable or by removing something unpleasant. In contrast, **punishment** *reduces* the frequency of an operant behaviour by presenting an unpleasant stimulus or removing a pleasant one. Shouting "No!" and swatting your dog when he begins chewing on the rug illustrates punishment that presents an unpleasant stimulus following a response. Taking away a child's TV privileges because of rude behaviour is a second kind of punishment—sometimes called *penalty*—that removes a positive stimulus (see Figure 6.10).

Punishment is often confused with negative reinforcement, but they are actually quite different. Reinforcement of any sort always *strengthens* behaviour; punishment weakens it. If shock is *turned off* when a rat presses a lever, that is negative reinforcement. It increases the chances that the rat will press the lever when shock occurs again. But if shock is *turned on* when the rat presses the lever, that is punishment. The rat will be less likely to press the lever again.

Punishment can certainly alter behaviour, but it has several potential drawbacks (Gershoff, 2002). First, it does not "erase" an undesirable habit; it merely suppresses it. This suppression usually occurs in the presence of stimuli (such as a parent or teacher) that were around at the time of punishment. In other words, people may repeat previously punished acts when they think they can avoid detection. This tendency is summed up in the adage "When the cat's away, the mice will play." Second, punishment sometimes produces unwanted side effects. For example, if you severely punish a child for swearing, the child may associate punishment with the punisher and end up fearing you. Third, punishment is often ineffective unless it is given immediately after the response and each time the response is made. This is especially true in relation to animals or young children. If a child gets into a cookie jar and enjoys a few cookies before being discovered and punished, the effect of the punishment will be greatly reduced. Similarly, if a child confesses to misbehaviour

punishment Presentation of an aversive stimulus or the removal of a pleasant stimulus.

and is then punished, the punishment may discourage honesty rather than eliminate undesirable behaviour. Fourth, physical punishment can become aggression and even abuse if administered in anger. Fifth, because children tend to imitate what they see, children who are frequently punished may be more likely to behave aggressively themselves (Gilbert, 1997). Finally, although punishment signals that inappropriate behaviour occurred, it does not specify what should be done instead. An "F" on a term paper says the assignment was poorly done, but the grade alone tells the student nothing about how to improve.

In the 1970s and 1980s, concerns over these drawbacks led many professionals to discourage parents from using spanking and other forms of punishment with their children (Rosellini, 1998). The debate about punishment has been reopened more recently by studies suggesting that spanking can be an effective way to control the behaviour of children who are between three and thirteen years of age. These studies found that occasional spanking does not harm children's development, if used in combination with other disciplinary practices. These other practices include requiring that the children pay some penalty for their misdeeds, having them provide some sort of restitution to the victims of their actions, and making them aware of what they did wrong (Gunnoe & Mariner, 1997; Larzelere, 1996).

When used *properly*, then, punishment can be a valuable tool (Baumrind, Larzelere, & Cowan, 2002). Occasionally, it may be the only alternative. For example, some children suffer developmental disabilities in which they hit or mutilate themselves or display other potentially life-threatening behaviours. As shown in Figure 6.11, punishing these behaviours has sometimes proven to be the only effective treatment (e.g., Flavell et al., 1982). Whatever the case, punishment is most effective when it is administered in accordance with several guidelines. First, the person giving punishment should specify why it is being given and that its purpose is to change the person's behaviour, not to harm or demean the person. This step helps prevent a general fear of the punisher. Second, without being abusive, punishment should be immediate and noticeable enough to eliminate the undesirable behaviour. A halfhearted "Quit it" may actually reinforce a child's misbehaviour, because almost any attention is reinforcing to some children. Moreover, if children become habituated to very mild punishment, the parent may end up using substantially more severe punishment to stop inappropriate behaviour than would have been necessary if a stern, but moderate, punishment had been used in the first place. (You may have witnessed this *escalation effect* in grocery stores or restaurants, where parents are often not initially firm enough in dealing with their children's misbehaviour.) Finally, the use of punishment alone is usually not enough to change behaviour in the long

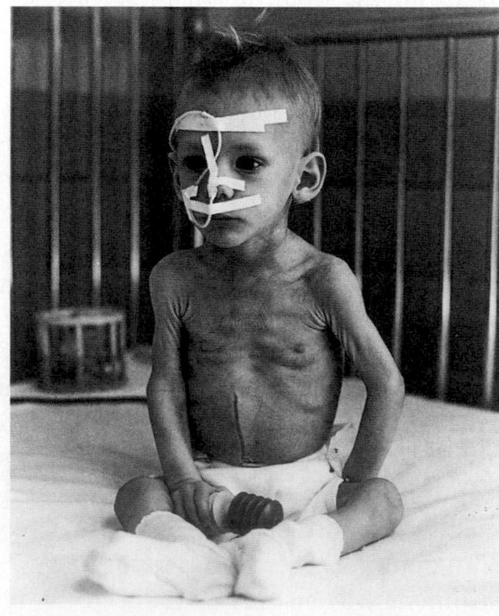

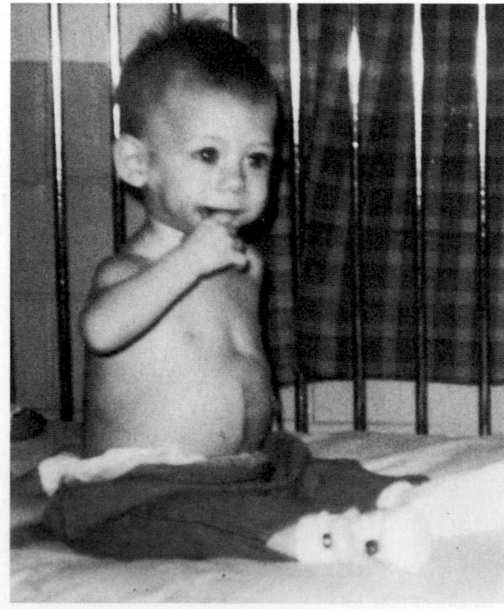

figure 6.11

Life-Saving Punishment

This child suffered from chronic ruminative disorder, a condition in which he vomited everything he ate. At left, the boy was approximately one year old and had been vomiting for four months. At right is the same child thirteen days after punishment with electric shock had eliminated the vomiting behaviour. His weight had increased 26 percent. He was physically and psychologically healthy when tested six months, one year, and two years later (Lang & Melamed, 1969).

Source: Lang & Melamed (1969).

in review Reinforcement and Punishment

Concept	Description	Example or Comment
Positive reinforcement	Increasing the frequency of a behaviour by following it with the presentation of a positive reinforcer—a pleasant, positive stimulus or experience	You say "Good job!" after someone works hard to perform a task.
Negative reinforcement	Increasing the frequency of a behaviour by following it with the removal of an unpleasant stimulus or experience	You learn to use the "mute" button on the TV remote control to remove the sound of an obnoxious commercial.
Escape conditioning	Learning to make a response that removes an unpleasant stimulus	A little boy learns that crying will cut short the time that he must stay in his room.
Avoidance conditioning	Learning to make a response that avoids an unpleasant stimulus	You slow your car to the speed limit when you spot a police car, thus avoiding being stopped and reducing the fear of a fine; very resistant to extinction.
Punishment	Decreasing the frequency of a behaviour by either presenting an unpleasant stimulus (punishment 1) or removing a pleasant one (punishment 2, or penalty)	You swat the dog after it steals food from the table, or you take a favourite toy away from a child who misbehaves. A number of cautions should be kept in mind before using punishment.

PsychAssist: Learned Helplessness; Shaping; Reinforcement and Punishment

run. It is important also to identify what the person should do instead of the punished act and then to reinforce the appropriate behaviour when it occurs. As the frequency of appropriate behaviour increases through reinforcement, the frequency of undesirable responses (and the need for further punishment) should decline.

When these guidelines are not followed, the potentially beneficial effects of punishment may disappear or be only temporary (Hyman, 1995). As illustrated in many countries' justice systems, punishment for criminal acts is typically administered long after the acts have occurred, and initial punishments are often relatively mild—as when offenders are repeatedly given probation. Even being sent to prison rarely leads to rehabilitation, because this punishment is usually not supplemented by efforts to teach and reinforce noncriminal lifestyles (Brennan & Mednick, 1994; Cassel & Bernstein, 2001). It is no wonder, then, that the reconviction rate of all federal offenders who were released between April 1994 and March 1995 was 44 percent (Government of Canada, 2003).

Some Applications of Operant Conditioning

Principles of operant conditioning were originally developed with animals in the laboratory, but they are valuable for understanding human behaviour in an endless variety of everyday situations. ("In Review: Reinforcement and Punishment" summarizes some key principles of operant conditioning.) The unscientific but effective use of rewards and punishments by parents, teachers, and peers is vital to helping children learn what is and is not appropriate behaviour at the dinner table, in the classroom, or at a birthday party. People learn how to be "civilized" in their own culture partly through positive ("Good!") and negative ("Stop that!") responses from others. As described in the chapter on human development, differing patterns of rewards and punishments for boys and girls also underlie the development of behaviours that fit culturally approved *gender roles*.

Learning Cultural Values As described in the chapter on social behaviour, the prevalence of aggressive behaviour varies considerably from culture to culture, partly because some cultures reward it more than others. In some Inuit cultures, for example, aggressive behaviour is actively discouraged and extremely rare (Banta, 1997). In many other cultures, it is all too common.

The scientific study of operant conditioning has led to numerous treatment programs for modifying problematic behaviour. These programs combine rewards for appropriate behaviours with extinction methods, or carefully administered punishment, for inappropriate behaviours. They have helped countless mental patients, mentally challenged individuals, severely autistic children, and hard-to-manage preschoolers to develop the behaviour patterns they need to live happier and more productive lives (e.g., Alberto, Troutman, & Feagin, 2002; Pear & Martin, 2002). Dave Korotkov of St. Thomas University in New Brunswick and his colleagues Ian Gilmour, Debra Charboneau, and Paula Berry from the Community Mental Health Clinic in Guelph, Ontario, produced a hypothetical example, based on their combined practical experience, of how operant conditioning could be used to modify a person's behaviour in a clinical setting. In the scenario, Sam is a developmentally challenged, 38-year-old individual living in a group home. Sam had been observed engaging in inappropriate sexual behaviour, such as the inappropriate touching of female staff members. The staff implement operant conditioning techniques to eliminate Sam's unwanted behaviour by reinforcing appropriate touching behaviours, rewarding a handshake with a trip to the bowling alley, and punishing inappropriate behaviours by using reprimands or the removal of Sam's privileges (Korotkov et al. 2001). These same methods have been used successfully to help keep former drug addicts drug free and to help patients with alcohol-related memory problems to recognize and remember new faces and names—including those of their own grandchildren (Hochhalter et al., 2001; Silverman et al., 2001). Many self-help books also incorporate principles of positive reinforcement, recommending self-reward following each small victory in efforts to lose weight, stop smoking, avoid procrastination, or reach other goals (e.g., Grant & Kim, 2002; Rachlin, 2000).

When people can't do anything about the consequences of a behaviour, discriminative stimuli may hold the key to changing the behaviour. For example, people trying to quit smoking often find it easier to do so if they stay away from bars and other places where there are discriminative stimuli for smoking. Stimulus control can also help alleviate insomnia. Insomniacs tend to use their beds for activities such as watching television, writing letters, reading magazines, worrying, and so on. Soon the bedroom becomes a discriminative stimulus for so many activities that relaxation and sleep become less and less likely. *Stimulus control therapy* encourages insomniacs to use their beds only for sleeping, and perhaps sex, making it more likely that they will sleep better when in bed (Edinger et al., 2001).

The Spanking Law In 2004 the Supreme Court of Canada decided to uphold an 1892 law stating that caregivers cannot be charged with physical abuse if they are using reasonable force to correct a child. Opponents argue that the law invites the use of excessive force. Proponents argue that parents need to be able to correct their child's behaviour as they see fit without the fear of accusations of physical abuse (Canadian Press, 2004).

Cognitive Processes in Learning

During the first half of the twentieth century, psychologists in North America tended to look at classical and operant conditioning through the lens of behaviourism, the theoretical approach that was dominant in psychology at the time. As described in the chapter on introducing psychology, behaviourism stresses the importance of empirical observation of lawful relationships in animal and human behaviour. Behaviourists tried to identify the stimuli, responses, and consequences that build and alter overt behaviour. In other words, they saw learning as resulting from the automatic, unthinking formation or modification of associations between observable events. Behaviourists paid almost no attention to the role of conscious mental activity that might accompany the learning process.

This strictly behavioural view of classical and operant conditioning is challenged by the cognitive approach, which has become increasingly influential in recent decades. Cognitive psychologists see a common thread in these apparently different forms of learning. Both classical and operant conditioning, they argue, help animals and people to detect causality—to understand what causes what (Schwartz & Robbins, 1995). By extension, both types of conditioning may result not only from automatic associations but also from more complex mental processes that underlie our adaptation to, and understanding of, the world around us (Dickinson, 2001).

Certainly there is evidence that cognitive processes—how people represent, store, and use information—play an important role in learning. This evidence comes from research on learned helplessness, latent learning, cognitive maps, insight, and observational learning.

Learned Helplessness

Babies learn that crying attracts attention. Children learn which button turns on the TV, and adults learn what behaviours bring success (or punishment) in the workplace. On the basis of this learning, people come to expect that certain actions on their part cause certain consequences. But sometimes events are beyond our control. What happens when behaviour has no effects on events, and especially when escape or avoidance behaviours fail? If such ineffectiveness is prolonged, one result may be **learned helplessness,** a tendency to give up any effort to control the environment (Overmier, 2002; Seligman, 1975).

learned helplessness Learning that responses do not affect consequences, resulting in failure to try to exert control over the environment.

Learned helplessness was first demonstrated in animals. As described earlier, dogs placed in a shuttle box (see Figure 6.7) will normally learn to jump over a barrier to escape a shock. However, if these dogs first receive shocks that they cannot escape, they later do not even try to escape when a shock is turned on in the shuttle box (Overmier & Seligman, 1967). It is as if the animals had learned that "shock happens, and there is nothing I can do to control it."

FOCUS ON RESEARCH METHODS

A Two-Factor Experiment on Human Helplessness

The results of animal studies on learned helplessness led psychologists to wonder whether learned helplessness might play a role in human psychological problems, but they had to deal with more basic questions first. One of the most important of these questions is whether lack of control over the environment can lead to helplessness in humans.

- **What was the researcher's question?**

Donald Hiroto (1974) conducted an experiment to test the hypothesis that people would develop learned helplessness after either experiencing lack of control or simply being told that their control was limited.

- **How did the researcher answer the question?**

Hiroto assigned research participants to one of three groups. One group heard a series of thirty random bursts of loud, obnoxious noise and, like dogs receiving inescapable shock, they had no way to stop it. A second group could control the noise by pressing a button to turn it off. The third group heard no noise at all.

After this preliminary phase, all three groups were exposed to eighteen additional bursts of noise, each preceded by a red warning light. During this second phase, *all* participants could stop the noise by pushing a lever. However, they didn't know whether to push the lever to the left or the right on any given trial. Still, they could prevent the noise if they acted quickly enough.

Before these new trials began, the experimenter led half the participants in each group to expect that avoiding or escaping the noise depended on their skill. The other half were led to expect that their success would be a matter of chance. So this was a *two-factor experiment,* because the dependent variable—the participants' efforts to control noise—could be affected by either or both of two independent variables: prior experience with noise (control, lack of control, or no noise) and expectation (skill or chance) about the ability to influence the noise.

- **What did the researcher find?**

On the average, participants who had previously experienced lack of control now failed to control noise on almost four times as many trials (50 percent vs. 13 percent) as did participants who had earlier been in control. *Expectation* of control also had an effect on behaviour. Regardless of whether participants had experienced control before, those who expected noise control to depend on their skill exerted control on significantly more trials than did those who expected chance to govern the outcome.

- **What do the results mean?**

These results supported Hiroto's hypothesis that people, like animals, tend to make less effort to control their environment when prior experience leads them to expect their efforts will be in vain. Unlike animals, though, people can develop expectations of helplessness either by personally experiencing lack of control or by being *told* that they are powerless. Hiroto's (1974) results appear to reflect a general phenomenon: When people's prior experience leads them to *believe* that nothing they do can change their lives or control their destiny, they generally stop trying to improve their lot (Faulkner, 2001; LoLordo, 2001; Peterson, Maier, & Seligman, 1993). Instead, they tend to passively endure aversive situations.

• What do we still need to know?

Further research is needed on when and how learned helplessness affects people's thoughts, feelings, and actions. For example, could learned helplessness explain why some battered women remain with abusive partners? We do know that learned-helplessness experiences are associated with the development of a generally pessimistic way of thinking that can produce depression and other mental disorders (Peterson & Seligman, 1984). People with this *pessimistic explanatory style* see the good things that happen to them as temporary and due to chance and the bad things as permanent and due to internal factors (e.g., lack of ability). This explanatory style has, in fact, been associated with poor grades, inadequate sales performance, health problems, and other negative outcomes (Bennett & Elliott, 2002; Seligman & Schulman, 1986; S. E. Taylor, 2002). The exact mechanisms responsible for this connection are still unknown, but understanding how pessimistic (or optimistic) explanatory styles can lead to negative (or positive) consequences remains an important focus of research (e.g., Brennan & Charnetski, 2000).

Does repeated success at controlling events create a sense of "learned mastery" that supports efforts to exert control in new situations? Animal experiments suggest that this is the case (Volpicelli et al., 1983). Further, people with a history of successful control appear more likely than others to develop the *optimistic cognitive style,* hopefulness, and resilience that lead to even more success and healthier lives (Gillham, 2000). (We discuss this cognitive style in the chapter on health, stress, and coping.) Accordingly, research is focusing on how best to minimize learned helplessness and maximize learned optimism in areas such as education, parenting, and psychotherapy (e.g., Jackson, Sellers, & Peterson, 2002). One option being evaluated at the moment is "resiliency training" for children at risk for depression (Cardemil, Reivich, & Seligman, 2002). Time will tell if such training leads to beneficial outcomes.

Latent Learning and Cognitive Maps

The study of cognitive processes in learning goes back at least to the 1920s and Edward Tolman's research on maze learning in rats. The rats' task was to find the goal box of the maze, where food awaited them. The animals typically took lots of wrong turns, but over the course of many trials they made fewer and fewer mistakes. The behavioural interpretation was that the rats learned a long chain of turning responses that were ultimately reinforced by the food. Tolman disagreed and offered evidence for a cognitive interpretation.

In one of Tolman's studies, three groups of rats were placed in the same maze once a day for several consecutive days (Tolman & Honzik, 1930). For Group A, food was placed in the goal box on each trial. As shown in Figure 6.12, these rats gradually improved their performance so that by the end of the experiment, they made only one or two mistakes as they ran through the maze. Group B also ran the maze once a day, but there was never any food in their goal box. These animals continued to make many errors throughout the experiment. Neither of these results is surprising, and each is consistent with a behavioural view of learning.

The third group of rats, Group C, was the critical one. For the first ten days, they received no reinforcement for running the maze and continued to make many mistakes. But on the eleventh day, food was placed in their goal box for the first time. Then a surprising thing happened: On the day after receiving reinforcement, these rats made almost no mistakes. In fact, their performance was as good as that of the rats who had been reinforced every day. In other words, for Group C the single reinforcement trial on day 11 produced a dramatic change in performance the next day.

Tolman argued that these results supported two conclusions. First, the reinforcement on day 11 could not have significantly affected the rats' *learning* of the

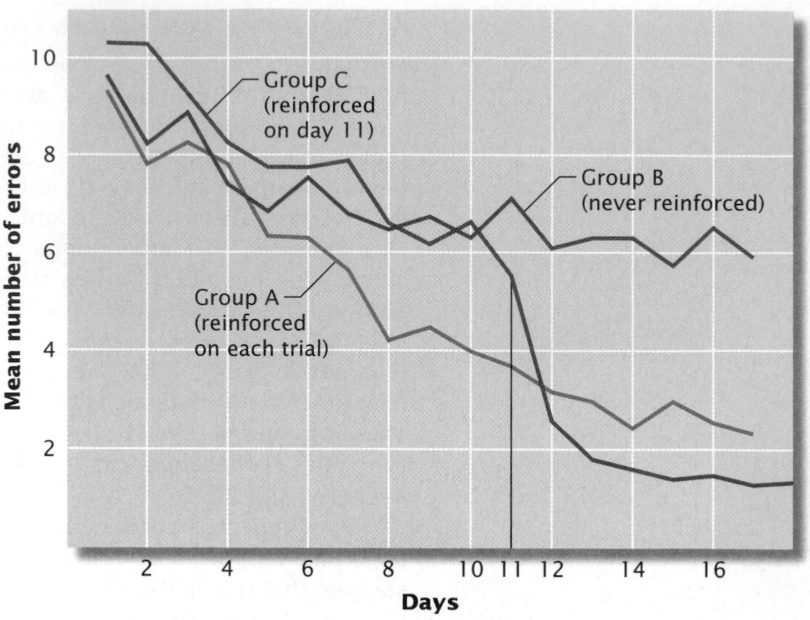

figure 6.12

Latent Learning

Notice that when rats in Group C did not receive food reinforcement, they continued to make many errors in locating the goal box of a maze. The day after first finding food there, however, they took almost no wrong turns! The reinforcement, argued Tolman, affected only the rats' performance; they must have learned the maze earlier, without reinforcement.

maze; it simply changed their later *performance*. They must have learned the maze earlier as they wandered around making mistakes on their way to the end of the maze. These rats demonstrated **latent learning**—learning that is not evident when it first occurs. (Latent learning occurs in humans, too; after years of experience in your neighbourhood, you could probably tell a visitor that the corner drugstore is closed on Sundays, even if you had never tried to go there on a Sunday yourself.)

Second, because the rats' performance changed immediately after the first reinforcement trial, the results obtained could occur only if the rats had earlier developed a **cognitive map**—that is, a mental representation of how the maze was arranged. Tolman concluded that cognitive maps develop naturally through experience with the world, even if there is no overt response or reinforcement. Research on learning in the natural environment has supported these views. For example, we develop mental maps of shopping malls and city streets, even when we receive no direct reward for doing so (Tversky & Kahneman, 1991). Having such a map allows you to tell that visitor to your neighbourhood exactly how to get to the corner drugstore from where you are standing.

Much as the Gestalt psychologists argued that the whole of a perception is different from the sum of its parts (see the chapter on perception), cognitive views hold that learning is more than just the combined effects of associations, reinforcements, and punishments. And just as perception may depend on the meaning attached to sensations, some forms of learning involve higher mental processes and depend on how the learner attaches meaning to events. To take just one example, being praised by a boss we respect may be more reinforcing than getting the same good evaluation from someone we dislike.

Insight and Learning

Wolfgang Köhler was a Gestalt psychologist whose work on the cognitive aspects of learning came about almost by accident. He was visiting the island of Tenerife when World War I broke out in 1914. As a German in an area controlled by Germany's enemy, Britain, he was confined to the island for the duration of the war, and he devoted his time to studying problem solving by chimpanzees housed there (Köhler, 1924).

For example, Köhler would put a chimpanzee in a cage and place a piece of fruit so that it was visible but out of the animal's reach. He sometimes hung the fruit from

latent learning Learning that is not demonstrated at the time it occurs.

cognitive map A mental representation of the environment.

figure 6.13

Insight

Here are three impressive examples of problem solving by chimpanzees. At left, the animal fixed a fifteen-foot pole in the ground, climbed to the top, and dropped down after grabbing fruit that had been out of reach. In the centre photo, the chimp stacked two boxes from different areas of the compound, climbed to the top, and used a pole to knock down the fruit. The chimp at right stacked three boxes and climbed them to reach the fruit.

Source: Köhler (1976).

a string too high to reach or laid it on the ground too far outside the cage to be retrieved. Many of the chimps overcame these obstacles easily. If the fruit was out of reach on the ground outside the cage, some chimps looked around the cage and, finding a long stick, used it to rake in the fruit. Surprised that the chimpanzees could solve these problems, Köhler tried more difficult tasks. Again, the chimps proved their skills, as Figure 6.13 illustrates.

In contrast to Thorndike, who thought that animals learn gradually through the consequences of their actions, Köhler argued that animals' problem solving does not have to depend on automatic associations developing slowly through trial and error. He supported his claim with three observations. First, once a chimpanzee solved a particular problem, it would immediately do the same thing in a similar situation. In other words, it acted as if it understood the problem. Second, Köhler's chimpanzees rarely tried a solution that didn't work. Apparently, the solution was not discovered randomly but "thought out" ahead of time and then acted out successfully. Third, the animals often reached a solution suddenly. When confronted with a piece of fruit hanging from a string, for example, a chimp might jump for it several times. Then it would stop jumping, look up, and pace back and forth. Finally it would run over to a wooden crate, place it directly under the fruit, and climb on top of it to reach the fruit. Once, when there were no other objects available, a chimp went over to Köhler, dragged him by the arm until he stood beneath the fruit, and then started climbing up his back!

Köhler believed that the only explanation for these results was that the chimpanzees had sudden **insight,** an understanding of the problem as a whole. The animals did not, he said, solve the problem simply by forming associations between responses and consequences. However, demonstrating that a particular performance is the

insight A sudden understanding about what is required to solve a problem.

IN THE BLEACHERS By Steve Moore

Painful learning experiences.

Despite the power of observational learning, some people just have to learn things the hard way.

product of sudden insight requires experiments that are more sophisticated than those conducted by Köhler. Some cases of "insight" might actually be the result of a process known as *learning to learn,* in which previous experiences in problem solving are applied to new ones in a way that makes their solution seem to be instantaneous (Harlow, 1949). In other cases, according to some cognitive psychologists, insight may actually result from a "mental trial-and-error" process in which people (and some animals) envision a course of action, mentally simulate its results, compare it with the imagined outcome of other alternatives, and settle on the course of action most likely to aid complex problem solving and decision making (Klein, 1993).

Observational Learning: Learning by Imitation

Research on the role of cognitive processes in learning has been further stimulated by the finding that learning can occur not only by doing but also by observing what others do. Learning by watching others—called **observational learning,** or *social learning*—is efficient and adaptive. It occurs in both animals and humans. For example, young chimpanzees learn how to use a stone to crack open nuts by watching their mothers perform this action (Inoue-Nakamura & Matsuzawa, 1997). And we don't have to find out for ourselves that a door is locked or an iron is hot if we have just seen someone else try the door or suffer a burn.

Children are particularly influenced by the adults and peers who act as models for appropriate behaviour in various situations. In one classic experiment, Albert Bandura showed nursery school children a film featuring an adult and a large, inflatable, bottom-heavy "Bobo" doll (Bandura, 1965). The adult in the film punched the Bobo doll in the nose, kicked it, threw objects at it, and hit its head with a hammer while saying things like "Sockeroo!" There were different endings to the film. Some children saw an ending in which the aggressive adult was called a "champion" by a second adult and rewarded with candy and soft drinks. Some saw the aggressor scolded and called a "bad person." Some saw a neutral ending in which there was neither reward nor punishment. After the film, each child was allowed to play alone with a Bobo doll. How the children played in this and similar studies led to some important conclusions about learning and about the role of cognitive factors in it.

Albert Bandura Albert Bandura was born in Mundare, Alberta, and was educated at the University of British Columbia and the University of Iowa. He later took a position at Stanford University where he has been teaching ever since. Bandura is known for the classic Bobo doll experiments and the development of his social learning theory (Pajares, 2004).

observational learning Learning how to perform new behaviours by watching others.

vicarious conditioning Learning conditioned responses by watching what happens to others.

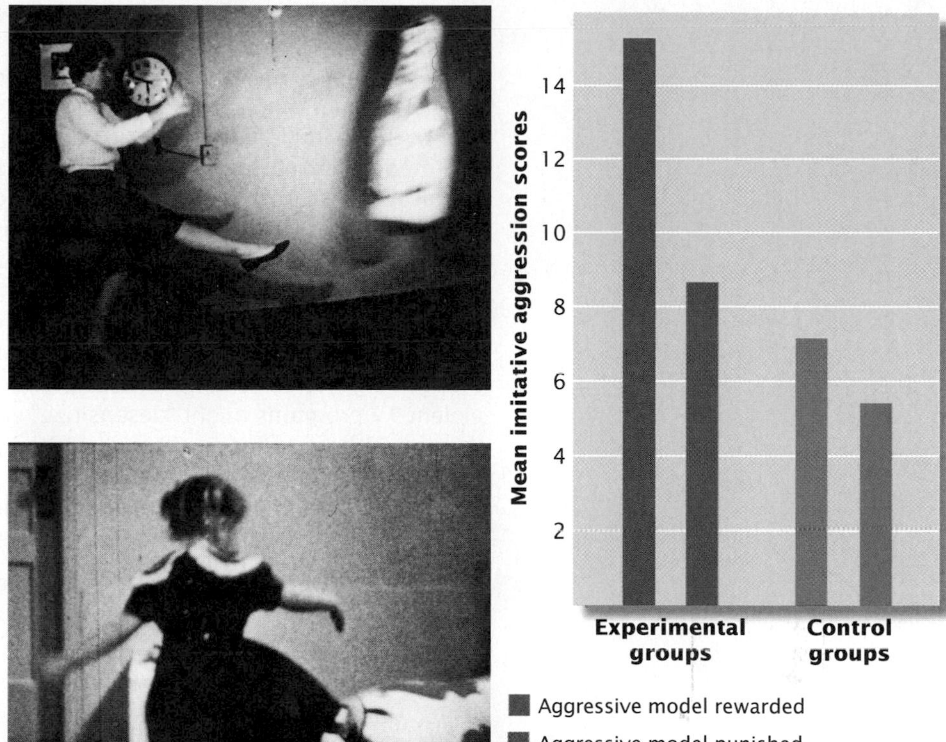

figure 6.14

Observational Learning

Albert Bandura found that after observing an aggressive model, many children imitate the model's acts precisely, especially if the model's aggression was rewarded.

Source: Bandura, Ross, & Ross (1963).

Bandura found that children who saw the adult rewarded for aggression showed the most aggressive acts in play (see Figure 6.14). They had received **vicarious conditioning,** a kind of observational learning in which a person is influenced by seeing or hearing about the consequences of other people's behaviour. Those who had seen the adult punished for aggressive acts showed less aggression, but they still learned something. When later offered rewards for all the aggressive acts they could perform, these children displayed just as many as the children who had watched the rewarded adult. Observational learning can occur even when there are no vicarious consequences; many children in the neutral condition also imitated the model's aggression.

LINKAGES (a link to Psychological Disorders)

Observational learning seems to be a powerful source of the *socialization* process through which children learn about which behaviours are—and are not—appropriate in their culture (Bandura, 1999). Experiments show, for example, that children are more willing to help and share after seeing a demonstration of helping by a friendly, impressive model—even after some months have elapsed (Schroeder et al., 1995). As described in the chapter on psychological disorders, other studies suggest that phobias can be learned partly through seeing fearfulness in others (Kleinknecht, 1991).

THINKING CRITICALLY

Does Watching Violence on Television Make People More Violent?

If observational learning is important, then surely television, and televised violence, must teach children a great deal. It is estimated that the average Canadian child spends approximately 15.5 hours a week watching television (Statistics Canada, 2001). Forty-five percent of the time Canadians are watching foreign programming (Statistics Canada, 2003). Canada is one of the largest importers of programming from the United States (Media Awareness Network, 2006). Prime time entertainment programs from the United States present an average of five acts of simulated violence per hour. Some American Saturday-morning cartoons include more than twenty per hour (American Psychological Association, 1993; Gerbner, Morgan, & Signorielli, 1994). Comparable Canadian programming produces 23.4% fewer violent acts than its American counterpart (Gosselin et al., 1997). It has been estimated, however, that a typical Canadian child will have witnessed approximately 12 000 violent deaths on television before his or her twelfth birthday (Chidley, 1996).

Psychologists have speculated that watching so much violence might be emotionally arousing, making the viewers more likely to react violently to frustration (Huston & Wright, 1989). Televised violence might also provide models that viewers imitate, particularly if the violence is carried out by attractive, impressive models—the "good guys," for example (Huesmann et al., 2003). Finally, prolonged viewing of violent TV programs might "desensitize" viewers, making them less distressed when they see others suffer and less disturbed about inflicting pain on others (Aronson, 1999; Donnerstein, Shabby, & Eron, 1995). Concern over the influence of violence on television led to the development of the violence-blocking V-Chip for new television sets in Canada (Canadian Intellectual Property Office, 2004).

- **What am I being asked to believe or accept?**

Many have argued that, through one or more of the mechanisms just listed, watching violence on television causes violent behaviour in viewers (Anderson et al., 2003; Anderson & Bushman, 2002b; Bushman & Huesmann, 2000; Eron et al., 1996; Husemann, 1998). A review of past research, conducted for the Canadian Paediatric Society, has demonstrated that over 1000 studies have linked violent television to increased aggressive behaviour, and that this link is particularly prevalent in boys (Psychosocial Paediatrics Committee, 2003).

- **What evidence is available to support the assertion?**

Three types of evidence support the claim that watching violent television programs increases violent behaviour. First, there is evidence from anecdotes and case studies. Children have poked one another in the eye after watching the Three Stooges appear to do so on television, and adults have claimed that watching TV shows prompted them to commit murders or other violent acts matching those seen on the shows (Werner, 2003).

Second, many correlational studies have found a relationship between watching violent television programs and later acts of aggression and violence (Johnson, Coehn, et al., 2002). One such study tracked people from the time they were six or seven (in 1977) until they reached their early twenties (in 1992). Those who had watched more violent television as children were significantly more aggressive as adults (Huesmann et al., 1997; Huesmann et al., 2003) and more likely to engage in criminal activity (Huesmann, 1995). They were also more likely to use physical punishment on their own children, who themselves tended to be much more aggressive than average. These latter results have been found not only in the United States but also in Israel, Australia, Poland, the Netherlands, and even Finland, where the number of violent TV shows is very small (Centrewall, 1990; Huesmann & Eron, 1986).

Finally, the results of numerous experiments also support the view that TV violence increases aggression among viewers (Josephson, 1995; Paik & Comstock, 1994; Psychosocial Paediatrics Committee, 2003; Reiss & Roth, 1993). Wendy Josephson, of the University of Winnipeg in Manitoba, studied two groups of boys who watched either violent or nonviolent programs in a controlled setting and then played floor hockey (Josephson, 1987). Boys who had watched the violent shows were more likely than those who had watched nonviolent programs to behave aggressively on the hockey floor. This effect was greatest for those boys who had the most aggressive tendencies to begin with. More extensive experiments, in which children are exposed for long periods to carefully controlled types of television programs, also suggest that exposure to large amounts of violent activity on television results in aggressive behaviour (Eron et al., 1996).

Are there alternative ways of interpreting the evidence?

To some researchers, like Wendy Josephson, this evidence leaves no doubt that media violence causes increases in aggressive and violent behaviour (Josephson, 1995). Others, like Joseph Freedman of the University of Toronto in Ontario, suggest the evidence is not conclusive and is open to some qualifications and alternate interpretations (Freedman, 2002).

Anecdotal reports and case studies are particularly suspect. When people face imprisonment or execution for their violent acts, how much confidence can we place in their claims that these acts were triggered by television programs? And how many other people might say that the same programs made them *less* likely to be violent? Anecdotes alone do not provide a good basis for drawing solid scientific conclusions.

What about the correlational evidence from studies that followed children over time? As discussed in the chapter on research in psychology, a *correlation* between two variables does not necessarily mean that one is *causing* an effect on the other. Both might be affected by a third factor. Why, for example, are certain people watching so much television violence in the first place? This question suggests a possible third factor that might account for the observed relationship between watching TV violence and acting aggressively: People who tend to be aggressive may prefer to watch more violent TV programs *and* may behave aggressively toward others. In other words, personality may partly account for the observed correlations (e.g., Aluja-Fabregat & Torrubia-Beltri, 1998).

The results of controlled experiments on the effects of televised violence have been criticized as well (Freedman, 2002; Geen, 1998a). The major objection is that both the independent and dependent variables in these experiments are artificial, so they may not apply beyond the laboratory (Anderson, Lindsay, & Bushman, 1999). For example, the kinds of violent shows viewed by the participants during some of these experiments, as well as the ways in which their aggression has been measured, may not reflect what goes on in the real-world situations we most want to know about.

What additional evidence would help to evaluate the alternatives?

Given the difficulty of interpreting correlational evidence, it would be useful to have evidence from controlled experiments in which equivalent groups of people were exposed for years to differing "doses" of the violence actually portrayed on TV and in which the effects on their later behaviour were observed in real-world situations. Such experiments could also explore the circumstances under which different people (e.g., children vs. adults) were affected by various forms of violence. However, studies like these create an ethical dilemma. If watching violent television programs really does cause violent behaviour, are psychologists justified in creating conditions that might lead some people to be more violent? If such violence occurred, would the researchers be partly responsible to the victims and to society? Difficulty in answering questions like these is one reason why there are so many short-term experiments and correlational studies in this area and why there is still some uncertainty about the effects of television violence. The violence that may affect children's aggressive behaviour may not be limited to what they see on television and in video games.

"I have HAD it with you two and your violent video games!"

Close to Home ©2003 John McPherson. Reprinted with Permission of Universal Press Syndicate. All rights reserved.

What conclusions are most reasonable?

The evidence collected so far makes it reasonable to conclude that watching TV violence may be one cause of violent behaviour, especially in some children (Anderson & Bushman, 2002b; Bushman & Anderson, 2001; Huesmann et al., 1997; Robinson et al., 2001; Smith & Donnerstein, 1998). Playing violent video games may be another (Anderson, 2004; Anderson & Bushman, 2001). However, a causal relationship between watching TV violence and acting violently is not inevitable, and there are many circumstances in which the effect does not occur (Charleton, Gunter, & Coles, 1998; Freedman, 1992, 2002). Parents, peers, and other environmental influences, along with personality factors, may dampen or amplify the effect of watching televised violence. Indeed, not every viewer interprets violence in the same way, and not every viewer is equally vulnerable (Ferguson, 2002; Wood, Wong, & Chachere, 1991).

Those most likely to be affected by TV violence may be those who are most aggressive or violence-prone in the first place, a trait that could well have been acquired by observing the behaviour of parents or peers (Huesmann et al., 1997). Still, the fact that violence on television *can* have a causal impact on violent behaviour is reason for serious concern and continues to influence public debate about what should and should not be aired on television.

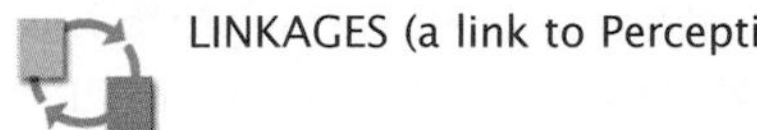

LINKAGES
Neural Networks and Learning

LINKAGES (a link to Perception)

Taking a cognitive approach to learning does not mean that associations are unimportant in the learning process. Associations between conditioned stimuli and reflexes or between responses and their consequences play an important role even in the mental processes that allow us to understand which events predict which other events. As a result of experience, some things remind us of other things, which remind us of still others, and so on.

How are associations actually stored in the brain? No one yet knows for sure, but neural network models provide a good way of thinking about this process. Networks of neural connections in the brain are believed to play a critical role not only in the rapid and accurate recognition of objects (Hintzman, 1991) but also in the learning process itself (Hergenhahn & Olson, 1997). These associative networks can be very complex. Consider the word *dog.* As shown in Figure 6.15, each person's experience builds many associations to this word, and the strength of each association will reflect the frequency with which *dog* has been mentally linked to the other objects, events, and ideas in that person's life.

Using what they know about the laws of learning and about the way neurons communicate and alter their synaptic connections, psychologists have been trying to develop models of how these associations are established (Messinger et al., 2001). We discuss some of these efforts in the chapters on perception and memory in terms of *neural networks* and *parallel distributed processing* models. A crucial aspect of such models is the idea of distributed memory or distributed knowledge. These models suggest, for example, that the knowledge of "dog" does not lie in a single location, or node, within your brain. Instead, knowledge is distributed throughout the network of associations that connect the letters *D, O,* and *G,* along with other dog-related experiences. In addition, as shown in Figure 6.15, each of the interconnected nodes that make up your knowledge of "dog" is connected to

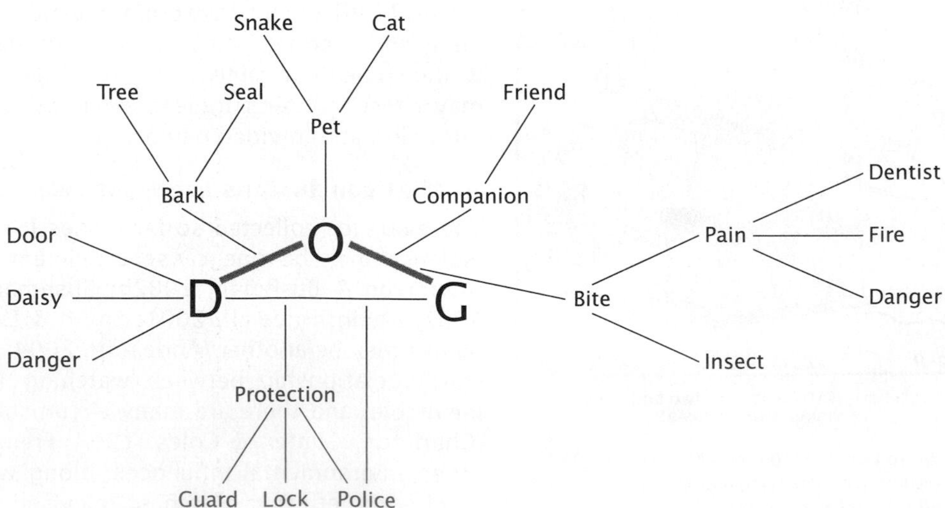

figure 6.15

An Associative Network

Here is an example of a network of associations to the word "dog." Network theorists suggest that the connections shown here represent patterns of neural connections in the brain.

many other nodes as well. So the letter *D* will be connected to "Daisy," "Danger," and a host of other concepts. Networks of connections also appear to be the key to explaining how people come to understand the words and sentences they read (Wolman, van den Broek, & Lorch, 1997).

Neural network models of learning focus on how these connections are developed through experience (Hanson & Burr, 1990). For example, suppose you are learning a new word in a foreign language. Each time you read the word and associate it with its English equivalent, you strengthen the neural connections between the sight of the letters forming that word and all of the nodes activated when its English equivalent is brought to mind. Neural network, or *connectionist,* models of learning predict how much the strength of each linkage grows (in terms of the likelihood of neural communication between the two connected nodes) each time the two words are experienced together.

The details of various theories about how these connections grow are very complex, but a theme common to many of them is that the weaker the connection between two items, the greater the increase in connection strength when they are experienced together. So in a simple classical conditioning experiment, the connections between the nodes characterizing the conditioned stimulus and those characterizing the unconditioned stimulus will show the greatest increase in strength during the first few learning trials. Notice that this prediction nicely matches the typical learning curve shown in Figure 6.3 (Rescorla & Wagner, 1972).

Neural network models have yet to fully explain the learning of complex tasks, nor can they easily account for how people adapt when the "rules of the game" are suddenly changed and old habits must be unlearned and replaced. Nevertheless, a better understanding of what we mean by *associations* may very well lie in future research on neural network models (Anthony & Bartlett, 1999; Goldblum, 2001).

Using Research on Learning to Help People Learn

Teaching and training—explicit efforts to assist learners in mastering a specific skill or body of material—are major aspects of socialization in virtually every culture. So the study of how people learn has important implications for improved teaching in our schools (Azar, 2002; Lambert, 1999; Woolfolk-Hoy, 1999) and for helping people develop skills ranging from typing to tennis.

Reciprocal Teaching Ann Brown and her colleagues (Brown et al., 1992) demonstrated the success of reciprocal teaching, in which children take turns teaching each other. This technique is similar to the cooperative arrangements seen in Japanese education.

Classrooms Across Cultures

The media is filled with concern for the educational system in Canada. Many people believe that schools in Canada are not doing a very good job. However, the average performance of 15-year-old Canadian students on tests of reading, math and science has tended to be strong when compared to 32 other countries. Canadian students scored second in reading, third in mathematics, and fifth in science overall (Bussière, et al., 2004).

Although Canada has scored well, we can still try to learn from those countries that have performed better. In science, for example, Finland, Japan, Hong Kong-China, and Korea out-performed the Canadian students (Bussière, et al., 2004). In a typical Canadian classroom session, teachers talked to students as a group. The students then worked at their desks independently. Reinforcement or other feedback about performance on their work was usually delayed until the next day or, often, not provided at all. In contrast, the typical Japanese classroom placed greater emphasis on cooperative work among students (Kristof, 1997). Teachers provided more immediate feedback on a one-to-one basis and there was an emphasis on creating teams of students with varying abilities, an arrangement in which faster learners help teach slower ones. However, before concluding that the difference in the science performance is the result of social factors alone, we must consider another important distinction: The Japanese children practise more. They spend more days in school during the year and, on average, spent more hours doing homework.

Psychologists and educators are also considering how other principles of learning can be applied to improve education (Azar, 2002; Bransford, Brown, & Cocking, 1999; Woolfolk-Hoy, 1999). Anecdotal and experimental evidence suggests that some of the most successful educational techniques are those that apply basic principles of operant conditioning, offering frequent testing, positive reinforcement for correct performance, and immediate corrective feedback following mistakes (Kass, 1999; Oppel, 2000; Walberg, 1987). Research in cognitive psychology (e.g., Bjork, 1979, 1999) also suggests that students are more likely to retain what they learn if they engage in numerous study sessions rather than in a single "cramming" session on the night before a quiz or exam. To encourage this more beneficial "distributed practice" pattern, researchers say, teachers should give enough exams and quizzes (some unannounced, perhaps) that students will be reading and studying more or less continuously. And because learning is aided by repeated opportunities to use new information, these exams and quizzes should cover material from throughout the term, not just from recent classes. Such recommendations are not necessarily popular with students, but there is good evidence that they promote long-term retention of course material (e.g., Bjork, 1999).

Active Learning

The importance of cognitive processes in learning is apparent in instructional methods that emphasize *active learning* (Bonwell & Eison, 1991). These methods take many forms, such as small-group problem-solving tasks, discussion of "one-minute essays" written in class, use of "thumbs up" or "thumbs down" to indicate agreement or disagreement with the instructor's lecture, and multiple-choice questions that give students feedback about their understanding of the previous fifteen minutes of lecture (Goss Lucas & Bernstein, 2005; Heward, 1997). There is little doubt that for many students, the inclusion of active learning experiences makes classes more interesting and enjoyable (Moran, 2000; Murray, 2000). Active learning methods also provide immediate reinforcement and help students to go beyond memorizing isolated facts by encouraging them to think more deeply about new information, consider how it relates to what they already know, and apply it in new

Active Learning Field trips provide students with firsthand opportunities to see and interact with the things they study in the classroom. Such experiences are just one example of the active learning exercises that can help students become more deeply involved in the learning process.

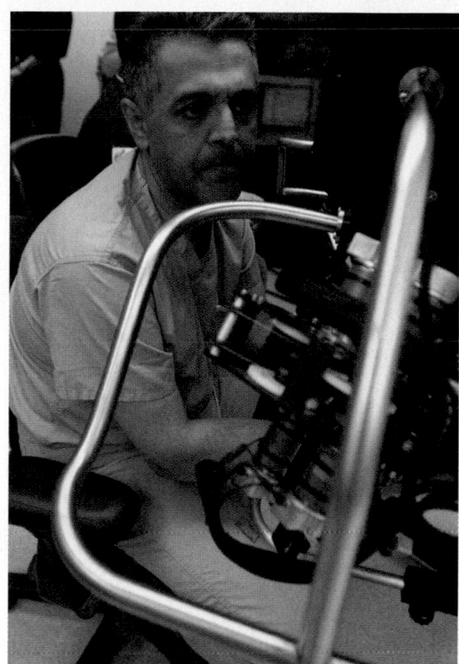

Virtual Surgery Mehran Anvari is a Canadian surgeon working with NASA on what could one day be surgery in space. He had to train himself to operate in a virtual environment that included a 2-second delay resulting from the time it takes for his signal to travel between his work station and the space station.

situations. The more elaborate mental processing associated with active learning makes new information not only more personally meaningful but also easier to remember.

Active learning strategies have been found to be superior to passive teaching methods in a number of studies with children and adults. In one study, a grade five science teacher spent some class periods calling on only those students whose hands were raised; the rest listened passively. On other days, all students were required to answer every question by holding up a card on which they had written their response. Scores on next-day quizzes and biweekly tests showed that students remembered more of the material covered on the active learning days than on the "passive" days (Gardner, Heward, & Grossi, 1994). Studies with students in high school, as well as with community college and university students, have found that active learning approaches result in better test performance and greater class participation compared with standard instructional techniques (e.g., Kellum, Carr, & Dozier, 2001). For example, students who passively listened to a physics lecture received significantly lower scores on a test of lecture content than did those who participated in a virtual reality lab that allowed them to "interact" actively with the physical forces covered in the lecture (Brelsford, 1993). Results like these have fuelled the development of other science education programs that place students in virtual laboratory environments where they can actively manipulate materials and test hypotheses (e.g., Horwitz & Christie, 2000). Despite the enthusiasm generated by active learning methods, rigorous experimental research is still needed to compare their short- and long-term effects with those of more traditional methods in teaching various kinds of course content.

Skill Learning

The complex action sequences, or *skills,* that people learn to perform in everyday life—tying a shoe, opening a door, operating a computer, shooting a basketball, driving a car—develop through direct and vicarious learning processes involving imitation, instructions, reinforcement, and, of course, lots of practice. Some skills, such as those of a basketball player or violinist, demand exceptional perceptual-motor coordination. Others, such as those involved in scientific thinking, have a large cognitive component, requiring rapid understanding. In either case, the learning of skills usually involves practice and feedback.

Practice—the repeated performance of a skill—is the most critical component of skill learning (Howe, Davidson, & Sloboda, 1998). For perceptual-motor skills, both physical and mental practice are beneficial (Druckman & Bjork, 1994). To be most effective, practice should continue past the point of correct performance until the skill can be performed automatically, with little or no need for attention. As mentioned earlier, in learning many cognitive skills, what counts most seems to be practice in retrieving relevant information from memory. Trying to recall and write down facts that you have read, for example, is a more effective learning tool than simply reading the facts a second time.

Try It This Way Good coaches provide enough guidance and performance feedback to help budding athletes develop their skills to the fullest, but not so much that the guidance interferes with the learning process. Striking this delicate balance is one of the greatest challenges faced by coaches and by teachers in general (Goodman & Wood, 2004).

Feedback about the correctness of responses is also necessary. As with any learning process, the feedback should come soon enough to be effective, but not so quickly that it interferes with the learner's efforts to learn independently. Large amounts of guidance may produce very good performance during practice, but too much guidance may impair later performance (Kluger & DeNisi, 1998; Wickens, 1992). Coaching students about correct responses in math, for example, may impair their ability to retrieve the correct response later on their own from memory. And in coaching athletes, if feedback is given too soon after an action occurs or while it is still taking place, it may divert the learner's attention from understanding how that action was achieved and what it felt like to perform it (Schmidt & Bjork, 1992). Independent practice at retrieving previously learned responses or information requires more effort, but it is critical for skill development (Ericsson & Charness, 1994).

LINKAGES

As noted in the chapter on introducing psychology, all of psychology's many subfields are related to one another. Our discussion of neural networks as possible models of learning illustrates just one way in which the topic of this chapter, learning, is linked to the subfield of perception, which is covered in the chapter by that name. The Linkages diagram shows ties to two other subfields as well, and there are many more ties throughout the book. Looking for linkages among subfields will help you see how they all fit together and better appreciate the big picture that is psychology.

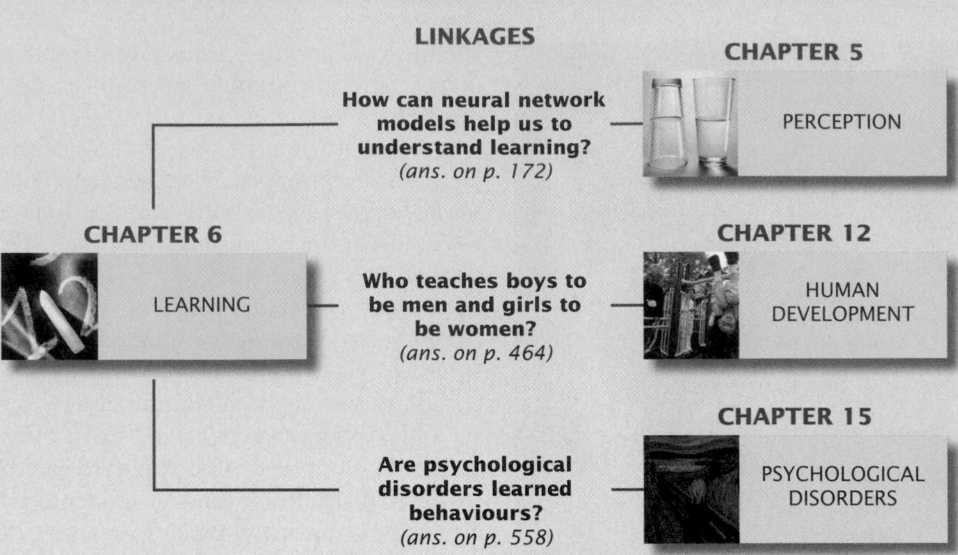

LINKAGES
CHAPTER 6
LEARNING
How can neural network models help us to understand learning?
(ans. on p. 172)
CHAPTER 5
PERCEPTION
Who teaches boys to be men and girls to be women?
(ans. on p. 464)
CHAPTER 12
HUMAN DEVELOPMENT
Are psychological disorders learned behaviours?
(ans. on p. 558)
CHAPTER 15
PSYCHOLOGICAL DISORDERS

SUMMARY

Individuals adapt to changes in the environment through the process of *learning*, which is the modification through experience of pre-existing behaviour and understanding.

Learning About Stimuli

One kind of learning is *habituation*, which is reduced responsiveness to a repeated stimulus. According to Richard Solomon's opponent-process theory, habituation results as two processes balance each other. The first process is a relatively automatic response to some stimulus. The second, or opponent, process follows and counteracts the first. This theory may help explain drug tolerance and some overdose cases.

Classical Conditioning: Learning Signals and Associations

Pavlov's Discovery

One form of associative learning is *classical conditioning*. It occurs when a *conditioned stimulus*, or *CS* (such as a tone), is repeatedly paired with an *unconditioned stimulus*, or *UCS* (such as meat powder on a dog's tongue), which naturally brings about an *unconditioned response*, or *UCR* (such as salivation). Eventually the conditioned stimulus will elicit a response, known as the *conditioned response*, or *CR*, even when the unconditioned stimulus is not presented.

Conditioned Responses over Time: Extinction and Spontaneous Recovery

In general, the strength of a conditioned response grows as CS-UCS pairings continue. If the conditioned stimulus is repeatedly presented without being paired with the unconditioned stimulus, the conditioned response eventually disappears; this is *extinction*. Following extinction, the conditioned response often reappears if the conditioned stimulus is presented after some time; this is *spontaneous recovery*. In addition, if the conditioned and unconditioned stimuli are paired once or twice after extinction, *reconditioning* occurs. That is, the conditioned response regains its original strength.

Stimulus Generalization and Discrimination

Because of *stimulus generalization*, conditioned responses are elicited by stimuli that are similar, but not identical, to conditioned stimuli. Generalization is limited by *stimulus discrimination*, which reduces conditioned responses to stimuli that are substantially different from the conditioned stimulus.

The Signalling of Significant Events

Classical conditioning involves learning that the conditioned stimulus is an event that predicts the occurrence of another event, the unconditioned stimulus. The conditioned response is not just an automatic reflex but also a means through which animals and people develop mental models of the relationships between events. Classical conditioning works best when the conditioned stimulus precedes the unconditioned stimulus, an arrangement known as *forward conditioning*. Conditioned responses develop best when the conditioned stimulus precedes the unconditioned stimulus by intervals ranging from less than a second to a minute or more, depending on the stimuli involved. Conditioning is also more likely when the conditioned stimulus reliably signals the unconditioned stimulus.

In general, the strength of a conditioned response and the speed of conditioning increase as the intensity of the unconditioned stimulus increases. Stronger conditioned stimuli also speed conditioning. The particular conditioned stimulus likely to be linked to a subsequent unconditioned stimulus depends in part on which stimulus was being attended to when the unconditioned stimulus occurred. *Second-order conditioning* occurs when a conditioned stimulus becomes powerful enough to function as an unconditioned stimulus for another stimulus associated with it. Some stimuli are easier to associate than others; organisms seem to be biologically prepared to learn certain associations, as exemplified by taste aversions.

Some Applications of Classical Conditioning

Classical conditioning plays a role in the development and treatment of phobias, in the humane control of predators in the wild, and in procedures for identifying people at risk for Alzheimer's disease.

Instrumental and Operant Conditioning: Learning the Consequences of Behaviour

Learning occurs not only through associating stimuli but also through associating behaviour with its consequences.

From the Puzzle Box to the Skinner Box

Edward L. Thorndike's *law of effect* holds that any response that produces satisfaction becomes more likely to occur again when the same stimulus is encountered, and any response that produces discomfort becomes less likely to occur again. Thorndike called this type of learning *instrumental conditioning*. B. F. Skinner called the same basic process *operant conditioning*. In operant conditioning the organism is free to respond at any time, and conditioning is measured by the rate of responding.

Basic Components of Operant Conditioning

An *operant* is a response that has some effect on the world. A *reinforcer* increases the probability that the operant preceding it will occur again. In other words, reinforcers strengthen behaviour. There are two types of reinforcers: *positive reinforcers,* which are pleasant stimuli that strengthen a response if they are presented after that response occurs, and *negative reinforcers,* which are the removal of an unpleasant stimulus following some response. Both kinds of reinforcers strengthen the behaviours that precede them. *Escape conditioning* results when behaviour terminates an aversive event. *Avoidance conditioning* results when behaviour prevents or avoids an aversive stimulus; it reflects both classical and operant conditioning. Behaviours learned through avoidance conditioning are highly resistant to extinction. *Discriminative stimuli* indicate whether reinforcement is available for a particular behaviour.

Forming and Strengthening Operant Behaviour

Complex responses can be learned through *shaping,* which involves reinforcing successive approximations of the desired response. *Primary reinforcers* are innately rewarding; *secondary reinforcers* are rewards that people or animals learn to like because of their association with primary reinforcers. In general, operant conditioning proceeds more quickly when the delay in receiving reinforcement is short rather than long and when the reinforcer is large rather than small. Reinforcement may be delivered on a *continuous reinforcement schedule* or on one of four basic types of *partial reinforcement schedules* (also called intermittent reinforcement schedules): *fixed-ratio (FR) schedules, variable-ratio (VR) schedules, fixed-interval (FI) schedules,* and *variable-interval (VI) schedules*. Ratio schedules lead to a rapid rate of responding. Behaviour learned through partial reinforcement, particularly through variable schedules, is very resistant to extinction; this phenomenon is called the *partial reinforcement extinction effect*. Partial reinforcement is involved in superstitious behaviour, which results when a response is coincidentally followed by a reinforcer.

Why Reinforcers Work

Research suggests that reinforcers are rewarding because they provide an organism with the opportunity to engage in desirable activities, which may change from one situation to the next. Another possibility is that activity in the brain's pleasure centres plays a role in reinforcement.

Punishment

The frequency of a behaviour can be decreased through *punishment,* in which the behaviour is followed by either an unpleasant stimulus or the removal of a pleasant stimulus. Punishment modifies behaviour but has several drawbacks. It suppresses behaviour without erasing it; fear of punishment may generalize to the person doing the punishing; it is ineffective when delayed; it can be physically harmful and may teach aggressiveness; and it teaches only what not to do, not what should be done to obtain reinforcement.

Some Applications of Operant Conditioning

The principles of operant conditioning have been used in many areas of life, including the teaching of everyday social skills, the treatment of sleep disorders, the development of self-control, and the improvement of classroom education.

Cognitive Processes in Learning

Cognitive processes—how people represent, store, and use information—play an important role in learning.

Learned Helplessness

Learned helplessness appears to result when people believe that their behaviour has no effect on the world.

Latent Learning and Cognitive Maps

Both animals and humans display *latent learning,* learning that is not obvious at the time it occurs. They also form *cognitive maps* of their environments, even in the absence of any reinforcement for doing so.

Insight and Learning

Experiments on *insight* also support the idea that cognitive processes and learned strategies play an important role in learning, perhaps even by animals.

Observational Learning: Learning by Imitation

The process of learning by watching others is called *observational learning,* or social learning. Some observational learning occurs through *vicarious conditioning,* in which an individual is influenced by seeing or hearing about the consequences of others' behaviour. Observational learning is more likely to occur when the person observed is rewarded for the observed behaviour. Observational learning is a powerful source of socialization.

Using Research on Learning to Help People Learn

Research on how people learn has implications for improved teaching and for the development of a wide range of skills.

Classrooms Across Cultures

The degree to which immediate reinforcement and extended practice are used in teaching varies considerably from culture to culture, but research suggests that the application of these and other basic learning principles is important to promoting effective teaching and learning.

Active Learning

The importance of cognitive processes in learning is seen in active learning methods designed to encourage people to think deeply about and apply new information instead of just memorizing isolated facts.

Skill Learning

Observational learning, practice, and corrective feedback play important roles in the learning of skills.

Memory

7

Have you ever forgotten someone's name five seconds after you were introduced? What happened to that memory, and why you lost it, are just two of the many questions that memory researchers study. In this chapter, we'll review what they have discovered about memory so far, and we'll suggest some ideas for improving your own memory. Here's how we have organized our presentation:

During the 2005 Gomery Inquiry into the Liberal sponsorship scandal, Justice John H. Gomery, the head of the inquiry, was continually frustrated by the testimony of Jean Lafleur, a former advertising executive with Lafleur Communications. Gomery kept pressing Lafleur, asking him to recall whether or not in 1997 he had asked his employees to make donations to the Liberal Party and then reimbursed them. Lafleur responded that he had no recollection of the event and, throughout the inquiry, his response never changed (CBC, 2005).

Is it possible for someone to forget such an incident so completely? Certainly, it would be hard for anyone to remember in vivid detail even significant events in the course of our lives. Moreover, memory is full of contradictions. It is common, for example, for adults to remember the name of their grade one teacher but not the phone number they just called. Like perception, memory is selective. It is also made up of many different abilities, some of which may operate much more effectively, or less efficiently, than others.

Memory plays a critical role in your life. Without memory, you would not know how to shut off your alarm clock, take a shower, get dressed, or recognize objects. You would be unable to communicate with other people, because you would not remember what words mean, or even what you had just said. You would be unaware of your own likes and dislikes, and you would have no idea of who you are (Craik et al., 1999). In this chapter we describe what is known about both memory and forgetting. First, we discuss what memory is the different kinds of memory and the different ways we remember things. Then we examine how new memories are formed and later recalled, and why they are sometimes forgotten. We continue with a discussion of the biological bases of memory, and we conclude with some practical advice for improving your memory and study skills.

The Nature of Memory

Mathematician John Griffith estimated that in an average lifetime, each of us will have stored roughly five hundred times as much information as can be found in all the volumes of the *Encyclopaedia Britannica* (Hunt, 1982). The impressive capacity of human memory depends on the operation of a complex mental system (Schacter, 1999).

Basic Memory Processes

Memory depends on three basic processes: encoding, storage, and retrieval (see Figure 7.1).

First, information must be put into memory, a step that requires **encoding.** Just as incoming sensory information must be coded so that it can be communicated to the brain, information to be remembered must be put in a form that the memory system can accept and use. Sensory information is put into various *memory codes,* which are mental representations of physical stimuli. Suppose you see a billboard that reads "Huey's Going-Out-of-Business Sale," and you want to remember it so you can take advantage of the sale later. If you encode the sound of the words as if they had been spoken, you are using **acoustic encoding,** and the information is represented in your memory as a sequence of sounds. If you encode the image of the letters as they were arranged on the sign, you are using **visual encoding,** and the information is represented in your memory as a picture. Finally, if you encode just the fact that you saw an ad for Huey's, you are using **semantic encoding,** and the information is represented in your memory by its general meaning. The type of encoding used can influence what is remembered. For example, semantic encoding

encoding The process of acquiring information and entering it into memory.

acoustic encoding The mental representation of information as a sequence of sounds.

visual encoding The mental representation of information as images.

semantic encoding The mental representation of an experience by its general meaning.

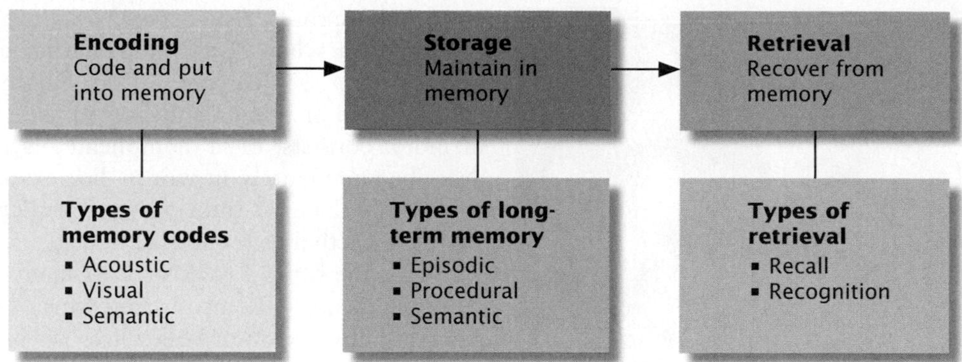

figure 7.1

Basic Memory Processes

Remembering something requires, first, that the item be encoded—put in a form that can be placed in memory. It must then be stored and, finally, retrieved, or brought into awareness. If any of these processes fails, forgetting will occur.

might allow you to remember that a car was parked in your neighbours' driveway just before their house was robbed. If there was little or no other encoding, however, you might not be able to remember the make, model, or colour of the car.

The second basic memory process is **storage,** which refers to keeping information in memory over time—often over a very long time. When you find that you can still use a pogo stick that you haven't seen since you were a child or that you can recall a vacation from many years ago, you are depending on the storage capacity of your memory.

The third process, **retrieval,** occurs when you locate information stored in memory and bring it into consciousness. Retrieving stored information such as your address or telephone number is usually so fast and effortless that it seems automatic. Only when you try to retrieve other kinds of information—such as the answer to a quiz question that you know but cannot quite recall at that moment—do you become aware of the searching process. Retrieval processes include both recall and recognition. To *recall* information, you have to retrieve it from memory without much help. This is what is required when you answer an essay test question or play *Jeopardy!* In *recognition,* retrieval is aided by clues, such as the response alternatives given on multiple-choice tests and the questions on *Who Wants to Be a Millionaire.* Accordingly, recognition tends to be easier than recall.

Types of Memory

When was the last time you charged something on your credit card? What part of speech is used to modify a noun? How do you keep your balance when you are skiing? To answer these questions, you must use your memory. However, each answer may require a different type of memory (Baddeley, 1998). To answer the first question, you must remember a particular event in your life. To answer the second one, you must recall a piece of general knowledge that is unlikely to be tied to a specific event. And the answer to the final question is difficult to put into words but appears in the form of remembered actions when you are on skis. How many types of memory are there? No one is sure, but most research suggests that there are at least three basic types. Each type is named for the kind of information it handles: episodic, semantic, and procedural (Roediger, Marsh, & Lee, 2002).

Endel Tulving of the University of Toronto has been instrumental in helping to distinguish between the three different types of memory listed above. For example, he defines **episodic memory** as a memory of a specific event that happened while you were present—that is, during an "episode" in your life (Tulving, 1983, 2002). Remembering what you had for dinner yesterday, what you did last summer, or where you were last Friday night all require episodic memory. Generalized knowledge of the world that does not involve memory of a specific event is called **semantic memory.** For instance, you can answer a question such as "Are wrenches pets or tools?" without remembering any specific event in which you learned that

storage The process of maintaining information in memory over time.

retrieval The process of recalling information stored in memory.

episodic memory Memory of an event that happened while one was present.

semantic memory A type of memory containing generalized knowledge of the world.

How Does She Do That? As she practises, this young violinist is developing procedural memories of how to play her instrument that will be difficult to put into words. To appreciate the special nature of procedural memory, try writing a step-by-step description of exactly how you tie a shoe.

wrenches are tools. As a general rule, people convey episodic memories by saying, "I remember when . . .," whereas they convey semantic memories by saying, "I know that. . . ." (Tulving, 2000). Finally, memory of how to do things, such as riding a bike or tying a shoelace, is called **procedural memory.** Often, procedural memory consists of a complicated sequence of movements that cannot be described adequately in words. For example, a gymnast might find it impossible to describe the exact motions in a particular routine.

Many activities require all three types of memory. Consider the game of tennis. Knowing the official rules or how many sets are needed to win a match involves semantic memory. Remembering which side served last requires episodic memory. Knowing how to lob or volley involves procedural memory.

Explicit and Implicit Memory

Recalling these three kinds of memories can be either intentional or unintentional. For example, you make use of **explicit memory** when you intentionally try to remember something and are consciously aware of doing so (Masson & MacLeod, 1992). Suppose someone asks you about your last vacation. As you think about where you went, you are using explicit memory to recall this episode from your past. Similarly, when responding to an exam question, you use explicit memory to retrieve the information needed to give a correct answer. In contrast, **implicit memory** is the unintentional recognition and influence of prior experiences (McDermott, 2002; Nelson, 1999). For example, if you were to read this chapter a second time, implicit memories of its content would help you to read it more quickly than you did the first time. For the same reason, you can solve a puzzle faster if you have solved it in the past. This facilitation of performance (often called *priming*) is automatic, and it occurs without conscious effort. Perhaps you've found yourself disliking someone you just met, but you didn't know why. One explanation is that implicit memory may have been at work. Specifically, you may have reacted as you did because the person bore a resemblance to someone from your past who treated you badly. In such instances, people are usually unable to recall the person from the past and are unaware of any connection between the two individuals (Lewicki, 1985). Episodic, semantic, and procedural memories can be explicit or implicit, but procedural memory usually operates implicitly. This is the reason that, for example, you can skillfully ride a bike even though you cannot explicitly remember all the procedures necessary to do so.

It is not surprising that experience affects how people behave. The surprising thing is that they are often unaware that their actions have been influenced by previous events. Because some influential events cannot be recalled even when people try to do so, implicit memory has been said to involve "retention without remembering" (Roediger, 1990).

LINKAGES (a link to Human Development)

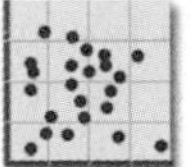

FOCUS ON RESEARCH METHODS

Measuring Explicit Versus Implicit Memory

Endel Tulving and his colleagues undertook a series of experiments to map the differences between explicit and implicit memory (Tulving, Schacter, & Stark, 1982).

- **What was the researcher's question?**

Tulving knew he could measure explicit memory by giving a recognition test. On such a test, participants are given a set of words and asked to say whether they remember seeing each of the words on a previous list. The question was, How would it be possible to measure implicit memory?

procedural memory A type of memory containing information about how to do things.

explicit memory The process in which people intentionally try to remember something.

implicit memory The unintentional influence of prior experiences.

Making Implicit Memories By the time they reach adulthood, these boys may have no explicit memories of the interactions they had in early childhood with friends from differing ethnic groups. Research suggests, however, that their implicit memories of such experiences could have an unconscious effect on their attitudes toward and judgments about members of those groups.

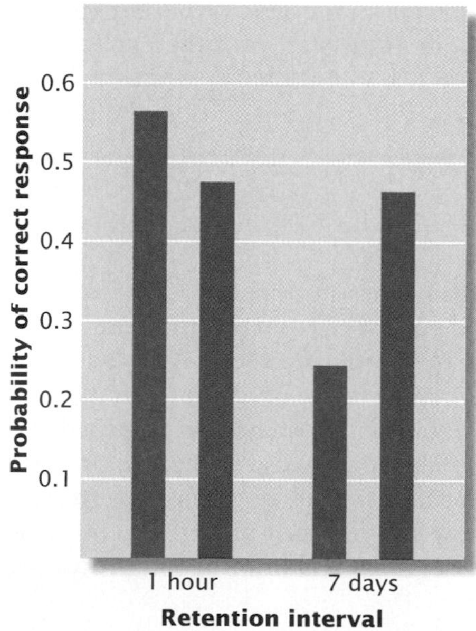

figure 7.2

Measures of Explicit and Implicit Memory

This experiment showed that the passage of time greatly affected people's recognition (explicit memory) of a word list but left fragment completion (implicit memory) essentially intact. Results such as these suggest that explicit and implicit memory may be different memory systems.

How did the researcher answer the question?

First, Tulving asked the participants in his experiment to study a long list of words—the "study list." An hour later, they took a recognition test involving explicit memory—saying which words on a new list had been on the original study list. Then, to test their implicit memory, Tulving asked them to perform a "fragment completion" task (Warrington & Weiskrantz, 1970). In this task, participants were shown a "test list" of word fragments, such as *d_li__u_*, and asked to complete the word (in this case, *delirium*). On the basis of priming studies such as those described in the chapter on consciousness, Tulving assumed that memory from a previous exposure to the correct word would improve the participants' ability to complete the fragment, even if they were unable to consciously recall having seen the word before. A week later, all participants took a second test of their explicit memory (recognition) and implicit memory (fragment completion) of the study list. Some of the words on this second test list had been on the original study list, but none had been used in the first set of memory tests. The independent variable in this experiment, then, was the amount of time that had elapsed since the participants read the study list (one hour versus one week), and the dependent variable was performance on each of the two types of memory tests, explicit and implicit.

What did the researcher find?

As shown in Figure 7.2, explicit memory for the study list decreased dramatically over time, but implicit memory (or priming) was virtually unchanged. Results from several other experiments also show that the passage of time affects explicit memory more than implicit memory (Komatsu & Naito, 1992; Mitchell, 1991). For example, it appears that the aging process has fewer negative effects on implicit memory than on explicit memory (Light, 1991).

What do the results mean?

The work of Tulving and others supports the idea of a dissociation, or independence, between explicit and implicit memory, suggesting that the two may operate on different principles (Gabrieli et al., 1995). In fact, some researchers believe that explicit and implicit memory may involve the activity of distinct neural systems in the brain (Squire, 1987; Tulving & Schacter, 1990). Others argue that the two types of memory are best described as requiring different cognitive processes (Nelson, McKinney, & Bennett, 1999; Roediger & McDermott, 1992).

What do we still need to know?

Psychologists have studied the role of implicit memory (and dissociations between explicit and implicit memory) in such important psychological phenomena as amnesia (Schacter, Church, & Treadwell, 1994; Tulving, 1993), depression (Elliott & Greene, 1992), problem solving (Jacoby, Marriott, & Collins, 1990), prejudice and stereotyping (Fiske, 1998), the development of self-concept in childhood (Nelson, 1993), and even the power of ads to associate brand names with good feelings (Duke & Carlson, 1994). The results of these studies are helping to shed new light on implicit memory and how it operates in the real world.

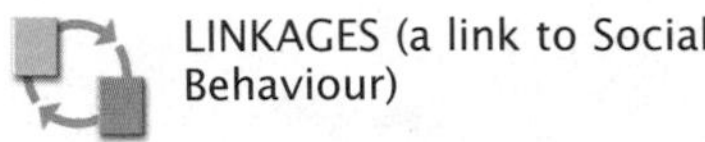
LINKAGES (a link to Social Behaviour)

For example, some social psychologists are trying to determine whether consciously held attitudes are independent of *implicit social cognitions*—past experiences that unconsciously influence a person's judgments about a group of people (Greenwald & Banaji, 1995). A case in point would be a person whose explicit thoughts about members of some ethnic group are positive but whose implicit thoughts are negative. Early work on implicit memory for stereotypes seemed to indicate that explicit and implicit stereotypes are independent (Devine, 1989), but more recent research suggests that they are related to some extent (Lepore & Brown, 1997). Further research is needed to determine what mechanisms are responsible for implicit versus explicit memory and how these two kinds of memory are related to one another (Lustig & Hasher, 2001; Nelson et al., 1998). That research will be facilitated by functional neuro-imaging techniques. As described later, these techniques allow scientists to observe brain activity during various memory tasks and to determine which areas are associated with the explicit and implicit cognitive processes involved in these tasks (Buckner & Wheeler, 2001; McDermott, 2002).

Models of Memory

We remember some information far better than other information. For example, suppose your friends throw a surprise party for you. When you enter the room, you might barely notice, and later fail to recall, the flash from a camera. And you might forget in a few seconds the name of a person you met at the party. But if you live to be a hundred, you will never forget where the party took place or how surprised and pleased you were. Why do some stimuli leave no more than a fleeting impression and others remain in memory forever? Each of four models of memory provides a somewhat different explanation. Let's see how the levels-of-processing, transfer-appropriate processing, parallel distributed processing, and information-processing models look at memory.

levels-of-processing model A view stating that how well something is remembered depends on the degree to which incoming information is mentally processed.

maintenance rehearsal Repeating information over and over to keep it active in short-term memory.

elaborative rehearsal A memorization method that involves thinking about how new information relates to information already stored in long-term memory.

Levels of Processing The **levels-of-processing model** suggests that the most important determinant of memory is how extensively information is encoded or processed when it is first received (Craik & Lockhart, 1972; Craik & Tulving, 1975). Consider situations in which you try to memorize something by mentally rehearsing it. There appear to be two basic types of mental rehearsal: maintenance and elaborative. **Maintenance rehearsal** involves simply repeating an item over and over. This method can be effective for remembering information for a short time. If you look up a phone number, pick up the phone, and then make the call, maintenance rehearsal works just fine. But what if you need to remember something for hours or months or years? In these cases, you are better off using **elaborative rehearsal,** which involves thinking about how new material relates to information already stored in memory. For example, instead of trying to remember a new

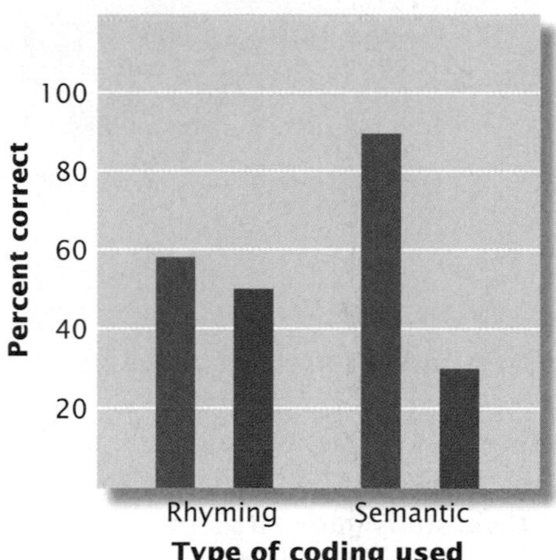

Recognition test

Identification test

figure 7.3

Matching Encoding and Retrieval Processes

People who were asked to recognize words seen earlier did better if they had encoded the words on the basis of their meaning (semantic coding) rather than on the basis of what they rhymed with. But if asked to identify words that *rhymed* with those seen before, they did better on those that had been encoded using a rhyming code. These results support the transfer-appropriate processing model of memory.

person's name by simply repeating it to yourself, try thinking about how the name is related to something you already know. If you are introduced to a man named Jim Crews, for example, you might think, "He is as tall as my Uncle Jim, who always wears a crew cut."

Study after study has shown that memory is improved when people use elaborative rather than maintenance rehearsal (Jahnke & Nowaczyk, 1998). According to the levels-of-processing model, this enhancement occurs because of the degree or "depth" to which incoming information is mentally processed during elaborative rehearsal (Lockhart & Craik, 1990; Roediger & Gallo, 2001). The more you think about new information, organize it, and relate it to existing knowledge, the "deeper" the processing, and the better your memory of it becomes. Teachers use this idea when they ask their students not only to define a new word but also to use it in a sentence. Figuring out how to use the new word takes deeper processing than merely defining it. (The next time you come across an unfamiliar word in this book, don't just read its definition. Try using the word in a sentence by coming up with an example of the concept that relates to your knowledge and experience.)

Transfer-Appropriate Processing The level of processing is not the only factor affecting what we remember (Baddeley, 1992). Another critical factor, suggested by the **transfer-appropriate processing model,** is how well the processes involved during retrieval match the way in which the information was first encoded. Consider an experiment in which people were shown sentences with a word missing and were then asked one of two types of questions about the missing word (Morris, Bransford, & Franks, 1977). Some questions were designed so that participants would encode the target word by its meaning (semantic encoding). For example, one sentence read, "A _______ is a building," and participants were asked whether the target word *house* could meaningfully go in the blank space. Other questions were designed to create a rhyming code. For example, participants were shown the sentence "_______ rhymes with legal" and asked whether the target word *eagle* rhymed with *legal.*

Later, the participants were given two kinds of memory tasks. On one task, they were asked to select from a list the target words they had been shown earlier. As Figure 7.3 shows, the participants did much better at recognizing the words for which they had used a semantic code rather than a rhyming code. On the other task, they were asked to pick out words that *rhymed* with the ones they had seen (e.g., *grouse*, which rhymes with *house*). Here, they did much better at identifying words that rhymed with those for which they had used a rhyming code rather than a semantic code.

In another study, half the students in a class were told that an upcoming exam would contain multiple-choice questions. The rest were told to expect essay questions. Only half the students actually got the type of exam they expected, however. These students did much better on the exam than those who took an unexpected type of exam. Apparently, in studying for the exam, the two groups used encoding strategies that were most appropriate to the type of exam they expected. Those who tried to retrieve the information in a way that did not match their encoding method had a harder time (d'Ydewalle & Rosselle, 1978). Results such as these illustrate that the match between encoding and retrieval processes can be as important as depth of processing in memory.

Parallel Distributed Processing A third approach to memory is based on **parallel distributed processing (PDP) models** of memory (Rumelhart & McClelland, 1986). These models suggest that new experiences don't just provide new facts that are later retrieved individually. Those facts are also integrated with existing knowledge or memories, changing our overall knowledge base and altering in a more general way our understanding of the world and how it operates. For example, when students first arrive on campus, they learn specific facts, such as

transfer-appropriate processing model A model of memory that suggests that a critical determinant of memory is how well the retrieval process matches the original encoding process.

parallel distributed processing (PDP) models Memory models in which new experiences change one's overall knowledge base.

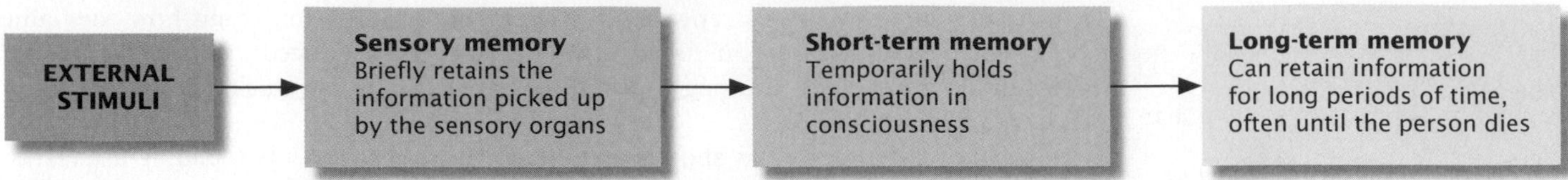
EXTERNAL STIMULI
Sensory memory
Briefly retains the information picked up by the sensory organs
Short-term memory
Temporarily holds information in consciousness
Long-term memory
Can retain information for long periods of time, often until the person dies

figure 7.4

Three Stages of Memory

The traditional information-processing model describes three stages in the memory system.

where classes are held, what time the library closes, and where to get the best pizza. Over time, these and many other facts of university life form a network of information that creates a more general understanding of how the whole system works. Developing this network makes students more knowledgeable, but also more sophisticated. It allows them to, say, allocate their study time so as to do well in their most important courses and to plan a schedule that avoids conflicts between classes, work, and recreational activities. Your own knowledge of university life probably changes day by day in a way that is much more general than any single new fact you learned.

PDP models of memory reflect this notion of knowledge networks. PDP memory theorists begin by considering how *neural networks* might provide the framework for a functional memory system (Anderson, 1990). As described in the chapters on perception, learning, and biological aspects of psychology, the structure of neural networks allows each part to be linked to every other part. When this network model is applied to memory, each unit of knowledge is seen as connected to every other unit, and the connections between units are seen as getting stronger the more often the units are experienced together. From this perspective, then, "knowledge" is distributed across a dense network of associations. When this network is activated, *parallel processing* occurs. That is, different portions of the network operate simultaneously, allowing people to quickly and efficiently draw inferences and make generalizations. Just seeing the word *sofa,* for example, allows us immediately to gain access to knowledge about what a sofa looks like, what it is used for, where it tends to be located, who might buy one, and the like. PDP models of memory explain this process very effectively.

Information Processing Historically, the most influential and comprehensive theories of memory have been based on a general **information-processing model** (Roediger, 1990). The information-processing model originally suggested that in order for information to become firmly embedded in memory, it must pass through three stages of mental processing: sensory memory, short-term memory, and long-term memory (Atkinson & Shiffrin, 1968; see Figure 7.4).

In *sensory memory,* information from the senses—sights or sounds, for example—is held in sensory registers for a very brief period of time, often for less than a second. Information in the sensory registers might be attended to, analyzed, and encoded as a meaningful pattern. This is the process of perception, as discussed in the chapter on that topic. If the information in sensory memory is perceived, it can enter short-term memory. If nothing further is done, the information will disappear in less than twenty seconds. But if the information in short-term memory is processed further, it may be encoded into long-term memory, where it might remain indefinitely.

The act of reading illustrates all three stages of memory processing. As you read any sentence in this book, light energy reflected from the page reaches your eyes, where it is converted to neural activity and registered in your sensory memory. If you pay attention to these visual stimuli, your perception of the patterns of light can be held in short-term memory. This stage of memory holds the early parts of the sentence so that they can be integrated and understood as you read the rest of the sentence. As you read, you are constantly recognizing words by matching your

information-processing model A model of memory in which information is seen as passing through sensory memory, short-term memory, and long-term memory.

figure 7.5

The Role of Memory in Comprehension Read the paragraph shown here, then turn away and try to recall as much of it as possible. Then read the footnote on page 241 and reread the paragraph. The second reading probably made a lot more sense and was much easier to remember because knowing the title of the paragraph allowed you to retrieve your knowledge about the topic from long-term memory (Bransford & Johnson, 1972).

The procedure is actually quite simple. First, you arrange items into different groups. Of course, one pile may be sufficient, depending on how much there is to do. If you have to go somewhere else due to lack of facilities that is the next step; otherwise, you are pretty well set. It is important not to overdo things. That is, it is better to do too few things at once than too many. In the short run, this may not seem important, but complications can easily arise. A mistake can be expensive as well. At first, the whole procedure will seem complicated. Soon, however, it will become just another facet of life. It is difficult to foresee any end to the necessity for this task in the immediate future, but then, one never can tell. After the procedure is completed, one arranges the materials into different groups again. Then they can be put into their appropriate places. Eventually they will be used once more, and the whole cycle will then have to be repeated. However, that is part of life.

perceptions of them with the patterns and meanings you have stored in long-term memory. In short, all three stages of memory are necessary for you to understand a sentence.

Today's versions of the information-processing model emphasize these constant interactions among sensory, short-term, and long-term memory (Massaro & Cowan, 1993; Wagner, 1999). For example, sensory memory can be thought of as that part of your knowledge base (or long-term memory) that is momentarily activated by information sent to the brain via the sensory nerves. And short-term memory can be thought of as that part of your knowledge base that is the focus of attention at any given moment. Like perception, memory is an active process, and what is already in long-term memory influences how new information is encoded (Cowan, 1988). To understand this interaction better, try the exercise in Figure 7.5.

For a summary of the four models we have discussed, see "In Review: Models of Memory." Each of these models provides an explanation of why we remember some things and forget others. Which one offers the best explanation? The answer is that more than one model may be required to understand memory. Just as it is helpful for physicists to characterize light in terms of both waves and particles, psychologists find it useful to think of memory both as a serial or sequential process, as suggested by the information-processing model, and as a parallel process, as suggested by parallel distributed processing models.

Sensory Memory at Work In a darkened room, ask a friend to hold a small flashlight and move it slowly in a circle. You will see a moving point of light. If it appears to have a "tail," like a comet, that is your sensory memory of the light before it fades from your sensory register. Now ask your friend to speed up the movement. You should now see a complete circle of light, because as the light moves, its impression on your sensory memory does not have time to fade before the circle is completed. A similar process allows us to see "sparkler circles."

in review Models of Memory

Model	Assumptions
Levels of processing	The more deeply material is processed, the better the memory of it.
Transfer-appropriate processing	Retrieval is improved when we try to recall material in a way that matches how the material was encoded.
Parallel distributed processing (PDP)	New experiences add to and alter our overall knowledge base; they are not separate, unconnected facts. PDP networks allow us to draw inferences and make generalizations about the world.
Information processing	Information is processed in three stages: sensory, short-term, and long-term memory.

Storing New Memories

The information-processing model suggests that sensory, short-term, and long-term memory each provide a different type of storage system.

Sensory Memory

To recognize incoming stimuli, the brain must analyze and compare them with what is already stored in long-term memory. Although this process is very quick, it still takes time. The major function of **sensory memory** is to hold information long enough for it to be processed further (Nairne, 2003). This maintenance is the job of the **sensory registers**, which act as temporary storage bins. There is a separate register for each of the five senses, and every register is capable of storing a relatively large amount of stimulus information. Memories held in the sensory registers are fleeting, but they last long enough for stimulus identification to begin (Eysenck & Keane, 1995).

Sensory memory helps bring coherence and continuity to your world. To appreciate this fact, turn your head slowly from left to right. It may seem as though your eyes are moving smoothly, like a movie camera scanning a scene, but that's not what is happening. Instead, your eyes fixate at one point for about one-fourth of a second and then rapidly jump to a new position. The sensation of smooth movement through the visual field occurs because you hold each scene in your visual sensory register until your eyes fixate again. Similarly, when you listen to someone speak, the auditory sensory register allows you to experience a smooth flow of information. Information persists for varying amounts of time in the five sensory registers. For example, information in the auditory sensory register lasts longer than information in the visual sensory register.

The fact that sensory memories quickly fade if they are not processed further is an adaptive characteristic of the memory system (Baddeley, 1998). You simply could not deal with all of the sights, sounds, odours, tastes, and tactile sensations that impinge on your sense organs at any given moment. As mentioned in the chapter on perception, **selective attention** focuses mental resources on only part of the stimulus field, thus controlling what information is processed further. It is through the process of perception that the elusive impressions of sensory memory are captured and transferred to short-term memory.

Short-Term Memory and Working Memory

The sensory registers allow your memory system to develop a representation of a stimulus. However, they can't perform the more thorough representation and analysis that is needed if the information is going to be used in some way. These functions are accomplished by short-term memory and working memory.

Short-term memory (STM) is the part of our memory system that stores limited amounts of information for a limited amount of time. When you check the television listings for the channel number of a show you want to watch, and then switch to that channel, you are using short-term memory. **Working memory** is the part of the memory system that allows us to mentally work with, or manipulate, the information being held in short-term memory. So short-term memory is actually a component of working memory. Together, they enable us to do many kinds of mental work (Baddeley, 2003; Engle & Oransky, 1999). Suppose you are buying something for 83 cents, and you go through your change and pick out two quarters, two dimes, two nickels, and three pennies. To do this, you use both short-term and working memory to remember the price, retrieve the rules of addition from long-term memory, *and* keep a running count of how much change you have so far. Now try to recall how many windows there are on the front of the house or apartment where you grew up. In attempting to answer this question, you probably formed a mental

sensory memory A type of memory that holds large amounts of incoming information very briefly, but long enough to connect one impression to the next.

sensory registers Memory systems that hold incoming information long enough for it to be processed further.

selective attention The focusing of mental resources on only part of the stimulus field.

short-term memory (STM) The maintenance component of working memory, which holds unrehearsed information for a limited time.

working memory The part of the memory system that allows us to mentally work with, or manipulate, information being held in short-term memory.

image of the building, which required one kind of working-memory process, and then, while maintaining that image in short-term memory, you "worked" on it by counting the windows. So working memory has at least two components: *maintenance* (holding information in short-term memory) and *manipulation* (working on that information).

Encoding in Short-Term Memory The encoding of information in short-term memory is much more elaborate and varied than that in the sensory registers (Brandimonte, Hitch, & Bishop, 1992). *Acoustic encoding* (by sound) seems to dominate. Evidence in support of this assertion comes from analyzing the mistakes people make when encoding information in short-term memory. These mistakes tend to be acoustically related, which means that they involve the substitution of similar sounds. For example, Robert Conrad (1964) showed people strings of letters and asked them to repeat the letters immediately. Their mistakes tended to involve replacing the correct letter (say, *C*) with another that *sounded* like it (such as *D, P,* or *T*). These mistakes occurred even though the letters were presented visually, without any sound.

Evidence for acoustic coding in short-term memory also comes from studies showing that items are more difficult to remember if their spoken sounds are similar. For example, native English speakers do less well when asked to remember a string of letters such as *ECVTGB* (which all have similar sounds) than when asked to remember one like *KRLDQS* (which have distinct sounds). Encoding in short-term memory is not *always* acoustic, however. Visual codes are also used (Zhang & Simon, 1985), but information coded visually tends to fade much more quickly from short-term memory than information that is encoded acoustically (Cornoldi, DeBeni, & Baldi, 1989). There is also evidence for kinesthetic encoding, which involves physical movements (Best, 1999). In one study, deaf people were shown a list of words and then asked to immediately write them down from memory (Shand, 1982). When these people made errors, they wrote words that are expressed through similar *hand movements* in American Sign Language, rather than words that *sounded* similar to the correct words. Apparently, these individuals had encoded the words on the basis of the movements they would use when making the signs for them.

Storage Capacity of Short-Term Memory You can easily determine the capacity of short-term memory by conducting the simple experiment shown in Figure 7.6 (Howard, 1983). Your **immediate memory span** is the maximum number of items you are able to recall perfectly after one presentation. If your memory span is like most people's, you can repeat about six or seven items from the test in this figure. The interesting thing is that you should come up with about the same number whether you estimate your immediate memory span with digits, letters, words, or virtually any type of unit (Pollack, 1953). George Miller (1956) noticed that studies of a wide variety of tasks showed the same limit on the ability to process information. This "magic number," which is seven plus or minus two, appears to be the capacity of short-term memory. In addition, the "magic number" refers not only to discrete elements, such as words or digits, but also to meaningful *groupings* of information, called **chunks.**

To appreciate the difference between discrete elements and chunks, read the following letters to a friend, pausing at each dash: *FB-IAO-LM-TVI-BMB-MW.* The chances are very good that your friend will not be able to repeat this string of letters perfectly. Why? There are fifteen letters, which exceeds most people's immediate memory span. Now, give your friend the test again, but group the letters like this: *FBI-AOL-MTV-IBM-BMW.* Your friend will probably repeat that string easily

The title of the paragraph in Figure 7.5 is "Washing Clothes."

immediate memory span The maximum number of items a person can recall perfectly after one presentation of the items.

chunks Stimuli that are perceived as one unit or as a meaningful grouping of information.

figure 7.6

Capacity of Short-Term Memory

Here is a test of your immediate memory span. Ask someone to read you the numbers in the top row at the rate of about one per second. Then try to repeat them back in the same order. Do the same test on the next row, and the one after that, until you make a mistake. Your immediate memory span is the maximum number of items you can repeat back perfectly. Similar tests can be performed using the rows of letters and words.

9 2 5
8 6 4 2
3 7 6 5 4
6 2 7 4 1 8
0 4 0 1 4 7 3
1 9 2 2 3 5 3 0
4 8 6 8 5 4 3 3 2
2 5 3 1 9 7 1 7 6 8
8 5 1 2 9 6 1 9 4 5 0
9 1 8 5 4 6 9 4 2 9 3 7

G M N
S L R R
V O E P G
X W D X Q O
E P H H J A E
Z D O F W D S V
D T Y N R H E H Q
K H W D A G R O F Z
U D F F W H D Q D G E
Q M R H X Z D P R R E H

CAT BOAT RUG
RUN BEACH PLANT LIGHT
SUIT WATCH CUT STAIRS CAR
JUNK LONE GAME CALL WOOD HEART
FRAME PATCH CROSS DRUG DESK HORSE LAW
CLOTHES CHOOSE GIFT DRIVE BOOK TREE HAIR THIS
DRESS CLERK FILM BASE SPEND SERVE BOOK LOW TIME
STONE ALL NAIL DOOR HOPE EARL FEEL BUY COPE GRAPE
AGE SOFT FALL STORE PUT TRUE SMALL FREE CHECK MAIL LEAF
LOG DAY TIME CHESS LAKE CUT BIRD SHEET YOUR SEE STREET WHEEL

because, even though the same fifteen letters are involved, they will be processed as only five meaningful chunks of information (Bower, 1975).

The Power of Chunking Chunks of information can become very complex. If someone says, "The boy in the red shirt kicked his mother in the shin," you could probably repeat the sentence very easily. Yet it contains twelve words and forty-three letters. How can you repeat the sentence so effortlessly? The answer is that people can build bigger and bigger chunks of information (Ericsson & Staszewski, 1989). In this case, you might have represented "the boy in the red shirt" as one chunk of information rather than as six words or nineteen letters. Similarly, "kicked his mother" and "in the shin" could be represented as just two chunks of information.

Learning to use bigger and bigger chunks of information can enhance short-term memory. Children's memories improve partly because they gradually become able to hold as many as seven chunks in memory, but also because they get better at grouping information into chunks (Servan-Schreiber & Anderson, 1990). Adults, too, can greatly increase the capacity of their short-term memory by more appropriate chunking (Waldrop, 1987). One university student increased his immediate memory span from seven digits to eighty digits (Neisser, 2000). In short, although the capacity of short-term memory is more or less constant—five to nine chunks of meaningful information—the size of those chunks can vary tremendously.

Duration of Short-Term Memory Imagine how hard it would be to, say, mentally calculate the tip you should leave in a restaurant if your short-term memory were cluttered with every other bill you had ever paid, every phone number you had ever called, and every conversation you had ever heard. This problem doesn't come up because—unless you continue repeating information to yourself (maintenance rehearsal) or use elaborative rehearsal to transfer it to long-term memory—information in short-term memory is usually forgotten quickly. You may have experienced this adaptive, although sometimes inconvenient, phenomenon if you

Brown-Peterson procedure A method for determining how long unrehearsed information remains in short-term memory.

long-term memory (LTM) A relatively long-lasting stage of memory whose capacity to store new information is believed to be unlimited.

Chunking in Action Those who provide instantaneous translation of speeches—such as this one by Stephen Harper in the house of commons—must store long, often complicated segments of speech in short-term memory while searching long-term memory for the equivalent second-language expressions. The task is made easier by chunking the speaker's words into phrases and sentences.

have ever been interrupted while repeating to yourself a new phone number you were about to call, and then couldn't remember the number.

How long does unrehearsed information remain in short-term memory? To answer this question, John Brown (1958) and Lloyd and Margaret Peterson (1959) devised the **Brown-Peterson procedure**, which is a method for preventing rehearsal. A person is presented with a group of three letters, such as GRB, and then counts backward by threes from some number until a signal is given. Counting prevents the person from rehearsing the letters. At the signal, the person stops counting and tries to recall the letters. By varying the number of seconds that the person counts backward, the experimenter can determine how much forgetting takes place over a certain amount of time. As you can see in Figure 7.7, information in short-term memory is forgotten gradually but rapidly: After 18 seconds, participants can remember almost nothing. Evidence from these and other experiments suggests that unrehearsed information can be maintained in short-term memory for no more than about 18 seconds. However, if the information is rehearsed or processed further, it may be encoded into long-term memory.

Percentage of items recalled: 100, 90, 80, 70, 60, 50, 40, 30, 20, 10

Recall interval (in seconds): 3, 6, 9, 12, 15, 18

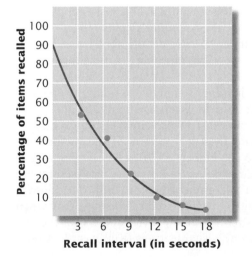

figure 7.7

Forgetting in Short-Term Memory

This graph shows the percentage of items recalled after various intervals during which rehearsal was prevented. Notice that virtually complete forgetting occurred after a delay of 18 seconds.

Source: Data from Peterson & Peterson (1959).

Long-Term Memory

When people talk about memory, they are usually talking about **long-term memory (LTM)**, the part of the memory system whose encoding and storage capabilities can produce memories that last a lifetime.

Encoding in Long-Term Memory Some information is encoded into long-term memory without any conscious attempt to memorize it (Ellis, 1991). However, putting information into long-term memory is often the result of more elaborate and conscious processing, which usually involves some degree of *semantic encoding*. In other words, encoding in long-term memory often ignores details and instead encodes the general, underlying meaning of the information.

Jacqueline Sachs (1967) demonstrated the dominance of semantic encoding in long-term memory in a classic study. She first asked research participants to listen to tape recordings of people speaking. She then showed them sentences and asked

(A)

(B)

(C)

(D)

figure 7.8

Encoding into Long-Term Memory

Which is the correct image of a penny? (See page 246 for the answer.) Most people often cannot explicitly remember the specific details of information stored in long-term memory, but priming studies suggest that they do retain some implicit memory of them (e.g., Srinivas, 1993).

Source: Figure designed by Mary MacLean of St. Thomas University, New Brunswick.

them to say which contained the exact wording heard on the tape. People did very well when they were tested immediately (using mainly short-term memory). However, after only 27 seconds, at which point the information had to be retrieved from long-term memory, they could not determine which of two sentences they had heard if both sentences expressed the same meaning. For example, they could not determine whether they had heard "He sent a letter about it to Galileo, the great Italian scientist" or "A letter about it was sent to Galileo, the great Italian scientist." In short, they remembered the general meaning of what they had heard, but not the exact wording.

Perhaps you are thinking, "So what?" After all, the two sentences mean the same thing. However, psychologists have found that when people encode the general meaning of information, they may make mistakes about the specifics of what they have heard. For example, after hearing "The karate champion hit the cinder block," people often remember having heard "The karate champion broke the cinder block" (Brewer, 1977). When recalling exact words is important—such as in the courtroom, during business negotiations, and in discussions between students and professors about previous agreements—people are often wrong about what someone actually said. As discussed later in this chapter, these errors occur partly because people encode into long-term memory not only the general meaning of information but also what they think and assume about that information (Hannigan & Reinitz, 2001). Those expectations and assumptions—that karate champions always break what they hit, for example—may alter what is recalled.

Counterfeiters depend on the fact that people encode only the general meaning of visual, as well as auditory, stimuli. For example, look at Figure 7.8, and find the correct picture of the penny. Most people are unsuccessful at this task; people from Great Britain do just as poorly at recognizing their country's coins (Jones, 1990). Research showing that people fail to remember specific details about visual information has prompted some countries to begin using more distinctive drawings on the paper currencies it distributes.

Although long-term memory normally involves semantic encoding, people can also use visual encoding to process images into long-term memory. In one study, people viewed 2500 pictures. It took 16 hours just to present the stimuli, but the participants later correctly recognized more than 90 percent of the pictures on which they were tested (Standing, Conezio, & Haber, 1970). *Dual coding theory* suggests that pictures tend to be remembered better than words because pictures are represented in two codes—visual and verbal—rather than in only one (Paivio, 1986). This suggestion is supported by neuro-imaging studies showing that when people are asked to memorize pictures, they tend to create a verbal label for the picture (e.g., *frog*), as well as look at the drawing's visual features (Kelley et al., 1998).

Storage Capacity of Long-Term Memory Whereas the capacity of short-term memory is limited, the capacity of long-term memory is extremely large. In fact, most memory theorists believe it to be unlimited (Matlin, 1998). The unlimited capacity of long-term memory is impossible to prove, but there are no cases of people being unable to learn something new because they had too much information stored in long-term memory. We do know for sure that people store vast quantities of information in long-term memory and that they often remember it remarkably well for long periods of time. For example, people are amazingly

A Remarkable Memory Franco Magnani had been away from his hometown in Italy for more than thirty years, but he could still paint it from memory with impressive accuracy (see comparison photo; Sacks, 1992). People like Magnani display *eidetic imagery,* commonly called *photographic memory.* It is not actually photographic, but it does create automatic, detailed, and vivid images of virtually everything they have ever seen. About 5 percent of all school-age children have eidetic imagery, but almost no adults have it (Haber, 1979).

accurate at recognizing the faces of their high school classmates after not having seen them for over 25 years (Bruck, Cavanagh, & Ceci, 1991). They also do surprisingly well on tests of a foreign language or high school algebra 50 years after having formally studied these subjects (Bahrick & Hall, 1991; Bahrick et al., 1994).

However, long-term memories are also subject to distortion. In one study, university students were asked to recall their high school grades. Even though the students were motivated to be accurate, they correctly remembered 89 percent of their A grades but only 29 percent of their D grades. And you might not be surprised to learn that when they recalled grades incorrectly, the errors usually involved remembering grades as being higher than they actually were (Bahrick, Hall, & Berger, 1996). In another study, students were asked to describe where they were and what they were doing when they heard about the verdict in the O. J. Simpson murder trial (Schmolck, Buffalo, & Squire, 2000). The students reported their recollections three times, first just three days after the verdict, and then again after fifteen and after thirty-two months. Only half the recollections reported at 15 months were accurate, and 11 percent contained major errors or distortions. Among those reporting after 32 months, 71 percent of their recollections were inaccurate, and just over 40 percent contained major errors or distortions. For example, three days after the verdict, one student said he heard about it while in a campus lounge with other students. Thirty-two months later, the same student recalled hearing the news in the living room of his home with his father and sister. Most of the students whose memories had been substantially distorted over time were unaware that this distortion had occurred. In fact, they were very confident that their reports were accurate. Later, we will see that such over-confidence can also appear in courtroom testimony by eyewitnesses to crime.

Distinguishing Between Short-Term and Long-Term Memory

Some psychologists claim that there is no need to distinguish between short-term and long-term memory. They say that what we call short-term (and working) memory is simply that part of memory that we happen to be thinking about at any particular time, whereas long-term memory is the part of memory that we are not thinking about at any given moment. ("In Review: Storing New Memories"

in review Storing New Memories

Storage System	Function	Capacity	Duration
Sensory memory	Briefly holds representations of stimuli from each sense for further processing	Large: absorbs all sensory input from a particular stimulus	Less than 1 second
Short-term and working memory	Holds information in awareness and manipulates it to accomplish mental work	Five to nine distinct items or chunks of information	About 18 seconds
Long-term memory	Stores new information indefinitely	Unlimited	Unlimited

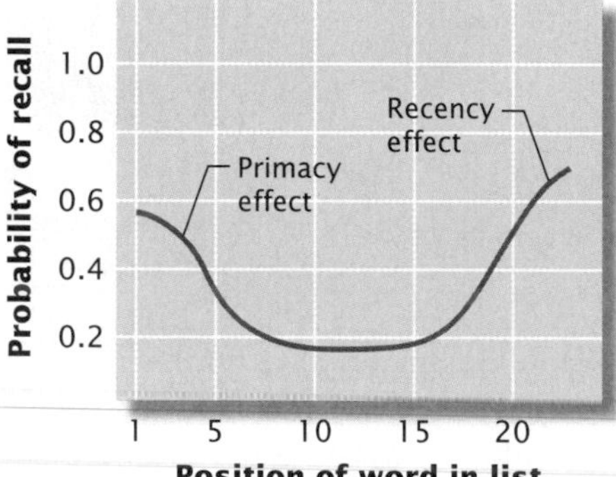

figure 7.9

A Serial-Position Curve

The probability of recalling an item is plotted here as a function of its serial position in a list of items. Generally, the first several items and the last several items are most likely to be recalled.

summarizes the characteristics of these systems.) However, other psychologists argue that short-term and long-term memory are fundamentally different—that they obey different laws (Cowan, 1988). Evidence that information is transferred from short-term memory to a distinct storage system comes from experiments on recall.

Experiments on Recall To conduct your own recall experiment, look at the following list of words for 30 seconds, then look away and write down as many of the words as you can, in any order: desk, chalk, pencil, chair, paperclip, book, eraser, folder, briefcase, essays. Which words you remember depends in part on their *serial position*—that is, where the words are in the list, as Figure 7.9 shows. This figure is a *serial-position curve,* which shows the chances of recalling words appearing in each position in a list. For the first two or three words in a list, recall tends to be very good—a characteristic that is called the **primacy effect.** The probability of recall decreases for words in the middle of the list and then rises dramatically for the last few words. The ease of recalling words near the end of a list is called the **recency effect.** It has been suggested that the primacy effect reflects rehearsal that puts early words into long-term memory, and that the recency effect occurs because the last few words are still in short-term memory when we try to recall the list (Glanzer & Cunitz, 1966; Koppenaal & Glanzer, 1990).

Retrieving Memories

Have you ever been unable to recall the name of an old television show or movie star, only to think of it the next day? Remembering something requires not only that it be appropriately encoded and stored but also that you have the ability to bring it into consciousness—in other words, to *retrieve* it.

Retrieval Cues and Encoding Specificity

Stimuli that help people retrieve information from long-term memory are called **retrieval cues.** They allow people to recall things that were once forgotten and help them to recognize information stored in memory. In general, recognition tasks are easier than recall tasks, because they contain more retrieval cues. As noted earlier, it is usually easier to recognize the correct alternative on a multiple-choice exam than to recall material for an essay test. The effectiveness of cues in aiding retrieval depends on the degree to which they tap into information that was encoded at the time of learning (Tulving, 1983). This rule, known as the **encoding specificity principle,** is consistent with the transfer-appropriate processing model of memory. Because long-term memories are often encoded semantically, cues related to the *meaning* of the

primacy effect A characteristic of memory in which recall of the first two or three items in a list is particularly good.

recency effect A characteristic of memory in which recall is particularly good for the last few items in a list.

retrieval cues Stimuli that aid the recall or recognition of information stored in memory.

encoding specificity principle A principle stating that the ability of a cue to aid retrieval depends on the degree to which it taps into information that was encoded at the time of the original learning.

Drawing (B) shows the correct penny image in Figure 7.8.

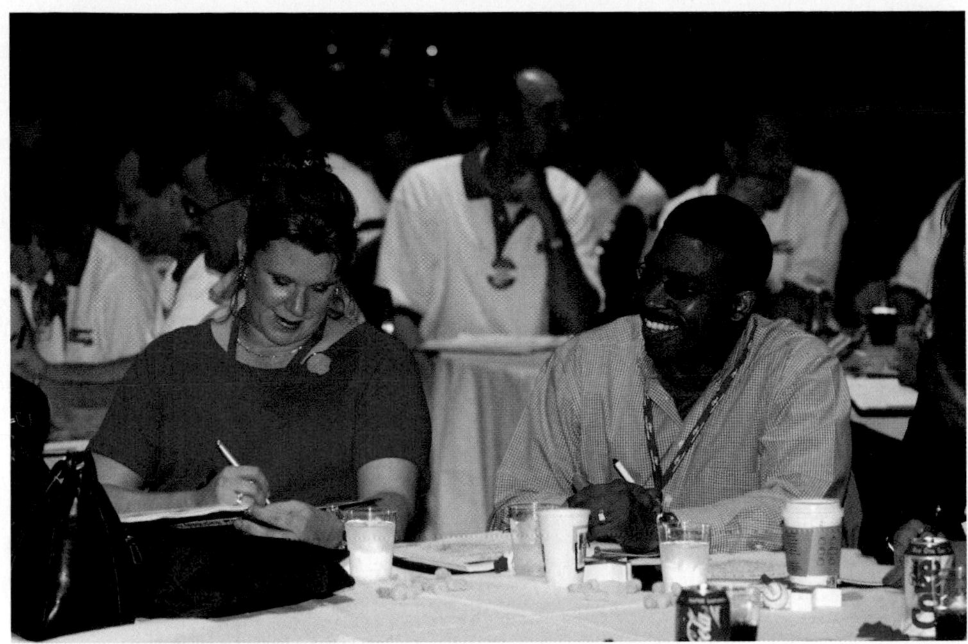

Context-Dependent Memories Many people attending a reunion at their old high school find that being in the building again provides context cues that help bring back memories of their school days.

stored information tend to work best. For example, imagine you have learned a long list of sentences, one of which is either (1) "The man lifted the piano" or (2) "The man tuned the piano." Having the cue "something heavy" during a recall test would probably help you remember the first sentence, because you probably encoded something about the weight of a piano, but "something heavy" would probably not help you recall the second sentence. Similarly, the cue "makes nice sounds" would be likely to help you recall the second sentence, but not the first (Barclay et al., 1974).

Context and State Dependence

Have you ever taken a test in a classroom other than the one in which you learned the material for that test? If so, your performance may have been affected (Smith, Glenberg, & Bjork, 1978). In general, people remember more of what they learned when the conditions during recall are the same as those during learning. This effect may appear because we tend to encode features of the environment in which the learning occurred, and these features may later serve as retrieval cues (Richardson-Klavehn & Bjork, 1988). In one experiment, people studied a series of photos while in the presence of a particular odour. Later, they reviewed a larger set of photos and tried to identify the ones they had seen earlier. Half of these people were tested in the presence of the original odour and half in the presence of a different odour. Those who smelled the same odour during learning and testing did significantly better on the recognition task than those who were tested in the presence of a different odour. The matching odour served as a powerful retrieval cue (Cann & Ross, 1989).

When memory is helped or hindered by the environment, it is called **context-dependent memory.** This context-dependency effect is not always strong (Saufley, Otaka, & Bavaresco, 1985; Smith, Vela, & Williamson, 1988), but some students do find it helpful to study for a test in the classroom in which the test will be given.

Like the external environment, the internal environment can be encoded during learning, and thus it can act as a retrieval cue. When a person's internal state can aid or hamper retrieval, the person has what is called **state-dependent memory.** For example, if people learn new material while under the influence of marijuana, they tend to recall it better if they are also tested under the influence of marijuana (Eich et al., 1975). Similar effects have been found with alcohol and other drugs (Eich, 1989; Overton, 1984), although memory is best overall when people are not

context-dependent memory Memory that can be helped or hindered by similarities or differences between the context in which it is learned and the context in which it is recalled.

state-dependent memory Memory that is aided or impeded by a person's internal state.

in review Factors Affecting Retrieval from Long-Term Memory

Process	Effect on Memory
Encoding specificity	Retrieval cues are effective only to the extent that they tap into information that was originally encoded.
Context dependence	Retrieval is most successful when people are in the same psychological state as when they originally learned the information.
State dependence	Retrieval is most successful when it occurs in the same environment in which the information was originally learned.

under the influence of any drug during encoding or retrieval! Mood states, too, can affect memory (Eich & Macaulay, 2000). People tend to remember more positive incidents from their past when they are in a positive mood at the time of recall and more negative events when they are in a negative mood (Ehrlichman & Halpern, 1988; Lewinsohn & Rosenbaum, 1987). These *mood congruency effects* are strongest when people try to recall personally meaningful episodes, because such events were most likely to be coloured by their moods (Eich & Metcalfe, 1989).

Retrieval from Semantic Memory

All of the retrieval situations we have discussed so far are relevant to episodic memory. ("In Review: Factors Affecting Retrieval from Long-Term Memory" summarizes this material.) But how do we retrieve information from semantic memory, in which our general knowledge about the world is stored? Researchers studying this process typically ask participants general-knowledge questions, such as (1) Are fish minerals? (2) Is a beagle a dog? (3) Do birds fly? and (4) Does a car have legs? As you might imagine, most people respond correctly to such questions. By measuring the amount of time people take to answer the questions, however, psychologists have found important clues about how semantic memory is organized and how we retrieve information from it.

Semantic Networks One of the most influential theories of semantic memory is based on the parallel distributed processing model discussed earlier. *Semantic network theory* suggests that all the concepts we have learned are represented in a dense network of associations (Collins & Loftus, 1975). Figure 7.10 presents just a tiny part of what such a *semantic memory network* might look like. In general, semantic network theory suggests that information is retrieved from memory through **spreading activation** (Medin, Ross, & Markman, 2001). So whenever you think about some concept, that concept becomes activated in the network, and this activation—in the form of neural energy—begins to spread along all the paths related to it. For example, if a person is asked to say whether "A robin is a bird" is true or false, the concepts of both "robin" and "bird" will become activated, and the spreading activation from each will intersect in the middle of the path between them.

Some associations within the network are stronger than others. Differing strengths are depicted by the varying thicknesses of the lines in Figure 7.10. Spreading activation travels faster along thick paths than along thin ones. For example, most people probably have a stronger association between "bat" and "can fly" or "haswings" than between "bat" and "is a mammal." Accordingly, most people respond more quickly to "Can a bat fly?" than to "Is a bat a mammal?"

spreading activation A principle that explains how information is retrieved in semantic network theories of memory.

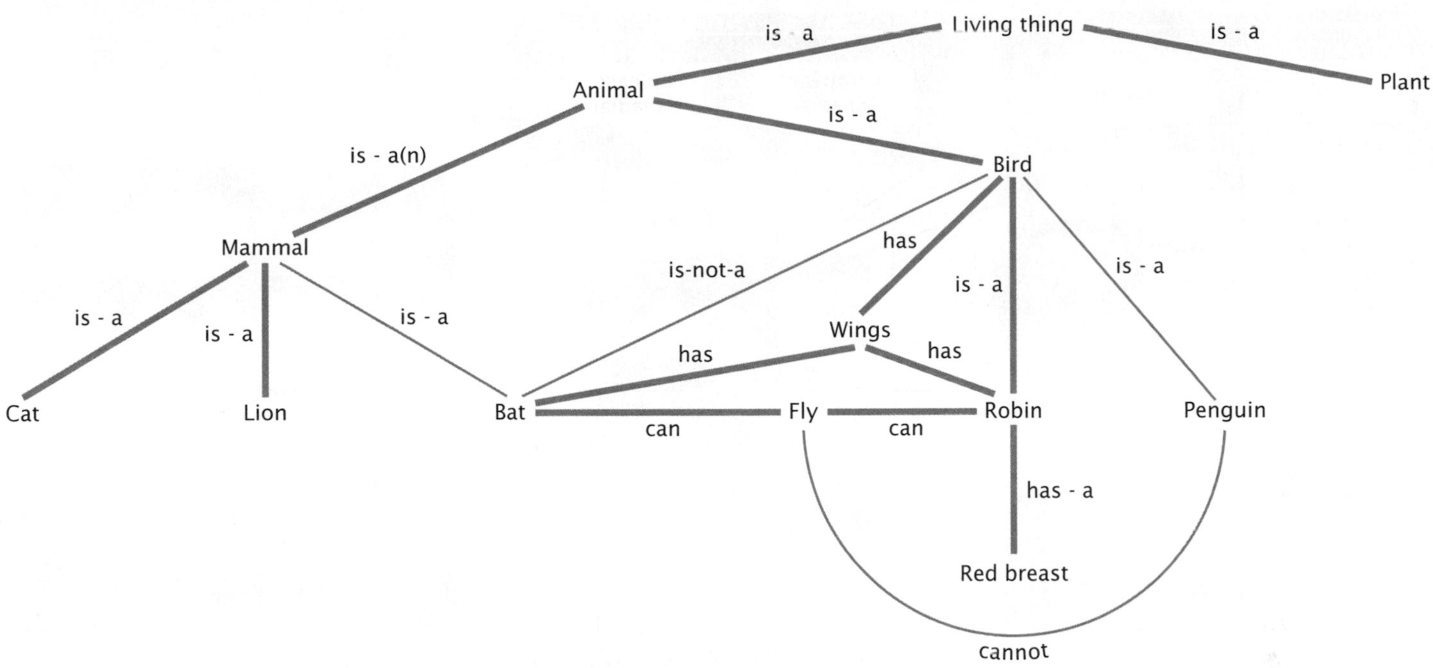

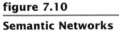

figure 7.10

Semantic Networks

This drawing represents just a small part of a network of semantic associations. Semantic network theories suggest that networks like this allow us to retrieve specific pieces of previously learned information and to make new inferences about concepts.

Because of the tight organization of semantic networks and the speed at which activation spreads through them, we have quick and easy access to an enormous body of knowledge about the world. We can retrieve not only the facts we have learned directly but also the knowledge that allows us to infer or compute other facts about the world (Matlin, 1998). For example, imagine answering the following two questions: (1) Is a robin a bird? and (2) Is a robin a living thing? You can probably answer the first question "directly," because you probably learned this fact at some point in your life. However, you may never have consciously thought about the second question, so answering it requires you to make an inference. Figure 7.10 illustrates the path to that inference. Because you know that a robin is a bird, a bird is an animal, and animals are living things, you can infer that a robin must be a living thing. As you might expect, however, it takes slightly longer to answer the second question than the first.

Retrieving Incomplete Knowledge Figure 7.10 also shows that concepts such as "bird" are represented in semantic memory as collections of features or characteristics. When you can retrieve some features of a concept from your semantic network, but not enough of them to identify what the concept is, you are said to have retrieved *incomplete knowledge*. For example, you might know that there is an animal that is not a bird but that has wings and can fly. Yet you might be unable to retrieve its name (*bat*) at the moment (Connor, Balota, & Neely, 1992).

You have probably experienced a particular example of incomplete knowledge called the *tip-of-the-tongue phenomenon*. In a typical experiment on this phenomenon, people listen to dictionary definitions of words and are then asked to name each defined word (Brown & McNeill, 1966). If they cannot recall a particular word, they are asked whether they can recall any feature of it, such as its first letter or how many syllables it has. People are surprisingly good at this task, indicating that they are able to retrieve at least some knowledge of the word (Brennen et al., 1990). Most people—especially older people—tend to experience the tip-of-the-tongue phenomenon about once a week (Brown, 1991; Brown & Nix, 1996).

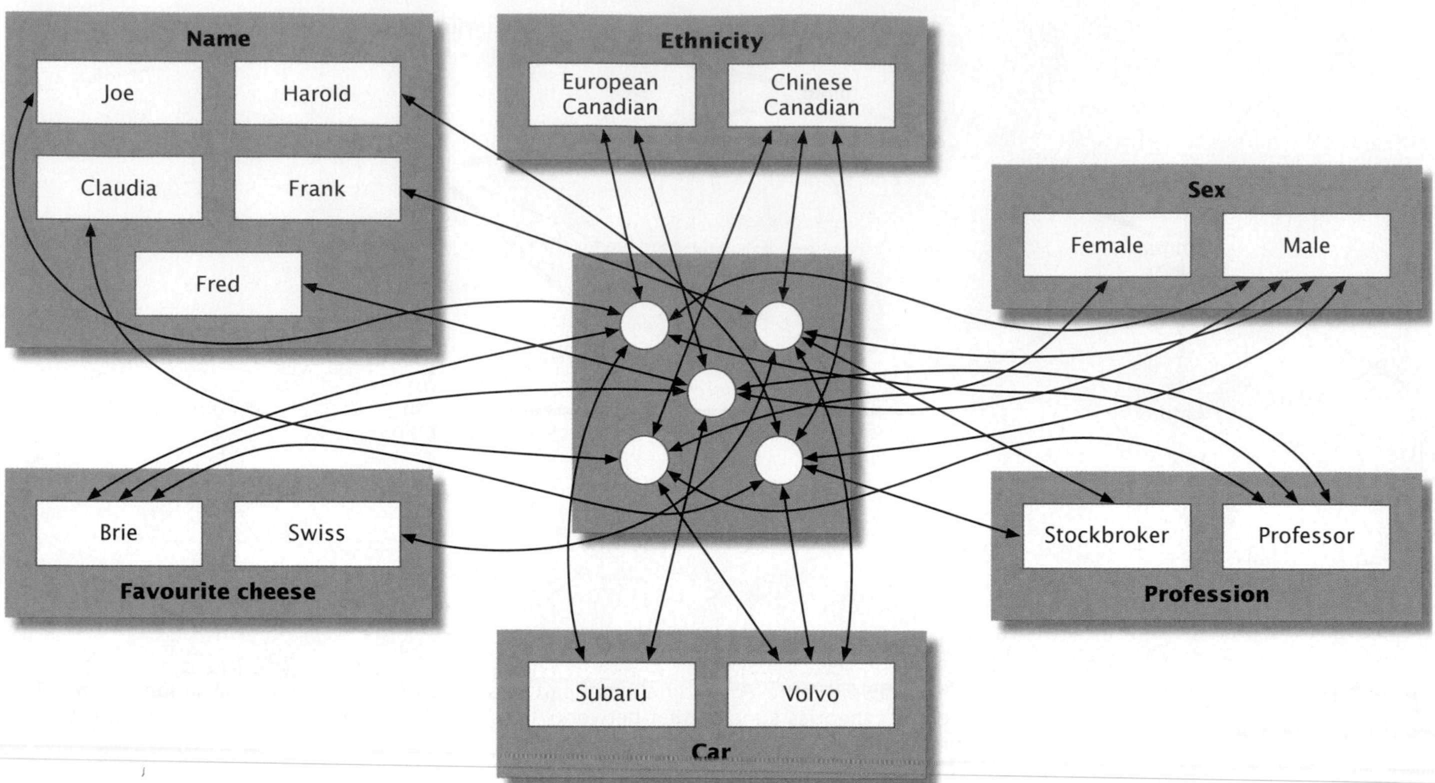

figure 7.11

A PDP Network Model

This simple parallel distributed processing network model represents what someone knows about the characteristics of five people and how these characteristics are related to one another. Each arrow between a rectangle and a circle connects a characteristic with a person. More complex versions of such networks are capable of accounting not only for what people know but also for the inferences and generalizations they tend to make.

Source: From *Cognitive Psychology,* 1st Edition, by C. Martindale, © 1991. Reprinted with permission of Wadsworth Publishing, a division of International Thomson Publishing. Fax 800-730-2215.

Another example of retrieving incomplete knowledge is the *feeling-of-knowing experience,* which is often studied by asking people trivia questions (Reder & Ritter, 1992). When they cannot answer a question, they are asked to say how likely it is that they could recognize the correct answer among several options. Again, people are remarkably good at this task. Even though they cannot recall the answer, they can retrieve enough knowledge to determine whether the answer is actually stored in their memory (Costermans, Lories, & Ansay, 1992).

A PDP Model of Memory

Relating Semantic and Episodic Memory: PDP Models Parallel distributed processing models offer one way of explaining how semantic and episodic information become integrated in developing memories. As mentioned earlier, PDP models suggest that newly learned facts alter our general knowledge of what the world is like. Figure 7.11 shows a simple PDP network model of just a tiny part of someone's knowledge of the world (Martindale, 1991). At its centre lie the intersections of several learned associations between specific facts about five people, each of whom is represented by a circle. This network "knows" that Joe is a Canadian male professor of European background who likes Brie cheese and drives a Subaru. It also "knows" that Claudia is a female Chinese-Canadian professor who drives a Volvo. Notice that the network has never learned what type of cheese she prefers.

schemas Mental representations of categories of objects, events, and people.

PDP Models and Constructive Memory If you hear "our basketball team won last night," your schema about basketball might cause you to encode, and later retrieve, though sometimes incorrectly, the fact that the players were men.

Suppose Figure 7.11 represents your memory, and you now think about Claudia. Because of the connections in the network, the facts that she is a female Chinese-Canadian professor and drives a Volvo would be activated. You would automatically remember these facts about her. However, "likes Brie cheese" would also be activated to some extent, because it is linked to other professors in the network. If there were only a few such links, the activation for Brie cheese would be low, and the idea that Claudia likes Brie might be considered a hypothesis or an educated guess. But suppose every other professor you know likes Brie. In that case, the connection between "professors" and "likes Brie cheese" would be so strong that you would be confident that Claudia, too, likes Brie (Rumelhart & McClelland, 1986). In short, you would have constructed a memory about Claudia.

PDP networks also produce spontaneous generalizations. For example, suppose a friend tells you she just bought a new car. You would know without asking that—like all other cars you have seen—it has four wheels. However, spontaneous generalizations can create errors if the network is based on limited or biased experience with a class of objects. So if the network in Figure 7.11 were asked what Canadian males of European background were like, it would think that all of them drove Japanese cars.

If it occurs to you that ethnic prejudice can result from spontaneous generalization errors, you are right (Greenwald & Banaji, 1995). Researchers are actually encouraged by this prejudicial aspect of PDP networks, though, because it accurately reflects human thought and memory. Virtually all people make spontaneous generalizations about males, females, Aboriginal Canadians, Chinese-Canadians, the young, the old, and many other categories (Rudman et al., 1999). Is prejudice, then, a process that we have no choice in or control over? Not necessarily. Relatively unprejudiced people tend to recognize that they are making generalizations and consciously try to ignore or suppress them (Monteith, Sherman, & Devine, 1998).

Schemas Parallel distributed processing models also help us better understand memory by explaining the operation of the schemas that guide it. **Schemas** are mental representations of categories of objects, events, and people. For example, among people who have a schema for *hockey,* simply hearing the word is likely to activate whole clusters of information in long-term memory, including the rules of the game, images of players, sticks, pucks, an icy rink, winter mornings, and perhaps hot dogs and beer. The generalized knowledge contained in schemas provides a basis for making inferences about incoming information during the encoding stage. Suppose you hear that a hockey player was injured. Your schema about hockey might lead you to assume the incident was game-related and to encode it that way, even though the cause was not mentioned. As a result, you are likely to recall the injury as having occurred during a game (see Figure 7.12 for another example).

figure 7.12

The Effect of Schemas on Recall

In a classic experiment, participants were shown figures like these, along with labels designed to activate certain schemas (Carmichael, Hogan, & Walter, 1932). For example, when showing the top figure, the experimenter said either "This resembles eyeglasses" or "This resembles a dumbbell." When the participants were asked to copy the figures from memory, their drawings tended to resemble the items mentioned by the experimenter. In other words, the labels activated their schemas, and the schemas altered their memories.

	Group 1		**Group 2**	
Figure shown to participants	Label given	Figure drawn by participants	Label given	Figure drawn by participants
	Eyeglasses		Dumbbell	
	Hourglass		Table	
	Seven		Four	
	Gun		Broom	

LINKAGES
Memory, Perception, and Eyewitness Testimony

There are few situations in which accurate retrieval of memories is more important, and filling in of memory gaps is more dangerous, than when an eyewitness testifies in court about a crime. Eyewitnesses provide the most compelling evidence in many trials, but they can sometimes be mistaken (Loftus & Ketcham, 1991; Wells, Olson, & Charman, 2002). In 1969, for example, Gail Miller, a twenty-two-year-old nursing assistant, was murdered in Saskatoon, Saskatchewan. Sixteen-year-old David Milgaard was charged and convicted of the murder based largely on the eyewitness recollections of a group of his friends. Two of his friends first corroborated David's story that he was with them the entire day Gail Miller was murdered. After intensive interrogation, however, they began to change their stories and one of his friends even confessed to seeing David stab Gail Miller, although later in court she said she couldn't remember the incident. In 1997, after 22 years behind bars, David was exonerated based on DNA evidence that proved he was innocent of the crime (Nadeau, 2000). What happened and why did his friends' stories change so dramatically? Let's consider the accuracy of eyewitness memory and how it can be distorted.

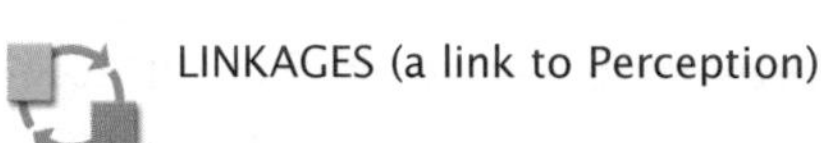

Like the rest of us, eyewitnesses can remember only what they perceive, and they can perceive only what they attend to (Backman & Nilsson, 1991). As described in the perception chapter, perception is influenced by a combination of the stimulus features we find "out there" in the world and what we already know, expect, or want—that is, by both bottom-up and top-down processing.

Witnesses are asked to report exactly what they saw or heard; but no matter how hard they try to be accurate, there are limits to how faithful their reports can be (Kassin, Rigby, & Castillo, 1991). For one thing, as mentioned earlier, the semantic encoding typical of long-term memory can cause the loss of certain important details (Fahsing, Ask, & Granhag, 2004). Further, the appearance of new information, including information contained in questions posed by police or lawyers, can alter a witness's memory (Belli & Loftus, 1996). In one study, when witnesses were asked, "How fast were the cars going when they *smashed into* each other?" they were likely to recall a higher speed than when they were asked, "How fast were the cars going when they *hit* each other?" (Loftus & Palmer, 1974; see Figure 7.13). There is also evidence that an object mentioned during questioning about an incident is often mistakenly remembered as having been there during the incident (Dodson & Reisberg, 1991). So if a lawyer says that a screwdriver was lying on the ground (when it was not), witnesses often recall with great certainty having seen it (Ryan & Geiselman, 1991). This *misinformation effect* can occur in several ways (Loftus & Hoffman, 1989). In some cases, hearing new information can make it harder to retrieve the original memory (Tversky & Tuchin, 1989). In others, the new information may be integrated into the old memory, making it impossible to distinguish the new information from what was originally seen (Loftus, 1992). In still others, an eyewitness report might be influenced by the person's assumption that if a lawyer or police officer says an object was there or that something happened, it must be true. Kim Roberts of Wilfrid Laurier University in Ontario also points out that there is a whole set of different circumstances that needs to be taken into consideration if the eyewitness is a child (c.f. Roberts, 2002).

A jury's belief in a witness's testimony often depends as much (or even more) on *how* the witness presents evidence as on the content or relevance of that evidence (Leippe, Manion, & Romanczyk, 1992). Many jurors are impressed, for example, by witnesses who give lots of details about what they saw or heard. Extremely detailed testimony from prosecution witnesses is especially likely to lead to guilty verdicts, even when the details reported are irrelevant (Bell & Loftus, 1989). When a witness gives highly detailed testimony, such as the exact time of the crime or the colour of the perpetrator's shoes, jurors apparently assume that the witness paid especially close attention or has a particularly accurate memory. At first

figure 7.13

The Impact of Questioning on Eyewitness Memory

After seeing a filmed traffic accident, people were asked, "About how fast were the cars going when they (smashed into, hit, or contacted) each other?" As shown here, the witnesses' responses were influenced by the verb used in the question; "smashed" was associated with the highest average speed estimates. A week later, people who heard the "smashed" question remembered the accident as being more violent than did people in the other two groups (Loftus & Palmer, 1974).

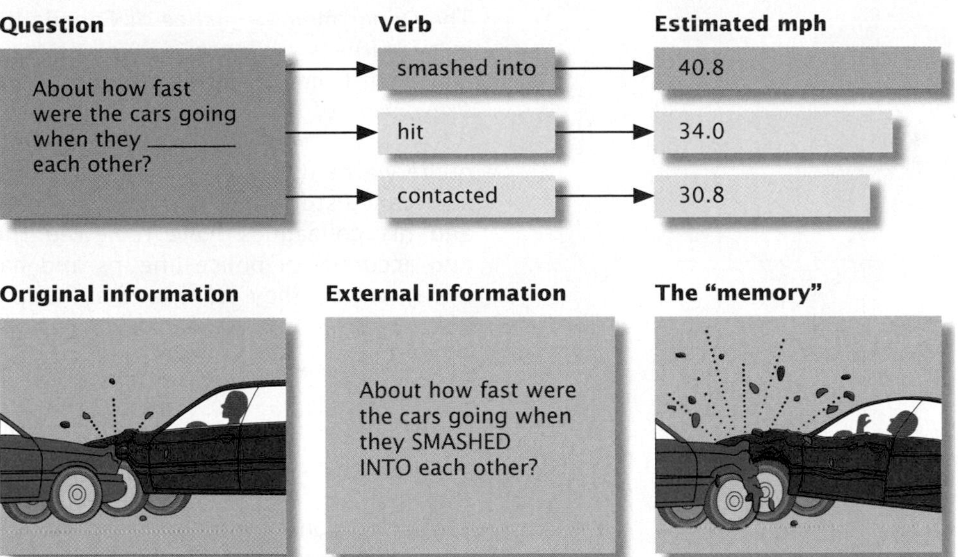

glance, these assumptions seem reasonable. However, as discussed in the chapter on perception, the ability to divide attention is limited. As a result, witnesses might be able to focus attention on the crime and the criminal, or on the surrounding details, but probably not on both—particularly if they were emotionally aroused and the crime happened quickly. So witnesses who accurately remember unimportant details of a crime scene may not accurately recall more important ones, such as the criminal's facial features (Backman & Nilsson, 1991).

Juries also tend to believe witnesses who are confident (Leippe, Manion, & Romanczyk, 1992). Unfortunately, witnesses' confidence in their testimony often exceeds its accuracy (Shaw, 1996). Repeated exposure to misinformation and the repeated recall of misinformation can increase a witness's confidence in testimony, whether or not it is accurate (Lamb, 1998; Mitchell & Zaragoza, 1996; Roediger, Jacoby, & McDermott, 1996). In other words, as in the Gail Miller case, even witnesses who are confident about their testimony are not always correct.

The weaknesses inherent in eyewitness memory can be amplified by the use of police lineups and certain other criminal identification procedures (Wells & Olson, 2003). In one study, for example, participants watched a videotaped crime and then tried to identify the criminal from a set of photographs (Wells & Bradfield, 1999). None of the photos showed the person who had committed the crime, but some participants nevertheless identified one of them as the criminal they saw on tape. When these mistaken participants were led to believe that they had correctly identified the criminal, they became even more confident in the accuracy of their false identification (Semmler, Brewer, & Wells, 2004; Wells, Olson, & Charman, 2003). These incorrect, but confident, witnesses became more likely than other participants to claim that it had been easy for them to identify the criminal from the photos because they had had a good view of him and had paid careful attention to him.

Barry Morrison, a lawyer from Saint John, New Brunswick, and Ian Fraser, a psychologist at St. Thomas University in New Brunswick, refer to a study commissioned by the Department of Justice of Canada that estimates that 78 percent of the 130 people exonerated by DNA evidence were convicted based mainly on faulty, eyewitness testimony (Morrison & Fraser, 2005). DNA evidence freed David Milgaard and later helped convict Larry Fisher of the murder of Gail Miller. The Province of Saskatchewan and the Government of Canada offered a compensation package totalling 10 million dollars to David Milgaard for having served 22 years in prison for a crime he did not commit (Nadeau, 2000).

HERMAN

"Can you identify the man who punched you in the knee?"

This is exactly the sort of biased police lineup that *Report on the Prevention of Miscarriages of Justice* (2004) is designed to avoid. Based on research in memory and perception, the guide recommends that no one in a lineup should stand out from the others, that police should not suggest that the real criminal is in the lineup, and that witnesses should not be encouraged to "guess" when making an identification.

The Department of Justice of Canada has acknowledged the potential for errors in eyewitness evidence, as well as the dangers of asking witnesses to identify suspects from lineups and photo arrays. The result is the *Report on the Prevention of the Miscarriages of Justice* (The Department of Justice of Canada, 2004) a guide for police and prosecutors who work with eyewitnesses. The guide warns these officials that asking leading questions about what witnesses saw can distort their memories. John Turtle of Ryerson University in Ontario and his colleagues have reviewed the wide range of literature on the use and accuracy of police lineups and have developed a series of recommendations, which they believe may help improve eyewitness accuracy. (Turtle, Lindsay, & Wells, 2003).

Forgetting

The frustrations of forgetting—where you left your keys, the answer to a test question, an anniversary—are apparent to most people nearly every day (Neisser, 2000). In this section we look more closely at the nature of forgetting and at some of the mechanisms that are responsible for it.

How Do We Forget?

In the late 1800s, Hermann Ebbinghaus, a German psychologist, began the systematic study of memory and forgetting by conducting research on his own memory. His aim was to study memory in its "pure" form, uncontaminated by emotional reactions and other pre-existing associations between new material and what was already in memory. To eliminate any such associations, Ebbinghaus created the *nonsense syllable,* a meaningless set of two consonants and a vowel, such as *POF, XEM,* and *QAL.* He read a list of nonsense syllables aloud at a constant rate and then tried to recall the syllables.

To measure forgetting, Ebbinghaus devised the **method of savings,** which involves computing the difference between the number of trials needed to learn a list of items and the number of trials needed to relearn it after some time has elapsed. This difference is called the *savings.* If it took Ebbinghaus ten trials to learn a list and ten more trials to relearn it, there would be no savings, and forgetting would have been complete. If it took him ten trials to learn the list and only five trials to relearn it, there would be a savings of 50 percent.

As you can see in Figure 7.14, Ebbinghaus found a decline in savings (and a corresponding increase in forgetting) as time passes. However, the most dramatic drop

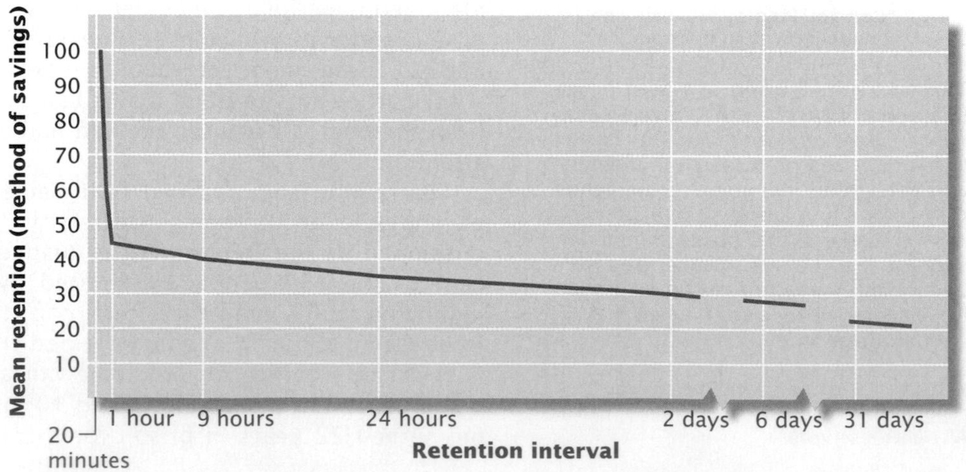

figure 7.14

Ebbinghaus's Curve of Forgetting

Select 30 words at random from a dictionary and spend a few minutes memorizing them. After an hour, write down as many words as you can remember, but don't look at the original list again. Do the same self-test eight hours later, a day later, and two days later. Now look at the original list, and see how well you did on each recall test. Ebbinghaus found that most forgetting occurs during the first nine hours after learning, and especially during the first hour. If this was not the case for you, why do you think your results were different?

Durable Memories This man probably hadn't used a pogo stick since he was ten. His memory of how to do it is not entirely gone, however, so he showed some "savings." That is, it took him less time to relearn the skill than it did to learn it originally.

in what people retain in long-term memory occurs during the first nine hours, especially in the first hour. After this initial decline, the rate of forgetting slows down considerably. In Ebbinghaus's study, some savings existed even 31 days after the original learning.

Ebbinghaus's research had some limitations, but it produced two lasting discoveries. One is the shape of the forgetting curve, shown in Figure 7.14. Psychologists have repeated some of his work, substituting words, sentences, and even stories for nonsense syllables. In virtually all cases the forgetting curve shows the same strong initial drop in memory, followed by a much more moderate decrease over time (Slamecka & McElree, 1983; Wixted, 2004). Of course, people remember sensible stories better than nonsense syllables, but the shape of the curve is the same no matter what type of material is involved (Davis & Moore, 1935). Even the forgetting of events from daily life tends to follow Ebbinghaus's forgetting curve (Thomson, 1982).

The second of Ebbinghaus's important discoveries is just how long-lasting savings in long-term memory can be. Psychologists now know from the method of savings that information about everything from algebra to bike riding is often retained for decades (Matlin, 1998). You may forget something you have learned if you do not use the information, but it is easy to relearn the material if the need arises, indicating that the forgetting was not complete (Hall & Bahrick, 1998).

Why Do We Forget? The Roles of Decay and Interference

We have seen how forgetting occurs, but nothing we have said so far explains *why* it occurs. In principle, either of two processes can be responsible. One process is **decay,** the gradual disappearance of the mental representation of a stimulus. Decay occurs in memory much as the inscription engraved on a ring or bracelet wears away and becomes less distinct over time. Forgetting might also occur because of **interference,** a process through which either the storage or retrieval of information is impaired by the presence of other information. Interference might occur either because one piece of information actually *displaces* other information, pushing it out of memory, or because one piece of information makes storing or recalling other information more difficult.

In the case of short-term memory, we noted that if an item is not rehearsed or elaborated, memory of it decreases consistently over the course of about 18 seconds. So decay appears to play a prominent role in forgetting information in short-term memory. But interference through displacement can also produce forgetting from short-term memory. Like a desktop, short-term memory can hold only so much. When additional items are added, the old ones tend to "fall off" and are no longer available (Haberlandt, 1999). Displacement is one reason why the phone number you just looked up is likely to drop out of short-term memory if you read another number before making your call. Rehearsal prevents displacement by continually re-entering the same information into short-term memory.

The cause of forgetting from long-term memory seems to be more directly tied to interference, but it is also more complicated because there can be two kinds of interference. In **retroactive interference,** learning of new information interferes with recall of older information. In **proactive interference,** old information interferes with learning or remembering new information. For example, retroactive interference would help explain why studying French vocabulary this term might make it more difficult to remember the Spanish words you learned last term. And because of proactive interference, the French words you are learning now might make it harder to learn German next term. Figure 7.15 outlines the types of experiments that are used to study the influence of each form of interference in long-term memory.

Suppose a person learns something and then, when tested on it after various intervals, remembers less and less as the delay becomes longer. Is the forgetting due

method of savings Measuring forgetting by computing the difference between the number of repetitions needed to learn and, after a delay, relearn the same material.

decay The gradual disappearance of the mental representation of a stimulus.

interference The process through which either the storage or the retrieval of information is impaired by the presence of other information.

retroactive interference A cause of forgetting in which new information placed in memory interferes with the ability to recall information already in memory.

proactive interference A cause of forgetting in which information already in memory interferes with the ability to remember new information.

PROACTIVE INTERFERENCE

Group	Time 1	Time 2	Time 3	Result
Experimental	Learn list A	Learn list B	Recall list B	The experimental group will suffer from proactive interference, and the control group will be able to recall more material from list B.
Control		Learn list B	Recall list B	

RETROACTIVE INTERFERENCE

Group	Time 1	Time 2	Time 3	Result
Experimental	Learn list A	Learn list B	Recall list A	The experimental group will suffer from retroactive interference, and the control group will be able to recall more material from list A.
Control	Learn list A		Recall list A	

figure 7.15

Procedures for Studying Interference

To recall the two types of interference, remember that the prefixes *pro* and *retro* indicate directions in time. *Pro* means "forward," and *retro* means "backward." In *pro*active interference, previously learned material "comes forward" to interfere with new learning. *Retro*active interference occurs when new information "goes back" to interfere with the recall of past learning.

to decay or to interference? It is not easy to tell, because longer delays produce both more decay and more retroactive interference as the person is exposed to further information while waiting. To separate the effects of decay from those of interference, Karl Dallenbach created situations in which time passed but there was no accompanying interference. Evidence of forgetting in such situations would suggest that decay, not interference, was operating.

In one of Dallenbach's studies, university students learned a list of nonsense syllables and then either continued with their usual routine or were sheltered from interference by going to sleep (Jenkins & Dallenbach, 1924). Although the delay (and thus the potential for decay) was held constant for both groups, the greater interference associated with being awake produced much more forgetting (see Figure 7.16).

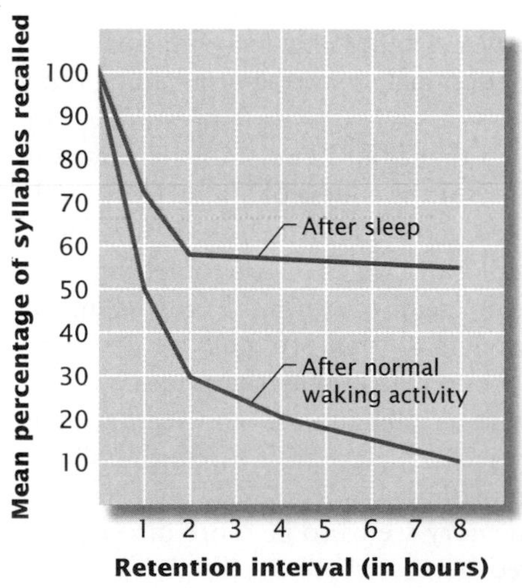

figure 7.16

Interference and Forgetting

In this study, university students' forgetting was more rapid if they engaged in normal activity after learning than if they spent the time asleep. These results suggest that interference is more important than decay in forgetting information in long-term memory.

Source: Minimi & Dallenbach (1946).

Results such as these suggest that although decay sometimes occurs, interference is the major cause of forgetting from long-term memory. But does interference actually push the forgotten information out of memory, or does it just impair the retrieval process? To find out, Endel Tulving and Joseph Psotka (1971) presented people with different numbers of word lists. Each list contained words from one of six categories, such as types of buildings (*hut, cottage, tent, hotel*) or earth formations (*cliff, river, hill, volcano*). Some people learned a list and then recalled as many of the words as possible. Other groups learned the first list and then learned different numbers of other lists before trying to recall the first one.

The results were dramatic. As the number of intervening lists increased, the number of words that people could recall from the original list declined. This finding reflected strong retroactive interference. Then the researchers gave a second test, in which they provided people with a *retrieval cue* by telling them the category of the words (such as "types of buildings") to be recalled. Now the number of intervening lists had almost no effect on the number of words recalled from the original list, as Figure 7.17 shows. These results indicate that the words were still in long-term memory. They had not been pushed out, but the participants had been unable to recall them without appropriate retrieval cues. In other words, the original forgetting was due to a failure in retrieval. So putting more and more information into long-term memory may be like putting more and more CDs into a storage cabinet.

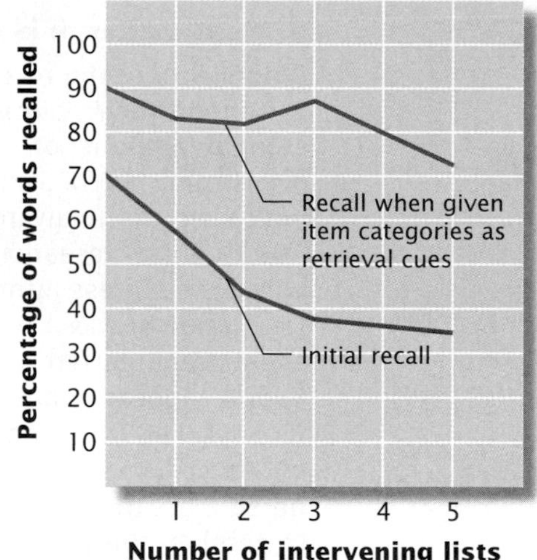

figure 7.17

Retrieval Failures and Forgetting

Tulving and Psotka found that people's ability to recall a list of items was strongly affected by the number of other lists they learned before being tested on the first one. When item-category (retrieval) cues were provided on a second test, however, retroactive interference from the intervening lists almost disappeared.

Source: Tulving & Psotka (1971).

None of the CDs disappears, but it becomes increasingly difficult to find the one you are looking for.

Data such as these suggest to some memory theorists that all forgetting from long-term memory is due to some form of retrieval failure (Ratcliff & McKoon, 1989). Does this mean that everything in long-term memory remains there for life, even if you cannot always, or ever, recall it? No one knows for sure, but as described in the Thinking Critically section, this question lies at the heart of some highly controversial court cases.

THINKING CRITICALLY

Can Traumatic Memories Be Repressed, Then Recovered?

LINKAGES (a link to Consciousness)

In the summer of 1991, Adriaan Mak, a retired elementary school teacher, was informed by his son that he was going into therapy to straighten himself out. In the winter of the same year Mak's son phoned him from Toronto and asked to meet with him. During the meeting, Mak's son informed him that his therapy sessions had helped him to recover a repressed memory and then confronted his father with the allegation that his father had raped him when he was a child. Mak was devastated and promptly denied that such an incident ever took place. The two eventually reconciled. Mak, however, began investigating such cases and has estimated that there have been 240 court cases in Canada alone where the evidence was based on recovered memories (Mak, 2006). The debate concerning use of recovered memory as evidence in court cases has continued to intensify in Canada and involves not only psychologists but the Canadian legal system as well. The controversy centres on the validity of claims of recovered memory. Some psychologists accept the idea that it is possible for people to repress, or push into unconsciousness, memories of traumatic incidents and then recover these memories many years later. Other psychologists are skeptical about recovered memory claims.

- **What am I being asked to believe or accept?**

Prosecutors in recovered memory cases, argue that accusers have repressed and later recovered their memories for the event. The juries in these trials often accept the assertion that repression can keep all memory of shocking events out of awareness for decades, yet leave them potentially subject to accurate recollections (Hyman, 2000). It has been estimated, for example, that of the 240 court cases in Canada based on recovered memories, 40 people have been incarcerated based on the evidence (Mc Dougall, 2002).

- **What evidence is available to support the assertion?**

Proponents of the recovered memory argument point to several lines of evidence to support their claims. First, as discussed in the chapter on consciousness, a substantial amount of mental activity occurs outside of conscious awareness (Kihlstrom, 1999). Second, research on implicit memory shows that information of which we are unaware can influence our behaviour (Schacter, Chiu, & Ochsner, 1993). Third, research on *motivated forgetting* suggests that people are able to willfully suppress information so that it is no longer accessible on a later memory test (Anderson & Green, 2001). Even suppressing one's emotional reactions to events can interfere with memories of those events (Richards & Gross, 2000). And people appear more likely to forget unpleasant rather than pleasant events (Erdelyi, 1985). In one study, a psychologist kept a detailed record of his daily life over a six-year period. When he later tried to recall those experiences, he remembered more than half of the positive ones, but only one-third of the negative ones. In another study, 38 percent of women who, as children, had been brought to a hospital because of sexual abuse did not report the incident as adults (Williams, 1994). Fourth, retrieval cues can help people recall memories that had previously been inaccessible to conscious awareness (Andrews et al., 2000; Landsdale & Laming, 1995). For example, these cues have helped soldiers remember for the first time the circumstances under which they had been wounded many years before (Karon & Widener, 1997). Finally, there is the confidence with which people report recovered memories; they say they are just too vivid to be anything but real.

- **Are there alternative ways of interpreting the evidence?**

Those who are skeptical about recovered memories do not deny the operation of subconscious memory and retrieval processes (Kihlstrom, 1999). They also recognize that, sadly, child abuse and other traumas are all too common. But to these psychologists, the available evidence is not strong enough to support the conclusion that traumatic memories can be repressed and then accurately recalled. Any given "recovered" memory, they say, might actually be a distorted, or constructed, memory (Clancy et al., 2000; Hyman, 2000; Loftus, 1998). As already mentioned, our recall of past events is affected by what happened at the time, what we knew beforehand, and everything we have experienced since.

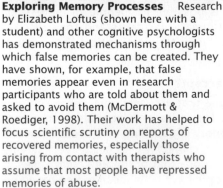

Exploring Memory Processes Research by Elizabeth Loftus (shown here with a student) and other cognitive psychologists has demonstrated mechanisms through which false memories can be created. They have shown, for example, that false memories appear even in research participants who are told about them and asked to avoid them (McDermott & Roediger, 1998). Their work has helped to focus scientific scrutiny on reports of recovered memories, especially those arising from contact with therapists who assume that most people have repressed memories of abuse.

Research shows that *false memories*—distortions of actual events and the recall of events that didn't actually happen—can be at least as vivid as accurate ones and that people can be just as confident in them (Brainerd & Reyna, 1998; Brainerd et al., 2003; Loftus, 2004; Nourkova, Bernstein, & Loftus, 2004; Roediger & McDermott, 1995, 2000). Most of us have experienced everyday versions of false memories. It is not unusual for people to "remember" turning off the coffeepot or mailing the rent cheque, only to discover later that they did not. Researchers have demonstrated that false memories can occur in relation to more emotional events, too. In one case study, a teenager named Chris was given descriptions of four incidents from his childhood and asked to write about each of them every day for five days (Loftus, 1997a). One of those incidents—being lost in a shopping mall at age five—never really happened. Yet Chris not only eventually "remembered" this event but added many details about the mall and the stranger whose hand he was supposedly found holding. He also rated this (false) memory as being more vivid than two of the other three (real) incidents. Similar results occurred in about half of 77 child participants in a more recent set of case studies (Porter, Yuille, & Lehman, 1999). The same pattern of results has appeared in formal experiments on the planting of emotion-laden false memories (Hyman & Pentland, 1996). Researchers have been able to create vivid and striking, but completely false, memories of events that people thought they experienced when they were one day old (DuBreuil, Garry, & Loftus, 1998). In other experiments, children who were repeatedly asked about a nonexistent trauma (getting a hand caught in a mousetrap) eventually developed a vivid and unshakable false memory of experiencing it (Ceci et al., 1994).

In other words, people sometimes have a difficult time distinguishing between what has happened to them and what they have only imagined, or have come to believe, has happened (Henkel, 2004; Johnson & Raye, 1998; Mazzoni & Memon, 2003; Zaragoza et al., 2001). Some studies indicate that people who score high on tests of introversion, fantasy-proneness, and dissociation (which includes a tendency toward lapses of memory and attention) are more likely than others to develop false memories and may also be more likely to report the recovery of repressed memories (McNally, 2003, McNally et al., 2000a, 2000b; Porter et al., 2000). Two other studies have found that women who have suffered physical or sexual abuse are more likely to falsely remember words on a laboratory recall test (Bremner, Shobe, & Kihlstrom, 2000; Zoellner et al., 2000). This tendency appears strongest among abused women who show signs of posttraumatic stress disorder (Bremner, Shobe, & Kihlstrom, 2000). Another study found that susceptibility to false memory in a word recall task was greater in women who reported recovered memories of sexual abuse than in nonabused women or in those who had always remembered the abuse they suffered (Clancy et al., 2000). False memories on this laboratory recall task are also more common among people who claim to have been abducted by space aliens than among other people (Clancy et al., 2002).

Why would anyone "remember" a traumatic event that did not actually occur? Elizabeth Loftus (1997b) suggests that, for one thing, popular books such as *The Courage to Heal* (Bass & Davis, 1994) and *Secret Survivors* (Blume, 1998) may lead people to believe that anyone who experiences guilt, depression, low self-esteem, overemotionality, or any of a long list of other problems is harbouring repressed memories of abuse. This message, says Loftus, tends to be reinforced and extended by therapists who specialize in using guided imagination, hypnosis, and other methods to "help" clients recover repressed memories (Lindsay et al., 2004; Polusny & Follette, 1996; Poole et al., 1995). These therapists may influence people to construct false memories by encouraging them to imagine experiencing events that might never have actually occurred or that occurred only in a dream (Mazzoni & Loftus, 1996; Olio, 1994). As one client described her therapy, "I was rapidly losing the ability to differentiate between my imagination and my real memory" (Loftus & Ketcham, 1994, p. 25). To such therapists, a client's failure to recover memories of abuse or refusal to accept their existence is evidence of "denial" of the truth (Loftus, 1997a; Tavris, 2003).

The possibility that recovered memories might actually be false memories has prompted the Canadian Psychological Association and Alan Gold, the President of the Canadian Criminal Lawyers Association, to urge the Minister of Justice to hold an inquiry into criminal convictions based solely on the use of repressed memories (CPA, 1998; Golds, 1998).

● What additional evidence would help to evaluate the alternatives?

Evaluating reports of recovered memories would be easier if we had more information about whether it is possible for people to repress traumatic events. If it *is* possible, we also need to know how common it is and how accurate recovered memories might be. So far, we know that some people apparently do forget intense emotional experiences, but that most people's memories of them are vivid and long lasting (McGaugh, 2003; Pope et al., 1998). Some are called *flashbulb memories* because they preserve particular experiences in great detail (Brown & Kulik, 1977). In fact, many people who live through trauma are *unable* to forget it but wish they could (Henig, 2004). In the sexual abuse study mentioned earlier, for example (Williams, 1994), 62 percent of the abuse victims did recall their trauma. A similar study of a different group of adults found that 81 percent of them recalled their documented childhood abuse (Goodman et al., 2003). The true recall figures might actually be higher in such studies, because some people who remember abuse may not wish to talk about it.

In any case, more research such as this—research that tracks the fate of memories in known abuse cases—would not only help to estimate the prevalence of this kind of forgetting but also might offer clues as to the kinds of people and events most likely to be associated with it.

It would also be valuable to know more about the processes through which repression might occur and how they are related to empirically established theories and models of human memory. Is there a mechanism that specifically pushes traumatic memories out of awareness, then keeps them at a subconscious level for long periods and allows them to be accurately recalled? Despite some suggestive results (Anderson & Green, 2001; Anderson et al., 2004; DePrince & Freyd, 2004), cognitive psychologists have so far not found reliable evidence for such a mechanism (Loftus, 1997a; McNally, 2003; McNally, Clancy, & Schacter, 2001; McNally et al., 2000a; Pope et al., 1998).

- **What conclusions are most reasonable?**

An objective reading of the available research evidence supports the view that recovery of memories of trauma is at least possible, but that the implantation of false memories is also possible—and has been demonstrated experimentally. Accordingly, it is difficult, and sometimes impossible, to decide whether any particular case is an instance of recovered memory or false memory, especially in the absence of objective corroborating evidence.

The intense conflict between those who uncritically accept claims of recovered memories and those who are more wary about the accuracy of such claims reflects a fundamental disagreement about evidence (Tavris, 2003). Client reports constitute "proof" for therapists who deal daily with victims of sexual abuse and other traumas and who rely more on personal experiences than on scientific research findings. Those reports are viewed with far more skepticism by psychologists who engage in, or rely on, empirical research on the processes of memory and forgetting (Loftus, 2003, 2004; Pope, 1998). They are looking for additional sources of evidence, including brain activity "signatures" that might distinguish true memories from false ones (e.g., Gonsalves et al., 2004; Slotnick & Schacter, 2004).

So whether or not you believe a claim of recovered memory may be determined by the relative weight you assign to personal experiences and intuition versus empirical evidence from controlled experiments. Still, the apparent ease with which false memories can be created should lead judges, juries, and the general public to exercise great caution before accepting as valid unverified memories of traumatic events. At the same time, we should not automatically and uncritically reject the claims of people who appear to have recovered memories. Perhaps the wisest course is to use all the scientific and circumstantial evidence available to carefully and critically examine such claims. This careful, scientific approach is vital if we are to protect the rights and welfare of those who report recovered memories, as well as of those who face accusations arising from them.

Biological Bases of Memory

Many psychologists who study memory focus on explicit and implicit mental processes. Others explore the physical, electrical, and chemical changes that take place in the brain when people encode, store, and retrieve information (Cavallaro et al., 2002; Mitchell, Heatherton, & Macrae, 2002; Otten, Henson, & Rugg, 2002; Simons & Spiers, 2003; Vogel & Machizawa, 2004). The story of the scientific search for the biological bases of memory begins with the work of Karl Lashley and Donald Hebb, who spent many years studying how memory is related to brain structures and processes. Lashley (1950) taught rats new behaviours and then observed how damage to various parts of the rats' brains changed their ability to perform the tasks they had learned. Lashley hoped that his work would identify the brain area that contained the "engram"—the physical manifestation of memory in the brain. However, after many experiments, he concluded that memories are not localized in one specific region, but instead are distributed throughout large areas of brain tissue (Lashley, 1950).

Hebb, who was a student of Lashley's, proposed another biological theory of memory. Hebb believed that each memory is represented by a group of interconnected neurons in the brain. These neurons, which he called a *cell assembly,* form a network in the cortex. The connections among these neurons are strengthened, he said, when the neurons are simultaneously stimulated through sensory experiences (Hebb, 1949). Although not correct in all its details, Hebb's theory stimulated research and contributed to an understanding of the physical basis of memory. His theory is also consistent, in many respects, with contemporary parallel distributed processing models of memory (Hergenhahn & Olson, 1997).

Let's consider more recent research on the biochemical mechanisms and brain structures that are most directly involved in memory processes.

The Biochemistry of Memory

As described in the chapter on biological aspects of psychology, communication among brain cells takes place at the synapses between axons and dendrites, and it depends on chemicals, called *neurotransmitters,* released at the synapses. The formation and storage of new memories are associated with at least two kinds of changes in synapses.

The first kind of change occurs when stimulation from the environment promotes the formation of new synapses, thus increasing the complexity of the communication networks through which neurons receive information (Black & Greenough, 1991; Rosenzweig & Bennett, 1996). Scientists can now actually see this process occur. As shown in Figure 7.18, repeatedly sending signals across a particular synapse increases the number of special little branches, called *spines,* that appear on the receiving cell's dendrites (Toni et al., 1999).

The second kind of change occurs as new experiences alter the functioning of existing synapses. Researchers have discovered that when two neurons fire at the same time and together stimulate a third neuron, that third neuron will later be more responsive than before to stimulation by either neuron alone (Sejnowski, Chattarji, & Stanton, 1990). This process of "sensitizing" synapses is called *long-term potentiation* (Li, Cullen, et al., 2003; Rioult-Pedotti, Friedman, & Donoghue, 2000). Changing patterns of electrical stimulation can also weaken synaptic connections (Malenka, 1995). Such changes in sensitivity could account for the development of conditioned responses and other types of learning.

In the hippocampus (see Figure 7.19), these changes appear to occur at synapses that use the neurotransmitter glutamate (Malenka & Nicoll, 1999). Other neurotransmitters, such as acetylcholine, also play important roles in memory formation

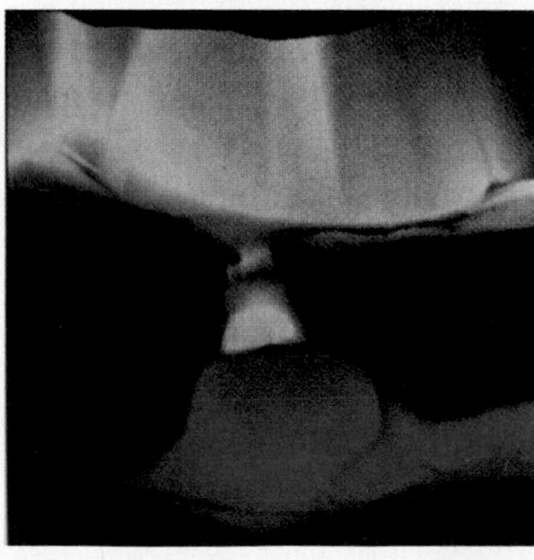

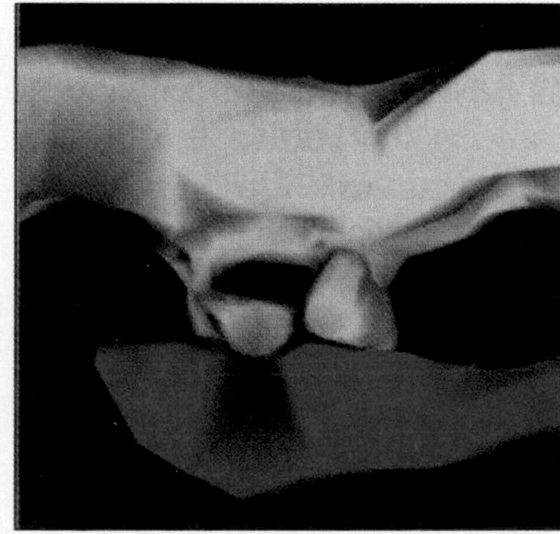

figure 7.18

Building Memories

These models of synapses are based on electron microscope images of neurons in the brain. Notice that before signals were repeatedly sent across the synapse, just one spine (shown in white) appears on this part of the dendrite. Afterward, there are two spines. The creation and changing of many individual synapses in the brain appears to underlie the formation and storage of new memories.

Source: Toni et al. (1999).

(e.g., Furey, Pietrini, & Haxby, 2000; Li, Cullen, et al., 2003). The memory problems seen in people with Alzheimer's disease are related to a deficiency in neurons that use acetylcholine and send fibres to the hippocampus and the cortex (Muir, 1997). Drugs that interfere with the action of acetylcholine impair memory, and drugs that increase the amount of acetylcholine in synapses improve memory in aging animals and humans (Pettit, Shao, & Yakel, 2001; Sirvio, 1999).

In short, research has shown that the formation of memories is associated with changes in many individual synapses that, together, strengthen and improve the communication in networks of neurons (Malleret et al., 2001; Rosenzweig & Bennett, 1996). These findings provide some support for the ideas formulated by Hebb many years ago.

Brain Structures and Memory

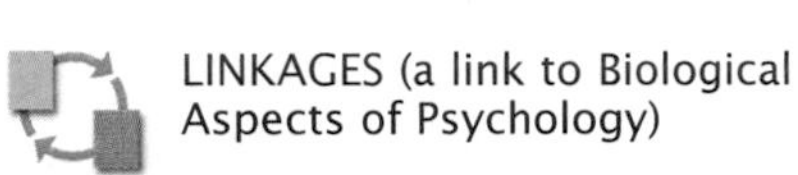
LINKAGES (a link to Biological Aspects of Psychology)

Are the biochemical processes involved in memory concentrated in certain regions, or are they distributed throughout the brain? The latest research suggests that memory involves both specialized regions for various types of memory formation and widespread areas for storage. Several of the brain regions shown in Figure 7.19, including the hippocampus and nearby parts of the cortex and the thalamus, are vital to the formation of new memories. Evidence for the memory-related functions of these regions comes from two main sources. First, there are case studies of patients with brain injuries that allow neuropsychologists to determine how damage to specific brain areas is related to specific kinds of memory problems. Second, studies using PET scans, functional MRI, and other neuro-imaging methods (described in the chapter on biological aspects of psychology) have allowed neuroscientists to observe where brain activity is concentrated as normal people perform various memory tasks. Data from these two sources are leading to an ever-growing understanding of how the brain encodes and retrieves memories.

The Impact of Brain Damage Research has confirmed that the hippocampus, which is part of the limbic system, is among the brain regions involved in the formation of new memories. Damage to the hippocampus often results in **anterograde amnesia,** a loss of memory for any event occurring after the injury. The case of H. M. provides a striking example of anterograde amnesia (Milner, 1966). When H. M. was 27 years old, part of his hippocampus was removed to end his

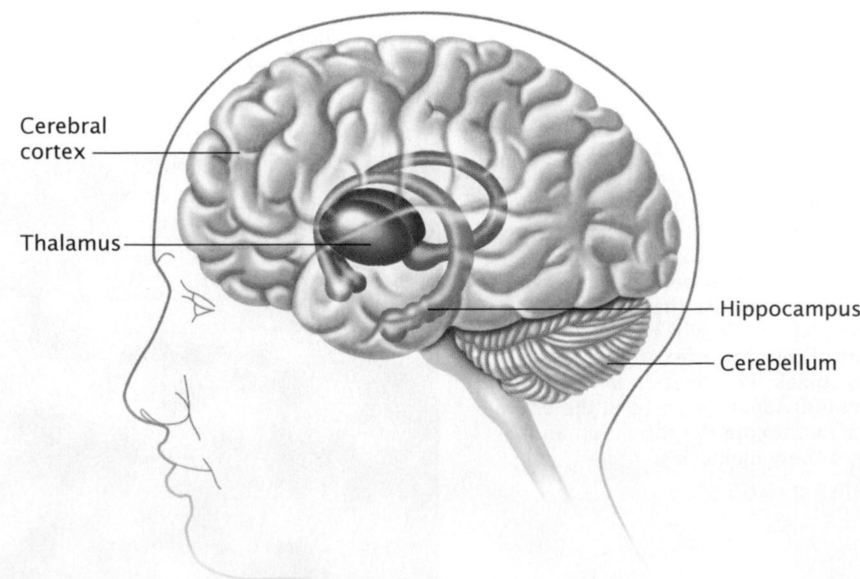

figure 7.19

Some Brain Structures Involved in Memory

Combined neural activity in many parts of the brain allows us to encode, store, and retrieve memories. The complexity of the biological bases of these processes is underscored by research showing that different aspects of a memory—such as the sights and sounds associated with some event—are stored in different parts of the cerebral cortex.

severe epileptic seizures. Afterward, both his long-term and short-term memory appeared normal, but he had a severe problem. Two years after the operation, he still believed that he was 27. When his family moved into a new house, H. M. could not remember the new address or even how to get there. When told that his uncle had died, he grieved in a normal way. But soon afterward, he began to ask why his uncle had not visited him. He had to be repeatedly reminded of the death and, each time, he became just as upset as when he was first told. The surgery had apparently destroyed the mechanism that transfers information from short-term to long-term memory. Now in his 70s, H. M. lives in a nursing home, where his only long-term memories are from 50 years ago, before the operation. He is still unable to recall events and facts he has experienced since then—not even the names of people he sees every day (Corkin, 2002; Hathaway, 2002).

Although patients with anterograde amnesia cannot form episodic memories following hippocampal damage, they may still be able to form implicit memories. For example, H. M. was presented with a complicated puzzle on which mistakes are common and performance gradually improves with practice. Over several days his performance steadily improved, just as it does with normal people, and eventually it became virtually perfect. But each time he tried the puzzle, he insisted that he had never seen it before (Cohen & Corkin, 1981; see Figure 9.4 for another example). A musician with a similar kind of brain damage was able to use his implicit memory to continue leading choral groups (Vattano, 2000). Other researchers, too, have found intact implicit memory in patients who have anterograde amnesia for new episodic material (Squire & McKee, 1992; Tulving, Hayman, & Macdonald, 1991). These patients are also able to keep information temporarily in working memory, which depends on the activity of dopamine neurons in the prefrontal cortex (Williams & Goldman-Rakic, 1995). So the hippocampus is crucial in the formation of new episodic memories, but implicit memory, procedural memory, and working memory appear to be governed by other regions of the brain (Squire, 1992).

Retrograde amnesia involves a loss of memory for events that occurred *before* a brain injury. This condition is also consistent with the idea that memory processes are widely distributed. Often, a person with retrograde amnesia is unable to remember anything that took place in the months, or even years, before the injury (Kapur, 1999). In 1994, head injuries from a car crash left 36-year-old Perlene Griffith-Barwell with retrograde amnesia so severe that she forgot virtually everything she had learned about everything and everybody over the previous 20 years. She thought she was still 16 and did not recognize her husband, Malcolm, or her four children. She said, "The children were sweet, but they didn't seem like mine," and she "didn't feel anything" for Malcolm. Her memories of the 20 years before the accident have never fully returned. She is divorced, but she still lives with her children and holds a job in a bank (Weinstein, 1999). Unlike Perlene, most victims of retrograde amnesia gradually recover their memories (Riccio, Millin, & Gisquet-Verrier, 2003). The most distant events are recalled first, and the person gradually regains memory for events leading up to the injury.

Recovery is seldom complete, however, and the person may never remember the last few seconds before the injury (Baddeley, 1982). Cases of retrograde amnesia that covers the minutes or hours before a blow to the head have led researchers to suggest that as memories are transferred from short-term memory to long-term memory, they are initially unstable and therefore vulnerable to disruption (Dudai, 2004). It may take minutes, hours, or days before these memories are fully solidified, or *consolidated* (Donegan & Thompson, 1991).

This consolidation process appears to depend on movement of electrochemical impulses within clusters of neurons in the brain (Berman, 1991; Taubenfeld et al., 2001). Accordingly, conditions that suppress neural activity in the brain may also disrupt the transfer of information from short-term to long-term memory. These conditions include anesthetic drugs, poisoning by carbon monoxide or other toxins, and strong electrical impulses such as those in the electroconvulsive therapy that is

anterograde amnesia A loss of memory for any event that occurs after a brain injury.

retrograde amnesia A loss of memory for events prior to a brain injury.

A Famous Case of Retrograde Amnesia After Ralf Schumacher slammed his race car into a wall during the United States Grand Prix in June of 2004, he sustained a severe concussion that left him with no memory of the crash. Retrograde amnesia is relatively common following concussions, so if you ride a motorcycle, wear that helmet!

sometimes used to treat cases of severe depression (see the chapter on treatment of psychological disorders).

An additional clue to the role of specific brain areas in memory comes from research on people with *Korsakoff's syndrome,* a disorder that usually occurs in chronic alcoholics. These people's brains become unable to use glucose as fuel, resulting in severe and widespread brain damage. Damage to the mediodoursal nucleus of the thalamus is particularly implicated in the memory problems typical of these patients, which can include both anterograde and retrograde amnesia (Squire, Amara, & Press, 1992). Moreover, like patients with hippocampal damage, Korsakoff's patients show impairments in the ability to form new episodic memories but retain some implicit memory abilities. Research has demonstrated that damage to the prefrontal cortex (also common in Korsakoff's patients) is related to disruptions in remembering the order in which events occur (Squire, 1992). Other studies have found that regions within the prefrontal cortex are involved in working memory in both animals and humans (D'Esposito et al., 1995; Goldman-Rakic, 1994; Smith, 2000).

Applications of Memory Research

Some questions remain about what memory is and how it works, but the results of memory research offer many valuable guidelines to help people improve their memories and function more effectively (Neisser, 2000).

Improving Your Memory

The most valuable memory enhancement strategies are based on the elaboration of incoming information, and especially on linking new information to what you already know.

Mnemonics Psychologists have found that people with normal memory skills, and even those with brain damage, can improve their memory through the use of **mnemonics** (pronounced "nee-MON-ix"). Named for Mnemosyne, the Greek goddess of memory, mnemonics are strategies for placing information into an organized context in order to remember it. For example, to remember the names of

mnemonics Strategies for placing information in an organized context in order to remember it.

the Great Lakes, you might use the acronym HOMES (for Huron, Ontario, Michigan, Erie, and Superior). Verbal organization is the basis for many mnemonics. You can link items by weaving them into a story, a sentence, or a rhyme. To help customers remember where they have parked their cars, some large garages have replaced section designations such as "A1" or "G8" with labels that use colours, animal names, or months. Customers can then tie the location of their cars to information already in long-term memory—for example, "I parked in the month of my mother's birthday."

One simple but powerful mnemonic is called the *method of loci* (pronounced "LOW-sigh"), or the method of places. To use this method, first think about a set of familiar locations—in your home, for example. You might imagine walking through the front door, around all four corners of the living room, and through each of the other rooms. Next, imagine that each item to be remembered is in one of these locations. Whenever you want to remember a list, use the same locations, in the same order. Creating vivid, unusual images of how these items appear in each location seems to be particularly effective (Kline & Groninger, 1991). For example, tomatoes smashed against the front door or bananas hanging from the bedroom ceiling might be helpful in recalling these items on a grocery list.

Guidelines for More Effective Studying The success of mnemonic strategies demonstrates again the importance of relating new information to knowledge already stored in memory. All mnemonic systems require that you have a well-learned body of knowledge (such as locations) that can be used to provide a context for organizing incoming information (Hilton, 1986). When you want to remember more complex material, such as a textbook chapter, the same principles apply (Palmisano & Herrmann, 1991). You can improve your memory for text material by first creating an outline or some other overall context for learning, rather than by just reading and rereading (Glover et al., 1990). Repetition may *seem* effective, because it keeps material in short-term memory; but for retaining information over long periods, repetition alone tends to be ineffective, no matter how much time you spend on it (Bjork, 1999; Bjorklund & Green, 1992). In short, "work smarter, not harder."

In addition, spend your time wisely. *Distributed practice* is much more effective than *massed practice* for learning new information. If you are going to spend ten hours studying for a test, you will be much better off studying for ten one-hour blocks (separated by periods of sleep and other activity) than "cramming" for one ten-hour block. By scheduling more study sessions, you will stay fresh and tend to think about the material from a new perspective at each session. This method will help you elaborate on the material (elaborative rehearsal) and remember it better.

Reading a Textbook More specific advice for remembering textbook material comes from a study that examined how successful and unsuccessful university students approach their reading (Whimbey, 1976). Unsuccessful students tend to read the material straight through. They do not slow down when they reach a difficult section, and they keep going even when they don't understand what they are reading. In contrast, successful students monitor their understanding, reread difficult sections, and stop now and then to review what they have learned. In other words, effective learners engage in a deep level of processing. They are active learners, thinking of each new fact in relation to other material, and they develop a context in which many new facts can be organized effectively.

Research on memory suggests two specific guidelines for reading a textbook. First, make sure that you understand what you are reading before moving on (Herrmann & Searleman, 1992). Second, use the *PQ4R method* (Thomas & Robinson, 1972), which is one of the most successful strategies for remembering textbook material (Anderson, 1990; Chastain & Thurber, 1989). PQ4R stands for six activities to engage in when you read a chapter: *preview, question, read, reflect, recite,* and *review*. These activities are designed to increase the depth to which you process the information you read and should be done as follows:

1. ***Preview.*** First, take a few minutes to skim the chapter. Look at the section headings and any boldfaced or italicized terms. Get a general idea of what material will be discussed, the way it is organized, and how its topics relate to one another and to what you already know. Some students find it useful to survey the entire chapter once and then survey each major section in a little more detail before reading it.
2. ***Question.*** Before reading each section, ask yourself what content will be covered and what information you should be getting from it.
3. ***Read.*** Now read the text, but *think about* the material as you read. Are you understanding the material? Are the questions you raised earlier being answered?
4. ***Reflect.*** As you read, think of your own examples—and create visual images—of the concepts and phenomena you encounter. Ask yourself what the material means, and consider how each section relates to other sections in the chapter and to other chapters in the book (this book's Linkages features are designed to promote this kind of reflection).
5. ***Recite.*** At the end of each section, recite the major points. Resist the temptation to be passive and say, "Oh, I'll remember that." Be active. Put the ideas into your own words by reciting them aloud.
6. ***Review.*** Finally, at the end of the chapter, review all the material. You should see connections not only within each section but also among sections. The objective is to see how the material is organized. Once you grasp the organization, the individual facts will be far easier to remember.

By following these procedures you will learn and remember the material better, and you will also save yourself considerable time.

Lecture Notes Effective note-taking during lectures is a vital skill that can be learned and that improves with practice (Pauk, 2002). Research on memory suggests some simple strategies for taking and using notes effectively.

Realize first that when taking notes, more is not necessarily better. Taking detailed notes of everything you hear requires that you pay close attention to unimportant, as well as important, content, leaving little time for thinking about the material. Note-takers who concentrate on expressing the major ideas in relatively few words remember more than those who try to catch every detail (Pauk & Fiore, 2000). The best way to take notes is to think about what is being said, draw connections with other material in the lecture, and then summarize the major points clearly and concisely (Kiewra, 1989).

Once you have a set of lecture notes, review them as soon as possible after the lecture so that you can fill in missing details. (Remember that most forgetting from long-term memory occurs within the first few hours after learning.) When the time comes for serious study, use your notes as if they were a chapter in a textbook. Write a detailed outline. Think about how various points are related. Once you have organized the material, the details will make more sense and will be much easier to remember. ("In Review: Improving Your Memory" summarizes tips for studying.)

Understand and Remember Research on memory suggests that students who simply read their textbooks will not remember as much as those who, like this woman, read for understanding using the PQ4R method. Further, memory for the material is likely to be better if you read and study it over a number of weeks rather than in one marathon session on the night before a test.

Design for Memory

The scientific study of memory has influenced the design of the electronic and mechanical devices that play an increasingly important role in our lives. Those who design computers, MP3 and DVD players, digital cameras, and even microwave ovens are faced with a choice: Either place the operating instructions on the devices

in review Improving Your Memory

Goal	Helpful Techniques
Remembering lists of items	Use mnemonics. Look for meaningful acronyms. Try the method of loci.
Remembering textbook material	Follow the PQ4R system. Allocate your time to allow for distributed practice. Read actively, not passively.
Taking lecture notes	Take notes, but record only the main points. Think about the overall organization of the material. Review your notes as soon after the lecture as possible in order to fill in missing points.
Studying for exams	Write a detailed outline of your lecture notes rather than passively reading them.

themselves, or assume that users will remember how to operate them. Understanding the limits of both working memory and long-term memory has helped designers distinguish between information that is likely to be stored in (and easily retrieved from) the user's memory and information that should be presented in the form of labels, instructions, or other cues that reduce memory demands (Norman, 1988). Placing unfamiliar or hard-to-recall information in plain view makes it easier to use the device as intended and with fewer chances for errors (Segal & Suri, 1999).

Psychologists have influenced advertisers and designers to create many other "user-friendly" systems (Wickens, Gordon, & Liu, 1998). As a result, toll-free numbers are designed to take advantage of chunking, which, as mentioned earlier, provides an efficient way to maintain information in working memory. Which do you think would be easier to remember: 1-800-438-4357 or 1-800-GET-HELP? Obviously, the more meaningful "get help" number is more memorable (there are Web sites that can help you translate any phone number into words or a phrase). Designers ensure that on-board auto navigation systems provide audible reminders about where to turn and that turn signals emit an audible cue when activated. Features such as these help reduce your memory load while driving and leave you with enough working memory capacity to keep in mind that there is a car in your "blind spot."

As ever more complex devices appear in the marketplace, it will be increasingly important that instructions about how to operate them are presented clearly and memorably. With guidance from research on memory, it should be possible for almost anyone to operate these devices efficiently.

LINKAGES

As noted in the chapter on introducing psychology, all of psychology's subfields are related to one another. Our discussion of the accuracy of eyewitnesses' memories illustrates just one way in which the topic of this chapter, memory, is linked to the subfield of perception (see the chapter on perception). The Linkages diagram shows ties to two other subfields as well, and there are many more ties throughout the book. Looking for linkages among subfields will help you see how they all fit together and help you better appreciate the big picture that is psychology.

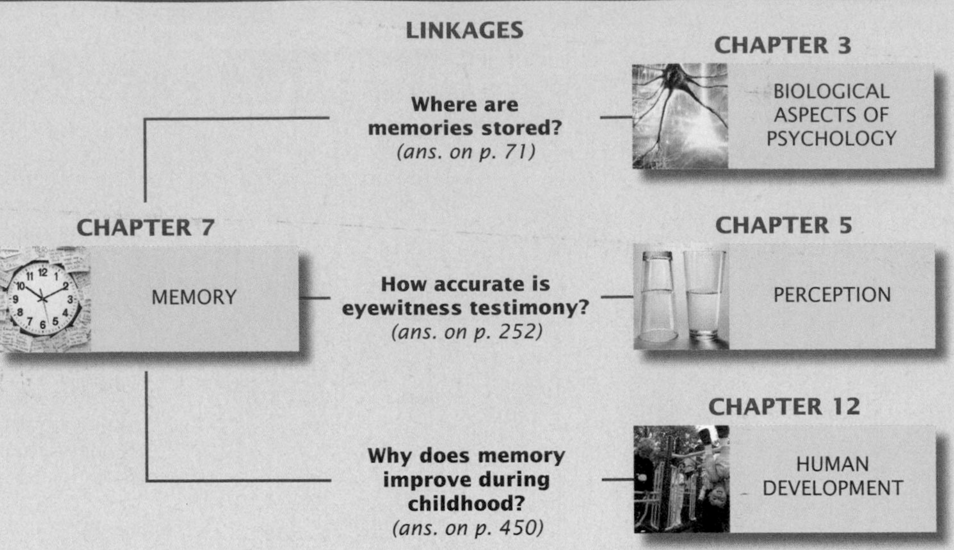

LINKAGES
CHAPTER 7
MEMORY
Where are memories stored?
(ans. on p. 71)
CHAPTER 3
BIOLOGICAL ASPECTS OF PSYCHOLOGY
How accurate is eyewitness testimony?
(ans. on p. 252)
CHAPTER 5
PERCEPTION
Why does memory improve during childhood?
(ans. on p. 450)
CHAPTER 12
HUMAN DEVELOPMENT

SUMMARY

The Nature of Memory

Human memory depends on a complex mental system.

Basic Memory Processes

There are three basic memory processes. *Encoding* transforms information into some type of mental representation. Encoding can be *acoustic* (by sound), *visual* (by appearance), or *semantic* (by meaning). *Storage* maintains information in the memory system over time. *Retrieval* is the process of gaining access to previously stored information.

Types of Memory

Most psychologists agree that there are at least three types of memory. *Episodic memory* contains information about specific events in a person's life. *Semantic memory* contains generalized knowledge about the world. *Procedural memory* contains information about how to do various things.

Explicit and Implicit Memory

Some research on memory concerns *explicit memory*, the processes through which people intentionally try to remember something. Psychologists also examine *implicit memory*, which refers to the unintentional influence of prior experiences.

Models of Memory

Four theoretical models of memory have guided most research. According to the *levels-of-processing model*, the most important determinant of memory is how extensively information is encoded or processed when it is first received. In general, *elaborative rehearsal* is more effective than *maintenance rehearsal* in learning new information, because it represents a deeper level of processing. According to the *transfer-appropriate processing model*, the critical determinant of memory is not how deeply information is encoded but whether processes used during retrieval match those used during encoding. *Parallel distributed processing (PDP) models* of memory suggest that new experiences not only provide specific information but also become part of, and alter, a whole network of associations. And the *information-processing model* suggests that in order for information to become firmly embedded in memory, it must pass through three stages of processing: sensory memory, short-term memory, and long-term memory.

Storing New Memories

Sensory Memory

Sensory memory maintains incoming information in the *sensory registers* for a very brief time. *Selective attention*, which focuses mental resources on only part of the stimulus field, controls what information in the sensory registers is actually perceived and transferred to short-term and working memory.

Short-Term Memory and Working Memory

Working memory is a system that allows us to store, organize, and manipulate information in order to think, solve problems, and make decisions. The storage, or maintenance, component of working memory is referred to as *short-term memory*. Remembering a phone number long enough to call it involves simple maintenance of the information in short-term memory.

Various memory codes can be used in short-term memory, but acoustic codes seem to dominate in most verbal tasks. Studies of the *immediate memory span* indicate that the storage capacity of short-term memory is approximately seven *chunks*, or meaningful groupings of information. Studies using the *Brown-Peterson procedure* show that information in short-term memory is usually forgotten within about 18 seconds if it is not rehearsed.

Long-Term Memory

Long-term memory normally involves semantic encoding, which means that people tend to encode the general meaning of information, not specific details, in long-term memory. The capacity of long-term memory to store new information is extremely large, and perhaps even unlimited.

Distinguishing Between Short-Term and Long-Term Memory

According to some psychologists, there is no need to distinguish between short-term and long-term memory. Still, some evidence suggests that these systems are distinct. For example, the *primacy* and *recency effects* that occur when people try to recall a list of words may indicate the presence of two different systems.

Retrieving Memories

Retrieval Cues and Encoding Specificity

Retrieval cues help people remember things that they would otherwise not be able to recall. The effectiveness of retrieval cues follows the *encoding specificity principle*: Cues help retrieval only if they match some feature of the information that was originally encoded.

Context and State Dependence

All else being equal, memory may be better when one attempts to retrieve information in the same environment in which it was learned; this is called *context-dependent memory*. When a person's internal state can aid or impede retrieval, the person is said to have *state-dependent memory*.

Retrieval from Semantic Memory

Researchers usually study retrieval from semantic memory by examining how long it takes people to answer general knowledge questions. It appears that ideas are represented as associations in a dense semantic memory network and that the retrieval of information occurs by a process of *spreading activation*. Each concept in the network is represented as a collection of features or attributes. The tip-of-the-tongue phenomenon and the feeling-of-knowing experience represent the retrieval of incomplete knowledge.

A PDP Model of Memory

In the process of developing memory, people often use their existing knowledge to fill in gaps in the information they encode and retrieve. Parallel distributed processing models provide one explanation of how people make spontaneous generalizations about the world. They also explain the *schemas* that shape the memories people construct.

Forgetting

How Do We Forget?

In his research on long-term memory and forgetting, Hermann Ebbinghaus introduced the *method of savings*. He found that most forgetting from long-term memory occurs during the first several hours after learning and that savings can be extremely long lasting.

Why Do We Forget? The Roles of Decay and Interference

Decay and *interference* are two mechanisms of forgetting. Although there is evidence of both decay and interference in short-term memory, it appears that most forgetting from long-term memory is due to either *retroactive interference* or *proactive interference*.

Biological Bases of Memory

The Biochemistry of Memory

Research has shown that memory can result as new synapses are formed in the brain and as communication at existing synapses is improved. Several neurotransmitters appear to be involved in the strengthening that occurs at synapses.

Brain Structures and Memory

Neuro-imaging studies of normal people, as well as research with patients with *anterograde amnesia, retrograde amnesia,* Korsakoff's syndrome, and other memory problems, provide valuable information about the brain structures involved in memory. The hippocampus and thalamus are known to play a role in the formation of memories. These structures send nerve fibres to the cerebral cortex, in which memories are probably stored and which is activated during memory retrieval. Memories appear to be both localized and distributed throughout the brain.

Applications of Memory Research

Improving Your Memory

Among the many applications of memory research are *mnemonics,* devices that are used to remember things better. One of the simplest but most powerful mnemonics is the method of loci. It is useful because it provides a context for organizing material more effectively. Guidelines for effective studying have also been derived from memory research. For example, the key to remembering textbook material is to read actively rather than passively. One of the most effective ways to do this is to follow the PQ4R method: preview, question, read, reflect, recite, and review. To take good lecture notes and to study them effectively, organize the points into a meaningful framework and think about how each main point relates to the others.

Design for Memory

Research on the limits of memory has helped product designers to create more user-friendly electronic and mechanical systems and devices.

8 Cognition and Language

What are you thinking right now? This is actually a hard question because thoughts don't come to us in clear, complete sentences. We have to construct those sentences—using the language we've learned—from the words, images, ideas, and other mental materials in our minds. In this chapter, we explore what thoughts are, what language is, and how we translate one into the other as we reason, make decisions, and solve problems. Here's how we have organized the discussion:

In the early fall of 2005, a mysterious illness claimed the lives of six residents at a Toronto area nursing home. At least 77 other residents and some staff members had symptoms which included high fever, cough, chills, muscle pain, and headaches. The Ontario Public Health Lab issued a press release on October 3 stating that testing had been conducted for over a dozen different viruses and bacteria including influenza, avian flu, and SARS, but none of the tests had yielded positive results (CBC Unlocked, 2005). The nursing home was closed to visitors and new residents while the investigation continued. Finally, after autopsy results were obtained, the illness was identified as Legionnaire's Disease. This illness is caused by bacteria that grow in warm water and is contracted by breathing air contaminated by water droplets. Investigators determined that a faulty ventilation system in the nursing home was to blame for the outbreak (City of Toronto, 2005). To solve this mystery, doctors relied on their ability to think, solve problems, and to make judgments and decisions. They used these higher mental processes to weigh the pros and cons of various hypotheses and to reach decisions about what tests to order and how to interpret them. They also consulted with patients and other physicians, using that remarkable human ability known as *language*.

As described in the chapter on the biological aspects of psychology, these vital skills depend on the proper functioning of the brain. Anything that disrupts that functioning can drastically impair cognitive abilities. For example, "Elliot," an intelligent and successful young businessman, had a cancerous tumour removed from the frontal area of his brain. After the surgery, neurologist Antonio Damasio found that Elliot's language, memory, and perceptual processes remained intact but that his ability to make complex business decisions and rational plans was virtually gone. In fact, a series of reckless, impulsive business schemes had already forced him into bankruptcy (Damasio, 1994).

These cases highlight the fact that our success in life depends largely on our cognitive and language skills. When those skills are impaired, by biological or other factors, we become vulnerable to all sorts of failures and errors. What pitfalls threaten the effectiveness of human cognition? What factors influence our success? How are our thoughts transformed into language? Many of the answers to these questions come from **cognitive psychology,** the study of the mental processes by which the information humans receive from their environment is modified, made meaningful, stored, retrieved, used, and communicated to others (Neisser, 1967; Reed, 2004). Many cognitive psychologists are working with biological psychologists and other neuroscientists to study the brain activity involved in these mental processes. Their collaboration in the rapidly developing field of *cognitive neuroscience* (e.g., D'Esposito, 2003) is leading to a better understanding of the relationship between mind and brain.

In this chapter we examine two major aspects of human cognition: thought and language. First we consider what thought is and what functions it serves. Then we examine the basic ingredients of thought and the cognitive processes people use as they interact with their environment. These cognitive processes include reasoning, problem solving, and decision making. Next, we discuss language and how it is acquired and used. We discuss thought and language in the same chapter because thinking and communicating often involve the same cognitive processes. Learning about thought helps us to better understand language, and learning about language helps us to better understand thought.

Basic Functions of Thought

cognitive psychology The study of the mental processes by which information from the environment is modified, made meaningful, stored, retrieved, used, and communicated to others.

Let's begin our exploration of human cognition by considering the five core functions of thought, which are to *describe, elaborate, decide, plan,* and *guide action.* These functions can be seen as forming a *circle of thought* (see Figure 8.1).

The Circle of Thought

Consider how the circle of thought operated in the doctors examining the mystery illness. It began when they received the information about symptoms that allowed them to *describe* the problem. Next, they *elaborated* on this information by using their knowledge and experience to consider what disorders might cause such symptoms. Then they made a *decision* to investigate a possible cause, such as influenza. To implement this decision, they made a *plan*—to order tests—and then *acted* on that plan. But the circle of thought did not stop there. Information from the tests provided new descriptive information, which the doctors elaborated further to reach another decision, create a new plan, and guide their next action. Each stage in the circle of thought was also influenced by *intention*—in this case, to find and cure the patients' problem.

Usually, the circle of thought spins so quickly, and its processes are so complex, that slowing it down enough for scientific analysis might seem impossible. Some psychologists approach this difficult task by studying thought processes as if they were part of a computer-like information-processing system. An **information-processing system** receives information, represents the information with symbols, and then manipulates those representations. In this information-processing model, then, **thinking** is defined as the manipulation of mental representations. Figure 8.2 shows how an information-processing model might view the sequence of events that form one spin around the circle of thought. Notice that according to this model, information from the world is transformed somewhat as it passes through each stage of processing (Wickens, Gordon, & Liu, 1998).

In the first stage, information about the world reaches the brain by way of the sensory receptors described in the chapter on sensation. This stage does not require attention. In the second stage, the information must be perceived and recognized, using the attentional and perceptual processes described in the chapter on perception. It is also during this stage that the information is consciously elaborated, using short-term and working memory processes that allow us to think about it in relation to knowledge stored in long-term memory. Once the information has been elaborated in this way, we must decide what to do with it. This third stage—decision making—also demands attention. The decision may be simply to store the information in memory. If, however,

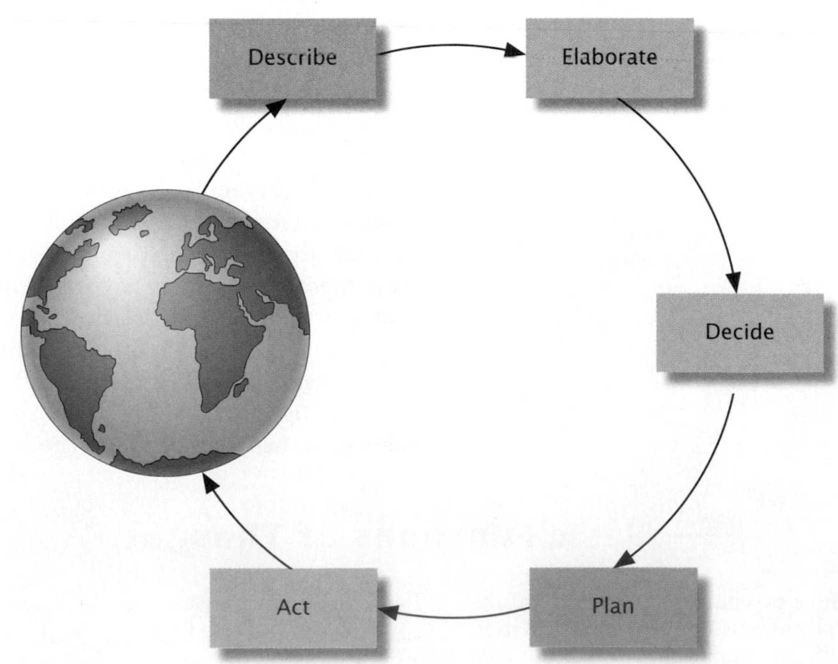

figure 8.1

The Circle of Thought

The circle of thought begins as our sensory systems take in information from the world. Our perceptual system describes and elaborates this information, which is represented in the brain in ways that allow us to make decisions, formulate plans, and guide our actions. As those actions change our world, we receive new information—and the circle of thought begins again.

information-processing system Mechanisms for receiving information, representing it with symbols, and manipulating it.

thinking The manipulation of mental representations.

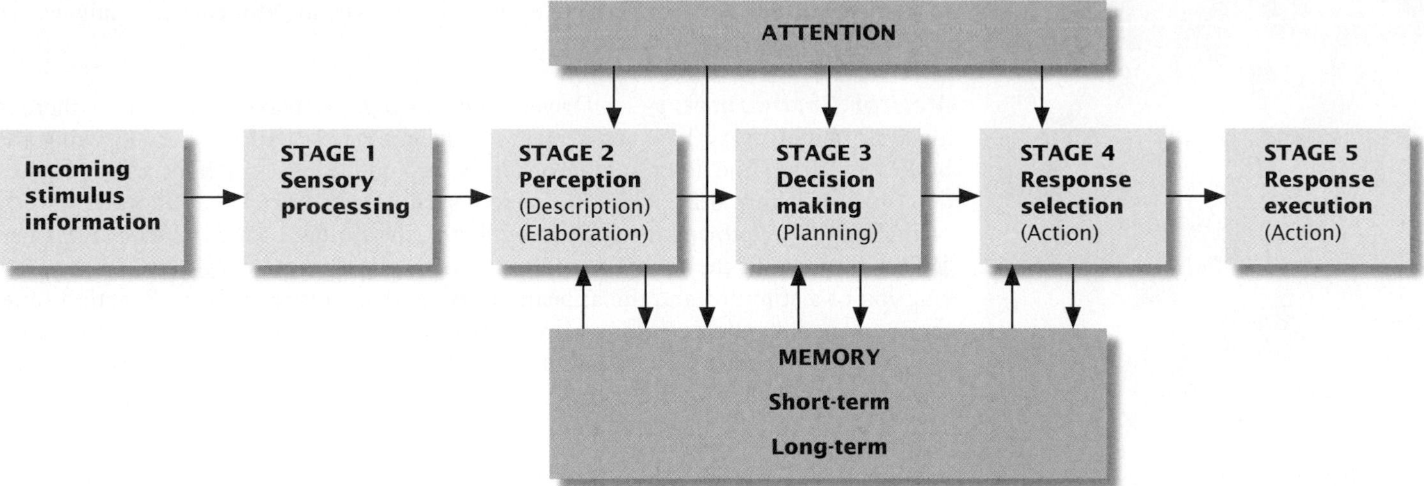

figure 8.2

An Information-Processing Model

According to the information-processing model, each stage in the circle of thought takes a certain amount of time. Some stages depend heavily on both short-term and long-term memory and require some attention—that limited supply of mental energy required for information processing to be carried out efficiently.

a decision is made to take some action, a response must be planned in the third stage and then carried out through a coordinated pattern of responses—the action itself—in the fourth and fifth stages. As suggested in Figure 8.1, this action usually affects the environment, providing new information that is "fed back" to the system for processing in the ongoing circle of thought.

Measuring Information Processing

The brain damage suffered by Dr. Damasio's patient Elliot appeared to have mainly affected the decision-making and response-selection stages of information processing. Analyzing the effects of brain damage is just one of several methods that scientists use

"Automatic" Thinking The sensory, perceptual, decision-making, and response-planning components that make up the circle of thought can occur so rapidly that—as when playing a game—we may be unaware of anything other than incoming information and our quick response to it. In such cases, our thinking processes become so well practised that they are virtually automatic.

Reaction Time When encountering heavy traffic in an unfamiliar city, drivers must make complex decisions quickly. The number of options available and the speed of the traffic often results in visitors to large cities missing their exits and becoming thoroughly lost and confused! Such mistakes are much less likely to happen when driving in a familiar place demanding fewer split-second decisions.

to study the details of how the entire information-processing sequence normally works and what can interfere with it.

Mental Chronometry Drivers and video-game players know that there is always a slight delay between seeing a red light or a "bad guy" and hitting the brakes or firing the laser gun. The delay occurs because each of the processes described in Figure 8.2 takes some time. Psychologists began the laboratory study of thinking by exploring *mental chronometry*, the timing of mental events (Posner, 1978). Specifically, they examined **reaction time,** the time elapsing between the presentation of a stimulus and the appearance of an overt response to it. Reaction time, they reasoned, would give us an idea of how long it takes for all the processes shown in Figure 8.2 to occur. In a typical reaction-time experiment, a person is asked to say a word or to push a button as rapidly as possible after a stimulus appears. Even in such simple situations, several factors influence reaction times (Wickens, Gordon, & Liu, 1998).

One important factor in reaction time is the *complexity* of the decision. The more options we have in responding to a set of stimuli, the longer the reaction time. The tennis player who knows that her opponent usually serves to a particular spot on the court will have a simple decision to make when the serve is completed and will react rapidly. But if she faces an opponent whose serve is less predictable, her reaction will be slower, because a more complex decision about which way to move is now required.

Expectancy, too, affects reaction time. People respond faster to stimuli that they are expecting and more slowly to stimuli that surprise them. So your reaction time will be shorter when braking for a traffic light that you knew might turn red than when dodging a ball thrown at you unexpectedly.

Reaction time is also influenced by *stimulus-response compatibility*. If the relationship between a set of stimuli and possible responses is a natural or compatible one, reaction time will be fast. If not, reaction time will be slower. Figure 8.3 illustrates compatible and incompatible relationships. Incompatible stimulus-response relationships are major culprits in causing errors in the use of all kinds of equipment, especially if it is unfamiliar or if the operator is under stress (Casey, 1993; Proctor & Van Zandt, 1994; Segal & Suri, 1999).

Finally, in any reaction-time task, there is a *speed-accuracy tradeoff*. If you try to respond quickly, errors increase. If you try for an error-free performance, reaction time increases (Wickens & Carswell, 1997). At a swimming meet, for example, contestants who try too hard to anticipate the starting gun may have especially quick starts but may also have especially frequent false starts that disqualify them.

Evoked Brain Potentials Research on reaction time has helped establish the time required for information processing to occur. It has also revealed how the

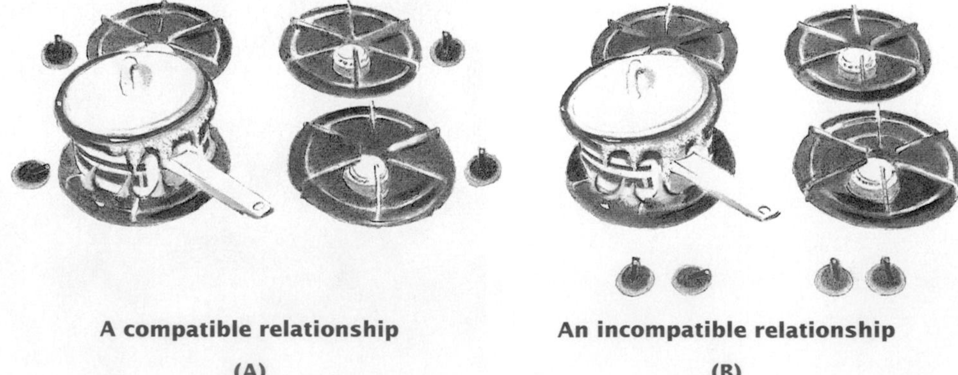

figure 8.3

Stimulus-Response Compatibility

Imagine standing in front of an unfamiliar stove when a pot starts to boil over. Your reaction time in turning down the heat will depend in part on the stove's design. The response you make will be quicker on the stove in Part A, because each knob is next to the burner it controls. There is compatibility between the source of the stimulus and the location of the response. The stove in Part B shows less compatibility. Here, which knob you should turn is not as obvious, so your reaction time will be slower.

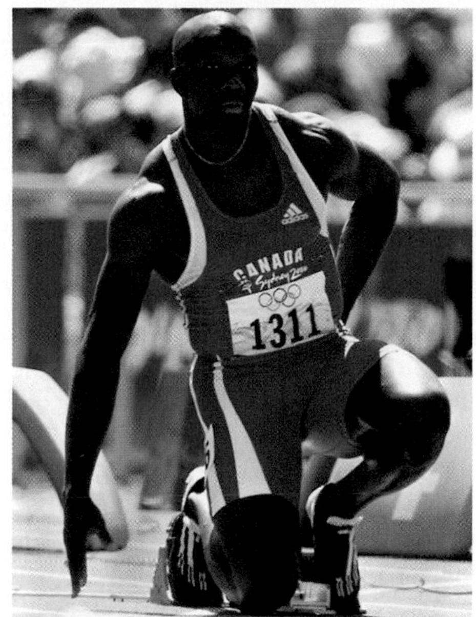

On Your Mark . . . The runner who reacts quickest to the starting gun will have an advantage over other competitors, but too much eagerness can cause an athlete to literally jump the gun and lose the race before it starts. Yet trying too hard to avoid a false start can slow reaction time and cost precious time in getting off the mark. Canadian runner, Donovan Bailey, shown in this picture, is known for his false start at the 2000 Summer Olympics. Once the world's fastest man, he finished last in his heat. This is the speed-accuracy tradeoff in action.

entire sequence can be made faster or slower. But reaction times alone cannot provide a detailed picture of what goes on between the presentation of a stimulus and the execution of a response. They do not tell us, for example, how long the perception stage lasts. Nor do they tell us whether we respond more quickly to an expected stimulus because we perceive it faster or because we make a decision about it faster. Reaction-time measures have been used in many ingenious efforts to make inferences about such things (Coles, 1989); but to analyze mental events more directly, psychologists have turned to other methods, such as the analysis of evoked brain potentials.

The **evoked brain potential** is a small, temporary change in voltage on an *electroencephalogram* (EEG) that occurs in response to specific events (Rugg & Coles, 1995). Figure 8.4 shows an example. Each peak on the EEG reflects the firing of large groups of neurons, within different regions of the brain, at different times during the information-processing sequence. The pattern of the peaks provides information that is more precise than overall reaction time. For example, a large positive peak, called the P300, occurs 300 to 500 milliseconds (thousandths of a second) after a stimulus is presented. The exact delay before a P300 occurs is a sensitive measure of how long it takes to complete the first two stages of information processing shown in Figure 8.2. Further, the size of the P300 reflects the operation of attention in the second of those stages. For example, P300s are normally larger in response to unusual or surprising stimuli than to monotonous or predictable ones. If this were not the case, there may be a problem, as was revealed in a study of university students who had suffered concussions. Although these students showed no obvious symptoms of brain damage, their P300s to surprising stimuli were abnormally small, which suggested some lingering disruption in their brains' information processing capacity (Lavoie et al., 2004).

Neuro-imaging Using positron emission tomography (PET), functional magnetic resonance imaging (fMRI), and other neuro-imaging techniques described in the chapter on biological aspects of psychology, cognitive neuroscientists can now watch what happens in the brain during information processing (e.g., Miller & Cohen, 2001; Posner & DiGirolamo, 2001). In one study, for example, participants performed a task that required complex problem-solving skills. As shown by the red-shaded areas in Figure 8.5, the frontal lobe of the brain was especially active when this task was still relatively new and difficult. As the participants learned the skills, however, this frontal lobe involvement decreased. When the task was well learned, the hippocampus became especially active (see the green-shaded areas in the bottom panel of Figure 8.5). Activation in the hippocampus suggests that the participants were no longer struggling with a problem-solving task but instead were performing it from memory.

A number of other studies of brain activity during the performance of cognitive tasks have also found that the frontal lobes are especially important for problem solving and other cognitive tasks that place heavy demands on attention and working memory (Duncan & Owen, 2000; Wallis, Anderson, & Miller, 2001; this chapter's Focus on Research Methods shows another example). These tasks involve coordinated activity in many other brain areas, too (Andrés, 2003), but it is certainly no wonder that damage to Elliot's frontal area disrupted his decision-making abilities.

Mental Representations: The Ingredients of Thought

Just as measuring, stirring, and baking are only part of the story of making cookies, describing the processes involved in thinking tells only part of the story behind the circle of thought. To understand thinking more fully, we also need to know what it is that these processes manipulate. Most psychologists describe the ingredients of thought as *information.* But this is like saying that you make cookies with "stuff." What specific forms does information take in our minds? In other words, how do we mentally represent information? Researchers in cognitive psychology have found that

reaction time The time between the presentation of a stimulus and an overt response to it.

evoked brain potential A small, temporary change in EEG voltage that is evoked by some stimulus.

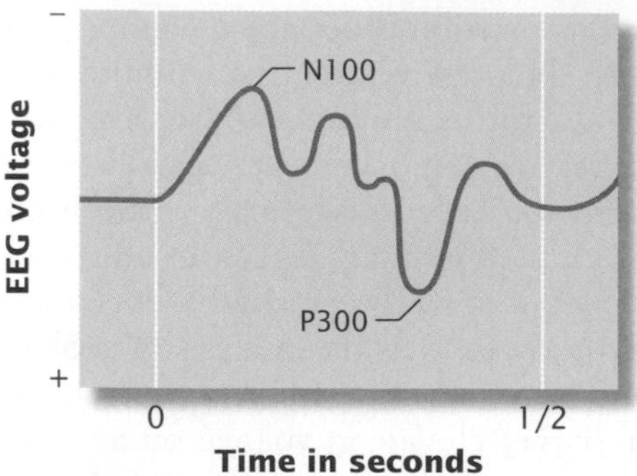

figure 8.4

Evoked Potentials

Here is the average EEG, or brain wave, tracing produced from several trials on which a participant's name was presented. Evoked potentials are averaged in this way so as to eliminate random variations in the tracings. The result is the appearance of a *negative* peak (N100) followed by a large *positive* peak (P300). Traditionally, positive peaks are shown as decreases on such tracings, whereas negative ones are shown as increases.

information can be mentally represented in many ways, including as *concepts, propositions, schemas, scripts, mental models, images,* and *cognitive maps.* Let's consider each of these ingredients of thought and how we manipulate them as we think.

Concepts

When you think about anything—dogs, happiness, sex, movies, pizza—you are manipulating a basic ingredient of thought called *concepts.* **Concepts** are categories of objects, events, or ideas with common properties (Jahnke & Nowaczyk, 1998; Katz & Fodor, 1963). To "have a concept" is to recognize the properties, or *features,* that tend to be shared by the members of the category. For example, the concept "bird" includes such properties as having feathers, laying eggs, and being able to fly. The concept "scissors" includes such properties as having two blades, a connecting hinge, and a pair of finger holes. Concepts allow you to relate each object, event, or idea you encounter to a category you already know. Using concepts, you can say, "No, that's not a dog," or "Yes, that's a car." Concepts also make it possible to think logically. If you have the concepts "whale" and "bird," you can decide whether a whale is bigger than a bird without having either creature in the room with you.

Types of Concepts Some concepts—called **formal concepts**—can be clearly defined by a set of rules or properties such that members of the concept have all of the defining properties and nonmembers don't. For example, the concept "square" can be defined as "a shape with four equal sides and four right-angle corners." Any object that does not have all of these features simply is not a square, and any object with all these features is a square. To study concept learning in the laboratory, psychologists often use formal concepts, because the members of the concept can be neatly defined (Trabasso & Bower, 1968).

figure 8.5

Watching People Think

Cognitive psychologists and other cognitive neuroscientists have found ways to actually watch information processing as it takes place in the brain. These fMRI pictures show activity in two "slices" of the brain of a research participant who was practising a complex problem-solving task. The areas shown in red were activated early in the learning process. As skill developed, the areas shown in green became activated.

(a)

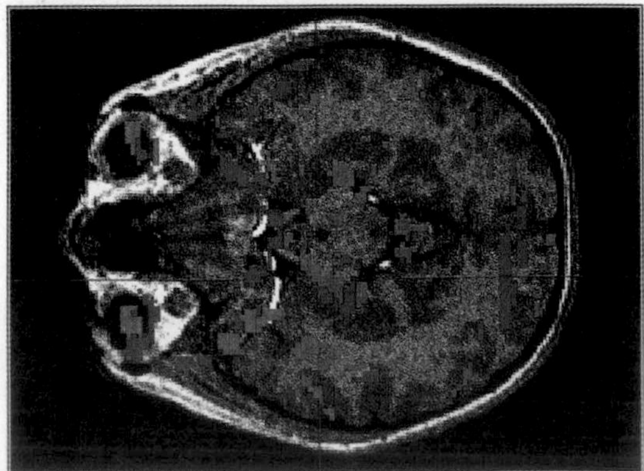

concept A category of objects, events, or ideas that have common properties.

formal concept A concept that can be clearly defined by a set of rules or properties.

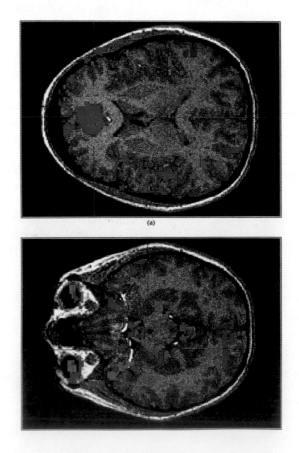

There are many other concepts, though, that can't be defined by a fixed set of necessary features (Wittgenstein, 1953). For example, try listing a small set of features that precisely defines the concept of "game." True, most games are competitive, but some—such as pitch-and-catch or ring-around-the-rosey—are not. And although most games require more than one player, those such as pinball and solitaire don't. Similarly, "home" can be defined as the place where you were born, the house in which you grew up, your current residence, your country of origin, the place where you are most comfortable, and so on. These are just two examples of **natural concepts,** concepts that have no fixed set of defining features but instead have a set of typical, or characteristic, features. Members of a natural concept need not have all of these characteristic features. One characteristic feature of the natural concept "bird," for example, is the ability to fly; but an ostrich is a bird even though it cannot fly. It's a bird because it possesses enough other characteristic features of "bird" (feathers, wings, and the like). Having just one bird property is not enough. A snake lays eggs and a bat flies, but neither one is a bird. It is usually a combination of properties that defines a concept. Outside the laboratory, most of the concepts people use in thinking are natural rather than formal concepts. Natural concepts include relatively concrete object categories, such as "bird" or "house"; abstract idea categories, such as "honesty" or "justice"; and temporary goal-related categories that help people make plans, such as "things I need to pack for my trip" (Barsalou, 1991, 1993).

The boundaries of a natural concept are fuzzy, and some members of it are better examples of the concept than others because they share more of its characteristic features (Rosch, 1975). A robin, a chicken, an ostrich, and a penguin are all birds. But a robin is the best example, because a robin can fly and is closer to the size and shape of what most people have learned to think of as a typical bird. A member of a natural concept that possesses all or most of its characteristic features is called a **prototype,** or is said to be *prototypical* (Smith, 1998). A robin, then, is a prototypical bird. The more prototypical a member of a concept is, the more quickly people can decide if it is an example of the concept. As a result, it takes less time to answer the question "Is a robin a bird?" than "Is a penguin a bird?"

According to Bruce Whittlesea and Jason Leboe at Simon Fraser University in Burnaby, British Columbia, people make judgments about whether a specific item fits into a concept based upon three factors: *fluency, generation,* and *resemblance.*

A Natural Concept A space shuttle and a hot-air balloon are two examples of the natural concept "aircraft," but most people think of the space shuttle, with its wings, as the better example. A prototype of the concept is probably an airplane.

natural concept A concept that has no fixed set of defining features but has a set of characteristic features.

prototype A member of a natural concept that possesses all or most of its characteristic features.

You Can't Judge a Book by Its Cover Our schemas tell us what to expect about objects, events, and people, but those expectations can sometimes be wrong. The person above is Rick Tobias, one of the leaders of Los Silverados motorcycle club and President and CEO of Yonge Street Mission, which is a 110-year-old church-based agency that is dedicated to serving the needs of the poor in Toronto's inner city. Rick also holds an honorary doctorate of divinity from McMaster University, is a graduate of Acadia Divinity College (M.Div.), and is qualified to be ordained as a clergy leader.

Fluency refers to deciding how familiar the object seems to be, *generation* is defined as recalling the context of past experience with the item, and *resemblance* is based on how similar the new item is to other items previously encountered. For example, when you come across a new item in the produce section at the grocery store, you would probably try to figure out what it is. Using the fluency heuristic, you might realize that the item seems familiar. The generation heuristic might lead you to recall that you once ate a fruit salad that contained the item. Finally, using the resemblance heuristic, you notice that the item looks a lot like a cantaloupe. Based on these heuristics, you conclude that the item is some kind of melon (Whittlesea & Leboe, 2000).

Propositions

We often combine concepts in units known as **propositions.** A proposition is a mental representation that expresses a relationship between concepts. Propositions can be true or false. Suppose you hear someone say that your friend Heather broke up with her boyfriend, Jason. Your mental representation of this event will include a proposition that links your concepts of "Heather" and "Jason" in a particular way. This proposition could be diagrammed (using unscientific terms) as follows: Heather→dumped→Jason.

The diagram looks like a sentence, but it isn't one. Propositions can be expressed as sentences, but they are actually general ideas that can be conveyed in any number of specific ways. In this case, "Jason was dumped by Heather" and "Heather is not dating Jason anymore" would all express the same proposition. If you later discover that it was Jason who caused the breakup, your proposition about the event would change to reflect this new information, shown here as reversed arrows: Heather←dumped←Jason.

Propositions are part of the network of associations that many psychologists see as the basis for our knowledge of the world (see Figures 7.10 and 7.11 in the chapter on memory). So hearing the name "Heather," for example, will activate lots of associated information about her, including the proposition about her relationship to Jason.

Schemas, Scripts, and Mental Models

Sets of propositions are often so closely associated that they form more complex mental representations called **schemas.** As described in the chapters on perception, memory, and human development, schemas are generalizations that we develop about categories of objects, places, events, and people. Our schemas help us to understand the world. If you borrow a friend's car, your "car" schema will give you a good idea of where to put the ignition key, where the accelerator and brake are, and how to raise and lower the windows. Schemas also generate expectations about objects, places, events, and people—telling us that stereo systems have speakers, that picnics occur in the summer, that rock concerts are loud, and so on.

Scripts Schemas about familiar activities, such as going to a restaurant, are known as **scripts** (Anderson, 2000). Your "restaurant" script represents the sequence of events you can expect when you go out to eat (see Figure 8.6). That script tells you what to do when you are in a restaurant and helps you to understand stories involving restaurants (Whitney, 2001). Scripts also shape your interpretation of events. For example, on your first day of university, you no doubt assumed that the person standing at the front of the class was a teacher, not a mugger.

If our scripts are violated, however, it is easy to misinterpret events. A heart-attack victim in London, England, lay in the hallway of an apartment building for nine hours after an ambulance crew smelled alcohol on his breath and assumed he was "sleeping it off." The crew's script for what happens in the poorer sections of big cities told them that someone slumped in a hallway is drunk, not sick. Because

proposition A mental representation of the relationship between concepts.

schema A generalization about categories of objects, places, events, and people.

script A mental representation of familiar sequences of activity.

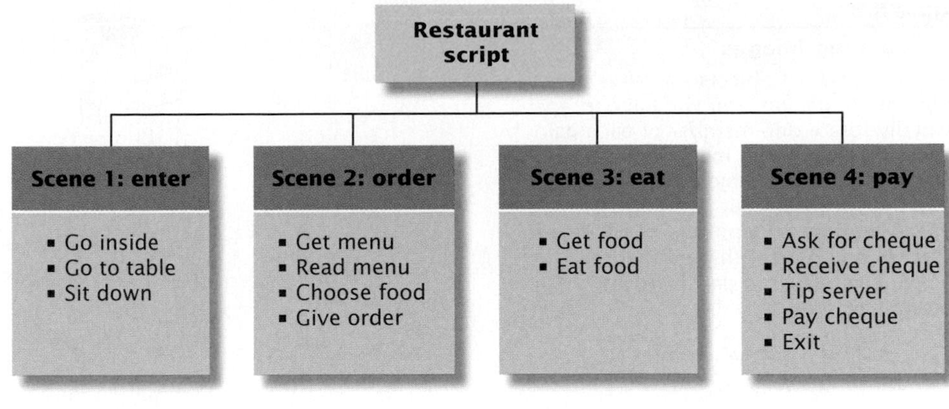

figure 8.6

Eating at a Restaurant

Schemas about what happens in restaurants and how to behave in them take the form of a *script*, represented here in four "scenes." Scripts guide our actions in all sorts of familiar situations and also help us to understand descriptions of events occurring in those situations (e.g., "Our service was really slow").

Source: Whitney (1998).

script-violating events are unexpected, our reactions to them tend to be slower and less effective than are our reactions to expected events. Your "grocery shopping" script, for example, probably includes pushing a cart, putting items in it, going to the checkout stand, and paying for your purchases. But suppose you are at the back of the store when a robber near the entrance fires a gun and shouts at the manager to open the safe. People sometimes ignore these script-violating events, interpreting gunshots as a car backfiring and shouted orders as "someone fooling around." Others simply "freeze," unsure of what to do.

Mental Models Sets of propositions can be organized not only as schemas and scripts but also as **mental models** (Johnson-Laird, 1983). For example, suppose someone tells you, "My living room has blue walls, a white ceiling, and an oval window across from the door." You will mentally represent this information as propositions about how the concepts "wall," "blue," "ceiling," "white," "door," "oval," and "window" are related. However, you will also combine these propositions to create in your mind a three-dimensional model of the room. As more information about the world becomes available, either from existing memories or from new information we receive, our mental models become more complete.

Accurate mental models are excellent guides for thinking about, and interacting with, many of the things we encounter (Galotti, 1999). If a mental model is incorrect, however, we are likely to make mistakes (see Figure 8.7). For example, people who hold an incorrect mental model of how physical illness is cured might stop taking an antibiotic when their symptoms begin to disappear. This is well before the bacteria causing those symptoms have been eliminated, so the symptoms soon reappear (Medin, Ross, & Markman, 2001). Others overdose on medication because according to their faulty mental model, "if taking three pills a day is good, taking six would be even better."

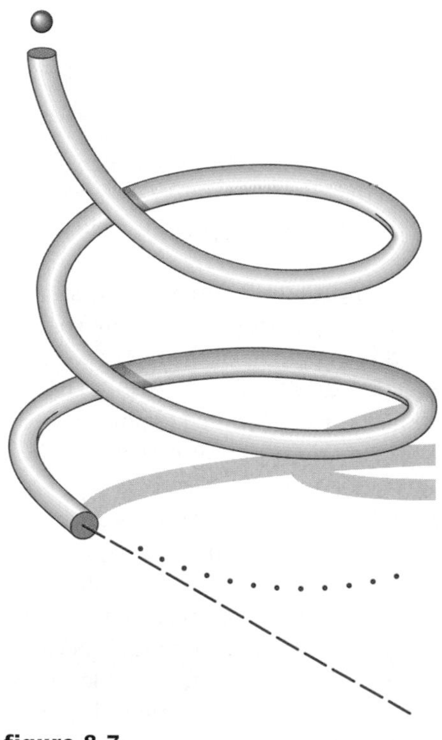

figure 8.7

Applying a Mental Model

Try to imagine the path that the marble will follow when it leaves the curved tube. In one study, most people drew the incorrect (curved) path indicated by the dotted line, rather than the correct (straight) path indicated by the dashed line (McCloskey, 1983). Their error was based on a faulty mental model of the behaviour of physical objects.

Images and Cognitive Maps

Think about how your best friend would look in a clown suit. The "mental picture" you just got illustrates that thinking often involves the manipulation of **images**—which are mental representations of visual information. Cognitive psychologists refer to mental images as *analogical representations,* because we manipulate these images in a way that is similar, or *analogous,* to manipulating the objects themselves (Reed, 2000). This similarity was demonstrated in a classic study by Roger Shepard and Jacqueline Metzler (1971). They measured how long it took people to decide whether pairs of objects such as those in Figure 8.8 were the same or different. They found that the amount of decision time depended on how far one object had to be "mentally rotated" to compare it with the other. The more rotation required, the longer the decision took. In other words, rotating the

mental model A cluster of propositions representing our understanding of objects and processes that guides our interaction with those things.

image A mental representation of visual information.

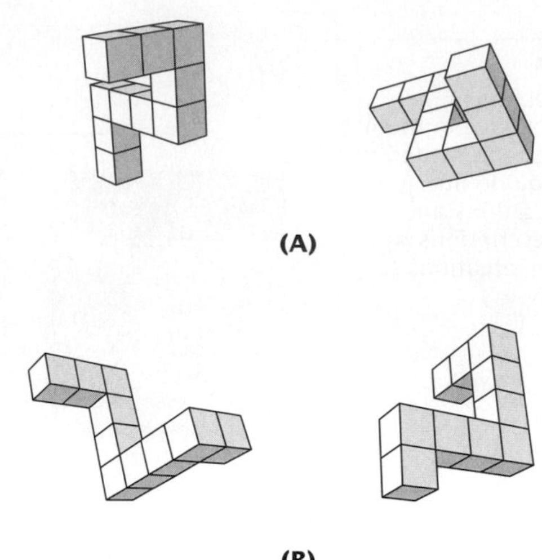

figure 8.8

Manipulating Images

Are these pairs of objects the same or different? To decide, you will have to mentally rotate one member of each pair. Because manipulating mental images, like manipulating actual objects, takes some time, the speed of your decision will depend on how far you have to rotate one object to line it up with the other for comparison. (The top pair matches; the bottom pair does not.)

Source: Shepard & Metzler (1971).

mental image of an object was like rotating the real object. More recent studies using neuro-imaging have confirmed that manipulating mental images activates some of the same areas of the brain that are active during comparable tasks with real objects (Farah, 2000).

Our ability to think using images extends beyond the manipulation of stimuli such as those in Figure 8.8. We also create mental images from written or spoken descriptions of scenes. In fact, brain areas involved in vision are activated as we construct mental images of those scenes (Mazoyer et al., 2002). You probably created a mental image a minute ago when you read about that blue-walled room, and you would do the same thing when someone gives you directions to that new pizza place in town. In the latter case, you would scan your **cognitive map**—a mental representation of familiar parts of your world—to find the location. In doing so, you would use a mental process similar to the visual process of scanning a paper map (Anderson, 2000; Taylor & Tversky, 1992). Manipulating images on a different cognitive map would help you if a power failure left your home pitch dark. Even though you couldn't see a thing, you could still find a flashlight or candle, because your cognitive map would show the floor plan, furniture placement, door locations, and other physical features of your home. You would not have this mental map in an unfamiliar house. There, you would have to walk slowly, arms outstretched, to avoid wrong turns and painful collisions.

According to Alinda Friedman and colleagues, cognitive maps of geographical locations tend to be organized around familiar landmarks. For example, when Canadians were asked to estimate the location of Mexican cities, they thought that the cities were located much closer to the equator than they actually are. Since the equator is a well-known landmark, people use it as a reference point and assume that cities south of them must be close to the equator (Friedman, et al., in press). In the chapter on learning we describe how experience shapes the cognitive maps that help animals navigate mazes and people navigate shopping malls.

Thinking Strategies

We have seen that our thinking capacity is based largely on our ability to manipulate mental representations—the ingredients of thought—much as a baker manipulates the ingredients of cookies (see "In Review: Ingredients of Thought" for a summary of these representations). But whereas the baker's food-processing system combines and transforms flour, sugar, milk, eggs, and chocolate into a delicious

cognitive map A mental representation of familiar parts of the environment.

in review Ingredients of Thought

Ingredient	Description	Examples
Concepts	Categories of objects, events, or ideas with common properties; basic building blocks of thought	"Square" (a formal concept); "game" (a natural concept).
Propositions	Mental representations that express relationships between concepts; can be true or false	Assertions such as "The cow jumped over the moon."
Schemas	Sets of propositions that create generalizations and expectations about categories of objects, places, events, and people	A schema might suggest that all grandmothers are elderly, grey-haired, and bake a lot of cookies.
Scripts	Schemas about familiar activities and situations; guide behaviour in those situations	You pay before eating in fast-food restaurants and after eating in fancier restaurants.
Mental models	Sets of propositions about how things relate to each other in the real world; can be correct or incorrect	Assuming that airflow around an open car will send thrown objects upward.
Images	Mental representations of visual information	Hearing a description of your blind date creates a mental picture of him or her.
Cognitive maps	Mental representations of familiar parts of the world	You can get to class by an alternate route even if your usual route is blocked by construction.

PsychAssist: Rotating Mental Objects

treat, our information-processing system combines, transforms, and elaborates mental representations in ways that allow us to engage in reasoning, problem solving, and decision making. Let's begin our discussion of these thinking strategies by considering **reasoning,** the process through which we generate and evaluate arguments, as well as reach conclusions about them.

Formal Reasoning

Astronomers tell us that the temperature at the core of the sun is about 27 million degrees Fahrenheit. They can't put a temperature probe inside the sun, so how can they be so confident about this assertion? Their estimate is based on *inferences* from other things that they know about the sun and about physical objects in general. Telescopic observations of the sun's volume and mass allowed astronomers to calculate its density, using the formula Density = Mass ÷ Volume. These observations also enabled them to measure the energy coming from one small region of the sun and—using what geometry told them about the surface area of spheres—to estimate the energy output from the sun as a whole. Further calculations told them how hot a body would have to be to generate that much energy.

In other words, the astronomers' highly educated guess about the sun's core temperature was based on **formal reasoning** (also called *logical reasoning*), the process of following a set of rigorous procedures to reach valid, or correct, conclusions. Some of these procedures included the application of specific mathematical formulas to existing data in order to generate new data. Such formulas are examples of **algorithms,** systematic methods that always produce a correct solution to a problem, if a solution exists (Jahnke & Nowaczyk, 1998). The astronomers also followed the **rules of logic,** sets of statements that provide a

reasoning The process by which people generate and evaluate arguments and reach conclusions about them.

formal reasoning The process of following a set of rigorous procedures for reaching valid conclusions.

algorithm A systematic procedure that cannot fail to produce a correct solution to a problem, if a solution exists.

rules of logic Sets of statements that provide a formula for drawing valid conclusions.

formula for drawing valid conclusions about the world. For example, each step in the astronomers' thinking took the form of "if-then" statements: If we know how much energy comes from one part of the sun's surface, and if we know how big the whole surface is, then we can calculate the total energy output. You use the same formal reasoning processes when you conclude, for example, that if your friend José is two years older than you are, then his twin brother, Juan, will be two years older, too. This kind of reasoning is called *deductive* because it takes a general rule (e.g., twins are the same age) and applies it to deduce conclusions about specific cases (e.g., José and Juan).

The rules of logic, which are traceable to the Greek philosopher Aristotle, have evolved into a system for drawing correct conclusions from a set of statements known as *premises*. Consider, for example, what conclusion can be drawn from the following premises:

Premise 1: *People who study hard do well in this course.*

Premise 2: *You have studied hard.*

According to the rules of logic, it would be valid to conclude that you will do well in this course. Logical arguments containing two or more premises and a conclusion are known as **syllogisms** (pronounced "SILL-o-jisms"). Notice that the conclusion in a syllogism goes beyond what the premises actually say. The conclusion is an inference based on the premises and on the rules of logic. In this case, the logical rule was this: If something is true of all members of a category, and if A is in that category, then that something will also be true of A.

Your ability to make everyday decisions and solve everyday problems depends heavily on your ability to draw correct inferences about facts. For example, if a course you want to take is open only to fourth-year students and you are in second year, you'll infer that it would be a waste of time to try to get in. Here, the syllogism would be:

Premise 1: *This class is open only to fourth-year students.*

Premise 2: *I am not in fourth-year.*

Conclusion: *I can't take this class.*

Logical reasoning skills can be so well learned that they seem to come naturally, but there are some tendencies toward errors in reasoning that seem to come naturally, too. These common pitfalls can lead us astray in our problem solving and decision making (Ashcraft, 2002).Two of the most important of these pitfalls are *belief bias* and *limits on working memory*:

1. ***Belief bias.*** Donna Torrens at the University of Saskatchewan found that people tend to judge a conclusion as accurate because it is believable rather than because it is logical. This tendency is known as the "belief bias effect" (Torrens, Thompson, & Cramer, 1999). For example, consider this syllogism:

   Premise 1: *Some professors wear ties.*

   Premise 2: *Some men wear ties.*

   Conclusion: *Some professors are men.*

   The conclusion happens to be true, but it doesn't actually follow logically from these premises. Conclusions such as this one *look* logical and valid only because they conform to our beliefs about the world. The impact of belief bias in this syllogism is easy to see if you substitute the word *scarecrows* for *men* in Premise 2. The syllogism now reads: *Some professors wear ties. Some scarecrows wear ties. Therefore, some professors are scarecrows.* No matter what you think of your professors, you would probably not accept this new conclusion as valid.

syllogism An argument made up of two propositions, called premises, and a conclusion based on those premises.

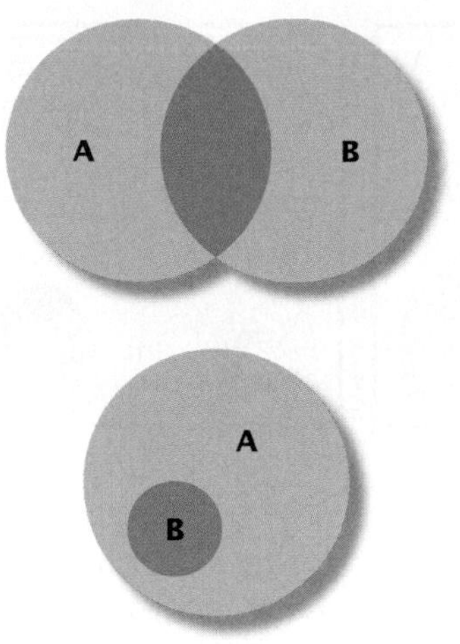

figure 8.9

Two Versions of the Same Premise

As these drawings show, the same premise—"Some As are Bs"—can be represented in more than one way. Keeping in mind two or more versions of a premise, or of two premises, can tax short-term memory. As a result, people tend to work with only one version of each premise. If they don't choose the right ones, it may be difficult or impossible to reach a valid conclusion.

Belief bias is related to a more general problem in human reasoning, called **confirmation bias**—a tendency to seek evidence and reach conclusions that are consistent with our existing beliefs. Confirmation bias can affect thinking in many situations. When people first fall in love, they often focus only on their loved one's best qualities and ignore evidence of less desirable ones. In the courtroom, jurors may pay little attention to evidence of a defendant's guilt if that defendant is, say, a beloved celebrity or a harmless-looking senior citizen. In such cases, prosecutors' logical arguments based on true premises may not lead to conviction, because the logical conclusion ("guilty") does not match jurors' beliefs about celebrities, the elderly, or some other favoured group. Similarly, if jurors believe the defendant represents a category of people who tend to commit crimes, they may not be swayed much by evidence suggesting innocence. In other words, the conclusions that people reach are often based on both logical and wishful thinking (Evans et al., 1999).

2. ***Limits on working memory.*** *Some As are B. All Bs are C. Therefore, some As are C.* Do you agree? This syllogism is correct, but evaluating it requires you to hold a lot of material in short-term memory while mentally manipulating it. This task is particularly difficult if elements in a syllogism involve negatives, as in *No dogs are non-animals.* There is also the related problem of trying to keep in mind several possible versions of the same premise (see Figure 8.9). If the amount of material to be mentally manipulated exceeds the capacity of short-term memory, logical errors can easily result (e.g., Bara, Bucciarelli, & Johnson-Laird, 1995).

Informal Reasoning

The use of logic to discover new facts and draw inferences is only one kind of reasoning. A second kind, **informal reasoning,** comes into play when we are trying to assess the *believability* of a conclusion based on the evidence available to support it. Informal reasoning is also known as *inductive reasoning,* because its goal is to induce a general conclusion to appear on the basis of specific facts or examples. Psychologists use this kind of reasoning when they design experiments and other research methods whose results will provide evidence for (or against) a theory. Jurors use informal reasoning when weighing evidence for the guilt or innocence of a defendant. And investigators used it to discover what caused the space shuttle *Columbia* to disintegrate as it returned to Earth in February 2003, killing its seven astronauts (Broad & Revkin, 2003).

Formal reasoning is guided by algorithms and the rules of logic, but there are no foolproof methods for informal reasoning. Consider, for example, how many white swans you would have to see before concluding that all swans were white. Fifty? A hundred? A million? A strictly formal, algorithmic approach would require that you observe every swan in existence to be sure they are all white, but such a task would be impossible. A more practical approach is to base your conclusion on the number of observations that you believe to be "enough." In other words, you would take a mental "shortcut" to reach a conclusion that is probably, but not necessarily, correct (there are, in fact, black swans). Such mental shortcuts are called **heuristics** (pronounced "hyoor-IST-ix").

Suppose you are about to leave home but can't find your watch. Applying an algorithm would mean searching in every possible location, room by room, until you find the watch. But you can reach the same outcome more quickly by using a heuristic—that is, by searching only where your experience suggests you might have left the watch. In short, heuristics are often valuable in guiding judgments about which events are probable or which hypotheses are likely to be true. They are easy to use and frequently work well (Gigerenzer et al., 2000).

confirmation bias The tendency to pay more attention to evidence in support of one's hypothesis than to evidence that refutes that hypothesis.

informal reasoning The process of evaluating a conclusion, theory, or course of action on the basis of the believability of evidence.

heuristics Time-saving mental shortcuts used in reasoning.

Formal reasoning follows the rules of logic, but there are no foolproof rules for informal reasoning, as this fool demonstrates.

However, heuristics can also bias cognitive processes and result in errors. For example, if a heuristic leads you to vote for only the candidates in a particular political party instead of researching the views of each candidate, you might help elect someone with whom you strongly disagree. The extent to which heuristics are responsible for important errors in judgment and decision making is a matter of continuing research and debate by cognitive psychologists (Hilton, 2002; Medin & Bazerman, 1999). Amos Tversky and Daniel Kahneman (1974, 1993) have described three potentially problematic heuristics that people seem to use intuitively in making judgments: the anchoring heuristic, the representativeness heuristic, and the availability heuristic.

Anchoring to a Price The anchoring heuristic operates in many bargaining situations. The asking price of this house, for example, has probably anchored the sellers' perception of its value. As a result, they may be reluctant to accept a lower price, even if information from their sales agent suggests they should. The buyers' judgment of the house's value will also be anchored to some extent by the seller's asking price. Even if they discover the house needs some repairs, they are more likely to offer 90 percent of the price rather than 50 percent.

The Anchoring Heuristic People use the **anchoring heuristic** when they estimate the probability of an event not by starting from scratch but by adjusting an earlier estimate (Rottenstreich & Tversky, 1997). This strategy sounds reasonable, but the starting point biases the final estimate. Specifically, once people have established that starting point, their adjustments to it tend to be too small. It is as if they have dropped a "mental anchor" that keeps them from moving very far from their original judgment. For example, if you were asked whether the average annual number of murders in Toronto was higher or lower than 200, and then asked to estimate the actual number, your estimate would probably be somewhere around 200. However, if you were asked whether the annual average was higher or lower than 50, and then asked to estimate the actual number, your estimate would probably be closer to 50. So, your estimate would reflect a bias based on the starting point you were given. In the second case, your estimate would be closer to the correct number of 60, which is the approximate annual average for the number of homicides in the city of Toronto (Toronto Police Service, 2003).

The anchoring heuristic presents a challenge for defense attorneys because once jurors have been affected by the prosecution's evidence (which is presented first), it may be difficult to alter their belief in a criminal defendant's guilt or in the amount of money the defendant in a civil case should have to pay (Greene & Loftus, 1998; Hogarth & Einhorn, 1992). In much the same way, our first impressions of people are not easily shifted by later evidence (see the chapter on social behaviour).

The Representativeness Heuristic Using the **representativeness heuristic,** people decide whether an example belongs in a certain class on the basis of how similar it is to other items in that class. This can be a sensible way to make decisions, but can lead to errors in judgment. Suppose, for example, you were given descriptions of two young men and asked which one is most likely to have a successful career in the NHL. Both are Canadians born in Laval, Quebec, in 1975. However, there are several key differences between these two men. The first had an impressive junior hockey career, accumulating 110 points in 66 games and being named Rookie of the Year in 1992. He set several records as a junior and was compared to Wayne Gretzky by sportswriters at the time. At 183 cm (6 feet) and 90.7 k (200 pounds), he was an average-sized hockey player with superior skills. In 1993, he was drafted first overall by the Ottawa Senators. The second man, on the

anchoring heuristic A mental shortcut that involves basing judgments on existing information.

representativeness heuristic A mental shortcut that involves judging whether something belongs in a given class on the basis of its similarity to other members of that class.

A Memorable Outcome The availability heuristic can have a strong impact on people's judgments about the chances of winning a lottery. Splashy media coverage makes it far easier to recall the few people who have won big prizes than the millions whose tickets turned out to be worthless.

other hand, was small at 175 cm (5 feet 9 inches) and 81.6 k (180 pounds). He did not play junior hockey in Canada, opting instead to play college hockey in the US. He was never drafted but finally signed with the Calgary Flames as a free agent in 1998. He was later released by the Flames and signed as a free agent with the Tampa Bay Lightning. Using the representativeness heuristic, most people would conclude that the first one had the more successful professional hockey career because he fits more closely with our notion of the ideal hockey player. However, in this example, that judgment would be false. The first player described is Alexandre Daigle (The Internet Hockey Database, 2006) who never lived up to early predictions of success. The second is Martin St. Louis (National Hockey Players Association, 2006) who, in 2003–04 won the Art Ross Trophy (scoring leader), Hart Memorial Trophy (Most Valuable Player), and was on the team that won the Stanley Cup, making him the first player since Wayne Gretzky to win all three in one year.

The impact of the representativeness heuristic can be seen in many real-life judgments and decisions. One study found, for example, that jurors' decisions to convict or acquit a defendant may depend partly on the degree to which the defendant's actions were representative of a crime category. Someone who abducts a child and asks for ransom (actions that clearly fit the category of "kidnapping") is more likely to be convicted than someone who abducts an adult and demands no ransom—even though both crimes constitute kidnapping and the evidence is equally strong in each case (Smith, 1991).

The Availability Heuristic A third heuristic that can bias people's thinking is the **availability heuristic,** which involves judging the likelihood of an event or the correctness of a hypothesis based on how easily that hypothesis or examples of that event come to mind (Reed, 2000). In other words, people tend to choose the hypothesis or predict the event that is most mentally "available" to them, much as they might select the box of cereal that is at the front of the supermarket shelf.

Like other heuristics, this shortcut tends to work well. After all, what people remember most easily are frequent events or likely hypotheses. However, the availability heuristic can lead to biased judgments, especially when mental availability does not reflect actual frequency. For example, many people are nervous on airplanes but very few experience any sense of anxiety when riding in a car. Air travel is perceived as being more dangerous partly because whenever a plane crash occurs,

availability heuristic A mental shortcut through which judgments are based on information that is most easily brought to mind.

media coverage is extensive with numerous updates on the number of fatalities being flashed across television screens nationwide. The fact that plane crashes receive so much attention makes them easy to recall and leads us to assume that they are more common than they really are. In this example, the availability heuristic leads to a false judgment regarding the relative danger as evident in statistics from Transport Canada indicating that approximately 60 Canadians die in plane crashes each year whereas nearly 3000 deaths occur as a result of traffic accidents (Transport Canada, 2003).

The heuristics we have discussed represent only three of the many mental shortcuts that people use more or less automatically in making judgments, and they describe only some of the biases and limitations that affect human reasoning (Hogarth & Einhorn, 1992). Some other biases and limitations are described in the following sections, as we consider two important goals of thinking: problem solving and decision making.

Problem Solving

If where you are is not where you want to be, and when the path to getting there is not obvious, you have a *problem*. As suggested by the circle of thought, the most efficient approach to problem solving would be first to diagnose the problem in the elaboration stage, then to come up with a plan for solving it, then to execute the plan, and finally to evaluate the results to determine whether the problem remains (Bransford & Stein, 1993). But people's problem-solving efforts are not always so systematic, which is one reason that medical tests are sometimes given unnecessarily, diseases are sometimes misdiagnosed, and auto parts are sometimes replaced when there is nothing wrong with them.

Strategies for Problem Solving

When you are trying to get from a starting point to some goal, the best path may not necessarily be a straight line. In fact, obstacles may force you to go in the opposite direction temporarily. So it is with problem solving. Sometimes, the best strategy is not to take mental steps aimed straight at your goal. For example, when a problem is especially difficult, it can sometimes be helpful to allow it to "incubate" by setting it aside for a while. A solution that once seemed out of reach may suddenly appear after you think about other things for a while. The benefits of incubation probably arise from forgetting incorrect ideas that may have been blocking the path to a correct solution (Anderson, 2000). Psychologists have identified several other useful problem-solving strategies.

Means-End Analysis One of the most general of these strategies is called *means-end analysis*. It involves continuously asking where you are in relation to your final goal, and then deciding on the means by which you can get one step closer to it (Newell & Simon, 1972). In other words, rather than trying to solve the problem all at once, you identify a subgoal that will take you toward a solution (this process is referred to as *decomposition*). After reaching that subgoal, you identify another one that will get you even closer to the solution, and you continue this step-by-step process until the problem is solved. Some students apply this approach to the problem of writing a major term paper. The task might seem overwhelming at first, but their first subgoal is simply to write an outline of what they think the paper should cover. When the outline is complete, they decide whether a paper based on it will satisfy the assignment. If so, the next subgoal might be to search the library and the Internet for information about each section. If they decide that this information is adequate, the next subgoal would be to write a rough draft of the introduction, and so on.

Simply knowing about problem-solving strategies, such as means-end analysis, is not enough. As described in the chapter on motivation and emotion, people must believe that the required effort is worth the rewards it can bring.

Calvin and Hobbes by Bill Watterson

Working Backward A second problem-solving strategy is to *work backward.* Many problems are like a tree. The trunk is the information you are given. The solution is a twig on one of the limbs. If you work forward by taking the "givens" of the problem and trying to find the solution, it will be easy to branch off in the wrong direction. A more efficient approach may be to start at the twig end and work backward toward your goal (Galotti, 1999). Consider, for example, the problem of planning a climb to the summit of Mount Everest. The best strategy is to figure out, first, what equipment and supplies are needed at the highest camp on the night before the summit attempt. Next, you have to establish how many people are needed to stock that camp the day before, how many people are needed to supply those who must stock the camp, and so on until a plan for the entire expedition is complete. It is easy to overlook the working-backward strategy, however, because it runs counter to the way most of us have learned to think. It is hard to imagine that the first step in solving a problem could be to assume that you have already solved it. Unfortunately, six climbers died on Mount Everest in 1996 in part because of failure to apply this strategy (Krakauer, 1997).

Working Backward to Forge Ahead Whether you are organizing a family vacation or, as Claire Cayley and Drew Osborne did, a canoe trip from the Alberta Rockies to Montreal along a famed fur-trading route, working backward from the final goal through all the steps necessary to reach that goal is a helpful approach to solving complex problems.

Using Analogies A third problem-solving strategy is trying to find *analogies*, or similarities between today's problem and others you have encountered before. An office manager may find, for example, that a seemingly hopeless problem between employees can be resolved using the same compromise that worked during a recent family squabble. To take advantage of analogies, we must first recognize the similarities between current and previous problems and then recall the solution that worked before. Most people are surprisingly poor at recognizing such similarities (Anderson, 2000). They tend to concentrate on the surface features that make problems appear different.

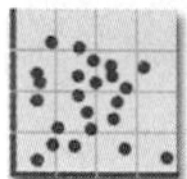

FOCUS ON RESEARCH METHODS

Locating Analogical Thinking

The value of using analogies in problem solving was beautifully illustrated after the Hubble Space Telescope was placed in orbit around the Earth in 1990. It was designed to take detailed photographs of distant galaxies, but because its main mirror was not focusing light properly, the pictures were blurry. Then NASA engineer James Crocker happened to notice the way a hotel room showerhead pivoted, and it gave him the idea for a system of movable mirrors to correct for the flaw in the Hubble's mirror. When shuttle astronauts installed these mirrors in 1993, the problem was solved (Stein, 1993).

- **What was the researchers' question?**

Charles Wharton and his colleagues wanted to know what goes on in the brain when people do this kind of analogical mapping—recognizing similarities between things that appear to be different and even unrelated (Wharton et al., 2000).

- **How did the researchers answer the question?**

The researchers knew that PET scan technology could show brain activity while participants performed an analogy task, but how could the researchers separate the activity associated with analogical mapping from everything else going on in the brain at the same time? Their answer was to use a *subtraction technique.* They asked people to perform two tasks—one after the other—that involved making comparisons between patterns of rectangles, ovals, triangles, and other shapes. Both tasks placed similar demands on the brain, but only one of them required the participants to *make analogies* between the patterns (see Figure 8.10). The researchers then compared the resulting PET scans, looking for areas of the brain that were active in the analogy task but not in the other one. What their computers did, in essence, was to take all the brain activity that occurred during the analogy task and "subtract" from it all the activity that occurred during the other task. The activity remaining was presumed to reflect analogical mapping.

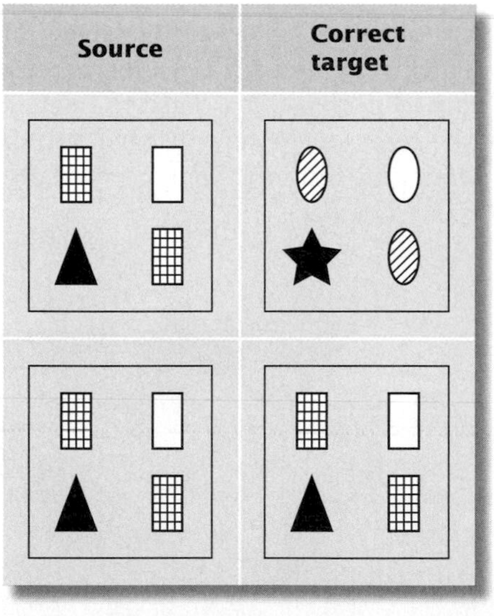

Source
Correct target

figure 8.10

Comparing Stimulus Patterns

The top row shows an example of the stimulus patterns that were compared in an analogy task. Participants had to say whether the pattern on the right is similar, or *analogous,* to the one on the left. (In this case it is, because even though the specific shapes used in one pattern differ from those in the other pattern, their shading and physical arrangement are similar.) The bottom row shows an example of the patterns that were compared in a "same-different" task. Here, participants were asked only to decide whether the two patterns are *exactly the same* (Wharton et al., 2000).

- **What did the researchers find?**

As you can see in Figure 8.11, the brain areas activated only during the analogy task were in the left hemisphere, particularly in the frontal and parietal areas. Other neuro-imaging studies have shown activation of similar areas during abstract problem solving and reasoning (e.g., Osherson et al., 1998).

- **What do the results mean?**

These results show that it is possible to locate specific brain activities associated with a specific kind of cognitive activity. They also fit well into what we already know about where certain brain functions are localized. As mentioned earlier, the frontal areas of the brain are involved in complex processing tasks, including those requiring coordination of information in working memory with information coming from the senses. There is also evidence that parietal areas are involved in our ability to perceive the arrangements of objects and relationships among them.

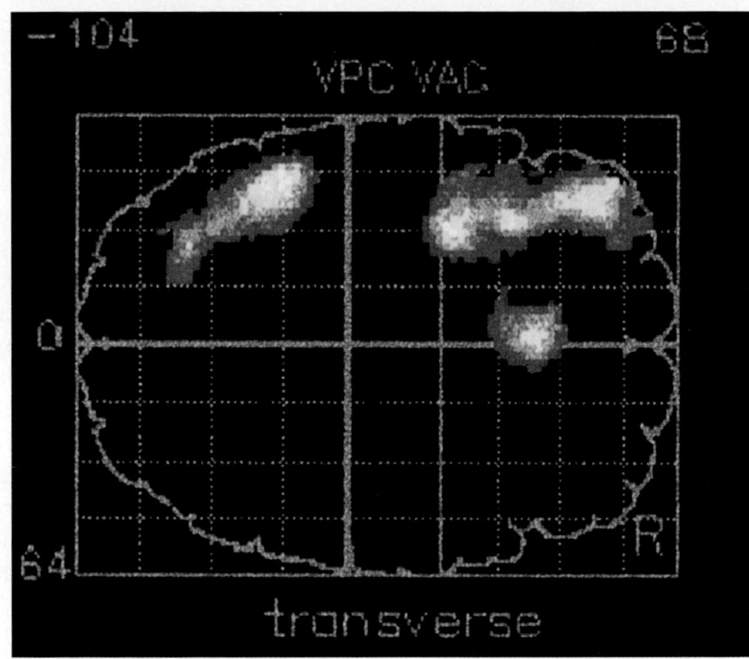

figure 8.11

Brain Activity During Analogical Mapping

Comparing PET scans of brain activity during an analogy task and a task not requiring analogical thinking revealed that making analogies appears to involve areas of the left frontal and parietal lobes, as seen here from below and highlighted in red.

Source: Wharton et al (2000).

Both of these regions were activated during the analogy task in this experiment, suggesting that this task required both kinds of abilities.

- **What do we still need to know?**

There is no doubt that Wharton and his colleagues devised a clever way to examine the analogical mapping process as it occurs in the human brain, but are the brain areas identified the only ones involved in analogies? Would the same results appear if the analogy task had been verbal instead of visual, requiring participants to make analogies such as "Dark is to light as cold is to ________"? It will take additional research to answer this question.

Consider also that even though the analogy task used in this study involved processing visual-spatial information (shape, shading, and location) rather than verbal information (words), the PET scans showed activation only on the left side of the brain. This is surprising, because as mentioned in the chapter on biological aspects of psychology, visual-spatial processing is usually handled mainly in the brain's right hemisphere. One reason for this unexpected pattern may be that, as also noted in that chapter, the right hemisphere actually does have some verbal processing abilities. However, the results also warn us to be careful about misinterpreting PET scan activity. Increased activity in a particular brain region doesn't always mean that the region is performing the processing we are trying to locate. The activity observed might also result if the area were being suppressed so as not to interfere with processing going on elsewhere. The study of brain activity during higher-level thinking is still quite new, so it will take some time, and a lot more research, to learn how to correctly interpret the data coming from neuro-imaging techniques (Luo et al., 2003; Ruff et al., 2003).

Obstacles to Problem Solving

Failing to use analogies is just one example of the obstacles that face problem solvers every day. Difficulties frequently occur at the beginning, during the diagnosis stage, when a person forms and then tests hypotheses about a problem.

As a case in point, consider this true story: In September 1998, John Gatiss was in the kitchen of his rented house in Cheltenham, England, when he heard a faint meowing sound. He couldn't find the source of the sound, but he assumed that a kitten had become trapped in the walls or under the flooring, so he called for the fire brigade to rescue the animal. The sound seemed to be coming from the electric oven, so the rescuers dismantled it, disconnecting the power cord in the process. The sound stopped, but everyone assumed that wherever the kitten was, it had become too frightened to meow. The search was reluctantly abandoned, and the oven was reconnected. Four days later, though, the meowing began again. This time, Gatiss and his landlord called the Royal Society for the Prevention of Cruelty to Animals (RSPCA), whose inspectors heard the kitten in distress and asked the fire brigade to return. They spent the next three days searching for the cat. First, they tore down parts of the kitchen walls and ripped up the floorboards. Next, they called in plumbing and drainage specialists, who used cables tipped with fibre-optic cameras to search remote cavities where a kitten might hide. Rescuers then brought in a disaster search team, which tried to find the kitten using acoustic and ultrasonic equipment designed to locate victims trapped in the debris of earthquakes and explosions. Not a sound could be heard. Increasingly concerned about how much longer the kitten could survive, the fire brigade tried to coax it from hiding with the finest quality fish, but to no avail. Suddenly, there was a burst of "purring," which to everyone's surprise (and the landlord's dismay), the ultrasonic equipment traced to the clock in the electric oven! Later, the landlord commented that everyone had assumed that Gatiss's hypothesis was correct—that the meowing sound came from a cat trapped somewhere in the kitchen. "I just let them carry on. If there is an animal in there, you have to do what it takes. The funniest thing was that it seemed to reply when we called out to it" (*London Daily Telegraph*, 1998).

How could fifteen fire-rescue workers, three RSPCA inspectors, four drainage workers, and two acoustics experts waste eight days and cause nearly $2,000 in damage to a house in pursuit of a nonexistent kitten? The answer lies in the fact that they, like the rest of us, are prone to four main obstacles to efficient problem solving, described in the following sections.

Multiple Hypotheses Often, people begin to solve a problem with only a vague notion of which hypotheses to test. Suppose you heard a strange sound in your kitchen. It could be caused by several things, but which hypotheses should you test, and in what order?

People have a difficult time considering more than two or three hypotheses at a time (Mehle, 1982). The limited capacity of short-term memory may be part of the reason. As discussed in the chapter on memory, we can hold only about seven chunks of information in short-term memory. A single hypothesis, let alone two or three, might include many more than seven chunks, so it might be difficult or impossible to keep them all in mind at once. As a result, the correct hypothesis is often neglected. Which hypothesis a person considers may depend on the availability heuristic. In other words, the hypothesis considered first may be the one that most easily comes to mind, not the one most likely to be correct (Tversky & Kahneman, 1974). So Mr. Gatiss diagnosed the sound he heard as a kitten, not a clock, because such sounds usually come from kittens, not clocks.

Mental Sets Sometimes people are so blinded by one hypothesis or strategy that they continue to apply it even when better alternatives should be obvious (a clear case of the anchoring heuristic at work). Once Gatiss reported hearing a "trapped kitten," his description created an assumption that everyone else accepted and no one challenged.

A laboratory example of this phenomenon devised by Abraham Luchins (1942) is shown in Figure 8.12. In each problem shown in the figure, the task is to use three jars of varying sizes to end up with a certain amount of water. For example, in the first problem you are to obtain 21 litres by using 3 jars that can hold 8, 35, and 3 litres, respectively. The solution is to fill Jar B to its capacity, 35 litres, and then

mental set The tendency for old patterns of problem solving to persist, even when they might not always be the most efficient alternative.

functional fixedness A tendency to think about familiar objects in familiar ways that may prevent using them in other ways.

figure 8.12

The Luchins Jar Problem

The problem is to obtain the quantities of water listed in the first column by filling jars with the capacities shown in the next three columns. Each line represents a different problem. In dealing with such problems, people often fall prey to mental sets that prevent them from using the most efficient solution. After solving all the problems shown here, read on to see if your performance, too, was affected by a mental set.

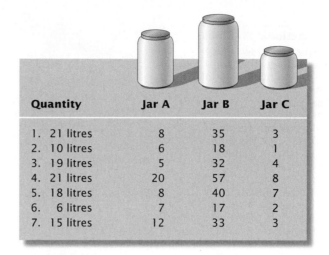

Quantity	Jar A	Jar B	Jar C
1. 21 litres	8	35	3
2. 10 litres	6	18	1
3. 19 litres	5	32	4
4. 21 litres	20	57	8
5. 18 litres	8	40	7
6. 6 litres	7	17	2
7. 15 litres	12	33	3

use its contents to fill Jar A to its capacity of 8 litres, leaving 27 litres in Jar B. Then pour liquid from Jar B to fill Jar C to its capacity twice, leaving 21 litres in Jar B [27 − (2 × 3) = 21]. In other words, the general solution formula is B − A − 2C. To confirm this, solve the rest of the problems before reading further.

As you worked, did you notice anything unusual about Problem 7? By the time you reached that one, you had probably developed a **mental set,** a tendency for old patterns of problem solving to persist (Sweller & Gee, 1978). That mental set may have caused you to use the standard solution formula (B − A − 2C) for Problem 7 even though a simpler one (A + C) would have worked just as well. Figures 8.13 and 8.15 show that a mental set can also restrict your perception of the problem itself.

A related restriction on problem solving may come from our experience with objects. Once people are accustomed to using an object for one purpose, they may be blinded to its other possible functions. Long experience may produce **functional fixedness,** a tendency to use familiar objects in familiar rather than creative ways. Figure 8.14 illustrates an example. An incubation strategy often helps to break mental sets.

Ignoring Negative Evidence In 1981, Susan Nelles, a nurse at Toronto's Hospital for Sick Children, was charged with murder when several babies at the hospital died, apparently from an overdose of a drug administered to them. The evidence against the young nurse was compelling and the media and the public were swift to condemn her as a baby killer. After a gruelling ordeal, Nelles' case was dismissed. A key piece of evidence that led to her exoneration was that Nelles was not even on duty when some of the babies died. However, investigators ignored the negative evidence and focused only on evidence that pointed to her guilt (Harris, 1999).

Cases such as this one remind us that the absence of signs, symptoms, or events can provide important evidence for or against a hypothesis. Compared with evidence that is present, however, the absence of evidence is less likely to be noticed (Hunt & Rouse, 1981). As a result, people have a difficult time using missing evidence to help eliminate hypotheses from consideration (Ashcraft, 1989). In the "trapped kitten" case, when the "meowing" stopped for several days after the stove was reconnected, rescuers assumed that the animal was frightened into silence. They ignored the possibility that their hypothesis was incorrect in the first place.

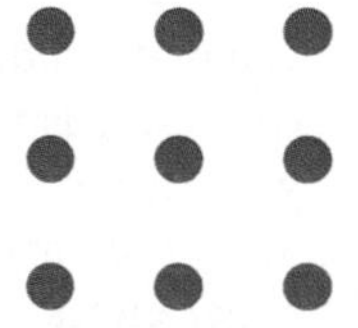

figure 8.13

The Nine-Dot Problem

The problem is to draw no more than four straight lines that run through all nine dots on the page without lifting your pencil from the paper. Figure 8.15 shows two ways of going beyond mental sets to solve this problem.

Confirmation Bias Anyone who has had a series of medical tests knows that diagnosis is not a one-shot decision. Instead, physicians choose their first hypothesis on the basis of observed symptoms and then order tests or evaluate additional symptoms to confirm or reject that hypothesis (Trillin, 2001). This process

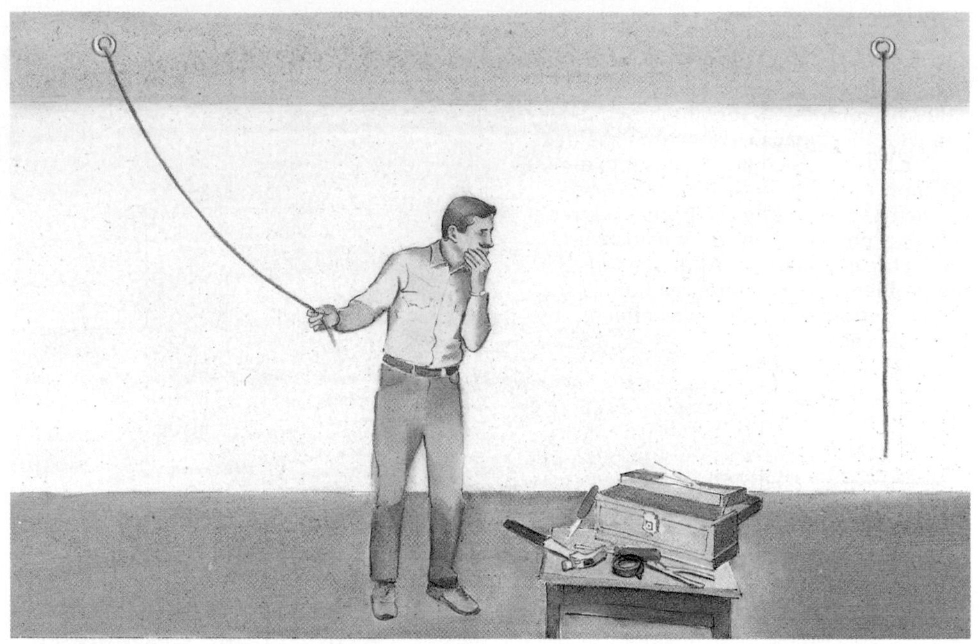

figure 8.14

An Example of Functional Fixedness

Before reading further, consider how you would fasten together two strings that are hanging from the ceiling but are out of reach of each other. Several tools are available, yet most people do not think of attaching, say, the vise-grip to one string and swinging it like a pendulum until it can be reached while holding the other string. This solution is not obvious because we tend to fixate on the function of a vise-grip as a tool rather than as a weight. People are more likely to solve this problem if the tools are scattered around the room. When the pliers are in a toolbox, their function as a tool is emphasized, and functional fixedness becomes nearly impossible to break.

can be distorted by the *confirmation bias* mentioned earlier: Humans have a strong bias to confirm rather than to reject the hypothesis they have chosen, even in the face of strong evidence against it (Aronson, Wilson, & Akert, 1999; Groopman, 2000). Confirmation bias can be seen as a form of the anchoring heuristic, in that it involves "anchoring" to an initial hypothesis and being unwilling to abandon it. The would-be rescuers of the "trapped kitten" were so intent on their efforts to locate it that they never stopped to question its existence. Similarly, as described in the chapter on social behaviour, when evaluating other people's behaviour or abilities we tend to look for, and pay extra attention to, information that is consistent with any prior beliefs we have about them. This tendency can create positive or negative bias in, say, a teacher's impressions of children's mental abilities or an interviewer's impressions of job candidate's skills (Jussim & Eccles, 1992; Reich, 2004).

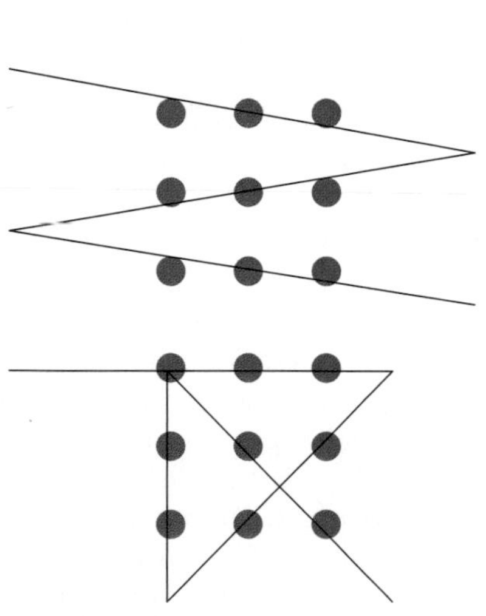

figure 8.15

Two Creative Solutions to the Nine-Dot Problem

Many people find puzzles such as this difficult because their mental sets create artificial constraints on the range of possible solutions. In this case, the mental sets involve the tendency to draw within the frame of the dots and to draw through the middle of each dot. As shown here, however, there are other possibilities.

Building Problem-Solving Skills

Some psychologists suggest that it should be possible to train people to avoid the biases that impair problem solving, and their efforts to do so have produced some modest benefits. In one study, cautioning people against their tendency to anchor on a hypothesis reduced the magnitude of confirmation bias and increased participants' openness to alternative evidence (Lopes, 1982).

How do experts avoid obstacles to problem solving? What do they bring to a situation that a beginner does not? Knowledge based on experience is particularly important (Mayer, 1992). Experts frequently proceed by looking for analogies between current and past problems. Compared with beginners, they are better able to relate new information and new experiences to past experiences and existing knowledge (Anderson, 1995; Bedard & Chi, 1992). Accordingly, experts can use existing knowledge to organize new information into chunks, a process described in the chapter on memory. By chunking many elements of a problem into a smaller number of units, experts are better than beginners at visualizing problems clearly and efficiently (Reingold et al., 2001).

Experts can use their experience as a guide because they tend to perceive the similarity between new and old problems more deeply than beginners do

(Hardimann, Dufresne, & Mestre, 1989). James Tanaka at the University of Victoria in British Columbia found that experts focus on more detailed (or subordinate level) features than beginners who focus only on surface features (Tanaka, Curran, & Sheinberg, 2005). Therefore, experts are able to see the similarity of underlying principles, whereas beginners perceive similarity only in surface features.

As a result, experts can more quickly and easily apply these principles to solve the new problem. In one study, expert physicists and beginning physics students sorted physics problems into groups (Chi, Feltovitch, & Glaser, 1981). The beginners grouped together problems that looked similar (such as those involving blocks lying on an inclined plane), whereas the experts grouped together problems that could be solved by the same principle (such as Newton's second law of motion). Finally, expert problem solvers can explain each step in their solutions, and they can remain aware of precisely what is and is not understood along the way (Medin, Ross, & Markman, 2001).

Although experts are often better problem solvers than beginners, expertise also carries a danger: Their extensive experience may create mental sets. Top-down, knowledge-driven processes can bias them toward seeing what they expect or want to see and prevent them from seeing a problem in new ways. As in the case of the "trapped kitten," confirmation bias sometimes prevents experts from appreciating that a proposed solution is incorrect. Several studies have shown that although experts may be more confident in their solutions (Payne, Bettman, & Johnson, 1992), they are not always more accurate than others in such areas as medical diagnosis, accounting, and pilot judgment (Wickens et al., 1992).

In other words, there is a fine line between using past experience and being trapped by it. Experience alone does not ensure excellence at problem solving, and practice may not make perfect (see Table 8.1). (For a summary of our discussion of human problem solving, see "In Review: Solving Problems.")

table 8.1

Experts typically have a large store of knowledge about their area of expertise, but even confidently stated opinions based on this knowledge can turn out to be wrong. In 1768, one expert critic called William Shakespeare's now-revered play *Hamlet* "the work of a drunken savage" (Henderson & Bernard, 1998). Here are some equally incorrect expert pronouncements from *The Experts Speak* (Cerf & Navasky, 1998).

Some Expert Opinions
On the possibility of painless surgery through anesthesia: "'Knife' and 'pain' are two words in surgery that must forever be associated. . . . To this compulsory combination we shall have to adjust ourselves." (Dr. Alfred Velpeau, professor of surgery, Paris Faculty of Medicine, 1839)
On the hazards of cigarette smoking: "If excessive smoking actually plays a role in the production of lung cancer, it seems to be a minor one." (Dr. W. C. Heuper, National Cancer Institute, 1954)
On the stock market (one week before the disastrous 1929 crash that wiped out over $50 billion in investments): "Stocks have reached what looks like a permanently high plateau." (Irving Fisher, professor of economics, Yale University, 1929)
On the prospects of war with Japan (three years before the December 1941 Japanese attack on Pearl Harbor): "A Japanese attack on Pearl Harbor is a strategic impossibility." (Maj. George F. Eliot, military science writer, 1938)
On the value of personal computers: "There is no reason for any individual to have a computer in their home." (Ken Olson, president, Digital Equipment Corporation, 1977)
On the concept of the airplane: "Heavier-than-air flying machines are impossible." (Lord Kelvin, mathematician, physicist, and president of the British Royal Society, 1895)

in review Solving Problems

Steps	Pitfalls	Remedies
Define the problem	Inexperience: the tendency to see each problem as unique.	Gain experience and practice in seeing the similarity between present problems and previous problems.
Form hypotheses about solutions	Availability heuristic: the tendency to recall the hypothesis or solution that is most available to memory.	Force yourself to entertain different hypotheses.
	Anchoring heuristic or mental set: the tendency to anchor on the first solution or hypothesis and not adjust your beliefs in light of new evidence or failures of the current approach.	Break the mental set, stop, and try a fresh approach.
Test hypotheses	The tendency to ignore negative evidence.	In evaluating a hypothesis, consider the things you should be seeing (but are not) if the hypothesis is true.
	Confirmation bias: the tendency to seek only evidence that confirms your hypothesis.	Look for disconfirming evidence that, if found, would show your hypothesis to be false.

PsychAssist: Common Heuristics

Problem Solving by Computer

Medical and scientific researchers have created artificial limbs, retinas, cochleas, and even hearts to help disabled people move, see, hear, and live more normally. They are developing artificial brains, too, in the form of computer systems that not only see, hear, and manipulate objects but also reason and solve problems. These systems are the product of research in **artificial intelligence (AI)**, a field that seeks to develop computers that imitate the processes of human perception and thought. For example, computerized *expert systems* can already perform as well as humans, and sometimes better (e.g., Gawande, 1998a; Khan et al., 2001).

Symbolic Reasoning and Computer Logic Early efforts at developing artificial intelligence focused on computers' enormous capabilities for formal reasoning and symbol manipulation and on their abilities to follow general problem-solving strategies, such as working backward (Newell & Simon, 1972). Valuable as it is, this logic-based approach to AI has important limitations. For one thing, expert systems are successful only in narrowly defined fields. And even within a specific domain, computers show limited ability. There are no ways of putting into computer code all aspects of the reasoning of human experts. Sometimes, the experts can only say, "I know it when I see it, but I can't put it into words." Second, the vital ability to draw analogies and make other connections among remote knowledge domains is still beyond the grasp of current expert systems, partly because the builders of the systems seldom know ahead of time which other areas of knowledge might lead to insight. They can't always tell computers where to look for new ideas or how to use them. Finally, logic-based AI systems depend on "if-then" rules, and it is often difficult to tell a computer how to recognize the "if" condition in the real world (Dreyfus & Dreyfus, 1988). Consider just one example: *If it's a clock, then set it.* Humans can recognize all kinds of clocks because they have the natural concept of "clock," but computers perform this task very poorly. As discussed earlier, forming natural concepts requires putting into the same category many examples that may have very different physical features—from a bedside digital alarm clock to Big Ben.

artificial intelligence (AI) The field that studies how to program computers to imitate the products of human perception, understanding, and thought.

Neural Network Models Recognizing the problems posed by the need to teach computers to form natural concepts, many researchers in AI have shifted to the *connectionist,* or *neural network,* approach discussed in other chapters (Anderson, 1995). This approach simulates the information processing taking place at many different, but interconnected, locations in the brain. It is very effective for modelling many aspects of perceptual recognition. It has contributed to the development of computers that are able to recognize voices, understand speech, read print, guide missiles, and perform many other complex tasks. Some of these computer simulations are being used to test theories of how speech recognition is learned by infants (e.g., Roy & Pentland, 2002). Other programs have been used to improve on human decision making in areas ranging from judging the quality of meat to predicting the reappearance of cancer (Berg, Engel, & Forrest, 1998; Burke et al., 1998). For example, one program, called PAPNET, actually outperforms human technicians at detecting abnormal cells in smears collected during cervical examinations (Kok & Boon, 1996).

The capacities of current computer models of neural networks still fall well short of those of the human perceptual system, however. For example, computers are slow to learn how to classify visual patterns, which has led to disappointment in efforts to develop computerized face recognition systems capable of identifying terrorists and other criminals in public places (Feder, 2004). Computers may also fail to show sudden insight when a key common feature is identified. But even though neural networks are far from perfect "thinking machines," they are sure to play an important role in psychologists' efforts to build ever more intelligent systems and to better understand the principles of human problem solving.

Computer-Assisted Problem Solving One approach to minimizing the limitations of both computers and humans is to have them work together in ways that create a better outcome than either could achieve alone. In medical diagnosis, for example, the human's role is to establish the presence and nature of a patient's symptoms. The computer then combines this information in a completely unbiased way to identify the most likely diagnosis (Swets, Dawes, & Monahan, 2000). Similarly, laboratory technologists who examine blood samples for the causes of

Artificial Intelligence In 2004, 16-year-old Mark Bluvshtein of Toronto was named Canadian Chess Player of the Year and became the youngest Canadian ever to achieve the status of Grandmaster (Chess Federation of Canada, 2005). Although modern technology has led to the development of sophisticated chess programs that have proven challenging even for grandmasters, computers still cannot perceive and think about the world anywhere near as well as humans can. Some observers believe that this situation will eventually change as progress in computer technology and a deepening understanding of human cognitive processes lead to dramatic breakthroughs in artificial intelligence.

disease are assisted by computer programs that serve to reduce errors and memory lapses by (1) keeping track of the findings from previous tests, (2) listing possible tests that remain to be tried, and (3) indicating either that certain tests have been left undone or that a new sequence of tests should be done (Guerlain, 1993, 1995). This kind of human-machine teamwork can also help in the assessment of psychological problems (Nietzel et al., 2003).

Decision Making

Administrators at the Toronto nursing home where deaths were occurring faced a simple decision: repair the faulty ventilation system or risk the deaths of additional residents and staff. Most decisions are not so easy. Patients must decide whether to undergo a dangerous operation; a college graduate must choose a career; a corporate executive must decide whether to shut down a factory. Unlike the high-speed decisions discussed earlier, these decisions require considerable time, planning, and mental effort.

Even carefully considered decisions sometimes lead to undesirable outcomes, however, because the world is uncertain. Decisions made when the outcome is uncertain are called *risky decisions* or *decisions under uncertainty*. Psychologists have discovered many reasons why human decisions may lead to unsatisfactory outcomes, and we describe some of them here.

Evaluating Options

Suppose that you have to choose between (1) an academic major you love but that is unlikely to lead to a good job and (2) a boring major that virtually guarantees a high-paying job. The fact that each option has positive and negative features, or *attributes,* greatly complicates decision making. Deciding which car to buy, which college to attend, or even how to spend the evening are all examples of *multi-attribute decision making* (Edwards, 1987). Often these decisions are further complicated by difficulties in comparing the attributes and in estimating the probabilities of various outcomes.

Comparing Attributes Part of the difficulty in making multi-attribute decisions lies in the limited capacity of short-term memory. Sometimes, we simply can't keep in mind all of the attributes of all of our options long enough to compare them (Bettman, Johnson, & Payne, 1990). Instead, we tend to focus on the one attribute that is most important to us (Kardes, 1999; Tversky, 1972). If, for instance, finishing a degree quickly is most important to you, then you might choose courses based mainly on graduation requirements, without giving much consideration to professors' reputations. (Listing the pros and cons of each option offers a helpful way of keeping them all in mind as you think about decisions.)

Furthermore, in most important decisions, it may be impossible to compare the attributes of our options in terms of money or other objective criteria. In other words, we are often forced to compare "apples and oranges." Psychologists use the term **utility** to describe the subjective value that each attribute holds for each of us. In deciding on a major, for example, you have to think about the positive and negative utilities of each attribute—such as the job prospects and interest level—of each major. Then you must somehow weigh and combine these utilities. Will the positive utility of enjoying your courses be higher than the negative utility of risking unemployment?

Estimating Probabilities Uncertainty adds other difficulties to the decision-making process: To make a good decision, you should take into account not only the attributes of each option but also the probabilities and risks of their possible outcomes. For example, the economy could change by the time you graduate, closing

utility A subjective measure of value.

many of today's job opportunities in one of the majors you are considering and perhaps opening opportunities in another.

In studying risky decision making, psychologists begin by assuming that the best decision is the one that maximizes **expected value,** or the average benefit you could expect if the decision were repeated on several occasions. Suppose someone asks you to buy a charity raffle ticket. You know that it costs $2 to enter the raffle and that the probability of winning the $100 prize is one in ten (.10). Assuming you are more interested in the prize money than in donating to the charity, should you enter the raffle? The expected value of entering is determined by multiplying the probability of gain (.10) by the size of the gain ($100). The result is the average benefit you would receive if you entered the raffle many times. Next, from this product you subtract the probability of loss, which is 1.0 (the entry fee is a certain loss), multiplied by the amount of the loss ($2). That is, $(.10 \times \$100) - (1.0 \times \$2) = \$8$. Because this $8 expected value is greater than the expected value of not entering (which is zero), you should enter. However, if the odds of winning the raffle were one in a hundred (.01), then the expected value of entering would be $(.01 \times \$100) - (1.0 \times \$2) = -\$1$. In this case, the expected value is negative, so you should not enter the raffle.

Biases and Flaws in Decision Making

Most people think of themselves as logical and rational, but in making decisions about everything from giving up smoking to investing in the stock market, they do not always act in ways that maximize expected value (Arkes & Ayton, 1999; Gilovich, 1997; Shiller, 2001). Why not?

Gains, Losses, and Probabilities For one thing, positive utilities are not mirror images of negative utilities. People usually feel worse about losing a certain amount than they feel good about gaining the same amount. This phenomenon is known as *loss aversion* (Dawes, 1998; Tversky & Kahneman, 1991). They may be willing to exert more effort to try to collect a $100 debt, for example, than to try to win a $100 prize.

It also appears that the utility of a specific gain depends not on how large the gain actually is but on what the starting point was. Suppose you can do something to receive a coupon for a free dinner worth $10. Does this gain have the same utility as having an extra $10 added to your paycheque? The amount of gain is the same, but people tend to behave as if the difference in utility between $0 and $10 is much greater than the difference between, say, $300 and $310. So the person who refuses to do an after-work errand across town for an extra $10 on payday might gladly make the same trip to pick up a $10 coupon. This tendency conforms to Weber's law of psychophysics, discussed in the chapter on perception. The subjective value of a gain depends on how much you already have (Dawes, 1998); the more you have, the less it means. Understanding these biases, and how they affect people's purchasing patterns and other economic decisions, has proven so important that psychologist Daniel Kahneman received the 2002 Nobel Prize in economics for his research in this area.

People are also biased in how they perceive probability, and this bias may lead to less-than-optimal decisions. One kind of probability bias comes into play when making decisions about extremely likely or extremely unlikely events. In such cases, we tend to overestimate the probability of the unlikely events and to underestimate the probability of the likely ones (Kahneman & Tversky, 1984). This bias helps explain why people gamble and enter lotteries, even though the odds are against them and the decision to do so has a negative expected value. According to the formula for expected value, buying a $1 lottery ticket when the probability of winning $4 million is 1 in 10 million yields an expected value of minus 60 cents. But because people overestimate the probability of winning, they believe there is a positive expected value. The tendency to overestimate the likelihood of unlikely events is

expected value The total benefit to be expected if a decision were to be repeated several times.

amplified by the availability heuristic: Vivid memories of rare gambling successes and the publicity given to lottery winners help people recall gains rather than losses when deciding about future gambles.

Another bias relating to probability is called the *gambler's fallacy*: People believe that future events in a random process will be changed by past events. This belief is false. For example, if you flip a coin and it comes up heads ten times in a row, the chance that it will come up heads on the eleventh try is still 50 percent. Some gamblers, however, will continue feeding a slot machine that hasn't paid off much for hours, assuming it is "due." This assumption may be partly responsible for the persistence of gambling and other behaviours that are only rewarded now and then. We discuss this phenomenon, called the *partial reinforcement extinction effect,* in the chapter on learning.

LINKAGES

Group Processes in Problem Solving and Decision Making

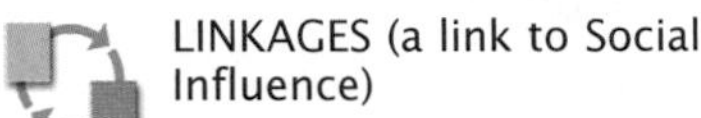

The processes that influence an individual's problem solving and decision making continue to operate when the individual is in a group, but group interactions also shape the outcome. When groups are trying to make a decision, for example, they usually begin by considering the preferences or opinions stated by various members. Not all of these views have equal influence, though. Views that are shared by the greatest number of group members will have the greatest impact on the group's final decision (Tindale & Kameda, 2000). This means that extreme proposals or opinions will usually have less effect on group decisions than those that are more representative of the majority's views.

Nevertheless, group discussions sometimes result in decisions that are more extreme than the group members would make individually. This tendency toward extreme decisions by groups, called *group polarization* (Rodrigo & Ato, 2002), appears to result from two mechanisms. First, most arguments presented during the discussion favour the majority view. Most criticisms are directed at the minority view, and (influenced by confirmation bias) group members tend to seek additional information that supports the majority position (Schulz-Hardt et al., 2000). In this atmosphere, it seems rational to those favouring the majority view to adopt an even stronger version of it (Stasser, 1991). Second, once some group members begin to agree that a particular decision is desirable, other members may try to associate themselves with that decision, perhaps by advocating an even more extreme version (Kaplan & Miller, 1987).

Are people better at problem solving and decision making when they work in groups than when on their own? This is one of the questions about human thought studied by social psychologists. In a typical experiment, a group of people is asked to solve a problem such as the one in Figure 8.13 or to make a decision about the guilt or innocence of a defendant in a fictional court case. Each person is asked to work alone and then to join with the others to try to agree on a decision. These studies have found that when problems have solutions that can be demonstrated easily to all members, groups will usually outperform individuals at solving them (Laughlin, 1999). When problems have less obvious solutions, groups may be somewhat better at solving them than their average member, but usually no better than their most talented member (Hackman, 1998). And because of a phenomenon called *social loafing* (discussed in the chapter on social behaviour), people working in a group are often less productive than people working alone (Williams & Sommer, 1997).

Other research (e.g., Stasser, Stewart, & Wittenbaum, 1995) suggests that a critical element in successful group problem solving is the sharing of individual members' unique information and expertise. For example, when asked to diagnose an illness, groups of physicians were much more accurate when they pooled their knowledge (Larson et al., 1998). However, *brainstorming,* a popular strategy that supposedly encourages group members to generate innovative solutions to a problem, may actually produce fewer ideas than are generated by individuals working alone (Kerr & Tindale, 2004). This result may occur because the lively and freewheeling discussion associated with brainstorming impairs each member's ability to think clearly and productively. In other words, running comments from the group can interfere with the creative process in individuals (Nijstad, Stroebe, & Lodewijkx, 2003). Further, some participants in a brainstorming session may be reluctant to offer an idea, even a good one, for fear it will be rejected or ridiculed by the group (Kerr & Tindale, 2004). To prevent these problems, some brainstorming groups today meet electronically, using computers to present and comment on ideas. Participants in these meetings can offer their suggestions anonymously and without being interrupted, yet still have access to the ideas of all the other members. Because this arrangement allows people to think more clearly and express even "oddball" ideas without fear, specially arranged electronic brainstorming groups may actually outperform groups that meet face to face (Nijstad, Stroebe, & Lodewijkx, 2003).

As they work to solve a problem, the members of a group manipulate their own concepts, propositions, images, and other mental representations. How does each member share these private events so as to help the group perform its task? The answer lies in the use of language.

Language

Language is the primary means through which we communicate our thoughts to others. We use language not only to share the thoughts we have at the moment but also to pass on cultural information and traditions from one generation to the next. In this section, we describe the elements that make up a language, the ways that people use language to communicate, the means by which language is learned, and how language influences our thinking.

The Elements of Language

A **language** has two basic elements: (1) symbols, such as words, and (2) a set of rules, called **grammar,** for combining those symbols. With their knowledge of approximately 50 000 to 100 000 words (Miller, 1991), humans can create and understand an infinite number of sentences. All of the sentences ever spoken are built from just a few dozen categories of sounds. The power of language comes from the way these rather unimpressive raw materials are organized according to certain rules. This organization occurs at several levels.

From Sounds to Sentences Organization occurs first at the level of sounds. A **phoneme** is the smallest unit of sound that affects the meaning of speech. Changing a phoneme changes the meaning of a spoken word, much as changing a letter in a printed word changes its meaning. *Tea* has a meaning different from *sea,* and *sight* is different from *sigh*.

The number of phonemes in the world's languages varies from a low of 13 (Hawaiian) to a high of over 60 (Hindi). Most languages have between 30 and 50 phonemes; English uses about 40. With 40 basic sounds and an alphabet of only 26 letters, you can see that the same letters must sometimes signal different sounds. For example, the letter *a* stands for different phonemes in the words *cat* and *cake*.

Although changing a phoneme affects the meaning of speech, phonemes themselves are not meaningful. We combine them to form a higher level of organization:

language Symbols and a set of rules for combining them that provides a vehicle for communication.

grammar A set of rules for combining the words used in a given language.

phoneme The smallest unit of sound that affects the meaning of speech.

morphemes. A **morpheme** is the smallest unit of language that has meaning. For example, because they have meaning, *dog* and *run* are morphemes; but so are prefixes such as *un-* and suffixes such as *-ed,* because they, too, have meaning, even though they cannot stand alone.

Words are made up of one or more morphemes (e.g., Devlin et al., 2004). Words, in turn, are combined to form phrases and sentences according to a set of grammatical rules called **syntax.** According to English syntax, a subject and a verb must be combined in a sentence, adjectives typically appear before the nouns that they modify, and so on. Compare the following sentences:

Fatal accidents deter careful drivers.

Snows sudden floods melting cause.

The first sentence makes sense, but the second sentence violates English syntax. If the words were reordered, however, they would produce the perfectly acceptable sentence "Melting snows cause sudden floods."

Even if you use English phonemes combined in proper ways to form morphemes strung together according to the laws of English syntax, you may still not end up with an acceptable sentence. Consider the sentence "Rapid bouquets deter sudden neighbours." It somehow sounds right, but it is nonsense. Why? It has syntax, but it ignores the set of rules, called **semantics,** that govern the meaning of words and sentences. For example, because of its meaning, the noun *bouquets* cannot be modified by the word *rapid.*

Surface Structure and Deep Structure So far, we have discussed elements of language that are apparent in the sentences people produce. These elements were the focus of study by linguists for many decades. Then, in 1965, Noam Chomsky started a revolution in the study of language. He argued that if linguists looked only at the language that people produce, they would never uncover the principles that account for all aspects of language. They could not explain,

Making sure that the surface structures we create accurately convey the deep structures we intend is one of the greatest challenges people face when communicating through language.

morpheme The smallest unit of language that has meaning.

word Unit of language composed of one or more morphemes.

syntax The set of rules that govern the formation of phrases and sentences in a language.

semantics Rules governing the meaning of words and sentences.

figure 8.16

Surface Structure and Deep Structure

The listener on the right has interpreted the speaker's message in a way that differs from the speaker's intended deep structure. Obviously, identical surface structures can correspond to quite different deep structures.

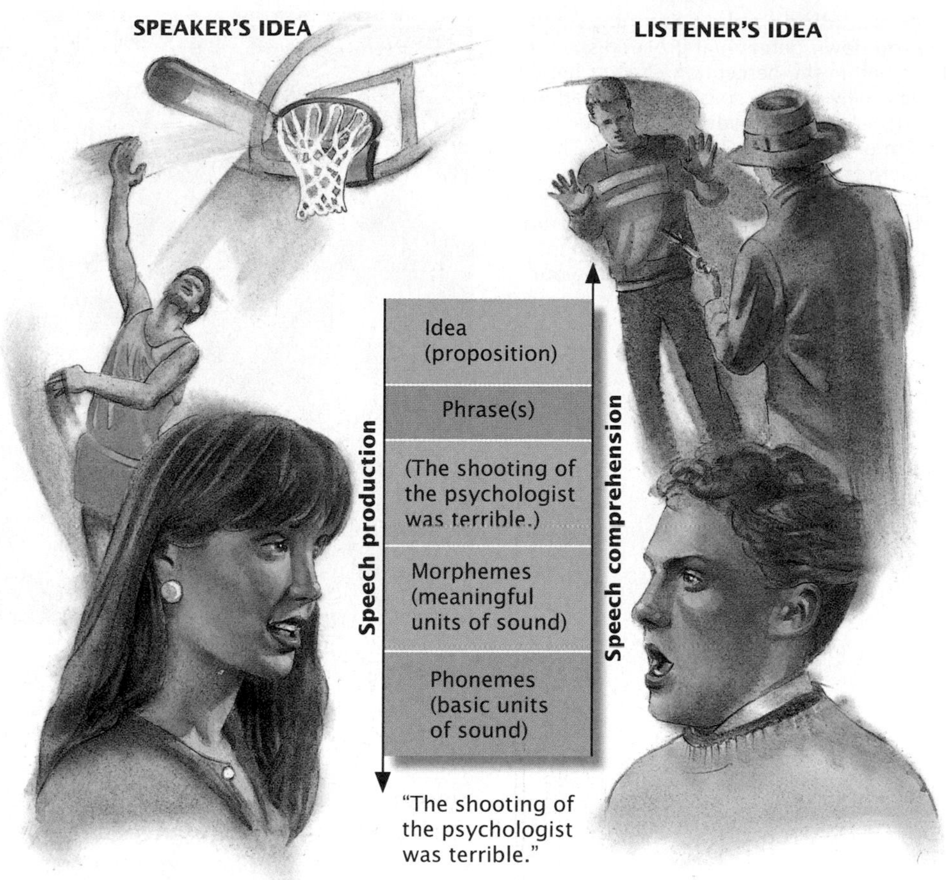

for example, how the sentence "This is my old friend" has more than one meaning. Nor could they account for the close relationship between the meanings of such sentences as "Don't give up just because things look bad" and "It ain't over 'til it's over."

To take these aspects of language into account, Chomsky proposed a more abstract level of analysis. He said that behind the strings of words people produce, called **surface structures**, there is a **deep structure**, an abstract representation of the relationships expressed in a sentence. For example, as Figure 8.16 illustrates, the surface structure "The shooting of the psychologist was terrible" can represent either of two deep structures: (1) that the psychologist had terrible aim or (2) that it was terrible that someone shot the psychologist. Chomsky's original analysis of deep and surface structures was important because it encouraged psychologists to analyze not just verbal behaviour and grammatical rules but also mental representations.

Understanding Speech

When someone speaks to you in your own language, your sensory, perceptual, and other cognitive systems reconstruct the sounds of speech in a way that allows you to detect, recognize, and understand what the person is saying. The process may seem effortless, but it involves amazingly complex feats of information processing.

Scientists trying to develop speech-recognition software systems have discovered just how complex the process is. After decades of effort, the accuracy and efficiency of these systems are still not much better than those of the average five-year-old child. What makes understanding speech so complicated?

surface structure The order in which words are arranged in sentences.

deep structure An abstract representation of the underlying meanings of a given sentence.

Understanding Spoken Language The top-down perceptual processes described in the perception chapter help explain why people speaking an unfamiliar language seem to produce a continuous stream of abnormally rapid speech. The problem is that you don't know where each word starts and stops. Without any perceived gaps, the sounds of speech run together, creating the impression of rapid-fire "chatter." People unfamiliar with your language think you are speaking extremely fast, too!

One factor is that the physical features of a particular speech sound are not always the same. This phenomenon is illustrated in Figure 8.17, which shows how the sounds of particular letters differ depending on the sounds that follow them. A second factor complicating our understanding of speech is that each of us creates slightly different speech sounds, even when saying the same words. Third, as people speak, their words are not usually separated by silence. So if the speech spectrograms in Figure 8.17 showed whole sentences, you would not be able to tell where one word ended and the next began.

Perceiving Words and Sentences Despite these challenges, humans can instantly recognize and understand the words and sentences produced by almost anyone speaking a familiar language. In contrast, even the best voice-recognition software must learn to recognize words spoken by a new voice, and even then it may make many mistakes.

Scientists have yet to discover all the details about how people overcome the challenges of understanding speech, but some general answers are emerging. Just as we recognize objects by analyzing their visual features (see the chapter on perception), it appears that humans identify and recognize the specific—and changing—features of the sounds created when someone speaks. And as in visual perception, this *bottom-up processing* of stimulus features combines with *top-down processing* guided by knowledge-based factors, such as context and expectation, to aid understanding (Samuel, 2001). For example, knowing the general topic of conversation helps you to recognize individual words that might otherwise be hard to understand (Cole & Jakimik, 1978).

In addition, speech comprehension is often guided by nonverbal cues. The frown, the enthusiastic nod, or the bored yawn that accompanies speech each carries information that helps you understand what the person is saying. So if someone says "Wow, are you smart!" but really means "I think you're a jerk," you will detect the true meaning based on the context, facial expression, and tone of voice. No wonder it is usually easier to understand someone in a face-to-face conversation than on the telephone or via email (Massaro & Stork, 1998).

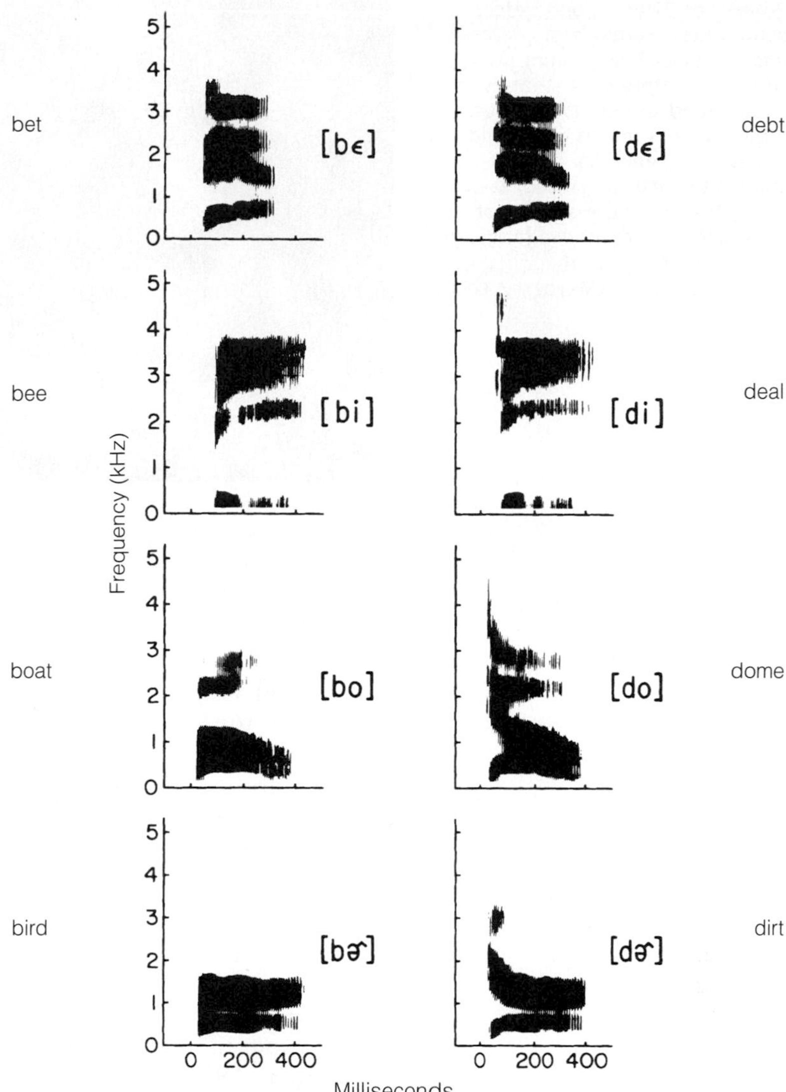

figure 8.17

Speech Spectrograms

These speech spectrograms show what the sound frequencies of speech look like as people say various words. Notice how the shape of the whole speech signal differs from one word to another, even when the initial consonant (*b* or *d*) is the same.

Source: Jusczyk et al. 1981.

The Development of Language

Children the world over develop language with impressive speed. The average six-year-old already has a vocabulary of about 13 000 words (Pinker, 1994). But acquiring a language involves more than just learning vocabulary. We also have to learn how words are combined and how to produce and understand sentences. Psychologists who study the development of language have found that the process begins in the earliest days of a child's life and follows some predictable steps (Saffran, Senghas, & Trueswell, 2001).

The First Year Janet Werker, of the University of British Columbia, is a well-known researcher in the field of infant speech perception. She and her colleagues have found that early in the first year of life, babies can tell the difference between the sounds of their native language and those of other languages. Furthermore, by ten months of age, infants pay closer attention to speech in their native language (Werker & Tees, 1999). In the first year, then, infants become more and more attuned to the sounds that will be important in acquiring their native language. In fact, this early experience with language appears to be vital. Without it, language acquisition can be impaired (Mayberry & Lock, 2003).

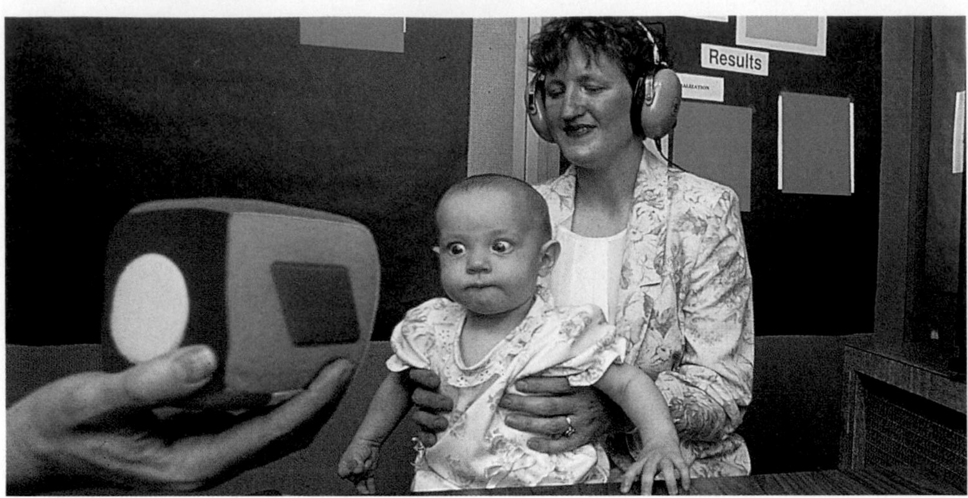

Getting Ready to Talk Long before they utter their first words, babies are getting ready to talk. Experiments in Patricia Kuhl's laboratory show that even six-month-olds tend to look longer at faces whose lip movements match the sounds of spoken words. This tendency reflects babies' abilities to focus on, recognize, and discriminate among the sounds of speech, especially in their native language. These abilities are crucial to the development of language (Mayberry, Lock, & Kazmi, 2002).

LINKAGES (a link to Human Development)

The first year is also the time when babies begin to produce **babblings,** which are patterns of meaningless sounds that resemble speech. Infants of all nationalities begin with the same set of babbling sounds. At about nine months, however, babies who hear only English start to lose their German gutturals and French nasals. At this time, babbling becomes more complex and begins to sound like "sentences" in the babies' native language (Goldstein, King, & West, 2003). Starting around this time, too, babies who hear English begin to shorten some of their vocalizations to "da," "duh," and "ma." These sounds seem very much like language, and babies use them in specific contexts and with obvious purpose (Blake & de Boysson-Bardies, 1992). Accompanied by appropriate gestures, they may be used to express joy ("oohwow") or anger ("uh-uh-uh"), to get something that is out of reach ("engh-engh"), or to point out something interesting ("dah!"). Interestingly, in research conducted at McGill University in Montreal, Laura Petitto and Paula Marentette found evidence that deaf babies exposed to sign language from birth babble using their hands (Petitto & Marentette, 1991).

By 10 to 12 months of age, babies can understand several words—certainly more words than they can say (Fenson et al., 1994). Proper names and object labels are among the earliest words they understand. Often the first word they understand is a pet's name. Proper names and object words—such as *mama, daddy, cookie, doggy,* and *car*—are also among the first words children are likely to say when, at around 12 months of age, they begin to talk (some do this a little earlier and some a little later). Nouns for simple object categories (*dog, flower*) are acquired before more general nouns (*animal, plant*) or more specific names (*collie, rose;* Rosch et al., 1976).

Of course, these early words do not sound exactly like adult language. English-speaking babies usually reduce them to a shorter, easier form, such as "duh" for *duck* or "mih" for *milk*. Children make themselves understood, however, by using gestures, tone of voice, facial expressions, and endless repetitions. If they have a word for an object, they may "overextend" it to cover more ground. So they might use *dog* for cats, bears, and horses. They might use *fly* for all insects and perhaps for other small things like raisins and M&Ms (Clark, 1983, 1993). Children make these "errors" because their vocabularies are limited, not because they fail to notice the difference between dogs and cats or because they want to eat a fly (Fremgen & Fay, 1980; Rescorla, 1981).

Until they can say the correct words for objects, children overextend the words they have, use all-purpose sounds (such as "dat" or "dis"), and coin new words (such as *pepping* for "shaking the pepper shaker"; Becker, 1994). Being around

babblings The first sounds infants make that resemble speech.

people who don't understand these overextensions encourages children to learn and use more precise words (Markman, 1994). During this period, children build up their vocabularies one word at a time. They also use their limited vocabulary one word at a time; they cannot yet put words together into sentences.

The Second Year The **one-word stage** of speech lasts for about six months. Then, sometime around 18 months of age, children's vocabularies expand dramatically (Gleitman & Landau, 1994). They may learn several new words each day, and by the age of two, most youngsters can use 50 to well over 100 words. They also start using two-word combinations to form efficient little sentences. These two-word sentences are called *telegraphic* because they are brief and to the point, leaving out anything that is not absolutely essential. So if she wants her mother to give her a book, a 20-month-old might first say, "Give book," then "Mommy give," and if that does not work, "Mommy book." The child also uses rising tones to indicate a question ("Go out?") and puts stress on certain words to indicate location ("Play *park*") or new information ("*Big* car").

Three-word sentences come next in the development of language. They are still telegraphic, but more nearly complete: "Mommy give book." The child can now speak in sentences that have the usual subject-verb-object form of adult sentences. Other words and word endings begin appearing, too, such as the suffix *-ing*, the prepositions *in* and *on*, the plural *-s*, and irregular past tenses ("It broke," "I ate"; Brown, 1973; Dale, 1976). Children learn to use the suffix *-ed* for the past tense ("I walked"), but then they often overapply this rule to irregular verbs that they previously used correctly. They'll say, for example, "It breaked," "It broked," or "I eated" (Marcus, 1996).

Children also expand their sentences with adjectives, although at first they make some mistakes. For instance, they are likely to use both *less* and *more* to mean "more" or both *tall* and *short* to mean "tall" (Smith & Sera, 1992).

The Third Year and Beyond By age three or so, children begin to use auxiliary verbs ("Adam is going") and to ask questions using *wh-* words, such as *what, where, who,* and *why*. They begin to put together clauses to form complex sentences ("Here's the ball I was looking for"). By age five, children have acquired most of the grammatical rules of their native language.

How Is Language Acquired?

Despite all that has been discovered about the steps children follow in acquiring language, mystery and debate still surround the question of just *how* they do it. Obviously, children pick up the specific content of language from the speech they hear around them: English children learn English, and Italian children learn Italian. As parents and children share meals, playtime, and conversations, children learn that words refer to objects and actions and what the labels for them are. But how do children learn syntax, the rules of grammar?

Conditioning, Imitation, and Rules Our discussion of conditioning in the chapter on learning would suggest that children learn syntax because their parents reward them for using it. This sounds reasonable, but observational studies show that positive reinforcement does not tell the whole story. Parents are usually more concerned about what is said than about its grammatical form (Hirsch-Pasek, Treiman, & Schneiderman, 1984). So when the little boy with chocolate crumbs on his face says, "I not eat cookie," his mother is more likely to say, "Yes, you did" than to ask the child to say, "I did not eat the cookie" and then praise him for grammatical correctness.

one-word stage A stage of language development during which children tend to use one word at a time.

Learning through modelling, or imitation, appears to be more influential. Children learn grammar most rapidly when adults demonstrate the correct syntax in the course of a conversation, as in the following example:

CHILD: Mommy fix.

MOTHER: Okay, Mommy will fix the truck.

CHILD: It breaked.

MOTHER: Yes, it broke.

CHILD: Truck broke.

MOTHER: Let's see if we can fix it.

But if children learn syntax by imitation, why would they overgeneralize rules, such as the rule for making the past tense? Why, for example, do children who at one time said "I went" later say "I goed"? Adults never use this form of speech. Its sudden appearance indicates that the child either has mastered the rule of adding *-ed* or has generalized from similar-sounding words (such as *mowed* or *rowed*). In short, neither conditioning nor imitation seems entirely adequate to explain how children learn language. Children must still analyze for themselves the underlying patterns in the language examples they hear around them (Bloom, 1995).

Biological Bases for Language Acquisition The ease with which children everywhere discover these underlying patterns and learn language has led some to argue that language acquisition is at least partly innate. For example, Chomsky believes that we have a built-in *universal grammar,* a mechanism that allows us to identify the basic dimensions of language (Baker, 2002; Chomsky, 1986; Nowak, Komarova, & Niyogi, 2001). One of these dimensions is how important word order is in the syntax of a particular language. In English, for example, word order tells us who is doing what to whom (the sentences "Heather dumped Jason" and "Jason dumped Heather" contain the same words, but they have different meanings). In languages such as Russian, however, word order is less important than the modifiers attached to the word, also called *inflections*. According to Chomsky, a child's universal grammar might initially be "set" to assume that word order is important to syntax, but it would change if the child hears language in which word order is not crucial. In Chomsky's system, then, we don't entirely learn language—we develop it as genetic predispositions interact with experience (Senghas & Coppola, 2001). Evidence that supports claims of a genetic predisposition for language comes from studies of *specific language impairment* (*SLI*). Children displaying SLI have trouble acquiring language despite having otherwise normal mental abilities, normal hearing, and adequate early exposure to language sounds (Gopnik & Crago, 1991). Because SLI runs in families, several investigators have proposed that it reflects a defect in the genes that normally provide us with our universal grammar (e.g., Pinker, 1994; Van der Lely, 1994). This is a controversial idea, though, partly because of evidence that people with SLI have specific deficiencies in auditory processing that might account for their difficulty in acquiring grammar (e.g., Bishop, 1997).

Indeed, other theorists argue that the development of language reflects the development of more general cognitive skills rather than innate, language-specific mechanisms (e.g., Bates, 1993). But even if Chomsky overestimated the role of genetics in language acquisition, there is other evidence to support the existence of more general biological contributions. For example, the unique speech-generating properties of the human mouth and throat, the language-related brain regions such as Broca's area and Wernicke's area (see Figure 3.17), and recent genetic research all suggest that humans are innately "prewired," or biologically programmed, for language (Buxhoeveden et al., 2001; Lai et al., 2001). In addition, there appears to be

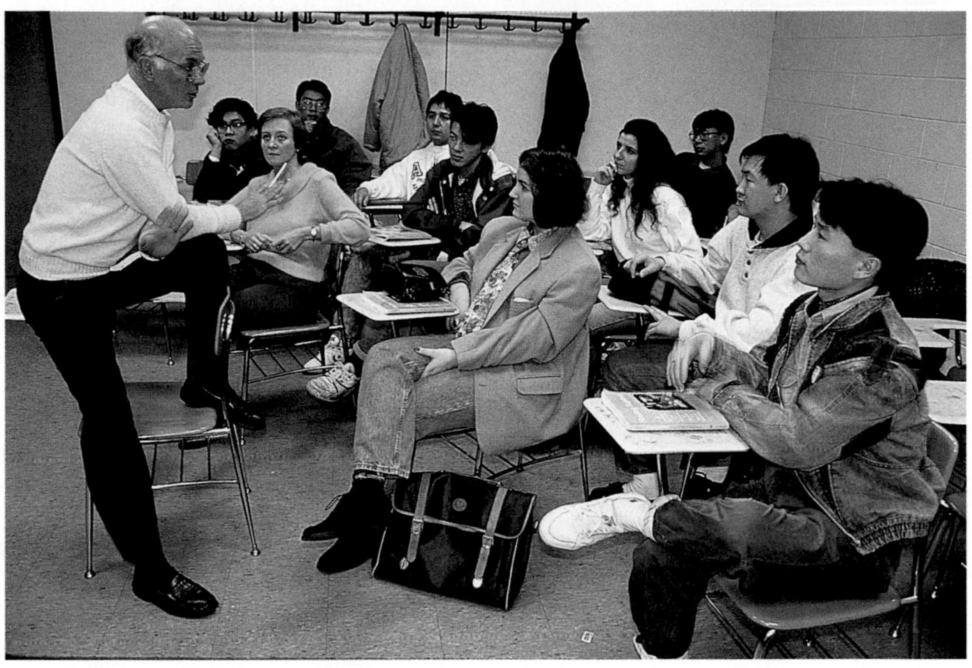

Learning a Second Language The notion of a critical period for language acquisition is supported by the fact that after the age of 13 or 14, people learn a second language more slowly (Johnson & Newport, 1989) and virtually never learn to speak it without an accent (Lenneberg, 1967).

a *critical period* in childhood during which we can learn language more easily than at any other time (Ridley, 2000). The existence of this critical period is supported by the difficulties adults have in learning a second language (e.g., Lenneberg, 1967) and also by cases in which unfortunate children spent their early years in isolation from human contact and the sound of adult language. Even after years of therapy and language training, these individuals are not able to combine ideas into sentences (Rymer, 1993). These cases suggest that, as mentioned earlier, acquiring the complex features of language depends on being exposed to speech before a certain age.

Bilingualism Does trying to learn two languages at once, even before the critical period is over, impair the learning of either? Research suggests just the opposite. Although their early language utterances may be confused or delayed, children who are raised in a bilingual environment before the end of the critical period seem to show enhanced performance in each language (De Houwer, 1995). There is also some evidence that *balanced bilinguals*—people who developed roughly equal mastery of two languages as children—are superior to others in cognitive flexibility, concept formation, and creativity. It is as if each language offers a slightly different perspective on thinking, and this dual perspective makes the brain more flexible (Hong et al., 2000).

The apparent benefits of bilingualism have important implications for Canadian school systems, in which children from English-speaking homes are often enrolled in immersion programmes where they receive instruction in French. Although lack of control over school environments makes it difficult to perform true experiments on the effects of this practice, available evidence suggests that these bilingual programs facilitate educational achievement (Bialystok et al., 2005).

THINKING CRITICALLY
Can Nonhumans Use Language?

Some psychologists say that it is our ability to acquire and use language that sets humans apart from all other creatures. Yet those creatures, too, use symbols to communicate. Bees perform a dance that tells other bees where they found sources of nectar; killer whales signal each other as they hunt in groups; and the grunts and gestures of chimpanzees signify varying desires and emotions. These forms of communication do not necessarily have the grammatical characteristics of language, however (Povinelli & Bering, 2002; Rendall, Cheney, & Seyfarth, 2000). Are any animals other than humans capable of learning language?

- **What am I being asked to believe or accept?**

Over the past 40 years, several researchers have asserted that nonhumans can master language. Chimpanzees and gorillas have been the most popular targets of study, because at maturity they are estimated to have the intelligence of two- or three-year-old children, who are usually well on their way to learning language. Dolphins, too, have been studied because they have a complex communication system and exceptionally large brains relative to their body size (Janik, 2000; Reiss & Marino, 2001). It would seem that if these animals were unable to learn language, their general intelligence could not be blamed. Instead, failure would be attributed to the absence of a genetic makeup that permits language learning.

- **What evidence is available to support the assertion?**

The question of whether nonhuman mammals can learn to use language is not a simple one, for at least two reasons. First, language is more than just communication, but defining just when animals are exhibiting that "something more" is a source of debate. What seems to set human language apart from the gestures, grunts, chirps, whistles, or cries of other animals is grammar—a formal set of rules for combining words. Also, because of their anatomical structures, nonhuman mammals will never be able to "speak" in the same way that humans do (Lieberman, 1991; Nishimura et al., 2003). To test these animals' ability to learn language, investigators therefore must devise novel ways for them to communicate.

David and Ann Premack taught their chimp, Sarah, to communicate by placing differently shaped chips, each symbolizing a word, on a magnetic board (Premack, 1971). Lana, a chimpanzee studied by Duane Rumbaugh (1977), learned to communicate by pressing keys on a specially designed computer. American Sign Language (ASL), the hand-gesture language used by people who are deaf, has been used by Beatrice and Allen Gardner with the chimp Washoe, by Herbert Terrace with Nim Chimsky, a chimp named after Noam Chomsky, and by Penny Patterson with a gorilla named Koko. Finally, Kanzi, a bonobo, or pygmy chimpanzee, studied by Sue Savage-Rumbaugh (1990; Savage-Rumbaugh et al., 1993), learned to recognize spoken words and to communicate by both gesturing and pressing word-symbol keys on a computer that would "speak" them. Kanzi was a special case: He learned to communicate by listening and watching as his mother, Matata, was being taught and then used what he had learned to interact with her trainers.

Studies of these animals suggested that they could use combinations of words to refer to things that were not present. Washoe, Lana, Sarah, Nim, and Kanzi all mastered between 130 and 500 words. Their vocabulary included names for concrete objects, such as *apple* or *me*; verbs, such as *tickle* and *eat*; adjectives, such as *happy* and *big*; and adverbs, such as *again*. The animals combined the words in sentences, expressing wishes such as "You tickle me" or "If Sarah good, then apple." Sometimes the sentences referred to things in the past. When an investigator called attention to a wound that Kanzi had received, the animal produced the sentence "Matata hurt," referring to a disciplinary bite his mother had recently given him (Savage-Rumbaugh, 1990). Finally, all these animals seemed to enjoy their communication tools and used them spontaneously to interact with their caretakers and with other animals.

Most of the investigators mentioned here have argued that their animals mastered a crude grammar (Premack & Premack, 1983; Savage-Rumbaugh, Shanker, & Taylor, 2001). For example, if Washoe wanted to be tickled, she would gesture, "You tickle Washoe." But if she wanted to do the tickling, she would gesture, "Washoe tickle you." The correct placement of object and subject in these sentences suggested that Washoe was following a set of rules for word combination—in other words, a grammar (Gardner & Gardner, 1978). Louis Herman and his colleagues documented similar grammatical sensitivity in dolphins, who rarely confused subject-verb order in following instructions given by human hand signals (Herman, Richards, & Wolz, 1984). Furthermore, Savage-Rumbaugh observed several hundred instances in which Kanzi understood sentences he had never heard before. Once, for example, while his back was turned to the speaker, Kanzi heard the sentence "Jeanie hid the pine needles in her shirt." He turned around, approached Jeanie, and searched her shirt to find the pine needles. His actions would seem to indicate that he understood this new sentence the first time he heard it.

● Are there alternative ways of interpreting the evidence?

Many of the early conclusions about primate language learning were challenged by Herbert Terrace and his colleagues in their investigation of Nim (Terrace et al., 1979). Terrace noticed many subtle characteristics of Nim's communications that seemed quite different from a child's use of language, and he argued that animals in other studies demonstrated these same characteristics.

First, he said, their sentences were always very short. Nim could combine two or three gestures but never used strings that conveyed more sophisticated messages. The ape was never able to say anything equivalent to a three-year-old child's "I want to go to Wendy's for a hamburger, OK?" Second, Terrace questioned whether the animals' use of language demonstrated the spontaneity, creativity, and expanding complexity characteristic of children's language. Many of the animals' sentences were requests for food, tickling, baths, pets, and other pleasurable objects and experiences. Is such behaviour different from the kind of behaviour shown by the family dog who learns to sit up and beg for table scraps? Other researchers also pointed out that chimps are not naturally predisposed to associate seen objects with heard words, as human infants are (Savage-Rumbaugh et al., 1983).

Finally, Terrace questioned whether experimenter bias influenced the reports of the chimps' communications. Consciously or not, experimenters who want to conclude that chimps learn language might tend to ignore strings of symbols that violate grammatical order or to reinterpret ambiguous strings so that they make grammatical sense. If Nim sees someone holding a banana and signs, "Nim banana," the experimenter might assume the word order is correct and means "Nim wants the banana" rather than, for example, "That banana belongs to Nim," in which case the word order would be wrong.

● What additional evidence would help to evaluate the alternatives?

Studies of animals' ability to learn language are expensive and take many years. Accordingly, the amount of evidence in the area is small—just a handful of studies, each based on a few animals. Obviously, more data are needed from more studies that use a common methodology.

It is important, as well, to study the extent to which limits on the length of primates' spontaneous sentences result from limits on short-term and working memory (Savage-Rumbaugh & Brakke, 1996). If memory is in fact the main limiting factor, then the failure to produce progressively longer sentences does not necessarily reflect an inability to master language.

Research on how primates might spontaneously acquire language by listening and imitating, as Kanzi did, as well as naturalistic observations of communications among primates in their natural habitat, would also help scientists better understand primates' capacity to communicate (Savage-Rumbaugh et al., 2001; Sevcik & Savage-Rumbaugh, 1994).

● What conclusions are most reasonable?

Psychologists are still not in full agreement about whether our sophisticated mammalian cousins can learn language. Two things are clear, however. First, whatever the chimp, gorilla, and dolphin have learned is a much more primitive and limited form of communication than that learned by children. Second, their level of communication does not do justice to their overall intelligence; these animals are smarter than their "language" production suggests. In short, the evidence to date

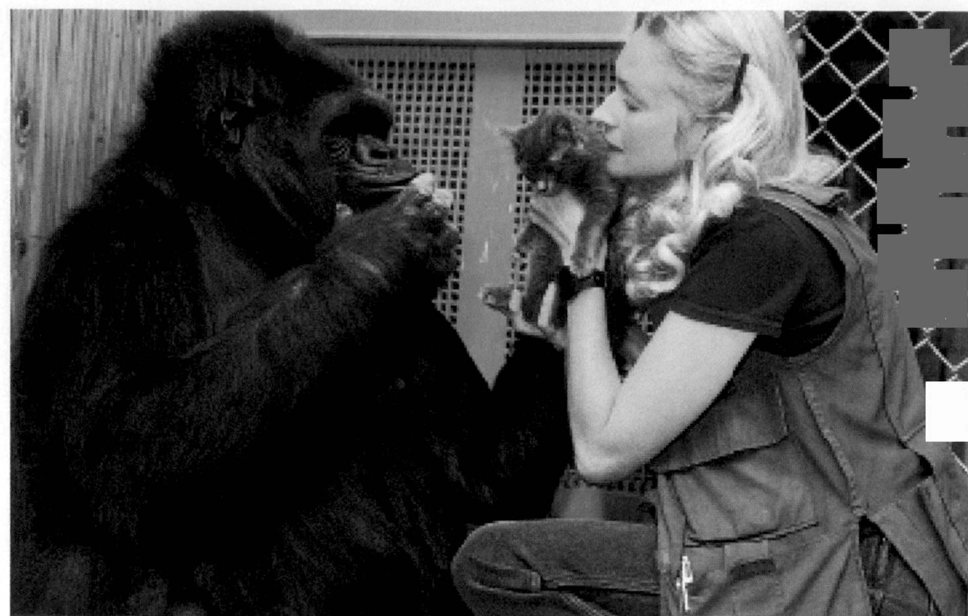

Animal Language? Here, a gorilla named Koko makes the American Sign Language (ASL) gesture for "smoke" as her trainer, Penny Patterson, holds Smoky the cat. In 1998, Patterson made Koko available for an Internet chat session. She relayed online questions to Koko in ASL, and a typist sent back Koko's signed responses.

favours the view that humans have language abilities that are unique (Buxhoeveden et al., 2001), but that under the right circumstances, and with the right tools, other animals can master many language-like skills.

Culture, Language, and Thought

When ideas from one language are translated into another, the intended meaning can easily be distorted, as shown in Table 8.2. But differences in language and culture may have more serious and important implications as well. The language that people speak forms part of their knowledge of the world, and that knowledge, as noted in the chapter on perception, guides perceptions. This relationship raises the question of whether differences among languages create differences in the ways that people perceive and think about the world.

Benjamin Whorf (1956) claimed that language actually determines how we can think, a process he called *linguistic determinism*. He noted, for example, that the Inuit have several different words for "snow" and proposed that this feature of their language should lead to a greater perceptual ability to discriminate among varieties of snow. When these discrimination abilities of the Inuit and other people are compared, there are indeed significant differences. But are these differences in perception the *result* of differences in language?

table 8.2

Sometimes a lack of familiarity with the formal and informal aspects of other languages gets North American advertisers in trouble. Here are three examples.

Lost in Translation
When the Clairol Company introduced its "Mist Stick" curling iron in Germany, it was unaware that *mist* is a German slang word meaning "manure." Not many people wanted to buy a manure stick.
In Chinese, the Kentucky Fried Chicken slogan "Finger lickin' good" came out as "Eat your fingers off."
In Chinese, the slogan for Pepsi, "Come alive with the Pepsi Generation," became "Pepsi brings your ancestors back from the grave."

One of the most interesting tests of Whorf's ideas was conducted by Eleanor Rosch (1975). She compared the perception of colours by North Americans with that by members of the Dani tribe of New Guinea. In the language of the Dani, there are only two colour names—one for dark, "cold" colours and one for lighter, "warm" ones. In contrast, English speakers have names for a vast number of different hues. Of these, it is possible to identify 11 focal colours; these are prototypes, the particular wavelengths of light that are the best examples of the 11 major categories (red, yellow, green, blue, black, grey, white, purple, orange, pink, and brown). Fire-engine red is the focal colour for red. Rosch reasoned that if Whorf's views were correct, then English speakers, who have verbal labels for focal colours, should recognize them better than nonfocal colours. For the Dani, the focal-nonfocal distinction should make no difference. In fact, however, Rosch found that both the Dani and the English-speaking North Americans perceived focal colours more efficiently than nonfocal ones (Heider, 1972).

This study was long seen as providing conclusive evidence against Whorf's linguistic-determinism hypothesis. Recently, though, some psychologists have suggested that language may have some effects on our thinking and that we shouldn't discount some weaker versions of Whorf's hypothesis (e.g., Gordon, 2004; Özgen, 2004; Özgen & Davies, 2002). Their point is that our language may not determine what we think about, but it may still influence how we think. For example, having words for particular concepts can make it easy to remember things based on verbal labels for those concepts. This verbal labelling can affect colour memory, if not colour perception (Lau, Lee, & Chiu, 2004).

Another example of the influence of language on thinking comes from a study of children's understanding of mathematics (Miura et al., 1993). The study found that compared with children who speak Japanese or Korean, children who speak English or French have more trouble understanding the concept of "place value"—such as that the number *eleven* means "one 10 and one 1." As described in the chapter on human development, one important reason for this difference is that some languages make place values more obvious than others. The Korean word for *eleven,* which is *shib-il,* means "ten-one." English speakers have to remember what *eleven* refers to every time they hear it.

Even within a culture, language can affect reasoning, problem solving, and decision making. For example, consider whether you would choose A or B in each of the following situations:

> *The government is preparing for the outbreak of an unusual disease, which you know will kill 600 people if nothing is done. Two programs are proposed. If program A is adopted, 200 people will be saved. If program B is adopted, there is a one-third chance that all 600 people will be saved and a two-thirds chance that no people will be saved.*
>
> *A ship hits a mine in the middle of the ocean, and 600 passengers on board will die if action is not taken immediately. There are two options. If option A is adopted, 400 passengers will die. If option B is adopted, there is a one-third chance that no passengers will die and a two-thirds chance that no passengers will be saved.*

The logic of each situation is the same (program A and option A will both save 200 lives), so people who choose program A in one case should choose option A in the other. But this is not what happens. In one study, 72 percent of participants chose program A in the disease situation, but 78 percent chose option B in the shipwreck situation (Kahneman & Tversky, 1984). Their choices were not logically consistent, because people's thinking tends to be influenced by the words used to describe situations. Here, program A was framed in terms of lives saved; option B was framed in terms of lives lost. Advertisers are well aware of how this *framing effect* alters decisions; as a result, your grocer stocks ground beef labelled as "75 percent lean," not "25 percent fat."

LINKAGES

As noted in the chapter on introducing psychology, all of psychology's subfields are related to one another. Our discussion of group processes in problem solving illustrates just one way in which the topic of this chapter, cognition and language, is linked to the subfield of social psychology (especially to the chapter on social influence). The Linkages diagram shows ties to two other subfields as well, and there are many more ties throughout the book. Looking for linkages among subfields will help you see how they all fit together and help you better appreciate the big picture that is psychology.

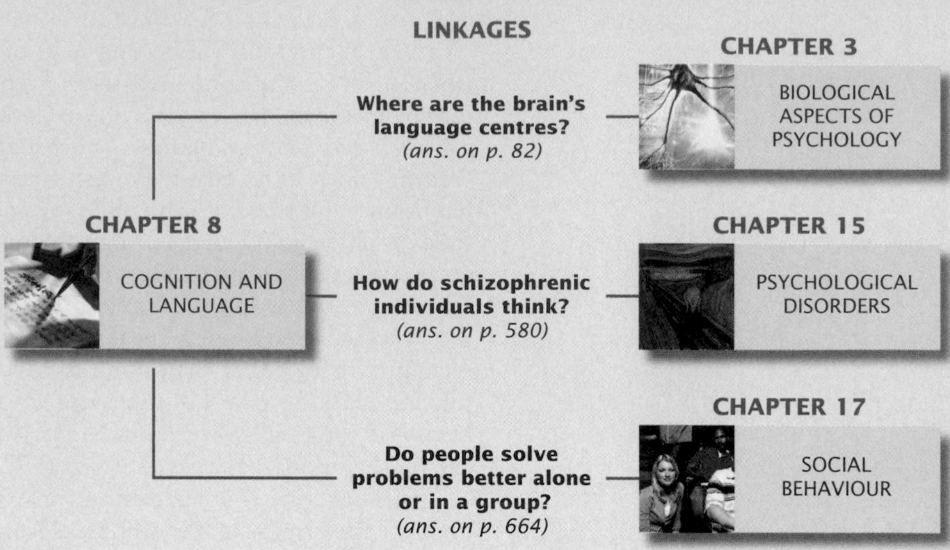

LINKAGES
CHAPTER 8
COGNITION AND LANGUAGE
Where are the brain's language centres?
(ans. on p. 82)
CHAPTER 3
BIOLOGICAL ASPECTS OF PSYCHOLOGY
How do schizophrenic individuals think?
(ans. on p. 580)
CHAPTER 15
PSYCHOLOGICAL DISORDERS
Do people solve problems better alone or in a group?
(ans. on p. 664)
CHAPTER 17
SOCIAL BEHAVIOUR

SUMMARY

Cognitive psychology is the study of the mental processes by which the information we receive from the environment is modified, made meaningful, stored, retrieved, used, and communicated to others.

Basic Functions of Thought

The five core functions of thought are to describe, elaborate, decide, plan, and guide action.

The Circle of Thought

Many psychologists think of the components of the circle of thought as constituting an *information-processing system* that receives, represents, transforms, and acts on incoming stimuli. *Thinking,* then, is defined as the manipulation of mental representations by this system.

Measuring Information Processing

The time elapsing between the presentation of a stimulus and an overt response to it is the *reaction time*. Among the factors affecting reaction times are the complexity of the choice of a response, stimulus-response compatibility, expectancy, and the tradeoff between speed and accuracy. Using methods such as the EEG and neuro-imaging techniques, psychologists can also measure mental events as reflected in *evoked brain potentials* and other brain activity.

Mental Representations: The Ingredients of Thought

Mental representations take the form of concepts, propositions, schemas, scripts, mental models, images, and cognitive maps.

Concepts

Concepts are categories of objects, events, or ideas with common properties. They may be formal or natural. *Formal concepts* are precisely defined by the presence or absence of certain features. *Natural concepts* are fuzzy; no fixed set of defining properties determines membership in a natural concept. A member of a natural concept that displays all or most of its characteristic features is called a *prototype*.

Propositions

Propositions are assertions that state how concepts are related. Propositions can be true or false.

Schemas, Scripts, and Mental Models

Schemas are sets of propositions that serve as generalized mental representations of concepts and also generate expectations about them. *Scripts* are schemas of familiar activities that help people to think about those activities and to interpret new events. *Mental models* are clusters of propositions that represent physical objects and processes, as well as guide our thinking about those things. Mental models may be accurate or inaccurate.

Images and Cognitive Maps

Information can be represented as *images* and can be mentally rotated, inspected, and otherwise manipulated. *Cognitive maps* are mental representations of the spatial arrangements in familiar parts of the world.

Thinking Strategies

By combining and transforming mental representations, our information-processing system makes it possible for us to reason, solve problems, and make decisions. *Reasoning* is the process through which people generate and evaluate arguments, as well as reach conclusions about them.

Formal Reasoning

Formal reasoning seeks valid conclusions through the application of rigorous procedures. These procedures include formulas, or *algorithms,* which are guaranteed to produce correct solutions if they exist, and the *rules of logic,* which are useful in evaluating sets of premises and conclusions called *syllogisms*. To reach a sound conclusion, we must consider both the truth or falsity of the premises and the logic of the argument itself. People are prone to logical errors; their belief in a conclusion is often affected by the extent to which the conclusion is consistent with their attitudes, as well as by other factors, including *confirmation bias* and limits on working memory.

Informal Reasoning

People use *informal reasoning* to assess the believability of a conclusion based on the evidence for it. Errors in informal reasoning often stem from the misuse of *heuristics,* or mental shortcuts. Three important heuristics are the *anchoring heuristic* (estimating the probability of an event by adjusting a starting value), the *representativeness heuristic* (categorizing an event by how representative it is of a category), and the *availability heuristic* (estimating probability by how available an event is in memory).

Problem Solving

Steps in problem solving include diagnosing the problem and then planning, executing, and evaluating a solution.

Strategies for Problem Solving

Especially when solutions are not obvious, problem solving can be aided by the use of strategies such as incubation, means-end analysis, working backward, and using analogies.

Obstacles to Problem Solving

Many of the difficulties that people experience in solving problems arise when they are dealing with hypotheses. People do not easily entertain multiple hypotheses. Because of *mental sets,* people may stick to a particular hypothesis even when it is unsuccessful and, through *functional fixedness,* may tend to miss opportunities to use familiar objects in unusual ways. Confirmation bias may lead people to be reluctant to revise or abandon hypotheses, especially cherished ones, on the basis of new evidence, and they may fail to use the absence of information as evidence in solving problems.

Building Problem-Solving Skills

Experts are usually superior to beginners in problem solving because of their knowledge and experience. They can draw on knowledge of similar problems, visualize related components of a problem as a single chunk, and perceive relations among problems in terms of underlying principles rather than surface features. Extensive knowledge is the main component of expertise, yet expertise itself can prevent the expert from seeing problems in new ways.

Problem Solving by Computer

Some specific problems can be solved by computer programs known as expert systems. These systems are one application of *artificial intelligence* (*AI*). One approach to AI focuses on programming computers to imitate the logical manipulation of symbols that occurs in human thought. Another approach (involving connectionist, or neural network, models) attempts to imitate the connections among neurons in the human brain. Current problem-solving computer systems deal most successfully with specific domains. Often, the best outcomes occur when humans and computers work together.

Decision Making

Evaluating Options

Decisions are sometimes difficult because there are too many alternatives and too many attributes of each alternative to consider at the same time. Furthermore, decisions often involve comparisons of subjective *utility,* not objective value. Decision making is also complicated by the fact that the world is unpredictable, which makes decisions risky. In risky decision making, the best decision is one that maximizes *expected value.*

Biases and Flaws in Decision Making

People often fail to maximize expected value in their decisions for two reasons. First, losses are perceived differently from gains of equal size. Second, people tend to overestimate the probability of unlikely events, to underestimate the probability of likely events, and to feel overconfident in the accuracy of their forecasts. The gambler's fallacy leads people to believe that future events in a random process are affected by previous events. People sometimes make decisions aimed at goals other than maximizing expected value. These goals may be determined by personal and cultural factors.

Language

The Elements of Language

Language consists of symbols such as words and rules for their combination—a *grammar*. Spoken *words* are made up of *phonemes*, which are combined to make *morphemes*. Combinations of words must have both *syntax* (grammar) and *semantics* (meaning). Behind the word strings, or *surface structures,* is an underlying representation, or *deep structure,* that expresses the relationship among the ideas in a sentence. Ambiguous sentences occur when one surface structure reflects two or more deep structures.

Understanding Speech

When people listen to speech in a familiar language, their perceptual system allows them to perceive gaps between words, even when those gaps are not physically present. To understand language generally, and conversations in particular, people use their knowledge of the context and of the world. In addition, understanding is guided by nonverbal cues.

The Development of Language

Children develop grammar according to an orderly pattern. *Babblings* and the *one-word stage* of speech come first, then telegraphic two-word sentences. Next come three-word sentences and certain grammatical forms that appear in a somewhat predictable order. Once children learn certain regular verb forms and plural endings, they may overgeneralize rules. Children acquire most of the syntax of their native language by the time they are five years old.

How Is Language Acquired?

Conditioning and imitation both play a role in a child's acquisition of language, but neither can provide a complete explanation of how children acquire syntax. Humans may be biologically programmed to learn language. In any event, it appears that language must be learned during a certain critical period if normal language is to occur. The critical-period notion is supported by research on second-language acquisition.

Culture, Language, and Thought

Research across cultures, and within North American culture, suggests that although language does not determine what we can think, it does influence how we think, solve problems, and make decisions.

Consciousness

In this chapter, we delve into the topic of consciousness and describe research on altered states of consciousness. We'll examine sleep and dreams, hypnosis, and meditation and how they differ from normal waking consciousness. We'll also look at how consciousness is affected by psychoactive drugs. We have organized the chapter as follows:

There is a *Sesame Street* episode in which Ernie is trying to find out whether Bert is asleep or awake. Ernie observes that Bert's eyes are closed, and he comments that Bert usually closes his eyes when he is asleep. Ernie also notes that when Bert is asleep, he does not respond to pokes, so naturally, he delivers a few pokes. At first, Bert does not respond. After being poked a few times, though, he awakes, very annoyed, and yells at Ernie for waking him. Ernie then informs Bert that he just wanted to let him know it was time for his nap.

Analyzing Consciousness

Doctors face a similar situation in dealing with the more than 30 million people each year who receive general anesthesia during surgery. These patients certainly appear to go to sleep, but there is no completely reliable way of knowing whether they are actually unconscious. Glenys Caseley-Rondi at Ontario's University of Waterloo found that patients under general anesthesia were able to perceive auditory information played on a cassette tape recorder during surgery, meaning that they retained some degree of consciousness during the surgical procedure (Caseley-Rondi, Merikle, & Bowers, 1994). In rare cases, patients have conscious awareness of surgical pain and remember it later. Although their surgical incisions heal, these people may be psychologically scarred by the experience and may even show symptoms of post-traumatic stress disorder (Schwender et al., 1995).

The fact that people can be conscious while "asleep" under the influence of powerful anesthetic drugs obviously makes defining consciousness quite difficult (Edelman, 2003). In fact, after decades of discussion and research by philosophers, psychologists, and even physicists, some believe that consciousness is still not yet understood well enough to be precisely defined (Crick & Koch, 1998; King & Pribram, 1995). Given the ethical and legal concerns raised by the need to ensure that patients are not subjected to pain during surgery, doctors tend to define *consciousness* as awareness that is demonstrated by either explicit or implicit recall (Schwender et al., 1995). In psychology, the definition is somewhat broader: **Consciousness** is generally defined as your awareness of the outside world and of your thoughts, feelings, perceptions, and other mental processes (Metzinger, 2000; Zeman, 2001).

In this chapter we consider the nature of consciousness and the ways in which it affects our mental activity and behaviour. Then we examine what happens when consciousness is altered by sleep, hypnosis, and meditation. Finally, we explore the changes in consciousness that occur when people use certain drugs.

Keeping an Eye Out Humans are not the only creatures capable of processing information while apparently unconscious. While ducks sleep, one hemisphere of their brains can process visual information from an eye that remains open. Birds positioned where they are most vulnerable to predators, such as at the end of a row, may spend twice as much time in this "alert" sleep than do birds in more protected positions (Rattenborg, Lima, & Amlaner, 1999).

Some Functions of Consciousness

Francis Crick and Christof Koch have suggested that one function of consciousness is to produce the best current interpretation of sensory information in light of past experience and to make this interpretation available to the parts of the brain that can act on it (Crick & Koch, 2003). They say that having a *single* conscious representation, rather than multiple ones, allows us to be more decisive in taking action. From this perspective, the conscious brain experiences a representation of the world that is the result of many complex computations. It has access to the results of these computational processes but not to the processes themselves. Some of those processes occur so quickly that our conscious experience can't keep up with them. For example, people playing tennis or a computer game can respond to a fast serve or a threatening alien even before they consciously "see" these stimuli. Although conscious processing is not always the fastest processing available, when dealing with life's most complex problems, consciousness allows the most adaptive and efficient blending of sensory input, motor responses, and knowledge resources in the brain (Baars, 2002).

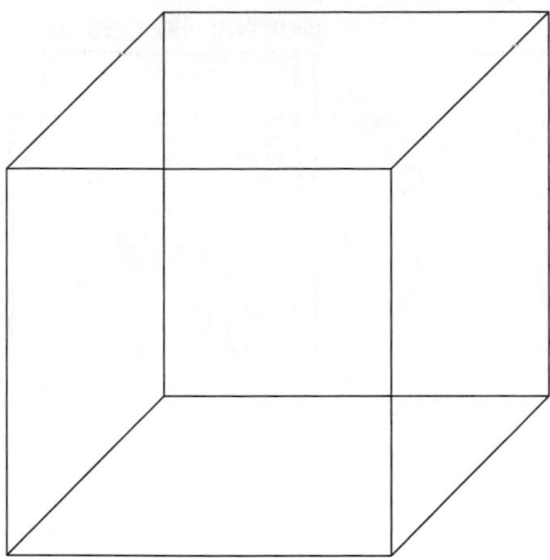

figure 9.1

The Necker Cube

Each of the two squares in the Necker cube can be perceived as either the front or rear surface of the cube. Try to make the cube switch back and forth between these two orientations. Now try to hold only one orientation. You probably cannot maintain the whole cube in consciousness for longer than about three seconds before it "flips" from one orientation to the other.

As described in the chapter on memory, the contents of consciousness at any given moment are limited by the capacity of short-term memory, but the overall process of consciousness allows access to a vast store of memories and other information. In one study, for example, participants paid brief conscious attention to ten thousand different pictures over several days. A week later they were able to recognize more than 90 percent of the photographs. Evidently, mere consciousness of an event helps to store a recognizable memory that can later be brought into consciousness (Kosslyn, 1994).

Over a century ago, psychologist William James compared consciousness to a stream, describing it as ever changing, multilayered, and varying in both quantity and quality. Variations in quantity—in the degree to which one is aware of mental events—result in different *levels of consciousness.* Variations in quality—in the nature of the mental processing available to awareness—lead to different *states of consciousness* (Tassi & Muzet, 2001). Appreciating the difference between levels of consciousness and states of consciousness takes a little thought. When you are alert and aware of your mental activity and of incoming sensations, you are fully conscious. At the same time, however, other mental activity is taking place within your brain at varying "distances" from your conscious awareness. These activities are occurring at differing *levels* of consciousness. It is when your experience of yourself varies in focus and clarity—as when you sleep or are under the influence of a mind-altering drug—that there are variations in your *state* of consciousness. Let's first consider various levels of consciousness.

Levels of Consciousness

At any moment, the mental events that you are aware of are said to exist at the **conscious level.** For example, look at the Necker cube in Figure 9.1. If you are like most people, you can hold the cube in one orientation for only a few seconds before the other orientation "pops out" at you. The orientation that you experience at any moment is at your conscious level of awareness for that moment.

LINKAGES (a link to Sensation)

Some mental events, however, cannot be experienced consciously. For example, you are not directly aware of the fact that your brain is regulating your blood pressure. Such mental processing occurs at the **nonconscious level,** totally removed from conscious awareness. Other mental events are not conscious, but they can either become conscious or influence conscious experience. These mental events make up the *cognitive unconscious* (Reber, 1992), which is further divided into preconscious and unconscious (or subconscious) levels. Mental events at the **preconscious level** are outside of awareness but can easily be brought into awareness. For example, what did you have for dinner last night? The information you needed to answer this question was probably not at a conscious level, but it was at a preconscious level and ready to be brought into awareness. Varying amounts of effort may be required to bring preconscious information into consciousness. When playing a trivia game, for example, it is sometimes easy and sometimes difficult to draw on your storehouse of preconscious memories to come up with obscure facts.

There are still other mental activities that can alter thoughts, feelings, and actions but that are more difficult to bring into awareness (Ratner, 1994). As described in the chapter on personality, Freud suggested that mental events at the **unconscious level**—especially those involving unacceptable sexual and aggressive urges—are actively kept out of consciousness. Many psychologists do not accept this view but still use the term *unconscious* (or *subconscious*) to describe the level of mental activity that influences consciousness but that is not conscious.

consciousness Awareness of external stimuli and one's own mental activity.

conscious level The level at which mental activities that people are normally aware of occur.

nonconscious level A level of mental activity that is inaccessible to conscious awareness.

preconscious level A level of mental activity that is not currently conscious but of which we can easily become conscious.

unconscious level A level of mental activity that influences consciousness but is not conscious.

Mental Processing Without Awareness

A fascinating demonstration of mental processing without awareness was provided by an experiment with patients who had surgery under general anesthesia.

Evidence for the operation of subconscious mental processing includes research showing that surgery patients may be able to hear and later comply with instructions or suggestions given while they are under anesthesia and of which they have no memory (Bennett, Giannini, & Davis, 1985). Other research shows that people display physiological arousal to emotionally charged words even when they are not paying attention to them (Von Wright, Anderson, & Stenman, 1975)

BLOOM COUNTY **by Berke Breathed**

While they were still unconscious in the recovery room, an audiotape of 15 word pairs was played over and over. After regaining consciousness, these patients could not say what words had been played—or even whether a tape had been played at all. Yet when given one word from each of the word pairs on the tape and asked to say the first word that came to mind, the patients were able to produce the other member of the word pair (Cork, Kihlstrom, & Hameroff, 1992).

Even when people are conscious and alert, information can sometimes be processed and used without their awareness (Rensink, 2004). In one study of this phenomenon, participants watched a computer screen as an X flashed in one of four locations. The participants' task was to indicate where the X appeared by rapidly pushing one of four buttons. The X's location seemed to vary randomly, but the movement sequence actually followed a set of complex rules, such as "If the X moves horizontally twice in a row, then it will move vertically next." The participants' responses became progressively faster and more accurate, but their performance instantly deteriorated when the rules were dropped and the Xs began appearing in truly random locations. Without being aware of doing so, these participants had apparently learned a complex, rule-bound strategy to improve their performance. However, even when offered $100 to state the rules that had guided the movement sequence, they could not do so, nor were they sure that any such rules existed (Lewicki, 1992).

Visual processing without awareness can also occur in cases of blindness caused by damage that is limited to the primary visual cortex. In such cases, fibres from the eyes are still connected to other brain areas that process visual information. Some of these surviving pathways may permit visual processing without visual awareness—a condition known as *blindsight* (Ro et al., 2004; Weiskrantz, 2004). Even though such patients say they see nothing, if forced to guess, they can still locate visual targets, identify the direction and orientation of moving images, reach for objects, name the colour of lights, and even discriminate happy from fearful faces that they cannot consciously see (Morris et al., 2001).

According to research conducted by Jim Cheesman at the University of Saskatchewan, research on *priming* also demonstrates mental processing without awareness (Cheesman & Merikle, 1981). In a typical priming study, people tend to respond faster or more accurately to previously seen stimuli, even when they cannot consciously recall having seen those stimuli (Abrams & Greenwald, 2000; Arndt et al., 1997; Bar & Biederman, 1998). In one study, people were asked to look at a set of drawings such as those in Figure 9.2 and decide which of the objects could actually exist in three-dimensional space and which could not. The participants were better at classifying pictures that they had seen before, even when they could not remember having seen them (Cooper et al., 1992; Schacter et al., 1991).

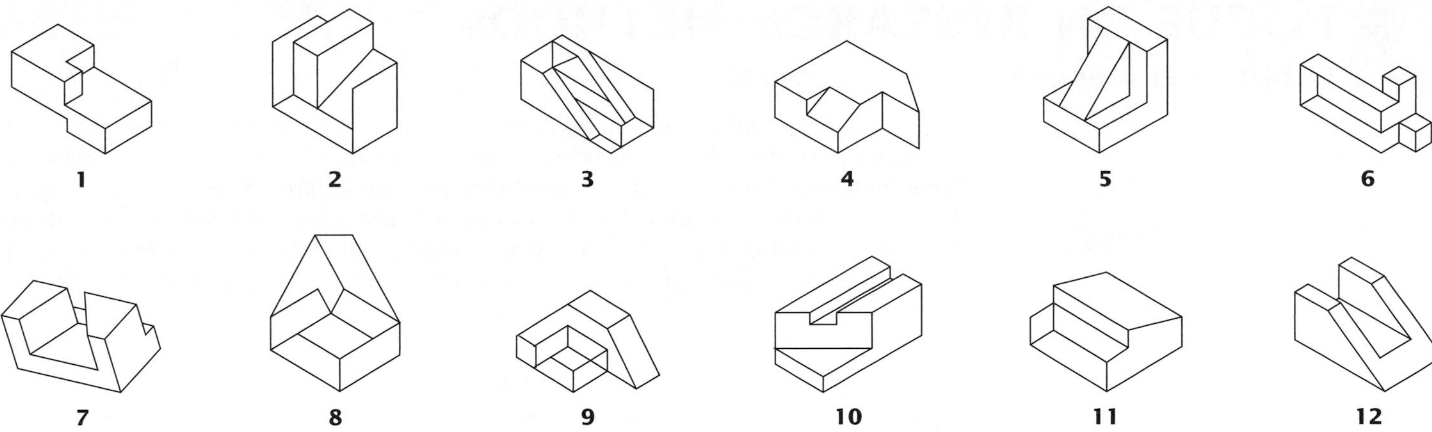

figure 9.2

Possible or Impossible?

Look at these figures and decide, as quickly as you can, whether each can actually exist. Priming studies show that this task would be easier for figures you have seen in the past, even if you don't recall seeing them. How did you do?

(The correct answers appear on page 321.)

Source: Schacter et al. (1991).

LINKAGES (a link to Social Behaviour)

Other studies show how priming can alter certain behaviours even when participants are not consciously aware of being influenced. In one such study, for example (Bargh, Chen, & Burrows, 1996), participants were asked to unscramble scrambled sentences (e.g., "Finds he it instantly"). For one group of participants, the scrambled sentences all contained words associated with rudeness (e.g., *bother,* and *annoying*). A second group read sentences whose scrambled words were associated with politeness (e.g., *respect, honour,* and *polite*). The scrambled words read by a third group were neutral (e.g., *normally, sends,* and *rapidly*). After completing the unscrambling task, each participant was asked to go to another room to get further instructions from the experimenter. But by design, the experimenter was always found talking to a research assistant. The dependent variable in this experiment was whether participants in the three conditions would interrupt the experimenter. As shown in Figure 9.3, the participants in the "rude priming" condition were most likely to interrupt, whereas those in the "polite priming" condition were least likely to do so. Those in the "neutral" condition fell in between the other two groups.

The results of priming studies challenge some of the traditional Freudian views about the unconscious. According to Freud, unconscious processes function mainly to protect us from painful or frightening thoughts, feelings, and memories by keeping them out of consciousness (Pervin, 1996). However, many psychologists studying unconscious processes now believe that, in fact, one of the primary functions of these processes is to help us more effectively carry out mundane, day-to-day mental activities.

Many questions about the relationship between conscious and unconscious processes remain to be answered. One of the most significant of these questions is whether conscious and unconscious thoughts occur independently of each other Priming studies seem to suggest that they are independent, but other research suggests that they may not be. For example, one study found a correlation between unconscious indicators of age prejudice—as seen in implicit memory for negative stereotypes about the elderly—and consciously held attitudes toward the elderly (Hense, Penner, & Nelson, 1995). Another study (Lepore & Brown, 1997) also found similarity between unconscious and conscious forms of ethnic prejudice. Overall, however, if there is a relationship between explicit and implicit cognitions, it appears to be weak and not yet clearly understood (Dovidio, Kawakami, & Beach, 2001). We consider this issue further in the chapter on social behaviour.

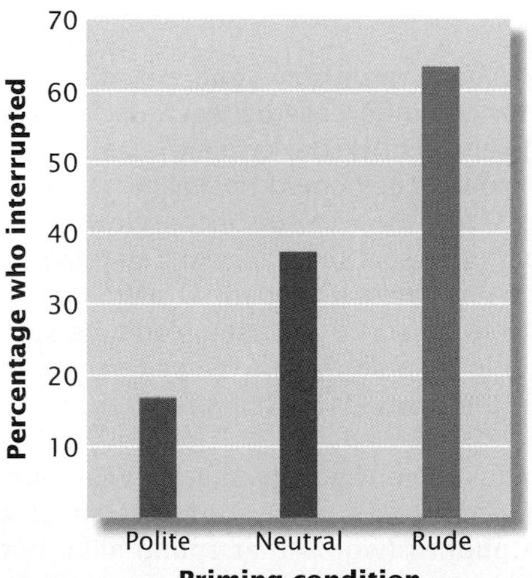

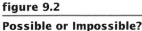

figure 9.3

Priming Behaviour without Awareness

Participants in this study were primed with rude, polite, or neutral words before being confronted with the problem of interrupting a conversation. Although not consciously aware of the priming process, participants who had been exposed to rude words were most likely to interrupt, whereas those previously exposed to polite words were least likely to do so.

Source: Bargh, Chen, & Burrows (1996, Figure 1).

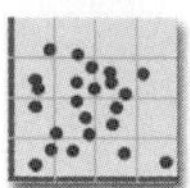

FOCUS ON RESEARCH METHODS

Subliminal Messages in Rock Music

According to various Internet Web sites, Satanic or drug-related messages have been embedded in the recorded music of rock bands such as Marilyn Manson, Nine Inch Nails, Judas Priest, Led Zeppelin, and the Rolling Stones. The story goes that because these alleged messages were recorded backward, they are *subliminal* (not consciously perceived), but they have supposedly influenced listeners to commit suicide or murder. For this claim to be true, however, the subliminal backward message would have to be perceived at some level of consciousness.

What was the researchers' question?

There is no good evidence that backward messages are actually present in most of the music cited. However, John R. Vokey at Alberta's University of Lethbridge and his colleague J. Don Read (1985) asked whether any backward messages that might exist could be perceived and understood when the music is playing forward. They also asked whether such messages have any effect on behaviour.

How did the researchers answer the question?

Vokey and Read conducted a series of multiple case studies of the impact of backward-recorded messages. They first recorded readings of portions of the Bible's twenty-third psalm and Lewis Carroll's poem "Jabberwocky." This poem includes many nonsense words, but it follows the rules of grammar (e.g., "'Twas brillig and the slithy toves did gyre and gimble in the wabe. . ."). These recordings were then played backward to college students. The students were asked to judge whether the recordings would have been nonsensical or meaningful if played forward.

What did the researchers find?

When the students heard the material played backward, they could not discriminate sense from nonsense. They could not tell the difference between declarative sentences and questions. They could not even identify the original material on which the recordings were based. In other words, they could not make sense of the backward messages at a conscious level. Could they do so subconsciously? To find out, the researchers asked the participants to sort the backward statements they heard into one of five categories: nursery rhymes, Christian, Satanic, pornographic, or advertising. They reasoned that if some sort of meaning could be subconsciously understood, the participants would be able to sort the statements in some logical way. As it turned out, however, the participants did no better at this task than random chance would predict.

Can even *unperceived* backward messages unconsciously shape behaviour? To answer this question, Vokey and Read presented a backward version of a message whose sentences contained homophones (words that sound alike but have two spellings and two different meanings, such as *feat* and *feet*). When heard in the normal forward direction, such messages affect people's spelling of ambiguous words that are read aloud to them at a later time. (For example, people tend to spell out *f-e-a-t* rather than *f-e-e-t* if they previously heard the sentence "It was a great feat of strength.") This example of priming occurs even if people do not recall having heard the message. After hearing a backward version of the message, however, the participants in this study did not show the expected spelling bias.

What do the results mean?

Obviously, it wasn't possible for the participants to subconsciously understand meaning in the backward messages. Backward messages are evidently not consciously or unconsciously understood, nor do they influence behaviour (Vokey, 2002).

- **What do we still need to know?**

Researchers would like to understand why the incorrect idea persists that backward messages can influence behaviour. Beliefs and suspicions do not simply disappear in the face of contrary scientific evidence (Vyse, 2000; Winer et al., 2002). Perhaps the evidence must be publicized more widely in order to lay the misconceptions to rest, but it seems likely that some people so deeply want to believe in the existence and power of backward messages in rock music that such beliefs will forever hold the status of folk myths in Western culture.

The Neuropsychology of Consciousness

The nature of various levels of consciousness and the role of the brain regions that support them have been illuminated by studies of the results of brain damage. Consider the case of Karen Ann Quinlan. After drug-induced heart failure starved her brain of oxygen, Quinlan remained unconscious and unresponsive, and her doctors said that she would never regain consciousness. Her parents got a court order allowing them to shut off their daughter's life-support machines, but Karen continued to live in a vegetative state for ten more years. A detailed study of her autopsied brain revealed that it had sustained damage mainly in the thalamus (Kinney et al., 1994; see Figure 3.14 in the chapter on biological aspects of psychology). Some researchers see such findings as supporting the idea that parts of the thalamus may be critical for the experience of consciousness (e.g., Bogen, 1995).

Other kinds of brain damage cause less extensive impairments in consciousness. A condition known as *prosopagnosia* (pronounced "proh-sop-ag-NO-see-ah") provides an example. People with prosopagnosia cannot consciously recognize faces—not even their own reflection—yet they can still see and recognize many other objects and can still recognize people by their voices (Stone & Valentine, 2003). This condition may be part of a more general inability to recognize familiar objects (e.g., types of cars), but in practice the problem is relatively specific for faces. One farmer with prosopagnosia could recognize and name his sheep, but he never was able to recognize humans (McNeil & Warrington, 1993). Still, when such people see a familiar—but not consciously recognized—face, they show eye movement patterns, changes in brain activity, and autonomic nervous system responses that do not occur when viewing an unfamiliar face (Barton, Cherkasova, & O'Connor, 2001; Bauer, 1984; Bruyer, 1991).These responses are especially strong when the face shows an emotional expression (de Gelder et al., 2003). So some vestige of face recognition can be preserved in prosopagnosia, but it remains unavailable to conscious experience.

The effects of brain damage on conscious access to other mental abilities has been studied extensively by Endel Tulving at the University of Toronto. For example, anterograde amnesia, the inability to form new memories, often accompanies damage to the hippocampus (Tulving, 2002). Anterograde amnesics seem unable to remember any new information, even about the passage of time. One man who developed this condition in 1957 still needed to be reminded more than 30 years later that it was no longer 1957 (Smith, 1988). Yet as Figure 9.4 shows, anterograde amnesics can learn new skills, even though they cannot consciously recall the practice sessions (Milner, 1965). Their brain activity, too, shows different reactions to words they have recently studied than to other words, even though they have no memory of studying them (Düzel et al., 2001).

Answer key for Figure 9.2: Figures 1, 4, 5, 7, 10, and 12 can exist in three-dimensional space.

figure 9.4

Memory Formation in Anterograde Amnesia

Brenda Milner at the Montreal Neurological Institute conducted a famous case study of H.M., a man with anterograde amnesia. In one of the tests she used, H.M. was asked to trace the outline of an object while using only a mirror (which reverses left and right) to guide him. His performance on this difficult task improved daily, indicating that he learned and remembered how to do the task. Yet he had no conscious memory of the practice sessions that allowed his skill to develop (Milner, 1965).

Source: Data from Milner (1965)

Mirror-tracing task

(A)

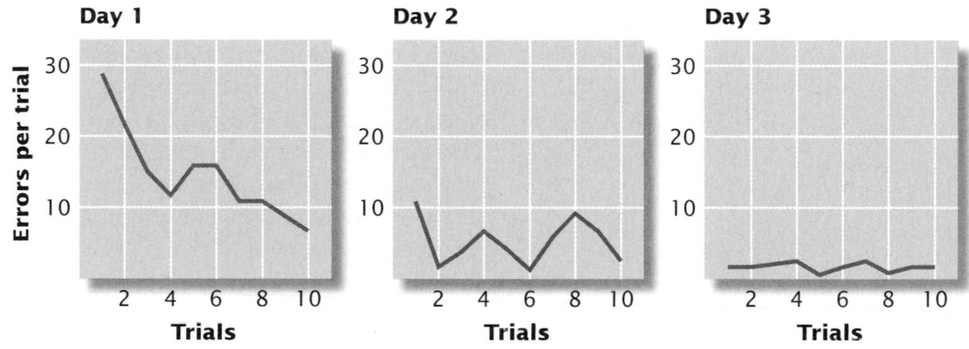

Performance of H.M. on mirror-tracing task

(B)

States of Consciousness

Mental activity is always changing. The features of consciousness at any instant—what reaches your awareness, the decisions you are making, and so on—make up your **state of consciousness** at that moment (Tassi & Muzet, 2001). States of consciousness can range from deep sleep to alert wakefulness; they can also be affected by drugs and other influences. Consider, for example, the varying states of consciousness that might occur aboard an airplane en route from Halifax to Vancouver. In the cockpit, the pilot calmly scans instrument displays while talking to an air-traffic controller. In seat 9B, a lawyer has just finished her second cocktail while planning a courtroom strategy. Nearby, a young father gazes out a window, daydreaming, while his small daughter sleeps in his lap, dreaming dreams of her own.

state of consciousness The characteristics of consciousness at any particular moment.

All these people are experiencing different states of consciousness. Some states are active and some are passive. The daydreaming father is letting his mind wander, passively noting images, memories, and other mental events that come unbidden to mind. The lawyer is actively directing her mental activity, evaluating various options, and considering their likely outcomes.

Most people spend most of their time in a waking state of consciousness. Mental processing in this state varies with changes in attention or arousal (Taylor, 2002). While reading, for example, you may temporarily ignore sounds around you. Similarly, if you are upset, or bored, or talking on a cell phone, you may miss important environmental cues, making it dangerous to drive a car.

When changes in mental processes are great enough for you or others to notice significant differences in how you function, you have entered an **altered state of consciousness.** In an altered state, mental processing shows distinct changes unique to that state. Cognitive processes or perceptions of yourself or the world may change, and normal inhibitions or self-control may weaken (Martindale, 1981).

The phrase *altered states of consciousness* recognizes waking consciousness as the most common state, a baseline against which "altered" states are compared. However, this is not to say that waking consciousness is universally considered more normal, proper, or valued than other states. In fact, value judgments about different states of consciousness vary considerably across cultures (Ward, 1994).

Consider, for instance, *hallucinations,* which are perceptual experiences—such as hearing voices—that occur in the absence of sensory stimuli. According to Ihsan Al-Issa at the University of Calgary, attitudes toward hallucinations vary by culture (Al-Issa, 1995). In North America, for example, hallucinations are considered so undesirable that even normal people who develop visual hallucinations due to an eye disorder may be reluctant to seek the medical help they need to solve the problem (Menon et al., 2003). Among mental patients, those who hallucinate often feel stress and self-blame and may choose not to report their hallucinations. Patients who do report them tend to be considered more disturbed and may receive more drastic treatments than those who keep their hallucinations to themselves (Wilson, Nathan, et al., 1996). Among the Moche of Peru, however, hallucinations have a culturally approved place. When someone is beset by illness or misfortune, a healer conducts an elaborate ritual to find causes and treatments. During the ceremony, the healer ingests mescaline, a drug that causes hallucinations. These hallucinations are thought to give the healer spiritual insight into the patient's problems (de Rios, 1992). In the context of many other tribal cultures, too, purposeful hallucinations are revered, not demeaned (Grob & Dobkin-de-Rios, 1992).

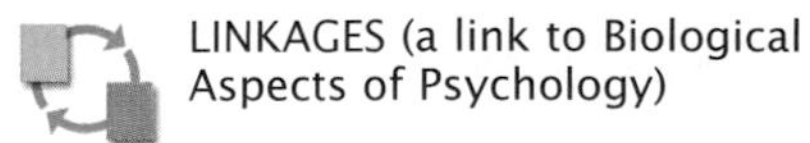

In other words, states of consciousness differ not only in their basic characteristics but also in their value to members of particular cultures. In the sections to follow, we describe some of the most interesting altered states of consciousness, beginning with the most common one, sleep.

Sleeping and Dreaming

According to ancient myths, sleepers lose control of their minds, flirting with death as their souls wander freely. Early researchers thought sleep was a time of mental inactivity. In fact, however, sleep is an active, complex state.

Stages of Sleep

Sleep researchers monitor the brain's electrical activity during sleep by taping tiny discs to a person's scalp and connecting them to an *electroencephalograph,* or *EEG.* The resulting EEG recordings, often called *brain waves,* show changes in height (amplitude) and speed (frequency) as behaviour or mental processes change. The brain waves of an awake, alert person have high frequency and low amplitude. They appear as small, closely spaced, irregular EEG spikes. A relaxed person with closed eyes shows *alpha waves,* which are more rhythmic brain waves occurring at speeds of eight to twelve cycles per second. During a normal night's sleep, your brain waves

altered state of consciousness A condition in which changes in mental processes are extensive enough that a person or others notice significant differences in psychological and behavioural functioning.

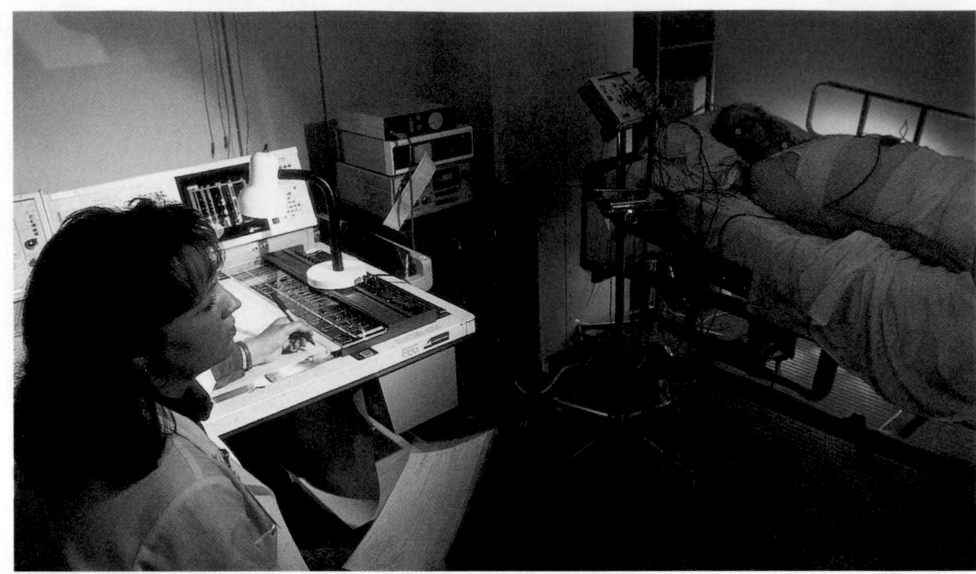

A Sleep Lab The electroencephalograph (EEG) allows scientists to record brain activity through small discs attached to the scalp. The development of this technology in the 1950s opened the door to the scientific study of sleep.

show distinctive and systematic changes in amplitude and frequency as you pass through various stages of sleep (Guevara et al., 1995).

Slow-Wave Sleep Imagine that you are participating in a sleep study at McGill University's sleep lab in Montreal. You are hooked up to an EEG and various monitors, and a video camera watches as you sleep through the night. If you were to review the results, here's what you'd see: At first, you are relaxed, with eyes closed, but awake. At this point, your muscle tone and eye movements are normal, and your EEG shows the slow brain waves associated with relaxation. As you then drift into sleep, your breathing deepens, your heartbeat slows, and your blood pressure drops.

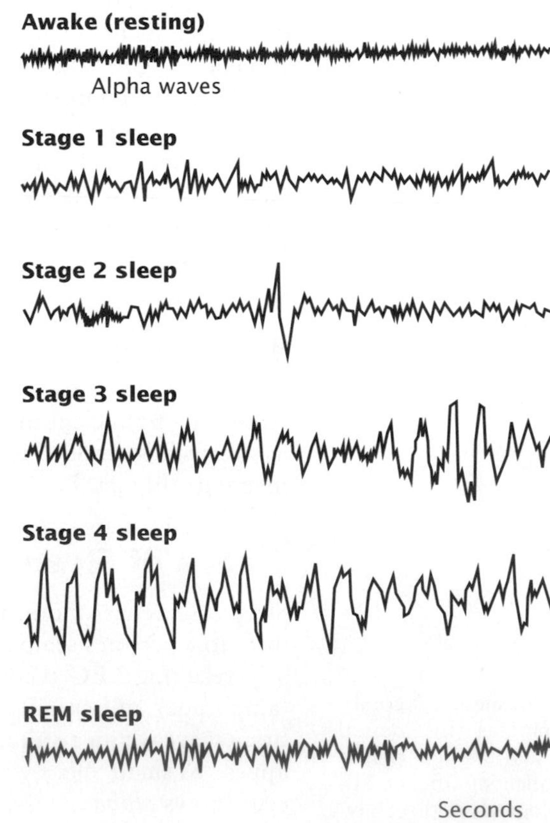

figure 9.5

EEG During Sleep

EEG recordings of brain wave activity show four relatively distinct stages of sleep. Notice the regular patterns of alpha waves that occur just before a person goes to sleep, followed by the slowing of brain waves as sleep becomes deeper (stages 1 through 4). In REM (rapid eye movement) sleep, the frequency of brain waves increases dramatically and in some ways resembles patterns seen in people who are awake.

Source: Horne (1988).

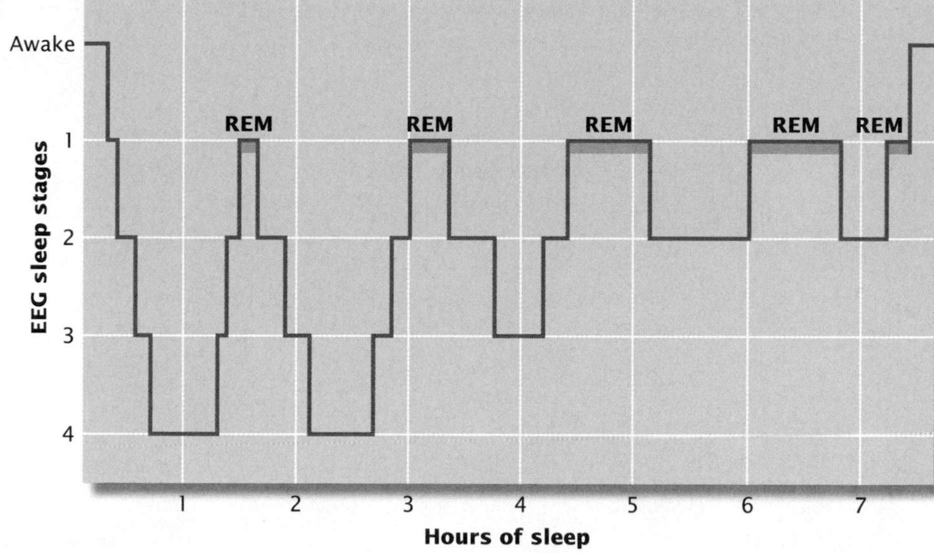

figure 9.6

A Night's Sleep

During a typical night a sleeper goes through this sequence of EEG stages. Notice that sleep is deepest during the first part of the night and more shallow later on, when REM sleep becomes more prominent.

Source: Cartwright (1978).

Over the next half hour, you descend through four stages of sleep that are characterized by even slower brain waves with even higher amplitude (see Figure 9.5). The last two of these, stages 3 and 4, are called **slow-wave sleep.** When you reach stage 4, the deepest stage of slow-wave sleep, it is quite difficult to be awakened. If you were roused from this stage of deep sleep, you would be groggy and confused.

REM Sleep After 30 to 45 minutes in stage 4, you quickly return to stage 2 and then enter a special stage in which your eyes move rapidly under their closed eyelids. This is called **rapid eye movement (REM) sleep,** or *paradoxical sleep*. It is called *paradoxical* because its characteristics pose a paradox, or contradiction. In REM sleep, your EEG resembles that of an awake, alert person, and your physiological arousal—heart rate, breathing, and blood pressure—is also similar to when you are awake. However, your muscles are nearly paralyzed. Sudden, twitchy spasms appear, especially in your face and hands, but your brain actively suppresses other movements (Blumberg & Lucas, 1994).

In other words, there are two distinctly different types of sleep, REM sleep and *non-REM,* or *NREM,* sleep.

A Night's Sleep Most people pass through the cycle of sleep stages four to six times each night. Each cycle lasts about 90 minutes, but with a somewhat changing pattern of stages and stage duration. Early in the night, most of the time is spent in slow-wave sleep, with only a few minutes in REM sleep (see Figure 9.6). As sleep continues, though, it is dominated by stage 2 and REM sleep, from which sleepers finally awaken.

LINKAGES (a link to Human Development)

Sleep patterns change with time; overall, people sleep less as they age (Floyd, 2002). The average infant sleeps about sixteen hours a day. The average seventy-year-old sleeps only about six hours (Roffwarg, Muzio, & Dement, 1966), and elderly people tend to wake more often during the night than younger people do (Floyd, 2002). The composition of sleep changes, too (see Figure 9.7). REM sleep accounts for half of total sleep time at birth but less than 25 percent in young adults and even less in the elderly (Darchia, Campbell, & Feinberg, 2003). Individuals may vary widely from these averages, however. Some people feel well rested after four hours of sleep, whereas others of similar age require ten hours to feel satisfied (Clausen, Sersen, & Lidsky, 1974). There are also wide variations among cultural and socioeconomic groups in the tendency to take daytime naps. Contrary to stereotypes about the popularity of siestas in Latin and South American countries, urban Mexican college students actually nap less than many other college populations (Valencia-Flores et al., 1998). Sleep patterns are also partly a matter of choice or

slow-wave sleep Sleep stages 3 and 4, which are accompanied by slow, deep breathing; a calm, regular heartbeat; and reduced blood pressure.

rapid eye movement (REM) sleep A stage of sleep in which brain activity and other functions resemble the waking state but that is accompanied by rapid eye movements and virtual muscle paralysis.

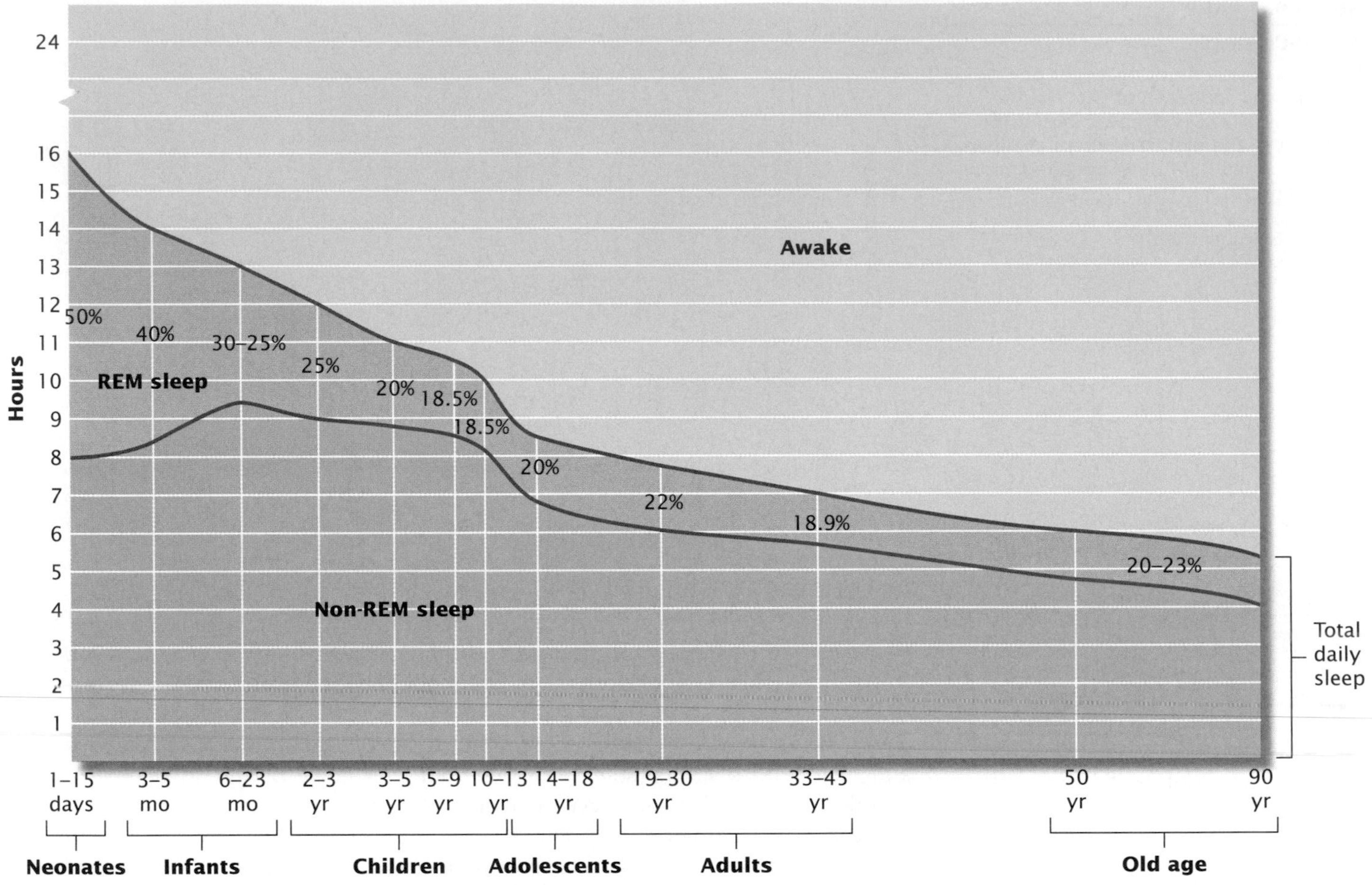

figure 9.7

Sleep and Dreaming over the Life Span

People tend to sleep less as they get older. There is also a sharp reduction in the percentage of REM sleep, from about eight hours per day in infancy to about an hour per day by age seventy. Non-REM sleep time also decreases but, compared with the drop in REM, remains relatively stable. After age twenty, however, non-REM sleep contains less and less of the deepest, or stage 4, sleep.

Note: Percentages indicate portion of total sleep time in REM sleep.

Source: Roffwarg, Muzio, & Dement (1966/1969).

necessity. For example, North American college students get less sleep than other people their age (Hicks, Fernandez, & Pellegrini, 2001). This trend has grown over the last 30 years as students deal with academic and job responsibilities, along with family obligations and a variety of recreational activities—including late-night sessions of playing computer games or surfing the Internet. You have probably noticed the results of sleep deprivation as your classmates (or you?) struggle to stay awake during lectures.

Sleep Disorders

Most people experience sleep-related problems at some point in their lives (Krahn, 2003; Silber, 2001). These problems range from occasional nights of tossing and turning to more serious and long-term *sleep disorders.* The most common sleeping problem is **insomnia**, in which people experience daytime fatigue due to trouble falling asleep or staying asleep. If you have difficulty getting to sleep or staying asleep that persists for longer than one month at a time, you may be suffering from insomnia. Besides being tiring, insomnia is tied to mental distress and impaired functioning. Insomnia is especially associated with depressive and anxiety disorders

insomnia A sleep disorder in which a person feels tired during the day because of trouble falling asleep or staying asleep at night.

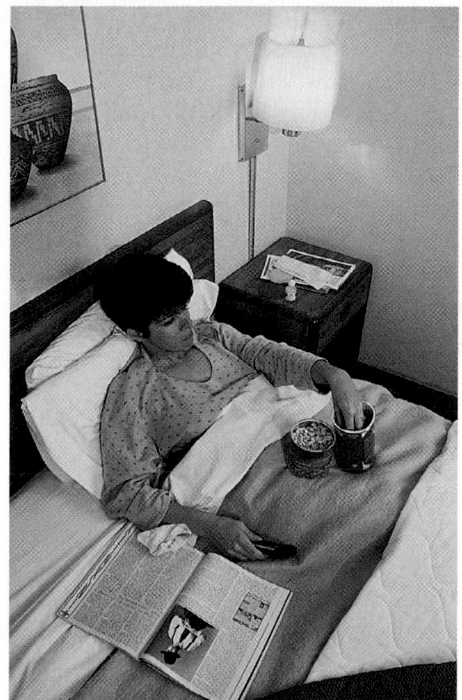

Stimulus Control Therapy Insomnia can often be reduced through a combination of relaxation techniques and *stimulus control therapy,* in which the person goes to bed only when sleepy and gets out of bed if sleep does not come within fifteen to twenty minutes. The goal is for the bed to become a stimulus associated with sleeping, and perhaps sex, but not with reading, eating, watching television, worrying, or anything else that is incompatible with sleep (Edinger et al., 2001).

(The Canadian Sleep Society, 2004). It is unclear from such correlations, however, whether insomnia causes mental disorders, mental disorders cause insomnia, or some other factor causes both.

Sleeping pills can relieve insomnia, but they interact dangerously with alcohol, disturb REM sleep, and may eventually lead to *increased* sleeplessness (Ashton, 1995; Poyares et al., 2004). In the long run, methods based on learning principles may be more helpful (Perlis et al., 2001; Stepanski & Perlis, 2000). For example, stress management techniques such as relaxation training have been shown to help reduce tension and other stress reactions, thus allowing sleep (Bernstein, Borkovec, & Hazlett-Stevens, 2000). Taking short daytime naps and engaging in moderate evening exercise may also help some people get to sleep more easily, sleep better, and experience better mood and performance the next day (Tanaka et al., 2001). And cognitive-behaviour therapy, a learning-based treatment described in the chapter on treatment of psychological disorders, has been found more effective for insomnia than sleeping pills (Jacobs et al., 2004).

Narcolepsy is a disturbing daytime sleep disorder that usually begins when a person is between 15 and 25 years old (Beuckmann & Yanagisawa, 2002; Choo & Guilleminault, 1998). Its victims abruptly switch from active, often emotional waking states into a few minutes of REM sleep. Because of the loss of muscle tone in REM, the narcoleptic may experience *cataplexy*, which means that they collapse and remain briefly immobile even after awakening. The most common cause of narcolepsy appears to be the absence or deficiency of a newly discovered neurotransmitter called *orexin,* also known as *hypocretin* (Beuckmann & Yanagisawa, 2002; Mieda et al., 2004; Naumann & Daum, 2003; Siegel, 2004). Planning regularly scheduled daily naps can be a helpful treatment, as can combinations of certain drugs (Rogers, Aldrich, & Lin, 2001). One of these, *modafinil,* appears to be effective not only for narcolepsy but also for counteracting the effects of sleep deprivation (Silber, 2001).

People suffering from **sleep apnea** briefly stop breathing hundreds of times every night, waking up each time long enough to resume breathing. In the morning, they do not recall the awakenings, but they feel tired and tend to show reduced attention and learning ability (Naëgelé et al., 1995). In one tragic case, two members of a train crew—both of whom had apnea—fell asleep on the job, resulting in a collision that killed two people (Pickler, 2002). Research conducted by Leslie Raschka at the Clarke Institute of Psychiatry in Toronto has shown that sleep apnea may even lead to violent daytime behaviour (Raschka, 1984).

Sleep apnea has many causes, including genetic predisposition, obesity, failure of brain mechanisms controlling breathing, and compression of the windpipe (Kadotani et al., 2001; Richards et al., 2002; Young, Skatrud, & Peppard, 2004). Effective treatments include weight loss and use of a nasal mask that provides a steady stream of air (Davies & Stradling, 2000; Gupta & Reiter, 2004; Peppard et al., 2000). It may be necessary in some cases to surgically widen the air passageway in the upper throat (Friedman et al., 2003; Patel et al., 2003).

In cases of **sudden infant death syndrome (SIDS),** sleeping infants stop breathing and die for no apparent reason. It is the most common cause of unexpected infant death in Western countries (Daley, 2004). SIDS is only diagnosed when no cause of death can be determined and therefore is more of a *non*-diagnosis, not a specific illness. In Canada, SIDS strikes about one of every 2000 infants, usually when they are two to four months old (Canadian Foundation for the Study of Infant Deaths, 2004). Although the cause is unknown, risk factors associated with SIDS include exposure to cigarette smoke prenatally or second-hand smoke after birth, over-heating caused by being too warmly dressed or tightly swaddled during sleep, and sleeping in a face-down position. SIDS is not contagious (Public Health Agency of Canada, 2002).

Nightmares are frightening REM sleep dreams that occur in 4 to 8 percent of the general population, but in a much higher percentage of people who suffer from post-traumatic stress disorder following military combat or rape (Kryger, Roth, &

narcolepsy A daytime sleep disorder in which a person switches abruptly from an active, often emotional waking state into several minutes of REM sleep.

sleep apnea A sleep disorder in which people briefly but repeatedly stop breathing during the night.

sudden infant death syndrome (SIDS) A disorder in which a sleeping baby stops breathing and dies.

nightmare Frightening dream that takes place during REM sleep.

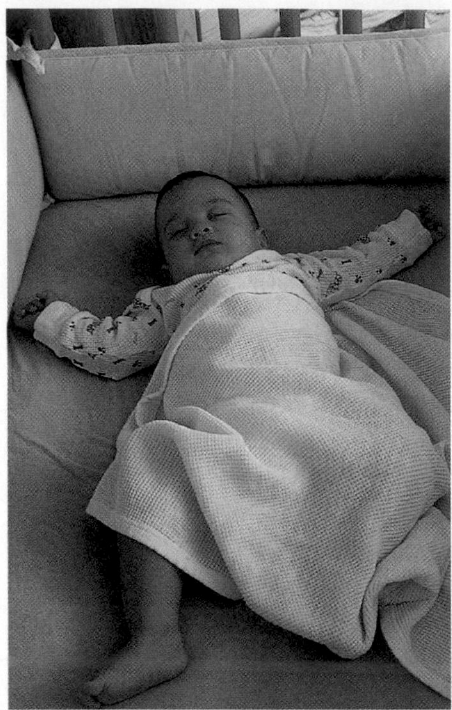

Sudden Infant Death Syndrome (SIDS) In SIDS cases, seemingly healthy infants stop breathing while asleep in their cribs. All the causes of SIDS are not known, but health authorities now urge parents to ensure that infants sleep on their backs, as this baby demonstrates.

Dement, 2000). Imagery therapy, in which people repeatedly imagine new and less frightening outcomes to their nightmares, has been effective in reducing their frequency (Forbes, Phelps, & McHugh, 2001; Krakow et al., 2001). Whereas nightmares occur during REM sleep, **night terrors** are horrific dream images that occur during stage 4 sleep. Sleepers often awake from a night terror with a blood-curdling scream and remain intensely frightened for up to 30 minutes, yet they may not recall the episode in the morning. Night terrors are especially common in boys, but adults can suffer milder versions. The condition is sometimes treatable with drugs (Lillywhite, Wilson, & Nutt, 1994).

Like night terrors, **sleepwalking** occurs during non-REM sleep, usually in childhood (Masand, Popli, & Welburg, 1995). By morning, most sleepwalkers have forgotten their travels. Despite myths to the contrary, waking a sleepwalker is not harmful. One adult sleepwalker was cured after his wife blew a whistle whenever he began a nocturnal stroll (Meyer, 1975). Drugs help reduce sleepwalking, but most children simply outgrow the problem.

Why Do People Sleep?

In trying to understand sleep, psychologists have studied both the functions that sleep serves and the ways in which brain mechanisms shape its characteristics.

Sleep as a Circadian Rhythm The sleep-wake cycle is one example of the rhythmic nature of life. Almost all animals, including humans, display cycles of behaviour and physiology that repeat about every 24 hours. These cyclical patterns are called **circadian rhythms** (from the Latin *circa dies,* meaning "about a day"). Longer and shorter rhythms also occur, but they are less common. Circadian (pronounced "sir-KAY-dee-en") rhythms are linked, or *entrained,* to signals such as the light and dark of day and night, but most of them continue even when no such cues are available. Volunteers living for months without external time cues maintain daily rhythms in sleeping and waking, hormone release, eating, urination, and other physiological functions. Under such conditions, these cycles repeat about every 24 hours (Czeisler et al., 1999).

Disrupting the sleep-wake cycle can create problems. For example, air travel across several time zones often causes **jet lag**—a pattern of fatigue, irritability, inattention, and sleeping problems that can last several days. The traveller's body feels ready to sleep at the wrong time for the new locale. Because it tends to be easier to stay awake longer than usual than to go to sleep earlier than usual, sleep-wake rhythms readjust to altered light-dark cycles more easily when sleep is shifted to a later, rather than an earlier, time (Lemmer et al., 2002). As a result, people usually experience more intense symptoms of jet lag after eastward travel (when time is lost) than after westward travel (when time is gained). Symptoms similar to those of jet lag affect workers who must repeatedly change between day and night shifts. Disrupted circadian rhythms may also explain the Monday morning "blues" that people experience after trying to go to bed early on Sunday night following a weekend of later-than-usual bedtimes (Yang & Spielman, 2001). There are also people who suffer because their circadian rhythms are never quite in synch with the local light-dark cycle (Ando, Kripke, & Ancoli-Israel, 2002).

Because circadian-like rhythms continue without external cues, an internal "biological clock" in the brain must keep track of time. This clock, which has been studied in detail by Michael Antle and colleagues at the University of Calgary, is in the *suprachiasmatic nuclei* (*SCN*) of the hypothalamus (Antle, Kriegsfeld, & Silver 2005), as shown in Figure 9.8. The SCN receives light information from a special set of ganglion cells in the retina that act as photoreceptors (Berson, Dunn, & Takao, 2002) and sends that information to areas in the hindbrain that promote sleep or wakefulness (Moore, 1997). SCN neurons show a rhythm of activity that repeats itself every 24 to 25 hours, even if the neurons are removed from the

night terror Horrific dream that causes rapid awakening from stage 3 or 4 sleep and intense fear for up to 30 minutes.

sleepwalking A phenomenon primarily occurring in non-REM sleep in which people walk while asleep.

circadian rhythm A cycle, such as waking and sleeping, that repeats about once a day.

jet lag A syndrome of fatigue, irritability, inattention, and sleeping problems caused by air travel across several time zones.

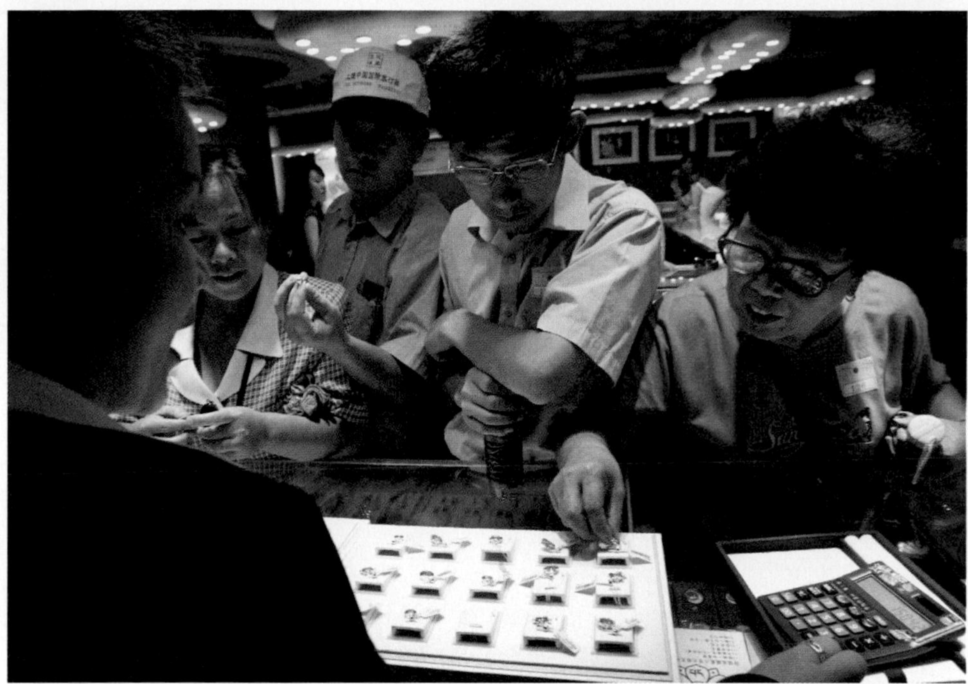

The Cost of Jet Lag Twice a year, thousands of exhibitors freshly arrived from around the world groggily set up dazzling displays at Asia's largest jewelry show. Then they try to wait on customers while keeping track of their treasures. Taking advantage of these jet-lagged travellers' inattentiveness, thieves steal millions of dollars of merchandise at every show (Fowler, 2004).

brain and put in a laboratory dish (Gillette, 1986; Yamaguchi et al., 2003). When animals with SCN damage receive transplanted SCN cells from another animal, their new circadian rhythms are similar to those of the donor animal (Menaker & Vogelbaum, 1993). SCN neurons also regulate the release of the hormone *melatonin* from the pineal gland. Melatonin, in turn, appears to be important in maintaining circadian rhythms (Beaumont et al., 2004; Cardinali et al., 2002). In fact, many of the symptoms associated with jet lag and other disruptions in sleep-wake cycles can be prevented or treated by taking melatonin.

The length of circadian rhythms can vary from person to person. Some have a natural tendency to stay up later at night ("owls") or to wake up earlier in the morning ("larks"). Scientists have discovered that extreme variations in these rhythms are associated with mutations in the genes that code for biological clock proteins and that certain variations can help in distinguishing Alzheimer's disease from other brain disorders (Harper et al., 2001; Toh et al., 2001).

The Functions of Sleep Examining the effects of sleep deprivation may help explain why people sleep at all. People who go without sleep for as long as a week usually do not suffer serious long-term effects, but prolonged sleeplessness does lead to fatigue, irritability, and inattention (Drummond et al., 2000). The effects of short-term sleep deprivation—which is a common condition among busy adolescents and adults—can also take their toll (Heuer et al., 2004; Stapleton, 2001). For example, the performance of doctors who must work through the night can be impaired when caring for patients the next day (Gaba & Howard, 2002; Landrigan et al., 2004), and according to Transport Canada (2003), driver fatigue is a significant cause of fatal car accidents. Learning, too, is more difficult after sleep deprivation, but certain parts of the cerebral cortex actually increase their activity when a sleep-deprived person faces a learning task, so the person is able to compensate for a while (Drummond et al., 2000).

Some researchers suggest that sleep helps restore the body and the brain for future activity and helps to consolidate memories of newly learned facts (Beuckmann & Yanagisawa, 2002; Gais & Born, 2004; Wagner et al., 2004). For example, in research conducted at the University of Manitoba by Marc Nesca and David Koulack, university students who were allowed to sleep after studying performed better on a test the next day than students who did not sleep between studying and writing the test

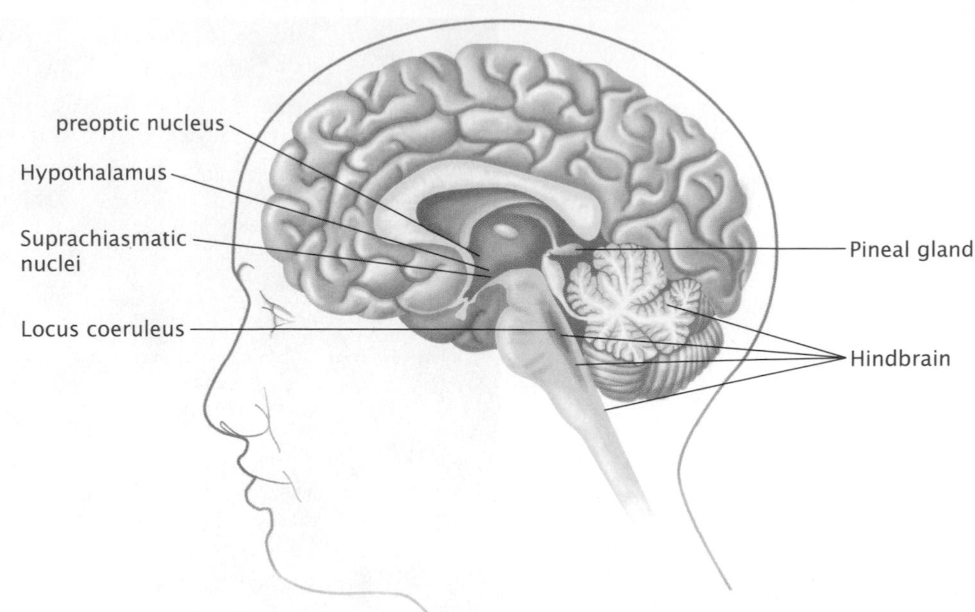

figure 9.8

Sleep, Dreaming, and the Brain

Here are some of the brain structures thought to be involved in sleep, dreaming, and other altered states of consciousness discussed later in the chapter. Scientists have discovered two specialized areas in the hypothalamus that appear to coordinate sleep and wakefulness. The preoptic nucleus appears to promote sleep. People with damage in this hypothalamic region find it difficult to ever go to sleep. The posterior lateral hypothalamus appears to promote wakefulness. Damage here causes continuous sleeping from which the person can be awakened only briefly (Salin-Pascual et al., 2001; Saper, Chou, & Scammerll, 2001).

(Nesca & Koulack, 1994). Restorative functions are especially associated with non-REM sleep, which would help explain why most people get their non-REM sleep in the first part of the night (see Figure 9.6). Sleep-deprived people do not make up lost sleep hour for hour. Instead, they sleep about 50 percent more than usual, then awake feeling rested. But if people are deprived only of REM sleep, they later compensate more directly. In a classic study, participants were awakened whenever their EEG tracings showed REM sleep. When allowed to sleep uninterrupted the next night, the participants "rebounded," nearly doubling the percentage of time spent in REM sleep (Dement, 1960). Even after *total* sleep deprivation, the next night of uninterrupted sleep includes an unusually high percentage of REM sleep (Feinberg & Campbell, 1993). This apparent need for REM sleep suggests that it has special functions.

What these special functions might be is still unclear, but there are several possibilities. First, REM sleep may improve the functioning of neurons that use norepinephrine (Siegel & Rogawski, 1988). Norepinephrine is a neurotransmitter

The Effects of Sleep Deprivation

Here, scientists at Loughborough University, England, test the effects of sleep deprivation on motor coordination. Driving while sleep-deprived can be so dangerous that at least one US state (New Jersey) has expanded the definition of reckless driving to include "driving while fatigued" (i.e., having had no sleep in the previous 24 hours). Some other functions may not suffer as much (Jennings, Monk, & van der Molen, 2003). One man reportedly stayed awake for 231 hours and was still lucid and capable of serious intellectual work, including the creation of a lovely poem on his tenth day without sleep (Katz & Landis, 1935).

released by cells in the *locus coeruleus* (pronounced "lo-kus seh-ROO-lee-us"; see Figure 9.8). During waking hours, norepinephrine affects alertness and mood. But the brain's neurons lose sensitivity to norepinephrine if it is released continuously for too long. Because the locus coeruleus is almost completely inactive during REM sleep, researchers suggest that REM helps restore sensitivity to norepinephrine and thus its ability to keep us alert (Steriade & McCarley, 1990). Animals deprived of REM sleep show unusually high norepinephrine levels and decreased daytime alertness (Brock et al., 1994).

REM sleep may also be a time for creating and solidifying connections between nerve cells in the brain (Graves, Pack, & Abel, 2001; Maquet, 2001; Peigneux et al., 2001; Roffwarg, Muzio, & Dement, 1966). If so, it would explain why children and infants, whose brains are still developing, spend so much time in REM sleep (see Figure 9.7). Evidence favouring this possibility comes from research showing that REM sleep enhances the creation of neural connections in response to altered visual experience during the development of the visual cortex (Frank et al., 2001). REM sleep may also help solidify and absorb the day's experiences, including newly learned skills (Fenn, Nusbaum, & Margoliash, 2003; Fischer et al., 2002; Sejnowski & Destexhe, 2000; Stickgold et al., 2000). In one study, people who were REM deprived showed poorer retention of a skill learned the day before than people who were either deprived of non-REM sleep or allowed to sleep normally (Karni et al., 1994). In another study, establishing memories of emotional information was particularly dependent on REM sleep (Wagner, Gais, & Born, 2001).

Dreams and Dreaming

We have seen that the brain is active in all sleep stages (for a summary of our discussion, see "In Review: Sleep and Sleep Disorders"). Some of this activity is experienced as the storylike sensations and perceptions known as dreams. **Dreams** can last from seconds to minutes and can be organized or chaotic, realistic or fantastic, peaceful or exciting (Hobson & Stickgold, 1994). Sometimes, dreams lead to creative insights. For example, after trying for days to write a story about good and evil in the same person, author Robert Louis Stevenson dreamed about a man who drank a potion that turned him into a monster (Hill, 1968). This dream inspired *The Strange Case of Dr. Jekyll and Mr. Hyde.* However, there is no scientific evidence that dreams lead to insights that are any more creative than those coming from waking thoughts.

Some dreaming occurs during non-REM sleep, but most dreams—and the most bizarre and vivid dreams—occur during REM sleep (Casagrande et al., 1996; Dement & Kleitman, 1957; Stickgold, Rittenhouse, & Hobson, 1994). Even when they seem to make no sense, dreams may contain a certain amount of logic. In one study, for example, when segments from some dream reports were scrambled, readers could correctly say which reports had been rearranged and which were intact (Stickgold, Rittenhouse, & Hobson, 1994). And although dreams often involve one person becoming another person or one object turning into another object, it is rare that objects become people or vice versa (Stickgold, Rittenhouse, & Hobson, 1994).

Daytime activities may influence the content of dreams to some degree (Foulkes, 1985; Wegner, Wenzlaff, & Kozak, 2004). When people were asked to wear red-tinted goggles for a few minutes before going to sleep, they reported more red images in their dreams than people who had not worn the goggles (Roffwarg, Hermann, & Bowe-Anders, 1978). It is also sometimes possible to intentionally direct dream content, especially during **lucid dreaming,** in which the sleeper is aware of dreaming while a dream is happening (Stickgold et al., 2000).

Research leaves little doubt that everyone dreams during every night of normal sleep. Even blind people dream, although their perceptual experiences are usually not visual. Whether you remember a dream depends on how you sleep and wake up. You'll remember more if you awaken abruptly and lie quietly while writing or tape-recording your recollections.

dream Story-like sequence of images, sensations, and perceptions occurring mainly during REM sleep.

lucid dreaming Awareness that a dream is a dream while it is happening.

in review Sleep and Sleep Disorders

Types of Sleep	Characteristics	Possible Functions
Slow wave (stages 3 and 4)	The deepest stages of sleep, characterized by slowed heart rate and breathing, reduced blood pressure and low-frequency, high-amplitude brain waves	Refreshing of body and brain; memory consolidation
Rapid eye movement (REM) sleep	Characterized by eye movements, waking levels of heart rate, breathing, blood pressure, and brain waves, but near-paralysis in muscles; most dreaming occurs during REM	Restoring sensitivity to norepinephrine, thus improving waking alertness; creating and solidifying nerve cell connections; consolidating memories and new skills
Sleep Disorders	**Characteristics**	**Possible Causes**
Insomnia	Difficulty (lasting at least a month) in falling asleep or staying asleep	Worry, anxiety
Narcolepsy	Sudden switching from a waking state to REM sleep	Absence or deficiency in *orexin* (*hypocretin*)
Sleep apnea	Frequent episodes of interrupted breathing while asleep	Genetic predisposition, obesity, faulty breathing-related brain mechanisms, windpipe compression
Sudden infant death syndrome (SIDS)	Interruption of an infant's breathing, resulting in death	Genetic predisposition, faulty breathing-related brain mechanisms
Nightmares	Frightening dreams during REM sleep	Stressful or traumatic events or experiences
Night terrors	Frightening dream images during non-REM sleep	Stressful or traumatic events or experiences
REM behaviour disorder	Lack of paralysis during REM sleep allows dreams to be enacted, sometimes with harmful consequences	Malfunction of brain mechanism normally creating REM paralysis

PsychAssist: Priming; EEG and Different Stages of Sleep

There are many theories about why we dream (Antrobus, 2001; Domhoff, 2001). Some researchers see dreaming as a fundamental process by which all mammals analyze and consolidate information that has personal significance or survival value (Porte & Hobson, 1996). This view is supported by the fact that dreaming appears to occur in most mammals, as indicated by the appearance of REM sleep. For example, after researchers disabled the neurons that cause REM sleep paralysis, sleeping cats ran around and attacked, or seemed alarmed by, unseen objects, presumably the images from dreams (Winson, 1990).

According to Freud (1900), dreams are a disguised form of *wish fulfillment,* a way to satisfy unconscious urges or resolve unconscious conflicts that are too upsetting to deal with consciously. So sexual desires might appear in a dream as the rhythmic motions of a horseback ride. Conflicting feelings about a parent might appear as a dream about a fight. Seeing patients' dreams as a "royal road to a knowledge of the unconscious," Freud interpreted their meaning as part of his psychoanalytic therapy (see the chapter on treatment of psychological disorders).

In contrast, the *activation-synthesis theory* describes dreams as the meaningless by-products of REM sleep (Hobson, 1997). According to this theory, hindbrain arousal during REM sleep creates random messages that *activate* the brain, especially the cerebral cortex. Dreams result as the cortex combines, or *synthesizes,* these random messages as best it can, using stored memories and current feelings to impose a coherent perceptual organization on confusingly random inputs. From this perspective, dreams arise as the brain attempts to make sense of meaningless stimulation during sleep, much as it does during waking hours when trying to find meaningful shapes in cloud formations (Bernstein & Roberts, 1995).

Even if dreams stem from random physiological activity, their content can still have psychological significance. Some psychologists believe that dreams give people a chance to review and address some of the problems they face during waking hours (Cartwright, 1993). This view is supported by evidence that people's current concerns can affect both the content of their dreams and the ways in which dreams are organized and recalled (Domhoff, 1996; Stevens, 1996). However, research using brain imaging techniques shows that while we are asleep, brain areas involved in emotion tend to be overactive, whereas areas controlling logical thought tend to be suppressed (Braun, Balkin, & Wesensten, 1998; Hobson et al., 1998). In fact, as we reach deeper sleep stages, and then enter REM, thinking subsides and hallucinations increase (Fosse, Stickgold, & Hobson, 2001). This is probably why dreams rarely provide realistic, logical solutions to our problems (Blagrove, 1996).

Hypnosis

The word *hypnosis* comes from the Greek word *hypnos,* meaning "sleep," but hypnotized people are not sleeping. People who have been hypnotized say that their bodies felt "asleep," but their minds were active and alert. **Hypnosis** has traditionally been defined as an altered state of consciousness brought on by special techniques and producing responsiveness to suggestions for changes in experience and behaviour (Kirsch, 1994b). Most hypnotized people do not feel forced to follow the hypnotist's instructions; they simply see no reason to refuse (Hilgard, 1965). In fact, a desire to cooperate with the hypnotist greatly increases the likelihood that a person will experience hypnosis (Lynn et al., 2002).

Experiencing Hypnosis

Usually, hypnosis begins with suggestions that the participant feels relaxed and sleepy. The hypnotist then gradually focuses the participant's attention on a particular, often monotonous set of stimuli while suggesting that the participant should ignore everything else and imagine certain feelings.

Not everyone can be hypnotized. There are special tests to measure *hypnotic susceptibility,* the degree to which people respond to hypnotic suggestions (Gfeller, 1994). Such tests reveal that about 10 percent of adults are difficult or impossible to hypnotize (Hilgard, 1982). At the other extreme are highly susceptible individuals who report vivid hypnotic experiences. In research conducted at Carleton University in Ottawa, Nicholas Spanos studied various factors that contribute to a person's susceptibility to hypnotic suggestions. He, and other researchers in this area, have found that hypnotically susceptible people typically differ from others in several ways. They have greater ability to focus attention and ignore distraction (Crawford, Brown, & Moon, 1993), a more active imagination (Spanos, Burnley, & Cross, 1993), a tendency to fantasize (Lynn & Rhue, 1986), a capacity for processing information quickly and easily (Dixon, Brunet, & Lawrence, 1990), a tendency to be suggestible (Kirsch & Braffman, 2001), and more positive attitudes toward hypnosis (Gfeller, 1994; Spanos et al., 1993). As suggested earlier, their *willingness* to be hypnotized is the most important factor of all. Contrary to myth, people cannot be hypnotized against their will.

hypnosis A phenomenon brought on by special induction techniques and characterized by varying degrees of responsiveness to suggestions for changes in experience and behaviour.

The results of hypnosis can be fascinating. People told that their eyes are sealed shut may struggle unsuccessfully to open them. They may appear deaf or blind or insensitive to pain. They may be unable to say their own names. Some appear to remember forgotten things. Others show *age regression,* apparently recalling or reenacting their childhood (see Figure 9.9). Hypnotic effects can last for hours or days through *posthypnotic suggestions*—instructions about behaviour that is to take place after hypnosis has ended (such as smiling whenever someone says "England"). Some people show *posthypnotic amnesia,* an inability to recall what happened while they were hypnotized, even after being told what happened.

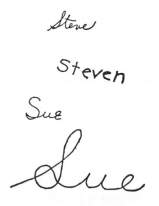

Ernest Hilgard (1965, 1992) described the main changes that people display during hypnosis.

1. Hypnotized people show *reduced planfulness.* They tend not to begin actions on their own, waiting instead for the hypnotist's instructions. One participant said, "I was trying to decide if my legs were crossed, but I couldn't tell, and didn't quite have the initiative to move to find out" (Hilgard, 1965, p. 6).
2. They tend to ignore all but the hypnotist's voice and whatever it points out; their *attention is redistributed.*
3. Hypnosis enhances the *ability to fantasize,* so participants more vividly imagine a scene or relive a memory.
4. Hypnotized people display *increased role taking;* they more easily act like a person of a different age or a member of the opposite sex, for example.
5. Hypnotic participants show *reduced reality testing,* tending not to question if statements are true and more willingly accepting apparent distortions of reality. A hypnotized person might shiver in a warm room if a hypnotist says it is snowing.

Inducing Hypnosis In the late 1700s, an Austrian physician named Franz Anton Mesmer became famous for his treatment of physical disorders using *mesmerism,* a forerunner of hypnosis. His patients touched their afflicted body parts to magnetized metal rods extending from a tub of water and then, when touched by Mesmer, fell into a curative "crisis" or trance, sometimes accompanied by convulsions. We now know that hypnosis can be induced far more easily, often simply by asking a person to stare at an object.

Explaining Hypnosis

Hypnotized people and nonhypnotized people act differently and may look different, too (Hilgard, 1965). Do these differences reflect an altered state of consciousness?

Advocates of the **state theory** of hypnosis say that they do. They point to the dramatic effects that hypnosis can produce, including insensitivity to pain and the disappearance of warts (Noll, 1994). They also note that there are subtle differences in the way hypnotized and nonhypnotized people carry out suggestions. In one study, hypnotized people and those who had been asked to simulate hypnosis were told to run their hands through their hair whenever they heard the word *experiment* (Orne, Sheehan, & Evans, 1968). Simulators did so only when the hypnotist said the cue word. Hypnotized participants complied no matter who said it. Another study found that hypnotized people complied more often than simulators with a posthypnotic suggestion to mail postcards to the experimenter (Barnier & McConkey, 1998).

Proponents of the **role theory** of hypnosis argue that hypnosis is *not* a special state of consciousness. They say that hypnotized people are merely complying with social demands and acting in accordance with a special social role (Kirsch, 1994a). From this perspective, then, hypnosis simply provides a socially acceptable reason to follow certain suggestions, much as a medical examination provides a socially acceptable reason to remove clothing on command.

Support for role theory comes from several sources. For example, laboratory experiments show that motivated, but nonhypnotized, volunteers can duplicate many, if not all, aspects of hypnotic behaviour, from arm rigidity to age regression (Dasgupta et al., 1995; Orne & Evans, 1965). Other studies using special tests have found that people rendered blind or deaf by hypnosis can still see or hear, even though their actions and beliefs suggest that they cannot (Bryant & McConkey, 1989; Pattie, 1935; see Figure 9.10).

Hilgard's (1992) **dissociation theory** of hypnosis blends role and state theories. He suggested that hypnosis is not a specific state but a general condition that temporarily

Steve

Steven

Sue

Sue

figure 9.9

Hypnotic Age Regression

Here are the signatures of two adults before hypnotically induced age regression (top of each pair) and while age regressed (bottom of each pair). The lower signatures in each pair look less mature, but was the change due to hypnosis? To find out, ask a friend to write his or her name on a blank sheet of paper, first as usual, and then as if he or she were five years old. If the two signatures look significantly different, what does this say about the cause of certain age-regression effects? *Source:* Hilgard (1965).

figure 9.10

Can Hypnosis Produce Blindness?

The top row looks like gibberish, but if you closed one eye while wearing special glasses, you could detect within it the numbers and letters shown in the bottom row. Yet when hypnotized people wore such glasses and were told that they were blind in one eye, they were unable to read the display. This result indicated that, despite the hypnotic suggestion, both their eyes were working normally (Pattie, 1935).

Source: Pattie (1935).

FHNV XTMI2 DN 6 NCLVDA

reorganizes or breaks down our normal control over thoughts and actions. Hypnosis, he said, activates a process called *dissociation,* meaning a split in consciousness (Hilgard, 1979). As a result, body movements normally under voluntary control can occur on their own, and normally involuntary processes (such as reactions to pain) can be controlled voluntarily. Hilgard argued that this relaxation of central control occurs as part of a *social agreement* to share control with the hypnotist. In other words, people usually decide for themselves how to act or what to attend to, perceive, or remember, but during hypnosis, the hypnotist is "allowed" to control some of these experiences and actions. So Hilgard saw hypnosis as a socially agreed-upon display of dissociated mental functions. Compliance with a social role may account for part of the story, he said, but hypnosis also leads to significant changes in mental processes.

Evidence for dissociation theory comes from a study in which hypnotized participants immersed one hand in ice water after being told that they would feel no pain (Hilgard, Morgan, & MacDonald, 1975). With the other hand, participants were to press a key to indicate if "any part of them" felt pain. Participants' oral reports indicated almost no pain, but their key pressing told a different story. Hilgard concluded that a "hidden observer" was reporting on pain that was reaching the person but had been separated, or dissociated, from conscious awareness (Hilgard, 1977).

Much remains to be learned about the nature of hypnosis. Contemporary research continues to test the validity of various explanatory theories of hypnosis, but traditional distinctions between state and role theories have become less relevant as the focus shifts to larger questions, such as the impact of social and cognitive factors in hypnotic phenomena, the nature of the hypnotic experience, and the psychological and physiological basis for hypnotic susceptibility (Kirsch & Lynn, 1995).

Surgery under Hypnosis Bernadine Coady, of Wimblington, England, has a condition that makes it dangerous for her to have general anesthesia. In April 1999, when a hypnotherapist failed to show up to help her through a painful foot operation, she used self-hypnosis as her only anesthetic. She imagined the pain as "waves lashing against a sea wall ... [and] going away, like the tide." Coady's report that the operation was painless is believable because, in December 2000, she underwent the same operation on her other foot, again using only self-hypnosis for pain control (Morris, 2000).

Applications of Hypnosis

Perry Campbell, in research conducted at Concordia University in Montreal, found hypnosis to be effective in treating symptoms associated with asthma, skin problems, burns, and some forms of cancer (Campbell, Laurence, & Nadon, 1988). In addition, hypnosis seems to be the only anesthetic some people need to block the pain of dental work, childbirth, and abdominal surgery (Morris, 2000; Van Sickel, 1992). For others, hypnosis relieves chronic pain from arthritis, nerve damage, and migraine headaches (Nolan et al., 1995). Functional MRI studies of hypnotized pain patients show altered activity in the anterior cingulate cortex, a brain region mentioned in the chapter on sensation as being associated with the emotional component of pain (Faymonville et al., 2000). Hypnotic suggestions can also reduce nausea and vomiting due to chemotherapy (Redd, 1984), help reduce surgical bleeding (Gerschman, Reade, & Burrows, 1980), and shorten postoperative recovery times (Astin, 2004).

Other applications of hypnosis are more controversial, especially the use of hypnosis to aid memory. For example, hypnotic age regression is sometimes attempted in an effort to help people recover lost memories. However, the memories of past events reported by age-regressed individuals are not as accurate as those of nonhypnotized individuals (Lynn, Myers, & Malinoski, 1997). It is

state theory A theory that hypnosis is an altered state of consciousness.

role theory A theory that hypnotized people act in accordance with a special social role that provides a socially acceptable reason to follow the hypnotist's suggestions.

dissociation theory A theory defining hypnosis as a socially agreed-upon opportunity to display one's ability to let mental functions become dissociated.

doubtful, then, that hypnosis can improve the ability of witnesses to recall details of a crime. In fact, their positive expectations about the value of hypnosis may lead them to unintentionally distort or reconstruct memories of what they saw and heard (Garry & Loftus, 1994; Weekes et al., 1992; Wells & Olson, 2003). So although hypnosis may not enhance people's memory for information, it might make them more confident about their reports, even if they are inaccurate. As discussed in the chapter on memory, confident witnesses tend to be especially impressive to juries.

LINKAGES
Meditation, Health, and Stress

LINKAGES (a link to Health, Stress, and Coping)

Meditation is intended to create an altered state of consciousness characterized by inner peace and tranquility (Shapiro & Walsh, 1984). Some claim that meditation increases people's awareness and understanding of themselves and their environment, reduces anxiety, improves health, and aids performance in everything from work to tennis (Bodian, 1999; Davidson et al., 2003; Mahesh Yogi, 1994).

The techniques used to achieve a meditative state differ, depending on belief and philosophy (for example, Eastern meditation, Sufism, yoga, or prayer). However, in the most common meditation methods, attention is focused on just one thing—a word, sound, or object—until the meditator stops thinking about anything and experiences nothing but "pure awareness" (Benson, 1975). In this way, the individual becomes more fully aware of the present moment rather than being caught up in the past or the future.

What a meditator focuses on is far less important than doing so with a passive attitude. To organize attention, meditators might inwardly name every sound or thought that reaches consciousness, focus on the sound of their own breathing, or slowly repeat a *mantra,* which is a soothing word or phrase. During a typical meditation session, breathing, heart rate, muscle tension, blood pressure, and oxygen

Memories recalled under hypnosis are generally not considered reliable evidence in court. However, in some cases, hypnosis has been used as a helpful tool in conducting criminal investigations. For example, in investigating the murder of Helen Betty Osbourne, a First Nations woman murdered in Manitoba, RCMP used hypnosis to help a witness recall the licence plate number of a car that was driven by one of her killers. The car contained several other key pieces of evidence that eventually led to a conviction in 1987, 16 years after her death.

"Are you not thinking what I'm not thinking?"

consumption decrease (Wallace & Benson, 1972), while in the brain blood flow to the thalamus and frontal lobes increases (Newberg et al., 2001). Meditation also increases the brain's level of dopamine, a neurotransmitter thought to be involved in the experience of reward or pleasure (Kjaer et al., 2002). Most forms of meditation induce alpha-wave EEG activity, the brain wave pattern commonly found in a relaxed, eyes-closed, waking state (see Figure 9.5).

Meditation has several potential benefits. For example, Linda Carlson and colleagues at the University of Calgary have successfully used meditation to treat sleep disturbances common in cancer patients (Carlson & Garland, 2005). In addition, meditators report significant reductions in stress-related problems such as general anxiety, high blood pressure, headache, back pain, and insomnia (Astin et al., 2003; Beauchamp-Turner & Levinson, 1992). More generally, meditators' scores on personality tests indicate increases in overall mental health, self-esteem, and social openness (Janowiak & Hackman, 1994; Sakairi, 1992). Exactly how meditation produces these benefits is unclear, though its effects on dopamine may tell an important part of the story. Whatever the mechanism, it is probably not unique to meditation. The same benefits have been associated with other techniques such as biofeedback, hypnosis, tai chi, and just relaxing (Beyerstein, 1999; Wang, Collet, & Lau, 2004).

Psychoactive Drugs

Every day, most people in the world use drugs that alter brain activity and consciousness (Levinthal, 1996). For example, 80 to 90 percent of people in North America use caffeine, the stimulant found in coffee (Gilbert, 1984). A drug is a chemical that is not usually needed for physiological activity and that can affect the body upon entering it. (Some people use the word *drug* to mean therapeutic medicines but refer to nonmedicinal drugs as *substances*, as in *substance abuse*). Drugs that affect the brain, changing consciousness and other psychological processes, are called **psychoactive drugs.** The study of psychoactive drugs is called **psychopharmacology.**

figure 9.11

Agonists and Antagonists

In part (A), a molecule of neurotransmitter interacts with a receptor on a neuron's dendrites by fitting into and stimulating it. Part (B) shows a drug molecule acting as an *agonist,* affecting the receptor in the same way a neurotransmitter would. Part (C) depicts an *antagonist* drug molecule blocking a natural neurotransmitter from reaching and acting upon the receptor.

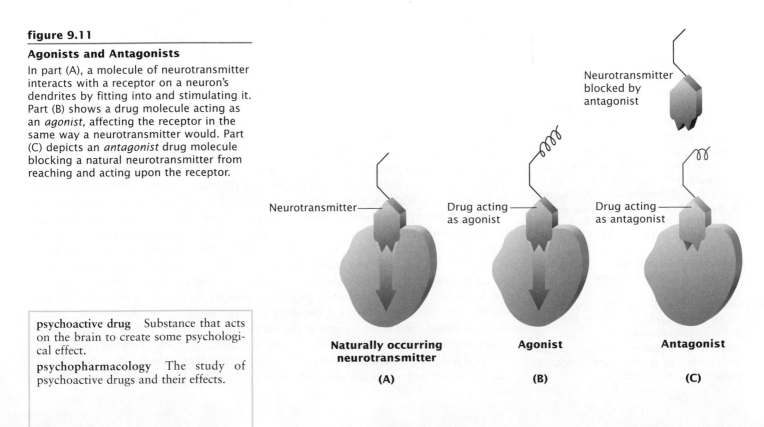

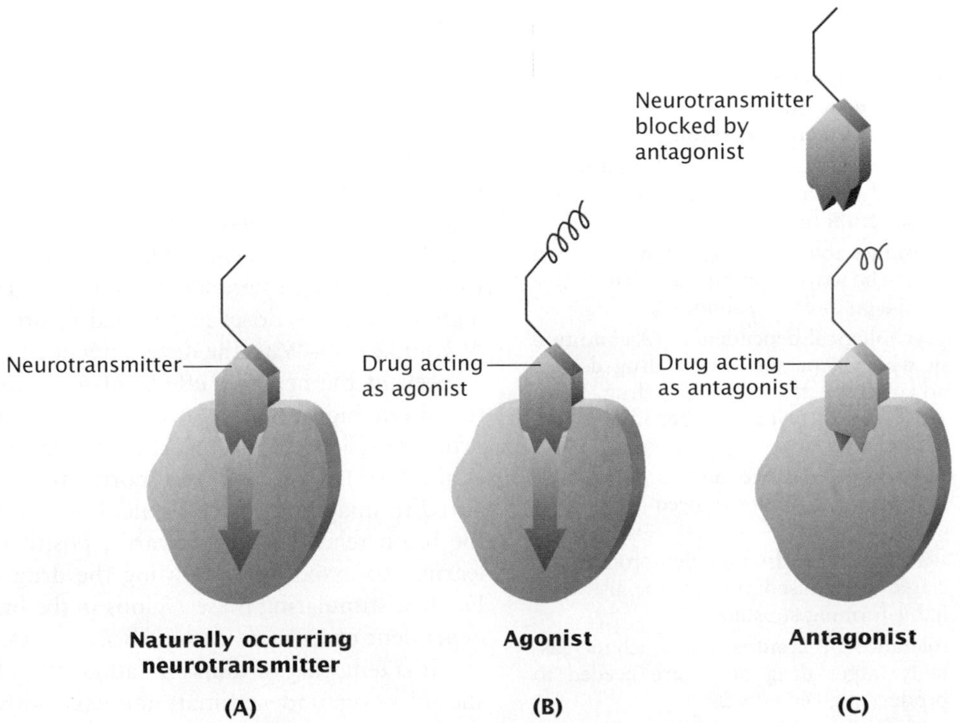

psychoactive drug Substance that acts on the brain to create some psychological effect.

psychopharmacology The study of psychoactive drugs and their effects.

Psychopharmacology

Most psychoactive drugs affect the brain by altering the interactions between neurotransmitters and receptors, as described in the chapter on biological aspects of psychology. To create their effects, these drugs must cross the **blood-brain barrier,** a feature of blood vessels in the brain that prevents some substances from entering brain tissue (Neuwelt, 2004). Once past this barrier, a psychoactive drug's effects depend on several factors: With which neurotransmitter systems does the drug interact? How does the drug affect these neurotransmitters or their receptors? What psychological functions are normally performed by the brain systems that use these neurotransmitters?

Drugs can affect neurotransmitters or their receptors through several mechanisms. As shown in Figure 9.11, neurotransmitters fit into their own receptors. However, some drugs are similar enough to a particular neurotransmitter to fool its receptors. These drugs, called **agonists,** bind to the receptor and mimic the effects of the normal neurotransmitter. Other drugs are similar enough to a neurotransmitter to occupy its receptors but cannot mimic its effects. So they bind to a receptor and prevent the normal neurotransmitter from binding. These drugs are called **antagonists.** Still other drugs work by increasing or decreasing the release of a specific neurotransmitter. Finally, some drugs work by speeding or slowing the *removal* of a neurotransmitter from synapses.

Predicting a drug's behavioural effects is complicated by the fact that most psychoactive drugs interact with many neurotransmitter systems. Also, the nervous system may compensate for a drug's effects. For example, repeated exposure to a drug that blocks receptors for a certain neurotransmitter often leads to an increase in the number of receptors available to accept that neurotransmitter.

The Varying Effects of Drugs

The medically desirable *main effects* of drugs, such as pain relief, are often accompanied by undesirable *side effects,* which may include the potential for abuse. **Substance abuse** is a pattern of use that causes serious social, legal, or interpersonal problems for the user (American Psychiatric Association, 2000).

Substance abuse may lead to psychological or physical dependence. **Psychological dependence** is a condition in which a person continues to use the drug despite its adverse effects, needs the drug for a sense of well-being, and becomes preoccupied with obtaining the drug. However, the person can still function without the drug. Psychological dependence can occur with or without **physical dependence,** or **addiction,** which is a physiological state in which continued drug use becomes necessary in order to prevent an unpleasant **withdrawal syndrome.** Withdrawal symptoms vary depending on the drug, but they often include an intense craving for the drug and physical effects generally opposite to those of the drug itself. Eventually, drug tolerance may appear. **Tolerance** is a condition in which increasingly larger drug doses are needed to produce the same effect (Sokolowska, Siegel, & Kim, 2002). With the development of tolerance, many addicts need the drug just to prevent the negative effects of not taking it. However, most researchers believe that a craving for the positive effects of drugs is what keeps addicts coming back to drug use (Ciccociopppo, Martin-Fardon, & Weiss, 2004; George et al., 2001; Weiss et al., 2001). This view is supported by functional MRI studies of addicts who were asked to imagine cocaine or alcohol use. The resulting craving activated regions of the brain related to the rewards, positive emotions, and other pleasures they had learned to associate with using the drug (George et al., 2001; Kilts et al., 2001). Further, stimulating these regions in the brains of rats that had once been physically dependent on cocaine causes them to seek out the drug again (Vorel et al., 2001).

It is tempting to think of "addicts" as being different from the rest of us, but we should never underestimate the ease with which drug dependence can develop in

blood-brain barrier A feature of blood vessels supplying the brain that allows only certain substances to leave the blood and interact with brain tissue.

agonist Drug that mimics the effects of the neurotransmitter that normally binds to a neural receptor.

antagonist Drug that binds to a receptor and prevents the normal neurotransmitter from binding.

substance abuse The self-administration of psychoactive drugs in ways that deviate from a culture's social norms.

psychological dependence A condition in which a person uses a drug despite adverse effects, needs the drug for a sense of well-being, and becomes preoccupied with obtaining it.

physical dependence (addiction) Development of a physical need for a psychoactive drug.

withdrawal syndrome Symptoms associated with discontinuing the use of a habit-forming substance.

tolerance A condition in which increasingly larger drug doses are needed to produce a given effect.

anyone, including ourselves. Physical dependence can develop gradually, without a person's awareness. In fact, scientists now believe that the changes in the brain that underlie addiction may be similar to those that occur during learning (Nestler, 2001; Overton et al., 1999). All addictive drugs stimulate the brain's "pleasure centres," regions that are sensitive to the neurotransmitter dopamine. Neuronal activity in these areas produces intensely pleasurable feelings; it also helps generate the pleasant feelings of a good meal, a "runner's high," or sex (Grunberg, 1994; Harris & Aston-Jones, 1995). Neuroscientists long believed that these feelings stem directly from the action of dopamine itself, but activity in dopamine systems may actually be more involved in responding to the novelty associated with pleasurable events than in actually creating the experience of pleasure (Bevins, 2001; Garris et al., 1999). In any case, by affecting dopamine regulation and related biochemical processes in pleasure centres, addictive drugs have the capacity to create tremendously rewarding effects in most people (Kelley & Berridge, 2002).

Expectations and Drug Effects Drug effects are determined by more than biochemistry (Crombag & Robinson, 2004). *Learned expectations* also play a role (Cumsille, Sayer, & Graham, 2000; Goldman, Del Boca, & Darkes, 1999; Stein, Goldman, & Del Boca, 2000). According to Heather MacLatchy-Gaudet and Sherry Stewart at Dalhousie University in Halifax, these expectations can be either positive or negative. For example, they found that university undergraduate women associated alcohol with positive social and sexual outcomes (MacLatchy-Gaudet & Stewart, 2001). Several experiments have shown that people who consume alcohol-free drinks that they *think* contain alcohol are likely to behave in line with their expectations about alcohol's effects. So they tend to feel drunk and to become more aggressive, more interested in violent and sexual material, and more easily sexually aroused (Darkes & Goldman, 1993; George & Marlatt, 1986; Lang et al., 1975; Lansky & Wilson, 1981). And because they know that alcohol impairs memory, these people are more vulnerable to developing false memories about a crime they witnessed on videotape (Assefi & Garry, 2003).

Expectations about drug effects develop, in part, as people watch other people react to drugs (Sher et al., 1996). Because what they see can be different from one individual and culture to the next, drug effects vary considerably throughout the world (MacAndrew & Edgerton, 1969). In North America, for example, loss of inhibition, increased anger and violence, and sexual promiscuity are commonly associated with drinking alcohol. These effects are not seen in all cultures, however. In Bolivia's Camba culture, people engage in extended bouts of drinking a brew that is 89 percent alcohol (178 proof). During their binges, the Camba repeatedly pass out, wake up, and start drinking again—all the while maintaining tranquil social relations. Other studies have shown that learned expectations also contribute to the effects of heroin, cocaine, and marijuana (Robbins & Everitt, 1999; Schafer & Brown, 1991; Smith et al., 1992).

The learned nature of responses to alcohol is also demonstrated by cases in which people are exposed to new ideas about the drug's effects. When Europeans brought alcohol to Tahiti in the 1700s, the Tahitians who drank it just became relaxed and disoriented, much as when consuming *kava,* their traditional nonalcoholic tranquilizing drink. But after years of watching European sailors' drunken violence, Tahitian alcohol drinkers became violent themselves. Fortunately, subsequent learning experiences have moderated their response to alcohol (MacAndrew & Edgerton, 1969).

Expectations about a drug's effects can also influence how much of it people will consume (Goldman, Darkes, & Del Boca, 1999). In one study, for example, participants took part in a memory experiment whose real purpose was to prime their positive expectations about the effects of alcohol (Roehrich & Goldman, 1995). The priming was done in one or both of two unobtrusive ways, so the participants were unaware of it. In the first, participants watched an episode of *Cheers,* a television

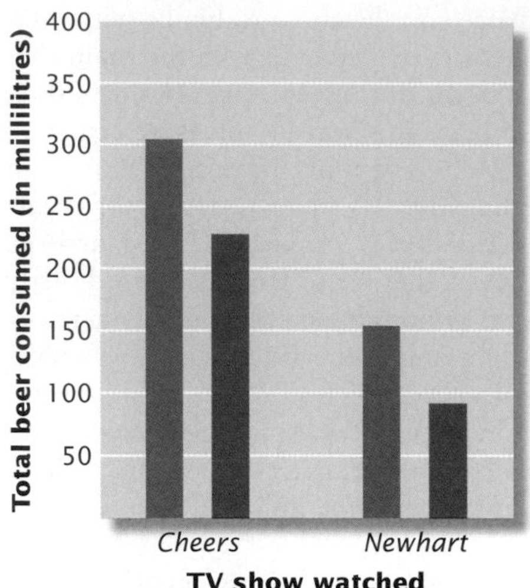

figure 9.12

Expectancies and Alcohol Consumption

People may drink more when their expectancies about the positive effects of alcohol have been primed. In this study, participants who (1) watched a TV show in which characters enjoyed drinking alcohol and (2) were exposed to adjectives associated with the positive effects of alcohol drank more (nonalcoholic) beer than participants who watched a show not alcohol-related and who were not exposed to the alcohol-positive adjectives.

Source: Roehrich & Goldman (1995, Figure 1).

show that portrays alcohol consumption in a positive light. In the second, participants were exposed to adjectives that are associated with the positive effects of alcohol consumption (e.g., *funny, happy,* and *talkative*). Later, the participants were given an opportunity to drink what they thought was alcohol (but was actually nonalcoholic beer) as part of a separate "taste-rating study." Figure 9.12 shows the results of this experiment. Although the participants saw no connection between the priming stages of the study and the later taste test, those who had watched *Cheers* drank more than those who had watched a TV show that wasn't related to alcohol. Those who were exposed to the positive alcohol-consumption adjectives drank more than those who were exposed to adjectives unrelated to alcohol.

These examples and experiments show that the effects of psychoactive drugs are complex and variable. In the chapter on treatment of psychological disorders, we discuss some of the psychoactive drugs being used to help troubled people. Here, we consider several categories of psychoactive drugs that are used primarily for the alterations they produce in consciousness. They include depressants, stimulants, opiates, and hallucinogens.

Depressants

Depressants are drugs that reduce the activity of the central nervous system. Examples are alcohol and barbiturates, both of which bring about their depressant effects by affecting a neurotransmitter called GABA. As described in the chapter on biological aspects of psychology, GABA reduces, or inhibits, neuron activity. Depressants increase the availability of GABA, which, in turn, reduces the activity of many neural circuits. So the results of using depressants include relaxation, drowsiness, and sometimes depression (Hanson & Venturelli, 1995).

Alcohol According to the Canadian Addictions Survey (Centre for Addictions Research of British Columbia, 2004), approximately 79 percent of adults in Canada drink alcohol. It is equally popular worldwide (Alvarez, Delrio, & Prada, 1995; Leigh & Stacy, 2004). Alcohol affects several neurotransmitters, including dopamine, endorphins, glutamate, serotonin, and most notably, GABA (Daglish & Nutt, 2003; Enoch, 2003). For this reason, drugs that interact with GABA receptors can block some of alcohol's effects, as shown in Figure 9.13 (Suzdak et al., 1986). Alcohol also enhances the effect of endorphins (the body's natural painkillers, described in the chapter on sensation). This action may underlie the "high" that people feel when drinking alcohol and may explain why *naltrexone* and *naloxone,* which

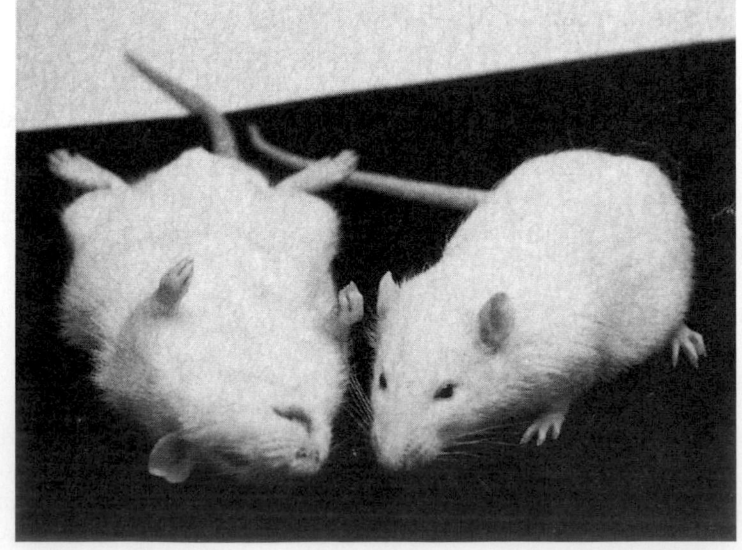

figure 9.13

GABA Receptors and Alcohol

These rats each received the same amount of alcohol, enough to incapacitate them with drunkenness. The rat on the right then received a drug that reverses alcohol's intoxicating effects by blocking the ability of alcohol to stimulate GABA receptors. Within two minutes, the animal was acting utterly sober. There is a serious problem with the drug, though: It did not reverse the effects of alcohol on the brain's breathing centres. So a person who took the drug could consume a fatal overdose of alcohol without ever feeling drunk. Needless to say, the drug's manufacturer has discontinued its development.

depressant Psychoactive drug that inhibits the functioning of the central nervous system.

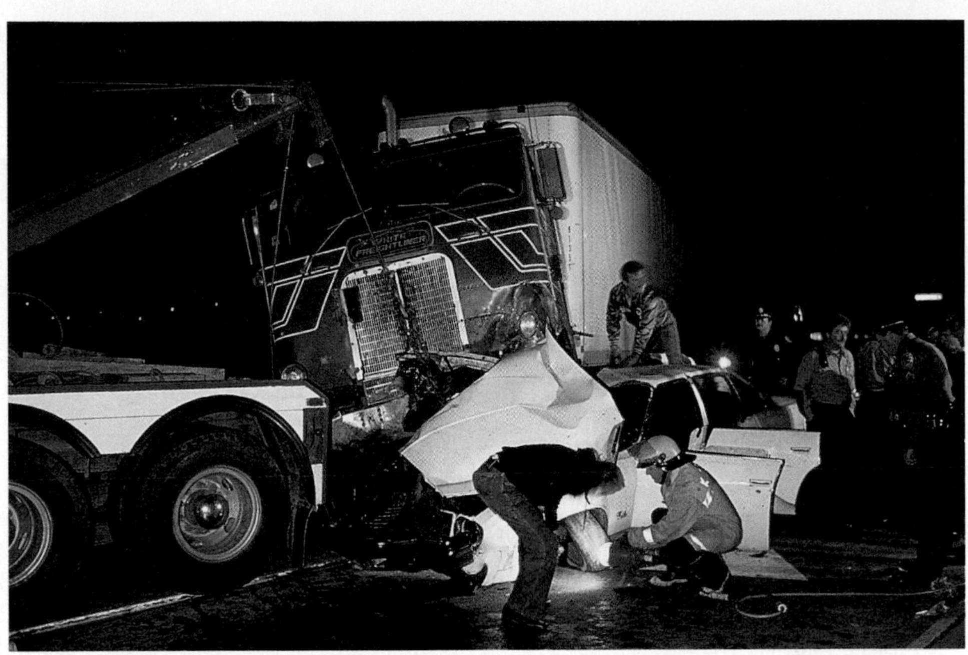

Drinking and Driving Don't Mix Although practice makes it seem easy, driving a car is a complex information-processing task. As described in the chapter on cognition and language, such tasks require constant vigilance, quick decisions, and skillful execution of responses. Alcohol can impair all these processes, as well as the ability to judge the degree of impairment—thus making drinking and driving a deadly combination. In 2003, Transport Canada recorded 1049 deaths and over 3000 serious injuries resulting from car accidents in which the driver had been drinking alcohol (Traffic Injury Research Foundation of Canada, 2005).

block endorphins, are better than placebos at reducing alcohol craving and relapse rates in recovering alcoholics (Balldin et al., 2003; Salloum et al., 1998). Alcohol also interacts with dopamine systems, a component of the brain's pleasure and reward mechanisms (Thanos et al., 2001). Prolonged alcohol use can have lasting effects on the brain's ability to regulate dopamine levels (Tiihonen et al., 1995). Dopamine agonists reduce alcohol craving and withdrawal effects (Lawford et al., 1995).

Alcohol affects specific brain regions. For example, it depresses activity in the locus coeruleus, an area that helps activate the cerebral cortex (Koob & Bloom, 1988). This reduced activity, in turn, tends to cause cognitive changes and a release of culturally prescribed inhibitions (Casbon et al., 2003). Some drinkers begin talking loudly, acting silly, or telling others what they think of them. Emotional reactions range from giddy happiness to deep despair. Normally shy people may become impulsive or violent. Alcohol's impairment of the hippocampus causes memory problems, making it more difficult to form new memories (Givens, 1995). And its suppression of the cerebellum causes poor motor coordination (Rogers et al., 1986). Alcohol's ability to depress hindbrain mechanisms that control breathing and heartbeat can make overdoses fatal.

As mentioned earlier, some effects of alcohol—such as anger and aggressiveness—depend on both biochemical factors and learned expectations (Goldman, Darkes, & Del Boca, 1999; Kushner et al., 2000). But other effects—especially disruptions in motor coordination, speech, and thought—result from biochemical factors alone. These biological effects depend on the amount of alcohol the blood carries to the brain. It takes the liver about an hour to break down one ounce of alcohol (the amount in one average drink), so alcohol has milder effects if consumed slowly. Effects increase with faster drinking, or with drinking on an empty stomach, thereby speeding the absorption of alcohol into the blood. Even after allowing for differences in average male and female body weight, researchers have found metabolic differences that allow males to tolerate somewhat higher amounts of alcohol. As a result, equal doses of alcohol may create greater effects in women compared with men (York & Welte, 1994).

Genetics also seems to play a role in determining the biochemical effects of alcohol. Some people appear to have a genetic predisposition toward alcohol dependence (Agarwal, 1997; Enoch, 2003), although the specific genes involved have not yet been identified. Others, such as the Japanese, may have inherited metabolic characteristics that increase the adverse effects of alcohol, thus possibly inhibiting the development of alcohol abuse (Iwahashi et al., 1995).

Barbiturates Sometimes called "downers" or "sleeping pills," *barbiturates* are extremely addictive. Small doses cause relaxation, feelings of well-being, loss of muscle coordination, and reduced attention. Higher doses cause deep sleep, but continued use actually distorts sleep patterns (Kales & Kales, 1973). So long-term use of barbiturates as sleeping pills is unwise. Overdoses can be fatal. Withdrawal symptoms are among the most severe for any drug and can include intense agitation, violent outbursts, convulsions, hallucinations, and even sudden death.

GHB *Gamma hydroxybutyrate,* or *GHB,* is a naturally occurring substance similar to the neurotransmitter GABA (Wong, Gibson, & Snead, 2004). Introduced many years ago as a nutritional supplement, a laboratory-manufactured version of GHB (also known as "G") has recently become a popular "club drug," known for inducing relaxation, elation, loss of inhibition, and increased sex drive.

Unfortunately, it can also cause nausea and vomiting, headaches, dizziness, loss of muscle control or paralysis, breathing problems, and even death—especially when combined with alcohol or other drugs (Miotto et al., 2001; Stillwell, 2002). Nearly half of those who use GHB report occasions on which it caused loss of memory, and two-thirds report having lost consciousness (Miotto et al., 2001). Because of these effects, GHB has sometimes been used by rapists to facilitate a sexual assault (Stillwell, 2002). As with other depressants, long-term use of GHB can lead to dependence, and suddenly stopping the drug can cause a withdrawal syndrome that can include seizures, hallucinations, agitation, and even coma or death (Tarabar & Nelson, 2004).

Stimulants

Whereas depressants slow down central nervous system activity, **stimulants** speed it up. Amphetamines, cocaine, caffeine, and nicotine are all examples of stimulants.

Amphetamines Also called "uppers" or "speed," *amphetamines* (such as Benzedrine) increase the release and decrease the removal of norepinephrine and dopamine at synapses, causing increased activity at these neurotransmitters' receptors (Bonci et al., 2003). This increased activity results in alertness, arousal, and appetite suppression. These effects are further enhanced by the fact that amphetamines also reduce activity of the inhibitory neurotransmitter GABA (Centonze et al., 2002). The rewarding properties of these drugs are probably due in part to their activation of dopamine systems, because taking dopamine antagonists reduces amphetamine use (Holman, 1994).

Amphetamines stimulate both the brain and the sympathetic branch of the autonomic nervous system, raising heart rate and blood pressure, constricting blood vessels, shrinking mucous membranes (relieving stuffy noses), and reducing appetite. Amphetamines also increase response speed, especially in tasks requiring prolonged attention (Koelega, 1993), and they may improve memory for verbal material (Soetens et al., 1995).

Abuse of amphetamines usually begins as an effort to lose weight, stay awake, or experience a "high." Continued use leads to anxiety, insomnia, heart problems, brain damage, movement disorders, confusion, paranoia, nonstop talking, and psychological and physical dependence (Thompson et al., 2004; Volkow et al., 2001). In some cases, the symptoms of amphetamine abuse are virtually identical to those of paranoid schizophrenia, a serious mental disorder associated with malfunctioning dopamine systems.

stimulant Psychoactive drug that has the ability to increase behavioural and mental activity.

Cocaine Like amphetamines, *cocaine* increases norepinephrine and dopamine activity and decreases GABA activity, so it produces many amphetamine-like effects

(Kolb et al., 2003). Cocaine's particularly quick and powerful effect on dopamine activity may underlie its remarkably addictive nature (Bonci et al., 2003; Ciccocioppo, Martin-Fardon, & Weiss, 2004; Ungless et al., 2001). Drugs with rapid onset and short duration are generally more addictive than others (Kato, Wakasa, & Yamagita, 1987), which may explain why *crack*—a purified, fast-acting, highly potent, smokable form of cocaine—is especially addictive.

Cocaine stimulates self-confidence, a sense of well-being, and optimism. But continued use brings nausea, overactivity, insomnia, paranoia, a sudden depressive "crash," hallucinations, sexual dysfunction, and seizures (Lacayo, 1995). Overdoses, especially of crack, can be deadly, and even small doses can cause a fatal heart attack or stroke (Klausner & Lewandowsky, 2002; Marzuk et al., 1995). Using cocaine during pregnancy harms the fetus (Hurt et al., 1995; Konkol et al., 1994; Snodgrass, 1994), but many of the severe, long-term behavioural problems seen in "cocaine babies" may have at least as much to do with poverty and neglect after birth as with the mother's cocaine use beforehand. Early intervention can reduce the effects of both cocaine and the hostile environment that confronts most cocaine babies (Mayes et al., 2003; Singer et al., 2004; Wren, 1998).

Ending a cocaine addiction is difficult. One possible treatment involves *buprenorphine,* an opiate antagonist that suppresses cocaine self-administration in addicted monkeys (Montoya et al., 2004). Other drugs that affect selective types of dopamine receptors have been found effective in preventing relapse when mice previously addicted to cocaine were exposed to drug-related cues, but these drugs have not yet been shown to be effective in humans (Beardsley et al., 2001; Kleber, 2003). Still another approach is to use *baclofen,* a drug that reduces the stimulating effects of cocaine by enhancing the inhibitory neurotransmitter GABA (Dobrovitsky et al., 2002). Baclofen has been shown to help reduce cocaine use in addicted people (Shoptaw et al., 2003). The results of other methods have been mixed; fewer than 25 percent of human cocaine addicts who have undergone even long-term pharmacological and psychological treatments are drug-free five years later (*Harvard Mental Health Letter,* 2001).

Deadly Drug Use Comedian and actor Chris Farley, a popular alumnus of Canada's SCTV comedy network, died of an apparent cocaine overdose in 1997 at the age 33. He joined a long list of celebrities (including fellow actor John Belushi and Righteous Brother Bobby Hatfield) and an even longer list of ordinary people whose lives have been destroyed by the abuse of cocaine or other drugs.

Caffeine *Caffeine* is probably the world's most popular drug. It is found in coffee, tea, chocolate, and many soft drinks. Caffeine reduces drowsiness and can enhance cognitive performance and vigilance (Beaumont et al., 2001; Lorist & Tops, 2003). For example, it improves problem solving, increases the capacity for physical work, and raises urine production (Warburton, 1995). At high doses it creates tremors and anxiety. Long-term caffeine use can result in tolerance, as well as physical dependence (Strain et al., 1994). Withdrawal symptoms—including headaches, fatigue, anxiety, shakiness, and craving—appear on the first day of abstinence and last about a week (Silverman et al., 1992). Caffeine may make it harder for women to become pregnant and may increase the risk of miscarriage, stillbirth, or a low-birth-weight baby (Alderete, Eskenazi, & Sholtz, 1995; Balat et al., 2003; Cnattingius et al., 2000; Rasch, 2003). Moderate daily caffeine use may also cause slight increases in blood pressure (James, 2004), but otherwise it appears to have few, if any, negative effects (Kleemola et al., 2000; Thompson, 1995).

Nicotine A powerful stimulant of the autonomic nervous system (ANS), nicotine is the main psychoactive ingredient in tobacco. Nicotine enhances the action of acetylcholine, increases the release of glutamate, the brain's primary excitatory neurotransmitter (McGehee et al., 1995), and activates the brain's dopamine-related pleasure system (Balfour, 2002). According to Michael Houlihan at St. Thomas University in Fredericton, New Brunswick, nicotine has many psychoactive effects, including ANS arousal, elevated mood, and improved memory and attention (Houlihan, Pritchard, & Robinson, 2002). Its ability to create physical dependence has been suggested by studies showing evidence of a nicotine withdrawal syndrome that includes craving, anxiety, irritability, lowered heart rate, and weight gain

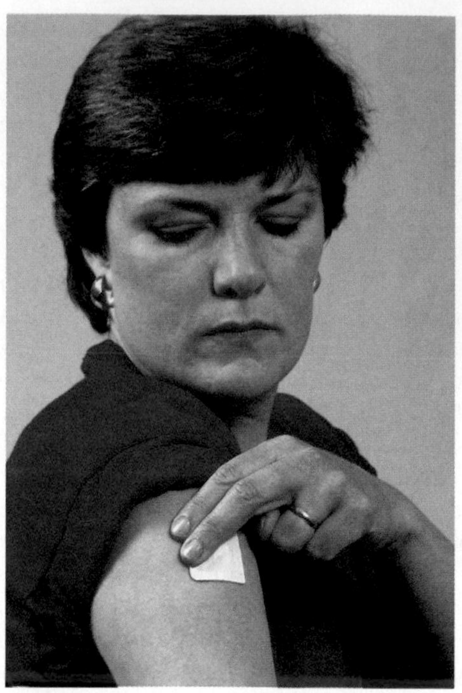

Giving Up Smoking The chemical effects of nicotine, combined with strongly learned associations between smoking and relaxation, stimulation, mealtimes, alcohol, and a wide variety of pleasant social interactions, make it extremely difficult for most smokers to give up their dangerous habit. One of the more promising treatment programs in use today combines nicotine replacement (through a patch such as the one this woman is wearing) with antidepressant medication and behavioural training in how to cope with smoking-related situations—and with the stress of quitting.

(Hughes, Higgins, & Bickel, 1994; White, 1998). And although nicotine does not create the "rush" characteristic of many drugs of abuse, withdrawal from it reduces activity in the brain's reward pathways (Epping-Jordan et al., 1998). Other research suggests that nicotine creates more psychological than physical dependence (Robinson & Pritchard, 1995), but whatever blend of physical and psychological dependence may be involved, there is no doubt that smoking is a difficult habit for most smokers to break (Breteler et al., 2004; Shiffman et al., 1997). As discussed in the chapter on health, stress, and coping, smoking is also clearly recognized as a major risk factor for cancer, heart disease, and respiratory disorders (Health Canada, 2005).

MDMA "Ecstasy," or *MDMA* (short for 3,4-methylenedioxymethamphetamine), is a popular drug on college campuses in Canada (Barrett, Gross, Garand, & Pihl, 2005). It creates increased energy and sex drive, a sense of well-being, and a feeling of greater closeness to others. Unfortunately, it also causes visual hallucinations, dry mouth, hyperactivity, jaw muscle spasms that can result in "lockjaw," elevated blood pressure, fever, and dangerously abnormal heart rhythms (Smith, Larive, & Romananelli, 2002). Because MDMA increases the activity of dopamine-releasing neurons, it leads to some of the same effects as those produced by cocaine and amphetamines (Steele, McCann, & Ricaurte, 1994). At serotonin synapses, MDMA is a receptor agonist and also causes neurotransmitter release, thus possibly accounting for the drug's hallucinatory effects (Green, Cross, & Goodwin, 1995). On the day after using MDMA—also known by names such as "XTC," "clarity," "essence," "E," and "Adam"—people often experience muscle aches, fatigue, depression, and poor concentration (Peroutka, Newman, & Harris, 1988). With continued use, MDMA's positive effects decrease, but its negative effects persist.

According to Sean Barrett at McGill University in Montreal, MDMA is a dangerous, potentially deadly drug. The most dangerous side-effects of MDMA use are dehydration and hyperthermia (high fever in excess of 40° C) that can lead to organ failure and death (Barrett, Gross, Garand, & Pihl, 2005). Between 1998 and 2000, complications from the use of MDMA led to the deaths of 14 Canadians, mostly in their early 20s (Oh, 2000). Research also suggests that it permanently damages the brain, killing neurons that use serotonin (Green, Cross, & Goodwin, 1995); the damage increases at higher doses and with continued use (Battaglia, Yeh, & De Souza,

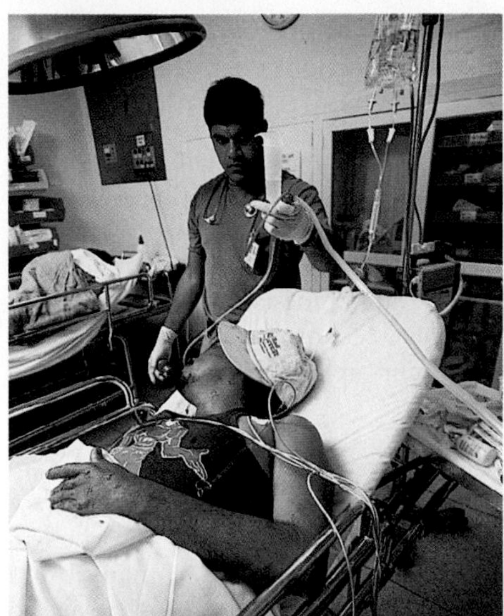

Another Drug Danger Oxycodone, a morphine-like drug prescribed by doctors under the label *OxyContin,* has become popular among recreational substance abusers. It was designed as a timed-release painkiller, but when people crush OxyContin tablets and then inject or inhale the drug, they get a much stronger and potentially lethal dose. Deaths from OxyContin abuse are already on the rise in Canada, particularly in the Atlantic Provinces (Gillis, 2004).

1988). At common recreational doses, MDMA also kills cells that use dopamine. This effect could eventually lead to shakiness and other symptoms similar to those of Parkinson's disease (Ricaurte et al., 2002). MDMA impairs memory, even after its use is discontinued (Reneman et al., 2001; Rodgers, 2000; Zakzanis & Young, 2001), and users may develop *panic disorder,* a problem whose symptoms include intense anxiety and a sense of impending doom (see the chapter on psychological disorders).

Opiates

The **opiates** (opium, morphine, heroin, and codeine) are unique in their capacity for inducing sleep and relieving pain (Julien, 2001). *Opium,* derived from the poppy plant, relieves pain and causes feelings of well-being and dreamy relaxation (Cowan et al., 2001). One of its most active ingredients, *morphine,* was first isolated in the early 1800s and is used worldwide for pain relief. Percodan and Demerol are two common morphine-like drugs. *Heroin* is derived from morphine but is three times more powerful, causing intensely pleasurable reactions when first taken.

Opiates have complex effects on consciousness. Drowsy, cloudy feelings occur because opiates depress activity in areas of the cerebral cortex. But they also create excitation in other parts, causing some users to experience euphoria, or elation (Bozarth & Wise, 1984). Opiates exert many of their effects through their role as agonists for endorphins. When opiates activate endorphin receptors, they are "tricking" the brain into an exaggerated activation of its painkilling and mood-altering systems (Julien, 2001).

Opiates are highly addictive, perhaps because they stimulate a particular type of glutamate receptor in the brain that can bring physical changes in a neuron's structure. It may be, then, that opiates alter neurons so that they come to require the drug to function properly. Supporting this idea are data showing that glutamate antagonists appear to prevent morphine dependence yet leave the drug's painkilling effects intact (Trujillo & Akil, 1991). Beyond the hazards of addiction itself, heroin addicts risk death through overdoses, contaminated drugs, or AIDS contracted by sharing drug-injection needles (Hser et al., 2001).

Hallucinogens

Hallucinogens, also called *psychedelics,* create a loss of contact with reality and alter other aspects of emotion, perception, and thought. They can cause distortions in body image (the user may feel gigantic or tiny), loss of identity (confusion about who one actually is), dream-like fantasies, and hallucinations. Because these effects resemble many severe forms of mental disorder, hallucinogens are also called *psychotomimetics* (mimicking psychosis).

LSD One of the most powerful psychedelics is *lysergic acid diethylamide,* or *LSD,* first synthesized from a rye fungus by Swiss chemist Albert Hofmann. In 1938, after Hofmann accidentally ingested a tiny amount of the substance, he discovered the drug's strange effects in the world's first LSD "trip" (Julien, 2001). LSD hallucinations can be quite bizarre. Time may seem distorted, sounds may cause visual sensations, and users may feel as if they have left their bodies. LSD's hallucinatory effects are probably due to its ability to stimulate a specific type of receptor in the forebrain, called 5-HT2a receptors, that normally respond to serotonin (Carlson, 1998; Leonard, 1992). Supporting this assertion is evidence that serotonin antagonists greatly reduce LSD's hallucinatory effects (Leonard, 1992).

The precise effects of LSD on a particular individual are unpredictable. Unpleasant hallucinations and delusions can occur during a person's first—or two hundredth—LSD experience. Although LSD is not addictive, tolerance to its effects does develop. Some users suffer lasting adverse effects, including severe short-term memory loss, paranoia, violent outbursts, nightmares, and panic attacks (Gold, 1994). Distortions in visual sensations can remain for years after heavy use has ended

opiate Psychoactive drug, such as opium, morphine, or heroin, that produces sleep-inducing and pain-relieving effects.

hallucinogen Psychoactive drug that alters consciousness by producing a temporary loss of contact with reality and changes in emotion, perception, and thought.

The Cannabis Controversy Marijuana for recreational use is illegal in Canada and in many other places, too, but the question of whether it should remain so is a matter of hot debate between those who see the drug as a dangerous gateway to more addictive substances and those who view it as a harmless source of pleasure that can have other benefits. Marc Emery, shown in this photograph, has been a long-time Canadian advocate for the decriminalization of marijuana.

(Abraham & Wolf, 1988). Sometimes flashbacks occur, in which a person suddenly returns to an LSD-like state of consciousness weeks or even years after using the drug.

Ketamine *Ketamine* is an anesthetic widely used by veterinarians to ease pain in animals. But because it also has hallucinogenic effects, ketamine is being stolen and sold as a recreational drug known as "Special K." Its effects include dissociative feelings that create what some users describe as an "out-of-body" or "near-death" experience. Unfortunately, ketamine can also cause enduring amnesia and other memory problems (Curran & Monaghan, 2001; Smith, Larive, & Romananelli, 2002). These adverse effects appear to result from damage to memory-related brain structures such as the hippocampus (Jevtovic-Todorovic et al., 2001).

Marijuana A mixture of crushed leaves, flowers, and stems from the hemp plant (*Cannabis sativa*) makes up *marijuana*. The active ingredient is *tetrahydrocannabinol*, or THC (Wachtel et al., 2002). When inhaled, THC is absorbed in minutes by many organs, including the brain. It alters blood flow to many brain regions (O'Leary et al., 2002) and continues to affect consciousness for several hours. Low doses of marijuana may initially create restlessness and hilarity, followed by a dreamy, carefree relaxation, an expanded sense of space and time, more vivid sensations, food cravings, and subtle changes in thinking (Kelly et al., 1990).

THC tends to collect in fatty deposits of the brain and reproductive organs, where it can be detected for weeks. The brain contains several receptors for THC. The first to be discovered was named *ananda* (from a Sanskrit word meaning "bliss") and is normally activated by a naturally occurring brain substance called anandamide (Fride & Mechoulam, 1993). Researchers have since discovered that the body produces a number of its own "endogenous cannaboids" whose receptors in the brain also respond to THC (Onaivi et al., 2002). Armed with knowledge of these receptors, scientists have developed a drug that acts as a cannabinoid antagonist. It may hold promise as an aid to helping people stop smoking marijuana (Huestis et al., 2001).

THINKING CRITICALLY
Is Marijuana Dangerous?

A large-scale study of Canadians aged 15 and over indicated a dramatic rise in their use of marijuana between 1989 and 2002, with the greatest increases among teenagers. Approximately three out of every ten Canadians between 15 and 17 years old, and 40 percent of 18- and 19-year-olds reported using cannabis (i.e., marijuana or hashish) in 2002. More than 10 million Canadians, or 41 percent of the population, over age 15 have tried marijuana at least once (Statistics Canada, 2004).

In 2001, Canada became the first country to legalize the use of marijuana for medical treatment of terminal illnesses as well as epilepsy, arthritis, and other chronic conditions if the drug was needed to ease their symptoms. For legal permission to use marijuana, patients must apply to the federal government (Ali & Wood, 2001).

The use of marijuana even for medical purposes is controversial. Opponents argue that medical legalization of marijuana is premature, because its medicinal value has not been clearly established (Bennet, 1994). They point out, too, that—even though patients may prefer marijuana-based drugs—other medications may be equally effective and less dangerous (e.g., Campbell et al., 2001; Fox et al., 2004; Hall & Degenhardt, 2003).

- **What am I being asked to believe or accept?**

Those who see marijuana as dangerous usually assert four beliefs: (1) that marijuana is addictive; (2) that it leads to the use of "hard drugs," such as heroin; (3) that marijuana intoxication endangers the user and other individuals; and

(4) that long-term marijuana use leads to undesirable behavioural changes, disruption of brain functions, and other adverse effects on health.

● What evidence is available to support the assertion?

Without a doubt, some people do use marijuana to such an extent that it disrupts their lives. According to the criteria normally used to define alcohol abuse, these people are dependent on marijuana—at least psychologically (Stephens, Roffman, & Simpson, 1994). The question of physical dependence (addiction) is less clear, inasmuch as withdrawal from chronic marijuana use has long been thought not to produce any severe physical symptoms. However, some evidence of a mild withdrawal syndrome has been reported in rats. In humans, withdrawal from marijuana may be accompanied by increases in anxiety, depression, and aggressiveness (Budney et al., 2001; Budney et al., 2003; Haney et al., 1999; Kouri, Pope, & Lukas, 1999; Rodriguez de Fonseca et al., 1997; Smith, 2002). Other research (e.g., Tanda, Pontieri, & Di Chiara, 1997) has found that marijuana interacts with the same dopamine and opiate receptors as does heroin, implying that marijuana could be a "gateway drug" to the use of more addictive drugs (Lynskey et al., 2003).

Regardless of whether marijuana is addicting or leads to "harder drugs," it can create a number of problems. It disrupts memory formation, making it difficult to carry out complex tasks (Lichtman, Dimen, & Martin, 1995; Pope et al., 2001). And despite the fact that people may feel more creative while using marijuana, the drug appears to actually reduce creativity (Bourassa & Vaugeois, 2001). Because marijuana affects muscle coordination, driving while under its influence is quite hazardous. Compounding the danger is the fact that motor impairment continues long after the obvious effects of the drug have worn off. In one study, for example, pilots had difficulty landing a simulated aircraft even a full day after smoking one marijuana cigarette (Yesavage et al., 1985). As for marijuana's effects on intellectual and cognitive performance, long-term use can lead to lasting impairments in reasoning and memory (Bolla et al., 2002; Solowij et al., 2002). One study found that adults who frequently used marijuana scored lower on a 12th-grade academic achievement test than did non-users with the same IQs (Block & Ghoneim,1993). Among long-term users, impairments in memory and attention can persist for years after their drug use has stopped (Solowij et al., 2002). Heavy use of marijuana in teenagers has also been associated with the later appearance of anxiety, depression, and other mental disorders as severe as schizophrenia (Arsenault et al., 2004; Patton et al., 2002; Zammit et al., 2002).

● Are there alternative ways of interpreting the evidence?

Those who see marijuana as a harmless or even beneficial substance criticize studies such as those just mentioned as providing an inaccurate or incomplete picture of marijuana's effects (Grinspoon, 1999). They argue, for example, that the same dopamine receptors activated by marijuana and heroin are also activated by sex and chocolate—and that few people would call for the criminalization of those pleasures (Grinspoon et al., 1997). Moreover, the correlation between early marijuana use and later use of "hard drugs" could be due more to the people with whom marijuana users become involved than to any property of the drug itself (Fergusson & Horwood, 1997).

The question of marijuana's long-term effects on memory and reasoning is also difficult to resolve, partly because studies of academic achievement scores and marijuana use tend to be correlational in nature. As noted in the chapter on research in psychology, cause and effect cannot easily be determined in such studies. Does marijuana use lead to poor academic performance, or does poor academic performance lead to increased marijuana use? Both possibilities are credible. The same can be said of the correlation between marijuana and mental disorder. Heavy use of marijuana could be a reaction to, or an early symptom of, mental disorder, not necessarily its cause.

● What additional evidence would help to evaluate the alternatives?

We obviously need more definitive evidence about marijuana's short- and long-term effects, and it should be based on well-controlled experiments with large and representative samples of participants. Still, evaluating the meaning of even the best possible evidence will be difficult. The issues in the marijuana debate involve questions of degree and relative risk. For example, is the risk of marijuana dependence greater than that of alcohol dependence? And what about individual differences? Some people are at much greater risk than others for negative consequences from marijuana use. So far, however, we have not determined what personal characteristics account for these differences. Nor do we know why some people use marijuana only occasionally, whereas others use it so often and in such quantities that it seriously disrupts their ability to function. The physical and psychological factors underlying these differences have yet to be identified.

What conclusions are most reasonable?

Those who would decriminalize the use of marijuana argue that when marijuana was declared illegal, there was no evidence that it was any more harmful than alcohol or tobacco. Scientific evidence supports that claim, but more by illuminating the dangers of alcohol and tobacco than by declaring marijuana safe. In fact, although marijuana is less dangerous than, say, cocaine or heroin, it is by no means harmless. Marijuana easily reaches a developing fetus and should not be used by pregnant women (Fried, Watkinson, & Gray, 1992); it suppresses some immune functions in humans (Cabral & Dove Pettit, 1998); and marijuana smoke is as irritating to lungs as tobacco smoke (Roth et al., 1998). Further, because possession of marijuana is still a crime in many countries throughout the world, it would be foolish to flaunt existing laws without regard for the legal consequences.

However, in Canada, it is legal to use marijuana for medicinal purposes, and despite federal laws to the contrary, the same is true in ten US states. Although the American Medical Association has recently rejected the idea of medical uses for marijuana, scientists are intent on objectively studying its potential value in the treatment of certain diseases, as well as its dangers (or lack thereof). Their work is being encouraged by bodies such as the National Institute of Medicine (Joy, Watson, & Benson, 1999), and drug companies are working to develop new cannabis-based medicines (Altman, 2000; Tuller, 2004). The United Nations, too, has recommended that governments worldwide sponsor additional work on the medical uses of marijuana (Wren, 1999). Ultimately, the most reasonable conclusions about marijuana use must await the outcome of this research.

LINKAGES

As noted in the chapter on introducing psychology, all of psychology's subfields are related to one another. Our discussion of meditation, health, and stress illustrates just one way in which the topic of this chapter, consciousness, is linked to the subfield of health psychology (which is a focus of the chapter on health, stress, and coping). The Linkages diagram shows ties to two other subfields as well, and there are many more ties throughout the book. Looking for linkages among subfields will help you see how they all fit together and help you better appreciate the big picture that is psychology.

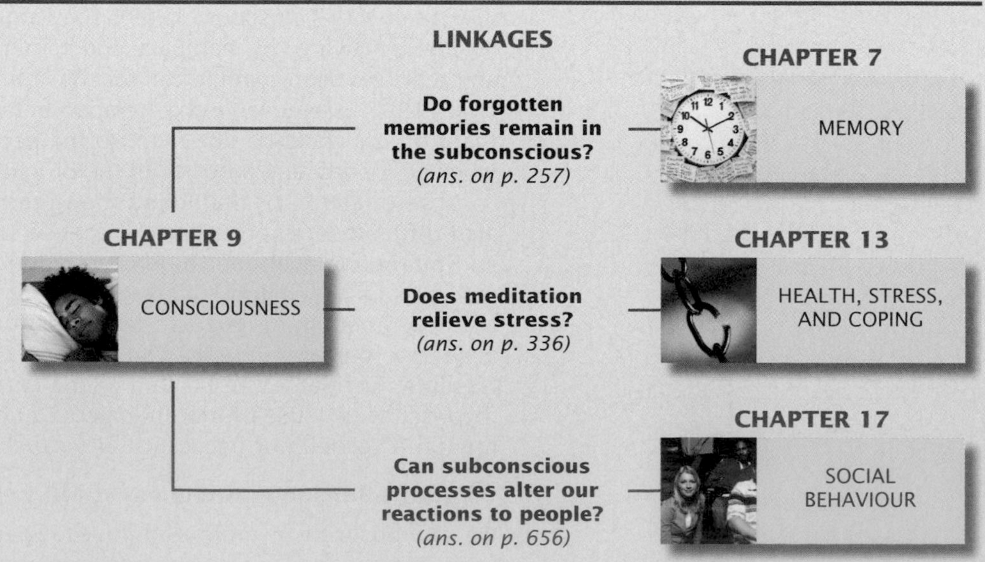

LINKAGES
CHAPTER 7
Do forgotten memories remain in the subconscious?
(ans. on p. 257)
MEMORY
CHAPTER 9
CONSCIOUSNESS
CHAPTER 13
Does meditation relieve stress?
(ans. on p. 336)
HEALTH, STRESS, AND COPING
CHAPTER 17
Can subconscious processes alter our reactions to people?
(ans. on p. 656)
SOCIAL BEHAVIOUR

SUMMARY

Consciousness can be defined as awareness of the outside world and of one's own thoughts, feelings, perceptions, and other mental processes.

Analyzing Consciousness

Current research on consciousness focuses on three main questions. First, what is the relationship between the mind and the brain? Second, does consciousness occur as a single "point" in mental processing or as several parallel and independent mental operations? Third, what mental processes are outside awareness, and how do they affect conscious processes?

Some Functions of Consciousness

Consciousness produces the best current interpretation of sensory information in light of past experience and makes this interpretation available to the parts of the brain that plan voluntary actions and speech.

Levels of Consciousness

Variations in how much awareness you have for a mental function are described by different levels of consciousness. The *preconscious level* includes mental activities that are outside of awareness but can easily be brought to the *conscious level.* At the *unconscious level* are thoughts, memories, and processes that are more difficult to bring to awareness. Mental processes that cannot be brought into awareness are said to occur at the *nonconscious level.*

Mental Processing Without Awareness

Awareness is not always required for mental operations. Priming studies show that people's responses to some stimuli can be speeded, improved, or modified, even when the people are not consciously aware of the priming stimuli.

The Neuropsychology of Consciousness

The thalamus and the cerebral cortex are among the brain structures involved in the experience of consciousness. Brain injuries can impair consciousness and reveal ways in which mental processing can occur without conscious awareness.

States of Consciousness

A person's *state of consciousness* is constantly changing. When the changes are particularly noticeable, they are called *altered states of consciousness.* Examples include sleep, hypnosis, meditation, and some drug-induced conditions. Cultures vary considerably in the value they place on different states of consciousness.

Sleeping and Dreaming

Sleep is an active and complex state.

Stages of Sleep

Different stages of sleep are defined on the basis of changes in brain activity (as recorded by an electroencephalograph, or EEG) and physiological arousal. Sleep normally begins with stage 1 sleep and progresses gradually to stage 4 sleep. Sleep stages 3 and 4 constitute *slow-wave sleep,* which is part of non-REM sleep. After passing back to stage 2, people enter *rapid eye movement* (*REM*) sleep, or paradoxical sleep. The sleeper passes through these stages several times each night, gradually spending more time in stage 2 and REM sleep later in the night.

Sleep Disorders

Sleep disorders can disrupt the natural rhythm of sleep. Among the most common is *insomnia,* in which one feels tired because of trouble falling asleep or staying asleep. *Narcolepsy* produces sudden daytime sleeping episodes. In *sleep apnea,* people briefly, but repeatedly, stop breathing during sleep. *Sudden infant death syndrome* (*SIDS*) may be due to brain abnormalities or accidental suffocation. *Nightmares* and *night terrors* are different kinds of frightening dreams. *Sleepwalking* occurs most frequently during childhood. *REM behaviour disorder* is potentially dangerous because it allows people to act out REM dreams.

Why Do People Sleep?

The cycle of waking and sleeping is a natural *circadian rhythm,* controlled by the suprachiasmatic nuclei in the brain. *Jet lag* can be one result of disrupting the normal sleep-wake cycle. The purpose of sleep is still being debated. Non-REM sleep may aid bodily rest and repair. REM sleep may help maintain activity in brain areas that provide daytime alertness, and it may allow the brain to solidify and absorb the day's experiences.

Dreams and Dreaming

Dreams are story-like sequences of images, sensations, and perceptions that occur during sleep, most commonly during REM sleep. Evidence from research on *lucid dreaming* suggests that people may sometimes be able to control the content of their dreams. According to activation-synthesis theory, dreams are the meaningless byproducts of brain activity, but they may still have psychological significance.

Hypnosis

Hypnosis is a well-known but still poorly understood phenomenon.

Experiencing Hypnosis

Tests of hypnotic susceptibility suggest that some people cannot be hypnotized. Hypnotized people tend to focus attention on the hypnotist and passively follow instructions. Their ability to fantasize and take roles shows improvement, and they may exhibit apparent age regression, experience posthypnotic amnesia, and obey posthypnotic suggestions.

Explaining Hypnosis

According to *state theory,* hypnosis is a special state of consciousness. *Role theory* suggests that hypnosis creates a special social role that gives people permission to act in unusual ways. *Dissociation theory* combines aspects of role and state theories, suggesting that hypnotic participants enter into a social contract with the hypnotist to allow normally integrated mental processes to become dissociated and to share control over these processes.

Applications of Hypnosis

Hypnosis is useful in the control of pain and the reduction of nausea associated with cancer chemotherapy. Its use as a memory aid is open to serious question.

Psychoactive Drugs

Psychoactive drugs affect the brain, changing consciousness and other psychological processes. *Psychopharmacology* is the field that studies drug effects and their mechanisms.

Psychopharmacology

Psychoactive drugs exert their effects primarily by influencing specific neurotransmitter systems and, hence, certain brain activities. To reach brain tissue, drugs must cross the *blood-brain barrier.* Drugs that mimic the receptor effects of a neurotransmitter are called *agonists,* and drugs that block the receptor effects of a neurotransmitter are called *antagonists.* Some drugs alter the release or removal of specific neurotransmitters, thus affecting the amount of neurotransmitter available for receptor effects.

The Varying Effects of Drugs

Adverse effects such as *substance abuse* often accompany the use of psychoactive drugs. *Psychological dependence, physical dependence (addiction), tolerance,* and a *withdrawal syndrome* may result. Drugs that produce dependence share the property of directly stimulating certain areas of the brain known as pleasure centres. The consequences of using a psychoactive drug depend both on how the drug affects neurotransmitters and on the user's expectations.

Depressants

Alcohol and barbiturates are examples of *depressants.* They reduce activity in the central nervous system, often by enhancing the action of inhibitory neurotransmitters. They have considerable potential for producing both psychological and physical dependence.

Stimulants

Stimulants such as amphetamines and cocaine increase behavioural and mental activity mainly by increasing the action of dopamine and norepinephrine and decreasing GABA activity. These drugs can produce both psychological and physical dependence. Caffeine, one of the world's most popular stimulants, can also create dependency. Nicotine is a potent stimulant. MDMA is one of several psychoactive drugs that can permanently damage brain tissue.

Opiates

Opiates such as opium, morphine, and heroin are highly addictive drugs that induce sleep and relieve pain.

Hallucinogens

LSD, ketamine, and marijuana are examples of *hallucinogens,* or psychedelics. Hallucinogens alter consciousness by producing a temporary loss of contact with reality and changes in emotion, perception, and thought.

Cognitive Abilities

Have you ever taken an IQ test? In theory, these tests measure intelligence, but what does that mean? What, exactly, is "intelligence," where does it come from, and how good are the tests that are used to measure it? These are some of the questions that we explore in this chapter on cognitive abilities. We have organized the material as follows:

Testing for Intelligence
A Brief History of Intelligence Tests
Intelligence Tests Today
Aptitude and Achievement Tests

Measuring the Quality of Tests
Reliability
Validity

Evaluating Intelligence Tests
The Reliability and Validity of Intelligence Tests

LINKAGES: Emotionality and the Measurement of Cognitive Abilities

IQ Scores as a Measure of Innate Ability
Group Differences in IQ Scores
Conditions That Can Raise IQ Scores
IQ Scores in the Classroom

THINKING CRITICALLY: Are Intelligence Tests Unfairly Biased Against Certain Groups?

Understanding Intelligence
The Psychometric Approach
The Information-Processing Approach
The Triarchic Theory of Intelligence
Multiple Intelligences

FOCUS ON RESEARCH METHODS: Tracking Cognitive Abilities over a Life Span

Diversity in Cognitive Abilities
Creativity
Unusual Cognitive Ability

Linkages

Summary

Consider the following sketches of four university students and their varying abilities and interests. Do any of these descriptions remind you of anyone you know? Do any of them sound like you?

Jack's big-city "street smarts" were not reflected in his high school grades. After testing revealed a learning disability, Jack worked to compensate for it, graduating with a 75 percent average. He attended a local university, where he was given extra time to complete exams because of his learning disability. He held a part-time job throughout all four years, and his GPA was 3.0. When he completes his undergraduate degree, Jack will apply to master's degree programs in special education.

Deneace earned straight As in elementary school. She attended a private high school, where she placed in the top fifth of her class and played the violin. After graduating from high school, Deneace was accepted at several small universities, but not at major research ones. She is enrolled in a pre-med program, and, with a GPA of 3.90, Deneace is hoping to be accepted by a medical school.

Ruthie has a wide range of interests and many friends, loves physical activities, and can talk to anybody about almost anything. Her high school grades, however, were only fair, but she played four sports, was captain of the provincial champion volleyball team, and was vice president of her grade 12 class. She received an athletic scholarship at a large university. She majored in sociology and minored in sport psychology. Focusing on just one sport helped her achieve a 3.40 GPA. She has applied to graduate schools but has also looked into a job as a city recreation director.

George showed an early interest in computers. In high school, he earned straight As in art and information technology, but his other grades were average, and he didn't get along with other students. Everyone was surprised when he went on to major in math and computer science at a large university. His grades suffered at first as he began to spend time with people who shared his interests, but his GPA is now 3.70. He writes computer animation software and has applied to graduate programs in fields relating to artificial intelligence and human factors engineering.

Before reading further, rank these four people on **cognitive ability**—the capacity to reason, remember, understand, solve problems, and make decisions. Who came out on top? Now ask a friend to do the same, and see if your rankings match. They may not, because each of the four students is outstanding in different ways.

Deneace might score highest on general intelligence tests, which emphasize remembering, reasoning, and verbal and mathematical abilities. But would these tests measure Ruthie's social skills, Jack's street smarts, or George's computer skills and artistic abilities? If you were hiring an employee or evaluating a student, what characteristics would you want a test to measure? Can test scores be compared without considering the social and academic background of the people who took the tests? The answers to these questions are important because, as our examples illustrate, measures of cognitive abilities often determine the educational and employment opportunities people have or don't have.

There are many kinds of cognitive abilities, but in this chapter we will focus mainly on the abilities that have come to be known as *intelligence*. We can't use X-rays or brain scans to see intelligence itself, so we have to draw conclusions about people's intelligence from what can be observed and measured (Borkenau et al., 2004). This usually means looking at scores on tests designed to measure intelligence.

cognitive ability The capacity to reason, remember, understand, solve problems, and make decisions.

Testing for Intelligence

Delroy Paulhus and Monica Landolt at the University of British Columbia asked undergraduate students to name one famous person they considered intelligent. Answers included politicians, scientists, writers, business tycoons, pop stars, sports heroes, and religious leaders. These results indicate that a wide variety of abilites are considered indicative of intelligence (Paulhus & Landolt, 2000). In fact, there is no universally agreed-upon definition of intelligence, even among experts, but Robert Sternberg (1997) has offered one that is accepted by many psychologists. Sternberg says that **intelligence** includes three main characteristics: (1) being able to learn, remember, reason, and perform other *information-processing skills,* (2) using those skills to *solve problems,* and (3) being able to *alter or adapt to* new or changing environments. Standard tests of intelligence measure some of these characteristics, but they don't address all of them. Accordingly, some psychologists argue that these tools are not able to capture all that should be tested if we want to get a complete picture of someone's intelligence in its broadest sense. To better understand the controversy, let's take a look at how standard intelligence tests were created, what they are designed to measure, and how well they do their job. Later, we will consider some alternative intelligence tests that have been proposed by those who find fault with traditional ones.

A Brief History of Intelligence Tests

The story of modern intelligence tests begins in France in 1904, when the French government appointed psychologist Alfred Binet (pronounced "bih-NAY") to a committee whose job was to identify, study, and provide special educational programs for children who were not doing well in school. As part of his work, Binet developed a set of test items that provided the model for today's intelligence tests. Binet assumed that reasoning, thinking, and problem solving all depend on intelligence, so he looked for tasks that would highlight differences in children's ability to do these things (Binet & Simon, 1905). His test included tasks such as unwrapping a piece of candy, repeating numbers or sentences from memory, and identifying familiar objects (Rogers, 1995).

Binet also assumed that children's abilities increase with age. He tested the items on children of various ages and then categorized items according to the age at which the typical child could respond correctly. For example, a "six-year-old item" was one that a large majority of six-year-olds could answer. In other words, Binet's test contained a set of *age-graded* items. It measured a child's "mental level"—later called *mental age*—by determining the age level of the most advanced items a child could consistently answer correctly. Children whose mental age equalled their actual age, or *chronological age,* were considered to be of "regular" intelligence (Schultz & Schultz, 2000).

About a decade after Binet published his test, Lewis Terman at Stanford University developed an English version known as the **Stanford-Binet** (Terman, 1916). Table 10.1 gives examples of the kinds of items included on this test. Terman added items to measure the intelligence of adults and revised the scoring procedure. Mental age was divided by chronological age, and the result, multiplied by 100, was called the *intelligence quotient,* or IQ. So a child whose mental age and chronological age were equal would have an IQ of 100, which is considered "average" intelligence. A ten-year-old who scored at the mental age of twelve would have an IQ of 12/10 100 = 120. From this method of scoring came the term **IQ test,** a name that is widely used for any test designed to measure intelligence on an objective, standardized scale.

This scoring method allowed testers to rank people on IQ, which was seen as an important advantage by Terman and others who promoted the test. Unlike Binet—who believed that intelligence improved with education and training—they saw intelligence as a fixed and inherited entity, and they believed that IQ tests could

intelligence Those attributes that centre around skill at information processing, problem solving, and adapting to new or changing situations.

Stanford-Binet A test for determining a person's intelligence quotient, or IQ.

IQ test A test designed to measure intelligence on an objective, standardized scale.

table 10.1

Here are samples of the types of items included on Lewis Terman's original Stanford-Binet test. As in Alfred Binet's test, an age level was assigned to each item

The Stanford-Binet

Age	Task
2	Place geometric shapes into corresponding openings; identify body parts; stack blocks; identify common objects.
4	Name objects from memory; complete analogies (e.g., fire is hot; ice is ________); identify objects of similar shape; answer simple questions (e.g., "Why do we have schools?").
6	Define simple words; explain differences (e.g., between a fish and a horse); identify missing parts of a picture; count out objects.
8	Answer questions about a simple story; identify absurdities (e.g., in statements like "John had to walk on crutches because he hurt his arm"); explain similarities and differences among objects; tell how to handle certain situations (e.g., finding a stray puppy).
10	Define more difficult words; give explanations (e.g., about why people should be quiet in a library); list as many words as possible; repeat 6-digit numbers.
12	Identify more difficult verbal and pictured absurdities; repeat 5-digit numbers in reverse order; define abstract words (e.g., *sorrow*); fill in a missing word in a sentence.
14	Solve reasoning problems; identify relationships among points of the compass; find similarities in apparently opposite concepts (e.g., "high" and "low"); predict the number of holes that will appear when folded paper is cut and then opened.
Adult	Supply several missing words for incomplete sentences; repeat 6-digit numbers in reverse order; create a sentence, using several unrelated words (e.g., *forest, businesslike,* and *dismayed*); describe similarities between concepts (e.g., "teaching" and "business").

Source: Nietzel & Bernstein (1987)

pinpoint who did and who did not have a suitable amount of intelligence. These beliefs were controversial because in some instances, they led to prejudice and discrimination against certain people as enthusiasm for testing outpaced understanding of what was being tested.

In 1928, the Province of Alberta passed a highly controversial piece of legislation known as *The Sexual Sterilization Act* that led to the forced sterilization of people deemed *mentally defective* or *feeble-minded*. The act was justified as a means to prevent individuals of low intelligence from passing on their inferior mental abilities to a future generation. This act was not repealed until 1972. In 1995, Leilani Muir took the Province of Alberta to court over this issue, claiming that the mandatory sterilization inflicted on her had irreparably damaged her future happiness. Madam Justice Joanne B. Veit of the Court of Queen's Bench ruled that the Province of Alberta had wrongly sterilized Muir, awarding her damages close to $750 000, plus legal costs. More civil suits against the Alberta government followed this precedent-setting case (Wahlsten, 1997).

In the late 1930s, David Wechsler (1939, 1949) developed new tests designed to improve on the earlier ones in three key ways. First, the new tests included both verbal and nonverbal subtests. Second, the tests were constructed so that success depended less on having formal schooling. Third, each subtest was scored separately, producing a profile that described an individual's performance on all the subtests. Special versions of these tests were developed for adults (the Wechsler Adult Intelligence Scale, or WAIS) and for children (the Wechsler Intelligence Scale for Children, or WISC).

Intelligence Tests Today

Today's editions of the Wechsler tests and the Stanford-Binet are the most widely used individually administered intelligence tests. The Wechsler Intelligence Scale for Children–Fourth Edition (WISC-IV; Wechsler, 2003) includes ten standard and five supplemental subtests, grouped into four clusters. Tests in the *verbal comprehension* cluster require children to define vocabulary words, explain the meaning of sayings or sentences, and identify similarities between words (for example, In what way are an apple and an orange alike?). The *perceptual reasoning* cluster includes tasks such as assembling blocks, solving mazes, and reasoning about pictures (see Figure 10.1). Tests in the *working memory* cluster ask children to recall a series of numbers, to put a random sequence of numbers into a logical order, and the like. The *processing speed* cluster includes tests of children's ability to search for particular symbols on a page and to figure out the meaning of simple coded messages. Using the WISC-IV, the tester can calculate a score for each of the four subtest clusters, as well as an overall composite, or full-scale IQ.

Like the Wechsler scales, the new fifth edition of the Stanford-Binet (SB5; Roid, 2003) also consists of ten main subtests. However, the SB5 subtests are designed to measure five different abilities: *fluid reasoning* (e.g., completing verbal analogies), *knowledge* (e.g., defining words, detecting absurdities in pictures), *quantitative reasoning* (e.g., solving math problems), *visual-spatial processing* (e.g., assembling a puzzle), and *working memory* (e.g., repeating a sentence). Each of these five abilities is measured by one verbal and one nonverbal subtest, so it is possible to calculate a score for each of the five abilities, a total score on all the verbal tests, a total score on all the nonverbal tests, and an overall score for all ten tests combined.

IQ scores are no longer calculated by dividing mental age by chronological age. If you take an IQ test today, the points you earn for each correct answer are added up. That total score is then compared with the scores earned by other people. The average score obtained by people at each age level is assigned the IQ value of 100. Other scores are given IQ values that reflect how far each score deviates from that

Picture completion
What part is missing from this picture?

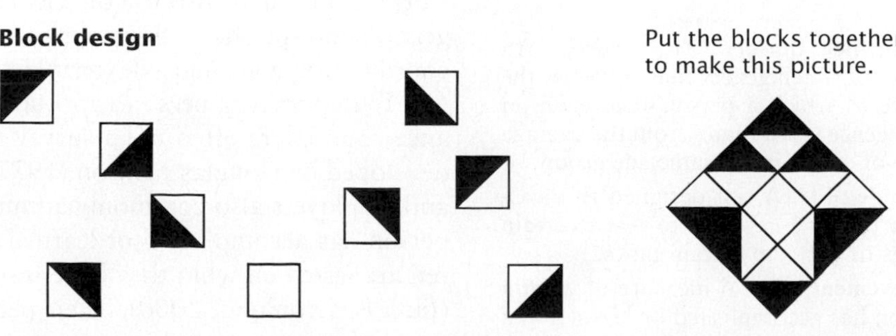
Block design
Put the blocks together to make this picture.

figure 10.1

Performance Items Similar to Those on the Wechsler Intelligence Scale for Children (WISC-IV)

Items such as these are designed to measure aspects of intelligence that involve little or no obvious verbal ability.

Source: Simulated items similar to those in the Wechsler Intelligence Scales for Adults and Children. Copyright © 1949, 1955, 1974, 1981, 1991 by the Psychological Corporation. Reproduced by permission. All rights reserved.

Taking a New Intelligence Test New intelligence tests are always being developed to measure newly identified aspects of cognitive abilities (Carroll, 1993). This child is taking the Woodcock-Johnson Tests of Cognitive Abilities, developed in 1997 and currently in its third edition (WJ-III; Woodcock, McGrew, & Mather, 2001). The WJ-III measures eight abilities that are somewhat more specific than those assessed by the Stanford-Binet and Wechsler tests. These eight abilities include fluid reasoning, verbal comprehension and knowledge, quantitative ability, visual-spatial thinking, short-term memory, retrieval from long-term memory, processing of auditory information, and mental processing speed. Testing results in an overall ability score, as well as a profile of scores on these eight abilities.

average. If you do better on the test than the average person in your age group, you will receive an IQ score above 100; how far above depends on how much better than average you do. Similarly, a person scoring below the age-group average will have an IQ below 100. This procedure is based on a well-documented assumption about many characteristics: Most people's scores fall in the middle of the range of possible scores, creating a bell-shaped curve that approximates the normal distribution shown in Figure 10.2. (The appendix on statistics provides a fuller explanation of the normal distribution and how IQ tests are scored.) As a result of this scoring method, your **intelligence quotient,** or **IQ score,** reflects your *relative* standing within a population of your age.

Aptitude and Achievement Tests

Closely related to intelligence tests are aptitude and achievement tests. **Aptitude tests** are designed to measure a person's readiness to learn certain things or perform certain tasks (Corno et al., 2002). Although such tests may contain questions about what you already know, their ultimate goal is to assess your *potential* to learn or to perform well in some future situation. Performing well in university or graduate school, for example, requires well-developed reading and mathematics skills, among other things. The *Graduate Record Examination (GRE)* is the aptitude test most commonly used by graduate schools to help guide decisions about which applicants to admit (e.g., Kuncel, Hezlett, & Ones, 2001; Powers, 2004). Corporations also use aptitude tests as part of the process of selecting new employees. These tests usually involve brief assessments of cognitive abilities; examples include the Otis-Lennon Mental Abilities Test and the Wonderlic Personnel Test (Aiken, 1994). Corporations may also use the General Aptitude Test Battery (GATB) to assess both general and specific skills ranging from learning ability and verbal aptitude to motor coordination and finger dexterity at computer or clerical tasks.

To determine a person's aptitude for different types of occupations, school guidance counsellors often use a survey such as the Jackson Vocational Interest Survey, developed by Douglas Jackson (1977) at the University of Western Ontario. Schools and employers also commonly administer **achievement tests,** which measure what a person has accomplished or learned in a particular area. For example, schoolchildren are tested on what they have learned about language, mathematics, and reading (Linn & Gronlund, 2000). Their performance on these tests is then compared with the performance of other students in the same grade to evaluate their educational

intelligence quotient (IQ score) An index of intelligence that reflects the degree to which a person's score on an intelligence test deviates from the average score of others in the same age group.

aptitude test A test designed to measure a person's capacity to learn certain things or perform certain tasks.

achievement test A measure of what a person has accomplished or learned in a particular area.

figure 10.2

The Normal Distribution of IQ Scores in a Population

When the IQ scores in the overall population are plotted on a graph, a bell-shaped curve appears. The average IQ score of any given age group is 100. Half of the scores are higher than 100, and half are lower than 100. Approximately 68 percent of the IQ scores of any age group fall between 84 and 116; about 16 percent fall below 84, and about 16 percent fall above 116.

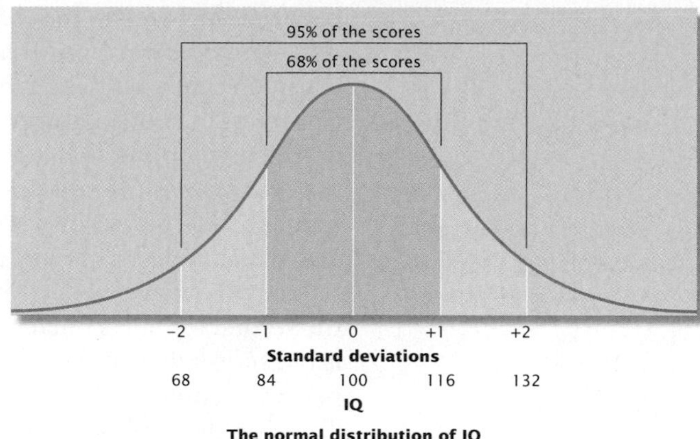

progress. Similarly, university students' scores on the Graduate Record Examination's Subject Tests assess how much they have learned about the field in which they wish to pursue graduate work.

Measuring the Quality of Tests

What does your IQ or SAT score say about you? Can it predict your performance in school or on the job? Is it a fair summary of your mental abilities? To scientifically answer questions like these, we have to measure the quality of the tests that yield these scores, using the same criteria that apply to tests of personality, language skills, driving, or anything else. Let's review these criteria and then see how they are used to evaluate IQ tests.

A **test** is a systematic procedure for observing behaviour in a standard situation and describing it with the help of a numerical scale or a system of categories (Cronbach, 1990). Tests have two major advantages over interviews and other means of evaluating people. First, they are *standardized;* that is, conditions surrounding a test are as similar as possible for everyone who takes it. Standardization helps ensure, for example, that test results will not be significantly affected by who gives and scores the test. Because the biases of those giving or scoring the test do not influence the results, a standardized test is said to be *objective.* Second, tests summarize the test-taker's performance with a specific number, known as a *score.* Scores, in turn, allow the calculation of **norms,** which describe the frequency of particular scores. Norms tell us, for example, what percentage of university students obtained each possible score on a law school entrance exam. They also allow us to say whether a person's overall test performance was above or below average and whether that person is particularly strong or weak in certain skill areas, such as verbal reasoning or mathematics.

Any test, including IQ tests, should fairly and accurately measure a person's performance. The two most important things to know about when determining the value of a test are its reliability and validity.

LINKAGES (a link to Personality)

Reliability

If you stepped on a scale, checked your weight, stepped off, stepped back on, and found that your weight had increased by ten kilos, you would know it was time to buy a new scale. A good scale, like a good test, must have **reliability;** in other words, the results must be repeatable or stable. If you received a very high score on a reasoning test the first time you took it but a very low score when the test was repeated the next day, the test is probably unreliable. The higher the reliability of a test, the less likely it is that its scores will be affected by temperature, hunger, or other irrelevant changes in the environment or the test taker.

To estimate the reliability of a test, researchers usually get two sets of scores on the same test from the same people and then compute a *correlation coefficient*

test A systematic procedure for observing behaviour in a standard situation and describing it with the help of a numerical scale or a category system.

norm A description of the frequency at which particular scores occur, allowing scores to be compared statistically.

reliability The degree to which a test can be repeated with the same results.

between the two (see the chapter on research in psychology and the statistics appendix). If the correlation is high and positive (usually above .80 or so), the test is considered reliable. The two sets of scores can be obtained in several ways. In the *test-retest* method, a group of people take the same test twice. This method is based on the assumption that whatever is being measured will not change much between the two testings. If you practised on your keyboard before taking a second test of typing skill, your second score would be higher than the first, but not because the test was unreliable. Using an *alternate form* of the test at the second testing can reduce this practice effect, but great care must be taken to ensure that the tasks on the second test are similar to those on the first. Perhaps the most common approach is the *split-half* method, in which a correlation coefficient is calculated between each person's scores on two comparable halves of the test (Thorndike & Dinnel, 2001). To be on the safe side, some researchers employ more than one of these methods to check the reliability of their tests.

Validity

Imagine that your scale is reliable, giving you the same reading every time you step on it, but that it says you weigh 15 kilos. Unless you are a small child, this scale would provide a reliable but incorrect, or *invalid,* measure of your weight. Like weight readings from a broken scale, even the most reliable scores from a test might not provide a correct, or valid, measure of intelligence, or anxiety, or typing skill, or whatever else we are interested in. Unlike a scale, whose weighing mechanism can be examined for accuracy, tests do not have "high" or "low" validity built into them.

Suppose you are teaching English to native Japanese speakers who are studying for their Canadian citizenship test. On the first day of class, you give your students a test of their ability to understand a magazine article written in English and find that their scores are quite low. Was the test valid? The answer depends on how you interpret its results. The scores are probably a valid measure of your students' ability to understand written English, but probably not a valid measure of their verbal intelligence. If you had given the test using an article written in Japanese, the resulting scores would have been a valid indicator of verbal intelligence, but not a valid measure of English comprehension.

In other words, we can't say that a test itself is "valid" or "invalid." Instead, **validity** refers to the degree to which test scores are interpreted appropriately and used properly (Cronbach, 1990; Messick, 1989). As in our English-comprehension example, a test score can be valid for one purpose but invalid for another.

Evidence about the validity of test scores can be gathered in several ways. For example, we can look at *content validity,* the degree to which the content of a test is a fair and representative sample of what the test is supposed to measure. If an instructor spends only five minutes out of forty lectures discussing the mating behaviour of the tree frog and then devotes half of the final exam to this topic, that exam would be low on content validity. It would not allow us to draw accurate conclusions about what students learned in the course as a whole. Similarly, a test that measures only math skills would not have acceptable content validity as an intelligence test. A content-valid test includes items relating to the entire area of interest, not just a narrow slice of it (Linn & Gronlund, 2000).

Another way to evaluate validity is to determine how well test scores correlate with an independent measure of whatever the test is supposed to assess. This independent measure is called a *criterion.* For example, a test of eye-hand coordination would have high *criterion validity* for hiring diamond cutters if scores on the test correlated highly with a test of actual skill at diamond cutting. Why give a test if there is an independent criterion we can measure? The reasons often relate to convenience and cost. It would be silly to hire all applicants for airport security jobs and then fire those who are unskilled if a 20-minute performance test could identify the best candidates. Criterion validity is called *predictive validity* when test scores are correlated with a

validity The degree to which test scores are interpreted correctly and used appropriately.

criterion that cannot be measured until some time in the future—such as success in a pilot training program or grade-point average at graduation.

We can also look at *construct validity*, the extent to which scores suggest that a test is actually measuring the theoretical construct, such as anxiety, that it claims to measure (Messick, 1989). Suppose you are developing a test of anxiety, and you know that various theories predict that anxiety occurs when people are uncertain about the future. With these theories in mind, you would expect that people waiting for the results of an important medical test should score higher on your test than those who know they are healthy. If this is not the case, then scores on your test would have low construct validity, at least with regard to most theories of anxiety (Borsboom, Mellenbergh, & van Heerden, 2004).

Evaluating Intelligence Tests

Criteria for assessing the reliability and validity of tests have been incorporated into the testing standards established by the Canadian Psychological Association and other organizations (American Educational Research Association, American Psychological Association, and National Council on Measurement in Education, 1999). These standards are designed to maintain quality in educational and psychological testing by providing guidelines for the administration, interpretation, and application of tests in such areas as therapy, education, employment, certification or licensing, and program evaluation (Turner et al., 2001). The standards tell us that in evaluating intelligence tests, we must take into account not only the reliability and validity of test scores but also a number of socio-cultural factors that might influence those scores.

The Reliability and Validity of Intelligence Tests

The reliability and validity of intelligence tests are generally evaluated on the basis of the stability, or consistency, of IQ scores (reliability) and the accuracy of these scores in measuring cognitive abilities associated with intelligence (validity).

How Reliable Are Intelligence Tests? IQ scores obtained before the age of seven typically do not correlate very well with scores on intelligence tests given later, for two key reasons: (1) Test items used with very young children are different from those used with older children, and (2) in the early years, cognitive abilities change rapidly and at different rates for different children (see the chapter on human development). During the school years, however, IQ scores tend to remain stable (Mayer & Sutton, 1996). For teenagers and adults, the stability of IQ scores is high, generally above .85.

Of course, a person's score may vary from one time to another if testing conditions, motivation or anxiety, health status, or other factors change. Scores will also vary across different intelligence tests because each presents a somewhat different collection of items. So a child's scores on the WISC-IV and the SB5 would probably differ somewhat. Accordingly, testers do not usually make decisions about a person's abilities on the basis of a single IQ score. Overall, though, modern intelligence tests usually provide exceptionally consistent results—especially compared with most other kinds of mental tests.

How Valid Are Intelligence Tests? If everyone agreed on exactly what intelligence is (having a good memory, for example), we could evaluate the validity of intelligence test scores simply by correlating people's IQs with their performance on particular tasks (in this case, memory tasks). The tests whose scores correlated most highly with scores on memory tests would be the most valid for measuring intelligence. But because psychologists do not fully agree on a single definition of

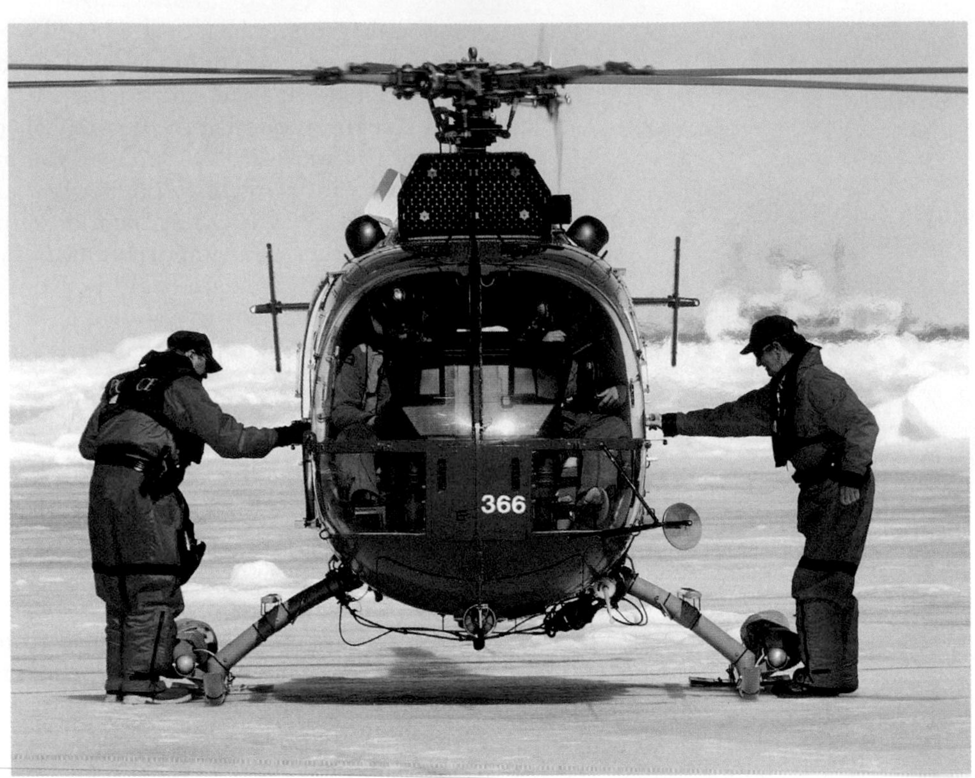

IQ and Job Performance IQ scores are reasonably good at predicting the ability to learn job-relevant information and to deal with unpredictable, changing aspects of the work environment—characteristics that are needed for success in complex jobs such as the ones held by these RCMP officers.

intelligence, they don't have a single standard against which to compare intelligence tests. Therefore, they cannot say whether intelligence tests are valid measures of intelligence. Instead, they can only assess the validity of intelligence test scores for *specific purposes.*

Intelligence test scores appear to be most valid for assessing aspects of intelligence that are related to schoolwork, such as abstract reasoning and verbal comprehension. The validity of individually administered tests—as measured by correlating IQ scores with high school grades—is reasonably good, about .50 (Brody & Ehrlichman, 1998). Scores on the Cognitive Abilities Test (Lohman & Hagen, 2001a) and other group-administered tests that focus more specifically on reasoning skills show even higher correlations with school performance (Kuncel, Hezlett, & Ones, 2004).

In addition, there is evidence that employees who score high on tests of verbal and mathematical reasoning tend to perform better on the job (and are paid more) than those who earned lower scores (Borman, Hanson, & Hedge, 1997; Johnson & Neal, 1998). Later, we describe a study that kept track of people for 60 years and found that children with high IQ scores tended to be well above average in terms of academic and financial success in adulthood (Cronbach, 1996; Oden, 1968; Terman & Oden, 1947). IQ scores also appear to be highly correlated with performance on "real-life" tasks such as reading medicine labels and using the telephone book (Gottfredson, 1997, 2004). So, by the standard measures for judging psychological tests, scores on intelligence tests have good reliability and reasonably good validity for predicting success in school and in many occupations (Schmidt & Hunter, 2004).

How Fair Are IQ Tests? As noted earlier, though, an IQ score is not a perfect measure of how "smart" a person is. Because intelligence tests do not measure the full array of cognitive abilities, a particular test score tells only part of the story, and even that part may be distorted. Many factors other than cognitive ability—including one's response to the tester—can influence test performance on a particular day. Children might not do as well if they are suspicious of strangers, for example (Jones & Appelbaum, 1989). And if older adults worry about making mistakes in unfamiliar situations, they may fail to even try to answer some questions, thus artificially lowering their IQ scores.

Test scores can also be affected by anxiety, physical disabilities, and language differences and other cultural barriers (Fagan, 2000; Steele, 1997). Early efforts at intelligence testing probably underestimated the abilities of people who were unfamiliar with English or with the vocabulary and experiences associated mainly with middle-class culture at the time. For example, consider the question "Which is most similar to a xylophone? (violin, tuba, drum, marimba, piano)." No matter how intelligent children are, if they have never had a chance to see an orchestra or to learn about these instruments, they may miss this question. One problem encountered in Canada is that most commonly used intelligence tests, such as the Wechsler tests, were developed in the United States, meaning that they may be biased in favour of Americans. To combat this problem, Canadian norms have been developed for some of these tests. Donald Saklofske at the University of Saskatchewan recommends that test scores for Canadian children be compared with Canadian norms rather than with the American norms provided in the testing manual (Saklofske, Tulsky, Wilkins & Weiss, 2003).

The solutions to many of the technical problems in intelligence tests, however, have not resolved the controversy over the fairness of intelligence *testing*. The debate continues partly because results of intelligence tests can have important consequences (Messick, 1982, 1989, 2000). Students who score well above average on these tests may receive advanced educational opportunities that set them on the road to further high achievement. Those whose relatively low test scores identify them as having special educational needs may find themselves in separate classes that isolate them from other students and carry negative social labels. Obviously, the social consequences of testing can be evaluated separately from the quality of the tests themselves; but those consequences cannot be ignored, especially if they tend to affect some groups more than others.

LINKAGES
Emotionality and the Measurement of Cognitive Abilities

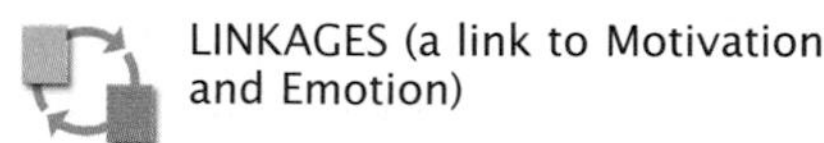

LINKAGES (a link to Motivation and Emotion)

Emotional arousal is one of the most important noncognitive factors that can potentially influence scores on cognitive ability tests. As described in the chapter on motivation and emotion, people tend to perform best when their arousal level is moderate. Too much arousal, or even too little, tends to result in decreased performance. People whose overarousal impairs their ability to do well in testing situations are said to suffer from *test anxiety.*

These people fear that they will do poorly on the test and that others will think they are "stupid." In a testing situation, they may experience physical symptoms such as heart palpitations and sweating, as well as negative thoughts such as "I am going to blow this exam" or "They are going to think I am a real idiot." In the most severe cases of test anxiety, individuals may be so distressed that they are unable to successfully complete the test.

Test anxiety may affect up to 40 percent of elementary school students and about the same percentage of university students. It afflicts boys and girls equally (Turner et al., 1993). High test anxiety is correlated with lower IQ scores, and even among people with high IQ scores, those who experience severe test anxiety tend to do poorly on tests. Test-anxious elementary school students are likely to receive low grades and to perform poorly on evaluated tasks and on those that require new learning (Campbell, 1986). Some children with test anxiety refuse to attend school, or they "play sick" on test days, creating a vicious circle that further harms their grades and their performance on standardized achievement tests.

Anxiety, frustration, and other emotions may also be at work in a testing phenomenon that Claude Steele and his colleagues have identified as *stereotype threat* (Steele & Aronson, 2000). In one study, women with good math skills were randomly assigned to one of two groups. The first group was given information that

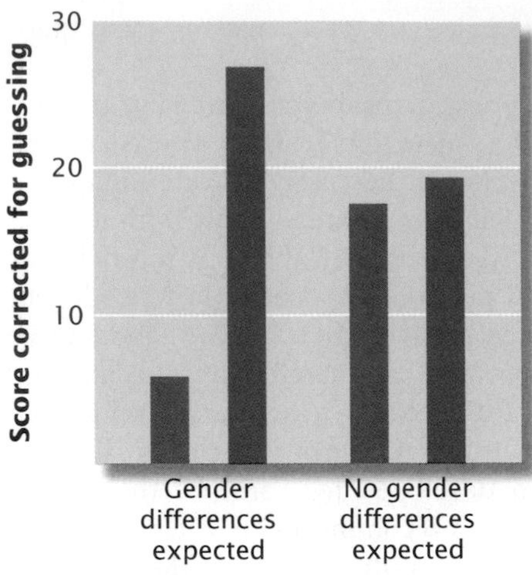

figure 10.3

The Stereotype Threat Effect

In this experiment, male and female college students took a difficult math test. Beforehand, some of the students were told that men usually outscore women on such tests. Women who heard this gender-stereotype information scored lower than those who did not hear it; they also scored lower than the men, even though their mathematical ability was equal to that of the men. Men's scores were not significantly affected by gender-stereotype information.

created concern over the stereotype that women aren't as good as men at math. In fact, they were told that men usually do better than women on the difficult math test they were about to take. The second group was not given this information. As shown in Figure 10.3, the women in the second group performed much better on the test than did those in the first. In fact, their performance was about equal to that of men who took the same test (Spencer, Steele, & Quinn, 1997). According to Steele, concern over negative stereotypes about the cognitive abilities of the group to which they belong can impair the performance of some women—and some members of ethnic minorities—such that the test scores they earn underestimate their cognitive abilities (Blascovich et al., 2001; Inzlicht & Ben-Zeev, 2000).

The good news for people who suffer from test anxiety is that the counselling centres at most universities have effective programs for dealing with it. Test anxiety can be remedied through some of the same procedures used to treat other anxiety disorders (see the chapter on treatment of psychological disorders). These and other research findings indicate that the relationship between anxiety and test performance is a complex one, but one generalization seems to hold true: People who are severely test anxious do not perform to the best of their ability on intelligence tests.

IQ Scores as a Measure of Innate Ability

Concern over the fairness of intelligence tests is based partly on the assumption that a good intelligence test should be able to see through the surface ripples created by an individual's cultural background, experience, and motivation to discover the innate cognitive abilities that lie beneath. Many researchers who study human intelligence argue that this is an impossible task for any test (Cronbach, 1990; Lohman, 1989). Years of research have led them to conclude that intelligence is *developed ability,* influenced partly by genetics but also by educational, cultural, and other life experiences that shape the very knowledge, reasoning, and other skills that intelligence tests measure (Garlick, 2003; Plomin & Spinath, 2004). For example, by asking many questions, bright children help generate an enriching environment for themselves; thus innate abilities allow people to take better advantage of their environment (Scarr & Carter-Saltzman, 1982; Scarr, 1997). In addition, if their own biologically influenced intelligence allows bright parents to give their children an environment that helps the development of intelligence, their children are favoured by both heredity and environment.

Psychologists have explored the influence of genetics on individual differences in intelligence by comparing the correlation between the IQ scores of people who have differing degrees of similarity in their genetic makeup and environment. For example, they have examined the IQ scores of identical twins—pairs with exactly the same genes—who were separated when very young and raised in different environments. They have also examined the scores of identical twins raised together. (You may want to review the Linkages section of the chapter on research in psychology, as well as the appendix on behavioural genetics, for more on the research designs typically used to analyze hereditary and environmental influences.)

These studies find, first, that hereditary factors are strongly related to IQ scores. When identical twins who were separated at birth and adopted by different families are tested many years later, the correlation between their scores is usually high and positive, at least +.60 (e.g., Bouchard & Pedersen, 1999). If one twin receives a high IQ score, the other probably will, too; if one is low, the other is likely to be low as well. However, studies of IQ correlations also highlight the importance of the environment (Scarr, 1998). Consider any two people—twins, siblings, or unrelated children—brought together in a foster home. No matter what the degree of genetic similarity in these pairs, the correlation between their IQ scores is higher if they share the same home than if they are raised in different environments, as Figure 10.4 shows (Scarr & Carter-Saltzman, 1982).

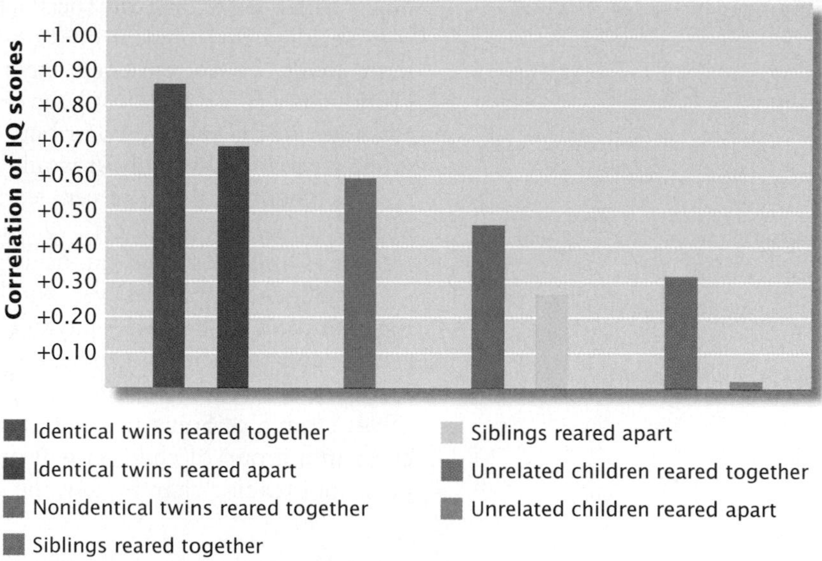

figure 10.4

Correlations of IQ Scores

The correlation in IQ between pairs increases with increasing similarity in heredity or environment.

Source: Reprinted with permission from "Familial Studies of Intelligence: A Review," T. Bouchard et al., *Science,* Vol. 212, #4498, pp. 1055–9, 29 May 1981. Copyright © 1981 American Association for the Advancement of Science.

The role of environmental influences is also seen in the results of studies that compare children's IQ scores before and after environmental changes such as adoption. Generally, when children from relatively impoverished backgrounds were adopted into homes offering a more enriching intellectual environment—including interesting materials and experiences, as well as a supportive, responsive adult—they showed modest increases in IQ scores (Weinberg, Scarr, & Waldman, 1992).

A study of French children who were adopted soon after birth demonstrates the importance of both genetic and environmental influences. These children were tested after years of living in their adopted homes. Children whose biological parents were from upper socioeconomic groups (in which higher IQ scores are more common) had higher IQ scores than children whose biological parents came from lower socioeconomic groups, regardless of the socioeconomic status of the adoptive homes (Capron & Duyme, 1989, 1996). These findings were supported by data from the Colorado Adoption Project (Cardon & Fulker, 1993; Cardon et al., 1992), and they suggest that a genetic component of children's cognitive abilities continues to exert an influence even in their adoptive environment (Petrill et al., 2004). At the same time, when children from low socioeconomic backgrounds were adopted by parents who provided academically enriched environments, their IQ scores rose by 12 to 15 points (Capron & Duyme, 1989). Other studies have also found that the IQ scores of adopted children were an average of 14 points higher than those of siblings who remained with their biological parents in poorer, less enriching environments (Schiff et al., 1978).

Other factors that can have negative effects on cognitive abilities include poor nutrition, exposure to lead or alcohol, low birth weight, and complications during birth (Matte et al., 2001; Strathearn et al., 2001). In contrast, exposure to early interventions that improve school readiness and academic ability tend to improve children's scores on tests of intelligence (Neisser et al., 1996; Ripple et al., 1999). These intervention programs, some of which are described later, may be responsible for the steady increase in average IQ scores throughout the world over the past six decades (Flynn, 1999; Neisser, 1998).

Some researchers have concluded that the influence of heredity and environment on differences in cognitive abilities appears to be about equal; others see a somewhat larger role for heredity (Herrnstein & Murray, 1994; Loehlin, 1989; Petrill et al., 1998, 2004; Plomin, 1994b). One research team has even suggested that specific genes are associated with extremely high IQs (Chorney et al., 1998). Still other researchers have suggested that the relative influence of heredity and environment might differ depending on social class. It may be, for example, that living in an impoverished environment does more to impair the development of cognitive skills than living in an enriched environment does to enhance that development (Turkheimer et al., 2003). Whatever the case, it is important to understand that any estimates of the relative contributions of heredity and environment apply only to groups, not to individuals. It would be inaccurate to say that 50 percent of your IQ score is inherited and 50 percent learned. It is far more accurate to say that about half of the *variability* in the IQ scores of a group of people can be attributed to hereditary influences and about half can be attributed to environmental influences.

Intelligence provides yet another example of nature and nurture working together to shape human behaviour and mental processes. It also illustrates how the relative contributions of genetic and environmental influences can change over time. Environmental influences, for example, seem to be greater at younger ages (Plomin, 1994; Plomin & Spinath, 2004) and tend to diminish over the years. So IQ differences in a group of children will probably be affected more by parental help with preschool reading than by, say, the courses they take in grade nine, ten years later.

Conditions That Can Raise IQ Scores

A number of environmental conditions can help or deter cognitive development (see the chapter on human development). For example, lack of caring attention or of normal intellectual stimulation can inhibit a child's mental growth. Low test scores have been linked to poverty, chaos, and noise in the home; poor schools; and inadequate nutrition and health care (Alaimo, Olson, & Frongillo, 2001; Kwate, 2001; Serpell, 2000; Weinberg, 1989). Can the effects of bad environments be reversed? Not always, but efforts to intervene in the lives of children and enrich their environments have had some success. Conditions for improving children's performance include rewards for progress, encouragement of effort, and creation of expectations for success.

In the United States, the best-known attempt to enrich children's environments is Project Head Start, a set of programs established by the federal government in the 1960s to help preschoolers from lower-income backgrounds. In some of these programs, teachers visit the home and work with the child and parents on cognitive skills. In others, the children attend classes in nursery schools. Some programs emphasize health and nutrition and family mental health and social skills as well. The Canadian government established a Head Start program in 1995, modelled after its American counterpart, aimed at improving school-readiness among Métis and Inuit preschool children. The program was initially launched in urban centres and northern communities. The program was expanded in 1998 to include First Nations children living on reserves. The Aboriginal Head Start program is run by Health Canada in partnership with non-profit community groups. In addition to school readiness skills, such as letter and number recognition, the program covers a wide range of social, emotional, and physical development opportunities. A key feature of the Aboriginal Head Start program is its focus on First Nations culture and language with the goal of enhancing the children's sense of pride in their heritage. Parents are also involved in various aspects of the program (Health Canada, 1998). Long-term studies on the benefits of the Aboriginal Head Start program in Canada have yet to be conducted, but evaluation of the American program suggests that Head Start has brought measurable benefits to children's health, as well as improvements in their academic and intellectual skills (Barnett, 1998; Lee, Brooks-Gunn, & Schnur, 1988; Ramey, 1999).

Do the gains achieved by preschool enrichment programs last? Although program developers sometimes claim long-term benefits (Schweinhart & Weikart, 1991), these claims are disputed (Spitz, 1991). Various findings from more than a thousand such programs are often contradictory, but the effect on IQ scores typically diminishes after a year or two (Woodhead, 1988). A study evaluating two of the better preschool programs concluded that their effects are at best only temporary (Locurto, 1991a). These fading effects reflect the fact that IQ scores describe a person's performance compared with others of the same age. To keep the same IQ score, a child must keep improving at the same rate as other children in the same age group (Kanaya, Scullin, & Ceci, 2003). So IQ scores will drop from year to year in children whose rate of cognitive growth falls behind that of their age mates.

Fading effects have also been seen in programs such as the Abecedarian Project, an early intervention program for children from low socioeconomic backgrounds (Ramey, 1992). Children at risk for mental retardation were identified while they were still in the womb. They then received five years of intense interventions to improve their chances of success once they entered school. When they started school, children in this enrichment program had IQ scores that were seven points higher than the scores of at-risk children who were not in the program. At age 12, they still scored higher on intelligence tests, but the size of the difference at that time was just five points. This difference was still evident nearly a decade later, when the participants were assessed at the age of 21 (Campbell et al., 2001).

Martin Woodhead (1988) concluded that the primary benefit of early enrichment programs probably lies in improving children's attitudes toward school. This can be an important benefit because, especially in borderline cases, children with favourable attitudes toward school may be less likely to be held back or placed in special-education classes. Children who have taken part in enrichment programs are also slightly less likely to be held back in school or to need special-education programs (Locurto, 1991b; Palmer & Anderson, 1979). Avoiding these experiences may, in turn, help children to retain positive attitudes about school and enter a cycle in which gains due to early enrichment are maintained and amplified on a long-term basis.

IQ Scores in the Classroom

IQ scores do not provide a crystal ball that can predict a person's destiny, nor are they a measure of some fixed quantity of cognitive ability. But might they affect how people are treated and how they behave? Decades ago, Robert Rosenthal and Lenore Jacobson (1968) argued that labels placed on students create teacher expectancies that can become self-fulfilling prophecies. They made this claim on the basis of a study in which they gave elementary school teachers the names of students who were about to enter a "blooming" period of rapid academic growth. These students had supposedly scored high on a special test, but the researchers had actually selected the "bloomers" at random. Nevertheless, the IQ scores of two-thirds of the bloomers dramatically increased during the following year. Only one-quarter of the other children showed the same increase. Apparently, the teachers' expectancies about certain children influenced those children in ways that showed up on IQ tests.

Several attempts to replicate these findings have failed, and researchers who reanalyzed the data concluded that they did not support Rosenthal and Jacobson's claims (Elashoff, 1979; Fielder, Cohen, & Feeney, 1971; Thorndike, 1968). Others have found that the effect of teacher expectancies may be statistically significant but that it is relatively small (Jussim, 1989; Snow, 1995). Still, there is little doubt that IQ-based teacher expectancies can have an effect on teachers' interactions with students (Rosenthal, 1994). To find out how, Alan Chaiken and his colleagues (Chaiken, Sigler, & Derlega, 1974) videotaped teacher-child interactions in a classroom in which teachers had been informed (falsely) that certain pupils were particularly bright. They found that the teachers tended to favour the supposedly brighter students—smiling at them more often than at other students, making more eye contact, and reacting more positively to their comments. Children receiving this extra social reinforcement not only get more intense teaching but are also more likely to enjoy school, to have their mistakes corrected, and to continue trying to improve. Later research found that teachers provide a wider range of classroom activities for students for whom they have higher expectations, suggesting another way in which expectancies might influence students' academic achievement and, indirectly, their IQ scores (Blatchford et al., 1989).

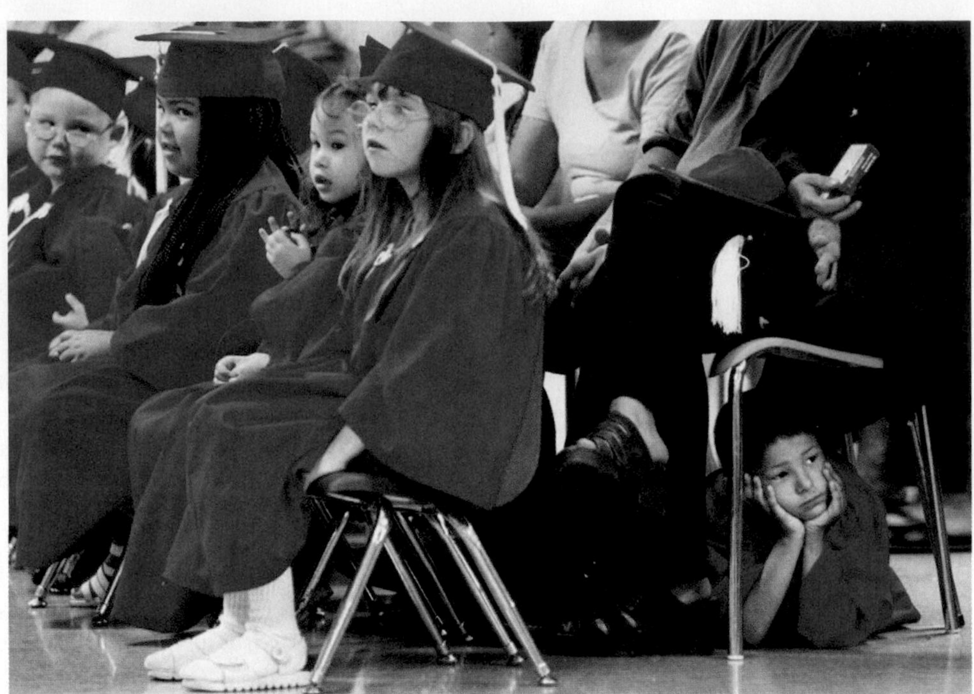

Head Start These children of the Niwasa Head Start Preschool in Hamilton, Ontario, took part in a Head Start program offering classes in both the Ojbway and Mohawk languages for Métis, status, and non-status Aboriginal preschoolers.

These results suggest that the "rich get richer." Those perceived to be blessed with better cognitive abilities are given better opportunities to improve those abilities. There may also be a "poor get poorer" effect. Some studies have found that teachers tend to be less patient, less encouraging, and less likely to try teaching as much material to students whom they do not consider bright (Cooper, 1979; Trujillo, 1986). Other studies indicate that teachers simply favour students who are most like themselves. Teachers who themselves had difficulty in math, for example, may favour students who have similar difficulties. Further, differential expectations among teachers—and even parents—about the academic potential of boys and girls may contribute to gender differences in performance in certain areas, such as science (e.g., Crowley et al., 2001). In summary, the operation of teacher expectancies is probably far more complex than Rosenthal and Jacobson originally thought (Snow, 1995).

in review Influences on IQ Scores

Source of Effect	Description	Examples of Evidence for Effect
Genetics	Genes appear to play a significant role in differences among people on intelligence test performance.	IQ scores have risen among children who are adopted into homes that offer a stimulating, enriching environment. Correlations between IQs of identical twins reared together are higher than for those reared apart.
Environment	The IQ scores of siblings who share no common environment are positively correlated. There is a greater correlation between scores of identical twins than between those of nonidentical twins.	Environmental conditions interact with genetic inheritance. Nutrition, medical care, sensory and intellectual stimulation, interpersonal relations, and influences on motivation are all significant features of the environment.

PsychAssist: Determining IQ—Stanford-Binet and IQ Tests; Wechsler Performance and Verbal Scale Simulation

IQ tests have been criticized for being biased and for labelling people on the basis of scores or profiles. ("In Review: Influences on IQ Scores" lists the factors that can shape IQ scores.) "Summarizing" a person through an IQ score does indeed run the risk of oversimplifying reality and making errors, but intelligence tests can also *prevent* errors by reducing the number of important educational and employment decisions that are made on the basis of inaccurate stereotypes, false preconceptions, and faulty generalizations. For example, boredom or lack of motivation at school might make a child appear mentally slow, or even challenged (retarded). But a test of cognitive abilities conducted under the right conditions is likely to reveal the child's potential. The test can prevent the mistake of moving a child of average intelligence to a class for the mentally handicapped. And as Alfred Binet had hoped, intelligence tests have been enormously helpful in identifying children who need special educational attention. So despite their limitations and potential for bias, IQ tests can minimize the likelihood of assigning children to remedial work they do not need or to advanced work they cannot yet handle.

THINKING CRITICALLY

Are Intelligence Tests Unfairly Biased Against Certain Groups?

We have seen that intelligence tests can undoubtedly have great value, but there is also great concern over the fact that IQ scores can be negatively affected by poverty, inferior educational opportunities, and other environmental factors. This concern focuses on the fact that members of some groups have not had an equal chance to develop the knowledge and skills that are required to achieve high IQ scores.

- **What am I being asked to believe or accept?**

Some critics claim that standard intelligence tests are not fair. They argue that a disproportionately large number of people in some ethnic minority groups receive low scores on intelligence tests for reasons that are unrelated to cognitive ability, job potential, or other criteria that the tests are supposed to predict (Helms, 1992, 1997; Kwate, 2001; Neisser et al., 1996). They say that using ability and aptitude tests to make decisions about people may unfairly deprive members of some ethnic minority groups of equal employment or educational opportunities.

- **What evidence is available to support the assertion?**

Research reveals several possible sources of bias in tests of cognitive abilities. First, as noted earlier, noncognitive factors such as motivation, trust, and anxiety can have an influence on test performance and may put certain individuals at a disadvantage. For example, children from some minority groups may be less motivated to perform well on standardized tests and less likely to trust the adult tester (Steele, 1997). Consequently, differences in test scores may partly reflect motivational differences among various groups during the testing process.

Second, many test items inevitably reflect the vocabulary and experiences of the dominant middle-class culture. Those who are less familiar with the knowledge and skills valued by that culture will not score as well as those who are more familiar with them. Not all cultures value the same things, however (Serpell, 1994; Sternberg & Grigorenko, 2004b). A study of Cree adults in northern Ontario revealed that words and phrases associated with *competence* included *good sense of direction*; at the *incompetent* end of the scale was the phrase *lives like a white person* (Berry & Bennett, 1992). A Canadian of European decent might not perform well on a Cree intelligence test based on these criteria. In fact, as illustrated in Table 10.2, poor performance on a culture-specific test is probably due more to unfamiliarity with culture-based concepts than to lack of cognitive ability. Compared with more traditional measures, "culture-fair" tests—such as the Universal Nonverbal Intelligence Test—that reduce dependence on oral skills do produce smaller differences between native English speakers and English-language learners (Bracken & McCallum, 1998).

Third, some tests may reward those who interpret questions as expected by the test designer. Conventional intelligence tests have clearly defined "right" and "wrong" answers. Yet a person may interpret test questions in a manner that is "intelligent" or "correct," but that produces a "wrong" answer. For example, when one child was asked, "In what way are an apple and a banana alike?" he replied, "Both give me diarrhea." The fact that you don't give the answer that the test designer was looking for does not mean that you *can't*.

- **Are there alternative ways of interpreting the evidence?**

This same evidence might be interpreted as showing that although intelligence tests do not provide a pure measure of innate cognitive ability, they do provide a fair picture of whether a person has developed the skills necessary to succeed in school or in certain jobs. When some people have had more opportunity than others to develop their abilities, the difference will be reflected in IQ scores. From this point of view, intelligence tests are fair measures of the cognitive abilities developed by people living in a society that, unfortunately, contains some unfair elements. In other words, the tests may be accurately detecting knowledge and skills that are not represented equally in all groups, but this doesn't mean that the tests discriminate *unfairly* among those groups.

To some observers, concern over cultural bias in intelligence tests stems from a tendency to think of IQ scores as measures of innate ability rather than of ability that is developed and expressed in a cultural context—much as athletes develop the physical skills needed to play certain sports (Lohman, 2004). Attempting to eliminate language and other cultural elements from intelligence tests, they say, would eliminate a vital part of what is meant by the term *intelligence* in any culture (Sternberg, 2004). This may be why "culture-fair" tests do not predict academic achievement as well as conventional intelligence tests do (Aiken, 1994; Lohman, in press). Perhaps familiarity with the culture reflected in intelligence tests is just as important for success at school or work in that culture as it is for success on the tests themselves. After all, the ranking among groups on measures of academic achievement is similar to the ranking for average IQ scores (Sue & Okazaki, 1990).

- **What additional evidence would help to evaluate the alternatives?**

If the problem of test bias is really a reflection of differences between various groups' opportunities to develop their cognitive skills, it will be important to conduct research on interventions that can reduce those differences. Making "unfair" tests fairer by enhancing the skill development opportunities of traditionally disadvantaged groups should lead to smaller differences between groups on tests of cognitive ability (Martinez, 2000).

At the same time, alternative tests of cognitive ability must also be explored, particularly those that include assessment of problem-solving skills and other abilities not measured by most intelligence tests (e.g., Sternberg & Kaufman,

table 10.2

How did you do on this "intelligence test"? If, like most people, you are unfamiliar with the material being tested by these rather obscure questions, your score was probably low. Would it be fair to say, then, that you are not very intelligent?

An Intelligence Test?

Take a minute to answer each of these questions, and check your answers against the key below.

1. What fictional detective was created by Leslie Charteris?
2. What vegetable yields the most pounds of produce per acre?
3. What was the infamous pseudonym of broadcaster Iva Toguri d'Aquino?
4. What kind of animal is Dr. Dolittle's pushmi-pullyu?

Answers: (1) Simon Templar (2) Cabbage (3) Tokyo Rose (4) A two-headed llama

1998). If new tests show smaller between-group differences than traditional tests but have equal or better predictive validity, many of the issues discussed in this section will have been resolved.

• What conclusions are most reasonable?

The effort to reduce unfair cultural biases in tests is well founded, but "culture-fair" tests will be of little benefit if they fail to predict success as well as conventional tests do (Anastasi & Urbina, 1997; Sternberg, 1985). Whether one considers this circumstance good or bad, fair or unfair, it is important for people to have information and skills that are valued by the culture in which they live and work. As long as this is the case, tests designed to predict success in such areas are reasonable insofar as they measure a person's skills and access to the information valued by that culture.

In other words, there is probably no value-free, experience-free, or culture-free way to measure the construct known as intelligence when that construct is defined by the behaviours that a culture values and that are developed through experience in that culture (Sternberg, 1985, 2004; Laboratory of Comparative Human Cognition, 1982). This conclusion has led some researchers to worry less about how cultural influences might "contaminate" tests of innate cognitive abilities and to focus instead on how to help people develop the abilities that are required for success in school and society. As mentioned earlier, if more attention were focused on combating poverty, poor schools, inadequate nutrition, inadequate health care, and other conditions that result in lower average IQ scores and reduced economic opportunities for certain groups of people, many of the reasons for concern about test bias might be eliminated.

Understanding Intelligence

We have seen that people who are skilled at using and understanding language, at learning and remembering, and at thinking, problem-solving, and other information-processing tasks are likely to score well on standard intelligence tests such as the Stanford-Binet and the Wechsler. But these standard tests do not measure all the abilities highlighted by other approaches to the concept of "intelligence" (Berry & Bennett, 1992; Carroll, 1993; Eysenck, 1986; Gardner, 1999; Hunt, 1983; Kanazawa, 2004; Meyer & Salovey, 1997; Sternberg, 1996; Sternberg, Lautrey, & Lubart, 2003). Let's consider these approaches and a few of the nontraditional intelligence tests that have emerged from some of them.

The Psychometric Approach

Standard intelligence tests are associated with the **psychometric approach,** which is a way of studying intelligence that emphasizes the *products* of intelligence, including IQ scores. Researchers taking this approach ask whether intelligence is one general trait or a bundle of more specific abilities. The answer matters, because if intelligence is a single trait, then an employer might assume that someone with a low IQ could not do any tasks well. But if intelligence is composed of many abilities that are somewhat independent of each other, then a poor showing in one area—say, spatial abilities—would not rule out good performance in others, such as understanding information or solving word problems.

psychometric approach A way of studying intelligence that emphasizes analysis of the products of intelligence, especially scores on intelligence tests.

g A general intelligence factor that Charles Spearman postulated as accounting for positive correlations between people's scores on all sorts of cognitive ability tests.

Early in the twentieth century, statistician Charles Spearman made a suggestion that began the modern debate about the nature of intelligence. Spearman noticed that scores on almost all tests of cognitive abilities were positively correlated (Spearman, 1904, 1927). That is, people who did well on one test also tended to do well on all of the others. Spearman concluded that these correlations were created by general cognitive ability, which he called **g**, for *general intelligence,* and a group of special intelligences, which he collectively referred to as *s*. The *s*-factors, he said, are the specific information and skills needed for particular tasks.

Spearman argued that people's scores on a particular test depend on both *g* and *s*. Further examination of test scores, however, revealed correlations that could not be explained by either *g* or *s*; these were called *group factors*. Although Spearman modified his theory to accommodate these group factors, he continued to claim that *g* represented a measure of mental force, or intellectual power.

In 1938, L. L. Thurstone published a paper criticizing Spearman's mathematical methods. Using the statistical technique of factor analysis, Thurstone analyzed the correlations among intelligence tests to identify the underlying factors, or abilities, being measured by those tests. His analyses did not reveal a single, dominating *g*-factor. Instead, he found seven relatively independent *primary mental abilities*: numerical ability, reasoning, verbal fluency, spatial visualization, perceptual ability, memory, and verbal comprehension. Thurstone did not deny that *g* exists, but he argued that it was not as important as these primary mental abilities in describing a particular person. Similarly, Spearman did not deny the existence of special abilities, but he maintained that *g* tells us most of what we need to know about a person's cognitive ability.

Raymond B. Cattell (1963) agreed with Spearman, but his own factor analyses suggested that there are two kinds of *g*, which he labeled *fluid* and *crystallized*. **Fluid intelligence,** he said, is the basic power of reasoning and problem solving. **Crystallized intelligence,** in contrast, involves specific knowledge gained as a result of applying fluid intelligence. It produces, for example, a good vocabulary and familiarity with the multiplication tables.

Who is right? After decades of research and debate, most psychologists today agree that there is a positive correlation among various tests of cognitive ability, a correlation that is due to a factor known as *g* (e.g., Frey & Detterman, 2004). However, the brain probably does not contain some unified "thing" corresponding to what people call intelligence. Instead, cognitive abilities appear to be organized in "layers," beginning with as many as 50 or 60 narrow and specific skills that can be grouped into seven or eight more general ability factors, all of which combine into *g*, the broadest and most general of all (Carroll, 1993; Gustafsson & Undheim, 1996; Lubinski, 2004).

The Information-Processing Approach

The **information-processing approach** tries to identify the mental *processes* involved in intelligent behaviour, not the traits (such as verbal ability) that result in test scores and other *products* of intelligence (Das, 2002; Hunt, 1983; Lohman, 2000; Sternberg, 2000). Researchers taking this approach ask: What mental operations are necessary to perform intellectual tasks? What aspects depend on past learning, and what aspects depend on attention, working memory, and processing speed? In other words, the information-processing approach relates the basic mental processes discussed in the chapters on perception, learning, memory, and cognition to the concept of intelligence. Are there individual differences in these processes that correlate with measures of intelligence? More specifically, are measures of intelligence related to differences in the amount of attention people have available for basic mental processes or in the speed of those processes?

The notion that intelligence may be related to attention builds on the results of research by Earl Hunt and others (Ackerman, 1994; Ackerman, Beier, & Boyle, 2002; Eysenck, 1987; Hunt, 1980). As discussed in the chapter on perception, attention represents a pool of resources or mental energy. When people perform difficult tasks or perform more than one task at a time, they must call on greater amounts of these resources. Does intelligent behaviour depend on the amount of attention that can be mobilized? Early research by Hunt (1980) suggests that it does—that people with greater intellectual ability have more attentional resources available.

s A group of special abilities that Charles Spearman saw as accompanying general intelligence (*g*).

fluid intelligence The basic power of reasoning and problem solving.

crystallized intelligence The specific knowledge gained as a result of applying fluid intelligence.

information-processing approach An approach to the study of intelligence that focuses on mental operations, such as attention and memory, that underlie intelligent behaviour.

There is also evidence of a positive correlation between IQ scores and performance on tasks requiring attention, such as silently counting the number of words in the "animal" category while reading a list of varied terms aloud (Stankov, 1989).

Another possible link between differences in information processing and differences in intelligence relates to processing speed. Perhaps intelligent people have "faster brains" than other people—perhaps they carry out basic mental processes more quickly. When a task is complex, having a "fast brain" might reduce the chance that information will disappear from memory before it can be used (Jensen, 1993; Larson & Saccuzzo, 1989). In research conducted at the University of Western Ontario, Linda Miller and Philip A. Vernon found that a fast brain might also allow people to do a better job of mastering material in everyday life and therefore to build up a good knowledge base (Miller & Vernon, 1992). Hans Eysenck (1986) even proposed that intelligence can be defined as the error-free transmission of information through the brain. Following his lead, some researchers have attempted to measure various aspects of intelligence by looking at electrical activity in particular parts of the brain (Deary & Caryl, 1993; Eysenck, 1994; Garlick, 2002; Haier, White, & Alkire, 2003). Others have emphasized the importance of working-memory resources in intelligent thinking (e.g., Engel et al., 1999; Gray, Chabris, & Braver, 2003; Kyllonen & Christal, 1990; Süss et al., 2002). In fact some of these researchers conclude that *g* is nothing more than working memory (Jensen, 1998), whereas others believe that *g* is more than memory alone (Ackerman et al., 2002; Mackintosh & Bennett, 2003).

Hypotheses about the role of information-processing skills in intelligence certainly sound reasonable. Research suggests, however, that only a portion of the variation seen in people's performance on general cognitive abilities tests can be accounted for by differences in their speed of access to long-term memory, the capacity of short-term and working memory, or other information-processing abilities (Baker, Vernon, & Ho, 1991; Miller & Vernon, 1992).

The Triarchic Theory of Intelligence

According to Robert Sternberg (1988b, 1999), a complete theory of intelligence must deal with three different types of intelligence: analytic, creative, and practical. *Analytic intelligence,* the kind that is measured by traditional intelligence tests, would help you solve a physics problem; *creative intelligence* is what you would use

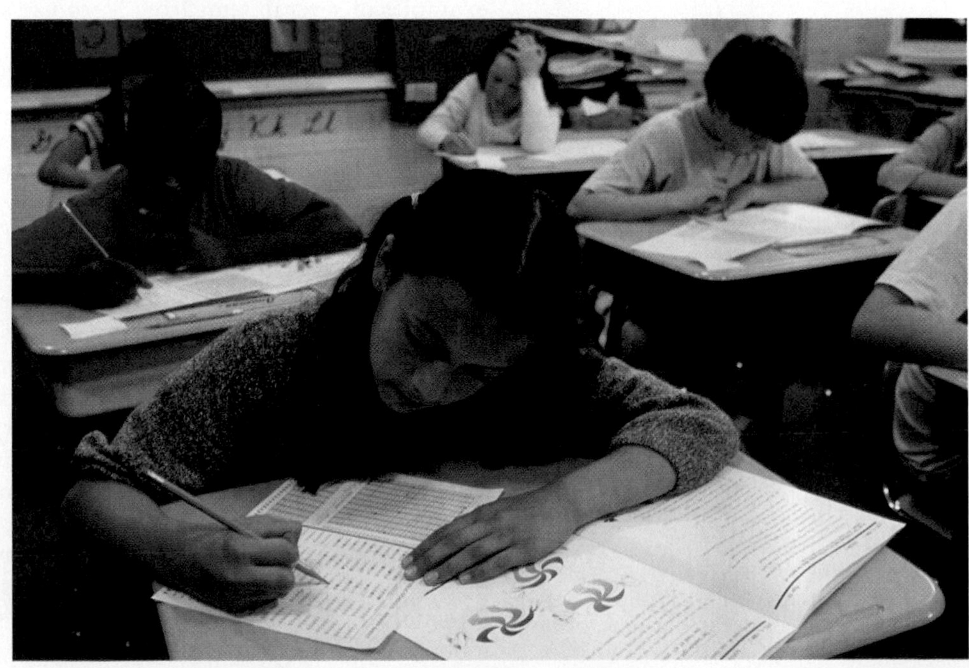

Brainpower and Intelligence The information-processing approach to intelligence suggests that people with the most rapid information processors—the "fastest" brains—should do best on cognitive ability tests, including intelligence tests. Research suggests that there is more to intelligent behaviour than sheer processing speed, though.

to compose music; and you would draw on *practical intelligence* to figure out what to do if you were stranded on a lonely road during a blizzard. Sternberg's **triarchic theory of intelligence** deals with all three types of intelligence.

Sternberg acknowledges the importance of analytic intelligence for success at school and in other areas, but he argues that graduate schools and employers should not select people solely on the basis of tests of this kind of intelligence (Sternberg, 1996; Sternberg & Williams, 1997). Why? Because the tasks posed by tests of analytic intelligence are often of little interest to the people taking them and typically have little relationship to their daily experience. For one thing, each task is usually clearly defined and comes with all the information needed to find the one right answer (Neisser et al., 1996), a situation that seldom occurs in the real world. The practical problems people face every day are generally of personal interest and are related to more common life experiences. That is, they are ill-defined and do not contain all the information necessary to solve them; they typically have more than one correct solution; and there may be several methods by which one can arrive at a solution (Sternberg et al., 1995).

It is no wonder, then, that children who do poorly in school may nevertheless show high degrees of practical intelligence. Some Brazilian street children, for example, are capable of doing the math required for their street business, despite having failed mathematics in school (Carraher, Carraher, & Schliemann, 1985). And a study of expert racetrack bettors revealed that even those whose IQ scores were as low as 82 were very good at predicting race odds at post time by combining many different kinds of complex information about horses, jockeys, and track conditions (Ceci & Liker, 1986). In other words, these people's practical intelligence is unrelated to measures of their IQ.

Sternberg's theory is important because it extends the concept of intelligence into areas that most psychologists traditionally have not examined and because it emphasizes what intelligence means in everyday life. The theory is so broad, however, that many parts of it are difficult to test. For example, methods for measuring practical "street smarts" have been proposed (Sternberg, 2001; Sternberg et al., 1995), but they remain controversial (Gottfredson, 2003). Sternberg and his colleagues have also developed new intelligence tests designed to assess analytic, practical, and creative intelligence, and there is some evidence that scores on these tests can predict success at some jobs at least as well as standard IQ tests (Leonhardt, 2000; Sternberg & Kaufman, 1998; Sternberg et al., 1995). Figure 10.5 provides examples of several items from Sternberg's test that are designed to measure practical and creative aspects of intelligence.

Multiple Intelligences

Some people whose IQ scores are only average, or even below average, may have exceptional ability in certain specific areas (Miller, 1999). One child whose IQ score was just 50 could correctly state the day of the week for any date between 1880 and 1950 (Scheerer, Rothmann, & Goldstein, 1945). He could also play melodies on the piano by ear and sing Italian operatic pieces he had heard. In addition, he could spell—forward or backward—any word spoken to him and could memorize long speeches, although he had no understanding of what he was doing.

Cases of remarkable ability in specific areas constitute part of the evidence cited by Howard Gardner in support of his theory of **multiple intelligences** (Gardner, 1993, 2002). To study intelligence, Gardner focused on how people learn and use symbol systems such as language, mathematics, and music. He asked, Do these systems all require the same abilities and processes, the same "intelligence"? According to Gardner, the answer is no. All people, he says, possess a number of intellectual potentials, or intelligences, each of which involves a somewhat different set of skills. Biology provides raw capacities; cultures provide symbolic systems—such as language—to mobilize those raw capacities. Although the intelligences normally interact, they can

triarchic theory of intelligence Robert Sternberg's theory that describes intelligence as having analytic, creative, and practical dimensions.

multiple intelligences Eight semi-independent kinds of intelligence postulated by Howard Gardner.

figure 10.5

Testing for Practical and Creative Intelligence

Robert Sternberg argues that traditional tests measure mainly analytic intelligence. Here are sample items from tests he developed to measure both practical and creative intelligence. The answers are given at the bottom of the figure. How did you do?

Source: Sternberg (1996).

PRACTICAL

1. Think of a problem that you are currently experiencing in real life. Briefly describe the problem, including how long it has been present and who else is involved (if anyone). Then describe three different practical things you could do to try to solve the problem. *(Students are given up to 15 minutes and up to 2 pages.)*

2. Choose the answer that provides the **best** solution, given the specific situation and desired outcome.
   John's family moved to Alberta from Ontario during grade 11. He enrolled as a new student in the local high school two months ago but still has not made friends and feels bored and lonely. One of his favourite activities is writing stories. What is likely to be the most effective solution to this problem?
   A. Volunteer to work on the school newspaper staff.
   B. Spend more time at home writing columns for the school newsletter.
   C. Try to convince his parents to move back to Ontario.
   D. Invite a friend from Ontario to visit during Christmas break.

3. Each question asks you to use information about everyday things. Read each question carefully and choose the best answer.

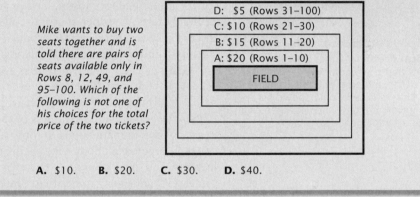

Mike wants to buy two seats together and is told there are pairs of seats available only in Rows 8, 12, 49, and 95–100. Which of the following is not one of his choices for the total price of the two tickets?

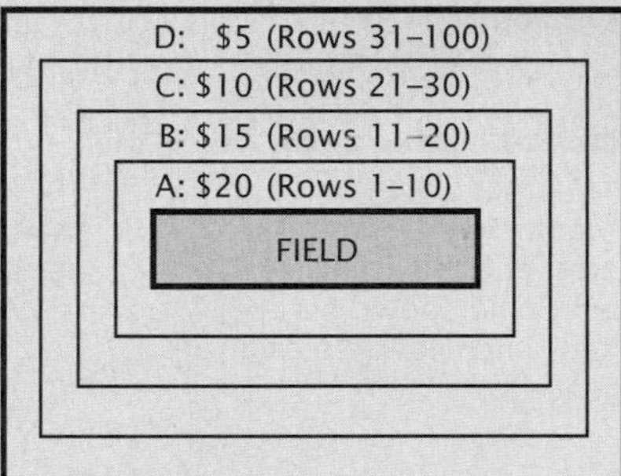

A. $10. **B.** $20. **C.** $30. **D.** $40.

CREATIVE

1. Suppose you are the student representative to a committee that has the power and the money to reform your school system. Describe your ideal school system, including buildings, teachers, curriculum, and any other aspects you feel are important. *(Students are given up to 15 minutes and up to 2 pages.)*

2. Each question has a "Pretend" statement. You must suppose that this statement is true. Decide which word goes with the third underlined word in the same way that the first two underlined words go together.
   Colours are audible.
   flavour is to tongue as shade is to
   A. ear. **B.** light. **C.** sound. **D.** hue.

3. First, read how the operation is defined. Then, decide what is the correct answer to the question.
   There is a new mathematical operation called ***flix.***
   It is defined as follows:
   $A \text{ flix } B = A + B, \text{ if } A > B$
   but $A \text{ flix } B = A \times B, \text{ if } A < B$
   and $A \text{ flix } B = A / B, \text{ if } A = B$
   How much is 4 flix 7?
   A. 28. **B.** 11. **C.** 3. **D.** -11.

ANSWERS. Practical: (2) A, (3) B. Creative: (2) A, (3) A.

A Musical Prodigy? According to Gardner's theory of multiple intelligences, skilled artists, athletes, and musicians—such as that of Glenn Gould shown here—display forms of intelligence not assessed by standard intelligence tests.

function with some independence, and individuals may develop certain intelligences further than others. ("In Review: Analyzing Cognitive Abilities" summarizes Gardner's theory, along with the other views of intelligence we have discussed.)

The specific intelligences that Gardner (1999) proposes are (1) *linguistic* intelligence (reflected in good vocabulary and reading comprehension), (2) *logical-mathematical* intelligence (as indicated by skill at arithmetic and certain kinds of reasoning), (3) *spatial* intelligence (seen in understanding relationships between objects), (4) *musical* intelligence (as in abilities involving rhythm, tempo, and sound identification), (5) *body-kinesthetic* intelligence (reflected in skill at dancing, athletics, and eye-hand coordination), (6) *intrapersonal* intelligence (displayed by self-understanding), (7) *interpersonal* intelligence (seen in the ability to understand and interact with others), and (8) *naturalistic* intelligence (the ability to see patterns in nature). Other researchers, such as Derek Dawda at Simon Fraser University in Burnaby, BC, have suggested that people also possess *emotional intelligence,* which involves the capacity to perceive emotions and to link them to one's thinking (Dawda, 2000, Meyer & Salovey, 1997). Gardner says that traditional intelligence tests sample only the first three of these intelligences, mainly because these are the forms of intelligence most valued in school. To measure intelligences not tapped by standard tests, Gardner suggests collecting samples of children's writing, assessing their ability to appreciate or produce music, and obtaining teacher reports of their strengths and weaknesses in athletic and social skills.

Gardner's view of intelligence is appealing, partly because it allows virtually everyone to be highly intelligent in at least one way. However, critics, such as Perry Klein at the University of Western Ontario, argue that including athletic or musical skill dilutes the validity and usefulness of the intelligence concept, especially as it is applied in school and in many kinds of jobs (Klein, 1998). They point out, too, that intrapersonal, interpersonal, body-kinesthetic, or naturalistic abilities are best described as collections of specific skills. Therefore it makes more sense to speak of, say, "interpersonal skills" rather than "interpersonal intelligence." Research on Gardner's theory has been hampered by a lack of dependable measures of the various intelligences he proposes (Lubinski & Benbow, 1995), but his theory is notable for its emphasis on the diversity in abilities that is easily ignored by focusing on general intelligence alone.

in review Analyzing Cognitive Abilities

Approach	Method	Key Findings or Propositions
Psychometric	Define the structure of intelligence by examining factor analyses of the correlations between scores on tests of mental abilities.	Performance on many tests of cognitive abilities is highly correlated, but this correlation, represented by *g*, reflects a bundle of abilities, not just one trait.
Information processing	Understand intelligence by examining the mental operations involved in intelligent behaviour.	The speed of basic processes and the amount of attentional resources available make significant contributions to performance on IQ tests.
Sternberg's triarchic theory	Understand intelligence by examining the information processing involved in thinking, changes with experience, and effects in different environments.	There are three distinct kinds of intelligence: analytic, creative, and practical. IQ tests measure only analytic intelligence, but creative intelligence (which involves dealing with new problems) and practical intelligence (which involves adapting to one's environment) may also be important to success in school and at work.
Gardner's theory of multiple intelligences	Understand intelligence by examining test scores, information processing, biological and developmental research, the skills valued by different cultures, and exceptional people.	Biology provides the capacity for eight distinct "intelligences": linguistic, logical-mathematical, spatial, musical, body-kinesthetic, intrapersonal, interpersonal, and naturalistic.

FOCUS ON RESEARCH METHODS

Tracking Cognitive Abilities over the Life Span

As described in the chapter on human development, significant changes in cognitive abilities occur from infancy through adolescence, but development does not stop there. Roger Dixon at the University of Alberta and his colleagues are conducting a major study on the changes in cognitive ability during adulthood. This study, known as the Victoria Longitudinal Study, has yielded interesting findings regarding the cognitive skills of older adults (Dixon & de Frais, 2004).

What was the researchers' question?

The researchers began by asking what appears to be a relatively simple question: How do adults' cognitive abilities change over time?

How did the researchers answer the question?

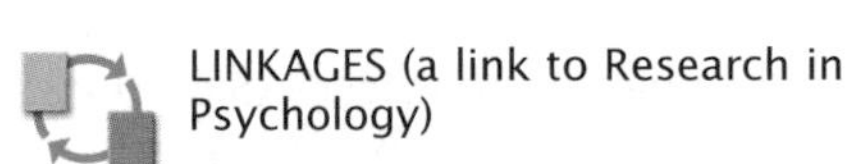

LINKAGES (a link to Research in Psychology)

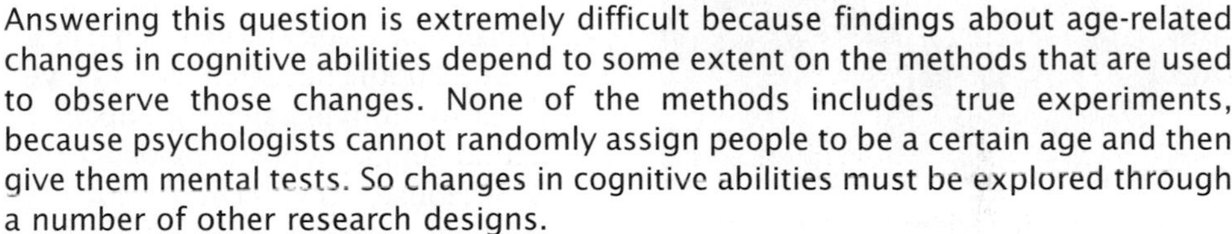

Answering this question is extremely difficult because findings about age-related changes in cognitive abilities depend to some extent on the methods that are used to observe those changes. None of the methods includes true experiments, because psychologists cannot randomly assign people to be a certain age and then give them mental tests. So changes in cognitive abilities must be explored through a number of other research designs.

One of these, the *cross-sectional study,* compares data collected at the same point in time from people of different ages. However, cross-sectional studies contain a major confounding variable: Because people are born at different times, they may have had very different educational, cultural, nutritional, and medical experiences. This confounding variable is referred to as a *cohort effect.* Suppose two cohorts, or age groups, are tested on their ability to imagine the rotation of an object in space. The cohort born around 1940 might not do as well as the one born around 1980, but does the difference reflect declining spatial ability in the older people? It might, but it might also be due in part to the younger group's greater experience with video games and other spatial tasks. In other words, differences in experience, and not just age, could account for differences in ability between older and younger people in a cross-sectional study.

Changes associated with age can also be examined through *longitudinal studies,* in which a group of people is repeatedly tested as its members grow older. But longitudinal designs, too, have some built-in problems. For one thing, fewer and fewer members of an age cohort can be tested over time as death, physical disability, relocation, and lack of interest reduce the sample size. Researchers call this problem the *mortality effect.* Further, the remaining members are likely to be the healthiest in the group and may also have retained better mental powers than the dropouts (Botwinick, 1977). As a result, longitudinal studies may underestimate the degree to which abilities decline with age. Another confounding factor can come from the *history effect.* Here, some event—such as a reduction in health care benefits for senior citizens—might have an effect on cognitive ability scores that is mistakenly attributed to age. Finally, longitudinal studies may be confounded by *testing effects,* meaning that participants may improve over time because of what they learn during repeated testing procedures. People who become "test wise" in this way might even remember answers from one testing session to the next.

One method used to combat the problems associated with the cross-sectional and longitudinal designs, used in the Victoria Longitudinal Study and others like it, is to combine cross-sectional with longitudinal methods in what is called a *cross-sequential with resampling design.* In a cross-sequential design, people from two or more age groups are compared initially (i.e., the cross-sectional component) and then the groups are compared again after a period of time has passed (i.e., the longitudinal component). This method allows the researcher to take advantage of the benefits of both the cross-sectional and longitudinal methods.

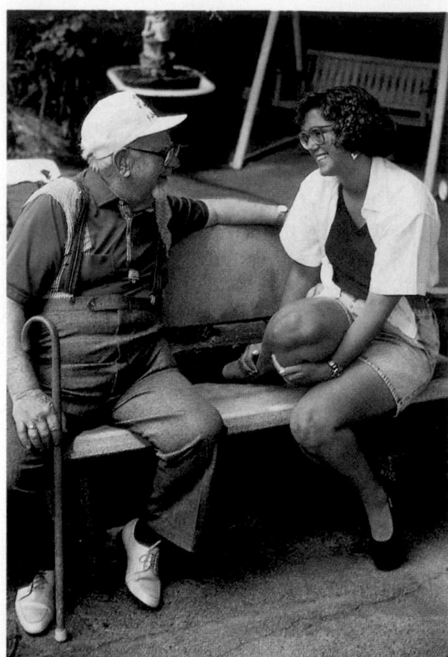

The Voice of Experience Even in old age, people's crystallized intelligence may remain intact. Their extensive storehouse of knowledge, experience, and wisdom makes older people a valuable resource for the young.

• What did the researchers find?

The results of the Victoria Longitudinal Study and other similar studies suggest a reasonably consistent conclusion: Unless people are impaired by Alzheimer's disease or other brain disorders, their cognitive abilities usually decline very slightly between early adulthood and old age (Dixon, 2003). Some aspects of *crystallized intelligence,* which depends on retrieving information and facts about the world from long-term memory, may remain robust well into old age. Other components of intelligence, however, may have failed quite noticeably by the time people reach sixty-five or seventy. *Fluid intelligence,* which involves rapid and flexible manipulations of ideas and symbols, is the most likely to decline (Horn, 1982; Schaie, 1996; see Figure 12.5 in the chapter on human development). The decline shows up in the following areas:

1. *Working memory.* The ability to hold and organize material in working memory declines beyond age 50 or 60, particularly when attention must be redirected (Parkin & Walter, 1991).

2. *Processing speed.* There is a general slowing of all mental processes (Salthouse, 1996, 2000). Research has not yet isolated whether this slowing is due to reduced storage capacity, impaired processing efficiency, problems in coordinating simultaneous activities, or some combination of these factors (Babcock & Salthouse, 1990; Li et al., 2004; Salthouse, 1990). For many tasks, this slowing does not create obstacles. But if a problem requires manipulating material in working memory, quick processing of information is critical (Rabbitt, 1977). To multiply two 2-digit numbers mentally, for example, you must combine the subsums before you forget them. In some cases, internal distractions may interfere with older people's processing efficiency (Li et al., 2004).

3. *Organization.* Older people seem to be less likely to solve problems by adopting specific strategies, or mental shortcuts (Charness, 1987, 2000; Young, 1971). For example, to locate a wiring problem, you might perform a test that narrows down the regions where the problem might be. The tests carried out by older people tend to be more random and haphazard (Young, 1971). This result may occur partly because many older people are out of practice at solving such problems.

4. *Flexibility.* Older people tend to be less flexible in problem solving than their younger counterparts. They are less likely to consider alternative solutions (Salthouse & Prill, 1987), and they require more information before making a tentative decision (Ackerman, Beier, & Boyle, 2002; Rabbitt, 1977). Laboratory studies suggest that older people are also more likely than younger ones to choose conservative, risk-free options (Botwinick, 1966).

5. *Control of attention.* The ability to direct or control attention declines with age (Kramer et al., 1999). When required to switch their attention from one task to another, older participants typically perform less well than younger ones.

• What do the results mean?

Findings from this area of research indicates that different kinds of cognitive abilities change in different ways throughout our lifetimes. In general, there is a gradual, continual accumulation of knowledge about the world, some systematic changes in the limits of cognitive processes, and changes in the way those processes are carried out. This finding suggests that a general decline in cognitive abilities during adulthood is neither inevitable nor universal (Richards et al., 2004).

• What do we still need to know?

There is an important question that the Schaie (1993) study doesn't answer: Why do age-related changes in cognitive abilities occur? Some researchers suggest that these changes are largely due to a decline in the speed and accuracy with which older people process information (Li et al., 2004; Salthouse, 2000). If this interpretation is correct, it would explain why some older people are less successful than younger ones at tasks that require rapidly integrating several pieces of information in working memory prior to making a choice or a decision.

It is also vital to learn why some people do *not* show declines in cognitive abilities—even when they reach their 80s. By understanding the biological and psychological factors responsible for these exceptions to the general rule, we might be able to reverse or delay some of the intellectual consequences of growing old.

Diversity in Cognitive Abilities

Although psychologists still don't agree on the details of what intelligence is, the study of intelligence tests and intelligent behaviour has yielded many insights into human cognitive abilities. It also has highlighted the diversity of those abilities. In this section we briefly examine some of that diversity.

Creativity

If you watch *The Simpsons* on television, you have probably noticed that Bart writes a different "punishment" sentence on the blackboard at the beginning of every episode. To maintain this tradition, the show's writers have had to create a unique—and funny—sentence for each of the more than two hundred shows that have aired since 1989. In every area of human endeavour, there are people who demonstrate **creativity,** the ability to produce new, high-quality ideas or products (Simonton, 1999; Sternberg & Grigorenko, 2004a). Whether a corporate executive or a homemaker, a scientist or an artist, everyone is more or less creative (Klahr & Simon, 1999). Yet like the concept of intelligence, the concept of creativity is difficult to define (Amabile, Goldfarb, & Brackfield, 1990). Does creativity include innovation based on previous ideas, or must it be utterly new? And must it be new to the world, as in Pablo Picasso's paintings, or only new to the creator, as when a child "makes up" the word *waterbird* without having heard it before? As with intelligence, psychologists have not defined *creativity* as a "thing" that people have or don't have. They have defined it instead as a process or cognitive activity that can be inferred from performance on creativity tests, as well as from the books and computer programs and artwork and other products that result from the creative process (Sternberg & Dess, 2001).

To measure creativity, some psychologists have devised tests of **divergent thinking,** the ability to think along many paths to generate many solutions to a problem (Diakidoy & Spanoudis, 2002; Guilford & Hoepfner, 1971). The Consequences Test is an example. It contains items such as "Imagine all of the things that might possibly happen if all national and local laws were suddenly abolished" (Guilford, 1959). Divergent-thinking tests are scored by counting the number of reasonable responses that a person can list for each item and how many of those responses differ from other people's responses. Unfortunately, these tests may underestimate creativity, because even creative people may find it difficult to create on demand in the same way they could, say, spell words or do multiplication problems when asked. Further, there is no guarantee that having the ability to come up with different answers or different ways of looking at a situation will lead to creative products. Creative behaviour requires divergent thinking that is appropriate for a given situation or problem. To be productive rather than just weird, a creative person must be firmly anchored to reality, understand society's needs, and learn from the experience and knowledge of others (Sternberg & Lubart, 1992). Teresa Amabile has identified three kinds of cognitive and

creativity The capacity to produce new, high-quality ideas or products.

divergent thinking The ability to think along many alternative paths to generate many different solutions to a problem.

personality characteristics necessary for creativity (Amabile, 1996; Amabile, Hennessey, & Grossman, 1986):

1. ***Expertise*** in the field of endeavour, which is directly tied to what a person has learned. For example, a painter or composer must know the paints, techniques, or instruments available.

2. A set of ***creative skills,*** including willingness to work hard, persistence at problem solving, capacity for divergent thinking, ability to break out of old problem-solving habits, and willingness to take risks. Amabile believes that training can influence many of these skills (some of which are closely linked to the strategies for problem solving discussed in the chapter on cognition and language).

3. The ***motivation*** to pursue creative production for internal reasons, such as satisfaction, rather than for external reasons, such as prize money. In fact, Amabile and her colleagues found that external rewards can deter creativity (e.g., Amabile, Hennessey, & Grossman, 1986). In one study, they asked groups of children or adults to create artistic products such as paintings or stories. Some were simply asked to work on the project. Others were told that their project would be judged for its creativity and excellence and that rewards would be given or winners announced. Experts—who did not know which products were created by which group—judged the work of the "reward" group to be significantly less creative. Similar effects have been found in other studies (Deci, Koestner, & Ryan, 1999, 2001), though research by Robert Eisenberger suggests that there may also be circumstances in which rewarding people's creativity can strengthen it—in much the same way that positive reinforcement strengthens any other behaviour (Eisenberger & Rhoades, 2001; Eisenberger & Shanock, 2003).

Is creativity inherited? To some extent, perhaps it is; but there is evidence that a person's environment—including the social, economic, and political forces within it—can influence creative behaviour at least as much as it influences intelligence (Amabile, 2001; Nakamura & Csikszentmihalyi, 2001). For example, the correlation between the creativity scores of identical twins reared apart is lower than that between their IQ scores (Nichols, 1978). Environmental factors, such as growing up around musicians or scientists, may focus one's creativity in a particular area, such as writing music or doing research. There are some notable exceptions, but most people who are creative in one domain are not especially creative in others.

Do you have to be smart to be creative? Creativity does appear to require a certain degree of intelligence (Simonton, 1984, 2002; Sternberg, 2001), but not necessarily an extremely high IQ score (Simonton, 1984). Correlations between scores on intelligence tests and on tests of creativity are only modest, between .10 and .30 (Barron & Harrington, 1981; Rushton, 1990; Simonton, 1999). This result is not surprising, because creativity as psychologists measure it requires broad, divergent thinking, whereas traditional intelligence tests measure **convergent thinking**—the ability to apply logic and knowledge in order to narrow down the number of possible solutions to a problem. The pace of research on creativity, and its relationship to intelligence, has picked up in recent years (Sternberg & Dess, 2001). One result of that research has been to define the combination of intelligence and creativity in the same person as *wisdom* (Sternberg, 2001; Sternberg & O'Hara, 1999).

convergent thinking The ability to apply logic and knowledge to narrow down the number of possible solutions to a problem or perform some other complex cognitive task.

Unusual Cognitive Ability

Our understanding of cognitive abilities has been advanced by research on people whose cognitive abilities are unusual—people who are gifted, mentally challenged, or have learning disabilities (Robinson, Zigler, & Gallagher, 2000).

Giftedness Bruce Shore, an internationally recognized expert at McGill University in Montreal, has spent over 30 years studying the factors associated with giftedness (e.g., Shore & Delcourt, 1996; Shore & Irving, 2005). Simply put, people who show remarkably high levels of accomplishment in particular domains, or who show promise for such accomplishment, are often referred to as *gifted*. Giftedness is typically measured by school achievement and other evidence of unusually high achievement, such as outstanding science projects, written products, and the like. The potential for this kind of accomplishment is usually measured with intelligence or scholastic aptitude tests. Researchers caution, though, against predicting academic potential from a single measure, such as an IQ score (Hagen, 1980; Lohman & Hagen, 2001b; Thorndike & Hagen, 1996).

In fact, people with unusually high IQs do not necessarily become famous and successful in their chosen fields. One of the best-known studies of the intellectually gifted was conducted by Louis Terman and his colleagues (Oden, 1968; Sears, 1977; Terman & Oden, 1947, 1959). This study began in 1921 with the identification of more than 1500 children whose IQ scores were very high—most higher than 135 by age ten. Interviews and tests conducted over the next 60 years revealed that few, if any, became truly creative geniuses—such as world-famous inventors, authors, artists, or composers—but that only 11 failed to graduate from high school and that more than two-thirds graduated from post-secondary education. Ninety-seven earned Ph.D.s; 92, law degrees; and 57, medical degrees. In 1955 their median family income was well above the national average (Terman & Oden, 1959). In general, they were physically and mentally healthier than non-gifted people and appear to have led happier, or at least more fortunate, lives. These results are consistent with more recent studies showing that people with higher IQ scores tend to live longer (Deary et al., 2004; Gottfredson, 2004; Hart et al., 2003), perhaps because they have the reasoning and problem-solving skills that lead them to take better care of themselves (Gottfredson & Deary, 2004; see the Focus on Research Methods section of the chapter on health, stress, and coping).

In short, although high IQ scores tend to predict longer, more successful lives, an extremely high IQ does not guarantee special distinction. Some research suggests that gifted children are not fundamentally different from other children; they just have "more" of the same basic cognitive abilities seen in all children (Dark & Benbow, 1993). Other work suggests that there may be other differences as well, such as an unusually intense motivation to master certain tasks or areas of intellectual endeavour (Lubinski et al., 2001; Winner, 2000).

Mental Retardation People whose IQ scores are less than about 70 *and* who fail to display the skill at daily living, communication, and other tasks expected of those their age have traditionally been described as *mentally retarded* (American Psychiatric Association, 1994). They now are often referred to as *developmentally disabled* or *mentally challenged*. People within this very broad category differ greatly in their cognitive abilities, as well as in their ability to function independently in daily life. Table 10.3 shows a classification that divides the range of low IQ scores into categories that reflect these differences.

Some cases of mental retardation have a clearly identifiable cause. The best-known example is *Down syndrome,* which occurs when an abnormality during conception results in an extra 21st chromosome (Hattori et al., 2000). Children with Down syndrome typically have IQ scores in the range of 40 to 55, though some may score higher than that. There are also several inherited causes of mental retardation.

The most common of these is *Fragile X syndrome,* caused by a defect on chromosome 23 (known as the *X chromosome*). More rarely, retardation is caused by inheriting *Williams syndrome* (a defect on chromosome 7) or by inheriting a gene for *phenylketonuria,* or PKU (which causes the body to create toxins out of milk and other foods). Retardation can also result from environmental causes, such as

table 10.3

These categories are approximate. Especially at the upper end of the scale, many retarded persons can be taught to handle tasks well beyond what their IQ scores might suggest. Furthermore, IQ is not the only diagnostic criterion for retardation. Many people with IQs lower than 70 can function adequately in their communities and so would not be classified as mentally retarded.

Categories of Mental Retardation

Level of Retardation	IQ Scores	Characteristics
Mild	50–70	A majority of all the mentally retarded. Usually show no physical symptoms of abnormality. Individuals with higher IQs can marry, maintain a family, and work in unskilled jobs. Abstract reasoning is difficult for those with the lower IQs of this category. Capable of some academic learning to a grade six level.
Moderate	35–49	Often lack physical coordination. Can be trained to take care of themselves and to acquire some reading and writing skills. Abilities of a 4- to 7-year-old. Capable of living outside an institution with their families.
Severe	20–34	Only a few can benefit from any schooling. Can communicate vocally after extensive training. Most require constant supervision.
Profound	Below 20	Mental age less than 3. Very limited communication. Require constant supervision. Can learn to walk, utter a few simple phrases, and feed themselves.

exposure to German measles (rubella) or alcohol or other toxins before birth; oxygen deprivation during birth; and head injuries, brain tumours, and infectious diseases (such as meningitis or encephalitis) in childhood (Public Health Agency of Canada, 2002).

Familial retardation refers to the 30 to 40 percent of (usually mild) cases in which there is no obvious genetic or environmental cause (American Psychiatric Association, 1994). In these cases, retardation appears to result from a complex, and as yet unknown, interaction between heredity and environment that researchers are continuing to explore (Croen, Grether, & Selvin, 2001; Spinath et al., 2004).

Mildly mentally retarded people are just as good as others at recognizing simple stimuli, and their rate of forgetting information from short-term memory is no more rapid (Belmont & Butterfield, 1971). But their cognitive abilities differ from other people in three important ways (Campione, Brown, & Ferrara, 1982):

1. They perform certain mental operations more slowly, such as retrieving information from long-term memory. When asked to repeat something they have learned, they are not as quick as a person of normal intelligence.

2. They simply know fewer facts about the world. It is likely that this deficiency is caused by the third problem.

3. They are not very good at remembering to use mental strategies that may be important in learning and problem solving. For example, they do not remember to rehearse material that must be held in short-term memory, even though they know how to do so.

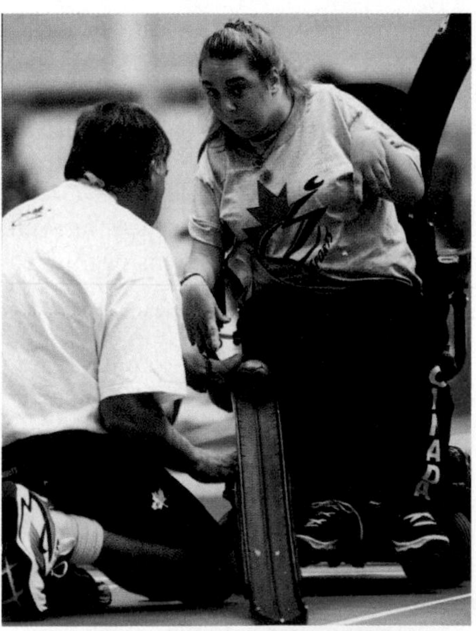

Endless Possibilities Special Olympics Canada provides an opportunity for athletes with intellectual disabilities to participate in national and international sporting events. As we come to better understand the potential, not just the limitations, of mentally retarded people, their opportunities and their role in society will continue to expand.

What are the reasons for these deficiencies? In some ways, the differences between normal and retarded children resemble the differences between older and younger children discussed in the chapter on human development. Both younger children and retarded children show deficiencies in *metamemory*—the knowledge of how their memory works. More generally, retarded children are deficient in **metacognition:** the knowledge of what strategies to apply, when to apply them, and

metacognition The knowledge of what strategies to apply, when to apply them, and how to use them in new situations.

Evaluating Intelligence Tests

The Reliability and Validity of Intelligence Tests

Intelligence tests are reasonably reliable, and they do a good job of predicting academic success. However, these tests assess only some of the abilities that might be considered aspects of intelligence, and they may favour people most familiar with middle-class culture. Nonetheless, this familiarity is important for academic and occupational success.

IQ Scores as a Measure of Innate Ability

Both heredity and the environment influence IQ scores, and their effects interact. The influence of heredity is shown by the high correlation between IQ scores of identical twins raised in separate households and by the similarity in the IQ scores of children adopted at birth and their biological parents. The influence of the environment is revealed by the higher correlation of IQ scores among siblings who share the same environment than among siblings who do not, as well as by the effects of environmental changes such as adoption.

Conditions That Can Raise IQ Scores

An enriched environment sometimes raises preschool children's IQ scores. Initial gains in cognitive performance that result from interventions such as Project Head Start may decline over time, but the programs may improve children's attitudes toward school.

IQ Scores in the Classroom

Like any label, an IQ score can generate expectations that affect both how other people respond to a person and how that person behaves. Children labelled with low IQ scores may be offered fewer or lower-quality educational opportunities. However, IQ scores help educators to identify a student's strengths and weaknesses and to offer the curriculum that will best serve that student.

Understanding Intelligence

The Psychometric Approach

The *psychometric approach* attempts to analyze the structure of intelligence by examining correlations between tests of cognitive ability. Because scores on almost all tests of cognitive ability are positively correlated, Charles Spearman concluded that such tests measure a general factor of mental ability, called *g*, as well as more specific factors, called *s*. As a result of factor analysis, other researchers have concluded that intelligence is not a single general ability but a collection of abilities and subskills needed to succeed on any test of intelligence. Raymond B. Cattell distinguished between *fluid intelligence,* the basic power of reasoning and problem solving, and *crystallized intelligence,* the specific knowledge gained as a result of applying fluid intelligence. Modern theories of intelligence describe it as a hierarchy that is based on a host of specific abilities that fit into about eight groups that themselves combine into a single, general category of cognitive ability.

The Information-Processing Approach

The *information-processing approach* to intelligence focuses on the process of intelligent behaviour. Varying degrees of correlation have been found between IQ scores and measures of the flexibility and capacity of attention and between IQ scores and measures of the speed of information processing. This approach has helped deepen our understanding of the processes that create individual differences in intelligence.

The Triarchic Theory of Intelligence

According to Robert Sternberg's *triarchic theory of intelligence,* there are three different types of intelligence: analytic, creative, and practical. Intelligence tests typically focus on analytic intelligence, but recent research has suggested ways to assess practical and creative intelligence, too.

Multiple Intelligences

Howard Gardner's approach to intelligence suggests that biology equips us with the capacities for *multiple intelligences* that can function with some independence—specifically, linguistic, logical-mathematical, spatial, musical, body-kinesthetic, intrapersonal, interpersonal, and naturalistic intelligences.

Diversity in Cognitive Abilities

Creativity

Tests of *divergent thinking* are used to measure differences in *creativity*. In contrast, intelligence tests typically require *convergent thinking*. Although creativity and IQ scores are not highly correlated, creative behaviour requires a certain amount of intelligence, along with expertise in a creative field, skills at problem solving and divergent thinking, and motivation to pursue a creative endeavour for its own sake.

Unusual Cognitive Ability

Knowledge about cognitive abilities has been expanded by research on giftedness, mental retardation, and learning disabilities. People with very high IQ scores tend to be successful in life, but they are not necessarily geniuses. People are considered mentally retarded if their IQ score is below about 70 and if their communication and daily living skills are less than expected of people their age. Some cases of retardation have a known cause; in familial retardation the mix of genetic and environmental causes is unknown. Compared with people of normal intelligence, retarded people process information more slowly, know fewer facts, and are deficient at *metacognition*—that is, at knowing and using mental strategies. Mentally retarded people can be taught strategies, but they must also be taught how and when to use those strategies. People who show a significant discrepancy between their measured intelligence and their academic performance may have a learning disability. Learning disabilities can take several forms and must be carefully diagnosed.

11 Motivation and Emotion

When your alarm clock goes off in the morning, do you jump out of bed, eager to face the day, or do you bury your head in the blankets? Once you're at your job or on campus, do you always do your best, or do you work just hard enough to get by? Are you generally happy? Do you sometimes worry, or experience sadness or anxiety? In this chapter, we explore the physical, mental, and social factors that motivate many aspects of human behaviour. We also examine the emotions that accompany our motivations and how they are expressed. Here's how we have organized this material:

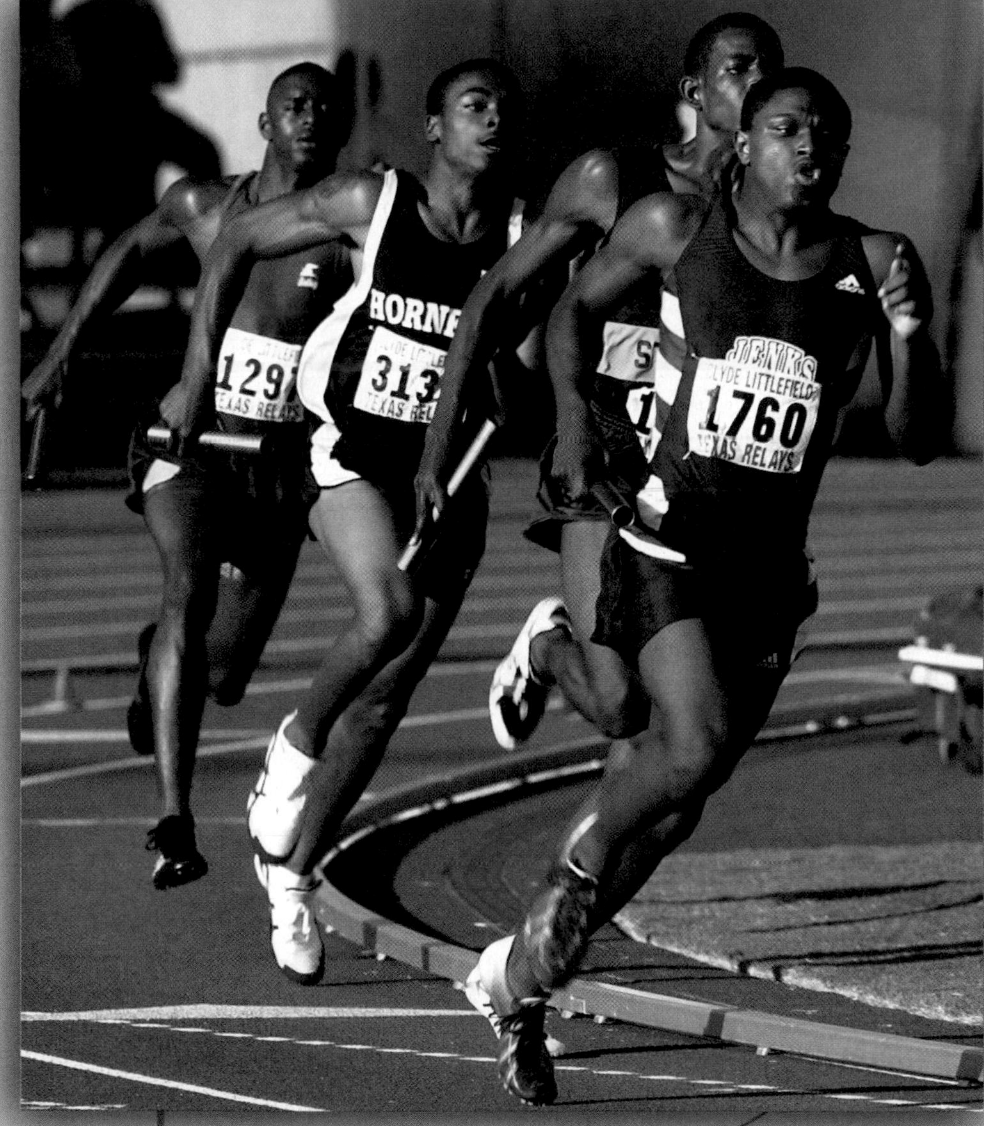

To raise money for cancer research, 21-year-old Terry Fox began his renowned run across Canada; Terry had lost most of his right leg to cancer two years before. His plan in the fall of 1979 was to raise one dollar for each Canadian, roughly $24 million in total. The goal: begin 12 April 1980 on the East Coast and conclude five months later on Vancouver Island. Terry set out from St. John's in April, arrived in Nova Scotia in May, and before June entered Saint John, running 48 km a day. After 73 days of running, Terry arrived in Quebec and took his first day off. He entered Ontario in early July and despite soaring heat (38°C), he continued at 42 km a day. Two hours north of Toronto, the people of Gravenhurst helped Terry celebrate his 22nd birthday on 28 July with over $14,000 in donations. Despite raising over $11M and now at the halfway point (Sudbury, Ontario, by 12 August), Terry was wearing down. On 31 August, just 25 km outside Thunder Bay, Terry learned his cancer had invaded his lungs—he had run almost 5400 km (the equivalent of 129 marathons), but had to cut his run short to be hospitalized. The donations continued. By February 1981, they totalled $24.17M, surpassing Canada's population. Terry Fox died on 28 June 1981. Today, in Canada and around the world, Terry Fox's Marathon of Hope is held every year to raise money for cancer research and treatment.

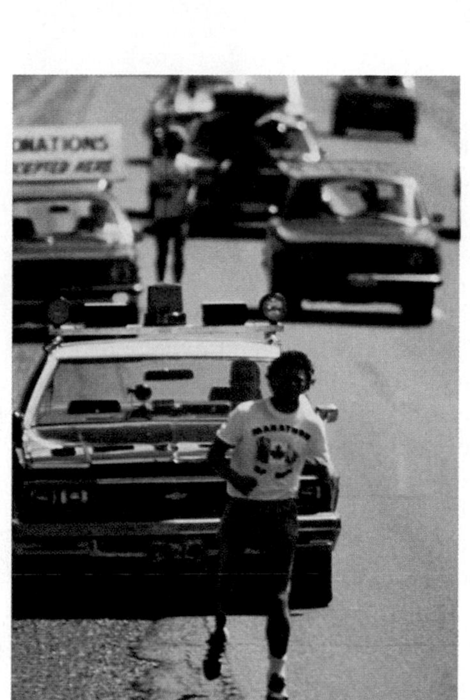

Terry Fox and the Marathon of Hope
What motivates people to jump from an airplane, to paint a giant fresco, or to earn a 4-year bachelor's degree? What motivated Terry Fox to run across thousands of kilometres of Canada's highways, raising money for cancer?

How can an individual choose to suffer through such harsh conditions for such a distant goal? Seeking a university degree is quite similar, reading page after page and chapter after chapter for course after course, all for a degree you hope to receive in four years. It all comes down to a question of **motivation,** or the factors that influence the initiation, direction, intensity, and persistence of behaviour (Reeve, 1996). Like the study of *how* people behave and think, the puzzle of *why* they do so has intrigued psychologists for many decades. Why do we help others or ignore them, eat what we want or stick to a diet, haunt art museums or sleazy bars, attend college or drop out of high school? Why, for that matter, do any of us do whatever it is that we do? In studying motivation, psychologists have noticed that behaviour is based partly on the desire to feel certain emotions, such as the joy that comes with winning a contest or climbing a mountain or becoming a parent. They've found, too, that motivation affects emotion, as when hunger makes you irritable. In short, motivation and emotion are closely intertwined.

Let's consider what psychologists have learned so far about motivation. We'll begin with some general theories of motivation and then discuss three specific motives—hunger, sexual desire, and the need for achievement. Next, we examine the nature of human emotion, as well as some theories of how and why certain emotions are experienced. We conclude with a discussion of how people communicate their emotions to one another.

Concepts and Theories of Motivation

The concept of motivation helps psychologists accomplish what Albert Einstein once called the whole purpose of science: to discover unity in diversity. Suppose that a man works two jobs, refuses party invitations, wears old clothes, drives a beat-up car, eats food others leave behind at lunch, never gives to charity, and keeps his house at 15°C in the dead of winter. In trying to explain why he does what he does, you could propose a separate reason for each behaviour: Perhaps he likes to work hard, is afraid of people, hates shopping, is sentimental about his car, doesn't want food to go to waste, thinks the poor should take care of themselves, and feels better when it's cold. Or you could suggest a **motive,** a reason or purpose that provides a single explanation for this man's diverse and apparently unrelated behaviours. That unifying motive might be his desire to save as much money as possible.

motivation The influences that account for the initiation, direction, intensity, and persistence of behaviour.

motive A reason or purpose for behaviour.

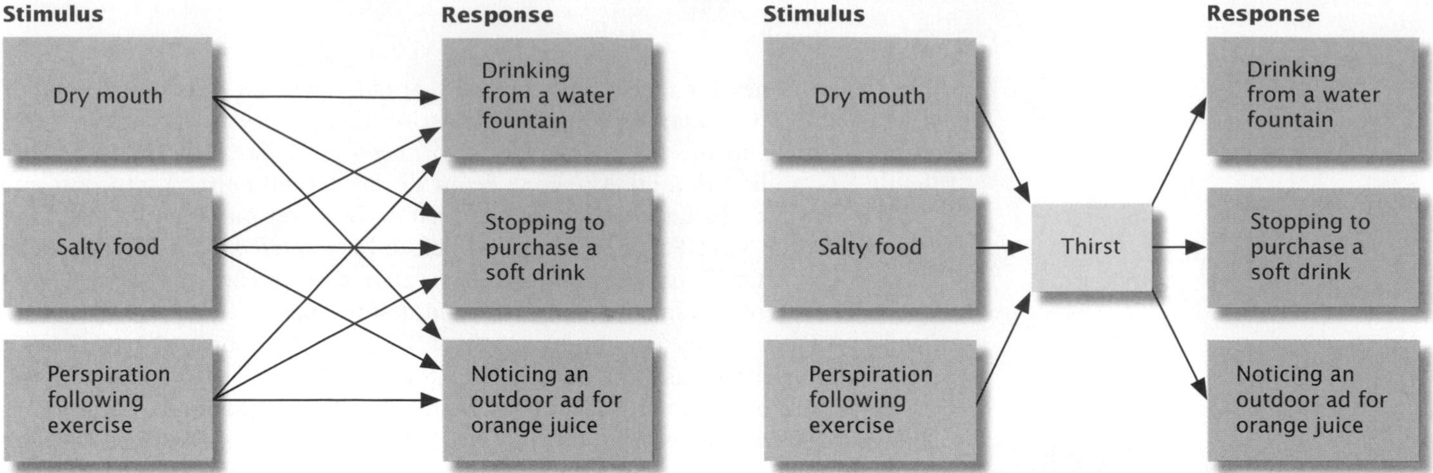

figure 11.1

Motives as Intervening Variables

Motives can explain the links between stimuli and responses that, in some cases, might seem unrelated. In this example, inferring the motive of thirst provides an explanation for why each stimulus triggers the responses shown.

This example illustrates the fact that motivation cannot be observed directly. We have to infer, or presume, that motivation is present from what we *can* observe. So psychologists think of motivation, whether it be hunger or thirst or love or greed, as an *intervening variable*—something that is used to explain the relationships between environmental stimuli and behavioural responses. The three different responses shown in Figure 11.1, for example, can be understood as guided by a single unifying motive: thirst. In order for an intervening variable to be considered a motive, it must have the power to change behaviour in some way. For example, suppose we arrange for some party guests to eat only salted peanuts and other guests to eat only unsalted peanuts. We will probably find that the people who ate salted peanuts drink more than do those who ate the unsalted nuts. In this situation, we can explain the observed differences in drinking in terms of differences in the motive known as thirst.

Figure 11.1 shows that motives can help explain why different stimuli can lead to the same response and why the same stimulus can cause different responses.

Motivation also helps explain why behaviour varies over time. For example, many people cannot bring themselves to lose weight, quit smoking, or exercise until they have a heart attack or symptoms of other serious health problems. At that point, these people may suddenly start eating a healthier diet, give up tobacco, and exercise regularly. In other words, because of changes in motivation, particular stimuli—such as ice cream, cigarettes, and health clubs—trigger different responses at different times.

Motivation and Emotion The link between motivation and emotion is obvious in many everyday situations. For example, Jennifer Heil's motivation to win the Olympic gold medal in Torino's 2006 freestyle mogul competition creates strong emotions. Sometimes, it is emotion that creates motivation, as when anger leads a parent to become aggressive toward a child or when love leads the parent to provide for that child.

Sources of Motivation

The number of possible motives for human behaviour seems endless, but psychologists see them as falling into four somewhat overlapping categories. First, human behaviour is motivated by basic *biological factors,* particularly the need for food, water, sex, and temperature regulation (Tinbergen, 1989). *Emotional factors* are a second source of motivation (Izard, 1993). Panic, fear, anger, love, and hatred can influence behaviour ranging from selfless giving to brutal murder. Third, *cognitive factors* can motivate human behaviour (Weiner, 1993). People behave in certain ways—becoming arrogant or timid, for example—partly because of these cognitive factors, which include their perceptions of the world, their beliefs about what they can or cannot do, and their expectations about how others will respond to them. You are more likely to try out for a talent show, for example, if you have confidence in your ability to sing or dance. Fourth, motivation may stem from *social factors,* that is, from reactions to parents, teachers, siblings, friends, television, and other sociocultural forces. The combined influence of these social factors in motivation has a profound effect on almost all human behaviour (Baumeister & Leary, 1995). For example, have you ever bought a jacket or tried a particular hairstyle not because you liked it but because it was in fashion?

Psychologists have combined these factors in various ways to develop four prominent theories of human motivation. None of these theories can fully explain all aspects of how and why we behave as we do, but each of them—instinct theory, drive reduction theory, arousal theory, and incentive theory—helps tell part of the story.

Instinct Theory and Its Descendants

In the early 1900s, many psychologists favoured **instinct theory** as an explanation for the motivation of both humans and animals. **Instincts** are automatic, involuntary behaviour patterns consistently triggered, or "released," by particular stimuli (Tinbergen, 1989). Such behaviours are often called *fixed-action patterns* because they are unlearned, genetically coded responses to specific "releaser" stimuli. For example, releaser stimuli cause birds to build nests or engage in complex mating dances, and the birds do so perfectly the first time they try.

In 1908, William McDougall listed 18 human instincts, including self-assertion, reproduction, pugnacity (aggressiveness), and gregariousness (sociability). Within a few years, McDougall and others had named more than 10 000 more, prompting one critic to suggest that his colleagues had "an instinct to produce instincts" (Bernard, 1924). The problem was that instincts had become labels that do little more than describe what people do. Saying that someone gambles because of a gambling instinct, golfs because of a golfing instinct, and works because of a work instinct explains nothing about why these behaviours appear in some people and not others and how they develop.

Despite the shortcomings of early instinct theories, psychologists have continued to explore the possibility that at least some aspects of human motivation are innate. Their interest has been stimulated partly by research showing that a number of human behaviours are present at birth. Among these are sucking and other reflexes, as well as certain facial expressions, such as smiling. There is also the fact that people do not have to learn to be hungry or thirsty and—as discussed in the chapters on learning and psychological disorders—that they appear to be biologically prepared to fear snakes and other potentially dangerous stimuli. Psychologists who take the evolutionary approach suggest that all such behaviours have evolved because they were adaptive for promoting individual survival. That is, the individuals who possessed these behavioural predispositions were more likely than others to father or give birth to offspring. We are the descendants of these ancestral human survivors, so to the extent that our ancestors' behavioural predispositions were transmitted genetically, we should show similar predispositions. Even many aspects of human social behaviour, such as helping and aggression, are seen by evolutionary psychologists as motivated by inborn factors—especially by the desire to maximize our genetic contribution to the next generation (Buss, 1999). We may not be aware of this specific desire, they say, but we nevertheless behave in ways that promote it (Geary, 2000). So you are more likely to hear someone say "I can't wait to have children" than to say "I want to pass on my genes."

The evolutionary approach suggests, for example, that the choice of a marriage partner has a biological basis. Heterosexual love and marriage are seen as the result of inborn desires to create and nurture offspring so that parents' genes will survive in their children. According to this view, the mating strategies of males and females differ in ways that reflect traditional differences in how much males and females invest in their offspring. Because women can produce relatively few children in their

instinct theory A view that explains human behaviour as motivated by automatic, involuntary, and unlearned responses.

instincts Innate, automatic dispositions toward responding in a particular way when confronted with a specific stimulus.

Fixed-Action Patterns The male three-spined stickleback fish attacks aggressively when it sees the red underbelly of another male. This automatic response is called a *fixed-action pattern* because it can be triggered by almost any red stimulus. These fish have been known to fly into an aggressive frenzy in response to a wooden fish model sporting a red spot, or even to a red mail truck driving past a window near their tank!

lifetimes, they are more psychologically invested than men are in the survival and development of those children (Townsend, Kline, & Wasserman, 1995). This greater investment motivates women to choose mates cautiously, seeking males who are not only genetically fit but also able to provide the protection and resources necessary to ensure children's survival.

The search for genetic fitness, say evolutionary psychologists, helps account for the fact that women tend to prefer men who display athleticism and facial symmetry (Barber, 1995; Gangestad & Thornhill, 1997). And the desire to find a "good provider," say these psychologists, helps explain why women are drawn to men who have demonstrated an ability to amass resources, as signified by maturity, ambition, and earning power. It takes some time to assess these resource-related characteristics (he drives a nice car, but can he afford it?), which is why, according to the evolutionary view, women are more likely than men to prefer a period of courtship prior to mating. Men tend to want to begin a sexual relationship sooner than women (Buss & Schmitt, 1993) because, compared with their female partners, they have little to lose from doing so. On the contrary, their eagerness to engage in sex early in a relationship is seen as reflecting their evolutionary ancestors' tendency toward casual sex as a means of maximizing their genetic contribution to the next generation. In fact, evolutionary psychologists see the desire to produce as many children as possible as motivating males' preference to mate with women whose reproductive capacity and genetic fitness are signified by youth, attractiveness, and good health (Symons, 1995).

These controversial ideas have received some support. For instance, according to a survey of more than 10 000 men and women in 33 countries on six continents and five isolated islands, males generally preferred youth and good health in prospective female mates, and females generally preferred males who were mature and wealthy (Kenrick, 1994). One example of this sex difference is illustrated in Figure 11.2, which shows the age preferences of men and women who advertised for dates in the personal sections of newspapers in the United States. In general, men were interested in women younger than themselves, but women were interested in older men (Kenrick et al., 1995).

Critics argue that such preferences could stem from cultural traditions, not genetic programming. Among the Zulu of South Africa, where women are expected to build houses, carry water, and perform other physically demanding tasks, men tend to value maturity and ambition in a mate more than women do (Buss, 1989). The fact that women have been systematically denied economic and political power in many cultures may also account for their tendency to rely on the security and economic power provided by men (Silverstein, 1996). Evolutionary theorists acknowledge the role of cultural forces and traditions in shaping behaviour, but they ask whether evolutionary factors might have contributed to the appearance of these forces and traditions.

figure 11.2

Age Preferences in Personal Advertisements

An analysis of 486 personal newspaper ads showed a sex difference in age preferences. As men got older, their preferences for younger women increased, whereas women, regardless of age, preferred men who were about their own age or older. Wood and Eagly (2000; Eagly & Wood, 1999) analyzed the mate preferences data from men and women sampled from 37 different cultures around the globe. They found that men's preferences for a mate centred around not merely youth, but her ability to provide a good clean home. However, women's preferences for a mate centred around not merely advanced age, but also relatively strong earning capacity. In other words, beyond merely age, we see across cultures the judgment of attractiveness in a mate based on breadwinners (males) and homemakers (females).

Source: Kenrick et al. (1995, Figure 1).

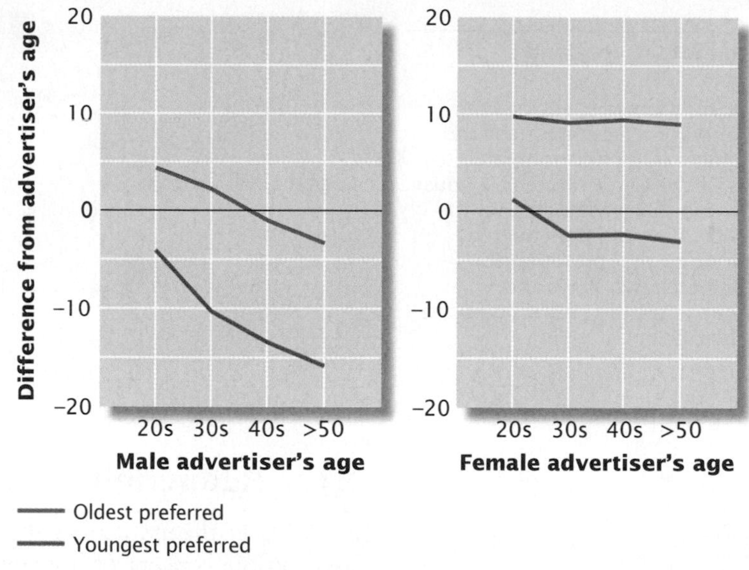

By emphasizing genetic dispositions and innate tendencies to promote the survival of our genes, modern versions of instinct theory seek to identify the ultimate, long-term reasons behind much human behaviour. The theories of motivation discussed next highlight influences that serve as more immediate causes of behaviour (Alcock, 2001).

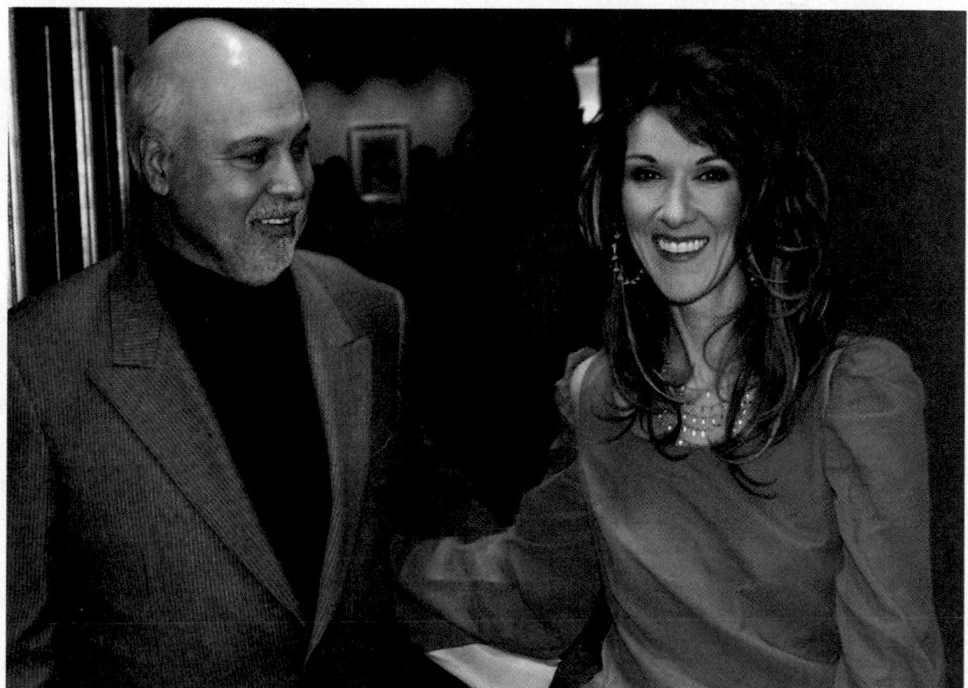

Evolution at Work? The marriage of Celine Dion and Rene Angelil, her manager who is several years older than her, illustrates the worldwide tendency for older men to prefer younger women, and vice versa. This tendency has been interpreted as evidence supporting an evolutionary explanation of mate selection, but skeptics see social and economic forces at work in establishing these preference patterns.

figure 11.3

Drive Reduction Theory and Homeostasis

Homeostatic mechanisms, such as the regulation of body temperature or food and water intake, are often compared to thermostats. If the temperature in a house drops below the thermostat setting, the furnace comes on and brings the temperature up to that preset level, achieving homeostasis. When the temperature reaches the preset point, the furnace shuts off.

Drive Reduction Theory

Like instinct theory, drive reduction theory emphasizes biological factors, but it is based on the concept of homeostasis. **Homeostasis** (pronounced "ho-me-oh-STAY-sis") is the tendency to keep physiological systems at a steady level, or *equilibrium,* by constantly making adjustments in response to change. We describe a version of this concept in the chapter on biological aspects of psychology, in relation to feedback loops that keep hormones at desirable levels.

According to **drive reduction theory,** an imbalance in homeostasis creates a **need**—a biological requirement for well-being. The brain responds to such needs by creating a psychological state called a **drive**—a feeling of arousal that prompts an organism to take action, restore the balance, and, as a result, reduce the drive (Hull, 1943). For example, if you have had no water for some time, the chemical balance of your body fluids is disturbed, creating a biological need for water. One consequence of this need is a drive—thirst—that motivates you to find and drink water. After you drink, the need for water is met, so the drive to drink is reduced. In other words, drives push people to satisfy needs, thereby reducing the drives and the arousal they create (see Figure 11.3).

Drive reduction theory recognizes the influence of learning on motivation by distinguishing between primary and secondary drives. **Primary drives** stem from biological needs, such as the need for food or water. (In the chapter on learning, we note that food, water, and other things that satisfy primary drives are called *primary reinforcers.*) People do not have to learn either these basic biological needs or the primary drives to satisfy them (Hull, 1951). However, we do learn other drives, called **secondary drives.** Once we learn them, secondary drives motivate us to act as if we have an unmet basic need. For example, as people learn to associate money with the ability to satisfy primary drives for food, shelter, and so on, having money may become a secondary drive. Having too little money then motivates many behaviours—from hard work to borrowing to theft—aimed at getting more of it.

Optimal Arousal and Personality
People whose optimal arousal is high are likely to smoke, drink alcohol, engage in frequent sexual activity, listen to loud music, eat spicy foods, and do things that are novel and risky (Farley, 1986; Zuckerman, 1979). Those with lower optimal arousal tend to take fewer risks and behave in ways that are less stimulating. Most of the differences in optimal arousal have a strong biological basis and, as discussed in the chapter on personality, may help shape other characteristics, such as whether we tend to be introverted or extraverted.

Arousal Theory

Drive reduction theory can account for a wide range of motivated behaviours. But humans and animals often go to great lengths to do things that don't appear to reduce any drive. Consider curiosity. Animals explore and manipulate their surroundings, even though these activities do not lead to drive reduction. They will also exert considerable effort simply to enter a new environment, especially if it is complex and full of novel objects (Bolles, 1975; Loewenstein, 1994). People are no less curious. Most of us can't resist checking out anything new or unusual. We go to the new mall, read the newspaper, surf the Internet, and travel the world just to see what there is to see. People also go out of their way to ride roller coasters, skydive, drive racecars, and do countless other things that, like curiosity-motivated behaviours, do

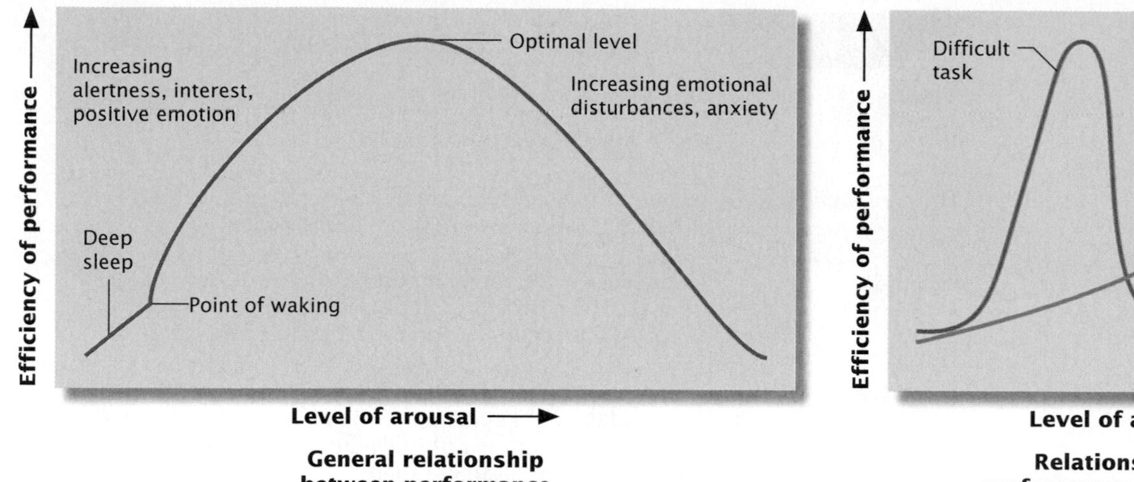

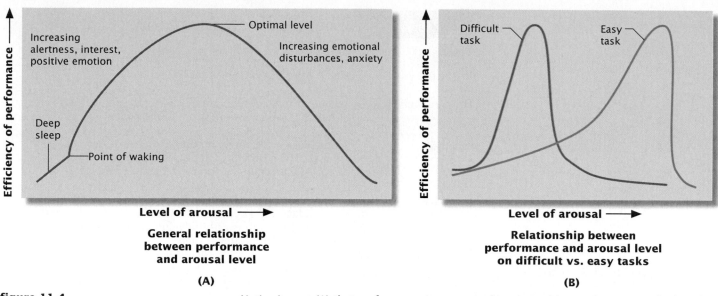

figure 11.4

The Arousal-Performance Relationship

Notice in part (A) that performance is poorest when arousal is very low or very high and best when arousal is at a moderate level. When you are either nearly asleep or overly excited, for example, it may be difficult to think clearly or to be physically coordinated. In general, optimal performance comes at a lower level of arousal on difficult or complex tasks and at a higher level of arousal on easy tasks, as shown in part (B). Even a relatively small amount of over-arousal can cause students to perform far below their potential on difficult tests (Sarason, 1984). Because animal research early in this century by Robert Yerkes and his colleagues provided supportive evidence, this arousal-performance relationship is sometimes referred to as the *Yerkes-Dodson law,* even though Yerkes never actually discussed performance as a function of arousal (Teigen, 1994).

LINKAGES (a link to Cognitive Abilities)

not reduce any known drive (Zuckerman, 1996). In fact, these behaviours *increase* people's levels of activation, or arousal. The realization that people sometimes try to decrease arousal and sometimes try to increase it has led some psychologists to argue that motivation is tied to the *regulation of arousal.*

Most of these theorists think of **arousal** as a general level of activation reflected in the state of several physiological systems (Plutchik & Conte, 1997). Your level of arousal can be measured by electrical activity in your brain, by heart rate, or by muscle tension. Normally, arousal is lowest during deep sleep and highest during panic or great excitement. Many factors increase arousal, including hunger, thirst, intense stimuli, unexpected events, and stimulant drugs such as amphetamines. It is interesting to note that people who tend to actively seek novelty and excitement also tend to be at increased risk for abusing stimulants. This phenomenon may be related to individual differences in the brain's dopamine system, which is activated both by novelty and by most drugs of abuse (Bardo, Donohew, & Harrington, 1996; Berns et al., 2001). Brain imaging studies have revealed that the dopamine system is activated even when a person gambles or plays a video game (Breiter et al., 2001; Koepp et al., 1998).

People perform best, and may feel best, when arousal is moderate (Teigen, 1994). Figure 11.4 illustrates the general relationship between arousal and performance. Overarousal can harm performance of all kinds, from intellectual tasks to athletic competition (Penner & Craiger, 1992; Smith et al., 2000; Wright et al., 1995).

Arousal theories of motivation suggest that people are motivated to behave in ways that keep them at their own *optimal* level of arousal (Hebb, 1955). This optimal level is higher for some people than for others (Zuckerman, 1984). Generally, however, people try to increase arousal when it is too low and decrease it when it is too high. They seek excitement when bored and relaxation when overaroused. After a day of dull classes and intense studying, for example, you

homeostasis The tendency for organisms to keep their physiological systems at a stable, steady level by constantly adjusting themselves in response to change.

drive reduction theory A theory of motivation stating that motivation arises from imbalances in homeostasis.

need A biological requirement for well-being that is created by an imbalance in homeostasis.

drive A psychological state of arousal created by an imbalance in homeostasis that prompts an organism to take action to restore the balance and reduce the drive.

primary drives Drives that arise from basic biological needs.

secondary drives Stimuli that acquire the motivational properties of primary drives through classical conditioning or other learning mechanisms.

arousal A general level of activation that is reflected in several physiological systems.

arousal theories Theories of motivation stating that people are motivated to behave in ways that maintain what is, for them, an optimal level of arousal.

in review Theories of Motivation

Theory	Main Points
Instinct	Innate biological instincts guide behaviour.
Drive reduction	Behaviour is guided by biological needs and learned ways of reducing drives arising from those needs.
Arousal	People seek to maintain an optimal level of physiological arousal, which differs from person to person. Maximum performance occurs at optimal arousal levels.
Incentive	Behaviour is guided by the lure of positive incentives and the avoidance of negative incentives. Cognitive factors influence expectations of the value of various rewards and the likelihood of attaining them.

may want to see an exciting movie. But if your day was spent playing baseball, debating a political issue, and helping a friend move, an evening of quiet relaxation may seem ideal.

Incentive Theory

Instinct, drive reduction, and arousal theories of motivation all focus on internal processes that prompt people to behave in certain ways. By contrast, **incentive theory** emphasizes the role of environmental stimuli that can motivate behaviour by pulling us toward them or pushing us away from them. From this point of view, people behave in a certain way in order to get positive incentives and avoid negative incentives. So differences in behaviour from one person to another, or in the same person from one situation to another, can be traced to the incentives available and the value a person places on them at the time. If you expect a behaviour (such as buying a lottery ticket) to lead to a valued outcome (winning lots of money), you will want to engage in that behaviour. The value of an incentive is influenced by biological, as well as cognitive, factors. For example, food is a more motivating incentive when you are hungry than when you are full (Balleine & Dickinson, 1994).

Incentive theorists distinguish between two incentive-related systems: wanting and liking. *Wanting* is the process of being attracted to stimuli, whereas *liking* is the immediate evaluation of how pleasurable a stimulus is (Berridge, 1999). Studies with animals have shown that these two systems involve activity in separate parts of the brain. They have also revealed that the wanting system guides behaviour to a greater extent than does the liking system and that the operation of the wanting system varies according to whether an individual has been deprived or not (Nader, Bechara, & Van der Kooy, 1997). So although you might like apple pie, your motivation to eat some would be affected by different brain regions, depending on whether the pie is served as an appetizer (when you are hungry) or as a dessert (when you are full).

The theoretical approaches we have outlined (see "In Review: Theories of Motivation") complement one another. Each emphasizes different sources of motivation, and each has helped to guide research into motivated behaviours, including eating, sex, and achievement-related activities, which are the topics of the next three sections.

incentive theory A theory of motivation stating that behaviour is directed toward attaining desirable stimuli and avoiding unwanted stimuli.

Hunger and Eating

Hunger is deceptively simple; you get hungry when you don't eat. Much as a car needs gas, you need fuel from food. Is there a bodily mechanism that, like a car's gas gauge, signals the need for fuel? What causes hunger? What determines which foods you eat, and how do you know when to stop? The answers to these questions involve interactions between the brain and the rest of the body, but they also involve learning, social, and environmental factors (Hill & Peters, 1998).

Biological Signals for Hunger and Satiety

A variety of mechanisms underlie **hunger,** the general state of wanting to eat, and **satiety** (pronounced "se-TY-a-tee"), the general state of no longer wanting to eat. In order to maintain body weight, we must have ways to regulate food intake over the short term (a question of how often we eat and when we stop eating a given meal) and to regulate the body's stored energy reserves (fat) over the long term.

Signals from the Stomach The stomach would seem to be a logical source of signals for hunger and satiety. After all, people say they feel "hunger pangs" from an "empty" stomach, and they complain of a "full stomach" after overeating. True, the stomach does contract during hunger pangs, and increased pressure within the stomach can reduce appetite (Cannon & Washburn, 1912; Houpt, 1994). But people with cancer who have had their stomachs removed still get hungry when they don't eat, and they still eat normal amounts of food (Janowitz, 1967). So stomach cues affect eating, but they do not play a major role in the normal control of eating. These cues appear to operate mainly when you are very hungry or very full.

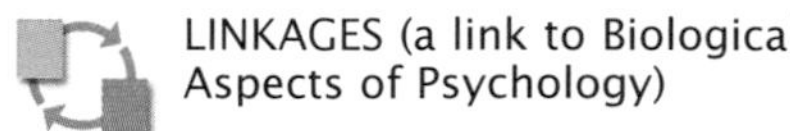

Signals from the Blood The most important signals about the body's fuel level and nutrient needs are sent to the brain from the blood. The brain's ability to "read" blood-borne signals about the body's nutritional needs was shown years ago when researchers deprived rats of food and then injected them with blood from rats that had just eaten. When offered food, the injected rats ate little or nothing (Davis et al., 1969); something in the injected blood of the well-fed animals apparently signaled the hungry rats' brains that there was no need to eat. What sent that satiety signal? More recent research has shown that the brain constantly monitors both the level of food *nutrients* absorbed into the bloodstream from the stomach and the level of *hormones* released into the blood in response to those nutrients and from stored fat (Korner & Leibel, 2003).

The nutrients that the brain monitors include *glucose,* the main form of sugar used by body cells. Decades ago, researchers noticed that when the level of blood glucose drops, eating increases sharply (e.g., Mogenson, 1976). More recent work has shown that glucose acts indirectly by affecting certain chemical messengers. For example, when glucose levels rise, the pancreas releases *insulin,* a hormone that most body cells need in order to use the glucose they receive. Insulin itself may also provide a satiety signal by acting directly on brain cells (Brüning et al., 2000; Schwartz et al., 2000).

The long-term regulation of fat stores involves a hormone called *leptin* (from the Greek word *leptos,* meaning "thin"). The process works like this: Cells that store fat have genes that produce leptin in response to increases in fat supplies. The leptin is released into the bloodstream, and when it reaches special receptors for it in the hypothalamus, it provides information to the brain about the increasing fat supplies (Farooqi et al., 2001; Margetic et al., 2002). When leptin levels are high, hunger decreases, helping to reduce food intake. When leptin levels are low, hunger increases, as illustrated in animals that are obese because of defects in leptin-producing genes (Bouret, Draper, & Simerly, 2004; Zhang et al., 1994). Researchers

hunger The general state of wanting to eat.

satiety The condition of no longer wanting to eat.

have found that injections of leptin cause these animals to lose weight and body fat rapidly, with no effect on muscle or other body tissue (Forbes et al., 2001). Leptin injections can produce the same effects in normal animals, too (Fox & Olster, 2000). At first, these results raised hope that leptin might be a "magic bullet" for treating *obesity,* or severe overweight, in humans, but this is not the case. It can help those rare individuals who are obese because their cells make no leptin (Farooqi et al., 1999), but leptin injections are far less effective for people whose obesity results from excessive intake and/or a high-fat diet (Gura, 1999; Heymsfield et al., 1999). In these far more common cases of obesity, the brain appears to become less sensitive to leptin's signals (Ahima & Flier, 2000; Lin et al., 2000; Lustig et al., 2004).

Hunger and the Brain

Many parts of the brain contribute to the control of hunger and eating, but research has focused on several regions of the hypothalamus that may play primary roles in detecting and reacting to the blood's signals about the need to eat (see Figure 11.5). Activity in a part of the network that passes through the *ventromedial nucleus* of the hypothalamus (much like a brake pedal) tells an animal that there is no need to eat. So if a rat's ventromedial nucleus is electrically or chemically stimulated, the animal will stop eating (Kent et al., 1994). However, if the ventromedial nucleus is destroyed, the animal will eat continuously, increasing its weight up to threefold.

In contrast, the *lateral hypothalamus* contains networks that stimulate eating (much like a gas pedal). When the lateral hypothalamus is electrically or chemically stimulated, rats eat huge quantities, even if they just had a large meal (Stanley et al., 1993). When the lateral hypothalamus is destroyed, however, rats stop eating almost entirely.

Years ago, these findings led some researchers to conclude that activity in the ventromedial and lateral areas of the hypothalamus combine to maintain some

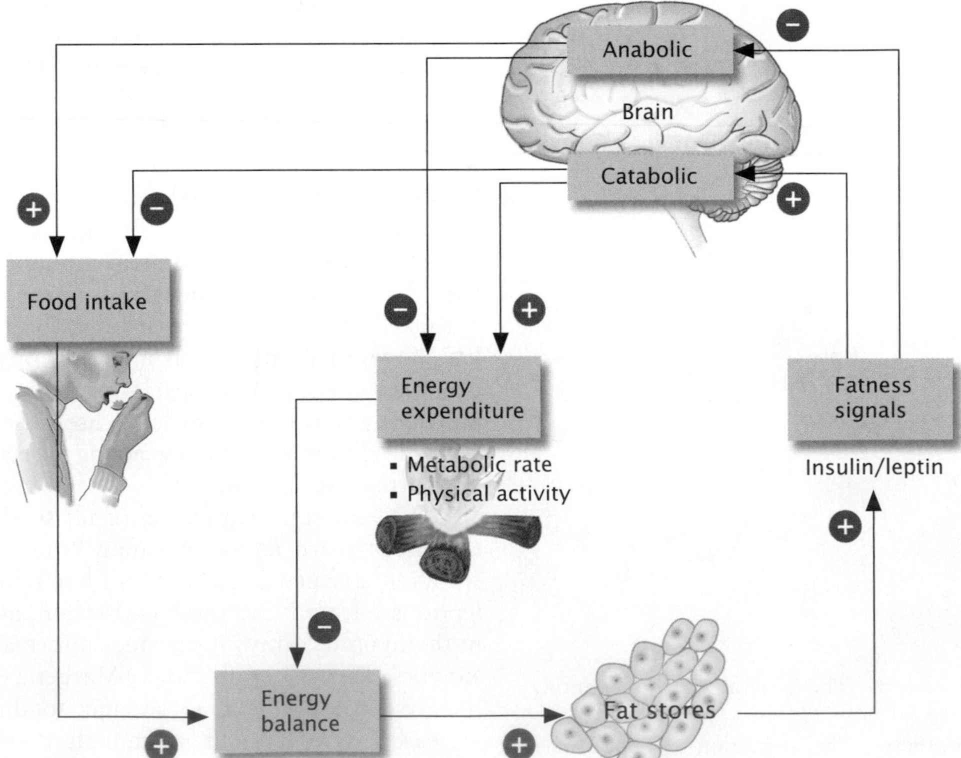

figure 11.5

The Hypothalamus and Hunger

Regions of the hypothalamus generate signals that either increase hunger and reduce energy expenditure, called *anabolic effects,* or reduce hunger and increase energy expenditure, called *catabolic effects.*

Source: Adapted from Schwartz et al. (2000).

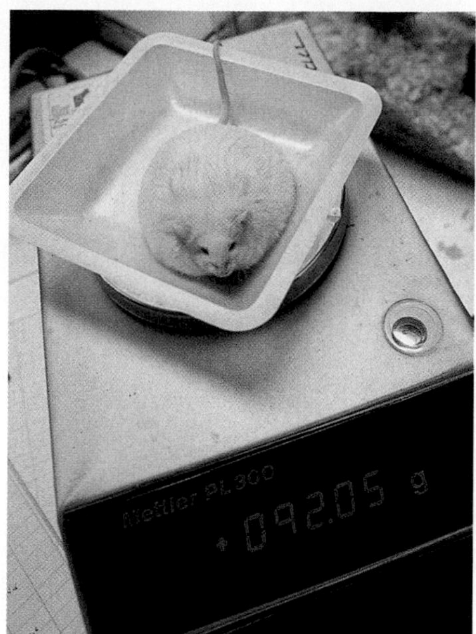

One Fat Mouse After surgical destruction of its ventromedial nucleus, this mouse ate enough to triple its body weight. Such animals become picky eaters, choosing only foods that taste good and ignoring all others.

homeostatic level, or *set point,* based on food intake, body weight, or other eating-related signals (Powley & Keesey, 1970). According to this application of drive reduction theory, normal animals eat until their set point is reached, then stop eating until desirable intake falls below the set point (Cabanac & Morrissette, 1992). In other words, several brain regions and many chemicals help to regulate hunger and eating. These regulatory processes are not set in stone, however. They can easily be overridden by other, nonbiological factors.

Flavour, Cultural Learning, and Food Selection

One factor that can override a set point is the *flavour* of food—the combination of its taste and smell (Carlson, 2001). In one experiment, some animals were offered just a single type of food, whereas others were offered foods of several different flavours. The group getting the varied menu ate nearly four times more than the one-food group. As each new food appeared, the animals began to eat voraciously, regardless of how much they had already eaten (Peck, 1978). Humans behave in similar ways. All things being equal, people eat more food during a multicourse meal than when only one food is served (Raynor & Epstein, 2001). Apparently, the flavour of any particular food becomes less enjoyable as more of it is eaten (Swithers & Hall, 1994). In one study, for example, people rated how much they liked four kinds of food. Then they ate one of the foods and rated all four again. The food they had just eaten now got a lower rating, whereas liking increased for all the rest (Johnson & Vickers, 1993).

Another factor that can override blood-borne signals about satiety is *appetite,* the motivation to seek food's pleasures. For example, the appearance and aroma of certain foods create conditioned physiological responses—such as secretion of saliva, gastric juices, and insulin—in anticipation of eating those foods. (The process is based on the principles of classical conditioning described in the chapter on learning.) These responses then increase appetite. So merely seeing a pizza on television can prompt you to order one—even if you hadn't been feeling hungry—and if you see a delicious-looking cookie, you do not have to be hungry to start eating it. In other words, people eat not only to satisfy nutritional needs but also to experience enjoyment.

A different mechanism appears to be responsible for *specific hungers,* or desires for particular foods at particular times. These hungers appear to reflect the biological need for the nutrients contained in certain foods. In one study, rats were allowed to eat from a bowl of food that contained carbohydrates but no protein and also from a bowl of food that contained protein but no carbohydrates. These animals came to eat from both bowls in amounts that gave them a proper balance of carbohydrates and protein (Miller & Teates, 1985). In another study, rats were given three bowls of tasty, protein-free food and one bowl of food that tasted bad but was rich in protein. Again, the rats learned to eat enough of the bad-tasting food to get a proper supply of dietary protein (Galef & Wright, 1995). These results are remarkable in part because food nutrients such as carbohydrates, fats, and proteins have no taste or odour.

The role of learning in food selection is also seen in the social rules and cultural traditions that influence eating. Munching popcorn at movies and hot dogs at baseball games are examples from North American culture of how certain social situations can stimulate appetite for particular food items. Similarly, how much you eat may depend on what others do. Courtesy or custom might lead you to eat foods you might otherwise have avoided. The mere presence of other people, even strangers, tends to increase our food consumption (Clendenen, Herman, & Polivy, 1995; Redd & de Castro, 1992). But we may also eat less than we otherwise would if others stop eating, especially if we want to impress them with our self-control (Herman, Roth, & Polivy, 2003).

Eating and food selection are central to the way people function within their cultures. Celebrations, holidays, vacations, and even daily family interactions often revolve around food and what has been called a *food culture* (Rozin, 1996). As any world traveller knows, there are wide cultural and subcultural variations in food selection. For example, chewing coca leaves is popular in the Bolivian highlands but illegal in the United States (Burchard, 1992). In China, people in urban areas eat a high-cholesterol diet rich in animal meat, whereas those in rural areas eat so little meat as to be cholesterol deficient (Tian et al., 1995). And the insects known as *palm weevils,* a popular food for people in Papua New Guinea (Paoletti, 1995), are regarded by many Westerners as disgusting (Springer & Belk, 1994).

Eating Disorders

Problems in the processes regulating hunger and eating may cause an *eating disorder.* The most common and dangerous examples are obesity, anorexia nervosa, and bulimia nervosa.

Obesity Both Health Canada and the World Health Organization define **obesity** as a condition in which a person's body-mass index, or BMI, is greater than 30. People whose BMI is 25 to 29.9 are considered to be overweight. (BMI is determined by dividing a person's weight in kilograms by the square of the person's height in metres. So someone who is 157.5 cm (5 feet 2 inches) tall and weighs 74.4 k (164 pounds) would be classified as obese, as would someone 177.8 cm (5 feet 10 inches) tall who weighs 93.9 (207 pounds). BMI calculators appear on Web sites such as www.hc-sc.gc.ca/fn-an/index_e.html. (Search for BMI in index.)

Two recent surveys of Canadian's health have followed respondents' over a longer period in an effort to track trends in weight changes to the population. First, the 2004 *Canadian Community Health Survey* (Statistics Canada, 2005) examined the nutritional habits of over 35 000 respondents between January and December of 2004, including both height and weight. This same survey had been conducted 25 years earlier (1978–1979), and the proportion of overweight and obese Canadians had grown dramatically. In the earlier study 3 percent of children (2–17 years old) were obese; that number is now 8 percent (2004, or an estimated half a million kids). But a more dramatic increase occurred among adults—14 percent were obese in 1978–1979 compared with 23 percent (5.5 million adults) in 2004. Sadly, the rates tripled for adolescent Canadians over those 25 years—from 3 percent to 9 percent (12–17 years). Although we should always be concerned when overweight and obesity trends are on the rise, it's more disturbing in youth because these trends typically persist into adulthood. Despite these alarming numbers, the rate remains lower than for our neighbours to the south—arguably the fattest nation in the world—whereas 23 percent of Canadian adults were obese in 2004, the American rate was 31 percent.

The second survey of its kind was based on longitudinal data taken from the *National Population Health Survey* (Statistics Canada, 2005) that followed participants every two years for eight years. At the start, participants ranged from 20 to 56 years of age and were 28 to 64 by the end of the study. Like the previous survey, their results showed that our weight gain appears to be a growing trend. If participants were overweight in 1994–1995, one in four were obese by 2002–2003 (that's 1.1 million additional adult cases of Canadian obesity), but only one in ten were of normal weight. In other words, it's harder to take off the weight rather than pack more on—an ounce of prevention really is worth a pound of cure. When we look closer at the numbers, we see that 38 percent of men and 28 percent of women had become overweight during those eight years, but women were more likely to become obese (28 percent) compared with men (20 percent). That translates into 600,000 new cases of male obesity and 500 000 new cases of female obesity in just eight years.

What predicted whether participants became overweight or obese in eight years? Age was a factor—obesity was more likely for men in their 20s and 30s than in their 50s. Smoking was a factor as well—overweight smokers were about

obesity A condition in which a person is severely overweight, as measured by a body-mass index greater than 30.

Bon Appétit! The definition of "delicacy" differs from culture to culture. At this elegant restaurant in Mexico, diners pay to feast on baby alligators, insects, and other dishes that some people from other cultures would not eat even if the restaurant paid *them*. To appreciate your own food culture, make a list of foods that are traditionally valued by your family or cultural group but that people from other groups do not, or might even be unwilling, to eat.

50 percent more likely to be obese in 2002–2003 than those who had never smoked. Family income was another factor—both men and women were less likely to become obese if they lived in a high-income household. And finally, physical activity was a factor—restricted daily activities typically led to higher risk of obesity.

Beyond Canadian borders, obesity appears to be on the rise among adults and children in regions as diverse as Europe, Asia, South America, Africa, and especially in the United States (e.g., Hedley et al., 2004; Manson et al., 2004; McCarthy, Ellis, & Cole, 2003; Sorof et al., 2004; Sturm, 2003; World Health Organization, 2002a). From 1994 to 2002, the percentage of overweight adults in the United States increased from 55.9 to 65.7 percent, and the percentage of obese adults rose from 22.9 to 30.6 percent (Flegal et al., 2002; Hedley et al., 2004; Mokdad et al., 2003). The problem has become so common that even the funeral industry has had to adjust by offering larger than normal coffins and ordering wider hearses (St. John, 2003). Obesity is associated with disability and health problems such as diabetes, high blood pressure, pancreatic cancer, and increased risk of heart attack (Field et al., 2001; Lakdawalla, Bhattacharya, & Goldman, 2004; Michaud et al., 2001; Sturm & Wells, 2001). The precise reasons for this obesity epidemic are unknown, but possible causes include increased portion sizes at fast-food outlets, greater prevalence of high-fat foods, and decreases in physical activity associated with both work and recreation (e.g., Slentz et al., 2004). These are important factors, because the body maintains a given weight through a combination of food intake and energy output (Keesey & Powley, 1986). Obese people get more energy from food than their body *metabolizes,* or "burns up"; the excess energy, measured in *calories,* is stored as fat. Metabolism declines during sleep and rises with physical activity. Because women tend to have a lower metabolic rate than men, even when equally active, they tend to gain weight more easily than do men with similar diets (Ferraro et al., 1992). Most obese people have normal resting metabolic rates, but they tend to eat above-average amounts of high-calorie, tasty foods and below-average amounts of less tasty foods (Kauffman, Herman, & Polivy, 1995; Peck, 1978).

But the picture is far from complete because not everyone who is inactive and eats a high-fat diet becomes obese, and some obese people are as active as lean people; other factors must be involved (Blundell & Cooling, 2000). Some people probably have a genetic predisposition toward obesity (Branson et al., 2003; Farooqi & O'Rahilly, 2004). For example, although most obese people have the genes to make leptin, they may not be sensitive to its weight-suppressing effects—perhaps because of a genetic defect in leptin receptors in the hypothalamus. Recent brain-imaging studies also suggest that obese people's brains may be slower to "read" satiety signals coming from their blood, thus causing them to continue eating when leaner people would have stopped (Liu et al., 2000). These factors, along with the presence of one or more recently discovered viruses in the body (Dhurandhar et al., 2000), may help explain obese people's tendency to eat more, to accumulate fat, and to feel more hunger than lean people.

Psychological explanations for obesity focus on factors such as learning from examples set by parents who overeat (Hood et al., 2000) and maladaptive reactions to stress. Many people do tend to eat more when under stress, a reaction that may be especially extreme among those who become obese (Dallman et al., 2003; Friedman & Brownell, 1995).

Losing weight and keeping it off are extremely difficult for many people, especially those who are obese (Lewis et al., 2000; McTigue et al., 2003). Part of the problem may be due to metabolic changes that accompany weight loss. When food intake is reduced, the process of homeostasis leads to a drop in metabolic rate, which saves energy and curbs weight loss (Leibel, Rosenbaum, & Hirsch, 1995). This response makes evolutionary sense. Conservation of energy during famine, for example, is adaptive for survival. But when obese people try to lose weight, their

Thin Is In In Western cultures today, thinness is a much-sought-after ideal, especially among young women who are dissatisfied with their appearance. That ideal is seen in fashion models whose body mass index has decreased from the "normal" range of 20 to 25 in the 1920s to an "undernourished" 18.5 more recently (Rubinstein & Caballero, 2000; Voracek & Fisher, 2002).

metabolic rate drops below normal. As a result, they can gain weight even while eating amounts that would maintain constant weight in other people.

To achieve the kind of gradual weight loss that is most likely to last, obese people are advised to increase exercise, because it burns calories without slowing metabolism (Tremblay & Bueman, 1995). In fact, a regular regimen of aerobic exercise and weight training *raises* the metabolic rate (Binzen, Swan, & Manore, 2001; McCarty, 1995). The most effective weight-loss programs include components designed to reduce food intake, change eating habits and attitudes toward food, and increase energy expenditure through exercise (Bray & Tartaglia, 2000; National Task Force on the Prevention and Treatment of Obesity, 2000; Stice & Shaw, 2004; Wadden et al., 2001).

We've been talking principally about disordered overeating. But beyond obesity, let's now review the statistics on other types of disordered eating and the eating disorders that often result. In Canada, 80 percent of females have issues with their body and food, and 37 percent of 11-year-old, 42 percent of 13-year-old, and 48 percent of 15-year-old Canadian females say they need to lose weight (Health and Welfare Canada, 1992). In one other study of 2279 females aged 10 to 14 years living in southern Ontario (McVey, Tween, & Blackmore, 2004), 29 percent were trying to lose weight and 11 percent were beyond the clinical threshold for disordered eating (McVey et al., 2004). Finally, a study of almost 2500 Ontario female students aged 12 to 18 years (Jones et al., 2001) showed warning signs for the development of eating disorders; that is, whereas dieting was the most prevalent means for weight loss, unhealthy behaviours such as self-induced vomiting were selected to achieve the same aim (Jones et al., 2001).

Anorexia Nervosa **Anorexia nervosa** is an eating disorder characterized by some combination of self-starvation, self-induced vomiting, and laxative use that results in weight loss to below 85 percent of normal (Kaye et al., 2000). About 95 percent of people who suffer from anorexia are young females. Anorexic individuals often feel hungry, and many are obsessed with food and its preparation, yet they refuse to eat. Anorexic self-starvation causes serious, often irreversible physical damage, including reduction in bone density that enhances the risk of fractures (Grinspoon et al., 2000). Between 4 and 30 percent of anorexics die of starvation, biochemical imbalances, or suicide. Their risk of death is 12 times higher than that of other young women (Herzog et al., 2000; Sullivan, 1995). Anorexia tends to emerge in adolescence, when concern over appearance becomes intense. The incidence of anorexia appears to be on the increase; it now affects between 0.5 percent to 4.0 percent of young women in Canada and is a growing problem in many other industrialized nations as well (American Psychiatric Association Work Group on Eating Disorders, 2000; Health Canada, 2006; Rome et al., 2003).

The causes of anorexia are not yet clear, but they probably involve a combination of factors, including genetic predispositions, biochemical imbalances, social influences, and psychological characteristics (Bulik et al., 2000; Jacobi et al., 2004; Kaye et al., 2000; Keel & Klump, 2003). Psychological factors that may contribute to the problem include a self-punishing, perfectionistic personality and a culturally reinforced obsession with thinness and attractiveness (Bulik et al., 2003; Ricciardelli & McCabe, 2004; Thompson & Stice, 2001). Anorexics appear to develop a fear of being fat, which they take to dangerous extremes (de Castro & Goldstein, 1995). Many anorexics continue to view themselves as fat or misshapen even as they are wasting away (Feingold & Mazzella, 1998). Drugs, hospitalization, and psychotherapy are all used to treat anorexia. In many cases, treatment brings recovery and maintenance of normal weight (National Institutes of Health, 2001; Pike et al., 2003), but more effective treatment methods are still needed (Agras et al., 2004).

anorexia nervosa An eating disorder characterized by self-starvation and dramatic weight loss.

in review Major Factors Controlling Hunger and Eating

	Stimulate Eating	Inhibit Eating
Biological factors	Levels of glucose and insulin in the blood provide signals that stimulate eating. Stomach contractions are associated with subjective feelings of hunger, but they do not play a substantial role in the stimulation of eating.	Hormones released into the bloodstream produce signals that inhibit eating; hormones such as leptin and insulin affect neurons in the hypothalamus and inhibit eating. The ventromedial nucleus of the hypothalamus may be a "satiety centre" that monitors these hormones.
Nonbiological factors	Sights and smells of particular foods elicit eating because of prior associations; family customs and social occasions often include norms for eating in particular ways; stress is often associated with eating more.	Values in contemporary North American society encourage thinness and thus can inhibit eating.

Bulimia Nervosa Like anorexia, bulimia nervosa involves intense fear of being fat, but the person may be thin, normal in weight, or even overweight (U.S. Surgeon General, 1999). **Bulimia nervosa** is characterized by the consumption of huge amounts of food (a binge—several boxes of cookies, a half-gallon of ice cream, and a bucket of fried chicken) and then getting rid of the food (a purge) through self-induced vomiting or strong laxatives. These "binge-purge" episodes may occur as often as twice a day (Weltzin et al., 1995).

Like people with anorexia, bulimic individuals are usually female, and like anorexia, bulimia usually begins with a desire to be slender. However, bulimia and anorexia are separate disorders (Pryor, 1995). For one thing, most bulimics see their eating habits as problematic, whereas most anorexics do not. In addition, bulimia nervosa is usually not life threatening (Thompson, 1996). There are consequences, however, including dehydration, nutritional problems, and intestinal damage. Many bulimics develop dental problems from the acids associated with vomiting. Frequent vomiting and the insertion of objects to trigger it can also cause damage to the throat. More generally, a preoccupation with eating and avoiding weight gain prevents many bulimics from working productively (Herzog, 1982).

Estimates of the frequency of bulimia range from one to four percent of Canadian adolescent and college-age women (Health Canada, 2006; Bruce & Agras, 1992). It appears to be caused by a combination of factors, including perfectionism, low self-esteem, stress, culturally encouraged preoccupation with being thin, depression and other emotional problems, and as-yet-undetermined biological problems that might include defective satiety mechanisms (Crowther et al., 2001; Steiger et al., 2001; Stice & Fairburn, 2003; Wade, Martin, & Tiggemann, 1998). Treatment for bulimia typically includes individual or group therapy and, sometimes, antidepressant drugs. These treatments help the vast majority of bulimic people to eat more normally (Herzog et al., 1999; Wilson et al., 1999).

(For a summary of the processes involved in hunger and eating, see "In Review: Major Factors Controlling Hunger and Eating.")

Sexual Behaviour

bulimia nervosa An eating disorder that involves eating massive amounts of food and then eliminating the food by self-induced vomiting or the use of strong laxatives.

Unlike food, sex is not necessary for individual survival. A strong desire for reproduction does help ensure the survival of a species, however. The various factors shaping sexual motivation and behaviour differ in strength across species, but they often include a combination of the individual's physiology, learned behaviour, and the physical and social environment. For example, one species of desert bird requires adequate sex hormones, a suitable mate, and a particular environment before it begins sexual behaviour. During the dry season, it shows no interest in sex, but within ten minutes of the first rain shower the birds copulate vigorously.

Rainfall is obviously much less influential as a sexual trigger for humans. People show a staggering diversity of *sexual scripts,* or patterns of behaviour that lead to sex. One survey of college-age men and women identified 122 specific acts and 34 different tactics used for promoting sexual encounters (Greer & Buss, 1994). What happens next? The matter is difficult to address scientifically, because most people are reluctant to respond to specific questions about their sexual practices, let alone to allow researchers to observe their sexual behaviour (Bancroft, 1997). Yet having valid information about the nature of human sexual behaviour is a vital first step for psychologists and other scientists who study such topics as individual differences in sexuality, gender differences in sexual motivation and behaviour (Peplau, 2003; Chivers et al., 2004), sources of sexual orientation, types of sexual dysfunctions, and the pathways through which sexually transmitted diseases (STDs) reach new victims. This information also has important implications for helping people understand themselves, alleviating sexual problems, and curbing the spread of STDs.

FOCUS ON RESEARCH METHODS

A Survey of Human Sexual Behaviour

One of the first extensive studies of sexual behaviour was done by Alfred Kinsey during the late 1940s and early 1950s (Kinsey, Pomeroy, & Martin, 1948; Kinsey et al., 1953). These were followed in the 1960s by the work of William Masters and Virginia Johnson (1966). Kinsey conducted surveys of people's sex lives; Masters and Johnson actually measured sexual arousal and behaviour in volunteers who received natural or artificial stimulation in a laboratory. Together, these studies broke new ground in the exploration of human sexuality, but the people who volunteered for them were probably not a representative sample of the American adult population. Accordingly, the results—and any conclusions drawn from them—may not apply to people in general or to Canadian youth in particular. The results of more recent surveys, such as reader polls in *Cosmopolitan* and other magazines, are also flawed by the use of unrepresentative samples (Davis & Smith, 1990).

- **What was the researchers' question?**

Is there a way to gather data on sexual behaviour that is more representative and therefore more revealing about people in general? A team of researchers at Queen's University in Kingston and the University of Toronto believe there is, so they undertook two ambitious surveys on the subject of sexual behaviour, attitudes to HIV/AIDS, among Canadian youth (Boyce et al., 2003; King et al., 1988; Rotermann, 2005). Both studies asked very similar questions about sexual behaviour and included large samples of Grade 9 (approximately age 14) and Grade 11 (approximately age 16) Canadian school students.

- **How did the researchers answer the question?**

The *Canada, Youth and AIDS Study* (King et al., 1988) conducted in 1988 and the *Canadian Youth, Sexual Health and HIV/AIDS Study* (Boyce et al., 2003) conducted in 2002 provide two readily comparable datasets that provide some indication of the trend in the percentage of Canadian youth at different age and grade levels who have engaged in sexual intercourse. These surveys included important features of their design typically neglected in most other surveys of sexual behaviour. To begin, these studies did not depend on self-selected volunteers; instead, respondents were drawn from a more diverse sociocultural makeup representative of the Canadian population in terms of gender, ethnicity, socioeconomic status, geographical location, and the like.

• What did the researchers find?

Comparison of the results from these two studies suggests that contrary to the common belief that recent cohorts of teens are more likely to have intercourse than older peers (see the table below), the percentage of Canadian youth from 1988 to 2002 who had experienced sexual intercourse did not increase.

Percentages of Grade 9 and Grade 11 School Students Reporting That They Have Had Sexual Intercourse at Least Once

	Males 1988	Males 2002	Females 1988	Females 2002
Grade 9	31	23	21	19
Grade 11	49	40	46	46

Results also showed that the age of first intercourse was roughly identical for females and males—16.5 years. It is worth noting however that this number has fallen steadily in surveys of older individuals. That is, those respondents presently aged 25 to 34 years had their first intercourse experience almost eighteen months later (17.9 years on average); this was later for those presently aged 35 to 44 years (18.7 years on average), and later still for those presently aged 45 to 59 years (19.2 years on average). The table below shows that over 50 percent of sexually active Grade 9 students responded that they have had intercourse once or "a few times," and over 40 percent of sexually active Grade 11 students responded that they have had intercourse once or "a few times." Although most Canadian young people have their first sexual intercourse experience during their teenage years, only a minority of sexually active adolescents in their early and middle teen years have intercourse on a regular basis.

Frequency of Sexual Intercourse Among Canadian Youth Who Have Had Intercourse One or A Few Times

	Once	A few times	Often
Grade 9			
Males	30%	32%	39%
Females	29%	34%	37%
Grade 11			
Males	19%	33%	48%
Females	13%	28%	59%

The 2003 *Canadian Community Health Survey* also asked sexually active respondents how many sexual partners they had had in the previous 12 months (Rotermann, 2005). Among sexually active Canadian youth aged 15 to 19, the percentage that reported more than one sexual partner in the previous 12 months was just over a third (35 percent). As shown in the table on the next page, sexually active males in both age categories were more likely than sexually active females to report having more than one sexual partner in the previous 12 months.

Percentage of Sexually Active 15 to 17 and 18 to 19 Year-Old Canadian Youth Reporting More Than One Sexual Partner in the Previous Twelve Months

	15–17 years	18–19 years
Male	14%	29%
Female	29%	31%

- **What do the results mean?**

These surveys challenge some of the cultural and media images of sexuality in Canada. In particular, it suggests that people in Canada may be more sexually conservative than one might think on the basis of magazine reader polls and the testimony of guests on daytime talk shows.

- **What do we still need to know?**

Many questions remain. These surveys did not ask about some of the more controversial aspects of human sexuality, such as the effects of pornography, the prevalence of pedophilia (sexual attraction to children), and the role in sexual activity of sexual fetishes such as shoes or other clothing. Had the researchers asked about such topics, their results might have painted a less conservative picture.

The results of even the best survey methods—like the results of all research methods—usually raise as many questions as they answer. When do people become interested in sex, and why? How do they choose to express these desires, and why? What determines their sexual likes and dislikes? How do learning and sociocultural factors modify the biological forces that seem to provide the raw material of human sexual motivation? These are some of the questions about human sexual behaviour that a survey cannot easily or accurately explore (Benson, 2003).

The Biology of Sex

Some aspects of the sexual behaviour observed by Masters and Johnson in their laboratory may not have reflected exactly what goes on when people have sex in more familiar surroundings. Still, those observations led to important findings about the **sexual response cycle,** the pattern of physiological arousal during and after sexual activity (see Figure 11.6).

People's motivation to engage in sexual activity has biological roots in **sex hormones.** The female sex hormones are **estrogens** and **progestins;** the main ones are *estradiol* and *progesterone.* The male hormones are **androgens;** the principal example is *testosterone.* Each sex hormone flows in the blood of both sexes, but males have relatively more androgens, and women have relatively more estrogens and progestins. Sex hormones have both organizational and activational effects. The *organizational* effects are permanent changes in the brain that alter the way a person responds to hormones. The *activational* effects are temporary behavioural changes that last only as long as a hormone level remains elevated, such as during puberty or in the ovulation phase of the monthly menstrual cycle.

Rising levels of sex hormones during puberty have activational effects, resulting in increased sexual desire and interest in sexual behaviour. Generally, estrogens and androgens stimulate females' sexual interest (Burleson, Gregory, & Trevarthen, 1995; Sherwin & Gelfand, 1987). Androgens raise males' sexual interest (Davidson, Camargo, & Smith, 1979). The activational effects of hormones are also seen in reduced sexual motivation and behaviour among people whose hormone-secreting

sexual response cycle The pattern of physiological arousal during and after sexual activity.

sex hormones Chemicals in the blood of males and females that have both organizational and activational effects on sexual behaviour.

estrogens Feminine sex hormones that circulate in the bloodstream of both men and women; relatively more estrogens circulate in women.

progestins Feminine sex hormones that circulate in the bloodstream of both men and women; relatively more progestins circulate in women.

androgens Masculine sex hormones that circulate in the bloodstream in both sexes; relatively more androgens circulate in men than in women.

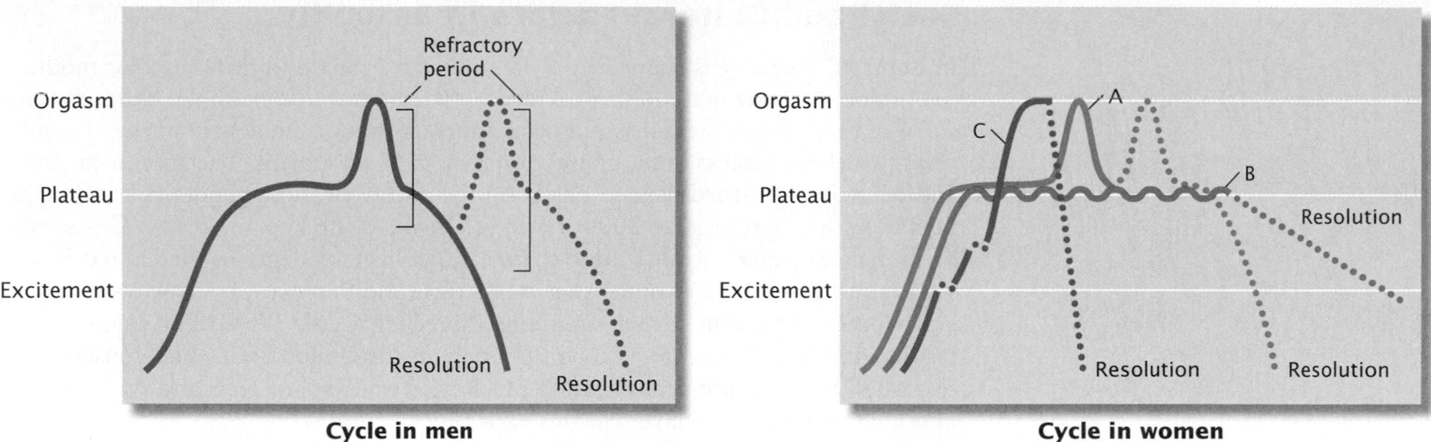

figure 11.6

The Sexual Response Cycle

As shown at left, Masters and Johnson (1966) found that men display one main pattern of sexual response. Women display at least three different patterns from time to time; these are labelled A, B, and C in the right-hand graph. For both men and women, the *excitement* phase begins with sexual stimulation from the environment or one's own thoughts. Continued stimulation leads to intensified excitement in the *plateau* phase, and if stimulation continues, to the intensely pleasurable release of tension in the *orgasmic* stage. During the *resolution* phase, both men and women experience a state of relaxation. Following resolution, men enter a *refractory* phase, during which they are unresponsive to sexual stimulation. Women are capable of immediately repeating the cycle.

Source: Adapted from Masters & Johnson (1966).

ovaries or testes have been removed for medical reasons. Injections of hormones help restore these people's sexual interest and activity.

Generally, hormones affect sexual *desire,* not the physical ability to have sex (Wallen & Lovejoy, 1993). This fact may explain why castration does not prevent sex crimes in male offenders. Men with low testosterone levels due to medical problems or castration show less sexual desire, but they still show physiological responses to erotic stimuli (Kwan et al., 1983). So a sex offender treated with androgen antagonists or castration would be less likely to seek out sex, but he would still respond as before to his favourite sexual stimuli (Wickham, 2001).

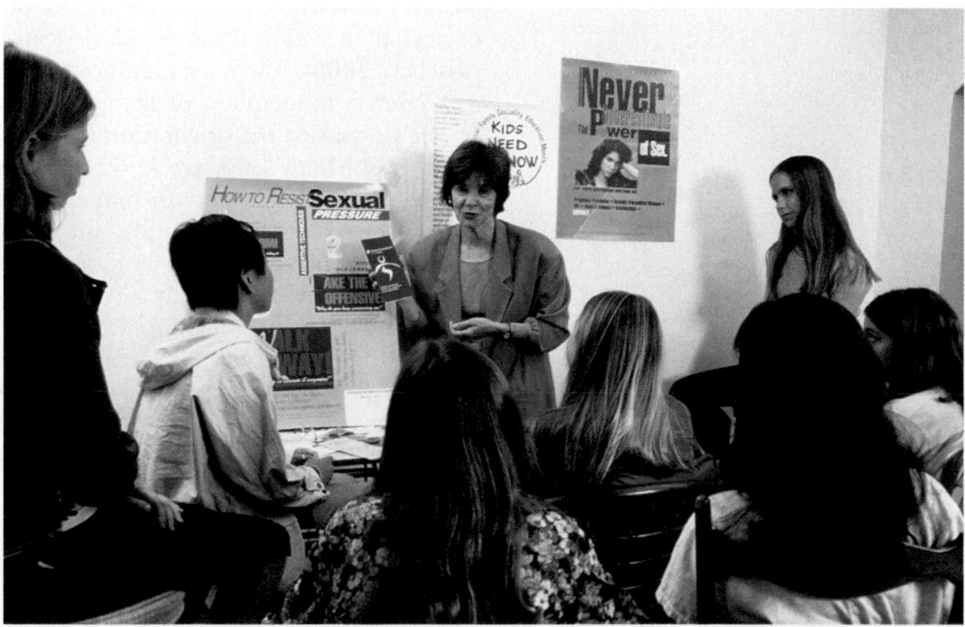

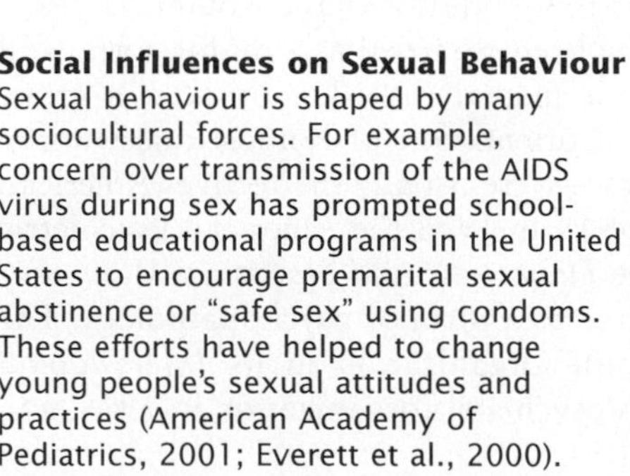

Social Influences on Sexual Behaviour Sexual behaviour is shaped by many sociocultural forces. For example, concern over transmission of the AIDS virus during sex has prompted school-based educational programs in the United States to encourage premarital sexual abstinence or "safe sex" using condoms. These efforts have helped to change young people's sexual attitudes and practices (American Academy of Pediatrics, 2001; Everett et al., 2000).

Social and Cultural Factors in Sexuality

In humans, sexuality is shaped by a lifetime of learning and thinking that modifies the biological "raw materials" provided by hormones. For example, children learn some of their sexual attitudes and behaviours as part of the development of *gender roles,* which we discuss in the chapter on human development. The specific attitudes and behaviours learned depend partly on the nature of those gender roles in a particular culture (Baumeister, 2000; Hyde & Durik, 2000; Peplau, 2003). One survey of the sexual experiences of more than 1500 college students in the United States, Japan, and Russia found numerous cross-cultural differences in the ways that men and women behave in sexual situations (Sprecher et al., 1994). For example, the results indicated that more women than men in the United States had consented to sex when they did not really want it. In Russia and Japan, men and women were about equally likely to have had this experience.

There are gender differences, too, in what people find sexually appealing. For example, in many cultures, men are far more interested in, and responsive to, pornographic films and other erotic stimuli than women are (Symons, 1979; Herz & Cahill, 1997). The difference in responsiveness was demonstrated recently in an MRI study that scanned the brain activity of males and females while they looked at erotic photographs (Hamann et al., 2004). As expected, the males showed greater activity in the amygdala and hypothalamus than the females. This result seems to reflect a gender difference in the way male and female brains are "wired." However, it is also important to note that the male and female participants rated the photos to be equally attractive and sexually arousing. In other words, differences in the biological underpinnings of sexual behaviour can be amplified, or dampened, by cultural learning. As women in Western cultures have learned to enjoy greater sexual freedom and expressiveness in recent decades, their responsiveness to erotic visual stimuli may have expanded, too. The growing popularity of male "strip clubs" certainly suggests that visual erotic stimulation can be of interest to both genders.

Indeed, gender-role learning interacts so deeply with biologically based characteristics that, as in many other aspects of human behaviour and mental processes, it is impossible to separate their influences on sexuality. Nowhere is this point clearer than in the case of sexual orientation.

Sexual Orientation

Sexual orientation refers to the nature of a person's enduring emotional, romantic, or sexual attraction to others (American Psychological Association, 2002a; Ellis & Mitchell, 2000). The most common sexual orientation is **heterosexual,** in which the attraction is to members of the opposite sex. When attraction focuses on members of one's own sex, the orientation is called **homosexual.** People who are attracted to members of both sexes are said to have a **bisexual** orientation. Sexual orientation involves feelings that may or may not be translated into corresponding patterns of sexual behaviour. For example, some people whose orientation is homosexual or bisexual may have sex only with opposite-sex partners. Similarly, people whose orientation is heterosexual may have had one or more homosexual encounters.

In many cultures, heterosexuality has long been regarded as a moral norm, and homosexuality has been seen as a disease, a mental disorder, or even a crime (Hooker, 1993). Attempts to alter the sexual orientation of homosexuals—using psychotherapy, brain surgery, or electric shock—were usually ineffective (American Psychiatric Association, 1999; Haldeman, 1994). In 1973 the American Psychiatric Association dropped homosexuality from the *Diagnostic and Statistical Manual of Mental Disorders,* thus ending its official status as a form of psychopathology. The same change was made by the World Health Organization in its *International Classification of Diseases* in 1993, by Japan's psychiatric organization in 1995, and by the Chinese Psychiatric Association in 2001.

heterosexual Referring to sexual motivation that is focused on members of the opposite sex.

homosexual Referring to sexual motivation that is focused on members of one's own sex.

bisexual Referring to sexual motivation that is focused on members of both sexes.

Nevertheless, some people still disapprove of homosexuality. Because homosexuals and bisexuals are often the victims of discrimination and even hate crimes, many are reluctant to let their sexual orientation be known (Bernat et al., 2001). It is difficult, therefore, to paint an accurate picture of the mix of heterosexual, homosexual, and bisexual orientations in the general population. In the Canadian surveys mentioned earlier, 1.6 percent of women and 3.3 percent of men identified themselves as exclusively homosexual, figures much lower than the 10 percent found in Kinsey's studies. However, that survey did not allow respondents to give anonymous answers to questions about sexual orientation. It has been suggested that if anonymous responses to those questions had been permitted, the prevalence figures for homosexual and bisexual orientations would have been higher (Bullough, 1995). In fact, studies that have allowed anonymous responding estimate the percentage of homosexual people in the United States, Canada, and Western Europe at between 2 and 15 percent (Aaron et al., 2003; Bagley & Tremblay, 1998; Binson et al., 1995; Sell, Wells, & Wypij, 1995).

THINKING CRITICALLY

Does Biology Determine Sexual Orientation?

The question of where sexual orientation comes from is a topic of intense debate in scientific circles, on talk shows, and in everyday conversations.

- **What am I being asked to believe or accept?**

One point of view suggests that genes dictate sexual orientation. According to this view, we do not learn a sexual orientation but rather are born with it.

- **What evidence is available to support the assertion?**

In 1995, a report by a respected research group suggested that one kind of sexual orientation—namely, homosexuality in males—was associated with a particular gene on the X chromosome (Hu et al., 1995). This finding was not supported by later studies (Rice et al., 1999), but a growing body of evidence from research in behavioural genetics suggests that genes might indeed influence sexual orientation (Kendler et al., 2000; Pillard & Bailey, 1998). One study examined pairs of monozygotic male twins (whose genes are identical), nonidentical twin pairs (whose genes are no more alike than those of any brothers), and pairs of adopted brothers (who are genetically unrelated). To participate in this study, at least one brother in each pair had to be homosexual. As it turned out, the other brother was also homosexual or bisexual in 52 percent of the identical-twin pairs. This was the case in only 22 percent of the nonidentical twin pairs and in just 11 percent of the pairs of adopted brothers (Bailey & Pillard, 1991). Similar findings have been reported for male identical twins raised apart, whose shared sexual orientation cannot be attributed to the effects of a shared environment (Whitam, Diamond, & Martin, 1993). The few available studies of female sexual orientation have yielded similar results (Bailey & Benishay, 1993; Bailey, Dunne, & Martin, 2000).

Evidence for the role of other biological factors in sexual orientation comes from research on the impact of sex hormones. In adults, differences in the levels of these hormones are not generally associated with differences in sexual orientation. However, hormonal differences during prenatal development might be involved in the shaping of sexual orientation (Lalumière, Blanchard, & Zucker, 2000; Lippa, 2003; Williams et al., 2000). Support for this view is provided by research on a disorder that causes the adrenal glands to secrete extremely high levels of androgens prior to birth (Carlson, 1998). Women exposed to high androgen levels because of this disorder were much more likely to become lesbians than their sisters who had not been exposed (Meyer et al., 1995). In animals, such hormonal influences alter the structure of the hypothalamus, a brain region known to underlie some aspects of sexual functioning (Swaab & Hofman, 1995). In humans,

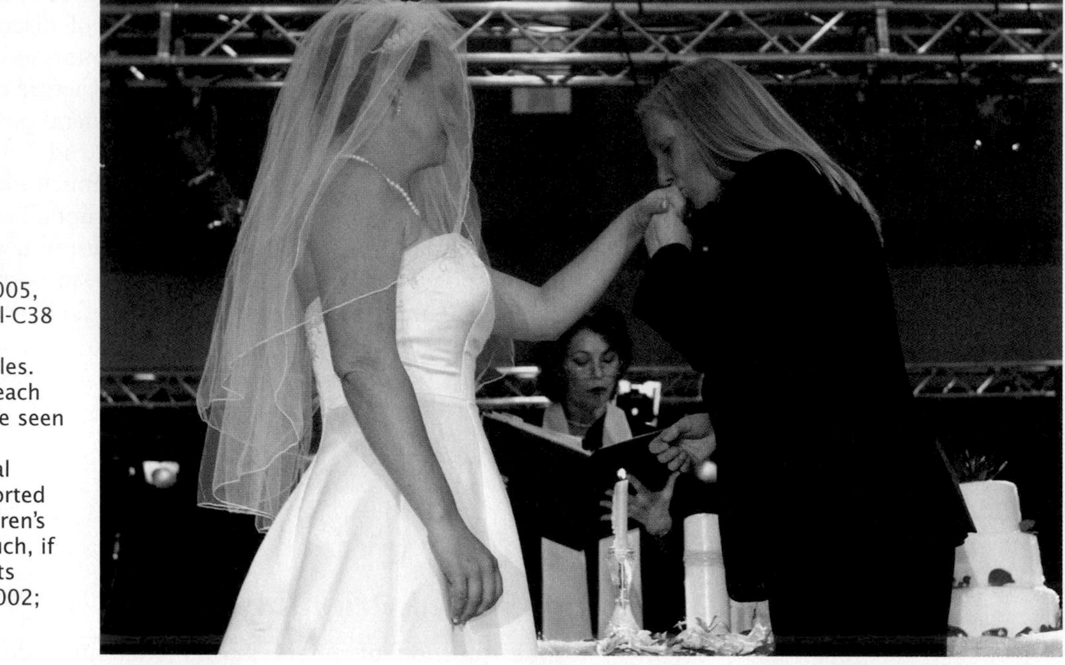

A Committed Relationship In 2005, the Canadian Government passed Bill-C38 that permitted the marriage (beyond merely civil union) of same-sex couples. These gay women's commitment to each other for the long haul might even be seen in their decision to adopt children together. The strong role of biological factors in sexual orientation is supported by research showing that these children's orientation will not be influenced much, if at all, by that of their adopted parents (e.g., Anderssen, Amlie, & Ytteroy, 2002; Stacey & Biblarz, 2001; Tasker & Golombok, 1995).

prenatal exposure to hormones and other chemicals may likewise be responsible for anatomical differences in the hypothalamus that are seen not only in males versus females but also in homosexual versus heterosexual men (Bogaert, 2003; LeVay, 1991; Swaab et al., 2001). The anterior commissure, an area near the hypothalamus, also appears to differ in people with differing sexual orientations (Allen & Gorski, 1992; Gladue, 1994).

Finally, a biological basis for sexual orientation is suggested by the fact that it is relatively unaffected by environmental factors. Several studies have shown, for example, that the sexual orientation of children's caregivers has little or no effect on those children's own sexual orientation (Anderssen, Amlie, & Ytteroy, 2002; Stacey & Biblarz, 2001).

Are there alternative ways of interpreting the evidence?

Correlations between genetics and sexual orientation, like all correlations, are open to alternative interpretations. As discussed in the chapter on research in psychology, a correlation describes the strength and direction of a relationship between variables, but it does not guarantee that one variable is actually influencing the other. Consider again the data showing that brothers who shared the most genes were also most likely to share a homosexual orientation. It is possible that what the brothers shared was not a gene for homosexuality but rather a set of genes that influenced their activity levels, emotionality, aggressiveness, or the like. One example is "gender nonconformity" in childhood, the tendency for some boys to display "feminine" behaviours and for some girls to behave in "masculine" ways (Bailey, Dunne, & Martin, 2000). It could be such general aspects of temperament or personality—and other people's reactions to them—that influence the likelihood of a particular sexual orientation (Bem, 1996). In other words, sexual orientation could arise as a reaction to the way people respond to a genetically determined, but nonsexual, aspect of personality. Prenatal hormone levels, too, could influence sexual orientation by shaping aggressiveness or other nonsexual aspects of behaviour.

It is also important to look at behavioural genetics evidence for what it can tell us about the role of *environmental factors* in sexual orientation. When we read that both members of identical twin pairs have a homosexual or bisexual orientation 52 percent of the time, it is easy to ignore the fact that the orientation of the twin pair members was *different* in nearly half the cases. Viewed in this way, the results suggest that genes do not tell the entire story of sexual orientation.

So even if sexual orientation has a biological base, it is probably not determined by genetic and hormonal forces alone. As described in the chapter on biological aspects of psychology, the brains and bodies we inherit are quite responsive to environmental input. The behaviours we engage in and the environmental experiences we have result in physical changes in the brain and elsewhere (Wang et al., 1995). Every time we form a new memory, for example, changes occur in the brain's synapses. So differences in the brains of people with differing sexual orientations could be the effect, not the cause, of their behaviour or experiences.

- **What additional evidence would help to evaluate the alternatives?**

Much more evidence is needed about the extent to which genetic characteristics directly determine sexual orientation. We also have much to learn about the extent to which genes and hormones shape physical and psychological characteristics that lead to the social construction of various sexual orientations. In studying this issue, researchers will want to know more not only about the genetic characteristics of people with different sexual orientations but also about their mental and behavioural styles. Are there personality characteristics associated with different sexual orientations? If so, do those characteristics have a strong genetic component? To what extent are heterosexuals, bisexuals, and homosexuals similar—and to what extent are they different—in terms of cognitive styles, biases, coping skills, developmental histories, and the like? And are there any differences in how sexual orientation is shaped in males versus females (Bailey, Dunne, & Martin, 2000)?

- **What conclusions are most reasonable?**

Given the antagonism and physical danger often faced by people with other than heterosexual orientations (Cramer, 1999), it seems unlikely that sexual orientation is entirely a matter of choice. In fact, much of the evidence reviewed suggests that our sexual orientation chooses us, rather than the other way around. In light of this evidence, a reasonable hypothesis is that genetic factors, probably operating through prenatal hormones, create differences in the brains of people with different sexual orientations. Even if this hypothesis is correct, however, the manner in which a person expresses a genetically influenced sexual orientation will be profoundly shaped by what that person learns through social and cultural experiences (Bancroft, 1994). In short, sexual orientation most likely results from the complex interplay of both genetic and nongenetic mechanisms—both nature and nurture. Those who characterize sexual orientation as being either all "in the genes" or entirely a matter of choice are probably wrong.

Sexual Dysfunctions

The same biological, social, and psychological factors that shape human sexual behaviour can also result in **sexual dysfunctions,** problems in a person's desire for or ability to have satisfying sexual activity (Goldstein & Rosen, 2002). According to the *Society for Obstetricians and Gynaecologists of Canada*, more than 40 percent of women and 30 percent of men suffer from some type of sexual difficulty, such as no interest in sex, inability to achieve orgasm, painful intercourse, or premature ejaculation. Researchers routinely find a strong link between sexual dysfunction and impaired quality of life including significantly reduced individual psychological health and well-being and quality of couple relationships. In fact, a wide variety of medical conditions including breast cancer, gynecological conditions and cancer, diabetes, multiple sclerosis, and depression constitute risk factors for the development of sexual dysfunction among women.

sexual dysfunctions Problems with sex that involve sexual motivation, arousal, or orgasmic response.

A common problem for men is *erectile disorder* (once called *impotence*), a persistent inability to have or maintain an erection adequate for sex. Physical causes—

such as fatigue, diabetes, hypertension, aging, alcohol or other drugs, and perhaps even genetics—account for some cases, but psychological causes such as anxiety are also common (Everaerd & Laan, 1994; Fischer et al., 2004; Heiman, 2002). Viagra, Cialis, Levitra, and other drugs that increase blood flow in the penis are effectively treating many cases of erectile disorder (Lue, 2000). Still other drugs are in development (Nehra & Kulaksizoglu, 2002). For Canadian men under 40 years of age, the key sexual complaint is premature ejaculation, wherein about 25 percent of males achieve orgasm sooner than the man or his partner desires. Most men experience episodes of at least one of these problems at some point in their lives, but such episodes are considered dysfunctions only if they become a distressing obstacle to sexual functioning (American Psychiatric Association, 1994; Mercer et al., 2003).

The most common sexual dysfunction for women aged 15 to 54 years is *arousal disorder* (once called *frigidity*), which is characterized by a recurring inability to become physiologically aroused during sexual activity (Phillips, 2000; Wilson et al., 1996). Arousal disorder can stem from inadequate genital stimulation, hormonal imbalances, insufficient vaginal lubrication, or inadequate blood flow to the clitoris (Anastasiadis et al., 2002; Mansfield, Voda, & Koch, 1995; Wilson et al., 1996). However, it is also often tied to psychological factors such as guilt or self-consciousness, which can affect men as well as women (Davidson & Moore, 1994; Laan et al., 1993).

Achievement Motivation

This sentence was written at 6 A.M. on a beautiful Sunday in March. Why would someone get up that early to work on a weekend? Why do people take their work seriously and try to do the best that they can? People work hard partly due to *extrinsic motivation,* a desire for external rewards such as money. But work and other human behaviours also reflect *intrinsic motivation,* a desire to attain internal satisfaction.

The next time you visit someone's home or office, look at the mementos displayed there. You may see framed diplomas and awards, trophies and ribbons, pictures of memorable personal events, and photos of children and grandchildren.

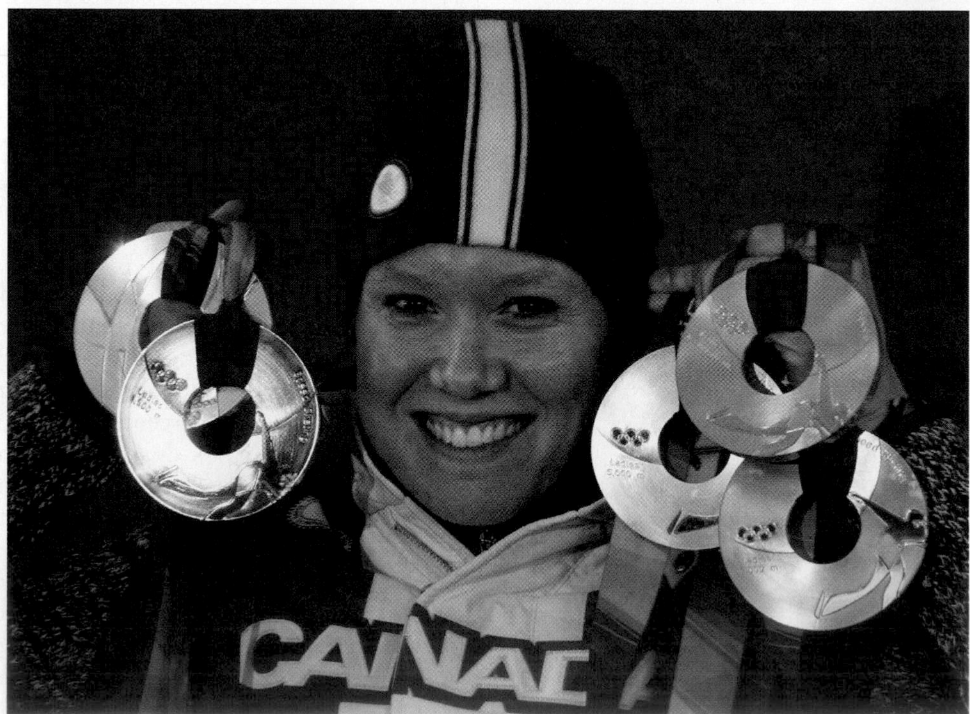

Cindy Klassen She captured five Olympic medals for Canada at Turin in 2006. Do you think she trained hard because of personal intrinsic goals or for something more external, like fame and fortune?

figure 11.7

Assessing Need Achievement

This picture is similar to those included in the Thematic Apperception Test, or TAT (Morgan & Murray, 1935). The strength of people's achievement motivation is inferred from the stories they tell about TAT pictures. A response such as "The young woman is hoping to make her grandmother proud of her" would be seen as reflecting high achievement motivation.

These badges of achievement affirm that a person has accomplished tasks that merit approval or establish worth. Much of our behaviour is motivated by a desire for approval, admiration, and achievement—in short, for *esteem*—from others and from ourselves. In this section, we examine two of the most common avenues to esteem: achievement in general and a job in particular.

Need for Achievement

Many athletes who already hold world records still train intensely; many people who have built multimillion-dollar businesses still work 14-hour days. What motivates these people?

One answer is a motive called **need achievement** (Murray, 1938). People with a high need for achievement seek to master tasks—be they sports, business ventures, intellectual puzzles, or artistic creations—and feel intense satisfaction from doing so. They strive for excellence, enjoy themselves in the process, and take great pride in achieving at a high level (McClelland, 1985).

Individual Differences How do people with strong achievement motivation differ from others? To find out, researchers gave children a test to measure their need for achievement (Figure 11.7 shows a test for adults) and then asked them to play a ring-toss game. Children scoring low on the need-achievement test usually stood either so close to the ring-toss target that they couldn't fail or so far away that they couldn't succeed. In contrast, children scoring high on the need-achievement test stood at a moderate distance from the target, making the game challenging but not impossible (McClelland, 1958). These and other experiments suggest that people with high achievement needs tend to set challenging—but realistic—goals. They actively seek success, take risks when necessary, and are intensely satisfied when they succeed. But if they feel they have tried their best, people with high achievement motivation are not too upset by failure. Those with low achievement motivation also like to succeed, but instead of joy, success tends to bring them relief at having avoided failure (Winter, 1996).

Differences in achievement motivation also appear in people's goals in achievement-related situations (Molden & Dweck, 2000). Some people tend to adopt *learning goals*. When they play golf, take piano lessons, work at puzzles and problems, go to school, and get involved in other achievement-oriented activities, they do so mainly to get better at those activities. Realizing that they may not yet have the skills necessary to achieve at a high level, they tend to learn by watching others and to struggle with problems on their own rather than asking for help (Mayer & Sutton, 1996). When they do seek help, people with learning goals are likely to ask for explanations, hints, and other forms of task-related information, not for quick, easy answers that remove the challenge from the situation. In contrast, people who adopt *performance goals* are usually more concerned with demonstrating the skill they believe they already have. They tend to seek information about how well they have performed compared with others rather than about how to improve their performance (Butler, 1998). When they seek help, it is usually to ask for the right answer rather than for tips on how to find that answer themselves. Because their primary goal is to demonstrate their competence, people with performance goals tend to avoid new challenges if they are not confident that they will be successful, and they tend to quit in response to failure (Grant & Dweck, 2003; Weiner, 1980). Individuals may also vary by their planning abilities, so that some are better at parcelling out the correct amount of time to complete a task or project. Roger Buehler and colleagues at Wilfrid Laurier University in Ontario explain why many of us are often enthusiastic and ambitious about when projects will be completed. It can occur on a small scale (like a term paper) or on a large scale (like repaving a stretch of highway). Why do some of us have this optimistic bias? Called the *planning fallacy*, Buehler explains that many of us tend to be overly optimistic as to how long it takes to complete our

need achievement A motive reflected in the degree to which a person establishes specific goals, cares about meeting those goals, and experiences feelings of satisfaction by doing so.

goals, largely because we focus too narrowly on the future plans of the target task and neglect various obstacles that can surface. That is, although we readily expect to complete jobs well before they are due, we are not so confident in those around us. Just ask yourself how soon a friend or stranger could complete the same term paper (Buehler & Griffin, 2003; Buehler, Griffin, & Ross, 2002; Buehler, Messervey, & Griffin, 2005; Lam, Buehler, McFraland, Ross, & Cheung, 2005).

Development of Achievement Motivation Achievement motivation tends to be learned in early childhood, especially from parents. For example, in one study young boys were given a difficult task at which they were sure to fail. Fathers whose sons scored low on achievement motivation tests often became annoyed as they watched their boys. They discouraged them from continuing, interfered, or even completed the task themselves (Rosen & D'Andrade, 1959). A different pattern of behaviour appeared among parents of children who scored high on tests of achievement motivation. Those parents tended to (1) encourage the child to try difficult tasks, especially new ones; (2) give praise and other rewards for success; (3) encourage the child to find ways to succeed rather than merely complaining about failure; and (4) prompt the child to go on to the next, more difficult challenge (McClelland, 1985). Other research with adults shows that even the slightest cues that bring a parent to mind can boost people's efforts to achieve a goal (Shah, 2003).

More general cultural influences also affect the development of achievement motivation. For example, subtle messages about a culture's view of how achievement occurs often appear in the books children read and the stories they hear. Does the story's main character work hard and overcome obstacles, thus creating expectations of a payoff for persistence? Is the character a loafer who wins the lottery, suggesting that rewards come randomly, regardless of effort? If the main character succeeds, is it the result of personal initiative, as is typical of stories in individualist cultures? Or is success based on ties to a cooperative and supportive group, as is typical of stories in collectivist cultures? These themes appear to act as blueprints for reaching culturally approved goals. It should not be surprising, then, that ideas about how people achieve differ from culture to culture. Achievement motivation is also influenced by how much a particular culture values achievement. For example, the motivation to excel is likely to be especially strong in cultures in which demanding standards lead students to fear rejection if they fail to attain high grades (Eaton & Dembo, 1997; Hess, Chih-Mei, & McDevitt, 1987).

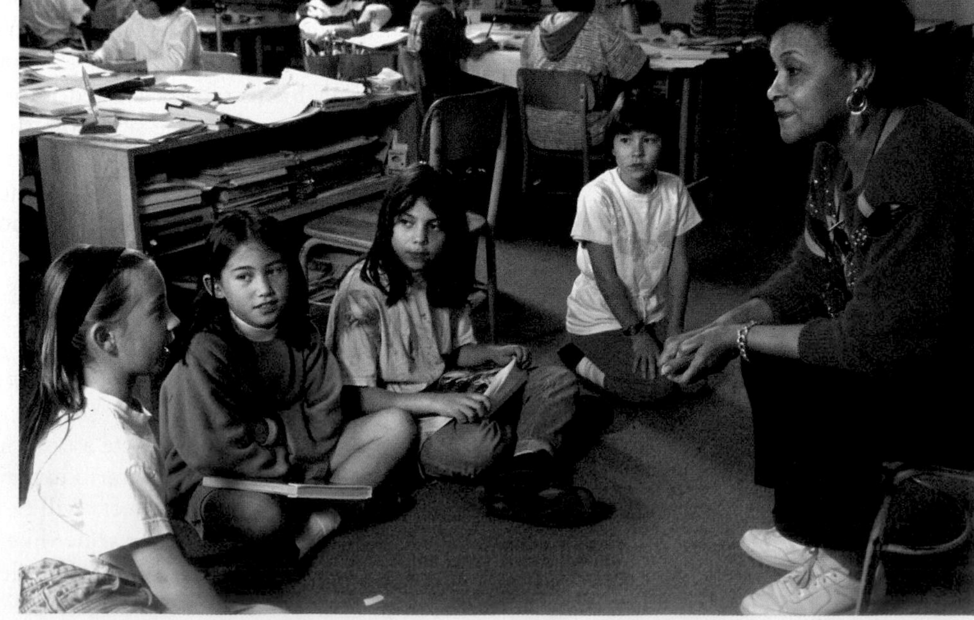

Helping Them Do Their Best Learning-oriented goals are especially appropriate in classrooms, where students typically have little knowledge of the subject matter. This is why most teachers tolerate errors and reward gradual improvement. They do not usually encourage performance goals, which emphasize doing better than others and demonstrating immediate competence (Reeve, 1996). Still, to help students do their best in the long run, teachers sometimes promote performance goals, too. The proper combination of both kinds of goals may be more motivating than either kind alone (Barron & Harackiewicz, 2001).

Children raised in environments that support the development of strong achievement motivation tend not to give up on difficult tasks—even if all the king's horses and all the king's men do!

"Maybe they didn't try hard enough."

It is possible to increase achievement motivation among people whose cultural training did not foster it in childhood (Mayer & Sutton, 1996). In one study, high school and college students with low achievement motivation were helped to develop fantasies about their own success. They imagined setting goals that were difficult, but not impossible. Then they imagined themselves concentrating on breaking a complex problem into small, manageable steps. They fantasized about working hard, failing but not being discouraged, continuing to work, and finally feeling elated at success. Afterward, the students' grades and academic success improved, suggesting an increase in their achievement motivation (McClelland, 1985). In short, achievement motivation is strongly influenced by social and cultural learning experiences, as well as by the beliefs about oneself that these experiences help to create. People who come to believe in their ability to achieve are more likely to do so than those who expect to fail (Butler, 1998; Dweck, 1998; Tuckman, 2003; Wigfield & Eccles, 2000).

Goal Setting and Achievement Motivation

Why are you reading this chapter instead of watching television or hanging out with your friends? Your motivation to study is probably based on your goal of doing well in a psychology course, which relates to broader goals, such as earning a degree, having a career, and the like. Psychologists have found that we set goals when we recognize a discrepancy between our current situation and how we want that situation to be (Oettingen, Pak, & Schnetter, 2001). Establishing a goal motivates us to engage in behaviours designed to reduce the discrepancy we have identified. The kinds of goals we set can influence the amount of effort, persistence, attention, and planning we devote to a task.

In general, the more difficult the goal, the harder people will try to reach it. This rule assumes, of course, that the goal is seen as attainable. Goals that are impossibly difficult may not motivate maximum effort. It also assumes that the person values the goal. If a difficult goal is set by someone else—as when a parent assigns a teenager to keep a large lawn and garden trimmed and weeded—people may not accept it as their own and may not work very hard to attain it. Setting goals that are clear and specific tends to increase people's motivation to persist at a task (Locke & Latham, 2002). For example, you are more likely to keep reading this chapter if your goal is to "read the motivation section of the motivation and emotion chapter today" than if it is to "do some studying." Clarifying your goal makes it easier to know when you have reached it, and when it is time to stop. Without clear goals, a person can be more easily distracted by fatigue, boredom, or frustration and more likely to give up before completing a task. Goals, especially clear goals, also tend to focus people's attention on creating plans for pursuing them, on the activities they believe will lead to goal attainment, and on evaluating their progress. In short, the process of goal setting is more than just wishful thinking. It is an important first step in motivating all kinds of behaviour.

Achievement and Success in the Workplace

In the workplace, there is usually less concern with employees' general level of achievement motivation than with their motivation to work hard during business hours. In fact, employers tend to set up jobs in accordance with their ideas about how intrinsic and extrinsic motivation combine to shape their employees' performance (Riggio, 1989). Employers who see workers as lazy, dishonest creatures with no ambition tend to offer highly structured, heavily supervised jobs that give employees little say in deciding what to do or how to do it. These employers assume that workers are motivated mainly by extrinsic rewards—money, in particular. So they tend to be surprised when, in spite of good pay and benefits, employees sometimes express dissatisfaction with their jobs and show little motivation to work hard (Diener & Seligman, 2004; Igalens & Roussel, 2000).

If good pay and benefits alone do not bring job satisfaction and the desire to excel on the job, what does? Research suggests that low worker motivation in Western cultures comes largely from the feeling of having little or no control over the work environment (Rosen, 1991). Compared with those in rigidly structured jobs, workers tend to be more satisfied and productive if they are (1) encouraged to participate in decisions about how work should be done; (2) given problems to solve, without being told how to solve them; (3) taught more than one skill; (4) given individual responsibility; and (5) given public recognition, not just money, for good performance (Fisher, 2000).

Allowing people to set and achieve clear goals is one way to increase both job performance and job satisfaction (Abramis, 1994). As suggested by our earlier discussion, some goals are especially effective at maintaining work motivation (Katzell & Thompson, 1990). First, effective goals are personally meaningful. When a form letter from a remote administrator decrees that employees should increase production, the employees tend to feel put upon and not particularly motivated to meet the goal. Before assigning difficult goals, good managers try to ensure that employees accept those goals (Klein et al., 1999). They include employees in the goal-setting process, make sure that the employees have the skills and resources to reach the goal, and emphasize the benefits to be gained from success—perhaps including financial incentives (Jenkins et al., 1998; Locke & Latham, 1990). Second, effective goals are specific and concrete. The goal of "doing better" is usually not a strong motivator, because it provides no direction about how to proceed and it fails to specify when the goal has been met. A specific target, such as increasing sales by 10 percent, is a far more motivating goal. It can be measured objectively, allowing feedback on progress, and it tells workers whether the goal has been reached (Locke, 2000). Finally, goals are most effective if management supports the workers' own goal setting, offers special rewards for reaching goals, and gives encouragement for renewed efforts after failure (Kluger & DeNisi, 1998).

In summary, motivating jobs offer personal challenges, independence, and both intrinsic and extrinsic rewards. They provide enough satisfaction for people to feel excitement and pleasure in working hard. For employers, meanwhile, the rewards are more productivity, less absenteeism, and greater employee loyalty (Ilgen & Pulakos, 1999).

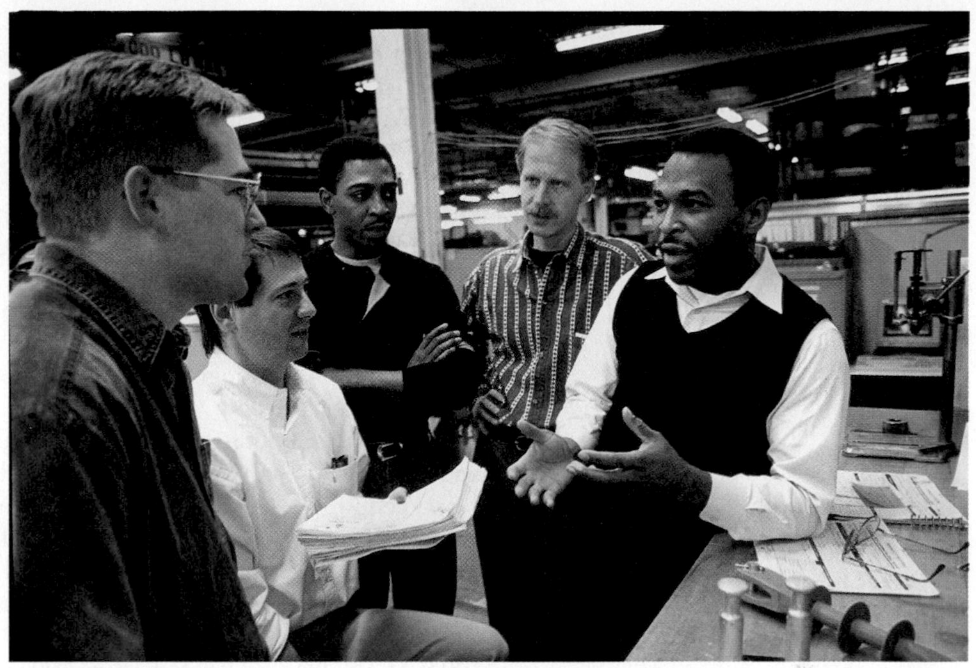

Teamwork Pays Off Many companies have followed Japanese examples by redesigning jobs to increase workers' responsibility and flexibility. The goal is to increase productivity and job satisfaction by creating teams in which employees are responsible for solving production problems and making decisions about how best to do their jobs. Team members are publicly recognized for outstanding work, and part of their pay depends on the quality (not just the number) of their products and on the profitability of the company as a whole.

Achievement and Subjective Well-Being

Some people believe that the more they achieve at work and elsewhere, and the more money and other material goods they amass as a result, the happier they will be. Will they? Researchers interested in *positive psychology* (Seligman & Csikszentmihalyi, 2000; Sheldon & King, 2001) have been studying what it actually takes to achieve happiness, or more formally, subjective well-being. **Subjective well-being** is a combination of a cognitive judgment of satisfaction with life, the frequent experiencing of positive moods and emotions, and the relatively infrequent experiencing of unpleasant moods and emotions (Diener, 2000; Diener & Biswas-Diener, 2002; Seligman, 2002; Urry et al., 2004).

Research on subjective well-being indicates that, as you might expect, people living in extreme poverty or in war-torn or politically chaotic countries are not as happy as people in better circumstances. And people everywhere react to good or bad events with corresponding changes in mood. As described in the chapter on health, stress, and coping, for example, severe or long-lasting stressors—such as the death of a loved one—can lead to psychological and physical problems. But although events do have an impact, the saddening or elevating effects of major changes, such as being promoted or fired, or even being imprisoned or seriously injured, tend not to last as long as we might think they would. In other words, how happy you are may have less to do with what happens to you than you might expect (Bonanno, 2004; Gilbert & Wilson, 1998; Lyubomirsky, 2001).

Most event-related changes in mood subside within days or weeks, and most people then return to their previous level of happiness (Suh, Diener, & Fujita, 1996). Even when events create permanent changes in circumstances, most people adapt by changing their expectancies and goals, not by radically and permanently changing their baseline level of happiness. For example, people may be thrilled after getting a big salary increase, but as they get used to having it, the thrill fades, and they may eventually feel just as underpaid as before. In fact, although people's level of subjective well-being can certainly change (Lucas et al., 2004), it tends to be relatively stable throughout their lives. This baseline level may be related to temperament, or personality, and it has been likened to a set point for body weight (Lykken, 1999). Like many other aspects of temperament, our baseline level of happiness may be

subjective well-being A combination of a cognitive judgment of satisfaction with life, the frequent experiencing of positive moods and emotions, and the relatively infrequent experiencing of unpleasant moods and emotions.

influenced by genetics. Twin studies have shown, for example, that individual differences in happiness are more strongly associated with inherited personality characteristics than with environmental factors such as money, popularity, or physical attractiveness (Lykken, 1999; Tellegen et al., 1988).

Beyond inherited tendencies, the things that appear to matter most in generating happiness are close social ties (especially a satisfying marriage or partnership and good friends), religious faith, and having the resources necessary to allow progress toward one's goals (Diener, 2000; Myers, 2000). So you don't have to be a rich, physically attractive high achiever to be happy, and it turns out that most people in Western cultures are relatively happy (Diener & Diener, 1995).

These results are consistent with the views expressed over many centuries by philosophers, psychologists, and wise people in all cultures. For example, decades ago, Abraham Maslow (1908–1970) noted that when people in Western cultures experience unhappiness and psychological problems, those problems can often be traced to a *deficiency orientation.* He said that these people seek happiness by trying to acquire the goods and reach the status they don't currently have—but think they need—rather than by appreciating life itself and the material and other riches they already have. Others have amplified this point, suggesting that efforts to get more of the things we think will bring happiness may actually contribute to unhappiness if what we get is never "enough" (Diener & Seligman, 2004; Nickerson et al., 2003; Srivastava, Locke, & Bartol, 2001).

Relations and Conflicts Among Motives

Maslow's ideas about deficiency motivation were part of his more general view of human behaviour as reflecting a hierarchy of needs, or motives (see Figure 11.8). Needs at the lowest level of the hierarchy, he said, must be at least partially satisfied before people can be motivated by higher-level goals. From the bottom to the top of Maslow's hierarchy, these five motives are as follows:

1. ***Biological,*** such as the need for food, water, oxygen, activity, and sleep.
2. ***Safety,*** such as the need to be cared for as a child and have a secure income as an adult.
3. ***Belongingness and love,*** such as the need to be part of groups and to participate in affectionate sexual and nonsexual relationships.
4. ***Esteem,*** such as the need to be respected as a useful, honourable individual.

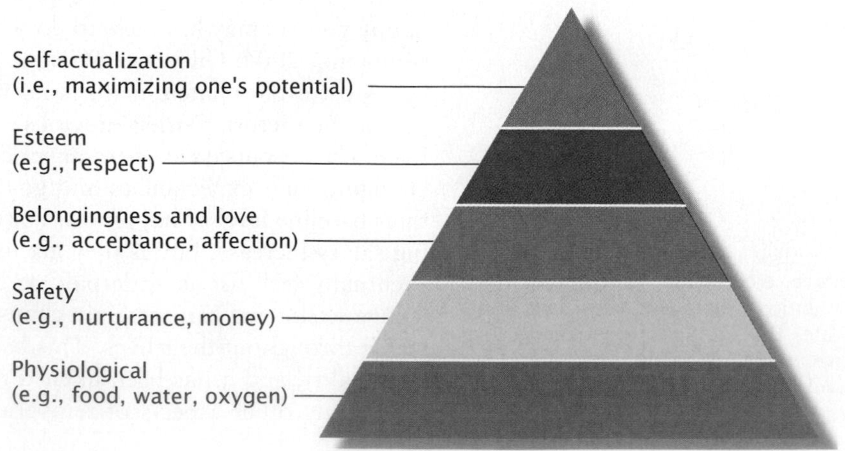

figure 11.8

Maslow's Hierarchy of Motives

Abraham Maslow (1908–1970) saw human motives as organized in a hierarchy in which those at lower levels take precedence over those at higher levels. According to this view, self-actualization is the essence of mental health. Take a moment to consider which level of Maslow's hierarchy you are focused on at this point in your life. Which level do you ultimately hope to reach?

Source: Adapted from Maslow (1943).

Choices based on Maslow's proposed hierarchy of needs are not usually this clear, nor are they always dictated strictly by that hierarchy.

5. ***Self-actualization,*** which means reaching one's fullest potential. People motivated by this need explore and enhance relationships with others; follow interests for intrinsic pleasure rather than for money, status, or esteem; and are concerned with issues affecting all people, not just themselves.

Maslow's hierarchy has been very influential over the years, but critics see it as far too simplistic (Hall, Lindzey, & Campbell, 1998; Neher, 1991). It does not predict or explain, for example, the motivation of people who starve themselves to death to draw attention to political or moral causes. In addition, although many people believe you should love yourself before you can love others, Maslow's model recommends the reverse. Further, people may not have to satisfy one kind of need before addressing others; we can seek several needs at once. And though the needs associated with basic survival and security do generally take precedence over those related to self-enhancement or personal growth (Baumeister & Leary, 1995; Oishi et al., 1999), the needs that are most important to people's satisfaction with life do not always correspond to Maslow's hierarchy.

LINKAGES
Conflicting Motives and Stress

LINKAGES (a link to Health, Stress, and Coping)

As in the case of hunger strikes, human motives can sometimes conflict. The usual result is some degree of discomfort. For example, imagine that you are alone and bored on a Saturday night, and you think about going to the store to buy some snacks. What are your motives? Hunger might prompt you to go out, as might the prospect of increased arousal that a change of scene will provide. Even sexual motivation might be involved, as you fantasize about meeting someone exciting in the snack-food aisle. But safety-related motives may also kick in—what if you get mugged? An esteem motive might come into play, too, making you hesitate to be seen alone on a weekend night.

These are just a few motives that may shape a trivial decision. When the decision is more important, the number and strength of motivational pushes and pulls are often greater, creating far more internal conflict. Four basic types of motivational conflict have been identified (Miller, 1959):

1. *Approach-approach conflicts:* when a person must choose only one of two desirable activities—say, going with friends to a movie or to a party. As the importance of the choice increases, so does the difficulty of making it.

A Stressful Conflict Think back to the time when you were deciding where to go for post-secondary education. Was the decision easy and obvious, or did it create a motivational conflict? If there was a conflict, was it an approach-approach, approach-avoidance, or multiple approach-avoidance conflict? What factors were most important in deciding how to resolve the conflict, and what emotions and signs of stress did you experience?

2. *Avoidance-avoidance conflicts:* when a person must pick one of two undesirable alternatives, like someone forced either to sell the house or to declare bankruptcy. Such conflicts are very difficult to resolve and often create intense emotions.
3. *Approach-avoidance conflicts:* when a single event or activity has both attractive and unattractive features. For example, consider if someone you couldn't stand had tickets to your favourite group's sold-out concert and invited you to come along, what would you do? Conflicts of this type are also difficult to resolve and often result in long periods of indecision.
4. *Multiple approach-avoidance conflicts.* Suppose you must choose between two jobs. One offers a good salary with a well-known company, but it requires long hours and relocation to a miserable climate. The other boasts advancement opportunities, fringe benefits, and a better climate, but also lower pay and an unpredictable work schedule. Note that two or more alternatives each have both positive and negative features. Such conflicts are difficult to resolve partly because it may be hard to compare the features of each option. For example, how much more money per year does it take to compensate you for living in a bad climate?

Each of these conflicts can create a significant amount of stress, a topic described in the chapter on health, stress, and coping. Most people in the midst of motivational conflicts are tense, irritable, and more vulnerable than usual to physical and psychological problems. These reactions are especially likely when there is no obviously "right" choice, when conflicting motives have approximately equal strength, and when the choice can have serious consequences (as in decisions to marry, to divorce, or to put an elderly parent in a nursing home). People may take a long time to resolve these conflicts, or they may act impulsively and thoughtlessly, if only to end the discomfort of uncertainty. And even after a conflict is resolved, stress responses may continue in the form of anxiety about the wisdom of the decision or self-blame over bad choices. These and other consequences of conflicting motives can even lead to depression or other serious disorders.

The Nature of Emotion

Everyone seems to agree that joy, sorrow, anger, fear, love, and hate are emotions, but it is hard to identify exactly what it is that makes these experiences emotions rather than, say, thoughts or impulses. In fact, some cultures see emotion and thought as the same thing. The Chewong of Malaysia, for example, consider the liver the seat of both what we call thoughts and feelings (Russell, 1991).

Defining Characteristics

Most psychologists in Western cultures see emotions as organized psychological and physiological reactions to changes in our relationship to the world. These reactions are partly private, or *subjective,* experiences and partly objectively measurable patterns of behaviour and physiological arousal. The subjective experience of emotion has several characteristics:

1. Emotion is usually *temporary;* it tends to have a relatively clear beginning and end, as well as a relatively short duration. Moods, by contrast, tend to last longer.

2. Emotional experience is either *positive* or *negative,* that is, pleasant or unpleasant.

3. Emotional experience is triggered partly by your thoughts, your mental assessment of how a situation relates to your goals. The same event can bring about different emotions depending on your cognitive interpretation of what the event means. An exam score of 75 percent could excite you if your previous score had been 50 percent, but it might upset you if you had never before scored below 90 percent and you saw the result as a disaster.

4. Emotional experience *alters thought processes,* often by directing attention toward some things and away from others. Negative emotions tend to narrow attention, and positive emotions tend to broaden it. Anxiety, for example, narrows our attention to focus on potential threats in the environment (Craske, 1999). The anguish of Donna French, mother of 15-year-old St. Catharines resident Kristin French, who was kidnapped and murdered in 1992 by apprehended serial rapist Paul Bernardo, for example, might cause her to focus intensely on the need to prevent kidnapping and to strengthen laws regarding sexual predators.

5. Emotional experience triggers an *action tendency,* the motivation to behave in certain ways. Positive emotions, such as joy, contentment, and pride, often lead to playfulness, creativity, and exploration of the environment (Cacioppo, Gardner & Berntson, 1999). These behaviours, in turn, can generate further positive emotions by creating stronger social ties, greater skill at problem solving, and the like. The result may be an "upward spiral" of positivity (Fredrickson & Joiner, 2002). Negative emotions, such as sadness and fear, often promote withdrawal from threatening situations, whereas anger might lead to actions aimed at revenge or constructive change. Grieving parents' anger, for example, might motivate them to harm their child's killer.

6. Emotional experiences are *passions* that happen to you, usually whether you want them to or not. You can exert at least some control over emotions in the sense that they depend partly on how you interpret situations (Gross, 2001). For example, your emotional reaction might be less extreme after a house fire if you remind yourself that no one was hurt and that you are insured. Still, such control is limited. You cannot *decide* to experience joy or sorrow; instead, you "fall in love" or "explode in anger" or are "overcome by grief." Emotional experiences, much like personality traits, have a different relation to the self than do conscious thoughts.

In other words, the subjective aspects of emotions are both *triggered* by the thinking self and felt as *happening* to the self. They reveal each individual as both agent and object, both I and me, both the controller of thoughts and the recipient of passions. The extent to which we are "victims" of our passions versus rational designers of our emotions is a central dilemma of human existence, as much a subject of literature as of psychology.

The *objective* aspects of emotion include learned and innate *expressive displays* and *physiological responses.* Expressive displays—such as a smile or a frown—communicate feelings to others. Physiological responses—such as changes in heart rate—are the biological adjustments needed to perform the action tendencies generated by emotional experience. If you throw a temper tantrum or jump for joy, your heart must deliver additional oxygen and fuel to your muscles.

In summary, an **emotion** is a temporary experience with either positive or negative qualities. It is felt with some intensity as happening to the self, generated in part by a cognitive interpretation of situations, and accompanied by both learned and innate physical responses. Through emotion, people communicate their internal states and intentions to others, but emotion also functions to direct and energize a person's own thoughts and actions. Emotion often disrupts thinking and behaviour, but it also triggers and guides thinking and organizes, motivates, and sustains behaviour and social relations.

The Biology of Emotion

The role of biology in emotion can be seen in mechanisms of the central nervous system and the autonomic nervous system. In the *central nervous system,* specific brain areas are involved in the generation of emotions, as well as in our experience of those emotions. The *autonomic nervous system* gives rise to many of the physiological changes associated with emotional arousal.

Brain Mechanisms Although many questions remain, researchers have described three basic features of the brain's control of emotion. First, it appears that activity in the *limbic system,* especially in the amygdala, is central to various aspects of emotion (Kensinger & Corkin, 2004; LeDoux, 1996; see Figure 11.9). Disruption of the amygdala's functioning prevents animals from being able to associate fear

Canada Brings Home the Gold! For members of the Women's Hockey Team, how might the six characteristics of emotions (short-lasting, positive or negative, personal interpretation, change in mental experience, change in behaviour, and a passionate event) be used to explain their emotions?

emotion A transitory positive or negative experience that is felt as happening to the self, is generated in part by cognitive appraisal of a situation, and is accompanied by both learned and reflexive physical responses.

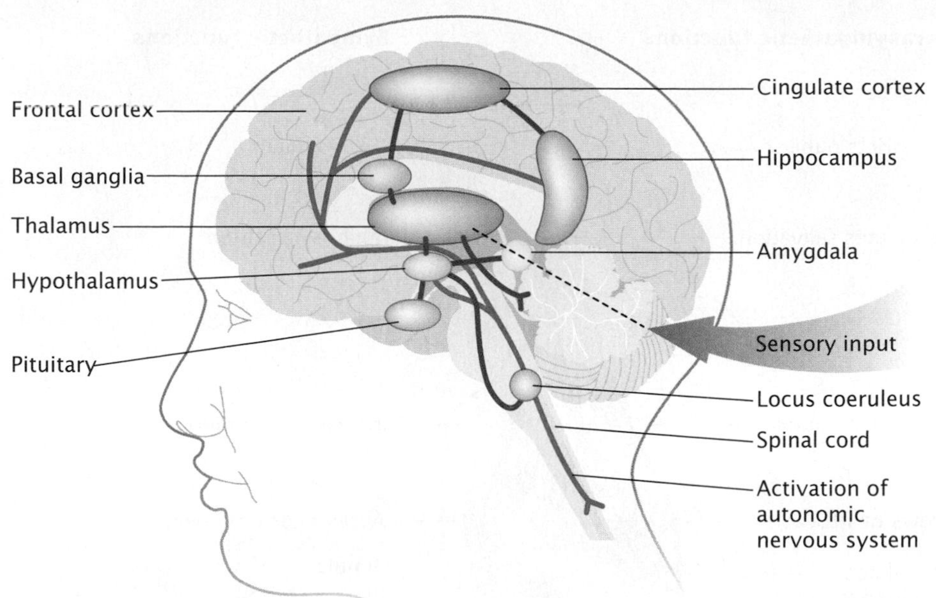

figure 11.9

Brain Regions Involved in Emotion

Incoming sensory information alerts the brain to an emotion-evoking situation. Most of the information goes through the thalamus. The cingulate cortex and hippocampus are involved in the interpretation of this sensory input. Output from these areas goes to the amygdala and hypothalamus, which control the autonomic nervous system via brainstem connections. There are also connections from the thalamus directly to the amygdala. The locus coeruleus is an area of the brainstem that causes both widespread arousal of cortical areas and changes in autonomic activity.

with a negative stimulus (Davis et al., 1993). In humans, too, the amygdala plays a critical role in the ability to learn emotional associations, recognize emotional expressions, and perceive emotionally charged words (e.g., Anderson & Phelps, 2001). In one brain imaging study, when researchers paired an uncomfortably loud noise with pictures of faces, the participants' brains showed activation of the amygdala while the noise-picture association was being learned (LaBar et al., 1998). In another study, victims of a disease that destroys only the amygdala were found to be unable to judge other people's emotional states by looking at their faces (Adolphs et al., 1994). Faces that normal people rated as expressing strong negative emotions were rated by the amygdala-damaged individuals as approachable and trustworthy (Adolphs, Tranel, & Damasio, 1998).

A second aspect of the brain's role in emotion is revealed by research on the cerebral cortex. It turns out that its two hemispheres make somewhat different contributions to the perception, experience, and expression of emotion (Davidson, 2000; Davidson, Shackman, & Maxwell, 2004). For example, after suffering damage to the right, but not the left, hemisphere, people no longer laugh at jokes—even though they can still understand the jokes' words, their logic (or illogic), and their punch lines (Critchley, 1991). Further, when people are asked to name the emotions shown in slides of facial expressions, blood flow increases in the right hemisphere more than in the left hemisphere (Gur, Skolnic, & Gur, 1994). People are also faster and more accurate at this emotion-naming task when the facial expressions are presented to the brain's right hemisphere than when they are presented to the left (Hahdahl, Iversen, & Jonsen, 1993). Finally, compared with normal people, depressed people display greater electrical activity in the right frontal cortex (Schaffer, Davidson, & Saron, 1983) and perform more poorly on tasks that depend especially on the right hemisphere (Banich et al., 1992; Heller, Etienne, & Miller, 1995).

If the right hemisphere is relatively dominant in emotion, which side of the face would you expect to be somewhat more involved in expressing emotion? If you said the left side, you are correct, because movements of each side of the body are controlled by the opposite side of the brain (see the chapter on biological aspects of psychology).

Mechanisms of the Autonomic Nervous System The autonomic nervous system (ANS) is involved in many of the physiological changes that accompany emotions (Vernet, Robin, & Dittmar, 1995). If your hands get cold and

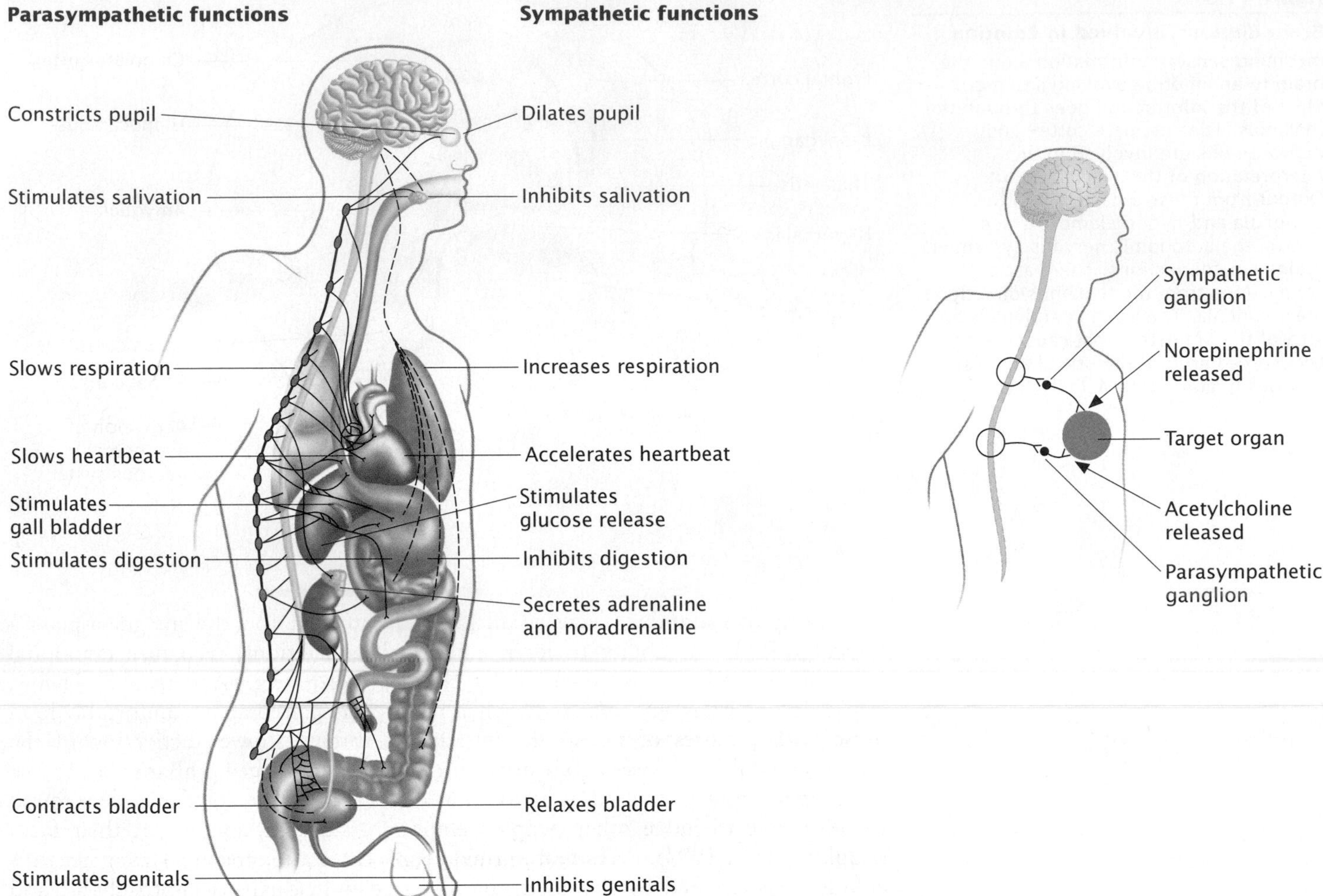

figure 11.10

The Autonomic Nervous System

Emotional responses involve activation of the autonomic nervous system, which includes sympathetic and parasympathetic subsystems. Which of the bodily responses depicted here do you associate with emotional experiences?

clammy when you are nervous, it is because the ANS has increased perspiration and decreased the blood flow in your hands.

As described in the chapter on biological aspects of psychology, the ANS carries information between the brain and most organs of the body—the heart and blood vessels, the digestive system, and so on (see Figure 11.10). Each of these organs has its own ongoing activity, but ANS input increases or decreases this activity. By doing so, the ANS coordinates the functioning of these organs to meet the body's general needs and to prepare it for change (Porges, Doussard, & Maita, 1995). If you are aroused to take action—to run to catch a bus, say—you need more glucose to fuel your muscles. The ANS frees needed energy by stimulating secretion of glucose-generating hormones and promoting blood flow to the muscles.

As shown in Figure 11.10, the autonomic nervous system is organized into two divisions: the **sympathetic nervous system** and the **parasympathetic nervous system.** Emotions can activate either of these divisions, both of which send axon fibres to each organ in the body. Generally, the sympathetic and parasympathetic fibres have opposite effects on these *target organs.* Axons from the parasympathetic system release *acetylcholine* onto target organs, leading to activity related to the protection, nourishment, and growth of the body. For example, parasympathetic activity increases digestion by stimulating movement of the intestinal system so that more nutrients

sympathetic nervous system The subsystem of the autonomic nervous system that usually prepares the organism for vigorous activity.

parasympathetic nervous system The subsystem of the autonomic nervous system that typically influences activity related to the protection, nourishment, and growth of the body.

are taken from food. Axons from the sympathetic system release a different neurotransmitter, *norepinephrine,* onto target organs, helping to prepare the body for vigorous activity. When one part of the sympathetic system is stimulated, other parts are activated "in sympathy" with it (Gellhorn & Loofbourrow, 1963). For example, input from sympathetic neurons to the adrenal medulla causes that gland to release norepinephrine and epinephrine into the bloodstream, thereby activating all sympathetic target organs (see Figure 13.3 in the health, stress, and coping chapter). The result is the **fight-or-flight syndrome,** a pattern of increased heart rate and blood pressure, rapid or irregular breathing, dilated pupils, perspiration, dry mouth, increased blood sugar, pilo-erection ("goose bumps"), and other changes that help prepare the body to combat or run from a threat.

The ANS is not directly connected to brain areas involved in consciousness, so sensations about organ activity reach the brain at a nonconscious level. You may hear your stomach grumble, but you can't actually feel it secrete acids. Similarly, you can't consciously experience the brain mechanisms that alter the activity of your autonomic nervous system. This is why most people cannot exert direct, conscious control over blood pressure or other aspects of ANS activity. However, there are things you can do to indirectly affect the ANS. For example, to create autonomic stimulation of your sex organs, you might imagine an erotic situation. To raise your blood pressure, you might hold your breath or strain your muscles; to lower it, you can lie down, relax, and think calming thoughts.

Theories of Emotion

How does all this activity in the brain and the autonomic nervous system relate to the emotions we actually experience? Are autonomic responses to events enough to *create* the experience of emotion, or are those responses the *result* of emotional experiences that begin in the brain? And how does our cognitive interpretation of events affect our emotional reactions to them? For over a century now, psychologists have worked at finding the answers to these questions. In the process, they have developed a number of theories that explain emotion mainly in terms of biological or cognitive factors. The main biological theories are those of William James and Walter Cannon. The most prominent cognitive theories are those of Stanley Schachter and Richard Lazarus. In this section we review these theories, along with some research designed to evaluate them.

James's Peripheral Theory

Suppose you are camping in the woods when a huge bear approaches your tent. Scared to death, you run for dear life. Do you run because you are afraid, or are you afraid because you run? The example and the question come from William James, who, in the late 1800s, offered one of the first formal accounts of how physiological responses relate to emotional experience. James argued that you are afraid because you run. Your running and the physiological responses associated with it, he said, follow directly from your perception of the bear. Without these physiological responses, you would feel no fear, because, said James, recognition of physiological responses *is* fear. Because James saw activity in the peripheral nervous system as the cause of emotional experience, his theory is known as a *peripheral theory* of emotion.

At first glance, James's theory might seem ridiculous. It doesn't make sense to run from something unless you already fear it. James concluded otherwise after examining his own mental processes. He decided that once you strip away all physiological responses, nothing remains of the experience of an emotion (James, 1890). Emotion, he reasoned, must therefore be the result of experiencing a particular set of physiological responses. A similar argument was offered by Carle Lange, a Danish physician, so James's view is sometimes called the *James-Lange theory* of emotion.

fight-or-flight syndrome The physical reactions initiated by the sympathetic nervous system that prepare the body to fight or to run from a threatening situation.

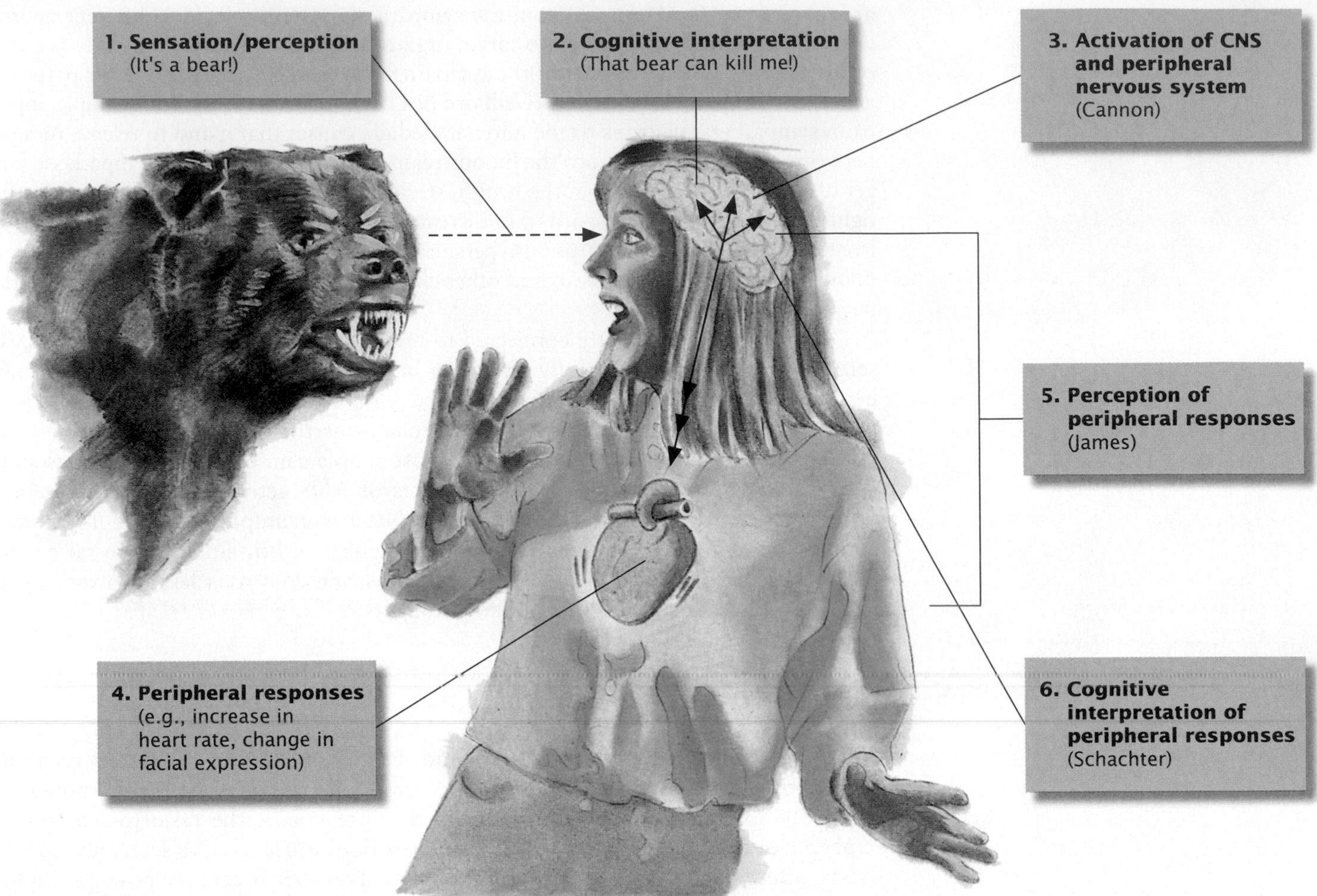

figure 11.11

Components of Emotion

Emotion is associated with activity in the central nervous system (the brain and spinal cord), with responses elsewhere in the body (called *peripheral* responses), and with cognitive interpretations of events. Emotion theorists have differed about which of these components is essential for emotion. William James focused on the perception of peripheral responses, such as changes in heart rate. Walter Cannon said that emotion could occur entirely within the brain. Stanley Schachter emphasized cognitive factors, including how we interpret events and how we label our peripheral responses to them.

Observing Peripheral Responses Figure 11.11 outlines the components of emotional experience, including those emphasized by James. First, a perception affects the cerebral cortex, said James; "then quick as a flash, reflex currents pass down through their pre-ordained channels, alter the condition of muscle, skin, and viscus; and these alterations, perceived, like the original object, in as many portions of the cortex, combine with it in consciousness and transform it from an object-simply-apprehended into an object-emotionally-felt" (James, 1890, p. 759). In other words, the brain interprets a situation and automatically directs a particular set of peripheral physiological changes—a palpitating heart, sinking stomach, facial grimace, perspiration, and certain patterns of blood flow. We are not conscious of the process, said James, until we become aware of these bodily changes; at that point, we experience an emotion. So, James's theory holds that reflexive peripheral responses appear before the subjective experience of emotion. It also implies that each particular emotion is created by a particular pattern of physiological responses. For example, fear would follow from one pattern of bodily responses, and anger would follow from a different pattern.

Notice that according to James's view, emotional experience is not generated by activity in the brain alone. There is no special "emotion centre" in the brain where the firing of neurons creates a direct experience of emotion. If this theory is accurate, it might account for the difficulty we sometimes have in knowing our true feelings: We must figure out what emotions we feel by perceiving subtle differences in specific physiological response patterns.

Evaluating James's Theory There are more than 500 labels for emotions in the English language (Averill, 1980). Does a different pattern of physiological activity precede each of these specific emotions? Probably not, but research shows that certain more general emotional states are indeed associated with certain patterns of autonomic activity (Craig, 2002; Damasio et al., 2000; Keltner & Buswell, 1996; Sinha & Parsons, 1996). For example, blood flow to the hands and feet increases in association with anger and declines in association with fear (Levenson, Ekman, & Friesen, 1990). So fear involves "cold feet"; anger does not. A pattern of activity associated with disgust includes increased muscle activity but no change in heart rate. Even when people mentally relive different kinds of emotional experiences, they show different patterns of autonomic activity (Ekman, Levenson, & Friesen, 1983). These emotion-specific patterns of physiological activity have been found in widely different cultures (Levenson et al., 1992). It also turns out that people who are keenly aware of physiological changes in their bodies are likely to experience emotions more intensely than those who are less aware of such changes (Barrett et al., 2004; Schneider, Ring, & Katkin, 1998; Wiens, Mezzacappa, & Katkin, 2000). It has even been suggested that the "gut feelings" that cause us to approach or avoid certain situations might be the result of physiological changes

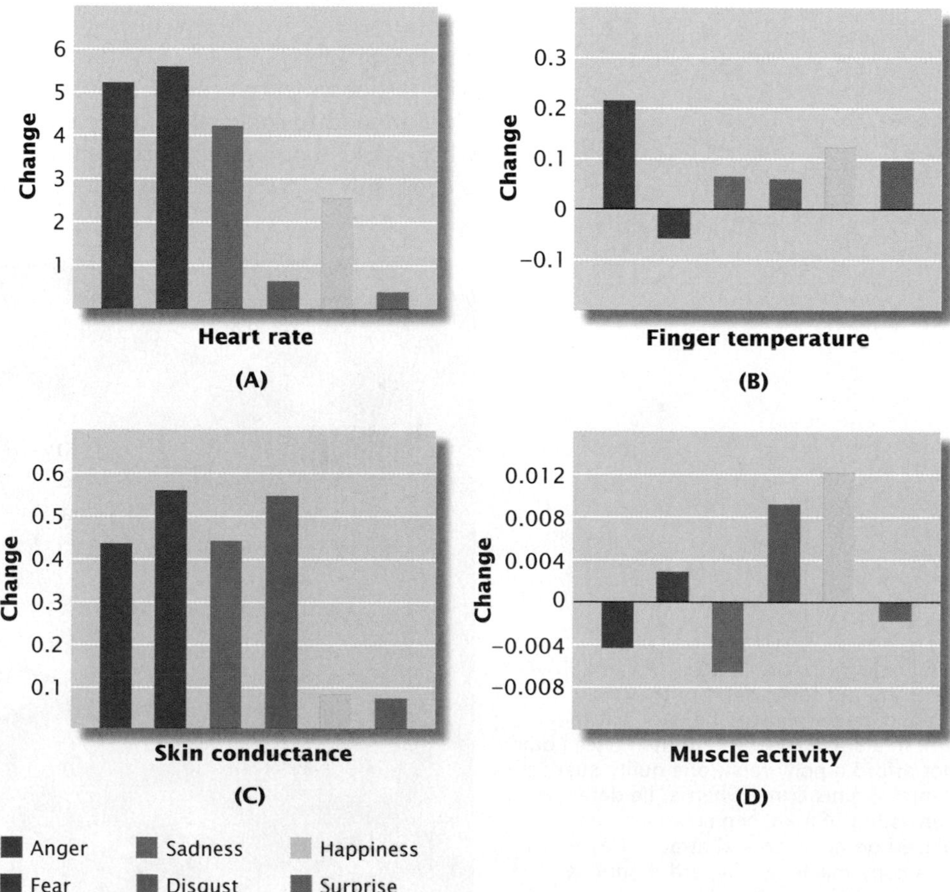

figure 11.12

Physiological Changes Associated with Different Emotions

In this experiment, facial movements characteristic of different emotions produced different patterns of change in (A) heart rate; (B) peripheral blood flow, as measured by finger temperature; (C) skin conductance; and (D) muscle activity (Levenson, Ekman, & Friesen, 1990). For example, making an angry face caused heart rate and finger temperature to rise, whereas making a fearful face raised heart rate but lowered finger temperature.

Source: Levenson, Ekman, & Friesen (1990).

that are perceived without conscious awareness (Bechara et al., 1997; Damasio, 1994; Katkin, Wiens, & Öhman, 2001; Winkielman & Berridge, 2004).

James's theory implies that the experience of emotion would be blocked if a person were unable to detect physiological changes occurring in the body's periphery. So spinal cord injuries that reduce feedback from peripheral responses should reduce the intensity of emotional experiences. Yet research shows that when people with spinal injuries continue to pursue their life goals, they experience a full range of emotions, including as much happiness as noninjured people (Bermond et al., 1991; Cobos et al., 2004). These people report that their emotional experiences are just as intense as before their injuries, even though they notice less intense physiological changes associated with their emotions.

Such reports seem to contradict James's theory. But spinal cord injuries do not usually affect facial expressions, which James included among the bodily responses that are experienced as emotions. Some researchers have proposed a variant of James's theory, the *facial feedback hypothesis,* which maintains that involuntary facial movements provide enough peripheral information to create emotional experience (Ekman & Davidson, 1993). This hypothesis helps to explain why posed facial expressions generate the emotions normally associated with them. (The next time you want to cheer yourself up, it might help to smile—even though you don't feel like it.)

Lie Detection James's view that different patterns of physiological activity are associated with different emotions forms the basis for the lie detection industry. If people experience anxiety or guilt when they lie, specific patterns of physiological activity accompanying these emotions should be detectable on instruments, called *polygraphs,* that record heart rate, breathing, perspiration, and other autonomic responses.

To identify the perpetrator of a crime using the *control question test,* a polygraph operator would ask questions specific to the crime, such as "Did you stab anyone on July 3, 2004?" Responses to such *relevant questions* are then compared with responses to *control questions,* such as "Have you ever lied to get out of trouble?" Innocent people might have lied at some time in the past and might feel guilty when asked about it, but they should have no reason to feel guilty about what they did on July 3, 2004. So an innocent person should have a stronger emotional

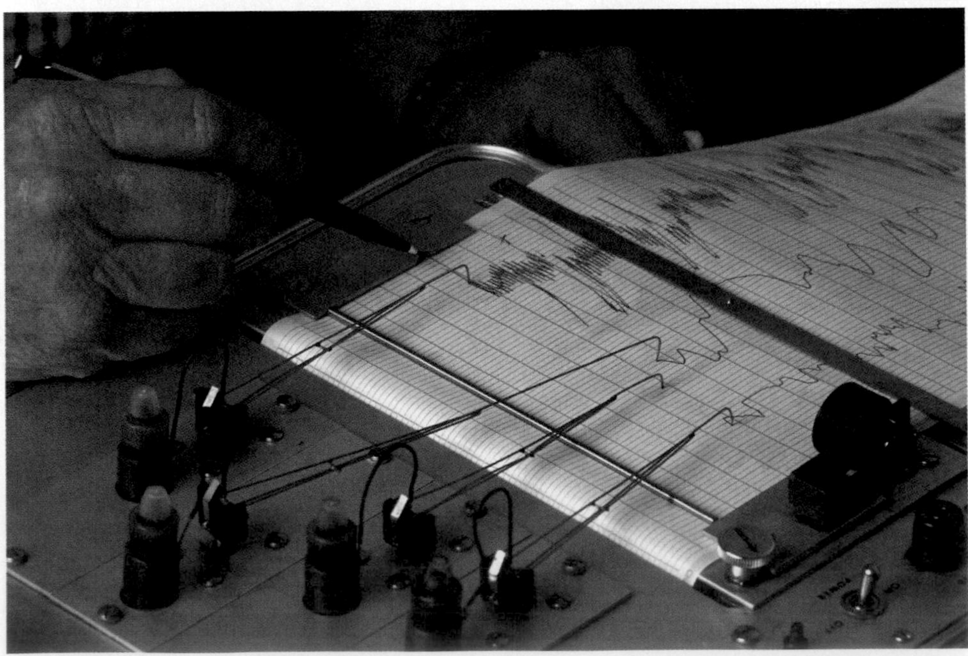

Searching for the Truth Polygraph tests are not foolproof, but they may intimidate people who believe that they are. In a small town where the police could not afford a polygraph, one guilty suspect confessed his crime when a "lie detector" consisting of a kitchen colander was placed on his head and attached by wires to a copy machine (Shepard, Kohut, & Sweet, 1989).

response to control questions than to relevant questions (Rosenfeld, 1995). Another approach, called the *directed lie test,* compares a person's physiological reactions when asked to lie about something and when telling what is known to be the truth. Finally, the *guilty knowledge test* seeks to determine if a person reacts in a notable way to information about a crime that only the criminal would know (Ben-Shakhar, Bar-Hillel, & Kremnitzer, 2002).

Most people do have emotional responses when they lie, but statistics about the accuracy of polygraphs are difficult to obtain. Estimates vary widely, from those suggesting that polygraphs detect 90 percent of guilty, lying individuals (Honts & Quick, 1995; Kircher, Horowitz, & Raskin, 1988; Raskin, 1986) to those suggesting that polygraphs mislabel as many as 40 percent of truthful, innocent persons as guilty liars (Ben-Shakhar & Furedy, 1990; Saxe & Ben-Shakhar, 1999). Obviously, the results of a polygraph test are not determined entirely by whether a person is telling the truth. What people think about the act of lying and about the value of the test can also influence the accuracy of its results. For example, people who consider lying to be acceptable—and who do not believe in the power of polygraphs—are unlikely to display emotion-related physiological responses while lying during the test. However, an innocent person who believes in such tests and who thinks that "everything always goes wrong" might show a large fear response when asked about a crime, thus wrongly suggesting guilt.

Polygraphs can catch some liars, but most researchers agree that a guilty person can "fool" a polygraph lie detector and that some innocent people can be mislabelled as guilty (Lykken, 1998). After reviewing the relevant research literature, a panel of distinguished psychologists expressed serious reservations about the value of polygraph tests in detecting deception and argued against their use as evidence in court or in employee screening and selection (Committee to Review the Scientific Evidence on the Polygraph, 2003). Other lie-detecting devices now being investigated focus on brain activity and other measures that do not depend on a link between deception and autonomic nervous system responses (Kozel, Padgett, & George, 2004; Lee et al., 2002; Preston, 2002; Zhou et al., 2000).

Cannon's Central Theory

James said the experience of emotion depends on feedback from physiological responses occurring outside the brain, but Walter Cannon disagreed (Cannon, 1927–1987). According to Cannon, you feel fear at the sight of a wild bear even before you start to run. He said that emotional experience starts in the central nervous system—specifically, in the thalamus, the brain structure that relays information from most sense organs to the cortex.

According to Cannon's *central theory* (also known as the *Cannon-Bard theory,* in recognition of Philip Bard's contribution), when the thalamus receives sensory information about emotional events and situations, it sends signals to the autonomic nervous system and—at the same time—to the cerebral cortex, where the emotion becomes conscious. So when you see a bear, the brain receives sensory information about it, perceives it as a bear, and *directly* creates the experience of fear while at the same time sending messages to the heart, lungs, and muscles to do what it takes to run away. In other words, Cannon said that the experience of emotion appears directly in the brain, with or without feedback from peripheral responses (see Figure 11.12).

Updating Cannon's Theory Research conducted since Cannon proposed his theory indicates that the thalamus is actually not the "seat" of emotion but that, through its connections to the amygdala (see Figure 11.9), the thalamus does participate in some aspects of emotional processing (Lang, 1995). For example, studies in animals and humans show that the emotion of fear is generated by connections from the thalamus to the amygdala (Anderson & Phelps, 2000; LeDoux, 1995). The implication is that strong emotions can sometimes bypass the cortex without requiring conscious thought to activate them. One study showed, for example, that people presented with stimuli such as angry faces display physiological signs of arousal even if they are not conscious of seeing those stimuli (Morris et al., 1998). The same processes might explain why people find it so difficult to overcome an intense fear, or phobia, even though they may consciously know the fear is irrational. Still, there is evidence to support the main thrust of Cannon's theory: that emotion occurs through the activation of specific parts of the central nervous system. What Cannon did not foresee is that different parts of the central nervous system may be activated for different emotions and for different aspects of the total emotional experience.

Cognitive Theories

Suppose you are about to be interviewed for your first job or to go out on a blind date or to take your first ride in a hot-air balloon. In situations such as these, it is not always easy to know exactly what you are feeling. Is it fear, excitement, anticipation, worry, happiness, dread, or what? Stanley Schachter suggested that the emotions we experience every day are shaped partly by how we interpret the arousal we feel. His cognitive theory of emotion, known as the *Schachter-Singer theory* in recognition of the contributions of Jerome Singer, took shape in the early 1960s, when many psychologists were raising questions about the validity of James's theory of emotion. Schachter argued that the theory was essentially correct—but required a few modifications (Cornelius, 1996). In Schachter's view, feedback about physiological changes may not vary enough to create the many shades of emotion that people can experience. He argued instead that emotions emerge from a combination of feedback from peripheral responses and the *cognitive interpretation* of the nature and cause of those responses (Schachter & Singer, 1962). Cognitive interpretation first comes into play, said Schachter, when you perceive the stimulus that leads to bodily responses ("It's a bear!"). Interpretation occurs again when you identify feedback from those responses as a particular emotion (see Figure 11.12). The same physiological responses might be given many different labels, depending on how you interpret those responses. So, according to Schachter, when that bear approaches your campsite, the emotion you experience might be fear, excitement, astonishment, or surprise, depending on how you label your bodily reactions.

Schachter also said that the labelling of arousal depends on **attribution,** the process of identifying the cause of an event. Physiological arousal might be attributed to one of several emotions depending on the information available about the situation. If you are watching the final seconds of a close ball game, you might attribute your racing heart, rapid breathing, and perspiration to excitement. You might attribute the same physiological reactions to anxiety if you are waiting for a big exam to begin. Schachter predicted that our emotional experiences will be less intense if we attribute arousal to a nonemotional cause. So if you notice your heart pounding before an exam but say to yourself, "Sure my heart's racing—I just drank five cups of coffee!" then you should feel "wired" from caffeine rather than afraid or worried. This prediction has received some support (Mezzacappa, Katkin, & Palmer, 1999; Sinclair et al., 1994), but other aspects of Schachter's theory have not.

Few researchers today fully accept the Schachter-Singer theory, but it did stimulate an enormous amount of valuable research, including studies of **excitation transfer,** a phenomenon in which physiological arousal from one experience carries over to affect emotion in an independent situation (Reisenzein, 1983; Zillman, 1984). For example, people who have been aroused by physical exercise become more angry when provoked, or experience more intense sexual feelings when in the company of an attractive person, than do people who have been less physically active (Allen et al., 1989). Arousal from fear, like arousal from exercise, can also enhance emotions, including sexual feelings. One study of this transfer took

attribution The process of explaining the causes of an event.

excitation transfer A process in which arousal from one experience carries over to affect emotion in an independent situation.

in review Theories of Emotion

Theory	Source of Emotions	Example
James-Lange	Emotions are created by awareness of specific patterns of peripheral (autonomic) responses.	Anger is associated with increased blood flow in the hands and feet; fear is associated with decreased blood flow in these areas.
Cannon-Bard	The brain generates direct experiences of emotion.	Stimulation of certain brain areas can create pleasant or unpleasant emotions.
Cognitive (Schachter-Singer and Lazarus)	Cognitive interpretation of events, and of physiological reactions to them, shapes emotional experiences.	Autonomic arousal can be experienced as anxiety or excitement, depending on how it is labelled. A single event can lead to different emotions, depending on whether it is perceived as threatening or challenging.

PsychAssist: Homeostasis and Drive Reduction Theory

place in Vancouver (Dutton & Aron, 1972), on either a swinging bridge suspended high over the Capilano River; or a sturdy wooden bridge just three metres above a gentle stream. A female researcher asked men who had just crossed either bridge to fill out a questionnaire that included a measure of sexual imagery. The men who met the woman after crossing the more dangerous bridge had much higher sexual imagery scores than the men who had crossed the stable bridge. Furthermore, they were more likely to rate the researcher as attractive. When the person giving out the questionnaire was a male, however, the type of bridge crossed had no effect on sexual imagery. To test the possibility that the men who crossed the dangerous bridge were simply more adventurous in both bridge crossing and heterosexual encounters, the researcher repeated the study, but with one change. This time, the woman approached the men farther down the trail, long after arousal from the bridge crossing had subsided. Now, the apparently adventurous men were no more likely than others to rate the woman as attractive. So it was probably excitation transfer, not just adventurousness, that produced the original result.

"In Review: Theories of Emotion" summarizes key elements of the theories we have discussed. It appears that both peripheral autonomic responses (including facial responses) and the cognitive interpretation of those responses add to emotional experience. So does cognitive appraisal of events themselves. In addition, the brain can apparently generate emotional experience on its own, independent of physiological arousal. In short, emotion is probably both in the heart and in the head (including the face). The most basic emotions probably occur directly within the brain, whereas the many shades of discernible emotions probably arise from attributions and other cognitive interpretations of physiological responses and environmental events. No theory has completely resolved the issue of which, if any, component of emotion is primary. However, the theories we have discussed have helped psychologists better understand how these components interact to produce emotional experience.

The Universal Smile The idea that some emotional expressions are innate is supported by the fact that the facial movement pattern we call a smile is related to happiness, pleasure, and other positive emotions in cultures throughout the world.

Communicating Emotion

So far, we have described emotion from the inside, as people experience their own emotions. Let's now consider how people communicate emotions to one another. One way they do this is through words. Some people describe their feelings relatively simply, and mainly in terms of pleasantness or unpleasantness. Others include information about the intensity of their emotions (Barrett, 1995; Barrett et al., 2001). In general, women are more likely than men to talk about their emotions and the complexity of their feelings (Barrett et al., 2000; Kring & Gordon, 1998). But humans also communicate emotion through the movement and posture of their bodies (Hadjikhani & de Gelder, 2003), through their tone of voice, and especially through their facial movements and expressions.

Imagine a woman watching television. You can see her face, but not what she sees on the screen. She might be engaged in complex thought, perhaps comparing her investments with those of the experts on CBC's *Venture*. Or she might be thinking of nothing at all as she loses herself in a rerun of *Third Rock from the Sun*. In other words, you won't be able to tell much about what the woman is thinking. But if the TV program creates an emotional experience, you will be able to make a reasonably accurate guess about what she is feeling simply by looking at the expression on her face. The human face can create thousands of different expressions (Zajonc, 1998), and people are good at detecting them. Observers can notice even tiny facial movements—a twitch of the mouth or eyebrow can carry a lot of information. Females consistently outperform males in identifying and interpreting the nonverbal emotion cues conveyed by facial expressions (Hall, 1984). This gender difference also appears in adolescents, children, and even infants (McClure, 2000), suggesting that it may be rooted in biology, as well as in gender-specific socialization. Are emotional facial expressions innate as well, or are they learned? And how are they used in communicating emotion?

Innate Expressions of Emotion

Charles Darwin observed that some facial expressions seem to be universal (Darwin, 1872/1965). He proposed that these expressions are genetically determined, passed on biologically from one generation to the next. The facial expressions seen today, said Darwin, are those that have been most effective at telling others something about how a person is feeling. If someone is scowling with teeth clenched, for example, you will

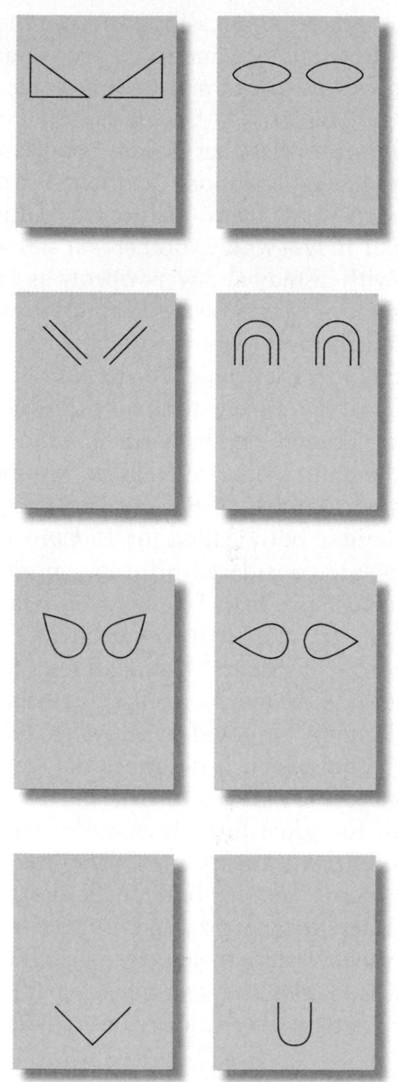

figure 11.13

Threat Elements of Ceremonial Masks

Certain geometric patterns are common to threatening masks in many cultures. When people in various cultures were asked which member of each of these pairs was more threatening, they consistently chose those, shown here on the left, containing triangular and diagonal elements. "Scary" Halloween pumpkins tend to have such elements as well.

probably assume that this person is angry, and you will be unlikely to choose that particular moment to ask for a loan.

Infants provide one source of evidence that some facial expressions are innate. Newborns do not need to be taught to grimace in pain or to smile in pleasure or to blink when startled (Balaban, 1995). Even blind infants, who cannot imitate adults' expressions, show the same emotional expressions as do sighted infants (Goodenough, 1932).

A second line of evidence for innate facial expressions comes from studies showing that for the most basic emotions, people in all cultures show similar facial responses to similar emotional stimuli (Hejmadi, Davidson, & Rozin, 2000; Zajonc, 1998). Participants in these studies look at photographs of people's faces and then try to name the emotion each person is feeling. Although there may be some subtle differences from culture to culture (Marsh, Elfenbein, & Ambady, 2003), the overall pattern of facial movements we call a smile, for example, is universally related to positive emotions. Sadness is almost always accompanied by slackened muscle tone and a "long" face. Likewise, in almost all cultures, people contort their faces in a similar way when shown something they find disgusting. And a furrowed brow is frequently associated with frustration (Ekman, 1994).

Anger is also linked with a facial expression recognized by almost all cultures. One study examined artwork—including ceremonial masks—of various Western and non-Western cultures (Aronoff, Barclay, & Stevenson, 1988). The angry, threatening masks of all 18 cultures contained similar elements, such as triangular eyes and diagonal lines on the cheeks. In particular, angular and diagonal elements carry the impression of threat (see Figure 11.13). One study with high school students found that threat is conveyed most strongly by the eyebrows, followed by the mouth and eyes (Lundqvist, Esteves, & Öhman, 1999).

Social and Cultural Influences on Emotional Expression

Some basic emotional expressions are innate, but many others are neither innate nor universal (Ekman, 1993). Even innate expressions are flexible and modifiable, changing as necessary in the social contexts within which they occur (Fernández-Dols & Ruiz-Belda, 1995). For example, facial expressions become more intense and change more frequently while people are imagining social scenes as opposed to solitary scenes (Fridlund et al., 1990). Similarly, facial expressions in response to odours tend to be more intense when others are watching than when people are alone (Jancke & Kaufmann, 1994).

Further, although a core of emotional responses is recognized by all cultures (Hejmadi, Davidson, & Rozin, 2000), there is a certain degree of cultural variation in recognizing some emotions (Russell, 1995). In one study, for example, Japanese and North American people agreed about which facial expressions signalled happiness, surprise, and sadness, but they frequently disagreed about which faces showed anger, disgust, and fear (Matsumoto & Ekman, 1989). Members of preliterate cultures, such as the Fore of New Guinea, agree even less with people in Western cultures on the labelling of facial expressions (Russell, 1994). In addition, there are variations in how people in different cultures interpret emotions expressed by tone of voice (Mesquita & Frijda, 1992). For instance, Taiwanese participants were best at recognizing a sad tone of voice, whereas Dutch participants were best at recognizing happy tones (Van Bezooijen, Otto, & Heenan, 1983).

People learn how to express certain emotions in particular ways, as specified by cultural rules. Suppose you say, "I just bought a new car," and all your friends stick their tongues out at you. In North America, this would mean that they are envious or resentful. But in some regions of China, such a display expresses surprise.

Learning About Emotions The effects of learning are seen in a child's growing range of emotional expressions. Although infants begin with an innate set of emotional responses, they soon learn to imitate facial expressions and use them for more and more emotions. In time, these expressions become more precise and personalized, so that a particular expression conveys a clear emotional message to anyone who knows that person well.

As children grow, they learn an *emotion culture*—rules that govern what emotions are appropriate in what circumstances and what emotional expressions are allowed. These rules can vary between genders and from culture to culture (LaFrance, Hecht, & Paluck, 2003). However, in Italy—where mother-son ties are particularly strong—many male soldiers wailed with dismay and wept openly as they left for military service. In a laboratory study, when viewing a distressing movie with a group of peers, Japanese students exhibited much more control over their facial expressions than did North American students. When they watched the film while alone, however, the Japanese students' faces showed the same emotional expressions as those of the North American students (Ekman, Friesen, & Ellsworth, 1972).

Emotion cultures shape how people describe and categorize feelings, resulting in both similarities and differences across cultures (Russell, 1991). At least five of the seven basic emotions listed in an ancient Chinese book called the *Li Chi*—joy, anger, sadness, fear, love, disliking, and liking—are considered primary emotions by most Western theorists. Yet whereas English has more than 500 emotion-related words, some emotion words in other languages have no English equivalent. The Czech word *litost* apparently has no English word equivalent: "It designates a feeling as infinite as an open accordion, a feeling that is the synthesis of many others: grief, sympathy, remorse, and an indefinable longing" (quoted in Russell, 1991). The Japanese word *ijirashii* also has no English equivalent; it describes the feeling of seeing a praiseworthy person overcoming an obstacle (Russell, 1991).

Similarly, other cultures have no equivalent for some English emotion words. Many cultures do not see anger and sadness as different, for example. The Ilongot, a Philippine head-hunting group, have only one word, *liget,* for both anger and grief (Russell, 1991). Tahitians have words for 46 different types of anger but no word for sadness and, apparently, no concept of it. One Westerner described a Tahitian man as sad over separation from his wife and child, but the man himself felt *pe'a pe'a*—a general term for feeling ill, troubled, or fatigued—and did not attribute it to the separation.

LINKAGES

As noted in the chapter on introducing psychology, all of psychology's many subfields are related to one another. Our discussion of conflicting motives and stress illustrates just one way in which the topic of this chapter, motivation and emotion, is linked to the subfield of health psychology (which is discussed in the chapter on health, stress, and coping). The Linkages diagram shows ties to two other subfields as well, and there are many more ties throughout the book. Looking for linkages among subfields will help you see how they all fit together and better appreciate the big picture that is psychology.

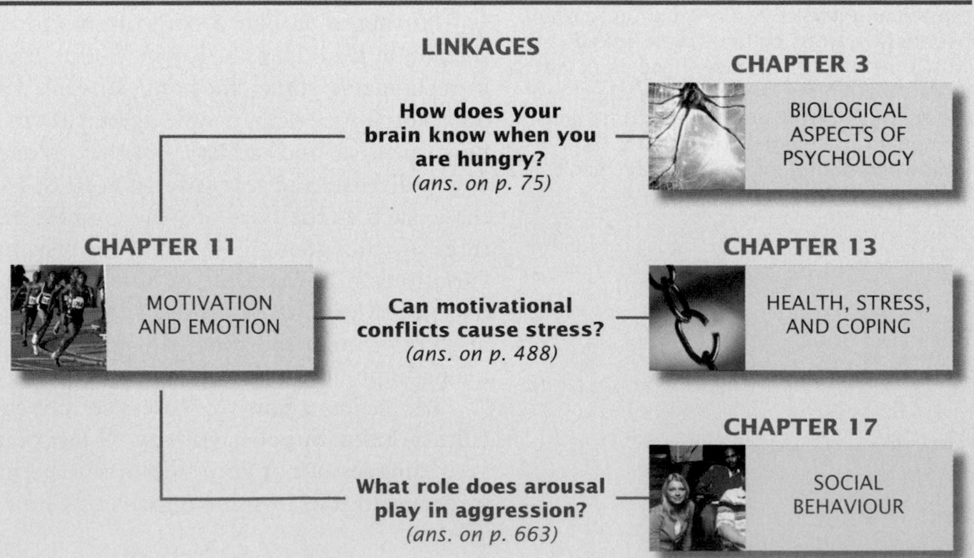
LINKAGES
CHAPTER 3
How does your brain know when you are hungry?
(ans. on p. 75)
BIOLOGICAL ASPECTS OF PSYCHOLOGY
CHAPTER 11
MOTIVATION AND EMOTION
CHAPTER 13
Can motivational conflicts cause stress?
(ans. on p. 488)
HEALTH, STRESS, AND COPING
CHAPTER 17
What role does arousal play in aggression?
(ans. on p. 663)
SOCIAL BEHAVIOUR

SUMMARY

Motivation refers to factors that influence the initiation, direction, intensity, and persistence of behaviour. Emotion and motivation are often linked: Motivation can influence emotion, and people are often motivated to seek certain emotions.

Concepts and Theories of Motivation

Focusing on a *motive* often reveals a single theme within apparently diverse behaviours. Motivation is said to be an intervening variable, a way of linking various stimuli to the behaviours that follow them.

Sources of Motivation

The many sources of motivation fall into four categories: biological factors, emotional factors, cognitive factors, and social factors.

Instinct Theory and Its Descendants

An early argument held that motivation follows from *instincts,* which are automatic, involuntary, and unlearned behaviour patterns consistently "released" by particular stimuli. Modern versions of *instinct theory* are seen in evolutionary accounts of helping, aggression, mate selection, and other aspects of social behaviour.

Drive Reduction Theory

Drive reduction theory is based on *homeostasis,* a tendency to maintain equilibrium in a physical or behavioural process. When disruption of equilibrium creates a *need* of some kind, people are motivated to reduce the resulting *drive* by behaving in some way that satisfies the need and restores balance. *Primary drives* are unlearned; *secondary drives* are learned.

Arousal Theory

According to *arousal theories* of motivation, people are motivated to behave in ways that maintain a level of *arousal* that is optimal for their functioning.

Incentive Theory

Incentive theory highlights behaviours that are motivated by attaining desired stimuli (positive incentives) and avoiding undesirable ones (negative incentives).

Hunger and Eating

Hunger and eating are controlled by a complex mixture of learning, culture, and biology.

Biological Signals for Hunger and Satiety

The desire to eat (*hunger*) or to stop eating (*satiety*) depends primarily on signals from blood-borne substances such as glucose, insulin, and leptin.

Hunger and the Brain

Activity in the ventromedial nucleus of the hypothalamus results in satiety, whereas activity in the lateral hypothalamus results in hunger. These brain regions might be acting together to maintain a set point of body weight, but control of eating is more complex than that.

Flavour, Cultural Learning, and Food Selection

Eating may also be influenced by the flavour of food and by appetite for the pleasure of food. Food selection is influenced by biological needs (specific hungers) for certain nutrients, as well as by food cravings, social contexts, and cultural traditions.

Eating Disorders

Obesity has been linked to overconsumption of certain kinds of foods, to low energy metabolism, and to genetic factors. People suffering from *anorexia nervosa* starve themselves to avoid becoming fat. Those who suffer from *bulimia nervosa* engage in binge eating, followed by purging through self-induced vomiting or laxatives.

Sexual Behaviour

Sexual motivation and behaviour result from a rich interplay of biology and culture.

The Biology of Sex

Sexual stimulation generally produces a stereotyped *sexual response cycle,* a pattern of physiological arousal during and after sexual activity. *Sex hormones,* which include male hormones (*androgens*) and female hormones (*estrogens* and *progestins*), occur in different relative amounts in both sexes. They can have organizational effects, such as physical differences in the brain, and activational effects, such as increased desire for sex.

Social and Cultural Factors in Sexuality

Gender-role learning and educational experiences are examples of cultural factors that can bring about variations in sexual attitudes and behaviours.

Sexual Orientation

Sexual orientation—*heterosexual, homosexual,* or *bisexual*—is increasingly viewed as a sociocultural variable that affects many other aspects of behaviour and mental processes. Though undoubtedly shaped by a lifetime of learning, sexual orientation appears to have strong biological roots.

Sexual Dysfunctions

Common male *sexual dysfunctions* include erectile disorder and premature ejaculation. Females may experience such problems as arousal disorder.

Achievement Motivation

People gain esteem from achievement in many areas, including the workplace.

Need for Achievement

The motive to succeed is called *need achievement.* Individuals with high achievement motivation strive for excellence, persist despite failures, and set challenging but realistic goals.

Goal Setting and Achievement Motivation

Goals influence motivation, especially the amount of effort, persistence, attention, and planning we devote to a task.

Achievement and Success in the Workplace

Workers are most satisfied when they are working toward their own goals and are getting concrete feedback. Jobs that offer clear and specific goals, a variety of tasks, individual responsibility, and other intrinsic rewards are the most motivating.

Achievement and Subjective Well-Being

People tend to have a characteristic level of happiness, or *subjective well-being,* which is not necessarily related to the attainment of money, status, or other material goals.

Relations and Conflicts Among Motives

Human behaviour reflects many motives, some of which may be in conflict. Abraham Maslow proposed a hierarchy of five classes of human motives, from meeting basic biological needs to attaining a state of self-actualization. Motives at the lowest levels, according to Maslow, must be at least partially satisfied before people can be motivated by higher-level goals.

The Nature of Emotion

Defining Characteristics

An *emotion* is a temporary experience with positive or negative qualities that is felt with some intensity as happening to the self, is generated in part by a cognitive appraisal of a situation, and is accompanied by both learned and reflexive physical responses.

The Biology of Emotion

Several brain mechanisms are involved in emotion. The amygdala, in the limbic system, is deeply involved in various aspects of emotion. The brain's right and left hemispheres play somewhat different roles in emotional expression. In addition to specific brain mechanisms, both branches of the autonomic nervous system, the *sympathetic nervous system* and the *parasympathetic nervous system,* are involved in physiological changes that accompany emotional activation. The *fight-or-flight syndrome,* for example, follows from activation of the sympathetic system.

Theories of Emotion

James's Peripheral Theory

William James's theory of emotion holds that peripheral physiological responses are the primary source of emotion and that awareness of these responses constitutes emotional experience. James's theory is supported by evidence that, at least for several basic emotions, physiological responses are distinguishable enough for emotions to be generated in this way. Distinct facial expressions are linked to particular patterns of physiological change.

Cannon's Central Theory

Walter Cannon's theory of emotion proposes that emotional experience occurs independent of peripheral physiological responses and that there is a direct experience of emotion based on activity of the central nervous system. Updated versions of this theory suggest that various parts of the central nervous system may be involved in different emotions and different aspects of emotional experience. Some pathways in the brain, such as that from the thalamus to the amygdala, allow strong emotions to occur before conscious thought can take place. And specific parts of the brain appear to be responsible for the feelings of pleasure or pain in emotion.

Cognitive Theories

Stanley Schachter's modification of James's theory proposes that physiological responses are primary sources of emotion but that the cognitive labelling of those responses—a process that depends partly on *attribution*—strongly influences the emotions we experience. Schachter's theory stimulated research on *excitation transfer.*

Communicating Emotion

Humans communicate emotions mainly through facial movement and expressions, but also through voice tones and bodily movements.

Innate Expressions of Emotion

Charles Darwin suggested that certain facial expressions of emotion are innate and universal and that these expressions evolved because they effectively communicate one creature's emotional condition to other creatures. Some facial expressions of basic emotions, such as happiness, do appear to be innate.

Social and Cultural Influences on Emotional Expression

Many emotional expressions are learned, and even innate expressions are modified by learning and social contexts. As children grow, they learn an emotion culture, the rules of emotional expression appropriate to their culture. Accordingly, the same emotion may be communicated by different facial expressions in different cultures.

Human Development

12

Infancy, childhood, adolescence, adulthood, and old age. These words can be read in seconds, but the stages they represent take a lifetime to play out. The story of development is different for each of us, but there are some common threads that developmental psychologists are exploring. In this chapter, we describe what they have discovered so far about how people change and grow over the course of the life span. Here's how we have organized the material:

When Pamela Robinson was offered an assistant professor job at the University of Prince Edward Island, she was excited—until she toured the university's childcare facility. The daycare did not meet the standards she and her husband expected for their three-year-old daughter. So, she did not take the job, electing to stay in Toronto instead where her daughter had better childcare. UPEI has since opened a new childcare facility, but Pamela Robinson's story illustrates the value Canadian parents place on quality care for their children (*Toronto Star*, 2006). However, Canadians do not agree on what constitutes quality care. Standards for daycare centres vary across provinces, and regions within provinces, sparking great debate among the public and government officials as to what are reasonable standards. Other questions that have been raised are whether daycare has a positive or negative impact on children and their families, and whether the impact differs depending on the age of the child and the number of hours spent in daycare each week. In addition, some Canadians believe that young children benefit more from spending their preschool years at home under the care of a parent, not in an institutionalized daycare at all. Researchers who study human development are also interested in these questions.

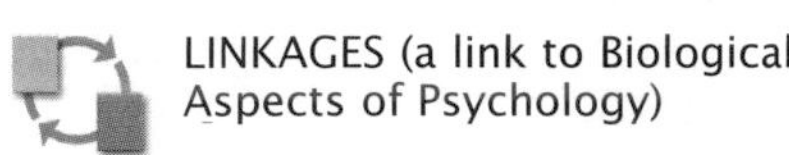

Human development is the topic addressed by researchers who specialize in developmental psychology. Developmental psychologists study changes in various areas such as physical growth, the senses (vision, hearing, and so on), thinking and reasoning skills, language, social interaction, morality, and self-concept. Some of the questions that developmental psychologists attempt to answer include: Does drinking coffee during pregnancy affect the baby's brain? Do newborn babies see colours in the same way as older children and adults? Does watching violence on television have a negative impact on children and adolescents? How do children and adults immigrating to a new country adjust to cultural differences? How do children and adults learn a second language? How do adolescents cope with the transition from high school to university? How do adults react to changes associated with mid-life? What are the particular challenges and joys of the older years? Developmental psychologists also investigate when certain behaviours first appear and how they change with age. They explore how development in one area, such as moral reasoning, relates to development in other areas, such as aggressive behaviour. They attempt to discover whether most people develop at the same rate and, if not, whether slow starters ever catch up to early bloomers. They ask why some children become well-adjusted, socially competent, nurturing, and empathic individuals, whereas others become murderers; why some adolescents go on to win honours in university, whereas others drop out of high school. They seek to explain how development throughout the life span is affected by both genetics and the environment, analyzing the extent to which development is a product of what we arrive with at birth (our inherited, biological *nature*) and the extent to which it is a product of what the world provides (the *nurture* of the environment). And they pursue development into adulthood, examining the changes that occur over the years and determining how these changes are related to earlier abilities and later events. In short, **developmental psychology** is concerned with the course and causes of the developmental changes that take place over a person's entire lifetime.

In this chapter we examine many such changes. We begin by describing the physical and biological changes that occur from the moment of conception to the time a child is born. Then we discuss cognitive, social, and emotional development during infancy and childhood. Next, we examine the changes and challenges that confront humans during their adolescence. And we conclude by considering the significant physical, intellectual, and social changes that occur as people move through early, middle, and late adulthood.

developmental psychology The psychological specialty that documents the course of physical, social, emotional, moral, and intellectual development over the life span.

Exploring Human Development

The question of whether development is the result of nature or nurture was the subject of philosophical debate centuries before psychologists began studying it scientifically. In essays published in the 1690s, British philosopher John Locke argued for nurture. He believed that experiences provided by the environment during childhood have a profound and permanent effect. As mentioned in the chapter on introducing psychology, Locke thought of the newborn as a blank slate, or *tabula rasa.* Adults write on that slate, he said, as they teach children about the world and how to behave in it. Some 70 years later, French philosopher Jean-Jacques Rousseau (pronounced "roo-SOH") made the opposite argument. He claimed that children are capable of discovering how the world operates and how they should behave without instruction from adults. According to Rousseau, children should be allowed to grow as their natures dictate, with little guidance or pressure from parents.

The first psychologist to systematically investigate the role of nature in behaviour was Arnold Gesell. In the early 1900s, Gesell (pronounced "geh-ZELL") observed many children of all ages. He found that their motor skills, such as standing and walking, picking up a cube, and throwing a ball, developed in a fixed sequence of stages, as Figure 12.1 illustrates. The order of the stages and the age at

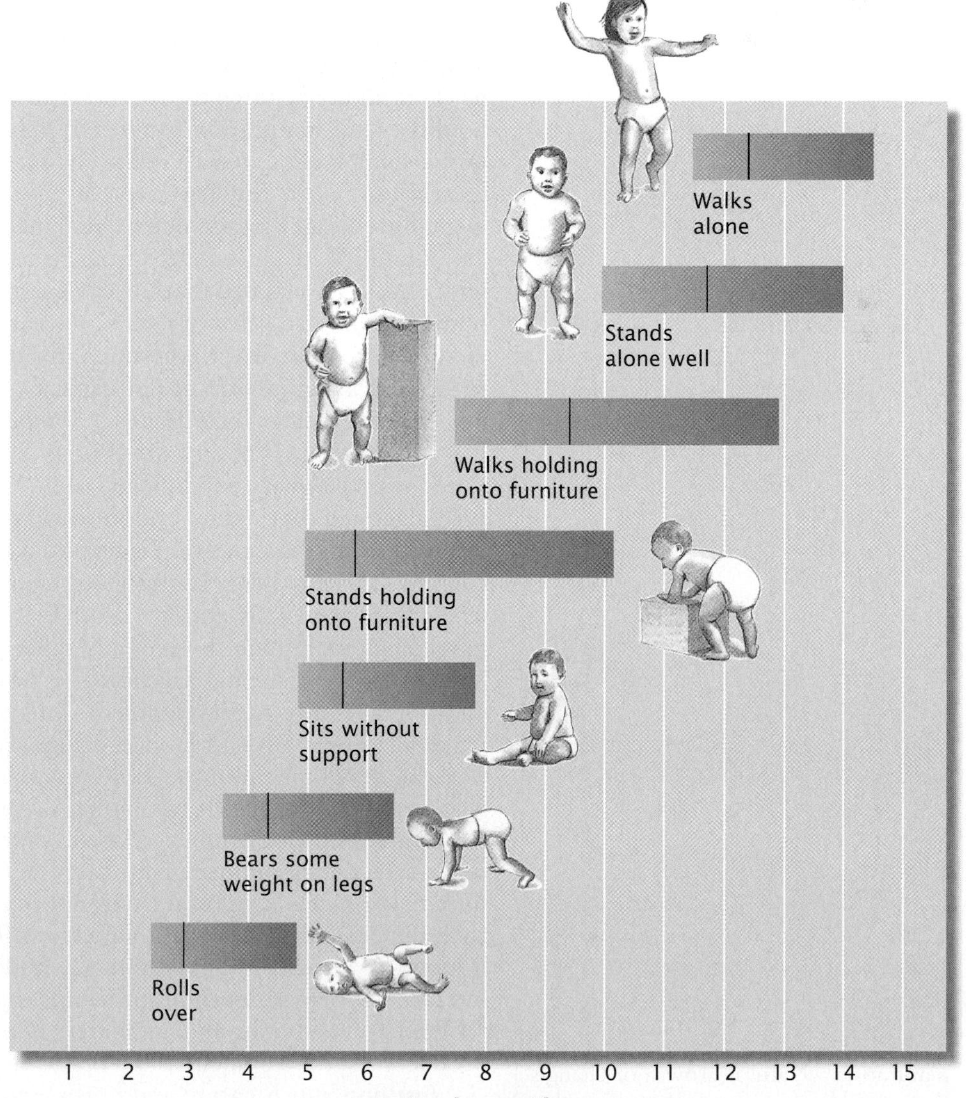

figure 12.1

Motor Development

When did you start walking? The left end of each bar indicates the age at which 25 percent of the infants tested were able to perform a particular behaviour; 50 percent of the babies were performing the behaviour at the age indicated by the vertical line in the bars. The right end of each bar indicates the age at which 90 percent could do so (Frankenberg & Dodds, 1967). Although different infants, especially in different cultures, achieve milestones of motor development at slightly different ages, all infants—regardless of their ethnicity, social class, or temperament—achieve them in the same order.

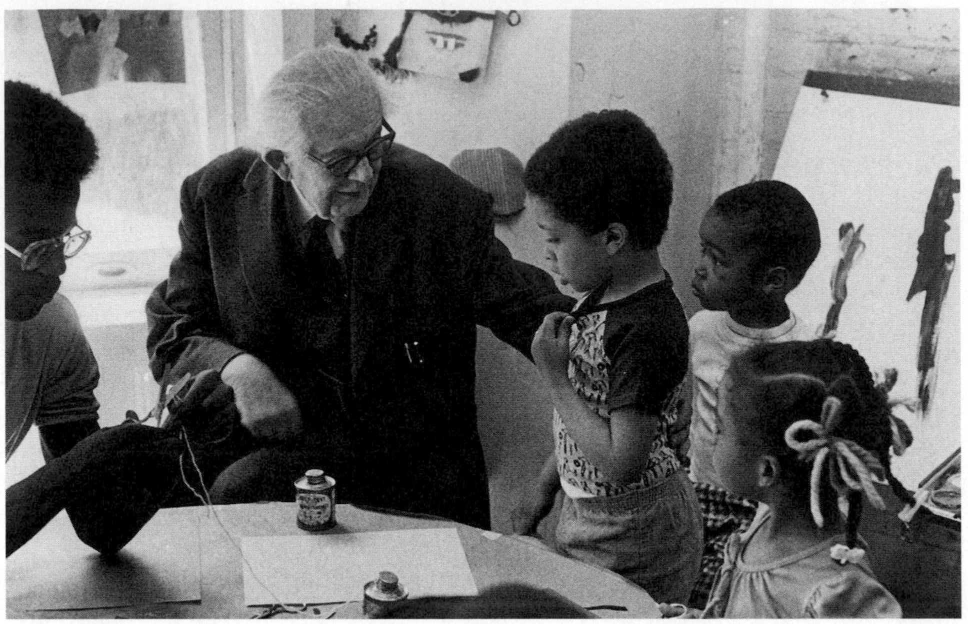

A Pioneer in the Study of Cognitive Development Using a variety of research procedures, including his remarkable observational skills, Jean Piaget (1896–1980) investigated the development of cognitive processes in children, including his own son and daughters. He wove his observations and inferences into the most comprehensive and influential theory that had yet been formulated about how thought and knowledge develop from infancy to adolescence.

which they develop, he suggested, are determined by nature and relatively unaffected by nurture. Only under extreme conditions, such as famine, war, or poverty, he claimed, are children thrown off their biologically programmed timetable. Gesell used the term **maturation** to refer to this type of natural growth or change, which unfolds in a fixed sequence relatively independent of the environment. The broader term *development* encompasses not only maturation but also the behavioural and mental processes that are due to learning.

John B. Watson, founder of the behaviourist approach to psychology, disagreed with Gesell. He claimed that the environment, not nature, moulds and shapes development. His research with children early in the twentieth century left Watson convinced that we learn everything, from skills to fears. In his words, "there is no such thing as an inheritance of capacity, talent, temperament, mental constitution and characteristics. These things . . . depend on training that goes on mainly in the cradle" (Watson, 1925, pp. 74–75).

It was the Swiss psychologist Jean Piaget (pronounced "pea-ah-ZHAY") who first suggested that nature and nurture work together and that their influences are inseparable and interactive. Piaget had a lifelong interest in human intellectual and cognitive development. His ideas, presented in numerous books and articles published from the 1920s until his death in 1980, influenced the field of developmental psychology more than those of any other person before or since.

Most developmental psychologists now accept the idea that nature and nurture contribute jointly to development—in two ways. First, they operate together to make all people alike as human beings. For example, we all achieve milestones of physical development in the same order and at roughly the same rate. This pattern is a result of the nature of biological maturation supported by the nurture of basic care, nutrition, and exercise. Second, nature and nurture also both operate to make each person unique. The nature of inherited genes and the nurture of widely different family and cultural environments produce differences among individuals in such dimensions as athletic abilities, intelligence, language ability, and personality (Plomin et al., 2002; Spinath et al., 2004). Heredity creates *predispositions* that interact with environmental influences, including family and teachers, friends and random events, books and computers (Caspi et al., 2002). It is this interaction that produces the developmental outcomes we see in individuals.

Just how much nature and nurture contribute varies from one characteristic to another. Nature shapes some characteristics, such as physical size and appearance,

maturation Natural growth or change that unfolds in a fixed sequence relatively independent of the environment.

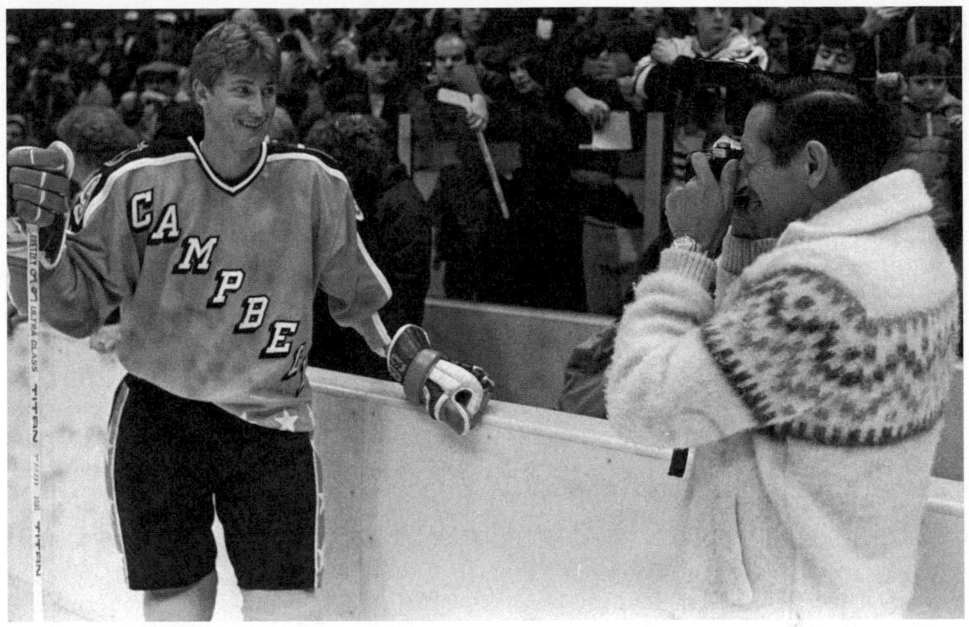

A Winning Combination The development of human behaviour is shaped by both heredity and environment—by nature and nurture. The combined and inseparable influence of these two factors in development is nicely illustrated in the case of hockey legend Wayne Gretzky. Here is the young Gretzky with his father, who not only provided some of The Great One's genes but also served as his first coach.

so strongly that only extreme environmental conditions can affect them. Variation in height, for example, has been estimated to be 80 to 95 percent genetic. This means that 80 to 95 percent of the differences in height that we see among people are due to their genes. Less than 20 percent of the differences are due to prenatal or postnatal diet or to early illness or other growth-stunting environmental factors. Nature's influence on other characteristics, such as intelligence or personality, is not as strong. Complex traits such as these are influenced by genes, but by many environmental factors as well.

It is impossible for researchers to identify the separate influences that nature and nurture exert on such complex traits, partly because heredity and environment are *correlated.* For instance, highly intelligent biological parents give their children genes for intelligence and typically also provide a stimulating environment. Heredity and environment also influence each other. Just as the environment promotes or hampers an individual's abilities, those inherited abilities to some extent determine the individual's environment. For example, a stimulating environment full of toys, books, and lessons encourages children's mental development and increases the chances that their full inherited intelligence will emerge. At the same time, more intelligent children seek out environments that are more stimulating, ask more questions, draw more attention from adults, and ultimately learn more from these experiences.

Beginnings

Nowhere are the intertwined effects of nature and nurture clearer than in the womb, as a single fertilized egg becomes a functioning infant.

Prenatal Development

The process of development begins when a sperm from the father-to-be penetrates, or fertilizes, the ovum of the mother-to-be, and a brand-new cell, called a **zygote,** is formed. This new cell carries a genetic heritage from both mother and father (see the appendix on behavioural genetics).

zygote A new cell, formed from a father's sperm and a mother's ovum.

Stages of Development In the first stage of prenatal development, called the *germinal stage,* the zygote divides into many more cells, which by the end of the

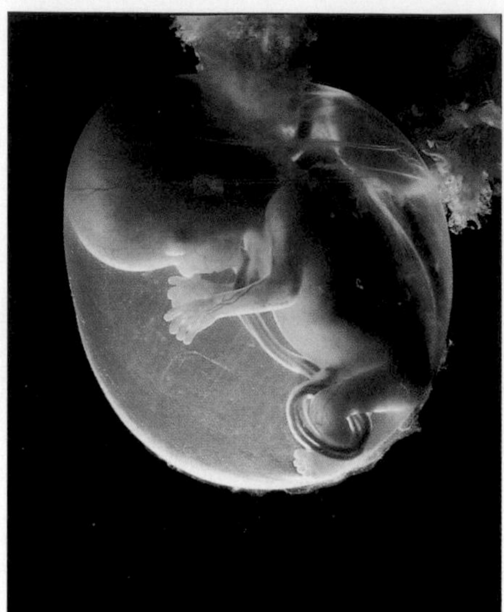

A Fetus at Twelve Weeks At this point in prenatal development, the fetus can kick its legs, curl its toes, make a fist, turn its head, squint, open its mouth, swallow, and take a few "breaths" of amniotic fluid.

second week have formed an **embryo** (pronounced "EM-bree-oh"). What follows is the *embryonic stage* of development, during which the embryo quickly develops a heart, nervous system, stomach, esophagus, and ovaries or testes. By two months after conception, when the embryonic stage ends, the inch-long embryo has developed eyes, ears, a nose, a jaw, a mouth, and lips. The tiny arms have elbows, hands, and stubby fingers; the legs have knees, ankles, and toes.

During the remaining seven-month period until birth, called the *fetal stage* of prenatal development, the organs grow and start to function. By the end of the third month, the **fetus** can kick, make a fist, turn its head, open its mouth, swallow, and frown. In the sixth month, the eyelids, which have been sealed, open. The fetus now has taste buds and a well-developed grasp and, if born prematurely, can breathe regularly for as long as 24 hours at a time. By the end of the seventh month, the organ systems, though immature, are all functional. In the eighth and ninth months, fetuses respond to light and touch, and they can hear what is going on outside. They can also learn. According to Barbara Kisilevsky and her colleagues at Queen's University in Kingston, Ontario, when fetuses hear their mother's familiar voice, their heart beats a little faster, but it slows if they hear a stranger (Kisilevsky et al., 2003).

Prenatal Risks Nature determines the timing and stages of prenatal development, but that development is also affected by the nurture provided by the environment of the womb. During prenatal development, a spongy organ called the *placenta,* formed from the outside layer of the zygote, sends nutrients from the mother to the fetus and carries away wastes. It also screens out many potentially harmful substances, including most bacteria. This screening is imperfect, however: Gases and viruses, as well as nicotine, alcohol, and other drugs, can pass through. Severe damage can occur if the baby's mother takes certain drugs, is exposed to toxic substances, or has certain illnesses during pregnancy.

Harmful external substances that invade the womb and result in birth defects are called **teratogens** (pronounced "ta-RAT-a-jens"). Teratogens are especially damaging during the embryonic stage, because it is a **critical period** in prenatal development, a time when certain kinds of growth must occur if the infant's development is to proceed normally. If the heart, eyes, ears, hands, and feet do not appear during this period, they cannot form later on. If they form incorrectly, the defects are permanent. So even before a mother knows she is pregnant, she may accidentally damage her infant by exposing it to teratogens. For example, a baby whose mother has rubella (German measles) during the third or fourth week after conception has a 50 percent chance of being blind, deaf, or mentally retarded or of having a malformed heart. If the mother has rubella later in the pregnancy, after the infant's eyes, ears, brain, and heart have formed, the likelihood that the baby will have one of these defects is much lower. Later, during the fetal stage, teratogens affect the baby's size, behaviour, intelligence, and health, rather than the formation of organs and limbs.

Of special concern today are the effects of drugs on infants' development (e.g., Gendle et al., 2004). Pregnant women who use substances such as cocaine create a substantial risk for their fetuses, which do not yet have the enzymes necessary to break down the drugs. "Cocaine babies" or "crack babies" may be born premature, underweight, tense, and fussy (Inciardi, Surratt, & Saum, 1997).They may also suffer delayed physical growth and motor development (Tarr & Pyfer, 1996). Current research suggests, however, that although cocaine babies are more likely to have behavioural and learning problems (Singer et al., 2001, 2002; Tan-Laxa et al., 2004), their mental abilities are not necessarily different from those of any baby born into an impoverished environment (Frank et al., 2001). How well these children ultimately do in school depends on how supportive that environment turns out to be (Begley, 1997; Messinger et al., 2004).

Alcohol is another dangerous teratogen, because it interferes with infants' brain development (Avaria et al., 2004). Almost half the children born to expectant

embryo The developing individual from the fourteenth day after fertilization until the end of the second month after conception.

fetus The developing individual from the third month after conception until birth.

teratogens Harmful substances that can cause birth defects.

critical period An interval during which certain kinds of growth must occur if development is to proceed normally.

mothers who abuse alcohol will develop **fetal alcohol syndrome,** a pattern of defects that includes mental retardation and malformations of the face (Jenkins & Culbertson, 1996). Pregnant women who drink as little as a glass or two of wine a day can harm their infants' intellectual functioning (Streissguth et al., 1999). According to Susan Harris of the University of British Columbia, prenatal exposure to alcohol may also be associated with the development of autism (Harris, 1995). Mothers who engage in bouts of heavy drinking triple the odds that their child will develop alcohol-related problems by the age of 21 (Baer et al., 2003).

Peter Fried and his colleagues at Carleton University in Ottawa have found that smoking, too, can affect the developing fetus (Fried, Watkinson, & Gray). Babies of women who smoke often suffer from respiratory problems, irritability, and attention problems, and they are at greater risk for nicotine addiction in adolescence and adulthood (Buka, Shenassa, & Niaura, 2003; Gilliland, Li, & Peters, 2001; Griesler, Kandel, & Davies, 1998; Law et al., 2003; Milberger et al., 1997; Niaura et al., 2001). Worse, they may be born prematurely, and they are usually underweight. Babies who are premature and/or underweight—for whatever reason—are likely to have cognitive and behavioural problems that continue throughout their lives (Bhutta et al., 2002; Jefferis, Power, & Hertzman, 2002).

Defects due to teratogens are most likely to appear when the negative effects of nature and nurture combine. The worst-case scenario is one in which a genetically susceptible infant receives a strong dose of a damaging substance during a critical period of prenatal development. The risk of behavioural and psychological difficulties in later life is also increased for children whose mothers were under significant stress during the first six months of pregnancy (Huizink, Mulder, & Buitelaar, 2004). Fortunately, mental or physical problems resulting from all harmful prenatal factors affect fewer than 10 percent of the babies born in Western nations. Mechanisms built into the human organism maintain normal development under all but the most adverse conditions. The vast majority of fetuses arrive at the end of their nine-month gestation averaging a healthy three-and-a-half kilos ready to continue a normal course of development in the world.

The Newborn

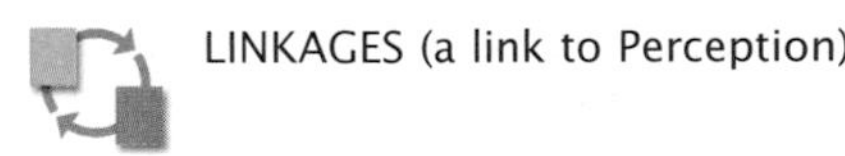

Determining what newborns are able to see, hear, and do is one of the most fascinating—and frustrating—research challenges in developmental psychology. Young infants are very difficult to study. About 70 percent of the time, they are asleep. When they aren't sleeping, they may be drowsy, crying, or restlessly moving about. It is only when they are in a state of quiet alertness, which occurs infrequently and only for a few minutes at a time, that researchers can assess infants' abilities.

During these brief periods, psychologists show infants objects or pictures, or present sounds to them, and watch where they look and for how long. They film the infants' eye movements and record changes in their heart rates, sucking rates, brain waves, body movements, and skin conductance (a measure of perspiration associated with emotion) to learn what infants can see and hear (Kellman & Banks, 1998).

Vision and Other Senses Infants can see at birth, but their vision is blurry. According to Daphne Maurer and Terri Lewis at McMaster University in Hamilton, Ontario, newborns' vision ranges from approximately 20/400 to 20/800 (Maurer & Lewis, 2001). In other words, an object 20 feet away looks as clear as it would if viewed from 400 to 800 feet away by an adult with normal vision. The reason infants' vision is so limited is that their eyes and brains still need time to grow and develop. Newborns' eyes are smaller than those of adults, and the cells in their foveas— the area of each retina on which images are focused—are fewer and far less

fetal alcohol syndrome A pattern of physical and mental defects found in babies born to women who abused alcohol during pregnancy.

A Baby's-Eye View of the World The photograph on the left simulates what the mother on the right looks like to her newborn infant. Although their vision is blurry, infants particularly seem to enjoy looking at faces. As mentioned in the chapter on perception, their eyes will follow a moving face-like drawing (Johnson et al.,1991), and they will stare at a human face longer than at other figures (Valenza et al., 1996).

sensitive. Their eye movements are slow and jerky. And pathways connecting the eyes to the brain are still inefficient, as is the processing of visual information within the brain.

Although infants cannot see small objects on the other side of the room, they are able to see large objects close up. They stare longest at objects that have large visible elements, movement, clear contours, and a lot of contrast—all qualities that exist in the human face (Turati, 2004). In fact, from the time they are born, infants will redirect their eyes to follow a moving drawing of a face, and they stare at a human face longer than at other figures (Johnson et al., 1991; Valenza et al., 1996). They are particularly interested in eyes, as shown in their preference for faces that are looking directly at them (Farroni et al., 2002). Megan Easterbrook, at Nipissing University in North Bay, Ontario, has found that infants can tell the difference between accurate drawings of a face and a face with the features placed in random positions (Easterbrook, Kisilevsky, Muir, & Laplante, 1999). Taken together, these studies show that infants are especially sensitive to the human face as an important feature of their environment.

Infants also experience a certain degree of *size constancy.* This means that objects will appear as the same size despite changes in the size of their image on the eye's retina (see the chapter on perception). So a baby perceives its mother's face as remaining about the same size, whether she is looking over the edge of the crib or is close enough to kiss the baby's cheek. Newborns do not experience normal *depth perception* until some time later, however. It takes about seven months before they develop the ability to use the pictorial cues to depth described in the chapter on perception.

The course of development for hearing is similar to that of vision. A newborn baby's hearing is similar to that of an adult with a head cold. At two or three days of age, they can hear soft voices and notice the difference between tones about one note apart on the musical scale; they also turn their heads toward sounds (Clifton, 1992). But their hearing is not as sharp as that of adults until well into childhood. Infants' hearing is particularly attuned to the sounds of speech. When they hear voices, babies open their eyes wider and look for the speaker. By four months of age, they can discriminate differences among almost all of the more than 50 phonetic contrasts in adult languages (Hespos & Spelke, 2004). Infants also prefer certain kinds of speech. They like rising tones spoken by women or children, and they like speech that is high pitched, exaggerated, and expressive. In other words, they like to hear the "baby talk" used by most adults when they talk to babies.

Newborns' sense of smell is similar to that of adults, but again, less developed. Certain smells and tastes appeal to them more than others. For instance, they like the smell of flowers and the taste of sweet drinks (Ganchrow, Steiner, & Daher, 1983). Research indicates that within a few days after birth, breastfed babies prefer the odour of their own mothers to the odours of other mothers (Porter et al., 1992).

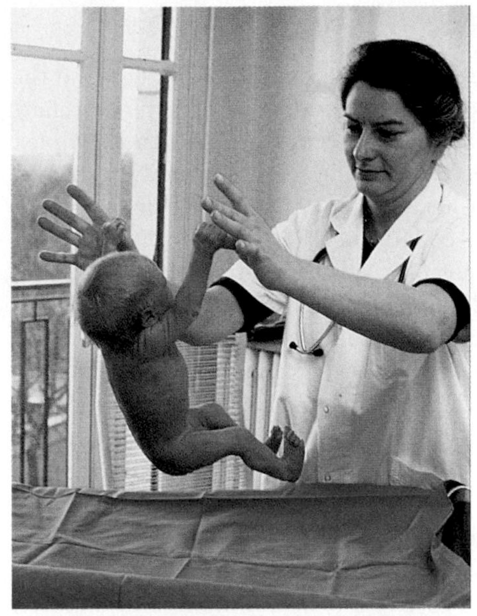

Reflexes in the Newborn When a finger is pressed into a newborn's palm, the *grasping reflex* causes the infant to hold on tightly enough to suspend its entire weight. And when a newborn is held upright over a flat surface, the *stepping reflex* leads to walking movements.

They also develop preferences for the food flavours consumed by their mothers (Mennella & Beauchamp, 1996).

Although limited, an infant's inborn sensory abilities are important for survival and development because they focus the infant's attention on the caregiver. For example, the attraction of newborns to the sweet smell and taste of mother's milk helps them locate appropriate food and identify their caregiver. Their sensitivity to speech allows them to focus on language and encourages the caregiver to talk to them. And because their vision is limited to the distance at which most interaction with a caregiver takes place and is tuned to the special qualities of faces, the caregiver's face is especially noticeable to them. Accordingly, infants are exposed to emotional expressions and come to recognize the caregiver by sight, further encouraging the caregiver to interact. As infants physically mature and learn from their environment, their sensory capacities become more complex and adult-like.

Reflexes and Motor Skills In the first few weeks and months after birth, babies demonstrate involuntary, unlearned motor behaviours called *reflexes.* These are swift, automatic movements that occur in response to external stimuli. The photo illustrates the *grasping reflex*; several other reflexes have been observed in newborn infants. For example, the *rooting reflex* causes the infant to turn its mouth toward a nipple (or anything else) that touches its cheek, and the *sucking reflex* causes the newborn to suck on anything that touches its lips. Most reflexes disappear after the first three or four months, when infants' brain development allows them to control their muscles voluntarily. At that point, infants can develop motor skills, so they are soon able to roll over, sit up, crawl, stand, and by the end of the year, walk (see Figure 12.1).

Infancy and Childhood: Cognitive Development

LINKAGES (a link to Social Behaviour)

Over the first ten years of life, the tiny infant becomes a competent child who can read a book, write a poem, and argue for access to the family's new computer. Researchers who study *cognitive development* are exploring the dramatic shifts in thinking, knowing, and remembering that occur between early infancy and later childhood.

Changes in the Brain

One factor that underlies the cognitive leaps of infancy and childhood is the continued growth and development of the brain. When infants are born, they already have a full quota of brain cells, but the neural networks connecting the cells are immature. With time, the connections grow increasingly complex and then, with pruning, more efficient. Studies reveal how, as different regions of the brain develop more complex and efficient neural networks, new cognitive abilities appear (Nelson, 1997).

In the first few months of infancy, the cerebellum is the most mature area of the brain. Its early maturation allows infants to display simple associative abilities, such as sucking more when they see their mother's face or hear her voice. Between six and twelve months of age, neurological development in the medial temporal lobe of the cerebral cortex makes it possible for infants to remember and imitate an action they have seen earlier or to recognize a picture of an object they have never seen but have held in their hands. And neurological development in the frontal cortex, which occurs later in childhood, allows for the development of higher cognitive functions such as reasoning. In other words, brain structures provide the "hardware" for cognitive development. How does the "software" of thinking develop, and how does it modify the "wiring" of the brain's "hardware"? These questions have been pursued by many developmental psychologists, beginning with Piaget.

The Development of Knowledge: Piaget's Theory

Piaget dedicated his life to a search for the origins of intelligence in infancy and the factors that lead to changes in knowledge over the life span. He was the first to chart the fascinating journey from the simple reflexes of the newborn to the complex understandings of the adolescent. Piaget's theory was not correct in every respect—later we discuss some of its weaknesses—but his ideas about cognitive development still guide much research in the field (Fischer & Hencke,1996).

Piaget proposed that cognitive development proceeds through a series of distinct *periods* or *stages* (see Table 12.1). He believed that all children's thinking goes through the same stages, in the same order, without skipping—building on previous stages, then moving to higher ones. According to Piaget, the thinking of infants is different from the thinking of children, and the thinking of children is different from that of adolescents. Entering each stage involves a *qualitative* change from the previous stage, much as a caterpillar is transformed into a butterfly. What drives children to higher stages is their constant struggle to make sense of their experiences. They are active thinkers who are always trying to construct more advanced understandings of the world.

Building Blocks of Development To explain how infants and children move to ever-higher stages of understanding and knowledge, Piaget used the concept

table 12.1

According to Piaget, a predictable set of features characterizes each period of children's cognitive development. The ages associated with the stages are approximate; Piaget realized that some children move through the stages slightly faster or slower than others.

Piaget's Periods of Cognitive Development

Period	Activities and Achievements
Sensorimotor Birth–2 years	Infants discover aspects of the world through their sensory impressions, motor activities, and coordination of the two. They learn to differentiate themselves from the external world. They learn that objects exist even when they are not visible and that objects are independent of the infant's own actions. They gain some appreciation of cause and effect.
Preoperational 2–4 years	Children cannot yet manipulate and transform information in logical ways, but they now can think in images and symbols.
4–7 years	They become able to represent items using different objects (e.g., pretending that a shoe is a telephone), acquire language, and play games that involve pretending. Intelligence at this stage is said to be intuitive, because children cannot make general, logical statements.
Concrete operational 7–11 years	They can appreciate that certain properties of an object remain the same despite changes in appearance, and they can sort objects into categories. They can appreciate the perspective of someone else. They can think about two concepts, such as longer and wider, at the same time. Children can understand logical principles that apply to concrete external objects.
Formal operational Over 11 years	Only adolescents and adults can think logically about abstractions, can speculate, and can consider what might or what ought to be. They can work in probabilities and possibilities. They can imagine other worlds, especially ideal ones. They can reason about purely verbal or logical statements. They can relate one element or statement to another, manipulate variables in a scientific experiment, and deal with proportions and analogies. They reflect on their own activity of thinking.

of **schemas.** As noted in the chapters on perception, memory, and cognition, schemas are the generalizations that form as people experience the world. Schemas organize past experiences and provide a framework for understanding future experiences. Piaget saw schemas as organized patterns of action or thought that children construct as they adapt to the environment; they are the basic units of knowledge, the building blocks of intellectual development. Schemas, he said, can involve behaviours (such as tying a shoelace or sucking), mental symbols (such as words or images), or mental activities (e.g., doing arithmetic "in our head" or imagining actions).

At first, infants form simple schemas. For example, a sucking schema consolidates their experiences of sucking into images of what objects can be sucked on (bottles, fingers, pacifiers) and what kinds of sucking can be done (soft and slow, speedy and vigorous). Later, children form more complex schemas, such as a schema for tying a knot or making a bed. Still later, adolescents form schemas about what it is to be in love.

Two complementary processes guide the development of schemas: assimilation and accommodation. In the process of **assimilation,** infants and children take in information about new objects by using existing schemas that will fit the new objects. An infant is given a new toy. He sucks on it, assimilating it into the sucking schema he has developed with his bottle and pacifier. A toddler sees a butterfly for the first time. It's colourful and flies, like a bird, so she assimilates it into her "birdie" schema. An older child encounters a large dog. How she assimilates this new creature depends on her existing schema of dogs. If she has had positive experiences with a friendly family pet, she will expect the dog to behave the same, and she will greet it enthusiastically. If she has been frightened by dogs in the past, she may have a negative schema and react with fear to the dog she has just met.

Sometimes, like Cinderella's stepsisters trying to squeeze their oversized feet into the glass slipper, people distort information about a new object to make it fit their existing schema. When squeezing won't work, though, they are forced to change, or accommodate, their schema to the new object. In **accommodation,** a person finds that a familiar schema cannot be made to fit a new object and changes the schema (see Figure 12.2). So when the infant discovers that another new toy—a squeaker—is more fun when it makes a noise, he accommodates his sucking schema and starts munching on the squeaker instead. When the toddler realizes that butterflies are not birds because they don't have beaks and feathers, she accommodates her "birdie" schema to include two kinds of "flying animals"—birds and butterflies. And if the child with the positive "doggie" schema meets a snarling stray, she discovers that her original schema does not extend to all dogs, and she refines it to distinguish between friendly dogs and aggressive ones. Through assimilation and accommodation, said Piaget, we build our knowledge of the world, block by block.

Sensorimotor Development Piaget (1952) called the first stage of cognitive development the **sensorimotor period** because, he claimed, the infant's mental activity and schemas are confined to sensory functions, such as seeing and hearing, and motor skills, such as grasping and sucking. According to Piaget, during this stage, infants can form schemas only of objects and actions that are present—things they can see or hear or touch. They cannot think about absent objects because they cannot act on them. For infants, then, thinking is doing. They do not lie in the crib thinking about their mother or their teddy bear, because they are not yet able to form schemas that are *mental representations* of objects and actions.

The sensorimotor period ends when infants can form mental representations. Now they can think about objects and actions even while the objects are not visible or the actions are not occurring. This is a remarkable milestone, according to Piaget; it frees the child from the here-and-now of the sensory environment and allows for the development of thought. One sign that children have reached this milestone is their ability to find a hidden object. This behaviour was of particular interest to

schemas Generalizations based on experience that form the basic units of knowledge.

assimilation The process of trying out existing schemas on objects that fit those schemas.

accommodation The process of modifying schemas when familiar schemas do not work.

sensorimotor period The first of Piaget's stages of cognitive development, when the infant's mental activity is confined to sensory perception and motor skills.

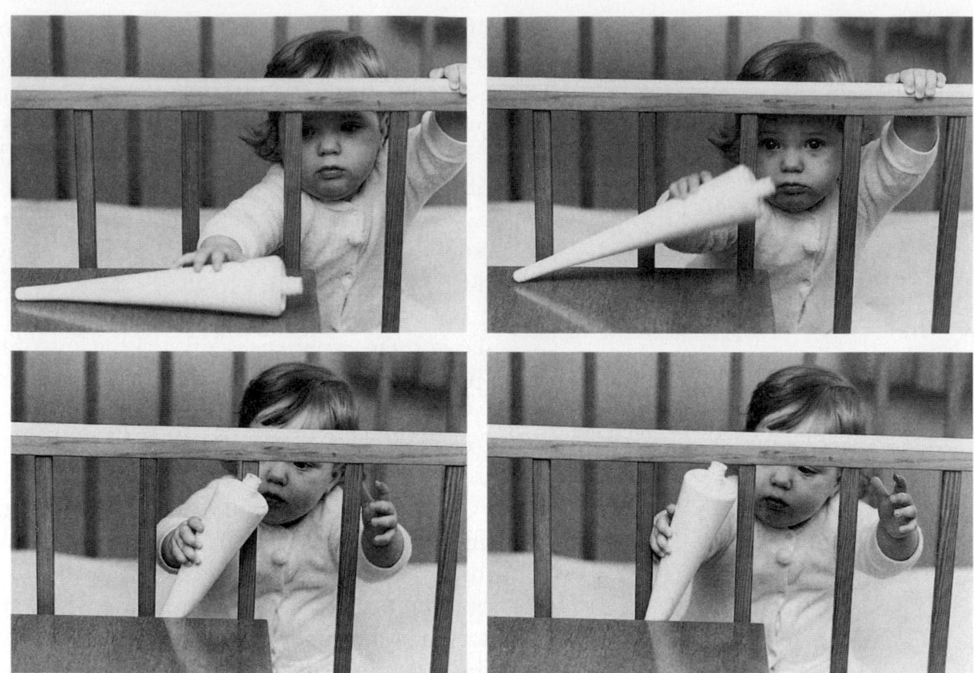

figure 12.2

Accommodation

Because the bars of the playpen are in the way, this child discovers that her schema for grasping and pulling objects toward her will not work. She then adjusts, or accommodates, her schema in order to achieve her goal.

Piaget because, for him, it reflected infants' knowledge that they don't have to look at, touch, or suck an object to know that it exists. They know it exists even when it's out of sight. Piaget called this knowledge **object permanence.**

Before they acquire knowledge of object permanence, infants do not search for objects that are placed out of their sight. They act as if out of sight is literally out of mind. The first evidence of developing object permanence appears when infants are four to eight months old. At this age, for the first time, they recognize a familiar object even if part of it is hidden. They know it's their bottle even if they can see only the nipple peeking out from under the blanket. In Piaget's view, infants now have some primitive mental representation of objects. If an object is completely hidden, however, they will not search for it.

Several months later, infants will search briefly for a hidden object, but their search is random and ineffective. Not until they are 18 to 24 months old, said Piaget, do infants appear able to picture and follow events in their minds. They look for the object in places other than where they saw it last, sometimes in completely new places. According to Piaget, their concept of the object as permanent is now fully developed. They have a mental representation of the object that is completely separate from their immediate perception of it.

New Views of Infants' Cognitive Development In the years since Piaget's death, psychologists have found new ways to measure what is going on in infants' minds. They use infrared photography to record infants' eye movements, time-lapse photography to detect subtle hand movements, special equipment to measure infants' sucking rates, and computer technology to track and analyze it all. Their research shows that infants know a lot more, and know it sooner, than Piaget ever thought they did.

Infants are not just sensing and moving during the sensorimotor period; they are already thinking as well. For example, Barbara Morrongiello, at the University of Guelph, Ontario, and Kimberley Fenwick, at St. Thomas University in Fredericton, New Brunswick, found that infants are not just experiencing isolated sights and sounds but combining these experiences. In one study, infants were shown two different videos at the same time, but they heard the soundtrack for only one of them coming from a speaker placed between the two video screens. The infants tended to

object permanence The knowledge that objects exist even when they are not in view.

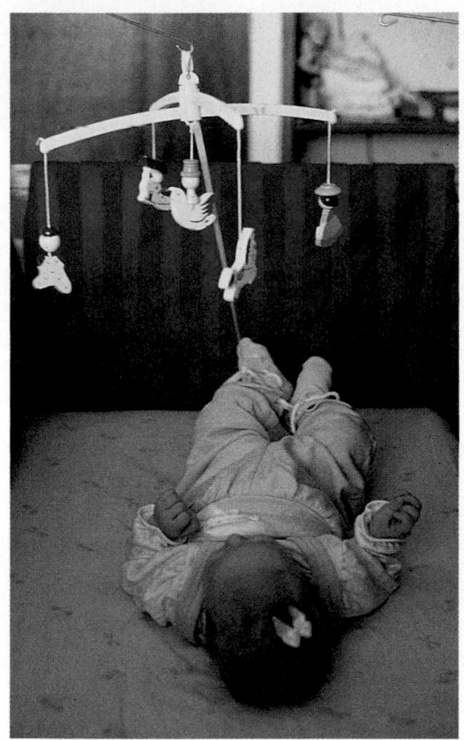

Infant Memory This three-month-old infant learned to move a mobile by kicking her left foot, which is tied to the mobile with a ribbon. Even a month later, the baby will show recognition of this particular mobile by kicking more vigorously when she sees it than when she sees another one.

look at the video that went with the soundtrack (Morrongiello & Fenwick, 1991). Infants can remember, too. At as young as two to three months of age, they can recall a particular mobile that was hung over their cribs a few days before (Rovee-Collier, 1999). They can also solve simple problems, such as how to use a little "bridge" to leave a raised platform. Infants in this laboratory situation could think ahead and work out a plan of attack. When the bridge was wide, they strode across. When it was narrow, they lingered on the platform, explored the bridge with their hands or feet, clung to the handrail with both hands, and took lots of tiny steps or sidled along (Berger & Adolph, 2003).

Young babies also seem to have a sense of object permanence. Piaget had required infants to demonstrate object permanence through rather grand movements, such as removing a cover that had been placed over a hidden object. However, when experimenters simply turn off the lights, infants as young as five months of age will reach for now-unseen objects in the dark (Clifton et al., 1991). Researchers now recognize that finding a hidden object under a cover requires several abilities: mentally representing the hidden object, figuring out where it might be, and pulling off the cover. Piaget's tests did not allow for the possibility that infants know a hidden object still exists but do not have adequate strategies for finding it or memory skills for remembering it while they search. When researchers have created situations in which infants merely have to stare to indicate that they know where an object is hidden, even infants under the age of one have demonstrated this cognitive ability (Ahmed & Ruffman, 1998; Hespos & Baillargeon, 2001).

In summary, developmental psychologists now generally agree that infants develop some mental representations earlier than Piaget had suggested. They disagree, however, about whether this knowledge is "programmed" in infants (Spelke et al., 1992), whether it quickly develops through interactions with the outside world (Baillargeon, 1995), or whether it is constructed through the recombination of old schemas into new ones (Fischer & Bidell, 1991).

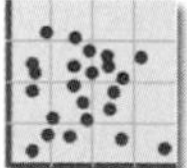

FOCUS ON RESEARCH METHODS

Experiments on Developing Minds

To explore how infants develop mental representations, Renée Baillargeon (pronounced "by-ar-ZHAN") investigated infants' early understanding of the principles of physics. Whether you realize it or not, you know a lot about physics. You know about gravity and balance, for example. But when did you first understand that "what goes up must come down" and that an unbalanced tray will tip over? Are these things you have always known, or did you figure them out through trial and error?

What was the researcher's question?

Baillargeon wanted to know when and how babies first develop knowledge about balance and gravity—specifically, about the tendency of unsupported objects to fall.

How did the researcher answer the question?

Baillargeon (1994, 2002) devised a creative experimental method to probe infants' knowledge. She showed infants pairs of events, one of which was physically possible and the other, physically impossible. She then determined the infants' interest in each kind of event by measuring the amount of time they spent looking at it. Their tendency to look longer at unexpected events provided an indication of which events violated what the babies knew about the world. Using this method, Baillargeon studied infants' knowledge of balance and gravity.

The independent variable in her studies was the amount of physical support objects had. The dependent variable was the length of time infants spent looking

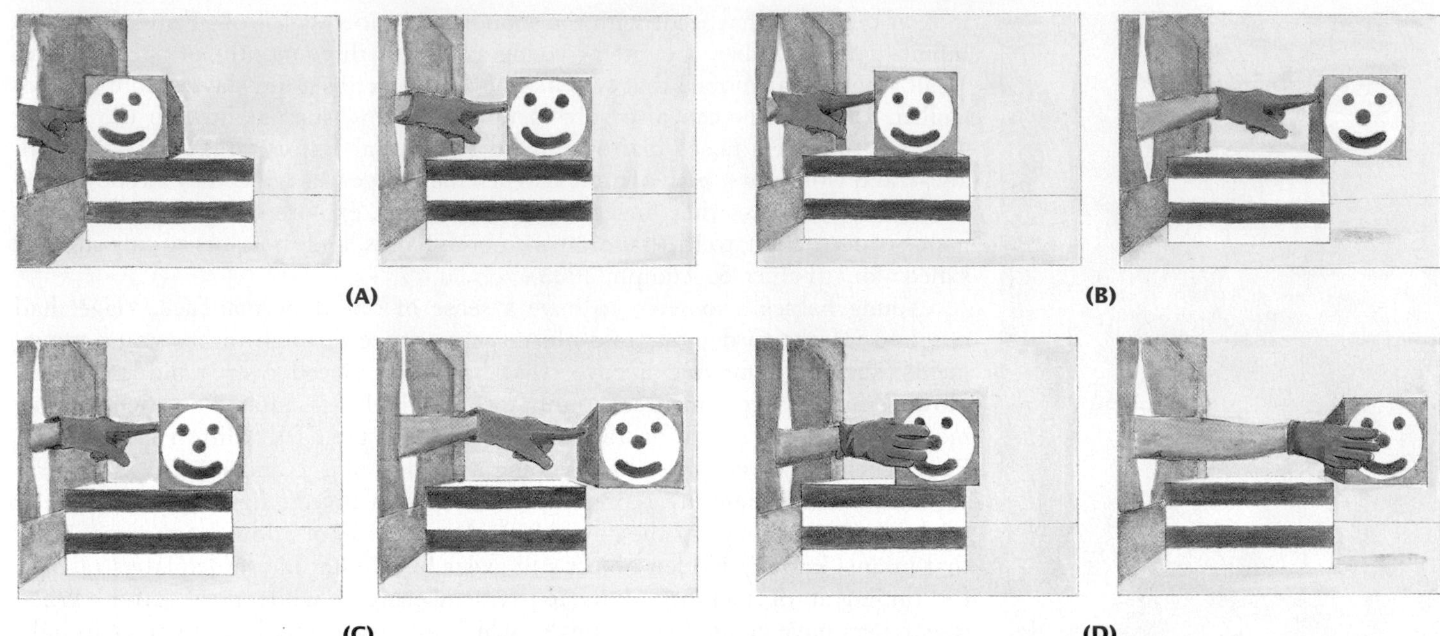

figure 12.3

Visual Events Testing Infants' Knowledge of Physics

Infants look longer at things that interest them—that is, at new things rather than things they have seen before and find boring. In her research on the development of knowledge, Renée Baillargeon (1995) has found that physically impossible events (B) and (C)—made possible by an experimenter reaching through a hidden door to support a moving box—attract the most attention from infants. These results suggest that humans understand some basic laws of physics quite early in life.

Source: Baillargeon (1992).

at these objects. Specifically, the infants viewed a red-gloved hand pushing a box from left to right along the top of a platform. On some trials, they saw physically possible events. For example, the hand pushed the box until its edge reached the end of the platform (see event A in Figure 12.3). On other trials, they saw impossible events, as when the hand pushed the box until only the end of its bottom surface rested on the platform or the box was beyond the platform altogether (see events B and C in the figure). On still other trials, the gloved hand held onto the box while pushing it beyond the edge of the platform (as shown in event D). Trials continued until the infants had seen at least four pairs of possible and impossible events in alternating order.

- **What did the researcher find?**

Baillargeon found that three-month-old infants looked longest at impossible event C, in which the box was entirely off the platform, whereas they were not particularly interested in either event D (box held by the gloved hand) or event A (box still on the platform). At six and a half months, infants stared intently at both event C (box off the platform) and event B (in which only the end of the box was resting on the platform).

- **What do the results mean?**

According to Baillargeon, these results suggest that three-month-old babies know something about physical support. They expect the box to fall if it is entirely off the platform and act surprised when it doesn't. But they do not yet know that a box should fall if its centre of gravity is unsupported, as in event B. By the time they are six and a half months old, however, infants apparently know about centres of gravity—that most of the box must be on the platform or it will fall.

Other researchers have questioned whether infants' tendency to stare longer at a particular display necessarily indicates "surprise" (Bogartz, Shinskey, & Speaker,

1997). Perhaps they simply recognize that the image is different from what they remember it to be or find the impossible image more noticeable.

What do we still need to know?

The question remains as to which of these interpretations is correct. Do infants possess fundamental knowledge about the world that includes an understanding of complex physical principles, or are they just staring at something because it is novel or vivid? The answer to this question will require further research using varied visual stimuli that allows researchers to determine whether infants stare longer at physically possible events that are just as novel and vivid as physically impossible events.

Whether or not such research confirms Baillargeon's view, psychologists are still faced with the task of discovering *how* babies know about physics (Johnson, Amso, & Slemmer, 2003). Does their increasing understanding of physical principles result from their experience with objects, or is the knowledge innate?

In an attempt to answer this question, Baillargeon conducted another experiment in which she manipulated object-experience (the independent variable). After identifying infants ranging in age from three months to six and a half months, she randomly assigned them to receive either normal or extra experience with objects. She then observed the effect of this experience on the infants' understanding of gravity (the dependent variable). After only a few demonstrations in which unsupported objects fell off platforms, infants in the extra-object-experience group stared longer at a display of an unsupported object that did not fall. Other studies found similar results (Needham & Baillargeon, 1999).

It is still too early to say for sure whether Baillargeon's hypothesis about the importance of experience in developing knowledge is correct, but her results seem to support it (Baillargeon, 2004).

Preoperational Development According to Piaget, the sensorimotor stage of development is followed by the **preoperational period.** During the first half of this period, children begin to understand, create, and use *symbols* (words, images, and objects) to represent things that are not present. As described in the chapter on cognition and language, they begin to use words to stand for objects: *Mommy, cup, me.* They also begin to play "pretend." They make their fingers "walk" and use a spoon to make a bridge. By the age of three or four, children can symbolize roles and play "house" or "doctor." They also can use drawing symbolically: Pointing to their scribble, they might say, "This is Mommy and Daddy and me going for a walk." The ability to use and understand symbols opens up vast new domains for two- to four-year-olds.

During the second half of the preoperational stage, according to Piaget, four- to seven-year-olds begin to make intuitive guesses about the world as they try to figure out how things work. They claim that dreams are real: "Last night there was a circus in my room." And they believe that inanimate objects are alive and have intentions, feelings, and consciousness, a belief called *animism*: "Clouds go slowly because they have no legs" and "Empty cars feel lonely." In short, said Piaget, preoperational children cannot distinguish between the seen and the unseen, between the physical world and the mental world. They are also highly *egocentric,* meaning that they appear to believe that the way things look to them is also how they look to everyone else. (This helps to explain why they may stand between you and the TV screen and assume you can still see it, or ask "What's this?" as they look at a picture book in the back seat of the car you're driving.)

Children's thinking is so dominated by what they can see and touch for themselves, Piaget said, that they do not realize that something is the same if its appearance changes. In one study, for example, preoperational children thought that a cat wearing a dog mask was actually a dog—because that's what it looked like (DeVries, 1969). These children do not yet have what Piaget called **conservation,** the ability

preoperational period According to Piaget, the second stage of cognitive development, during which children begin to use symbols to represent things that are not present.

conservation The ability to recognize that the important properties of a substance remain constant despite changes in shape, length, or position.

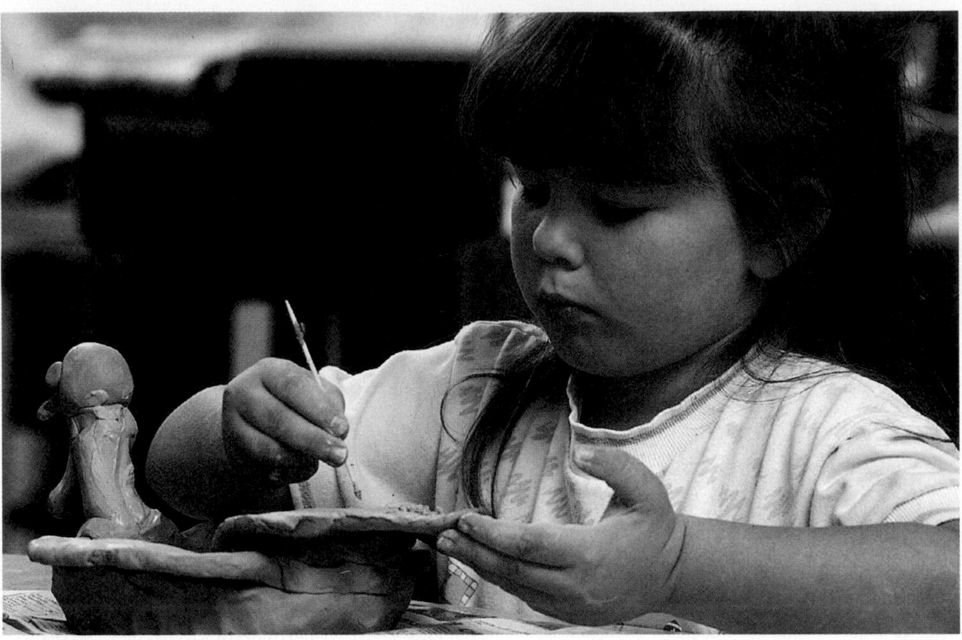

Testing for Conservation If you know a child who is between the ages of four and seven, get parental permission to test the child for what Piaget called *conservation.* Show the child two identical lumps of clay and ask which lump is bigger. The child will probably say they are the same. Now roll one lump into a long "rope" and again ask which lump is bigger. If the child says that they are still the same, this is evidence of conservation. If the longer one is seen as bigger, conservation has not yet developed—at least not for this task. The older the child, the more likely it is that conservation will appear, but some children display conservation earlier than Piaget thought was possible.

to recognize that important properties of a substance or object—including its volume, weight, and species—remain constant despite changes in its shape.

During the second half of the pre-operational period, according to Piaget, children believe that inanimate objects are alive and have feelings, intentions, and consciousness.

In a test of conservation, Piaget first showed children equal amounts of water in two identical containers. He then poured one of them into a tall, thin glass and the other into a short, wide glass and asked whether one glass contained more water than the other. Children at the preoperational stage of development said that one glass (usually the taller one) contained more. Their conclusion was dominated by the evidence of their eyes. If the glass looked bigger, they thought it contained more. In other words, they did not understand the logical concepts of *reversibility* (you just poured the water from one container to another, so you can pour it back, and it will still be the same amount) or *complementarity* (one glass is taller but also narrower; the other is shorter but also wider). Piaget named this stage "*pre*operational" because children at this stage do not yet understand logical mental operations such as these.

Concrete and Formal Operational Thought Sometime around the age of six or seven, Piaget observed, children do develop the ability to conserve number and amount. When this happens, they enter what Piaget called the stage of **concrete operations.** Now, he said, they can count, measure, add, and subtract. Their thinking is no longer dominated by the appearance of things. They can use simple logic and perform simple mental manipulations and mental operations on things. They can also sort objects into classes (such as tools, fruit, and vehicles) or series (such as largest to smallest).

Still, concrete operational children can perform their logical operations only on real, concrete objects—sticks and glasses, tools and fruit—not on abstract concepts such as justice and freedom. They can reason about what *is,* but not yet about what is *possible.* The ability to think logically about abstract ideas comes in the next stage of cognitive development, as children enter adolescence. This new stage is called the **formal operational period,** and it is marked by the ability to engage in hypothetical

concrete operations According to Piaget, the third stage of cognitive development, during which children's thinking is no longer dominated by visual appearances.

formal operational period According to Piaget, the fourth stage in cognitive development, usually beginning around age 11, when abstract thinking first appears.

thinking, including the imagining of logical consequences. For example, adolescents who have reached this level can consider various strategies for finding a part-time job and recognize that some methods are more likely to succeed than others. They can form general concepts and understand the impact of the past on the present and the present on the future. They can question social institutions; think about the world as it might be and ought to be; and consider the consequences and complexities of love, work, politics, and religion. They can think logically and systematically about symbols and propositions.

Piaget explored adolescents' formal operational abilities by asking them to perform science experiments that involved formulating and investigating hypotheses. Research indicates that only about half the people in Western cultures ever reach the formal operational level necessary to succeed in Piaget's experiments. People who have not studied high school level science and math are less likely to do well in those experiments (Keating, 1990). In adulthood, people are more likely to use formal operations for problems based on their own occupations; this is one reason that people whose logic is impeccable at work may still become victims of a home-repair or investment scam (Cialdini, 2001).

Modifying Piaget's Theory

Piaget was right in pointing out that there are significant shifts with age in children's thinking and that thinking becomes more systematic, consistent, and integrated as children get older. His idea that children are active explorers and constructors of knowledge has been absorbed into contemporary ways of thinking about childhood. And he inspired many other psychologists to test his findings and theory with experiments of their own. The results of these experiments have suggested that Piaget's theory needs some modification.

What needs to be modified most is Piaget's notion of developmental stages. Researchers have shown that changes from one stage to the next are less consistent and global than Piaget thought. For example, three-year-olds can sometimes make the distinction between physical and mental phenomena; they know the characteristics of real dogs versus pretend dogs (Woolley, 1997). Moreover, they are not always egocentric. In one study, children of this age knew that a white card, which looked pink to them because they were wearing rose-coloured glasses, still looked white to someone who was not wearing the glasses (Liben, 1978). Preoperational children can even do conservation tasks if they are allowed to count the number of objects or have been trained to focus on relevant dimensions such as number, height, and width (Gelman & Baillargeon, 1983).

Taken together, these studies suggest that children's knowledge and mental strategies develop at different ages in different areas and in "pockets" rather than at global levels of understanding (Sternberg, 1989). Knowledge in particular areas is demonstrated sooner in children who are given specific experience in those areas or who are presented with very simple questions and tasks. Children's reasoning depends not only on their general level of development but also on (1) how easy the task is, (2) how familiar they are with the objects involved, (3) how well they understand the language being used, and (4) what experiences they have had in similar situations (Siegal, 1997). Research has also shown that the level of a child's thinking varies from day to day and may even shift when the child solves the same problem twice in the same day (Siegler, 1994).

In summary, psychologists today tend to think of cognitive development in terms of rising and falling "waves," not fixed stages—in terms of changing frequencies in children's use of different ways of thinking, not sudden, permanent shifts from one way of thinking to another (Chen & Siegler, 2000). Psychologists now suggest that children systematically try out many different solutions to problems and gradually come to select the best of them.

Information Processing During Childhood

LINKAGES (a link to Memory)

An alternative to Piaget's theory of cognitive development is based on the *information-processing approach* discussed in the chapters on memory and on cognition and language. This approach describes cognitive activities in terms of how people take in information, use it, and remember it. Developmental psychologists taking this approach focus on gradual increases in children's mental capacities rather than on dramatic changes in their stages of development. Their research demonstrates that as children get older, their information-processing skills gradually get better, and they can perform more complex tasks faster and more easily.

First, older children have longer attention spans and are better at filtering out irrelevant information. These skills help them overcome distractions and concentrate intently on a variety of tasks, from hobbies to homework. Second, older children take in information faster and can shift their attention from one task to another more quickly. (This is how they manage to do their homework while watching TV.) Third, older children can process the information they take in more rapidly and efficiently (Halford et al., 1994; Miller & Vernon, 1997). Compared with younger children, they code information into fewer dimensions and divide tasks into steps that can be processed one after another. This helps them to organize and complete their homework assignments.

Children's memory also markedly improves with age (Gathercole et al., 2004; Schneider & Bjorklund, 1998). Whereas preschoolers can keep only two or three pieces of information in their short-term memory at the same time, older children can hold four or five pieces of information. Older children can also put more information into their long-term memory storage, so they remember things longer than younger children. After about age seven, children can remember information that is more complex and abstract, such as the gist of what several people have said during a conversation. Their memories are more accurate, extensive, and well organized. And because they have accumulated more knowledge during their years of learning about the world, older children can integrate new information into a more complete network of facts. This makes it easier for them to understand and remember new information. (See "In Review: Milestones of Cognitive Development in Infancy and Childhood.")

What accounts for these increases in children's attention, information processing, and memory capacities? It should not be surprising that it's nature plus nurture. As mentioned earlier, maturation of the brain contributes to better and faster information processing as children grow older. Experience contributes, too. The importance of experience has been demonstrated by researchers who have tested children's cognitive abilities using familiar versus unfamiliar materials. In one study, for example, Mayan children in Mexico lagged behind their age-mates in the United States on standard memory tests for pictures and nouns that the Mexican children had not seen before. But the children did much better when researchers gave them a more familiar task, such as recalling the objects they saw in a model of a Mayan village (Rogoff & Waddell, 1982). The children's memory for these familiar objects was better, presumably because they could process information about them more easily and quickly.

Knowing how to memorize also improves children's memories. To a great extent, children acquire memorization strategies in school. They learn to repeat information over and over to help fix it in memory, to place information into categories, and to use memory aids such as "*i* before *e* except after *c*" to help them remember. They also learn what situations call for deliberate memorization and what factors, such as the length of a list, affect memory.

Culture and Cognitive Development

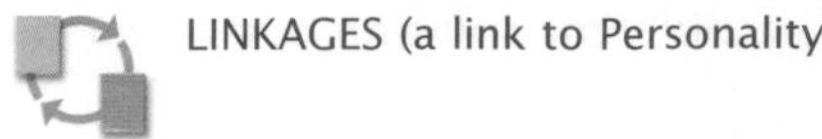
LINKAGES (a link to Personality)

To explain cognitive development, Piaget focused on the physical world of objects. Russian psychologist Lev Vygotsky (pronounced "vah-GOT-ski") focused on the social world of people. He viewed cognitive abilities as the product of cultural

in review Milestones of Cognitive Development in Infancy and Childhood

Age*	Achievement	Description
3–4 months	Maturation of senses	Immaturities that limit the newborn's vision and hearing are overcome.
	Voluntary movement	Infants begin to gain voluntary control over their movements.
12–18 months	Mental representation	Infants can form images of objects and actions in their minds.
	Object permanence	Infants understand that objects exist even when out of sight.
18–24 months	Symbolic thought	Young children use symbols to represent things that are not present in their pretend play, drawing, and talk.
4 years	Intuitive thought	Children reason about events, real and imagined, by guessing rather than by engaging in logical analysis.
6–7 years	Concrete operations Conservation	Children can apply simple logical operations to real objects. For example, they recognize that important properties of a substance, such as number or amount, remain constant despite changes in shape or position.
7–8 years	Information processing	Children can remember more information; they begin to learn strategies for memorization.

*These ages are approximate; they indicate the order in which children first reach these milestones of cognitive development rather than the exact ages.

PsychAssist: Preoperational Inability to Conserve Matter

history. The child's mind, said Vygotsky, grows through interaction with other minds. Dramatic support for this idea comes from cases such as the "Wild Boy of Aveyron," a French child who, in the late 1700s, was apparently lost or abandoned by his parents at an early age and had grown up with animals. At about 11 years of age, he was captured by hunters and sent to Paris, where scientists observed him. What the scientists saw was a dirty, frightened creature who trotted like a wild animal and spent most of his time silently rocking. Although the scientists worked with the boy for more than ten years, he was never able to live unsupervised among other people, and he never learned to speak.

Consistent with Vygotsky's ideas, this tragic case suggests that without society, children's minds would not develop much beyond those of animals—that children acquire their ideas through interaction with parents, teachers, and other agents of their culture. Vygotsky's followers have studied the effects of the social world on children's cognitive development—how participation in social routines affects children's developing knowledge of the world (Gauvain, 2001). In Western societies, those routines include shopping, eating at McDonald's, going to birthday parties, and attending religious services. In other cultures they might include helping to make pottery, going hunting, and weaving baskets (Larson & Verma, 1999). Quite early, children develop mental representations, called *scripts*, for these activities (see the chapter on cognition and language). By the time they are three, children can accurately describe the scripts for their routine activities (Nelson,1986). Scripts, in turn, affect children's knowledge and understanding of cognitive tasks. So suburban children can understand conservation problems earlier than inner-city children if the problems are presented, as Piaget's were, like miniature science experiments. But the performance of inner-city children is improved when the task is presented through a more familiar script, such as one involving what a "slick trickster" would do to fool someone (White & Glick, 1978).

From a remarkably young age, children's cognitive abilities are influenced by the language of their culture. Consider, for instance, the way people think about relations between objects in space. Children who learn a language that has no words for spatial concepts—such as *in, on, in front of, behind, to the left,* and *to the right*—will acquire cognitive categories that are different from those of people in North America. Such individuals do, in fact, have difficulty distinguishing between the left and right sides of objects, and they tend not to use the symbolic associations with left and right hands that North Americans do (Bowerman, 1996; Levinson, 1996).

As a cultural tool, language can also affect academic achievement. For example, Korean and Chinese children show exceptional ability at adding and subtracting large numbers (Miller et al., 1995). In grade three, they can do in their heads three-digit problems (such as 702 minus 125) that would stump most North American children. The difference seems due in part to the clear way that Asian languages label numbers from 11 to 19. In English, the meaning of the words 11 and 12, for instance, is not as clear as the Asian *ten-one* and *ten-two*. In addition, Asians use a manual computing device, called the *abacus*, that is structured around the number ten. Korean math textbooks emphasize this tens structure by presenting the ones digits in red, the tens in blue, and the hundreds in green. Above all, in Asian cultures, educational achievement, especially in mathematics, is encouraged at home and strongly encouraged in school (Naito & Miura, 2001). In short, children's cognitive development is affected in ways large and small by the culture in which they live (Tomasello, 2000).

Variations in Cognitive Development

Even within a single culture, some children are mentally advanced, whereas others lag behind their peers. Why? As already suggested, heredity is an important factor, but experience also plays a role. To explore the significance of that role, psychologists have studied the cognitive development of children who are exposed to differing environments.

Cognitive development is seriously delayed if children are raised in environments that deprive them of the everyday sights, sounds, and feelings provided by conversation and loving interaction with family members, by pictures and books, even by toys and television. Children subjected to this kind of severe deprivation show marked impairment in intellectual development by the time they are two or three years old. And they may never fully recover, even if they are given special attention later on. These effects were seen in the "Wild Boy" and also in more recent cases of youngsters whose abusive parents deliberately isolated them from contact with the world (Rymer, 1993) or who spent their early years in the understaffed and understimulating orphanages of Russia and Romania (Rutter, O'Connor, & the ERA Study Team, 2004). Cognitive development is also impaired by less extreme conditions of deprivation. One study found that children raised in poverty scored nine points lower on IQ tests by the time they were five years old than did children in families whose incomes were twice the poverty level (Duncan, Brooks-Gunn, & Klebanov, 1994). These differences continue as poor

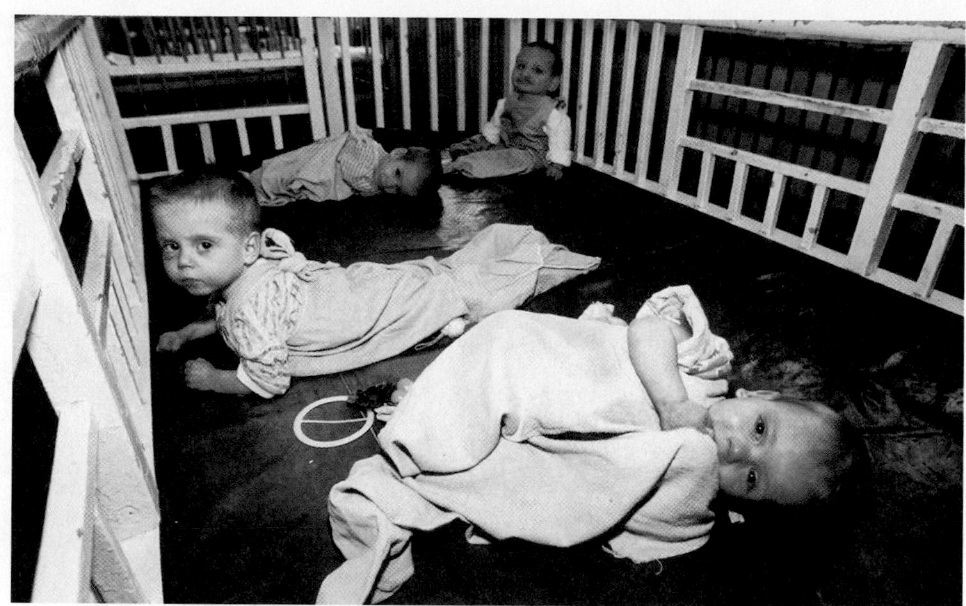

Babies at Risk The cognitive development of infants raised in this understaffed Russian orphanage will be permanently impaired if they are not given far more stimulation in the orphanage or, better yet, adopted into a loving family at a young age.

children enter school. Children who remain in poverty have lower IQs and poorer school achievement (McLoyd, 1998; Stipek & Ryan, 1997). In fact, one study of more than 10 000 children found that the economic status of a child's family is a much better predictor of the child's later cognitive development than are physical risk factors, such as low birth weight (Jefferis et al., 2002). The effects of poverty come from a buildup of problems that often begins with prenatal complications and continues through childhood with lack of cognitive stimulation and harsh and inconsistent parenting.

In families above the poverty line, too, children's cognitive development is related to their surroundings, their experiences, and most notably, their parents' behaviour. One longitudinal study, for instance, revealed that the parents of gifted children started stimulating their children's cognitive activity very early on (Gottfried, 1997). When they were infants, the parents read to them. When they were toddlers, the parents provided them with reference books, computerized teaching aids, and trips to museums. And when they were preschoolers and older, the parents drew out their children's natural curiosity about the world and encouraged their tendency to seek out new learning opportunities themselves. Another study examined how interactions between parents and children are related to IQ scores (Fagot & Gauvain, 1997). When the children were 18 to 30 months old, they were asked to solve a problem—specifically, to use a hook to remove a stuffed animal from a box. The researchers recorded how the mothers interacted with their children during this task. Later, at the age of five, the children were given IQ tests. It turned out that the mothers of children with the highest IQ scores had been the ones who provided cognitive guidance by offering numerous hints and suggestions. In contrast, the mothers of children with the lowest IQ scores had forcefully told them what they needed to do to complete the task.

To improve the cognitive skills of children who do not get the optimum stimulation and guidance at home, developmental psychologists have provided extra lessons, materials, and educational contact with sensitive adults. In a variety of such programs, ranging from weekly home visits to daily preschools, children's cognitive abilities have been enhanced (Ramey & Ramey, 1998), and some effects can last into adulthood (Campbell et al., 2001). Music lessons can also promote children's cognitive development, especially verbal memory (Ho, Cheung, & Chan, 2003; Rauscher et al., 1997). Even electronic games, although no substitute for adult attention, can provide opportunities for school-age children to hone spatial skills

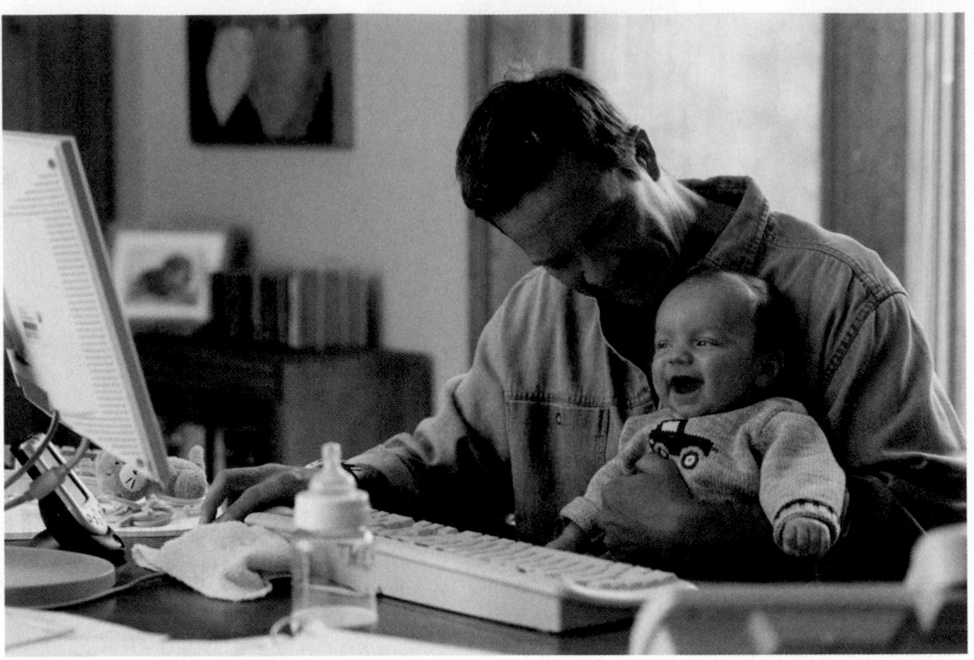

When Does Stimulation Become Overstimulation? A child's cognitive development is enhanced by a stimulating environment, but can there be too much stimulation? In the face of an avalanche of electronic media aimed specifically at babies and toddlers, some people are beginning to wonder. These stimulating media include computer "lapware," such as this baby is enjoying, videos and DVDs for even the tiniest infants, and, of course, the television. Many babies in Western countries are immersed in electronic media for hours each day. We don't yet know how all this well-intentioned electronic stimulation is affecting young children because we don't yet have enough evidence on which to base conclusions.

that help improve their performance in math and science (Green & Bavelier, 2003; Subrahmanyam & Greenfield, 1994). It appears that the earlier the stimulation begins, the better; and for some cognitive abilities, stimulation affects both the brain and behaviour throughout much of the life span (Greenough, 1997).

Infancy and Childhood: Social and Emotional Development

Life for the child is more than learning about objects, doing math problems, and getting good grades. It is also about social relationships and emotional reactions. From the first months onward, infants are sensitive to those around them (Mumme & Fernald, 2003), and they are both attracted by and attractive to other people.

During the first hour or so after birth, mothers gaze into their infants' eyes and give them gentle touches (Klaus & Kennell, 1976). This is the first opportunity for the mother to display her *bond* to her infant—an emotional tie that begins even before the baby is born. Psychologists once believed that this immediate contact was critical—that the mother-infant bond would never be strong if the opportunity for early interaction was missed. Research has revealed, however, that such interaction in the first few hours is not a requirement for a close relationship (Myers, 1987). With or without early contact, mothers and fathers, whether biological or adoptive, come to form close attachments to their infants by interacting with them day after day.

As the mother gazes at her baby, the baby is gazing back (Klaus & Kennell, 1976). By the time infants are two days old, they recognize—and like—their mother's face; they will suck more vigorously to see a videotaped image of her face than to see that of a stranger (Walton, Bower, & Bower, 1992). Soon, they begin to respond to the mother's facial expressions as well. By the time they are a year old, children use their mothers' emotional expressions to guide their own behaviour in uncertain situations (Saarni, Mummer, & Campos, 1998; Hertenstein & Campos, 2004). If the mother looks frightened when a stranger approaches, for example, the child is more likely to avoid the stranger. This phenomenon is called *social referencing*. Children can pick up emotion cues from many sources, including television. In one study, after seeing a video in which an adult showed fear of an object, infants later avoided that object (Mumme & Fernald, 2003). As described in the chapter on learning, observational learning can sometimes lead to fears, and even phobias.

Infants communicate feelings as well as recognize them. They do so by crying and screaming, but also by more subtle behaviour. When they want to interact, they look and smile; when they do not want to interact, they turn away and some suck their thumbs (Tronick,1989).

Individual Temperament

From the moment infants are born, they differ from one another in the emotions they express most often. Some infants are happy, active, and vigorous; they splash, thrash, and wriggle. Others are usually quiet. Some infants approach new objects with enthusiasm; others turn away or fuss. Some infants whimper; others kick, scream, and wail. Characteristics such as these make up the infant's temperament. **Temperament** refers to the infant's individual style and frequency of expressing needs and emotions. Although temperament mainly reflects nature's contribution to the beginning of an individual's personality, it can also be affected by the prenatal environment, including—as noted earlier—the mother's stress level, smoking, and drug use.

In some of the earliest research on infant temperament, Alexander Thomas and Stella Chess found that most babies fall into one of three general temperament patterns (Thomas & Chess, 1977). *Easy babies* are the most common kind. They get hungry and sleepy at predictable times, react to new situations cheerfully, and seldom fuss. In contrast, *difficult babies* are irregular and irritable. And *slow-to-warm-up babies* react warily to new situations but eventually come to enjoy them. Later research has shown that traces of these early temperament patterns weave their way throughout childhood (Rothbart, Ahadi, & Evans, 2000). Easy infants usually stay easy (Zhou et al., 2004); difficult infants often remain difficult, sometimes developing attention and aggression problems in childhood (Guerin, Gottfried, & Thomas, 1997); timid, or slow-to-warm-up, toddlers tend to be shy as preschoolers, restrained and inhibited as eight-year-olds, and somewhat anxious as teenagers (Roberts, Caspi, & Moffitt, 2001). The differences even seem to extend into adulthood. In one study, the brains of adults who were timid toddlers reacted especially strongly to novel stimuli (Schwartz et al., 2003).

However, these tendencies are not set in stone. In temperament, as in cognitive development, nature interacts with nurture. Many events take place between infancy and adulthood that can shift an individual's development in one direction or another. For instance, if parents are patient enough to allow their difficult baby to respond to changes in daily routines at a more relaxed pace, the child may become less difficult over time.

The Infant Grows Attached

During the first year of life, as infants and caregivers watch and respond to one another, the infant begins to form an **attachment**—a deep, affectionate, close, and enduring relationship—to these important figures. John Bowlby, a British psychoanalyst, drew attention to the importance of attachment after he observed children who had been orphaned in World War II. These children's depression and other emotional scars led Bowlby to develop a theory about the importance of developing a strong attachment to one's primary caregivers, a tie that normally keeps infants close to their caregivers and, therefore, safe (Bowlby, 1973). Soon after Bowlby first described his theory, researchers began to investigate how such attachments are formed and what happens when they are not formed, or when they are broken by loss or separation. Some of the most dramatic of these studies were conducted by Harry Harlow.

temperament An individual's basic disposition, which is evident from infancy.

attachment A deep and enduring relationship with the person with whom a baby has shared many experiences.

Motherless Monkeys—and Children Harlow (1959) explored two hypotheses about what leads infants to develop attachments to their mothers. The first hypothesis was that attachment occurs because mothers feed their babies. Perhaps food, along with the experience of being fed, creates an emotional bond to the mother. Harlow's second hypothesis was that attachment is based on the warm, comforting contact the baby gets from the mother. To evaluate these hypotheses, Harlow separated newborn monkeys from their mothers and raised them in cages containing two artificial mothers. One "mother" was made of wire, but it had a rubber nipple from which the infant could get milk (see photo). In other words, it provided food but no physical comfort. The other artificial mother had no nipple but was made of soft, comfortable terrycloth. Harlow found that the infants preferred the terrycloth mother, spending most of their time with it, especially when frightened. The terrycloth mother provided feelings of softness and cuddling, which were things the infants needed when they sensed danger.

Harlow also investigated what happens when attachments do not form. He isolated some newborn monkeys from all social contact. After a year of this isolation, the monkeys showed dramatic disturbances. When visited by normally active, playful monkeys, they withdrew to a corner, huddling or rocking for hours. As adults, they were unable to have normal sexual relations. When some of the females did have babies (through artificial insemination), they tended to ignore them. When their infants became distressed, the mothers physically abused and sometimes even killed them.

Humans who spend their first few years without a consistent caregiver react in a tragically similar manner. For examples, at Romanian and Russian orphanages, where many children were neglected by institutional caregivers, visitors discovered that the children, like Harlow's deprived monkeys, were withdrawn and engaged in constant rocking (Holden, 1996). These effects continued even after the children were adopted. Kim MacLean, a professor at St. Francis Xavier University in Antigonish, Nova Scotia, and her colleagues, observed four-year-old children who had been in a Romanian orphanage for at least eight months before being adopted. The behaviour of these children was compared with the behaviour of children in two other groups matched for age and gender: Those who had been adopted before the age of four months and those who had remained with their biological parents (MacLean, 2003). The late-adopted children were found to have many more serious problems. Depressed or withdrawn, they stared blankly, demanded attention, and could not control their tempers (Holden, 1996). They also interacted poorly with their adopted mothers but were indiscriminately friendly with strangers, trying to cuddle and kiss them. At age six, a third of late-adopted children still showed no preference for their parents or any tendency to look to them when stressed (Rutter et al., 2004). Neurologists suggest that the dramatic problems observed in isolated monkeys and humans are the result of developmental brain dysfunction or damage brought on by a lack of touch and body movement in infancy and by the absence of early play, conversation, and other normal childhood experiences early in development (Prescott, 1996; Rutter et al., 2004).

Wire and Terrycloth "Mothers" Here are the two types of artificial mothers used in Harlow's research. Although baby monkeys received milk from the wire mother, they spent most of their time with the terrycloth version, and they clung to it when frightened.

Forming an Attachment Fortunately, most infants do have a consistent caregiver, usually their birth or adoptive mother, to whom they can form an attachment. They learn to recognize her and are able to distinguish her from a stranger at an early age. By the age of six or seven months, infants show signs of preferring their mothers to anyone else—watching her closely, crawling after her, clambering up into her lap, protesting when she leaves, and brightening when she returns (Ainsworth, 1973).

After an attachment has been formed, separation from the mother for even 30 minutes can be a stressful experience (Larson, Gunnar, & Hertsgaard, 1991).

Later on, infants develop attachments to their fathers as well (Lamb, 1997). However, interactions with fathers are typically less frequent, and of a somewhat different nature, than with mothers (Parke, 2002). Mothers tend to feed, bathe, dress, cuddle, and talk to their infants, whereas fathers are more likely to play with, jiggle, and toss them, especially sons.

Variations in Attachment The amount of closeness and contact infants seek with either their mothers or fathers depends to some extent on the infants. Those who are ill, tired, or slow to warm up may require more closeness. Closeness also depends to some extent on the parents. An infant whose parent has been absent, aloof, or unresponsive is likely to need more closeness than one whose parent is accessible and responsive.

Researchers have studied the differences in infants' attachments in a special situation that simulates the natural comings and goings of parents—the so-called *Strange Situation* (Ainsworth et al., 1978). This test occurs in an unfamiliar playroom where the infant interacts with the mother and an unfamiliar woman in brief episodes: The infant plays with the mother and the stranger, the mother leaves the baby with the stranger for a few minutes, the mother and the stranger leave the baby alone in the room briefly, and the mother returns to the room.

Videotapes of these sessions show that most infants display a *secure attachment* to the mother in the Strange Situation (Thompson, 1998). In the unfamiliar room, they use the mother as a home base, leaving her side to explore and play but returning to her periodically for comfort or contact. When the mother returns after the brief separation, the infant is happy to see her and receptive when she initiates contact. These mother-child pairs also tend to have harmonious interactions at home. According to Greg Moran, David Pederson, and Anne Krupka at the University of Western Ontario, the mothers themselves are generally sensitive and responsive to their babies' needs and signals (Moran, Pederson, & Krupka, 2005).

Some infants, however, display an *insecure attachment.* If the relationship is *avoidant,* they avoid or ignore their mothers when they return after the brief separation. If the relationship is *ambivalent,* they greet their mothers when they return but then act angry and reject the mothers' efforts at contact. If the relationship is *disorganized,* their behaviour is inconsistent, disturbed, and disturbing; they may begin to cry after the mothers have returned and comforted them, or they may reach out for the mothers while looking away from them (Moss et al., 2004).

Cultural Differences in Parent-Child Relations Variations in the intimacy of family interactions, including whether infants sleep in their parents' bed, may contribute to cross-cultural differences in attachment patterns.

The nature of a child's attachment to parents can have long-term and far-reaching effects. For example, unless disrupted by the loss of a parent, abuse by a family member, chronic depression in the mother, or some other severe negative event (Weinfield, Sroufe, & Egeland, 2000), an infant's secure attachment continues into young adulthood—and probably throughout life (Hamilton, 2000; Mattanah, Hancock, & Brand, 2004; Waters et al., 2000). A secure attachment to the mother is also reflected in relationships with other people. Children who are securely attached receive more positive reactions from other children when they are toddlers (Fagot, 1997) and have better relations with peers in middle childhood and adolescence (Carlson, Sroufe, & Egeland, 2004; Schneider, Atkinson, & Tardif, 2001). Attachment to the mother also affects the way children process emotional information. Securely attached children tend to remember positive events more accurately than negative events, whereas insecurely attached children tend to do the opposite (Belsky, Spritz, & Crnic, 1996).

Patterns of attachment vary widely in different parts of the world and are related to how parents treat their children. In northern Germany, for example, where parents promote children's independence with strict discipline, the proportion of infants who display avoidant attachments is quite high (Spangler, Fremmer-Bombik, & Grossman, 1996). Kibbutz babies in Israel, who sleep in infant houses away from their parents, are likely to show insecure attachment, as well as other attachment difficulties, later in life (Aviezer et al., 1999). And in Japan, where mothers are completely devoted to their young children and are seldom apart from them, including at night, children develop an attachment relationship that emphasizes harmony and union (Rothbaum et al., 2000).

THINKING CRITICALLY

Does Daycare Harm the Emotional Development of Infants?

With about 70 percent of mothers in Canada working outside the home (Friendly, Beach, & Turiano, 2002), concern has been expressed about how daily separations from their mothers might affect children, especially infants. Some have argued that leaving infants with a baby sitter or putting them in a daycare centre damages the quality of the mother-infant relationship and increases the babies' risk for psychological problems later on (Gallagher, 1998).

- **What am I being asked to believe or accept?**

The claim to be evaluated is that daily separations brought about by the need for daycare undermine the infant's ability to form a secure attachment, as well as inflict emotional harm.

- **What evidence is available to support the assertion?**

There is clear evidence that separation from the mother is painful for young children. Furthermore, if separation lasts a week or more, young children may become apathetic and mournful and eventually lose interest in the missing mother (Robertson & Robertson, 1971). But daycare does not involve such lasting separations, and research has shown that infants in daycare do form attachments to their mothers. In fact, they prefer their mothers to their daytime caregivers (Clarke-Stewart & Fein, 1983).

But are their attachments as secure as the attachments formed by infants whose mothers do not work outside the home? Researchers first examined this question by comparing infants' behaviour in the Strange Situation test. A review of the data showed that, on average, infants in full-time daycare were somewhat more likely to be classified as insecurely attached. Specifically, 36 percent of the infants in full-time care received this classification, compared with 29 percent of the infants not in full-time daycare (Clarke-Stewart, 1989). These results appear to support the suggestion that daycare may hinder the development of infants' attachments to their mothers.

- **Are there alternative ways of interpreting the evidence?**

Perhaps factors other than daycare could explain this difference between infants in daycare and those at home with their mothers. One such factor could be the method used to assess attachment—the Strange Situation test. Infants in these studies were judged insecure if they did not run to their mothers after a brief separation. But maybe infants who experience daily separations from their mothers are less disturbed by the separations in the Strange Situation test and therefore seek out less closeness with their mothers. A second factor could be differences between the infants' mothers: Perhaps mothers who value independence in themselves and in their children are more likely to be working and to place their children in daycare, whereas mothers who emphasize closeness with their children are more likely to stay home.

- **What additional evidence would help to evaluate the alternatives?**

Finding insecure attachment to be more common among the infants of working mothers does not, by itself, prove that daycare is harmful. To judge the effects of daycare, we must use other measures of emotional adjustment. If infants in daycare show consistent signs of troubled emotional relations in other situations (at home, say) and with other caregivers (such as the father), this evidence would

The Effects of Daycare Parents are understandably concerned that leaving their infants in a daycare centre all day might interfere with the mother-infant attachment or with other aspects of the children's development. Research shows that most infants in daycare do form healthy bonds with their parents.

support the argument that daycare harms children's emotional development. Another useful method would be to control statistically for differences in the attitudes and behaviours of parents who do and do not use daycare and then examine the differences in their children.

In fact, this research design has already been employed. In 1990 the US government funded a study of infant daycare in ten sites around the country. The psychological and physical development of more than 1,300 randomly selected infants was tracked from birth through age three. The results showed that when factors such as parents' education, income, and attitudes were controlled for statistically, infants in daycare were no more likely to have emotional problems or to be insecurely attached to their mothers than infants not in daycare. However, in cases in which infants were placed in poor-quality daycare with caregivers who were insensitive and unresponsive, and in which mothers were insensitive to their babies' needs at home, the infants were less likely to develop a secure attachment to their mothers (NICHD Early Child Care Research Network, 2005). A study of this magnitude has not yet been conducted in Canada but Canadian researchers suggest that high quality daycare has several benefits for children's intellectual and social development (Public Health Agency of Canada, 2004).

- **What conclusions are most reasonable?**

Based on available evidence, the most reasonable conclusion appears to be that daycare by itself does not lead to insecure attachment or cause emotional harm to infants. But if the care is of poor quality, it can worsen a risky situation at home and increase the likelihood that infants will have problems forming a secure attachment to their mothers. The US government study is still underway, and the children's progress is being followed into adolescence. Time will tell if other problems develop in the future.

Relationships with Parents and Peers

Erik Erikson (1968) saw the first year of life as the time at which infants develop a feeling of basic trust (or mistrust) about the world. According to his theory, an infant's first year represents the first of eight stages of lifelong psychosocial development (see Table 12.2). Each stage focuses on an issue or crisis that is especially important at that time of life. Erikson believed that the ways in which people resolve these issues shape their personalities and social relationships. Positive resolution of

table 12.2

In each of Erikson's stages of development, a different psychological issue presents a new crisis for the person to resolve. The person focuses attention on that issue and, by the end of the period, has worked through the crisis and resolved it either positively, in the direction of healthy development, or negatively, hindering further psychological development.

Erikson's Stages of Psychosocial Development

Age	Central Psychological Issue or Crisis
First year	**Trust versus mistrust** Infants learn to trust that their needs will be met by the world, especially by the mother—or they learn to mistrust the world.
Second year	**Autonomy versus shame and doubt** Children learn to exercise will, to make choices, and to control themselves—or they become uncertain and doubt that they can do things by themselves.
Third to fifth year	**Initiative versus guilt** Children learn to initiate activities and enjoy their accomplishments, acquiring direction and purpose. Or, if they are not allowed initiative, they feel guilty for their attempts at independence.
Sixth year through puberty	**Industry versus inferiority** Children develop a sense of industry and curiosity and are eager to learn—or they feel inferior and lose interest in the tasks before them.
Adolescence	**Identity versus role confusion** Adolescents come to see themselves as unique and integrated persons with an ideology—or they become confused about what they want out of life.
Early adulthood	**Intimacy versus isolation** Young people become able to commit themselves to another person—or they develop a sense of isolation and feel they have no one in the world but themselves.
Middle age	**Generativity versus stagnation** Adults are willing to have and care for children and to devote themselves to their work and the common good—or they become self-centred and inactive.
Old age	**Integrity versus despair** Older people enter a period of reflection, becoming assured that their lives have been meaningful and ready to face death with acceptance and dignity. Or they are in despair for their unaccomplished goals, failures, and ill-spent lives.

an issue provides the foundation for characteristics such as trust, independence, initiative, and industry. But if the crisis is not resolved positively, according to Erikson, the person will be psychologically troubled and cope less effectively with later crises. In Erikson's theory, then, forming basic feelings of trust during infancy is the bedrock for all future emotional development.

After children have formed strong emotional attachments to their parents, their next psychological task is to begin to develop a more independent, or autonomous, relationship with them. This task is part of Erikson's second stage, when children begin to exercise their wills, develop some independence from their parents, and start activities on their own. According to Erikson, children who are not allowed to exercise their wills or begin their own activities will feel uncertain about doing things for themselves and guilty about seeking independence. The extent to which parents allow or encourage their children's autonomy depends largely on their parenting style.

Parenting Styles Parents try to channel children's impulses into socially accepted outlets and teach them the skills and rules needed to function in their society. This process, called *socialization,* is shaped by cultural values. Parents in Eastern countries such as China, for example, tend to be influenced by the collectivist tradition, in which family and community interests are emphasized over individual goals. Children in these cultures are expected to respect and obey their elders and to do less of the questioning, negotiating, and arguing that is encouraged—or at least allowed—in many middle-class Canadian families (Lam, 2001). When families from China immigrate to Canada, the parents may find that some of their values conflict with those of their adolescent children, especially if their children become more immersed in Canadian culture than the parents (Tardif & Geva, 2006).

North American parents tend to employ one of three distinct parenting styles, as described by Diana Baumrind (1971). **Authoritarian parents** are relatively strict, punitive, and unsympathetic. They value obedience and try to shape their children's behaviour to meet a set standard and to curb the children's wills. They do not encourage independence. They are detached and seldom praise their youngsters. In contrast, **permissive parents** are lax in disciplining their children and give them a great deal of freedom. **Authoritative parents** fall between these two extremes. They reason with their children, encouraging give and take. They allow the children increasing responsibility as they get older and better at making decisions. They are firm but understanding. They set limits but also encourage independence. Their demands are reasonable, rational, and consistent.

In her research with middle-class parents, Baumrind found that these three parenting styles were related to young children's social and emotional development. The children of authoritarian parents tended to be unfriendly, distrustful, and withdrawn. Children of permissive parents tended to be immature, dependent, and unhappy; they were likely to have tantrums or to ask for help when they encountered even slight difficulties. Children raised by authoritative parents tended to be friendly, cooperative, self-reliant, and socially responsible (Baumrind, 1986).

According to Lynne Jackson at King's University College in London, Ontario, authoritative parenting is associated with higher levels of optimism in adolescents (Jackson, Pratt, Hunsberger, & Pancer, 2005). Other researchers have found authoritative parenting styles to be associated with additional positive outcomes, including better school achievement (Steinberg et al., 1994), greater popularity (Hinshaw et al., 1997), and better psychological adjustment to parental divorce (Hetherington & Clingempeel, 1992). In contrast, children of authoritarian parents are more likely to cheat and to be aggressive and less likely to be empathic or to experience guilt or accept blame after doing something wrong (Eisenberg & Fabes, 1998).

The results of these studies of parenting styles are interesting, but they have some limitations. First, they involve correlations, which, as discussed in the chapter on research in psychology, do not prove causation. Finding consistent correlations between parenting styles and children's behaviour does not establish that the parents' behaviour is *causing* the differences seen in their children. In fact, parents' behaviour is, itself, often shaped by their children to some extent. For example, parents may react differently to children of different ages. Children's temperament, size, and appearance may also influence the way parents treat them (Bugental & Goodnow, 1998) and may alter the effects of parenting styles (Zhou et al., 2004). Second, some psychologists have suggested that it is not the parents' behaviour itself that influences children but rather how the children perceive the discipline they receive—as stricter or more lenient than what an older sibling received, for example (Reiss et al., 2000).

A third limitation of these studies is that the correlations between parenting styles and children's behaviour, though statistically significant, are usually not terribly large. Expected relationships between parenting styles and children's behaviour

authoritarian parents Firm, punitive, and unsympathetic parents who value obedience from the child and authority for themselves.

permissive parents Parents who are lax in disciplining their child and give them great freedom.

authoritative parents Parents who reason with the child, encourage give and take, and are firm but understanding.

do not always appear. For example, Baumrind (1971) found a small group of "harmonious" families in which she never observed the parents disciplining the children, yet the children were thriving. In all likelihood, it is the "fit" between parenting style and children's characteristics that affects children the most.

Relationships with Peers Social development over the years of childhood occurs in a world that broadens to include brothers, sisters, playmates, and classmates. Relationships with other children start early (Rubin, Bukowski, & Parker, 1998). Ann Bigelow and her colleagues at St. Francis Xavier University in Antigonish, Nova Scotia, have studied the early development of peer relationships. They found that by two months of age, infants engage in mutual gazing. By six months, they vocalize and smile at each other. By eight months, they prefer to look at another child rather than at an adult (Bigelow et al., 1990). So people are interested in one another, even as infants, but it's a long journey from interest to intimacy.

Observations of two-year-olds show that the most they can do with their peers is to look at them, imitate them, and exchange—or grab—toys. By age four, they begin to play "pretend" together, agreeing about roles and themes. This "sociodramatic" play is important because it provides a new context for communicating desires and feelings and offers an opportunity to form first "friendships" (Dunn & Hughes, 2001; Rubin et al., 1998).

In research conducted at the University of Western Ontario, Lynne Zarbatany and her colleagues have found that during the school years, peer interaction becomes more frequent, complex, and structured (Zarbatany, Hartmann, & Rankin, 1990; Zarbatany, McDougall, & Hymel, 2000). Children play games with rules, join teams, tutor each other, and cooperate—or compete—in achieving goals. Friends become more important and friendships longer lasting as school-age children find that friends are a source of companionship, stimulation, support, and affection (Hartup & Stevens, 1997). In fact, companionship and fun are the most important aspects of friendship for children at this age. Psychological intimacy does not enter the picture until adolescence (Parker et al., 2001).

Friends also help children to establish their sense of self-worth. For example, through friendships children can compare their own strengths and weaknesses with those of others in a supportive and accepting atmosphere. Unfortunately, about 10 percent of school-age children do not have friends, and without friends, children tend to feel unlikeable. These children report extremely high levels of loneliness and rejection (Asher & Hopmeyer, 2001). They often do poorly in school and usually experience psychological and behaviour problems in later life (Asher & Hopmeyer, 2001; Bagwell, Newcomb, & Bukowski, 1998; Ladd & Troop-Gordon, 2003). It appears that having just one close, stable friend can protect schoolchildren from loneliness and other problems (Parker et al., 2001); having more than one friend does not seem to provide further benefits.

Social Skills

The changes in peer interactions and the formation of friendships over the years of childhood can be traced in part to children's increasing social competencies and skills. *Social skills,* like cognitive skills, must be learned (Rubin et al., 1998).

One important social skill is the ability to engage in sustained, responsive interactions with peers. These interactions require cooperation, sharing, and taking turns—behaviours that first appear in the preschool years. Parents can help their children to develop these skills by engaging them in lots of "pretend" play and other prosocial activities (Ladd, 2005) and by encouraging them to express their emotions constructively (Eisenberg, 1998). Older siblings, too, can help by acting out social roles during play and by talking about their feelings (Ruffman et al., 1998). Children who have been abused by their parents tend to lack these

Children's Friendships Though relationships with peers may not always be this cordial, they are often among the closest and most positive in a child's life. Friends are more interactive than nonfriends; they smile and laugh together more, pay closer attention to equality in their conversation, and talk about mutual goals, not just personal ones. Having at least one close friend in childhood predicts good psychological functioning later on.

important interaction skills and are thus more likely to be victimized by their peers (Bolger & Patterson, 2001; Crick, 1997).

A second social skill that children learn is the ability to detect and correctly interpret other people's emotional signals. In fact, effective performance in social situations depends on this ability (Slomkowski & Dunn, 1996). Children who understand another person's perspective, who appreciate how that person might be feeling, and who behave accordingly tend to be the most popular members of a peer group (Izard et al., 2001; Rubin et al., 1998). Children who do not have these skills are rejected or neglected; they may become bullies or the victims of bullies.

LINKAGES (a link to Social Cognition)

A related set of social skills involves the ability to feel what another person is feeling, or something close to it (*empathy*), and to respond with comfort or help if the person is in distress. Affectionate mothers who discuss emotions openly and who provide clear messages about the consequences of their child's hurtful behaviour effectively encourage the child to be empathic (Eisenberg, 1997).

A third social skill that develops in childhood is the ability to control one's emotions and behaviour—an ability known as **self-regulation** (Rothbart & Bates, 1998; Campos, Frankel, & Camras, 2004). In the first few years of life, children learn to calm or console themselves by sucking their thumbs or cuddling their favourite blanket. Later, they learn more sophisticated strategies of self-regulation, such as counting to ten, planning ahead to avoid a problem (for example, getting on the first bus if the school bully usually takes the second one), and recruiting social support (for example, casually joining a group of big kids to walk past the bully on the playground). Children who cannot regulate their emotions tend to experience anxiety and distress and have trouble recovering from stressful events. They become emotionally overaroused when they see someone in distress and are often unsympathetic and unhelpful (Eisenberg & Fabes, 1998). Further, boys who are easily aroused and have difficulty regulating this arousal become less and less popular with their peers and may develop problems with aggressiveness (Eisenberg et al., 2004; Fabes et al., 1997).

Self-regulation is most effectively learned by children who experience harmonious interactions at home under the guidance of supportive and competent parents (Saarni et al., 1998). One study revealed that children skilled at regulating their emotions had parents who had soothed them in infancy by holding them, talking to them, and providing distractions. As the children grew older, the parents gradually began to introduce them to new and potentially uncomfortable events (such as their first haircut), all the while remaining close by as a safe base (Fox, 1997). Another

self-regulation The ability to control one's emotions and behaviour.

study, specifically involving North American children, found that self-regulation and empathy are fostered by parents who talk about their own feelings and encourage their children to express emotions (Eisenberg, 1997). This phenomenon is not universal, however. For example, Japanese children are usually better emotion regulators than North American children, even though Japanese parents tend not to encourage the expression of strong emotion (Zahn-Waxler et al., 1996).

Emphasis on the development of social skills varies from culture to culture. In China, Zambia, and Kenya, for example, the concept of intelligence includes the social skills of being understanding, respectful, responsible, and considerate (Benson, 2003). For the past decade, psychologists have been encouraging schools to help teach children social skills, including self-regulation, understanding, empathy, and cooperation (Goleman, 1995; Salovey & Sluyter, 1997). It is their hope that this "emotional literacy" will reduce the prevalence of childhood depression and aggression.

Gender Roles

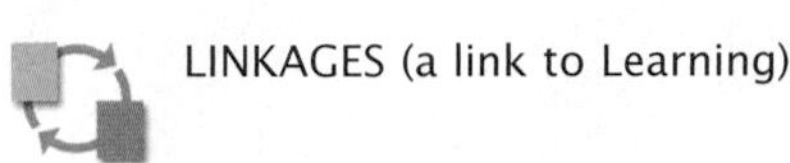

An important aspect of understanding other people and being socially skilled is knowing about social roles, including **gender roles**—the general patterns of work, appearance, and behaviour associated with being a man or a woman. Gender roles appear in every culture, but they are more pronounced in cultures in which there are greater male-female differences in social status (Wood & Eagly, 2002). One survey of gender roles in 25 countries found that children learn these roles earliest in Muslim countries, where gender roles are perhaps most extreme (Williams & Best, 1990). Gender roles persist because they are deeply rooted in both nature and nurture.

Small physical and behavioural differences between the sexes are evident early on and tend to increase over the years (Eagly, 1996). Girls tend to speak and write earlier and to be better at grammar and spelling than boys (Halpern, 1997). Boys tend to be more skilled than girls at manipulating objects, constructing three-dimensional forms, and mentally manipulating complex figures and pictures (Choi & Silverman, 2003). Girls are more attracted than boys are to baby faces (Maestripieri, 2004), and by four months of age, the average duration of mutual gazing between girls and women is four times longer than that between boys and women (Leeb & Rejskind, 2004). Girls are also able to read emotional signals at younger ages than boys (Dunn et al., 1991). Girls are likely to be more kind, considerate, and empathic. Friendships between girls are private and important affairs, and girls worry about them more than boys do (Benenson & Christakos, 2003). Thoughts of suicide are nearly twice as likely among girls with few friends than among boys with few friends (Bearman & Moody, 2004). Girls are likely to play in pairs, whereas boys tend to play in groups (Fabes, Martin, & Hanish, 2003). Boys are more physically active and aggressive; they play in larger spaces, enjoying noisier, more strenuous physical games. From the age of two, boys engage in riskier behaviours and are injured at a rate that is two to four times that of girls (Morrongiello & Hogg, 2004). On the playground, boys are the overtly aggressive ones; they push and they punch (Hyde, 1986). Among girls, the aggression is less obvious and more "relational." Although unlikely to hit other children, girls hurt with nasty words and threats to withdraw friendship (Crick, Casas, & Mosher, 1997; Crick et al., 1999; Zuger, 1998). Given all these differences, it is not surprising to find that girls are more sensitive and boys more competitive (Fabes et al., 2003).

Biological Factors A biological contribution to these male-female differences is suggested by several lines of evidence. First are studies showing gender differences in anatomy, hormones, and brain organization and functioning (Geary, 1999; Ruble & Martin, 1998). Second, cross-cultural research reveals consistent gender patterns even in the face of differing socialization practices (Simpson & Kenrick, 1997). Finally, research with nonhuman primates has found sex differences that parallel those seen in human children. In one study, young female animals

gender roles Patterns of work, appearance, and behaviour that a society associates with being male or female.

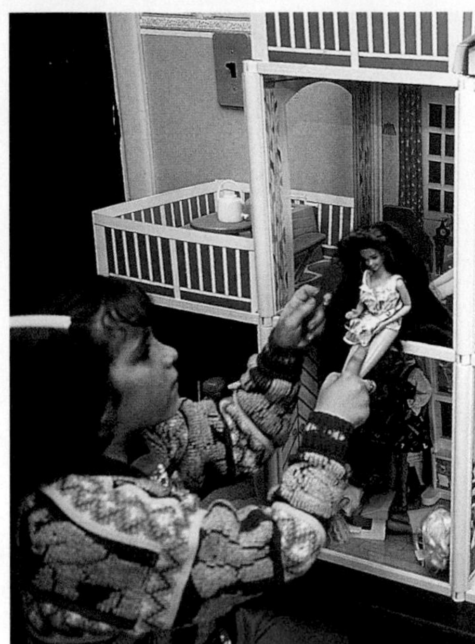

Learning Gender Roles Socialization by parents and others typically encourages interests and activities traditionally associated with a child's own gender.

preferred playing with dolls and young males preferred playing with a toy car (Alexander & Hines, 2002).

Social Factors There is no doubt, though, that socialization also influences gender roles, partly by exaggerating whatever gender differences may already exist. From the moment they are born, boys and girls are treated differently. Adults usually play more gently and talk more to infants they believe to be girls than to infants they believe to be boys. They often shower their daughters with dolls and doll clothes, their sons with trucks and tools. They tend to encourage boys to achieve, compete, explore, control their feelings, act independently, and assume personal responsibility. They encourage girls to be reflective, dependent, domestic, obedient, and unselfish (Ruble & Martin, 1998). Mothers speak with more feeling to girls and in more supportive ways (Kitamura & Burnham, 2003; Leaper, Anderson, & Sanders, 1998). And when asked to imagine that their child has been injured, it takes a less severe injury to cause concern about daughters than about sons (Morrongiello & Hogg, 2004). In these and many other ways, parents, teachers, and television role models consciously or inadvertently pass on their ideas about "appropriate" behaviours for boys and girls (Witt, 1997). They also convey information about gender-appropriate interests. For example, girls and boys in grade six express equal interest in science and earn the same grades. Yet parents underestimate their daughters' interest in science, believe that science is difficult for them, and are less likely to give them scientific explanations when working on a physics task (Tenenbaum & Leaper, 2003).

Children also pick up notions of what is gender-appropriate behaviour from their peers (Martin & Fabes, 2001). For example, one reason boys tend to be better than girls at computer and video games (Greenfield, 1994) is that boys encourage and reward each other for skilled performance at these games more than girls do (Law, Pellegrino, & Hunt, 1993). Children are also more likely to play with other children of the same sex, and to act in gender-typical ways, when they are on the playground than when they are at home or in the classroom (Luria, 1992).

Cognitive Factors Because most children want to be accepted, especially by peers, they become "gender detectives," always searching for clues about who should do what, who can play with whom, and in what ways girls and boys are different (Martin & Ruble, 2004). In the process, they develop **gender schemas,** which are generalizations about what toys and activities are "appropriate" for boys versus girls and what jobs are "meant" for men versus women (Fagot, 1995). For example, by the time they are three years old, children tend to believe that dolls are for girls and trucks are for boys. Once they have developed these gender schemas and know that they themselves are male or female, children tend to choose activities, toys, and behaviours that are "appropriate" for their own gender (Ruble & Martin, 1998). They become "sexist self-socializers" as they work at developing the masculine or feminine attributes they view as consistent with their self-image as a male or a female. By the age of eight or nine, they may have become more flexible about what's okay for members of each sex to do—but most still say they wouldn't be friends with a boy who wore lipstick or a girl who played football (Levy, Taylor, & Gelman, 1995). And later in elementary school, when most girls outperform boys in language arts, math, science, and social studies, girls think of themselves as good only in language arts, because that's what they are "supposed" to be good at (Pomerantz, Altermatt, & Saxon, 2002).

In summary, social training by both adults and peers, along with the child's own cognitions about the world, tends to bolster and amplify any biological predispositions that distinguish boys and girls. This process, in turn, creates gender roles that are the joint—and inextricably linked—products of nature and nurture. This and other elements of early development are summarized in "In Review: Social and Emotional Development During Infancy and Childhood."

gender schemas The generalizations children develop about what toys, activities, and occupations are "appropriate" for males versus females.

in review Social and Emotional Development During Infancy and Childhood

Age	Relationships with Parents	Relationships with Other Children	Social Understanding
Birth–2 years	Infants form an attachment to the primary caregiver.	Play focuses on toys, not on other children.	Infants respond to emotional expressions of others.
2–4 years	Children become more autonomous and no longer need their parents' constant attention.	Toys are a way of eliciting responses from other children.	Young children can recognize emotions of others.
4–10 years	Parents actively socialize their children.	Children begin to cooperate, compete, play games, and form friendships with peers.	Children learn social rules, like politeness, and roles, like being a male or female; they learn to control their emotions.

PsychAssist: Strange Situation Test and Attachment

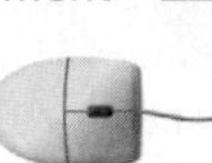

The efforts of some parents to deemphasize gender roles in their children's upbringing may help to reduce the magnitude of gender differences in areas such as verbal and quantitative skills. However, some observers believe that other gender differences—such as males' greater ability to visualize the rotation of objects in space and females' greater ability to read facial expressions—are unlikely to change much. In particular, those who adopt the evolutionary approach see these differences as deeply rooted in the distant past, when males' major activity was hunting and females' was child rearing (Buss, 1999). Other psychologists have suggested that prenatal exposure to male or female hormones influences the organization of male and female brains in ways that make boys more receptive to spatial activities and motion and girls more susceptible to social exchanges (Halpern, 1997). Still others see such differences as reflecting social inequality, not just biological destiny (Wood & Eagly, 2002).

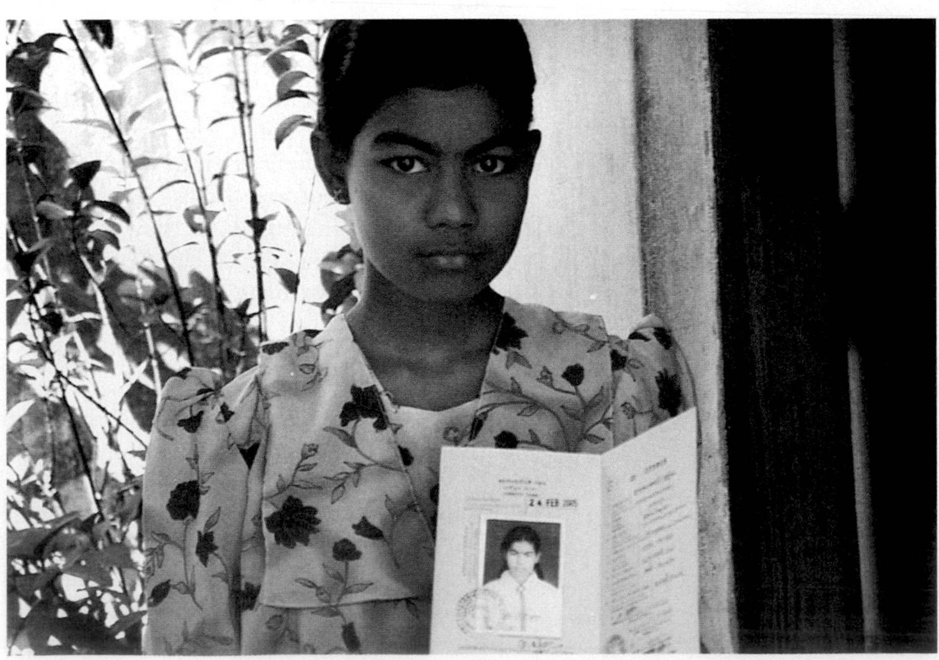

Beating the Odds Some children are able to overcome the difficulties and risks associated with poverty, war, family violence, homelessness, and other circumstances to make a success of their lives. These children are said to be *resilient*. This 15-year-old girl grew up in a war zone but retains her dream of becoming a doctor.

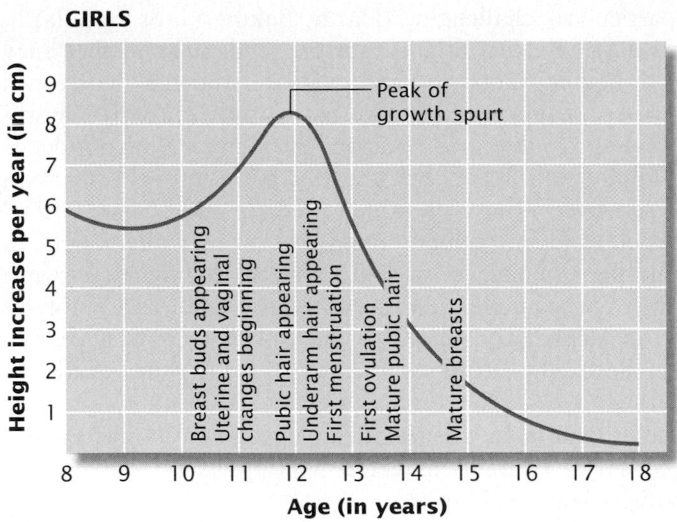

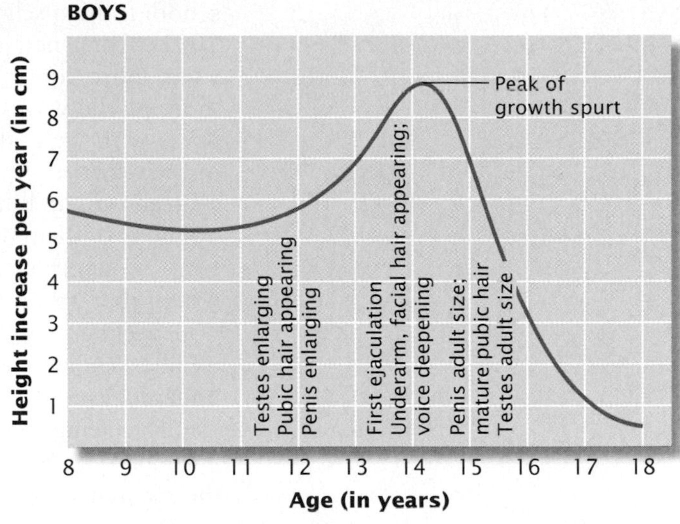

figure 12.4

Physical Changes in Adolescence

At about ten and a half years of age, girls begin their growth spurt, and by age twelve, they are taller than their male peers. Boys begin their growth spurt at about twelve and a half years of age and usually grow faster and for a longer period of time than girls. Adolescents may grow as much as 12.7 centimetres a year. The development of sexual characteristics accompanies these changes in height. The ages at which these changes occur vary considerably across individuals, but their sequence is the same.

Adolescence

A sudden spurt in physical growth is the most visible sign that adolescence has begun. This growth spurt peaks at about age 12 for girls and age 14 for boys (Tanner, 1978; see Figure 12.4). Suddenly, adolescents find themselves in new bodies. At the end of the growth spurt, females begin to menstruate, and males produce live sperm. This state of being able for the first time to reproduce is called **puberty.**

puberty The condition of being able, for the first time, to reproduce.

The Challenges of Change

In Western cultures, *early adolescence,* the period from ages 11 to 14 or so, is filled with challenges. Sexual interest stirs, and there are opportunities to smoke, drink alcohol, and take other drugs (Patton et al., 2004). All of this can be disorienting. Adolescents—especially early maturing girls—may experience bouts of depression and other psychological problems (Ge, Conger, & Elder, 2001; Ohring, Graber, & Brooks-Gunn, 2002). This is also the time when eating disorders are likely to first appear (Wilson et al., 1996) and when the incidence of attempted and completed suicides rises (Centers for Disease Control and Prevention, 1999a). For some, early adolescence marks the beginning of a downward spiral that ends up in academic failure, delinquency, and substance abuse. According to Canadian statistics, just under 10 percent of adolescents drop out of school (Statistics Canada, 2005a), with approximately the same number coming in contact with the law for violations of the *Criminal Code* each year (Public Health Agency of Canada, 2005). About 20 percent of 15- to 19-year-olds smoke (Heart and Stroke Foundation of Canada, 2002), and roughly the same number describe themselves as frequent drinkers (Health Canada, 1995). Approximately 35 percent report using marijuana or hashish (Statistics Canada, 2004).

Many of the problems of adolescence are associated with challenges to young people's *self-esteem,* their sense of being worthy, capable, and deserving of respect (Harter, 1998). Adolescents are especially vulnerable if many stressors occur at the same time (DuBois et al., 1992; Kling et al., 1999). According to Cindy Hardy and her colleagues at Concordia University in Montreal, the switch from elementary school to high school is particularly challenging (Hardy, Bukowski, & Sippola, L, 2002). Their new teachers may have less time to nurture students, and they may exert more control, impose higher standards, and evaluate students' work in a more public way. Under these circumstances, grades may drop, especially for students who were already having trouble in school or who don't have confidence in their own abilities (Rudolph et al., 2001). But grades don't affect self-esteem in all teens. Some base their self-esteem more on athletic success and on their peers' opinions of them than on their academic achievement (Crocker & Wolfe, 2001). In fact, adolescents' academic performance is strongly affected by the peers with whom they spend their time. For example, adolescents whose grades and motivation decline from the end of elementary school to the end of their first year in middle school tend to be those who affiliated themselves with other academic underachievers (Ryan, 2001).

The changes and pressures of adolescence are often played out at home, as adolescents try to have a greater say in a parent-child relationship once ruled mainly by their parents. Serious conflicts may lead to serious problems, including running away, pregnancy, stealing, drug taking, or even suicide—especially among teens who do not feel close to their parents (Blum, Beuhring, & Rinehart, 2000). Fortunately, although the bond with parents deteriorates during the transition from early to mid-adolescence, most adolescents and young adults maintain a reasonably good relationship with their parents (van Wel, ter Bogt, & Raaijmakers, 2002).

Sexual Activity among Adolescents Research suggests that the percentage of Canadian adolescents who report experience with sexual intercourse is declining. For example, between 1998 and 2002, the percentage of sexually active grade nine males declined from 31 percent to 23 percent. During the same time period, the percentage of sexually active females in the same grade declined from 21 percent to 19 percent. The percentage of sexually active males in grade 11 declined from 49 percent to 40 percent between 1998 and 2002, whereas the percentage for female grade 11 students remained stable at 46 percent (Boyce, Doherty, Fortin, & Mackinnon, 2003). Teenagers have higher rates of gonorrhea, chlamydia, pelvic inflammatory disease, and other sexually transmitted diseases than any other age group (Health Canada, 2004). Just under 2 percent of Canadian teenage girls gave birth in 2000, and just over 2 percent had an abortion that year (Statistics Canada, 2003).

A teenage pregnancy can create problems for the mother, the baby, and others in the family. For one thing, babies of teenage mothers are less likely than babies of older mothers to survive their first year (Phipps, Blume, & DeMonner, 2002). Teenage parents tend to be less positive and stimulating with their children, and more likely to abuse them, than older parents (Brooks-Gunn & Chase-Lansdale, 2002). The children of teenage parents, in turn, are more likely to develop behaviour problems and to do poorly in school than those whose parents are older (Furstenberg, Brooks-Gunn, & Chase-Lansdale, 1989; Moffitt, 2002). They do better if they have strong attachments to their fathers and if their mothers are prepared for maternal responsibilities and know about children and parenting even before the baby is born (Miller et al., 1996; Whitman et al., 2001). The younger sisters of teenage mothers are also affected by the birth. Often, they must take time away from schoolwork to help care for the child, and they are at increased risk for drug and alcohol use and for becoming pregnant themselves (East & Jacobson, 2001).

Violent Adolescents As described at the beginning of this chapter, some youngsters respond to the challenges of adolescence with violence. And as in the case of early and risky sexual behaviour, the roots of teenage violence can be found in childhood. Among the childhood factors that increase the risk of violent behaviour in adolescence are fearlessness, low intelligence, lack of empathy, lack of emotional self-regulation, and aggressiveness (Eisenberg et al., 2004; Hay et al., 2003; Rutter, 2003). In one study, for example, one-third of children who were described

table 12.3

Kohlberg's stages of moral reasoning describe differences in how people think about moral issues. Here are some examples of answers that people at different stages of development might give to the "Heinz dilemma" described in the text. This dilemma is more realistic than you might think. In 1994, a man was arrested for robbing a bank after being turned down for a loan to pay for his wife's cancer treatments; a similar case occurred in 2004.

Kohlberg's Stages of Moral Development

Stage	What Is Right?	Should Heinz Steal the Drug?
Preconventional		
1	Obeying, and avoiding punishment from a superior authority	Heinz should not steal the drug because he will be jailed.
2	Making a fair exchange, a good deal	Heinz should steal the drug because his wife will repay him later.
Conventional		
3	Pleasing others and getting their approval	Heinz should steal the drug because he loves his wife and because she and the rest of the family will approve.
4	Doing your duty, following rules and social order	Heinz should steal the drug for his wife because he has a duty to care for her, or he should not steal the drug because stealing is illegal.
Postconventional		
5	Respecting rules and laws, but recognizing that they may have limits	Heinz should steal the drug because life is more important than property.
6	Following universal ethical principles, such as justice, reciprocity, equality, and respect for human life and rights	Heinz should steal the drug because of the principle of preserving and respecting life.

to think logically and reason about abstract concepts. Adolescents are also capable of applying their advanced cognitive skills to questions of morality. According to Lawrence Walker and colleagues at the University of British Columbia, moral reasoning is an important aspect of development that changes with both age and experience (Walker, Gustafson, & Hennig, 2001).

Kohlberg's Stages of Moral Reasoning To examine how people think about morality, psychologists have asked them how they would resolve various moral dilemmas. Perhaps the most famous of these is the "Heinz dilemma." It requires people to decide whether a man named Heinz should steal a rare and unaffordable drug in order to save his wife from cancer. Using moral dilemmas such as this one, Lawrence Kohlberg found that the reasons people give for their moral choices change systematically and consistently with age (Kohlberg & Gilligan, 1971). Kohlberg proposed that moral reasoning develops in six stages, summarized in Table 12.3. These stages, he said, are not tightly linked to a person's age. There is a range of ages for reaching each stage, and not everyone reaches the highest level.

Stage 1 and Stage 2 moral judgments, which are most typical of children under the age of nine, tend to be selfish. Kohlberg called this level **preconventional moral reasoning** because reasoning at this level is not yet based on the conventions or rules that guide social interactions in society. People at this level of moral development are concerned with avoiding punishment or following rules when it is to their own advantage. At the **conventional moral reasoning** level, Stages 3 and 4, people are

preconventional moral reasoning Reasoning that is not yet based on the conventions or rules that guide social interactions in society.

concerned about other people; they believe that morality consists of following rules and conventions such as duty to the family, to marriage vows, and to the country. A conventional thinker would never think it was proper to burn the flag in protest, for example. The moral reasoning of children and adolescents from ages nine to nineteen is most often at this level. Stages 5 and 6 represent the highest level of moral reasoning, which Kohlberg called **postconventional moral reasoning** because it occurs after conventional reasoning. Moral judgments at this level are based on personal standards or universal principles of justice, equality, and respect for human life rather than on the demands of authority figures or society. People who have reached this level view rules and laws as arbitrary but respect them because they protect human welfare. They believe that individual rights can sometimes justify violating these laws if the laws become destructive. People do not usually reach this level until sometime in young adulthood—if at all. Stage 6 is seen only rarely in extraordinary individuals. Studies of Kohlberg's stages generally support the sequence he proposed (Colby et al., 1983; Walker, 1989).

Limitations of Kohlberg's Stages Kohlberg's first four stages appear to be universal. Evidence of them has been found in 27 cultures from Alaska to Zambia. Stages 5 and 6, however, do not always appear (Snarey, 1987). Further, moral judgments made in some cultures do not always fit neatly into Kohlberg's stages. Some people in collectivist cultures—Papua New Guinea, Taiwan, and Israeli kibbutzim, for example—explained their answers to moral dilemmas by pointing to the importance of the community rather than to personal standards. People in India included in their moral reasoning the importance of acting in accordance with one's gender and caste and with maintaining personal purity (Shweder et al., 1994). As in other areas of cognitive development, culture plays a significant role in shaping moral judgments.

Gender may also play a role. Carol Gilligan (1982, 1993) has suggested that for females, the moral ideal is not the abstract, impersonal concept of justice that Kohlberg found in males but, rather, the need to protect enduring relationships and fulfill human needs. Gilligan questioned Kohlberg's assumption that the highest level of morality is based on justice. When she asked her research participants about moral conflicts, the majority of men focused on justice, but only half of the women did. The other half focused on caring. Although this difference between men and women has not been found in many studies (Jaffe & Hyde, 2000), there does seem to be an overall tendency for females to focus on caring more than males do and for males to focus on justice more than females do when they are resolving hypothetical moral dilemmas (Turiel, 1998). When resolving real-life moral issues, both men and women focus more on caring than on justice (Walker, 1995).

Taken together, the results of research in many countries and with both genders suggest that moral ideals are not absolute and universal. Moral development is apparently an adaptation to the moral world in which one lives, a world that differs from place to place (Bersoff, 1999). Formal operational reasoning may be necessary for people to reach the highest level of moral reasoning, but formal operational reasoning alone is not sufficient. To some extent, at the highest levels, moral reasoning is a product of culture and history.

Moral Reasoning and Moral Action There is some evidence that moral reasoning is related to moral behaviour. In one study, adolescents who committed crimes ranging from burglary to murder tended to see obedience to laws mainly as a way of avoiding jail—a Stage 1 belief. Their nondelinquent peers, who showed Stage 4 reasoning, believed that one should obey laws because they prevent chaos in society (Gregg, Gibbs, & Basinger, 1994). But having high moral reasoning ability is no guarantee that a person will always act morally; other factors, such as the likelihood of being caught, also affect behaviour (Krebs, 1967).

conventional moral reasoning Reasoning that reflects the belief that morality consists of following rules and conventions.

postconventional moral reasoning Reasoning that reflects moral judgments based on personal standards or universal principles of justice, equality, and respect for human life.

Children and adolescents can be encouraged to move to higher levels of moral reasoning through exposure to arguments at a higher stage, perhaps as they argue about issues with one another. Hearing about moral reasoning that is one stage higher than their own or encountering a situation that requires more advanced reasoning seems to push people into moral reasoning at a higher level (Enright, Lapsley, & Levy, 1983). The development of moral behaviour takes more than abstract knowledge, however. Consider a study of inner-city adolescents who were required to take a high school class that involved community service—working at a soup kitchen for the needy (Youniss & Yates, 1997). As part of the course they also had to write essays on their experience. Over time, the students' essays became more sophisticated, going beyond discussion of, say, homelessness to observations about the distribution of wealth in society and other ideological matters. By the end of the course, the behaviour of the students had also changed; they were going to the soup kitchen more often than the course required.

For children and adolescents, learning to behave in moral ways requires (1) consistent modelling of moral reasoning and behaviour by parents and peers, (2) parents and teachers who promote moral behaviour, (3) real-life experience with moral issues, and (4) situational factors that support moral actions. Moral reasoning and moral behaviour both tend to be lower when situational factors—such as excessive use of alcohol—do not support them (Denton & Krebs, 1990). Not only do we sometimes fail to act at the highest level of which we are capable, but we also sometimes fail even to reason at this level (Batson & Thompson, 2001).

Adulthood

Development does not end with adolescence. Adults, too, go through transitions and experience physical, cognitive, and social changes. It has been suggested that adulthood emerges as early as age 18 (Arnett, 2000), but for our purposes, adulthood can be divided into three periods: early adulthood (ages 20 to 39), middle adulthood (ages 40 to 65), and late adulthood (older than age 65).

Physical Changes

In *early adulthood,* physical growth continues. Shoulder width, height, and chest size increase. People continue to develop their athletic abilities. For most people, the years of early adulthood are the prime of life.

In *middle adulthood,* one of the most common physical changes is the loss of sensory sharpness (Fozard et al., 1977). By this time, nearly everyone shows some hearing impairment. People in their early 40s become less sensitive to light, and their vision deteriorates somewhat. Increased farsightedness is an inevitable change that usually results in a need for reading glasses. Inside the body, bone mass is dwindling, the risk of heart disease is increasing, and fertility declines. In their late 40s or early 50s, women generally experience the shutdown of reproductive capability, a process known as **menopause.** Estrogen and progesterone levels drop, and the menstrual cycle eventually ceases.

In *late adulthood,* men shrink about an inch, and women about two inches, as their posture changes and cartilage disks between the spinal vertebrae become thinner. Hardening of the arteries and a buildup of fat deposits on the artery walls may lead to heart disease. The digestive system slows down and becomes less efficient. In addition, the brain shrinks and the flow of blood to the brain slows. The few reflexes that remained after infancy (such as the knee-jerk reflex) weaken or disappear. Bedtime comes earlier, and naps are more frequent (Park et al., 2002). But as in earlier years, declines in physical functioning can be delayed or diminished by a healthy diet and exercise (Brach et al., 2003; Seeman, & Chen, 2002).

menopause The process whereby a woman's reproductive capacity ceases.

Cognitive Changes

Adulthood is marked by increases, as well as decreases, in cognitive abilities. Abilities that involve intensive information processing begin to decline in early adulthood, but those that depend on accumulated knowledge and experience increase until beginning to tail off in old age, if at all. In fact, older adults can function as well as, or better than, younger adults in situations that tap their long-term memories and well-learned skills. The experienced teacher may deal with an unruly child more skillfully than the novice, and the senior lawyer may understand the implications of a new law more quickly than the recent graduate. Their years of accumulating and organizing information can make older adults practised, skillful, and wise.

Early and Middle Adulthood In early and middle adulthood, until age 60 at least, important cognitive abilities improve. During this period, adults do better on tests of vocabulary, comprehension, and general knowledge, especially if they use these abilities in their daily lives (Eichorn et al., 1981; Park, 2001). Young and middle-aged adults learn new information and new skills; they remember old information and hone old skills. It is in their 40s through their early 60s that people tend to put in the best performance of their lives on complex mental tasks such as reasoning, verbal memory, and vocabulary (Willis & Schaie, 1999).

The nature of thought may also change during adulthood. Adult thought is often more complex and adaptive than adolescent thought (Labouvie-Vief, 1992). Adults can understand, as adolescents cannot, the contradictions inherent in thinking. They see both the possibilities and the problems in every course of action (Riegel, 1975)—in deciding whether to start a new business or to move to a new house, for example. Middle-aged adults are more adept than adolescents or young adults at making rational decisions and at relating logic and abstractions to actions, emotions, social issues, and personal relationships (Tversky & Kahneman, 1981). As they appreciate these relationships, their thought becomes more global, more concerned with broad moral and practical concerns (Labouvie-Vief, 1982). It has been suggested that the achievement of these new kinds of thinking reflects a stage of cognitive development that goes beyond Piaget's formal operational period (Lutz & Sternberg, 1999). In this stage, people's thinking becomes *dialectical,* which means they understand that knowledge is relative, not absolute—such that what is seen as wise today may have been thought foolish in times past. They see life's contradictions as an inevitable part of reality, and they tend to weigh various solutions to problems rather than just accepting the first one that springs to mind.

Late Adulthood It is not until late adulthood—after 65 or so—that intellectual abilities decline noticeably. Generally, the abilities most severely affected are those that require rapid and flexible manipulation of ideas and symbols, active thinking and reasoning, and sheer mental effort (Baltes, 1993, 1994; Finkel et al., 2003; see Figure 12.5). Older adults do just as well as younger ones at tasks they know well, like naming familiar objects (Radvansky, 1999). It is when they are asked to perform an unfamiliar task or to solve a complex problem they have not seen before that older adults are generally slower and less effective than younger ones (Craik & Rabinowitz, 1984). When facing complex problems, older people apparently suffer from having too much information to sift through. They have trouble considering, choosing, and executing solutions (Arenberg, 1982). As people age, they grow less efficient at organizing the elements of a problem and at holding and manipulating more than one idea at a time. They have difficulty doing tasks that require them to divide their attention between two activities (Smith et al., 2001) and are slower at shifting their attention back and forth between two activities (Korteling, 1991). If older adults have enough time, though, and can separate the two activities, they can perform just as well as younger adults (Hawkins, Kramer, & Capaldi, 1993).

figure 12.5

Mental Abilities over the Life Span

Mental abilities collectively known as "fluid" intelligence—speed and accuracy of information processing, for example—begin to decline quite early in adult life. Changes in these biologically based aspects of thinking are usually not marked until late adulthood, however. "Crystallized" abilities learned over a lifetime—such as reading, writing, comprehension of language, and professional skills—decline, too, but later, and at a slower pace (Li et al., 2004).

Source: Adapted from Baltes (1994).

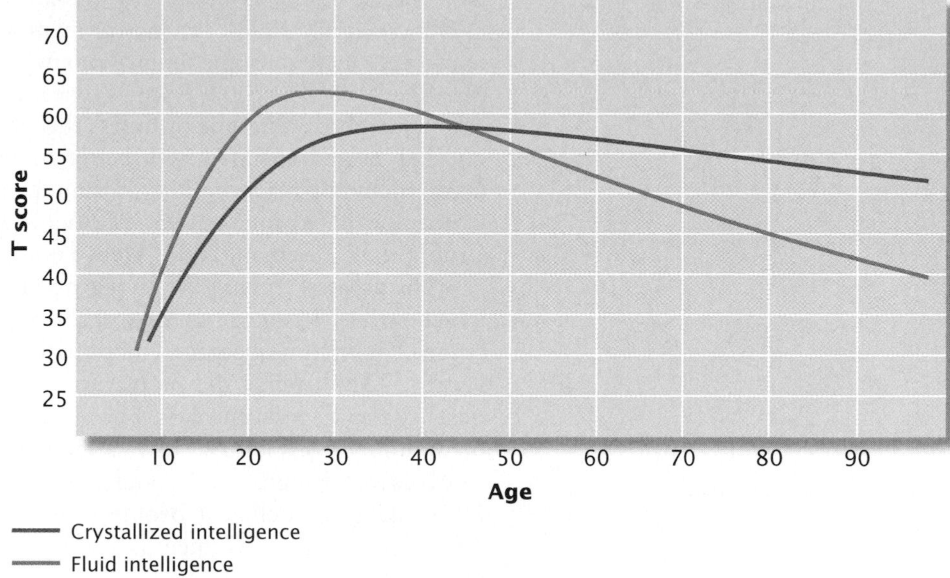

Older people also have the ability to think deeply and wisely about life. Psychologists define *wisdom* as expert knowledge in the fundamental, practical aspects of life, permitting exceptional insight and judgment involving complex and uncertain matters of the human condition (Smith & Baltes, 1990). Old age does not guarantee wisdom, but if it is combined with experiences conducive to the accumulation and refinement of wisdom-related knowledge, growing old can be associated with high levels of wisdom (Baltes et al., 1995). Researchers have found that one component of wisdom—the ability to infer what other people are thinking—remains intact and sometimes even improves over the later adult years. For example, when asked to explain why a burglary suspect in a story surrendered to the police, 70-year-olds gave better answers than younger adults. Their answers included inferences about the suspect's motives, such as "the burglar surrendered because he thought the policeman knew he had robbed the shop" (Happe, Winner, & Brownell, 1998).

Usually the loss of intellectual abilities in older adults is slow and need not cause major problems (Bashore & Ridderinkhoff, 2002). A study of Swedish adults (Nilsson, 1996) found that memory problems among older adults are largely confined to *episodic memory* (e.g., what they ate for lunch yesterday) rather than to *semantic memory* (general knowledge, such as the name of the capital of Spain). In short, everyday competencies that involve verbal processes are likely to remain intact into advanced old age (Freedman, Aykan, & Martin, 2001; Willis & Schaie, 1999). Unfortunately, however, there is one way in which older adults' declining memories can have negative effects: They may be more likely than younger adults to recall false information as being true (Park, 2001), making some of them especially prone to victimization by scam artists. For example, the more warnings they hear about a false medical claim—such as that shark cartilage supposedly cures arthritis—the more familiar it becomes, and the more likely they are to believe it. As described in the chapter on memory, younger people are also vulnerable to memory distortions, but they are more likely to remember that false information is false, even when it is familiar.

The risk of cognitive decline is much lower for people who are healthy and psychologically flexible; who have a high level of education, income, and occupation; and who live in an intellectually stimulating environment with mentally able spouses or companions (Albert et al., 1995; Shimamura et al., 1995). Continued mental exercise—such as doing puzzles, painting, and talking to intelligent friends—can help older adults continue to think and remember effectively and creatively (Verghese et al., 2003). Practice at memory and other information-processing tasks may even lead to some improvement in skills impaired by old age and disuse (Kramer & Willis, 2002; Rapp, Brenes, & Marsh, 2002). Continued physical exercise helps, too. A lifetime of fitness through dancing or other forms of aerobic exercise has been associated with better maintenance of skills on a variety of mental tasks, including reaction time, reasoning, and divided attention (Abbott et al., 2004; Colcombe & Kramer, 2003; McAuley, Kramer, & Colcombe, 2004; Tabbarah, Crimmins, & Seeman, 2002; Weuve et al, 2004).

The greatest threat to cognitive abilities in late adulthood is *Alzheimer's disease,* which strikes 3 percent of the world's population by age 75. As the disease runs its course, its victims become emotionally flat, then disoriented, and then mentally vacant. They usually die prematurely. The average duration of the disease, from onset to death, is seven years. But the age of onset and rate of deterioration depends on a number of factors, such as intelligence (Rentz et al., 2004), gender (Molsa, Marttila, & Rinne, 1995), and education (Mortimer, Snowdon, & Markesbery, 2003). Highly intelligent people show clinical signs of Alzheimer's later than the general population. Women and well-educated people of either gender deteriorate more slowly.

One ongoing study of the risk factors for Alzheimer's disease is focused on a group of nuns from the School Sisters of Notre Dame. When they took their vows, at ages ranging from 18 to 32, they had written autobiographies. Years later, when the women were 75 to 95 years old, they were given cognitive tests, and they gave permission for their brains to be examined after death.

The Nun Study has found that the women whose autobiographies indicated more limited language abilities did less well on the cognitive tests, were more likely to develop Alzheimer's, and died at younger ages than those with richer linguistic abilities (Kemper et al., 2001). Similar findings appeared in a Scottish study of childhood mental ability and dementia in late adulthood (Whalley et al., 2000). These results suggest that the seeds of Alzheimer's disease may be planted early in life, even though it may not appear for many decades.

Staying Alert, Staying Active, Staying Alive Sisters Alcantara, 91, Claverine, 87, and Nicolette, 94, of the School Sisters of Notre Dame convent, stay alert by reading, solving puzzles, playing cards, and participating in vocabulary quizzes. Along with the other nuns at this convent, these women are participating in a study of aging and the brain.

Social Changes

In adulthood, people develop new relationships, assume new positions, and take on new roles. These changes do not come in neat, predictable stages but instead follow various paths, depending on each individual's experiences (Lieberman, 1996). Transitions—such as filing for divorce, getting fired from a job, going back to school, remarrying, losing a spouse to death, being hospitalized, getting arrested, or retiring—are turning points that can redirect a person's life path and lead to changes in personality (Caspi, 1998; Roberts, Helson, & Klohnen, 2002). Sometimes these events create radical turnarounds. More often, they involve gradual and incremental change.

Early Adulthood Men and women in industrialized cultures typically enter the adult world in their 20s. The process may begin with an "emerging adulthood" period during which they explore life's possibilities through education, dating, and travel before they settle into stable adult roles and responsibilities (Arnett, 2000; Roisman et al., 2004). Gradually, they become more conscientious, organized, disciplined, and able to plan, as they decide on an occupation, or at least take a job, and become preoccupied with their careers (Srivastava et al., 2003). They also become more controlled and confident and less angry and alienated (Roberts et al., 2001). Nevertheless, by age 25 about 20 percent of young adults are still living with their parents, and just under half are still financially dependent (Cohen et al., 2003).

In their 20s, young adults also become more concerned with matters of romantic love (Whitbourne et al., 1992). Having reached the sixth of Erikson's stages of psychosocial development noted in Table 12.2 (intimacy versus isolation), they begin to focus on forming mature, committed relationships based on sexual intimacy, friendship, or mutual intellectual stimulation. The nature of these relationships is predictable in part from the nature of the person's earlier relations with parents, including the attachment pattern that developed in infancy (Horowitz, Rosenberg, & Bartholomew, 1993; Scharf, Mayseless, & Kivenson-Baron, 2004; Treboux, Crowell, & Waters, 2004). Young adults whose view of relationships reflects a secure attachment tend to feel valued and worthy of support and affection. They develop closeness easily and have relationships characterized by joy, trust, and commitment. If their view reflects an insecure attachment, however, they tend to be preoccupied with relationships and may feel misunderstood, underappreciated, and worried about being abandoned. Their relationships are often negative, obsessive, and promiscuous. Overall, young adults whose parents have been accepting and supportive tend to develop warm and supportive romantic relationships (Conger et al., 2000; Dresner & Grolnick, 1996). Age also can help people develop loving relationships: Most individuals become more agreeable during their 30s—warm, generous, and helpful (Srivastava et al., 2003).

For many young adults, the experience of becoming parents represents entry into a major new developmental phase that is accompanied by personal, social, and occupational changes (Palkovitz, Copes, & Woolfolk, 2001).This milestone is usually reached earlier for young adults from lower income backgrounds, who are more likely to be in full-time employment and less likely to be living at home (Cohen et al., 2003). Often, satisfaction with the marriage or partnership declines once a baby is born (Belsky & Kelly, 1994). Young mothers may experience particular dissatisfaction, especially if they resent the constraints infants bring, if they see their careers as important, if the infants are temperamentally difficult, if the partnerships are not strong, and if the partners are not supportive (Shapiro, Gottman, & Carrere, 2000). Researchers have found that when the father does not do his share of child care, both mothers and fathers are dissatisfied (Levy-Shiff, 1994). The ability of young parents to provide adequate care for their babies is related to their own attachment histories. New mothers whose attachments to their own mothers were secure tend to be more responsive to their infants, and the infants, in turn, are more likely to develop secure attachments to them (Adam, Gunnar, & Tanaka, 2004; van IJzendoorn, 1995).

The challenges of young adulthood are complicated by the nature of family life in the twenty-first century. Forty years ago, about half of North American households consisted of married couples in their 20s and 30s—a breadwinner husband and a homemaker wife— raising at least two children together. This picture now describes only about 10 percent of households (Demo, Allen, & Fine, 2000; Hernandez, 1997). Today, parents are older because young adults are delaying marriage longer and waiting longer to have children. And many are having children without marrying (Weinraub, Horuath, & Gringlas, 2002). Most of these women become pregnant the "old-fashioned" way, but some are taking advantage of technological advances that allow them to conceive through *in vitro fertilization* (Hahn & DiPietro, 2001). Many gay men and lesbians are becoming parents, too. Statistics Canada reported that in the 2001 census, 34 200 couples identified themselves as same-sex common-law couples. Approximately 15 percent of the female couples had at least one child living with them, whereas only 3 percent of the male couples were living with a child (Statistics Canada, 2002). Young adult homosexuals face special challenges in making the transition to parenthood. They often confront prejudice in health care organizations and employer policies that do not recognize their parental role. They may also experience pervasive hostility, even from members of their own extended families.

Whether they are homosexual or heterosexual, mothers who hold full-time jobs outside the home often find that the demands of children and career pull them in opposite directions. Devotion to their jobs leaves many of these mothers feeling guilty about spending too little time with their children (Booth et al., 2002), but placing too much emphasis on home life may reduce their productivity at work and threaten their advancement. This stressful balancing act can lead to anxiety, frustration, and conflicts at home and on the job. It affects fathers, too. The husbands of employed women are more involved in child care (Booth et al., 2002), and their contributions to housework have doubled since 1970 (Coltrane, 2001). They can be effective caregivers (Parke, 2002), but mothers still do most of the child care and housework (Bureau of Labor Statistics, 2004). Research indicates that gay and lesbian parents share duties more equally—and are more satisfied with the division of labour—than is typically the case in heterosexual families (Patterson, 2002).

Nearly 40 percent of all marriages in Canada end in divorce (Statistics Canada, 2004), creating yet another set of challenges for adults (Clarke-Stewart & Brentano, 2005). Although it frees people from bad relationships, divorce can leave them feeling anxious, guilty, incompetent, depressed, and lonely. Divorce is also correlated with health problems and, ultimately, with earlier mortality. Often, divorce creates new stressors, including money problems, changes in living circumstances and working hours, and, for custodial parents, a dramatic increase in housework and childcare tasks. One study found that two years after divorcing, most women were happier than they were during the final year of their marriage but more distressed than were mothers in two-parent families (Hetherington & Stanley-Hagan, 2002). How effectively divorced people deal with these stressors depends on many factors, such as social support, their general psychological stability and coping skills, their ability to form new relationships, and whether or not they continue to have conflicts with their ex-spouses.

In short, the changes seen in families and family life over the past several decades have made it more challenging than ever to successfully navigate the years of early adulthood.

midlife transition A point at around age 40 when adults take stock of their lives.

Middle Adulthood At around age 40, people go through a **midlife transition,** during which they may reappraise and modify their lives and relationships.

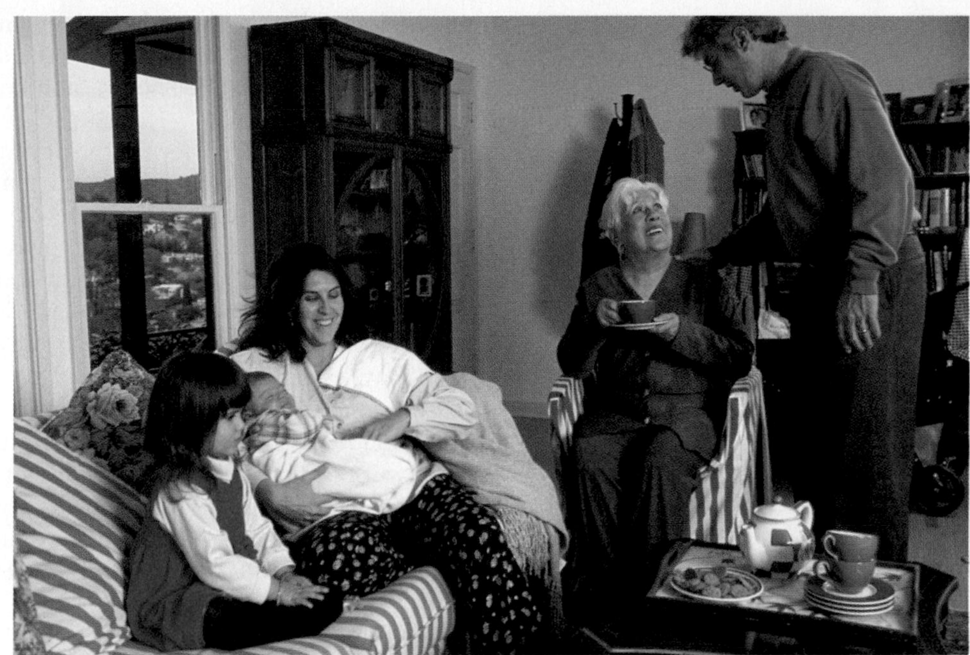

The "Sandwich" Generation During their midlife transition, many people feel "sandwiched" between generations—pressured by the social, emotional, and financial needs of their children on one side and of their aging parents on the other.

Many feel invigorated and liberated; some may feel upset and have a "midlife crisis" (Beck, 1992; Levinson et al., 1978). The contrast between youth and middle age may be especially upsetting for men who matured early in adolescence and were sociable and athletic rather than intellectual (Block, 1971). Women who chose a career over a family now hear the biological clock ticking out their last childbearing years. Women who have had children, however, become more independent and confident and more oriented toward achievement and events outside the family (Helson & Moane, 1987). For both men and women, the emerging sexuality of their teenage children, the emptiness of the nest as children leave home, or the declining health of a parent can precipitate a crisis. Results from a study of more than 7000 adults suggest that the degree of happiness and healthiness people experience during middle adulthood depends on how much control they feel they have over their work, finances, marriage, children, and sex life, as well as how many years of education they completed and what kind of job they have (Azar, 1996).

Following the midlife transition, the middle years of adulthood are often a time of satisfaction and happiness (MacArthur Foundation, 1999). Many people become concerned with producing something that will outlast them—usually through parenthood or job achievements. Erikson called this concern the crisis of **generativity,** because people begin to focus on producing or generating something. If they do not resolve this crisis, he suggested, people stagnate. Research shows that after the age of 40 people are indeed more likely than before to strive for generativity goals (Sheldon & Kasser, 2001; Zucker, Ostrove, & Stewart, 2002). These might include writing a book, helping those in need, developing closer relationships with children and being a good role model for them, and trying to make a lasting contribution to society.

In their 50s, many people become grandparents (Smith & Drew, 2002).This new status often amazes them. One study of professionals in their 50s found that they could not quite believe they were no longer young (Karp, 1991). Most described themselves as healthy but acknowledged that their bodies were slowing down. At this age, spending time caring for young grandchildren can be stressful. One recent study found that grandmothers who spent more time providing care for their grandchildren were at increased risk of coronary heart disease (Lee et al., 2003). Caring for grown children can be stressful, too. Most people in their 60s

generativity Adult concerns about producing or generating something.

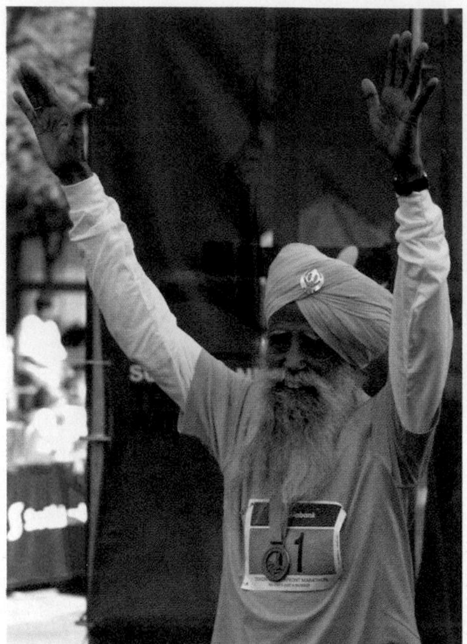

Still on a Roll At the age of 93, Fauja Singh made history at the Toronto Waterfront Marathon on September 26, 2004, when he crossed the finish line after running the half marathon in 5 hours and 40 minutes, breaking his own world record for people over 90.

want their children to be independent and perhaps even ready to support their parents, if necessary. They may have mixed feelings toward adult children who still need financial support (Pillemer & Suitor, 2002).

Late Adulthood Even when they are 65 to 75, most people think of themselves as middle-aged, not old (Neugarten, 1977). They are active and influential politically and socially; they often are physically vigorous. Ratings of life satisfaction, well-being, and self-esteem are, on average, as high in old age as during any other period of adulthood (Ben-Zur, 2002; Hamarat et al., 2002; Sheldon & Kasser, 2001; Volz, 2000). Those who experienced abundant parental support during childhood are particularly likely to have good physical and mental health in late adulthood (Shaw et al., 2004).

This is the time when men and women usually retire from their jobs, but research shows that many people underestimate older people's ability and willingness to work (Clay, 1996). This misperception was once codified in laws that forced workers to retire at 65 regardless of their abilities. Thanks to changes in those laws in several provinces, many Canadians can now continue working as long as they wish (CBC News, 2005). Being forced to retire can result in psychological and physical problems. In one study of cardiovascular disease, men who retired involuntarily were found to be more depressed, less healthy, and less well-adjusted than those who retired voluntarily (Swan, 1996). Such problems may also occur when husbands retire before their wives do (Rubin, 1998). Men tend to view retirement as a time to wind down, whereas women see it as a time to try new things, to reinvent themselves (Helgesen, 1998). In one study that followed people from childhood through adulthood, researchers found that when previously employed women reached their 70s, they were more active and more concerned about maintaining their independence and continuing their achievements than women who had been homemakers. They were also happier, as well as less depressed and anxious (Holahan, 1994). In general, it seems, retirees are more likely to be satisfied with their lives than people who continue to work through their 60s and 70s (Moen et al., 2000).

More people than ever are reaching old age. Today, 170 000 people in Canada are more than 90 years old (Statistics Canada, 2005b). Old age is not necessarily a time of loneliness and desolation, but it is a time when people generally become more inward looking, cautious, and conforming (Reedy, 1983). It is a time when people develop coping strategies that increasingly take into account the limits of their control—accepting chronic health problems and other things they cannot change (Brandtstadter & Renner, 1990). One such coping strategy is to direct attention to positive thoughts, activities, and memories (Mather et al., 2004; Charles, Mather, & Carstensen, 2003).

In old age, people interact with others less frequently, but they enjoy their interactions more (Carstensen, 1997). They find relationships more satisfying, supportive, and fulfilling than they did earlier in life. As they sense that time is running out, they value positive interactions and become selective about their social partners. During the last 20 years of their lives, people gradually restrict their social network to loved ones. As long as there are at least three close friends or relatives in their network, they tend to be content.

Death and Dying

With the onset of old age, people become aware that death is approaching. They watch as their friends disappear. They feel their health deteriorating, their strength waning, and their intellectual capabilities declining. A few years or a few months before death, people may experience a sharp decline in mental functioning known as **terminal drop** (Small & Bäckman, 1999).

terminal drop A sharp decline in mental functioning that tends to occur in late adulthood, a few years or months before death.

The awareness of impending death brings about the last psychological crisis, according to Erikson's theory, in which people evaluate their lives and accomplishments and affirm them as meaningful (leading to a feeling of integrity) or meaningless (leading to a feeling of despair). People at this stage tend to become more philosophical and reflective. They attempt to put their lives into perspective. They reminisce, resolve past conflicts, and integrate past events. They may also become more interested in the religious and spiritual side of life. This "life review" can trigger anxiety, regret, guilt, and despair, or allow people to face their own deaths and the deaths of friends and relatives with a feeling of peace and acceptance (Lieberman & Tobin, 1983).

Even the actual confrontation with death does not have to bring despair and depression. People generally want to be told if they are dying (Hinton, 1967). When death finally is imminent, old people strive for a death with dignity, love, affection, physical contact, and no pain (Schulz, 1978). As they think about death, they are comforted by their religious faith, their achievements, and the love of their friends and family (Kastenbaum, Kastenbaum, & Morris, 1989).

Developmental Trajectories

The life-span development we have described is a bit like the flight of an airplane, beginning with a takeoff, cruising along for a while, and eventually entering its final descent. And like aircraft bound for differing destinations, the flight path, or trajectory, of our lives can be long or short, reach high or low altitudes, and be bumpy or smooth. There may be mid-course corrections during flight, of course, but researchers who have tracked developmental trajectories find a remarkable degree of stability from childhood through adulthood on many dimensions. For example, people who are intelligent and have good memories, who are good with numbers or poor at languages, tend to retain these advantages or disadvantages throughout their lifetimes (e.g., Anstey, Hofer, & Luszcz, 2003; Chodosh et al., 2002).

There are also consistencies in personality and social development (Roberts et al., 2001; Roberts et al., 2002; Shiner, Masten, & Roberts, 2003). Children who are creative, persistent, enthusiastic about their activities, and motivated to achieve are likely to become adults who take pleasure in their pursuits, enjoy challenges, work hard to succeed, and become effective leaders who handle stress well. Children who take their schoolwork seriously and finish their homework promptly are likely to become adults who are traditional in their views, who plan well, and who are not apt to take risks. Children who exhibit early social competence tend to have good romantic relationships and strong friendships as adults (Shiner et al., 2003). Those who are better able to empathize tend to become more prosocial (Eisenberg et al., 2002). Children who view social relationships as secure and trusting continue to do so in adulthood (Carlson et al., 2004). Boys who are aggressive in childhood tend to be antisocial in adulthood (Schaeffer et al., 2003). Adolescents who do well in school and have friends and social skills are more successful in work and romance in adulthood (Roisman et al., 2004). In other words, people tend to stay on relatively consistent developmental paths throughout their lives.

Longevity

The length of life's trajectory depends on a number of factors. Researchers have discovered, for example, that longevity is greater in women and in people without histories of heavy drinking or heart problems. Longevity is also related to personality characteristics such as conscientiousness as a child (Friedman et al., 1995a) and curiosity as an adult (Swan & Carmelli, 1996). In addition, adults who had more positive self-perceptions when they were in their 50s and 60s lived seven and one-half years longer than those with less positive self-perceptions. This cognitive factor was more predictive of longevity than health problems such as high blood pressure, high cholesterol, smoking, lack of exercise, or being overweight (Levy et al., 2002). However, the secret of extreme longevity—100 years or more—may lie in a group of genes on chromosome 4 that appears to somehow slow the aging process (Puca et al., 2001).

Older adults can be helped to feel better physically and psychologically if they continue to be socially active and useful. For example, old people who are given parties, plants, or pets are happier and more alert than those who receive less attention, and they do not die as soon (Clark et al., 2001). People who restrict their caloric intake, engage in regular physical and mental exercise, and have a sense of control over important aspects of their lives are also likely to live longer (Krause & Shaw, 2000; Yaffe et al., 2001). So eat your veggies, stay physically fit, and continue to think actively—not just to live longer later, but to live better now.

LINKAGES

As noted in the chapter on introducing psychology, all of psychology's many subfields are related to one another. Our discussion of child development illustrates just one way in which the topic of this chapter, human development, is linked to the subfield of intelligence (which is the focus of the cognitive abilities chapter). The Linkages diagram shows ties to two other subfields as well, and there are many more ties throughout the book. Looking for linkages among subfields will help you see how they all fit together and help you better appreciate the big picture that is psychology.

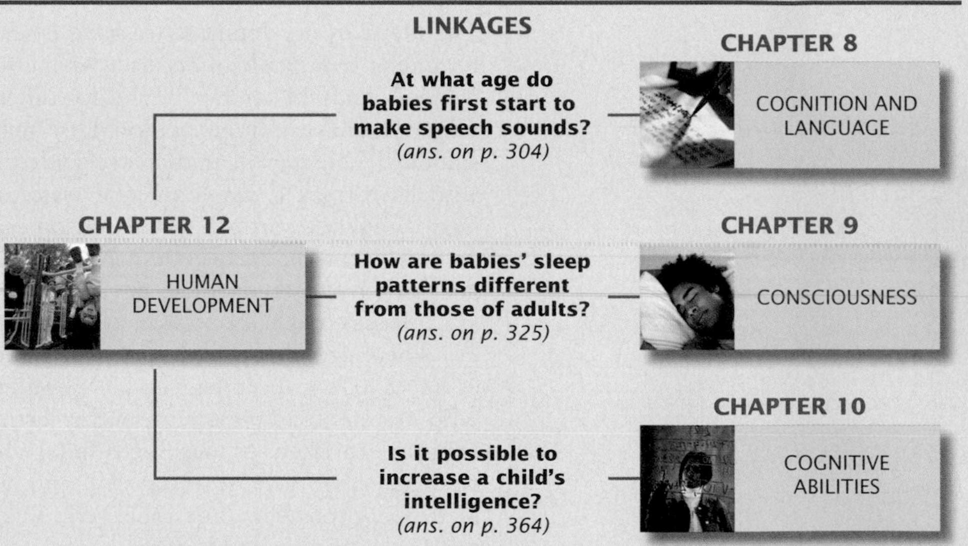
LINKAGES
CHAPTER 12
HUMAN DEVELOPMENT
At what age do babies first start to make speech sounds?
(ans. on p. 304)
CHAPTER 8
COGNITION AND LANGUAGE
How are babies' sleep patterns different from those of adults?
(ans. on p. 325)
CHAPTER 9
CONSCIOUSNESS
Is it possible to increase a child's intelligence?
(ans. on p. 364)
CHAPTER 10
COGNITIVE ABILITIES

SUMMARY

Developmental psychology is the study of the course and causes of age-related changes in mental abilities, social relationships, emotions, and moral understanding over the life span.

Exploring Human Development

A central question in developmental psychology concerns the relative influences of nature and nurture, a theme that has its origins in the philosophies of John Locke and Jean-Jacques Rousseau. In the twentieth century, Arnold Gesell stressed nature in his theory of development, proposing that development is *maturation*—the natural unfolding of abilities with age. John B. Watson took the opposite view, claiming that development is learning—shaped by the external environment. In his theory of cognitive development, Jean Piaget described how nature and nurture work together. Today we accept the notion that both nature and nurture affect development and ask how and to what extent each contributes.

Beginnings

Prenatal Development

Development begins with the union of an ovum and a sperm to form a *zygote,* which becomes an *embryo.* The embryonic stage is a *critical period* for development, a time when certain organs must develop properly or they never will. Development of organs at this stage is permanently affected by harmful *teratogens,* such as drugs and alcohol. After the embryo develops into a *fetus,* adverse conditions during the fetal stage may harm the infant's size, behaviour, intelligence, or health. Babies born to women who drink heavily have a strong chance of suffering from *fetal alcohol syndrome.*

The Newborn

Newborns have limited but effective senses of vision, hearing, taste, and smell. They exhibit many reflexes, or swift, automatic responses to external stimuli. Motor development proceeds as the nervous system matures, muscles grow, and the infant experiments with and selects the most efficient movement patterns.

Infancy and Childhood: Cognitive Development

Cognitive development includes the development of thinking, knowing, and remembering.

Changes in the Brain

The development of increasingly complex and efficient neural networks in various regions of the brain provides the "hardware" for the increasingly complex cognitive abilities that arise during infancy and childhood.

The Development of Knowledge: Piaget's Theory

According to Piaget, cognitive development occurs in a fixed sequence of stages, as *schemas* are modified through the complementary processes of *assimilation* (fitting new objects or events into existing schemas) and *accommodation* (changing schemas when new objects will not fit existing ones). During the *sensorimotor period,* infants progress from using only simple senses and reflexes to forming mental representations of objects and actions. Thus the child becomes capable of thinking about objects that are not present. The ability to recognize that objects continue to exist even when they are hidden from view is what Piaget called *object permanence.* During the *preoperational period,* children can use symbols, but they do not have the ability to think logically and rationally. Their understanding of the world is intuitive and egocentric. They do not understand the logical operations of reversibility or complementarity. When children develop the ability to think logically about concrete objects, they enter the period of *concrete operations.* At this time they can solve simple problems. They also have an understanding of *conservation,* recognizing that, for example, the amount of a substance is not altered even when its shape changes. The *formal operational period* begins in adolescence and allows thinking and logical reasoning about abstract ideas.

Modifying Piaget's Theory

Recent research reveals that Piaget underestimated infants' mental abilities. Developmental psychologists now also believe that new levels of cognition are reached not in sharply marked stages of global understanding but more gradually, and in specific areas. Children's reasoning is affected by factors such as task difficulty and degree of familiarity with the objects and language involved.

Information Processing During Childhood

Psychologists who explain cognitive development in terms of information processing have documented age-related improvements in children's attention, their abilities to explore and focus on features of the environment, and their memories.

Culture and Cognitive Development

The specific content of cognitive development, including the development of scripts, depends on the cultural context in which children live.

Variations in Cognitive Development

How fast children develop cognitive abilities depends to a certain extent on how stimulating and supportive their environments are. Children growing up in poverty are likely to have delayed or impaired cognitive abilities.

Infancy and Childhood: Social and Emotional Development

Infants and their caregivers, from the early months, respond to each other's emotional expressions. When an infant's behaviour in an ambiguous situation is affected by the caregiver's emotional expression, social referencing is said to have occurred.

Individual Temperament

Most infants can be classified as having easy, difficult, or slow-to-warm-up *temperaments.* Whether they retain these temperamental styles depends to some extent on their parents' expectations and demands.

The Infant Grows Attached

Over the first year of life, infants form a deep and abiding emotional *attachment* to their mothers or other primary caregivers. This attachment may be secure or insecure.

Relationships with Parents and Peers

Parents teach their children the skills and rules needed in their culture using various parenting styles. They can be described as *authoritarian, permissive,* or *authoritative parents.* In general, parents with an authoritative style tend to have more competent and cooperative children. Parenting styles depend upon the culture and conditions in which parents find themselves. Over the childhood years, interactions with peers evolve into cooperative and competitive encounters, and friendships become more important.

Social Skills

Children become increasingly able to interpret and understand social situations and emotional signals. They begin to express empathy and to engage in the *self-regulation* of their emotions and behaviours. They also learn social rules and roles.

Gender Roles

Children develop *gender roles* that are based both on biological differences between the sexes and on implicit and explicit socialization by parents, teachers, and peers. Children are also influenced by *gender schemas,* which affect their choices of activities and toys.

Adolescence

Adolescents undergo significant changes not only in size, shape, and physical capacity but also, typically, in their social lives, reasoning abilities, and views of themselves.

The Challenges of Change

Puberty brings about physical changes that lead to psychological changes. Early adolescence is a period of shaky self-esteem. It is also a time when conflict with parents, as well as closeness with and conformity to friends, is likely to rise. A particularly difficult challenge for adolescents is the transition from elementary school to high school. Older adolescents making the transition from high school to post-secondary education also face challenges in adjusting to new expectations and new responsibilities. According to Michael Pratt and colleagues at Wilfred Laurier University in Waterloo, Ontario, a supportive group of friends and involvement in organized student activities can be particularly helpful in making a smooth transition to this new stage of life (Pratt et al., 2000).

Identity and Development of the Self

Late adolescence focuses on finding an answer to the question, Who am I? Events such as graduating from high school and going to university challenge the adolescent's self-concept, precipitating an *identity crisis*. To resolve this crisis the adolescent must develop an integrated self-image as a unique person, an image that often includes *ethnic identity.*

Moral Reasoning

Principled moral judgment—shaped by gender and culture—becomes possible for the first time in adolescence. The development of moral reasoning may progress through *preconventional, conventional,* and *postconventional moral reasoning* stages. A person's moral reasoning may be reflected in moral action.

Adulthood

Physical, cognitive, and social changes occur throughout adulthood.

Physical Changes

Middle adulthood sees changes that include decreased acuity of the senses, increased risk of heart disease, and the end of fertility (*menopause*). Nevertheless, major health problems may not appear until late adulthood.

Cognitive Changes

The cognitive changes that occur in early and middle adulthood are generally positive, including improvements in reasoning and problem-solving ability. In late adulthood, some intellectual abilities decline—especially those involved in tasks that are unfamiliar, complex, or difficult. Other abilities, such as recalling facts or making wise decisions, tend not to decline. Individuals with Alzheimer's disease become disoriented and mentally vacant, and they die prematurely.

Social Changes

In their 20s, young adults begin to make occupational choices and form intimate commitments. In middle adulthood they become concerned with *generativity*—with producing something that will outlast them. Sometime around age 40, adults experience a *midlife transition,* which may or may not be a crisis. The 40s and 50s are often a time of satisfaction. In their 60s, people contend with retirement. They generally become more inward looking, cautious, and conforming. Adults' progress through these ages is influenced by the unique personal events that befall them.

Death and Dying

In their 70s and 80s, people confront their own mortality. They may become more philosophical and reflective as they review their lives. A few years or months before death, individuals may experience a sharp decline in mental functioning known as *terminal drop*. They strive for a death with dignity, love, and no pain.

Developmental Trajectories

Researchers who have tracked developmental trajectories have found stability from childhood through adulthood in terms of cognitive abilities, personality characteristics, and social skills.

Longevity

Death is inevitable, but certain factors—including healthy diets, exercise, personality qualities such as conscientiousness and curiosity, a sense of control over one's life, and genetics—are associated with living longer and happier lives. Older adults feel better and live longer if they receive attention from other people, maintain an open attitude toward new experiences, and keep their minds active.

Health, Stress, and Coping

How long will you live? To some extent, the answer lies in your genes, but it is also affected by how you behave, how you think, and what stressors you face. In this chapter, you will learn about several kinds of stressors, how people respond to them, and the relationship between stress reactions and illness. You'll also discover what you can do to protect your own health. We've organized the material as follows:

Twenty-five years ago, acquired immune deficiency syndrome (AIDS) was a rare and puzzling medical condition. Today, it threatens everyone and is one of the major causes of death in the world. In some African countries, the infection rate among adults from the human immunodeficiency virus (HIV), which causes AIDS, is as high as 20 percent (World Health Organization, 2003). As medical researchers race against time to find a cure for AIDS and a vaccine against HIV, others work to find ways to prolong the lives of people infected with HIV or suffering with AIDS.

One important factor that may affect how long AIDS patients live is their expectations about survival. Geoffrey Reed and his associates asked 74 male AIDS patients about the extent to which they had accepted their situation and prepared themselves for the worst (Reed et al., 1994). Acknowledging the reality of a terminal illness has been considered by some to be a psychologically healthy adaptation (e.g., Kübler-Ross, 1975). However, Reed and his associates found that the men who had accepted their situation and prepared themselves for death died an average of nine months earlier than those who had neither accepted nor resigned themselves to their situation. This statistically significant difference is all the more impressive because it cannot be accounted for by differences in the patients' general health status, immune system functioning, psychological distress, or other factors that might have affected the time of death. Here is evidence that, compared with those who are "fighters," terminally ill patients who resign themselves to decline and death might actually hasten both.

Research such as this has made psychologists and the medical community more aware than ever of psychological factors that can affect health and illness (Ray, 2004). It also reflects the growth of **health psychology,** "a field within psychology devoted to understanding psychological influences on how people stay healthy, why they become ill, and how they respond when they do get ill" (Taylor, 1999, p. 4). Health psychologists use knowledge from many subfields of psychology to enhance understanding of the psychological and behavioural processes associated with health and illness (Smith & Suls, 2004). Their work is part of the broader field of *behavioural medicine,* in which psychologists pursue their health-related goals in cooperation with physicians, nurses, public health workers, and other biomedical specialists. In this chapter we describe some of what has been discovered so far about psychological, social, and behavioural influences on health and how research in health psychology and behavioural medicine is being applied to prevent illness and promote better health. We begin by examining the nature of stressors and people's physical, psychological, and behavioural responses to stress. Then we consider factors that might alter the impact of stressful life events on a person. Next, we consider the psychological factors responsible for specific physical disorders and some behaviours that endanger people's health. We conclude by discussing health psychologists' recommendations for coping with stress and promoting health and some of their programs for doing so.

Health Psychology

Although the field of health psychology is relatively new, its underlying themes are ancient. For thousands of years, in many cultures around the world, people have believed that their mental state, their behaviour, and their health are linked. Today, there is scientific evidence to support this belief (Taylor, 2002). We know, for example, that through their impact on psychological and physical processes, the stresses of life can influence physical health. Researchers have also associated anger, hostility, pessimism, depression, and hopelessness with the appearance of physical illnesses and traits such as optimism with good health. Similarly, poor health has

health psychology A field in which psychologists conduct and apply research aimed at promoting human health and preventing illness.

table 13.1

This table shows seven of the leading causes of death in Canada today, along with behavioural factors that contribute to their development.

Lifestyle Behaviours That Affect the Leading Causes of Death in Canada

Cause of Death (Number of Deaths in 1997 %; total)	Contributing Behavioural Factor				
	Alcohol	**Smoking**	**Diet**	**Exercise**	**Stress**
Cancer (58 703; 27.2%)	x	X	x		?
Heart Disease (57 417; 26.6%)	x	X	x	X	X
Stroke (16 051; 7.4%)	x	X	x	?	?
Lung disease (9618; 4.5%)		X			
Accidents and injury (8626; 4.0%)	x	X		x	
Pneumonia & Influenza (8032; 3.7%)		X			x
Diabetes (5699; 2.6%)			X	x	x

Source: Statistics Canada, 2006.

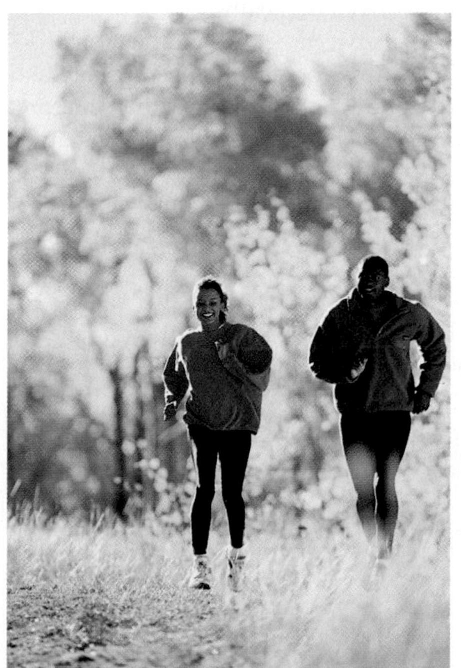

Running for Your Life Health psychologists have developed programs to help people increase exercise, stop smoking, eat healthier diets, and make other lifestyle changes that lower their risk of illness and death. They have even helped to ensure community blood supplies by finding ways to make blood donation less stressful (Bonk, France, & Taylor, 2001).

been linked to lack of exercise, inadequate diet, smoking, alcohol and drug abuse, and other behavioural factors. Good health has been associated with behaviours such as physical activity and following medical advice.

Health psychology has become increasingly prominent in North America, in part because of changing patterns of illness. Until the middle of the twentieth century, the major causes of illness and death in the United States and Canada were acute infectious diseases, such as influenza, tuberculosis, and pneumonia. With these afflictions now less threatening, chronic illnesses—such as coronary heart disease, cancer, and diabetes—have joined accidents and injuries as the leading causes of disability and death (Guyer et al., 2000). Further, psychological, lifestyle, and environmental factors play substantial roles in determining whether a person will fall victim to these modern-day killers (Taylor, 2002). For example, lifestyle choices, such as whether a person smokes, affect the risk of the five leading causes of death for men and women in Canada (Stats Canada, 2006; D'Agostino et al., 2001; see Table 13.1). The psychological and behavioural factors that contribute to these illnesses can be changed by intervention programs such as those that promote exercise, healthy eating, and not smoking (e.g., Bazzano et al., 2003; Kraus et al., 2002).

Health psychologists have been active in helping people understand the role they can play in controlling their own health and life expectancy (Nash et al., 2003; Nicassio, Meyerowitz, & Kerns, 2004). For example, they have promoted early detection of disease by educating people about the warning signs of cancer, heart disease, and other serious illnesses and encouraging them to seek medical attention while lifesaving treatment is still possible. Health psychologists also study, and help people to understand, the role played by stress in physical health and illness.

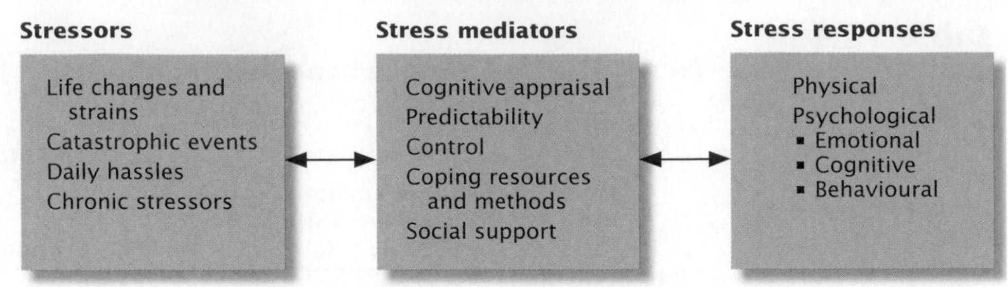

figure 13.1

The Process of Stress

Stressful events, stress reactions, and stress mediators are all important components of stress. Notice the two-way relationships in the stress process. For example, if a person has effective coping skills, stress responses will be less severe. Having milder stress responses can act as a "reward" that strengthens those skills. Further, as coping skills (such as refusing unreasonable demands) improve, certain stressors (such as a boss's unreasonable demands) may become less frequent.

Stress and Stressors

You have probably heard that death and taxes are the only two things you can be sure of in life. If there is a third, it must surely be stress. Stress is basic to life—no matter how wealthy, powerful, attractive, or happy you might be. It comes in many forms—a difficult exam, an automobile accident, waiting in a long line, a day on which everything goes wrong. Mild stress can be stimulating, motivating, and sometimes desirable. But as it becomes more severe, stress can bring on physical, psychological, and behavioural problems (Downing & Miyan, 2000).

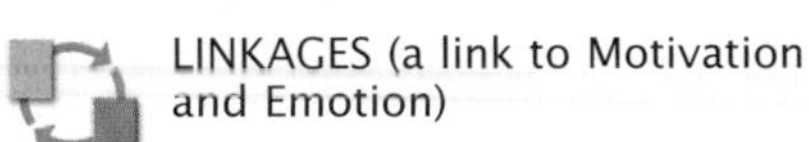

Stress is the negative emotional and physiological process that occurs as individuals try to adjust to or deal with **stressors**, which are environmental circumstances that disrupt, or threaten to disrupt, individuals' daily functioning and cause people to make adjustments (Taylor, 2002). In other words, stress involves a *transaction* between people and their environment. Figure 13.1 lists the main types of stressors and illustrates that when confronted by stressors, people respond physically (e.g., with nervousness, nausea, and fatigue), as well as psychologically.

As also shown in Figure 13.1, the transactions between people and their environments can be influenced by *stress mediators*. These mediators include such variables as the extent to which people can predict and control their stressors, how they interpret the threat involved, the amount of social support they perceive as available from family and friends, and their stress-coping skills. (We discuss these mediators in greater detail later.) Mediating factors can either dampen or magnify a stressor's impact. In other words, stress is not a specific event but a process in which the nature and intensity of stress responses depend to a large degree on factors such as the way people think about stressors and the skills and resources they have available to cope with them.

For humans, most stressors have both physical and psychological components. Students, for example, are challenged by psychological demands to do well in their courses, as well as by the physical fatigue that can result from a heavy load of classes, combined perhaps with a job and family responsibilities. Similarly, for victims of arthritis, AIDS, and other chronic illnesses, physical pain is accompanied by worry and other forms of psychological distress. Here, we focus on psychological stressors that can stimulate some of the same physiological responses as physical stressors (Cacioppo et al., 1995).

Psychological Stressors

Any event that forces people to accommodate or change can be a psychological stressor. Accordingly, even pleasant events can be stressful. For example, the increased salary and status associated with a promotion may be desirable, but the upgrade usually brings new pressures as well (Schaubroeck, Jones, & Xie, 2001). Similarly, vacations are supposed to be relaxing, but people often feel exhausted after returning home. Still, it is typically negative events that have the most adverse psychological and physical effects (Kessler, 1997). These circumstances include

stress The process of adjusting to circumstances that disrupt, or threaten to disrupt, a person's equilibrium.

stressors Events or situations to which people must adjust.

Coping with Catastrophe Catastrophic events such as explosions, hurricanes, plane crashes, school shootings, and other traumas are stressors that can be psychologically devastating for victims, their families, and rescue workers. Health psychologists and other professionals provide on-the-spot counselling and follow-up sessions to help people deal with the consequences of trauma.

A Daily Hassle Relatively minor daily hassles can combine to create significant physical and psychological stress responses. The frustrations of daily commuting in heavy traffic, for example, can become so intense for some drivers that they may display a pattern of anger and aggression called "road rage."

catastrophic events, life changes and strains, chronic stressors, and daily hassles (Baum, Gatchel, & Krantz, 1997).

Catastrophic events are sudden, unexpected, potentially life-threatening experiences or traumas, such as physical or sexual assault, military combat, natural disasters, terrorist attacks, and accidents. *Life changes* and *strains* include divorce, illness in the family, difficulties at work, moving to a new place, and other circumstances that create demands to which people must adjust (see Table 13.2). *Chronic stressors*—those that continue over a long period of time—include circumstances such as living near a noisy airport or in a high-crime neighbourhood, having a serious illness, being unable to earn a decent living, being the victim of discrimination, and even enduring years of academic pressure. *Daily hassles* include irritations, pressures, and annoyances that might not be significant stressors by themselves but whose cumulative effects can be significant. Although not the only

table 13.2

Here are some items from the Undergraduate Stress Questionnaire, which asks students to indicate whether various stressors have occurred during the previous week (Crandall, Preisler, & Aussprung, 1992).

The Undergraduate Stress Questionnaire

Has this stressful event happened to you at any time during the last week? If it has, please check the space next to it. If it has not, please leave it blank.

____ 1. Assignments in all classes due the same day

____ 2. Having roommate conflicts

____ 3. Lack of money

____ 4. Trying to decide on a major

____ 5. Can't understand your professor

____ 6. Stayed up late writing a paper

____ 7. Sat through a boring class

____ 8. Went into a test unprepared

____ 9. Parents getting divorced

____ 10. Incompetence at the registrar's office

measure of its kind, Kathryn Lafrienere at Windsor and Paul Kohn at York University developed an instrument to assess the day to day hassles in Canadian university students. Along with Jennifer Macdonald, Kohn has linked scores on the hassles scale to feelings of anxiety and recent life experiences (Kohn & Macdonald, 1992a, 1992b).

Measuring Stressors

Which stressors are most harmful? To study stress more precisely, psychologists have tried to measure the impact of particular stressors. In 1967, Thomas Holmes and Richard Rahe (pronounced "ray") made a pioneering effort to find a standard way of measuring the stress in a person's life. Working on the assumption that all change, positive or negative, is stressful, they asked a large number of people to rate—in terms of *life-change units,* or *LCUs*—the amount of change and demand for adjustment associated with events such as divorcing, being fired, retiring, losing a loved one, or becoming pregnant. (Getting married, the event against which raters were told to compare all other stressors, came in as slightly more stressful than losing one's job.) On the basis of these ratings, Holmes and Rahe created the *Social Readjustment Rating Scale,* or *SRRS.* People taking the SRRS receive a stress score equal to the sum of the LCUs for the events they have recently experienced (Holmes & Rahe, 1967).

Numerous studies show that people scoring high on the SRRS and other life-change scales are more likely to suffer physical or mental disorders than those with lower scores (e.g., Monroe, Thase, & Simons, 1992). However, other researchers questioned whether life changes alone tell the whole story about the effects of stress. Accordingly, investigators developed scales such as the *Life Experiences Survey,* or *LES* (Sarason, Johnson, & Siegel, 1978), that go beyond the SRRS to measure not just what life events have occurred but also people's perceptions, or cognitive appraisal, of how positive or negative the events were, how controllable they were, and how well they were able to cope with the events. This information is particularly important for understanding the impact of life experiences that may have different meanings to different individuals. For example, a woman eager to have a child is likely to see pregnancy as a blessing, but for someone who doesn't want a baby, or can't afford the costs, a positive pregnancy test can be a disaster. Still other researchers have measured stressors and their impact in face-to-face interviews (e.g., Dohrenwend et al., 1993). Different measures yield somewhat differing results (McQuaid et al., 2000; Steffen et al., 2003), but as you might expect, they generally show that events appraised as negative have a stronger negative impact on health than do those appraised as positive (De Benedittis, Lornenzetti, & Pieri, 1990).

The LES also gives respondents the opportunity to write in and rate any stressors they have experienced that are not on the printed list. This personalized approach is particularly valuable for capturing the differing impact and meaning that experiences may have for men compared with women and for individuals from various cultural or subcultural groups. Divorce, for example, may have very different meanings to people of different religious or cultural backgrounds. Similarly, members of certain ethnic groups are likely to experience stressors—such as prejudice and discrimination—that are not felt by other groups (Contrada et al., 2000; Moradi & Hasan, 2004).

Canadian researchers like Gordon Flett and Paul Hewitt at York University have been involved in differentiating between daily hassles and major life events (Flett, Hewitt, Blankstein, & Mosher, 1995). In one study, over 300 undergraduates read a scenario in which either a male or female faces a major life event (e.g., divorce) or daily hassles (e.g., lost keys, having to do laundry). Those facing major life events were more likely to seek and receive the support of loved ones around them (Flett, Blankstein, Hicken, & Watson, 1995).

Stress Responses

Physical and psychological responses to stress often occur together, especially as stressors become more intense. Furthermore, one type of stress response can set off other types. For example, a physical stress response—such as mild chest pain—may lead to the psychological stress response of worrying about having a heart attack. Still, it is useful to analyze separately each category of stress responses.

Physical Responses

If you have ever experienced a near accident or some other sudden, frightening event, you know that the physical responses to stressors include rapid breathing, increased heartbeat, sweating, and, a little later, shakiness. These reactions are part of a general pattern known as the *fight-or-flight syndrome.* As described in the chapters on biological aspects of psychology and on motivation and emotion, this syndrome prepares the body to face or to flee an immediate threat. When the danger has passed, fight-or-flight responses subside. However, when stressors are long lasting, these responses are only the beginning of a sequence of reactions.

The General Adaptation Syndrome Careful observation of animals and humans led McGill researcher Hans Selye (pronounced "SELL-yay") to suggest that the sequence of physical responses to stress occurs in a consistent pattern and is triggered by the effort to adapt to any stressor. Selye called this sequence the **general adaptation syndrome,** or **GAS** (Selye, 1956, 1976). The GAS has three stages, shown in Figure 13.2.

The first stage is the *alarm reaction,* which involves some version of the fight-or-flight syndrome. In the face of a mild stressor such as an overheated room, the reaction may simply involve changes in heart rate, respiration, and perspiration that helps the body regulate its temperature. More severe stressors prompt more dramatic alarm reactions, rapidly mobilizing the body's adaptive energy, much as a burglar alarm alerts the police to take action (Kiecolt-Glaser et al., 1998).

Alarm reactions are controlled by the sympathetic branch of the autonomic nervous system (ANS) through organs and glands that make up the *sympathoadreno medullary (SAM)* system. As shown on the right side of Figure 13.3, environmental demands (stressors) trigger a process in the brain in which the hypothalamus activates the sympathetic branch of the ANS, which stimulates the medulla (inner part) of the adrenal gland. The adrenal gland, in turn, secretes *catecholamines* (pronounced "kat-uh-KOH-luhmeens")—especially adrenaline and noradrenaline—which circulate in the bloodstream, activating various organs, including the liver, kidneys, heart, and lungs. The results are increased blood pressure, enhanced muscle tension, increased blood sugar, and other physical changes

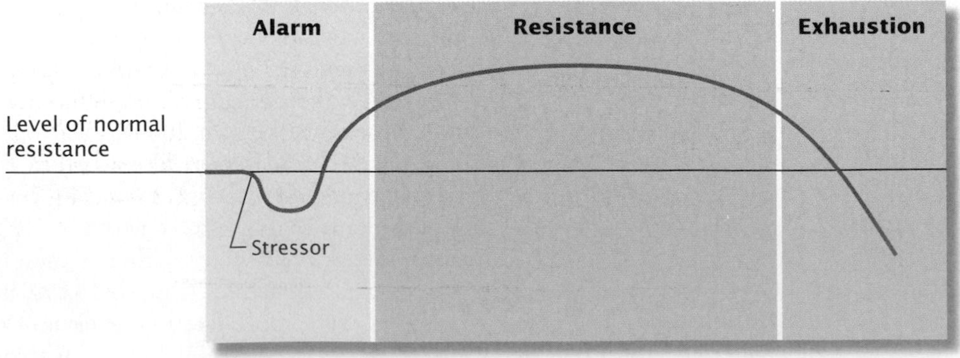

figure 13.2

The General Adaptation Syndrome

Hans Selye found that physical reactions to stressors include an initial alarm reaction, followed by resistance and then exhaustion. During the alarm reaction, the body's resistance to stress temporarily drops below normal as it absorbs a stressor's initial impact. Resistance increases and then levels off in the resistance stage, but it ultimately declines if the exhaustion stage is reached.

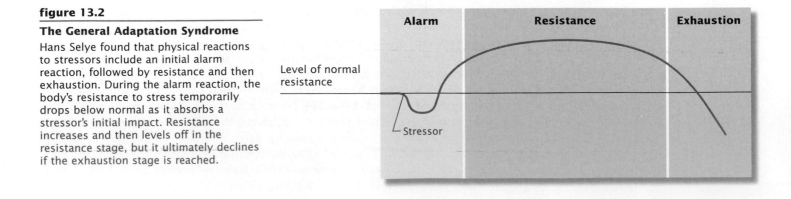

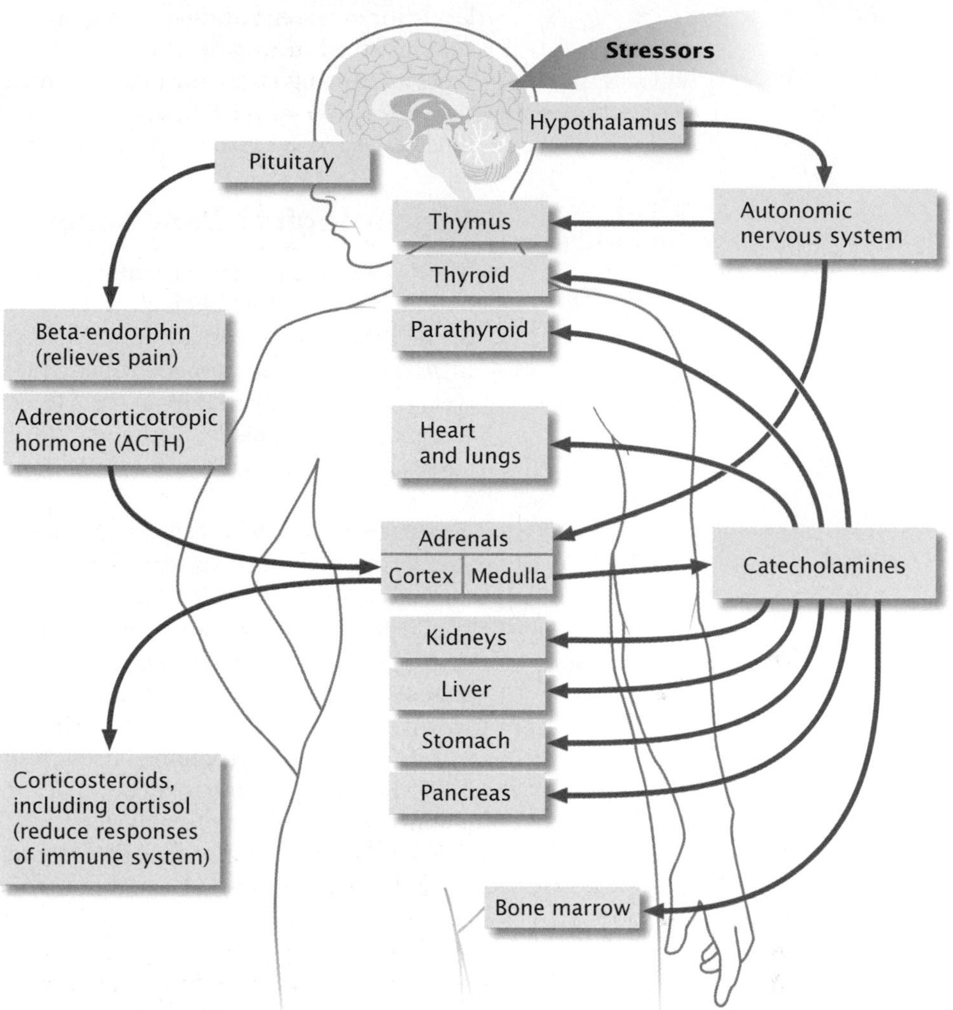

figure 13.3

Organ Systems Involved in the GAS

Stressors produce a variety of physiological responses that begin in the brain and spread to organs throughout the body. Through the hypothalamic-pituitaryadrenocortical system (HPA; purple arrows), for example, the hypothalamus causes the pituitary gland to trigger the release of endorphins, the body's natural painkillers. The HPA also stimulates the release of corticosteroids, which help resist stress but also tend to suppress the immune system. In the sympatho-adrenomedullary system (SAM; blue arrows) the hypothalamus stimulates the release of catecholamines, which mobilize the body for action. Some of these substances may interact with sex hormones to create different physical stress responses and coping methods in men and women (Taylor et al., 2000b).

needed to cope with stressors. Even brief exposure to a mild stressor can produce major changes in these coordinated physiological mechanisms (Cacioppo et al., 1995).

As shown on the left side of Figure 13.3, stressors also activate the *hypothalamic-pituitary-adrenocortical (HPA) system,* in which the hypothalamus stimulates the pituitary gland in the brain. The pituitary, in turn, secretes hormones such as adrenocorticotropic hormone (ACTH). Among other things, ACTH stimulates the cortex (outer surface) of the adrenal glands to secrete *corticosteroids;* these hormones release the body's energy supplies and fight inflammation. The pituitary gland also triggers the release of endorphins, the body's natural painkillers.

The overall effect of these stress systems is to generate emergency energy. The more stressors there are and the longer they last, the more resources the body must expend in response.

If stressors persist, the *resistance stage* of the GAS begins. Here, obvious signs of the initial alarm reaction fade as the body settles in to resist the stressor on a long-term basis. The drain on adaptive energy is slower during the resistance stage than it was during the alarm reaction, but the body is still working hard, physiologically, to cope.

This continued campaign of biochemical resistance is costly. It slowly but surely uses up the body's reserves of adaptive energy. The body then enters the third GAS stage, known as *exhaustion.* In extreme cases, such as prolonged exposure to freezing temperatures, the result is death. More commonly, the exhaustion stage brings signs of physical wear and tear, especially in organ systems that were weak in the first place or heavily involved in the resistance process. For example, if adrenaline and cortisol, which help fight stressors during the resistance stage, remain at high

diseases of adaptation Illnesses that are caused or worsened by stressors.

general adaptation syndrome (GAS) A three-stage pattern of responses triggered by the effort to adapt to any stressor.

levels for an extended time, they can damage the heart and blood vessels. They also suppress the functioning of the body's disease-fighting immune system and promote illnesses ranging from heart disease, high blood pressure, and arthritis to colds and flu (Carney et al., 1998; Light et al., 1999; McEwen, 1998). Selye referred to illnesses that are caused or worsened by stressors as **diseases of adaptation.**

Psychological Responses

Selye's model has been very influential, but it has also been criticized for underestimating the role of psychological factors in stress, such as a person's emotional state or the way a person thinks about stressors. These criticisms led to the development of *psychobiological models,* which emphasize the importance of psychological, as well as biological, variables in regulating and producing stress responses (Lazarus & Folkman, 1984; Suls & Rothman, 2004; Taylor, 2002). Psychological responses to stress can appear as changes in emotions, thoughts (cognitions), and behaviours.

Emotional Responses The physical stress responses we have described are usually accompanied by emotional stress responses. If someone pulls a gun and demands your money, you will no doubt experience the GAS alarm reaction, but you will also feel some strong emotion, probably fear and maybe anger. In fact, when people describe stress, they are more likely to say, "I was angry and frustrated!" than "My heart rate increased and my blood pressure went up." In other words, they are likely to mention changes in the emotions they are experiencing.

In most cases, emotional stress responses subside soon after the stressors are gone. However, if stressors continue for a long time or occur in a tight sequence, emotional stress reactions may persist. When people do not have a chance to recover their emotional equilibrium, they commonly report feeling tense, irritable, short-tempered, or anxious more and more of the time.

Cognitive Responses In 1995, in the busy, noisy intensive care unit of a hospital in London, England, a doctor misplaced a decimal point while calculating the amount of morphine a one-day-old premature baby should receive. The child

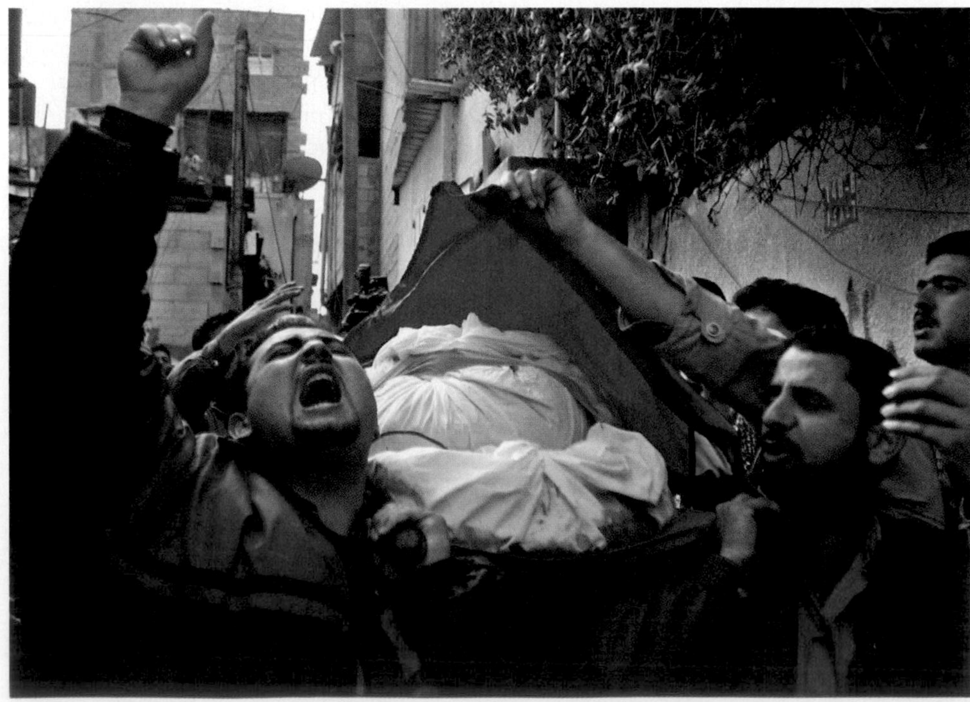

Another Funeral Even severe emotional stress responses usually ease eventually, but people plagued by numerous stressful events in quick succession—such as those living in strife-torn areas of the Middle East where violent death is all too frequent—may experience increasingly intense feelings of fear, sadness, and helplessness. These reactions can become severe enough to be diagnosed as generalized anxiety disorder, major depressive disorder, or other stress-related mental disorders described in the chapter on psychological disorders.

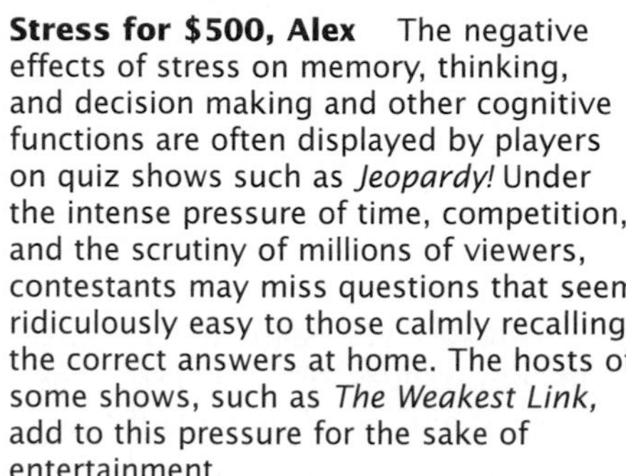
Stress for $500, Alex The negative effects of stress on memory, thinking, and decision making and other cognitive functions are often displayed by players on quiz shows such as *Jeopardy!* Under the intense pressure of time, competition, and the scrutiny of millions of viewers, contestants may miss questions that seem ridiculously easy to those calmly recalling the correct answers at home. The hosts of some shows, such as *The Weakest Link,* add to this pressure for the sake of entertainment.

died of a massive overdose (Davies, 1999). Reductions in the ability to concentrate, to think clearly, or to remember accurately are typical cognitive stress responses (Birnbaum et at., 2004; Hygge, Evans, & Bullinger, 2002). Sometimes, these problems appear because of *ruminative thinking,* the recurring intrusion of thoughts about stressful events (Lyubomirsky & Nolen-Hoeksema, 1995). Ruminative thoughts about problems in a romantic relationship, for example, can seriously interfere with studying for a test. A related phenomenon is *catastrophizing*, which means dwelling on and overemphasizing the potential consequences of negative events (Sarason et al., 1986). During examinations, test-anxious college students are likely to say to themselves, "I'm falling behind" or "Everyone else is doing better than I am." As catastrophizing or ruminative thinking impairs cognitive functioning, a person may experience anxiety and other emotional arousal that adds to the total stress response and further hampers performance (Dougall, Craig, & Baum, 1999).

Over-arousal created by stressors can also lead to a narrowing of attention, making it harder to scan the full range of possible solutions to complex problems (Craske, 1999; Keinan, Friedland, & Ben-Porath, 1987). In fact, stress-narrowed attention may increase the problem-solving errors described in the chapter on cognition and language. People under stress are more likely to cling to *mental sets,* which are well learned, but not always efficient, approaches to problems. Stress can also intensify *functional fixedness,* the tendency to use objects for only one purpose. Victims of hotel fires, for example, sometimes die trapped in their rooms because, in the stress of the moment, it did not occur to them to use the telephone or a piece of furniture to break a window.

Stressors may also impair decision making. People who normally consider all aspects of a situation before making a decision may, under stress, act impulsively and sometimes foolishly. High-pressure salespeople try to take advantage of this phenomenon by creating artificially time-limited offers or by telling customers that others are waiting to buy the item they are considering (Cialdini, 2001).

Behavioural Responses Clues about people's physical and emotional stress responses come from changes in how they look, act, or talk. Strained facial expressions, a shaky voice, tremors or spasms, and jumpiness are common behavioural stress responses. Posture can also convey information about stress, a fact well known to skilled interviewers.

Even more obvious behavioural stress responses appear as people attempt to escape or avoid stressors. Some quit their jobs, drop out of school, turn to alcohol, or even attempt suicide. Unfortunately, as discussed in the chapter on learning, escape and avoidance tactics deprive people of the opportunity to learn more adaptive ways of coping with stressful environments, including post-secondary education (Cooper et al., 1992). Aggression is another common behavioural response to stressors. All too often, this response is directed at members of one's own family (Polusny & Follette, 1995). For instance, in the wake of hurricanes and other natural disasters, it is not uncommon to see dramatic increases in the rate of domestic-violence reports in the devastated area (Curtis, Miller, & Berry, 2000; Rotton, 1990).

LINKAGES
Stress and Psychological Disorders

LINKAGES (a link to Psychological Disorders)

Physical, psychological, and behavioural stress responses sometimes appear together in patterns known as *burnout* and *post-traumatic stress disorder.* **Burnout** is an increasingly intense pattern of physical and psychological dysfunction in response to a continuous flow of stressors or to chronic stress (Maslach, 2003; Mas-lach & Goldberg, 1998). As burnout approaches, previously reliable workers or once-attentive spouses may become indifferent, disengaged, impulsive, or accident prone. They may miss work frequently; oversleep; perform their jobs poorly; abuse alcohol or other drugs; and become irritable, suspicious, withdrawn, depressed, and unwilling to talk about stress or anything else (Taylor, 2002). Burnout is particularly common among individuals who do "people work," such as teachers and nurses, and those who perceive themselves as being treated unjustly by employers (Elovainio, Kivimäki, & Vahtera, 2002; Schultz & Schultz, 1998). Each year, it accounts for a significant percentage of occupational disease claims by US workers (Schwartz, 2004).

Post-Traumatic Stress While a seasoned soldier and military professional, Romeo Dallaire suffered a breakdown after the enormous stresses of his experience of leading the UN peacekeeping mission in Rwanda.

burnout A gradually intensifying pattern of physical, psychological, and behavioural dysfunction in response to a continuous flow of stressors.

post-traumatic stress disorder (PTSD) A pattern of adverse and disruptive reactions following a traumatic event.

A different pattern of severe stress reactions is illustrated by the case of Romeo Dallaire. As Lieutenant General with UNAMIR, the United Nations peacekeeping force in Rwanda in 1993 and 1994, he witnessed a level of violence and aggression vastly beyond anything most of us could even imagine, much of which he later presented in his memoir, *Shake Hands with the Devil.* Included there are descriptions of machete-wielding warriors on a genocidal rampage, resulting in an estimated 800 000 deaths, some of which Dallaire witnessed first-hand. He also describes his feelings of powerlessess and responsibility as the military professional in charge of the peacekeeping forces.

On his return to Canada, Dallaire suffered from **post-traumatic stress disorder (PTSD),** a pattern of adverse reactions following a traumatic and threatening event. Among the characteristic reactions are anxiety, depression, irritability, jumpiness, inability to concentrate or work productively, and difficulty in getting along with others (e.g., Goenjian et al., 2001). People suffering from post-traumatic stress disorder may also experience sleep disturbances, intense startle responses to noise or other sudden stimuli, and long-term suppression of their immune systems (Goenjian et al., 2001; Johnson et al., 2002; Kawamura, Kim, & Asukai, 2001; Shalev et al., 2000). The most common feature of post-traumatic stress disorder is re-experiencing the trauma through nightmares or vivid memories. In rare cases, *flashbacks* occur in which the person behaves for minutes, hours, or days as if the trauma were occurring again. Post-traumatic stress disorder is most commonly associated with events such as war, terrorism, assault, or rape (Galea et al., 2002; Schnurr et al., 2000; Verger et al., 2004), but researchers now believe that some-PTSD symptoms can be triggered by any major stressor, from car accidents to being stalked (Ironson et al., 1997; Kamphuis & Emmelkamp, 2001). Heime Anisman and colleagues at Carleton University explain that the same physiological mechanisms at work in helping the individual cope with daily stresses and major life events are responsible for the prolonged response the body has to these crisis situations (Anisman, Griffiths, Matheson, Ravindran, & Merali, 2001; Anisman, Hayley, Turrin, & Merali, 2002; Hayley, Merali, & Anisman, 2003).

Post-traumatic stress disorder can appear immediately following a trauma, or it may not occur until weeks, months, or—rarely—even years later (Gilboa-Schechtman & Foa, 2001; Heim et al., 2000; Port, Engdahl, & Frazier, 2001). The majority of people affected require professional help, although some seem to recover without it. For most, improvement takes time; for nearly all, the support of family and friends is vital to recovery (Foa et al., 1999; Shalev, Bonne, & Eth, 1996).

Stress has also been implicated in the development of a number of other psychological disorders, including depression and schizophrenia (see the chapter on psychological disorders). The *diathesis-stress model* suggests that certain people are predisposed to these disorders but that whether or not individuals actually display them depends on the frequency, nature, and intensity of the stressors they encounter. If untreated, stress-related mental health problems can threaten physical health, too. For example, depression or anxiety may leave people unmotivated or forgetful when it comes to taking prescribed medication for high blood pressure or other medical conditions they may have. Similarly, some schizophrenia patients develop delusions that doctors, and the medicines they prescribe, will hurt them and thus begin to avoid both. As a result, all these people are likely to be at increased risk for worsening health.

Stress Mediators: Interactions Between People and Stressors

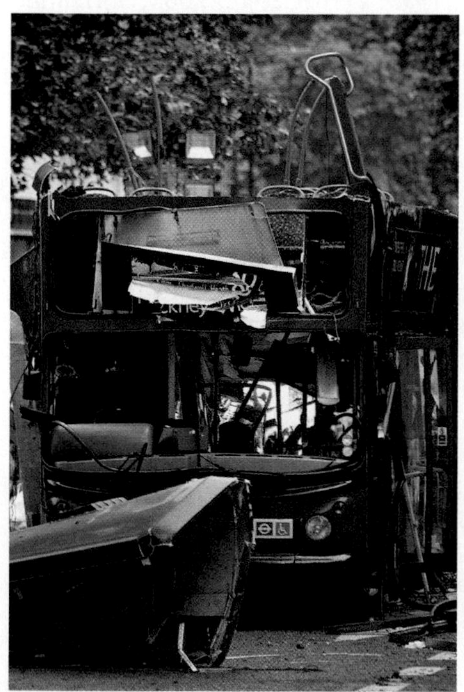

Life Hanging in the Balance
Symptoms of burnout and post-traumatic stress disorder often plague firefighters, police officers, emergency medical personnel, and others who are repeatedly exposed to time pressure, trauma, danger, and other stressors (Fullerton, Ursano, & Wang, 2004). Post-traumatic stress disorder can also occur following a single catastrophic event (DeLisi et al., 2003; Galea et al., 2002; Simeon et al., 2003).

Why does stress disrupt the performance of some people more than others? And why does one individual survive, and even thrive, under the same circumstances that lead another to break down, give up, and burn out? A number of the mediating factors listed in Figure 13.1 help determine how much impact a given stressor will have (Bonanno, 2004; Kemeny, 2003; McEwen & Seeman, 1999).

How Stressors Are Perceived

As discussed in the chapter on perception, our view of the world depends on which stimuli we attend to and how we interpret, or appraise, them. Any potential stressor, whether it is a crowded elevator or a deskful of work, usually has more negative impact on those who perceive it as a threat than on those who see it as a challenge (Goode et al., 1998; Lazarus, 1999; Maddi & Khoshaba, 2005).

Evidence for the effects of cognitive factors on stress responses comes from both laboratory experiments and surveys. Figure 13.4 shows the results of a classic experiment that demonstrated these effects. In this case, the intensity of physiological arousal during a film depended on how the viewers were instructed to think about the film (Lazarus et al., 1965). Similarly, physical and psychological symptoms associated with the stress of airport noise, of learning about toxins in local soil, or of bioterrorism threats are more common in people who engage in more catastrophic thinking about these problems (Kjellberg et al., 1996; Lerner et al., 2003; Matthies, Hoeger, & Guski, 2000; Speckhard, 2002).

The influence of cognitive factors weakens somewhat as stressors become more extreme. For example, chronic-pain patients who feel a sense of control over the pain tend to be more physically active, but this effect does not hold for those whose pain is severe (Jensen & Karoly, 1991). Still, even the impact of natural disasters or major stressors such as divorce may be lessened for those who think of them as challenges to be overcome. In other words, many stressful events are not inherently stressful. Their impact depends partly on how people perceive them (Wiedenfeld et al., 1990). An important aspect of this appraisal is the degree to which the stressors are perceived to be predictable or controllable.

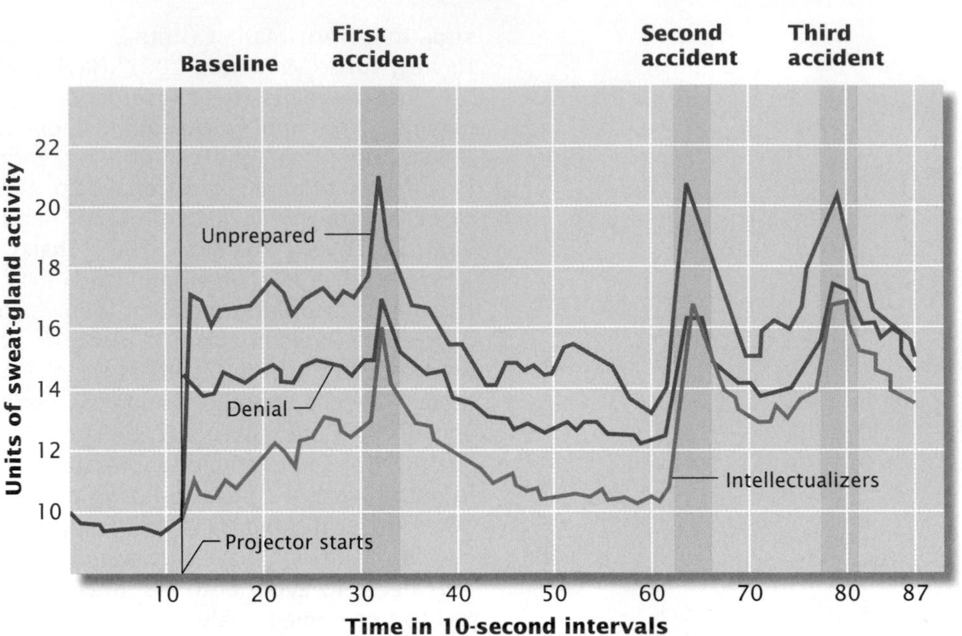

figure 13.4

Cognitive Influences on Stress Responses

Richard Lazarus and his colleagues found that students' physiological stress reactions to a film showing bloody industrial accidents was affected by the way they thought about the film. Those who had been instructed to remain detached from the film (the "intellectualizers") or to think of it as unreal (the "denial" group) were less upset—as measured by sweat-gland activity—than those in an "unprepared" group. These results were among the first to show that people's cognitive appraisal of stressors can affect their responses to those stressors (Lazarus et al., 1966).

Predictability and Control

Knowing that a particular stressor might occur but being uncertain whether it will tends to increase the stressor's impact (Boss, 1999; Lerner et al., 2003; Sorrentino & Roney, 2000). In other words, *predictable* stressors tend to have less impact than those that are unpredictable (Lazarus & Folkman, 1984; Pham, Taylor, & Seeman, 2001), especially when the stressors are intense and relatively brief (Abbott, Schoen, & Badia, 1984). Rats given a reliable warning signal every time they are to receive a shock show less severe physiological responses than animals given no warnings (Weinberg & Levine, 1980). Among humans, men and women whose spouses died suddenly tend to display more immediate disbelief, anxiety, and depression than those who had weeks or months to prepare for the loss (Schulz et al., 2001; Swarte et al., 2003). This is not to say that predictability provides total protection against stressors. Laboratory research with animals has shown that predictable stressors, even if relatively mild, can be more damaging than unpredictable ones if they occur over long periods of time (Abbott et al., 1984).

As Ken Cramer from Windsor and James Nickels from Manitoba explain, the *perception of control* can also mediate the effects of stressors (Cramer, Nickels, & Gural, 1997; Cramer & Perreault, 2006; Langlois, Cramer, & Mohagen, 2002; Nickels, Cramer, & Gural, 1992). If people can exert some control over them, stressors usually have less impact on health (e.g., Christensen, Stephens, & Townsend, 1998; Krause & Shaw, 2000). Studies of several thousand employees in the United States, Sweden, and the United Kingdom have found that workers who had little or no control over their work environments were more likely to suffer heart disease and other health problems than workers with a high degree of control over their work environments (Bosma et al., 1997; Cheng et al., 2000; Spector, 2002). In another study, researchers randomly selected a group of patients awaiting surgery and gave them a full explanation of the procedures that they could expect to undergo, along with information that would help them manage post-surgical pain (Egbert et al., 1964). After the surgery was over, patients who had been given this information and who felt they had at least some control over the pain they experienced not only were better adjusted than patients in a control group who received no special preparation but also healed faster and could be discharged from the hospital sooner. So impressive are findings such as these that, in many hospitals, it is now standard practice to teach patients how to manage or control the adverse effects of surgery (Broadbent et al., 2003; Chamberlin, 2000; Kiecolt-Glaser et al., 1998).

Simply believing that a stressor is controllable, even if it isn't, can also reduce its impact (Thompson et al., 1993). In one study of the cause of panic disorder (discussed in the chapter on psychological disorders), volunteer clients suffering this disorder inhaled a mixture of carbon dioxide and oxygen that typically causes them to experience fear and other symptoms of a panic attack (Sanderson, Rapee, & Barlow, 1989). Half the clients were led to believe (falsely) that they could control the concentration of the mixture. Compared with those who believed they had no control, significantly fewer of the "in control" clients experienced full-blown panic attacks during the session, and their panic symptoms were fewer and less severe.

People who feel they have no control over negative events appear especially prone to physical and psychological problems. They often experience feelings of helplessness and hopelessness that, in turn, may promote depression or other mental disorders (Taylor & Aspinwall, 1996).

Coping Resources and Coping Methods

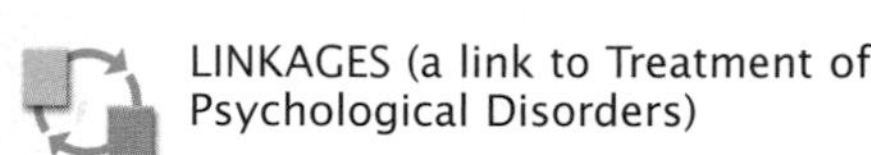

People usually suffer fewer ill effects from a stressor if they have adequate coping resources and effective coping methods. *Coping resources* include, for example, the money and time to deal with stressful events. So the physical and psychological responses you experience if your car breaks down are likely to be more negative if you are low on cash and pressed for time than if you have money for repairs and the freedom to take a day off from work.

The impact of stressors can also be reduced by the use of effective *coping methods* (Benight et al., 1999; Cote & Pepler, 2002; Poczwardowski & Conroy, 2002). Most of these methods can be classified as focusing either on problems or on emotions. *Problem-focused* coping involves efforts to alter or eliminate a source of stress, whereas *emotion-focused* techniques are aimed at regulating the negative emotional consequences of the stressor (Folkman et al., 1986). These two forms of coping sometimes work together. For example, you might deal with the problem of noise from a nearby airport by forming a community action group to push for tougher noise regulations and, at the same time, calm your anger when noise occurs by mentally focusing on the group's efforts to improve the situation (Folkman & Moskowitz, 2000; Hatfield et al., 2002). As mentioned earlier, coping efforts may not always be so adaptive. In the face of a financial crisis or impending exams, for example, some people rely on emotion-focused methods such as using alcohol or other drugs to ease anxiety but take no problem-focused steps to get out of debt or learn difficult material. These emotion-focused strategies might reduce distress in the short run, but the long-term result can be a financial or academic situation that is worse than it was before. Susan Folkman and Richard Lazarus (1988) have devised a widely used questionnaire to assess the specific ways in which people cope with stressors; Table 13.3 shows some examples of responses to their questionnaire.

Particularly when a stressor is difficult to control, it is sometimes helpful to express fully, and think about, the emotions you are experiencing in relation to the stressful event (Bower et al., 1999; Niederhoffer & Pennebaker, 2002). For example, although people may not be able to do very much about stressors such as the death of a family member, attempting to see the meaning of the death in relation to their own lives may help them cope more successfully (Bower et al., 1999). The benefits of this cognitive strategy have been observed among many individuals whose religious beliefs allow them to bring meaning to events that might otherwise be deemed senseless tragedies (Powell, Shahabi, & Thoreson, 2003; Seybold & Hill, 2001; VandeCreek et al., 2002). Similarly, women who focus on the fact that a diagnosis of breast cancer has at least brought their family closer together may adjust better to having the disease (Antoni et al., 2001; Carver & Antoni, 2004).

table 13.3

Coping is defined as the cognitive and behavioural efforts to manage specific demands that people perceive as taxing their resources (Folkman et al., 1986b). This table illustrates two major approaches to coping measured by the Ways of Coping questionnaire: problem-focused and emotion-focused coping. To get an idea of your own coping style, rank-order the skills under each major approach in terms of how often you tend to use each skill. Do you rely on just one or two, or do you adjust your coping strategies to fit different kinds of stressors?

Ways of Coping

Coping Skills	Example
Problem-focused coping	
Confronting	"I stood my ground and fought for what I wanted."
Seeking social support	"I talked to someone to find out more about the situation."
Planful problem solving	"I made a plan of action, and I followed it."
Emotion-focused coping	
Self-controlling	"I tried to keep my feelings to myself."
Distancing	"I didn't let it get to me; I tried not to think about it too much."
Positive reappraisal	"I changed my mind about myself."
Accepting responsibility	"I realized I brought the problem on myself."
Escape/avoidance (wishful thinking)	"I wished that the situation would go away or somehow be over with."

Source: Adapted from Folkman et al. (1986a); Taylor (1995).

Humour can also play a role. Some individuals who use humour to help them cope show better adjustment and lower physiological reactivity to stressful events (Martin, 2001; Moran, 2002).

Social Support

If you have ever benefited from the comforting presence of a good friend during troubled times, you know about another factor that mediates the impact of stressful events—*social support.* Social support consists of resources provided by other people. The friends and social contacts on whom you can depend for support constitute

You've Got a Friend Even when social support cannot eliminate stressors, it can help people, such as these breast cancer survivors, to feel less anxious, more optimistic, more capable of control, and more willing to try new ways of dealing with stressors (Trunzo & Pinto, 2003). Those who give social support may feel better, too (Brown et al., 2003).

your **social support network** (Burleson, Albrecht, & Sarason, 1994). Social support may take many forms, from eliminating the stressor (as when a friend helps you fix your car) to easing its impact with companionship, ideas for coping, or reassurance that you are cared about and valued and that everything will be all right (Sarason, Sarason, & Gurung, 1997).

The stress-reducing effects of social support have been documented for a wide range of stressors, including cancer, heart disease, military combat, loss of loved ones, natural disasters, arthritis, AIDS, and even ethnic discrimination (e.g., Foster, 2000; Gonzalez et al., 2004; Jason, Witter, & Torres-Harding, 2003; Mookadam & Arthur, 2004; Penner, Dovidio, & Albrecht, 2001; Savelkoul et al., 2000). Students clearly benefit from social support. Compared with those who are part of a supportive network, students with the least adequate social support suffer more emotional distress and are more vulnerable to upper respiratory infections during times of high academic stress (Lepore, 1995b). Some researchers have concluded that having inadequate social support can be as dangerous as smoking, obesity, or lack of exercise in that it nearly doubles a person's risk of dying from disease, suicide, or other causes (House, Landis, & Umberson, 1988; Kiecolt-Glaser & Newton, 2001; Mookadam & Arthur, 2004).

Having strong social support can reduce the likelihood of illness, improve recovery from existing illness, promote healthier behaviours (Grassi et al., 2000; Uchino, Uno, & Holt-Lunstad, 1999), and even reduce the intensity of stress responses. In laboratory studies, for example, participants tended to show smaller heart rate changes in response to a stressor if a friend was present than if they experienced the stressor alone (Gerin et al., 1995; Kamarck, Annunziato, & Amateau, 1995).

However, the relationship between social support and the impact of stressors is more complex than it might appear. First, just as the quality of social support may influence people's ability to cope with stress, the reverse may also be true: People's ability to cope may determine the quality of social support they receive (McLeod, Kessler, & Landis, 1992). For example, people who complain endlessly about stressors but never try to do anything about them may discourage social support, whereas those with an optimistic, action-oriented approach may attract support.

Second, *social support* refers not only to relationships with others but also to the recognition that others care and will help (Demaray & Malecki, 2002). Some relationships in a social support network may be stormy and fragile, resulting in interpersonal conflicts that can have an adverse effect on health (Ben-Ari & Gil, 2002; Malarkey et al., 1994).

Finally, having too much support or the wrong kind of support can be as bad as not having enough (Reynolds & Perrin, 2004). For example, people whose friends and family are overprotective may actually put less energy into coping efforts. And in one study of people with physical disabilities, nearly 40 percent of them were found to have experienced emotional distress in response to the well-intentioned help they received from their spouses. This distress, in turn, was a predictor of depression nearly a year later (Newsome & Schulz, 1998). Similarly, people living in crowded conditions might at first perceive the situation as providing lots of social support, but these conditions can eventually become an added source of stress (Lepore, Evans, & Schneider, 1991). Further, the value of social support may depend on the kind of stressor being encountered. So although having a friend present might reduce the impact of some stressors, it might amplify the impact of others. In one study, for example, participants faced with speaking in public experienced it as more threatening—and showed stronger physical and psychological stress responses—when a friend was watching than when they were alone (Stoney & Finney, 2000). In short, the efforts or presence of members of a social support network can sometimes become annoying, disruptive, or interfering, thereby increasing stress and intensifying psychological problems (Newsome, 1999; Newsome & Schulz, 1998).

social support network The friends and social contacts on whom one can depend for help and support.

Stress, Personality, and Gender

The impact of stress on health appears to depend not only on how people think about particular stressors but, to some extent, on how they think about and react to the world in general (Prior, 1999). For instance, stress-related health problems are more common among people whose "disease-prone" personalities lead them to be angry, anxious, or depressed; who persist at mentally evading perceived stressors; who perceive stressors as long-term, catastrophic threats that they brought on themselves; and who are pessimistic about their ability to overcome negative situations (e.g., Penninx et al., 2001; Peterson et al., 1998; Segerstrom et al., 1998; Suinn, 2001).

Other cognitive styles, such as those characteristic of "disease-resistant" personalities, help insulate people from the ill effects of stress. These people tend to think of stressors as temporary challenges to be overcome, not catastrophic threats, and they do not constantly blame themselves for bringing them about. Among the most important components of the disease-resistant personality are sociability (e.g., Cohen et al., 2003) and *dispositional optimism,* the belief or expectation that things will work out positively (Folkman & Moskowitz, 2000; Rosenkranz et al., 2003; Taylor et al., 2000a). Optimistic students, for example, experience fewer physical symptoms at the end of the academic term (Aspinwall & Taylor, 1992; Ebert,Tucker, & Roth, 2002). Optimistic coronary bypass surgery patients have been shown to heal faster than pessimists (Scheier et al., 1989) and to experience a higher quality of life following coronary surgery than those with less optimistic outlooks (Fitzgerald et al., 1993). And among HIV-positive men, dispositional optimism has been associated with less psychological distress, fewer worries, and lower perceived risk of acquiring full-blown AIDS (Johnson & Endler, 2002; Taylor et al., 1992). These effects appear to be due in part to optimists' tendency to use challenge-oriented, problem-focused coping strategies that attack stressors directly, in contrast to pessimists' tendency to use emotion-focused coping, such as denial and avoidance (Bosompra et al., 2001; Brenes et al., 2002).

Gender may also play a role in responses to stress. In a review of 200 studies of stress responses and coping methods, Shelley Taylor and her colleagues found that males under stress tended to get angry, avoid stressors, or both, whereas females were more likely to help others and to make use of their social support networks (Taylor et al., 2000b). This was not true in every case, of course, but why should a significant difference show up at all? The gender-role learning discussed in the chapter on human development surely plays a part (Eagly & Wood, 1999). But Taylor also proposes that women's "tend-and-befriend" style differs from the "fight-or-flight" pattern so often seen in men because of gender differences in how hormones combine under stress. For example, oxytocin (pronounced "oxsee-TOE-sin"), a hormone released in both sexes as part of the general adaptation syndrome, interacts differently with male and female sex hormones—amplifying men's physical stress responses and reducing women's. This difference could lead to the more intense emotional and behavioural stress responses typical of men, and it might be partly responsible for their greater vulnerability to heart disease and other stress-related illnesses. If that is the case, gender differences in stress responses may help to explain why women in North America live an average of 7.5 years longer than men.

FOCUS ON RESEARCH METHODS

Personality and Health

The way people think and act in the face of stressors, the ease with which they attract social support, and their tendency to be optimists or pessimists are but a few aspects of *personality*.

● What was the researchers' question?

Are there other personality characteristics that protect or threaten people's health? This was the research question asked by Howard Friedman and his associates

(Friedman et al., 1995a; Friedman et al., 1995b). In particular, they attempted to identify aspects of personality that increase the likelihood that people will develop heart disease or hypertension and die prematurely from these disorders.

● How did the researchers answer the question?

Friedman suspected that an answer might lie in earlier research—specifically, in the Terman Life Cycle Study of Intelligence, named after Louis Terman, author of the Stanford-Binet intelligence test. The study was originally designed to document the long-term development of 1528 gifted California children (856 boys and 672 girls)—nicknamed the "Termites" (Terman & Oden, 1947). Friedman and his colleagues found ways of using data from this study to explore the relationship between personality and health.

Starting in 1921, and every five to ten years thereafter, Terman's research team had gathered information about the Termites' personality traits, social relationships, stressors, health habits, and many other variables. The data were collected through questionnaires and interviews with the Termites themselves, as well as with their teachers, parents, and other family members. When, by the early 1990s, about half of the Termites had died, Friedman realized that the Terman Life Cycle Study was really a longitudinal study in health psychology. As in most such studies, the independent variable (in this case, personality characteristics) was not actually manipulated (the Termites had obviously not been randomly assigned different personalities by the researchers), but the various personality traits identified in these people could still be related to a dependent variable (namely, longevity—how long they lived). So Friedman and his colleagues gathered the death certificates of the Termites, noted the dates and causes of death, and then looked for associations between personality and longevity.

● What did the researchers find?

One of the most important predictors of long life turned out to be a personality dimension known as *conscientiousness,* or social dependability (described in the chapter on personality). Termites who, in childhood, had been seen as truthful, prudent, reliable, hard-working, and free from vanity tended to live longer than those whose parents and teachers had identified them as impulsive and lacking in self-control.

Friedman and his colleagues also used the Terman Life Cycle Study to investigate the relationship between social support and health. They compared the life spans of Termites whose parents had divorced or who had been in unstable marriages themselves with those who grew up in stable homes and who had stable marriages. The researchers found that people who had experienced parental divorce during childhood or who themselves had unstable marriages died an average of four years earlier than those whose close social relationships had been less stressful.

● What do the results mean?

The research of Friedman and his co-workers was based mainly on the analysis of correlations, so it is difficult to draw conclusions about whether differences in personality traits and social support actually caused the observed differences in life span. Nevertheless, Friedman and his colleagues searched the Terman data for clues to mechanisms through which personality and other factors might have exerted a causal influence on longevity (Peterson et al., 1998). For example, they evaluated the hypothesis that conscientious, dependable Termites who lived socially stable lives might have followed healthier lifestyles than their impulsive and socially stressed age-mates. People in the latter group did indeed tend to eat less healthy diets and were more likely to smoke, drink to excess, or use drugs. However, these behaviours alone did not fully account for their shorter average life spans. Another possible explanation is that conscientiousness and stability in social relationships create a general attitude of caution that goes beyond eating right and avoiding substance abuse. The researchers found some support for this idea in the Terman data. Termites who were impulsive or low on conscientiousness were somewhat more likely to die from accidents or violence than those who were less impulsive. (A similar finding is reported in the Focus on Research Methods section of the chapter on personality.)

- **What do we still need to know?**

Although the Terman Life Cycle Study cannot provide definite answers about the relationship between personality and health, it has generated some important clues and a number of intriguing hypotheses to be evaluated in future research with more representative samples of people. Further, Friedman's decision to reanalyze a set of data on psychosocial development as a way of exploring issues in health psychology stands as a fine example of how a creative researcher can pursue answers to complex questions that are difficult or impossible to study through controlled experiments.

Our review of personality and other factors that can alter the impact of stressors should make it obvious that what is stressful for a particular individual is not determined simply by predispositions, coping styles, or situations. (See "In Review: Stress Responses and Stress Mediators.") Even more important are interactions between the person and the situation, the mixture of each individual's coping resources and the specific characteristics of the situations encountered (Smith, 1993).

in review Stress Responses and Stress Mediators

Category	Examples
Responses	
Physical	Fight-or-flight syndrome (increased heart rate, respiration, and muscle tension; sweating; pupillary dilation); SAM and HPA activation (involving release of catecholamines and corticosteroids); eventual breakdown of organ systems involved in prolonged resistance to stressors.
Psychological	*Emotional:* anger, anxiety, depression, and other emotional states. *Cognitive:* inability to concentrate or think logically, ruminative thinking, catastrophizing. *Behavioural:* aggression and escape/avoidance tactics (including suicide attempts).
Mediators	
Appraisal	Thinking of a difficult new job as a challenge will create less discomfort than focusing on the threat of failure.
Predictability	A tornado that strikes without warning may have a more devastating emotional impact than a long-predicted hurricane.
Control	Repairing a disabled spacecraft may be less stressful for the astronauts doing the work than for their loved ones on Earth, who can do nothing to help.
Coping resources and methods	Having no effective way to relax after a hard day may prolong tension and other stress responses.
Social support	Having no one to talk to about a rape or other trauma may amplify the negative impact of the experience.

PsychAssist: Physical Reactions to Stressors—General Adaptation Syndrome

The Physiology and Psychology of Health and Illness

Several studies mentioned so far have suggested that stress shapes the development of physical illness by affecting cognitive, physiological, and behavioural processes. Those studies are part of a much larger body of research in health psychology that sheds light on the relationship between stress and illness. In the following sections we focus on some of the ways in which stress can, directly or indirectly, lead to physical illnesses by affecting the *immune system* and the *cardiovascular system.*

Stress, Illness, and the Immune System

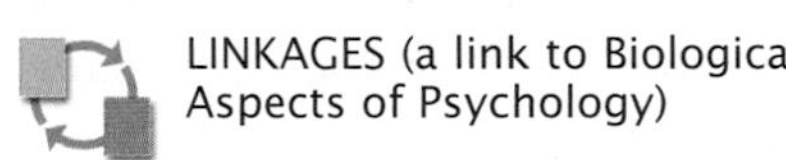

As described in the chapter on biological aspects of psychology, components of the immune system act as the body's first line of defence by killing or deactivating foreign or harmful substances in the body, such as viruses and bacteria (Simpson, Hurtley, & Marx, 2000).

The role of physiological stress responses in altering the body's ability to fight disease was demonstrated more than a century ago. On 19 March 1878, at a seminar before the Académie de Médecine de Paris, Louis Pasteur showed his distinguished audience three chickens. One healthy bird, the control chicken, had been raised normally. A second bird had been intentionally infected with bacteria but given no other treatment; it was also healthy. The third chicken Pasteur presented was dead. It had been infected with the same bacteria as the second bird, but it had also been stressed by being exposed to cold temperatures. As a result, the bacteria had killed it (Kelley, 1985).

Research conducted since Pasteur's time has greatly expanded knowledge about how stressors affect the body's reaction to disease. **Psychoneuroimmunology** is the field that examines the interaction of psychological, social, behavioural, neural, hormonal, and immune system processes that affect the body's ability to defend itself against disease (Ader, 2001).

The Immune System and Illness If the immune system is impaired—by stressors, for example—a person is left more vulnerable to colds, mononucleosis, and many other infectious diseases (Potter & Zautra, 1997). It is by disabling the immune system that HIV infection leads to AIDS and leaves the HIV-infected person defenceless against other infections or cancers.

There are many facets to the human immune system. One important component is the action of immune system cells, especially white blood cells, called *leukocytes* (pronounced "LU-koh-sites"), which are formed in the bone marrow and serve as the body's mobile defence units. Leukocytes are called into action when foreign substances are detected. Among the varied types of leukocytes are *B-cells,* which mature in the bone marrow, and *T-cells,* which mature in the thymus. Generally, T-cells kill other cells, and B-cells produce *antibodies,* which are circulating proteins that bind to specific toxins and other foreign cells and begin to deactivate them. *Natural killer cells,* another type of leukocyte, destroy a wide variety of foreign organisms, but they have particularly important antiviral and antitumour functions. Yet another type of immune system cell is the *macrophage* (pronounced "MACK-row-fayj). Macrophages engulf foreign cells and digest them in a process called *phagocytosis,* or "eating cells." These scavengers are able to squeeze out of the bloodstream and enter organs, where they destroy foreign cells.

The activity of immune system cells can be either strengthened or weakened by a number of systems, including the endocrine system and the central and autonomic nervous systems. It is through these connections that stress-related psychological and emotional factors can affect the functioning of the immune system (see Figure 3.25 in the chapter on biological aspects of psychology). The exact mechanisms by which the nervous system affects the immune system are not yet fully understood, but they

psychoneuroimmunology A field of research on the interaction of psychological, social, behavioural, neural, hormonal, and immune system processes that affect the body's defences against disease.

appear to involve both indirect and direct connections (Rosenkranz et al., 2003). The brain can influence the activity of the immune system indirectly by altering the secretion of hormones (including cortisol secretion by the adrenal gland) that stimulate receptors in circulating T-cells and B-cells. More direct influences occur as nerves affect immune organs, such as the thymus, where T-cells and B-cells are stored (Felten et al., 1991; Maier & Watkins, 2000).

The Immune System and Stress Researchers have found that people under stress are more likely than less stressed people to develop infectious diseases and to experience flare-ups of latent viruses responsible for oral herpes (cold sores) or genital herpes (Cohen & Herbert, 1996). For example, Sheldon Cohen and his colleagues in the United Kingdom (Cohen et al., 1995) exposed 394 healthy adult volunteers either to one of five respiratory viruses or to a placebo. The participants were then isolated and asked about the number and severity of life stresses they had experienced in the previous year. After controlling for factors such as prior history of colds, exposure to other viruses, and health practices, the researchers found that the more stress the participants had experienced, the greater was the likelihood that their exposure to a virus would result in colds and respiratory infections.

These findings are supported by other research showing that a variety of stressors lead to suppression of the immune system. The effects are especially strong in the elderly (Penedo & Dahn, 2004), but they occur in everyone (Kiecolt-Glaser & Glaser, 2001; Kiecolt-Glaser et al., 2002). For example, a study of first-year law students found that as these students participated in class, took exams, and experienced other stressful aspects of law school, they showed a decline in several measures of immune functioning (Segerstrom et al., 1998). Similarly, reduction in natural killer cell activity has been observed in both men and women following the deaths of their spouses (Irwin et al., 1987), and a variety of immune system impairments have been found in people suffering the effects of separation, divorce, lack of social support, and loneliness (Kiecolt-Glaser & Glaser, 1992). Providing care for an elderly relative who is mentally or physically incapacitated is a particularly stressful circumstance that has been reliably shown to diminish immune function (Cacioppo et al., 1998; Kiecolt-Glaser et al., 2003; Vitaliano, Zhang, & Scanlan, 2003).

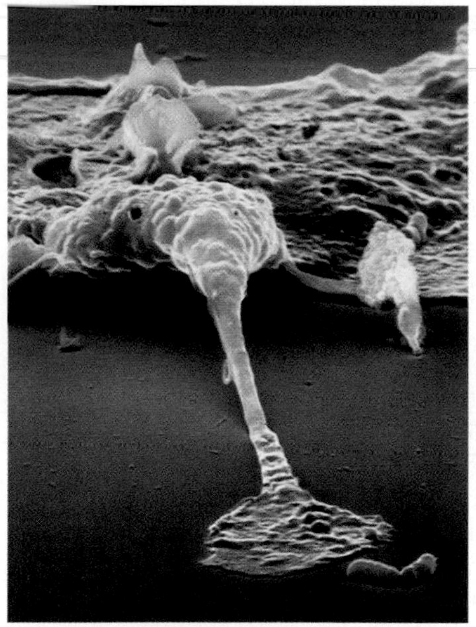

The First Line of Defence A patrolling immune system cell sends out an extension known as a *pseudopod* (pronounced "SUE-doh-pod") to engulf and destroy a bacterial cell before alerting more defenders. Psychological stressors can alter immune system functions through a number of mechanisms. For example, they can activate neural connections between the sympathetic nervous system and organs of the immune system through response systems that have direct suppressant effects on immune function. These suppressant effects are due largely to the release of cortisol and other corticosteroid hormones from the adrenal cortex (see Figure 13.3).

The relationship between stress and the immune system is especially important in persons who are HIV-positive but do not yet have AIDS. Because their immune systems are already seriously compromised, further stress-related impairments could be life threatening. Research indicates that psychological stressors are associated with the progression of HIV-related illnesses (e.g., Antoni et al., 2000; Heckman et al., 2004). Unfortunately, people with HIV (and AIDS) face a particularly heavy load of immune-suppressing psychological stressors, including bereavement, unemployment, uncertainty about the future, and daily reminders of serious illness. A lack of perceived control and resulting depression can further amplify their stress responses (Balbin, Ironson, & Solomon, 1999).

Moderators of Immune Function The effects of social support and other stress-moderating factors can be seen in the activity of the immune system. For example, immune system functioning among students who are able to get emotional assistance from friends during stressful periods appears better than among those with less adequate social support (Cohen & Herbert, 1996).

James Pennebaker (1995, 2002) suggests that social support may help prevent illness by providing the person under stress with an opportunity to express pent-up thoughts and emotions. Suppressing the emotions associated with stressors, says Pennebaker, is itself a stressor that can lead to further impairment of the immune system (Pennebaker, Colder, & Sharp, 1990; Pennebaker, Kiecolt-Glaser, & Glaser, 1988; Petrie et al., 1995; Petrie, Booth, & Pennebaker, 1998). For example, the spouses of suicide or accidental-death victims who do not or cannot confide their feelings to

Fighting a Deadly Disease The impact of psychological factors on immune system functioning can be seen in the progression of HIV/AIDS. Sustained depression, concealment of gay identity, negative expectancies, and reliance on passive, emotion-focused coping methods such as denial have all been related to faster disease progression. Openly expressing emotions; collaborating closely with doctors; having optimistic expectations, remaining involved in normal activities; finding meaning in the situation; and other active, problem-focused coping strategies have all been associated with slower disease progression (Balbin et al., 1999).

others are most likely to develop physical illnesses during the year following the death (Pennebaker & O'Heeron, 1984). Disclosing, even anonymously, the stresses and traumas one has experienced is associated with enhanced immune functioning, reduced physical symptoms, and decreased use of health services (Campbell & Pennebaker, 2003; Niederhoffer & Pennebaker, 2002; Richards et al., 2000; Rosenberg et al., 2002). This may explain why support groups for problems ranging from bereavement to overeating to alcohol and drug abuse tend to improve participants' quality of life and, to some extent, their physical health status (Taylor, Dickerson, & Klein, 2002). Future research in psychoneuroimmunology promises to reveal more about the complex chain of mental and physical events that determine whether people become ill or stay healthy (Rosenkrantz et al., 2003).

Stress, Illness, and the Cardiovascular System

Earlier we discussed the role played by the sympatho-adreno-medullary (SAM) system in mobilizing the body during times of threat. Because the SAM system is linked to the cardiovascular system, its repeated activation in response to stressors has been linked to the development of coronary heart disease (CHD), high blood pressure (hypertension), and stroke. The link appears especially strong in people who display strong physical reactivity to stressors (Andre-Petersson et al., 2001; Ming et al., 2004; Treiber et al., 2001). For example, among healthy young adult research participants, those whose blood pressure rose most dramatically in response to a mild stressor were the ones most likely to develop hypertension over the next three decades (Kasagi, Akahoshi, & Shimaoki, 1995; Light et al., 1999; Menkes et al., 1989).

As also mentioned earlier, these physical reactions to stressors—and the chances of suffering stress-related health problems—depend partly on personality factors, especially on how people tend to think about stressors and about life in general. For example, hostility has been associated with the appearance of coronary heart disease (Day & Jreige, 2002; Friedman & Rosenman, 1974; Krantz & McCeney, 2002; Smith, 2003a; Smith & Ruiz, 2002).

THINKING CRITICALLY

Does Hostility Increase the Risk of Heart Disease?

Health psychologists see hostility as characterized by suspiciousness, resentment, frequent anger, antagonism, and distrust of others (Helmers & Krantz, 1996; Krantz & McCeney, 2002; Williams, 2001). The identification of hostility as a risk factor for coronary heart disease and *myocardial infarction,* or *MI* (commonly known as heart attack), could be an important breakthrough in better understanding the chief cause of death in the United States and most other Western nations (Centers for Disease Control and Prevention, 2001; Hu et al., 2000). But is hostility as dangerous as health psychologists suspect?

- **What am I being asked to believe or accept?**

Many researchers claim that individuals displaying hostility are at increased risk for coronary heart disease and heart attack (e.g., Bleil et al., 2004; Boyle et al., 2004). This risk, they say, is independent of other risk factors such as heredity, diet, smoking, and drinking.

- **What evidence is available to support the assertion?**

The precise mechanism underlying the relationship between hostility and heart disease is not clear, but there are several possibilities (Helmers et al., 1995). The risk of CHD and MI may be elevated in hostile people because these people tend to display an unusually strong reaction to stressors, especially when challenged (Suls & Wan, 1993). During interpersonal conflicts, for example, people predisposed to hostile behaviour display not only overt hostility but also unusually large increases in blood pressure, heart rate, and other aspects of SAM reactivity (Brondolo et al., 2003; Suls & Wan, 1993). In addition, it takes hostile individuals longer than normal to get back to their resting levels of SAM functioning. Like a driver who damages a car by flooring the accelerator and applying the brakes at the same time, these "hot reactors" may create excessive wear and tear on the arteries of the heart as their increased heart rate forces blood through constricted vessels. Increased sympathetic nervous system activation not only puts a strain on the coronary arteries but also leads to surges of stress-related hormones from the adrenal glands, including the catecholamines (adrenaline and noradrenaline). High levels of these hormones are associated with increases in cholesterol and other fatty substances that are deposited in arteries and contribute to atherosclerosis (hardening of the arteries) and CHD (Bierhaus et al., 2003; Stoney & Hughes, 1999; Stoney, Bausserman, et al., 1999; Stoney, Niaura, et al., 1999). And in fact, cholesterol and triglycerides do appear to be elevated in hostile people, even when they are not under stress (Dujovne & Houston, 1991; Engebretson & Stoney, 1995).

Hostility might also affect heart disease risk less directly, through its impact on social support. Some evidence suggests that hostile people take less advantage of their social support networks (Lepore, 1995a). Failure to use this support—and possibly offending potential supporters in the process—may intensify the impact of stressful events on hostile people. The result may be increased anger, antagonism, and, ultimately, additional stress on the cardiovascular system (e.g., Hall & Davidson, 1996).

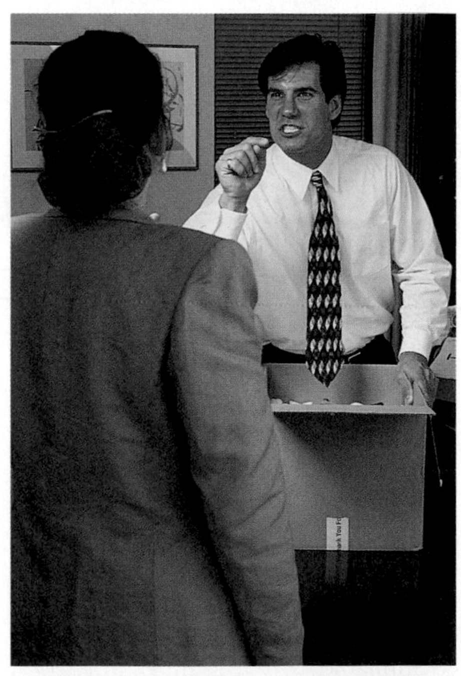

You Can't Fire Me—I Quit! For a time, researchers believed that anyone who displayed the pattern of aggressiveness, competitiveness, and nonstop work known as "Type A" behaviour was at elevated risk for heart disease. More recent research shows, however, that the danger lies not in these characteristics alone, but in hostility, a pattern seen in some, but not all, Type A people.

- **Are there alternative ways of interpreting the evidence?**

Studies suggesting that hostility causes CHD are not true experiments. Researchers cannot manipulate the independent variable, hostility, by creating it in some people but not others, nor can they create experimental conditions in which individuals who differ only in terms of hostility are compared on heart disease, the dependent variable. Accordingly, we have to consider other explanations of the hostility–CHD/MI relationship.

Some researchers suggest that higher CHD/MI rates among hostile people are due not to the impact of hostility on autonomic reactivity and hormone surges but, rather, to a third variable that accounts for the other two. Specifically, genetically determined autonomic reactivity might increase the likelihood of both hostility and heart disease (Krantz et al., 1988). Supporting this alternative interpretation is evidence that people with an inherited predisposition toward strong physiological responses to the stressors of everyday life not only have a higher risk for CHD but also tend to be more hostile (Cacioppo et al., 1998). It is at least plausible, then, that some individuals are biologically predisposed to exaggerated autonomic reactivity and to hostility, each of which is independent of the other.

- **What additional evidence would help to evaluate the alternatives?**

One way of testing whether hostile people's higher rates of CHD and MI are related to their hostility or to a more general tendency toward intense physiological arousal is to examine how hostile individuals react to stress when they are not angry. Researchers have done exactly this by observing the physiological reactions of hostile people as they undergo surgery. They have found that while enduring surgical stress under general anesthesia, hostile people show unusually strong autonomic reactivity (Krantz & Durel, 1983). Because these individuals are not conscious, it is more likely that oversensitivity to stressors, not hostile thinking, is causing this exaggerated response.

To more fully illuminate the role of hostility in the development of CHD and MI, future research will have to take into account a number of important possibilities: (1) Some individuals may be biologically predisposed to react to stress and challenge with hostility and increased cardiovascular activity, which in turn may contribute to heart disease; (2) hostile people may amplify and perpetuate their stress through aggressive thoughts and actions, which in turn may provoke others and elicit additional stressors; and (3) people high in hostility may harm their health to a greater extent than less hostile people by smoking, drinking, overeating, failing to exercise, and engaging in other high-risk behaviours (Houston & Vavac, 1991).

- **What conclusions are most reasonable?**

Although there is some inconsistency among various studies, most researchers continue to find that hostile individuals have a higher risk of heart disease and heart attacks than other people (Krantz & McCeney, 2002; Stansfeld & Marmot, 2002). However, the causal relationship is probably more complex than researchers first thought; it appears that many interacting factors affect the relationship between hostility and CHD.

We must also keep in mind that the relationship between heart problems and hostility may not be universal. The relationship does appear to hold for women, as well as for men, and for individuals in various ethnic groups (e.g., Davidson, Hall, & MacGregor, 1996; Nakano & Kitamura, 2001; Powch & Houston, 1996; Yoshimasu et al., 2002). However, final conclusions must await further research that examines the impact of gender, culture, and ethnicity on the link between hostility and CHD/MI.

Risking Your Life: Health-Endangering Behaviours

As we have seen, many of today's major health problems are caused or amplified by preventable behaviours such as those listed in Table 13.1.

Smoking Smoking is the single most preventable risk factor for fatal illnesses in Canada (Health Canada, 2006). Since the US Surgeon General outlined the harmful effects of smoking in the 1970s, the incidence of smoking has been on a steady decline. Despite this, in 2005 slightly fewer than 5 million Canadians aged 15 years or older were smokers (19 percent of the general population)—22 percent of the male population and 16 percent of the female population (CTUMS, 2006).

Overall, poorer, less educated people are particularly likely to smoke. In many other countries, particularly less developed countries, smoking is still the rule rather

table 13.4
Smoking Trends from 1981 to 2004 for Canadian Males and Females (All Ages)

	1981	1999	2001	2002	2004
Males	46%	27%	20%	21%	22%
Females	42%	29%	26%	23%	17%
TOTAL	44%	28%	23%	22%	20%

than the exception (Lam et al., 2001). Today, we're also seeing an alarming trend in the age of initiation—when Canadians are likely to begin smoking; Canadians are now starting at a younger age (just over 15). Compare that to their parents (born around 1955) who began just under 16 and their great-grandparents (born in 1910) when males began smoking at 18 and females at 27.

This is a critical finding because the earlier you start smoking, the greater the exposure to its adverse effects and the greater risk to your health. With a ten- to twenty-year latency period until you develop cardiovascular disease and cancer, decreased age of smoking initiation means added pressure on the health care system for a decade. Who are the heavy smokers? They are in their middle years (44 to 49), who in 1998 over 44 percent smoked 20 or more cigarettes a day. Compare that to 29 percent of younger adults (15 to 39) and 29 percent of those over 70 smoking 20 or more a day. Even more serious is the nature of premature death in this country due to smoking—it is by far the most important public health problem facing Canadians today. Statistics Canada estimates that at least one in every four deaths among Canadians 35–84 years of age were caused by smoking. In 1991, an estimated 45 000 deaths were attributed to tobacco use.

Smoking affects non-smokers, too. Non-smokers exposed to second-hand smoke are at an elevated risk of getting cancer and other lung diseases. In addition to cancer and heart disease, second-hand smoke has been identified as a factor in the development of asthma in children, and in the severity of asthma attacks. A recent study also suggests that second-hand smoke may increase a woman's risk of developing breast cancer. According to Health Canada, more than 300 non-smokers die each year from lung cancer because of second-hand smoke (Je et al., 1999; Otsuka et al., 2001; Whincup et al., 2004), a fact that has fuelled a militant nonsmokers' rights movement in North America. In fact, second-hand smoke is more dangerous than directly inhaled smoke (even when you cannot see or smell it) because that smoke releases the same chemicals (over 4000) as smoke directly inhaled, but in even greater quantity, and about 50 are known cancer-causing agents. Second-hand smoke is linked to the deaths of at least 1100 Canadians every year. In addition to the suffering and loss caused by second-hand smoke-related deaths and the direct medical costs associated with long-term illnesses, there are significant indirect costs related to second-hand smoke.

table 13.5
Smoking Trends from 1981 for Young (20 to 24 Years) Canadians

	1981	1999	2001	2002
Males	47%	40%	36%	31%
Females	50%	31%	32%	30%
TOTAL	48%	36%	34%	31%

Smoking is a difficult habit to break; only about 10 to 40 percent of people participating in the stop-smoking programs available today show long-term success (Riemsma et al., 2003). In North America, only about 4 percent of smokers who try to quit on their own remain abstinent, and only 27 to 30 percent of those using nicotine replacement and/or behaviour modification programs achieve long-term success (American Lung Association, 2002). Still, persistence can pay off: There are encouraging findings as well. Over 1.6 million Canadians (831 000 males and 778 000 females) had quit smoking in 1995. (Heart and Stroke Foundation of Canada, 2006). The highest incidence of quitting was for those aged 20 to 34, with 28 percent quitting. Those aged 12 to 19 and aged 65 and over had the lowest incidence of quitting, at 19 percent. Improving this success rate and preventing adolescents from taking up smoking remain among health psychology's greatest challenges.

Alcohol Like tobacco, alcohol is a potentially addicting substance that can lead to major health problems. In addition to its association with most leading causes of death, including heart disease, stroke, cancer, and liver disease, alcohol abuse contributes to permanent damage to brain tissue and to gastrointestinal illnesses, among many others (Centers for Disease Control and Prevention, 1999a). Both male and female alcohol abusers may experience disruption of their reproductive functions, such as early menopause in women and erectile disorder in men. Alcohol consumption by pregnant women is the most preventable cause of birth defects. For others, though, light to moderate alcohol consumption is associated with reduced risk of death from cardiovascular disease (Malinski et al., 2004), possibly because this modest level of consumption is part of a more generally healthy lifestyle. In fact, Health Canada (2006) recommends males consume two drinks and females consume one drink per day for its health benefits (to relieve stress). And although moderate use of alcohol is not harmful for some, excessive drinking can lead to a host of social and health problems. In 2000 there were over 1100 deaths attributed to alcohol-related liver diseases (mostly cirrhosis or scarring of the liver). In addition, many motor vehicle crashes involve impaired drivers. Approximately 1350 people die each year in alcohol-related motor vehicle crashes (32 percent of all driver fatalities). According to the National Population Health Survey of 1998–1999, 55 percent of Canadians 12 years of age or older drank alcohol at least once a month. Men were more likely to be drinkers than women, but for both sexes, the higher the level of education the more likely they were to be drinkers.

Unsafe Sex According to the Joint United Nations Programme on HIV/AIDS, about 40 million people worldwide are HIV-positive, and about 21 million have died from AIDS (Centers for Disease Control and Prevention, 2002b; Steinbrook, 2004a; World Health Organization, 2003). Testing for HIV began in November 1985, and up to 2002, approximately 56 000 Canadians were living with HIV (including those with

table 13.6

Proportion of Canadians 15 to 24 years of age who qualify as heavy weekly or monthly drinkers—5 or more drinks in men and 4 or more drinks in women—in one sitting

	Heavy Weekly Consumption		**Heavy Monthly Consumption**	
	15–19 years	20–24 years	15–19 years	20–24 years
Males	12%	16%	40%	47%
Females	6%	11%	27%	37%

(*Source:* National Population Health Survey, 1998–1999)

AIDS); and about 30 percent (17 000) were not aware of their infection. With almost 50 000 cases in 1999, that represents a 12 percent increase into 2002. In short, there are about 2500 to 5200 new HIV infections in Canada every year, with over 2500 in 2004. Since tracking began in 1985, there have been over 58,000 positive HIV tests reported, and almost 45 000 (75 percent) of those cases are male. In addition to incidence, even exposure to HIV varies by gender—whereas females typically become infected through heterosexual contact, males become infected chiefly through male-to-male intercourse (65 percent of the time; while that dropped to 36 percent in 2001, it rose again to 44 percent in 2004). There were (by June 2005) over 20 146 diagnosed cases of AIDS (18 169 male, 90 percent) in Canada, and at least 13 502 people have died. In fact, although the provinces of British Columbia, Alberta, Ontario, and Quebec account for 85 percent of the population, they represent 95 percent of the nation's AIDS diagnoses.

Although health professionals encourage the use of condoms to curb the spread of the infection, the 1994–1995 National Population Health Survey reported that among youth aged 15 to 19 years of age, 51 percent of sexually active females and 29 percent of sexually active males had sex in the previous year without a condom. For young adults 20 to 24 years of age, 53 percent of sexually active females and 44 percent of sexually active males had not used a condom. Beyond HIV infection, the extent of unprotected sex among youth is clearly seen in the transmission of other sexually transmitted diseases. For instance, the incidence of chlamydia and gonorrhea in Canada in 2002 was highest among females aged 15 to 19 years.

Promoting Healthy Behaviour

Health psychologists are deeply involved in the development of smoking cessation programs, in campaigns to prevent young people from taking up smoking, in alcohol-education efforts, and in the fight against the spread of HIV infection and AIDS (e.g., Carey et al., 2004; Latkin, Sherman, & Knowlton, 2003; Taylor, 2002). They have also helped promote early detection of disease. Encouraging women to perform breast self-examinations and men to do testicular self-examinations are just two examples of health psychology programs that can save thousands of lives each year (Taylor, 2002). Health psychologists have also explored the reasons behind some people's failure to follow treatment regimens that are vital to the control of diseases such as diabetes, heart disease, AIDS, and high blood pressure (Bartlett, 2002; Gonzalez et al., 2004). Understanding these reasons and devising procedures that encourage greater adherence to medical advice could speed recovery, prevent unnecessary suffering, and save many lives.

The process of preventing, reducing, or eliminating behaviours that pose risks to health and of increasing healthy behaviour patterns is called **health promotion** (Smith, Orleans, & Jenkins, 2004). Toward this end, many health psychologists have developed programs that teach children as young as nine or ten to develop healthy behaviours and avoid health-risky behaviours. School systems now offer a variety of these programs, including those that give children and adolescents the skills necessary to help them turn down cigarettes, drugs, and unprotected sex. To meet the more difficult challenge of modifying existing health-threatening behaviours, health psychologists go into workplaces and communities with the goal of altering diet, smoking, and exercise patterns and teaching stress-management techniques to help people develop healthier lifestyles (Langenberg et al., 2000; Tuomilehto et al., 2001). These programs may have the added advantage of creating savings in future medical treatment costs (Blumenthal et al., 2002; Schneider-man et al., 2001).

In their health-promotion efforts, many health psychologists also conduct and apply research on the cognitive factors associated with health-related behaviours. These psychologists have two goals: to better understand the thought processes that lead people to engage in health-endangering behaviours and to tailor intervention

health promotion The process of altering or eliminating behaviours that pose risks to health, as well as encouraging healthy behaviour patterns.

programs that alter those thought processes, or at least take them into account (Klepp, Kelder, & Perry, 1995).

Health Beliefs and Health Behaviours

This cognitive approach to health psychology is embodied in various *health-belief models*. One of the most influential of these models was developed by Irwin Rosenstock (1974). This model has been extensively tested (Aspinwall & Duran, 1999) and is based on the assumption that people's decisions about health-related behaviours (such as smoking) are guided by four main factors:

1. Perceiving a *personal threat* of, or susceptibility to, developing a specific health problem. (Do you believe that *you* will get lung cancer from smoking?)
2. Perceiving the seriousness of the illness and the consequences of having it. (How serious do *you* think lung cancer is, and what will happen if you get it?)
3. The belief that a particular behaviour change will reduce the threat. (Will giving up smoking prevent *you* from getting lung cancer?)
4. A comparison of the *perceived costs* of enacting a health-related behaviour change and the *benefits expected* from that change. (Will the reduced chance of getting cancer in the future be worth the discomfort and loss of pleasure associated with not smoking?)

This health-belief model suggests that the people most likely to quit smoking would be those who believe that they are susceptible to getting cancer from smoking, that cancer is serious and life threatening, that quitting will decrease their chances of getting cancer, and that the benefits of preventing cancer clearly outweigh the difficulties associated with quitting.

Other cognitive factors not included in Rosenstock's model may also be important, however. For cxample, people are unlikely to try to quit smoking unless they believe they can succeed. So *self-efficacy,* the belief that one is able to perform some behaviour, is an additional determinant of decisions about health behaviours (Bandura, 1992; Schwarzer, 2001). A related factor is the person's intention to engage in a behaviour designed to improve health or protect against illness (Albarracin et al., 2001; Schwarzer, 2001).

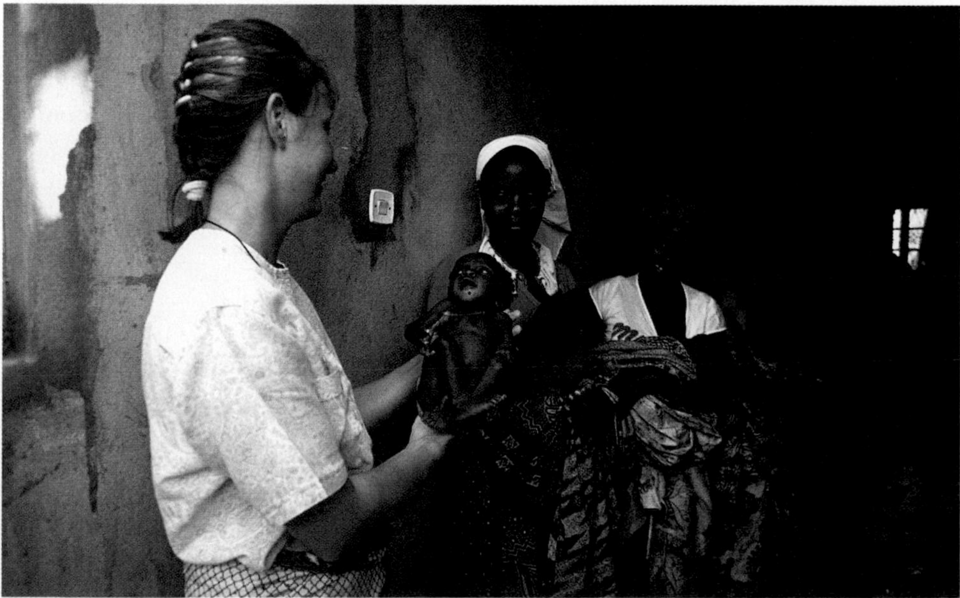

Doctor's Orders Despite their physicians' instructions, many patients fail to take their blood pressure medication and continue to eat unhealthy diets. Noncompliance with medical advice is especially common when cultural values and beliefs conflict with that advice. Aware of this problem, health psychologists are developing culture-sensitive approaches to health promotion and disease prevention (Kazarian & Evans, 2001).

table 13.7

Many successful programs for systematically coping with stress guide people through several stages and are aimed at removing stressors that can be changed and at reducing responses to stressors that cannot be changed (Taylor, 1999).

Stages in Coping with Stress

Stage	Task
1. Assessment	Identify the sources and effects of stress.
2. Goal setting	List the stressors and stress responses to be addressed. Designate which stressors are and are not changeable.
3. Planning	List the specific steps to be taken to cope with stress.
4. Action	Implement coping plans.
5. Evaluation	Determine the changes in stressors and stress responses that have occurred as a result of coping methods.
6. Adjustment	Alter coping methods to improve results, if necessary.

Health-belief models have been useful in predicting a variety of health behaviours, including exercise (McAuley, 1992), safe-sex practices among gay men at risk for AIDS (Fisher, Fisher, & Rye, 1995), adherence to medical regimens among diabetic adolescents (Bond, Aiken, & Somerville, 1992), and the decision to undergo mammography screening for breast cancer (Champion & Huster, 1995). These models have also guided researchers in the development of interventions to reduce certain health-risky behaviours and promote health-enhancing actions. For example, interventions with individuals at high risk for AIDS, particularly adolescents and African American women, include programs to improve knowledge about the disease and skill in demanding safe sex (e.g., DiClemente et al., 2004).

Changing Health Behaviours: Stages of Readiness

Changing health-related behaviours depends not only on a person's health beliefs but also on that person's readiness to change. According to James Prochaska and his colleagues, the process of successful change occurs in five stages (Prochaska, DiClemente, & Norcross, 1992):

1. ***Precontemplation.*** The person does not perceive a health-related problem and has no intention of changing in the foreseeable future.

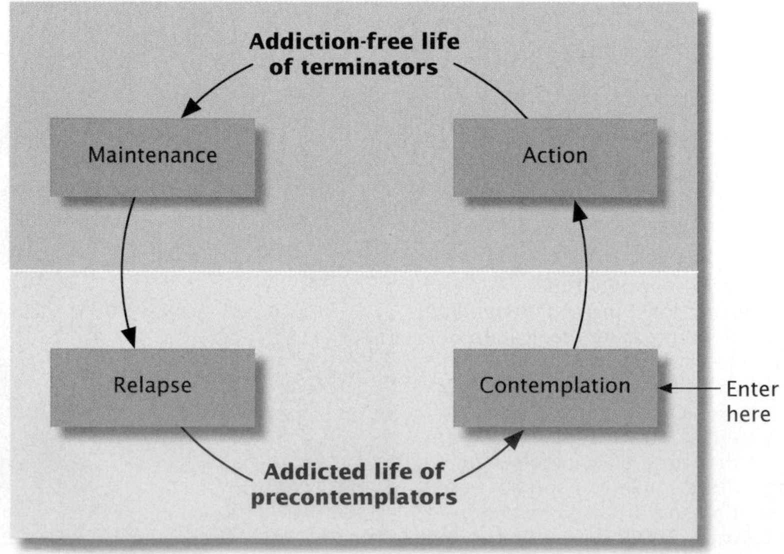

figure 13.5

Stages of Readiness to Change Health Behaviours

Many health psychologists are guided by Prochaska's theory that readiness to change health behaviours progresses through predictable stages. To help people quit smoking, for example, they use persuasive communications during the contemplation stage and relapse prevention techniques during the action stage (Witkiewitz & Marlatt, 2004). Tailoring interventions to each individual's history of progress through the stages of readiness may increase the likelihood of permanent changes in behaviour.

Source: Prochaska, DiClemente, & Norcross (1992).

2. *Contemplation.* The person is aware of a health-related behaviour that should be changed and is seriously thinking about changing it. People often get stuck here. Smokers, for example, have been known to spend years "thinking about" quitting.

3. *Preparation.* The person has a strong intention to change; has specific plans to do so; and may already have taken preliminary steps, such as cutting down on smoking.

4. *Action.* The person at this stage is engaging successfully in behaviour change. Because "backsliding," or relapse, is so common when trying to change health-related behaviours, people must remain successful for up to six months before they officially reach the final stage.

5. *Maintenance.* The person uses skills learned along the way to continue the healthy behaviour and to prevent relapse.

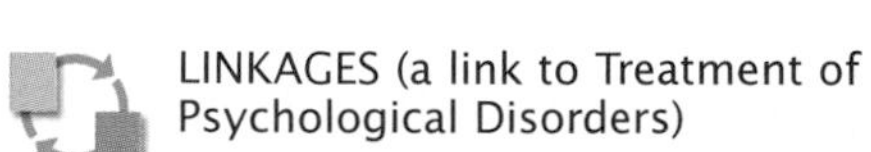
LINKAGES (a link to Treatment of Psychological Disorders)

The path from precontemplation through maintenance may not be a smooth one (Prochaska, 1994). Usually, people relapse and repeat one or more of the previous stages before finally achieving stability in the healthy behaviour they desire (Polivy & Herman, 2002; see Figure 13.5). For example, smokers typically require three to four cycles through the stages and up to seven years before they finally reach the maintenance stage.

What helps people to move from one stage to the next? Prochaska and his colleagues found that the factors facilitating progress at one stage may be different from the most important factors at another stage. However, *decisional balance*—the outcome of weighing the pros and cons of changing—is important for predicting progress at any stage (Prochaska et al., 1994). Incorporating these factors into intervention programs has helped people seek mammography on a regular basis (Rakowski et al., 1996), participate in exercise programs (Bock, Marcus, & Pinto, 2001; Courneya, 1995), eat healthy diets (Laforge, Greene, & Prochaska, 1994), quit smoking (Adelman et al., 2001), and engage in other healthy behaviours (Prochaska & DiClemente, 1992).

LINKAGES

As noted in the chapter on introducing psychology, all of psychology's many subfields are related to one another. Our discussion of post-traumatic stress disorder illustrates just one way in which the topic of this chapter, health, stress, and coping, is linked to the subfield of psychological disorders (which is the focus of the chapter by that name). The Linkages diagram shows ties to two other subfields as well, and there are many more ties throughout the book. Looking for linkages among subfields will help you see how they all fit together and help you better appreciate the big picture that is psychology.

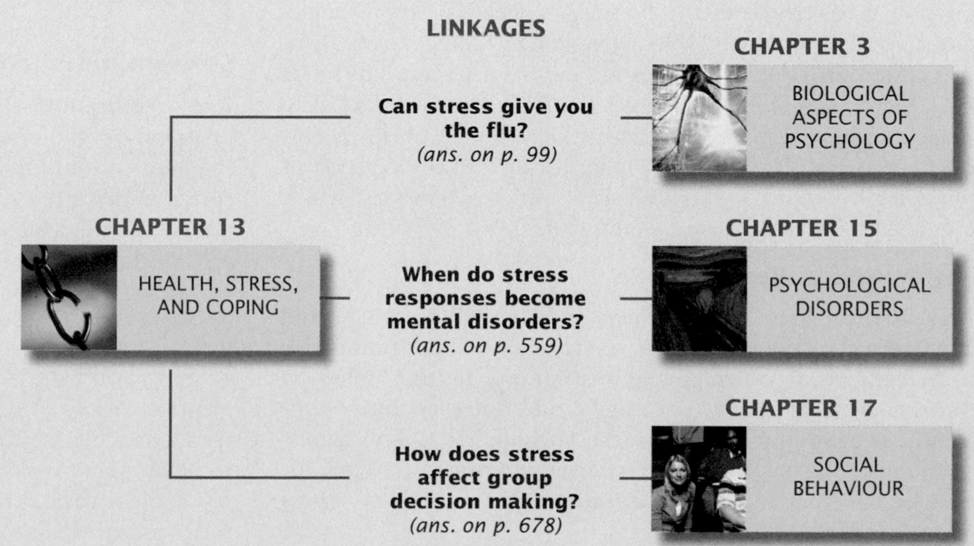
LINKAGES
CHAPTER 13
HEALTH, STRESS, AND COPING
Can stress give you the flu?
(ans. on p. 99)
CHAPTER 3
BIOLOGICAL ASPECTS OF PSYCHOLOGY
When do stress responses become mental disorders?
(ans. on p. 559)
CHAPTER 15
PSYCHOLOGICAL DISORDERS
How does stress affect group decision making?
(ans. on p. 678)
CHAPTER 17
SOCIAL BEHAVIOUR

SUMMARY

Health Psychology

The development of *health psychology* was prompted by recognition of the link between stress and illness, as well as the role of behaviours such as smoking, in elevating the risk of illness. Researchers in this field explore how psychological factors are related to physical disease and vice versa. Health psychologists also help people to behave in ways that prevent or minimize disease and promote health.

Stress and Stressors

The term *stress* refers in part to *stressors,* which are events and situations to which people must adjust. More generally, stress is viewed as an ongoing, interactive process that takes place as people adjust to and cope with their environment. Stressors may be physical or psychological.

Psychological Stressors

Psychological stressors include catastrophic events, life changes and strains, and daily hassles.

Measuring Stressors

Stressors can be measured by tests such as the Social Readjustment Rating Scale (SRRS) and the Life Experiences Survey (LES), as well as by surveys of daily hassles, but scores on such tests provide only a partial picture of the stress in an individual's life.

Stress Responses

Responses to stressors can be physical or psychological. They can occur alone or in combination, and the appearance of one response can stimulate others.

Physical Responses

Physical stress responses include changes in sympatho-adreno-medullary (SAM) activation, such as increases in heart rate, respiration, and many other processes, as well as hypothalamic-pituitary-adrenocortical (HPA) activation, including the release of corticosteroids. These responses are part of a pattern known as the *general adaptation syndrome,* or *GAS*. The GAS has three stages: alarm, resistance, and exhaustion. The GAS helps people resist stress, but if present too long, it can lead to depletion of physiological resources, as well as to physical illnesses, which Hans Selye called *diseases of adaptation.*

Psychological Responses

Psychological stress responses can be emotional, cognitive, and behavioural. Cognitive stress reactions include ruminative thinking; catastrophizing; and disruptions in the ability to think clearly, remember accurately, and solve problems efficiently. Behavioural stress responses include irritability, aggression, absenteeism, and even suicide attempts. Extreme or chronic stressors can lead to *burnout* or *post-traumatic stress disorder (PTSD).*

Stress Mediators: Interactions Between People and Stressors

The fact that different individuals react to the same stressors in different ways can be explained in part by stress mediators, such as the extent to which individuals can predict and control their stressors, how they interpret the threat involved, the social support they get, and their stress-coping skills.

How Stressors Are Perceived

Many stressors are not inherently stressful; their impact depends partly on how people perceive them. In particular, stressors appraised as threats are likely to have greater impact than those appraised as challenges.

Predictability and Control

Knowing that a particular stressor might occur but being uncertain whether it will occur tends to increase the stressor's impact, as does lack of control over stressors.

Coping Resources and Coping Methods

The people most likely to react strongly to a stressor are those whose coping resources and coping methods are inadequate.

Social Support

Social support, which consists of resources provided by other persons, can lessen the impact of stressors. The friends and social contacts on whom a person can depend for support constitute that person's *social support network.*

Stress, Personality, and Gender

Certain personality characteristics help insulate people from the ill effects of stress. One such characteristic appears to be dispositional optimism, the belief or expectation that things will work out positively. Gender can also play a role in stress responses.

The Physiology and Psychology of Health and Illness

Stress, Illness, and the Immune System

Psychoneuroimmunology is the field that examines the interaction of psychological and physiological processes that affect the body's ability to defend itself against disease. When a person is under stress, some of the hormones released from the adrenal gland, such as cortisol, reduce the effectiveness of the cells of the immune system (for example, T-cells, B-cells, natural killer cells, and macrophages) in combating foreign invaders such as viruses.

Stress, Illness, and the Cardiovascular System

Heart disease is a major cause of death in most Western countries, including the United States. People who are hostile appear to be at greater risk for heart disease than other people, possibly because their heightened reactivity to stressors can damage their cardiovascular system.

Risking Your Life: Health-Endangering Behaviours

Many of the major health problems in Western cultures are related to preventable behaviours such as smoking and drinking alcohol to excess. Having unsafe sex is a major risk factor for contracting HIV infection.

Promoting Healthy Behaviour

The process of altering or eliminating health-risky behaviours and fostering healthy behaviour patterns is called *health promotion.*

Health Beliefs and Health Behaviours

People's health-related behaviours are partly guided by their beliefs about health risks and what they can do about them.

Changing Health Behaviours: Stages of Readiness

The process of changing health-related behaviours may involve several stages, including precontemplation, contemplation, preparation, action, and maintenance. Understanding which stages people are in and helping them move through these stages are important tasks in health psychology.

14 Personality

Some people stay calm in a traffic jam. Others become so fearful and cautious that they worsen the congestion. Still others get so impatient that they can cause an accident. How people handle frustration is just one aspect of their personalities. In this chapter, we examine the concept of personality, review some of the tests that psychologists have developed to measure it, and look at how personality theories and research are being applied in everyday life. Here's how we have organized the material:

It has been estimated that North American businesses lose hundreds of billions of dollars each year as a result of employee theft (Gatewood & Feild, 2001). Millions more are spent on security and surveillance designed to curb these losses, but it would be far better if companies could simply avoid hiring dishonest employees in the first place. Some firms have tried to screen out potential thieves by requiring prospective employees to take "lie detector" polygraph tests. As described in the chapter on motivation and emotion, however, these tests may not be reliable or valid. In fact, the United States federal government has banned their use in most kinds of employee selection.

Thousands of companies have turned instead to paper-and-pencil "integrity" tests designed to identify job applicants who are likely to steal or behave in other dishonest or irresponsible ways (Wanek, Sackett, & Ones, 2003). Some of these tests simply ask applicants if they have stolen from previous employers and if they might steal in the future. Such questions can screen out people who are honest about their stealing, but most people who steal would probably also lie to conceal previous crimes or criminal intentions. Accordingly, some companies now use tests to assess applicants' general psychological characteristics and compare their scores with those of current or past employees. Applicants whose characteristics are most like the company's honest employees are hired; those who appear similar to dishonest employees are not hired.

Can undesirable employee behaviours be predicted on the basis of such tests? To some extent, they can (Ones, Viswesvaran, & Schmidt, 2003). For example, scores on the *Reliability Scale*—which includes questions about impulsivity and disruptive behaviour during school years—are significantly correlated with a broad range of undesirable activities in the workplace (Hogan & Ones, 1997). But psychological tests are far from perfect predictors of those activities (Mumford et al., 2001). Although better than polygraph tests, psychological tests still fail to detect dishonesty in some people, or worse, they may falsely identify some honest people as potential thieves. The best that companies can hope for is to find tests that will help reduce the overall likelihood of hiring dishonest people.

The use of psychological tests to help select honest employees is a more formal version of the process that most of us use when we meet someone new. We observe the person's behaviour, form impressions, and draw conclusions—often within just a few seconds (Borkenau et al., 2004)—about how that person will act at other times or under other circumstances. Like the employer, we are looking for clues to personality. Although there is no universally accepted definition, psychologists generally view **personality** as the unique pattern of enduring thoughts, feelings, and actions that characterizes a person (Hergenhahn, Olson, & Cramer, 2003). Personality research, in turn, focuses on understanding the origins or causes of the similarities and differences among people in their patterns of thinking, emotion, and behaviour.

With such a large agenda, personality researchers must incorporate information from many other areas of psychology. In fact, personality psychology lies at the crossroads of all psychological research (Funder, 2001a). It is the merging, in a particular individual, of all the psychological, behavioural, and biological processes discussed in this book. To gain a full understanding of anyone's personality, for example, you must know something about that person's developmental experiences (including cultural influences), genetic and other biological characteristics, perceptual and other information-processing habits and biases, typical patterns of emotional expression, and social skills. Psychologists also want to know about personality in general, such as how it develops and changes across the life span, why some people are usually optimistic whereas others are usually pessimistic, and how consistent or inconsistent people's behaviour tends to be from one situation to the next.

In this chapter we describe four approaches to the study of personality and some of the ways in which personality theory and research are being applied. We

personality The pattern of psychological and behavioural characteristics by which each person can be compared and contrasted with others.

begin by presenting the *psychodynamic approach,* developed by Sigmund Freud and later modified by a number of people he influenced. Next, we describe the *trait approach,* which focuses on the consistent patterns of thoughts, feelings, and actions that form individual personalities. Then we present the *social-cognitive approach,* which explores the roles of learning and cognition in shaping human behaviour. Finally, we consider the *humanistic approach,* with its emphasis on personality as a reflection of personal growth and the search for meaning in life. After reviewing these approaches, we describe how psychologists measure and compare people's personalities. We also give some examples of how psychological tests are being used in personality research and in other ways as well.

The Psychodynamic Approach

Some people think they can understand personality simply by watching people. Someone with an "obnoxious personality," for example, shows it by acting obnoxiously. But is that all there is to personality? Not according to Sigmund Freud, who described personality as being like an iceberg, whose tip is clearly visible but whose bulk is hidden under water.

Trained as a medical doctor in the late 1800s, Freud spent most of his life in Vienna, Austria, treating patients who displayed "neurotic" disorders, such as blindness or paralysis, for which there was no physical cause. Freud's experience with these patients, as well as his reading of the works of Charles Darwin and other scientists of his day, led him to believe that our personalities, behaviour, and behaviour disorders are determined mainly by basic drives and past psychological events (Schultz & Schultz, 2001). He agreed, too, with Sir Francis Galton and other nineteenth-century writers when he proposed that people may not know why they feel, think, or act the way they do, because these activities are partly controlled by the unconscious part of the personality—the part of which we are not normally aware (Funder, 2001b). From these ideas Freud created the **psychodynamic approach** to personality that assumes that our thoughts, feelings, and behaviour are determined by the interaction of various unconscious psychological processes.

Founder of the Psychodynamic Approach Here is Sigmund Freud with his daughter, Anna, who developed her own version of her father's psychodynamic theories of personality.

figure 14.1

Freud's Conception of the Personality Structure

According to Freud, some parts of the personality are conscious, whereas others are unconscious. Between these levels is the *preconscious,* which Freud saw as the location of memories and other material not usually in awareness but that can be brought into consciousness with little or no effort.

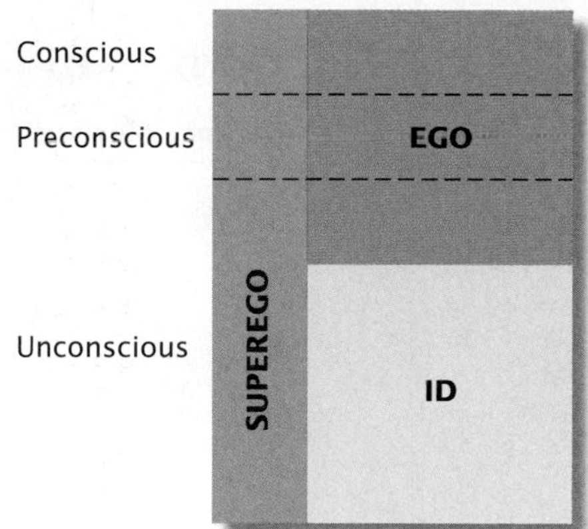

The Structure and Development of Personality

Freud believed that people have certain basic impulses or urges—related not only to food, water, and air but also to sex and aggression. In most translations of his writings, the term *instinct* is used to describe these impulses and urges, although Freud did not believe that they are all inborn and unchangeable, as the word *instinct* might imply (Schultz & Schultz, 2001). He did believe, however, that our desires for love, knowledge, security, and the like arise from these more basic impulses. He said that each of us faces the task of figuring out how to satisfy basic urges. Our personality develops, he claimed, as we struggle with that task, and it is reflected in the ways we go about satisfying a range of urges.

Id, Ego, and Superego As shown in Figure 14.1, Freud described the structure of personality as having three major components: the id, the ego, and the superego (Allen, 2003). He saw the **id** as the unconscious portion of personality, in which two kinds of "instincts" reside. There are life instincts, which he called *Eros.* They promote positive, constructive behaviour and reflect a source of energy (sometimes called *psychic energy*) known as **libido.** There are also death instincts, or *Thanatos,* which Freud saw as responsible for aggression and destructiveness (Westen & Gabbard, 1999). The id operates on the **pleasure principle,** seeking immediate satisfaction of both kinds of instincts, regardless of society's rules or the rights or feelings of others. A hungry person who pushes to the front of the line at McDonald's would be satisfying an id-driven impulse.

Parents, teachers, and others soon begin to place more and more restrictions on children's expression of their id impulses. In the face of these restrictions, a second part of the personality—the **ego**—develops from the id. The ego tries to find ways to get what a person wants in the real world, as opposed to the fantasy world of the id. Operating on the **reality principle,** the ego makes compromises between the id's unreasoning demands for immediate satisfaction and the practical limits imposed by the social world. The ego would lead that hungry person at McDonald's to wait in line and think about what to order rather than risk punishment by pushing ahead.

As children learn about the rules and values of society, they tend to adopt them. This process of *internalizing* parental and cultural values produces the third component of personality. It is called the **superego,** and it tells us what we should and should not do. The superego becomes our moral guide, and it is just as relentless and unreasonable as the id in its demand to be obeyed. It would make the pushy person at McDonald's feel guilty for even thinking about violating society's rules.

Conflicts and Defences Freud described the inner clashes among the three personality components as *intrapsychic* or *psychodynamic conflicts.* He believed that each person's personality is shaped by the number, nature, and

psychodynamic approach Freud's view that personality is based on the interplay of unconscious mental processes.

id The unconscious portion of personality that contains basic impulses and urges.

libido The psychic energy contained in the id.

pleasure principle The id's operating principle that guides people toward whatever feels good.

ego The part of the personality that mediates conflicts between and among the demands of the id, the superego, and the real world.

reality principle The operating principle of the ego that creates compromises between the id's demands and those of the real world.

superego The component of personality that tells people what they should and should not do.

table 14.1

According to Freud, defence mechanisms deflect anxiety or guilt in the short run, but they sap energy. Further, using them to avoid dealing with the source of problems can make those problems worse in the long run. Try listing some incidents in which you or someone you know might have used each of the defences described here. What questions would a critical thinker ask to determine whether these behaviours were unconscious defence mechanisms or actions motivated by conscious intentions?

Ego Defence Mechanisms

Defence Mechanism	Description
Repression	Unconsciously pushing threatening memories, urges, or ideas from conscious awareness: A person may experience loss of memory after witnessing a traumatic event like an accident.
Rationalization	Attempting to make actions or mistakes seem reasonable: The reasons or excuses given (e.g., "I spank my children because it is good for them") sound rational, but they are not the real reasons for the behaviour.
Projection	Unconsciously attributing one's own unacceptable thoughts or impulses to another person: Instead of recognizing that "I hate him," a person may feel that "He hates me."
Reaction formation	Defending against unacceptable impulses by acting opposite to them: Sexual interest in a married co-worker might appear as strong dislike instead.
Sublimation	Converting unacceptable impulses into socially acceptable actions, and perhaps symbolically expressing them: Sexual or aggressive desires may appear as artistic creativity or devotion to athletic excellence.
Displacement	Deflecting an impulse from its original target to a less threatening one: Anger at one's boss might be expressed through hostility toward a clerk, a family member, or even a pet.
Denial	Simply discounting the existence of threatening impulses: A person may vehemently deny ever having had even the slightest degree of physical attraction to a person of the same sex.
Compensation	Striving to make up for unconscious impulses or fears: A business executive's extreme competitiveness might be aimed at compensating for unconscious feelings of inferiority.

outcome of these conflicts. Freud said that the ego's primary function is to prevent the anxiety or guilt we would feel if we became aware of our socially unacceptable id impulses or if we thought about violating the superego's rules (Engler, 2003). Sometimes, the ego motivates sensible actions, as when a parent asks for help in dealing with impulses to abuse a child. However, the ego may also use **defence mechanisms,** which are unconscious tactics that protect against anxiety and guilt by either preventing threatening material from surfacing or disguising it when it does (see Table 14.1).

defence mechanisms Psychological responses that help protect a person from anxiety and guilt.

psychosexual stages Periods of personality development in which, according to Freud, conflicts focus on particular issues.

oral stage The first of Freud's psychosexual stages, in which the mouth is the centre of pleasure and conflict.

Stages in Personality Development Freud proposed that personality develops during childhood in a series of **psychosexual stages.** Failure to resolve the problems and conflicts that appear at a given stage can leave a person *fixated*—that is, unconsciously preoccupied with the area of pleasure associated with that stage. Freud believed that the stage at which a person became fixated in childhood can be seen in adult personality characteristics.

In Freud's theory, a child's first year or so is called the **oral stage,** because the mouth—which the infant uses to eat and explore—is the centre of pleasure during

The Oral Stage According to Freud, personality develops in a series of psychosexual stages. At each stage, a different part of the body becomes the primary focus of pleasure. This baby would appear to be in the oral stage.

this period. Freud said fixation at the oral stage can stem from weaning that is too early or too late and can result in adult characteristics ranging from overeating or childlike dependence (late weaning) to the use of "biting" sarcasm (early weaning).

The **anal stage** occurs during the second year, as the demand for toilet training shifts the focus of pleasure and conflict to the anal area. According to Freud, toilet training that is too harsh or begins too early can produce a kind of anal fixation that appears in adulthood as stinginess or preoccupation with neatness (thus symbolically withholding feces). If toilet training is too late or too lax, however, the result could be another kind of anal fixation, which is reflected in adults who are disorganized or impulsive (symbolically expelling feces at will).

The most controversial stage in Freud's theory of personality development occurs between the ages of three and five, when the child's focus of pleasure is said to shift to the genitals. Because Freud emphasized male psychosexual development, he called this period the **phallic stage** (*phallus* is another word for *penis*). He believed that during this stage, a boy experiences sexual desire for his mother and a desire to eliminate, or even kill, his father, with whom the boy competes for the mother's affection. (Freud named this pattern of impulses the **Oedipus complex** because it echoes the plot of *Oedipus Rex,* the classical Greek play in which Oedipus, upon returning to his homeland, unknowingly slays his father and marries his mother.) The boy's fantasies make him fear that his powerful "rival" (his father) will castrate him. To reduce this fear, the boy's ego represses his incestuous desires and leads him to "identify" with his father and try to be like him. It is during this stage that the male's superego begins to develop.

According to Freud, a girl begins the phallic stage with a strong attachment to her mother. When she realizes that boys have penises and girls don't, though, she supposedly develops *penis envy* and transfers her love to her father. To avoid her mother's disapproval, the girl identifies with and imitates her, thus forming the basis for her own superego.

Freud believed that unresolved conflicts from the phallic stage can lead to many problems in adulthood, including difficulties in dealing with authority figures and an inability to maintain a stable love relationship.

As the phallic stage draws to a close and its conflicts are dealt with by the ego, a peaceful interval begins. During this **latency period,** which lasts through childhood, sexual impulses stay in the background as the youngster focuses on education, same-sex peer play, and the development of social skills. When sexual impulses reappear during adolescence, the genitals again become the focus of pleasure, marking the beginning of the **genital stage,** which Freud said lasts for the rest of a person's life.

anal stage The second of Freud's psycho-sexual stages, usually occurring during the second year of life, in which the focus of pleasure and conflict shifts from the mouth to the anus.

phallic stage The third of Freud's psycho-sexual stages, in which the focus of pleasure and conflict shifts to the genital area.

Oedipus complex A pattern described by Freud in which a child has sexual desire for his or her opposite sex parent and wants to eliminate his or her same sex parent's competition for attention.

latency period The fourth of Freud's psychosexual stages, in which sexual impulses lie dormant.

genital stage The last of Freud's psycho-sexual stages, which begins during adolescence, when sexual impulses appear at the conscious level.

Variations on Freud's Personality Theory

Freud's ideas—especially those involving the Oedipus complex and the role of infantile sexuality—were, and still are, controversial. Even many of Freud's followers did not entirely agree with him. Some of these dissenters have been called *neo-Freudian* theorists, because they maintained many of the basic ideas in Freud's theory but developed their own approaches. Others are known as *ego psychologists,* because their ideas focused more on the ego than on the id (Larsen & Buss, 2005).

Jung's Analytic Psychology Carl Jung (pronounced "yoong") was the most prominent dissenter among Freud's early followers. Jung (1916) emphasized that libido is not just sexual instinct but rather a more general life force that includes an innate drive for creativity, for growth-oriented resolution of conflicts, and for the productive blending of basic impulses with real-world demands. Jung did not identify specific stages in personality development. He suggested instead that people gradually develop differing degrees of *introversion* (a tendency to reflect on one's own experiences) or *extraversion* (a tendency to focus on the social world), along with differing tendencies to rely on specific psychological functions, such as thinking versus feeling. Combinations of these differing tendencies, said Jung (1933), creates personalities that display distinctive and predictable patterns of behaviour.

Jung also claimed there is a *collective unconscious* that contains the memories we have inherited from our human and nonhuman ancestors (Carver & Scheier, 2004). According to Jung, we are not consciously aware of these memories, but they are responsible for our innate tendencies to react in particular ways to certain things. For example, Jung believed that our collective memory of mothers influences how each of us perceives our own mother. Canadians readily identify with the struggles of others in their part of the country to cope with intense cold, whether it is the routinely frigid temperatures of a Prairie winter, the 1998 ice storm in Montreal, or the massive snowstorm in Toronto in 2001. Although the notion of a collective unconscious is widely accepted by followers of Jung, there is no empirical evidence that it exists. In fact, Jung himself acknowledged that it would be impossible to objectively demonstrate the existence of a collective unconscious (Hergenhahn et al., 2003).

Other Neo-Freudian Theorists Jung was not the first or the only theorist to challenge Freud. Alfred Adler, once a loyal follower of Freudian theory, came to believe that the power behind the development of personality comes not from the id but from an innate desire to overcome infantile feelings of helplessness and to gain some control over the environment. Adler (1927–1963) referred to this process as striving for superiority, by which he meant a drive for fulfillment as a person, not just a desire to do better than others. Terry Fox symbolizes for many Canadians the opportunity to rise above considerable challenge (such as losing a leg to cancer) and still manage to run halfway across Canada, one of the widest countries in the world.

An Early Feminist After completing medical school at the University of Berlin in 1913, Karen Horney (1885–1952) trained as a Freudian psychoanalyst. She accepted some aspects of Freud's psychoanalytic views, including the idea of unconscious motivation, but she eventually developed her own neo-Freudian theory. She saw the need for security as more important than biological instincts in motivating infants' behaviour. She also rejected Freud's notion that the psychological development of females is influenced by penis envy.

The first feminist personality theorist, Karen Horney (pronounced "HORN-eye"), disputed Freud's view that women's lack of a penis causes them to envy men and feel inferior to them. Horney (1937) argued that, in fact, it is men who envy women: Realizing that they cannot bear children and that they often play only a small role in raising them, males see their lives as having less meaning or substance than women's. Horney called this condition *womb envy.* She argued further that when women feel inferior, it is because of the personal and political restrictions that men have placed upon them, not because of penis envy. Horney's position on this issue reflected her strong belief that cultural factors, rather than instincts, play a major role in personality development (Hergenhahn et al., 2003). This greater emphasis on cultural influences is one of the major theoretical differences between Freud and the neo-Freudians generally.

Contemporary Psychodynamic Theories

Some of the most influential psychodynamic approaches to personality now focus on *object relations*—that is, on how people's perceptions of themselves and others influence their view of, and reactions to, the world (Cristobal, 2003). According to early object relations theorists, the first relationships between infants and their love objects, usually the mother and other primary caregivers, are vitally important in the development of personality. In their view, these relationships shape a person's thoughts and feelings about social relationships later in life.

Today, object relations theory finds its clearest expression in research on the kinds of relationships, or *attachments,* that infants form with their primary caregivers. As University of Saskatchewan's Margaret McKim explains, the infant forms a secure early bond to the mother or some other caregiver, tolerates gradual separation from the object of attachment, and eventually develops the ability to relate to others as an independent, secure individual (Ainsworth, 1989; Bowlby, 1973). As described in the chapter on human development, however, some infants do not develop this *secure attachment*. Instead, they may display various kinds of *insecure attachments*. There is indeed evidence that the nature of early child-parent attachments is associated with differences in self-image, identity, security, and social relationships in adolescence, adulthood, and even old age (Consedine & Magai, 2003; Mattanah, Hancock, & Brand, 2004; Simpson & Rholes, 2000). In one study, women who had secure attachments to their parents in childhood were more likely to have happy marriages than women whose childhood attachments had been insecure (Klohnen & Bera, 1998). Another study found that people who tended to shy away from social situations in childhood were less supportive and comforting when they encountered a person in distress (Westmaas & Silver, 2001). A third study found that children, who because of abuse, neglect, or rejection, miss the opportunity to become securely attached to their mothers or other adults may suffer severe disturbances in their later relationships (Aizawa, 2002).

Evaluation of the Psychodynamic Approach

As with the other views we will consider, any overall evaluation of Freud and his theories must include both positive and negative features. There is no doubt that his views have influenced modern Western thinking about medicine, literature, religion, sociology, and anthropology, or that his contributions to the field of psychology have been considerable. That we hold stock in our dreams, that we believe early childhood experiences matter in later personality characteristics, that we believe talking about our problems can alleviate them, that we believe there is meaning behind those often embarrassing slips of the tongue can all be credited to Sigmund Freud. In fact, Freud's personality theory is probably the most comprehensive and influential psychological theory ever proposed. His ideas have also shaped a wide range of psychotherapy techniques and stimulated the development of several personality assessments, including the projective tests described later in this chapter. Further, contemporary theories and research have provided some limited support for certain aspects of Freud's theory. For example, psychologists have found that people do employ several of the defence mechanisms Freud described (Paulhus, Fridhandler, & Hayes, 1997), although it is unclear whether these always operate at an unconscious level. As mentioned in the chapter on consciousness, there is also evidence that people's thoughts and actions can be influenced by events and experiences that people do not recall (Andersen & Miranda, 2000; Andersen & Chen, 2002; Bargh & Ferguson, 2000) and perhaps by emotions they do not experience (Winkielman & Berridge, 2004). And some researchers believe that unconscious processes can affect people's health (Arndt et al., 2000).

However, Freud's psychodynamic theories have several weaknesses. For one thing, they are based almost entirely on case studies of a few individuals. As discussed in the chapter on research in psychology, conclusions drawn from case studies may not apply to people in general. Nor was Freud's sample representative of people in general. Most of his patients were upper-class Viennese women who not only had psychological problems but also were raised in a culture in which discussion of sex was considered to be uncivilized. Moreover, Freud's thinking about personality reflected Western European and North American values, which may or may not be helpful in understanding people in other cultures (Hergenhahn et al., 2003). For example, the concepts of ego and self that are so central to Freud's personality theory (and those of his followers) are based on the self-oriented values of individualist cultures. These values may be less central to personality development in the more collectivist cultures of, say, Asia and South America (Matsumoto, 2000).

Freud's focus on male psychosexual development and his notion that females envy male anatomy have also caused both female and male feminists to reject some or all of his ideas. In the tradition of Horney, some contemporary female neo-Freudians have proposed theories that focus specifically on the psychosexual development of women (Sayers, 1991).

Finally, as judged by today's standards, Freud's theory is not very scientific. His definitions of id, ego, unconscious conflict, and other concepts lack the precision required for scientific measurement and testing (Hergenhahn et al., 2003). His belief that human beings are driven mainly by unconscious desires ignores evidence that much human behaviour goes beyond impulse gratification. The conscious drive to reach personal, social, and spiritual goals is also an important determinant of behaviour, as is learning from others.

Some of the weaknesses in Freudian theory have been addressed by those who have altered some of Freud's concepts and devoted more attention to social influences on personality. Attempts have also been made to increase precision and objectivity in the measurement of psychodynamic concepts (e.g., Barber, Crits-Christoph, & Paul, 1993). Research on concepts from psychodynamic theory is, in fact, becoming more sophisticated and increasingly reflects interest in subjecting psychodynamic principles to experimental tests (e.g., Wegner, Wenzlaff, & Kozak, 2004). Still, the psychodynamic approach is better known for generating hypotheses about personality than for scientifically testing them. Accordingly, this approach to personality is now much less influential in mainstream psychology than it was in the past (Mischel, 2002; Robins, Gosling, & Craik, 2000).

The Trait Approach

If you were to describe the personality of someone you know, it would probably take the form of a small number of descriptive statements. Here is an example:

> *She is a truly caring person, a real extravert. She is generous with her time, and very conscientious about everything she does. Yet sometimes I think she is not very assertive or confident. She is submissive to other people's demands because she wants to be accepted by them.*

In other words, most people describe others by referring to the kind of people they are ("extravert," "conscientious"); to the thoughts, feelings, and actions that are most typical of them ("caring," "not very assertive," "generous"); or to their needs ("wants to be accepted"). Together, these statements describe personality *traits*—the inclinations or tendencies that help to direct how a person usually thinks and behaves (Carver & Scheier, 2004; Pervin & John, 2001).

The **trait approach** to personality makes three basic assumptions:

1. Personality traits are relatively stable and therefore predictable over time. So a gentle person tends to stay that way day after day, year after year (Costa & McCrae, 2002).
2. Personality traits are relatively stable across situations, and they can explain why people act in predictable ways in many different situations. A person who is competitive at work will probably also be competitive on the tennis court or at a party. We will see later how this assumption has not gone unchallenged.
3. People differ in how much of a particular personality trait they possess; no two people are exactly alike on all traits. The result is an endless variety of unique human personalities.

trait approach A perspective in which personality is seen as a combination of characteristics that people display over time and across situations.

Traits versus Types Theories about enduring differences in people's personality characteristics go back at least as far as Hippocrates, a physician of ancient Greece. He suggested that a certain temperament, or basic behavioural tendency, is associated with each of four bodily fluids, or humours: blood, phlegm, black bile, and yellow bile. Personality, said Hippocrates, depends on how much of each humour a person has. His terms for the four humour-based personalities—sanguine (optimistic), phlegmatic (slow, lethargic), melancholic (sad, depressive), and choleric (angry, irritable)—survive today.

Notice that Hippocrates was describing personality *types,* not traits. Traits involve *quantitative* differences among people—such as how much of a certain characteristic they possess. Types involve *qualitative* differences, such as whether someone possesses a certain characteristic at all. When people are "typed," they are said to belong to one class or another—such as male or female. Modern type theories of personality try to do the same by placing people in one category or another (Funder, 2001b). For example, Avshalom Caspi and his colleagues claim to have identified three qualitatively different basic personality types (Caspi, 1998; Robins, John, & Caspi, 1998). These include the *well-adjusted person,* who is flexible, resourceful, and successful with other people; the *maladjusted overcontrolling person,* who is too self-controlled to enjoy life and is difficult for others to deal with; and the *maladjusted undercontrolling person,* whose excessive impulsiveness can be dangerous both for the person and for others. (This chapter's Focus on Research Methods section contains more information on these and other types.)

Type theories have recently gained acceptance among some personality researchers, but the majority still doubt that it's possible to compress the dazzling range of human characteristics into just a few discrete types. Accordingly, the trait approach to personality remains much more influential. Trait theorists are interested in measuring the relative strength of the many personality characteristics that they believe are present in everyone (see Figure 14.2).

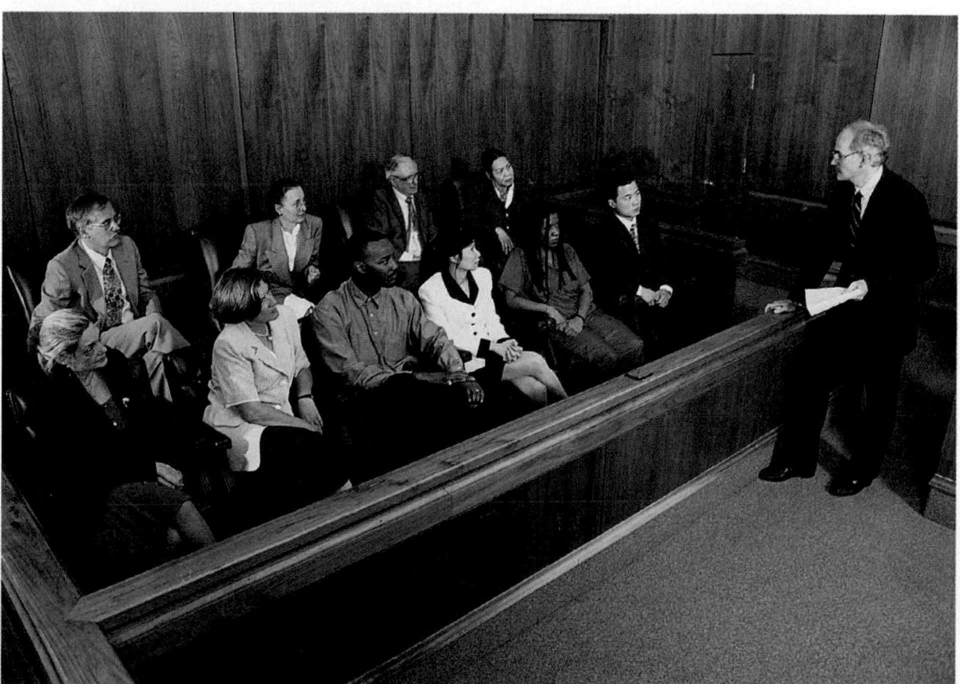

Selecting a Jury Some psychologists employ type and trait theories of personality in advising prosecution or defence attorneys about which potential jurors are most likely to be sympathetic to their side of a court case.

figure 14.2

Two Personality Profiles

Trait theory describes personality in terms of the strength of particular dimensions, or traits. Here are trait profiles for Rodney, an inner-city social worker, and James, a sales clerk. Compared with James, Rodney is about equally industrious; more generous; and less nervous, extraverted, and aggressive. Just for fun, mark this figure to indicate how strong you think you are on each of the listed traits. Trait theorists suggest that this should be easy for you to do because, they say, virtually everyone displays a certain amount of almost any personality characteristic.

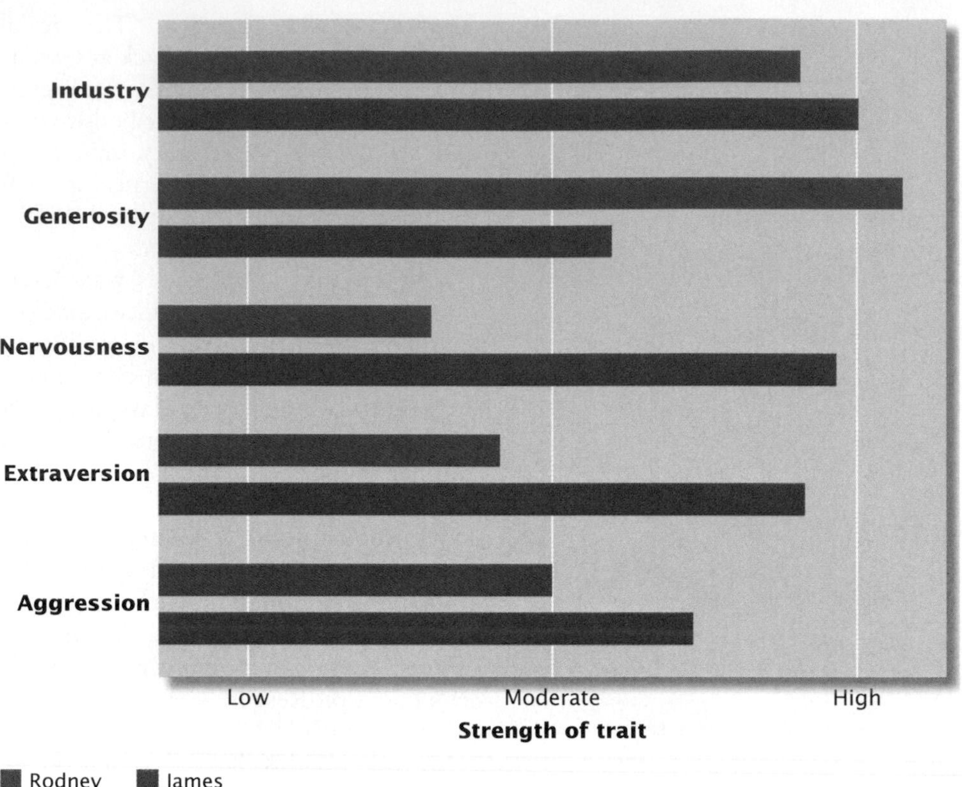

Allport's Trait Theory

Gordon Allport spent 30 years searching for the traits that combine to form personality (1961). He had found nearly 18 000 dictionary terms that can be used to describe human behaviour (Allport & Odbert, 1936), but he noticed that many of these terms referred to the same thing (e.g., *hostile, nasty,* and *mean* all convey a similar meaning). So if you were to jot down the personality traits that describe a close friend or relative, you would probably be able to capture that individual's personality using only about seven trait labels. Allport believed that the set of labels chosen to describe a particular person reflects that person's *central traits*—those that are usually obvious to others and that organize and control behaviour in many different situations. Central traits are roughly equivalent to the descriptive terms used in letters of recommendation (*reliable* or *distractible*, for example) that are meant to convey what can be expected from a person most of the time (Schultz & Schultz, 2001). Allport also believed that people possess *secondary traits*—those that are more specific to certain situations and control far less behaviour. "Dislikes crowds" is an example of a secondary trait.

Allport's research helped to lay the foundation for modern research on personality traits. However, his emphasis on the uniqueness of each individual personality made it difficult to draw conclusions about the structure of human personality in general (McAdams, 1997).

The Big-Five Model of Personality

In recent years, trait approaches have continued to focus on identifying and describing the core structure of personality. This work owes much to Allport and also to a British psychologist named Raymond Cattell. Cattell asked people to rate

table 14.2

Here is a list of the adjectives that define the big-five personality factors. You can more easily remember the names of these factors by noting that their first letters spell the word *ocean* or *canoe.*

The Big-Five Personality Dimensions

Dimension	Defining Descriptors
Openness to experience	Artistic, curious, imaginative, insightful, original, wide interests, unusual thought processes, intellectual interests
Conscientiousness	Efficient, organized, planful, reliable, thorough, dependable, ethical, productive
Extraversion	Active, assertive, energetic, outgoing, talkative, gesturally expressive, gregarious
Agreeableness	Appreciative, forgiving, generous, kind, trusting, uncritical, warm, compassionate, considerate, straightforward
Neuroticism	Anxious, self-pitying, tense, emotionally unstable, impulsive, vulnerable, touchy, worrying

Source: Adapted from McCrae & John (1992).

themselves and others on many of the trait-descriptive terms that Allport had identified. He then used a mathematical technique called *factor analysis* to study which of these terms were related to one another. Factor analysis can reveal, for example, whether someone who is moody is also likely to be anxious, rigid, and unsociable. Cattell believed that the sets of traits clustering together in this analysis would reflect a set of basic personality *factors* or dimensions. His analyses eventually identified 16 such factors, including shy versus bold, trusting versus suspicious, and relaxed versus tense. Cattell believed that these factors are found in everyone, and he measured their strength using a test called the *Sixteen Personality Factor Questionnaire,* or *16PF* (Cattell, Eber, & Tatsuoka, 1970).

More recent factor analyses by researchers such as Paul Costa and Robert McCrae have led many trait theorists to believe that personality is organized around only five basic factors (McCrae & Costa, 2004). The components of this so-called **big-five model,** or five-factor model, of personality are *openness to experience, conscientiousness, extraversion, agreeableness,* and *neuroticism* (see Table 14.2). The importance of the big-five model is suggested by the fact that different investigators, including Michael Ashton from Brock University, find these factors (or a set very similar to them) when they factor-analyze data from numerous sources, including personality inventories, peer ratings of personality characteristics, and checklists of descriptive adjectives (Ashton, Lee, & Goldberg, 2004; Costa & McCrae, 1995; John & Srivastava, 1999). The fact that some version of the big-five factors reliably appears in many countries and cultures—including Canada, China, the Czech Republic, Germany, Finland, India, Japan, Korea, the Philippines, Poland, and Turkey (Allik & McCrae, 2004; McCrae et al, 2004)—provides further evidence that these few dimensions may represent the basic components of human personality.

big-five model Five trait dimensions found in many factor-analytic studies of personality: neuroticism, extraversion, openness to experience, agreeableness, and conscientiousness.

Biological Trait Theories

Some personality theorists are interested not only in what traits form the core of human personality but also in why people differ on these traits. Their research suggests that trait differences reflect the operation of some important biological factors.

Animal Personalities The idea that personality can be described in terms of five main dimensions seems to hold for some animals as well as humans. The five animal dimensions vary from, but are still related to, human traits. For example, hyenas differ from one another in terms of dominance, excitability, agreeableness (toward people), sociability (toward each other), and curiosity. Some of these same traits have been observed in a wide variety of other species, including dogs, horses, and chimpanzees (Gosling, 2001; Gosling, Kwan, & John, 2003; Morris, Gale, & Duffy, 2002). Cat lovers often report such traits in their pets, too.

Eysenck's Biological Trait Theory Like Cattell, British psychologist Hans Eysenck (pronounced "EYE-sink") used factor analysis to study the structure of personality and thus helped lay the groundwork for the big-five model. Eysenck suggested that most people's traits could be described using two (and later three) main dimensions—*introversion-extraversion* and *emotionality-stability,* and later psychoticism (Eysenck 1990a, 1990b; see Figure 14.3):

1. ***Introversion-extraversion.*** Extraverts are sociable and outgoing, enjoy parties and other group activities, take risks, and love excitement and change. Introverts tend to be quiet, thoughtful, and reserved, enjoying solitary pursuits and avoiding excitement and social involvement.
2. ***Emotionality-stability.*** People at one extreme of the emotionality-stability dimension display such characteristics as moodiness, restlessness, worry, anxiety, and other negative emotions. Those at the opposite extreme are calm, even-tempered, relaxed, and emotionally stable. (This dimension is also often called *neuroticism.*)
3. ***Psychoticism.*** This dimension was added after 1985 when Eysenck found predictable and explainable leftovers after each factor analysis of his dataset of personality scores. Eysenck labelled it "psychoticism" and represents a "not-so-nice" dimension of personality. High scorers are cold, aloof, insensitive, and unempathic. Alternatively, low scorers are sensitive, warm, nurturing, and empathic.

Eysenck argued that the variations in personality characteristics that we see among individuals can be traced to inherited differences in their nervous systems, especially in their brains. These biological differences, he said, create variations in people's typical levels of physiological arousal and in their sensitivity to stress and other environmental stimulation. For example, as mentioned in the chapter on motivation and emotion, people who inherit a nervous system that normally operates below their optimum arousal level will always be on the lookout for excitement, change, and social contact in order to increase their arousal. As a result, these people will be *extraverted.* In contrast, people whose nervous system is normally "over-aroused" will tend to avoid excitement, change, and social contact in order to

figure 14.3

Eysenck's Main Personality Dimensions

According to Eysenck, varying degrees of emotionality-stability and introversion-extraversion combine to produce predictable trait patterns. Notice that an introverted but stable person is likely to be controlled and reliable, whereas an introverted emotional person is likely to be rigid and anxious. (The traits appearing in the quadrants created by crossing these two personality dimensions correspond roughly to Hippocrates' four temperaments.) Eysenck also identified a less influential third dimension, called *psychoticism*. People who score high on psychoticism show such traits as cruelty, hostility, coldness, oddness, and rejection of social customs.

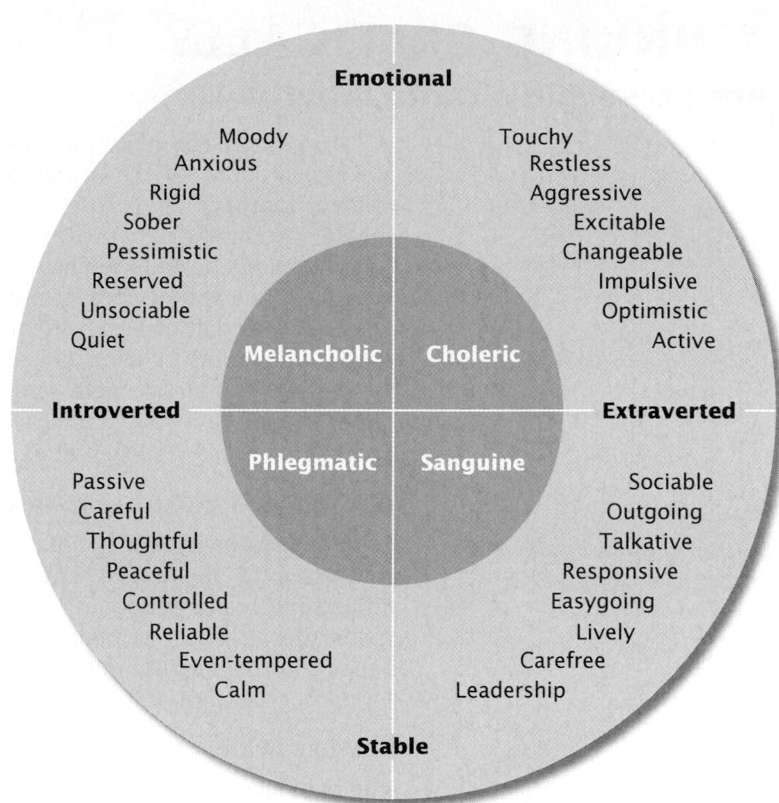

reduce arousal to their optimum level. In short, they will be *introverted*. What about the emotionality-stability dimension? Eysenck said that people who score toward the stability side have nervous systems that are relatively insensitive to stress; those who are more emotional have nervous systems that react more strongly to stress.

Gray's Approach-Inhibition Theory Jeffrey Gray, another British psychologist, agrees with Eysenck about the two basic dimensions of personality, but he offers a different explanation of the biological factors underlying them (Gray, 1991). According to Gray, differences among people in introversion-extraversion and emotionality-stability stem from two related systems in the brain: the behavioural approach system and the behavioural inhibition system. The *behavioural approach system,* or *BAS,* is made up of brain regions that affect people's sensitivity to rewards and their motivation to seek those rewards (Pickering & Gray, 1999). The BAS has been called a "go" system, because it is responsible for how impulsive or uninhibited a person is. The *behavioural inhibition system,* or *BIS,* involves brain regions that affect sensitivity to potential punishment and the motivation to avoid being punished. The BIS is a "stop" system that is responsible for how fearful or inhibited a person is. People with an active behavioural approach system tend to experience positive emotions; people with an active behavioural inhibition system are more likely to experience negative ones (Zelenski & Larsen, 1999).

In explaining Eysenck's personality dimensions, Gray sees extraverts as having a sensitive reward system (BAS) and an insensitive punishment system (BIS). Introverts are just the opposite—they are relatively insensitive to rewards but highly sensitive to punishment. Similarly, emotionally unstable people are much more sensitive to both rewards and punishments than are those who are emotionally stable.

Gray's theory has its critics (e.g., Corr, 2002), but it is now more widely accepted than Eysenck's theory—primarily because it is being supported by other research (e.g., Canli et al., 2001) and because it is more consistent with what neuroscientists know about brain structures, neurotransmitters, and how they operate (Avila, 2001; Larsen & Buss, 2002).

THINKING CRITICALLY

Are Personality Traits Inherited?

Gray's approach-inhibition theory is one of several new biologically oriented explanations of the origins of personality traits (e.g., Zuckerman, 2004). A related approach involves investigating the genetics of these traits. Think about the Rankin Family—a popular East Coast musical group made up of many musically gifted siblings. Could they have been born with these talents? Were they raised to have a unique appreciation of music? Consider also the case of identical twins who were separated at five weeks of age and did not meet again for 39 years. Both men drove Chevrolets, chain-smoked the same brand of cigarettes, had divorced women named Linda, were remarried to women named Betty, had sons named James Allan, had dogs named Toy, enjoyed similar hobbies, and had served as sheriff's deputies (Tellegen et al., 1988).

- **What am I being asked to believe or accept?**

Several personality researchers at the University of British Columbia (Jang, Livesley, & Vernon, 1996) have led the way to address these questions with key studies comparing twins' ratings on the Big-Five. Indeed, studies like these have helped focus the attention of behavioural geneticists on the possibility that some core aspects of personality might be partly, or even largely, inherited (Krueger, 2000; Johnson et al., 2004; Plomin, 2002).

- **What evidence is available to support the assertion?**

The evidence and the arguments regarding this assertion are much like those presented in the chapter on cognitive abilities, in which we discuss the origins of differences in intelligence. Stories about children who seem to "have" their parents' or grandparents' bad temper, generosity, or shyness are often presented in support of the heritability of personality. And in fact, family resemblances in personality do provide an important source of evidence. Several studies have found moderate but significant correlations between children's personality test scores and those of their parents and siblings (Davis, Luce, & Kraus, 1994; Loehlin, 1992).

Even stronger evidence comes from studies conducted around the world comparing identical twins raised together, identical twins raised apart, nonidentical twins raised together, and nonidentical twins raised apart (Grigorenko, 2002). Whether they are raised apart or together, identical twins (who have exactly the same genes) tend to be more alike in personality than nonidentical twins (whose genes are no more similar than those of other siblings). This research also shows that identical twins are more alike than nonidentical twins in general temperament, such as how active, sociable, anxious, and emotional they are (Pickering & Gray, 1999; Rowe, 1997). On the basis of such twin studies, behavioural geneticists have concluded that at least 30 percent, and perhaps as much as 60 percent, of the differences among people, in terms of their personality traits, are due to genetic factors (Borkenau et al., 2001; Wolf et al., 2004).

Family Resemblance Do children inherit personality traits in the same direct way as they may inherit facial features, colouration, and other physical characteristics? Research in behavioural genetics suggests that personality is the joint product of genetically influenced behavioural tendencies and the environmental conditions each child encounters.

- **Are there alternative ways of interpreting the evidence?**

Family personality resemblances could reflect genetic or social influence. An obvious alternative interpretation of this evidence, then, might be that family similarities come not from common genes but from a common environment, especially from the modelling that parents and siblings provide. Children learn many rules, skills, and behaviours by watching those around them; perhaps they learn their personalities as well (Funder, 2001b). The fact that siblings who aren't twins are less alike than twins may well result from what are called *nonshared environments* (Plomin & Caspi, 1999). A child's place in the family birth order, differences in the way parents treat each of their children, and accidents and illnesses that alter a particular child's life or health are examples of nonshared factors that can have a differential impact on each individual (Paulhus, Trapnell, & Chen, 1999). Nontwins are more likely than twins, especially identical twins, to be affected by nonshared environmental factors.

• What additional evidence would help to evaluate the alternatives?

One way to evaluate the degree to which personality is inherited would be to study people in infancy, before the environment has had a chance to exert its influence. If the environment were entirely responsible for personality, all newborns should be essentially alike. However, as discussed in the chapter on human development, they show immediate differences in *temperament*—varying markedly in activity, sensitivity to the environment, tendency to cry, and interest in new stimuli (Rothbart & Derryberry, 2002). These differences suggest biological and perhaps genetic influences.

To evaluate the relative contributions of nature and nurture beyond infancy, psychologists have examined the characteristics of adopted children. The argument for genetic influences on personality would be stronger if adopted children are more like their biological parents than their adoptive parents. If they are more like their adoptive families, a strong role for environmental factors in personality would be suggested. In actuality, adopted children's personalities tend to resemble the personalities of their biological parents and siblings more than those of the families in which they are raised (Plomin et al., 1998).

Despite this finding, further research is needed to determine more clearly what aspects of the environment are most important in shaping personality (Turkheimer & Waldron, 2000). So far, the evidence suggests that elements in the shared environment that affect all children in the family to varying degrees (socioeconomic status, for example) are probably not the main reason that identical twins show similar personalities. As mentioned earlier, however, nonshared environmental influences may be very important in personality development (Harris, 2000; Loehlin, Neiderhiser, & Reiss, 2003). In fact, some researchers believe that nonshared influences must be considered even when trying to explain the greater similarities between identical twins reared apart than among nontwin siblings reared together. Additional research on the role of nonshared factors in personality development and the ways in which these factors might affect twin and nontwin siblings' development differentially is obviously vital. It will also be important to investigate the ways in which the personalities of individual children might affect the nature of the environment in which they are raised (Krueger, Markon, & Bouchard, 2003; see also the behavioural genetics appendix).

• What conclusions are most reasonable?

Even those researchers, such as Robert Plomin, who support genetic theories of personality caution that we should not replace "simple-minded environmentalism" with the equally incorrect view that personality is almost completely biologically determined (Plomin & Crabbe, 2000). As with cognitive abilities, it is pointless to talk about heredity versus environment as causes of personality, because nature and nurture always intertwine to exert joint and simultaneous influences (Cacioppo et al., 2000; Caspi et al., 2002). For example, we know that genetic factors affect the environment in which people live (for example, their families) and how they react to their environment, but it also turns out that environmental factors can influence which of a person's genes are activated and how much those genes affect the person's behaviour (Cacioppo et al., 2000; Pickering & Gray, 1999).

With these findings in mind, we would be well advised to draw rather tentative conclusions about the sources of differences in people's personalities. The evidence available so far suggests that genetic influences do appear to contribute significantly to personality differences. However, it is important to understand the implications of this statement. No single gene is responsible for a specific personality trait (Plomin, 2002). The genetic contribution to personality most likely comes through genes' influence on people's nervous systems and on their general predispositions toward certain temperaments (Arbelle et al., 2003; Grigorenko, 2002). Temperamental factors—such as how active, emotional, and sociable a person is—combine with environmental factors, such as a person's interactions with other people, to produce specific features of personality (Caspi & Roberts, 1999). For example, children who inherit a tendency toward emotionality might play less with other children, withdraw from social interactions, and thereby fail to learn important social skills (Eisenberg, Fabes, & Murphy, 1995). These experiences and tendencies, in turn, might lead to the self-consciousness and shyness seen in introverted personalities.

Notice, though, that genetic predispositions toward particular personality characteristics may or may not appear in behaviour, depending on whether the environment supports or suppresses them. Changes in genetically influenced traits are not only possible but may actually be quite common as children grow (Cacioppo et al., 2000). So even though there is a strong genetic basis for shyness, many children learn to overcome this tendency and become rather outgoing (Rowe, 1997). In summary, it appears that rather than inheriting specific traits, people inherit the raw materials out of which personality is shaped by the world.

Evaluation of the Trait Approach

The trait approach, especially the big-five model, has gained such wide acceptance that it tends to dominate contemporary research in personality. Yet there are several problems and weaknesses associated with this approach.

For one thing, trait theories seem better at describing people than at understanding them. It is easy to say, for example, that Marilyn is nasty to others because she has a strong hostility trait; but other factors, such as the way people treat her, could also be responsible. In short, trait theories say a lot about how people behave, but they don't always explain why (Mischel, 2004). Trait theories also don't say much about how traits are related to the thoughts and feelings that precede, accompany, and follow behaviour. Do introverts and extraverts decide to act as they do, can they behave otherwise, and how do they feel about their actions and experiences (Cervone & Shoda, 1999)? Some personality psychologists are currently linking their research to that of cognitive psychologists in an effort to better understand how thoughts and emotions influence, and are influenced by, personality traits (e.g., Shoda & LeeTiernan, 2002). The trait approach has also been faulted for offering a short list of traits that provides, at best, a fixed and superficial description of personality but that fails to capture how traits combine to form a complex and dynamic individual (Block, 2001; Funder, 2001a). Also, some people have questioned whether there are exactly five core dimensions of personality and whether they are exactly the same in all cultures (Cross & Markus, 1999; Zuckerman, 1998). The University of Western Ontario's Sampo Paunonen suggests there may be as many as nine (not five) dimensions of personality. And even if the big-five model is correct and universal, its factors are not all-powerful, because situations also affect behaviour. For example, people high in extraversion are not always sociable. Whether they behave sociably depends, in part, on where they are and who else is present.

The Impact of Situations Like the rest of us, many public figures act very differently in different situations. When Peter C. Newman wrote *The Secret Mulroney Tapes: Unguarded Confessions of a Prime Minister*, he exposed a private side of Mulroney's personality that, previously, had only been seen by his friends and confidants. Mischel's theory of personality emphasizes that person-situation interaction are important in determining behaviour.

It wasn't long ago that psychologists questioned the very value of traits, given that we know that certain situations can overwhelm traits. For example, a hate-filled bigot will still rush to save a child of the "wrong" skin colour from an approaching vehicle. According to Walter Mischel, it's not that personality doesn't matter, but tends instead to interact with the situation to produce behaviour. Mischel refers to this perspective as an "if-then" theory, because he proposes that *if* people encounter a particular situation, *then* they will engage in the characteristic behaviours (what he calls *behavioural signatures*) they have learned to display in that situation (Mischel, Shoda, & Mendoza-Denton, 2002). In other words, Mischel argues that trait theorists underestimate the power of situations to alter behaviour and do not pay enough attention to relevant situational variables. In recent years, theorists have found a reconciliation with some widely accepted conclusions:

1. Personal dispositions (like traits) influence behaviour only in relevant situations. The trait of anxiousness, for example, may predict anxiety, but only in situations in which an anxious person feels threatened.

2. Personal dispositions can lead to behaviours that alter situations that, in turn, promote other behaviours. For example, a hostile child can trigger aggression in others and thus start a fight.
3. People choose to be in situations that are in tune with their personal dispositions. Introverts, for instance, are likely to choose quiet environments, whereas extraverts tend to seek out livelier, more social circumstances.
4. Personal dispositions are more important in some situations than in others. Under circumstances in which many different behaviours would all be appropriate—a picnic, for example—what people do may be predicted from their dispositions (extraverts will probably play games and socialize while introverts watch). However, in situations such as a funeral, in which fewer options are socially acceptable, personal dispositions will not differentiate one person from another; everyone is likely to be quiet and somber.

In fairness, early trait theorists, such as Allport, did implicitly acknowledge the importance of situations in influencing behaviour, but it is only recently that consideration of person-situation interactions has become an explicit part of trait-based approaches to personality. This change is largely the result of research conducted by psychologists who have taken a social-cognitive approach to personality, which we describe next.

The Social-Cognitive Approach

The **social-cognitive approach** to personality differs from the psychodynamic and trait approaches in two important ways. First, social-cognitive theorists look to *conscious* thoughts and emotions for clues to how people differ from one another and what guides their behaviour (Mischel, 2004). Second, the social-cognitive approach did not grow out of clinical cases or other descriptions of people's personalities. It was based instead on the principles of animal and human learning described in the chapter on learning. In fact, the founders of the social-cognitive approach were originally known as *social-learning theorists* because of their view that what we call *personality* consists mainly of the thoughts and actions we learn through observing and interacting with family and others in social situations (Bandura & Walters, 1963; Funder, 2001b).

Roots of the Social-Cognitive Approach

Elements of the social-cognitive approach can be traced back to the behaviourism of John B. Watson. As described in the chapter on introducing psychology, Watson (1925) used research on classical conditioning to support his claim that all human behaviour, from mental disorder to scientific skill, is determined by learning. B. F. Skinner broadened the behavioural approach by emphasizing the importance of operant conditioning in learning. Through what he called **functional analysis,** Skinner tried to understand behaviour in terms of the function it serves in obtaining rewards or avoiding punishment. For example, if observations show that a schoolboy's aggressive behaviour occurs mainly when a certain teacher is present, it may be that aggression is tolerated by that teacher, and might even be rewarded with special attention. Rather than describing personality traits, then, functional analysis summarizes what people find rewarding, what they are capable of doing, and what skills they lack.

The principles of classical and operant conditioning launched social-learning explanations of personality, but because they were focused on observable behaviour, they were of limited usefulness to researchers who wanted to explore the role of thoughts in guiding behaviour. As the social-learning approach evolved into the

social-cognitive approach An approach in which personality is seen as the patterns of thinking and behaviour that a person learns.

functional analysis Analyzing behaviour by studying what responses occur under what conditions of operant reward and punishment.

social-cognitive approach, it incorporated learning principles but also went beyond them.

Today, proponents of this very popular approach to personality seek to assess and understand how learned patterns of thoughts and feelings contribute to behaviour and how behaviour and its consequences alter cognitive activity, as well as future actions. In dealing with that aggressive schoolboy, for example, social-cognitive theorists would want to know not only what he has learned to do in certain situations (and how he learned it) but also what he thinks about himself, his teachers, his behaviour—and his expectations about each (Mischel & Shoda, 1999).

Prominent Social-Cognitive Theories

Julian Rotter, Albert Bandura, and Walter Mischel have presented the most influential social-cognitive personality theories.

Rotter's Expectancy Theory Julian Rotter (1982) argued that learning creates cognitions, known as *expectancies,* that guide behaviour. Specifically, he said that a person's decision to engage in a behaviour is determined by (1) what the person expects to happen following the behaviour and (2) the value the person places on the outcome. For example, people spend a lot of money on clothes to be worn at a job interview because (1) past learning leads them to expect that doing so will help get them the job, and (2) they place a high value on having the job. To Rotter, then, behaviour is determined not only by the kinds of consequences that Skinner called *positive reinforcers* but also by the expectation that a particular behaviour will result in those consequences (Mischel, Shoda, & Smith, 2004).

Rotter himself focused mainly on how expectations shape particular behaviours in particular situations, but several of the researchers he influenced also examined people's more general expectations about what controls life's rewards and punishments. Those researchers noticed that some people (*internals*) are inclined to expect events to be controlled by their own efforts. These individuals assume that what they achieve and the reinforcements they receive are due to efforts they make themselves. Others (*externals*) are more inclined to expect events to be determined by external forces over which they have no control. When externals succeed, they are likely to believe that the success was due to chance or luck.

Research on differences in generalized expectancies does show that they are correlated with differences in behaviour. For example, when threatened by a hurricane or other natural disaster, internals—in accordance with their belief that they can control what happens to them—are more likely than externals to buy bottled water and make other preparations (Sattler, Kaiser, & Hittner, 2000). When confronted with a personal problem, internals are more likely than externals to work to solve this problem. Externals are more likely to see it as being unsolvable (Gianakos, 2002). Internals also tend to work harder than externals at staying physically healthy. They are less likely to drink alcohol, or—if they do drink—less likely to drive while intoxicated (Cavaiola & Desordi, 2000). Among college students, internals tend to be better informed about the courses they take, including what they need to do to get a high grade. Perhaps as a result, students who are internals tend to get better grades than externals (Dollinger, 2000).

Bandura and Reciprocal Determinism In his social-cognitive theory, Albert Bandura (1999)—born and raised in Mundare, Alberta—sees personality as shaped by the ways in which thoughts, behaviour, and the environment interact and influence one another. He points out that whether people learn through direct experience with rewards and punishments or through the observational learning-processes described in the chapter on learning, their behaviour creates changes in their environment. Observing these changes, in turn, affects how they think, which then affects their behaviour, and so on in a constant web of mutual influence that Bandura calls *reciprocal determinism* (see Figure 14.4).

According to Bandura, an especially important cognitive element in this web of influence is perceived **self-efficacy**—the learned expectation of success. Bandura says that what we do, and what we try to do, is largely controlled by our perceptions or beliefs about our chances of success at a particular task or problem. The higher our perceived self-efficacy in relation to a particular situation or task, the greater our actual accomplishments in that situation or task (Zimmerman & Shunk, 2003). So going into a job interview with the belief that you have the skills necessary to be hired may lead to behaviours that help you get the job, or at least help you to deal with the impact of rejection.

Perceived self-efficacy about a specific behaviour can interact with a person's expectancies about the consequences of behaviour in general, thus helping to shape the person's psychological well-being (Maddux & Gosselin, 2003; see Figure 14.5). For example, if an unemployed person has low perceived self-efficacy about finding a job and also expects that nothing anyone does has much effect on the world, the result may be apathy. But if a person with low perceived self-efficacy also believes that other people are enjoying the benefits of their efforts, the result may be self-criticism and depression.

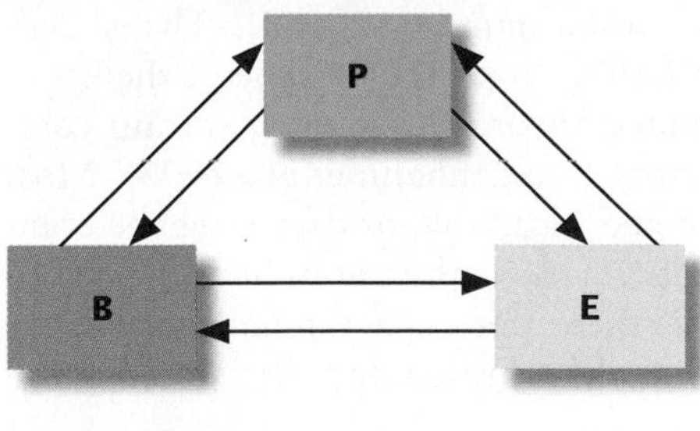

B = Behaviour

E = The external environment

P = Personal factors, such as thoughts, feelings, and biological events

figure 14.4

Reciprocal Determinism

Bandura's notion of reciprocal determinism suggests that personal factors (such as cognitions, or thoughts), behaviour, and the environment are constantly affecting one another. For example, a person's hostile thoughts may lead to hostile behaviour, which creates even more hostile thoughts. At the same time, the hostile behaviour offends other people, which creates a threatening environment that causes the person to think and act in even more negative ways. As increasingly negative thoughts alter the person's perceptions of the environment, that environment seems to be more threatening than ever.

Evaluation of the Social-Cognitive Approach

The original behavioural view of personality appealed to many people. It offered an objective, experimentally oriented approach that operationally defined its concepts, relied on empirical data for its basic principles, and based its applications on the results of empirical research (Pervin, 1996). However, its successor, the social-cognitive approach, has gained even wider acceptance because it blends theories from behavioural and cognitive psychology and applies them to such socially important areas as aggression, the effects of mass media on children, and the development of self-regulatory processes that enhance personal control over behaviour. The popularity of this approach also stems from the ease with which its principles can be translated into treatment procedures for many types of psychological disorders (O'Donohue, Fisher, & Hayes, 2003; see the chapter on treatment of psychological disorders).

Still, the social-cognitive approach has not escaped criticism. Psychodynamic theorists point out that social-cognitive theories leave no role for unconscious thoughts and feelings in determining behaviours (e.g., Westen, 1998). Some advocates of trait theory complain that social-cognitive theorists have focused more on explaining why traits are unimportant than on why situations are important and that they have failed to identify what it is about specific situations that bring out

figure 14.5

Self-Efficacy and Psychological Well-Being

According to Bandura, if people with high self-efficacy perceive the environment as unresponsive to their best efforts, they may become resentful and socially active protesters. If they perceive the environment as responsive to their efforts, they are more likely to be both active and self-assured.

self-efficacy According to Bandura, learned expectations about the probability of success in given situations.

certain behaviours (Friedman & Schustack, 2003; Funder, 2001a). The social-cognitive approach has also been faulted for failing to present a general theory of personality, offering instead a set of more limited theories that share certain common assumptions about the nature of personality (Hergenhahn et al., 2003). Most generally, the social-cognitive approach is deemed incapable of capturing the complexity, richness, and uniqueness that some critics see as inherent in human personality (Carver & Scheier, 2004). According to these critics, a far more attractive alternative is provided by the humanistic approach to personality.

The Humanistic Approach

Unlike theories that emphasize the instincts and learning processes that humans seem to share with other animals, the **humanistic approach** to personality focuses on mental capabilities that set humans apart: self-awareness, creativity, planning, decision making, and responsibility. Those who adopt the humanistic approach see human behaviour as motivated mainly by an innate drive toward growth that prompts people to fulfill their unique potential. And like the planted seed whose natural potential is to become a flower, people are seen as naturally inclined toward goodness, creativity, love, and joy. Humanistic psychologists also believe that to explain people's actions in any particular situation, it is more important to understand their view of the world than their instincts, traits, or learning experiences. To humanists, that world view is a bit different for each of us, and it is this unique *phenomenology,* or way of perceiving and interpreting the world, that shapes personality and guides behaviour (Kelly, 1980). From this perspective, then, no one can understand another person without somehow perceiving the world through that person's eyes. All behaviour, even seemingly weird behaviour, is presumed to be meaningful to the person displaying it. Because it emphasizes the importance of looking at people's perceptions, this approach is sometimes called the *phenomenological approach.*

What Is Reality? Each of these judges who provides ratings of Olympian figure skating pairs has a different perception of what he or she sees on the ice. Although the controversy over Canadian Olympic figure skaters Jamie Sale and David Pelletier was resolved after the French judge admitted to charges of corruption, Canadian viewers were baffled by the loss of their country's gold medal during the 2002 Games in Salt Lake. Disagreement about the "same" event illustrates phenomenology, each person's unique perceptions of the world. The humanistic approach sees these perceptions as shaping personality and guiding behaviour.

Seeking Self-Actualization According to Rogers, conditions of worth can make it harder for children to become aware of and accept aspects of themselves that conflict with their parents' values. Progress toward self-actualization can be enhanced by associating with those whose positive regard is not conditional on displaying any particular pattern of behaviour.

Prominent Humanistic Theories

By far, the most prominent humanistic theories of personality are those of Carl Rogers and Abraham Maslow.

Rogers's Self Theory In his extensive writings, Carl Rogers (e.g., 1961, 1970, 1980) emphasized the **actualizing tendency,** which he described as an innate inclination toward growth and fulfillment that motivates all human behaviour and is expressed in a unique way by each individual (Raskin & Rogers, 2001). Rogers saw personality as the expression of that actualizing tendency as it unfolds in each individual's uniquely perceived reality (Hergenhahn et al., 2003). The centrepiece of Rogers's theory is the *self,* the part of experience that a person identifies as "I" or "me." According to Rogers, those who accurately experience the self—with all its preferences, abilities, fantasies, shortcomings, and desires—are on the road to *self-actualization.* The progress of people whose experiences of the self become distorted, however, is likely to be slowed or stopped.

Rogers saw personality development beginning early, as children learn to need other people's approval, or *positive regard.* Evaluations by parents, teachers, and others soon begin to affect children's self-evaluations. When these evaluations are in agreement with a child's own self-evaluations, the child reacts in a way that matches, or is *congruent* with, self-experience. The child not only experiences positive regard but also evaluates the self as "good" for having earned approval. This positive self-experience becomes part of the **self-concept,** which is the way one thinks of oneself. But what if a positive self-experience is evaluated negatively by others, as when a little boy is teased by his father for having fun playing with dolls? In this case, the child must either do without a parent's positive regard or, more likely, reevaluate the self-experience—deciding perhaps that "I don't like dolls" or "Feeling good is bad."

In other words, said Rogers, personality is shaped partly by the actualizing tendency and partly by evaluations made by others. In this way, people come to like what they are "supposed" to like and to behave as they are "supposed" to behave. This socialization process is adaptive, because it helps people to function in society, but it often requires that they suppress their self-actualizing tendency and distort

humanistic approach A view in which personality develops through an actualizing tendency that unfolds in accordance with each person's unique perceptions of the world.

actualizing tendency According to Rogers, an innate inclination toward growth that motivates all people.

self-concept The way one thinks of oneself.

Parents are not usually this obvious about creating conditions of worth, but according to Rogers, the message gets through in many more subtle ways.

"Just remember, son, it doesn't matter whether you win or lose—unless you want Daddy's love."

their experience. Rogers argued that psychological discomfort, anxiety, or even mental disorder can result when the feelings people experience or express are *incongruent,* or at odds, with their true feelings.

Incongruence is likely, said Rogers, when parents and teachers act in ways that lead children to believe that their worth as people depends on displaying the "right" attitudes, behaviours, and values. These **conditions of worth** are created whenever *people* are evaluated instead of their behaviour. For example, parents who find their toddler smearing finger paint on the dog are unlikely to say, "I love you, but I don't approve of this particular behaviour." They are more likely to shout, "Bad boy!" or "Bad girl!" This reaction sends a subtle message that the child is lovable and worthwhile only when well behaved. As a result, the child's self-experience is not "I like painting Fang, but Mom and Dad don't approve," but instead, "Playing with paint is bad, and I am bad if I like it, so I don't like it," or "I like it, so I must be bad." The child may eventually display overly neat and tidy behaviours that do not reflect the real self but, rather, is part of the ideal self dictated by the parents.

As with Freud's concept of superego, conditions of worth are first set up by external pressure but eventually become part of the person's belief system. So Rogers saw rewards and punishments as important in personality development not just because they shape overt behaviour but also because they can so easily create distorted self-perceptions and incongruence.

conditions of worth According to Rogers, the feelings an individual experiences when the person, instead of the person's behaviour, is evaluated.

Maslow's Growth Theory Like Rogers, Abraham Maslow (1954, 1971) considered personality to be the expression of a basic human tendency toward growth and self-actualization. In fact, Maslow believed that self-actualization is not just a human capacity but a human need. As described in the chapter on motivation and emotion, he placed self-actualization as the highest in a hierarchy of motives, or needs. Yet, said Maslow, people are often distracted from seeking self-actualization because they focus on needs that are lower on the hierarchy.

The Joys of a Growth Orientation According to Maslow's theory of personality, the key to personal growth and fulfillment lies in focusing on what we have, not on what we don't have or on what we have lost. Rachel Barton could have let the accident that took her leg destroy her career as a concert violinist and, with it, her joy in life—but she didn't.

Maslow saw most people as controlled by a **deficiency orientation,** the preoccupation with perceived needs for material things. Ultimately, he said, deficiency-oriented people come to see life as a meaningless exercise in disappointment and boredom, and they may begin to behave in problematic ways. For example, in an attempt to satisfy the need for love and belongingness, people may focus on what love can give them (security), not on what they can give to another. This deficiency orientation may lead a person to be jealous and to focus on what is missing in relationships. As a result, the person will never truly experience either love or security.

In contrast, people with a **growth orientation** do not focus on what is missing but draw satisfaction from what they have, what they are, and what they can do. This orientation opens the door to what Maslow called *peak experiences*, in which people feel joy, even ecstasy, in the mere fact of being alive, being human, and knowing that they are utilizing their fullest potential.

Evaluation of the Humanistic Approach

The humanistic approach to personality is consistent with the way many people view themselves. It gives a central role to each person's immediate experiences and emphasizes the uniqueness of each individual. The humanistic approach and its phenomenological perspective inspired the person-centred therapy of Rogers and other forms of psychotherapy (see the chapter on treatment of psychological disorders). This approach also underlies various short-term personal growth experiences—such as sensitivity training and encounter groups designed to help people become more aware of themselves and the way they relate to others (e.g., Cain & Seeman, 2002). It has also led to programs designed to teach parents how to avoid creating conditions of worth while maximizing their children's potential. Further, the humanistic approach is consistent with the rapidly growing field of *positive psychology* (Engler, 2003), which, as described in the chapter on motivation and emotion, focuses on subjective well-being and other positive aspects of human thought and feelings (Diener, 2003).

Yet to some, the humanistic view is naive, romantic, and unrealistic. Are people all as inherently good and growth-oriented as this approach suggests? Critics wonder about that, and they also fault humanistic personality theories for paying too little attention to the importance of inherited characteristics, learning, situational influences, and unconscious motivation in shaping personality. The idea that everyone is directed only by an innate growth potential is viewed by these critics as an

deficiency orientation According to Maslow, a preoccupation with perceived needs for things a person does not have.

growth orientation According to Maslow, a tendency to draw satisfaction from what is available in life, rather than to focus on what is missing.

in review Major Approaches to Personality

Approach	Basic Assumptions About Behaviour	Typical Research Method
Psychodynamic	Determined by largely unconscious intrapsychic conflicts	Case studies
Trait	Determined by traits or needs	Analysis of tests for basic personality dimensions
Social-cognitive	Determined by learning, cognitive factors, and specific situations	Analysis of interactions between people and situations
Humanistic	Determined by innate growth tendency and individual perception of reality	Studies of relationships between perceptions and behaviour

oversimplification. So, too, is the assumption that all human problems stem from blocked actualization. Like the trait approach, humanistic theories seem to do a better job of describing personality than explaining it. And like many of the concepts in psychodynamic theories, humanistic concepts seem too vague to be tested empirically. Accordingly, the humanistic approach is not very popular among psychologists who rely on empirical research to learn about personality (Friedman & Schustack, 2003).

Finally, humanists' tendency to define ideal personality development in terms of personal growth, independence, and self-actualization has been criticized for emphasizing culture-specific ideas about mental health that may not apply outside North America and other Western cultures (Heine, 2003). As described in the next section, the individualist foundations of humanistic personality theories may be in direct conflict with the values of non-Western, collectivist cultures. ("In Review: Major Approaches to Personality" summarizes key features of the humanistic approach, along with those of the other approaches we have described.)

LINKAGES
Personality, Culture, and Human Development

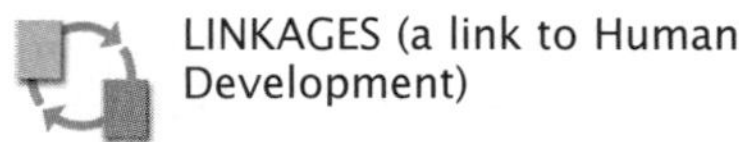

LINKAGES (a link to Human Development)

In many Western cultures, it is common to hear people encourage others to "stand up for yourself" or to "blow your own horn" in order to "get what you have coming to you." In middle-class North America, for example, the values of achievement and personal distinction are taught to children, particularly male children, very early in life (Markus & Kitayama, 1997). North American children are encouraged to feel special, to want self-esteem, and to feel good about themselves, partly because these characteristics are associated with happiness, popularity, and superior performance in school. Whether self-esteem is the cause or the result of these good outcomes (Baumeister et al., 2003), children who learn and display these values nevertheless tend to receive praise and encouragement for doing so. (The goal of esteem building is clear in daycare centres, summer camps, and other children's programs with names such as Starkids, Little Wonders, Superkids, and Precious Jewels.)

As a result of this cultural training, many people in North America and Europe develop personalities that are largely based on a sense of high self-worth. In a study by Hazel Markus and Shinobu Kitayama (1991), for example, 70 percent of a sample of students believed they were superior to their peers, and 60 percent believed they were in the top 10 percent on a wide variety of personal attributes! This tendency toward self-enhancement is evident as early as age four.

Culture and Personality In individualist cultures, most children learn early that personal distinction is valued by parents, teachers, and peers. In cultures that emphasize collectivist values, a strong sense of personal self-worth tends to be seen as a less important characteristic. In other words, the features of "normal" personality development vary from culture to culture.

As mentioned earlier, a sense of independence, uniqueness, and self-esteem is seen by many Western personality theorists as fundamental to mental health. Psychoanalyst Erik Erikson included the appearance of personal identity and self-esteem as part of normal psychosocial development (see the chapter on human development). Middle-class Americans who fail to value and strive for independence, self-promotion, and unique personal achievement may be seen as displaying a personality disorder, some form of depression, or other psychological problems.

Do these ideas reflect universal truths about personality development or, rather, the influence of the cultures that generated them? It is certainly clear that people in many non-Western cultures develop personal orientations very different from those of North Americans and Europeans (Cross & Markus, 1999). In China and Japan, for example, an independent, unique self is not emphasized (Ho & Chiu, 1998). Children there are encouraged to develop and maintain harmonious relations with others and not to stand out from the crowd, lest they diminish someone else. In fact, the Japanese word for "different" (*tigau*) also means "wrong" (Kitayama & Markus, 1992). So whereas children in Canada hear that "the squeaky wheel gets the grease," Japanese children are warned that "the nail that stands out gets pounded down" (Markus & Kitayama, 1997). From a very young age, they are taught to be modest, to play down the value of personal contributions, and to appreciate the joy and value of group work (Kitayama & Markus, 1992).

In contrast to the *independent* self-system prevalent in individualist cultures (e.g., Canada, the United States, and the United Kingdom), countries characterized by a more collectivist orientation (e.g., Japan, China, Brazil, and Nigeria) promote an *interdependent* self-system through which people see themselves as a small fraction of a social whole. Each person has little or no meaningful definition without reference to the group. These differences in self-systems may produce differences in what gives people a sense of well-being and satisfaction. In Canada, a sense of personal well-being is typically associated with the feeling of *having positive attributes*, such as intelligence, creativity, competitiveness, persistence, and so on. In Japan and other Asian countries it is more likely to be associated with the feeling of *having no negative attributes* (Eliot et al., 2001). Similarly, the results of studies conducted around the world indicate that in collectivist cultures, life satisfaction is associated with social approval and harmonious relations with others, whereas in individualist cultures, life satisfaction is associated with high self-esteem and feeling good about one's own life (Uchida et al., 2001).

Given that cultural factors shape notions about ideal personality development, it is important to evaluate various approaches to personality in terms of how well they apply to cultures other than the one in which they were developed (Cross & Markus, 1999). Their applicability to males and females must also be considered. Even within North American cultures, for example, there are gender differences in the development of self-esteem. Females tend to display an interdependent self-system, achieving their sense of self and self-esteem from attachments to others. By contrast, males' self-esteem tends to develop in relation to personal achievement, in a manner more in keeping with an independent self-system (Cross & Madson, 1997). Cross-gender and cross-cultural differences in the nature and determinants of a sense of self underscore the pervasive effects of gender and culture on the development of many aspects of human personality.

FOCUS ON RESEARCH METHODS

Longitudinal Studies of Temperament and Personality

Studying the development of personality over the life span requires longitudinal research, in which the same people are followed from infancy to adulthood so that their characteristics can be assessed at different points in their lives. A number of studies have used longitudinal methods to explore a variety of questions about changes in personality over time.

- **What was the researchers' question?**

The specific question addressed by Avshalom Caspi and his colleagues was whether the temperament children display at birth and in their early years predicts their personality and behaviour as adults (Caspi, 2000; Caspi & Silva, 1995; Caspi et al., 1997; Caspi et al., 1995; Caspi et al., 2003). As discussed in the chapter on human development, it is generally agreed that differences in temperament are influenced more by heredity than by the environment (Rowe, 1997).

- **How did the researchers answer the question?**

Caspi's research team studied all the children born in Dunedin, New Zealand, between April 1972 and March 1973—a total of about 1000 individuals. When the children were three years old, an examiner gave each of them a test of their cognitive abilities and motor skills and, using a three-point scale, rated their reactions to the testing situation. Some of the children displayed uncontrolled behaviours; some interacted easily; some were withdrawn and unresponsive. (To avoid bias while making their ratings, the examiners were told nothing about the children's typical behaviour outside of the testing room.) These observations were used to place each child into one of five temperament categories: *undercontrolled* (irritable, impatient, emotional), *inhibited* (shy, fearful, easily distracted), *confident* (eager to perform, responsive to questions), *reserved* (withdrawn, uncomfortable), and *well adjusted* (confident, friendly, well controlled). The children were observed and categorized again when they were five, seven, and nine years old. On each occasion, a different person did the ratings, thus ensuring that the observers' ratings would not be biased by earlier impressions. Almost all correlations among the independent ratings made at various ages were positive and statistically significant, indicating that the temperament classifications were stable across time.

When the participants were 18 years old, they completed a standard personality test, and then, at 21, they were interviewed about the degree to which they engaged in risky and unhealthy behaviours such as excessive drinking, violent crime, unprotected sexual activity, and unsafe driving habits. To avoid bias, the interviewers were given no information about the participants' temperament when they were children or about their scores on the personality test. Finally, at the age of 26, the participants again took a standard personality test and were also rated by their friends on the big-five personality dimensions.

• What did the researchers find?

Several significant differences were found among the average personality scores for the three temperament categories. For example, the average test scores of 26-year-olds who had been classified as "undercontrolled" in childhood showed that they were more alienated, uninhibited, and stressed than any other temperament group. Further, people who had been classified as "confident" or "well adjusted" as children tended to be better adjusted and more extraverted at 26 than people who had been classified as "inhibited" or "reserved" when they were children. Young adults who, as children, had been classified as "well adjusted" tended to be effective individuals who were likely to assume leadership roles. These findings held true for males and females alike.

Caspi and his colleagues also found small but significant correlations between early temperament and health-risky and criminal behaviours (Caspi et al., 2003). For example, people classified as "overcontrolled" were more likely to avoid dangerous and exciting activities at the age of 21 than were those who had been classified as "undercontrolled." In fact, participants classified as "undercontrolled" were significantly more likely than any of the other groups to engage in risky behaviours and to have criminal records. The relationship between temperament in childhood and health-risky behaviours in young adulthood was not a direct one, though. Statistical analyses revealed that temperament at age three affected personality at age 18, which in turn affected later behaviour patterns.

• What do the results mean?

The results of Caspi's studies provide persuasive empirical support for a hypothesis long endorsed by personality psychologists: that we can make relatively accurate predictions about adult personality and behaviour if we know about childhood temperament. However, the strength of these results should not be overstated. The relationships between temperament and personality, and between temperament and various problematic behaviours, though statistically significant, were also relatively modest. For example, not all the participants classified as "undercontrolled" at age three turned out to be aggressive or violent at age 21. The implication is that personality is influenced and shaped by temperament, but not completely determined by it.

The results of these studies also confirm a point made in the chapter on health, stress, and coping—that personality plays a significant role in health. Specifically, personality characteristics predispose people to engage in behaviours that can affect their mental and physical health.

• What do we still need to know?

Caspi's research has revealed some consistency between temperament in childhood and personality in adulthood, but it also leaves some unanswered questions (Roberts & Delvecchio, 2000). For example, what factors underlie this consistency? The fact that there are individual differences in adult behaviour within temperament groups shows that a child is not simply biologically programmed to display certain personality traits later. One explanation offered by Caspi and his colleagues draws heavily on social-cognitive theories, particularly on Bandura's notion of reciprocal determinism. These researchers believe that long-term consistencies in behaviour result from the mutual influence that temperament and environmental events have on one another. They propose, for example, that people tend to put themselves in situations that reinforce their temperament. So "undercontrolled" people might choose to spend time with people who accept and even encourage rude or impolite behaviour. And when such behaviour brings negative reactions, the world seems that much more hostile, and they become even more aggressive and negative. Caspi and his colleagues see the results of their studies as evidence that this process of mutual influence between personality and situations can continue over a lifetime (Caspi et al., 2003).

Assessing Personality

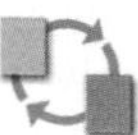
LINKAGES (a link to Personality)

Psychologists describe people's personalities using information from four main sources (Ozer, 1999): *life outcomes* (such as level of education, income, or marital status); *situational tests* (laboratory measurements of behavioural, emotional, and physiological reactions to conflict, frustration, and the like); *observer ratings* (judgments about a person made by family or friends); and *self-reports* (responses to interviews and personality tests). The data gathered through these methods are used for many purposes, including diagnosing psychological disorders, predicting dangerousness, selecting new employees, and even choosing astronaut candidates best suited to space travel (Meyer et al., 2001; Nietzel et al., 2003).

Observer ratings and situational tests allow direct assessment of many aspects of behaviour, including how often, how effectively, and how consistently various actions occur. *Interviews* provide a way to gather information about personality from the person's own point of view. Some interviews are *open ended,* meaning that questions are tailored to the intellectual level, emotional state, and special needs of the person being interviewed. Others are *structured,* meaning that the interviewer asks a fixed set of questions about specific topics in a particular order. Structured interviews are routinely used in personality research because they are sure to cover matters of special interest to the researcher.

Personality tests offer a way of gathering self-report information that is more standardized and economical than interviews. To be useful, however, a personality test must be reliable and valid. As described in the chapter on cognitive abilities, reliability refers to how stable or consistent the results of a test are; validity reflects the degree to which test scores are interpreted appropriately and used properly in making inferences about people. The many personality tests available today are traditionally classified as either *objective* or *projective.*

Objective Personality Tests

Objective personality tests contain clearly stated items that relate to a person's thoughts, feelings, or behaviour (such as "Do you like parties?"). The most common kind of objective personality test is similar in format to the multiple-choice or true-false examinations used in many classrooms. Like those exams, self-report personality tests can be administered to many people at the same time. They can also be machine scored. Howcvcr, whereas there is only one correct answer for each item on a classroom exam, the "correct" answers to an objective personality test depend on who is taking it. Each person is asked to respond in a way that best describes him or her.

The person's responses to an objective test's items are combined into a score. That score can be used to draw conclusions about the individual's personality, but only after it has been compared with the responses of thousands of other people who have taken the same test. For example, before interpreting your score of "77" on a self-report test of extraversion, a psychologist would compare that score with *norms,* or average scores from other individuals of your age and gender. Only if you were well above these averages would you be considered unusually extraverted.

Some self-report tests focus on one personality trait, such as optimism (Carver & Scheier, 2002). Others measure a set of related traits, such as empathy and social responsibility (Penner, 2002). Still others measure the strength of a wider variety of traits to reveal general psychological functioning. For example, the *Neuroticism Extraversion Openness Personality Inventory, Revised,* or NEO-PI-R (Costa & McCrae, 1992), is designed to measure the big-five personality traits described earlier. Table 14.3 shows how the test's results are presented. One innovative feature of the NEO-PI-R is its "private" and "public" versions. The first version asks for the respondent's self-assessment. The second version asks a person who knows the

objective personality tests Tests containing direct, unambiguous items relating to the individual being assessed.

table 14.3
Sample Summary of Results from the NEO-PI-R

The NEO-PI-R assesses the big-five personality dimensions. In this example of the results a respondent might receive, the five factors scored are, from the top row to the bottom row, neuroticism, extraversion, openness, agreeableness, and conscientiousness. Because people with different NEO profiles tend to have different psychological problems, this test has been used to aid in the diagnosis of personality disorders (Trull & Sher, 1994).

Compared with the responses of other people, your responses suggest that you can be described as:

☐ Sensitive, emotional, and prone to experience feelings that are upsetting.	☒ Generally calm and able to deal with stress, but you sometimes experience feelings of guilt, anger, or sadness.	☐ Secure, hardy, and generally relaxed even under stressful conditions.
☐ Extraverted, outgoing, active, and high-spirited. You prefer to be around people most of the time.	☐ Moderate in activity and enthusiasm. You enjoy the company of others, but you also value privacy.	☒ Introverted, reserved, and serious. You prefer to be alone or with a few close friends.
☐ Open to new experiences. You have broad interests and are very imaginative.	☐ Practical but willing to consider new ways of doing things. You seek a balance between the old and the new.	☒ Down-to-earth, practical, traditional, and pretty much set in your ways.
☐ Compassionate, good-natured, and eager to cooperate and avoid conflict.	☒ Generally warm, trusting, and agreeable, but you can sometimes be stubborn and competitive.	☐ Hardheaded, skeptical, proud, and competitive. You tend to express your anger directly.
☒ Conscientious and well organized. You have high standards and always strive to achieve your goals.	☐ Dependable and moderately well organized. You generally have clear goals but are able to set your work aside.	☐ Easygoing, not very well organized, and sometimes careless. You prefer not to make plans.

respondent to rate him or her on various dimensions. Personality descriptions based on the two versions are often quite similar, but discrepancies may indicate problems. For example, if a person's self-ratings are substantially different from those of a spouse, marital problems may be indicated. The nature of the discrepancies could suggest a focus for marital therapy.

The NEO-PI-R is quite reliable (Viswesvaran & Ones, 2000), and people's scores on its various dimensions have been successfully used to predict a number of behaviours, including performance on specific jobs and overall career success (Barrick & Mount, 1991; Siebert & Kraimer, 2001; Thoreson et al., 2004), social status (Anderson et al., 2001), and the likelihood that people will engage in criminal activities and risky sexual behaviours (Clower & Bothwell, 2001; Miller et al., 2004).

Projective Personality Tests

Unlike objective tests, **projective personality tests** contain relatively unstructured stimuli, such as inkblots, which can be perceived in many ways (Viglione & Rivera, 2003). Those who favour projective tests tend to take a psychodynamic approach to personality. They believe that people's responses to the tests' ambiguous stimuli are guided by unconscious needs, motives, fantasies, conflicts, thoughts, and other hidden aspects of personality. Some projective tests ask people to draw items such as a house, a person, or a tree (see Figure 14.6); to fill in the missing parts of incomplete pictures or sentences; or to say what they associate with a particular word. Projective techniques are sometimes used in basic personality research, but they are far more popular among clinical psychologists, who use them in the assessment of psychological disorders (Lilienfeld, Wood, & Garb, 2000).

projective personality tests Tests made up of unstructured stimuli that can be perceived and responded to in many ways.

figure 14.6

A Draw-a-Person Test

These drawings were done by an 18-year-old male who had been caught stealing a television set. A psychologist interpreted the muscular figure as the young man's attempt to boast of masculine prowess but saw the muscles' "puffy softness" as suggesting feelings of inadequacy. The drawing of the baby-like figure was seen to reveal vulnerability, dependency, and a need for affection. Appealing as these interpretations may be, research does not generally support the value of projective tests in personality assessment (Lilienfield, Wood, & Garb, 2000).

Source: Hammer (1968).

One prominent projective test, developed by Henry Murray and Christina Morgan, is called the *Thematic Apperception Test,* or *TAT.* As described in the chapter on motivation and emotion, the TAT is used to measure need for achievement (see Figure 11.7 in that chapter). It is also used to assess other needs (for example, for power or affiliation) that Murray and Morgan saw as the basis for personality. Another widely used projective test, the *Rorschach Inkblot Test,* asks people to say what they see in a series of inkblots (see Figure 14.7).

Advocates of projective tests claim that using ambiguous test items makes it difficult for respondents to detect what is being measured and what the "best" answers would be. They argue, therefore, that these tests can measure aggressive and sexual impulses and other personality features that people might otherwise be able to hide. However, in comparison with the results of objective tests, responses to projective tests are much more difficult to translate into numerical scores for scientific analysis. In an effort to reduce the subjectivity involved in projective-test interpretation, some psychologists have developed more structured—and thus potentially more reliable—scoring systems for instruments such as the Rorschach (Erdberg, 1990; Exner & Ona, 1995). And there are in fact specific instances—as in studies assessing implicit social motives with the TAT—in which projective tests show acceptable reliability and validity (Schultheiss & Rohde, 2002). Overall, though, projective personality tests are substantially less reliable and valid than objective tests (Hunsley, Lee, & Wood, 2003; Lilienfeld, Wood, & Garb, 2000). Because of their generally low predictive power, projective tests often add little information beyond what might be inferred from life outcome data, interviews, and objective personality tests (Hunsley, Lee, & Wood, 2003). ("In Review: Personality Tests" summarizes the characteristics of objective and projective tests, along with some of their advantages and disadvantages.)

Personality Tests and Employee Selection

How good are personality tests at selecting people for jobs? Most industrial/organizational psychologists believe these tests are valuable tools in the selection of good employees. The majority of personality tests used by large organizations are

figure 14.7

The Rorschach Inkblot Test

The Rorschach test consists of ten patterns, some in colour, others in black and white. The respondent is asked to tell what the blot might be and then to explain why. This pattern is similar to those in the Rorschach test. What do you see? Most scoring methods focus on (1) what part of the blot the person responds to; (2) what details, colours, or other features appear to determine each response; (3) the content of responses (such as seeing animals, maps, body parts); and (4) the popularity or commonness of the responses.

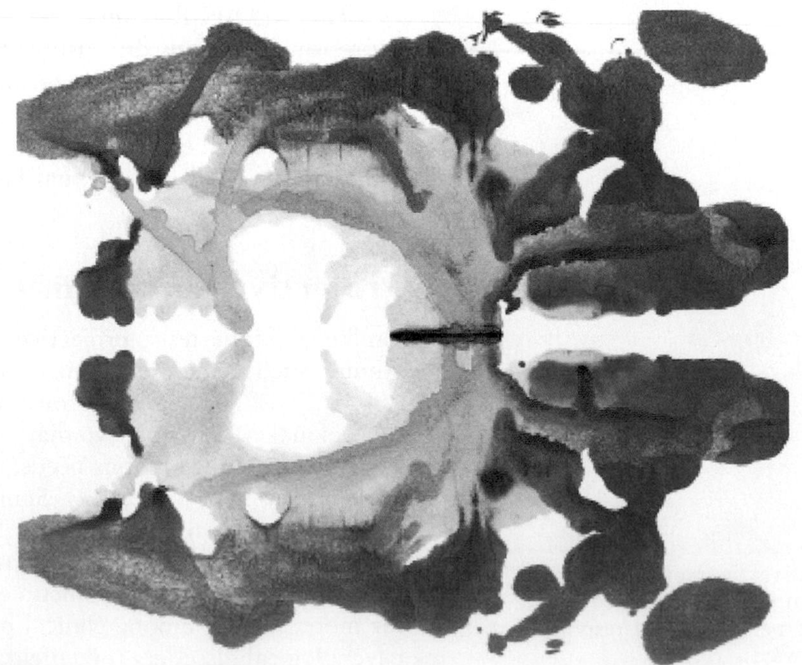

in review Personality Tests

Type of Test	Characteristics	Advantages	Disadvantages
Objective	Asks direct questions about a person; quantitatively scored	Efficiency, standardization	Subject to deliberate distortion
Projective	Unstructured stimuli create maximum freedom of response; scoring is subjective, though some objective methods exist	"Correct" answers not obvious; designed to tap unconscious impulses; flexible use	Reliability and validity lower than those of objective tests

those that measure the big-five personality dimensions or related characteristics (Borman, Hanson, & Hedge, 1997; Costa, 2001). Several researchers have found significant relationships between scores on these characteristics and measures of overall job performance and effective leadership (Kieffer, Schinka, & Curtiss, 2004; Lim & Ployhart, 2004; Silverthorne, 2001). A more general review of studies involving thousands of people has shown that objective personality tests are of value in helping businesses reduce thefts and other disruptive employee behaviours (Ones & Viswesvaran, 2001).

Still, personality tests are far from perfect predictors of behaviour, and as noted earlier, they sometimes lead to incorrect predictions. Many tests measure traits that may be too general to predict specific aspects of job performance (Furnham, 2001). Often, features of the work situation are better predictors of employee behaviour than are personality tests (Mumford et al., 2001). Further, some employees see personality tests as an invasion of their privacy. They worry also that test results in their personnel files might later be misinterpreted and hurt their chances for promotion or for employment by other companies. Concerns about privacy and other issues surrounding personality testing have also led the Canadian Psychological Association and other organizations to publish joint ethical standards relating to procedures for the development, dissemination, and use of all psychological tests. The goal is not only to improve the reliability and validity of tests but also to ensure that their results are properly used and do not infringe on individuals' rights (Turner et al., 2001).

LINKAGES

As noted in the chapter on introducing psychology, all of psychology's many subfields are related to one another. Our discussion of cultural factors and personality illustrates just one way in which the topic of this chapter, personality, is linked to the subfield of developmental psychology (which is the focus of the chapter on human development). The Linkages diagram shows ties to two other subfields as well, and there are many more ties throughout the book. Looking for linkages among subfields will help you see how they all fit together and better appreciate the big picture that is psychology.

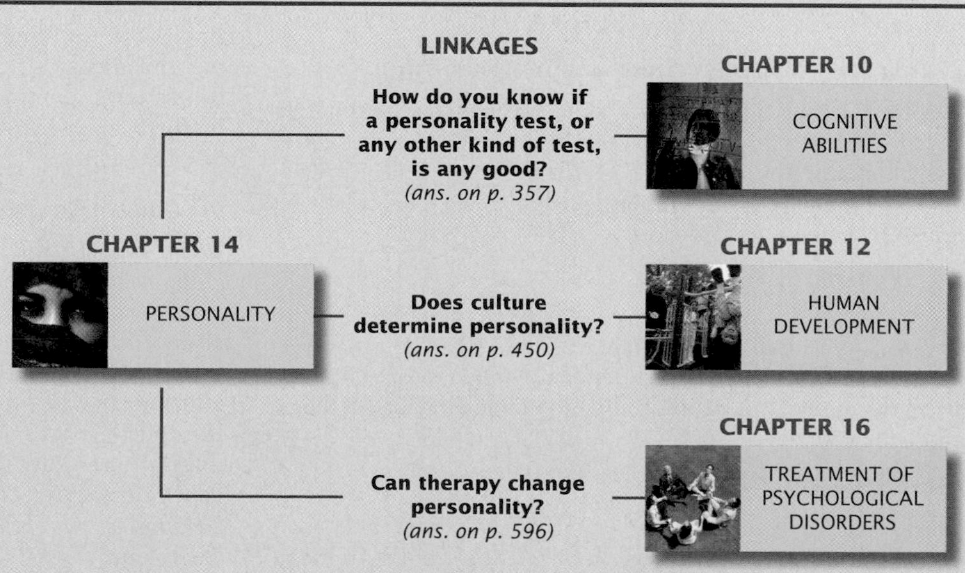
LINKAGES
CHAPTER 14
PERSONALITY
How do you know if a personality test, or any other kind of test, is any good?
(ans. on p. 357)
CHAPTER 10
COGNITIVE ABILITIES
Does culture determine personality?
(ans. on p. 450)
CHAPTER 12
HUMAN DEVELOPMENT
Can therapy change personality?
(ans. on p. 596)
CHAPTER 16
TREATMENT OF PSYCHOLOGICAL DISORDERS

SUMMARY

Personality refers to the unique pattern of psychological and behavioural characteristics by which each person can be compared and contrasted with other people. The four main theoretical approaches to personality are the psychodynamic, trait, social-cognitive, and humanistic approaches.

The Psychodynamic Approach

The *psychodynamic approach,* first proposed by Sigmund Freud, assumes that personality arises out of the interplay of various unconscious psychological processes.

The Structure and Development of Personality

Freud believed that personality has three components—the *id,* which has a reservoir of *libido* and operates according to the *pleasure principle;* the *ego,* which operates according to the *reality principle;* and the *superego,* which internalizes society's rules and values. The ego uses *defence mechanisms* to prevent unconscious conflicts among these components from becoming conscious and causing anxiety or guilt. Freud proposed that the focus of conflict changes as the child passes through *psychosexual stages* of development, called the *oral stage,* the *anal stage,* the *phallic stage* (during which the *Oedipus complex* arises), the *latency period,* and the *genital stage.*

Variations on Freud's Personality Theory

Many of Freud's early followers developed new theories that differed from his. Among these theorists were Carl Jung, Alfred Adler, and Karen Horney. These and other theorists tended to downplay the role of instincts and the unconscious, emphasizing instead the importance of conscious processes, ego functions, and social and cultural factors. Horney also challenged the male-oriented nature of Freud's original theory.

Contemporary Psychodynamic Theories

Current psychodynamic theories are derived from the neo-Freudians' emphasis on family and social relationships. According to object relations (attachment) theorists, personality development depends mainly on the nature of early interactions between individuals and their caregivers.

Evaluation of the Psychodynamic Approach

Despite evidence in support of some psychodynamic concepts and recent attempts to test psychodynamic theories more precisely and objectively, critics still fault the approach for its lack of a scientific base and for its view of human behaviour as driven by unmeasurable forces.

The Trait Approach

The *trait approach* to personality assumes that personality is made up of stable internal characteristics that appear at varying strengths in different people and guide their thoughts, feelings, and behaviour.

Allport's Trait Theory

Gordon Allport believed that personality is created by a small set of central traits and a larger number of secondary traits in each individual. He analyzed language to try to identify those traits, thus laying the foundation for modern research on personality traits.

The Big-Five Model of Personality

Building on the work of Allport and Raymond Cattell, contemporary researchers have used factor analysis to identify five basic dimensions of personality, collectively referred to as the *big-five model,* or five-factor model. These dimensions have been found in many different cultures.

Biological Trait Theories

Hans Eysenck believed that differences in nervous system arousal are responsible for differences in core dimensions of personality, especially introversion-extraversion and emotionality-stability. Newer biological theories have largely supplanted Eysenck's theory, and they suggest instead that these differences are due to biological differences in the sensitivity of brain systems involved with responsiveness to rewards and to punishments.

Evaluation of the Trait Approach

The trait approach has been criticized for being better at describing personality than at explaining it, for failing to consider mechanisms that motivate behaviour, and for underemphasizing the role of situational factors. Nevertheless, the trait approach—particularly the big-five model—currently dominates the field of personality.

The Social-Cognitive Approach

The *social-cognitive approach* to personality focuses on the thoughts and feelings that influence people's behaviour and assumes that personality is a label that summarizes the unique patterns of thinking and behaviour that a person learns in the social world.

Roots of the Social-Cognitive Approach

With roots in research on classical and operant conditioning (including Skinner's *functional analysis* of behaviour), the social-cognitive approach has expanded on traditional behavioural approaches by emphasizing the role of cognitive factors, such as observational learning, in personality development.

Prominent Social-Cognitive Theories

Julian Rotter's theory focuses on cognitive expectancies that guide behaviour, and it generated interest in assessing general beliefs about whether rewards occur because of personal efforts (internal control) or chance (external control). Albert Bandura believes that personality develops largely through cognitively mediated learning, including observational learning. He sees personality as reciprocally determined by interactions among cognition, environmental stimuli, and behaviour. Perceived *self-efficacy*—the belief in one's ability to accomplish a specific task—is an important determinant of behaviour.

Evaluation of the Social-Cognitive Approach

The social-cognitive approach has gained wide acceptance because it has merged theories from behavioural and cognitive psychology and used them to explain a wide range of important social behaviours. However, the approach has been criticized for failing both to provide one coherent theory of personality and to capture the complexity, richness, and uniqueness of human personalities.

The Humanistic Approach

The *humanistic approach* to personality is based on the assumption that people are primarily motivated by a desire to fulfill their natural potential in a uniquely perceived version of reality. So to understand a person, you have to understand the person's view of the world, which serves as the basis for personality and guides behaviour.

Prominent Humanistic Theories

Carl Rogers believed that personality development is driven by an innate *actualizing tendency,* but also that one's *self-concept* is shaped by social evaluations. He proposed that when people are free from the effects of *conditions of worth,* they will be psychologically healthy and achieve self-actualization. Abraham Maslow saw self-actualization as the highest in a hierarchy of needs. Personality development is healthiest, he said, when people have a *growth orientation* rather than a *deficiency orientation.*

Evaluation of the Humanistic Approach

Although it has a large following, the humanistic approach is faulted for being too idealistic, for failing to explain personality development, for being vague and unscientific, and for underplaying cultural differences in "ideal" personalities.

Assessing Personality

The information used in personality assessment comes from four main sources: life outcomes, situational tests, observer ratings, and self-reports. To be useful, personality assessments must be both reliable and valid.

Objective Personality Tests

Objective personality tests contain clearly worded items relating to the individual being assessed; individual scores can be compared with group norms. The NEO-PI-R is an example of an objective test.

Projective Personality Tests

Based on psychodynamic theories, *projective personality tests* present ambiguous stimuli in an attempt to tap unconscious personality characteristics. Two popular projective tests are the TAT and the Rorschach Inkblot Test. In general, projective personality tests are less reliable and valid than objective personality tests.

Personality Tests and Employee Selection

Objective personality tests are often used to identify the people best suited for certain occupations. Although such tests can be helpful in this regard, those who use them must be aware of the tests' limitations and take care not to violate the rights of test respondents.

15 Psychological Disorders

Many people pursue what other people consider to be odd hobbies, such as collecting tons of string, but when does oddness become abnormality? In this chapter, we discuss the ways in which society answers that question. We also describe the main types of psychological disorders, their possible causes, their legal status, and how they have been explained over the centuries. We have organized our presentation as follow:

During his first year at university, Mark began to worry about news stories describing the deadly illness known as SARS. He was frightened by images on the nightly news of people walking the streets of Toronto wearing surgical masks, and by reports of travel advisories warning tourists to stay home and hospitals restricting visitors. When the deaths of patients and health care workers who had contracted SARS was reported, he cancelled his spring break trip to Florida because he was concerned that someone on the plane might be carrying the virus that causes SARS. Further reports of suspicious cases in other parts of the country led Mark to conclude that no place was safe.

Given his growing fear, Mark concluded that the only way to protect himself was absolute cleanliness. Mark began to scrub himself whenever he touched door-knobs, money, walls, floors—anything. People with SARS, he thought, could have touched these things, or they might have coughed on the street and he might have tracked their infected saliva into his car and house and bathroom. Eventually he felt the need to scrub everything around him up to 40 times in each direction; it took him several exhausting hours just to shower and dress. He washed the shower knobs before touching them and, once in the shower, felt that he had to wash his body in cycles of 13 strokes. If his feet touched the bare floor, he had to wash them again before putting on his underwear to ensure that his feet would not contaminate the fabric. He was sure that his hands, rubbed raw from constant washing, were especially susceptible to infection, so he wore gloves at all times except in the summer, when he wrapped his fingers in flesh-coloured bandages. The process of protecting himself from infection was wearing him out and severely restricting his activities; he could not go anywhere without first considering the risk of infection.

Mark's case provides an example of someone who suffers from a psychological disorder, also called a *mental disorder* or *psychopathology.* **Psychopathology** is generally defined as patterns of thought, emotion, and behaviour that result in personal distress or a significant impairment in a person's social or occupational functioning. Identifying psychopathology, then, is a social as well as a personal matter, and deciding who "has it" depends in part on how a particular culture defines *normal* and *abnormal* (Castillo, 1997).

In Western cultures, these terms are defined in such a way that a large number of people can be said to display a psychological disorder. According to the Public Health Agency of Canada (2002a), approximately 20 percent of Canadians will be diagnosed with a psychological disorder at some point in their lifetime. In addition, about 15 percent of Canadian children display significant mental disorders in any given year (BC Partners for Mental Health and Addictions, 2002). Bear in mind that the actual rates may be higher than the percentages just cited, because major survey studies have examined fewer than half of all known psychological disorders. Research in 14 countries around the world shows that psychological disorders are a global problem. A recent study found that 24 percent of adults were actually suffering from a disorder and that another 31 percent displayed significant symptoms (World Health Organization, 2002b).

Psychological disorders are enormously costly in terms of human suffering, wasted potential, economic burden, and lost resources (Druss, Rosenheck, & Sledge, 2000; Lyons & McLoughlin, 2001; Marcotte & Wilcox-Goek, 2001; Stewart et al., 2003). Let's consider how abnormality is defined and classified.

Surveys of adults in Canada revealed that about 20 percent of them experience some form of mental disorder in any given year and that almost half of them have displayed a disorder at some time. The data shown in Table 15.1 summarize these findings by category of disorder. The same general patterns appear among the more than 400 million people worldwide who suffer from some form of psychological disorder (Andrade et al., 2002; Bjil et al., 2003; Liu et al., 2002; World Health Organization, 2002b; 2004).

psychopathology Patterns of thinking, feeling, and behaving that are maladaptive, disruptive, or uncomfortable for those who are affected or for those with whom they come in contact.

table 15.1
Estimated One-Year Prevalence of Mental Illnesses Among Adults in Canada

Mental Illness	Estimates of One-Year Prevalence
Mood Disorders	
Major (Unipolar) depression	4.1–4.6%
Bipolar disorder	0.2–0.6%
Dysthymia	0.8–3.1%
Schizophrenia	0.3%
Anxiety Disorders	12.2%
Personality Disorders	—
Eating Disorders	
Anorexia	Anorexia 0.7% women 0.2% men
Bulimia	Bulimia 1.5% women 0.1% men
Deaths from Suicide	12.2 per 100 000 (1998) 2% of all deaths 24% of all deaths among those aged 15–24 years 16% of all deaths among those aged 25–44 years

Source: http://www.phac-aspc.gc.ca/publicat/miic-mmac/chap_1_e.html

Defining Psychological Disorders

A woman's husband dies, and in her grief she stays in bed all day, weeping, refusing to eat, at times holding "conversations" with him. In India, a Hindu holy man on a pilgrimage rolls along the ground across a thousand miles of deserts and mountains, pelted by monsoon rains, until he reaches the sacred place he seeks. In research conducted at the University of Ottawa, Alain Paltry and Luc Pelletier found that of the 398 students surveyed, 48 percent believed in UFOs (Paltry & Pelletier, 2001), and hundreds of people around the world claim to have been abducted by space aliens (Appelle, Lynn, & Newman, 2000). These examples and countless others raise the question of where to draw the line between normality and abnormality, between eccentricity and mental disorder (Kanner, 1995).

What Is Abnormal?

There are several criteria for judging whether people's thinking, emotions, or behaviours are abnormal. Each criterion has value but also some flaws.

Infrequency If we define *normality* as what most people do, an obvious criterion for abnormality is *statistical infrequency*—that which is unusual. By this criterion, the few people who believe that space aliens are stealing their thoughts would be judged abnormal, and the many people who worry about crime or terrorism would not. But statistical infrequency alone is a poor criterion for abnormality, because some characteristics that appear only rarely—such as creative genius or world-class athletic ability—may be highly valued. Further, this definition implies that only those who conform to all aspects of the majority's standards are normal. Equating nonconformity with abnormality can result in the oppression of those who express minority views in a society. Finally, just how rare must a behaviour be in order to be "abnormal"? The dividing line is not easy to locate.

Is this man abnormal? William Lyon MacKenzie King served three terms as Prime Minister of Canada between 1921 and 1948, and is pictured on the Canadian fifty dollar bill. During his time in office, he developed an interest in spiritualism, and held seances with his friends and sometimes a medium. He regularly sought both personal and political advice from the spirits of his dead mother and his dog, Pat, as well as Sir Wilfred Laurier and Saints Luke and John. He was considered eccentric but was never diagnosed with a mental illness.

Norm Violation Abnormality can also be defined in terms of whether someone violates social norms—the cultural rules that tell us how we should and should not behave in various situations, especially in relation to others (see the chapter on social behaviour). According to this *norm violation criterion,* when people behave in ways that are bizarre, unusual, or disturbing enough to violate social norms, they may be described as abnormal.

Like infrequency, though, norm violation alone is an inadequate measure of abnormality. For one thing, some norm violations are better characterized as eccentric or illegal than as abnormal. People who seldom bathe or stand too close during a conversation violate social norms, but are they abnormal or merely annoying? Further, whose norms are we talking about? Social norms vary across cultures, subcultures, and historical eras, so actions that qualify as abnormal in one part of the world might be perfectly acceptable elsewhere (Giosan, Glovsky, & Haslam, 2001; Phelan et al., 2000).

Personal Suffering Another criterion for abnormality is *personal suffering.* In fact, experiencing distress is the criterion that people often use in deciding that their psychological problems are severe enough to require treatment. But personal suffering alone is an inadequate criterion for abnormality. It does not take into account the fact that people's distress might stem from events or characteristics that are not pathological (for example, the death of a loved one). Further, people can display psychological disorders without experiencing distress if the disorders have impaired their ability to recognize how maladaptive their behaviour is. Those who sexually abuse children, for example, create far more distress in victims and their families than they suffer themselves.

Behaviour in Context: A Practical Approach

Because no single criterion is entirely adequate for identifying abnormality, mental health practitioners and researchers tend to adopt a *practical approach* that combines aspects of all the criteria we've discussed. They consider the *content* of behaviour (what the person does); the socio-cultural *context* in which the person's behaviour occurs; and the *consequences* of the behaviour for that person, as well as for others. This practical approach pays special attention to whether a person's thoughts, behaviour, or emotions cause **impaired functioning**—that is, difficulty in fulfilling appropriate and expected family, social, and work-related roles (U.S. Surgeon General, 1999; Wakefield, 1999).

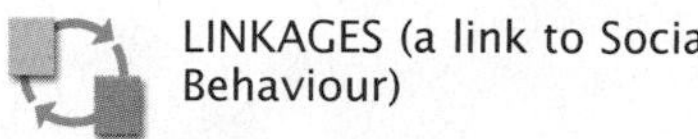

LINKAGES (a link to Social Behaviour)

What is "appropriate" and "expected" depends on age, gender, and culture, as well as on the particular situation and historical era in which people find themselves. For example, the same short attention span that is considered normal in a two-year-old would be considered inappropriate and problematic in an adult. There are gender-specific norms as well. In some countries, for example, it is more appropriate for women than for men to display emotion. Kisses, tears of happiness, and long embraces are common when women greet each other after a long absence. Men tend to simply shake hands or, at most, hug briefly. Because of cultural differences, hearing a dead relative's voice calling from the afterlife would be more acceptable among some Aboriginal communities than among, say, the white, middle-class families of suburban Toronto. Situational factors are important, too. Falling to the floor and speaking an unintelligible language is considered appropriate, even desirable, during the worship services of certain religious groups, but the same behaviour would be seen as inappropriate, and a sign of disorder, in a college classroom. Finally, judgments about behaviour are shaped by changes in social trends and cultural values. For example, the American Psychiatric Association once listed homosexuality as a mental disorder but dropped this category from its *Diagnostic and Statistical Manual of Mental Disorders* in 1973. In taking this step, it was responding to changing views of homosexuality that were prompted in part by the political and educational efforts of gay and lesbian rights groups.

impaired functioning Difficulty in fulfilling appropriate and expected family, social, and work-related roles.

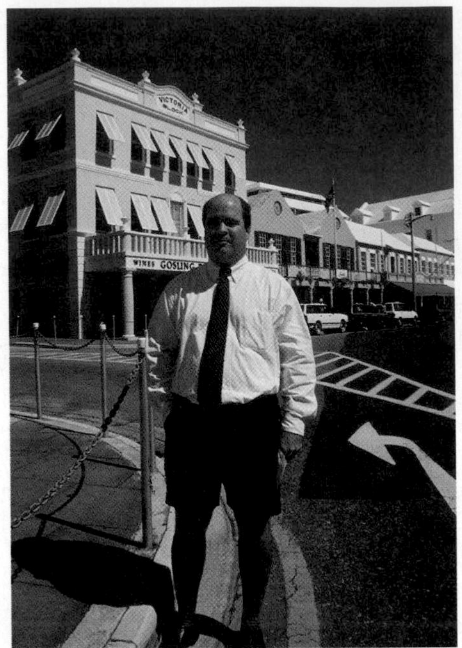

Is this normal business attire? The answer depends on the context. For example, if you saw this man on his way to work in Edmonton, Alberta, you would probably find his dress rather unusual, to say the least. However, if you lived in Bermuda, this man's attire would be considered perfectly normal for a day at the office.

In summary, it is difficult, and probably impossible, to define a specific set of behaviours that everyone, everywhere, will agree constitutes abnormality (Lilienfeld & Marino, 1999; Wakefield, 1999). The practical approach defines abnormality as including those patterns of thought, behaviour, and emotional reaction that significantly impair people's functioning within their culture (Wakefield, 1992).

Explaining Psychological Disorders

Since the dawn of civilization, people throughout the world have tried to understand the causes of psychological disorder. The earliest explanations of abnormal behaviour focused on possession by gods or demons. Disordered people were seen either as innocent victims of spirits or as social or moral deviants suffering supernatural punishment. In Europe during the late Middle Ages, for example, disbelief in established religious doctrine and other unusual behaviours were viewed as the work of the devil or other evil beings. Hundreds of "witches" were burned at the stake, and exorcisms were performed to rid people of their demons. Supernatural explanations of psychological disorders are still invoked today in many cultures around the world—including certain ethnic and religious subcultures in North America (Nickell, 2001; Tagliabue, 1999).

The Biopsychosocial Model

More generally, however, researchers in Western cultures attribute psychopathology to three other causes: biological factors, psychological processes, and socio-cultural contexts. For many decades, there was controversy over which of these three causes is most important, but it is now widely agreed that they can all be important. Accordingly, researchers have adopted a **biopsychosocial model** in which mental disorders are seen as caused by the combination and interaction of biological, psychological, and socio-cultural factors, each of which contributes in varying degrees to particular problems in particular people (U.S. Surgeon General, 1999).

Biological Factors The *biological factors* thought to be involved in causing mental disorders include physical illnesses, disruptions or imbalances in bodily processes, and genetic influences. This *medical model* of psychopathology has a long

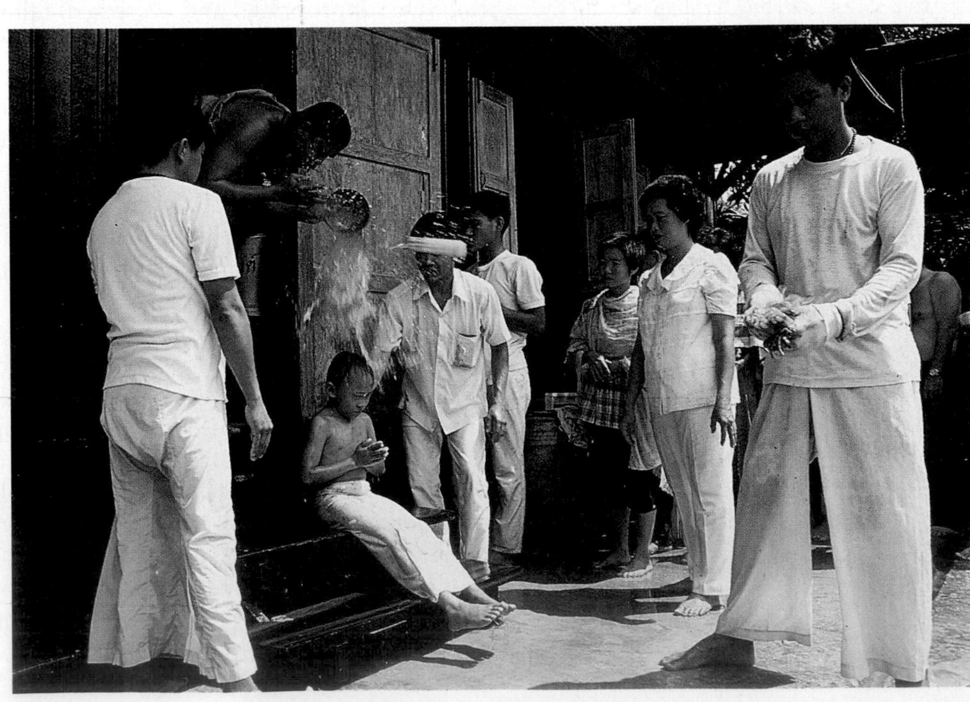

An Exorcism Supernatural explanations of mental disorder remain influential among religious groups in many cultures and subcultures around the world—including some in Canada and other Western countries (Fountain, 2000, Kirmayer, Fletcher, & Boothroyd, 1997). The exorcism being performed by this Buddhist monk in Thailand is designed to banish supernatural forces that are seen as causing this child's disorder.

biopsychosocial model A view of mental disorders as caused by a combination of interacting biological, psychological, and socio-cultural factors.

Visiting Bedlam As shown here in William Hogarth's portrayal of "Bedlam" (the slang name for London's St. Mary's of Bethlehem hospital), most eighteenth-century asylums were little more than prisons. Notice the well-dressed visitors; in those days, people could buy tickets to tour the cells and gawk at the patients.

history. For example, the ancient Greek physician Hippocrates said that psychological disorders resulted from imbalances among four *humours,* or bodily fluids (blood, phlegm, black bile, and yellow bile). According to Hippocrates, depression ("melancholia") resulted from an excess of black bile. In ancient Chinese cultures, psychological disorders were seen as resulting from an imbalance of *yin* and *yang,* the dual forces of the universe flowing in the physical body.

As the medical model gained prominence in Western cultures after the Middle Ages, specialized hospitals for the insane were established throughout Europe. Treatment in these early asylums consisted mainly of physical restraints, laxative purges, bleeding of "excess" blood, and induced vomiting. Cold baths, fasts, and other physical discomforts were also used in efforts to "shock" patients back to normality.

The medical model led to a view of abnormality as *mental illness,* and in fact, most people in Western cultures today still tend to seek medical doctors and hospitals for the diagnosis and treatment of psychological disorders. The medical model is now more properly called the **neurobiological model,** because it explains psychological disorders in terms of particular disturbances in the anatomy and chemistry of the brain and in other biological processes, including genetic influences (e.g., Plomin & McGuffin, 2003). Neuroscientists and others who adopt a neurobiological approach study the causes and treatment of these disorders as they would study any physical illness, seeing problematic symptoms stemming primarily from an underlying illness that can be diagnosed, treated, and cured.

The importance of biological factors in psychopathology has been demonstrated in many psychological disorders (Spitzer et al., 1992). *Dementia,* for example, is characterized by a loss of mental functions, including disturbances in memory, personality, and cognitive abilities. The most frequent causes of dementia are progressive deterioration of the brain as a result of aging or long-term alcohol abuse; acute diseases and disorders such as encephalitis, brain tumours, or head injury; and drug intoxication. Alzheimer's disease is a severe form of dementia seen mostly in the elderly. Research in neuroscience and behavioural genetics has also implicated biological factors in a number of other psychological disorders to be described later, including schizophrenia, bipolar disorders, some forms of anxiety disorder, and autism and attention deficit disorder (Kendler, 2001).

neurobiological model A modern name for the medical model, in which psychological disorders are seen as reflecting disturbances in the anatomy and chemistry of the brain and in other biological processes.

Psychological Processes If biological factors provide the "hardware" of mental disorders, the "software" includes psychological factors, such as our wants, needs, and emotions; our learning experiences; and our way of looking at the world. The roots of this **psychological model** of mental disorders can be seen in ancient Greek literature and drama dealing with the *psyche,* or mind—especially with the mind's struggles to resolve inner conflicts or to overcome the effects of stressful events. These ideas took centre stage in the late 1800s, when Sigmund Freud challenged the assumption that psychological disorders had only physical causes. As described in the chapter on personality, Freud's explanations of mental disorders were part of his *psychodynamic approach.* He believed that those disorders are the result of unresolved, mostly unconscious conflicts that begin in childhood. These conflicts pit people's inborn (id) impulses against the limits placed on those impulses by society. More recent psychodynamic explanations—such as *object relations* theory—focus less on unconscious urges and more on the role of attachment and other early interpersonal relationships (Schultz & Schultz, 2001).

LINKAGES (a link to Learning)

Other theories discussed in the chapter on personality suggest other psychological processes that can contribute to the development of mental disorders. For example, *social-cognitive* theorists, also known as *social-learning* theorists, see most psychological disorders as resulting from the interaction of past learning and current situations. Just as people learn to avoid hot grills after being burned, say these theorists, bad experiences in school or a dental office can "teach" people to fear such places. Social-cognitive theorists also emphasize that learned expectations, schemas, and other mental processes discussed in the chapter on cognition and language can influence the development of disorders. Depression, for example, is seen as stemming from negative events, such as losing a job, but also from the irrational or maladaptive thoughts that people have learned in relation to these events—thoughts such as "I never do anything right."

Finally, the *humanistic* approach to personality suggests that behaviour disorders appear when a person's natural tendency toward healthy growth is blocked, usually by a failure to be aware of, and to express, true feelings. When this happens, the person's perceptions of reality become distorted. The greater the distortion, the more serious the psychological disorder. Humanistic psychologists also focus on the meanings that people attach to events and how those meanings can lead to adaptive or maladaptive reactions.

Sociocultural Context Together, neurobiological and psychological factors can take us a long way toward explaining many forms of mental disorder. Still, these factors relate mainly to causes residing within the individual. The **sociocultural model** of disorder suggests that we cannot fully explain all forms of psychopathology without also looking outside the individual—especially at the social and cultural factors that form the background of abnormal behaviour. Looking for causes of disorders in this *sociocultural context* means paying attention to factors such as gender, age, and marital status; the physical, social, and economic situations in which people live; and the cultural values, traditions, and expectations in which they are immersed (Evans et al., 2000; Johnson et al., 1999; Whisman, 1999). Sociocultural context influences not only what is and is not labelled "abnormal" but also who displays what kind of disorder.

Consider gender, for instance. The greater tolerance in many cultures for the open expression of emotional distress among women, but not men, may contribute to the higher rates of depression seen in women compared with men (Nolen-Hoeksema, Larson, & Grayson, 1999). Similarly, the view held in many cultures that excessive alcohol consumption is less appropriate for women than for men is a sociocultural factor that may help explain higher rates of alcohol abuse among men in those cultures (Helzer et al., 1990).

Sociocultural factors also influence the form that abnormality takes (Kyrios et al., 2001). For example, depression is a *culture-general* disorder—appearing

psychological model A view in which mental disorder is seen as arising from psychological processes.

sociocultural model A way of looking at mental disorders in relation to gender, age, ethnicity, and other social and cultural factors.

virtually everywhere in the world—but its specific symptoms tend to differ depending on the disordered person's cultural background (Hopper & Wanderling, 2000). In Western cultures, emotional and physical components of disorders are generally viewed separately, so symptoms of depression tend to revolve around despair and other signs of emotional distress (Kleinman, 1991). But in China and certain other Asian cultures, emotional and physical experiences tend to be viewed as one, so a depressed person is as likely to report stomach or back pain as to complain of sadness (Kleinman, 2004; Parker, Gladstone, & Chee, 2001).

There are also culture-specific forms of disorder. For instance, Puerto Rican and Dominican Hispanic women sometimes experience *ataques de nervios* ("attack of nerves"), a unique way of reacting to stress that includes heart palpitations, shaking, shouting, nervousness, depression, and, on occasion, fainting or seizure-like episodes (Spiegel, 1994). In Asia, Khmer refugees sometimes suffer from *kyol goeu* ("wind overload"), a panic-related fainting disorder (Hinton, Um, & Ba, 2001). Another example can be found in Southeast Asia, southern China, and Malaysia, where a disorder called *koro* is occasionally observed. Victims of this condition, who are usually male, fear that their penis will shrivel, retract into the body, and cause death (in females, the fear relates to shrivelling of the breasts). *Koro* appears only in cultures that hold the specific supernatural beliefs that explain it. In such cultures, epidemics of *koro* are often triggered by economic hard times (Tseng et al., 1992).

In short, sociocultural factors create differing social roles, stressors, opportunities, and experiences for people who differ in age, gender, and cultural traditions. They also help shape the disorders and symptoms to which certain categories of people are prone, and they even affect responses to treatment. For example, among people diagnosed with schizophrenia, those living in a developing country such as India are much more likely to improve than those living in a more developed country (Hopper & Wanderling, 2000). We don't yet know what cultural factors might be responsible for this difference, but these data highlight the fact that any attempt to fully explain psychological disorders must take sociocultural factors into account.

Diathesis-Stress as an Integrative Explanation

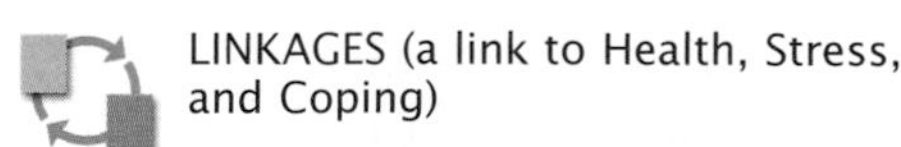

The biopsychosocial model is currently the most comprehensive and influential approach to explaining psychological disorders. It is prominent partly because it encompasses so many important causal factors, including biological imbalances, genetically inherited characteristics, brain damage, enduring psychological traits, socioculturally influenced learning experiences, stressful life events, and many more.

How do all these factors interact to actually create disorder? Most researchers believe that inherited characteristics, biological processes, and early learning experiences combine to create a predisposition, or *diathesis* (pronounced "dye-A-thuh-sis"), for a psychological disorder. Whether or not a person actually develops symptoms of disorder depends on the nature and amount of stress the person encounters (Turner & Lloyd, 2004; U.S. Surgeon General, 1999). For example, a person may have inherited a biological tendency toward depression or may have learned depressing patterns of thinking, but these predispositions may be expressed as a depressive disorder only after the person is faced with a financial crisis or suffers the loss of a loved one. If such circumstances don't occur, or if the person has adequate skills for coping with stress, depressive symptoms may never appear or may be quite mild.

This way of thinking about the biopsychosocial model is known as the **diathesis-stress approach.** It assumes that biological, psychological, and sociocultural factors can predispose us toward disorder but that it takes a certain amount of stress to actually trigger a disorder. For people with a strong diathesis, relatively mild stress might be enough to create a problem. People whose predisposition is weaker might not show signs of disorder until stress becomes extreme or prolonged. Another way to think about the notion of diathesis-stress is in terms of *risk:* The more risk factors for a

diathesis-stress approach Viewing psychological disorders as arising when a predisposition for a disorder combines with sufficient amounts of stress to trigger symptoms.

table 15.2

Here are the factors that would be considered by the biopsychosocial model, and combined in the diathesis-stress approach, to explain the case of José, a 55-year-old electronics technician. A healthy and vigorous father of two adult children, he was recently forced to take medical leave because of a series of sudden, uncontrollable panic attacks in which he experienced dizziness, heart palpitations, sweating, and fear of impending death. The attacks also kept him from his favourite pastime, scuba diving, but he has been able to maintain a part-time computer business out of his home. (Panic disorder is discussed in more detail later in this chapter; the outcome of this case is described in the chapter on treatment of psychological disorders.)

The Biopsychosocial Model of Psychopathology

Explanatory Domain	Possible Contributing Factors
Neurobiological/medical	José may have organic disorders (e.g., genetic tendency toward anxiety; brain tumour, endocrine dysfunction; neurotransmitter imbalance).
Psychological: psychodynamic	José has unconscious conflicts and desires. Instinctual impulses are breaking through ego defenses into consciousness, causing panic.
Psychological: social-cognitive	Physical stress symptoms are interpreted as signs of serious illness or impending death. Panic is rewarded by avoidance of work stress and the opportunity to stay home.
Psychological: humanistic	José fails to recognize his genuine feelings about work and his place in life, and he fears expressing himself.
Sociocultural	A culturally based belief that "a man should not show weakness" amplifies the intensity of stress reactions and delays José's decision to seek help.
Diathesis-stress summary	José has a biological (possibly genetic) predisposition to be overly responsive to stressors. The stress of work and extra activity exceeds his capacity to cope and triggers panic as a stress response.

disorder a person has—whether in the form of genetic tendencies, personality traits, cultural traditions, or stressful life events—the more likely it is that the person will display a form of psychological disorder associated with those risk factors.

Table 15.2 provides an example of how the diathesis-stress approach and the factors contained in the biopsychosocial model of disorder might explain a particular case of psychopathology. Throughout this chapter, you'll see how the biopsychosocial model and the diathesis-stress approach are applied to understanding the causes of several other psychological disorders.

Classifying Psychological Disorders

Although definitions of abnormality differ somewhat within and across cultures, there is a set of culture-general and culture-specific behaviour patterns that characterize what most mental health professionals consider to be psychopathology. Most of these behaviour patterns qualify as disorders because they result in impaired functioning, a main criterion of the practical approach to defining abnormality. It has long been the goal of those who study abnormal behaviour to organize these patterns into a system of diagnostic categories.

The main purpose of diagnosing psychological disorders is to determine the nature of people's problems. Once the characteristics of the problems are understood, the most appropriate method of treatment can be chosen. Diagnoses are also important for research on the causes of mental disorders. If researchers can accurately and reliably classify people into particular disorder categories, they will have a better chance of spotting genetic flaws, biological abnormalities, cognitive processes, and environmental experiences that people in the same category might share. Finding that people in a certain diagnostic category share a set of features that differs from those seen in other categories could provide clues about which features are related to the development of each disorder.

In 1952 the American Psychiatric Association published the first edition of what has become the official North American diagnostic classification system, the *Diagnostic and Statistical Manual of Mental Disorders (DSM)*. Each new edition of the *DSM* has included more categories of disorders. The latest editions, *DSM-IV* and *DSM-IV-TR* (which contains some text revisions), include more than three hundred specific diagnostic labels (American Psychiatric Association, 1994, 2000).

Mental health professionals outside North America diagnose mental disorders using the classification systems that appear in the tenth edition of the World Health Organization's *International Classification of Diseases (ICD-10)* and its companion volume, the second edition of the *International Classification of Impairments, Disabilities and Handicaps (ICIDH-2)*. To improve international communication about—and cross-cultural research on—psychopathology, *DSM-IV* was designed to be compatible with these manuals, and efforts are under way to remove inconsistencies existing between the systems (DeAngelis, 2001; Ottosson et al., 2002).

A Classification System: *DSM-IV*

DSM-IV describes the abnormal patterns of thinking, emotion, and behaviour that define various mental disorders. For each disorder, *DSM* provides specific criteria outlining the conditions that must be present before a person can be given that diagnostic label. Diagnosticians using *DSM-IV* can evaluate troubled people on as many as five dimensions, or *axes*. In keeping with the biopsychosocial model, evaluations on all relevant dimensions are combined to create a broad outline of the person's biological and psychological problems, as well as of any sociocultural factors that might contribute to them. As shown in Table 15.3, major mental disorders, such as schizophrenia or mood disorders, are recorded on Axis I, whereas evidence of personality disorders or mental retardation are noted on Axis II. Any medical conditions that might be important in understanding the person's cognitive, emotional, or behavioural problems are listed on Axis III. On Axis IV the diagnostician notes any psychosocial and environmental problems (such as the loss of a loved one, physical or sexual abuse, discrimination, unemployment, poverty, homelessness, inadequate health care, or conflict with religious or cultural traditions) that are important for understanding the person's psychological problems. Finally, a rating (from 100 down to 1) of the person's current level of psychological, social, and occupational functioning appears on Axis V. Here is a sample *DSM-IV* diagnosis for a person who received labels on all five axes:

Axis I Major depressive disorder, single episode; alcohol abuse.

Axis II Dependent personality disorder.

Axis III Alcoholic cirrhosis of the liver.

Axis IV Problems with primary support group (death of spouse).

Axis V Global assessment of functioning: 50.

The current system for diagnosing psychological disorders has not satisfied everyone, and it is unlikely that any system ever will. No shorthand diagnostic label can fully describe a person's problems or predict exactly how that person will behave. All that can be reasonably expected of a diagnostic system is that it is based on the latest research on psychopathology and that it provides informative, general descriptions of the types of problems displayed by people who have been placed in various categories (First et al., 2004).

We don't have the space to cover all the *DSM-IV* categories, so we will sample several of the most prevalent and socially significant ones. As you read, try not to catch "medical student's disease." Just as medical students often think they have the

table 15.3

The *Diagnostic and Statistical Manual of Mental Disorders (DSM)* of the American Psychiatric Association

Axis I of the fourth edition *(DSM-IV)* lists the major categories of mental disorders. Personality disorders and mental retardation are listed on Axis II.

Axis I (Clinical Syndromes)

1. ***Disorders usually first diagnosed in infancy, childhood, or adolescence.*** Problems such as hyperactivity, childhood fears, conduct disorders, frequent bed-wetting or soiling, and other problems in normal social and behavioural development. Autistic disorder (severe impairment in social, behavioural, and language development), as well as learning disorders.
2. ***Delirium, dementia, and amnestic and other cognitive disorders.*** Problems caused by physical deterioration of the brain due to aging, disease, drugs or other chemicals, or other possible unknown causes. These problems can appear as an inability to "think straight" (delirium) or as loss of memory and other intellectual functions (dementia).
3. ***Substance-related disorders.*** Psychological, behavioural, physical, social, or legal problems caused by dependence on, or abuse of, a variety of chemical substances, including alcohol, heroin, cocaine, amphetamines, hallucinogens, marijuana, and tobacco.
4. ***Schizophrenia and other psychotic disorders.*** Severe conditions characterized by abnormalities in thinking, perception, emotion, movement, and motivation that greatly interfere with daily functioning. Problems involving false beliefs (delusions).
5. ***Mood disorders (also called affective disorders).*** Severe disturbances of mood, especially depression, overexcitement (mania), or alternating episodes of each extreme (as in bipolar disorder).
6. ***Anxiety disorders.*** Specific fears (phobias); panic attacks; generalized feelings of dread; rituals of thought and action (obsessive-compulsive disorder) aimed at controlling anxiety; and problems caused by traumatic events, such as rape or military combat (see the chapter on health, stress, and coping for more on post-traumatic stress disorder).
7. ***Somatoform disorders.*** Physical symptoms, such as paralysis and blindness, that have no physical cause. Unusual preoccupation with physical health or with nonexistent physical problems (hypochondriasis, somatization disorder, pain disorder).
8. ***Factitious disorders.*** False mental disorders, which are intentionally produced to satisfy some psychological need.
9. ***Dissociative disorders.*** Psychologically caused problems of consciousness and self-identification—e.g., loss of memory (amnesia) or the development of more than one identity (multiple personality).
10. ***Sexual and gender identity disorders.*** Problems of (a) finding sexual arousal through unusual objects or situations (like shoes or exposing oneself), (b) unsatisfactory sexual activity (sexual dysfunction; see the chapter on motivation and emotion), or (c) identifying with the opposite gender.
11. ***Eating disorders.*** Problems associated with eating too little (anorexia nervosa) or binge eating followed by self-induced vomiting (bulimia nervosa). (See the chapter on motivation and emotion.)
12. ***Sleep disorders.*** Severe problems involving the sleep-wake cycle, especially an inability to sleep well at night or to stay awake during the day. (See the chapter on consciousness.)
13. ***Impulse control disorders.*** Compulsive gambling, stealing, or fire setting.
14. ***Adjustment disorders.*** Failure to adjust to, or deal well with, such stressors as divorce, financial problems, family discord, or other unhappy life events.

Axis II (Personality Disorders and Mental Retardation)

1. ***Personality disorders.*** Diagnostic labels given to individuals who may or may not receive an Axis I diagnosis but who show lifelong behaviour patterns that are unsatisfactory to them or that disturb other people. These patterns may involve unusual suspiciousness, unusual ways of thinking, self-centredness, shyness, overdependency, excessive concern with neatness and detail, or overemotionality, among others.
2. ***Mental retardation.*** As described in the chapter on cognitive abilities, the label of mental retardation is applied to individuals whose measured IQ is less than about 70 *and* who fail to display the skills at daily living, communication, and other tasks expected of people their age.

symptoms of every illness they read about, some psychology students worry that their behaviour (or that of a relative or friend) signals a mental disorder. Remember that everyone has problems sometimes. Before deciding that you or someone you know needs psychological help, consider whether the content, context, and functional impairment associated with the behaviour would qualify it as abnormal according to the criteria of the practical approach.

table 15.4

Phobia is the Greek word for "morbid fear," after the Greek god Phobos. Phobias are usually named by attaching the word *phobia* to the Greek word for the feared object or situation.

Some Phobias

Name	Feared Stimulus	Name	Feared Stimulus
Acrophobia	Heights	Aerophobia	Flying
Claustrophobia	Enclosed places	Entomophobia	Insects
Hematophobia	Blood	Gamophobia	Marriage
Gephyrophobia	Crossing a bridge	Ophidiphobia	Snakes
Kenophobia	Empty rooms	Xenophobia	Strangers
Cynophobia	Dogs	Melissophobia	Bees

Anxiety Disorders

If you have ever been tense before an exam, a date, or a job interview, you have some idea of what anxiety feels like. Increased heart rate, sweating, rapid breathing, a dry mouth, and a sense of dread are common features of anxiety. Brief episodes of moderate anxiety are a normal part of life for most people. But when anxiety is so intense and long-lasting that it impairs a person's daily functioning, it is called an **anxiety disorder.**

Types of Anxiety Disorders

Here we discuss four types of anxiety disorders: *phobia, generalized anxiety disorder, panic disorder,* and *obsessive-compulsive disorder.* Another type, called *posttraumatic stress disorder,* is described in the chapter on health, stress, and coping. Together, these are the most common psychological disorders in North America.

Phobia An intense, irrational fear of an object or situation that is not likely to be dangerous is called a **phobia.** People who experience phobias usually realize that their fears are groundless, but that's not enough to make the anxiety go away. The continuing discomfort and avoidance of the object or event may greatly interfere with daily life. Thousands of phobias have been described; Table 15.4 lists just a few.

DSM-IV classifies phobias into specific, social, and agoraphobia subtypes. **Specific phobias** include fear and avoidance of heights, blood, animals, automobile or air travel, and other specific stimuli and situations. In Canada and other developed nations, they are the most prevalent of the anxiety disorders, affecting 7 to 11 percent of adults and children (Public Health Agency of Canada, 2003). Here is an example:

> *Mr. L. was a 50-year-old office worker who became terrified whenever he had to drive over a bridge. For years, he avoided bridges by taking roundabout ways to and from work, and he refused to be a passenger in anyone else's car, just in case they might use a bridge. Even this very inconvenient adjustment failed when Mr. L. was transferred to a position requiring frequent automobile trips, many of which were over bridges. He refused the transfer and lost his job.*

Social phobias involve anxiety about being criticized by others or acting in a way that is embarrassing or humiliating. The anxiety is so intense and persistent that it impairs the person's normal functioning. Common social phobias are fear of public speaking or performance ("stage fright"), fear of eating in front of others, and fear of using public restrooms (Kleinknecht, 2000). *Generalized social phobia* is a more severe form in which fear occurs in virtually all social situations (Mannuzza et al.,

anxiety disorder A condition in which intense feelings of apprehension are longstanding and disruptive.

phobia An anxiety disorder involving strong, irrational fear of an object or situation that does not objectively justify such a reaction.

specific phobia An anxiety disorder involving fear and avoidance of heights, animals, and other specific stimuli and situations.

social phobia An anxiety disorder involving strong, irrational fears relating to social situations.

It's a Long Way Down Almost everyone is afraid of something, but as many as 11 percent of Canadian adults suffer from a specific phobia, in which fear interferes significantly with daily life. For example, people with acrophobia (fear of heights) could never even consider joining Calgary Mayor Dave Bronconnier here on the glass deck of the Calgary Tower.

1995). Sociocultural factors can alter the nature of social phobias. For example, in Japan, where cultural training emphasizes group-oriented values and goals, a common social phobia is *tai-jin kyofu sho,* fear of embarrassing those around you (Kleinknecht, 1994).

Agoraphobia is a strong fear of being away from a safe place, such as home; of being away from a familiar person, such as a spouse or close friend; or of being in a place (such as a crowded theatre or mall) that might be difficult to leave or where help may be unavailable. These fears can cause serious disruption. People who suffer from agoraphobia typically avoid social situations and refuse to shop, drive, or use public transportation. They may be unable to work and can easily become isolated. In severe cases, agoraphobia can make leaving home such a frightening prospect that people become housebound, unwilling to even try going out alone. Most individuals who display agoraphobia have a history of panic attacks, which we describe later. Their intense fear of public places occurs partly because they don't want to risk triggering an attack by going to places in which they had a previous attack or where they feel an attack would be dangerous or embarrassing.

Like other phobias in Western cultures, agoraphobia is more often reported by women. However, in other cultures, such as India, where being a housebound woman is considered less unusual, those diagnosed as agoraphobic tend to be male (Raguram & Bhide, 1985). Although agoraphobia occurs less frequently than specific phobias (affecting about 4 percent of the population in Canada), it is the phobia that most often leads people to seek treatment, mainly because it interferes so severely with everyday life (U.S. Surgeon General, 1999, Public Health Agency of Canada, 2003).

Generalized Anxiety Disorder Excessive and long-lasting anxiety that is not focused on any particular object or situation marks **generalized anxiety disorder.** Because the problem occurs in almost all situations and because the person cannot pinpoint its source, this type of anxiety is sometimes called *free-floating anxiety.* For weeks at a time, the person feels anxious and worried, sure that some disaster is about to happen. The person becomes jumpy and irritable; sound sleep is impossible. Fatigue, inability to concentrate, and physiological signs of anxiety are also common. Generalized anxiety disorder affects about 5 percent of the Canadian population at

On the Attack Against Panic Former Toronto Maple Leaf, Shayne Corson, has spoken openly about his experience of panic attacks.

agoraphobia An anxiety disorder involving strong fear of being alone or away from the security of home.

generalized anxiety disorder A condition that involves relatively mild but long-lasting anxiety that is not focused on any particular object or situation.

some point in their lives (Public Health Agency of Canada, 2003). It is more common in women, often accompanying other problems such as depression or substance abuse (Wittchen & Hoyer, 2001).

Panic Disorder For some people, anxiety takes the form of **panic disorder.** Like the man described in Table 15.2, people suffering from panic disorder experience recurrent, terrifying *panic attacks* that seem to come without warning or obvious cause. These attacks are marked by intense heart palpitations, pressure or pain in the chest, dizziness or unsteadiness, sweating, and a feeling of faintness. Often, victims believe they are having a heart attack. They may worry constantly about suffering future panic episodes and thus restrict their activities to avoid possible embarrassment (Carter & Barlow, 1995). (As noted earlier, fear of experiencing panic attacks while alone or away from home can lead to agoraphobia.) Panic disorder can continue for years, with periods of improvement followed by recurrence (Ehlers, 1995). Approximately 21 percent of Canadians aged 15 and over have experienced at least one panic attack at some point in their lives, but only about 4 percent of the population has been diagnosed with panic disorder (Statistics Canada, 2004). Here is one example:

> *Geri, a 32-year-old nurse, had her first panic attack while driving on a highway. Afterward, she would not drive on a highway. Her next attack occurred while with a patient and a doctor in a small examining room. A sense of impending doom flooded over her, and she burst out of the office and into the parking lot, where she felt immediate relief. From then on, fear of another attack made it impossible for her to tolerate any close quarters, including crowded shopping malls. She eventually quit her job because of terror of the examining rooms.*

Obsessive-Compulsive Disorder Anxiety is also at the root of **obsessive-compulsive disorder (OCD),** which affects about 2 percent of the population in any given year in Canada and elsewhere (American Psychiatric Association, 2000; Howarth & Weissman, 2000; U.S. Surgeon General, 1999; Public Health Agency of Canada, 2002b). Like Mark, whose story opened this chapter, people displaying obsessive-compulsive disorder are plagued by persistent, upsetting, and unwanted thoughts—called *obsessions*—that often centre on the possibility of infection, contamination, or doing harm to themselves or others. They do not actually carry out

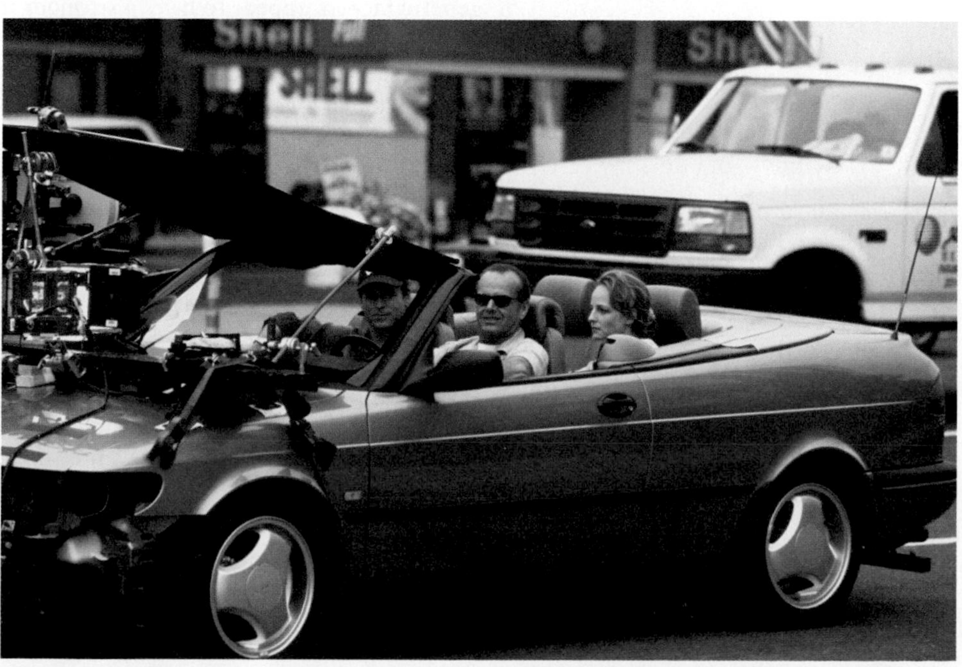

A Cleaning Compulsion In the 1997 movie, *As Good as It Gets*, Jack Nicholson played the role of a person diagnosed with Obsessive-Compulsive Disorder. Obsessive-compulsive disorder is diagnosed when a culturally expected degree of cleanliness becomes an obsessive preoccupation with germs and a disruptive compulsion to clean things. Though learning and stress appear to play the major role in shaping and triggering this and other anxiety disorders, biological factors, including genetically inherited characteristics and deficiencies in certain neurotransmitters in the brain, may result in an oversensitive nervous system and a predisposition toward anxiety.

panic disorder An anxiety disorder involving sudden panic attacks.

obsessive-compulsive disorder (OCD) An anxiety disorder involving repetitive thoughts and urges to perform certain rituals.

harmful acts, but the obsessive thoughts motivate ritualistic, repetitive behaviours—called *compulsions*—that are performed in an effort to avoid some dreaded outcome or to reduce feelings of anxiety associated with the obsessions (Foa & Kozak, 1995). For example, Mark engaged in incessant, ritualized cleaning to protect himself from infection. Other common compulsions include rituals such as checking locks; repeating words, images, or numbers; counting things; or arranging objects "just so." Obsessions and compulsions are much more intense than the familiar experience of having a repetitive thought or tune "in the back of your mind" or rechecking that a door is locked. In obsessive-compulsive disorder, the obsessions and compulsions are intense, disturbing, and often bizarre intrusions that can severely impair daily activities. (*DSM-IV* defines compulsions as taking up more than one hour a day.) Many people who display this disorder recognize that their thoughts and actions are irrational, but they still experience severe agitation and anxiety if they try to interrupt their obsessions or give up their compulsive behaviours.

Causes of Anxiety Disorders

As with all the forms of psychopathology we will consider, the exact causes of anxiety disorders are a matter of some debate. However, there is good evidence that biological, psychological, and social factors all contribute. Biological predispositions, distortions in thinking, and certain learning experiences appear to be particularly important (U.S. Surgeon General, 1999).

Biological Factors Most anxiety disorders, including panic disorder, obsessive-compulsive disorder, and generalized social phobia, appear to run in families (Kendler et al., 1995; Kendler, Myers, et al., 2001; Pauls et al., 1995; Skre et al., 2000; Wittchen et al., 1994). This tendency may be partly due to environmental factors that affect members of the same family, but it also suggests that people may inherit a predisposition to develop anxiety disorders. Genetic influences on these disorders are suggested by research showing that if one identical twin has an anxiety disorder, the other is more likely also to have an anxiety disorder than is the case in nonidentical twin pairs (Kendler, Neale, et al., 1992; Kendler, Jacobson, et al., 2002). Data from twin, family, and other studies suggest, for example, that genetic influences play a relatively strong role in panic disorder and generalized anxiety disorder (Hettema, Neale, & Kendler, 2001; Neumeister et al., 2004). In social phobia, genetic factors appear to have a stronger influence in males than in females (Kendler, Jacobson, et al., 2002).

People who display anxiety disorders may have inherited an autonomic nervous system that is oversensitive to stress, thus predisposing them to react with anxiety to a wide range of situations (Ahmad et al., 2002; Zinbarg & Barlow, 1996). There may be more specific predispositions as well. One study has found that identical twins were more likely than other siblings to share phobias about small animals and social situations but not about heights or enclosed spaces (Skre et al., 2000).

A predisposition for developing anxiety disorders may also stem from abnormalities in the brain's neurotransmitter systems, which are discussed in the chapter on the biological aspects of psychology. Excessive activity of norepinephrine in certain parts of the brain has been linked with panic disorder, and dysregulation of serotonin has been associated with obsessive-compulsive disorder. In addition, there is evidence that anxiety-generating neural impulses may run unchecked when the neurotransmitter GABA is prevented from exerting its normal inhibitory influence in certain neural pathways (Friedman, Clark, & Gershon, 1992; Zorumski & Isenberg, 1991).

Psychological Factors Although biological predispositions may set the stage for anxiety disorders, most researchers agree that environmental stressors and psychological factors, including cognitive processes and learning, are crucial to the development of most anxiety disorders (Ley, 1994; Schmidt et al., 2000; Stein, Chavira, & Jang, 2001). To see the effects of environmental stressors, one need only look at the dramatic rise in cases of post-traumatic stress disorder following natural disasters or terrorist attacks (Galea et al., 2002). The impact of learning can be seen in families in which parents don't socialize much, tend to be suspicious of others, and constantly exaggerate life's everyday dangers. These parents might unwittingly promote social anxiety in their children—especially children born with a tendency toward shyness—by influencing them to interpret social situations as threatening. Abuse or other traumatic childhood experiences also increase the risk of developing an anxiety disorder, particularly panic disorder (Safren et al., 2002).

People suffering from an anxiety disorder often exaggerate the dangers in their environment, thereby creating an unrealistic expectation that bad events are going to happen (Foa et al., 1996). In addition, they tend to underestimate their own capacity for dealing with threatening events, resulting in anxiety and desperation when feared events do occur (Beck & Emery, 1985). As an example, consider the development of a panic attack. Whereas the appearance of unexplained symptoms of physical arousal may make a panic attack more likely, the person's interpretation of those symptoms can determine whether or not the attack actually develops (Clark et al., 1997; Schmidt, Lerew, & Jackson, 1999). One study found that panic attacks were much less likely if panic-disorder patients believed they could control the source of their discomfort (Rapee et al., 1992). In another study, panic-disorder patients were asked to inhale carbon dioxide, which typically causes panic attacks in such patients. Those who inhaled this substance in the presence of a person they associated with safety were significantly less fearful than patients whose "safe person" was absent (Carter et al., 1995). Results like these suggest a role for cognitive factors in panic disorder.

LINKAGES
Anxiety Disorders and Learning

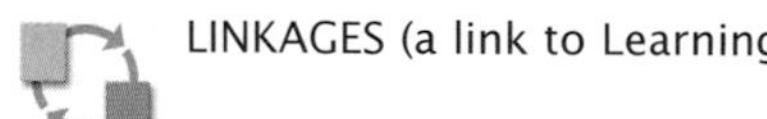

LINKAGES (a link to Learning)

The learning principles discussed in the chapter on learning also play an important role in anxiety disorders. For example, upsetting thoughts—about money or illness, for example—often create anxiety and worry, especially when people are already under stress or feel incapable of dealing with their problems. As the thoughts become more persistent, anxiety increases. If, say, cleaning the kitchen temporarily relieves the anxiety, that behaviour may be strengthened through the process of negative reinforcement discussed in the chapter on learning. But such actions cannot eliminate the obsessive thoughts, so they return, and the actions become compulsive, endlessly repeated rituals that keep the person trapped in a vicious circle of anxiety (Barlow, 1988). In other words, to social-cognitive theorists, obsessive-compulsive disorder is a pattern that is sparked by distressing thoughts and maintained by operant conditioning.

Phobias, too, may be partly based on learning, especially on the principles of classical conditioning and observational learning described in the learning chapter. The feared object becomes an aversive conditioned stimulus after being associated with a traumatic event that acts as an unconditioned stimulus (Öst, 1992). Fear of dogs, for example, may result from a dog attack. But fear can also be learned merely by seeing or hearing about other people's bad experiences (most people who fear flying have never been in a plane crash). Once phobias are learned, avoiding the feared object or situation prevents the person from finding out that there is nothing to fear. This cycle of avoidance helps explain why many phobias do not simply extinguish, or disappear, on their own.

Why are phobias about snakes and spiders so common, even though people are seldom harmed by them? And why are there so few cases of electrical-shock phobia, even though lots of people receive accidental electrical shocks? As

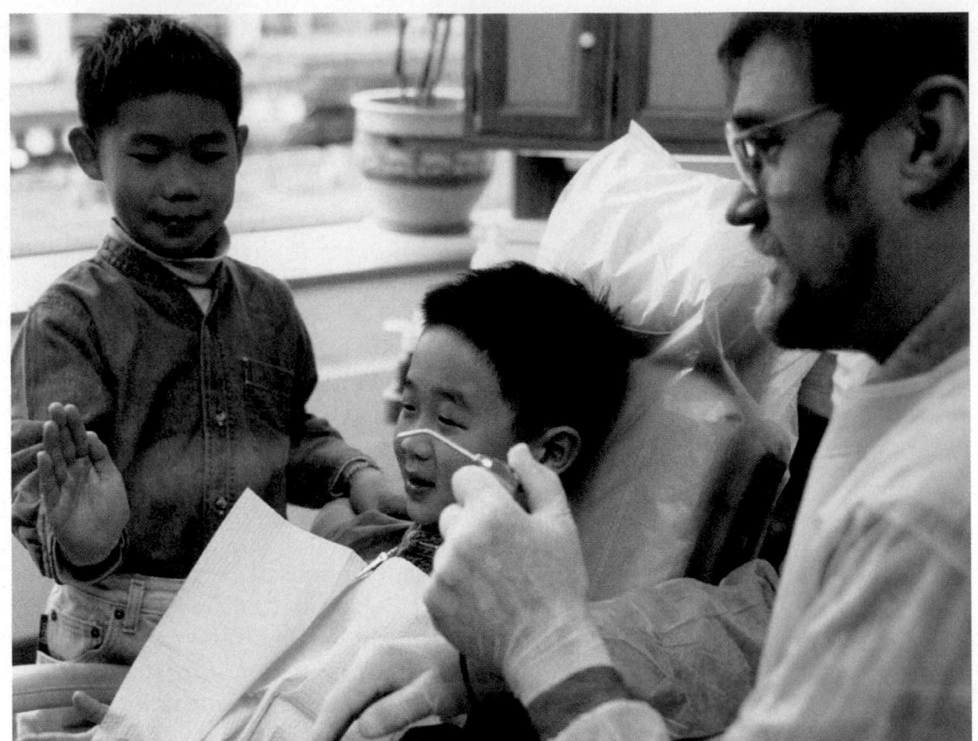

Learning by Watching Many phobias, including those involving needles, blood, and medical-related situations, are acquired vicariously—by what we see and hear. Fear developed through observational learning can be as strong as fear developed through direct experience, though direct conditioning is the more common pathway to phobia (Öst, 1992). Fearlessness can also be learned vicariously. By simply watching the boy in the dental chair as he learns to relax with his dentist, the other youngster is less likely to be distressed when it is his turn.

discussed in the chapter on learning, the answer may be that we are *biologically prepared* to learn associations between certain stimuli and certain responses. These stimuli and responses, then, would be especially easy to link through conditioning (Hamm, Vaitl, & Lang, 1989).

Some laboratory evidence supports the notion that people are biologically prepared to learn certain phobias. A group of Swedish psychologists attempted to condition people to fear certain stimuli by associating those stimuli with electrical

Biological Preparedness Being predisposed to learn to fear snakes and other potentially dangerous stimuli makes evolutionary sense. Animals (and humans) who rapidly learn a fear response to objects or situations that they see causing fright in their parents or peers are more likely to survive to pass on their genes to the next generation. Make a list of the things that you might be especially afraid of. How did these fears develop? And how many of them appear to have "survival value"?

shocks (Öhman, Dimberg, & Öst, 1985). The research participants developed approximately equal conditioned anxiety reactions to photos of houses, human faces, and snakes. Later, however, when they were tested without shock, their fear reaction to snakes remained long after their reaction to houses and faces had faded. A series of investigations with animals has also supported preparedness theory (Cook & Mineka, 1990). If a monkey sees another monkey behaving fearfully in the presence of a snake, it quickly develops a strong and persistent fear of snakes. However, if the snake is entwined in flowers, the observer monkeys come to fear only the snake, not the flowers. So the fear conditioning was selective, focusing only on potentially dangerous creatures such as snakes or crocodiles (Zinbarg & Mineka, 1991), not on harmless objects. Data such as these suggest that anxiety disorders probably arise through the combined effects of genetic predispositions and learning.

Somatoform Disorders

A young athlete began to suffer fainting spells that prevented her from competing in track and field events, but doctors could find nothing physically wrong. After a program of stress management, however, her symptoms disappeared, and she was able to rejoin her team (Lively, 2001). Sometimes people show symptoms of a *somatic*, or bodily, disorder, even though it has no physical cause. Because these conditions reflect psychological problems that take somatic form, they are called **somatoform disorders.** The classic example is **conversion disorder,** a condition in which a person appears to be, but is not, blind, deaf, paralyzed, or insensitive to pain in various parts of the body. (An earlier term for this disorder was *hysteria.*) Conversion disorders are rare, accounting for only about 2 percent of diagnoses (American Psychiatric Association, 1994, 2000). Although they can occur at any point in life, they usually appear in adolescence or early adulthood.

Conversion disorders differ from true physical disabilities in several ways. First, they tend to appear when a person is under severe stress. Second, they often help reduce that stress by allowing the person to avoid unpleasant or threatening situations. Third, the person may show remarkably little concern about what is apparently a rather serious problem. Finally, the symptoms may be neurologically impossible or improbable, as Figure 15.1 illustrates. One university student, for example, experienced visual impairment that began each Sunday evening and became total blindness by Monday morning. Her vision would begin to return on Friday evenings and was fully restored in time for weekend football games and other social activities. She expressed no particular concern over her condition (Holmes, 1991).

Can people who display a conversion disorder actually see and hear, even though they act as if they cannot? Experiments show that they can (Grosz & Zimmerman, 1970), but this does not necessarily mean that they are *malingering,* or faking. Research on consciousness suggests that people can use sensory input even when they are not consciously aware of doing so (e.g., Blake, 1998). Rather than destroying visual or auditory ability, the conversion process may prevent the person from being aware of information that the brain is still processing (Halligan & David, 1999).

Another somatoform disorder is **hypochondriasis** (pronounced "hye-poh-kon-DRY-a-sis"), a strong, unjustified fear that one has cancer, heart disease, AIDS, or other serious physical problems. The fear prompts frequent visits to physicians and reports of numerous symptoms. Their preoccupation with illness often leads hypochondriacs to become experts on their most feared diseases. In some ways, hypochondriasis is like an anxiety disorder that includes elements of phobia, panic, and obsessive-compulsiveness (Neziroglu, McKay, & Yaryura-Tobias, 2000). However, whereas a person suffering from anxiety disorder might have an irrational

somatoform disorders Psychological problems in which there are symptoms of a physical disorder without a physical cause.

conversion disorder A somatoform disorder in which a person displays blindness, deafness, or other symptoms of sensory or motor failure without a physical cause.

hypochondriasis A somatoform disorder involving strong, unjustified fear of having physical illness.

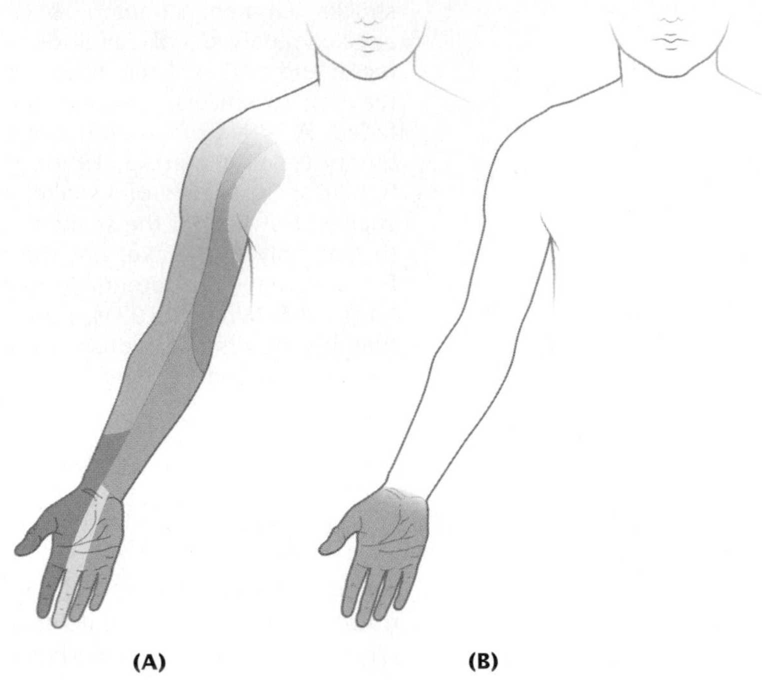

figure 15.1

Glove Anesthesia

In "glove anesthesia," a form of conversion disorder, lack of feeling stops abruptly at the wrist, as in Part B. But as shown in Part A, the nerves of the hand and arm blend, so if they were actually impaired, part of the arm would also lose sensitivity. Other neurologically impossible symptoms of conversion disorder include sleepwalking at night on legs that are "paralyzed" during the day.

fear of getting a serious illness, the person diagnosed with hypochondriasis is excessively concerned about already *having* the illness. A related condition, called **somatization disorder,** is characterized by dramatic, but vague, reports about a multitude of physical problems rather than any specific illness. Finally, **pain disorder** is marked by complaints of severe, often constant pain (typically in the neck, chest, or back) with no physical cause.

Some cases of somatoform disorder may be related to childhood experiences in which a person learns that symptoms of physical illness bring special attention, care, and privileges (Barsky et al., 1994). Others, including conversion disorder, may be triggered by severe stressors (Spiegel, 1994). Cognitive factors also come into play. When given information about their health, persons with hypochondriasis are strongly biased to focus on threat-confirming information but to ignore reassuring information (Smeets, de Jong, & Mayer, 2000).

Based on such findings, many researchers have adopted a diathesis-stress approach to explaining somatoform disorders. The results of their work suggest that certain people may have biological and psychological traits that make them especially vulnerable to somatoform disorders, particularly when combined with a history of physical illness. Among these traits are self-consciousness and oversensitivity to physical sensations. If such people experience a number of long-lasting stressors, intense emotional conflicts, or severe traumas, they are more likely than others to display physical symptoms in association with emotional arousal (Nietzel et al., 1998).

Sociocultural factors may also shape some somatoform disorders. For example, in many Asian, Latin American, and African cultures, it is not unusual for people to experience severe physical symptoms in association with psychological or interpersonal conflicts, whereas in North America such conflicts are more likely to result in anxiety or depression (Brislin, 1993). Genetic factors appear to play only a minor role in somatoform disorders.

Dissociative Disorders

If you have ever spent many hours driving on a boring highway, you may have suddenly realized that you had little or no recollection of what happened during the previous half-hour. This common experience does not signal a mental disorder, but when disruptions in a person's memory, consciousness, or identity are more intense

A Famous Case of Dissociative Identity Disorder In this scene from the film *Sybil*, Sally Field portrays a woman diagnosed with dissociative identity disorder, previously known as multiple personality disorder. Sybil appeared to have as many as 17 distinct personalities. The causes of such dramatic cases, and the reasons behind their increasing prevalence in recent years, is a matter of intense debate.

and long-lasting, they are known as **dissociative disorders.** These disruptions can come on gradually, but they usually occur suddenly and last from a few hours to many years.

Consider the case of John, a 30-year-old computer manufacturing executive. John was a meek person who was dependent on his wife for companionship and emotional support. It came as a jolt when she announced that she was leaving him to live with his younger brother. John did not go to work the next day. In fact, nothing was heard from him for two weeks until he was arrested for public drunkenness and assault in a city more than 300 miles from his home. During those two weeks, John lived under another name at a cheap hotel and worked selling tickets at a pornographic movie theatre. When he was interviewed, John did not know his real name or his home address, could not explain how he had reached his present location, and could not remember much about the previous two weeks.

John's case illustrates the dissociative disorder known as **dissociative fugue** (pronounced "fewg"), which is marked by a sudden loss of personal memory and the adoption of a new identity in a new locale. Another dissociative disorder, **dissociative amnesia,** also involves sudden memory loss. As in fugue, all personal identifying information may be forgotten, but the person does not leave home or create a new identity. These rare conditions attract intense publicity because they are so dramatic. As with other forms of disorder, the nature of dissociative disorders can vary from culture to culture. For instance, some dissociative-disorder patients in China, Malaysia, and India report being possessed by one of their religion's gods (Ng, 2000).

The most famous dissociative disorder is **dissociative identity disorder (DID),** formerly known as—and still commonly called—*multiple personality disorder (MPD)*. A person diagnosed with DID appears to have more than one identity, each of which speaks, acts, and writes in a different way. Each personality seems to have its own memories, wishes, and (often conflicting) impulses. Here is a case example:

> *Mary, a pleasant and introverted 35-year-old social worker, was referred to a psychiatrist for hypnotic treatment of chronic pain. At an early interview she mentioned the odd fact that though she had no memory of using her car after coming home from work, she often found that it had been driven 50 to 100 miles overnight. It turned out that she also had no memory of large parts of her childhood. Mary rapidly learned self-hypnosis for pain control, but during one hypnotic session, she suddenly began speaking in a hostile manner. She told the doctor her name was Marian, and that it was "she" who had been taking long evening drives. She also called Mary "pathetic" for "wasting time" trying to please other people. Eventually, six other identities emerged, some of whom told of having experienced parental abuse in childhood.* (Spitzer et al., 1994)

How do dissociative disorders develop? Psychodynamic theorists see massive repression of unwanted impulses or memories as the basis for creating a "new person" who acts out otherwise unacceptable impulses or recalls otherwise unbearable memories (Ross, 1997). Social-cognitive theorists focus on the fact that everyone is capable of behaving in different ways, depending on circumstances (e.g., rowdy in a bar, quiet in a museum); but in rare cases, they say, this variation can become so extreme that an individual feels— and is perceived by others as being—a "different person." Further, dissociative symptoms may be strengthened by reward as people find that a sudden memory loss or shift in behaviour allows them to escape stressful situations, responsibilities, or punishment for misbehaviour (Lilienfeld et al., 1999).

Evaluating these hypotheses has been difficult, partly because dissociative disorders have been so relatively rare. Recently, however, dissociative identity disorder has been diagnosed more frequently, either because clinicians are looking for it more carefully or because the conditions leading to it are more prevalent. Research available so far supports three conclusions. First, many people displaying DID have experienced events they would like to forget or avoid. The majority (some clinicians believe all) have suffered severe, unavoidable, persistent abuse in childhood (Ross et al., 1991).

somatization disorder Somatoform disorders in which there are numerous physical complaints without verifiable physical illness.

pain disorder A somatoform disorder marked by complaints of severe pain with no physical cause.

dissociative disorders Rare conditions that involve sudden and usually temporary disruptions in a person's memory, consciousness, or identity.

dissociative fugue A dissociative disorder involving sudden loss of memory and the assumption of a new identity in a new locale.

dissociative amnesia A dissociative disorder marked by a sudden loss of memory.

dissociative identity disorder (DID) A dissociative disorder in which a person reports having more than one identity.

in review Anxiety, Somatoform, and Dissociative Disorders

Disorder	Subtypes	Major Symptoms
Anxiety disorders	Phobias	Intense, irrational fear of objectively nondangerous situations or things, leading to disruptions of behaviour
	Generalized anxiety disorder	Excessive anxiety not focused on a specific situation or object; free-floating anxiety
	Panic disorder	Repeated attacks of intense fear involving physical symptoms such as faintness, dizziness, and nausea
	Obsessive-compulsive disorder	Persistent ideas or worries accompanied by ritualistic behaviours performed to neutralize anxiety-driven thoughts
Somatoform disorders	Conversion disorder	A loss of physical ability (e.g., sight, hearing) that is related to psychological factors
	Hypochondriasis	Preoccupation with, or belief that one has, a serious illness in the absence of any physical evidence
	Somatization disorder	Wide variety of somatic complaints that occur over several years and are not the result of a known physical disorder
	Pain disorder	Preoccupation with pain in the absence of physical reasons for the pain
Dissociative disorders	Dissociative amnesia/fugue	Sudden loss of memory, which may result in relocation and the assumption of a new identity
	Dissociative identity disorder (multiple personality disorder)	Appearance within the same person of two or more distinct identities, each with a unique way of thinking and behaving

PsychAssist: Disorders

Second, like Mary, most of these people appear to be skilled at self-hypnosis, through which they can induce a trance-like state. Third, most found that they could escape the trauma of abuse at least temporarily by creating "new personalities" to deal with stress (Spiegel, 1994). However, not all abused children display dissociative identity disorder, and there is evidence that some cases of dissociative identity disorder may have been triggered by media stories or by suggestions made to clients by their therapists (Spanos, 1996).

This evidence has led some skeptics to question the very existence of multiple personalities (Acocella, 1998; Merckelbach, Devilly, & Rassin, 2002). Others suggest that the increased incidence of dissociative identity disorder may simply reflect its status as a socioculturally approved method of expressing distress (Hacking, 1995; Spanos, 1994). In fact, it was observations such as these that prompted the official change in designation from *multiple personality disorder* to *dissociative identity disorder.* The authors of *DSM-IV* made this change partly to avoid perpetuating the notion that people harbour multiple personalities that can easily be "contacted" through hypnosis or related techniques. The new name was chosen to suggest, instead, that dissociation, or separation, between one's memories and other aspects of identity can be so dramatic that people experiencing it may come to believe that they have more than one personality (Gleaves, May, & Cardena, 2001; Spiegel, 1994). Research on the existence and alleged effects of repressed memories—discussed in the chapter on memory—is sure to have an impact on our understanding of, and the controversy over, the causes of dissociative identity disorder. ("In Review: Anxiety, Somatoform, and Dissociative Disorders" presents a summary of our discussion of these disorders.)

Mood Disorders

Everyone's mood, or *affect,* tends to rise and fall from time to time. However, when people experience extremes of mood—wild elation or deep depression—for long periods, when they shift from one extreme to another, and especially when their moods are not consistent with the events around them, they are said to show a **mood disorder** (also known as *affective disorder*). We will describe two main types: depressive disorders and bipolar disorders.

Depressive Disorders

Depression can range from occasional, normal "down" periods to episodes severe enough to require hospitalization. A person suffering **major depressive disorder** feels sad and overwhelmed for weeks or months, typically losing interest in activities and relationships and taking pleasure in nothing (Coryell et al., 1993; Sloan, Strauss, & Wisner, 2001). Exaggerated feelings of inadequacy, worthlessness, hopelessness, or guilt are common. Despite the person's best efforts, everything from conversation to bathing is an unbearable, exhausting effort (Solomon, 1998). Changes in eating habits resulting in weight loss or weight gain often accompany major depressive disorder, as does sleep disturbance or, less often, excessive sleeping. Problems in working, concentrating, making decisions, and thinking clearly are also common. More often than not, there are also symptoms of an accompanying anxiety disorder (Zimmerman, McDermut, & Mattia, 2000). In extreme cases, depressed people may express false beliefs, or **delusions**—worrying, for example, that the government is planning to punish them. Major depressive disorder can come on suddenly or gradually. It can consist of a single episode or, more commonly, repeated depressive periods. Here is a case example:

> *Mr. J. was a 51-one-year-old industrial engineer. . . . Since the death of his wife five years earlier, he had been suffering from continuing episodes of depression marked by extreme social withdrawal and occasional thoughts of suicide. . . . He drank and, when thoroughly intoxicated, would plead to his deceased wife for forgiveness. He lost all capacity for joy. . . . Once a gourmet, he now had no interest in food and good wine . . . and could barely manage to engage in small talk. As might be expected, his work record deteriorated markedly. Appointments were missed and projects haphazardly started and left unfinished.* (Davison & Neale, 1990, p. 221)

Depression is not always so extreme. In a less severe pattern of depression, called **dysthymic disorder,** the person experiences the sad mood, lack of interest, and loss of pleasure associated with major depression, but less intensely and for a longer period. (The duration must be at least two years to qualify as dysthymic disorder.) Mental and behavioural disruption are also less severe; people exhibiting dysthymic disorder rarely require hospitalization.

Major depressive disorder occurs at some time in the lives of approximately 17 percent of the North American and European populations (Kessler et al., 1994; Kessler et al., 2003; U.S. Surgeon General, 1999). The incidence of the disorder varies considerably across cultures and subcultures, however. For example, it occurs at much higher rates in urban Ireland than in urban Spain (Judd et al., 2002), though it is not always clear whether such differences reflect real differences in rates of depression or differences in the application of diagnostic criteria (Judd et al., 2002). There are gender differences in some cultures, too. In Canada and other Western countries, females are two to three times more likely than males to experience major depressive disorder; 10 to 25 percent of women and 5 to 12 percent of men will display this disorder during their lifetimes (American Psychiatric Association, 2000; Thommasen, Baggaley, Thommasen, & Zhang, 2005; Weissman et al., 1993). This difference does not appear in the less economically developed countries of the Middle East, Africa, and Asia (Ayuso-Mateos et al., 2001; Culbertson, 1997). According to Michelle Lafrance at St. Thomas University in

mood disorder Conditions in which a person experiences extreme moods, such as depression or mania.

major depressive disorder A mood disorder in which a person feels sad and hopeless for weeks or months.

delusions False beliefs, such as those experienced by people suffering from schizophrenia or extreme depression.

dysthymic disorder A mood disorder involving a pattern of comparatively mild depression that lasts for at least two years.

Singing the Blues Award-winning poet and musician Leonard Cohen has experienced episodes of major depression.

Fredericton, New Brunswick, and her colleague, Janet Stoppard at the University of New Brunswick, one reason Canadian women experience depression at higher rates than men is that women are expected to exert much of their time and energy caring for others, which may lead to neglect of their own needs (Lafrance & Stoppard, in press). Depression can occur at any age, but there appear to be two peaks of prevalence across the life span. The first occurs in late adolescence or young adulthood, and the second during old age (Cross-National Collaborative Group, 1992; Fassler & Dumas, 1997; Sowdon, 2001).

Suicide and Depression Suicide is associated with a variety of psychological disorders, but it is most closely tied to depression. Some form of depression has been implicated in 40 to 60 percent of suicides (Angst, Angst, & Stassen, 1999; Oquendo & Mann, 2001; Rihmer, 2001). In fact, thinking about suicide is a symptom of depressive disorders. Hopelessness about the future—another depressive symptom—and a desire to seek instant escape from problems are also related to suicide attempts (Beck et al., 1990; Brown et al., 2000).

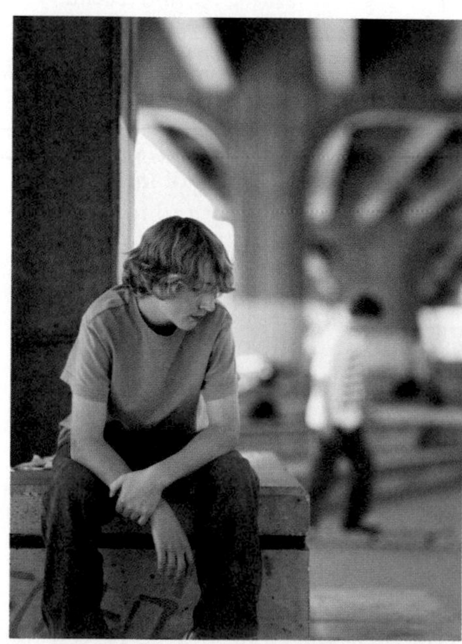

Depression in adolescents Depression is a serious problem which, in some cases, leads to suicide. Among Canadian adolescents, suicide is the second leading cause of death.

About 4000 people in Canada commit suicide each year (Canadian Mental Health Association, 2006). This puts the Canadian suicide rate at about 15 per 100 000 individuals, making suicide the 11th leading cause of death. Worldwide, the suicide rate is as high as 25 per 100 000 in some northern European countries and Japan (Lamar, 2000) and as low as 6 per 100 000 in countries with stronger religious prohibitions against suicide, such as Greece, Italy, Ireland, and the nations of the Middle East.

Suicide rates also differ considerably depending on sociocultural factors such as age, gender, and ethnicity (Canadian Mental Health Association, 2006; Centres for Disease Control and Prevention, 2002c, 2002d; Oquendo et al., 2001). In Canada, suicide is most common among people over 65 years old, especially men. The suicide rate for men who are 85 or older is 35 per 100 000 (BC Partners for Mental Health and Addictions Information, 2006; Centres for Disease Control and Prevention, 2004). However, since 1952, suicide among adolescents has increased five-fold. In Canada, suicide is now the second leading cause of death, after motor vehicle accidents, among people who are 15 to 24 years old. Women attempt suicide three times as often as men, but men are four times as likely to actually kill themselves (Canadian Mental Health Association, 2006). Close to 90 percent of Canadians who have taken their own lives suffered from depression or another psychological disorder (BC Partners for Mental Health and Addictions Information, 2006).

Battling the Enemy Within Canadian actress Margot Kidder, known for her role as Lois Lane opposite Christopher Reeve's Superman, is a well-known person with bipolar disorder.

Suicide rates also differ across ethnic groups. For example, suicide rates in Canada exceed the national average within First Nations communities, possibly due to deteriorating quality of life and a higher incidence of depression. One notable exception is the low suicide rates among First Nations elders. The elders in these communities may be less likely to take their own lives because of the respect with which their cultures traditionally view the aged members of their societies (BC Partners for Mental Health and Addictions Information, 2006).

It is often said that people who talk about suicide will never try it. This is a myth. On the contrary, those who say they are thinking of suicide are much more likely than other people to attempt suicide. In fact, according to Edwin Schneidman (1987), 80 percent of suicides are preceded by some kind of warning, whether direct ("I think I'm going to kill myself ") or vague ("Sometimes I wonder if life is worth living"). Although not everyone who threatens suicide follows through, if you suspect that someone you know is thinking about suicide, encourage the person to contact a mental health professional or a crisis hotline. If the danger is immediate, make the contact yourself, and ask for advice about what to do. Many suicide attempts—including those triggered by other suicides in the same town or school—can be prevented by social support and other forms of help for people at high risk (Centres for Disease Control and Prevention, 2004). According to Erin Boone and Bonnie Leadbeater at the University of Victoria in British Columbia, involvement in team sports is one factor that helps to reduce depression and prevent suicide among adolescents, both boys and girls (Boone & Leadbeater, 2006). For more information, visit suicide prevention-related Web sites, such as that of the Canadian Association for the Prevention of Suicide (www.thesupportnetwork.com/CASP/main.html).

Bipolar Disorders

The alternating appearance of two emotional extremes, or poles, characterizes *bipolar I disorder.* We have already described one emotional pole: depression. The other is **mania,** which is an extremely agitated, usually elated, emotional state. People in a manic state tend to be utterly optimistic, boundlessly energetic, certain of having extraordinary powers and abilities, and bursting with all sorts of ideas. They become irritated with anyone who tries to reason with them or "slow them down." During manic episodes individuals may make impulsive and unwise decisions, including spending their life savings on foolish schemes.

In **bipolar I disorder,** manic episodes may alternate with periods of deep depression. Sometimes, periods of relatively normal mood separate these extremes (Tohen et al., 2003). This pattern has also been called *manic depression.* Compared with major depressive disorder, bipolar I disorder is rare. It occurs in only about 1 percent of adults, and it affects men and women about equally. However, it can severely disrupt a person's ability to work or maintain social relationships (Goldberg, Harrow, & Grossman, 1995). Even less common is *bipolar II disorder,* in which major depressive episodes alternate with episodes known as *hypomania,* which are less severe than the manic phases seen in bipolar I disorder.

A somewhat more common mood disorder is *cyclothymic disorder,* the bipolar equivalent of dysthymia. Cyclothymic disorder involves episodes of depression and mania, but the intensity of both moods is less severe than in cases of bipolar I disorder. As with depression, bipolar disorders are often accompanied by anxiety disorders (Freeman, Freeman, & McElroy, 2002). ("In Review: Mood Disorders" summarizes the main types of mood disorders.)

mania An elated, very active emotional state.

bipolar I disorder A mood disorder in which a person alternates between deep depression and mania.

Causes of Mood Disorders

Research on the causes of mood disorders has focused on biological, psychological, and sociocultural risk factors. The more of these risk factors people have, the more likely they are to experience a mood disorder.

in review Mood Disorders

Type	Typical Symptoms	Related Features
Major depressive disorder	Deep sadness, feelings of worthlessness, changes in eating and sleeping habits, loss of interest and pleasure	Lasts weeks or months; may occur in repeating episodes; severe cases may include delusions; danger of suicide
Dysthymic disorder	Similar to major depressive disorder, but less severe and longer lasting	Hospitalization usually not necessary
Bipolar I disorder	Alternating extremes of mood, from deep depression to mania, and back	Manic episodes include impulsivity, unrealistic optimism, high energy, severe agitation
Cyclothymic disorder	Similar to bipolar disorder, but less severe	Hospitalization usually not necessary

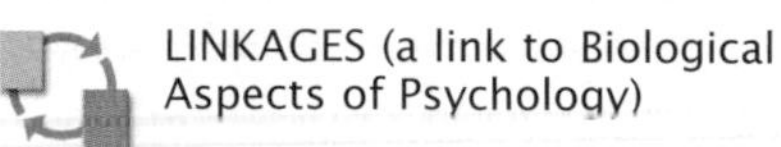
LINKAGES (a link to Biological Aspects of Psychology)

Biological Factors The role of genetics in mood disorders, especially in bipolar disorders, is suggested by twin studies and family studies (Kelsoe et al., 2001; Kieseppä et al., 2004). For example, bipolar disorder is much more likely to be seen in both members of genetically identical twin pairs than in fraternal, or nonidentical, twins (Bowman & Nurnberger, 1993; Egeland et al., 1987; McGuffin et al., 2003). Family studies also show that those who are closely related to people with a bipolar disorder are more likely than others to develop that disorder themselves (Blackwood, Visscher, & Muir, 2001). Major depressive disorder is also more likely to be shared among family members, and especially by identical twins (Kendler et al., 1995; Klein et al., 2001; Nurnberger, 1993). This genetic influence is especially strong in female twins (Bierut et al., 1999). Findings such as these suggest that genetic influences tend to be stronger for mood disorders, and especially for bipolar I disorder, than for most other disorders. Researchers are making progress at identifying regions on various chromosomes that appear related to the genetic transmission of vulnerability to bipolar disorder and other affective disorders (Blackwood et al., 2001; Caspi et al., 2003; Konradi et al., 2004).

Other potential biological causes of mood disorders include malfunctions in regions of the brain devoted to mood, imbalances in the brain's neurotransmitter systems, malfunctioning of the endocrine system, disruption of biological rhythms, and reduced brain development in the frontal lobes, hippocampus, or other areas (Cotter et al., 2001; Jacobs, 2004). All of these conditions may themselves be influenced by genetics. The brain regions involved in mood are many, including the prefrontal cortex, the hippocampus, the amygdala, and other components of the limbic system (Blumberg et al., 2003; MacQueen et al., 2003). There are so many of these regions, in fact, and so many different pathways through which their activity can be disrupted, that different mood disorders might reflect problems in different brain regions (Davidson et al., 2002; Elliott et al., 2002).

As for the role of neurotransmitters, norepinephrine, serotonin, and dopamine were implicated in mood disorders decades ago, when scientists discovered that drugs capable of altering these brain chemicals also relieved depression. Early research suggested that depression was triggered by too little of these neurotransmitters, whereas unusually high levels caused mania. However, the neurochemical causes now appear far more complex. For example, mood disorders may result in part from changes in the sensitivity of the neuronal receptors at which these chemicals have their effects in the brain. The precise nature of these neurotransmitter-receptor mechanisms, and just how they affect mood, is not yet fully understood.

Mood disorders have also been related to malfunctions in the endocrine system, especially the hypothalamic-pituitary-adrenocortical (HPA) system, described in the chapter on health, stress, and coping as being involved in the body's responses to stress. For example, research shows that as many as 70 percent of depressed people secrete abnormally high levels of the stress hormone cortisol (Dinan, 2001; Nemeroff, 1998; Posener et al., 2000).

The cycles of mood swings seen in bipolar disorders and in recurring episodes of major depressive disorder suggest that mood disorders may be related to stressful triggering events (Miklowitz & Alloy, 1999). They may also be related to disturbances in the body's biological clock, which is described in the chapter on consciousness (Goodwin & Jamison, 1990). This second possibility seems especially likely in the 15 percent of depressed people who consistently experience a calendar-linked pattern of depressive episodes known as *seasonal affective disorder* (SAD). During months of shorter daylight, these people slip into severe depression, accompanied by irritability and excessive sleeping (Blehar & Rosenthal, 1989). Their depression tends to lift as daylight hours lengthen (Faedda et al., 1993). Disruption of biological rhythms is also suggested by the fact that many depressed people tend to have trouble sleeping—perhaps partly because during the day their biological clocks are telling them it is the middle of the night. Resetting the biological clock through methods such as sleep deprivation or light stimulation has relieved depression in many cases (Kuhs & Tolle, 1991; Terman et al., 2001).

Psychological and Social Factors Researchers have come to recognize that whatever biological causes are involved in mood disorders, their effects are always combined with those of psychological and social causes (U.S. Surgeon General, 1999; Jacobs, 2004). As mentioned earlier, the very nature of depressive symptoms can depend on the culture in which a person lives. Biopsychosocial explanations of mood disorders also emphasize the impact of anxiety, negative thinking, and the other psychological and emotional responses triggered by trauma, losses, and other stressful events (Kendler, Hettema, et al., 2003; Kendler, Kuhn, & Prescott, 2004; Monroe et al., 1999). For example, the higher incidence of depression among females—and especially among poor, ethnic minority, single mothers—has been

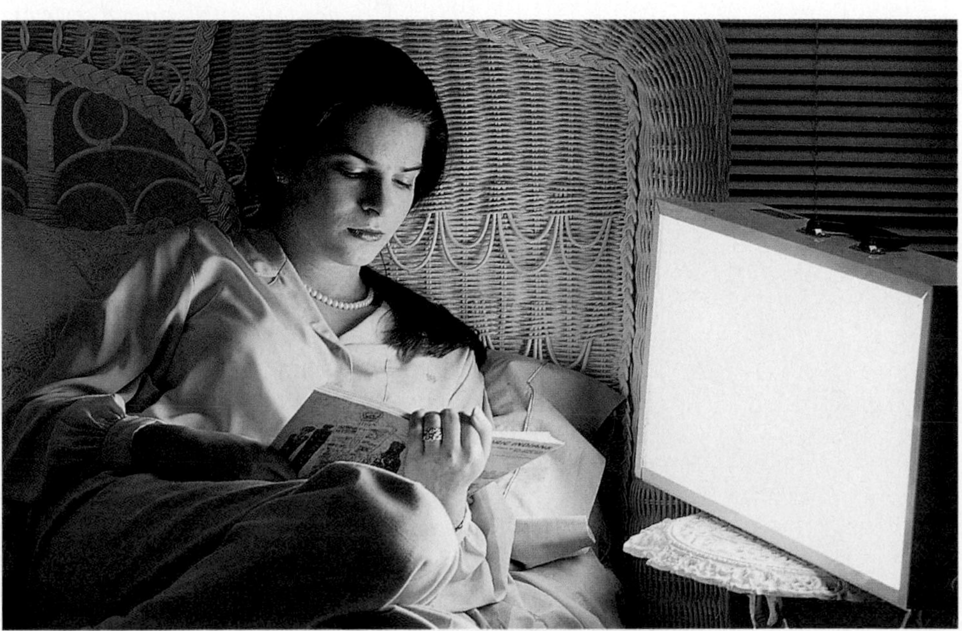

Treating SAD Seasonal affective disorder (SAD) can often be relieved by exposure to full-spectrum light for as little as a couple of hours a day (Campbell & Murphy, 1998; Sato, 1997).

attributed to their greater exposure to stressors of all kinds (Brown & Moran, 1997; Miranda & Green, 1999). Environmental stressors affect men, too, which may be one reason why gender differences in depression are smaller in countries in which men and women face equally stressful lives (Bierut et al., 1999; Maier et al., 1999). Still, differing stressors may not be the only source of these gender differences (Kendler, Thornton, & Prescott, 2001).

A variety of social-cognitive theories suggest that the way people think about their stressors can increase or decrease the likelihood of mood disorders. One of these theories stemmed from the research on *learned helplessness* described in the chapter on learning. Just as animals become inactive and appear depressed when they have no control over negative events (El Yacoubi et al., 2003), humans may experience depression as a result of feeling incapable of controlling their lives, especially the stressors confronting them (Klein & Seligman, 1976; Seligman, 1991). But most of us have limited control; why aren't we all depressed? The ways in which people learn to think about events in their lives may hold the key. For example, Aaron Beck's (1967, 1976) cognitive theory of depression suggests that depressed people develop mental habits of (1) blaming themselves when things go wrong; (2) focusing on and exaggerating the negative side of events; and (3) jumping to overly generalized, pessimistic conclusions. Such cognitive habits, says Beck, are errors that lead to depressing thoughts and other symptoms of depression (Beck & Beck, 1995). Depressed people, in fact, do think about significant negative events in ways that are likely to increase or prolong their depression (Gotlib & Hammen, 1992; Gotlib et al., 2004).

Social-cognitive theories of depression are somewhat consistent with the psychodynamically oriented *object relations* approach discussed in the chapter on personality (Blatt & Maroudas, 1992). Both views suggest that negative patterns of thinking can be acquired through maladaptive experiences in childhood. For example, research indicates that children whose early relationships with parents or other primary caregivers were characterized by deprivation or abuse are especially likely to develop depression in later life (Gotlib & Hammen, 1992). It may be that close, protective, predictable, and responsive early relationships are necessary if children are to form healthy views of themselves, positive expectations about others, and a sense of control over the environment (Bowlby, 1980; Main, 1996).

Severe, long-lasting depression is especially common among people who see their lack of control or other problems as caused by a permanent, generalized lack of personal competence rather than by a temporary lapse or external cause (Seligman et al., 1988). This *negative attributional style* may be another important cognitive factor in depression (Alloy, Abramson, & Francis, 1999; Ingram, Miranda, & Segal, 1998). People may be prone to depression when they attribute negative events to their own characteristics and believe they will never be capable of doing better.

Are depressed people's unusually negative beliefs about themselves actually helping to cause their depression, or are they merely symptoms of it? A number of studies have assessed the attributional styles of large samples of undepressed people and then kept in touch with them to see if, in the face of equivalent stressors, individuals with negative self-beliefs are more likely to become depressed. These longitudinal studies suggest that a negative attributional style is, in fact, a risk factor for depression, not just a result of being depressed (Garber, Keiley, & Martin, 2002; Runyon & Kenny, 2002; Gibb et al., 2004; Satterfield, Folkman, & Acree, 2002). In one study, for example, adolescents who held strong negative self-beliefs were more likely than other youngsters to develop depression when faced with stress later in life (Lewinsohn, Joiner, & Rohde, 2001).

Social-cognitive theorists also suggest that whether depression continues or worsens depends in part on how people respond once they start to feel depressed. Those who ruminate, or continuously dwell, on negative events, on why they occur, and even on the feelings of depression are likely to feel more and more depressed (Just & Alloy, 1997). According to Susan Nolen-Hoeksema (1990, 2001), this *rumi-*

native style is especially common in women and may help explain gender differences in the frequency of depression. When men start to feel sad, she says, they tend to use a *distracting style*. That is, they engage in activity that distracts them from their concerns and helps bring them out of their depressed mood (Hankin & Abramson, 2001; Just & Alloy, 1997; Nolen-Hoeksema, Morrow, & Fredrickson, 1993).

Notice that social-cognitive explanations of depression are consistent with the diathesis-stress approach to disorder (Hankin & Abramson, 2001). These explanations suggest that certain cognitive styles constitute a predisposition (or diathesis) that makes a person vulnerable to depression. The actual occurrence of depression is then made more likely by stressors. In fact, most episodes of major depressive disorder are preceded by the onset of major stressors, such as the loss of a loved one. As suggested in the chapter on health, stress, and coping, the depressing effects of these stressors are likely to be magnified in people who lack social support, who have inadequate coping skills, and who must face other stressful conditions such as poverty (e.g., Stice, Ragan, & Randall, 2004).

Given the number and complexity of biological, psychological, social, and situational factors potentially involved in causing mood disorders, the biopsychosocial model and the diathesis-stress approach appear to be especially appropriate guides to future research. Studies based on these guides are already bearing fruit. One study looked at the role of genetics and stressful events in shaping mood disorders in a large group of female twins. Both factors were associated with major depression. Specifically, the women at highest genetic risk were also the most likely to become depressed following a significant stressor (Kendler, Thornton, & Gardner, 2000, 2001). On the basis of studies like this one, Kenneth Kendler and his colleagues (Kendler, Gardner, & Prescott, 2002) have identified specific sets of risk factors for depression in women that appear at five developmental stages, including childhood, early adolescence, late adolescence, adulthood, and in the year preceding the diagnosis of depression.

In the final analysis, it may turn out that each subtype in the spectrum of mood disorders is caused by a unique combination of factors. The challenge for researchers is to identify these subtypes and map out their causal ingredients.

Schizophrenia

Here is part of a letter that arrived in the mail several years ago:

> *Dear Sirs:*
> *Pertaining to our continuing failure to prosecute violations of minor's rights to sovereign equality which are occurring in gestations being compromised by the ingestation of controlled substances, . . . the skewing of androgyny which continues in female juveniles even after separation from their mother's has occurred, and as a means of promulflagitating my paying Governor Hickel of Alaska for my employees to have personal services endorsements and controlled substance endorsements, . . . the Iraqi oil being released by the United Nations being identified as Kurdistanian oil, and the July, 1991 issue of the Siberian Review spells President Eltsin's name without a letter y.*

The disorganization and strange content of this letter suggest that its writer suffers from **schizophrenia** (pronounced "skit-so-FREE-nee-uh"), a pattern of extremely disturbed thinking, emotion, perception, and behaviour that seriously impairs the ability to communicate and relate to others and disrupts most other aspects of daily functioning (Freedman, 2003). Schizophrenia is one of the most severe and disabling of all mental disorders. Its core symptoms are seen virtually everywhere in the world, occurring in 1 to 2 percent of the population (American Psychiatric Association, 1994, 2000). It appears about equally in various ethnic

schizophrenia A severe and disabling pattern of disturbed thinking, emotion, perception, and behaviour.

groups, but like most disorders, it tends to be diagnosed more frequently in economically disadvantaged populations. Schizophrenia is seen about equally in men and women, although in women it may appear later in life, be less severe, and respond better to treatment (Aleman, Kahn, & Selten, 2003; American Psychiatric Association, 2000; U.S. Surgeon General, 1999).

Schizophrenia tends to develop in adolescence or early adulthood. About 75 percent of the time, its onset is gradual, with the earliest signs appearing as much as five years before the first major schizophrenic episode. In other cases, the onset is more rapid. About 40 percent of people with schizophrenia improve with treatment and are able to function reasonably well. The rest show continuous or intermittent symptoms that permanently disrupt their functioning (an der Heiden & Haefner, 2000; Hegarty et al., 1994). Those who also have a drug abuse problem are at increased risk for becoming homeless. It has been estimated that 10 to 13 percent of homeless individuals suffer from schizophrenia (Fischer & Breakey, 1991; Olfson et al., 1999).

One of the best predictors of the course of schizophrenia is *premorbid adjustment,* which is the level of functioning a person had achieved before schizophrenic symptoms first appeared. Improvement is more likely in those who had attained higher levels of education and occupation and who had established supportive relationships with family and friends (Rabinowitz et al., 2002; Watt & Saiz, 1991). Jean Addington and colleagues at the University of Toronto and the University of Calgary have developed a program to help families cope with the special challenges associated with providing care and support for relatives in the early stages of the illness (Addington, Collins, McCleery, & Addington, 2005).

Symptoms of Schizophrenia

People displaying schizophrenia have problems in how they think and what they think. The nineteenth-century psychiatrist Eugen Bleuler coined the word *schizophrenia,* or "split mind," to refer to the oddities of schizophrenic thinking. However, schizophrenia does not mean "split personality," as in dissociative identity disorder (multiple personality disorder). It refers instead to a splitting of normally integrated mental processes, such as thoughts and feelings. For instance, some schizophrenics may giggle while claiming to feel sad.

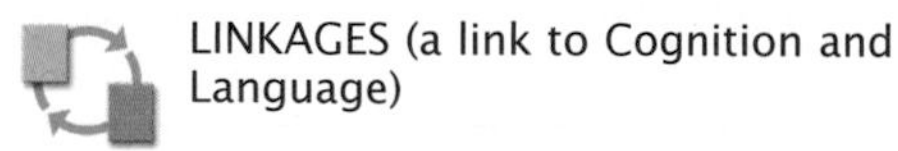

Schizophrenic thought and language are often disorganized. *Neologisms* ("new words" that have meaning only to the person speaking them) are common. The appearance of "promulflagitating" in the preceding letter is one example. That letter also illustrates *loose associations,* the tendency for one thought to be logically unconnected, or only slightly related, to the next. Sometimes the associations are based on double meanings or on the way words sound (*clang associations*). For example, "My true family name is Abel or A Bell. We descended from the clan of Abel, who originated the bell of rights, which we now call the bill of rights." In the most severe cases, a jumble of words known as *word salad* reflects utterly chaotic thoughts: "Upon the advisability of held keeping, environment of the seabeach gathering, to the forest stream, reinstatement to be placed, poling the paddleboat, of the swamp morass, to the forest compensation of the dunce" (Lehman, 1967, p. 627).

The *content* of schizophrenic thinking is also disturbed. Often it includes a bewildering assortment of delusions, especially delusions of persecution. Some patients claim that space aliens are trying to steal their internal organs or that the CIA has implanted a control device in their brains, and they may interpret everything from TV commercials to casual hand gestures as supporting these beliefs. Delusions that common events are somehow related to oneself are called *ideas of reference. Delusions of grandeur* may also appear; one man was convinced that the prime minister of Canada was trying to contact him for advice. Other types of delusions include (1) *thought broadcasting,* in which patients believe that their thoughts can be heard by others; (2) *thought blocking* or *withdrawal,* the belief that someone

hallucinations A symptom of disorder in which people perceive voices or other stimuli when there are no stimuli present.

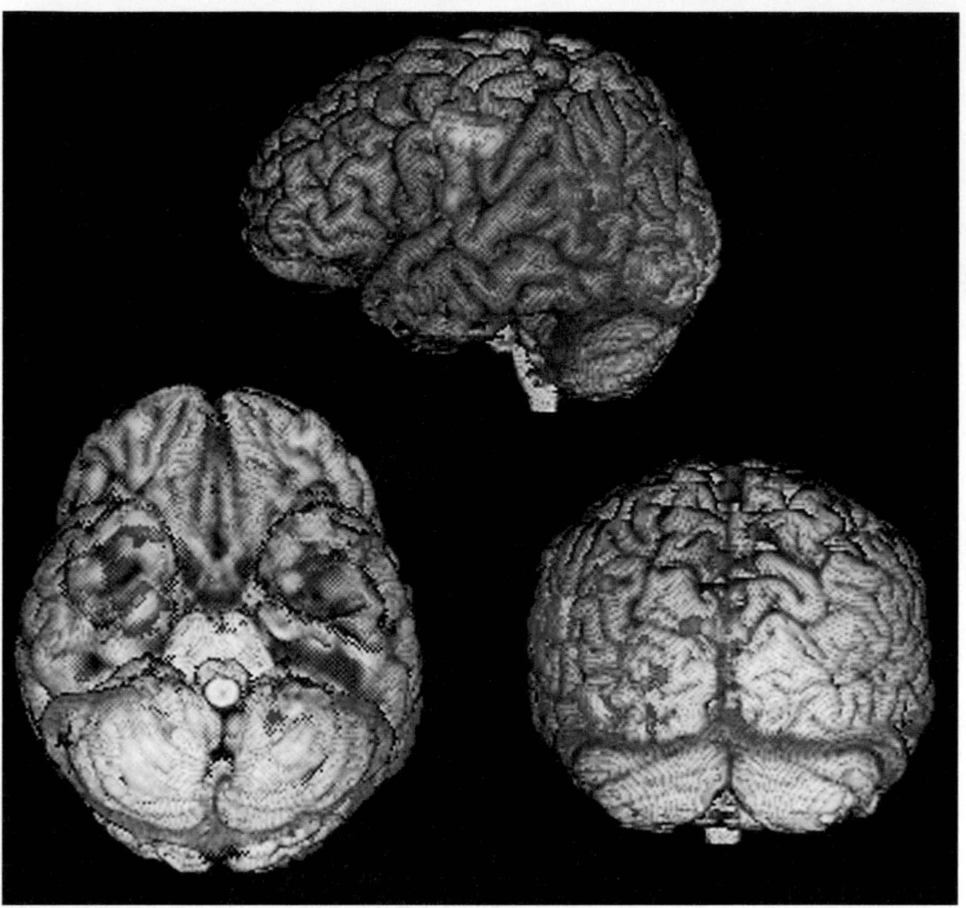

figure 15.2

Brain Activity During Hallucinations
Here are brain images of a 23-year-old schizophrenia patient who was hallucinating rolling, disembodied heads that spoke to him. PET scans revealed heightened activity in visual and auditory (language) *association* cortex, rather than in the *primary* cortex regions for these senses. The posterior cingulate cortex (part of the limbic system) was also activated; it is known to be affected by drugs that produce hallucinations (Silbersweig et al., 1995).

Catatonic Stupor The symptoms of schizophrenia often occur in characteristic patterns. This woman's lack of motivation and other negative symptoms of schizophrenia are severe enough that she appears to be in a catatonic stupor. Such patients may become rigid or, as in this case, show a waxy flexibility that allows them to be "posed" in virtually any position. Diagnosticians using the traditional subtype system would probably label her as displaying catatonic schizophrenia.

is either preventing thoughts or stealing them as they appear; and (3) *thought insertion,* the belief that other people's thoughts are appearing in one's own mind.

People with schizophrenia often report that they cannot focus their attention. They may feel overwhelmed as they try to attend to everything at once. Various perceptual disorders may also appear. The person may feel detached from the world and see other people as flat cutouts.The body may feel like a machine, or parts of it may seem to be dead or rotting. **Hallucinations,** or false perceptions, are common, often taking the form of voices. These voices may sound like an overheard conversation, or they may tell the person to do or not to do things. They may also comment on, narrate, or (most often) harshly criticize the person's actions or characteristics. Hallucinations can also create sights, smells, tastes, and touch sensations even when no external stimuli are present. As shown in Figure 15.2, the brain areas activated during hallucinations are related to those that respond to real sights and sounds (Shergill et al., 2000).

The emotional expressiveness of people with schizophrenia is often muted, but when they do show emotion, it is frequently exaggerated or inappropriate. They may cry for no apparent reason or fly into a rage in response to a simple question.

Some schizophrenia patients are extremely agitated, constantly moving their limbs, making facial grimaces, or pacing the floor in highly ritualistic sequences. Others become so withdrawn that they move very little. Lack of motivation and poor social skills, deteriorating personal hygiene, and an inability to function in everyday situations are other common characteristics of schizophrenia.

Categorizing Schizophrenia

DSM-IV lists five major subtypes of schizophrenia: paranoid, disorganized, catatonic, undifferentiated, and residual (see Table 15.5). These subtype labels convey a

table 15.5

Mental health professionals still use these *DSM-IV* subtypes when diagnosing schizophrenia, but many researchers now tend to categorize patients in terms of whether positive or negative symptoms of schizophrenia predominate in a given case.

Subtypes of Schizophrenia

Type	Frequency	Prominent Features
Paranoid schizophrenia	40 percent of schizophrenics; appears late in life (after age 25–30)	Delusions of grandeur or persecution; anger; anxiety; argumentativeness; extreme jealousy; onset often sudden; signs of impairment may be subtle.
Disorganized schizophrenia	5 percent of all schizophrenics; high prevalence in homeless population	Delusions; hallucinations; incoherent speech; facial grimaces; inappropriate laughter/giggling; neglected personal hygiene; loss of bladder/bowel control.
Catatonic schizophrenia	8 percent of all schizophrenics	Disordered movement, alternating between total immobility (stupor) and wild excitement. In stupor, the person does not speak or attend to communication; also, the body is rigid or can be posed in virtually any posture (a condition called *waxy flexibility*).
Undifferentiated schizophrenia	40 percent of all schizophrenics	Patterns of disordered behaviour, thought, and emotion that do not fall easily into any other subtype.
Residual schizophrenia	Varies	Applies to people who have had prior episodes of schizophrenia but are not currently displaying symptoms.

certain amount of useful information, but they don't always provide an accurate picture of patients' behaviour, because some symptoms appear in more than one subtype. Further, people originally diagnosed as suffering from one subtype might later display characteristics of another subtype. Finally, the *DSM-IV* subtypes may not be linked very closely to the various biological conditions thought to underlie schizophrenia (Fenton & McGlashan, 1991).

Accordingly, many researchers are now categorizing schizophrenia in ways that focus more precisely on the kinds of symptoms that patients display. One such method highlights the positive-negative symptom dimension in schizophrenia. Disorganized thoughts, delusions, and hallucinations are sometimes called **positive symptoms** of schizophrenia, because they appear as undesirable *additions* to a person's mental life (Andreasen et al., 1995; Racenstein et al., 2002). In contrast, the absence of pleasure and motivation, lack of emotional reactivity, social withdrawal, reduced speech, and other deficits seen in schizophrenia are sometimes called **negative symptoms**, because they appear to *subtract* elements from normal mental life (Nicholson & Neufeld, 1993). Describing patients in terms of positive and negative symptoms does not require that they be placed in one category or the other. In fact, many patients exhibit both positive and negative symptoms. However, it is important to know whether negative or positive symptoms predominate, because when symptoms are mainly negative, schizophrenia is usually more severe and less responsive to treatment. In such cases, patients typically experience long-term disability. Such disability has also been associated with positive symptoms if those symptoms are severe (e.g., Fenton & McGlashan, 1994; Racenstein et al., 2002). Another way of categorizing schizophrenia symptoms focuses on whether they are *psychotic* (hallucinations, delusions), *disorganized* (incoherent speech, chaotic behaviour, inappropriate affect), or *negative* (e.g., lack of speech or motivation). Other

positive symptoms Schizophrenic symptoms such as disorganized thoughts, hallucinations, and delusions.

negative symptoms Schizophrenic symptoms such as absence of pleasure, lack of speech, and flat affect.

researchers have suggested categorizing schizophrenia symptoms as positive, negative, or depressive (Haefner & Maurer, 2000). The fact that, like positive and negative symptoms, these dimensions of schizophrenia are to some extent independent from one another suggests to some researchers that each symptom cluster or dimension may ultimately be traceable to different causes. For this reason, schizophrenia is often referred to as the schizophrenia *spectrum,* implying that each cluster may develop differently and require different treatments (Tsuang, Stone, & Faraone, 2000).

Causes of Schizophrenia

The search for the causes of schizophrenia has been more intense than for any other psychological disorder. The findings so far confirm one thing: As with other disorders, there are biological, psychological, and social factors at work in causing or worsening all forms of schizophrenia (Sullivan, Kendler, & Neale, 2003).

Biological Factors Research in behavioural genetics shows that schizophrenia runs in families (Asarnow et al., 2001; Gottesman, 1991). One longitudinal family study found, for instance, that 16 percent of the children of schizophrenic mothers—compared with 2 percent of those of nonschizophrenic mothers—developed schizophrenia themselves over a 25-year period (Parnas et al., 1993). Even if they are adopted by families with no schizophrenia, the children of schizophrenic parents are ten times more likely to develop schizophrenia than adopted children whose biological parents are not schizophrenic (Kety et al., 1994). Still, it is unlikely that a single gene transmits schizophrenia (Kendler & Diehl, 1993; Plomin & McGuffin, 2003). Among identical twins in which one displays schizophrenia, 40 percent of the others will, too; but 60 percent will not (McGue, 1992). It is more likely that some people inherit a predisposition, or diathesis, for schizophrenia that involves many genes. This diathesis then combines with other genetic and nongenetic factors to cause the disorder (Moldin & Gottesman, 1997).

The search for biological causes of schizophrenia also focuses on a number of abnormalities in the structure, functioning, and chemistry of the brain that tend to appear in schizophrenics (e.g., Davis et al., 2003). For example, numerous brain imaging studies have shown that, compared with other mental patients, many schizophrenia patients have less tissue in thalamic regions, prefrontal cortex, and some subcortical areas (Conklin & Iacono, 2002; Csernansky et al., 2004; Highley et al., 2003; Pol et al., 2002; Selemon et al., 2003). As shown in Figure 15.3, shrinkage of tissue in these regions leads to corresponding enlargement in the brain's fluid-filled spaces, called *ventricles.* The brain areas in which anatomical abnormalities have been found are active in emotional expression, thinking, and information processing—functions that are disordered in schizophrenia. Enlarged ventricles and reduced prefrontal cortex are more often found in patients whose schizophrenic symptoms are predominantly negative (Sigmundsson et al., 2001). Continued tissue loss has been associated with worsening of negative symptoms (Ho et al., 2003; Mathalon et al., 2001). Patients with mainly positive symptoms tend to have essentially normal-looking brains (Andreasen, 1997).

Hundreds of studies of brain functioning in people diagnosed with schizophrenia provide general support for the idea that their impairments in information processing and other cognitive abilities are consistent with structural abnormalities (Gur et al., 2000; Jeon & Polich, 2003; Lee et al., 2003; Niznikiewicz et al., 1997). For example, patients with predominantly negative symptoms are especially likely to display cognitive deficits associated with prefrontal-cortex problems (Wible et al., 2001). This research provides important clues, but we still don't know the extent to which, or exactly how, specific structural abnormalities are related to the differing patterns of neurocognitive dysfunction seen in specific forms of schizophrenia (Allen, Goldstein, & Weiner, 2001). For one thing, not all schizophrenia patients show brain abnormalities, and some normal people do.

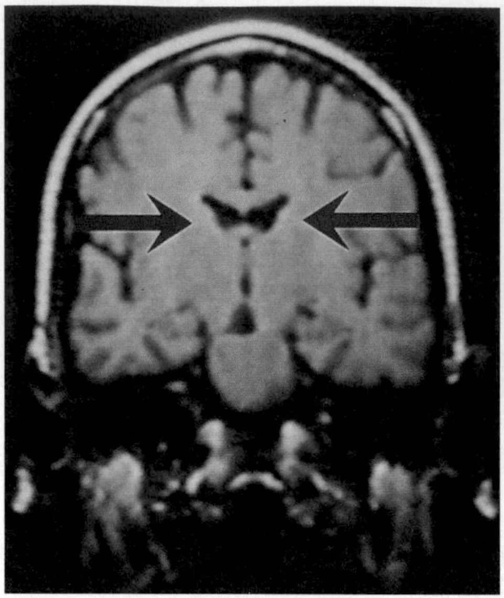
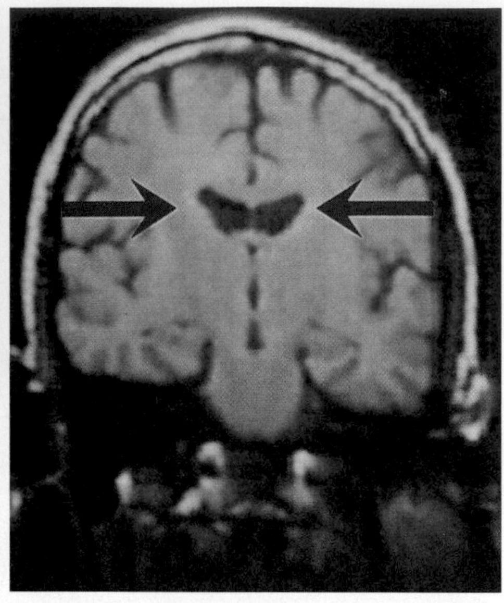

figure 15.3

Brain Abnormalities in Schizophrenia

Here is a magnetic resonance imaging (MRI) comparison of the brains of identical twins. The schizophrenic twin, on the right, has greatly enlarged ventricles (see arrows) and correspondingly less brain tissue, including in the hippocampal area, a region involved in memory and emotion. The same results appeared in 14 other identical twin pairs. By contrast, no significant differences appeared between members of a seven-pair control group of normal identical twins (Suddath et al., 1990). These results support the idea that brain abnormalities are associated with schizophrenia and, because identical twins have the same genes, that such abnormalities may stem from nongenetic factors (Baare et al., 2001).

Researchers are also investigating the possibility that abnormalities in brain chemistry—especially in neurotransmitter systems that use dopamine—play a role in causing or intensifying schizophrenic symptoms. Because drugs that block the brain's dopamine receptors often reduce hallucinations, delusions, disordered thinking, and other positive symptoms of schizophrenia, some investigators speculate that schizophrenia results from excess dopamine. However, the relationship between dopamine and schizophrenia appears to be quite complex (Albert et al., 2002; Koh et al., 2002). Some research suggests, for example, that excessive activity in dopamine systems may be related to the appearance of hallucinations, delusions, and other positive symptoms of schizophrenia. Abnormally low dopamine system activity, especially in prefrontal brain areas, has been associated with negative symptoms such as withdrawal (e.g., Cohen & Servan-Schreiber, 1992; Davis et al., 1991).

Some researchers are seeking to integrate genetic and environmental explanations of schizophrenia by looking for *neurodevelopmental abnormalities* (Cannon et al., 2002; Conklin & Iacono, 2002; Gur et al., 2000; Loeber, Cintron, & Yurgelun-Todd, 2001; McGlashan & Hoffman, 2000; Walbeck et al., 2001). Perhaps, they say, some forms of schizophrenia arise from disruptions in brain development during the period from before birth through childhood, when the brain is growing and its various functions are maturing. Studies have shown, for instance, that prenatal exposure to physical traumas, influenza, or other viral infections is associated with increased risk for developing schizophrenia (AbdelMalik et al., 2003; Brown et al., 2004; Malaspina et al., 2001). Similarly, low birthweight children are more likely to have the brain abnormalities described earlier. These abnormalities are especially likely in children of schizophrenic parents (Cannon et al., 1993; Lawrie et al., 2001). Even parental age may make a difference. Children whose fathers were older than 45 at the time the children were conceived appear to be at elevated risk for developing schizophrenia, possibly because of a sperm cell mutation (Dalman & Allebeck, 2002). The older the father, the greater the risk (Zammit et al., 2003). These neurodevelopmental factors may help explain why children of schizophrenic parents tend to show the kinds of subtle cognitive and intellectual problems associated with brain abnormalities (Ashe, Berry, & Boulton; 2001; Cannon et al., 1994; McGlashan & Hoffman, 2000; Neumann et al., 1995).

The expression of a genetically transmitted predisposition for brain abnormality may be enhanced by environmental factors such as maternal drug use during pregnancy, oxygen deprivation or other complications during birth, childhood malnutrition, and the like (Sorensen et al., 2003). For example, as mentioned earlier,

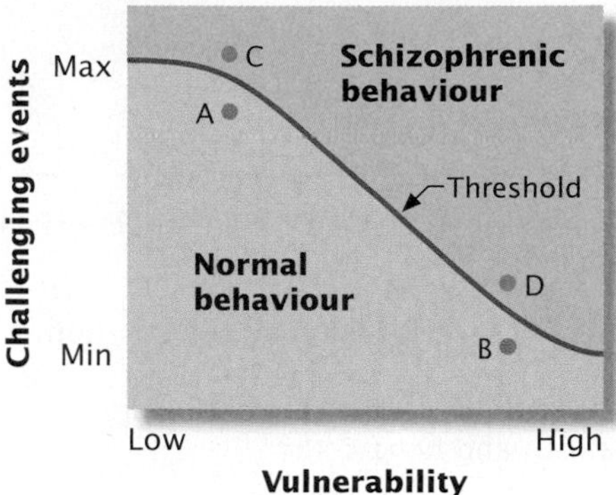

figure 15.4

The Vulnerability Theory of Schizophrenia

According to this theory, a person can cross the threshold into schizophrenia as a result of many combinations of predisposition and stress. A strong predisposition for schizophrenia and little environmental stress (point D), a weak predisposition and a lot of stress (point C), or any other sufficiently potent combination can lead to the disorder. Points A and B represent combinations of vulnerability and stress that would not lead to schizophrenia.

smaller-than-normal prefrontal lobes and other brain structures appear to constitute an inherited predisposition for schizophrenia. However, reduced brain growth alone is not sufficient to cause the disorder. When only one member of an identical twin pair has schizophrenia, both tend to have unusually small brains, but the schizophrenic twin's brain in each pair is the smaller of the two (Baare et al., 2001). This finding suggests that some environmental influence caused degeneration in an already underdeveloped brain, making it even more prone to function abnormally.

Psychological and Sociocultural Factors Psychological factors alone are not considered to be primary causes of schizophrenia (Bassett et al., 2001), but psychological processes and sociocultural influences can contribute to the appearance of schizophrenia and influence its course (Blackwood et al., 2001; Pitschel-Walz et al., 2001). These include maladaptive learning experiences, dysfunctional cognitive habits, and stressful family communication patterns. For example, schizophrenia patients living with relatives who are critical, unsupportive, or emotionally overinvolved are especially likely to relapse following improvement (Hooley, 2004; Rosenfarb et al., 2000; Wearden et al., 2000). Family members' negative attitudes can be a source of stress that actually increases the chances that disruptive or odd behaviours will persist or worsen (Rosenfarb et al., 1995). Patients who are helped to cope with these potentially damaging influences tend to have better long-term outcomes (Bustillo et al., 2001; Velligan et al., 2000).

Vulnerability Theory All the causal theories of schizophrenia we have discussed are consistent with the diathesis-stress approach, which assumes that various forms of stress can activate a person's predisposition for disorder. ("In Review: Schizophrenia" summarizes these theories, as well as the symptoms of schizophrenia.) The diathesis-stress approach is embodied in the *vulnerability theory* of schizophrenia (Cornblatt & Erlenmeyer-Kimling, 1985). This theory suggests that (1) vulnerability to schizophrenia is mainly biological; (2) different people have differing degrees of vulnerability; (3) vulnerability is influenced partly by genetic influences on development and partly by neurodevelopmental abnormalities associated with environmental risk factors; and (4) psychological components—such as exposure to poor parenting or high-stress families, having inadequate coping skills, and the like—may help determine whether schizophrenia actually appears and may also influence the course of the disorder (Walker & Diforio, 1998; Wearden et al., 2000).

in review Schizophrenia

Aspect	Key Features
Common Symptoms	
Disorders of thought	Disturbed content, including delusions; disorganization, including loose associations, neologisms, and word salad
Disorders of perception	Hallucinations, or false perceptions; poorly focused attention
Disorders of emotion	Flat affect; inappropriate tears, laughter, or anger
Possible Causes	
Biological	Genetics; abnormalities in brain structure; abnormalities in dopamine systems; neurodevelopmental problems
Psychological	Learned maladaptive behaviour; disturbed patterns of family communication

table 15.6

Here are brief descriptions of the ten personality disorders listed on Axis II of *DSM-IV*.

Personality Disorders

Type	Typical Features
Paranoid	Suspiciousness and distrust of others, all of whom are assumed to be hostile.
Schizoid	Detachment from social relationships; restricted range of emotion.
Schizotypal	Detachment from, and great discomfort in, social relationships; odd perceptions, thoughts, beliefs, and behaviours.
Dependent	Helplessness; excessive need to be taken care of; submissive and clinging behaviour; difficulty in making decisions.
Obsessive-compulsive	Preoccupation with orderliness, perfection, and control.
Avoidant	Inhibition in social situations; feelings of inadequacy; oversensitivity to criticism.
Histrionic	Excessive emotionality and preoccupation with being the centre of attention; emotional shallowness; overly dramatic behaviour.
Narcissistic	Exaggerated ideas of self-importance and achievements; preoccupation with fantasies of success; arrogance.
Borderline	Lack of stability in interpersonal relationships, self-image, and emotion; impulsivity; angry outbursts; intense fear of abandonment; recurring suicidal gestures.
Antisocial	Shameless disregard for, and violation of, other people's rights.

Many different blends of vulnerability and stress can lead to schizophrenia, as Figure 15.4 illustrates. People whose genetic characteristics or developmental influences leave them vulnerable to develop schizophrenia may be especially likely to do so if they are later exposed to learning experiences, family conflicts, and other stressors that trigger and maintain schizophrenic patterns of thought and action. Those same experiences and stressors would not be expected to lead to schizophrenia in people who are less vulnerable to developing the disorder. In other words, schizophrenia is a highly complex disorder—probably more than one disorder (Kirkpatrick et al., 2001; Tsuang, Stone, & Faraone, 2000)—whose origins lie in many biological, psychological, and social domains, some of which are yet to be discovered (Kapur, 2003; Thaker & Carpenter, 2001).

Personality Disorders

Personality disorders are long-standing, inflexible ways of behaving that are not so much severe mental disorders as dysfunctional styles of living (Shea et al., 2002). These disorders affect all areas of functioning and, beginning in childhood or adolescence, create problems for those who display them and for others (Millon & Davis, 1996). Some psychologists view personality disorders as interpersonal strategies (Kiesler, 1996) or as the extreme, rigid, and maladaptive expressions of personality traits (Widiger, 1997). The ten personality disorders listed on Axis II of *DSM-IV* are grouped into three clusters that share certain features (see Table 15.6).

The *odd-eccentric* cluster—often referred to as *cluster A*—includes paranoid, schizoid, and schizotypal personality disorders. People diagnosed as having schizo-

personality disorders Long-standing, inflexible ways of behaving that create a variety of problems.

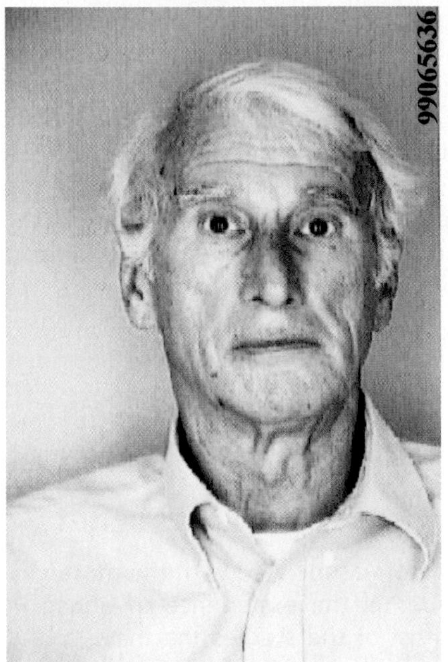

A Classic Case of Antisocial Personality Disorder Alfred Jack Oakley meets women through personal ads, claiming to be a millionaire movie producer, pilot, and novelist. In reality, he is a penniless con artist who uses smooth talk and charm to gain the women's trust so he can steal from them. In January 2000, after being convicted of stealing a Florida woman's Mercedes, Oakley complimented the prosecutor's skills and the jury's wisdom and claimed to feel remorseful. The judge appeared to see through this ploy ("I don't believe there is a sincere word that ever comes out of your mouth"), but it was still effective enough to get him probation instead of jail time!

typal personality disorder, for example, display some of the peculiarities seen in schizophrenia but are not disturbed enough to be labelled as schizophrenic. Rather than hallucinating, these people may report "illusions" of sights or sounds. They may also exhibit "magical thinking," including odd superstitions or beliefs (such as that they have extrasensory perception or that salt under the mattress will prevent insomnia).

The *dramatic-erratic* cluster—called *cluster B*—includes the histrionic, narcissistic, borderline, and antisocial personality disorders. The main characteristics of narcissistic personality disorder, for example, are an exaggerated sense of self-importance, extreme sensitivity to criticism, a constant need for attention, and a tendency to arrogantly overestimate personal abilities and achievements. People displaying this disorder feel entitled to special treatment by others but are markedly lacking in empathy *for* others.

The *anxious-fearful* cluster—*cluster C*—includes dependent, obsessive-compulsive, and avoidant personality disorders. Avoidant personality disorder, for example, is similar to social phobia in the sense that persons labelled with this disorder tend to be "loners" with a long-standing pattern of avoiding social situations and of being particularly sensitive to criticism or rejection. They want to be with others but are too inhibited.

From the perspective of public welfare and safety, the most serious, costly, and intensively studied personality disorder is **antisocial personality disorder** (e.g., Scott et al., 2001). It is marked by a long-term pattern of irresponsible, impulsive, unscrupulous, even criminal behaviour beginning in childhood or early adolescence.

In the 1800s, this pattern was called *moral insanity,* because the people displaying it appear to have no morals or common decency. Later, these people came to be called *psychopaths* or *sociopaths.* The current "antisocial personality" label more accurately portrays them as troublesome but not "insane" by the legal standards we will discuss shortly. About 3 percent of men and about 1 percent of women in North America fall into this diagnostic category (American Psychiatric Association, 1994, 2000; Public Health Agency of Canada, 2002c).

At their least troublesome, people exhibiting antisocial personality disorder are a nuisance. They are charming, intelligent, "fast talkers" who borrow money and fail to return it. They are arrogant and self-centred manipulators who con people into doing things for them, usually by lying and taking advantage of people's decency and trust. A hallmark of people with antisocial personality disorder is a lack of anxiety, remorse, or guilt, whether they have wrecked a borrowed car or killed an innocent person (Gray et al., 2003; Hare, 1993). Fortunately, these individuals tend to become less active and dangerous after the age of 40 or so (Stoff, Breiling, & Maser, 1997). No method has yet been found for permanently altering their behaviour (Rice, 1997), but research suggests that identification of antisocial personalities prior to the development of their more treatment-resistant traits may offer the best hope for dealing with this disorder (Crawford, Cohen, & Brooks, 2001; Lynam, 1996; Stoff et al., 1997).

As for the causes of antisocial personality disorder, theories abound. Some studies suggest a genetic predisposition (Slutske et al., 2001), possibly in the form of abnormal brain development or chronic under-arousal of both the autonomic and central nervous systems (Dolan & Park, 2002; Patrick, Cuthbert, & Lang, 1994; Raine et al., 2000). This under-arousal may render people less sensitive to punishment and more likely to seek exciting stimulation than is normally the case (Herpertz et al., 2001; Stoff et al. 1997). Other evidence suggests more specific information-processing defects. For example, on neuropsychological test batteries, people diagnosed with antisocial personality disorder perform more poorly than others do on tests of the ability to make plans (Dolan & Park, 2002). There seem to be specific problems, too, in the processing of fear-related information among people whose symptoms of antisocial personality disorder include extreme emotional detachment (Levenston et al., 2000; Patrick, Bradley, & Lang, 1993).

antisocial personality disorder A personality disorder involving impulsive, selfish, unscrupulous, even criminal behaviour.

Broken homes, rejection by parents, poor discipline, lack of good parental models, lack of attachment to early caregivers, impulsivity, conflict-filled childhoods, and poverty have all been suggested as psychological and social factors contributing to the development of antisocial personality disorder (Lahey et al., 1995; Raine, Brennan, & Mednick, 1994; Tremblay et al., 1994). The biopsychosocial model suggests that antisocial personality disorder results when these psychosocial and environmental conditions interact with genetic predispositions to low arousal and the sensation seeking and impulsivity associated with it (Gray et al., 2003; Rutter, 1997). Environmental and/or genetic factors can suppress the development of antisocial personality disorder, too. In one study, for example, boys whose environments heightened their risk of antisocial behaviour were less likely to display such behaviour if they had inherited a particular gene (Caspi et al., 2002).

FOCUS ON RESEARCH METHODS

Exploring Links Between Child Abuse and Antisocial Personality Disorder

One of the most prominent environmental factors associated with the more violent forms of antisocial personality disorder is the experience of abuse in childhood (MacMillan et al., 2001). However, most of the studies that have found a relationship between childhood abuse and antisocial personality disorder were based on potentially biased reports (Monane, Leichter, & Lewis, 1984; Rosenbaum & Bennett, 1986). People with antisocial personalities—especially those with criminal records—are likely to make up stories of abuse in order to shift blame for their behaviour onto others. Even if these people's reports were accurate, however, most of the studies lacked a control group of people from similar backgrounds who were not antisocial. Because of this research design flaw, it is virtually impossible to separate the effects of reported child abuse from the effects of poverty or other factors that might also have contributed to the development of antisocial personality disorder.

- **What was the researcher's question?**

Can childhood abuse cause antisocial personality disorder? To help answer this question and to correct some of the flaws in earlier studies, Cathy Widom (1989) used a prospective research design, first finding cases of childhood abuse and then looking for the effects of that abuse on adult behaviour.

- **How did the researcher answer the question?**

Widom began by identifying 416 adults whose backgrounds included official records of having been physically or sexually abused before the age of 11. She then explored the stories of these people's lives, as told in police and school records, as well as in two-hour diagnostic interviews. To reduce experimenter bias and distorted reporting, Widom ensured that the interviewers were unaware of the purpose of the study and that the respondents were told only that the researchers wanted to learn about people who had grown up in a midwestern US metropolitan area in the late 1960s and early 1970s. Widom also selected a comparison group of 283 people who had no history of abuse but who were similar to the abused sample in terms of age, gender, ethnicity, hospital of birth, schools attended, and area of residence. Her goal was to obtain a nonabused control group that had been exposed to approximately the same environmental risk factors and socioeconomic conditions as the abused children.

- **What did the researcher find?**

First, Widom (1989) tested the hypothesis that exposure to abuse in childhood is associated with criminality and/or violence in later life. She found that 26 percent of the abused youngsters went on to commit juvenile crimes, 29 percent were arrested as adults, and 11 percent committed violent crimes. These percentages were significantly higher than the figures for the nonabused group. The association between criminality and abuse was stronger for males than for females. And overall, victims of physical abuse were more likely to commit violent crimes as adults than were victims of sexual abuse.

Next, Widom tested the hypothesis that childhood abuse is associated with the development of antisocial personality disorder (Luntz & Widom, 1994). She found that the abused group exhibited a significantly higher rate of antisocial personality disorder (13.5 percent) than did the comparison group (7.1 percent). The apparent role of abuse in antisocial personality disorder was particularly pronounced in men, and it remained strong even when other factors—such as age, ethnicity, and socio-economic status—were accounted for in the statistical analyses. It is interesting to note that one other factor—failure to graduate from high school—was also strongly associated with the appearance of antisocial personality disorder, whether or not childhood abuse had occurred.

What do the results mean?

Widom's research supported earlier studies in finding an association between childhood abuse and criminality, violence, and antisocial personality disorder. Further, although her study did not permit a firm conclusion that abuse alone causes antisocial personality disorder, the data from its prospective design added strength to the argument that abuse may be an important causal factor (Widom, 2000). This interpretation is supported by the results of research by other investigators (Jaffee et al., 2004). Finally, Widom's work offers yet another reason—as if more reasons were needed—why it is so important to prevent the physical and sexual abuse of children. The long-term consequences of such abuse can be tragic not only for its immediate victims but also for those victimized by the violence, criminal actions, and antisocial behaviour perpetrated by some abused children as they grow up (Weiler & Widom, 1996).

What do we still need to know?

Widom's results suggest that one or more of the factors leading teenagers to drop out (or be thrown out) of high school might help create antisocial personality disorder even in children who were not abused. Some of her more recent work suggests, too, that exposure to poverty and other stressors can be as important as abuse in promoting antisocial personality disorder (Horwitz et al., 2001). Further research is needed to discover whether antisocial personality disorder stems from abuse itself, from one of the factors accompanying it, or from some other specific combination of known and still-unknown risk factors. The importance of combined and interacting risk factors is suggested by the fact that abuse is often part of a larger pool of experiences, such as exposure to deviant models, social rejection, poor supervision, and the like.

In fact, another of Widom's more recent studies (Horwitz et al., 2001) supported the conclusion that childhood abuse increases the likelihood of encountering later stressful life events and that it is some of these events that lead to an increased risk of antisocial personality disorder. In other words, childhood abuse might create general vulnerability for a variety of psychological disorders and life stressors, but the chain of events that promote the development of any particular disorder, such as antisocial personality disorder, are not yet fully understood.

We need to know more, too, about why such a small percentage of the abused children in Widom's sample displayed violence, criminal behaviour, and antisocial personality disorder. What genetic characteristics or environmental experiences serve to protect children from at least some of the devastating effects of abuse (Rind & Tromovitch, 1997; Rind, Tromovitch, & Bauserman, 1998)? As described in the chapter on human development, some clues have already been found (Caspi et al., 2002; Wills et al., 2001), but a better understanding of these protective elements is needed if there are to be effective programs for the prevention of antisocial personality disorder.

LINKAGES

As noted in the chapter on introducing psychology, all of psychology's many subfields are related to one another. Our discussion of how classical conditioning can lead to phobias illustrates just one way in which the topic of this chapter, psychological disorders, is linked to the subfield of learning (which is the focus of the chapter by that name). The Linkages diagram shows ties to two other subfields as well, and there are many more ties throughout the book. Looking for linkages among subfields will help you see how they all fit together and better appreciate the big picture that is psychology.

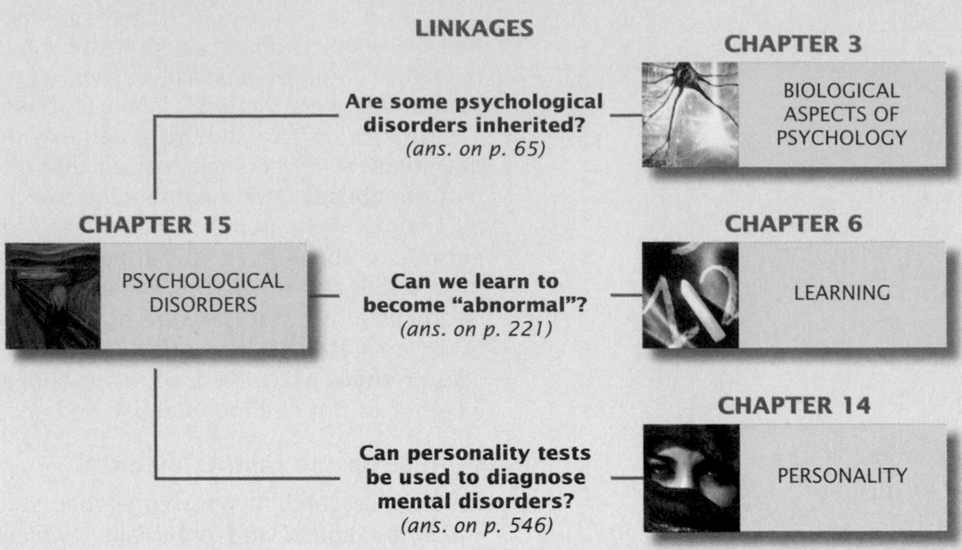

LINKAGES
CHAPTER 3
BIOLOGICAL ASPECTS OF PSYCHOLOGY
Are some psychological disorders inherited?
(ans. on p. 65)
CHAPTER 15
PSYCHOLOGICAL DISORDERS
CHAPTER 6
LEARNING
Can we learn to become "abnormal"?
(ans. on p. 221)
CHAPTER 14
PERSONALITY
Can personality tests be used to diagnose mental disorders?
(ans. on p. 546)

SUMMARY

Psychopathology involves patterns of thinking, feeling, and behaving that cause personal distress or that significantly impair a person's social or occupational functioning.

Defining Psychological Disorders

Some disorders show similarity across cultures, but the definition of abnormality is largely determined by social and cultural factors.

What Is Abnormal?

The criteria for judging abnormality include statistical infrequency (a comparison with what most people do), norm violation, and personal suffering. Each of these criteria is flawed to some extent.

Behaviour in Context: A Practical Approach

The practical approach to defining abnormality, which considers the content, context, and consequences of behaviour, emphasizes the question of whether individuals show *impaired functioning* in fulfilling the roles appropriate for particular people in particular settings, cultures, and historical eras.

Explaining Psychological Disorders

Abnormal behaviour has been attributed, at one time or another, to many different factors, including the action of supernatural forces.

The Biopsychosocial Model

In today's *biopsychosocial model*, mental disorders are attributed to the combination and interaction of biological, psychological, and sociocultural factors. Biological factors are emphasized by the medical model, or *neurobiological model*, which sees psychological disorders as reflecting disturbances in the anatomy and chemistry of the brain and in other biological processes. The causal factors emphasized by the *psychological model* of mental disorders include unconscious conflicts, maladaptive cognitive schemas, learning, or blocked actualizing tendencies. The *sociocultural model* focuses on factors that help define abnormality and influence the form that disorders take in different parts of the world.

Diathesis-Stress as an Integrative Explanation

No single aspect of the biopsychosocial model can adequately explain all psychological disorders. The *diathesis-stress approach* takes into account all the causal factors in that model by suggesting that biological, psychological, and sociocultural characteristics create predispositions for disorder and that the symptoms of a disorder appear only in the face of sufficient amounts of stress.

Classifying Psychological Disorders

There seems to be a set of behaviour patterns that roughly defines abnormality in most cultures. Classifying these patterns helps to identify the features, causes, and most effective methods of treating various psychological disorders.

A Classification System: *DSM-IV*

The dominant system for classifying abnormal behaviour in North America is the American Psychiatric Association's *Diagnostic and Statistical Manual of Mental Disorders (DSM-IV)* and its most recent text revision (*DSM-IV-TR*). It includes more than three hundred specific categories of mental disorders.

Anxiety Disorders

Long-standing and disruptive patterns of anxiety characterize *anxiety disorders.*

Types of Anxiety Disorders

The most prevalent type of anxiety disorder is *phobia*, which includes *specific phobias*, *social phobias*, and *agoraphobia*. Other anxiety disorders are *generalized anxiety disorder*, which involves nonspecific anxiety; *panic disorder*, which brings unpredictable attacks of intense anxiety; and *obsessive-compulsive disorder (OCD)*, in which uncontrollable repetitive thoughts and ritualistic actions occur.

Causes of Anxiety Disorders

The most influential explanations of anxiety disorders suggest that they may develop through the combination of a biological predisposition for strong anxiety reactions and the impact of fear-enhancing thought patterns and learned anxiety responses.

Somatoform Disorders

Somatoform disorders, including *conversion disorder*, involve physical problems that have no apparent physical cause. Other examples are *hypochondriasis*, an unjustified concern about being ill; *somatization disorder*, in which the person complains of numerous, unconfirmed physical complaints; and *pain disorder*, in which pain is felt in the absence of a known physical cause.

Dissociative Disorders

Dissociative disorders involve rare conditions such as *dissociative fugue*, *dissociative amnesia*, and *dissociative identity disorder*, or *DID* (multiple personality disorder), in which a person suffers memory loss or develops two or more identities.

Mood Disorders

Mood disorders, also known as affective disorders, involve extreme moods of long duration that may be inconsistent with events.

Depressive Disorders

Major depressive disorder is marked by feelings of inadequacy, worthlessness, and guilt; in extreme cases, *delusions* may also occur. *Dysthymic disorder* includes similar but less severe symptoms persisting for a long period. Suicide is often related to these disorders.

Bipolar Disorders

Alternating periods of depression and *mania* characterize bipolar I disorder, which is also known as *manic depression*. *Cyclothymic disorder*, an alternating pattern of less extreme mood swings, is more common.

Causes of Mood Disorders

Mood disorders have been attributed to biological causes such as genetics—which underlie disruptions in neurotransmitter and endocrine systems—and irregularities in biological rhythms. Both loss of significant sources of reward and maladaptive patterns of thinking are among the psychological causes proposed. A predisposition toward some of these disorders may be inherited, although their appearance may be determined by a diathesis-stress process.

Schizophrenia

Schizophrenia is perhaps the most severe and puzzling disorder of all.

Symptoms of Schizophrenia

Among the symptoms of schizophrenia are problems in thinking, perception (often including *hallucinations*), attention, emotion, movement, motivation, and daily functioning.

Categorizing Schizophrenia

Although *DSM-IV* lists five major subtypes of schizophrenia (paranoid, disorganized, catatonic, undifferentiated, and residual), many researchers today favour a descriptive system that focuses on whether patients display mainly *positive symptoms* (such as hallucinations and disorganized thoughts) or *negative symptoms* (such as lack of speech and restricted emotional expression). Each category of symptoms may be traceable to different causes. Predominantly negative symptoms tend to be associated with more severe disorder and less successful treatment outcomes.

Causes of Schizophrenia

Genetic factors, neurotransmitter problems, abnormalities in brain structure and functioning, and neurodevelopmental abnormalities are biological factors implicated in schizophrenia. Psychological explanations have focused on maladaptive learning experiences and disturbed family interactions. The diathesis-stress approach, often described in terms of the vulnerability model, remains a promising framework for research into the multiple causes of schizophrenia.

Personality Disorders

Personality disorders are long-term patterns of maladaptive behaviour that may be disturbing to the person displaying them and/or to others. Examples include schizotypal, avoidant, narcissistic, and *antisocial personality disorders*.

16 Treatment of Psychological Disorders

Many movies and television dramas include scenes in a psychotherapist's office, but even the best of them tell only part of the story of how psychological disorders can be treated. In this chapter we describe a wide range of treatment options, from "talking therapy" to drugs. We also summarize the results of research on the effectiveness of treatment and on efforts to prevent psychological disorders. Here's how we have organized the material

In the chapter on psychological disorders, we described José, an electronics technician who was forced to take medical leave from his job because of repeated panic attacks (see Table 15.2). After four months of diagnostic testing turned up no physical problems, José's physician suggested that he see a psychologist. José resisted at first, insisting that his condition was not "just in his head," but he eventually began psychological treatment. Within a few months, his panic attacks had stopped, and José had returned to all his old activities. After the psychologist helped him reconsider his workload, José decided to retire from his job in order to pursue more satisfying work at his home-based computer business.

José's case is not unusual. In Canada, about 12.5 percent of adults will receive treatment for a psychological disorder at some point in their lifetime (BC Partners for Mental Health and Addictions Information, 2003). Compared with untreated patients, those who receive treatment for psychological disorders typically need fewer mental and physical health services later on (American Psychological Association, 2002c; Chiles, Lambert, & Hatch, 1999; Clay, 2002b). In this chapter, we describe a variety of treatment methods, most of which are based on the theories of stress and coping, personality, and psychological disorders reviewed in the chapters on those topics.

First we examine the basic features common to all forms of treatment. Then we discuss approaches that rely on **psychotherapy**, the treatment of psychological disorders through psychological methods, such as talking about problems and exploring new ways of thinking and acting. These methods are based on psychodynamic, humanistic, or social-cognitive (behavioural) theories of disorder and treatment. We then consider biological approaches to treatment, which consist of prescribing drugs and other physical therapies.

Although we discuss different psychotherapy methods in separate sections, keep in mind that the majority of mental health professionals see themselves as *eclectic* therapists. In other words, they might lean toward one set of methods, but when working with particular clients or particular problems, they employ other methods as well (Hayes & Harris, 2000; Northcut & Heller, 1999; Slife & Reber, 2001). Further, many clients receive psychoactive drugs in addition to psychotherapy during the course of psychological treatment (Sammons & Schmidt, 2001).

Basic Features of Treatment

All treatments for psychological, as well as physical, disorders share certain basic features. These common features include a *client* or patient, a *therapist* who is accepted as being capable of helping the client, and the establishment of a *special relationship* between the client and therapist. In addition, all forms of treatment are based on some *theory* about the causes of the client's problems (Dumont & Corsini, 2000). That theory may presume causes ranging from magic spells to infections and everything in between (Frank & Frank, 1991). The theory, in turn, leads to procedures for dealing with the client's problems. So traditional healers combat supernatural forces with ceremonies and prayers, medical doctors treat chemical imbalances with drugs, and psychologists focus on altering psychological processes through psychotherapy.

People receiving treatment for psychological disorders can be inpatients or outpatients. *Inpatients* are treated in a hospital or other residential institution. They are voluntarily or involuntarily committed to these institutions because their impairments are severe enough to create a threat to their own well-being or the safety of others. Depending on their level of functioning, inpatients may stay in the hospital

psychotherapy The treatment of psychological disorders through talking and other psychological methods.

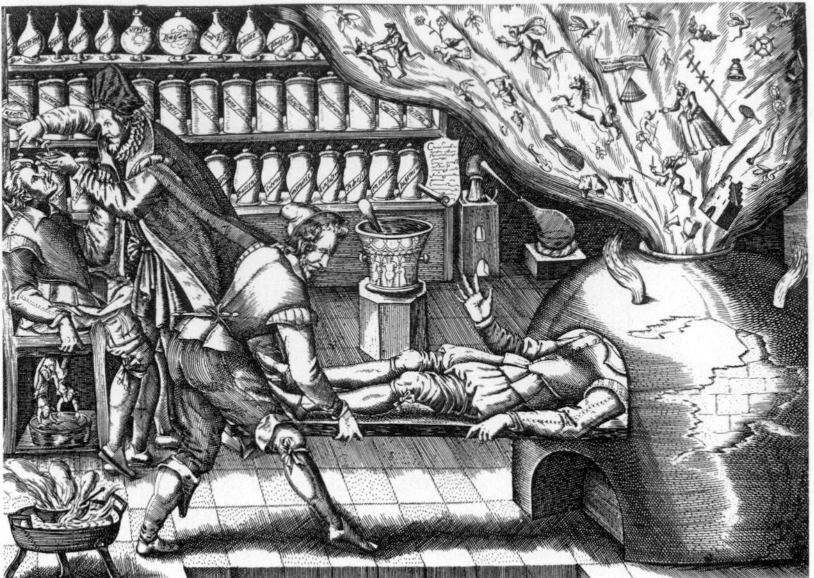

Medieval Treatment Methods
Methods used to treat psychological disorders have always been related to the presumed causes of those disorders. In medieval times, when demonic possession was widely blamed for abnormal behaviour, physician-priests tried to make the victim's body an uncomfortable place for evil spirits. Here, we see a depiction of demons fleeing as an afflicted person's head is placed in an oven.

for a few days or weeks or—in rare cases—several years. Their treatment almost always includes psychoactive drugs. *Outpatients* receive psychotherapy and/or drugs while living in the community. Compared with inpatients, outpatients tend to be younger, are more likely to be female, and typically come from the middle or upper socio-economic classes.

Those who provide psychological treatment are a diverse group. **Psychiatrists** are medical doctors who have completed specialty training in the treatment of psychological disorders. Like other physicians, they are authorized to prescribe drugs for the relief of psychological problems. **Psychologists** who offer psychotherapy have usually completed a doctoral degree in clinical or counselling psychology, often followed by additional specialized training. In Canada, psychologists are not authorized to prescribe drugs (Dittmann, 2003; Heiby, DeLeon, & Anderson, 2004; Mantell, Ortiz, & Planthara, 2004; Sammons, Paige, & Levant, 2003). Other therapy providers include *clinical social workers, marriage and family therapists,* and *licensed professional counsellors,* all of whom typically hold a master's degree in their respective professions and provide treatment in a variety of settings, such as hospitals, clinics, and private practice. *Psychiatric nurses, substance abuse counsellors,* members of the clergy working as *pastoral counsellors*, and a host of paraprofessionals also provide therapy services, often as part of a hospital or outpatient treatment team (Nietzel et al., 2003).

The general goal of treatment providers is to help troubled people change their thinking, feelings, and behaviour in ways that relieve discomfort, promote happiness, and improve their overall functioning as parents, students, workers, and the like. To reach this goal, some therapists try to help clients gain insight into the hidden causes of problems. Others seek to promote growth through more genuine self-expression, and still others help clients learn and practise new ways of thinking and acting. The particular methods used in each case—whether some form of psychotherapy, a drug treatment, or both—depend on the problems, preferences, and financial circumstances of the client; the time available for treatment; and the therapist's theoretical leanings, methodological preferences, and professional qualifications. Later, we will discuss drugs and other biological treatments; here, we consider several forms of psychotherapy, each of which is based on psychodynamic, humanistic, or behavioural explanations of mental disorder.

psychiatrists Medical doctors who have completed special training in the treatment of psychological disorders.

psychologists Among therapists, those whose education includes completion of a master's or (usually) a doctoral degree in clinical or counselling psychology, often followed by additional specialty training.

Group Therapy Some psychotherapy occurs in one-to-one office sessions, but treatment is also conducted with couples, families, and groups in hospitals, community health centres, and facilities for former mental hospital residents. Therapy is offered in prisons, at military bases, in drug and alcoholism treatment centres, and in many other places.

Psychodynamic Psychotherapy

The field of formal psychotherapy began in the late 1800s when, as described in the chapter on personality, Sigmund Freud established the psychodynamic approach to psychological disorders. Central to his approach, and to modern revisions of it, is the assumption that personality and behaviour reflect the efforts of the ego to referee conflicts, usually unconscious, among various components of the personality.

Freud's method of treatment, **psychoanalysis,** was aimed at understanding these unconscious conflicts and how they affect the client. His one-to-one method of studying and treating people, his search for relationships between an individual's life history and current problems, his emphasis on thoughts and emotions in treatment, and his focus on the client-therapist relationship have influenced almost all forms of psychotherapy. We describe Freud's original methods first, and then consider some more recently developed treatments that are rooted in his psychodynamic approach.

Classical Psychoanalysis

Classical psychoanalysis developed mainly out of Freud's medical practice. He was puzzled by patients who suffered from "hysterical" ailments—blindness, paralysis, or other symptoms that had no apparent physical cause. (As mentioned in the chapter on psychological disorders, these ailments are now considered to be symptoms of *conversion disorders*.) Inspired by his colleague Josef Breuer's dramatic success in using hypnosis to treat hysterical symptoms in a patient known as "Anna O." (Breuer & Freud, 1895/1974), Freud tried similar methods with other hysteria patients but found them to be only partially and temporarily successful. Eventually, Freud merely asked patients to lie on a couch and report whatever thoughts, memories, or images came to mind (a process Freud called *free association*).

The results of this "talking cure" were surprising. Freud was struck by how many of his patients reported childhood memories of sexual abuse, usually by a parent or other close relative (Esterson, 2001). Freud wondered whether child abuse was rampant in Vienna, whether he was seeing a biased sample of patients, or whether his patients' memories were being distorted in some way. He ultimately concluded that his patients' memories of abuse probably reflected unconscious childhood wishes and

psychoanalysis A method of psychotherapy that seeks to help clients gain insight by recognizing and understanding unconscious thoughts and emotions.

Freud's Consulting Room During psychoanalytic sessions, Freud's patients lay on this couch, free-associating or describing dreams and everyday events, while he sat in the chair behind them. According to Freud, even apparently trivial behaviour may carry messages from the unconscious. Forgetting a dream or missing a therapy appointment might reflect a client's unconscious resistance to treatment. Even accidents may be meaningful. The waiter who spills hot soup on an elderly male customer might be seen as acting out unconscious aggressive impulses against a father figure.

fantasies, not reality. Further, he believed that hysterical symptoms stem from unconscious conflicts over those wishes and fantasies. Accordingly, Freud focused psychoanalysis on an exploration of unconscious impulses and fantasies and the conflicts they create.

Classical psychoanalytic treatment aims to help clients gain insight into their problems by recognizing unconscious thoughts and emotions and then to discover, or *work through,* the many ways in which those unconscious elements affect their everyday lives. The treatment may require as many as three to five sessions per week, usually over several years. Generally, the psychoanalyst is compassionate but emotionally neutral as the client slowly develops an understanding of how past conflicts determine current problems (Auld & Hyman, 1991; Gabbard, 2000).

LINKAGES (a link to Personality)

To gain glimpses of the unconscious—and of the sexual and aggressive impulses he believed reside there—Freud looked for meaning in his patients' free associations, their dreams, their everyday behaviours, and their relationship with him. He believed that hidden beneath the obvious or *manifest content* of dreams is *latent content* that reflects the wishes, impulses, and fantasies that the dreamer's defense mechanisms keep out of consciousness during waking hours. He focused also on "Freudian slips" of the tongue (such as saying *beast* instead of *best*) and other seemingly insignificant, but potentially meaningful, behaviours. Similarly, when patients expressed dependency, hostility, or even love toward him, Freud saw it as an unconscious process in which childhood feelings and conflicts about parents and other significant people were being transferred to the therapist. Analysis of this *transference,* this "new edition" of the client's childhood conflicts and current problems, became another important psychoanalytic method. Freud believed that focusing on the transference allows clients to see how old conflicts haunt their lives and helps them to resolve these conflicts (Arlow, 1995).

Contemporary Variations on Psychoanalysis

Classical psychoanalysis is still practised, but not as much as it was several decades ago (Gabbard, 2000; Horgan, 1996). The decline is due to many factors, including disenchantment with Freud's personality theory; the expense of classical psychoanalysis (Moran, 2000); its limited usefulness with children; and the availability of many alternative forms of treatment, including variations on classical psychoanalysis.

Some of these variations were developed by the neo-Freudian theorists discussed in the chapter on personality. As noted there, those theorists tended to place less emphasis than Freud did on the past and on unconscious impulses stemming from

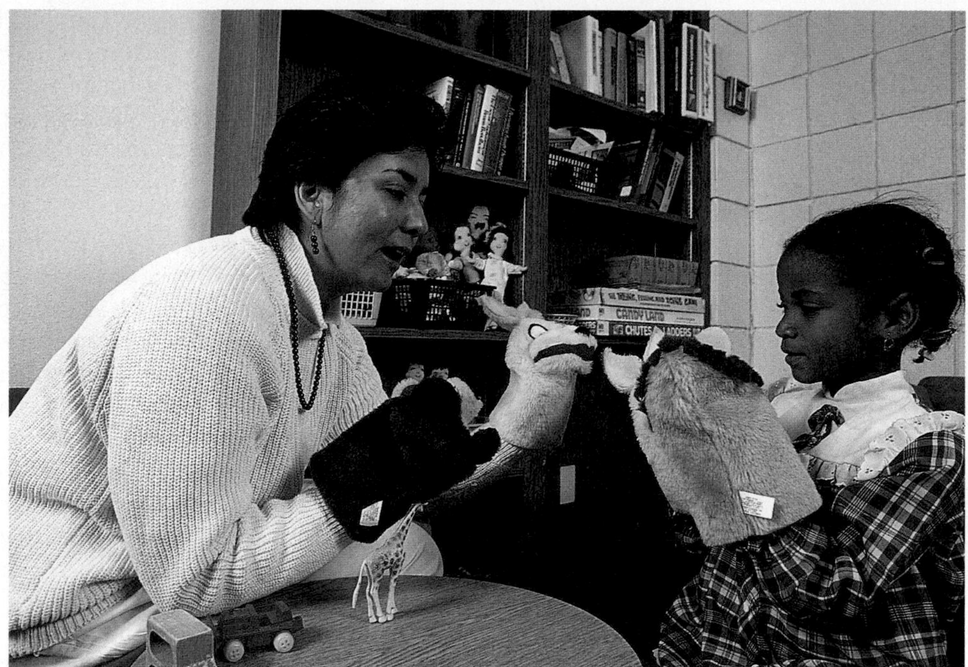

Play Therapy Modern versions of psychoanalytic treatment include fantasy play and other techniques that make the approach more useful with children. A child's behaviour and comments while playing with puppets representing family members, for example, are seen as a form of free association that the therapist hopes will reveal important unconscious material, such as fear of abandonment (Booth & Lindaman, 2000).

the id. They also tended to stress the role of social relationships in clients' problems and how the power of the ego can be harnessed to solve those problems. *Ego analysis* (Hartmann, 1958; Klein, 1960) and *individual analysis* (Adler, 1927/1963) were among the first treatments to be based on neo-Freudian theories. Some were designed for treating children (A. Freud, 1946; Klein, 1960).

More recent variants have come to be known as *short-term dynamic psychotherapy* because they aim to provide benefits in far less time than is required in classical psychoanalysis (Davanloo, 1999; Levenson, 2003). A particularly popular short-term dynamic approach is known as *object relations therapy* (Scharff & Scharff, 1998; St. Clair, 1999). (The term *object* refers to anything, including a person, that has had emotional significance in a client's life.) In object relations therapy, the powerful need for human contact and support takes centre stage. In fact, object relations therapists believe that most of the problems that bring clients to treatment ultimately stem from this need and how it plays out in their relationships with others—especially with their mothers or other early caregivers. Psychotherapists who adopt an object relations perspective take a much more active role in therapy sessions than classical analysts do—particularly by directing the client's attention to evidence of certain conflicts, rather than waiting for free association or other more subtle methods to reveal these conflicts. Object relations therapists work to develop a nurturing relationship with their clients, providing a "second chance" for them to receive the support that might have been lacking in infancy and to counteract some of the consequences of maladaptive early attachment patterns (Kahn & Rachman, 2000; Lieberman & Pawl, 1988; Wallerstein, 2002). For example, object relations therapists take pains to show that they will not abandon their clients, as might have happened to these people in the past. *Interpersonal therapy,* too, is rooted partly in neo-Freudian theory (Sullivan, 1954), but it focuses on helping clients explore and overcome the problematic effects of interpersonal events that occur *after* early childhood—events such as the loss of a loved one, conflicts with a parent or a spouse, job loss, or social isolation (Weissman, Markowitz, & Klerman, 2000).

Other variations on psychoanalysis retain more of Freud's ideas but alter the format of treatment so that it is less intense, less expensive, and more appropriate for a broader range of clients (Hoyt, 1995; Messer & Kaplan, 2004). For example, *psychoanalytically oriented psychotherapy* and *time-limited dynamic psychotherapy* employ classical psychoanalytic methods but use them more flexibly (Levenson & Strupp, 1997). The goal of treatment may range from giving psychological support to achieving basic changes in personality, and therapy may be completed in fewer than 30 sessions. A therapist using these briefer psychodynamic methods encourages clients to focus on concrete, specific goals. For example, the therapist might ask a client to describe how he or she would feel and act if a specific problem were suddenly solved.

Some version of transference analysis is seen in virtually all variations on classical psychoanalysis. In a short-term psychodynamic treatment called *supportive-expressive therapy,* for example, the therapist looks for a "core conflict" that appears repeatedly across a variety of relationships, including in the therapy relationship (Connolly, Crits-Cristoph, & Barber, 2000; Luborsky, 1997; Luborsky & Crits-Christoph, 1998). The core conflict in one young man, for example, centred on his desire to stand up for himself and his tendency to criticize himself for having that desire. (As a child, the client had been physically abused by his father.) The therapist watched for this core conflict to appear in the therapy relationship—as when assertiveness was tempered by fear of having done wrong—and then helped the client see the links among his fear of asserting himself, his fantasies of getting even, and his childhood abuse experiences. This interpretation is part of transference analysis (Luborsky, 1997). At the same time, the therapist supported the client's attempts to be more assertive with authority figures without having violent fantasies.

With their focus on interpersonal relationships rather than instincts, their emphasis on clients' potential for self-directed problem solving, and the reassurance and emotional support they provide, contemporary variants on classical psychoanalysis have helped the psychodynamic approach retain its influence among mental health professionals (Westen & Gabbard, 1999).

Humanistic Psychotherapy

Whereas some therapists revised Freud's ideas, others developed radical new therapies based on the humanistic approach to personality, which we describe in the chapter on personality. *Humanistic psychologists,* sometimes called *phenomenologists,* emphasize the ways in which people interpret the events in their lives. They see people as capable of consciously controlling their own actions and taking responsibility for their own decisions. Most humanistic therapists believe that human behaviour is motivated not by sexual or aggressive impulses but rather by an innate drive toward growth that is guided from moment to moment by the way people perceive their world. Disordered behaviour, they say, reflects a blockage of natural growth brought on by distorted perceptions or lack of awareness of feelings. Accordingly, humanistic (or phenomenological) therapy operates on the following assumptions:

1. Treatment is an encounter between equals, not a cure provided by an expert. It is a way to help clients restart their natural growth and to feel and behave more in line with that growth.
2. Clients will improve on their own, given the right conditions. These ideal conditions promote clients' awareness, acceptance, and expression of their feelings and perceptions. So, like psychodynamic therapy, humanistic therapy promotes insight, but it is insight into current feelings and perceptions, not into unconscious childhood conflicts.
3. Ideal conditions in therapy can best be established through a relationship in which clients feel fully accepted and supported as human beings, no matter how problematic or undesirable their behaviour may be. It is the client's

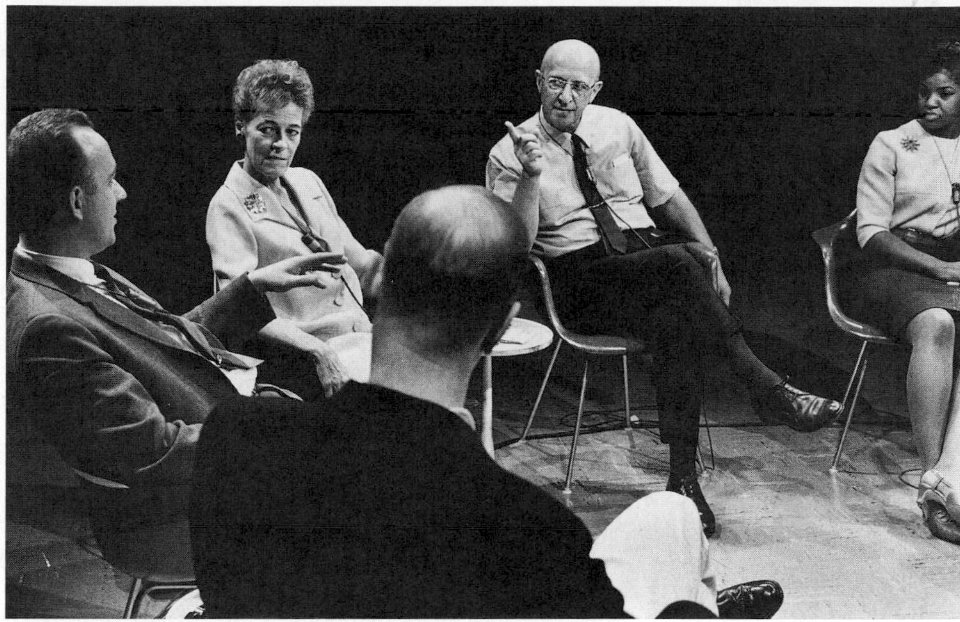

A Client-Centred Therapy Group
Carl Rogers (shown here in shirtsleeves) believed that, as successful treatment progresses, clients become more self-confident, more aware of their feelings, more accepting of themselves, more comfortable and genuine with other people, more reliant on self-evaluation than on the judgments of others, and more effective and relaxed.

experience of this relationship that brings beneficial changes. (As noted earlier, this assumption is also important in object relations therapy.)

4. Clients must remain responsible for choosing how they will think and behave.

Of the many humanistically oriented treatments in use today, the most influential are client-centred therapy, developed by Carl Rogers, and Gestalt therapy, developed by Frederick and Laura Perls (Cain & Seeman, 2002).

Client-Centred Therapy

Carl Rogers was trained in psychodynamic therapy methods during the 1930s, but he soon began to question their value. He especially disliked being a detached expert observer whose task was to "figure out" the client. Convinced that a less formal approach would be more effective for the client and more comfortable for the therapist, Rogers allowed his clients to decide what to talk about and when, without direction, judgment, or interpretation by the therapist (Raskin & Rogers, 1995). This approach, now called **client-centred therapy** or **person-centred therapy,** relies on the creation of a relationship that reflects three intertwined attitudes of the therapist: unconditional positive regard, empathy, and congruence.

Unconditional Positive Regard The attitude Rogers called **unconditional positive regard** consists of treating the client as a valued person, no matter what. It is communicated through the therapist's willingness to listen to what the client has to say, without interrupting or evaluating it. The therapist doesn't have to approve of everything the client says, but must accept each statement as reflecting the client's view of the world. Because they trust clients to solve their own problems, Rogerian therapists rarely give advice. Doing so, said Rogers, would send clients an unspoken message that they are incompetent, making them less confident and more dependent on help.

client-centred therapy (person-centred therapy) A therapy that allows the client to decide what to talk about, without direction, judgment, or interpretation from the therapist.

unconditional positive regard A therapist attitude that conveys a caring for, and acceptance of, the client as a valued person.

empathy The therapist's attempt to appreciate and understand how the world looks from the client's point of view.

Empathy Client-centred therapists also try to appreciate the client's point of view. This goes far beyond saying "I know what you mean." It involves an effort to see the world as each client sees it, and not to look at clients from the outside. In other words, client-centred therapists work at developing **empathy,** an emotional understanding of what the client might be thinking and feeling. They convey empathy by showing that they are *actively listening* to the client. Like other skillful interviewers, they make eye contact with the client, nod in recognition as the client speaks, and give other signs of careful attention. They also use **reflection,** a paraphrased summary of the client's words that emphasizes the feelings and meanings that appear to accompany them. Reflection confirms the communication, shows that the therapist is interested, and helps the client to perceive and focus on the thoughts and feelings being expressed. Here is an example:

CLIENT: *This has been such a bad day. I've felt ready to cry any minute, and I'm not even sure what's wrong!*

THERAPIST: *You really do feel so bad. The tears just seem to well up inside, and I wonder if it's a little scary to not even know why you feel this way.*

Notice that in rephrasing the client's statements, the therapist reflected back not only the obvious feelings of sadness but also the fear in the client's voice. Most clients respond to empathic reflection by elaborating on their feelings. In this example, the client went on to say, "It *is* scary, because I don't like to feel in the dark about myself. I have always prided myself on being in control." Clients do this, said Rogers, simply because the therapist expresses the desire to listen and understand without asking disruptive questions. Empathic listening tends to be so effective in promoting self-understanding and awareness that it is used across a wide range of therapies (Corsini & Wedding, 2001). Even outside the realm of therapy, people who are thought of as easy to talk to are usually "good listeners" who reflect back the important messages they hear from others.

Congruence Sometimes called *genuineness,* **congruence** refers to a consistency between the therapist's feelings and actions. When the therapist's unconditional positive regard and empathy are genuine, the client is able to see that relationships can be built on openness and honesty. Ideally, this experience will help the client become more congruent in other relationships.

Here is an excerpt that illustrates the three therapist attitudes we have described.

CLIENT: . . . *I cannot be the kind of person I want to be. I guess maybe I haven't the guts or the strength to kill myself, and if someone else would relieve me of the responsibility or I would be in an accident I, I . . . just don't want to live.*

THERAPIST: *At the present time things look so bad that you can't see much point in living.* [Note the use of empathic reflection and the absence of any criticism.]

CLIENT: *Yes. I wish I'd never started this therapy. I was happy when I was living in my dream world. There I could be the kind of person I wanted to be. But now there is such a wide, wide gap between my ideal and what I am. . . .* [Notice that the client responds to reflection by giving more information.]

THERAPIST: *It's really a tough struggle digging into this like you are, and at times the shelter of your dream world looks more attractive and comfortable.* [Note the use of reflection.]

CLIENT: *My dream world or suicide. . . . So I don't see why I should waste your time—coming in twice a week—I'm not worth it—what do you think?*

THERAPIST: *It's up to you. . . . It isn't wasting my time. I'd be glad to see you whenever you come but it's how you feel about it. . . .* [Note the congruence in stating an honest desire to see the client and the unconditional positive regard in trusting her capacity and responsibility for choice.]

CLIENT: *You're not going to suggest that I come in oftener? You're not alarmed and think I ought to come in every day until I get out of this?*

reflection An active listening method in which a therapist conveys empathy by paraphrasing clients' statements and noting accompanying feelings.

congruence A consistency between the way therapists feel and the way they act toward clients.

THERAPIST: *I believe you are able to make your own decision. I'll see you whenever you want to come.* [Note the unconditional positive regard.]

CLIENT: (With a note of awe in her voice) *I don't believe you are alarmed about—I see—I may be afraid of myself but you aren't afraid for me.* [Here the client experiences the therapist's confidence in her. Happily, she did not kill herself.] (Rogers, 1951, p. 49)

Nonverbal Cues in Gestalt Therapy Gestalt therapists pay particular attention to clients' "body language," especially when it appears to conflict with what they are saying. If this client had just said that she is looking forward to starting her new job, the therapist would probably challenge that statement in an effort to help the client become more aware of her mixed feelings.

Gestalt Therapy

Another form of humanistic treatment was developed by Frederick S. (Fritz) Perls, along with his wife, Laura. A European psychoanalyst, Perls was greatly influenced by research in *Gestalt psychology*. (As described in the chapter on perception, Gestalt psychologists emphasized the idea that people actively organize their perceptions of the world.) He believed that (1) people create their own versions of reality and (2) people's natural psychological growth continues only as long as they perceive, remain aware of, and act on their true feelings. Growth stops and symptoms appear, said Perls, when people are not aware of all aspects of themselves (Perls, 1969; Perls, Hefferline, & Goodman, 1951).

Fritz and Laura Perls based Gestalt therapy on these beliefs. Like client-centred therapy, **Gestalt therapy** seeks to create conditions in which clients can become more unified, self-aware, and self-accepting—and thus ready to grow again. However, Gestalt therapists use more direct and dramatic methods than do Rogerians. Often working in group settings, Gestalt therapists prod clients to become aware of feelings and impulses that they have disowned and to discard feelings, ideas, and values that are not really their own. For example, the therapist or other group members might point out inconsistencies between what clients say and how they behave. Gestalt therapists pay particular attention to clients' gestures and other kinds of "body language" that appear to conflict with what the clients are saying (Kepner, 2001). They may also ask clients to engage in imaginary dialogues, or "conversations," with other people, with parts of their own personalities, and even with objects (Elliott, Watson, & Goldman, 2004a, 2004b; Greenberg & Malcolm, 2002). Like a shy person who can be socially outgoing only while masked at a costume party, clients often find that these dialogues help to get them in touch with, and express, their feelings (Paivio & Greenberg, 1995).

Behaviour Therapy

Psychodynamic and humanistic approaches to therapy assume that if clients gain insight or self-awareness about underlying problems, the symptoms created by those problems will disappear. Behaviour therapists emphasize a different kind of client insight, namely that most psychological problems are *learned behaviours* that can be changed by taking action to learn new ones, not by searching for underlying problems (Martin & Pear, 2002; Miltenberger, 2003).

For example, suppose you have a panic attack every time you leave home and find relief only when you return. Making excuses when friends invite you out eases your anxiety temporarily but does nothing to solve the problem. Could you reduce your fear without discovering its "underlying meaning"? *Behaviour therapy* would offer just such an alternative by first identifying the signals, rewards and punishments, and other learning-based factors that maintain your fear and then helping you to develop new responses in feared situations.

These goals are based on both the *behavioural approach* to psychology and the *social-cognitive approach* to personality and disorder. As described in the chapters on introducing psychology, on personality, and on psychological disorders, these approaches emphasize the role of learning in the development of personality, as well

Gestalt therapy An active treatment designed to help clients get in touch with genuine feelings and disown foreign ones.

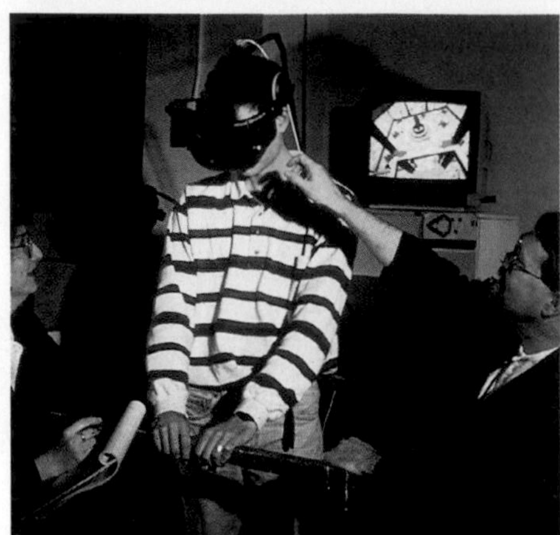

Virtual Desensitization This client fears heights. He is wearing a virtual reality display that creates the visual experience of being in a glass elevator which, under the therapists careful control, seems to gradually rise higher and higher. After learning to tolerate these realistic images without anxiety, clients are better able to fearlessly face the situations they once avoided.

as in most psychological disorders. Accordingly, behaviourists tend to see those disorders as examples of the maladaptive thoughts and actions that a client has learned. For instance, behaviour therapists believe that fear of leaving home (*agoraphobia*) develops through classically conditioned associations between being away from home and having panic attacks. The problem is maintained in part through operant conditioning: Staying home and making excuses for doing so are rewarded by reduced anxiety. Therapists adopting a behavioural approach argue that if learning experiences can create problems, they can also help to alleviate problems. So even if the experiences that led to today's problems began in the client's childhood, behaviour therapy seeks to solve those problems by creating beneficial new experiences using the principles discussed in the chapter on learning.

Inspired by John B. Watson, Ivan P. Pavlov, B. F. Skinner, and others who studied learning during the 1920s and 1930s, researchers in the late 1950s and early 1960s began to systematically apply the principles of classical conditioning, operant conditioning, and observational learning to alter disordered human behaviour (Ullmann & Krasner, 1965). By 1970, behavioural treatment had become a popular alternative to psychodynamic and humanistic methods.

Some of the most notable features of behavioural treatment include the following:

1. Development of a productive therapist-client relationship. As in other therapies, this relationship enhances clients' confidence that change is possible, makes it easier for them to be open about the nature and history of their problems, and increases their motivation to work toward improvement. In fact, behaviour therapists see the therapeutic relationship as central to the success of treatment because it provides the context in which adaptive new learning can take place (Cahill, Carrigan, & Evans, 1998; Wilson, 1995).

2. A careful listing of the behaviours and thoughts to be changed. This assessment—and the establishment of specific goals—sometimes replaces the formal diagnosis used in some other therapy approaches. So instead of treating "agoraphobia" or "depression" or "obsessive-compulsive disorder," behaviour therapists work to change the specific thoughts, behaviours, and emotional reactions that led to these diagnostic labels.

3. A therapist who acts as a kind of teacher/assistant by providing learning-based treatments, giving "homework" assignments, and helping the client take specific actions to deal with problems instead of just talking about them.

4. Continuous monitoring and evaluation of treatment, along with constant adjustments to any procedures that do not seem to be effective. (Because ineffective procedures are soon altered or abandoned, behavioural treatment tends to be one of the briefer approaches to therapy.)

Behavioural treatment can take many forms. By tradition, those methods that rely mainly on classical conditioning principles are usually referred to as **behaviour therapy.** Methods that focus on operant conditioning principles are usually called **behaviour modification.** And behavioural treatment that focuses on changing thinking patterns as well as overt behaviours is called **cognitive-behaviour therapy.**

behaviour therapy Treatments that use classical conditioning principles to change behaviour.

behaviour modification Treatments that use operant conditioning methods to change behaviour.

cognitive-behaviour therapy Learning-based treatment methods that help clients change the way they think, as well as the way they behave.

systematic desensitization A behavioural treatment for anxiety in which clients visualize a graduated series of anxiety-provoking stimuli while remaining relaxed.

Techniques for Modifying Behaviour

Some of the most important and commonly used behavioural treatment techniques are systematic desensitization, modelling, positive reinforcement, extinction, aversion conditioning, and punishment.

Systematic Desensitization José Wolpe (1958) developed one of the first behavioural methods for helping clients overcome phobias and other forms of anxiety. Called **systematic desensitization,** it is a method in which the client visualizes a

table 16.1

Desensitization hierarchies are lists of increasingly fear-provoking situations that clients visualize while using relaxation methods to remain calm. Here are a few items from the beginning and the end of a hierarchy that was used to help a client overcome fear of flying.

A Desensitization Hierarchy

1. You are reading a newspaper and notice an ad for an airline.
2. You are watching a television program that shows a group of people boarding a plane.
3. Your boss tells you that you need to take a business trip by air.
4. You are in your bedroom packing your suitcase for your trip.

.

.

.

12. Your plane begins to move as you hear the flight attendant say, "Be sure your seatbelt is securely fastened."
13. You look at the runway as the plane is readied for takeoff.
14. You look out the window as the plane rolls down the runway.
15. You look out the window as the plane leaves the ground.

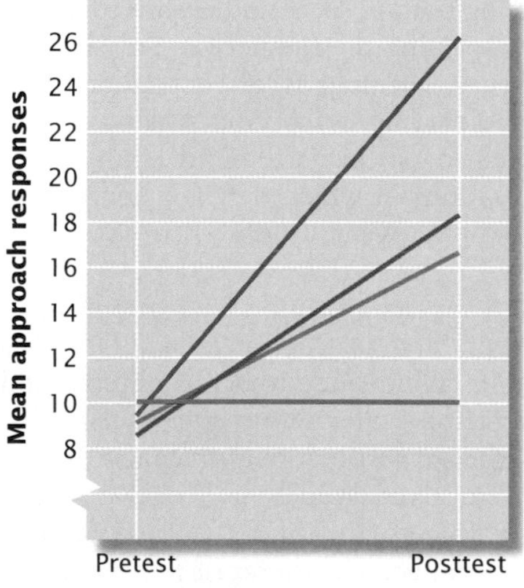

figure 16.1

Participant Modelling in the Treatment of Snake Phobia

In this study, participant modelling was compared with systematic desensitization, symbolic modelling (watching filmed models), and no treatment (control). Notice that, compared with no treatment, all three methods helped snake-phobic clients approach live snakes, but participant modelling was clearly the best. Ninety-two percent of the participants in that group were virtually free of any fear. The value of participant modelling has been repeatedly confirmed (e.g., Öst, Salkovskis, & Hellström, 1991).

series of anxiety-provoking stimuli while remaining relaxed. Wolpe believed that this process gradually weakens the learned association between anxiety and the feared object, until the fear disappears.

Wolpe first arranged for clients to do something that is incompatible with being afraid. He often used *progressive relaxation training* (described in the chapter on health, stress, and coping) to prevent anxiety. Then, while relaxed, the client would be asked to imagine an item from a *desensitization hierarchy,* a sequence of increasingly fear-provoking situations (see Table 16.1). The client would imagine one hierarchy item at a time, moving to a more difficult scene only after tolerating the previous one without distress. Wolpe found that once clients could calmly imagine being in feared situations, they were better able to deal with them in reality later on.

Desensitization appears especially effective if it slowly and carefully presents clients with real, rather than imagined, hierarchy items (Bouton, 2000; Chambless, 1990; Marks, 2002; McGlynn et al., 1999). This *in vivo,* or "real life," desensitization was once difficult to arrange or control, especially in cases involving fear of flying, heights, or highway driving, for example. However, a technique known as *virtual reality graded exposure* now makes it possible for clients to "experience" extremely vivid and precisely graduated versions of feared situations without actually being exposed to them. In one study, clients who feared heights wore a head-mounted virtual reality helmet that gave them the impression of standing on bridges of gradually increasing heights, on outdoor balconies at higher and higher floors, and in a glass elevator as it slowly rose 49 stories (Rothbaum et al., 1995). The same technology has been used successfully in the treatment of many other anxiety disorders, ranging from fear of spiders or air travel to social phobia and post-traumatic stress disorder (Anderson, Rothbaum, & Hodges, 2003; Choi et al, 2001; Gershon et al., 2002; Glantz, Rizzo, & Graap, 2003; Robbins, 2000; Maltby, Kirsch, & Mayers, 2002; Rothbaum et al., 1999, 2000, 2002).

Exactly why systematic desensitization works is not clear. Traditionally, clinicians believed that change occurs because of basic learning processes—either through classical conditioning of a new, calmer response to the fear-provoking stimulus or through extinction, as the object or situation that had been a conditioned fear stimulus repeatedly occurs without being paired with pain or any other aversive unconditioned stimulus (Rachman, 1990). More recent explanations emphasize that desensitization also modifies clients' cognitive processes, including their expectation that they can deal calmly and successfully with previously feared situations (Kehoe & Macrae, 1998).

Modelling Therapists often teach clients desirable behaviours by demonstrating those behaviours. In **modelling** treatments, the client watches the therapist or other people perform desired behaviours, thus learning skills vicariously, or secondhand, without going through a lengthy shaping process. In fear treatment, modelling can teach the client how to respond fearlessly while vicariously extinguishing conditioned fear responses. For example, one therapist showed a 24-year-old student with a severe spider phobia how to kill spiders with a fly swatter and had her practise this skill at home with rubber spiders (MacDonald & Bernstein, 1974). The combination of live modelling with gradual practice is called *participant modelling;* it is one of the most powerful treatments for fear (Bandura, Blanchard, & Ritter, 1969; Faust, Olson, & Rodriguez, 1991; see Figure 16.1).

Modelling is also a major part of **assertiveness training** and **social skills training,** which teach clients how to interact with people more comfortably and effectively. The goals of social skills training range from helping social-phobic singles make conversation on dates to rebuilding the abilities of mental patients to interact normally with people outside the hospital (Fairweather & Fergus, 1993; McQuaid et al, 2000; Spence, Donovan, & Brechman-Toussaint, 2000; Trower, 1995; Wong et al., 1993). In assertiveness training, the therapist helps clients learn to be more direct and expressive in social situations. *Assertiveness* does not require aggressiveness. Instead, it involves clearly and directly expressing both positive and negative feelings and standing up for one's own rights while respecting the rights of others (Alberti & Emmons, 1986; Ballou, 1995). Assertiveness training is often conducted in groups and involves both modelling and role playing of specific situations. For example, group assertiveness training has helped wheelchair-bound adults more comfortably handle the socially awkward situations in which they sometimes find themselves (Gleuckauf & Quittner, 1992; Weston & Went, 1999).

Positive Reinforcement Behaviour therapists also use systematic **positive reinforcement** to change problematic behaviours and to teach new skills in cases ranging from childhood tantrums and juvenile delinquency to schizophrenia and self-starvation. Using operant conditioning principles, they set up *contingencies,* or rules, that specify the behaviours to be strengthened through reinforcement. In one study, language-impaired autistic children were given grapes, popcorn, or other items they liked in return for saying "please," "thank you," and "you're welcome" while exchanging crayons and blocks with a therapist. The therapist first modelled the behaviour by saying the appropriate words. The children almost immediately began to utter the phrases themselves and were reinforced for doing so. The effects of positive reinforcement generalized to situations involving other toys, and as indicated in Figure 16.2, the new skills were still evident at a follow-up session six months later (Matson et al., 1990).

For severely retarded or disturbed clients in institutions, behaviour therapists sometimes establish a **token economy,** a system for rewarding desirable behaviours with coin-like tokens or points that can be exchanged later for snacks, access to television, or other reinforcers (Ayllon, 1999; Ayllon & Azrin, 1968; Paul & Lentz, 1977; Seegert, 2003).The goal is to shape behaviour patterns that will persist outside the institution (Kopelowicz, Liberman, & Zarate, 2002; Moore et al., 2001; Paul, 2000; Paul, Stuve, & Cross, 1997).

Extinction Just as reinforcement can make desirable behaviours more likely, other behavioural techniques can make undesirable behaviours less likely. In operant conditioning, **extinction** is the process of removing the reinforcers that normally follow a particular response. If you've ever given up trying to reach someone whose phone has been busy for hours, you know how extinction works: When a behaviour

modelling Demonstrating desirable behaviours as a way of teaching them to clients.

assertiveness training and social skills training Methods for teaching clients how to interact with others more comfortably and effectively.

positive reinforcement A therapy method that uses rewards to strengthen desirable behaviours.

token economy A system for improving the behaviour of institutionalized clients in which desirable behaviours are rewarded with tokens that can be exchanged for desired items or activities.

extinction The gradual disappearance of a conditioned response or operant behaviour through nonreinforcement.

figure 16.2

Positive Reinforcement for an Autistic Child

During each pretreatment baseline period, an autistic child rarely said "please," "thank you," or "you're welcome," but these statements began to occur once they were modelled, then reinforced. Did modelling and reinforcement actually cause the change? Probably, because each type of response did not start to increase until the therapist began demonstrating it.

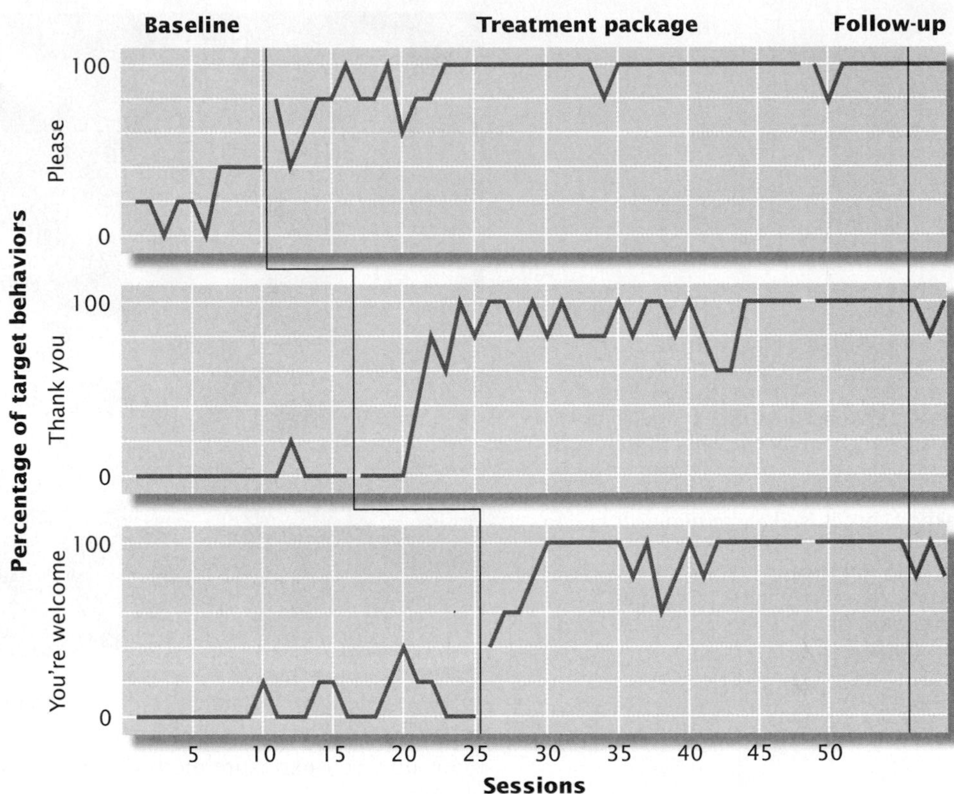

doesn't "pay off," people usually stop it. Extinction changes behaviour rather slowly, but it has been a popular way of treating children and retarded or seriously disturbed adults because it provides a gentle way to eliminate undesirable behaviours. For example, a client who gets attention by disrupting a classroom, damaging property, or violating hospital rules might be placed in a quiet, boring "time out" room for a few minutes in order to interrupt reinforcement for this misbehaviour (e.g., Kee, Hill, & Weist, 1999; Reitman & Drabman, 1999).

Extinction is also the basis of **flooding**, an anxiety-reduction treatment that keeps people in a feared but harmless situation and prevents them from engaging in their normally rewarding pattern of escape (Barlow, 1988). (Because they continuously expose clients to feared stimuli, flooding and other similar methods are also called *exposure techniques*.) When someone is kept in contact with a fear-eliciting conditioned stimulus (a snake, say) without experiencing pain, injury, or any other aversive unconditioned stimulus, the fear-provoking power of the conditioned stimulus eventually fades, and the conditioned fear response extinguishes (Basoglu, Livanou, & Salcioglu, 2003; Harris & Goetsch, 1990; Öst et al., 2001). In one study, 20 clients who feared needles were exposed for two hours to the sight and feel of needles, including mild finger pricks, harmless injections, and blood samplings (Öst, Hellström, & Kever, 1992). Afterward, all but one of these clients were able to have a blood sample drawn without experiencing significant anxiety.

Although often highly effective, flooding is equivalent to immediately exposing a fearful client to the most distressing item on a desensitization hierarchy. Therefore, some therapists and clients prefer more gradual exposure methods, especially when a client's fear is not focused on a specific stimulus (Hecker & Thorpe, 1992). In dealing with agoraphobia, for instance, the therapist might provide gradual exposure by escorting the client away from home for increasing periods and eventually venturing into shopping malls and other previously avoided places (Barlow, Raffa, & Cohen, 2002; Kleinknecht, 1991; Zuercher-White, 1997). Clients can also practise gradual exposure methods on their own. They might be instructed, for example, to spend a little more time each day looking at photos of some feared animal or to

flooding A procedure for reducing anxiety that involves keeping a person in a feared, but harmless, situation.

Treating Fear Through Flooding Flooding is designed to extinguish anxiety by allowing it to occur without the harmful consequences the person dreads. This man's fear of flying is obvious here, on takeoff, but it is likely to diminish during and after an uneventful flight. Like other behavioural treatments, flooding is based on the idea that phobias and other psychological disorders are learned and can thus be "unlearned."

spend some time alone in a dental chair or waiting room. In one study, clients suffering from various phobias made as much progress after six hours of instruction in gradual self-exposure methods and daily "homework" exercises as did those who received an additional nine hours of therapist-aided gradual exposure (Al-Kubaisy et al., 1992). Effective self-treatment using gradual exposure has also been reported in cases of panic disorder (Hecker et al., 1996) and obsessive-compulsive disorder (Fritzler, Hecker, & Losee, 1997).

Aversion Therapy Some unwanted behaviours—such as using addictive drugs, gambling, or engaging in certain sexual offenses—can become so habitual and temporarily rewarding that they must be made less attractive if the client is to have any chance of giving them up in favour of a more desirable alternative. Methods for reducing the appeal of certain stimuli are known as *aversion therapy*. The name reflects the fact that these methods rely on a classical conditioning principle called **aversion conditioning** to associate nausea, painful electrical shock, or some other unpleasant stimulus with the actions, thoughts, or situations the client wants to stop or avoid (e.g., Clapham & Abramson, 1985).

Because aversion therapy is unpleasant and uncomfortable, because it may not work with all clients (Flor et al., 2002), and because its effects are often temporary, behaviour therapists use this method relatively rarely, only when it is the best treatment choice, and only long enough to allow the client to learn more desirable alternative behaviours.

Punishment Sometimes the only way to eliminate a dangerous or disruptive behaviour is to punish it with an unpleasant but harmless stimulus, such as a shouted "No!" or a mild electrical shock. Unlike aversion therapy, in which the unpleasant stimulus occurs along with the behaviour that is to be eliminated (a classical conditioning approach), **punishment** is an operant conditioning technique. It presents the unpleasant stimulus *after* the undesirable response occurs. (Although technically distinct, the two methods may overlap.) Before behaviour therapists use mild shock or any other form of punishment with the institutionalized clients, other impaired adults, or children for whom it might be appropriate and beneficial, they must consider certain ethical and legal questions: Would the client's life be in danger without treatment? Have all other methods failed? Has an ethics committee reviewed and approved the procedures? And has the client or a close relative formally agreed to the treatment

aversion conditioning A method that uses classical conditioning to create a negative response to a particular stimulus.

punishment A therapy method that weakens undesirable behaviour by following it with an unpleasant stimulus.

(Kazdin, 1994a)? When the answer to these questions is yes, punishment can be an effective, sometimes lifesaving, treatment—as in the case illustrated in Figure 6.11 in the chapter on learning. Like extinction and aversion therapy, punishment is best used only long enough to eliminate undesirable behaviour and in combination with other behavioural methods designed to reinforce more appropriate behaviour.

Cognitive-Behaviour Therapy

Like psychodynamic and phenomenological therapists, behaviour therapists recognize that depression, anxiety, and many other behaviour disorders can stem from how clients think about themselves and the world. And like other therapists, behaviour therapists also try to change their clients' troublesome ways of thinking. However, the methods used by behaviour therapists—known collectively as *cognitive-behaviour therapy*—rely on learning principles to help clients change the way they think (e.g., Dobson, 2003; O'Donohue, Fisher, & Hayes, 2003). Suppose, for example, that a client suffers intense anxiety in social situations, despite having excellent social skills. In a case such as this, social skills training would be unnecessary. Instead, the behaviour therapist would use cognitive-behavioural methods designed to help the client identify the habitual thoughts (such as "I shouldn't draw attention to myself") that get in the way of self-expression and create discomfort. Once these cognitive obstacles are brought to light, the therapist models—and encourages the client to develop and practise—new and more adaptive ways of thinking. As these new cognitive skills are learned, it becomes easier and more rewarding for the client to behave in accordance with them (Meichenbaum, 1995).

Rational-Emotive Behaviour Therapy One prominent form of cognitive-behaviour therapy is **rational-emotive behaviour therapy (REBT).** Developed by Albert Ellis (1962, 1993, 1995, 2004a, 2004b), rational-emotive behaviour therapy is based on the principle that anxiety, guilt, depression, and other psychological problems are caused by how people think about events. Ellis's therapy aims first at identifying self-defeating beliefs such as "I must be loved or approved by everyone" or "I must be perfectly competent, adequate, and achieving to be worthwhile." After the client learns to recognize such beliefs and to see how they cause problems, the therapist uses modelling, encouragement, and logic to help the client replace them with beliefs and thoughts that are more realistic and adaptive. Here is part of a rational-emotive behaviour therapy session with a 39-year-old woman who suffered from panic attacks. She has just said that it would be "terrible" if she had an attack in a restaurant and that people "should be able to handle themselves!"

THERAPIST: . . . *The reality is that . . "shoulds" and "musts" are the rules that other people hand down to us, and we grow up accepting them as if they are the absolute truth, which they most assuredly aren't.*

CLIENT: *You mean it is perfectly okay to, you know, pass out in a restaurant?*

THERAPIST: *Sure!*

CLIENT: *But . . . I know I wouldn't like it to happen.*

THERAPIST: *I can certainly understand that. It would be unpleasant, awkward, inconvenient. But it is illogical to think that it would be terrible, or . . . that it somehow bears on your worth as a person.*

CLIENT: *What do you mean?*

THERAPIST: *Well, suppose one of your friends calls you up and invites you back to that restaurant. If you start telling yourself, "I might panic and pass out and people might make fun of me and that would be terrible," . . . you might find you are dreading going to the restaurant, and you probably won't enjoy the meal very much.*

rational-emotive behaviour therapy (REBT) A treatment designed to identify and change self-defeating thoughts that lead to anxiety and other symptoms of disorder.

Albert Ellis Rational-emotive behaviour therapy (REBT) focuses on altering the self-defeating thoughts that Ellis believes underlie people's behaviour disorders. Ellis argues, for example, that students do not get upset because they fail a test but because they have learned to believe that failure is a disaster that indicates they are worthless. Many of Ellis's ideas have been incorporated into various forms of cognitive-behaviour therapy, and they helped Ellis himself to deal rationally with the health problems he encountered when he reached his 80s (Ellis, 1997).

CLIENT: *Well, that is what usually happens.*

THERAPIST: *But it doesn't have to be that way. . . The way you feel, your reaction . . . depends on what you choose to believe or think, or say to yourself.* (Masters et al., 1987)

Cognitive-behaviour therapists use many techniques related to rational-emotive behaviour therapy to help clients learn to think and act in more adaptive ways. Behavioural techniques aimed at replacing upsetting thoughts with alternative thinking patterns are called *cognitive restructuring* (Lazarus, 1971). Using these techniques, clients develop calming thoughts that they can use as part of *self-instruction* during exams, tense discussions, and other anxiety-provoking situations. The calming thoughts might be something like "OK, relax; you can handle this if you just focus on the task and don't worry about being perfect" (Meichenbaum, 1977). Sometimes, the methods are expanded into *stress inoculation training,* in which clients imagine being in a stressful situation, then practise newly learned cognitive skills to remain calm (Meichenbaum, 1995). In one study of stress inoculation training, first-year law students tried out calming new thoughts during role-playing exercises that exposed them to stressful classroom-style questioning, unhelpful feedback, and a competitive learning atmosphere. Following training, these students showed reductions in troublesome responses to stressors and improved academic performance (Sheehy & Horan, 2004).

Beck's Cognitive Therapy Many behaviour therapists seek a different kind of cognitive restructuring using Aaron Beck's **cognitive therapy** (Beck, 1976, 1995; Beck & Beck, 1995). Beck's treatment approach is based on the idea that certain psychological disorders—especially those involving depression and anxiety—can often be traced to errors in logic (e.g., "If I fail my driver's test the first time, I'll never pass it"), false beliefs (e.g., "Everyone ignores me"), and thoughts that minimize personal accomplishments (e.g., "Anyone could do that"). Beck says that over time, these learned *cognitive distortions* occur so quickly and automatically that the client never stops to consider that they might not be true.

Cognitive therapy is an active, structured, problem-solving approach in which the therapist helps clients notice how certain negative thoughts precede anxiety and depression (see Table 16.2). Then, much as in the five-step critical thinking system illustrated throughout this book, those thoughts and beliefs are treated as hypotheses to be tested rather than as assertions to be uncritically accepted (Hatcher, Brown, & Gariglietti, 2001).

table 16.2

Here are just a few examples of the kinds of thoughts that cognitive-behaviour therapists see as underlying anxiety, depression, and other behaviour problems. After reading this list, try writing an alternative thought that clients could use to replace each of these ingrained cognitive habits. Then jot down a "homework assignment" that you would recommend to help clients challenge each maladaptive statement, and thus develop new ways of thinking about themselves.

Some Examples of Negative Thinking
"I shouldn't draw attention to myself."
"I will never be any good at this."
"It will be so awful if I don't know the answer."
"Everyone is smarter than I am."
"Nobody likes me."
"I should be able to do this job perfectly."
"What if I panic?"
"I'll never be happy."
"I should have accomplished more by this point in my life."

Accordingly, therapist and client take the role of "investigators" who develop ways to test beliefs such as "I'm no good around the house." They might decide on tasks that the client will attempt as "homework"—such as cleaning out the basement, cooking a meal, paying bills, or cutting the grass. Success at accomplishing even one of these tasks provides concrete evidence to challenge a false belief that has supported depression, thus helping to reduce it (Beck et al., 1992). As therapy progresses, clients become more skilled at recognizing, and then correcting, the cognitive distortions related to their problems.

As mentioned in the chapter on psychological disorders, however, the cognitive roots of depression may involve more than specific thoughts and beliefs about certain situations (Beck, 2002). Depression may be associated with a more general cognitive style that leads people to expect that the worst will always happen to them and to assume that negative events confirm that they are completely and permanently incompetent and worthless (Peterson, 1995; Peterson & Seligman, 1984). Accordingly, cognitive-behaviour therapists also help depressed clients to develop more optimistic ways of thinking and to reduce their tendency to blame themselves for negative outcomes (Persons, Davidson, & Tompkins, 2001). In some cases, cognitive restructuring is combined with practice at using logical thinking, anxiety management techniques, and skill training—all designed to help clients experience success and develop confidence in situations in which they had previously expected to fail (Beck & Beck, 1995). Some cognitive therapists have found that successful clients may be able to avoid further episodes of depression by combining what they have learned in cognitive therapy with a certain form of meditation (see the chapter on consciousness). This combined approach is called *mindfulness-based cognitive therapy* (Segal, Williams, & Teasdale, 2001; Ma & Teasdale, 2004).

Group, Family, and Couples Therapy

The psychodynamic, humanistic, and behavioural treatments we have described are often conducted with individuals, but they can also be adapted for use with groups of clients or with family units (Petrocelli, 2002; Rosen, Stukenbert, & Saeks, 2001; Thorngren & Kleist, 2002).

Group Therapy

Group therapy refers to the treatment of several unrelated clients under the guidance of a therapist who encourages helpful interactions among group members. Many groups are organized around a particular problem (such as alcoholism) or a particular type of client (such as adolescents). In most cases, six to twelve clients meet with their therapist at least once a week for about two hours. All group members agree to hold confidential everything that occurs during group sessions.

Group therapy offers several features not found in individual treatment (Yalom, 1995). First, group therapy allows the therapist to see clients interacting with one another. Second, clients discover that they are not alone as they listen to others and realize that many people struggle with difficulties at least as severe as their own. This realization tends to lift each client's expectations for improvement, a factor important in all forms of treatment. Third, group members can boost one another's self-confidence and self-acceptance as they come to trust and value one another and develop group cohesiveness. Fourth, clients learn from one another. They share ideas for solving problems and give one another honest feedback about how each member "comes across." Fifth, perhaps through mutual modelling, the group experience makes clients more willing to share their feelings and more sensitive to other people's needs, motives, and messages. Finally, group therapy allows clients to try out new skills in a supportive environment.

cognitive therapy A treatment in which the therapist helps clients to notice and change negative thoughts associated with anxiety and depression.
group therapy Psychotherapy involving several unrelated clients.

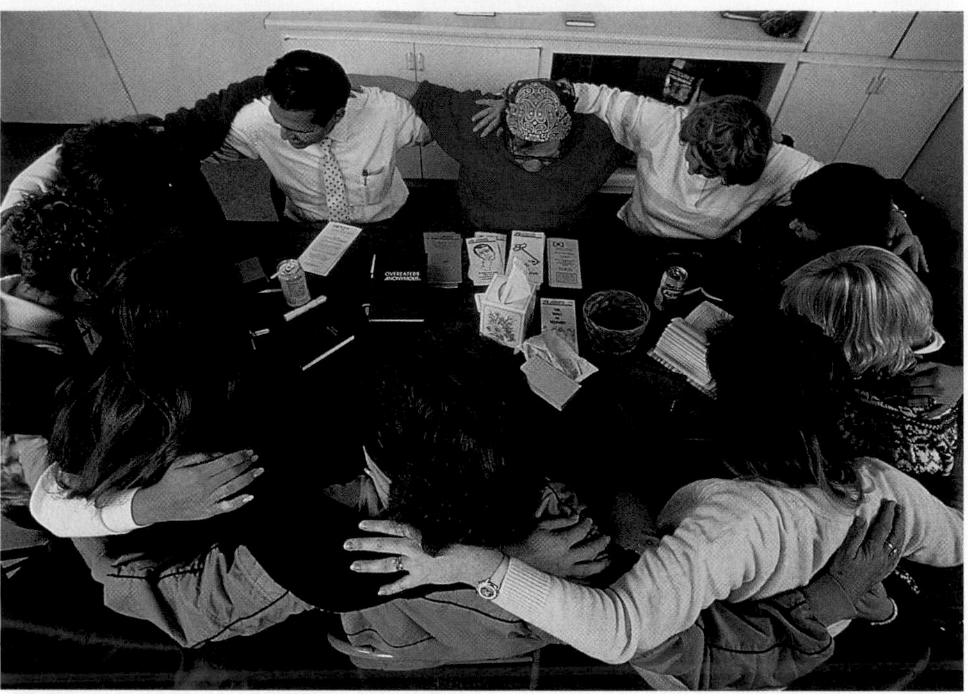

A Circle of Friends This meeting of Overeaters Anonymous is but one example of the self-help movement in North America, a growing network of inexpensive mental health and anti-addiction services offered by volunteer helpers, including friends and relatives of troubled people. A Toronto directory listed 170 local self-help groups focused on a wide variety of issues including alcohol and drug addictions, weight control, bereavement, among others (Romeder, 1990). The services provided by these nonprofessional groups make up about 20 percent of the total mental health and anti-addiction services offered in the United States (Borkman, 1997; Regier, Narrow, et al., 1993; Swindle et al., 2000). Similar statistics are not available for Canada but research has demonstrated a dramatic increase in the use of these services and supports by Canadians since 1980 (Romeder, 1990).

Some of the advantages of group therapy are also put to use in *self-help*, or *mutual-help, organizations*. Self-help groups, such as Alcoholics Anonymous (AA), are made up of people who share some problematic experience and meet to help one another (Nowinski, 1999; Zimmerman et al., 1991). There are self-help groups for a wide range of problems, including alcohol and drug addiction, childhood sexual abuse, cancer, overeating, over-spending, bereavement, compulsive gambling, and schizophrenia, among many others. The worldwide self-help movement has grown dramatically in recent decades, partly because many troubled people prefer to seek help from friends, teachers, or other "unofficial" helpers before turning to mental health practitioners (Swindle et al., 2000) and partly because some people have been dissatisfied with professional treatment. Dozens of self-help organizations operate through hundreds of thousands of local chapters, enrolling 10 to 15 million participants in the United States and about half a million in Canada (Barlow et al., 2000; Nietzel et al., 2003; Norcross et al., 2000; Swindle et al., 2000).

Lack of reliable data makes it difficult to assess the value of many self-help groups, but available information suggests that active members may obtain some moderate improvement in their lives (Kelly, 2003; Moos et al., 2001; Morganstern et al., 1997; Ouimette, Finney, & Moos, 1997). Some professional therapists view these groups with suspicion; others encourage clients to participate in them as part of their treatment or as a first step that might lead to more formal treatment (Haaga, 2000; Salzer, Rappaport, & Segre, 1999). This is especially true for clients with problems such as eating disorders, alcoholism, and other substance-related disorders (Dunne & Fitzpatrick, 1999; McCrady, Epstein, & Kahler, 2004).

Family and Couples Therapy

As its name implies, **family therapy** involves treatment of two or more individuals from the same family system, one of whom—often a troubled child or adolescent—is the initially identified client. The term *family system* highlights the idea that the problems displayed by one family member usually reflect problems in the functioning of the entire family (Beels, 2002; Cox & Paley, 2003; Pilling et al., 2002).

family therapy Treatment of two or more individuals from the same family.

couples therapy A form of therapy focusing on improving communication between partners.

Ultimately, the family becomes the client, and treatment involves as many members as possible. In fact, the goal of family therapy is not just to ease the identified client's problems but also to create harmony and balance within the family by helping each member understand family interaction patterns and the problems they create (Blow & Timm, 2002; Goldenberg & Goldenberg, 1995). As with group therapy, the family format gives the therapist a chance to see how the initially identified client interacts with others, thus providing a basis for discussion of topics that are important to the family.

Family therapists who emphasize object relations theory point out that if the parents in a family have not worked out conflicts with their own parents, these conflicts will surface in relation to their spouses and children. Accordingly, these family therapy sessions might focus on the parents' problems with their own parents and, when possible, include members of the older generation (Nugent, 1994). A related approach, called *structural family therapy,* concentrates on family communication patterns (Minuchin & Fishman, 1981). It focuses on changing the rigid patterns and rituals that create alliances (such as mother and child against father) that maintain conflicts and prevent the communication of love, support, or even anger. Structural family therapists argue that when dysfunctional communication patterns are eliminated, problematic behaviours decrease because family members no longer need them in order to survive in the family system.

Behaviour therapists often use family therapy sessions as meetings at which family members can discuss and agree on behavioural "contracts." Often based on operant conditioning principles, these contracts establish rules and reinforcement contingencies that help parents encourage their children's desirable behaviours (and discourage undesirable ones) and help spouses become more supportive of each other (O'Farrell, 1995; Sanders & Dadds, 1993).

Therapists of many theoretical persuasions also offer **couples therapy,** in which communication between partners is the most important focus of treatment (Christensen et al., 2004; Gurman & Jacobson, 2002). Discussion in couples therapy sessions is usually aimed at identifying and improving the miscommunication or lack of communication that is interfering with a couple's happiness and intimacy. Often, the sessions revolve around learning to abide by certain "rules for talking," such as those listed in Table 16.3. Some therapists also focus on helping couples talk to each other as a way of becoming closer, and behaviour therapists even offer programs designed to prevent marital problems in couples who are at high risk for

table 16.3

Many forms of couples therapy help partners improve communication through establishing rules such as these. Think about your own experience in relationships or your observations of couples as they interact, and then write down some rules you would add to this list. Why do you think it would be important for couples to follow the rules on your list?

Some "Rules for Talking" in Couples Therapy

1. Always begin with something positive when stating a problem.
2. Use specific behaviours rather than derogatory labels or overgeneralizations to describe what is bothersome about the other person.
3. Make connections between those specific behaviours and feelings that arise in response to them (e.g., "It makes me sad when you . . .").
4. Admit your own role in the development of the problem.
5. Be brief; don't lecture or harangue.
6. Maintain a focus on the present or the future; don't review all previous examples of the problem or ask "why" questions, such as "Why do you always . . . ?"
7. Talk about observable events; don't make inferences about them (e.g., say, "I get angry when you interrupt me" rather than "Stop trying to make me feel stupid").
8. Paraphrase what your partner has said, and check out your own perceptions of what was said before responding. (Note that this suggestion is based on the same principle as Rogers's empathic listening.)

developing such problems (Berger & Hannah, 1999; Jacobson et al., 2000). One such program, called *behavioural premarital intervention,* not only helps engaged couples head off relationship problems but also prepares them to deal effectively with problems that might arise.

Evaluating Psychotherapy

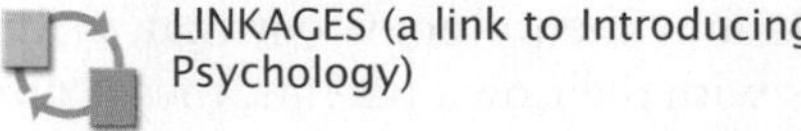
LINKAGES (a link to Introducing Psychology)

Psychotherapy has been available for more than a hundred years, and people are still asking if it works. Most psychotherapists and their clients believe in psychotherapy's effectiveness (*Consumer Reports,* 1995), but confirming this belief with experimental research has proved to be challenging and controversial (Beutler, 2002; Brock, Green, & Reich, 1998; Dawes, 1994; DeRubeis & Crits-Christoph, 1998; Lambert & Barley, 2001; Nathan, Stuart, & Dolan, 2000; Seligman, 1995, 1996).

The value of psychotherapy was first widely questioned in 1952, when British psychologist Hans Eysenck reviewed studies in which thousands of clients had received either traditional psychodynamic therapy, various other therapies, or no treatment. To the surprise and dismay of many therapists, Eysenck (1952) concluded that the percentage of clients who improved following any kind of psychotherapy was actually lower than that of people who received no treatment. He later offered additional evidence reaffirming this pattern of results (Eysenck, 1961, 1966).

Critics argued that in drawing his conclusions, Eysenck had ignored studies that supported the value of psychotherapy and that he had misinterpreted his data (Bergin, 1971; de Charms, Levy, & Wertheimer, 1954; Luborsky, 1972). They pointed out, for example, that untreated clients might have been less disturbed than those in treatment. Further, they said, untreated clients might have received informal treatment from their medical doctors. Finally, the physicians who judged untreated clients' progress might have used less demanding criteria than the psychotherapists who rated their own clients. In fact, when some of these critics conducted their own "box score" counts of successes and failures, they concluded that psychotherapy tends to be more helpful than no treatment (Bergin, 1971).

Debate over Eysenck's findings—and the contradictory reports that followed them—highlighted several reasons why it is so difficult to answer the apparently simple question, Does psychotherapy work? For one thing, there is the problem of how to measure improvement in psychotherapy. Should it be measured with psychological tests, behavioural observations, interviews, or a combination of all three? And what kinds of tests should be used? Where should clients be observed (and by whom)? And should equal weight be given to interviews with clients, friends, relatives, therapists, and teachers? The fact that these various measures don't always tell the same story about improvement makes it that much harder for researchers to compare or combine the results of different studies and draw conclusions about the overall effectiveness of treatment (Lambert & Hill, 1994; Mackay et al., 2003).

The question of effectiveness is further complicated by the broad range of clients, therapists, and treatments involved in psychotherapy. Clients differ not only in terms of their problems but also in terms of their motivation to solve them and in the amount of stress and social support present in their environments. Therapists differ too, not only in skill, experience, and personality but also in which of the hundreds of available treatment procedures they might select (Feltham, 2000). Further, differences in the nature and quality of the client-therapist relationship from one case to another can significantly alter the course of treatment, the clients' faith in the procedures, and their willingness to cooperate (Lambert & Barley, 2001). Because clients' responses to psychotherapy can be influenced by all these factors, results from any particular treatment evaluation study might not tell us much about how well different therapists, using different methods, would do with other kinds of clients and problems (Kazdin, 1994b). Consider the example of a study in which "kindly college professors" were found to be as effective as experienced psychotherapists in helping people solve their problems (Strupp & Hadley, 1979). This result would appear relevant to the question of psychotherapy's effectiveness, but a careful reading of the study shows that the clients were university students with minor problems, not severe psychological disorders. Further, the fact that these students already had a relationship with their professors might have given the professors an edge over unfamiliar therapists (Chambless & Hollon, 1998). So the outcome of this study probably does not apply to the outcome of professional psychotherapy in general.

THINKING CRITICALLY

Are All Forms of Therapy Equally Effective?

LINKAGES (a link to Personality)

In short, the general question of whether psychotherapy "works" is difficult or impossible to answer scientifically in a way that applies to all therapies for all disorders. However, the findings of several research reviews (Anderson & Lambert, 1995; Galatzer-Levy et al., 2000; Shadish et al., 2000; Smith, Glass, & Miller, 1980; Weisz & Jensen, 1999) have reinforced therapists' beliefs that psychotherapy does work (see Figure 16.3). In fact, most therapists believe that the theoretical approach and treatment methods *they* use are superior to those of other therapists (e.g., Giles, 1990; Mandelid, 2003). They can't all be right, of course, so what is going on?

- **What am I being asked to believe or accept?**

Some researchers argue that the success of psychotherapy doesn't have much to do with theories about the causes of psychopathology, or even with the specific treatment methods that are used in treatment. All approaches, they say, are equally effective. This has been called the "Dodo Bird Verdict," after the *Alice in Wonderland* character who, when called upon to judge who had won a race, answered, "Everybody has won and all must have prizes" (Luborsky, Singer, & Luborsky, 1975).

- **What evidence is available to support the assertion?**

Some evidence does suggest that there are no significant differences in the overall effectiveness of psychodynamic, humanistic, and behavioural therapies. Statistical methods, called *meta-analysis,* that combine the results of a large number of therapy studies have shown that the three treatment approaches are associated with about the same degree of success (Lambert & Bergin, 1994; Luborsky et al., 2002; Luborsky, Rosenthal, & Diguer, 2003; Shadish et al., 2000; Smith, Glass, & Miller, 1980).

- **Are there alternative ways of interpreting the evidence?**

It is possible, however, that evidence for the Dodo Bird Verdict is based on methods that cannot detect genuine differences among treatments. For example, a meta-analysis combining the results of many studies might not reveal important differences in the impact of particular treatments for particular problems

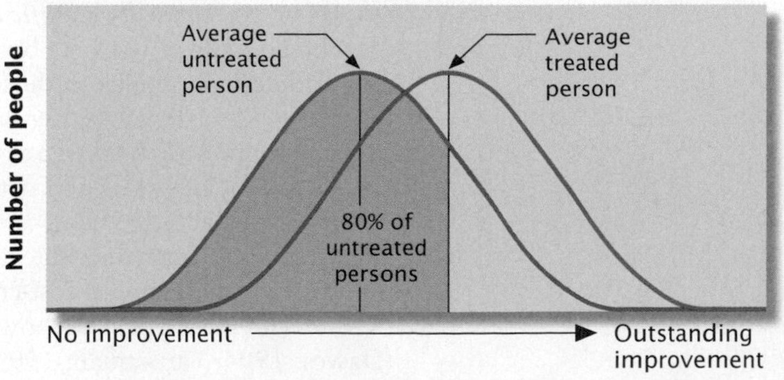

figure 16.3

An Analysis of Psychotherapy Effects

These curves show the results of one large-scale analysis of the effects of psychotherapy. Notice that on average, people who received therapy for their problems were better off than 80 percent of troubled people who did not. The overall effectiveness of psychotherapy has also been confirmed in a more recent analysis of 90 treatment outcome studies (Shadish et al., 2000).

(Beutler, 2002; Eysenck, 1978; Wilson, 1985; Rounsaville & Carroll, 2002). It may also be that some specific techniques are more successful than others but that when therapies are grouped by theoretical approach (psychodynamic, humanistic, or behavioural), rather than by specific procedures, the impact of those procedures might not be noticed (Giles, 1990; Marmar, 1990). For example, as described later, certain cognitive-behavioural techniques that are not used in other psychotherapy methods have been shown to be especially successful in the treatment of anxiety (Chambless & Ollendick, 2001).

Further, differences in the effects of specific procedures might be overshadowed by the beneficial features shared by almost all forms of therapy—such as the support of the therapist, the hope and expectancy for improvement that therapy creates, and the trust that develops between client and therapist (Barber et al., 2000; Duncan, 2002; Martin, Garske, & Davis, 2000). A therapist whose personal characteristics motivate a client to change might promote that change regardless of the therapeutic methods being used (Elkin, 1999; Hubble, Duncan, & Miller, 1999).

• What additional evidence would help to evaluate the alternatives?

Debate is likely to continue over the question of whether, on average, all forms of psychotherapy are about equally effective. But many researchers believe that this is the wrong question. In their view, it is pointless to compare the effects of psychodynamic, humanistic, and behavioural methods in general. It is more important, they say, to address what Gordon Paul called the "ultimate question" about psychotherapy: "What treatment, by whom, is most effective for this individual with that specific problem, under what set of circumstances?" (Paul, 1969, p. 44).

• What conclusions are most reasonable?

Statistical analyses show that various treatment approaches appear to be about equally effective overall. But this does not mean that every specific psychotherapy method works in the same way or that every psychotherapy experience will be equally beneficial. Clients entering therapy must realize that the success of their treatment can still be affected by how severe their problems are, by the quality of the relationship they form with a therapist, and by the appropriateness of the therapy methods chosen for their problems.

Like those seeking treatment, many clinical psychologists, too, are eager for more specific scientific evidence about the effectiveness of particular therapies for particular kinds of clients and disorders. These empirically oriented clinicians are concerned that all too often, a therapist's choice of therapy methods depends more heavily on personal preferences or current trends than on scientific evidence of effectiveness (Lynn, Lilienfeld, & Lohr, 2003; Nathan, Stuart, & Dolan, 2000; Peterson, 2003; Tavris, 2003). They believe that advocates of any treatment—whether it is object relations therapy or systematic desensitization—must demonstrate that its benefits are the result of the treatment itself and not just of the passage of time, the effects of repeatedly measuring progress, the client's motivation and personal characteristics, or other confounding factors. They also want to see evidence that the benefits of treatment are *clinically significant*. To be clinically significant, therapeutic changes must be not only measurable but also substantial enough to make treated clients' feelings and actions similar to those of people who have not experienced these clients' disorders (Kendall, 1999; Kendall & Sheldrick, 2000). For example, a reduction in treated clients' scores on an anxiety test might be *statistically significant*, but if those clients do not now feel and act more like people without an anxiety disorder, the change is probably not clinically significant (see Figure 16.4). In recent years, the need to demonstrate the clinical significance of treatment effects has become clearer than ever as increasingly cost-conscious clients—and their health insurance companies—decide whether, and how much, to pay for various psychotherapy services (Dawes, 1994; Farberman, 1999; Roberts, 2002).

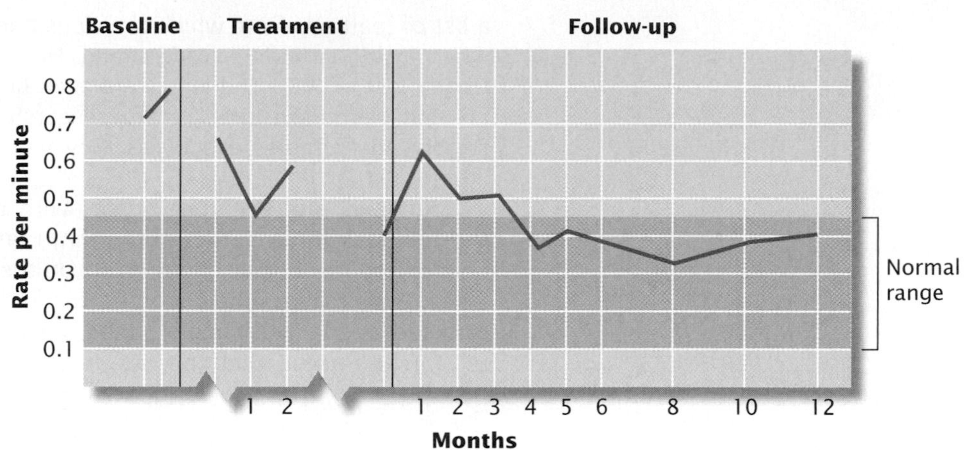

figure 16.4

Clinical Significance

Evaluations of psychological treatments must consider the clinical, as well as statistical, significance of observed changes. Here, the shaded area shows the range of deviant behaviours per minute displayed at home by normal boys. The solid line shows the average rate of deviant behaviours for boys in an operant conditioning treatment for severe behaviour problems. The improvement following reinforcement of appropriate behaviour was not only statistically significant (compared with the pretreatment baseline) but also clinically significant, inasmuch as the once-deviant behaviour came to resemble that of normal boys.

By scientific tradition, the ideal way to evaluate treatment effects is through experiments in which clients are randomly assigned to various treatments or control conditions and their progress is objectively measured over time.

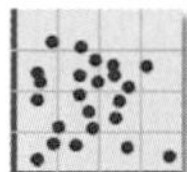

FOCUS ON RESEARCH METHODS

Which Therapies Work Best for Which Problems?

LINKAGES (a link to Research in Psychology)

To help clinicians select treatment methods on the basis of that kind of empirical evidence, the American Psychological Association's Division of Clinical Psychology created a task force on effective psychotherapies (Task Force on Promotion and Dissemination of Psychological Procedures, 1995).

- **What was the researchers' question?**

The question addressed by this task force was, What therapies have proven themselves most effective in treating various kinds of psychological disorders?

- **How did the researchers answer the question?**

Working with other empirically oriented clinical psychologists, members of this task force examined the outcomes of thousands of experiments that evaluated psychotherapy methods used to treat mental disorder, marital distress, and health-related behaviour problems in adults, children, and adolescents (Baucom et al., 1998; Chambless & Ollendick, 2001; Compas et al., 1998; DeRubeis & Crits-Christoph, 1998; Kazdin & Weisz, 1998; Kendall & Chambless, 1998; Norcross, 2001, 2002).

- **What did the researchers find?**

The task force found that a number of treatments—known as **empirically supported therapies,** or **ESTs**—have been validated by controlled experimental research (Chambless & Ollendick, 2001; DeRubeis & Crits-Christoph, 1998; Kendall & Chambless, 1998; Norcross, 2001, 2002). Table 16.4 contains some examples of these therapies. Notice that the treatments identified as effective for particular problems in adult clients are mainly behavioural, cognitive, and cognitive-behavioural methods but that certain psychodynamic therapies (for example, interpersonal therapy and brief dynamic therapy) also made the list (Chambless & Ollendick, 2001; Svartberg, Stiles, & Seltzer, 2004).

- **What do the results mean?**

The authors of the report on empirically supported therapies, as well as those who support their efforts, claim that by relying on analysis of experimental research, they have accomplished a scientific evaluation of various treatments and generated

empirically supported therapies (ESTs) Treatments whose effects have been validated by controlled experimental research.

a list of methods from which clinicians and consumers can choose with confidence when facing specific disorders (e.g., Hunsley & Rumstein-McKean, 1999; Kendall & Chambless, 1998). Therapists are even being urged to follow the treatment manuals that were used in successful research studies to help them deliver empirically supported therapies exactly as they were intended (Addis, 1997; Wade, Treat, & Stuart, 1998).

However, not everyone agrees with the conclusions or recommendations of the APA task force. Critics note, first, that treatment methods are not necessarily discredited just because they aren't on the latest list of empirically supported therapies; they have simply not been validated according to the efficacy criteria selected by the task force. Further, these critics take issue with some of those criteria. They argue that the list of empirically supported therapies is based on

table 16.4
Examples of Empirically Supported Therapies for Selected Disorders

Treatments listed as "efficacious and specific" were shown to be superior to no treatment, or to some alternative treatment, in at least two experiments in which clients were randomly assigned to various treatment conditions. These experiments are called *randomized clinical trials*, or *RCTs*. Also included in this category are treatments supported by scientific outcome measures from a large number of carefully conducted case studies. Treatments listed as "probably efficacious" are supported by at least one RCT or by a smaller number of rigorously evaluated case studies. Those listed as "possibly efficacious" are supported by a mixture of data, generally from single-case studies or other nonexperimental studies (Chambless & Ollendick, 2001).

Problem	Efficacious and Specific	Probably Efficacious	Possibly Efficacious
Major depressive disorder	Behaviour therapy Cognitive-behaviour therapy Interpersonal therapy	Brief dynamic therapy Social problem solving Self-control therapy	
Specific phobia	Exposure therapy	Systematic desensitization	
Agoraphobia/panic disorder	Cognitive-behavioural therapy	Couples training + exposure therapy	
Generalized anxiety disorder	Cognitive-behaviour therapy	Applied relaxation therapy	
Obsessive-compulsive disorder	Exposure therapy + response prevention	Cognitive therapy Family-assisted exposure therapy + response prevention + relaxation	Rational emotive behaviour therapy + exposure therapy
Posttraumatic stress disorder		Exposure Stress inoculation Cognitive therapy + stress inoculation + exposure	Structured psychodynamic treatment
Schizophrenia	Behavioural family therapy	Family systems therapy Social skills training Supportive group therapy	Cognitive therapy (for delusions)
Alcohol abuse and dependence	Community reinforcement	Cue exposure therapy Behavioural marital therapy + anti-alcohol drug, disulfiram Social skills training (with inpatients)	
Opiate abuse and dependence		Behaviour therapy Brief dynamic therapy Cognitive therapy	
Marital discord	Behavioural marital therapy	Insight-oriented marital therapy	

Source: Chambless & Ollendick (2001).

research that may not be relevant to clinicians practising in the real world. They point out, for example, that experimental studies of psychotherapy have focused mainly on the therapeutic procedures used rather than on the characteristics and interactions of therapists and clients (Garfield, 1998; Hilliard, Henry, & Strupp, 2000). This emphasis on procedure is a problem, they say, because the outcome of therapy in these experiments might have been affected by whether the random assignment of clients to therapists resulted in a match or a mismatch on certain personal characteristics. These critics say that in real clinical situations, clients and therapists are not paired up at random (Hohmann & Shear, 2002; Persons & Silberschatz, 1998; Seligman, 1995). Finally, because therapists participating in experimental research were required to follow standard treatment manuals, they were not free to adapt treatment methods, as they normally would, to the needs of particular clients (Garfield, 1998). Perhaps, say these critics, when there is less experimental control over the treatment situation, all therapies are about equally effective, as suggested by the statistical analyses of outcome research we mentioned earlier (Shadish et al., 2000; Smith, Glass, & Miller, 1980).

In short, critics reject the empirically supported therapies list as a useful guide. In fact, some see it as an incomplete, irrelevant, and ultimately misleading document. They worry that it is based on research designed to evaluate treatment effects without adequately taking into account either the personal qualities and theoretical biases of those who offer therapy or how those factors might interact with the characteristics of the clients who receive therapy (e.g., Henry, 1998). There is worry, too, that widespread use of treatment manuals would make psychotherapy too mechanical and less effective and that it might suppress therapists' creativity in developing new treatment methods (Addis & Krasnow, 2000; Beutler, 2000; Garfield, 1998; Najavits et al., 2004).

• What do we still need to know?

The efforts of the APA task force represent an important step in responding to Paul's (1969) "ultimate question" about psychotherapy: "What treatment, by whom, is most effective for this individual with that specific problem, under what set of circumstances?" We still have a long way to go, but—with research funding from the U.S. National Institute of Mental Health—empirically oriented clinical psychologists are determined to find scientific answers to this challenging question (Foxhall, 2000a). The work of at least three APA task forces will focus not only on the long-term efficacy of psychotherapy—in naturalistic as well as laboratory settings—but also on the role of the therapeutic relationship in promoting that efficacy (Morrison, Bradley, & Westen, 2003; Nathan, Stuart, & Dolan, 2000; Norcross, 2001; Wampold, Lichtenberg, & Waehler, 2002; Westen & Morrison, 2001).

Addressing the "Ultimate Question"

The combinations of treatment methods and therapist and client characteristics that are best suited to solving particular psychological problems have not yet been mapped out, but there are a few trends. For example, when differences show up in comparative studies of adult psychotherapy, they tend to reveal a small to moderate advantage for behavioural and cognitive-behavioural methods, especially in the treatment of phobias and certain other anxiety disorders (Barrowclough et al., 2001; Borkovec & Costello, 1993; DeRubeis & Crits-Christoph, 1998; Lambert & Bergin, 1994; Weisz et al., 1995), as well as bulimia nervosa, an eating disorder (Wilson, 1997). The same tends to be true for child and adolescent clients (Epstein et al., 1994; Weiss & Weisz, 1995; Weisz et al., 1995).

Further, the client-therapist relationship plays a consistent role in the success of all forms of treatment (Barber et al., 2000; Beutler, 2000; Brown & O'Leary, 2000; Elkin et al., 1999; Martin, Garske, & Davis, 2000; Messer & Wampold, 2002; Vocisano et al., 2004). Certain people seem to be particularly effective in forming productive human relationships. Even without formal training, these people can sometimes be as helpful as professional therapists because of personal qualities that are inspiring, healing, and soothing to others (Stein & Lambert, 1995). Their presence in self-help groups may well underlie some of the success of those groups and, among professionals, may help account for the success of many kinds of formal therapy. (It would be ideal if we could learn more about these people's qualities and, if possible, train others to develop them, too.)

Before choosing a therapist and treatment approach, then, clients should keep Paul's "ultimate question" in mind. They should carefully consider (1) what treatment approach, methods, and goals they find most comfortable and appealing; (2) information about the therapist's "track record" of clinically significant success with a particular method for treating problems similar to those they face; and (3) the likelihood of forming a productive relationship with the therapist. This last consideration assumes special importance when client and therapist do not share similar cultural backgrounds.

Cultural Factors in Psychotherapy

Imagine that after moving to an unfamiliar country to pursue your education or career, you become severely depressed. A friend there refers you to a therapist who specializes in depression. At your first session the therapist stares at you intently, touches your head for a moment, and says, "You have taken in a spirit from the river, and it is trying to get out. I will help." The therapist then begins chanting softly and appears to go into a trance. What would you think? Would you return for a second visit? If you are like most people raised in a Western culture, you probably wouldn't continue treatment, because this therapist probably does not share your beliefs and expectations about what is wrong with you and what should be done about it.

Similar sociocultural clashes can also occur within a particular country if clients bring to therapy a cultural or subcultural world view that is not shared by their therapist. For example, if a therapist assumes that a client's unexplained abdominal pain is a learned reaction to stress but the client is sure that it comes as punishment for having offended a long-dead ancestor, the client may not easily accept a treatment based on the principles of stress management (Wohl, 1995). Cultural clashes may be partly to blame for the underuse of, or withdrawal from, mental health services by recent immigrants, as well as members of other minority populations (Akutsu, Tsuru, & Chu, 2004; Gone, 2004; Sanders Thompson, Bazile, & Akbar, 2004). Often the problem lies in mismatched goals (e.g., Chien & Banerjee, 2002). A therapist who believes that people should confront and overcome life's problems may encounter a client who believes that one should work at calmly accepting such problems (Sundberg & Sue, 1989). The result may be much like two people singing a duet using the same music but different lyrics (Johnson & Thorpe, 1994).

In other words, cultural differences, including religious differences and differences in sexual orientation, can create enough miscommunication or mistrust to threaten the quality of the client-therapist relationship (Jones, Botsko, & Gorman, 2003). Major efforts are under way to ensure that cultural differences between clients and therapists do not interfere with the delivery of treatment to anyone who wants or needs it (Pachankis & Goldfried, 2004; Richards & Bergin, 2000; Sue et al., 1999). Virtually every psychotherapy training program in North America is seeking to recruit more students from traditionally underserved minority groups in order to make it easier to match clients with therapists from similar cultural backgrounds (e.g., Norcross, Hedges, & Prochaska, 2002).

In the meantime, minority group clients are still likely to encounter a therapist from a differing background, so researchers are also examining the value of matching therapy techniques with clients' culturally based expectations and preferences (Hays, 1995; Li & Kim, 2004; Preciado, 1994; Tanaka-Matsumi & Higginbotham, 1994). For example, many clients from collectivist cultures—in which the emphasis is on meeting the expectations of family and friends rather than satisfying personal desires—might expect to receive instructions from a therapist about how to overcome problems. How would such clients respond to a therapist whose client-centred treatment emphasizes more individualist goals, such as being independent and taking responsibility for the direction of change? David Sue and his students have investigated the hypothesis that the collectivist values of Asian cultures would lead Asians and Asian Americans to prefer a directive, problem-solving approach over nondirective, client-centred methods. Sue (1992) found that a preference for directive treatment was highest among foreign-born Asians compared with American-born Asians and Americans of European background. However, there are always individual differences. Two individuals from the same culture may react quite differently to a treatment that group research suggests should be ideal for both of them. In Sue's (1992) study, for example, more than a third of the foreign-born Asians preferred the nondirective approach, and 28 percent of the Americans of European background preferred the directive approach.

Today, psychotherapists are more sensitive than ever to the cultural values of particular groups and to the difficulties that can impair intercultural communication (Carrillo & Lopez, 2001; Hall, 2001; Knox et al., 2003). Training on the role of cultural factors helps clinicians appreciate, for example, that it is considered impolite in some cultures to make eye contact with a stranger. Having that information makes it easier for them to recognize that clients from those cultures are not necessarily depressed, lacking in self-esteem, or inappropriately submissive just because they look at the floor during an interview. Graduate students are receiving similar training and practical experience as part of their course work in clinical or counselling psychology (Clay, 2001; Norcross, Hedges, & Prochaska, 2002). According to Sarah Maiter at Wilfrid Laurier University in Waterloo, Ontario, the need for sensitivity to cultural differences in mental health workers is increasing as our country becomes more ethically diverse (Maiter, 2004).

There is no guarantee that cultural sensitivity training will improve treatment results (Pope-Davis et al., 1995; Quintana & Bernal, 1995; Ramirez et al., 1996), but there is some evidence that it can help (e.g., Razali, Aminah, & Umeed, 2002). And although it is unrealistic to expect all therapists to be equally effective with clients of every ethnic or religious background, cultural sensitivity training offers a

Preparing for Therapy Special pretreatment orientation programs may be offered to clients whose cultural or subcultural backgrounds leave them unfamiliar with the rules and procedures of psychotherapy. These programs provide a preview of what psychotherapy is, how it can help, and what the client is expected to do to make it more effective (Sue, Zane, & Young, 1994).

way to improve their *cultural competence,* an extension of Carl Rogers' concept of "empathy." When therapists appreciate the client's view of the world, it is easier for them to set goals that are in harmony with that view (Dyche & Zayas, 2001; Pedersen & Draguns, 2002; Stuart, 2004; Ulrich, Richards, & Bergin, 2000). Minimizing the chances of cultural misunderstanding and miscommunication is one of the many ethical obligations that therapists assume whenever they work with a client (Tomes, 1999). Let's consider some others.

Rules and Rights in the Therapeutic Relationship

Treatment can be an intensely emotional experience, and the relationship established with a therapist can profoundly affect a client's life. Professional ethics and common sense require the therapist to ensure that this relationship does not harm the client. For example, the Canadian Psychological Association's Canadian Code of Ethics for Psychologists forbids a sexual relationship between therapist and client because of the severe harm it can cause the client (Canadian Psychological Association, 2000).

Ethical standards also require therapists, with a few exceptions, to keep strictly confidential everything a client says in therapy. Confidentiality is one of the most important features of a successful therapeutic relationship, because it allows the client to discuss unpleasant or embarrassing feelings, behaviours, or events without fear that the therapist might disclose this information to others. Professionals sometimes do consult with one another about their clients, but they are required not to reveal information to outsiders (including members of the client's family) without the client's consent. The CPA's code of ethics even includes standards for protecting confidentiality for the growing number of clients who seek psychological services via *telehealth* or *e-health* channels, which include telephone, videophone, email, or other Internet links (Barnett & Scheetz, 2003; Christensen, Griffiths, & Jorm, 2004; Fisher & Fried, 2003; Ruskin et al., 2004). Among other things, these standards require therapists to inform clients that others might be able to gain access to their email messages and that no formal client-therapist relationship exists in email exchanges.

Professional ethics regarding confidentiality are backed up by laws recognizing that information revealed in therapy is privileged communication. This means that by asserting *privilege,* a therapist can refuse, even in court, to answer questions about a client or to provide personal notes or tape recordings from therapy sessions. According to a ruling of the Supreme Court of Canada, this type of *privilege* is extended to communications between psychologists and clients only when the following criteria, known as the *Wigmore test,* are met: (1) the client was assured of confidentiality before disclosing the information to the psychologist, (2) a guarantee of confidentiality is an essential component of the therapeutic relationship between the psychologist and client, (3) maintenance of the therapeutic relationship is desirable, and (4) the potential harm resulting from violation of confidentiality would outweigh the benefits (Judgments of the Supreme Court of Canada, 1995).

The last condition poses a dilemma. Suppose a client says, "Someday I'm going to kill that brother of mine!" Should the therapist consider this a serious threat and warn the brother? In most cases, the danger is not real, but there have been tragic exceptions. For example, Prosenjit Poddar, a graduate student receiving therapy at the University of California at Berkeley in 1969, revealed his intention to kill Tatiana Tarasoff, a young woman whom he had dated the previous year but who later rejected him. The therapist took the threat seriously and consulted his supervisor and the campus police. It was decided that there was no real danger, so neither Tarasoff nor her parents were warned. After dropping out of therapy, the client killed Tarasoff. Her parents sued the university, the campus police, and the therapist. They won their case, thus setting an important

Rights of the Mentally Ill In 2004, Martin Ostopovich shot and killed RCMP officer, Jim Galloway, in Spruce Grove, Alberta. Ostopovich was then shot and killed by police. At an inquiry into the deaths, his doctor, Jeffrey Moss, testified that Ostopovich had been diagnosed with paranoid schizophrenia several years earlier and believed that police were out to get him. He once tried to cut his own neck in an attempt to remove what he thought was a transmitter implanted there by RCMP officers. He had been admitted to a psychiatric hospital in 2002 but doctors could not keep him against his will as they did not have evidence that he posed a serious threat to others or himself. After his release from hospital, he was prescribed medication, which he did not take regularly. Dr. Moss said at the inquiry that little can be done when a patient refuses treatment, except in extreme cases in which the legal requirements for involuntary treatment are met. Cases such as this can be frustrating for mental health professionals when the rights of the mentally ill and the safety of the general public must be balanced.

precedent. As a result of this landmark case, changes were made to both American and Canadian laws regarding limits on confidentiality. According to Canadian law, therapists have a duty to protect people who are at risk of being harmed by a potentially dangerous client. The duty to protect may take the form of warning the intended victim, which would necessitate a breach of confidentiality (Truscott & Crook, 2004).

In Canada, people are protected from being casually committed to mental hospitals. Federal court decisions have given clients being considered for involuntary commitment the right to have written notice, an opportunity to prepare a defence with the help of an attorney, and a court hearing. Furthermore, before people can be forcibly committed, evidence that they are not only mentally ill but also gravely disabled or a significant danger to themselves or others must be provided. Most provinces now require a periodic review of every committed person's records to determine whether release is appropriate (Kelly, Dunbar, Gray, & O'Reilly, 2002). In addition, most provinces allow for conditional leave from hospital (Gray & O'Reilly, 2005).

While hospitalized, patients have the right to receive treatment, but they also have the right to refuse certain forms of treatment (Stromberg et al., 1988). These rules are designed to protect hospitalized mental patients from abuse, neglect, coercion, and exploitation, but they can also create difficulties and dangers. Consider the case of Scott Starson. He was diagnosed with bipolar disorder and admitted to a mental health treatment facility after making death threats for which he was judged *not criminally responsible due to mental illness,* which is Canada's equivalent to the insanity defence popularized in movies and television court dramas. While institutionalized, he refused drug treatment for his illness. Doctors determined that he was not capable of making treatment decisions and ordered that he be administered the prescribed drugs. Mr. Starson appealed this decision and eventually the Supreme Court of Canada ruled in his favour, stating that Mr. Starson's physicians did not establish, to the court's satisfaction, that he was indeed incapable of making decisions about his own treatment. This case, which became known as Starson vs. Swayze, led to the establishment of stricter guidelines for determining a patient's incapacity to make treatment decisions (Judgments of the Supreme Court of Canada, 2003).

Hospitalized patients who do not pose a danger to themselves or others—including those whose dangerous impulses are being suppressed by drug treatment—have the right to be subjected to minimal restriction of their freedom. Accordingly, they are released from mental hospitals, usually with a supply of medication that they are to take on their own. Unfortunately, not all these patients follow doctors' orders, sometimes with tragic results. In 2004, Martin Ostopovich, who had been diagnosed with paranoid schizophrenia, but was not taking medication, shot and killed RCMP officer Jim Galloway in a stand-off with police in Alberta. Police then shot and killed Ostopovich (D'Aliesio & Leeder, 2004). Ostopovich suffered from delusions involving suspicion and hatred of police and other authority figures, which was the apparent motive for his violent behaviour (Cormier, 2006).

In Ontario, legislation regarding ongoing treatment of psychiatric patients released from institutions into the community was enacted in 2000 in reaction to the death of an Ottawa sportscaster, Brian Smith. Smith was shot and killed in 1995 by Jeffrey Arenburg as Smith was leaving work. Arenburg had been diagnosed with paranoid schizophrenia but had refused treatment (Harris, 1999). His delusions led to an intense hatred of the media and he had been found guilty of assaulting a radio personality three years earlier (Caragata, 1995). An investigation into Smith's death and resulting recommendations led to new legislation in Ontario, known as *Brian's law,* which allows for mandatory treatment and care in the community following release from hospital (Ontario Ministry of Health and Long-Term Care, 2001).

Biological Treatments

Drugs that can ease the symptoms of psychological disorders are the latest in a long line of treatments based on the idea that psychological problems have physical causes. Hippocrates, a physician of ancient Greece, was among the first to propose this idea, and the treatments he prescribed included rest, special diets, laxatives, and abstinence from alcohol or sex. In the mental hospitals of Europe and North America during the sixteenth through eighteenth centuries, treatment of psychological disorders was based in part on Hippocrates' methods and consisted mainly of physical restraints, laxative purges, draining of "excess" blood, and induced vomiting. Cold baths, hunger, and other physical discomforts were also used in efforts to shock patients back to normality (Jones, 1923).

Biological treatments for psychological problems have advanced considerably since then, but they remain somewhat controversial. In this section we review the three main biological treatments that appeared in the twentieth century: brain surgery, electroconvulsive therapy, and psychoactive drugs. Drugs are the dominant form of medical treatment today, but in the mid-1900s, the most common biological method for treating severe psychological problems was to create seizures with electrical shock.

Electroconvulsive Therapy

In the 1930s, a Hungarian physician named Ladislaus Von Meduna used a drug to induce convulsions in schizophrenics. He believed, incorrectly, that because schizophrenia and epilepsy rarely occur in the same person, epileptic-like seizures might combat schizophrenia. In 1938, two Italian physicians—Ugo Cerletti and Lucio Bini—created seizures by briefly passing an electric current through the brains of schizophrenia patients. During the next 20 years or so, this procedure, called **electroconvulsive therapy (ECT)**, became a routine treatment for schizophrenia, depression, and sometimes mania. Upon awakening after an ECT session, the patient typically remembered nothing about the events just preceding the shock and experienced confusion. Although many patients improved, they often relapsed. The benefits of ECT also had to be weighed against its side effects, such as varying degrees of memory loss, speech disorders, and in some cases, death due to cardiac arrest or other problems (Lickey & Gordon, 1991; Shiwach, Reid, & Carmody, 2001).

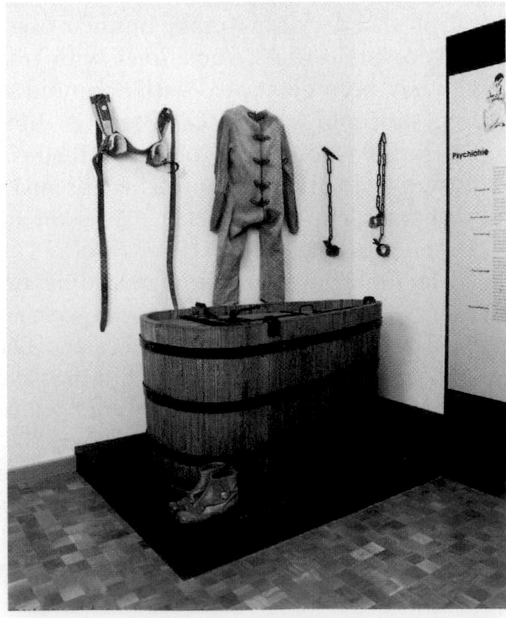

Hospital Restraints Here are examples of the chains, straitjackets, belts, and covered bathtubs that were used to restrain disruptive patients in North American and European mental hospitals in the 1800s and well into the 1900s. These devices were gentle compared with some of the methods endorsed in the late 1700s by Benjamin Rush. Known as the "father of American psychiatry," Rush advocated curing patients by frightening or disorienting them—for example, by placing them in a coffinlike box which was then briefly immersed in water.

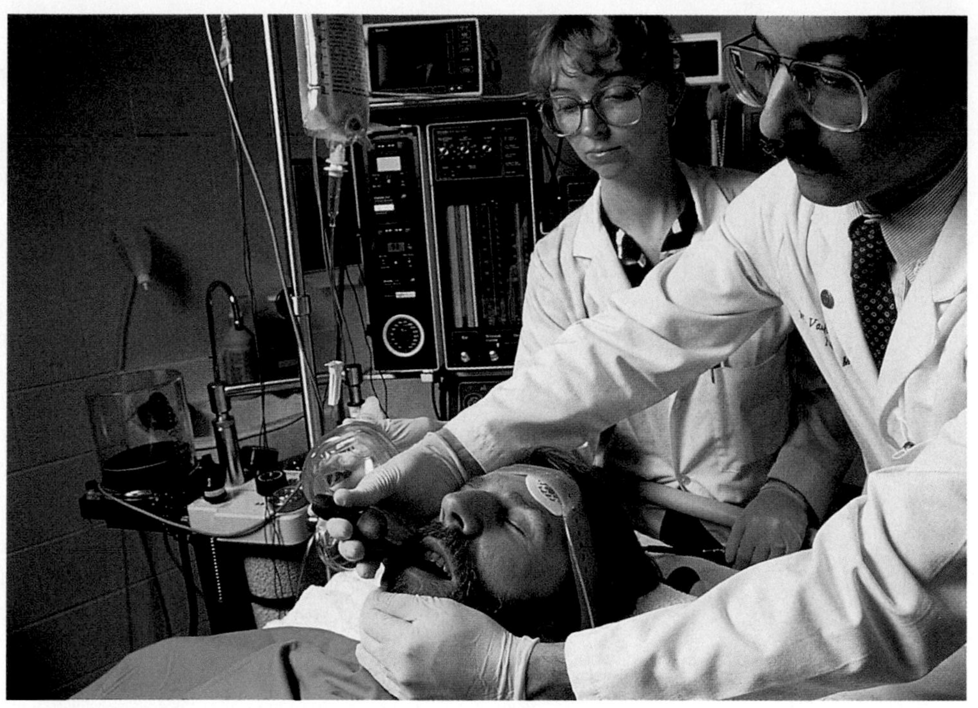

Electroconvulsive Therapy There are no national statistics on the use of ECT in Canada, but data have been collected in some provinces. For example, in 2000–2001, 13 000 ECT treatments were administered in Ontario and 7925 were administered in Quebec (Lyons, 2002). The use of ECT as a treatment for some disorders, including major depression, is endorsed by both the American and Canadian Psychiatric Associations (Enns & Reiss, 2006; Lyons, 2002). However, because of its dramatic and potentially dangerous nature, ECT remains a controversial method of treatment. Critics want it outlawed, but proponents of ECT argue that its benefits to certain patients outweigh its potential costs (Breggin, 1997; Fink, 1999).

To make ECT safer, patients are now given an anesthetic so that they are unconscious before the shock is delivered, along with a muscle relaxant to prevent bone fractures during convulsions. Also, the shock now lasts only about half a second and is usually delivered to only one side of the brain (e.g., Sackeim et al., 2000). Finally, in contrast to the dozens of treatments administered decades ago, patients now receive only about six to twelve shocks, one approximately every two days (Fink, 1999). *Magnetic seizure therapy (MST)* is currently being investigated as a potentially safer alternative to ECT (Lisanby, 2004). MST creates seizures not with electric shock but with timed pulses of magnetic energy (e.g., Lisanby et al., 2003). A related but less intense procedure called *repetitive transcranial magnetic stimulation (rTMS)* is also being studied. Compared with ECT, MST and rTMS appear to be more focused and controllable and may have fewer undesirable cognitive side effects (Fitzgerald et al., 2003; Gershon, Dannon, & Grunhaus, 2003; Hoffman et al., 2003; Lisanby, 2002). rTMS may be particularly effective for patients whose current episode of depression has been of relatively short duration (Holtzheimer, Russo, & Claypoole, 2004).

Today, ECT is used mainly for patients with severe depression (and occasionally with manic patients) who do not respond to less drastic treatments (Ciapparelli et al., 2001; Daly et al., 2001; Potter & Rudorfer, 1993; Rasmussen, 2003; Rosenbach, Hermann, & Dorwart, 1997). ECT can be effective in such cases—especially when followed up with medication—and does not appear to cause brain damage, even when administered repeatedly (e.g., Anghelescu et al., 2001; Carney, Cowen, & Geddes, 2003; Ende et al., 2000; McCall, Dunn, & Rosenquist, 2004; Rasmussen, 2003; Sackeim et al., 2001).

However, no one knows for sure how ECT works (Rudorfer, Henry, & Sackeim, 1997; Sackeim, 1994). Some suggest that it may somehow improve neurotransmitter functions and thereby alter mood (Julien, 2001; Kapur & Mann, 1993). Another view is that the neurotransmitters that help the brain recover from convulsions also reduce activity in areas of the brain associated with depression, thus relieving it (Nobler et al., 2001; Sackeim, 1985). Because shock affects many aspects of brain function, identifying the specific mechanisms underlying ECT's effects on depression is exceedingly difficult (Abrams, 1997).

electroconvulsive therapy (ECT) Brief electrical shock administered to the brain, usually to reduce depression that does not respond to drug treatments.

Psychosurgery

Procedures known as **psychosurgery** involve the destruction of brain tissue for the purpose of treating mental disorder. Among the first to try these procedures was a Portuguese neurosurgeon named António Egas Moniz. In 1935 he developed a technique, called *prefrontal lobotomy,* in which small holes are drilled in the forward portion of the skull and a sharp instrument is inserted and moved from side to side to cut connections between the prefrontal cortex and the rest of the brain (Freeman & Watts, 1942; Moniz, 1948). The theory was that emotional reactions in disturbed people become exaggerated due to neural processes in the frontal lobes and that the lobotomy disrupts these processes. During the 1940s and 1950s, psychosurgery became almost routine in the treatment of schizophrenia, depression, anxiety, aggressiveness, and obsessive-compulsive disorder (Valenstein, 1980). Unfortunately, brain surgery is risky, and sometimes fatal; its benefits are uncertain; and its side effects and complications, including epilepsy, are irreversible (Balon, 2004; Martin et al., 2001; Rueck, Andreewitch, & Flyckt, 2003). Today, psychosurgery is performed only in rare cases in which all else has failed, and—guided by brain-imaging techniques—it focuses on much smaller brain areas than those involved in lobotomies (Dougherty et al., 2002; Feldman & Goodrich, 2001).

Psychoactive Drugs

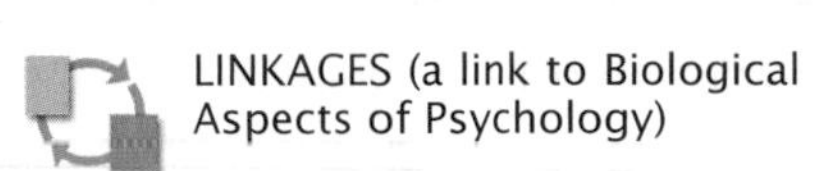
LINKAGES (a link to Biological Aspects of Psychology)

The use of psychosurgery and ECT declined after the 1950s, not only because of their complications and general distastefulness but also because *psychoactive drugs* had begun to emerge as more convenient and effective treatment alternatives. In the chapters on biological aspects of psychology and on consciousness, we discuss how psychoactive drugs affect neurotransmitter systems and consciousness. Here, we describe how drugs are used to combat schizophrenia, depression, mania, and anxiety.

Neuroleptics One group of drugs appearing in the early 1950s revolutionized the treatment of severe mental disorder. Called **neuroleptics** (or *antipsychotics*), these drugs dramatically reduced the intensity of psychotic symptoms such as hallucinations, delusions, paranoid suspiciousness, disordered thinking, and incoherence in many mental patients, especially those diagnosed with schizophrenia. As a result of taking these drugs, these patients became better able to care for themselves and more responsive to their environments. Thousands were able to leave the hospitals where they had been confined, some for many years. For those remaining, the drugs made straitjackets, padded cells, and other once-common restraints almost obsolete.

The most widely used neuroleptics are the *phenothiazines* (pronounced "fee-noh-THYE-uh-zeens"), of which the first, *chlorpromazine* (marketed as *Thorazine* in the United States and as *Largactil* in Canada and the United Kingdom), has been especially popular. Another neuroleptic called *haloperidol (Haldol)* is comparable to the phenothiazines in overall effectiveness, but it creates less sedation (Julien, 2001). Patients who do not respond to one of these neuroleptics may respond to the other (Davis, Chen, & Glick, 2003). Between 60 and 70 percent of patients receiving neuroleptics show improvement, though fewer than 30 percent respond well enough to live entirely on their own.

Unfortunately, neuroleptics have problematic side effects, the mildest of which include dry mouth, blurred vision, urinary retention, dizziness, and skin pigmentation problems. More serious side effects include symptoms similar to those of Parkinson's disease, such as muscle rigidity, restlessness, tremours, and slowed movement (Kane, 1989). Some of these side effects can be treated with medication, but the most serious one, called *tardive dyskinesia (TD),* is an irreversible disorder of the motor system that appears only after years of neuroleptic use (Janno et al., 2004). Affecting at least 25 percent of patients who take chlorpromazine or haloperidol for several years, TD

psychosurgery Surgical procedures that destroy tissue in small regions of the brain in an effort to treat psychological disorders.

neuroleptics Drugs that alleviate the symptoms of severe disorders such as schizophrenia.

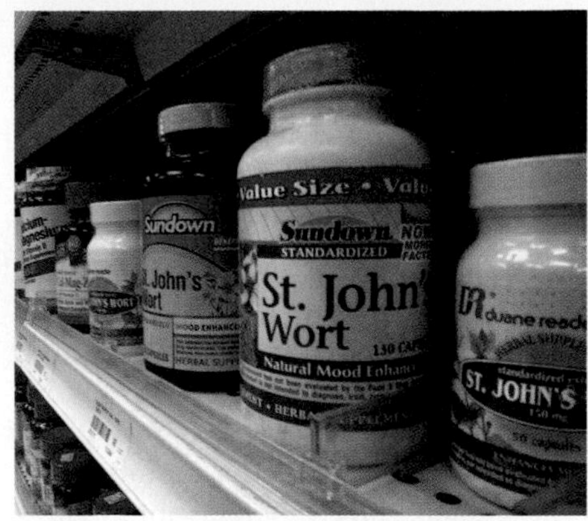

A Natural Cure? An herbal remedy from the plant called *Saint John's wort* has become a popular nonprescription treatment for depression. One of its active ingredients, ***hypericin,*** is thought to affect serotonin much as Prozac does (Butterweck, 2003). In double-blind, placebo-controlled studies, Saint John's wort has done as well as Prozac, but only for the mildest forms of depression (Brenner et al., 2000; Gaster & Holroyd, 2000; Hammerness, Basch, & Ulbricht, 2003; Hypericum Depression Trial Study Group, 2002; Lecrubier et al., 2002; Volz & Laux, 2000; Woelk, 2000). Some of these studies may be flawed, however (e.g., Spira, 2001), so final conclusions about the safety and effectiveness of Saint John's wort for even mild depression must await the results of further research (Gupta & Moller, 2003).

involves grotesque, uncontrollable, repetitive movements of the body, often including tic-like movements of the face and thrusting of the tongue. Sometimes the person's arms or legs flail unpredictably.

Among a newer generation of antipsychotic drugs (called *atypical neuroleptics*) is *clozapine (Clozaril),* which has effects similar to those of the phenothiazines but does not cause movement disorders. Although no more effective on average than the phenothiazines, clozapine has helped many patients who did not respond to the phenothiazines or haloperidol, and it may reduce suicide risk in schizophrenia (Green & Patel, 1996; Rabinowitz et al., 2001). Unfortunately, for about 1 or 2 percent of those who take it, clozapine greatly increases the risk of developing a fatal blood disease called *agranulocytosis,* which is marked by the loss of white blood cells and consequent susceptibility to infectious disease (Alvir et al., 1993). Weekly blood tests are required to detect early signs of this disease, thus greatly increasing the cost of using clozapine (Meltzer, 1997).

Several other atypical neuroleptics have been introduced recently, including *risperidone (Risperdal), olanzapine (Zyprexa), quetiapine (Seroquel), ziprasidone (Geodon),* and most recently, *aripiprazole (Abilify).* These newer medications are expensive, but they have even fewer side effects than clozapine, and they do not cause agranulocytosis (Correll, Leucht, & Kane, 2004). Like clozapine, they also appear to reduce the "negative" symptoms of schizophrenia, such as lack of emotion, social withdrawal, and reduced speech (e.g., Azorin et al., 2001; Bailey, 2002; Conley & Mahmoud, 2001; Davis, Chen, & Glick, 2003; Kane et al., 2003; Kapur, Sridhar & Remington, 2004; Lieberman et al., 2003; Potkin et al., 2003; Volavka et al., 2002).

Antidepressants Soon after antipsychotic drugs appeared, they were joined by **antidepressants**, a class of drugs that is now widely prescribed for relieving the symptoms of depression (Olfson et al., 2002). Although these drugs have almost immediate effects on neurotransmitters (usually increasing the availability of serotonin or norepinephrine), their effects on depressive symptoms do not appear for a week or two, and maximum effects take even longer (Quitkin et al., 2003). The mechanism underlying the effects of these drugs is consistent with some theories about the biology of depression discussed in the chapter on psychological disorders, but the time lag suggests that the effects occur through some sort of long-term compensatory process in the nervous system.

There are several classes of antidepressant drugs. The *monoamine oxidase inhibitors (MAOIs)* are effective in many cases of depression and in some cases of panic disorder, but they can produce severe high blood pressure if mixed with foods containing tyramine, a substance found in aged cheeses, red wine, and chicken livers (Julien, 2001). Fortunately, a new class of monoamine oxidase inhibitors is now available that does not carry this side effect risk (Julien, 2001).

Tricyclic antidepressants (TCAs) form another popular class of drugs for combating depression. The TCAs are prescribed more frequently than MAOI drugs because they seem to work somewhat better. They also have fewer side effects, though some patients stop taking tricyclics because of the sleepiness, dry mouth, dizziness, blurred vision, low blood pressure, constipation, and urinary retention they can cause. Further, the combination of tricyclics and alcohol can increase the effects of both, with potentially fatal results. Still, if side effects are controlled, tricyclics can be effective in treating depression and can also reduce the severity and frequency of panic attacks in some cases of panic disorder.

Today, the most popular medications for depression are those that affect serotonin. The most prominent drug in this group is *fluoxetine (Prozac).* Its popularity is due to the fact that it is as effective as older antidepressants and, in most cases, has milder side effects (Cookson & Duffett, 1998; Stokes, 1998). An improved version of Prozac, containing a purer active ingredient called *R-fluoxetine,* is currently being developed. Other, even newer antidepressants, including *venlafaxine (Effexor),*

antidepressants Drugs that relieve depression.

nefazodone (Serzone), bupropion (Wellbutrin), escitalopram (Lexapro), and *duloxetine (Cymbalta),* show similar promise (Appleton, 2000; Croft et al., 1999; Hirschfeld & Vornik, 2004, Quitkin et al., 2000).

About 50 to 60 percent of patients who take antidepressant drugs show improved mood, greater physical activity, increased appetite, and better sleep (Hollon, Thase, & Markowitz, 2002).This degree of improvement is seen in only 10 to 20 percent of the most severe cases of psychotic depression, however (Agency for Healthcare Research and Quality, 1999; U.S. Surgeon General, 1999). It has long been assumed that these results were due to the drugs' active ingredients, but critics have cast some doubt on this assumption. An analysis of clinical trial data submitted to the US Food and Drug Administration by the makers of six widely prescribed antidepressant drugs showed that in 57 percent of the trials, antidepressant drugs did only a little better than placebo medication ("sugar pills") at relieving depression (Kirsch et al., 2002). Defenders of antidepressant medications argue that even relatively small effects are better than none (e.g., Thase, 2002), whereas critics contend that those effects are too small to matter.

Lithium and Anticonvulsants Around 1970, it was discovered that a mineral salt of the element *lithium,* when taken regularly, could prevent both the depression and the mania associated with bipolar disorders in some patients. Administered as lithium carbonate, lithium is effective for 30 to 50 percent of patients with bipolar disorder (Baldessarini & Tondo, 2000; Geddes et al., 2004; Manji, Bowden, & Belmaker, 2000; Zornberg & Pope, 1993). Without lithium, the typical bipolar patient has a manic episode about every 14 months and a depressive episode about every 17 months (Lickey & Gordon, 1991). With lithium, attacks of mania occur as rarely as every nine years (Bowden, 2000; Geddes et al., 2004). The lithium dosage, however, must be exact and carefully controlled. Taking too much can cause nausea, vomiting, tremor, fatigue, slurred speech, and, if the overdose is severe, coma or death. Further, lithium is not useful for treating a manic episode in progress because, as in the case of antidepressants, it takes a week or two of regular use before its effects are seen. So, as with the antidepressants, lithium's effects probably occur through some form of long-term adaptation as the nervous system adjusts to the presence of the drug.

In recent years, anticonvulsant drugs such as *divalproex (Epival/Depakote)* and *lamotrigine (Lamictal)* have been used as an alternative to lithium in treating mania (Bowden, 2003b; Goodwin, Bowden, & Calabrese, 2004; McElroy, Zarate, & Cookson, 2004; Salzman, 2003). These drugs appear to cause fewer side effects, are less dangerous at higher doses, and are easier to regulate (Bowden et al., 2000, 2003a, 2003b; Hirschfeld et al., 1999). However, their long-term benefits in reducing mania and the risk of suicide are not as well established, so lithium is still considered the treatment of choice against which others are measured (Baldessarini et al., 2002; Dinan, 2002; Goodwin et al., 2003).

Anxiolytics During the 1950s, a new class of drugs called *tranquilizers* was shown to reduce mental and physical tension and other symptoms of anxiety. The first of these drugs, called *meprobamate (Miltown* or *Equanil),* acts somewhat like barbiturates, meaning that overdoses can be fatal. Because they do not pose this danger, the *benzodiazepines,* particularly *chlordiazepoxide (Librium)* and *diazepam (Valium),* became the worldwide drug treatment of choice for anxiety. Today, these and other anti-anxiety drugs, now called **anxiolytics** (pronounced "ang-zee-oh-LIT-iks"), continue to be the most widely prescribed and used of all legal drugs.

Anxiolytics have an immediate calming effect and are quite useful in reducing anxiety, including in cases of generalized anxiety disorder and post-traumatic stress disorder. One of the newest of the benzodiazepines, *alprazolam (Xanax),*

anxiolytics Drugs that reduce feelings of anxiety.

has also become especially popular for the treatment of panic disorder and agoraphobia (Greenblatt, Harmatz, & Shader, 1993). Another benzodiazepine, *clonazepam (Klonopin),* is also being used, alone or in combination with other anxiolytics, in the treatment of anxiety ranging from phobias to panic disorder (Worthington et al., 1998). But benzodiazepines can have bothersome side effects such as sedation, lightheadedness, and impaired psychomotor and mental functioning. Combining these drugs with alcohol can have fatal consequences, and continued use can lead to tolerance and physical dependence (Chouinard, 2004). After heavy or long-term use, attempts to stop taking benzodiazepines, particularly if the change is sudden, can result in severe withdrawal symptoms, including seizures and a return of anxiety more intense than the patient had initially experienced (Rickels et al., 1993).

An anxiolytic called *buspirone (BuSpar)* provides an alternative anxiety treatment that eliminates some of these problems, but it acts more slowly. As with the antidepressants, buspirone's effects do not occur for days or weeks after treatment begins. As a result, many patients stop taking it because they think it has no effect other than dizziness, headache, and nervousness (Lickey & Gordon, 1991; Stahl, 2002; Wagner et al., 2003). Yet buspirone can ultimately equal benzodiazepines in reducing generalized anxiety (Gorman, 2003; Rickels & Rynn, 2002; Schnabel, 1987; U.S. Surgeon General, 1999). Further, it does not seem to promote dependence, has fewer side effects than the benzodiazepines, and does not interact negatively with alcohol.

A number of antidepressant drugs that increase serotonin in the brain—including *fluoxetine (Prozac), paroxetine (Paxil), clomipramine (Anafranil), fluvoxamine (Luvox),* and *sertraline (Zoloft)*—have also been used in treating anxiety-related problems such as panic disorder, social phobia, obsessive-compulsive disorder, and post-traumatic stress disorder (Davidson et al., 2001; Gorman, 2002, 2003; Julien, 2001; Koran et al., 2002; Rickels et al., 2003; Stein et al., 2002; Todorov, Freeston, & Borgeat, 2000; U.S. Surgeon General, 1999; Van Ameringen et al., 2001; Walkup et al., 2001).

Table 16.5 lists the psychoactive drugs we have described, along with their uses, effects, and side effects.

Human Diversity and Drug Treatment So far, we have talked about drug treatment effects in general. However, these effects can differ significantly among people from different ethnic groups and between men and women, especially in terms of the psychoactive drug dose necessary to produce clinical effects. For example, Keh-Ming Lin, director of the Research Center on the Psychobiology of Ethnicity at the University of California at Los Angeles, has demonstrated that compared with Asians, Caucasians must take significantly higher doses of the benzodiazepines, haloperidol, clozapine, lithium, and possibly the tricyclic antidepressants in order to obtain equally beneficial effects (Lin & Poland, 1995; Matsuda et al., 1996). In addition, African Americans may show a faster response to tricyclic antidepressants than Americans of European background and may respond to lower doses of lithium (Strickland et al., 1991). There is also some evidence that compared with Americans of European background or African Americans, Hispanic Americans require lower doses of antipsychotic drugs to get the same benefits (Ruiz et al., 1999). Some of these ethnic differences are thought to be a function of genetically regulated differences in drug metabolism, whereas others may be due to diet.

Sex differences in drug response are also being investigated (e.g., Seeman, 2004). In the past, much of our knowledge about drug effects in women—and about women's health in general—was based on studies of men. Because drug responses can differ in women and men, however, the male-oriented approach can be potentially dangerous for women. Fortunately, we are now seeing rapid growth in

table 16.5

A Sampling of Psychoactive Drugs Used for Treating Psychological Disorders

Psychoactive drugs have been successful in dramatically reducing the symptoms of many psychological disorders. Critics point out that drugs can have troublesome side effects, however, and they may create dependence, especially after years of use (e.g., Breggin, 1997). They note, too, that drugs do not "cure" mental disorders (National Institute of Mental Health, 1995), that their effects are not always strong (Kirsch et al., 2002), and that temporary symptom relief may make some patients less likely to seek a permanent solution to their psychological problems.

For Schizophrenia: Neuroleptics (Antipsychotics)

Chemical Name	Trade Name	Effects and Side Effects
Chlorpromazine Haloperidol	Thorazine Haldol	Reduce hallucinations, delusions, incoherence, jumbled thought processes; cause movement-disorder side effects, including tardive dyskinesia
Clozapine	Clozaril	Reduces psychotic symptoms; causes no movement disorders, but raises risk of serious blood disease
Risperidone	Risperdal	Reduces positive and negative psychotic symptoms without risk of blood disease
Ziprasidone	Geodon	Reduces positive and negative psychotic symptoms without causing weight gain
Aripiprazole	Abilify	Reduces positive and negative psychotic symptoms without weight gain and with few side effects

For Mood Disorders: Antidepressants and Mood Elevators

Chemical Name	Trade Name	Effects and Side Effects
Tricyclics		
Imipramine	Tofranil	Act as antidepressants, but also have antipanic action; cause sleepiness and other moderate side effects; potentially dangerous if taken with alcohol
Amitriptyline	Elavil, Amitid	
Other Antidepressants		
Fluoxetine	Prozac	Have antidepressant, antipanic, and anti-obsessive action
Clomipramine	Anafranil	
Fluvoxamine	Luvox	
Sertraline	Zoloft	
Escitalopram	Lexapro	
Other Drugs		
Lithium carbonate	Carbolith, Lithizine	Calms mania; reduces mood swings of bipolar disorder; overdose harmful, potentially deadly
Divalproex	Depakote	Is effective against mania, with fewer side effects
Lamotrigine	Lamictal	Is effective in delaying relapse in bipolar disorder; most benefits associated with depression

For Anxiety Disorders: Anxiolytics

Chemical Name	Trade Name	Effects and Side Effects
Benzodiazepines		
Chlordiazepoxide Diazepam	Librium Valium	Act as potent anxiolytics for generalized anxiety, panic, stress; extended use may cause physical dependence and withdrawal syndrome if abruptly discontinued
Alprazolam	Xanax	Also has antidepressant effects; often used in agoraphobia (has high dependence potential)
Clonazepam	Klonopin	Often used in combination with other anxiolytics for panic disorder
Other Anti-anxiety Agents		
Buspirone	BuSpar	Has slow-acting anti-anxiety action; no known dependence problems

research focused specifically on matters relating to women's health, including their response to drugs. Some research shows, for example, that although males and females may respond in about the same way to tricyclic antidepressants (Wohlfarth et al., 2004), women may maintain higher blood levels of these and other therapeutic psychoactive drugs and may show better response to neuroleptics (Hildebrandt et al., 2003). They also may be more vulnerable to adverse effects such as tardive dyskinesia (Yonkers et al., 1992). It may be that hormonal and body-composition differences (such as the ratio of body fat to muscle) are among the factors responsible for sex differences in drug response (Dawkins & Potter, 1991; Yonkers et al., 1992). Continued research on these and other dimensions of human diversity will undoubtedly lead to more effective and safer drug treatments for psychological disorders (Thompson & Pollack, 2001).

Evaluating Psychoactive Drug Treatments

Despite the widespread success of psychoactive drugs in the treatment of psychological disorders, critics point out several problems with them. First, even if a disorder has physical components, drugs may mask the problem without curing it. For example, anti-anxiety drugs may be an aid to psychotherapy (Koenigsberg, 1994), but these drugs alone cannot teach people to cope with the source of their anxiety. Critics are concerned that psychiatrists, and especially general practitioners, rely too heavily on anxiolytics and other drugs to solve patients' psychological problems (Glenmullen, 2000). The antidepressant Prozac, for instance, is being widely prescribed—overprescribed, critics say—for problems ranging from hypersensitivity to criticism and fear of rejection to low self-esteem and premenstrual syndrome. Second, abuse of some drugs (such as the anti-anxiety benzodiazepines) can result in physical or psychological dependence. Third, side effects present a problem. Some are merely annoying, such as the thirst and dry mouth produced by some antidepressants. Other side effects, such as tardive dyskinesia, are far more serious. Although these side effects occur in a minority of patients, some are irreversible, and it is impossible to predict in advance who will develop them. For example, recent research on Prozac and similar antidepressant medications has prompted Health Canada to issue a warning about the potential for suicidal behaviour in some children and adolescents who take these drugs (Health Canada, 2003, 2004).

Still, research on psychoactive drugs holds the promise of creating better drugs, a fuller understanding of the origin and nature of some psychological disorders, and more informed prescription practices (Cryan et al., 2004; Lira et al., 2003; Shildkraut & Mooney, 2004). For example, advances in research on individual variations in the structure of the genes that create different types of dopamine receptors may explain why some schizophrenia patients respond to phenothiazines that bind primarily to one type of dopamine receptor. Other patients respond only to clozapine, which has a preference for another type of dopamine receptor (Van Tol et al., 1992). This research may guide the development of new drugs that are matched to specific receptors; the symptoms of schizophrenia then could be alleviated without the risk of movement disorders posed by the phenothiazines or the potentially lethal side effects of clozapine. Similarly, research on anxiolytics promises to reveal information about the chemical aspects of anxiety.

Drugs and Psychotherapy

We have seen that both drugs and psychotherapy can be effective in treating psychological disorders. Is one better than the other? Can they be effectively combined? A considerable amount of research is being conducted to address these questions.

Although occasionally a study does show that one approach or the other is more effective, there is no clear consensus. Overall, neither form of therapy is clearly superior for treating problems such as anxiety disorders and major depressive disorder (Antonuccio, Danton, & DeNelsky, 1995). For example, large-scale studies of treatment for severe depression found that cognitive-behaviour therapy and interpersonal psychotherapy were as effective as an antidepressant drug (DeRubeis et al., 1999; Hollon et al., Thase, & Markowitz, 2002; March et al., 2004; Nemeroff et al., 2003; Spanier et al., 1996). Cognitive-behaviour therapy has also equaled drug effects in the treatment of phobias (Clark et al., 2003; Davidson et al., 2004; Otto et al., 2000; Thom, Sartory, & Jöhren, 2000), panic disorder (Klosko et al., 1990), generalized anxiety disorder (Gould et al., 1997), and obsessive-compulsive disorder (Abramowitz, 1997; Kozak, Liebowitz, & Foa, 2000). Further, the dropout rate from psychotherapy may be lower than from drug therapies (Casacalenda, Perry, & Looper, 2002), and the benefits of many kinds of psychotherapy may last longer than those of drug therapies (e.g., Bovasso, Eaton, & Armenian, 1999; Hollon et al., 2002; Segal, Gemar, & Williams, 2000; Thom et al., 2000).

What about combining drugs and psychotherapy? One research team compared the effects of gradual exposure treatment and an anti-anxiety drug (Xanax) in the treatment of agoraphobia. Clients receiving gradual exposure alone showed better short- and long-term benefits than those getting either the drug alone or a combination of the drug and gradual exposure (Echeburua et al., 1993). Other studies, too, have found that combining drugs and psychotherapy may produce surprisingly little advantage (e.g., Davidson et al., 2004; Elkin, 1994; Nemeroff et al., 2003; Spiegel & Bruce, 1997). However, the combination of drugs and psychotherapy has been shown to be more effective than either method alone in treating certain disorders, including attention deficit hyperactivity disorder, obsessive-compulsive disorder, alcoholism, stammering, compulsive sexual behaviour, panic disorder, and chronic depression (Barlow et al., 2000; deBeurs et al., 1995; Engeland, 1993; Keller et al., 2000; March et al., 2004; Reynolds et al., 1999). This combined approach may be especially helpful for clients who are initially too distressed to cooperate in psychotherapy (Kahn, 1995). Another approach, already found successful with clients who have been taking drugs for panic disorder, is to use psychotherapy to prevent relapse and make further progress as drug treatment is discontinued (e.g., Bruce, Spiegel, & Hegel, 1999; Lam et al., 2003).

It has been suggested that the most conservative strategy for treating anxiety and depression is to begin with cognitive or interpersonal psychotherapy (which has no major negative side effects) and then to add or switch to drug treatment if psychotherapy alone is ineffective (Jacobs et al., 2004). Often, clients who do not respond to one method will be helped by the other.

LINKAGES

Biological Aspects of Psychology and the Treatment of Psychological Disorders

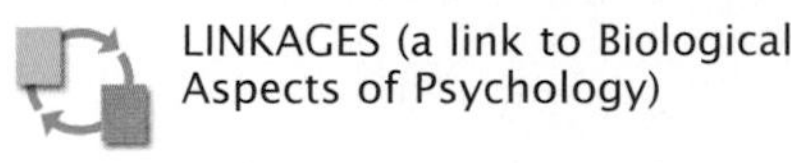

LINKAGES (a link to Biological Aspects of Psychology)

As noted in the chapter on biological aspects of psychology, human feelings, thoughts, and actions—whether normal or abnormal—are ultimately the result of biological processes, especially those in the brain, and most especially those involving neurotransmitters and their receptors. Alterations in the availability of these neurotransmitters, in the sensitivity of their receptors, and thus in the activity of the neural circuits they influence affect the ebb and flow of neural communication, the integration of information in the brain, and, ultimately, behaviour and mental processes. Because different neurotransmitters are especially prominent in particular brain regions or circuits (see Figure 3.23), altering the functioning of particular neurotransmitter systems will have relatively specific psychological and behavioural effects.

Some of the drugs that we have described for the treatment of psychological disorders were developed specifically to alter a neurotransmitter system that biological theories suggest might be involved in those disorders. In other cases, causal theories evolved from (often accidental) findings that drugs known to affect certain neurotransmitter systems help patients who display some disorder.

Let's consider in a little more detail some of the ways in which therapeutic psychoactive drugs affect neurotransmitters and their receptors. As described in the chapter on biological aspects of psychology, a given neuron can receive excitatory ("fire") or inhibitory ("don't fire") signals via neurotransmitters that facilitate or inhibit firing. Some therapeutic drugs amplify excitatory signals, whereas others increase inhibition. For example, the benzodiazepines (e.g., Valium and Xanax) exert their anti-anxiety effects by helping the inhibitory neurotransmitter GABA bind to postsynaptic receptors and, thus, suppress neuronal firing. This enhanced inhibitory effect acts as a sort of braking system that slows the activity of GABA-sensitive neurons involved in the experience of anxiety. However, benzodiazepines also slow the action of all neural systems that use GABA, including those associated with motor activity and mental processing, which are located throughout the brain. The result is the decreased psychomotor coordination and clouded thinking that appear as benzodiazepine's side effects. Research suggests that it might soon be possible to develop drugs that will bind only to certain kinds of GABA receptors and thus greatly reduce these side effects (Löw et al., 2000; Stahl, 2002).

Other therapeutic drugs reduce postsynaptic activity by serving as receptor antagonists (see Figure 9.11 in the chapter on consciousness), acting to block the receptor site normally used by a particular neurotransmitter. Some neuroleptics—the phenothiazines and haloperidol, for example—exert their antipsychotic effects by blocking receptors for dopamine, a neurotransmitter that, as described in the chapter on biological aspects of psychology, is important for movement. These drugs compete with dopamine, blocking the firing of neurons that normally use it. The fact that dopamine blockage can normalize the disordered thinking processes of many schizophrenics suggests that, as discussed in the chapter on psychological disorders, schizophrenia may be partly due to excess dopamine activity. Unfortunately, reducing this activity can create severe disorders—such as tardive dyskinesia—in the movement systems that are also controlled by dopamine.

Psychoactive drugs can also exert their therapeutic influence by increasing the amount of a neurotransmitter available at receptors, thereby maximizing the effects of that neurotransmitter. This enhanced availability can be accomplished either by stimulating production of the neurotransmitter or, as is more common in therapeutic drugs, by keeping the neurotransmitter in circulation in the synapse. Normally, after a neurotransmitter has been released, it flows back to the presynaptic terminal, where it is stored for later use. If this *reuptake* process is blocked, the neurotransmitter remains in the synapse, ready to work. The tricyclic antidepressants, for example, operate by blocking the reuptake of norepinephrine. Fluoxetine, clomipramine, and several other of the newer antidepressants are called *selective serotonin reuptake inhibitors* (or *SSRIs*) because they block the reuptake of serotonin. Others, such as venlafaxine, slow the reuptake of both serotonin and norepinephrine. These effects are consistent with biological theories suggesting that some cases of depression are traceable to faulty norepinephrine or serotonin systems.

Community Psychology: From Treatment to Prevention

It has long been argued that even if psychologists knew exactly how to treat every psychological problem, there would never be enough mental health professionals to help everyone who needs them (Albee, 1968). This view fostered the rise of **community psychology,** a movement that aims both to treat troubled people in their home communities and to promote social and environmental changes that can minimize or prevent psychological disorders. Graduate degrees in Community Psychology are offered in Canada at Wilfrid Laurier University in Waterloo, Ontario, and at Université Laval in Quebec.

One aspect of community psychology, the *community mental health movement,* arose during the 1960s as an attempt to make treatment available to people in their own communities. As antipsychotic drugs became available, and as concern grew that patients were not improving—and might be getting worse—after years of confinement in mental hospitals, thousands of these patients were released. The plan was that they would receive drugs and other mental health services in newly funded community mental health centres. This *deinstitutionalization* process did spare patients the boredom and isolation of the hospital environment, but the mental health services available in the community never matched the need for them. Some former hospital patients and many people whose disorders might once have sent them to mental hospitals are now living in halfway houses and other community-based facilities where they receive *psychosocial rehabilitation.* These community support services are not designed to "cure" them but to help them cope with their problems and develop the social and occupational skills necessary for semi-independent living (Hunter, 1995; Liberman et al., 1998). All too many others with severe psychological disorders are to be found enduring the dangers of homelessness on city streets or of confinement in jails and prisons (Ditton, 1999; U.S. Department of Health and Human Services, 2001a; World Health Organization World Mental Health Survey Consortium, 2004).

Community psychology also attempts to prevent psychological disorders by addressing unemployment, poverty, overcrowded substandard housing, and other stressful social problems that may underlie some disorders (Albee, 1985; Bracken & Thomas, 2001; Tucker & Herman, 2002; Weissberg, Kumpfer, & Seligman, 2003). Less ambitious, but perhaps even more significant, are efforts to detect psychological problems in their earliest stages and keep them from becoming worse (Sanders et al., 2000), as well as to minimize the long-term effects of psychological disorders and prevent their recurrence (e.g., Dadds et al., 1997; Sanders et al., 2000). Examples include prevention of depression and suicide (Beardslee et al., 2003; Freres et al., 2002; Garland & Zigler, 1993); programs, including Canada's Aboriginal Head Start Program, that help preschoolers whose backgrounds hurt their chances of doing well in school and put them at risk for delinquency (Public Health Agency of Canada, 2004; Tremblay et al., 1995; Zigler, Taussig, & Black, 1992); identification of children who are at risk for disorder or delinquency because of aggressiveness, parental divorce, or being rejected or victimized at school (e.g., Greenberg et al., 1999; Lochman & Wells, 2004; Martinez & Forgatch, 2001); interventions to head off anxiety disorders or schizophrenia in children and adults (August et al., 2001; McGorry et al., 2002; Raine et al., 2003); and programs designed to prevent drug abuse and promote health consciousness in ethnic minority communities (Borg, 2002; Hawkins, Cummins, & Marlatt, 2004).

community psychology A movement to minimize or prevent psychological disorders through changes in social systems and through community mental health programs.

LINKAGES

As noted in the chapter on introducing psychology, all of psychology's many subfields are related to one another. Our discussion of treating psychological disorders through the use of psychoactive drugs illustrates just one way in which the topic of this chapter, the treatment of psychological disorders, is linked to the subfield of biological psychology (see the chapter on that topic). The Linkages diagram shows ties to two other subfields as well, and there are many more ties throughout the book. Looking for linkages among subfields will help you see how they all fit together and better appreciate the big picture that is psychology.

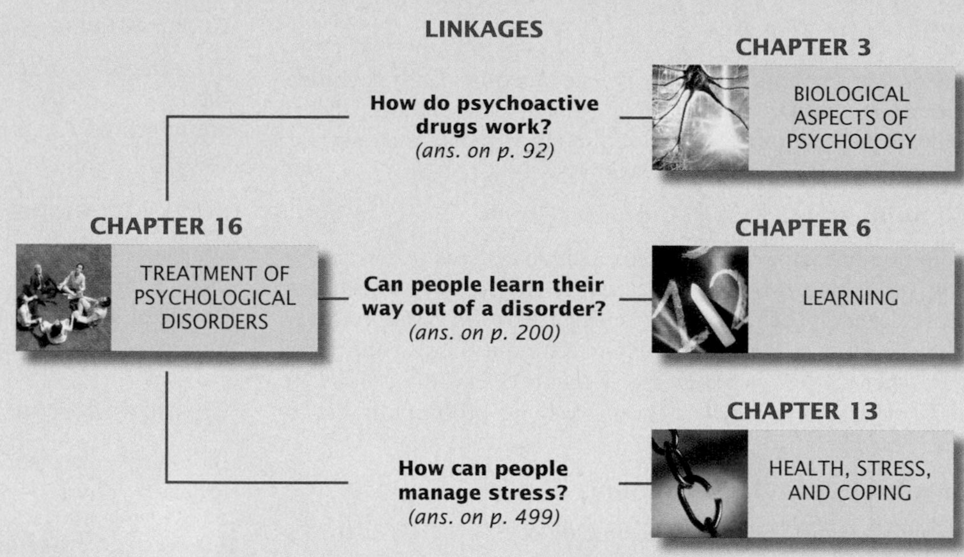
LINKAGES
CHAPTER 16
TREATMENT OF PSYCHOLOGICAL DISORDERS
How do psychoactive drugs work?
(ans. on p. 92)
CHAPTER 3
BIOLOGICAL ASPECTS OF PSYCHOLOGY
Can people learn their way out of a disorder?
(ans. on p. 200)
CHAPTER 6
LEARNING
How can people manage stress?
(ans. on p. 499)
CHAPTER 13
HEALTH, STRESS, AND COPING

SUMMARY

Psychotherapy for psychological disorders is usually based on psychodynamic, humanistic, or social-cognitive (behavioural) theories of personality and behaviour disorder. Most therapists combine features of these theories in an eclectic approach. The biological approach is reflected in the use of drugs and other physical treatment methods.

Basic Features of Treatment

All forms of treatment for psychological disorders include a client; a therapist; an underlying theory of behaviour disorder; a set of treatment procedures suggested by the underlying theory; and the development of a special relationship between the client and therapist, which may make it easier for improvement to occur. Therapy may be offered to inpatients and outpatients in many different settings by *psychologists, psychiatrists,* and other mental health professionals. The goal of treatment is to help people change their thinking, feelings, and behaviour so that they will be happier and function better. This goal may be pursued by promoting insight into hidden causes of behaviour problems, by fostering personal growth through genuine self-expression, or by helping clients learn new ways of thinking and acting.

Psychodynamic Psychotherapy

Psychodynamic psychotherapy, which began with Sigmund Freud's methods of *psychoanalysis,* seeks to help clients gain insight into unconscious conflicts and impulses and then to explore how those factors have created disorders.

Classical Psychoanalysis

Exploration of the unconscious is aided by the use of free association, dream interpretation, and analysis of transference.

Contemporary Variations on Psychoanalysis

Some variations on psychoanalysis focus less on the id, the unconscious, and the past and more on helping clients harness the ego to solve problems in the present. Other forms of psychodynamic treatment retain most of Freud's principles but use a more flexible format. Object relations therapy, for example, examines the effects of early relationships with caregivers and how those relationships affect current ones.

Humanistic Psychotherapy

Humanistic (or phenomenological) psychotherapy helps clients to become more aware of discrepancies between their feelings and their behaviour. According to the humanistic approach, these discrepancies are at the root of behaviour disorders and can be resolved by the client once they are brought to light in the context of a genuine, trusting relationship with the therapist.

Client-Centred Therapy

Therapists using Carl Rogers's *client-centred therapy,* also known as *person-centred therapy,* help mainly by adopting attitudes toward the client that express *unconditional positive regard, empathy,* and *congruence*. These attitudes create a nonjudgmental atmosphere that facilitates the client's honesty with the therapist, with himself or herself, and with others. One way of creating this atmosphere is through *reflection*.

Gestalt Therapy

Therapists employing the *Gestalt therapy* of Fritz and Laura Perls use more active techniques than do Rogerian therapists, often confronting and challenging clients.

Behaviour Therapy

Behaviour therapy, behaviour modification, and *cognitive-behaviour therapy* use learning principles to reduce clients' undesirable patterns of thought and behaviour and to strengthen more desirable alternatives.

Techniques for Modifying Behaviour

Common behavioural treatments include *systematic desensitization, modelling, assertiveness training,* and *social skills training.* More generally, behaviour therapists use *positive reinforcement* (sometimes in a *token economy*), techniques based on *extinction* (such as *flooding*), *aversion therapy,* and *punishment* to make desirable behaviours more likely or problematic behaviours less likely.

Cognitive-Behaviour Therapy

Many behaviour therapists also employ cognitive-behaviour therapy to help clients alter the way they think, as well as the way they behave. Among the specific cognitive-behaviour therapy methods are *rational-emotive behaviour therapy (REBT),* cognitive restructuring, stress inoculation training, and *cognitive therapy.*

Group, Family, and Couples Therapy

Therapists of all theoretical persuasions may offer therapy to several clients at once. Clients' interactions with one another can enhance the effects of treatment.

Group Therapy

Group therapy may involve a variety of people and problems, or it may focus on particular types of clients and problems. The group format is also adopted in many self-help, or mutual-help, organizations.

Family and Couples Therapy

Family therapy involves treatment of two or more individuals from the same family system. In *couples therapy,* the clients are spouses or other intimate partners. In both formats, treatment usually focuses on improving communication and other interactions between and among the people involved.

Evaluating Psychotherapy

There is some disagreement about exactly how to measure improvement following psychotherapy and how best to ensure that observed improvement was actually due to the treatment itself and not to some other factor. Meta-analyses have found that clients who receive psychotherapy are better off than most people who receive no treatment but that no single approach is uniformly better than all others for all clients and problems. Still, some methods appear effective enough in the treatment of particular disorders to have been listed by an American Psychological Association task force as *empirically supported therapies (ESTs).*

Addressing the "Ultimate Question"

Research is needed to discover which combinations of therapists, clients, and treatments are ideally suited to alleviating particular psychological problems. Several factors, including personal preferences, must be considered when choosing a treatment approach and a therapist.

Cultural Factors in Psychotherapy

The effects of cultural differences in values and goals between therapist and client have attracted increasing attention. Efforts are under way to minimize the problems that these differences can create.

Rules and Rights in the Therapeutic Relationship

Whatever the specific form of treatment, the client's rights include the right to confidentiality; the right to receive or, sometimes, to refuse treatment; and the right to protection from unnecessary confinement.

Biological Treatments

Biological treatment methods seek to relieve psychological disorders by physical rather than psychological means.

Electroconvulsive Therapy

In *electroconvulsive therapy (ECT),* an electric current is passed through the patient's brain, usually in an effort to relieve severe depression.

Psychosurgery

Psychosurgery procedures once involved mainly prefrontal lobotomy; when used today, usually as a last resort, they focus on more limited areas of the brain.

Psychoactive Drugs

Today the most prominent form of biological treatment is the prescription of psychoactive drugs, including drugs that are used to treat schizophrenia (the *neuroleptics,* or antipsychotics), mood disorders (*antidepressants, lithium,* and *anticonvulsants*), and anxiety disorders (*anxiolytics*). There appear to be significant differences among members of various ethnic groups and between men and women in the dosages of psychoactive drugs necessary to produce clinical effects.

Evaluating Psychoactive Drug Treatments

Psychoactive drugs have proven impressively effective in many cases, but critics point out a number of undesirable side effects associated with these drugs, the risks of abuse, and the dangers of overreliance on chemical approaches to human problems that might have other solutions.

Drugs and Psychotherapy

So far, neither psychotherapy nor drug treatment has been found clearly superior overall for treating problems such as anxiety or depression. Combining drugs and psychotherapy may help in some cases, but their joint effect may not be any greater than the effect of either one alone.

Community Psychology: From Treatment to Prevention

The realization that there will never be enough therapists to treat everyone who needs help prompted the development of *community psychology.* Community mental health programs and efforts to prevent mental disorders are the two main elements of community psychology.

Social Behaviour

17

Your view of yourself, and what you think about others, play major roles in shaping your behaviour every day. In this chapter, we explore the ways in which perception, learning, emotion, and other factors affect how people think about themselves and others. We'll consider topics such as how we form first impressions, how we develop attitudes—including prejudiced attitudes—and why we may like (or love) one person and dislike another. In addition, if you are like most people, there is probably at least one thing you do in private that you would never do when someone else is around. We also describe many other ways in which the presence and behaviour of other people affect our own behaviour, and how we, in turn, affect the behaviour of others. Here's how we have organized our presentation:

On September 11, 2001, terrorists who had hijacked American Airlines Flight 11 crashed the plane into the north tower of New York City's World Trade Center. Fifteen minutes later, another team of hijackers flew United Airlines Flight 175 into the Trade Center's south tower. Less than an hour later, a third group of terrorists flew American Airlines Flight 77 into the Pentagon building, in Washington, D.C. Another target in Washington was spared only because courageous passengers on a fourth hijacked plane realized what was happening and attacked the hijackers. That plane, United Airlines Flight 93, crashed in a Pennsylvania field, killing everyone aboard. The death toll in all four locations exceeded 3000.

Almost all of the questions that can be asked about this horrendous tragedy, and about terrorism in general, relate to human behaviour. For example, what could lead people to kill themselves, along with thousands of innocent people, in the name of political or religious beliefs? Why did hundreds of firefighters, police officers, emergency medical workers, and others enter the World Trade Center's burning towers to save the lives of others while risking, and some ultimately losing, their own? Why did some of the people who were fleeing the damaged buildings return to their offices after hearing an announcement telling them to do so? Is there any reason to hope that someday the hatred and distrust that brought about this disaster can be reduced or eliminated?

We may never have final answers to such questions, but some partial answers may come from **social psychology,** the scientific study of how people's thoughts and feelings influence their behaviour toward others and how the behaviour of others influences people's own thoughts, feelings, and behaviour. In this chapter we focus on **social cognition,** the mental processes associated with the ways in which people perceive and react to other individuals and groups (Wyer, 2004). Specifically, we will examine how people think about themselves and others, how they form and change attitudes, why and how they use stereotypes to judge other people (sometimes in unfair and biased ways), and why they like and dislike other people. We also describe how social factors affect individuals (**social influence**), helping to shape behaviours that range from despicable acts of aggression to inspiring acts of heroism and self-sacrifice.

Social Influences on the Self

In the chapters on human development and personality, we describe how each individual develops within a cultural context and the ways in which collectivist and individualist cultures emphasize different core values and encourage contrasting definitions of the self. In this section we highlight the processes whereby the people in each culture help to shape two important components of the self. The first is our **self-concept,** the beliefs we hold about who we are and what characteristics we have. The second is our **self-esteem,** the evaluations we make about how worthy we are as human beings (Crocker & Park, 2004).

social psychology The study of how people's thoughts, feelings, and behaviour influence, and are influenced by, the behaviour of others.

social cognition Mental processes associated with people's perceptions of, and reactions to, other people.

social influence The process whereby one person's behavoiur is affected by the words or actions of others

self-concept The way one thinks of oneself.

self-esteem The evaluations people make about how worthy they are as human beings.

Social Comparison

People spend a lot of time thinking about themselves, trying to evaluate their own perceptions, opinions, values, abilities, and the like (Mussweiler, 2003). Decades ago, Leon Festinger (1954) pointed out that self-evaluation involves two types of questions: those that can be answered by taking objective measurements and those that cannot. So you can determine your height or weight by measuring it, but how

The Muhammad Ali Effect When former heavyweight boxing champion of the world Muhammad Ali was once asked why he did so poorly on an intelligence test, he replied, "I only said I was the greatest, not the smartest." Research in the United States and in Holland suggests that most people, like Ali, consider it more important to be moral and honest than to be smart. They also believe that they are more honest than other people. This helps to maintain self-esteem (Van Lange & Sedikides, 1998).

do you answer questions about your mental ability, social skills, athletic talent, or the quality of your relationships? Here, there are no yardsticks to act as objective measurement criteria. In these cases, we make one of two types of comparisons. If we use a **temporal comparison**, we consider the way we are now in relation to how we were in the past (Wilson & Ross, 2000). Using a **social comparison,** we evaluate ourselves in relation to others. So if you use others as a basis for evaluating how intelligent, athletic, interesting, or attractive you are, you are using social comparison (Buunk & Ybema, 2003).

Who serves as your basis of comparison? Festinger said that people usually look to others who are similar to themselves. If you are curious about how good a swimmer you are, you are likely to compare yourself with the people you normally compete against, not with Olympic champions. In other words, you tend to choose swimmers at your own level of experience and ability (Mussweiler, 2003). The categories of people to which you see yourself belonging and to which you usually compare yourself are called **reference groups.**

An unfavourable comparison of your own status with that of others can produce **relative deprivation**—the belief that no matter how much you are getting in terms of recognition, status, money, and so forth, it is less than you deserve (Buunk et al., 2003). The concept of relative deprivation explains why an actor who receives $5 million to star in a film feels abused if a costar is receiving $10 million. It also explains the far more common situation in which employees become dissatisfied when they see themselves as underpaid or underappreciated in comparison to their co-workers (Feldman & Turnley, 2004). When large groups of people experience relative deprivation, political unrest may follow. Social and political turmoil usually begins after the members of a deprived group experience some improvement in their lives and begin to compare their circumstances with those in other groups (Worchel et al., 2000). With this improvement comes higher expectations about what they deserve. When these expectations are not met, violence may follow (Plous & Zimbardo, 2004).

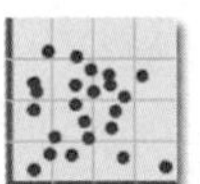

FOCUS ON RESEARCH METHODS

Self-Esteem and the Ultimate Terror

Why is self-esteem so important to so many people? An intriguing answer to this question comes from the *terror management theory* proposed by Jeff Greenberg, Tom Pyszczynski, and Sheldon Solomon. This theory is based on the notion that humans are the only creatures capable of thinking about the future. One result of this ability is the realization that we will all eventually die, and the sense of terror it may bring. We can't change this reality, but terror management theory suggests that humans cope with anxiety about death by developing a variety of self-protective psychological strategies, including efforts to establish and maintain high self-esteem (Greenberg, Pyszczynski, & Solomon, 2003; Pyszczynski et al., 2004).

- **What was the researchers' question?**

In one series of experiments, Jeff Greenberg and his colleagues (1992) asked whether high self-esteem would, in fact, serve as a buffer against anxiety—specifically, the anxiety brought on by thoughts about death and pain.

- **How did the researchers answer the question?**

About 150 students at several North American universities participated in these studies, each of which followed a similar format. The first step in each experiment was to manipulate the independent variable, in this case the participants' self-esteem. To do this, the researchers gave the students feedback on a test they had

temporal comparison Using one's previous performance or characteristics as a basis for judging oneself in the present.

social comparison Using other people as a basis of comparison for evaluating oneself.

reference groups Categories of people to which people compare themselves.

relative deprivation The belief that, in comparison to a reference group, one is getting less than is deserved.

taken earlier in the semester. Half the participants received esteem-building feedback, such as that their scores indicated high intelligence or a stable personality. The other half received feedback that was neutral (i.e., neither flattering nor demeaning). Next, the students' self-esteem was measured, and these measures showed that the positive feedback actually did produce higher self-esteem than the neutral feedback. In the third phase of each experiment, the researchers manipulated a second independent variable by provoking some anxiety in half of the participants in each of the two feedback groups. In one study, for example, anxiety was created by showing some students a film containing pictures of dead people and discussions of death. The others saw a film that did not arouse emotion. In two other experiments, anxiety was created by leading some of the participants to believe (falsely) that they would be receiving a mild electrical shock. Afterward, the participants' anxiety was measured by their self-reports or by monitoring galvanic skin resistance (GSR), an anxiety-related measure of perspiration (Dawson, Schell, & Fillon, 2000).

What did the researchers find?

Self-reports or GSR measures revealed that participants in all three experiments were significantly less upset by an anxiety-provoking experience (the death film or the threat of shock) if they had first received esteem-building feedback about their previous test performance.

What do the results mean?

The researchers concluded that these results offer support for terror management theory, and specifically for the notion that self-esteem is important as a buffer against anxiety and other negative feelings. The results may help explain why the maintenance of self-esteem is such a powerful human motive (Tesser, 2001). People do not like to feel anxious, and increased self-esteem reduces most people's anxiety.

What do we still need to know?

Additional research by Greenberg and his associates, as well as by others, has provided additional support for terror management theory. For instance, the theory predicts that when people are sensitized to the threat of death, they will seek to protect themselves by suppressing thoughts of death and also by doing prosocial things that increase the approval and support of others in the society in which they live. Consistent with this prediction, people have been found to make larger contributions to charity after they have been made more aware of their own mortality (Jonas et al., 2002). Similarly, dramatic increases in volunteering for charity work occurred after the events of September 11, 2001 (Penner et al., in press).

But which esteem-building strategies are people most likely to use, and why? Are some strategies more or less likely to be adopted at different times in a person's life or among people in certain cultures? Most of the research on terror management theory has been done in individualistic cultures such as North America, in which self-esteem is largely based on personal accomplishments.

However, terror management theory has also been supported by preliminary studies in Japan, aboriginal Australia, and other collectivist cultures in which feelings of self-worth tend to be more closely tied to the performance and status of the groups to which people belong (Halloran & Kashima, 2004; Heine, Harihara, & Niiya, 2002).

Researchers also wonder whether terror management theory offers the best explanation of why high self-esteem reduces anxiety. Perhaps people value self-esteem not because it makes them less afraid of death but simply because it is a flattering indicator (a sort of "sociometer") of their acceptance by others (Leary, 2004). According to sociometer theory, people want to have high self-esteem because it tells them that they are liked and accepted. Perhaps the goal of acceptance evolved because people who were excluded from the protective circle of their group were not likely to survive to reproduce. Compared with terror management

Social Identity With their tall hats, facial makeup, and colourful pajama suits, these fans must carry a deep sense of pride in both their province and their nation. They each identify very closely with their team, which is why they look alike and dress alike.

theory, sociometer theory is certainly a simpler and more plausible explanation of the desire for high self-esteem, but is it the best explanation? Both theories make similar predictions about the effects of self-esteem on anxiety, so it will take additional research to evaluate their relative merits.

Social Identity Theory

Stop reading for a moment, and fill in the blank in the following sentence: "I am a(n)____."

Some people complete the sentence by using characteristics such as "I am Canadian," "a hard worker," "a good sport," or some other aspect of their *personal* identity. However, many others identify themselves by using a word or phrase that reflects their nationality, gender, or religion (e.g., Lee & Yoo, 2004). These responses reflect **social identity,** our beliefs about the groups to which we belong. Our social identity is thus part of our self-concept (Troop & Wright, 2001).

Our social, or group, identity permits us to feel part of a larger whole (Ashmore, Deaux, & McLaughlin-Volpe, 2004). Its importance is seen in the pride that people feel when a member of their family graduates from college or when a local team wins a big game (Burris, Branscombe, & Klar, 1997). In wars between national, ethnic, or religious groups, individuals make sacrifices, and even die, for the sake of their group identity. A group identity is also one reason people donate money to those in need, support friends in a crisis, and display other helping behaviours toward those with whom they can identify. We will see later, though, that defining ourselves in terms of a group identity can create an "us-versus-them" mentality that sets the stage for prejudice, discrimination, intergroup conflict, and even terrorism (Brewer, 2001).

Self-Schemas

social identity The beliefs we hold about the groups to which we belong.

self-schemas Mental representations that people form of themselves.

Through social comparison and the formation of a social identity, people develop **self-schemas,** which are mental representations of their beliefs and views about themselves (Brehm, Kassin, & Fein, 2005). Like our social identity, self-schemas

All in the Family Many people find that their place in their family is a central aspect of their social identity. For others, their role in a political, religious, cultural, or business organization might be most vital to that identity. Whatever the specifics, social identity is an important part of people's self-concept, or view of themselves.

become part of our self-concept. Some people's self-schemas are relatively *unified.* That is, they tend to think of themselves as having more or less the same characteristics or attributes in every situation (at home, at a party, and so on) and in every role (as student, friend, or romantic partner). Other individuals have *differentiated* self-schemas. They tend to think of themselves as having different attributes in different roles or situations.

Social Perception

There is a story about a company president who was having lunch with a man being considered for an executive position. When the man salted his food without first tasting it, the president decided not to hire him. The reason, she explained, was that the company had no room for a person who acted before collecting all relevant information. The candidate lost his chance because of **social perception,** the process through which people interpret information about others, form impressions of them, and draw conclusions about the reasons for their behaviour. In this section we examine how and why social perception influences our thoughts, feelings, and actions.

The Role of Schemas

The perception of people follows many of the same laws that govern the perception of objects, including the Gestalt principles discussed in the chapter on perception. Consider Figure 17.1. Consistent with Gestalt principles, most people would describe it as "a square with a notch in one side," not as eight straight lines (Woodworth & Schlosberg, 1954). The reason is that they interpret new information using the mental representations, or *schemas,* they already have about squares. In short, they interpret this diagram as a square with a slight modification.

Schemas about people, too, can have a significant influence on our perception of them. First of all, schemas influence what we pay attention to and what we ignore. Characteristics or events that are consistent with our schema about another

social perception The processes through which people interpret information about others, draw inferences about them, and develop mental representations of them.

figure 17.1

A Schema-Plus-Correction

People who see an object like this tend to use a pre-existing mental representation (their schema of a square) and then correct or modify it in some way (here, with a notch).

person usually get more attention than those that are inconsistent with that schema. As a result, we tend to process information about the other person more quickly if it confirms our beliefs about, say, that person's gender or ethnic group than if it violates those beliefs (Smith & Queller, 2001). Second, schemas influence what we remember about others. One study demonstrated that if people thought a woman they saw in a videotape was a waitress, they later recalled that she had a beer with dinner and owned a TV set. If they thought she was a librarian, they remembered that she was wearing glasses and liked classical music (Cohen, 1981). Finally, schemas affect our judgment about other people's behaviour (Fiske, 1995). As an example, Thomas Hill and his colleagues (1989) found that participants' ratings of male and female friends' sadness were influenced not only by the friends' actual behaviour but also by the participants' general schemas about whether men or women experience more sadness.

So we don't usually ask our doctors or bus drivers to show us their credentials. Our schemas about these people lead us to perceive them as competent, confident, skilled, and experienced. And usually these perceptions are correct. It is only when our expectations are violated that we realize that schemas can create errors in our judgment about other people.

First Impressions

The schemas we have about people act as lenses that shape our first impressions of them. Those impressions, in turn, influence both our perceptions of their behaviours and our reactions to those behaviours. First impressions are formed quickly, usually change slowly, and typically have a long-lasting influence. No wonder first impressions are so important in the development of social relations (Brehm et al., 2005). How do people form impressions of other people? And why are they so resistant to change?

Forming Impressions Think about your first impression of a close friend. It probably formed rapidly, because as mentioned earlier, existing schemas create a tendency to automatically infer a great deal about a person on the basis of limited information (Smith & Queller, 2001). An ethnic name, for example, might have caused you to draw inferences about your friend's religion, food preferences, or temperament. Clothing or hairstyle might have led you to make assumptions about your friend's political views or taste in music. These inferences and assumptions may or may not have been accurate. How many turned out to be true in your friend's case?

One schema has a particularly strong influence on our first impressions: We tend to assume that people we meet will have attitudes and values similar to our own (Hoyle, 1993). So all else being equal, we are inclined to like other people. However, it doesn't take much negative information to change our minds. The main reason for this is that most of us don't expect other people to act negatively toward us. When unexpectedly negative behaviours do occur, they capture our attention and lead us to believe that these behaviours reflect something negative about the other person (Taylor, Peplau, & Sears, 2003). For example, we know that there are many reasons why people might be nice to us—because they are kind, because they like our best friends, or because they want to sell us a car. But if they do something negative—such as insult us or steal our lecture notes—the most likely explanation is that they are unfriendly or have other undesirable personality traits (Coovert & Reeder, 1990). In other words, negative behaviour carries more weight in shaping first impressions than does positive information (Smith & Mackie, 2000).

Lasting Impressions Does your friend seem the same today as when you met? First impressions can change, but the process is usually slow. One reason is that humans tend to be "cognitive misers" (Fiske, 1995). We cling to our beliefs

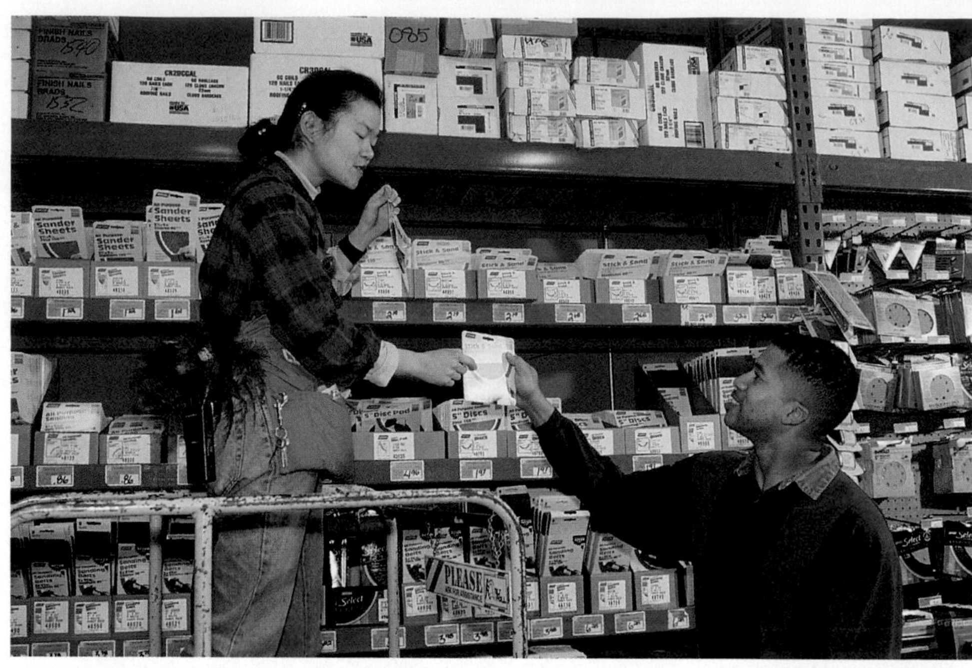

May I Help You? Schemas help us to quickly categorize people and respond appropriately to them, but they can also create narrow-mindedness and even prejudice. If this woman does not fulfill your schema—your mental representation—of how carpenters are supposed to look, you might be less likely to ask her advice on your home improvement project. One expert carpenter who manages the hardware department of a large home improvement store told us that most customers walk right past her in order to ask the advice of one of her less experienced male clerks.

about the world, often using our schemas to preserve a reality that fits our expectations. Holding on to existing impressions appears to be part of this effort. If your friend has recently said or done something that violates your expectations, your view of her probably did not change much, if at all. In fact, you may have acted to preserve your impression by thinking something like, "She's just not herself today." In other words, impressions are slow to change because the meaning we give to new information about people is shaped by what we already know or believe about them (Sherman & Klein, 1994).

Self-Fulfilling Prophecies in the Classroom If teachers inadvertently spend less time helping children who impressed them as "dull," those children may not learn as much, thus fulfilling the teachers' expectations. If the girl in the back row has not impressed this teacher as being bright, how likely do you think it is that she will be called on?

Self-Fulfilling Prophecies Another reason first impressions tend to be stable is that we often do things that cause others to confirm our impressions (Madon et al., 2001). If teachers expect particular students to do poorly in mathematics, those students may sense this expectation, exert less effort, and perform below their ability level. Similarly, if mothers expect their young children to eventually abuse alcohol, their children are more likely to do so than the children of mothers who didn't convey that expectation (Madon et al., 2003). When, without our awareness, schemas cause us to subtly lead people to behave in line with our expectations, a **self-fulfilling prophecy** is at work.

In one experiment on self-fulfilling prophecies, men and women participated in "get-acquainted" conversations over an intercom system. They could not see each other, but before the conversations took place, the men were shown photographs and told that they were pictures of their partners. Some saw a photograph of an obese woman, whereas others saw a picture of a woman of normal weight. In fact, the photographs bore no relationship to the women's actual appearance. Judges who had not seen any of the participants listened to tapes of the conversations and rated the women's behaviour and personalities. The women who had been portrayed as normal in weight were rated as more articulate, lively, interesting, exciting, and fun to be with. Apparently, when the men thought their partners were of normal weight, they were more friendly and engaging, and this behaviour drew more positive reactions from the women. In contrast, men who thought their partners were overweight behaved in ways that drew comparatively dull responses (Snyder & Haugen, 1995).

Self-fulfilling prophecies also help maintain judgments about groups. If you assume that members of a certain ethnic group are pushy or aggressive, for example, you might be defensive or even hostile toward them. Faced with this behaviour, members of the group might become frustrated and angry. In other words, their reactions would fulfill your prophecy and maintain the impressions that created it (Ross & Jackson, 1991).

Explaining Behaviour: Attribution

So far, we have considered how people form impressions about the characteristics of other people. But our perceptions of others include another key element: explanations of their behaviour. People tend to form *implicit theories* about why people (including themselves) behave as they do and about what behaviour to expect in the future. Psychologists use the term **attribution** to describe the process people go through to explain the causes of behaviour (including their own).

As an example, suppose a classmate fails to return some borrowed notes on time. You could attribute this behaviour to many causes, from an unavoidable emergency to simple selfishness. Which of these alternatives you choose is important because it will help you to *understand* your classmate's behaviour, *predict* what will happen if this person asks to borrow something in the future, and decide how to *control* the situation should it arise again. Similarly, whether a person attributes a spouse's nagging to temporary stress or to lack of affection can influence whether that person will work on the marriage or work to dissolve it.

People tend to attribute behaviour in a particular situation to either internal causes (characteristics of the person) or external causes (characteristics of the situation). If you thought your classmate's failure to return your notes was due to lack of consideration or laziness, you would be making an *internal attribution*. If you thought that the oversight was caused by time pressure or a family crisis, you would be making an *external attribution*. And if you failed an exam, you could explain it by concluding either that you're not very smart (internal attribution) or that your job responsibilities didn't leave you enough time to study (external attribution). The attribution that you make, in turn, might determine how much you study for the next exam or even whether you decide to stay in school.

self-fulfilling prophecy A process through which an initial impression of someone leads that person to behave in accordance with that impression.

attribution The process of explaining the causes of people's behaviour, including one's own.

Why Are They Helping? Helping occurs all around the world, but research shows that people's attributions, or explanations, about why it happens can differ from culture to culture.

Culture and Attribution Most theories of causal attribution were developed by North American psychologists who implicitly assumed that people all over the world use the same kinds of information to make similar kinds of attributions. However, there is substantial evidence to suggest that this may not be true (Lehman, Chiu, & Schaller, 2004). For example, Joan Miller and David Bersoff (1994) found that students from the United States and students from India made very different attributions about the reasons why people would do a favour for someone who had just helped them. The Americans attributed the behaviour to an external cause (feeling an obligation to repay a favour), but the Indians attributed it to an internal cause (liking to help people). Miller (1994) suggested that the differences in the two groups' responses reflected differences in their cultural experiences. The results of Miller and Bersoff's experiment highlight once again the danger of assuming that phenomena seen in the cultures of North Americans with European background can be generalized to all cultures. Cross-cultural differences in attribution and other aspects of social cognition may help to explain why people in different cultures sometimes have so much difficulty in understanding one another.

Biases in Attribution

Whatever their background, most people are usually logical in their attempts to explain behaviour (Trope, Cohen, & Alfieri, 1991). However, they are also sometimes prone to *attributional biases* that can distort their views of behaviour (Gilbert, 1998).

The Fundamental Attribution Error North American psychologists have paid special attention to the **fundamental attribution error,** a tendency to overattribute the behaviour of others to internal factors, such as personality traits (Gilbert & Malone, 1995). Imagine that you hear a student give an incorrect answer in class. You will probably attribute this behaviour to an internal cause and assume that the person is not very smart. In doing so, however, you might be failing to consider the possible influence of various external causes, such as lack of study time.

A related form of cognitive bias is called the **ultimate attribution error.** Through this error, when members of a social or ethnic *out-group* (people we see as "different") do something positive, we attribute their behaviour to luck or some other

fundamental attribution error A bias toward overattributing the behaviour of others to internal causes.

ultimate attribution error A bias wherein we overattribute internal causes to members of the out-group.

Attributional Bias Men whose thinking is coloured by the ultimate attribution error might assume that women who succeed at tasks associated with traditional male gender roles (e.g., fixing a car) are just lucky, but that men succeed at those tasks because of their skill (Deaux & LaFrance, 1998). When this attributional bias is in operation, people who are perceived as belonging to an out-group, whether on the basis of their gender, age, sexual orientation, religion, ethnicity, or other characteristics, may be denied fair evaluations and equal opportunities.

external cause. But we attribute their negative behaviour to an internal cause, such as dishonesty (Pettigrew, 1979). At the same time, when members of an *in-group* (people we see as like ourselves) do good deeds, we attribute the behaviour to integrity or other internal factors. If they do something bad, we attribute it to some external cause. Because of the ultimate attribution error, members of the out-group receive little credit for their positive actions, and members of the in-group get little blame for their negative actions. Biases such as the ultimate attribution error help maintain people's negative views of out-groups and positive views of their own in-group (Fiske, 1998).

Like other aspects of social cognition, the fundamental attribution error may not be universal (Sabini, Siepmann, & Stein, 2001). Researchers have found, for example, that people in collectivist cultures such as India, China, Japan, and Korea are less likely than those in the individualist cultures of North America and Europe to attribute people's behaviour to internal causes. Instead, these people tend to see behaviour as due to an interaction between individual characteristics and the situations or contexts in which the person is immersed (Lehman, Chiu, & Schaller, 2004).

Researchers have also pointed out that attributing behaviour to internal causes may not always be an "error." In some circumstances, an internal attribution may simply be the most reasonable attribution to make, given the information available to us (Sabini et al., 2001). Further, David Funder (2001b) has argued that, in many situations, personality characteristics and other internal factors are indeed the true causes of behaviour. In other words, according to Funder, social perception is much more accurate than many psychologists have previously recognized.

Other Attributional Biases The inclination toward internal attributions is much less pronounced when people explain their own behaviour. Here, in fact, another bias tends to come into play: the **actor-observer bias.** Whereas people often attribute other people's behaviour to internal causes, they tend to attribute their own behaviour to external factors, especially when the behaviour is inappropriate or inadequate (Knobe & Malle, 2002). For example, when you drive slowly, you're doing it because you are looking for an address, not because you're a dimwitted loser like that jerk who crawled along in front of you yesterday.

The actor-observer bias occurs mainly because people have different kinds of information about their own behaviour and about others' behaviour. When *you* are acting in a situation—giving a speech, perhaps—the stimuli that are most noticeable to you are likely to be external and situational, such as the temperature of the room and the size of the audience. You also have a lot of information about other external factors, such as the amount of time you had to prepare your talk or the upsetting argument that occurred this morning. If your speech is disorganized and boring, you can easily attribute it to one or all of these external causes. But when you observe someone else, the most noticeable stimulus in the situation is *that person.* You do not know what happened to the person last night or this morning, so you are likely to attribute whatever he or she does to enduring internal characteristics (Gilbert, 1998).

Of course, people do not always attribute their own behaviour to external forces. In fact, the degree to which they do so depends on whether the outcome of their behaviour is positive or negative. In one study, when people were asked what they saw as the cause of their good and bad experiences when shopping online, they tended to take personal credit for positive outcomes but to blame the computer for the negative ones (Moon, 2003). In other words, these people showed a **self-serving bias,** the tendency to take personal credit for success but to blame external causes for failure. This tendency has been found in almost all cultures, but as with the fundamental attribution error, it is usually more pronounced among people from individualistic Western cultures than among those from collectivist Eastern cultures (Mezulis et al., 2004).

actor-observer bias The tendency to attribute other people's behaviour to internal causes while attributing one's own behaviour (especially errors and failures) to external causes.

self-serving bias The tendency to attribute one's successes to internal characteristics while blaming one's failures on external causes.

in review Some Biases in Social Perception

Bias	Description
Importance of first impression	Ambiguous information is interpreted in line with a first impression, and the initial schema is recalled better and more vividly than any later correction to it. Actions based on this impression may elicit behaviour that confirms it.
Fundamental attribution error	The tendency to attribute the behaviour of others to internal factors.
Ultimate attribution error	The tendency to overattribute internal causes to members of the out-group.
Actor-observer bias	The tendency for actors to attribute their own behaviour to external causes and for observers to attribute the behaviour of others to internal factors.
Self-serving bias	The tendency to attribute one's successes to internal factors and one's failures to external factors.
Unrealistic optimism	The tendency to assume that positive events are more likely, and negative events are less likely, to occur to oneself than to others.

PsychAssist: Fundamental Attribution Error

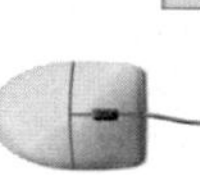

Attitudes

People's views about health or safety reflect their *attitudes,* an aspect of social cognition that social psychologists have studied longer and more intensely than any other. An **attitude** is the tendency to think, feel, or act positively or negatively toward objects in our environment (Ajzen, 2001; Eagly & Chaiken, 1998). Attitudes play an important role in guiding how we act toward other people, what political causes we support, which products we buy, and countless other daily decisions.

The Structure of Attitudes

Social psychologists have long viewed attitudes as having three components (Schwarz & Bohner, 2001; see Figure 17.2). The *cognitive* component is a set of beliefs about the attitude object. The emotional, or *affective,* component includes feelings about the object. The *behavioural* component is the way people act toward the object. If these components were always in harmony, we would be able to predict people's behaviour toward the homeless, for example, on the basis of the thoughts or feelings they express and vice versa. This is often not the case, however (Bohner & Schwarz, 2001). Many people's positive thoughts and supportive emotions regarding homeless people are never translated into actions aimed at helping them.

What determines whether people's behaviour will be consistent with the cognitive and affective components of their attitudes? Several factors are important. For one thing, consistency is more likely when the person's thoughts and feelings (cognitive and affective components) are themselves in agreement (Lord, 1997). Second, consistency is more likely when the behavioural component of the attitude is in line

attitude A predisposition toward a particular cognitive, emotional, or behavioural reaction to objects.

figure 17.2

Three Components of an Attitude

Although made up of various constituent components, the components of an attitude may or may not be consistent with one another. For example, people may think that drunken driving is wrong (cognitive component) and be upset by its tragic consequences (affective component), yet they may still get behind the wheel after drinking too much (behavioural component).

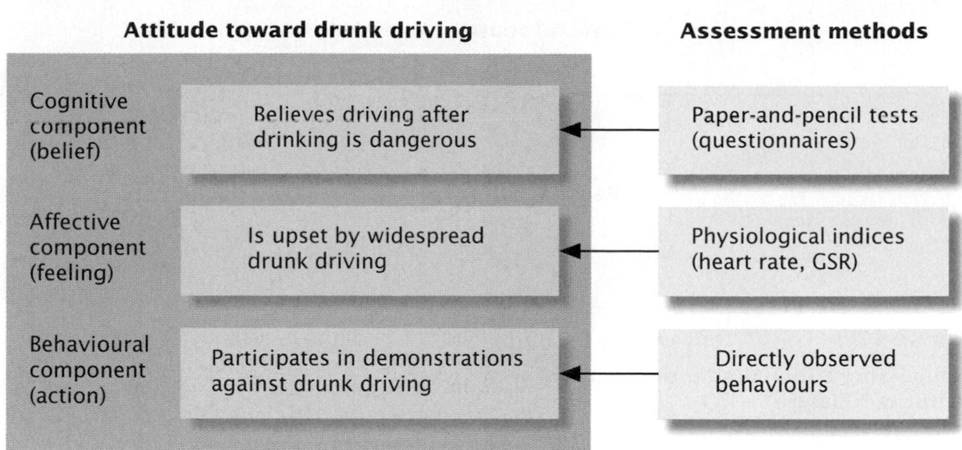

with a *subjective norm,* our view of how important people in our lives want us to act. Conflict between attitudes and subjective norms may cause us to behave in ways that are inconsistent with our attitudes (Ajzen, 2001). For example, someone who believes that the rights of gay men and lesbians should be protected might not campaign for this cause because doing so would upset family members or co-workers who are against it. Third, *direct experience* with the attitude object increases the likelihood of attitude-consistent behaviour (Bohner & Schwarz, 2001). This is because attitudes based on direct experiences are more stable and memorable and thus more likely to come into play when the attitude object is present. Accordingly, you might be more likely to actively support, and perhaps even participate in, efforts to help the homeless if you have come to know a homeless person on your campus than if you have only read about the plight of the homeless.

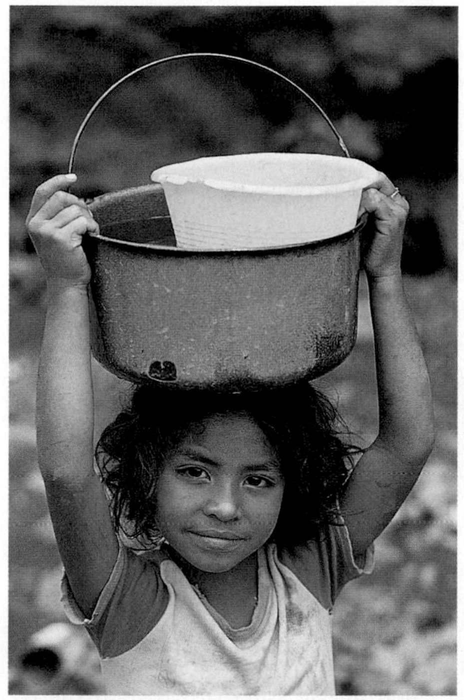

A Reminder about Poverty
Photographs such as this one are used by fund-raising organizations to remind us of the kind thoughts and charitable feelings we have toward needy people and other social causes. As a result, we may be more likely to behave in accordance with the cognitive and affective components of our attitudes and make a donation to these causes. Browse through several newspapers and popular magazines and calculate the percentage of such photos you find in ads for charitable organizations.

Forming Attitudes

People are not born with specific attitudes toward specific objects, but their attitudes about new objects begin to appear in early childhood and continue to emerge throughout life. How do attitudes form? Some of the variation we see in people's attitudes may reflect genetic influences inherited from their parents (Abrahamson, Baker, & Caspi, 2002), but what they *learn* from their parents and others appears to play the major role in attitude formation. In childhood, modelling and other forms of social learning are especially important. Children learn not only the names of objects but also what they should believe and feel about them and how they should act toward them. For example, a parent may teach a child not only that snakes are reptiles but also that they should be feared and avoided. So as children learn concepts such as "reptile" or "work," they learn attitudes about those concepts, too (Bohner & Schwarz, 2001).

Attitudes can also be influenced by classical and operant conditioning. In one study demonstrating this process, certain cartoon characters were associated with positive words (e.g., *excellent*) and images (e.g., an ice cream sundae), whereas others were associated with negative words and images (Olson & Fazio, 2001). Afterward, participants in this study liked the characters associated with the positive stimuli much more than those associated with the negative ones. No wonder so many advertisers present enjoyable music or attractive images in association with the products they are trying to sell (Aronson, Wilson, & Akert, 2002; Pratkanis & Aronson, 1991)! As for operant conditioning, parents, teachers, and peers actively shape children's attitudes by rewarding them for stating particular views. The *mere-exposure effect* is influential as well: All else being equal, attitudes toward an object will become more positive the more frequently people are exposed to it (Zajonc,

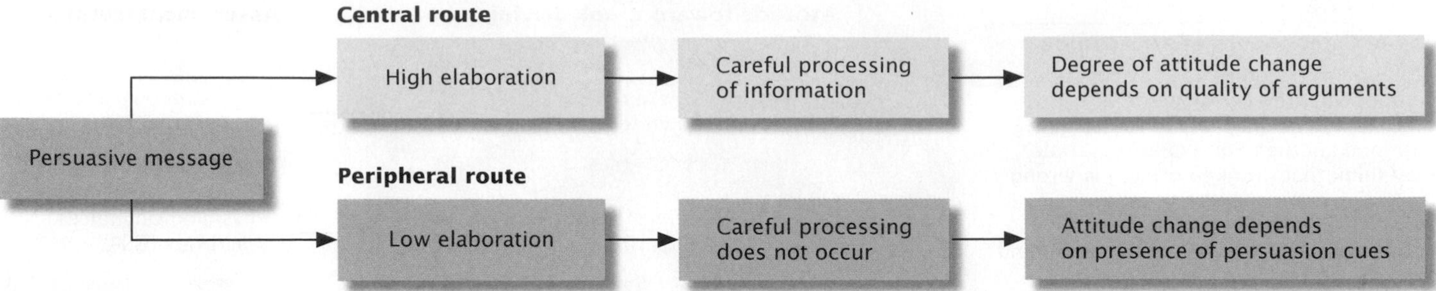

figure 17.3

The Elaboration Likelihood Model of Attitude Change

The central route to attitude change involves carefully processing and evaluating the content of a message (high elaboration). The peripheral route involves low elaboration, or processing, of the message and relying on persuasion cues such as the attractiveness of the person making the argument (Cacioppo, Petty, & Crites, 1993).

2001). One study found that even newborns showed a preference for stories that their mother had repeatedly read aloud while they were still in the womb (Cacioppo, Berntson, & Petty, 1997). The mere-exposure effect helps explain why we sometimes come to like a song only after hearing it several times—and why commercials are aired over and over.

Changing Attitudes

The $9.1 billion a year spent on advertising in Canada provides just one example of how people are constantly trying to change our attitudes (Interactive Advertising Bureau of Canada, 2006).

Stop for a moment and make a list of other examples, perhaps starting with the messages of groups concerned with global warming or recycling—and don't forget your friends who want you to think the way they do.

Two Routes to Attitude Change Whether a persuasive message succeeds in changing attitudes depends primarily on three factors: (1) the person communicating the message, (2) the content of the message, and (3) the audience who receives it (Bohner & Schwarz, 2001). The **elaboration likelihood model** of attitude change provides a framework for understanding when and how these factors affect attitude change. As shown in Figure 17.3, the model is based on the notion that persuasive messages can change people's attitudes through one of two main routes.

The first is called the *peripheral route* because, when it is activated, we devote little attention to the central content of the persuasive message. Instead, we tend to be affected by the *persuasion cues* that surround it, such as the confidence, attractiveness, or other characteristics of the person delivering the message. Persuasion cues influence attitude change even though they say nothing about the logic or validity of the message content. Commercials in which movie stars or other attractive non-experts praise pain relievers or political candidates are designed to operate via the peripheral route to attitude change.

By contrast, when the *central route* to attitude change is activated, the content of the message becomes more important than the characteristics of the communicator in determining attitude change. A person following the central route uses logical steps—such as those outlined in the Thinking Critically sections of this book—to rationally analyze the content of the persuasive message. This analysis considers the validity of the message's claims, determines whether the message leaves out important information, assesses alternative interpretations of evidence, and so on.

elaboration likelihood model A model suggesting that attitude change can be driven by evaluation of the content of a persuasive message (central route) or by irrelevant persuasion cues (peripheral route).

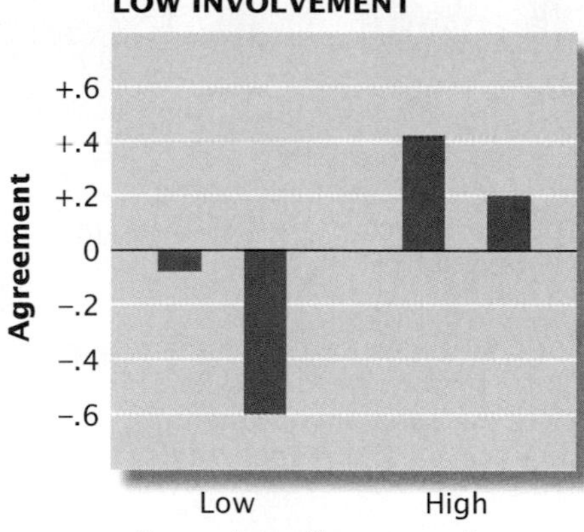

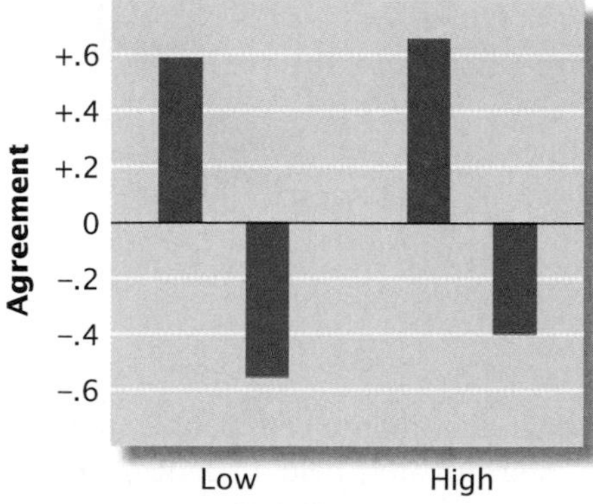

Strong arguments   Weak arguments

figure 17.4

Personal Involvement and Routes to Attitude Change

In the study represented here, students' reactions to messages supporting exit exams for students in fourth year depended on whether they thought the policy would begin immediately (high involvement) or only after they had graduated (low involvement). In the low-involvement condition, students followed a peripheral route to attitude change, agreeing with messages from expert communicators regardless of how logical they were. More involved students followed a central route, changing their minds only if the message contained a strong, logical argument.

Source: Data from Petty, Cacioppo, & Goldman

What determines which route people will follow? Personal involvement with the content of the message is one important factor. The elaboration likelihood model proposes that the more personally involving a topic is, the more likely it is that the central route will be activated (Petty & Wegener, 1998; Wood, 2000). Suppose, for example, that you heard someone arguing for the elimination of student loans in Chile. This message might persuade you via the peripheral route if it came from someone who looked attractive and sounded intelligent. However, you would be more likely to follow the central route if the message proposed doing away with student loans at your own school. You might be persuaded, but only if the logic of the message was undeniable (see Figure 17.4). This is why celebrity endorsements tend to be most effective when the products being advertised are relatively unimportant to the audience.

"Cognitive busyness" is another factor affecting which attitude-change route is activated. If you are busy thinking about other things while a message is being delivered, you will be unable to pay much attention to its content. In this case, activation of the peripheral route becomes more likely. Personality characteristics are also related to attitude-change processes. For example, people with a strong *need for cognition* like to engage in thoughtful mental activities and are therefore more likely to use the central route to attitude change (Suedfeld & Tetlock, 2001). In contrast, people whose discomfort with uncertainty creates a *need for closure* are more likely to use the peripheral route (Cacioppo et al., 1996).

Persuasive messages are not the only means of changing attitudes. Another approach is to get people to act in ways that are inconsistent with their current attitudes in the hope that they will adjust those attitudes to match their behaviour. Often, such adjustments do occur. Cognitive dissonance theory attempts to explain why.

Cognitive Dissonance Theory

Leon Festinger's (1957) classic **cognitive dissonance theory** holds that people want their thoughts, beliefs, and attitudes to be consistent with one another and with their behaviour. When people experience inconsistency, or *dissonance,* among these elements, they become anxious and are motivated to make them more consistent (Elliot & Devine, 1994; Harmon-Jones et al., 1996). For example, someone who believes that "smoking is unhealthy" but must also acknowledge that "I smoke" would be motivated to reduce the resulting dissonance. Because it is often difficult to change behaviour, people usually reduce cognitive dissonance by changing inconsistent attitudes. So rather than quit smoking, the smoker might decide that smoking is not so dangerous.

In one of the first studies of cognitive dissonance, Festinger and his colleague Merrill Carlsmith (Festinger & Carlsmith, 1959) asked people to turn pegs in a board, a very dull task. Later, some of these people were asked to persuade a person waiting to participate in the study that the task was "exciting and fun." Some were told that they would be paid $1 to tell this lie; others were promised $20. After they had talked to the waiting person, their attitudes toward the dull task were measured.

Figure 17.5 shows the surprising results. The people who were paid just $1 to lie liked the dull task more than those who were paid $20. Why? Festinger and Carlsmith (1959) argued that telling another person that a boring task is enjoyable will produce dissonance (between the thoughts "I think the task is boring" and "I am saying it is fun"). To reduce this dissonance, the people who were paid just $1 adopted a more favourable attitude toward the task, making their cognitions consistent: "I think the task is fun" and "I am saying it is fun." But if a person has adequate justification for the behaviour, any dissonance that exists will be reduced simply by thinking about the justification. The participants who were paid $20 thought they had adequate justification for lying and so did not need to change their attitudes toward the task.

cognitive dissonance theory A theory asserting that attitude change is driven by efforts to reduce tension caused by inconsistencies between attitudes and behaviours.

in review Forming and Changing Attitudes

Type of Influence	Description
Modelling and conditioning	Attitudes are usually formed through observation of how others behave and speak about an attitude object, as well as through classical and operant conditioning.
Elaboration likelihood model	People change attitudes through either a central or peripheral route, depending on factors such as personal involvement, "cognitive busyness," and personality characteristics.
Cognitive dissonance	Inconsistencies between attitudes and behaviours can produce attitude change.

PsychAssist: Cognitive Dissonance Theory

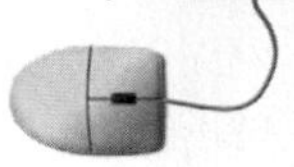

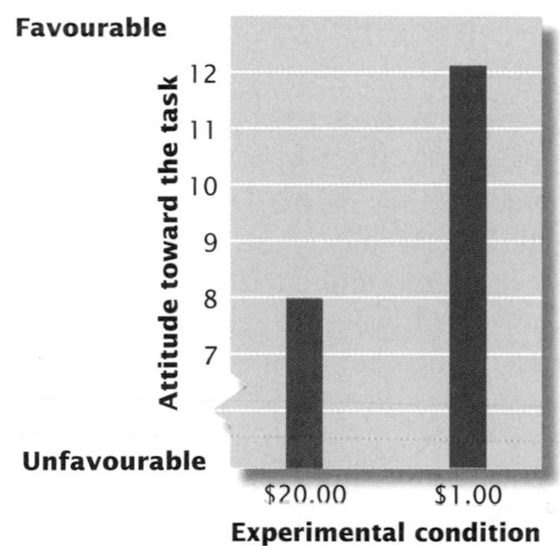

figure 17.5

Cognitive Dissonance and Attitude Change

According to cognitive dissonance theory, people who were paid $20 to say a boring task was enjoyable had clear justification for lying, so they should experience little dissonance between what they said and what they thought about the task. In fact, their attitudes toward the task did not change much. However, participants who received just $1 had little justification to lie and reduced their dissonance mainly by displaying a more positive attitude toward the task.

Hundreds of other experiments have also found that when people publicly engage in behaviours that are inconsistent with their privately held attitudes, they are likely to change their attitudes to be consistent with their behaviour (Stone & Cooper, 2001). These experiments have also found that behaviour-attitude inconsistency will produce attitude change when (1) the inconsistency causes some distress or discomfort and (2) changing attitudes will reduce this distress or discomfort. But what causes the discomfort in the first place? There is considerable debate among attitude researchers about this question (Wood, 2000).

Currently, the most popular of several possible answers is that discomfort results when people's positive self-concept is threatened by the recognition that they have done something inconsistent with that self-concept. For example, if they have encouraged another person to do something that they themselves didn't believe in or that they themselves wouldn't do, this inconsistency makes most people feel uncomfortable, so they change their attitudes to reduce or eliminate such feelings (Stone & Cooper, 2001; Stone, 2003). If people can persuade themselves that they really believed in what they did, the perceived inconsistency disappears, and their positive self-concepts are restored. Changing one's private attitude to match one's public actions is one way to accomplish this self-persuasion.

The impact of attitude-behaviour inconsistencies on attitude change may be greater in individualist cultures of Europe and North America than in collectivist cultures such as Japan and China (e.g., Heine & Lehman, 1997). Where group rather than individual identities are emphasized, behaving at odds with one's personal beliefs may create less discomfort—and thus less motivation for attitude change—because holding to those beliefs tends to be less important for self-esteem. However, a study by Shinobu Kitayama and his colleagues (Kitayama et al., 2004) suggests that people from a collectivist culture (Japan) are likely to experience dissonance and attitude change if they are sensitized to other people's possible reactions to their behaviour.

LINKAGES
Biological and Social Psychology

Social psychologists' research on thoughts, feelings, and behaviours was once entirely separate from research on the biological processes that underlie those thoughts, feelings, and behaviours (Winkielman, Berntson, & Cacioppo, 2001). Social psychologists believed that it was not possible to reduce complex social psychological processes to the firing of neurons or the secretion of hormones. For their part, biological psychologists, more commonly known as *neuroscientists,* viewed the study of social psychology as having little, if any, relevance to the understanding of behavioural genetics or the functioning of the nervous, endocrine, or immune systems. Recently, however, scientists in both subfields have begun to take a closer look at each other's research and how their subfields are related. The result has been the emergence of a new specialty called *social neuroscience* or *social cognitive neuroscience* (Adolphs, 2003; Cacioppo, 2002; Heatherton, Macrae, & Kelley, 2004). This new specialty focuses on the influence of social processes on biological processes and on the influence of biological processes on social psychological phenomena.

There are many reasons to believe that this approach will be valuable. For example, the chapter on health, stress, and coping contains numerous examples of how social stressors can have health-related biological consequences. Health psychologists have also found that the quality of a person's social relationships can affect biological processes ranging from the functioning of the immune system to the healing of wounds (Kiecolt-Glaser et al., 1998; Uchino, Cacioppo, & Kiecolt-Glaser, 1996; Robles & Kiecolt-Glaser, 2003). The social environment can affect even the way genes express themselves. In one study, for example, monkeys were selectively bred to react strongly to even mild stressors. These animals' oversensitivity appeared to be based on a specific gene, but researchers found it possible to modify the effects of this gene by changing the monkeys' social situation. When the animals were paired with a warm, nurturant foster mother, their oversensitivity diminished significantly, and it remained low even when they were later separated from her (Suomi, 1991, 1999).

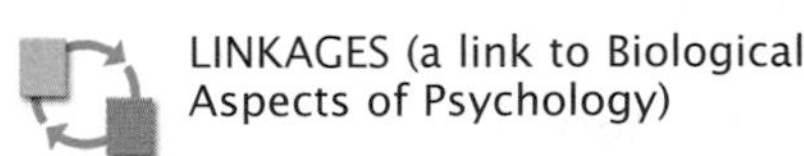

Researchers are also beginning to identify the biological underpinnings of many social processes. One example can be seen in studies of how the amygdala—a brain structure that plays a significant role in emotion—is related to the stereotypes and prejudice described in the next section. Using functional magnetic resonance imaging technology, researchers found that Americans of European background who were prejudiced against African Americans showed significantly more amygdala activity when looking at pictures of black people than when looking at pictures of white people (Hart et al., 2000; Phelps et al., 2000). More recently, researchers in Switzerland (de Quervain et al., 2004) have used positron emission tomography (PET scans) to study the brain activity associated with helping others. They found that the brain activity accompanying helpful acts is similar to that seen in people who are being rewarded, suggesting that engaging in such behaviours may be biologically rewarding. Social neuroscientists have also used electroencephalography (EEG) and other techniques to record the brain activity associated with positive and negative attitudes about people and objects (e.g., Amodio et al., 2004). Their research has shown that these evaluative reactions are associated with activity in specific brain regions (Cacioppo, Crites, & Gardner, 1996).

Social cognitive neuroscience is still in its infancy; the first conference devoted to research in this specialty did not occur until April 2001 (Ochsner & Lieberman, 2001). However, that research shows great promise for creating a better understanding of the linkages among social, cognitive, and biological phenomena, as well as a better understanding of complex social and physiological processes.

Prejudice and Stereotypes

All of the principles that underlie impression formation, attribution, and attitudes come together to create prejudice and stereotypes. As the cognitive component of prejudicial attitudes, **stereotypes** are the perceptions, beliefs, and expectations a person has about members of some group; they are schemas about entire groups of people (Dion, 2003). Usually, they involve the false assumption that all members of a group share the same characteristics. The characteristics that make up the stereotype can be positive, but they are usually negative. The most common and powerful stereotypes focus on observable personal attributes, particularly ethnicity, gender, and age (Operario & Fiske, 2001).

The stereotypes people hold can be so ingrained that their effects on behaviour can be automatic and unconscious (Banaji, Lemm, & Carpenter, 2001). In one study in the US, for example, Americans of European background and African American participants played a video game in which white or black men suddenly appeared on a screen holding objects that might be weapons (Correll et al., 2002; see Figure 17.6). The participants were instructed to immediately "shoot" an armed man, but not an unarmed one. Under this time pressure, the participants' errors were not random. If they "shot" an unarmed man, he was significantly more likely to be black than white. If they failed to "shoot" an armed man he was more likely to be white than black. These differences occurred among both Americans of European background and African American participants, but were most pronounced among those who held the strongest cultural stereotypes about blacks.

Stereotyping often leads to **prejudice** (the affective component), which is a positive or negative attitude toward an individual based simply on membership in some group (Dion, 2003). The literal meaning of the word *prejudice* is "prejudgment." Many theorists believe that prejudice, like other attitudes, has cognitive, affective, and behavioural components. Stereotyped thinking is the cognitive component of prejudicial attitudes. The hatred, admiration, anger, and other feelings people have about stereotyped groups make up the affective component. The behavioural component of prejudice involves **discrimination,** which is differing treatment of individuals who belong to different groups. As Western Ontario's Jim Olson and Brock University's Carolyn Hafer (2001) explain, discriminatory arrangements survive only because members within that arrangement come to accept it, and is often tolerated without much protest. Although this is a strong position, the authors support it based on (a) the members' belief that the world is a good and fair place, (b) the fact that members from the disadvantaged group rarely report discrimination, and (c) there are socially awkward implications of reporting incidents of discrimination. Even so, Wilfrid Laurier's Mindy Foster and Toronto's Kenneth Dion (2003, 2004) showed that the effect of discrimination seems to depend on the victim's personality.

Theories of Prejudice and Stereotyping

Prejudice and stereotyping may occur for several reasons (Duckitt, 1994). Let's consider three explanatory theories, each of which has empirical support and accounts for some, but not all, instances of stereotyping and prejudice.

Motivational Theories For some people, prejudice against certain groups might enhance their sense of security and help them meet certain personal needs. This idea was first proposed by Theodor Adorno and his associates more than 50 years ago (Adorno et al., 1950). It has since been revised and expanded by Bob Altemeyer (1996) at the University of Manitoba. Specifically, these researchers suggest that prejudice may be especially likely among people who display a personality trait called *authoritarianism.* According to Altemeyer, authoritarianism is composed of three elements: (1) an acceptance of conventional or traditional values, (2) a willingness to unquestioningly follow the orders of authority figures, and (3) an inclination to act

stereotypes False assumptions that all members of some group share the same characteristics; the cognitive component of prejudice.

prejudice A positive or negative attitude toward an entire group of people; the affective component of this attitude.

discrimination Differential treatment of various groups; the behavioural component of prejudice.

figure 17.6

The Impact of Stereotypes on Behaviour

When these men suddenly appeared on a video screen, participants were supposed to "shoot" them, but only if they appeared to be armed (Correll et al., 2002). Stereotypes about whether white men or black men are more likely to be armed significantly affected the errors made by participants in firing their video game "weapons." Cover each of these photos with an index card; then ask a few friends to watch as you reveal each of them for an instant before covering it again. Then ask your friends to say whether either man appeared to be armed. Was one individual more often seen as armed? If so, which one?

aggressively toward individuals or groups identified by these authority figures as threatening the values held by one's in-group. People with an authoritarian orientation tend to view the world as a threatening place (Winter, 1996), and one way to protect themselves from perceived threats is to identify strongly with their in-group and to reject, dislike, and perhaps even punish anyone who is a member of other groups. Looking down on, and discriminating against, out-groups—such as gay men and lesbians, African Canadians, or Aboriginals, for example—may help people with authoritarian tendencies to feel safer and feel better about themselves (Haddock & Zanna, 1998b).

A more recent motivational explanation of prejudice employs the concept of social identity discussed earlier. Recall that whether they are authoritarian or not, most people are motivated to identify with their in-group and tend to see it as better than other groups (Prentice & Miller, 2002). As a result, members of an in-group often see all members of out-groups as less attractive and less socially acceptable than in-group members and may thus treat them badly (Jackson, 2002). In other words, prejudice may result when people's motivation to enhance their own self-esteem causes them to disrespect other people.

Cognitive Theories Stereotyping and prejudice may also result from the social-cognitive processes people use in dealing with the world. There are so many other people, so many situations in which one meets them, and so many possible behaviours they might perform that we cannot possibly attend to and remember them all. Therefore, we use schemas and other cognitive shortcuts to organize and make sense out of our social world (Fiske, 1998). These cognitive processes allow us to draw accurate and useful conclusions about other people, but sometimes they lead to inaccurate stereotypes. For example, one effective way to deal with social complexity is to group people into *social categories.* Rather than remembering every detail about everyone we have ever encountered, we tend to put other people into categories, such as doctor, senior citizen, liberal, student, Italian, and the like (Dovidio, Kawakami, & Gaertner, 2000). To further simplify perception of these categories, we tend to see their members as being quite similar to one another. In fact, members of one ethnic group may find it harder to distinguish among specific faces within other ethnic groups than within their own group (Anthony, Cooper, & Mullen, 1992). People also tend to assume that all members of a different group share the same beliefs and values and that those beliefs and values differ from their own (Dion, 2003). Finally, as noted in the chapter on perception, people's attention tends to be drawn to distinctive stimuli. Rude behaviour by even a few members of an easily identified ethnic group may lead other people to see an *illusory correlation* between rudeness and ethnicity (Hamilton & Sherman, 1994). As a result, they may incorrectly believe that all members of that group are rude.

Learning Theories Like other attitudes, prejudice can be learned. Some prejudice is learned on the basis of conflicts between members of different groups, but people also develop negative attitudes toward groups with whom they have had little or no contact.

Learning theories suggest that children acquire prejudices just by watching and listening to parents, peers, and others (Rohan & Zanna, 1996). Movies and television may also portray ethnic or other groups in ways that teach stereotypes and prejudice (Smith & Mackie, 2000). Another American study revealed that local news coverage often gives the impression that African Americans are responsible for a higher percentage of crimes than is actually the case (Romer, Jamieson, & de Coteau, 1998). Consider the case of Saskatchewan Aboriginal Darrel Night (age 35 years) who spoke publically against the ill-treatment he received from two Saskatoon constables in the winter of 2000. Night was forced into a police cruiser and driven to the outskirts of the city before being dumped out in the freezing weather. Although the jury found the two veteran officers guilty of unlawful confinement, the Aboriginal

Schemas and Stereotypes The use of schemas to assign certain people to certain categories can be helpful when deciding who is a customer and who is a store employee, but it can also lead to inaccurate stereotypes. After the September 11, 2001, terrorist attacks on New York and Washington, D.C., many people began to think of all Muslims as potential terrorists and to discriminate against them. This false assumption and the problems it has created for Muslims around the world was one of the many awful side effects of the terrorist attacks.

community will likely still harbour negative beliefs about law enforcement in that province. Indeed, it is no wonder so many young children already know about the supposed negative characteristics of certain groups long before they ever meet members of those groups (Mackie et al., 1996; Quintana, 1998).

Reducing Prejudice

One clear implication of the cognitive and learning theories of prejudice and stereotyping is that members of one group are often ignorant or misinformed about the characteristics of people in other groups (Dovidio, Gaertner, & Kawakami, 2003). Before 1954, for example, most black and white children in the United States knew very little about one another because they went to separate schools. Then the Supreme Court declared that segregated public schools should be prohibited. By ruling segregation to be unconstitutional, the court created a real-life test of the **contact hypothesis,** which states that stereotypes and prejudice toward a group will diminish as contact with that group increases (Hewstone, 2003).

Did the desegregation of US schools confirm the contact hypothesis? In a few schools, integration was followed by a decrease in prejudice, but in most places either no change occurred or prejudice actually increased (Oskamp & Schultz, 1998). However, these results did not necessarily disprove the contact hypothesis. In-depth studies of schools in which desegregation was successful suggested that contact alone was not enough. Integration reduced prejudice only when certain social conditions were created (Pettigrew & Tropp, 2000). First, members of the two groups had to be of roughly equal social and economic status. Second, school authorities had to promote cooperation and interdependence between the members of different ethnic groups by having them work together on projects that required relying on one another to reach success. Third, the contact between group members had to occur on a one-on-one basis. It was only when people got to know one another as individuals that the errors contained in stereotypes became apparent. Finally, the members of each group had to be seen as typical and not unusual in any significant way. When these four conditions prevailed, the children's attitudes toward one another became more positive. The same effects have appeared in adults, and in other countries, too. In Italy, for example, people who had equal-status contact with black immigrants from North Africa displayed less prejudice against them than did Italians who had no contact with those immigrants (Kirchler & Zani, 1995).

contact hypothesis The idea that stereotypes and prejudice toward a group will diminish as contact with the group increases.

Elliot Aronson (1995) describes a teaching strategy, called the *jigsaw technique,* that helps create the conditions that reduce prejudice. The strategy calls for children

Fighting Ethnic Prejudice Negative attitudes about members of ethnic groups are often based on negative personal experiences or the negative experiences and attitudes people hear from others. Cooperative contact between equals can help promote mutual respect and reduce ethnic prejudice.

from several ethnic groups to work as a team to complete a task, such as writing a report about a famous person in history. Each child learns, and provides the team with, a separate piece of information about this person, such as place of birth (Aronson, 1990). Studies show that children from various ethnic groups who are exposed to the jigsaw technique and other cooperative learning experiences show substantial reductions in prejudice toward other groups (Aronson, 1997). The success reported in these studies has greatly increased the popularity of cooperative learning exercises in classrooms. Such exercises may not eliminate all aspects of ethnic prejudice in children, but they seem to be a step in the right direction.

Can friendly, cooperative, interdependent contact reduce the more entrenched forms of prejudice seen in adults? It may. When equal-status adults work jointly toward a common goal, bias and distrust can be reduced. This is especially true if they come to see themselves as members of the same group rather than as belonging to opposing groups (Dovidio, Kawakami, & Gaertner, 2000; Fiske, 2000). The challenge to be met in creating such cooperative experiences in the real world is that the participants must be of equal status—a challenge made more difficult in many countries by the sizable status differences that still exist among ethnic groups (Pettigrew & Tropp, 2000).

In the final analysis, contact provides only part of the solution to the problems of stereotyping, prejudice, and discrimination. To reduce ethnic prejudice, we must develop additional educational techniques that address the social cognitions and perceptions that lie at the core of bigotry and hatred toward people who are different from us (Monteith, Zuwerink, & Devine, 1994).

THINKING CRITICALLY

Is Ethnic Prejudice Too Ingrained Ever to Be Eliminated?

There is little doubt that overt forms of ethnic prejudice have decreased dramatically in North America over the past 40 to 50 years. For example, in the 1950s fewer than half of American university students of European background who were surveyed said they were willing to live in integrated neighbourhoods. Today, about 95 percent say they would be willing to do so. And four decades ago, fewer than 40 percent of respondents of European background from the United States said they would vote for a Black presidential candidate; over 95 percent now say they might do so (Dovidio & Gaertner, 1998). Despite these changes, research in social psychology suggests that more subtle manifestations of prejudice and discrimination may remain as entrenched in North America today as they were 15 or even 20 years ago (Dovidio & Gaertner, 2000).

● What am I being asked to believe or accept?

Even people who see themselves as unprejudiced and who disavow ethnic stereotypes and discrimination still hold negative stereotypes about ethnic out-groups and, in certain situations, will display prejudice and discrimination toward them (Dovidio, Kawakami, & Beach, 2001). Some people claim, therefore, that negative attitudes toward ethnic out-groups are so deeply ingrained in all of us that ethnic prejudice can never be eliminated.

● What evidence is available to support the assertion?

Evidence for this assertion focuses primarily on prejudice against African Americans by Americans of European background. It comes, first, from studies testing the theory of *aversive racism* (Dovidio & Gaertner, 1998). This theory holds that even though many Americans of European background consider ethnic prejudice to be unacceptable, or aversive, they will still sometimes display it—especially when they can do so without admitting, even to themselves, that they are prejudiced.

LINKAGES (a link to Consciousness)

In one test of this theory, a male experimenter telephoned male and female Americans of European background who were known to believe in ethnic equality. The man claimed to be a stranded motorist who was trying to call a service station from a pay phone. When told he had called the wrong number, the man replied that he was out of coins and asked the person he'd reached to call a service station for him. If people listened long enough to learn of the man's problem, they were just as likely to contact the service station whether the caller "sounded" European American or African American. However, if the caller "sounded" African American, these supposedly unprejudiced people were almost five times as likely to hang up even before the caller could ask for help (Gaertner & Dovidio, 1986). In other studies, female American university students of European background were asked to help another female student who was doing poorly on some task. When the student's poor performance was described as being due to the task's difficulty, the students agreed to help, regardless of the other student's ethnicity. But if the problem was said to be due to lack of effort, help was offered much more often to Americans of European background than to African Americans (Frey & Gaertner, 1986; McPhail & Penner, 1995). These findings suggest that even people who do not display prejudice in most situations may do so in others.

A second line of evidence for the entrenched nature of prejudice comes from research showing that many people hold negative stereotypes about ethnic minorities (and women) but are unaware that they do so. These negative stereotypes can also be *activated* without conscious awareness, even among people who believe they are free of prejudice (Banaji, Lemm, & Carpenter, 2001; Wheeler & Petty, 2001). To demonstrate these phenomena, researchers have used the priming procedures described in the chapter on consciousness to activate unconscious thoughts and feelings that can alter people's reactions to stimuli without their awareness. In one study, for example, white participants were exposed to subliminal presentations of pictures of Black individuals (Chen & Bargh, 1997). The participants were not consciously aware that they had seen these pictures, but when they interacted with a Black man soon afterward, those who had been primed with the pictures acted more negatively toward him and saw him as more hostile than did people who had not been primed. Priming apparently activated these participants' negative ethnic stereotypes. It is also possible to prime unconscious negative stereotypes about other groups, including women and the elderly (Glick & Fiske, 2001; Hense, Penner, & Nelson, 1995). All of these findings suggest that stereotypes are so well learned and so ingrained in people that they may be activated automatically and without their conscious awareness (Dovidio et al., 2001).

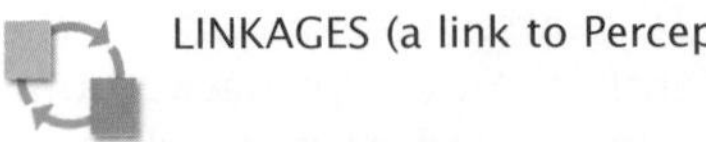

LINKAGES (a link to Perception)

- **Are there alternative ways of interpreting the evidence?**

The evidence presented so far suggests that it may be impossible to eliminate ethnic prejudice, because everyone harbours unconscious negative stereotypes about various groups. But this evidence does not necessarily mean that unconscious stereotypes affect everyone in the same way. Perhaps they have a greater impact on people who are more overtly prejudiced.

- **What additional evidence would help to evaluate the alternatives?**

One way to evaluate this possibility is to compare the responses of prejudiced and unprejudiced people in various experimental situations. In one mock-trial studying the US, for example, overtly prejudiced white jurors recommended the death penalty more often for Black defendants than for white defendants found guilty of the same crime. Low-prejudice white jurors showed this bias only when they believed that a Black member of the jury also favoured giving the death penalty (Dovidio et al., 1997). Priming studies, too, show that although negative stereotypes can be primed in both prejudiced and unprejudiced people, it is easier to do in people who openly display their ethnic bias (Dovidio, Kawakami, & Gaertner, 2000). Furthermore, activation of these stereotypes may be less likely to affect the conscious attitudes and behaviour of unprejudiced people. So when unconscious stereotypes are activated in unprejudiced people, the effects tend to appear in subtle ways, such as in facial expressions or other nonverbal behaviours (Kawakami, Dion, & Dovidio, 1998; Lepore & Brown, 1997; Vanman et al., 2004).

- **What conclusions are most reasonable?**

Taken together, research evidence presents a mixed picture regarding the possibility of eliminating ethnic prejudice. True, people in the United States are not nearly as colourblind as they might hope, and ethnic prejudice may be so ingrained in some people as to be subconscious. However, research suggests that it may still be possible to eliminate even subconscious stereotypes (Kawakami et al., 2000; Kurzban, Tooby, & Cosmides, 2001). It also appears that when unprejudiced people are made aware of their negative beliefs about some target group, they will actively work to prevent those beliefs from influencing their behaviour toward members of that group (Amodio et al., 2004; Devine, Plant, & Buswell, 2000). In short, prejudice is ingrained, but it can also be reduced, and it makes sense to do everything possible to reduce it. In any multicultural country, survival as a civilized society requires that we continue to fight against overt and covert forms of stereotyping, prejudice, and discrimination.

Interpersonal Attraction

Research on prejudice suggests some of the reasons why people, from childhood on, may come to dislike or even hate other people. An equally fascinating aspect of social cognition is why people like or love other people. Folklore tells us that "opposites attract," but also that "birds of a feather flock together." Although valid to some degree, neither of these statements is entirely accurate in all cases. We begin our coverage of interpersonal attraction by discussing the factors that lead to initial attraction. We then examine how liking sometimes develops into more intimate relationships.

Keys to Attraction

Whether you like someone or not depends partly on situational factors and partly on personal characteristics.

Proximity and Liking Research on environmental factors in attraction suggests that, barring bad first impressions, the more often we make contact with someone—as neighbours, classmates, or co-workers, for example—the more we tend to like that person. Does this principle apply in your life? To find out, think about how and where you met each of your closest friends. If you can think of cases in which proximity did not lead to liking, what do you think interfered with the formation of friendship?

The Environment One of the most important determinants of attraction is simple physical proximity (Berscheid & Reis, 1998). As long as you do not initially dislike a person, your liking for that person will increase with additional contact (Brehm et al., 2005). For example, Richard Moreland and Scott Beach (1992) varied the number of times that several experimental assistants (posing as students) attended a class. Even though none of the assistants ever spoke to anyone in the class, they were rated by the other students as more likable the more often they attended. A more recent study found that these higher ratings generalized to individuals who resembled the people who had been present (Rhodes, Halberstadt, & Brajkovich, 2001). This proximity phenomenon—another example of the mere-exposure effect mentioned earlier—helps account for the fact that next-door neighbours are usually more likely to become friends than people who live farther from one another. Chances are, most of your friends are people whom you met as neighbours, co-workers, or classmates.

The circumstances under which people first meet also influence attraction. In accordance with the conditioning principles discussed in the chapter on learning, you are much more likely to be attracted to a stranger if you meet in comfortable, rather than uncomfortable, physical conditions. Similarly, if you are rewarded in the presence of a stranger, the chances that you will like that stranger are increased, even if the stranger was not the one who gave the reward (Clark & Pataki, 1995). In one study, for example, an experimenter judged one person's creativity while another person watched. Compared with those who received a negative evaluation, participants who were evaluated positively tended to like the observer more (Griffitt & Guay, 1969). At least among strangers, then, liking can occur through associating someone with something pleasant.

Similarity People also tend to like those they perceive as similar to themselves on variables such as age, name, religion, smoking or drinking habits, or being a "morning" or "evening" person (Buston & Emlen, 2003; Jones et al., 2004). As shown in Figure 17.7, similarity in attitudes is an especially important influence on attraction. This relationship has been found among children, university students, adult workers, and senior citizens (Brehm et al., 2005).

One reason why we like people with similar views of the world is that we expect such people to think highly of us (Condon & Crano, 1988). Like many important relationships, it's hard to say whether attraction is a cause or an effect of similarity (Berscheid & Reis, 1998). For example, you might like someone because his attitudes are similar to yours, but it is also possible that as a result of liking him, your attitudes will become more similar to his (Davis & Rusbult, 2001). Even if your own attitudes don't change, you may change your *perceptions* of the liked person's attitudes such that those attitudes seem more similar to yours (Brehm, 1992).

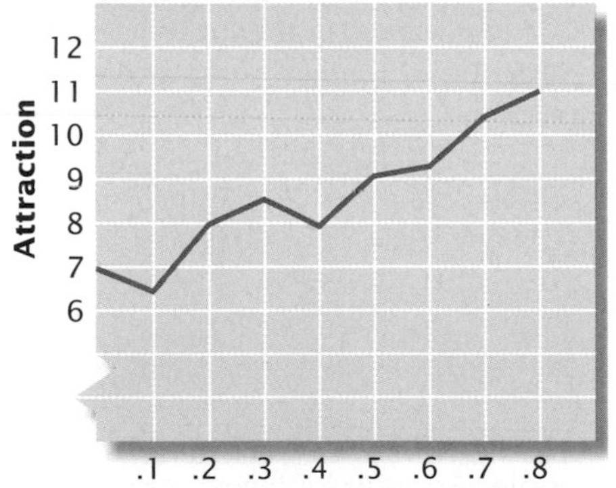

figure 17.7

Attitude Similarity and Attraction

This graph shows the results of a study in which participants learned about another person's attitudes. Their liking for that person was strongly related to the proportion of the other person's attitudes that were similar to the participants' own attitudes.

Source: Adapted from Byrne & Nelson (1965).

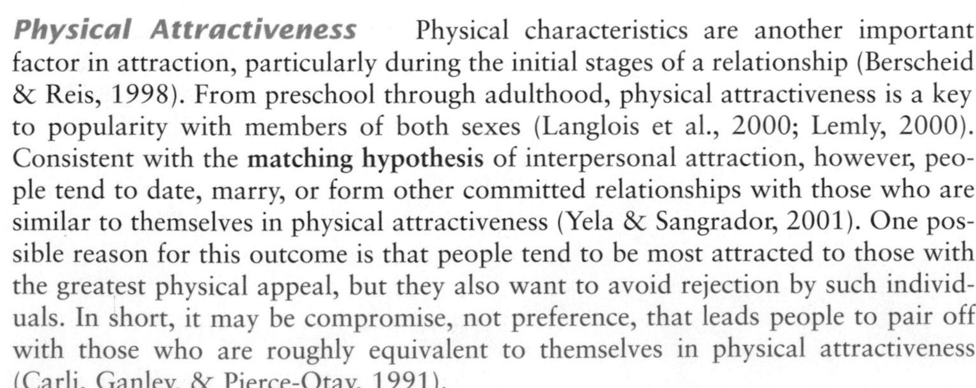

Physical Attractiveness Physical characteristics are another important factor in attraction, particularly during the initial stages of a relationship (Berscheid & Reis, 1998). From preschool through adulthood, physical attractiveness is a key to popularity with members of both sexes (Langlois et al., 2000; Lemly, 2000). Consistent with the **matching hypothesis** of interpersonal attraction, however, people tend to date, marry, or form other committed relationships with those who are similar to themselves in physical attractiveness (Yela & Sangrador, 2001). One possible reason for this outcome is that people tend to be most attracted to those with the greatest physical appeal, but they also want to avoid rejection by such individuals. In short, it may be compromise, not preference, that leads people to pair off with those who are roughly equivalent to themselves in physical attractiveness (Carli, Ganley, & Pierce-Otay, 1991).

figure 17.8

Sex Differences in Date and Mate Preferences

According to evolutionary psychologists, men and women have developed different strategies for selecting sexual partners. These psychologists say that women became more selective than men because they can have relatively few children and want a partner who is able to help care for those children. Here are some data supporting this idea. When asked about the intelligence of people they would choose for one-night stands, dating, and sexual relationships, women preferred much smarter partners than men did. Only when the choices concerned steady dating and marriage did the men's preference for bright partners equal that of the women. Critics of the evolutionary approach explain such sex differences as reflecting learned social norms and expectations of how men and women should behave (Eagly & Wood, 1999; Miller, Putcha-Bhagavatula, & Pedersen, 2002).

Source: Kenrick et al. (1993).

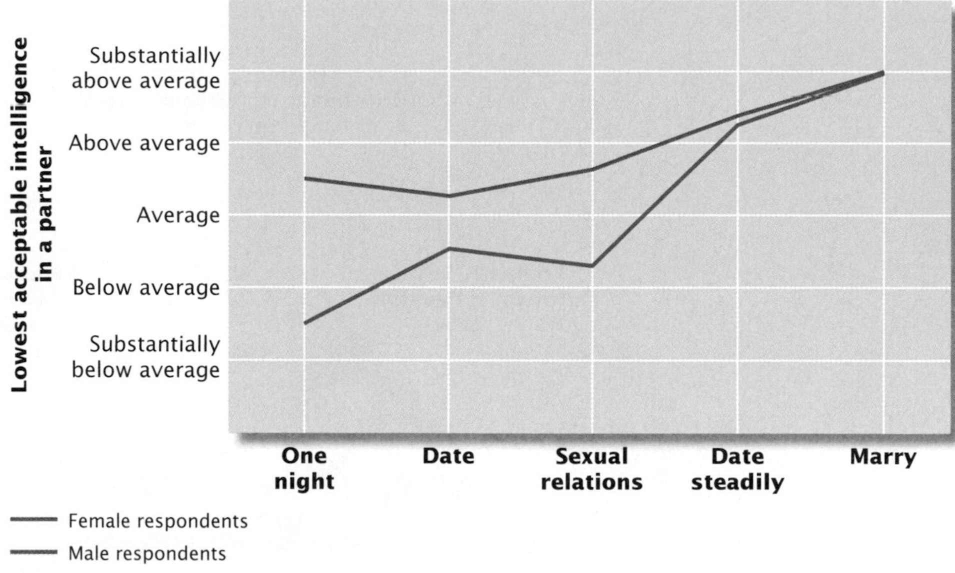

Intimate Relationships and Love

There is much about intimate relationships that psychologists do not—and may never—understand, but they are learning all the time. As mentioned in the chapter on motivation and emotion, evolutionary psychologists suggest that men and women employ different strategies to ensure the survival of their genes and that each gender looks for different attributes in a potential mate (Buss, 2004b; Kenrick, Neuberg, & Cialdini, 2002; Schmitt, 2003). For example, women may be much more concerned than men about the intelligence of their dating partners (Kenrick & Trost, 1997; see Figure 17.8).

Intimate Relationships Eventually, people who are attracted to each other usually become *interdependent,* which means that the thoughts, emotions, and behaviours of one person affect the thoughts, emotions, and behaviours of the other (Rusbult & Van Lange, 2003). Interdependence is one of the defining characteristics of intimate relationships. It occurs in large measure as the thoughts and values of one person become part of the self-concept of the other (Agnew et al., 1998).

Another key component of successful intimate relationships is *commitment,* which is the extent to which each party is psychologically attached to the relationship and wants to remain in it (Le & Agnew, 2003). People feel committed to a relationship when they are satisfied with the rewards they receive from it, when they have invested significant tangible and intangible resources in it, and when there are few attractive alternative relationships available to them (Bui, Peplau, & Hill, 1996).

Analyzing Love Affection, emotional expressiveness, social support, cohesiveness, and sexuality—these characteristics of intimate relationships are likely to bring something else to mind: love. Yet *intimacy* and *love* are not the same (Diamond, 2004). Most theorists agree that there are several different types of love (Brehm et al., 2005). One widely accepted view distinguishes between *passionate love* and *companionate love* (Hendrick & Hendrick, 2003). Passionate love is intense, arousing, and marked by both strong physical attraction and deep

matching hypothesis The notion that people are most likely to form relationships with those who are similar to themselves in physical attractiveness.

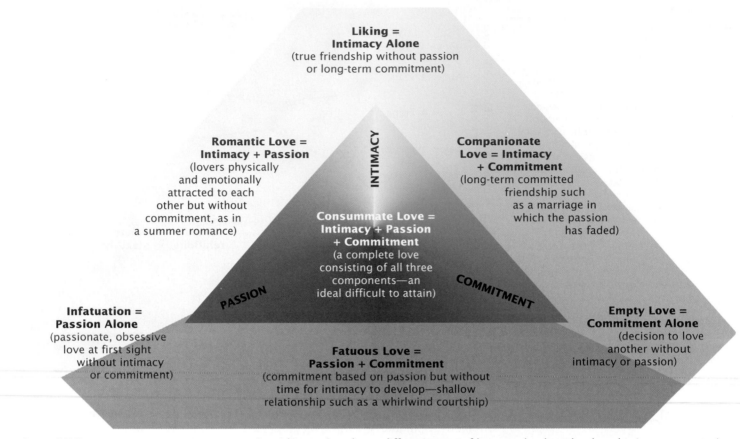

Liking =
Intimacy Alone
(true friendship without passion or long-term commitment)

Romantic Love =
Intimacy + Passion
(lovers physically and emotionally attracted to each other but without commitment, as in a summer romance)

INTIMACY

Companionate Love = Intimacy + Commitment
(long-term committed friendship such as a marriage in which the passion has faded)

Consummate Love =
Intimacy + Passion
+ Commitment
(a complete love consisting of all three components—an ideal difficult to attain)

PASSION

COMMITMENT

Infatuation =
Passion Alone
(passionate, obsessive love at first sight without intimacy or commitment)

Fatuous Love =
Passion + Commitment
(commitment based on passion but without time for intimacy to develop—shallow relationship such as a whirlwind courtship)

Empty Love =
Commitment Alone
(decision to love another without intimacy or passion)

Figure 17.9

A Triangular Theory of Love

According to Sternberg, different types of love result when the three basic components in his triangular theory occur in different combinations. Sternberg has also explored factors associated with falling in love (Sternberg, Hojjat, & Barnes, 2001). Preliminary results suggest that people who share similar views about what a loving relationship should be like are much more likely to fall in love with each other, and remain committed to the relationship, than are people whose views on love are dissimilar.

Source: Sternberg (1988).

A Wedding in India Most people in Western cultures tend to marry a person whom they choose on the basis of love, sometimes without regard for differences between them in religion, ethnicity, and financial or social status. In other cultures, however, these socio-cultural considerations—and even arrangements made by parents—may largely determine who marries whom. What factors do you think might have brought this couple together?

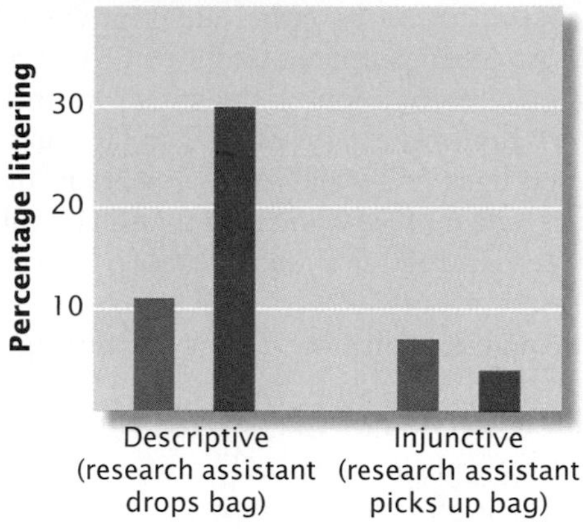

Clean environment
Littered environment

figure 17.10

Descriptive and Injunctive Norms

When both descriptive norms (a littered parking lot) and injunctive norms (a person discarding paper in the parking lot) were consistent with littering, 30 percent of the people crossing the parking lot also littered. But after seeing a person picking up a bag in the parking lot (creating an injunctive norm against littering), very few people engaged in littering, whether or not the lot was littered (Reno, Cialdini, & Kallgren, 1993). Applying these findings to combat alcohol abuse on campus, some student health campaigns now create descriptive norms for responsible drinking by citing statistics showing that most students drink in moderation (Zernike, 2000). Such campaigns might also change injunctive norms by portraying excessive drinking as socially unacceptable (Larimer et al., 2004).

Source: Adapted from Reno, Cialdini, & Kallgren (1993).

emotional attachment. Sexual feelings are strong, and thoughts of the loved one intrude on a person's awareness frequently. Companionate love is less arousing but psychologically more intimate. It is marked by mutual concern for the welfare of the other (Hendrick & Hendrick, 2003).

Robert Sternberg (1997) has offered a more comprehensive analysis of love. According to his *triangular theory,* the three basic components of love are *passion, intimacy,* and *commitment.* Various combinations of these components result in different types of love, as illustrated in Figure 17.9. For example, Sternberg suggests that *romantic love* involves a high degree of passion and intimacy, yet lacks substantial commitment to the other person. *Companionate love* is marked by a great deal of intimacy and commitment but little passion. *Consummate love* is the most complete and satisfying. It is the most complete because it includes a high level of all three components, and it is the most satisfying because the relationship is likely to fulfill many of the needs of each partner.

Cultural factors have a strong influence on the value that people place on love. In North America and the United Kingdom, for example, the vast majority of people believe that they should love the person they marry. By contrast, in India and Pakistan, about half the people interviewed in a survey said they would marry someone they did not love if that person had other qualities that they desired (Levine et al., 1995). In Russia, only 40 percent of respondents said that they married for love. Most reported marrying because of loneliness, shared interests, or an unplanned pregnancy (Baron & Byrne, 1994).

Social Influence

After the murderous rampage at Columbine High School in Littleton, Colorado, in April of 1999, a number of students at other high schools were arrested for threatening similar acts of violence (called "copycat crimes") against their classmates. This included the small town of Taber, Alberta, where one week after Columbine, a 14-year-old student opened fire with a .22-calibre rifle inside W.R. Myers High School. Jason Lang (17 years old) was killed, and another 17-year-old was wounded. Copycat, or imitative, crimes illustrate the effects of **social influence,** the process whereby a person's behaviour is directly or indirectly affected by the words or actions of other people. This section begins with a discussion of social influence itself, after which we consider several related aspects of how we are influenced by others, including the processes of conformity, compliance, and obedience. Then we explore the causes and consequences of helping and altruism.

Copycat crimes are but one illustration of the fact that people can influence the way other people think, feel, and act, even without specifically trying to do so (Cialdini & Goldstein, 2004). There are countless others. For example, simply asking people if they have thought about buying a car in the coming year dramatically increases the chance that they will actually purchase a car (Fitzsimons & Shiv, 2001; Fitzsimons & Williams, 2000). The most widespread, yet subtle, form of social influence is communicated through social norms.

Norms are learned, socially based rules that prescribe what people should or should not do in various situations (Cialdini & Trost, 1998). Norms are transmitted by parents, teachers, clergy, peers, and other agents of culture. Although they often cannot be verbalized, norms are so powerful that people usually follow them automatically. At movie theatres in North America, for example, norms tell us that we should get in line to buy a ticket rather than crowd around the ticket window; they also lead us to expect that others will do the same. By informing people of what is expected of them and others, norms make social situations less uncertain and more comfortable.

social influence The process whereby one person's behaviour is affected by the words or actions of others.

norms Socially based rules that prescribe what people should or should not do in various situations.

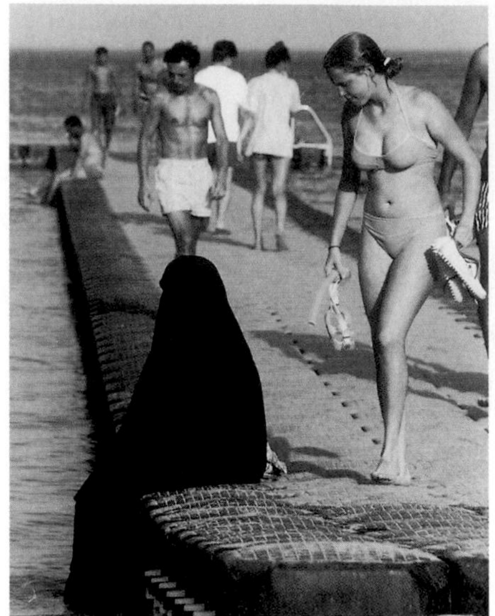

Clothing and Culture The social norms that guide how people dress and behave in various situations are part of the culturally determined socialization process described in the chapter on human development. The process is the same worldwide. Parents, teachers, peers, religious leaders, and others communicate their culture's social norms to children, but differences in those norms result in quite different behaviours from culture to culture.

Robert Cialdini (2003) has described social norms as either descriptive or injunctive. *Descriptive norms* indicate how most other people actually behave in a given situation. They tell a person what actions are common in the situation and thereby implicitly give the person permission to act in the same way. The fact that most people do not cross a street until the green light or "walk" sign appears is an example of a descriptive norm. *Injunctive norms* give more specific information about the actions that others find acceptable and those that they find unacceptable. Subtle pressure exists to behave in accordance with these norms. A sign with an icon of a red light surrounded by a circle with a line through it indicating "No right turn on red" is an example of an injunctive norm.

A study by Raymond Reno and his colleagues (Reno, Cialdini, & Kallgren, 1993) illustrates the differing effects of these two types of norms. The participants were people who walked through a parking lot just after being handed an advertising leaflet. The experimenters arranged for the participants to see another person (who was working with the experimenters) either toss a paper bag on the ground or pick one up from the ground. On half the trials of this experiment, the parking lot was littered with paper; on the other half, the lot was clean. As shown in Figure 17.10, the descriptive norm—seeing another person litter in an already dirty environment—appeared to communicate that "many people do this," and a relatively high percentage of people dropped their leaflets in the dirty parking lot. By contrast, the injunctive norm—seeing someone pick up litter—appeared to communicate that even though many people litter, it's not the right thing to do. When this norm was evident, fewer than 5 percent of the people dropped their leaflets in the dirty parking lot. Later research has shown that norms are most likely to actually reduce littering when a person focuses on and believes in the relevant norm (Kallgren, Reno, & Cialdini, 2000).

One very powerful injunctive norm is *reciprocity,* the tendency to respond to others as they have acted toward you (Cialdini & Goldstein, 2004). Restaurant servers often apply this norm by leaving some candy with the bill. Customers who receive this gift tend to reciprocate by leaving a larger tip than customers who don't get candy (Strohmetz et al., 2002). But norms are not universal (Miller, 2001), as illustrated by the fact that people around the world differ greatly in terms of the physical distance they maintain between themselves and others during conversation. For example, people from South America usually stand much closer to one another than do people from North America. And as suggested in the chapter on psychological disorders, behaviour considered normal and friendly in one culture may be seen as abnormal, and even offensive, in another.

The social influence exerted by norms creates orderly social behaviour. But social norms can also lead to a breakdown in order. For example, **deindividuation** is a phenomenon in which a person becomes "submerged in a group" and loses the sense of individuality (Cialdini & Goldstein, 2004). When people experience deindividuation, they become emotionally aroused and feel intense closeness with the group. This increased awareness of group membership may create greater adherence to the group's norms, even if those norms promote antisocial behaviour (Spears et al., 2001). In other words, through deindividuation, people appear to become "part of the herd," and they may perform acts that they would not do otherwise. Fans at rock concerts and athletic events have trampled one another to death in their frenzy to get the best seats. Normally mild-mannered people may find themselves throwing rocks or fire bombs at police during political protests.

The greater the sense of personal anonymity, the more influence the group appears to have (Lea, Speers, & de Groot, 2001). An analysis of newspaper accounts of lynchings in the United States over a 50-year period showed that larger lynch mobs were more savage and vicious than smaller ones (Mullen, 1986).

Deindividuation Bandanas and military uniforms help create deindividuation in these Aboriginal freedom fighters at Oka by focusing their attention on membership in their group and on its values. The bandanas also hide their identities, which reduces their sense of personal responsibility and accountability and makes it easier to engage in violent behaviour. Deindividuation operates in other groups, too, ranging from lynch mobs and terrorist cells to political protesters and urban rioters. In short, people who feel themselves to be anonymous members of a group may engage in antisocial acts that they might not perform on their own.

Deindividuation provides an example of how, given the right circumstances, quite normal people can engage in destructive, even violent, behaviour.

LINKAGES
Motivation and the Presence of Others

LINKAGES (a link to Motivation and Emotion)

In the chapter on motivation and emotion, we noted that social factors such as parental attitudes toward achievement often affect motivation. But a person's current motivational state is also affected by the mere presence of other people. As an illustration, consider what was probably the first experiment in social psychology, conducted by Norman Triplett in 1897.

Triplett noticed that bicycle racers tended to go faster when other racers were nearby than when they were alone. Did seeing one another remind the racers of the need to go faster to win? To test this possibility, Triplett arranged for bicyclists to complete a 25-mile [40 km] course under three conditions: riding alone in a race against the clock; riding with another cyclist, but not in competition; or competing directly with another rider. The cyclists went much faster when another rider was present than when they were simply racing against time. This was true even when they were not competing against the other person. Something about the presence of the other person, not just competition, produced increased speed.

The term **social facilitation** describes circumstances in which the mere presence of other people can improve performance (Aiello & Douthitt, 2001; Platania & Moran, 2001). This improvement does not always occur, however. The presence of other people sometimes hurts performance, a process known as **social impairment.** For decades these results seemed contradictory. Then Robert Zajonc (pronounced "ZYE-onze") suggested that both effects could be explained by one process: arousal.

deindividuation A psychological state occurring in group members that results in loss of individuality and a tendency to do things not normally done when alone.

social facilitation A phenomenon in which the presence of others improves a person's performance.

Social Facilitation Like many other professional athletes, Toronto Blue Jays slugger Carlos Delgado, shown here adding to his home run total, is able to perform at his best even when large crowds are present. In fact, the crowds probably help him hit well because the presence of others tends to increase arousal, which enhances the performance of familiar and well-learned skills, such as a batting swing. However, arousal created by an audience tends to interfere with the performance of unfamiliar and poorly developed skills. This is one reason why athletes who show flawless grace in front of thousands of fans are likely to freeze up or blow their lines in front of a small production crew when trying for the first time to tape a TV ad or a public service announcement.

The presence of other people, said Zajonc, increases a person's general level of arousal or motivation (Zajonc, 1965). Why? One reason is that being watched by others increases our sense of being evaluated, producing apprehension that in turn increases emotional arousal (Penner & Craiger, 1992). Arousal increases the tendency to perform those behaviours that are most *dominant*—the ones we know best—and this tendency can either help or hinder performance. If you are performing an easy, familiar task, such as riding a bike, the increased arousal caused by the presence of others should allow you to ride even faster than normal. But if the task is hard or unfamiliar—such as trying new dance steps or playing a piano piece you just learned—the most dominant responses may be incorrect and cause your performance to suffer. In other words, the impact of other people on performance depends on whether the task is easy or difficult. Research shows that this is true even when the "other person" is a machine that records one's errors at a task (Aiello & Kolb, 1995).

The presence of others may affect performance in other ways as well. For example, having an audience can distract us from the task at hand or cause us to focus on only one part of it, thus impairing performance (Aiello & Douthitt, 2001).

What if a person is not merely in the presence of others but is actually working on a task with them? Research indicates that the impact of their presence changes slightly (Murphy et al., 2003). In these situations, people typically exert less effort than they do when performing alone, a phenomenon called **social loafing** (Karau & Williams, 1997). Whether the task is pulling on a rope, clapping as loudly as possible, or trying to solve puzzles, people tend to work harder when performing alone than with others (Baron, Kerr, & Miller, 1992; Geen, 1991). There are at least three reasons behind this social loafing phenomenon. First, it is usually much harder to evaluate the performance of individuals when they are working as part of a group (Szymanski, Garczynski, & Harkins, 2000). As a result, it is simply easier to succeed at loafing when in a group. Second, rewards may come to a group whether or not every member exerts maximum effort. Third, a group's rewards are usually divided equally among its members rather than according to individual effort (Karau & Williams, 1997).

In North American and other Western countries, social loafing can be seen in all kinds of groups, from volunteer committees to search parties. Because social loafing can reduce productivity in business situations, it is important for managers to develop ways of evaluating the efforts of every individual in a work group, not just the overall output of the team (Shepperd, 1993). Social loafing can also be reduced by strategies that cause people to like the group and identify with it (Karau & Williams, 1997).

Social loafing is much less common in Eastern cultures, such as those of China and Japan. In fact, in collectivist cultures, working in a group usually produces *social striving*—defined as greater individual effort when working in a group (Matsumoto, 2000). This difference in the effects of group membership on individual efforts probably reflects the value that collectivist cultures place on coordinated and cooperative group activities. This orientation serves to discourage social loafing.

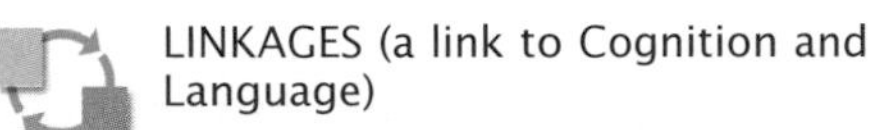

LINKAGES (a link to Cognition and Language)

Conformity and Compliance

Suppose you are with three of your friends. One says that Pierre Trudeau was the greatest prime minister in Canada's history. You think that the greatest PM was Sir John A. Macdonald, but before you can say anything, another friend agrees that it was Trudeau, and then the other one does as well. What would you do? Disagree with all three? Maintain your opinion but keep quiet? Change your mind?

When people change their behaviour or beliefs to match those of other members of a group, they are said to conform. **Conformity** occurs as a result of group pressure,

Mass Conformity The faithful who gather at Mecca, at the Vatican, and at other holy places around the world exemplify the power of religion and other social forces to produce conformity to group norms.

social impairment A reduction in performance due to the presence of other people.
social loafing Exerting less effort when performing a group task than when performing the same task alone.
conformity Changing one's behaviour or beliefs to match those of others, generally as a result of real or imagined, though unspoken, group pressure.
compliance Adjusting one's behaviour because of an explicit or implicit request.

real or imagined (Cialdini & Goldstein, 2004). You probably have experienced such group pressure when everyone around you stood to applaud a performance you thought was not that great. You might have conformed by standing as well, although no one told you to do so. The group's behaviour created a silent, but influential, pressure to follow suit. **Compliance,** in contrast, occurs when people adjust their behaviour because of a request. The request can be either *explicit,* such as your roommate saying, "Please pass the salt," or *implicit,* as when someone looks at you in a certain way to let you know it is time to start studying (Cialdini & Goldstein, 2004).

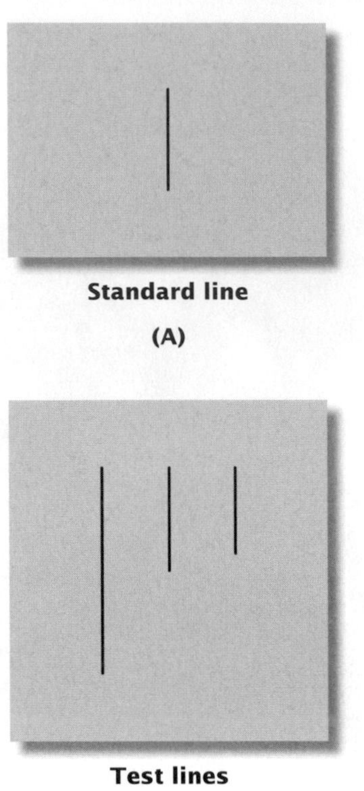

figure 17.11

Stimulus Lines for Conformity Studies

Participants in Asch's (1956) experiments saw a new set of lines like these on each trial. The middle line in Part B matches the one in Part A, but when several of Asch's assistants chose an incorrect line, so did many of the participants. Try re-creating this experiment with four friends. Secretly ask three of them to choose the line on the left when you show this drawing, then see if the fourth person conforms to the group norm. If not, do you think it was something about the person, the length of the incorrect line chosen, or both that led to noncomformity? Would conformity be more likely if the first three people were to choose the line on the right? (Read on for more about this possibility.)

Source: Asch (1955).

The Role of Norms

Conformity and compliance are usually generated by spoken or unspoken norms. In a classic experiment, Muzafer Sherif (1937) charted the formation of a group norm by taking advantage of a perceptual illusion, called the *autokinetic phenomenon*. In this illusion, a stationary point of light in a pitch dark room appears to move. Estimates of the amount of movement tend to stay the same over time—if an observer is alone. But when Sherif tested several people at once, asking each person to say aloud how far the light moved on repeated trials, their estimates tended to converge. They had established a group norm. Even more important, when the individuals from the group were later tested alone, they continued to be influenced by this norm.

In another classic experiment, Solomon Asch (1956) examined how people would respond when they faced a norm that already existed but was obviously wrong. The participants in this experiment saw a standard line like the one in Figure 17.11(A); then they saw a display like that in Figure 17.11(B). Their task was to pick out the line in the display that was the same length as the one they had first been shown.

Each participant performed this task in a small group of people who posed as fellow participants but who were actually the experimenter's assistants. There were two conditions. In the control condition, the real participant responded first. In the experimental condition, the participant did not respond until after the assistants did. The assistants chose the correct response on 6 trials, but on the other 12 trials they all gave the same obviously incorrect response. So on 12 trials, each participant was confronted with a "social reality" created by a group norm that conflicted with the physical reality created by what the person could clearly see. Only 5 percent of the participants in the control condition ever made a mistake on this easy task. However, among participants who heard the assistants' responses before giving their own, about 70 percent made at least one error by conforming to the group norm. An analysis of 133 studies conducted in 17 countries reveals that, in the United States, conformity in Asch-type situations has declined somewhat since the 1950s but that it still occurs. Furthermore, it is especially likely in collectivist cultures, in which conformity to group norms is emphasized (Cialdini et al., 2001).

Pressure for conformity can even affect reports about personal experiences. In one study that used a procedure similar to Asch's, participants were shown a number of objects. Later, the same objects were shown again, along with some new ones, and the participants were asked to say whether they had seen each object in the previous display. When tested alone, the participants' memories were quite accurate, but hearing another person's opinion about which objects had or had not been shown before strongly affected their memory of which objects they had seen (Hoffman et al., 2001).

Why Do People Conform?

Why did so many people in Asch's experiment, and others like it, give incorrect responses when they were capable of near-perfect performance? One possibility is that they displayed *public conformity,* giving an answer they did not believe simply because it was the socially desirable thing to do. Another possibility is that they experienced *private acceptance:* Perhaps the participants used other people's responses as legitimate evidence about reality, were convinced that their own perceptions were wrong, and actually changed their minds. Morton Deutsch and Harold Gerard (1955) reasoned that if conformity disappeared when people gave their responses without identifying themselves, then Asch's findings must reflect public conformity, not private acceptance. Actually, conformity does decrease when people respond anonymously instead of publicly, but it doesn't disappear (Deutsch & Gerard, 1955). So people sometimes say things in public that they don't believe, but hearing other people's responses also influences their private beliefs (Moscovici, 1985).

Why are group norms so powerful? Research suggests three influential factors (Cialdini & Trost, 1998). First, people want to be correct, and norms provide information about what is right and wrong. This factor may help explain why some extremely disturbed or distressed people consider stories about suicide to be "social proof " that self-destruction is a reasonable way out of their problems (Cialdini, 1993). Second, people want to be liked by others, and we generally like those who agree with us. Finally, norms influence the distribution of social rewards and punishments (Cialdini, 1995). From childhood on, people in many cultures learn that going along with group norms is good and earns rewards. (These positive outcomes presumably help compensate for not always being able to say or do exactly what we please.) People also learn that breaking a norm may bring punishments ranging from scoldings for small transgressions to imprisonment for violation of norms that have been translated into laws.

When Do People Conform?

People do not always conform to social influence. In the original Asch studies, for example, nearly 30 percent of the participants did not go along with the research assistants' obviously incorrect judgments. Countless experiments have probed the question of what combinations of people and circumstances do and do not lead to conformity.

Ambiguity of the Situation Ambiguity, or uncertainty, is very important in determining how much conformity will occur. As the physical reality of a situation becomes less certain, people rely more and more on others' opinions, and conformity to a group norm becomes increasingly likely (Cialdini & Goldstein, 2004).

You can demonstrate this aspect of conformity on any street corner. First, create an ambiguous situation by having several people look at the sky or the top of a building. When passersby ask what is going on, be sure everyone excitedly reports seeing something interesting but fleeting—perhaps a faint light or a tiny, shiny object. If you are especially successful, conforming newcomers will begin persuading other passersby that there is something fascinating to be seen.

Unanimity and Size of the Majority If ambiguity contributes so much to conformity, why did so many of Asch's participants conform to a judgment that was so clearly wrong? The answer has to do with the *unanimity* of the group's judgment and the number of people expressing it. Specifically, people experience great pressure to conform as long as the majority is unanimous. If even one other person in the group disagrees with the majority view, conformity drops greatly. When Asch (1951) arranged for just one assistant to disagree with the others, fewer than 10 percent of the real participants conformed. Once unanimity is broken, it becomes much easier to disagree with the majority, even if the other nonconformist does not agree with the person's own view (Turner, 1991).

Conformity also depends on the size of the group. Asch (1955) demonstrated this phenomenon by varying the number of assistants in the group from one to fifteen. Conformity to incorrect norms grew as the number of people in the group increased. But most of the growth in conformity occurred as the size of the majority rose from one to about three or four members. Further additions had little effect. Several years after Asch's research, Bibb Latané (pronounced "lat-a-NAY") sought to explain this phenomenon with his *social impact theory.* This theory holds that a group's impact on an individual depends not only on group size but also on how important and close the group is to the person.

And according to Latané (1981), the impact of increasing the size of a majority depends on how big the majority was originally. Increasing a majority from, say, two to three will have much more impact than increasing it from, say, sixty to sixty-one. The reason is that the increase from sixty to sixty-one is psychologically much smaller than the change from two to three; it attracts far less notice in relative terms. Does this explanation sound familiar? The principles underlying it are similar to those of Weber's law, which, as described in the chapter on perception, governs our experience of changes in brightness, weight, and other physical stimuli.

Minority Influence Conformity can also result from **minority influence,** by which a minority in a group influences the behaviour or beliefs of a majority (Taylor, Peplau, & Sears, 2000). This phenomenon is less common than majority influence, but minorities can be influential, especially when they are established members of the group, when they agree with one another, and when they persist in their views (David & Turner, 2001). William Crano and his associates have found that, whereas majority influence tends to affect people immediately and directly, minority influence is indirect. That is, minority-influenced change often takes a while to occur and may involve only a moderate adjustment of the majority view in the direction favoured by the minority (Alvaro & Crano, 1997; Crano & Chen, 1998).

Gender Early research on conformity suggested that women conform more than men, but this gender difference stemmed mainly from the fact that the tasks used in those experiments were often more familiar to men than to women. This fact is important because people are especially likely to conform when they are faced with an unfamiliar situation (Cialdini & Goldstein, 2004). No male-female differences in conformity have been found in subsequent research using materials that are equally familiar to both genders (Maupin & Fisher, 1989).

So why do some people still perceive women as more conforming than men despite evidence to the contrary? Part of the answer may lie in their perception of the relative social status of men and women. People who think of women as having lower social status than men in most social situations are likely to see women as easier to influence, even though men and women conform equally often (Eagly, 1987).

Inducing Compliance

In the conformity experiments we have described, the participants experienced psychological pressure to conform to the views or actions of others, even though no one specifically asked them to do so. In contrast, *compliance* involves changing what you say or do because of a request.

How is compliance brought about? Many people believe that the direct approach is always best: If you want something, ask for it. But salespeople, political strategists, social psychologists, and other experts have learned that often the best way to get something is to ask for something else. Three examples of this strategy are the foot-in-the-door technique, the door-in-the-face procedure, and the low-ball approach.

The *foot-in-the-door technique* works by getting a person to agree to a small request and then gradually presenting larger ones. In the original experiment on this strategy, homeowners were asked to do one of two things. Some were asked to allow a large, unattractive "Drive Carefully" sign to be placed on their front lawns. Approximately 17 percent of the people approached in this way complied with the request. In the foot-in-the-door condition, however, homeowners were first asked only to sign a petition supporting new laws aimed at reducing traffic accidents. Several weeks later, when a different researcher asked these same people to put the "Drive Carefully" sign on their lawns, 55 percent of them complied (Freedman & Fraser, 1966).

Why should the granting of small favours lead to granting larger ones? First, people are usually far more likely to comply with a request that costs little in time, money, effort, or inconvenience. Second, complying with a small request makes people think of themselves as being committed to the cause or issue involved (Burger & Guadagno, 2003). This change occurs through the processes of cognitive dissonance discussed earlier in this chapter. In the study just described, participants who signed the petition might have thought, "I must care enough about traffic safety to do something about it." Compliance with the higher-cost request (displaying the sign)

minority influence A phenomenon whereby members of a numerical minority in a group alter the view of the majority.

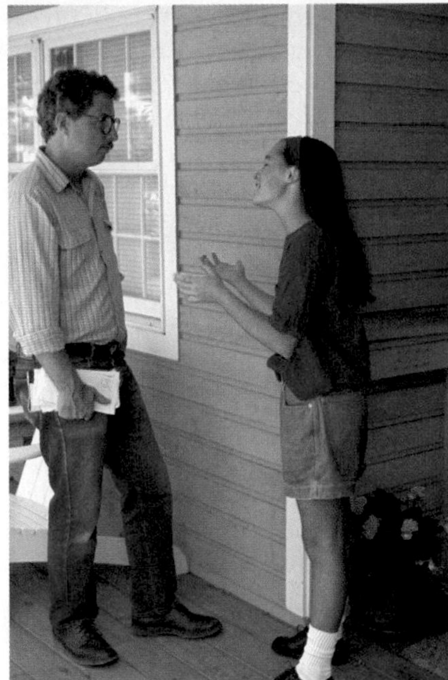

OK, OK, I'll Be Home by One! The door-in-the-face approach is sometimes used successfully by teenagers to influence parents to comply with many kinds of requests. After asking to stay out overnight, a youngster whose curfew is normally 11 P.M. might be allowed to stay out until 1 A.M.—a "compromise" that was actually the original goal.

then became more likely because it was consistent with these people's past actions (Burger & Caldwell, 2003).

The foot-in-the-door technique can be quite effective. Steven Sherman (1980) created a 700 percent increase in the rate at which people volunteered to work for a charity simply by first getting them to say that, in a hypothetical situation, they would volunteer if asked. In some sales situations, the foot in the door takes the form of a request that potential customers merely answer a few questions. The request to buy something comes later. In others, customers are offered a small gift, or "door opener," as salespeople call it. Acceptance of the gift not only allows a foot in the door but may also activate the reciprocity norm: Many people who get something free of charge feel obligated to reciprocate by buying something (Cialdini, 2001). Research suggests, however, that small favours don't always lead to bigger ones. If a request for a larger favour comes immediately after the first small one, people may be unlikely to comply with it (Guadagno et al., 2001).

The *door-in-the-face procedure* offers a second way of obtaining compliance (Cialdini, 2001; Reeves et al., 1991). This strategy begins by asking for a big favour or making some other request that is likely to be denied. After being turned down, the person making the request concedes that it was excessive and asks for something less—something the person really wanted in the first place! Because the person appears willing to compromise and because the new request seems modest in comparison with the first one, it is more likely to be granted than if it had been made at the outset. Here again, compliance appears to be due partly to activation of the reciprocity norm. The door-in-the-face strategy often lies at the heart of the bargaining that takes place among political groups and between labour and management.

A third technique for gaining compliance, called the *low-ball approach,* is commonly used by car dealers and other salepeople (Cialdini, 2001). The first step in this strategy is to obtain a person's oral commitment to do something, such as to purchase a car at a certain price. Once this commitment is made, the cost of fulfilling it is increased, often because of an "error" in computing the car's price. Why do buyers end up paying much more than originally planned for "low-balled" items? Apparently, once people say they will do something, they feel obligated to follow through, especially when the person who obtains the initial commitment also makes the higher-cost request (Burger & Cornelius, 2003). In other words, as described in relation to cognitive dissonance theory earlier in this chapter, people like to be consistent in their words and deeds. In this case, it appears that people try to maintain a positive self-image by behaving in accordance with their initial oral commitment, even though it may cost them a great deal to do so.

Obedience

Compliance involves a change in behaviour in response to a request. In the case of **obedience,** the behaviour change comes in response to a *demand* from an authority figure (Blass, 2004). In the 1960s, Stanley Milgram developed a laboratory procedure at Yale University to study obedience. In his first experiment, he used newspaper ads to recruit 40 male volunteers between the ages of 20 and 50. Among the participants were professionals, white-collar businessmen, and unskilled workers (Milgram, 1963).

Imagine you are one of the people who answered the ad. When you arrive for the experiment, you join a 50-year-old gentleman who has also volunteered and has been scheduled for the same session. The experimenter explains that the purpose of the experiment is to examine the effects of punishment on learning. One of you—the "teacher"—will help the "learner" remember a list of words by administering an electrical shock whenever he makes a mistake. Then the experimenter turns to you and asks you to draw one of two cards out of a hat. Your card says "TEACHER." You think to yourself that this must be your lucky day.

obedience Changing behaviour in response to a demand from an authority figure.

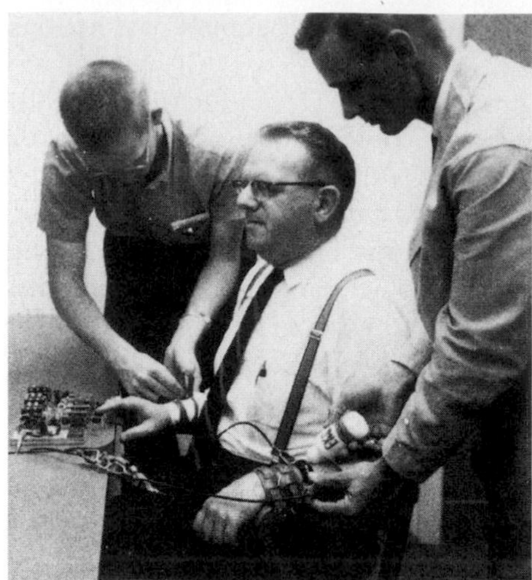

figure 17.12

Studying Obedience in the Laboratory

In this photograph from Milgram's original experiment, a man is being strapped into a chair with electrodes on his arm. Although participants in the experiment didn't know it, the man was actually one of the experimenter's research assistants and received no shock.

Now the learner is taken into another room and strapped into a chair, as shown in Figure 17.12. Electrodes are attached to his arms. Meanwhile, you are shown a shock generator featuring 30 switches. The experimenter explains that the switch on the far left administers a mild, 15-volt shock and that each succeeding switch increases the shock by 15 volts. The switch on the far right delivers 450 volts. The far left section of the shock generator is labelled "slight shock." Looking across the panel, you see "moderate shock," "very strong shock," and at the far right, "danger—severe shock." The last two switches are ominously labelled "XXX." The experimenter explains that you, the teacher, will begin by reading a list of word pairs to the learner. Then you will go through the list again, presenting just one word of each pair. It is the learner's task to say which word went with it. After the first mistake, you are to throw the switch to deliver 15 volts of shock. Each time the learner makes another mistake, you are to increase the shock by 15 volts.

You begin, following the experimenter's instructions. But after the learner makes his fifth mistake and you throw the switch to give him 75 volts, you hear a loud moan. At 90 volts, the learner cries out in pain. At 150 volts, he screams and asks to be let out of the experiment. You look to the experimenter, who says, "Proceed with the next word."

No shock was actually delivered in Milgram's experiments. The learner was always an employee of the experimenter, and the moans and other signs of pain came from a prerecorded tape. But you don't know that. What would you do in this situation? Suppose you continue and eventually deliver 180 volts. The learner screams that he cannot stand the pain any longer and starts banging on the wall. The experimenter says, "You have no other choice; you must go on." Would you continue? Would you keep going even when the learner begged to be let out of the experiment and then fell silent? Would you administer 450 volts of potentially deadly shock to a perfect stranger just because an experimenter demanded that you do so?

Figure 17.13 shows that only five participants in Milgram's experiment stopped before 300 volts, and 26 out of 40 participants (or 65 percent) went all the way to the 450-volt level. The decision to continue was difficult and stressful for the participants. Many protested repeatedly; but each time the experimenter told them to continue, they did so. Here is a partial transcript of what a typical participant said:

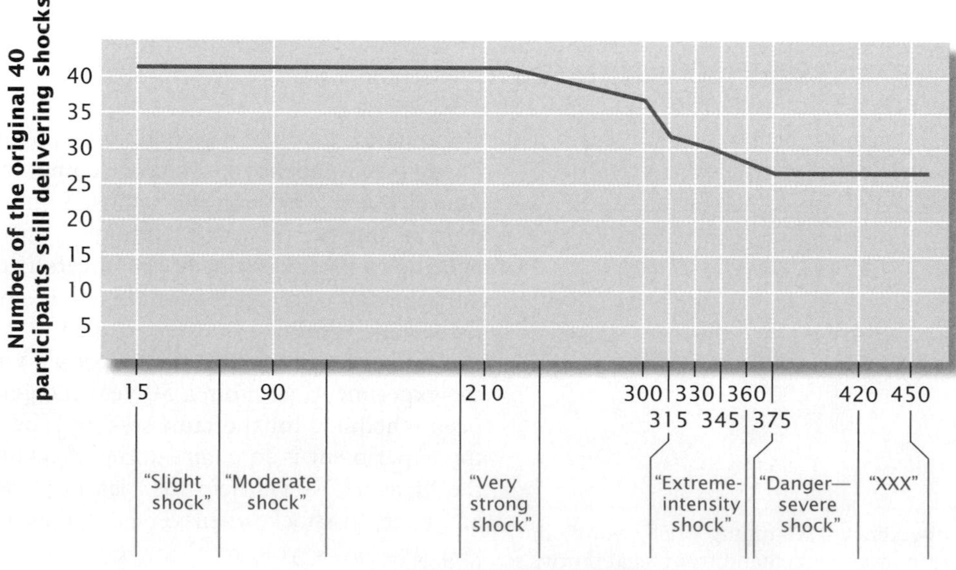

figure 17.13

Results of Milgram's Obedience Experiment

When Milgram asked a group of undergraduates and a group of psychiatrists to predict how participants in his experiment would respond, they estimated that no more than 2 percent would go all the way to 450 volts. In fact, 65 percent of the participants did so. What do you think you would have done in this situation?

Source: Milgram (1963).

Proximity and Obedience Milgram's research suggested that the close proximity of an authority figure enhances obedience to authority (Rada & Rogers, 1973). This principle is employed in the military, where no one is ever far away from the authority of a higher-ranking person.

[After throwing the 180-volt switch:] *He can't stand it. I'm not going to kill that man in there. Do you hear him hollering? He's hollering. He can't stand it. What if something happens to him? I'm not going to get that man sick in there. He's hollering in there. Do you know what I mean? I mean, I refuse to take responsibility. He's getting hurt in there. . . . Too many left here. Geez, if he gets them wrong. There are too many of them left. I mean, who is going to take responsibility if anything happens to that gentleman?*

[After the experimenter accepts responsibility:] *All right. . . .*

[After administering 240 volts:] *Oh, no, you mean I've got to keep going up the scale? No, sir, I'm not going to kill that man. I'm not going to give him 450 volts.*

[After the experimenter says, "The experiment requires that you go on":] *I know it does, but that man is hollering in there, sir.*

This participant administered shock up to 450 volts (Milgram, 1974, p. 74).

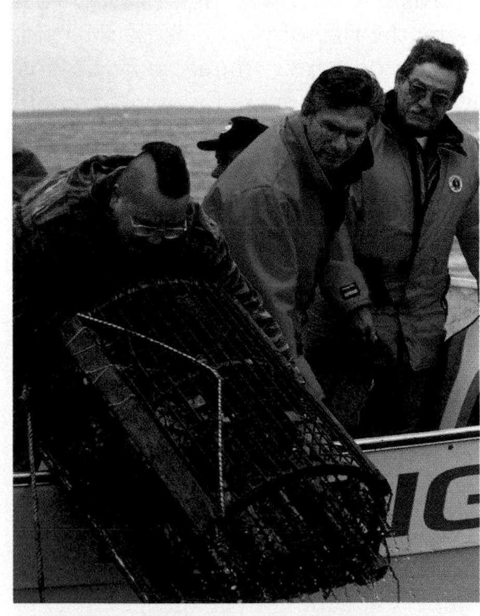

Civil Disobedience Not everyone is blindly obedient to authority. In August of 2000 (roughly 10 years after the Oka Crisis in Quebec), Mi'kmaq from the small fishing village of Burnt Church, New Brunswick, staged a protest claiming their treaty right to fish for lobster in full disregard of the Department of Fisheries and Oceans' mandate to regulate the fishery.

Factors Affecting Obedience

Milgram had not expected so many people to deliver such apparently intense shocks. Was there something about his procedure that produced this high level of obedience? To find out, Milgram and other researchers varied the original procedure in numerous ways. The overall level of obedience to an authority figure was usually quite high, but the degree of obedience was affected by several factors.

Experimenter Status and Prestige In Milgram's original study, the experimenter's status and prestige as a Yale University professor created two kinds of social power that affected the participants. The first was *expert social power,* which is the ability to influence people because they assume the person in power is a knowledgeable and responsible expert. The second was *legitimate social power,* which is the ability to influence people because they assume the person in power has the right or legitimate authority to tell them what to do (Blass & Schmitt, 2001).

To test the effects of reduced status and prestige, Milgram rented an office in a rundown building in Bridgeport, Connecticut. He then placed a newspaper ad for people to participate in research sponsored by a private firm. There was no mention of Yale. In all other ways, the experimental procedure was identical to the original. Under these less prestigious circumstances, the level of obedience dropped, but not

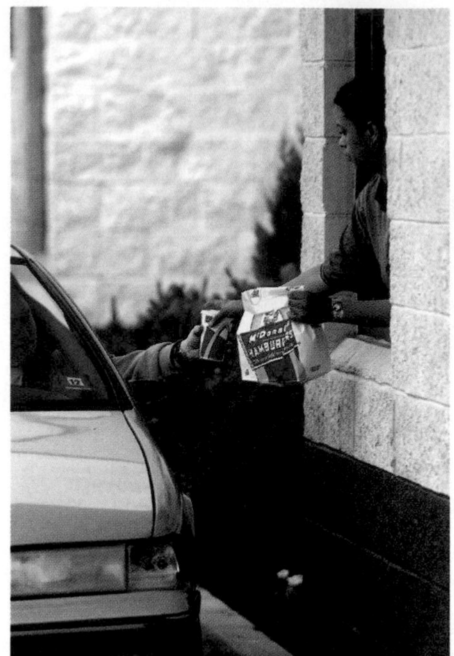

May I Take Your Order? In February of 2004, the managers of four fast-food restaurants in Boston, Massachusetts, received calls from someone claiming to be a police detective on the trail of a robbery suspect. The caller said the suspect might be one of the restaurant's employees and told the managers to strip-search all of them for evidence of guilt. The calls turned out to be hoaxes, but every manager obeyed this bizarre order, apparently because it appeared to come from a legitimate authority.

as much as you might expect; 48 percent of the participants continued to the maximum level of shock, compared with 65 percent in the original study. Milgram concluded that people still would obey instructions that could cause great harm to another even if the authority figure was not associated with a prestigious institution. Evidently, people's willingness to follow orders from an authority operates somewhat independently of the setting in which the orders are given.

The Behaviour of Others To study how the behaviour of fellow participants might affect obedience, Milgram (1965) created a situation in which there were apparently three teachers. Teacher 1 (in reality, a research assistant) read the words to the learner. Teacher 2 (another research assistant) indicated whether or not the learner's response was correct. Teacher 3 (the actual participant) was to deliver shock when mistakes were made. At 150 volts, when the learner began to complain that the shock was too painful, Teacher 1 said he would not participate any longer and left the room. The experimenter asked him to come back, but he refused. The experimenter then instructed Teachers 2 and 3 to continue by themselves. The experiment went on for several more trials. However, at 210 volts, Teacher 2 said that the learner was suffering too much and refused to participate further. The experimenter then told Teacher 3 (the actual participant) to continue the procedure. In this situation, only 10 percent of the participants (compared with 65 percent in the original study) continued to deliver shock all the way up to 450 volts. In other words, as research on conformity would suggest, the presence of others who disobey appears to be the most powerful factor in reducing obedience.

Personality Characteristics Were the participants in Milgram's original experiment heartless creatures who would have given strong shocks even if there had been no pressure on them to do so? Quite the opposite; most of them were nice people who were influenced by experimental situations to behave in apparently antisocial ways. In a later demonstration of the same phenomenon, college students playing the role of prison guards behaved with aggressive heartlessness toward other students who were playing the role of prisoners (Zimbardo, 1973). A real-life illustration of this phenomenon occurred among some US soldiers who were assigned to guard or interrogate Iraqi prisoners following the fall of Saddam Hussein's regime in 2003.

Still, not everyone is equally obedient to authority. For example, people high in *authoritarianism* (a characteristic discussed earlier in this chapter) are more likely than others to comply with an experimenter's request to shock the learner (Blass, 1991). Support for this idea comes from data suggesting that German soldiers who obeyed orders to kill Jews during World War II were higher on the authoritarianism scale than other German men of the same age and background (Steiner & Fahrenberg, 2000).

LINKAGES (a link to Introducing Psychology)

Evaluating Milgram's Studies

How relevant are Milgram's 35-year-old studies in today's world? Consider this fact: Many commercial airline accidents can be attributed to a phenomenon called "captainitis." This phenomenon occurs when the captain of an aircraft makes an obvious error, but none of the other crew members is willing to challenge the captain's authority by pointing out the mistake. As a result, planes have crashed and people have died (Kanki & Foushee, 1990). Obedience to authority may also have operated during the World Trade Center attack on September 11, 2001, when some people who had started for the exits returned to their offices after hearing an ill-advised public address announcement telling them to do so. Most of these people died as a result. Such events suggest that Milgram's findings are still relevant and important (Blass, 1999). Similar kinds of obedience have been observed

in review Types of Social Influence

Type	Definition	Key Findings
Conformity	A change in behaviour or beliefs to match those of others	In cases of ambiguity, people develop a group norm and then adhere to it. Conformity occurs because people want to be right, because they want to be liked by others, and because conformity to group norms is usually reinforced. Conformity usually increases with the ambiguity of the situation, as well as with the unanimity and psychological size of the majority.
Compliance	A change in what is said or done because of a request	Compliance increases with the foot-in-the-door technique, which begins with a small request and works up to a larger one. The door-in-the-face procedure can also be used. After making a large request that is denied, the person substitutes a less extreme alternative that was desired all along. The low-ball approach also elicits compliance. A person first obtains an oral commitment for something, then claims that only a higher-cost version of the original request will suffice.
Obedience	A change in behaviour in response to an explicit demand, typically from an authority figure	People may inflict great harm on others when an authority demands that they do so. Even though people obey orders to harm another person, they often agonize over the decision. People are most likely to disobey orders to harm someone else when they see another person disobey.

PsychAssist: Conformity and the Asch Experiment

in experiments conducted in many countries, from Europe to the Middle East, with female as well as male participants. In short, people appear to be as obedient today as they were when Milgram conducted his research (Blass, 1999; Smith & Bond, 1999).

Nevertheless, many aspects of Milgram's work still provoke debate. (For a summary of Milgram's results, plus those of studies on conformity and compliance, see "In Review: Types of Social Influence.")

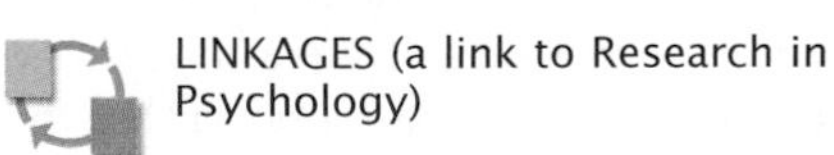

Ethical Questions Although the "learners" in Milgram's experiment suffered no discomfort, the participants did. Milgram (1963) saw participants "sweat, stutter, tremble, groan, bite their lips, and dig their fingernails into their flesh" (p. 375). Against the potential harm inflicted by Milgram's experiments stand the potential gains. For example, people who learn about Milgram's work often take his findings into account when deciding how to behave in social situations (Sherman, 1980). But even if social value has come from Milgram's studies, the question remains: Was it ethical for Milgram to treat his participants as he did?

In the years before his death in 1984, Milgram defended his experiments (e.g., Milgram, 1977). He argued that his debriefing of the participants after the experiment prevented any lasting harm. For example, to demonstrate that their behaviour was not unusual, Milgram told them that most people went all the way to the

450-volt level. He also explained that the learner did not experience any shock; in fact, the learner came in and chatted with each participant. On a later questionnaire, 84 percent of the participants said that they had learned something important about themselves and that the experience had been worthwhile. Milgram argued, therefore, that the experience was actually a positive one. Still, today's committees charged with protecting human participants in research would be unlikely to approve Milgram's experiments, and less controversial ways to study obedience have now been developed (Meeus & Raaijmakers, 1995).

Questions of Meaning Do Milgram's dramatic results mean that most people are putty in the hands of authority figures and that most of us would blindly follow inhumane orders from our leaders? Some critics have argued that other factors besides obedience to authority were responsible for the behaviour of Milgram's participants and that the social-influence processes identified in his studies might not explain obedience in the real world. For example, Leonard Berkowitz (1999) pointed out that Milgram's studies cannot explain why, during World War II, many German concentration camp guards not only obeyed their superiors' orders to kill prisoners but also carried out those orders in the most sadistic and inhumane manner possible. Their actions, Berkowitz said, went far beyond simple obedience to authority.

Most psychologists believe that Milgram did more than highlight the phenomenon of obedience. He appears to have demonstrated a basic truth about human behaviour—namely, that under certain circumstances, human beings are capable of unspeakable acts of brutality toward other humans. Sadly, examples abound. And one of the most horrifying aspects of human inhumanity—whether it is the Nazis' campaign of genocide against Jews 60 years ago or the campaigns of terror under way today—is that the perpetrators are not necessarily demented, sadistic fiends. Most of them are, in many respects, "normal" people who have been influenced by economic and political situations and the persuasive power of their leaders to behave in a demented and fiendish manner. In short, inhumanity can occur even without pressure for obedience. For example, a good deal of people's aggressiveness toward other people appears to come from within.

Altruism and Helping Behaviour

Called "the flood of the century," in the spring of 1997, the lower fifth of the province of Manitoba looked like an enormous lake from the air. Granted, any natural disaster like a tornado puts obvious strains on everyone in a community. But at the same time, these strains also help reveal some of the most inspiring examples of human behaviour at its best. Thousands of volunteers from all across Canada pitch in to sandbag, cook, evacuate livestock and patrol dikes. Along with fellow volunteers, Pauline from Pauline's Kitche*n* of Morden, Manitoba, made an average of 10 000 sandwiches a day to feed flood relief workers. Greater still were those who pitched in for flood relief—thousands attended a free outdoor concert led by Canadian actor and musician Tom Jackson and featured Randy Bachman and Burton Cummings; it raised over $2 million! A similar concert in Calgary sold over 7000 tickets at $10 each, all going to flood relief.

All of these actions are examples of **helping behaviour,** which is defined as any act that is intended to benefit another person. Helping can range from picking up dropped packages to donating a kidney. Closely related to helping is **altruism,** an unselfish concern for another's welfare (Penner, Dovidio, et al., in press). Let's consider some of the reasons for helping and altruism, along with some of the conditions under which people are most likely to help others.

helping behaviour Any act that is intended to benefit another person.

altruism An unselfish concern for another's welfare.

A Young Helper Even before their second birthday, some children offer help to those who are hurt or crying by snuggling, patting, or offering food or even their own teddy bears.

Why Do People Help?

The tendency to help others begins early, although at first it is not spontaneous. In most cultures, very young children generally help others only when they are asked to do so or are offered a reward (Grusec, Davidov, & Lundell, 2002). Still, Carolyn Zahn-Waxler and her associates (1992) found that almost half of the two-year-olds they observed acted helpfully toward a friend or family member. As they grow older, children use helping behaviour to gain social approval, and their efforts at helping become more elaborate. The role of social influence in the development of helping is seen as children follow examples set by people around them. Their helping behaviours are shaped by the norms established by their families and the broader culture (Grusec & Goodnow, 1994). In addition, children are praised and given other rewards for helpfulness but are scolded for selfishness. Eventually children come to believe that being helpful is good and that they are good when they are helpful. By the late teens, people often help others even when no one is watching and no one will know that they did so (Grusec et al., 2002). There are three major theories about why people help even when they cannot expect any external rewards for doing so.

Arousal: Cost-Reward Theory One approach to explaining why people help is called the **arousal: cost-reward theory** (Piliavin et al., 1981). This theory proposes that people find the sight of a victim distressing and anxiety provoking, which motivates them to do something to reduce the unpleasant arousal. Several studies have shown that, all else being equal, the more physiologically aroused bystanders are, the more likely they are to help someone in an emergency (Dovidio et al., 1991; Schroeder et al., 1995). Before rushing to a victim's aid, however, the bystander will first evaluate two aspects of the situation: the costs associated with helping and the costs (to the bystander and the other person) of not helping. Whether or not the bystander actually helps depends on the outcome of this evaluation (Dovidio et al., 1991). If the costs of helping are low (as when helping someone pick up a dropped grocery bag) and the costs of not helping are high (as when the other person is physically unable to do this alone), the bystander will almost certainly help. However, if the costs of helping are high (as when the task is to load a heavy box into a car) and the costs of not helping are low (as when the person is strong enough to manage the task alone), the bystander is unlikely to offer help. This theory is attractive partly because it is comprehensive enough to provide a framework for explaining research findings on the factors that affect helping.

One of these factors is the *clarity of the need for help*, which has a major impact on whether people provide help (Dovidio et al., 1991). In one study, undergraduate students were waiting alone in a campus building when a staged "accident" took place outside. A window washer screamed as he and his ladder fell to the ground. He then began to clutch his ankle and groan in pain. All of the students looked out a window to see what had happened, but only 29 percent of them did anything to help. Other students experienced the same situation with one important difference: The man *said* he was hurt and needed help. In this case, more than 80 percent of the students came to his aid (Yakimovich & Saltz, 1971). Why so many? Apparently, this one additional cue eliminated any uncertainty about whether the person needed help. This cue also raised the perceived costs to the victim of not offering help. As these costs become higher, helping becomes more likely.

The *presence of others* also has a strong influence on the tendency to help. Somewhat surprisingly, though, their presence actually tends to inhibit helping behaviour. One of the most highly publicized examples of this phenomenon was the Kitty Genovese incident, which occurred on a New York City street in 1964. During a 30-minute struggle, a man stabbed Genovese repeatedly, but none of the dozens of neighbours who witnessed the attack intervened or even called the police until it was too late to save her life. A similar case occurred in November 2000, in London, England, when a ten-year-old boy who had been stabbed by members of

arousal: cost-reward theory A theory attributing people's helping behaviour to their efforts to reduce the unpleasant arousal they feel in the face of someone's need or suffering.

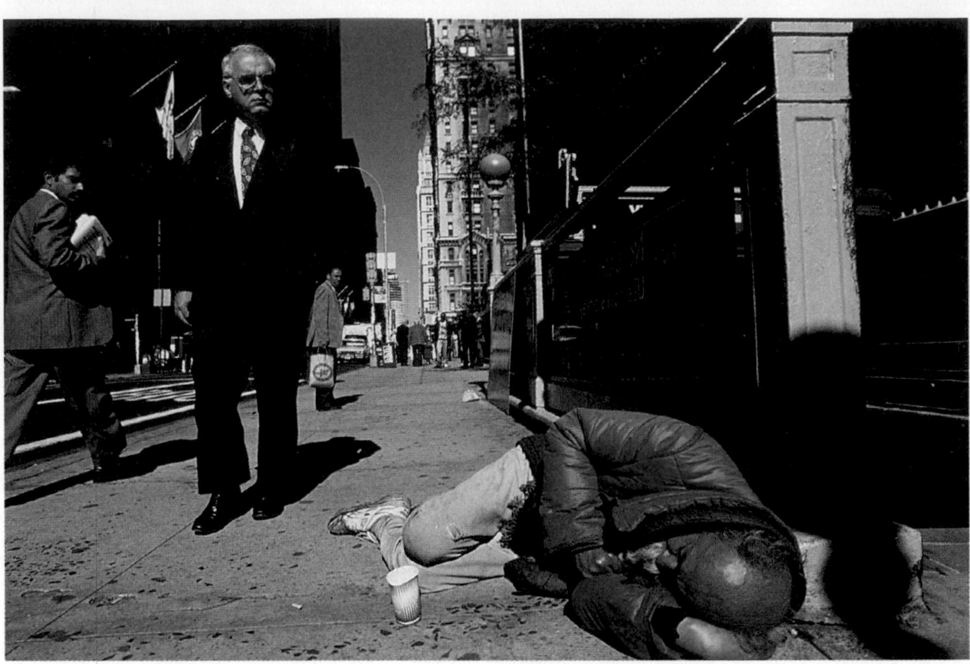

Diffusion of Responsibility Does the man on the sidewalk need help? The people nearby probably are not sure and might assume that, if he does, someone else will assist him. Research on factors affecting helping and altruism suggests that if you need help, especially if a number of others are present, it is important not only to clearly ask for help but also to tell a specific onlooker to take specific action (for example, "You, in the yellow shirt, please call an ambulance!").

a street gang lay ignored by passersby as he bled to death. After each case, journalists and social commentators expressed dismay about the apathy and callousness that seems to exist among people who live in big cities. But psychologists believe that something about the situation surrounding such events deters people from helping.

The numerous studies of helping behaviour stimulated by the Genovese case revealed a phenomenon that may explain the inaction of Genovese's neighbours and those passersby in London. This phenomenon is known as the **bystander effect:** Usually, as the number of people who witness an emergency increases, the likelihood that one of them will help decreases (Garcia et al., 2002). One explanation for why the presence of others often reduces helping is that each person thinks someone else will help the victim. That is, seeing other bystanders allows each individual to experience a *diffusion of responsibility* for taking action, which lowers the costs of not helping (Dovidio & Penner, 2001).

The degree to which the presence of other people inhibits helping may depend on who those other people are. When they are strangers, perhaps poor communication inhibits helping. People often have difficulty speaking to strangers, particularly in an emergency, and without speaking, they have difficulty knowing what the others intend to do. According to this logic, if people are with friends rather than strangers, they should be less uncomfortable, more willing to discuss the problem, and thus more likely to help.

Research suggests that the *personality of the helper* also plays a role in helping. Some people are simply more likely to help than others. Consider, for example, the Christians who risked their lives to save Jews from the Nazi Holocaust. Samuel and Pearl Oliner (1988) interviewed more than two hundred of these rescuers and compared their personalities with those of people who had a chance to save Jews but did not do so. The rescuers were found to have more empathy (the ability to understand or experience another's emotional state; Davis, 1994), more concern about others, a greater sense of responsibility for their own actions, and a greater sense of self-efficacy (confidence in the success of their efforts). Louis Penner and his associates (Penner & Finkelstein, 1998; Penner, 2002) have found that these kinds of personality traits predict a broad spectrum of helping behaviours, ranging from the speed with which bystanders intervene in an emergency to the amount of time volunteers spend helping AIDS victims. Consistent with the

bystander effect A phenomenon in which the chances that someone will help in an emergency decrease as the number of people present increases.

empathy-altruism theory A theory suggesting that people help others because of empathy with their needs.

in review Theories of Helping Behaviours

Theory	Basic Premise	Important Variables
Arousal: cost-reward	People help in order to reduce the unpleasant arousal caused by another person's distress. They attempt to minimize the costs of doing this.	Factors that affect the costs of helping and of not helping
Empathy-altruism	People sometimes help for utterly altruistic reasons. They are motivated by a desire to increase another person's well-being.	The amount of empathy that one person feels for another
Evolutionary	People help relatives because it increases the chances that the helper's genes will survive in future generations.	The biological relationship between the helper and the recipient of help

PsychAssist: Cooperation, Competition, and the Prisoner's Dilemma

arousal: cost-reward theory, these personality characteristics are also correlated with people's estimates of the costs of helping and not helping. For example, empathic individuals usually estimate the costs of not helping as high, and people with a sense of self-efficacy usually rate the costs of helping as low (Penner et al., 1995). These patterns of cost estimation may partially explain why such people tend to be especially helpful.

It is also difficult for the arousal: cost-reward theory to predict what bystanders will do when the cost of helping and the cost of not helping are *both* high. In these cases, helping (or not helping) may depend on several situational factors and, sometimes, on the personality of the potential helper. There may also be circumstances in which cost considerations may not be the major cause of a decision to help or not to help. A second approach to helping considers some of these circumstances.

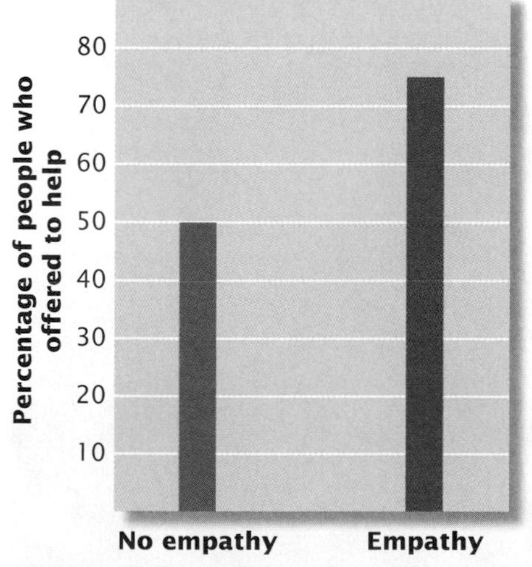

figure 17.14

The Effect of Empathy on Helping

After hearing a staged interview with a woman who supposedly needed to raise money for her family, participants in this experiment were asked to help her. Those who were led to empathize with the woman were much more likely to offer their help than those who did not empathize. These results are consistent with the empathy-altruism theory of helping.

Empathy-Altruism Theory The second approach to explaining helping is embodied in **empathy-altruism theory,** which maintains that people are more likely to engage in *altruistic,* or unselfish, helping—even when the cost of helping is high—if they feel empathy toward the person in need (Batson, 1998). In one experiment illustrating this phenomenon, participants listened to a tape-recorded interview with a female student. The student told the interviewer that her parents had been killed in an automobile accident, that they had no life insurance, and that she was now faced with the task of finishing college while taking care of a younger brother and sister. She said that these financial burdens might force her to quit school or give up her siblings for adoption. None of this was true, but the participants were told that it was. Further, before listening to the woman's story, half the participants were given additional information about her that was designed to promote strong empathy. Later, all the participants were asked to help the woman raise money for herself and her siblings (Batson et al., 1997). The critical question was whether the participants who heard the additional empathy-promoting information would help more than those who did not have that information. Consistent with the empathy-altruism theory, more participants in the empathy condition than in the nonempathy condition offered to help (see Figure 17.14).

Were those who offered help in this experiment being utterly altruistic, or could there be a different reason for their actions? This is a hotly debated question. Some researchers dispute the claim that this study illustrated truly altruistic helping. They suggest that people help in such situations for more selfish reasons, such as relieving the distress they experienced after hearing of the woman's problems (Maner et al., 2002). The final verdict on this question is not yet in.

LINKAGES (a link to Health, Stress, and Coping)

Evolutionary Theory The evolutionary approach to social psychology offers a third way of explaining helping. This approach views many human social behaviours as echoes of actions that contributed to the survival of our prehistoric ancestors (Buss, 2003). At first glance, it might not seem reasonable to apply evolutionary theory to helping and altruism, because helping others at the risk of one's own well-being doesn't appear adaptive. If we die while trying to save others, it will be their genes, not ours, that will survive. In fact, according to Charles Darwin's concept of the survival of the fittest, helpers—and their genes—should have disappeared long ago. Contemporary evolutionary theorists suggest, however, that Darwin's thinking about natural selection focused too much on the survival of the fittest *individuals* and not enough on the survival of their genes in others. Accordingly, the concept of survival of the fittest has been replaced by the concept of *inclusive fitness,* the survival of one's genes in future generations (Hamilton, 1964). Because we share genes with our relatives, helping or even dying for a cousin, a sibling, or, above all, our own child potentially increases the likelihood that at least some of our genetic characteristics will be passed on to the next generation through the beneficiary's future reproduction (Burnstein & Brannigan, 2001). So *kin selection*—helping a relative to survive—may produce genetic benefits for the helper (Kruger, 2003).

There is considerable evidence that kin selection occurs among birds, squirrels, and other animals. The more closely the animals are related, the more likely they are to risk their lives for one another.

Family Ties Research indicates that people are more likely to donate organs to family members than to strangers. This pattern may reflect greater attachment or a stronger sense of social obligation to relatives than to others. However, psychologists who take an evolutionary approach to helping suggest that when, as in the case of these sisters, one family member donates a kidney to save the life of another, the donor is helping to ensure the survival of the genes shared with the recipient.

LINKAGES

As noted in the chapter on introducing psychology, all of psychology's subfields are related to one another. Our discussion of how the presence of other people affects a person's motivation to perform illustrates just one way in which the topic of this chapter, social behaviour, is linked to the subfield of motivation and emotion (see the chapter on that topic). The Linkages diagram shows ties to two other subfields as well, and there are many more ties throughout the book. Looking for linkages among subfields will help you see how they all fit together and help you better appreciate the big picture that is psychology.

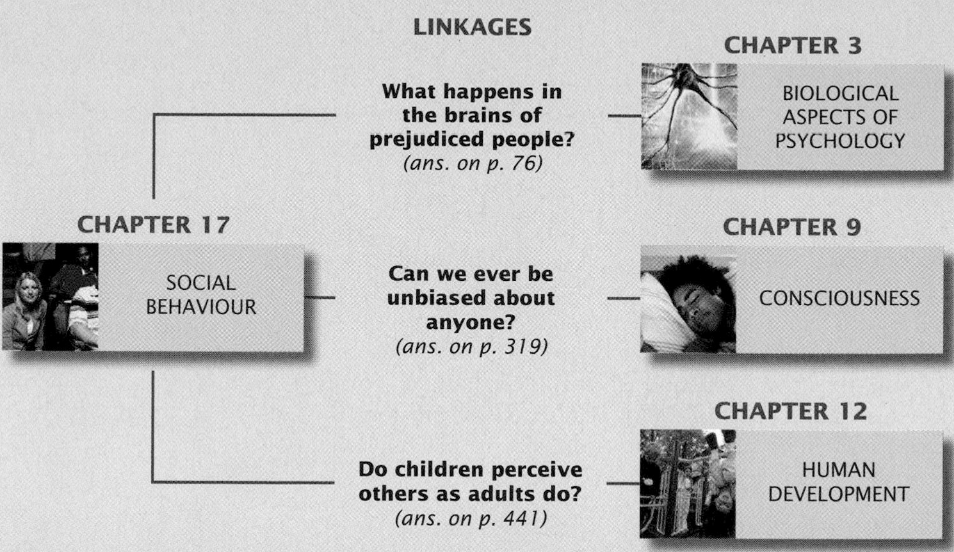

LINKAGES
CHAPTER 17
SOCIAL BEHAVIOUR
What happens in the brains of prejudiced people?
(ans. on p. 76)
CHAPTER 3
BIOLOGICAL ASPECTS OF PSYCHOLOGY
Can we ever be unbiased about anyone?
(ans. on p. 319)
CHAPTER 9
CONSCIOUSNESS
Do children perceive others as adults do?
(ans. on p. 441)
CHAPTER 12
HUMAN DEVELOPMENT

SUMMARY

Social cognition (the mental processes through which people perceive and react to others) is one aspect of *social psychology* (the study of how people influence, and are influenced by, other people).

Social Influences on the Self

People's social and cultural environments affect their thoughts and feelings about themselves, including their *self-esteem* and their *self-concept*.

Social Comparison

When people have no objective criteria by which to judge themselves, they engage in *social comparison* (using others) or *temporal comparison* (using themselves at an earlier time) as their standard. Such comparison can affect self-evaluation, or self-esteem. Comparison to groups sometimes produces *relative deprivation,* which in turn can cause personal and social turmoil.

Social Identity Theory

A person's *social identity* is formed from beliefs about the groups to which the person belongs. Social identity affects the beliefs we hold about ourselves. It permits us to feel part of a larger group, engendering loyalty and sacrifice from group members but also potentially creating bias and discrimination toward people who are not members of the group.

Self-Schemas

Through social comparison and the formation of social identity, people develop mental representations of their views and beliefs about themselves. These mental representations, called *self-schemas,* are part of one's self-concept. Self-schemas can affect people's emotional reactions to events.

Social Perception

Social perception concerns the processes by which people interpret information about others, form impressions of them, and draw conclusions about the reasons for their behaviour.

The Role of Schemas

Schemas, the mental representations about people and social situations that we carry into social interactions, affect what we pay attention to, what we remember, and how we judge people and events.

First Impressions

First impressions are formed easily and quickly, in part because people apply existing schemas to their perceptions of others. First impressions change slowly because people are "cognitive misers"; once we form an impression about another person, we try to maintain it. Schemas, however, can create *self-fulfilling prophecies,* leading people to act in ways that bring out in others behaviour that is consistent with expectations.

Explaining Behaviour: Attribution

Attribution is the process of explaining the causes of people's behaviour, including one's own. Observers tend to attribute behaviour to causes that are either internal or external to the actor. People from different cultures may sometimes reach different conclusions about the causes of an actor's behaviour.

Biases in Attribution

Attributions are affected by biases that systematically distort one's view of behaviour. The most common attributional biases are the *fundamental attribution error* (and its cousin, the ultimate attribution error), the *actor-observer bias,* and the *self-serving bias.* Personal and cultural factors can affect the extent to which people exhibit attributional biases.

Attitudes

An *attitude* is the tendency to respond positively or negatively to a particular object. Attitudes affect a wide range of behaviours.

The Structure of Attitudes

Many theorists believe that attitudes have three components: the cognitive (beliefs), affective (feelings), and behavioural (actions) components. However, it is often difficult to predict a specific behaviour from a person's beliefs or feelings about an object. Cognitive theories propose that attitudes consist of evaluations of an object that are stored in memory. This approach suggests that the likelihood of attitude-behaviour consistency depends on the accessibility of evaluations in memory, on subjective norms, on perceived control over the behaviour, and on prior direct experience with the attitude object.

Forming Attitudes

Attitudes can be learned through modelling, as well as through classical or operant conditioning. They are also subject to the mere-exposure effect: All else being equal, people develop greater liking for a new object the more often they are exposed to it.

Changing Attitudes

The effectiveness of a persuasive message in changing attitudes is influenced by the characteristics of the person who communicates it, by its content, and by the audience receiving it. The *elaboration likelihood model* suggests that attitude change can occur through either a peripheral or a central route, depending on a person's ability and motivation to carefully consider an argument. Another approach to attitude change is to change a person's behaviour in the hope that the person's attitude will be adjusted to match the behaviour. *Cognitive dissonance theory* holds that if inconsistency between attitudes and behaviour creates discomfort related to a person's self-concept or self-image, the person will be motivated to reduce that discomfort.

Prejudice and Stereotypes

Stereotypes often lead to *prejudice* and *discrimination.*

Theories of Prejudice and Stereotyping

Motivational theories of prejudice suggest that some people have a need to disrespect and dislike others. This need may stem from the trait of authoritarianism, as well as from a strong social identity. In either case, feeling superior to members of out-groups helps these people to feel better about themselves. As a result, in-group members tend to discriminate against members of out-groups. Cognitive theories suggest that people categorize others into groups in order to reduce social complexity. And learning theories maintain that stereotypes, prejudice, and discriminatory behaviours can be learned from parents, peers, and the media.

Reducing Prejudice

The *contact hypothesis* proposes that intergroup contact can reduce prejudice and lead to more favourable attitudes toward a stereotyped group—but only if the contact occurs under specific conditions, such as when there is equal status between group members. Helping diverse people to feel as if they belong to the same group can also reduce intergroup prejudice.

Interpersonal Attraction

Keys to Attraction

Interpersonal attraction is a function of many variables. Physical proximity is important because it allows people to meet. The situation in which they meet is important because positive or negative aspects of the situation tend to be associated with the other person. Characteristics of the other person are also important. Attraction tends to be greater when two people share similar attitudes and characteristics. Physical appearance plays a role in attraction. Initially, attraction is strongest to those who are most physically attractive. But for long-term relationships, the *matching hypothesis* applies: People tend to choose others whose physical attractiveness is about the same as theirs.

Intimate Relationships and Love

A defining characteristic of intimate relationships is interdependence, and a key component of successful relationships is commitment. Commitment, in turn, is affected by the rewards coming from the relationship, by the resources invested in it, and by the possible alternatives open to each party. Robert Sternberg's triangular theory suggests that love is a function of three components: passion, intimacy, and commitment. Varying combinations of these three components create different types of love.

Social Influence

Social influence is a process through which a person's behaviour is directly or indirectly affected by the words or actions of others. *Norms* establish the rules for what should and should not be done in a particular situation. Descriptive norms indicate what most other people do and create pressure to do the same. Injunctive norms provide specific information about what others approve or disapprove of. *Deindividuation* is a psychological state in which people in a group temporarily lose their individuality, focus on the group's norms, and may engage in antisocial acts that they would not normally perform. *Social facilitation, social impairment,* and *social loafing* provide three other examples of how the presence of other people can affect an individual's behaviour.

Conformity and Compliance

When behaviours or beliefs change as the result of unspoken or implicit group pressure, *conformity* has occurred; when the change is the result of a request, *compliance* has occurred.

The Role of Norms

People tend to follow the normative responses of others, and groups create norms when none already exist.

Why Do People Conform?

People sometimes exhibit public conformity without private acceptance. At other times, the responses of other people have a genuine impact on private beliefs. People conform because they want to be right, because they want to be liked, and because they tend to be rewarded for doing so.

When Do People Conform?

People are most likely to conform when the situation is ambiguous, as well as when others in the group are in unanimous agreement. Up to a point, conformity usually increases as the number of people holding the majority view grows larger. Persistent and unanimous *minority influence* can also produce some conformity.

Inducing Compliance

Effective strategies for inducing compliance include the foot-in-the-door technique, the door-in-the-face procedure, and the low-ball approach.

Obedience

Obedience involves complying with an explicit demand, typically from an authority figure. Research by Stanley Milgram indicates that levels of obedience are high even when obeying an authority appears to result in pain and suffering for another person.

Factors Affecting Obedience

People obey someone who has certain kinds of social power. Obedience declines when the status of the authority figure declines, as well as when others are observed to disobey. Some people may be more likely to obey orders than others.

Evaluating Milgram's Studies

Because participants in Milgram's studies experienced considerable stress, the experiments have been questioned on ethical grounds. Nevertheless, Milgram's research showed that even apparently "normal" people can be influenced to inflict pain on others.

Altruism and Helping Behaviour

Human behaviour is also characterized by *helping behaviour* and *altruism*.

Why Do People Help?

There are three major theories of why people help others. According to the *arousal: cost-reward theory,* people help in order to reduce the unpleasant arousal they experience when others are in distress. Their specific reaction to a suffering person depends on the costs associated with helping or not helping. Helping behaviour is most likely when the costs of helping are low and the costs of not helping are high. Perceptions of cost are affected by the clarity of the need for help, by the presence of others (which can create the diffusion of responsibility seen in the *bystander effect*), and by personality traits. Environmental factors also affect willingness to help. The *empathy-altruism theory* suggests that helping can be truly unselfish if the helper feels empathy for the person in need. Evolutionary theory suggests that humans have an innate tendency to help others, especially relatives, because doing so increases the likelihood that family genes will survive.

Appendix

Behavioural Genetics

Think about some trait that distinguishes you from other people, a trait on which you feel you are well above or well below average. Perhaps it relates to your skill at sports, languages, or music, or maybe to your fearfulness, sociability, or other aspects of your personality. Have you ever wondered what made you the way you are? If you are shy, for example, it is easy to think of possible environmental explanations. Perhaps you are shy because as a child you had few opportunities to meet new children or because you had embarrassing or unpleasant experiences when you did meet them. Maybe you have shy parents who served as the role models you imitated. Such environmental explanations are certainly reasonable, but it is also possible that you inherited a disposition toward shyness from your parents. It is even more likely that both inheritance and environment contributed to your shyness.

Topics such as these are addressed by researchers in the field of *behavioural genetics*, the study of how genes affect behaviour (see the chapter on research in psychology). These researchers have developed methods to explore genetic, as well as environmental, origins of behavioural differences among people. The results of behavioural genetics research make it clear that heredity has a significant influence, not just on shyness but on personality more generally, on cognitive abilities, on psychological disorders, and on many other aspects of human behaviour and mental processes. However, behavioural genetics is just as much the study of environment as of genetics. In the process of trying to disentangle genetic from environmental factors, researchers have made several important discoveries about the impact of the environment.

In this appendix, we discuss behavioural genetics in more detail than we did in the chapter on research in psychology. We begin with a review of the biochemical mechanisms underlying genetics and heredity. We then offer a brief history of genetic research in psychology, followed by a discussion of what research on genetic influences can and cannot tell us about the origins of human differences. Finally, we describe some findings from behavioural genetics research that illuminate several important aspects of human behaviour and mental processes.

The Biology of Genetics and Heredity

What does it mean to say that someone has inherited some physical feature or behavioural trait? The answer lies in **genetics**, the biology of inheritance. The story begins with the biochemistry of the human body and with the chromosomes contained within each of the body's cells. Most human cells contain 46 chromosomes, arranged in 23 matching pairs. These **chromosomes** are long, thin structures that are made up of thousands of genes. **Genes** are the biochemical units of heredity that govern the development of an individual by controlling the synthesis of protein. They are composed of **deoxyribonucleic acid (DNA)**—strands of sugar, phosphate, and four kinds of nitrogen-containing molecules twisted around each other in a double spiral (see Figure 1). It is the particular order in which the four nitrogen-containing molecules are arranged in the DNA that determines, through the production of *ribonucleic acid (RNA)*, which protein each gene will produce. Protein molecules, in turn, form the physical structure of each cell and also direct the activity of the cell. So as a function of DNA, the genes contain a coded message that provides a blueprint for constructing every aspect of a physical human being, including eye colour, height, blood type, inherited disorders, and the like—and all in less space than the period that ends this sentence.

genetics The biology of inheritance.

chromosomes Long, thin structures in every biological cell that contain genetic information.

genes The biological instructions, inherited from both parents and located on the chromosomes, that provide the blueprint for physical development.

deoxyribonucleic acid (DNA) The molecular structure of a gene that provides the genetic code.

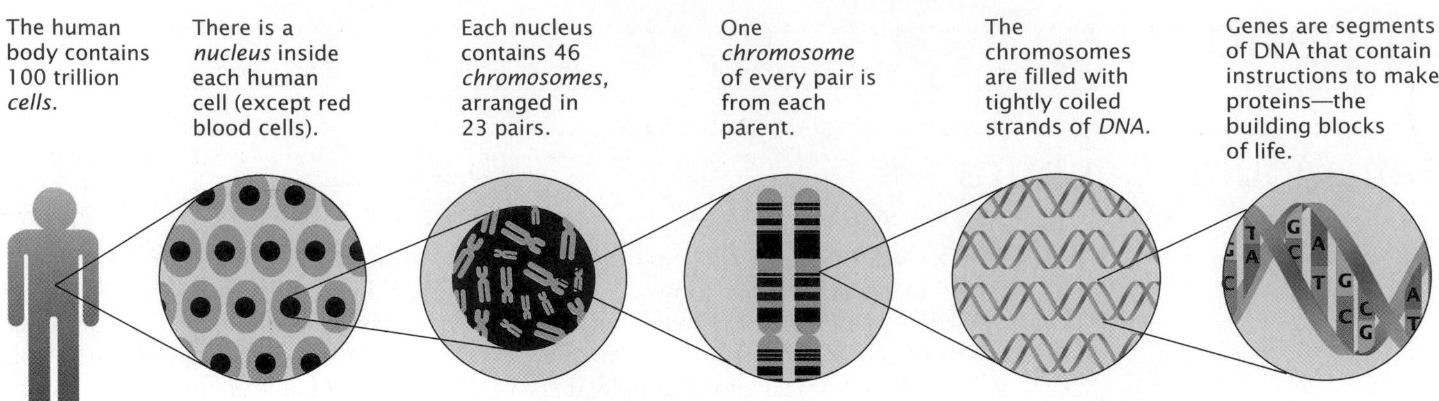
The human body contains 100 trillion *cells.*
There is a *nucleus* inside each human cell (except red blood cells).
Each nucleus contains 46 *chromosomes,* arranged in 23 pairs.
One *chromosome* of every pair is from each parent.
The chromosomes are filled with tightly coiled strands of *DNA.*
Genes are segments of DNA that contain instructions to make proteins—the building blocks of life.

figure 1
Genetic Building Blocks

Only about 3 percent of DNA contains genes that guide the production of proteins, but it nevertheless determines all aspects of our physical bodies, and influences many of our behavioural characteristics, too.

Source: "Genetic Building Blocks" from *Time*, January 17, 1994. Copyright © 1994 TIME, Inc. Reprinted with permission.

New cells are constantly being produced by the division of existing cells. Most of the body's cells divide through a process called *mitosis*, in which the cell's chromosomes duplicate themselves so that each new cell contains copies of the 23 pairs of chromosomes in the original.

A different kind of cell division occurs when a male's sperm cells and a female's egg cells (called *ova*) are formed. This process is called *meiosis*. In meiosis, the chromosome pairs are not copied. Instead, they are randomly split and rearranged, leaving each new sperm and egg cell with just one member of each chromosome pair, or 23 single chromosomes. No two of these special new cells are quite the same, and none contains an exact copy of the person who produced it. So at conception, when a male's sperm cell fertilizes the female's ovum, a truly new cell is formed. This fertilized cell, called a *zygote*, carries 23 pairs of chromosomes—half of each pair from the mother and half from the father. The zygote represents a unique heritage, a complete genetic code for a new person that combines genes from both parents. As described in the chapter on human development, the zygote divides first into copies of itself and then into the billions of specialized cells that form a new human being.

Whether or not genes express themselves in the individual who carries them depends on whether they are dominant or recessive. *Dominant* genes are outwardly expressed whenever they are present. *Recessive* genes are expressed only when they are paired with a similar gene from the other parent. For example, phenylketonuria (PKU)—a disorder seen in about 1 in 10 000 newborns—is caused by a recessive gene. When inherited from both parents, this gene disrupts the body's ability to control phenylalanine, an amino acid found in milk and other foods. As a result, this acid is converted into a toxic substance that can cause severe mental retardation. (Discovery of this genetic defect made it possible to prevent retardation in children with PKU simply by making sure they did not consume foods high in phenylalanine.) PKU is one of more than 4000 single-gene disorders, but in fact, relatively few human characteristics are controlled by just one gene. Most characteristics are **polygenic,** meaning that they are controlled by many genes. Even a person's eye colour and height are affected by more than one gene.

The genes contained in the chromosomes inherited from parents make up an individual's **genotype**. Because identical twins develop from one fertilized egg cell, they are described as *monozygotic*; they have exactly the same genotype. So why don't all identical twins look exactly alike? Because they do not have exactly the same environment. An individual's **phenotype** is the set of observable characteristics that result from the combination of heredity and environment. In twins and nontwins

polygenic A term describing characteristics that are determined by more than one gene.

genotype The full set of genes, inherited from both parents, contained in 23 pairs of chromosomes.

phenotype How an individual looks and acts, which depends on how inherited characteristics interact with the environment.

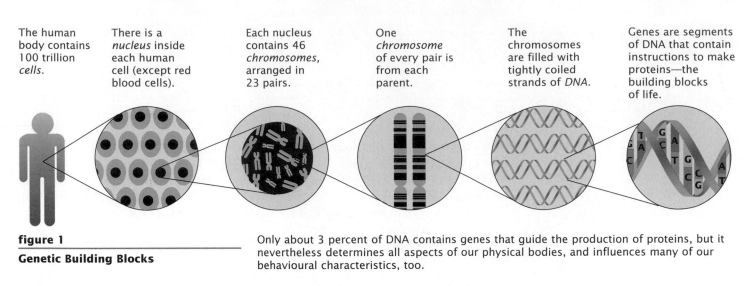

alike, the way people actually look and act is influenced by the combination of genes they carry, as well as by environmental factors—in other words, by both nature and nurture.

A Brief History of Genetic Research in Psychology

The field now known as behavioural genetics began in the late 1800s with the work of Sir Francis Galton. A cousin of Charles Darwin, Galton was so impressed with Darwin's book on evolution that he decided to study heredity in the human species, especially as it relates to human behaviour. Galton suggested the family, twin, and adoption study designs that are the mainstays of human behavioural genetics research today (see the chapter on research in psychology). He even coined the phrase *nature-nurture* to refer to genetic and environmental influences. Galton's most famous behavioural genetics study was one in which he showed that genius runs in families. Unfortunately, Galton went too far in interpreting the evidence from this family study when he concluded that "nature prevails enormously over nurture" (Galton, 1883, p. 241). As noted in the chapter on research in psychology, family members can be similar to each other because of environmental, as well as hereditary, factors. So similarity seen among family members with regard to characteristics such as genius could be traced to the environments family members share, to their shared genes, or both. Still, Galton's work helped to focus psychologists' interest on the influence of genetics and on the need to separate nature from nurture in drawing conclusions about why people resemble or differ from each other.

The first two studies aimed at separating nature and nurture by studying twins and adoptees were conducted in 1924. Both focused on IQ, and both suggested the existence of an important genetic contribution to intelligence. However, research on the influence of genetics on behaviour and mental processes was inhibited for a while because of two factors. The first was the impact of John B. Watson's behaviourism, which, as mentioned in the introductory chapter, suggested that we are only what we learn. In 1925, Watson insisted "that there is no such thing as an inheritance of capacity, talent, temperament, mental constitution and characteristics. These things again depend on training that goes on mainly in the cradle" (Watson, 1925, pp. 74–75). The second factor that discouraged attention to human genetics was its association with the view proclaimed by Adolf Hitler and his Nazis that certain groups of people were "genetically inferior." This view led to the Holocaust during World War II, a campaign of genocide during which millions of Jews and other allegedly "inferior" people were killed.

Genetic research on human behaviour was reduced to a trickle during the 1930s and 1940s, but research with animals led, in 1960, to publication of the first behavioural genetics textbook (Fuller & Thompson, 1960) and to signs of increased interest in human genetics. In 1963 an influential article reviewed family, twin, and adoption findings and concluded that genetic factors are an important influence on IQ (Erlenmeyer-Kimling & Jarvik, 1963). Around the same time, the first adoption study of schizophrenia pointed to a strong genetic contribution to that disorder (Heston, 1966).

In the early 1970s, however, interest in human behavioural genetics among psychologists faded again, this time because of reactions to two publications. The first was a paper by Arthur Jensen in which he suggested that differences in average IQ between blacks and whites might be partly due to genetic factors (Jensen, 1969). The second was a book by Richard Herrnstein in which he argued that genetics might contribute to social class differences (Herrnstein, 1973). The furious public and scientific response to these publications—which included branding the authors as racists—inhibited genetic research in psychology, even though very few behavioural geneticists were studying ethnic or class differences. It was not until later in the 1970s and into the 1980s that major genetic studies were again conducted in psychology.

Today most psychologists recognize the role of both genetics and environment in behaviour and mental processes, including the controversial area of cognitive abilities (Snyderman & Rothman, 1987). In fact, in 1992 the American Psychological Association selected behavioural genetics as one of two themes best representing the past, present, and especially the future of psychological research (Plomin & McClearn, 1993). To some, though, the study of human behavioural genetics still carries a hint of racism and class elitism. These concerns were resurrected about a decade ago by a book titled *The Bell Curve,* which considers the role of genetics in ethnic differences in intelligence and the implications of intelligence for social class structure (Herrnstein & Murray, 1994). Fortunately, reaction to that book has not altered the balanced perspective that recognizes the importance of nature as well as nurture in psychology (Neisser, 1997; Pinker, 2002).

The Focus of Research in Behavioural Genetics

Much of the controversy about behavioural genetics and about nature and nurture in general comes from misunderstandings about what behavioural genetics researchers study and, more specifically, what it means to say that genes influence behaviour.

For one thing, behavioural genetics is the study of genetic and environmental factors that are responsible for *differences* among individuals or groups of individuals, not for the characteristics of any single individual. Consider height, for example. Identical twins are much more similar in height than are fraternal twins (who share no more genes than other siblings), and individuals who are genetically related but raised separately are just as similar in height as are relatives who are raised together. Further, genetically unrelated individuals who are raised together are no more similar in height than random pairs of individuals. These data suggest, not surprisingly, that height is highly *heritable*. This means that much of the *variability* in height that we see among people—actually about 80 percent of it—can be explained by genetic differences among them rather than by environmental differences. (It does not mean that a person who is 182 cm tall grew 80 percent of that height because of genes and the other 20 percent because of environment!) It also follows that if a person is, say, shorter than average, genetic reasons are probably the primary cause. We say "probably" because finding a genetic influence on height involves referring only to the origins of average individual differences in the population. So although the difference in people's heights is attributable mainly to genetic factors, a particular person's height could be due mainly to an early illness or other growth-stunting environmental factors. For example, Hattie and Samantha Peters, a pair of identical twins, were exposed to a rare condition in their mother's womb that deprived Samantha of vital nutrients. As a result, Hattie is 162.4 cm tall, but Samantha is only 141.3 cm (Taggart, 2004).

To see how the logic of behavioural genetics applies to conclusions about psychological characteristics, suppose a researcher found that the heritability of a certain personality trait is 50 percent. This result would mean that approximately half of the differences among people on that trait are attributable to genetic factors. It would not mean that each person inherits half of the trait and gets the other half from environmental influences. As in our height example, behavioural geneticists want to know how much variability among people can be accounted for by genetic and environmental factors. The results of their research allow generalizations about the influence of nature and nurture on certain characteristics, but those generalizations do not necessarily apply to the origin of a particular person's characteristics.

Another misconception about genetic influences is that they are "hard-wired" and thus have inevitable effects. Complex traits—intelligence, for example—are influenced by many genes, as well as by many environmental factors. So genetic influence means just that—influence (Plomin, Owen, & McGuffin, 1994). Genes can affect a trait without completely determining whether or not it will appear.

The Role of Genetic Factors in Psychology

In the following sections, we consider behavioural genetics research results that tell a little more of the story about how genes can have an impact on behaviour and mental processes.

Genetic Influences over the Life Span

One particularly interesting finding about genetic influences on general cognitive ability is that these influences continue to increase throughout the life span (McGue et al., 1993; Plomin, 1986). That is, the proportion of individual differences (variance) in IQ scores that can be explained by genetic factors increases from 40 percent in childhood to 60 percent in adolescence and young adulthood and then to 80 percent later in life. This increase in the magnitude of genetic influence can be seen, for example, in the expanding difference between IQ correlations for identical twins and those for fraternal twins: Identical twins become more similar in IQ over the life span, whereas fraternal twins become less similar as the years go by. This finding is all the more interesting for overturning the common assumption that environmental influences become increasingly important as accidents, illnesses, and other experiences accumulate throughout life.

How can it be that genetic influences become more important over time? One possible explanation is that, as discussed later, genetic predispositions lead people to select, and even create, environments that foster the continued development of their genetically influenced abilities.

Genes Affecting Multiple Traits

Behavioural genetics research has also revealed that genes affecting one trait can sometimes affect others as well. For example, it appears that the same genetic factors that affect anxiety also affect depression (Kendler, Neale, et al., 1992; Kendler et al., 2003). So if we could identify specific genes responsible for genetic influences on anxiety, we would expect to find that the same genes were associated with the appearance of depression. Similarly, genetic factors affecting substance dependence are highly correlated with genetic factors affecting antisocial behaviour and impulsive style (Kendler et al., 2003; Krueger et al., 2002).

A similar finding has emerged for cognitive ability and scholastic achievement. Tests of scholastic achievement show almost as much genetic influence as do tests of cognitive ability. Moreover, tests of scholastic achievement correlate substantially with tests of cognitive ability. To what extent is a common set of genes responsible for this overlap? Research suggests that the answer is "almost entirely." It appears that the genes that influence performance on mental ability tests are the same ones that influence students' performance at school (Wadsworth, 1994).

Identifying Genes Related to Behaviour

One of the most exciting new developments in behavioural genetics involves identifying the specific genes responsible for genetic influences in psychology (Plomin & Crabbe, 2000). For example, there are hundreds of rare, single-gene disorders that affect behaviour. One of these is *Huntington's disease*, an ultimately fatal disorder that involves loss of motor control and progressive deterioration of the central nervous system. Huntington's disease emerges only in adulthood, beginning with personality changes, forgetfulness, and other behavioural problems. It is caused by a single dominant gene whose identification in 1983 made it possible to determine who will get this disease—even though the biochemical mechanisms underlying the disorder are still not fully understood and prevention is not yet possible.

Researchers are also tracking down the several genes involved in the appearance of Alzheimer's disease. (As described in the chapter on the biological aspects of psychology, this disease causes memory loss and increasing confusion in many older people.) One of these, a gene that contributes to the risk for late-onset Alzheimer's disease, was identified in 1993. This gene increases the risk for Alzheimer's disease about fivefold, but its presence is neither necessary nor sufficient for the disease to appear. That is, many people with Alzheimer's disease do not have the gene, and many people with the gene do not have the disease. Nonetheless, this gene is by far the strongest risk factor known for Alzheimer's disease, and its discovery marks the beginning of a new era in which specific genes—or regions of DNA near specific genes—will be identified as influencing disorders and psychological traits. Additional examples include reports of linkages between DNA and reading disability (Cardon et al., 1994) and hyperactivity (Faraone et al., 2001).

Progress in identifying specific genes in humans has been slower than expected, in part because research ethics and common sense prevent the use of selective breeding. Accordingly, human studies have lacked the statistical power needed to detect relatively weak but still potentially important genetic influences on behaviour (Plomin et al., 2002). However, the more powerful genetic research techniques available in studies of animals have identified several genes associated, for example, with fearfulness (Flint et al., 1995), with sensitivity to drugs such as alcohol (Crabbe et al., 1999), and with various aspects of learning and memory (Wahlsten, 1999).

Future efforts to identify genes related to human behaviour will be aided by advances flowing from the Human Genome Project, which in early 2001 succeeded in identifying the sequence of most of the three billion "letters" of DNA in the human genome. One of the most surprising findings of that project so far is that the human genome appears to contain only about 20 000 to 25 000 genes—less than half the number expected, and a number that is similar to the estimates for animals such as mice and worms (International Human Genome Sequencing Consortium, 2004). Does this smaller-than-expected number of human genes mean that there are too few to influence all aspects of human behaviour, and that the environment (nurture) must be even more important than we thought in this regard? Not necessarily. It may be that the greater complexity seen in human behaviour versus, say, mouse behaviour stems not from the number of genes we have but from the greater complexities involved in decoding our genes into proteins. Human genes, more than the genes of other species, are spliced in alternative ways to create a greater variety of proteins. It may be this more subtle variation in genes—not the number of genes—that is responsible for differences between mice and people. This possibility has important implications for behavioural genetics because if the obvious differences between humans and other species are due to subtle DNA differences, then individual differences *within* our species—in other words, among people—are likely to involve genetic factors that are even more subtle and hard to find.

Fortunately, new techniques are available that make it possible to detect DNA differences for many thousands of genes simultaneously. These techniques will help in identifying genes related to behaviour, a process which will fill in the causal picture about a variety of characteristics and disorders that are influenced by many genes and many environmental factors. But it might not just be the actions of multiple genes that have a major impact on behaviour. It might also be a gene-environment interaction—the combination of a specific gene in a specific environment—that has the greatest influence on behaviour. Examples of such interactions appear in research by Avshalom Caspi and his colleagues (Caspi et al., 2002; Caspi et al., 2003). In one study, they found that children living in an environment in which there is abuse or other maltreatment were at increased risk for displaying antisocial behaviour in later life. But the at-risk children who also had a particular gene did not become antisocial. It was as if the gene protected them against this common consequence of childhood maltreatment (Caspi et al., 2002). A second study showed that, although depression and suicide are often associated with stressful life events, variation in a particular gene could predict whether people became depressed and suicidal in response to such events (Caspi et al., 2003). Understanding how multiple genes combine to influence behaviour and analyzing gene-environment interactions will continue to be active and exciting areas of research in behavioural genetics.

Behavioural Genetics and Environmental Influences

As suggested earlier, research on genetic influences in psychology has also provided some of the best evidence for the importance of environmental influences. It has shown that even though genetic influences are important, they cannot explain everything about human behaviour.

For example, twin and adoption studies have provided evidence of the importance of genetic factors in schizophrenia (Gottesman, 1991; Sullivan, Kendler, & Neale, 2003), and as a result, many researchers are now trying to identify the specific genes responsible. Enthusiasm for genetic explanations of schizophrenia makes it easy to forget, however, that environmental factors can be at least as important as genes. As described in the chapter on psychological disorders, when one member of an identical twin pair is schizophrenic, the chances are about 40 percent that the other member of the pair is also schizophrenic, a rate that is much higher than the one percent rate of schizophrenia in the general population. This result surely provides evidence of a strong genetic contribution to schizophrenia, but it also suggests that schizophrenia is strongly influenced by the environment. After all, most of the time, the identical twin of a person with schizophrenia will not display the disorder. Such differences within pairs of identical twins can be due only to the operation of environmental factors.

In fact, research generally suggests that genetic factors account for only about half of the variance among individuals for psychological characteristics such as personality and psychopathology. This means that at least half of the variance among individuals on these characteristics is due to environmental factors. These environmental—or more properly, *nongenetic*—factors encompass everything other than genetic inheritance. They include such biological factors as prenatal events, nutrition, and illnesses, as well as more traditional environmental factors such as parenting, schooling, and peer influences.

In short, one of the most important findings to emerge from behavioural genetics research has concerned the environment, not genetics. That research suggests that the most important environmental influences are likely to be those that different family members do not share (Plomin, Asbury, & Dunn, 2001). Psychologists want to find out more about these *nonshared factors* and how they act to create differences in children—twins or not—who grow up in the same family (Turkheimer & Waldron, 2000).

So far, research on this topic has shown that children may grow up in the same family but that they experience quite different environments, especially in relation to their parents (Brody, 2004). Siblings perceive that their parents treat them very differently—and observational studies back up these perceptions of differential treatment (Plomin, Asbury, & Dunn, 2001). Even events such as parental divorce, which would seem to be shared by all children in the family, appear to be experienced differently by each child, depending especially on age, personality, and the nature of the relationship with each parent.

Research is also beginning to focus on environmental influences beyond the family—such as relationships with teachers or friends—which are even more likely than home-related factors to vary among siblings. If you have a brother or sister, think about a psychological trait on which you and your sibling differ—confidence, for example. Why do you think you two are different on that trait? Perhaps one of you experienced a loss of self-confidence when faced with the demands of an impatient elementary-school teacher or after being betrayed by a childhood friend. Did these differing experiences occur randomly and thus make you considerably more confident or less confident than your sibling? Or is it possible that differences in your genetic makeups helped bring about these different experiences? Unless you and your sibling are identical twins, you share only about 50 percent of your genes. Perhaps genetically influenced differences between the two of you—in emotionality or other aspects of temperament, for example—caused parents, peers, and others to respond to each of you differently. This brings us to the second major discovery about the environment to emerge from research on behavioural genetics: Environmental influences associated with differences between siblings might actually be the *result* of genetic differences between the siblings.

Most of the measures used by psychologists to assess what might be thought of as environmental factors have now been shown to be influenced by genetic factors (Plomin & Bergeman, 1991). These include measures such as adolescents' ratings of how their parents treated them, observations of parent-child interactions, and questionnaires about life events and social support. If scores on measures such as these reflected only environmental factors, then the scores of identical twins should be no more similar to each other than those of fraternal twins. By the same token, there should be little similarity in environmental-experience measures for genetically related individuals who grew up in different families.

The results reported by behavioural geneticists do not fit these expectations (Plomin, 1994; Reiss et al., 2000). For example, parents differ in terms of how responsive they are to their children, but these differences in responsiveness correlate with the children's cognitive ability—a trait that has a clear genetic component. So, as described in the chapters on cognitive abilities and human development, parental responsiveness can influence cognitive development, and—as behavioural genetics research suggests—children's inherited cognitive abilities can alter the responsiveness of their parents. That is, parents tend to be more responsive to bright children who ask lots of questions and are interested in the answers.

Outside the family, too, genetic factors appear to play a role in generating environmental experiences (Harris, 1998). For example, research on the characteristics of children's peer groups shows that children tend to choose their friends—and to be chosen as friends—partly on the basis of genetically influenced traits, such as mental ability and temperament (Manke et al., 1995). Several studies also suggest that genetic factors can increase or decrease the likelihood of family conflicts and other social stressors that threaten one's physical and psychological well-being (Reiss et al., 2000). In addition, genetic influences on personality can account for the genetic effects seen in adults' reports about their family environments when growing up (Krueger, Markon, & Bouchard, 2003).

An important implication of genetic influences on environmental events is that measuring the impact of family relationships, peer influences, and other environmental factors on behaviour and mental processes may be less straightforward than psychologists thought. A measure that is aimed at assessing an "environmental" factor may nonetheless be affected by the genetic characteristics of the people being studied.

In human development, nature and nurture work together. Children select, modify, and create environments that are correlated with their genetic inclinations. As developmental psychologists have long argued, children are not formless blobs of clay passively moulded by the environment. Rather, they are active participants in their experiences. The new findings we have described here suggest that genetics plays an important role in those experiences (Plomin, 1994).

SUMMARY

Behavioural genetics is the study of how genes affect behaviour.

The Biology of Genetics and Heredity

Research on the ways in which nature and nurture interact to shape behaviour and mental processes requires a knowledge of *genetics,* the biology of inheritance. The genetic code that transmits characteristics from one generation to the next is contained in the *deoxyribonucleic acid (DNA)* that makes up the *genes* that in turn make up *chromosomes*. Dominant genes are expressed whenever they are present; recessive genes are expressed only when inherited from both parents. Most human characteristics are controlled by more than one gene; they are *polygenic*. The genes in a person's 46 chromosomes make up the *genotype*. The *phenotype*—how people actually look and act—is influenced by genes and the environment.

A Brief History of Genetic Research in Psychology

Sir Francis Galton's work in the nineteenth century helped to stimulate psychologists' interest in the influence of genetics on behaviour. The popularity of research in this area has waxed and waned over the years, but today most psychologists recognize the role of genetic, as well as environmental, influences on many aspects of behaviour and mental processes.

The Focus of Research in Behavioural Genetics

Behavioural genetics research identifies the genetic and environmental factors responsible for differences among individuals, not for the characteristics of a particular person. Although genes can influence a trait, they may not completely determine whether that trait appears.

The Role of Genetic Factors in Psychology

Genetic factors probably influence, to some extent, every aspect of behaviour and mental processes.

Genetic Influences over the Life Span

Genetic influences on general cognitive ability appear to increase over time, possibly because genetic predispositions lead people to select and even create environments that foster the continued development of abilities that are in line with those predispositions.

Genes Affecting Multiple Traits

Genes that affect one trait, such as anxiety, can sometimes also affect other traits, such as depression.

Identifying Genes Related to Behaviour

Current research in behavioural genetics, aided by findings from the Human Genome Project, is identifying specific genes responsible for specific characteristics—especially rare, single-gene disorders such as Huntington's disease. It is also illuminating gene-environment interactions.

Behavioural Genetics and Environmental Influences

Research in behavioural genetics has actually provided evidence for the importance of environmental influences, too, because the research shows that genetics alone cannot account for such characteristics as intelligence, personality, and psychological disorders. Some of the most important environmental influences are likely to be those that members of the same family do not share. In short, neither nature nor nurture is conducting the performance of the other: They are playing a duet.

Appendix

Statistics in Psychological Research

Understanding and interpreting the results of psychological research depends on *statistical analyses,* which are methods for describing and drawing conclusions from data. The chapter on research in psychology introduced some terms and concepts associated with *descriptive statistics*—the numbers that psychologists use to describe and present their data—and with *inferential statistics*—the mathematical procedures used to draw conclusions from data and to make inferences about what they mean. Here, we present more details about these statistical analyses that will help you to evaluate research results.

Describing Data

To illustrate our discussion, consider a hypothetical experiment on the effects of incentives on performance. The experimenter presents a list of mathematics problems to two groups of participants. Each group must solve the problems within a fixed time, but for each correct answer, the low-incentive group is paid ten cents, whereas the high-incentive group gets one dollar. The hypothesis to be tested is the **null hypothesis**, the assertion that the independent variable manipulated by the experimenter will have no effect on the dependent variable measured by the experimenter. In this case, the null hypothesis is that the size of the incentive (the independent variable) will not affect performance on the mathematics task (the dependent variable).

Assume that the experimenter has gathered a representative sample of participants, assigned them randomly to the two groups, and done everything possible to avoid the confounds and other research problems discussed in the chapter on research in psychology. The experiment has been run, and the psychologist now has the data: a list of the number of correct answers given by each participant in each group. Now comes the first task of statistical analysis: describing the data in a way that makes them easy to understand.

The Frequency Histogram

The simplest way to describe the data is to draw up something like Table 1, in which all the numbers are simply listed. After examining the table, you might notice that the high-incentive group seems to have done better than the low-incentive group, but this is not immediately obvious. The difference might be even harder to see if more participants had been involved and if the scores included three-digit numbers. A picture is worth a thousand words, so a better way of presenting the same data is in a picture-like graphic known as a **frequency histogram** (see Figure 1).

Construction of a histogram is simple. First, divide the scale for measuring the dependent variable (in this case, the number of correct answers) into a number of categories, or "bins." The bins in our example are 1–2, 3–4, 5–6, 7–8, and 9–10. Next, sort the raw data into the appropriate bin. (For example, the score of a participant who had 5 correct answers would go into the 5–6 bin, a score of 8 would go into the 7–8 bin, and so on.) Finally, for each bin, count the number of scores in that bin and draw a bar up to the height of that number on the vertical axis of a graph. The resulting set of bars makes up the frequency histogram.

Because we are interested in comparing the scores of two groups, there are separate histograms in Figure 1: one for the high-incentive group and one for the low-incentive group. Now the difference between groups that was difficult to see in

null hypothesis The assertion that the independent variable manipulated by the experimenter will have no effect on the dependent variable measured by the experimenter.

frequency histogram A graphic presentation of data that consists of a set of bars, each of which represents how frequently different scores or values occur in a data set.

descriptive statistics Numbers that summarize a set of research data.

range A measure of variability that is the difference between the highest and the lowest values in a data set.

table 1

Here are the test scores obtained by thirteen participants performing under low-incentive conditions and thirteen participants performing under high-incentive conditions.

A Simple Data Set

Low Incentive	High Incentive
4	6
6	4
2	10
7	10
6	7
8	10
3	6
5	7
2	5
3	9
5	9
9	3
5	8

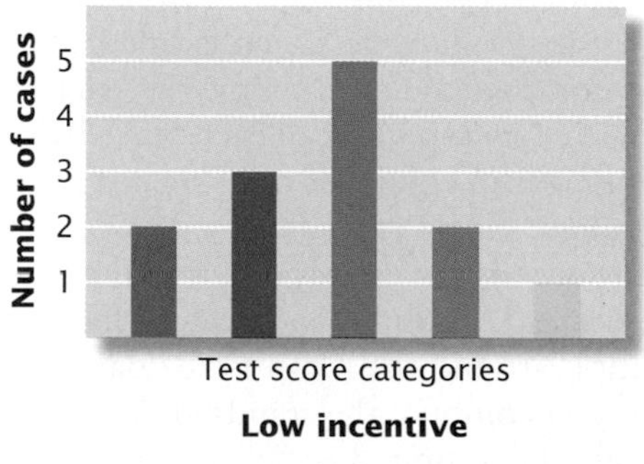

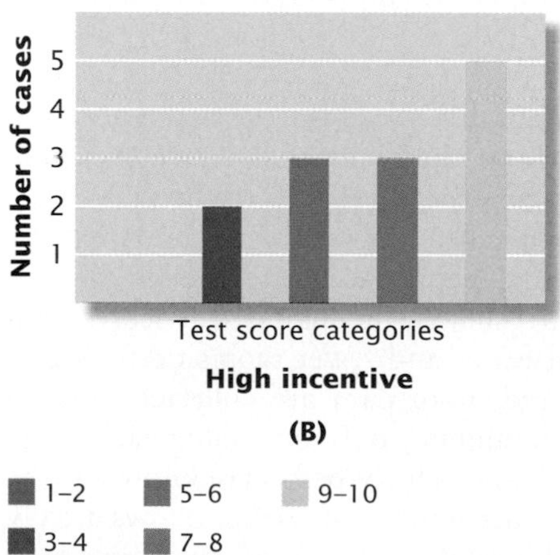

figure 1

Frequency Histograms

The height of each bar of a histogram represents the number of scores falling within each range of score values. The pattern formed by these bars gives a visual image of how research results are distributed.

Table 1 becomes clearly visible: High scores were more common among people in the high-incentive group than among people in the low-incentive group.

Histograms and other pictures of data are useful for visualizing and better understanding the "shape" of research results, but in order to analyze those results statistically, we need to use other ways of handling the data that make up these graphic presentations. For example, before we can tell whether two histograms are different statistically or just visually, the data they represent must be summarized using **descriptive statistics.**

Descriptive Statistics

The four basic categories of descriptive statistics (1) measure the number of observations made; (2) summarize the typical value of a set of data; (3) summarize the spread, or variability, in a set of data; and (4) express the correlation between two sets of data.

N The easiest statistic to compute, abbreviated as N, simply describes the number of observations that make up the data set. In Table 1, for example, $N = 13$ for each group, or 26 for the entire data set. Simple as it is, N plays a very important role in more sophisticated statistical analyses.

Measures of Central Tendency It is apparent in the histograms in Figure 1 that there is a difference in the pattern of scores between the two groups. But how much of a difference? What is the typical value, the *central tendency*, that represents each group's performance? As described in the chapter on research in psychology, there are three measures that capture this typical value: the mode, the median, and the mean. Recall that the *mode* is the value or score that occurs most frequently in the data set. The *median* is the halfway point in a set of data: Half the scores fall above the median, half fall below it. The *mean* is the arithmetic average. To find the mean, you add up the values of all the scores and divide that total by the number of scores.

Measures of Variability The variability, or spread, or dispersion of a set of data is often just as important as its central tendency. This variability can be quantified by measures known as the *range* and the *standard deviation*.

As described in the chapter on research in psychology, the **range** is simply the difference between the highest and the lowest values in a data set. For the data in

table 2

The standard deviation of a set of scores reflects the average degree to which those scores differ from the mean of the set.

Calculating the Standard Deviation

Raw Data	Difference from Mean = D	D^2
2	2 − 4 = − 2	4
2	2 − 4 = − 2	4
3	3 − 4 = − 1	1
4	4 − 4 = 0	0
9	9 − 4 = 5	25
Mean = 20/5 = 4		$\Sigma D^2 = 34$

$$\text{Standard deviation} = \sqrt{\frac{\Sigma D^2}{N}} = \sqrt{\frac{34}{5}} = \sqrt{6.8} = 2.6$$

Note: Σ means "the sum of."

Table 1, the range for the low-incentive group is 9 − 2 = 7; for the high-incentive group, the range is 10 − 3 = 7.

The **standard deviation**, or **SD**, measures the average difference between each score and the mean of the data set. To see how the standard deviation is calculated, consider the data in Table 2. The first step is to compute the mean of the set—in this case, 20/5 = 4. Second, calculate the difference, or *deviation* (D), of each score from the mean by subtracting the mean from each score, as in column 2 of Table 2. Third, find the average of these deviations. Notice, though, that if you calculated this average by finding the arithmetic mean, you would sum the deviations and find that the negative deviations exactly balance the positive ones, resulting in a mean difference of 0. Obviously there is more than zero variation around the mean in the data set. So, instead of employing the arithmetic mean, you compute the standard deviation by first squaring the deviations (which, as shown in column 3 of Table 2, removes any negative values). You then add up these squared deviations, divide the total by N, and then take the square root of the result. These simple steps are outlined in more detail in Table 2.

The Normal Distribution Now that we have described histograms and reviewed some descriptive statistics, let's re-examine how these methods of representing research data relate to some of the concepts discussed elsewhere in the book.

In most subfields in psychology, when researchers collect many measurements and plot their data in histograms, the resulting pattern often resembles the one shown for the low-incentive group in Figure 1. That is, the majority of scores tend to fall in the middle of the distribution, with fewer and fewer scores occurring as one moves toward the extremes. As more and more data are collected, and as smaller and smaller bins are used (perhaps containing only one value each), histograms tend to smooth out until they resemble the bell-shaped curve known as the **normal distribution**, or *normal curve*. When a distribution of scores follows a truly normal curve, its mean, median, and mode all have the same value. Furthermore, if the curve is normal, we can use its standard deviation to describe how any particular score stands in relation to the rest of the distribution.

IQ scores provide an example. They are distributed in a normal curve, with a mean, median, and mode of 100 and an SD of 16—as shown in Figure 2. In such a distribution, half of the population will have an IQ above 100, and half will be below 100. The shape of the true normal curve is such that 68 percent of the area

standard deviation (SD) A measure of variability that is the average difference between each score and the mean of the data set.

normal distribution A dispersion of scores such that the mean, median, and mode all have the same value. When a distribution has this property, the standard deviation can be used to describe how any particular score stands in relation to the rest of the distribution.

figure 2

The Normal Distribution

Many kinds of research data approximate the balanced, or symmetrical, shape of the normal curve, in which most scores fall toward the centre of the range.

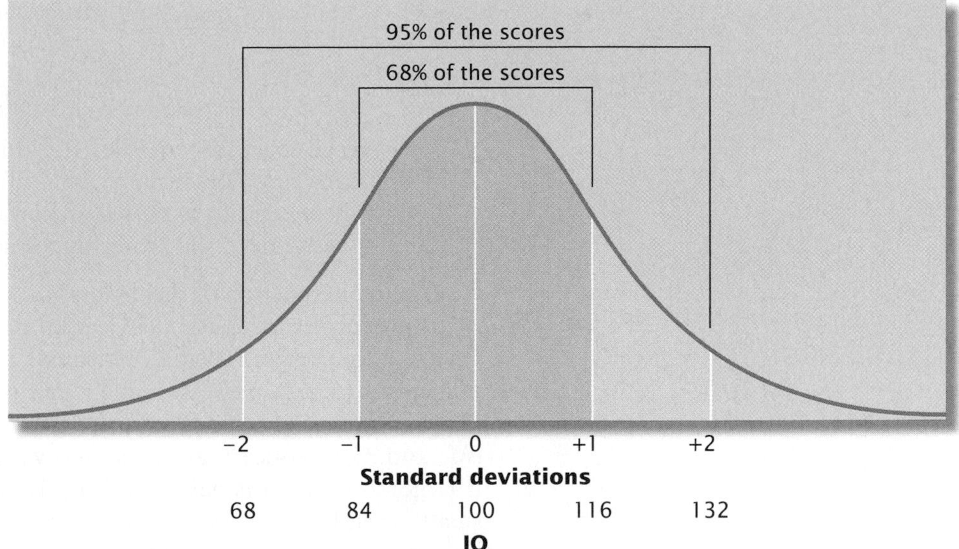

The normal distribution of IQ

under it lies in a range within one standard deviation above and below the mean. In terms of IQ, this means that 68 percent of the population has an IQ somewhere between 84 (100 minus 16) and 116 (100 plus 16). Of the remaining 32 percent of the population, half falls more than 1 SD above the mean, and half falls more than 1 SD below the mean. Thus, 16 percent of the population has an IQ above 116, and 16 percent scores below 84.

The normal curve is also the basis for percentiles. A **percentile score** indicates the percentage of people or observations that fall below a given score in a normal distribution. In Figure 2, for example, the mean score (which is also the median) lies at a point below which 50 percent of the scores fall. Thus the mean of a normal distribution is at the 50th percentile. What does this say about IQ? If you score 1 SD above the mean, your score is at a point above which only 16 percent of the population falls. This means that 84 percent of the population (100 percent minus 16 percent) must be below that score; so this IQ score is at the 84th percentile. A score at 2 SDs above the mean is at the 97.5 percentile, because only 2.5 percent of the scores are above it in a normal distribution.

Scores may also be expressed in terms of their distance in standard deviations from the mean, producing what are called **standard scores.** A standard score of 1.5, for example, is 1.5 standard deviations from the mean.

Correlation Histograms and measures of central tendency and variability describe certain characteristics of one dependent variable at a time. However, psychologists are often interested in describing the relationship between two variables. Measures of correlation are frequently used for this purpose. We discussed the interpretation of the *correlation coefficient* in the chapter on research in psychology; here we describe how to calculate it.

Recall that correlations are based on the relationship between two numbers that are associated with each participant or observation. The numbers might represent, say, a person's height and weight or the IQ scores of a parent and child. Table 3 contains this kind of data for four participants from our incentives study who took the test twice. (As you may recall from the chapter on cognitive abilities, the correlation between their scores would be a measure of test-retest reliability.) The formula for computing the Pearson product-moment correlation, or r, is as follows:

percentile score A value that indicates the percentage of people or observations that fall below a given point in a normal distribution.

standard score A value that indicates the distance, in standard deviations, between a given score and the mean of all the scores in a data set.

$$r = \frac{\Sigma(x - M_x)(y - M_y)}{\sqrt{\Sigma(x - M_x)^2 \, \Sigma(y - M_y)^2}}$$

where:

x = each score on variable 1 (in this case, test 1)
y = each score on variable 2 (in this case, test 2)
M_x = the mean of the scores on variable 1
M_y = the mean of the scores on variable 2

The main function of the denominator (bottom part) in this formula is to ensure that the coefficient ranges from +1.00 to −1.00, no matter how large or small the values of the variables being correlated. The "action element" of this formula is the numerator (or top part). It is the result of multiplying the amounts by which each of two observations (x and y) differ from the means of their respective distributions (M_x and M_y). Notice that, if the two variables "go together" (so that, if one score is large, the score it is paired with is also large, and if one is small, the other is also small), then both scores in each pair will tend to be above the mean of their distribution or both of them will tend to be below the mean of their distribution. When this is the case, $x - M_x$ and $y - M_y$ will both be positive, or they will both be negative. In either case, when you multiply one of them by the other, their product will always be positive, and the correlation coefficient will also be positive. If, on the other hand, the two variables go opposite to one another, such that, when one score in a pair is large, the other is small, one of them is likely to be smaller than the mean of its distribution, so that either $x - M_x$ or $y - M_y$ will have a negative sign, and the other will have a positive sign. Multiplying these differences together will always result in a product with a negative sign, and r will be negative as well.

Now compute the correlation coefficient for the data presented in Table 3. The first step (step *a* in the table) is to compute the mean (M) for each variable. M_x turns out to be 3 and M_y is 4. Next, calculate the numerator by finding the differences between each x and y value and its respective mean and by multiplying them (as in step *b* of Table 3). Notice that, in this example, the differences in each pair have like signs, so the correlation coefficient will be positive. The next step is to calculate the terms in the denominator; in this case, as shown in steps *c* and *d* in Table 3, they have values of 18 and 4. Finally, place all the terms in the formula and carry out the arithmetic (step *e*). The result in this case is an r of +.94, a high and positive correlation suggesting that performances on repeated tests are very closely related. A participant doing well the first time is very likely to do well again; a person doing poorly at first will probably do no better the second time.

table 3

Though it appears complex, calculation of the correlation coefficient is quite simple. The resulting r reflects the degree to which two sets of scores tend to be related, or to co-vary.

Calculating the Correlation Coefficient

Participant	Test 1	Test 2	$(x - M_x)(y - M_y)^{(b)}$
A	1	3	$(1-3)(3-4) = (-2)(-1) = +2$
B	1	3	$(1-3)(3-4) = (-2)(-1) = +2$
C	4	5	$(4-3)(5-4) = (1)(1) = +1$
D	6	5	$(6-3)(5-4) = (3)(1) = +3$
	$^{(a)}M_x = 3$	$M_y = 4$	$\Sigma(x - M_x)(y - M_y) = +8$

$^{(c)}\Sigma(x - M_x)^2 = 4 + 4 + 1 + 9 = 18$

$^{(d)}\Sigma(y - M_y)^2 = 1 + 1 + 1 + 1 = 4$

$$^{(e)}\, r = \frac{\Sigma(x - M_x)(y - M_y)}{\sqrt{\Sigma(x - M_x)^2\Sigma(y - M_y)^2}} = \frac{8}{\sqrt{18 \times 4}} = \frac{8}{\sqrt{72}} = \frac{8}{8.48} = +.94$$

Inferential Statistics

The descriptive statistics from the incentives experiment tell the experimenter that the performances of the high- and low-incentive groups differ. But there is some uncertainty. Is the difference large enough to be important? Does it represent a stable effect or a fluke? The researcher would like to have some *measure of confidence* that the difference between groups is genuine and reflects the effect of incentives on mental tasks in the real world, rather than the effect of random or uncontrolled factors. One way of determining confidence would be to run the experiment again with a new group of participants. Confidence that incentives produced differences in performance would grow stronger if the same or a larger between-group difference occurs again. In reality, psychologists rarely have the opportunity to repeat, or *replicate*, their experiments in exactly the same way three or four times. But **inferential statistics** provide a measure of how likely it was that results came about by chance. They put a precise mathematical value on the confidence or probability that rerunning the same experiment would yield similar (or even stronger) results.

Differences Between Means: The *t* Test

One of the most important tools of inferential statistics is the *t* test. It allows the researcher to ask how likely it is that the difference between two means occurred by chance rather than as a function of the effect of the independent variable. When the *t* test or other inferential statistic says that the probability of chance effects is small enough (usually less than 5 percent), the results are said to be *statistically significant*. Conducting a *t* test of statistical significance requires the use of three descriptive statistics.

The first component of the *t* test is the size of the observed effect, the difference between the means. Recall that the mean is calculated by summing a group's scores and dividing that total by the number of scores. In the example shown in Table 1, the mean of the high-incentive group is 94/13, or 7.23, and the mean of the low-incentive group is 65/13, or 5. So the difference between the means of the high- and low-incentive groups is $7.23 - 5 = 2.23$.

Second, we have to know the standard deviation of scores in each group. If the scores in a group are quite variable, the standard deviation will be large, indicating that chance may have played a large role in producing the results. The next replication of the study might generate a very different set of group scores. If the scores in a group are all very similar, however, the standard deviation will be small, which suggests that the same result would probably occur for that group if the study were repeated. In other words, the *difference* between groups is more likely to be significant when each group's standard deviation is small. If variability is high enough that the scores of two groups overlap, the mean difference, though large, may not be statistically significant. (In Table 1, for example, some people in the low-incentive group actually did better on the math test than some in the high-incentive group.)

Third, we need to take the sample size, *N*, into account. The larger the number of participants or observations, the more likely it is that an observed difference between means is significant. This is so because, with larger samples, random factors within a group—the unusual performance of a few people who were sleepy or anxious or hostile, for example—are more likely to be cancelled out by the majority, who better represent people in general. The same effect of sample size can be seen in coin tossing. If you toss a quarter five times, you might not be too surprised if heads comes up 80 percent of the time. If you get 80 percent heads after one hundred tosses, however, you might begin to suspect that this is probably not due to chance alone and that some other effect, perhaps some bias in the coin, is significant in producing the results. (For the same reason, even a relatively small correlation coefficient—between diet and grades, say—might be statistically significant if it were based on 50 000 students. As the number of participants increases, it becomes less likely that the correlation reflects the influence of a few oddball cases.)

inferential statistics A set of procedures that provides a measure of how likely it is that research results came about by chance.

To summarize, as the differences between the means get larger, as N increases, and as standard deviations get smaller, t increases. This increase in t raises the researcher's confidence in the significance of the difference between means.

Let's now calculate the t statistic and see how it is interpreted. The formula for t is:

$$t = \frac{(M_1 - M_2)}{\sqrt{\frac{(N_1 - 1)S_1^2 + (N_2 - 1)S_2^2}{N_1 + N_2 - 2}\left(\frac{N_1 + N_2}{N_1 N_2}\right)}}$$

where:

M_1 = mean of group 1
M_2 = mean of group 2
N_1 = number of scores or observations for group 1
N_2 = number of scores or observations for group 2
S_1 = standard deviation of group 1 scores
S_2 = standard deviation of group 2 scores

Despite appearances, this formula is quite simple. In the numerator is the difference between the two group means; t will get larger as this difference gets larger. The denominator contains an estimate of the standard deviation of the *differences* between group means; in other words, it suggests how much the difference between group means would vary if the experiment were repeated many times. Because this estimate is in the denominator, the value of t will get smaller as the standard deviation of group differences gets larger. For the data in Table 1,

$$t = \frac{(M_1 - M_2)}{\sqrt{\frac{(N_1 - 1)S_1^2 + (N_2 - 1)S_2^2}{N_1 + N_2 - 2}\left(\frac{N_1 + N_2}{N_1 N_2}\right)}}$$

$$= \frac{7.23 - 5}{\sqrt{\frac{(12)(5.09) + (12)(4.46)}{24}\left(\frac{26}{169}\right)}}$$

$$= \frac{2.23}{\sqrt{.735}} = 2.60 \text{ with 24 df}$$

To determine what a particular t means, we must use the value of N and a special statistical table called, appropriately enough, the *t table*. We have reproduced part of the t table in Table 4.

First, we have to find the computed values of t in the row corresponding to the **degrees of freedom,** or **df,** associated with the experiment. In this case, degrees of freedom are simply $N_1 + N_2 - 2$ (or two less than the total sample size or number of scores). Because our experiment had 13 participants per group, df = 13 + 13 − 2 = 24. In the row for 24 df in Table 4, you will find increasing values of t in each column. These columns correspond to decreasing p values, the probabilities that the difference between means occurred by chance. If an obtained t value is equal to or larger than one of the values in the t table (on the correct df line), then the difference between means that generated that t is said to be significant at the .10, .05, or .01 level of probability.

Suppose, for example, that an obtained t (with 19 df) was 2.00. Looking along the 19 df row, you find that 2.00 is larger than the value in the .05 column. This allows you to say that the probability that the difference between means occurred by chance was no greater than .05, or 5 in 100. If the t had been less than the value in the .05 column, the probability of a chance result would have been greater than .05. As noted earlier, when an obtained t is not large enough to exceed t table values at the .05 level, at least, it is not usually considered statistically significant.

degrees of freedom The total sample size or number of scores in a data set, less the number of experimental groups.

table 4

This table allows the researcher to determine whether an obtained *t* value is statistically significant. If the *t* value is larger than the one in the appropriate row in the .05 column, the difference between means that generated that *t* score is usually considered statistically significant.

The *t* Table

	p Value		
df	**.10 (10%)**	**.05 (5%)**	**.01 (1%)**
4	1.53	2.13	3.75
9	1.38	1.83	2.82
14	1.34	1.76	2.62
19	1.33	1.73	2.54
22	1.32	1.71	2.50
24	1.32	1.71	2.49

The *t* value from our experiment was 2.60, with 24 df. Because 2.60 is greater than all the values in the 24 df row, the difference between the high- and low-incentive groups would have occurred by chance less than 1 time in 100. In other words, the difference is statistically significant.

Beyond the *t* Test

Many experiments in psychology are considerably more complex than simple comparisons between two groups. They often involve three or more experimental and control groups. Some experiments also include more than one independent variable. For example, suppose we had been interested not only in the effect of incentive size on performance but also in the effect of problem difficulty. We might then create six groups whose members would perform easy, moderate, or difficult problems and would receive either low or high incentives.

In an experiment like this, the results might be due to the size of the incentive, the difficulty of the problems, or the combined effects (known as the *interaction*) of the two. Analyzing the size and source of these effects is typically accomplished through procedures known as *analysis of variance*. The details of analysis of variance are beyond the scope of this book. For now, note that the statistical significance of each effect is influenced by the size of the differences between means, by standard deviations, and by sample size in much the same way as we described for the *t* test. For more detailed information about how analysis of variance and other inferential statistics are used to understand and interpret the results of psychological research, consider taking courses in research methods and statistical or quantitative methods.

SUMMARY

Psychological research generates large quantities of data. Statistics are methods for describing and drawing conclusions from data.

Describing Data

Researchers often test the *null hypothesis*, which is the assertion that the independent variable will have no effect on the dependent variable.

The Frequency Histogram

Graphic representations such as *frequency histograms* provide visual descriptions of data, making the data easier to understand.

Descriptive Statistics

Numbers that summarize a set of data are called *descriptive statistics*. The easiest statistic to compute is *N*, which gives the number of observations made. A set of scores can be described by two other types of descriptive statistics: a measure of central tendency, which describes the typical value of a set of data, and a measure of variability. Measures of central tendency include the mean, median, and mode; variability is typically measured by the *range* and by the *standard deviation*. Sets of data often follow a *normal distribution*, which means that most scores fall in the middle of the range, with fewer and fewer scores occurring as one moves toward the extremes. In a truly normal distribution the mean, median, and mode are identical. When a set of data shows a normal distribution, a data point can be cited in terms of a *percentile score*, which indicates the percentage of people or observations falling below a certain score, and in terms of *standard scores*, which indicate the distance, in standard deviations, between any score and the mean of the distribution. Another type of descriptive statistic, a correlation coefficient, is used to measure the correlation between sets of scores.

Inferential Statistics

Researchers use *inferential statistics* to quantify the probability that conducting the same experiment again would yield similar results.

Differences Between Means: The *t* Test

One inferential statistic, the *t* test, assesses the likelihood that differences between two means occurred by chance or reflect the impact of an independent variable. Performing a *t* test requires using the difference between the means of two sets of data, the standard deviation of scores in each set, and the number of observations or participants. Interpreting a *t* test requires that *degrees of freedom* also be taken into account. When the *t* test indicates that the experimental results had a low probability of occurring by chance, the results are said to be statistically significant.

Beyond the *t* Test

When more than two groups must be compared, researchers typically rely on analysis of variance in order to interpret the results of an experiment.

REFERENCES

Aaron, D. J., Chang, Y.-F., Markovic, N., & LaPorte, R. E. (2003). Estimating the lesbian population: A capture-recapture approach. *Journal of Epidemiology and Community Health, 57,* 207–209.

Abbott, B. B., Schoen, L. S., & Badia, P. (1984). Predictable and unpredictable shock: Behavioral measures of aversion and physiological measures of stress. *Psychological Bulletin, 96,* 45–71.

Abbott, R. D., White, L. R., Ross, G. W., Masaki, K. H., Curb, J. D., & Petrovitch, H. (2004). Walking and dementia in physically capable elderly men. *Journal of the American Medical Association, 292,* 1447–1453.

Abdel Malik, P., Husted, J., Chow, E. W., & Bassett, A. S. (2003). Childhood head injury and expression of schizophrenia in multiply affected families. *Archives of General Psychiatry, 60,* 231–236.

Abi-Hashem, N. (2000). Psychology, time, and culture. *American Psychologist, 55,* 342–343.

Aboud, F. E., (2003). The formation of ingroup favoritism and outgroup prejudice in young children. *Developmental Psychology, 39,* 48–60.

Abraham, H. D., & Wolf, E. (1988). Visual function in past users of LSD: Psychophysical findings. *Journal of Abnormal Psychology,* 97, 443–447.

Abrahamson, A. C., Baker, L. A., & Caspi, A. (2002). Rebellious teens? Genetic and environmental influences on the social attitudes of adolescents. *Journal of Personality and Social Psychology, 83,* 1392–1408.

Abramis, D. J. (1994). Work role ambiguity, job satisfaction, and job performance: Meta-analyses and review. *Psychological Reports, 75,* 1411–1433.

Abramowitz, J. S. (1997). Effectiveness of psychological and pharmacological treatments for obsessive-compulsive disorder: A quantitative review. *Journal of Consulting and Clinical Psychology, 65,* 44–52.

Abrams, R. (1997). *Electroconvulsive therapy* (3rd ed.). New York: Oxford University Press.

Abrams, R. L., & Greenwald, A. G. (2000). Parts outweigh the whole (word) in unconscious analysis of meaning. *Psychological Science, 11,* 118–124.

Ackerman, D. (1995). *Mystery of the senses.* Boston: WGBH-TV/Washington, DC: WETA-TV.

Ackerman, P. L. (1994). Intelligence, attention, and learning: Maximal and typical performance. In D. K. Detterman (Ed.), *Current topics in human intelligence* (Vol. 4, pp. 1–27). Norwood, NJ: Ablex.

Ackerman, P. L., Beier, M. E., & Boyle, M. O. (2002). Individual differences in working memory within a nomological network of cognitive and perceptual speed abilities. *Journal of Experimental Psychology: General, 131,* 567–589.

Acocella, J. (1998, April 6). The politics of hysteria. *New Yorker,* pp. 64–79.

Adam, E. K., Gunnar, M. R., & Tanaka, A. (2004). Adult attachment, parent emotion, and observed parenting behavior: Mediator and moderator models. *Child Development, 75,* 110–122.

Adams, R. J., Courage, M. L., & Mercer, M. E. (1994). Systematic measurement of human neonatal color vision. *Vision Research, 34,* 1691–1701.

Addington, J., Collins, A., McCleery, A., & Addington, D. (2005). The role of family work in early psychosis. *Schizophrenia Research, 79,* 77–83.

Addis, M. E. (1997). Evaluating the treatment manual as a means of disseminating empirically validated psychotherapies. *Clinical Psychology: Science and Practice, 4,* 1–11.

Addis, M. E., & Krasnow, A. D. (2000) A national survey of practicing psychologists' attitudes toward psychotherapy treatment manuals. *Journal of Consulting and Clinical Psychology, 68,* 331–339.

Adelman, W. P., Duggan, A. K., Hauptman, P., & Joffe, A. (2001). Effectiveness of a high school smoking cessation program. *Pediatrics, 107,* E50.

Ader, R. (2001). Psychoneuroimmunology. *Current Directions in Psychological Science, 10,* 94–98.

Ader, R., Felten, D., & Cohen, N. (1990). Interactions between the brain and the immune system. *Review of Pharmacology and Toxicology, 30,* 561–602.

Adler, A. (1963). *The practice and theory of individual psychology.* Paterson, NJ: Littlefield Adams. (Original work published 1927) Adler, T. (1993, March). Bad mix: Combat stress, decisions. *APA Monitor,* p. 1.

Adolphs, R. (2003). Investigating the cognitive neuroscience of social behavior. *Neuropsychologia, 41,* 119–126.

Adolphs, R., Tranel, D., & Damasio, A. R. (1998). The human amygdala in social judgment. *Nature, 393*(6684), 470–474.

Adolphs, R., Tranel, D., & Damasio, H., & Damasio, A. (1994). Impaired recognition of emotion in facial expressions following bilateral damage to the human amygdala. *Nature, 372*(6507), 669–672.

Adorno, T. W., Frenkel-Brunswik, E., Levinson, D. J., & Sanford, R. N. (1950). *The authoritarian personality.* New York: Harper & Row.

Agarwal, D. P. (1997). Molecular genetic aspects of alcohol metabolism and alcoholism. *Pharmacopsychiatry, 30*(3), 79–84.

Agency for Healthcare Research and Quality (AHRQ). (1999). *Treatment of depression–newer pharmacotherapies* (Evidence Report/Technology Assessment, Number 7, Pub. No. 99–E014). Rockville, MD: Author.

Agnew, C. R., Van Lange, P. A. M., Rusbult, C. E., & Langston, C. A. (1998). Cognitive interdependence: Commitment and the mental representation of close relationships. *Journal of Personality and Social Psychology, 74,* 939–954.

Agras, W. S., Brandt, H. A., Bulik, C. M., Dolan-Sewell, R., Fairburn, C. G., Halmi, K. A., et al. (2004). Report of the National Institutes of Health workshop on overcoming barriers to treatment research in anorexia nervosa. *International Journal of Eating Disorders, 35,* 509–521.

Ahima, R. S., & Flier, J. S. (2000). Leptin. *Annual Review of Physiology, 62,* 413–437.

Ahmad, R. H., Venkata, S. M., Alessandro, T., Bhaskar, K., Francesco, F., Goldman, D., et al. (2002). Serotonin transporter genetic variation and the response of the human amygdala. *Science, 297,* 400–403.

Ahmed, A., & Ruffman, T. (1998). Why do infants make A not B errors in a search task, yet show memory for the location of hidden objects in a nonsearch task? *Developmental Psychology, 34,* 441–453.

Aiello, J. R., & Douthitt, E. A. (2001). Social facilitation from Triplett to electronic performance monitoring. *Group Dynamics, 5,* 163–180.

Aiello, J. R., & Kolb, K. J. (1995). Electronic performance monitoring and social context: Impact on productivity and stress. *Journal of Applied Psychology, 80,* 339–353.

Aiken, L. R. (1994). *Psychological testing and assessment* (8th ed.). Boston: Allyn & Bacon.

Ainsworth, M. D. S. (1973). The development of infant-mother attachment. In B. M. Caldwell & H. N. Ricciuti (Eds.), *Review of child development research* (Vol. 3, pp. 1–94). Chicago: University of Chicago Press.

Ainsworth, M. D. S. (1989). Attachments beyond infancy. *American Psychologist, 44,* 709–716.

Ainsworth, M. D. S., Blehar, M. D., Waters, E., & Wall, S. (1978). *Patterns of attachment: A psychological study of the Strange Situation.* Hillsdale, NJ: Erlbaum.

Aizawa, N. (2002). Grandiose traits and hypersensitive traits of the narcissistic personality. *Japanese Journal of Educational Psychology, 50,* 215–224.

Ajzen, I. (2001). Nature and operation of attitudes. *Annual Review of Psychology, 52,* 27–58.

Akutsu, P. D., Tsuru, G. K., & Chu, J. P. (2004). Predictors of nonattendance of intake appointments among five Asian American client groups. *Journal of Consulting and Clinical Psychology, 72,* 891–896.

Alaimo, K., Olson, C. M., & Frongillo, E. A., Jr. (2001). Food insufficiency and American school-aged children's cognitive, academic, and psychosocial development. *Pediatrics, 108,* 44–53.

Albarracin, D., Johnson, B. T., Fishbein, M., & Muellerleile, P. A. (2001). Theories of reasoned action and planned behavior as models of condom use: A meta-analysis. *Psychological Bulletin, 127,* 142–161.

Albee, G. W. (1968). Conceptual models and manpower requirements in psychology. *American Psychologist, 23,* 317–320.

Albee, G. W. (1985, February). The answer is prevention. *Psychology Today, 19,* 60–62.

Albert, K. A., Hemmings, H. C., Adamo, A. I. B., Potkin, S. G., Akbarian, S., Sandman, C. A. (2002). Evidence for decreased DARPP-32 in the prefrontal cortex of patients with schizophrenia. *Archives of General Psychiatry, 59,* 705–712.

Albert, M. S., Savage, C. R., Blazer, D., Jones, K., Berkman, L., & Seeman, T. (1995). Predictors of cognitive change in older persons: MacArthur studies of successful aging. *Psychology and Aging, 10,* 578–589.

Alberti, R. E., & Emmons, M. L. (1986). *Your perfect right: A guide to assertive living* (5th ed.). San Luis Obispo, CA: Impact.

Alberto, P. A., Troutman, A. C., & Feagin, J. R. (2002). *Applied behavior analysis for teachers* (6th ed.). Englewood Cliffs, NJ: Prentice Hall.

Alcock, J. (2001). *Animal behavior: An evolutionary approach* (7th ed.). Sunderland, MA: Sinauer.

Alderete, E., Eskenazi, B., & Sholtz, R. (1995). Effect of cigarette smoking and coffee drinking on time to conception. Epidemiology, 6(4), 403–408.

Aleman, A., Kahn, R. S., & Selten, J.-P. (2003). Sex differences in the risk of schizophrenia: Evidence from meta-analysis. *Archives of General Psychiatry, 60,* 565–571.

Alexander, G. M., & Hines, M. (2002). Sex differences in response to children's toys in nonhuman primates (*Cercopithecus aethiops sabaeus*). *Evolution and Human Behavior, 23,* 467–479.

Al-Issa, I. (1995). The illusion of reality or the reality of illusion: Hallucinations and culture. *British Journal of Psychiatry, 166,* 368–373.

Ali, A. & Wood, O. (2001). The need for weed: Medical marijuana. CBC News Online. Available: http://www.cbc.ca/news/background/marijuana/medical_marijuana.html

Al-Kubaisy, T., Marks, I. M., Logsdail, S., Marks, M. P., Lovell, K., Sungur, M., & Araya, R. (1992). Role of exposure homework in phobia reduction: A controlled study. *Behavior Therapy, 23,* 599–621.

Allen, B. P. (2003). *Personality theories: Development, growth, and diversity* (4th ed). Boston: Pearson Allyn & Bacon.

Allen, D. N., Goldstein, G., & Weiner, C. (2001). Differential neuropsychological patterns of frontal- and temporal-lobe dysfunction in patients with schizophrenia. *Schizophrenia Research, 48,* 7–15.

Allen, J. B., Kenrick, D. T., Linder, D. E., & McCall, M. A. (1989). Arousal and attraction: A response-facilitation alternative to misattribution and negative-reinforcement models. *Journal of Personality and Social Psychology, 57,* 261–270.

Allen, L. S., & Gorski, R. A. (1992). Sexual orientation and the size of the anterior commissure in the human brain. *Proceedings of the National Academy of Sciences of the United States of America, 89,* 7199–7202.

Allen, L. S., Hines, M., Shryne, J. E., & Gorski, R. A. (1989). Two sexually dimorphic cell groups in the human brain. *Journal of Neuroscience, 9,* 497–506.

Allik, J., & McCrae, R. R. (2004). Toward a geography of personality traits: Patterns of profiles across 36 cultures. *Journal of Cross-Cultural Psychology, 35,* 13–28.

Alloy, L. B., Abramson, L. Y., & Francis, E. L. (1999). Do negative cognitive styles confer vulnerability to depression? *Current Directions in Psychological Science, 8,* 128–132.

Allport, G. W., & Odbert, H. S. (1936). Trait names: A psycholexical study. *Psychological Monographs, 47*(1, Whole No. 211).

Altemeyer, B. (1996). *The authoritarian specter.* Cambridge: Harvard University Press.

Altman, J., & Das, G. D. (1965). Autoradiographic and histological evidence of postnatal hippocampal neurogenesis in rats. *Journal of Comparative Neurology, 124,* 319–335.

Altman, L. K. (2000, April 10). Company developing marijuana for medical uses. *New York Times.* Retrieved December 13, 2004, from http://www.mapinc.org/drugnews/v00/n474/a01.html

Aluja-Fabregat, A., & Torrubia-Beltri, R. (1998). Viewing of mass media violence, perception of violence, personality and academic achievement. *Personality and Individual Differences, 25,* 973–989.

Alvarez, F. J., Delrio, M. C., & Prada, R. (1995). Drinking and driving in Spain. *Journal of Studies on Alcohol, 56*(4), 403–407.

Alvaro, E. M., & Crano, W. D. (1997). Indirect minority influence: Evidence for leniency in source evaluation and counterargumentation. *Journal of Personality and Social Psychology, 72,* 949–964.

Alvir, J. M., Lieberman, J. A., Safferman, A. Z., Schwimmer, J. L., & Schaaf, J. A. (1993). Clozapine-induced agranulocytosis: Incidence and risk factors in the United States. *New England Journal of Medicine, 329,* 162–167.

Amabile, T. M. (1996). *Creativity in context: Update to "The Social Psychology of Creativity."* Boulder, CO: Westview.

Amabile, T. M. (2001). Beyond talent: John Irving and the passionate craft of creativity. *American Psychologist, 56,* 333–336.

Amabile, T. M., Goldfarb, P., & Brackfield, S. C. (1990). Social influences on creativity: Evaluation, coaction, and surveillance. *Creativity Research Journal, 3,* 6–21.

Amabile, T. M., Hennessey, B. A., & Grossman, B. S. (1986). Social influences on creativity: The effects of contracted-for reward. *Journal of Personality and Social Psychology, 50,* 14–23.

American Academy of Pediatrics. (2001). Condom use by adolescents. *Pediatrics, 107,* 1463–1469.

American Lung Association. (2002). *Trends in tobacco use.* Retrieved July 23, 2003, from http//www/lungusa.org/data/smoke/SMK1.pdf

American Psychiatric Association Work Group on Eating Disorders. (2000). Practice guidelines for the treatment of patients with eating disorders (revision). *American Journal of Psychiatry, 157,* 1–39.

American Psychiatric Association. (1994). *Diagnostic and statistical manual of mental disorders* (4th ed.). Washington, DC: Author.

American Psychiatric Association. (2000). *Diagnostic and statistical manual of mental disorders* (4th ed., rev.). Washington DC: Author.

American Psychiatric Association. (1999). Position statement on psychiatric treatment and sexual orientation. *American Journal of Psychiatry, 156,* 1131.

American Psychological Association. (1993). *Violence and youth: Psychology's response.* Washington: DC: Author.

American Psychological Association. (2002a). *Answers to your questions about sexual orientation and homosexuality.* Retrieved December 13, 2004, from http://www.apa.org/pubinfo/answers.html#whatis

American Psychological Association. (2002c). *Medical cost offset.* Retrieved December 13, 2004, from http://www.apa.org/practice/offset3.html

American Society for Microbiology. (2000, September 18). *America's dirty little secret—our hands.* Washington, DC: Author.

Amodio, D. M., Harmon-Jones, E., Devine, P. G., Curtin, J. J., Hartley, S. L., & Covert, A. E. (2004). Neural signals for the detection of unintentional race bias. *Psychological Science, 15,* 88–93.

an der Heiden, W., & Haefner, H. (2000). The epidemiology of onset and course of schizophrenia. *European Archives of Psychiatry and Clinical Neuroscience, 250,* 292–303.

Anastasi, A., & Urbina, S. (1997). *Psychological testing* (7th ed.). Upper Saddle River, NJ: Prentice-Hall.

Anastasiadis, A.G., Davis, A. R., Salomon, L., Burchardt, M., & Shabsigh, R. (2002). Hormonal factors in female sexual dysfunction. *Current Opinion in Urology, 12,* 503–507.

Andersen, S. M., & Chen, S. (2002). The relational self: An interpersonal social-cognitive theory. *Psychological Review, 109,* 619–645.

Andersen, S. M., & Miranda, R. (2000). Transference: How past relationships emerge in the present. *Psychologist, 13,* 608–609.

Anderson, A. K., & Phelps, E. A. (2001). Lesions of the human amygdala impair enhanced perception of emotionally salient events. *Nature, 411,* 305–309.

Anderson, B. L. (2004). The role of occlusion in the perception of depth, lightness, and opacity. *Psychological Review, 110,* 785–801.

Anderson, C. A. (2004). An update on the effects of playing violent video games. *Journal of Adolescence, 27,* 113–122.

Anderson, C. A., & Bushman, B. J. (2001). Effects of violent video games on aggressive behavior, aggressive cognition, aggressive affect, physiological arousal, and prosocial behavior: A meta-analytic review of the scientific literature. *Psychological Science, 12,* 353–359.

Anderson, C. A., & Bushman, B. J. (2002b). Media violence and the American public revisited. *American Psychologist, 57,* 448–450.

Anderson, C. A., Berkowitz, L., Donnerstein, E., Huesmann, L. R., Johnson, J. D., Linz, D., et al. (2003). The influence of media violence on youth. *Psychological Science in the Public Interest, 4,* 81–110.

Anderson, C. A., Lindsay, J. J., & Bushman, B. J. (1999). Research in the psychological laboratory: Truth or triviality? *Current Directions in Psychological Science, 8,* 3–9.

Anderson, C., John, O. P., Keltner, D., & Kring, A. M. (2001). Who attains social status? Effects of personality and physical attractiveness in social groups. *Journal of Personality and Social Psychology, 81,* 116–132.

Anderson, E. M., & Lambert, M. J. (1995). Short-term dynamically oriented psychotherapy: A review and meta-analysis. *Clinical Psychology Review, 9*(6), 503–514.

Anderson, J. R. (1990). *Cognitive psychology and its implications* (3rd ed.). New York: Freeman.

Anderson, J. R. (1995). *Learning and memory: An integrated approach.* New York: Wiley.

Anderson, J. R. (2000). *Cognitive psychology and its implications* (5th ed). New York: Worth.

Anderson, M. C., & Green, C. (2001). Suppressing unwanted memories by executive control. *Nature, 410,* 366–369.

Anderson, M. C., Ochsner, K. N., Kuhl, B., Cooper, J., Robertson, E., Gabrieli, S. W., et al. (2004). Neural systems underlying the suppression of unwanted memories. *Science, 303,* 232–235.

Anderson, P., Rothbaum, B. O., & Hodges, L. F. (2003). Virtual reality exposure in the treatment of social anxiety. *Cognitive and Behavioral Practice, 10*(3), 240–247.

Anderssen, N., Amlie, C., & Ytteroy, E. A. (2002). Outcomes for children with lesbian or gay parents: A review of studies from 1978 to 2000. *Scandinavian Journal of Psychology, 43,* 335–351.

Ando, K., Kripke, D. F., & Ancoli-Israel, S. (2002). Delayed and advanced sleep phase symptoms. *Israel Journal of Psychiatry and Related Sciences, 39,* 11–18.

Andrade, L., Walters, E. E., Gentil, V., & Laurenti, R. (2002). Prevalence of ICD-10 mental disorders in a catchment area in the city of San Paolo, Brazil. *Social Psychiatry and Psychiatric Epidemiology, 37,* 316–325.

Andreasen, N. C. (1997). Linking mind and brain in the study of mental illnesses: A project for a scientific psychopathology. *Science, 275,* 1586–1593.

Andreasen, N. C., Arndt, S., Alliger, R., Miller, D., & Flaum, M. (1995). Symptoms of schizophrenia. *Archives of General Psychiatry, 52,* 341–351.

Andre-Petersson, L., Engstroom, G., Hagberg, B., Janzon, L., Steen, G., Lane, D. A., et al. (2001). Adaptive behavior in stressful situations and stroke incidence in hypertensive men: Results from prospective cohort study "Men Born in 1914" in Malmo, Sweden. *Stroke, 32,* 1712–1720.

Andrés, P. (2003). Frontal cortex as the central executive of working memory: Time to revise our view. *Cortex, 39,* 871–895.

Andrew, D., & Craig, A. D. (2001). Spinothalamic lamina I neurons selectively sensitive to histamine: A central neural pathway for itch. *Nature Neuroscience, 4,* 72–77.

Andrews, B., Brewin, C., Ochera, J., Morton, J., Bekerian, D. A., Davies, G. M., & Mollon, P. (2000). The timing, triggers, and quality of recovered memories in therapy. *British Journal of Clinical Psychology, 39,* 11–26.

Anghelescu, I., Klawe, C. J., Bartenstein, P., & Szegedi, A. (2001). Normal PET after long-term ETC. *American Journal of Psychiatry, 158,* 1527.

Angst, J., Angst, F., & Stassen, H. H. (1999). Suicide risks in patients with major depressive disorder. *Journal of Clinical Psychiatry, 60* (Suppl. 2), 57–62.

Anisman, H., Griffiths, J., Matheson, K., Ravindran, A. V., & Merali, Z. (2001). Posttraumatic stress symptoms and salivary cortisol levels. *American Journal of Psychiatry, 158,* 1509–1511.

Anisman, H., Hayley, S., Turrin, N., & Merali, Z. (2002). Cytokines as a stressor: Implications for depressive illness. *International Journal of Neuropsychopharmacology, 5,* 357–373.

Anrep, G. V. (1920). Pitch discrimination in the dog. *Journal of Physiology, 53,* 367–385.

Anstey, K. J., Hofer, S. M., & Luszcz, M. A. (2003). Cross-sectional and longitudinal patterns of dedifferentiation in late-life cognitive and sensory function: The effects of age, ability, attrition, and occasion of measurement. *Journal of Experimental Psychology: General, 132,* 470–487.

Anthony, M., & Bartlett, P. L. (1999). *Neural network learning: Theoretical foundations.* Cambridge: Cambridge University Press.

Anthony, T., Cooper, C., & Mullen, B. (1992). Cross-racial facial identification: Five studies of sex differences in facial prominence. *Personality and Social Psychology Bulletin, 18,* 296–301.

Antle, M.C., Kriegsfeld, L.J., & Silver, R. (2005). Signaling within the master clock of the brain: Localized activation of mitogen-activated protein kinase by gastrin-releasing peptide. *Journal of Neuroscience, 25, 2447–2454.*

Antle, M. C., LeSauter, J., and Silvera, R. (2005). Neurogenesis and ontogeny of specific cell phenotypes within the hamster suprachiasmatic nucleus. *Developmental Brain Research, 157* (1), 8–18.

Antoni, M. H., Cruess, D. G., Cruess, S., Lutgendorf, S., Kumar, M., Ironson, G., et al. (2000). Cognitive-behavioral stress management intervention effects on anxiety, 24-hr urinary norepinephrine output, and t-cytotoxic/suppressor cells over time among symptomatic HIV-infected gay men. *Journal of Consulting and Clinical Psychology, 68,* 31–45.

Antoni, M. H., Lehman, J., Kilbourn, K., Boyers, A., Yount, S., Culver, J., et al. (2001). Cognitive-behavioral stress management intervention enhances optimism and the sense of positive contributions among women under treatment for early-stage breast cancer. *Health Psychology, 20,* 20–32.

Antonuccio, D. O., Danton, W. G., & DeNelsky, G. Y. (1995). Psychotherapy versus medication for depression: Challenging the conventional wisdom with data. *Professional Psychology: Research and Practice, 26,* 574–585.

Antrobus, J. (2001). Rethinking the fundamental process of dream and sleep mentation production: Defining new questions that avoid the distraction of REM versus NREM comparisons. *Sleep and Hypnosis, 3,* 1–8.

Appelle, S., Lynn, S. J., & Newman, L. (2000). Alien abduction experiences. In E. Cardena, S. J. Lynn, & S. Krippner (Eds.), *Varieties of anomalous experience: Examining the scientific evidence* (pp. 253–282). Washington, DC: American Psychological Association.

Appleton, W. S. (2000). *Prozac and the new antidepressants: What you need to know about Prozac, Zoloft, Paxil, Luvox, Wellbutrin, Effexor, Serzone, Vestra, Celexa, St. John's Wort, and others* (Rev. ed.). New York: Plume Books.

Arbelle, S., Benjamin, J., Golin, M., Kremer, I., Belmaker, R. H., & Ebstein, R. P. (2003). Relation of shyness in grade school children to the genotype for the long form of the serotonin transporter promoter region polymorphism. *American Journal of Psychiatry, 160,* 671–676.

Arenberg, D. (1982). Changes with age in problem solving. In F. I. M. Craik & S. Trehub (Eds.), *Aging and cognitive processes* (pp. 221–236). New York: Plenum.

Arkes, H. R., & Ayton, P. (1999). The sunk cost and Concorde effects: Are humans less rational than lower animals? *Psychological Bulletin, 125,* 591–600.

Arlow, J. (1995). Psychoanalysis. In R. J. Corsini & D. Wedding (Eds.), *Current psychotherapies* (5th ed., pp. 15–50). Itasca, IL: Peacock.

Arndt, J., Goldenberg, J., Greenberg, J., Pyszcynski, T., & Solomon, S. (2000). Death can be hazardous to your health: Adaptive and ironic consequences of defenses against the terror of death. In. R. P. Duberstein & J. Masling (Eds.), *Psychodynamic perspectives on sickness and health* (pp. 201–257). Washington, DC: American Psychological Association.

Arndt, J., Greenberg, J., Pyszczynski, T., & Solomon, S. (1997). Subliminal exposure to death-related stimuli increases defense of the cultural worldview. *Psychological Science, 8,* 379–385.

Arnett, J. J. (1999). Adolescent storm and stress, reconsidered. *American Psychologist, 54,* 317–326.

Arnett, J. J. (2000). Emerging adulthood: A theory of development from the late teens through the twenties. *American Psychologist, 55,* 469–480.

Aronoff, J., Barclay, A. M., & Stevenson, L. A. (1988). The recognition of threatening stimuli. *Journal of Personality and Social Psychology, 54, 647–655.*

Aronson, E. (1990). Applying social psychology to desegregation and energy conservation. *Personality and Social Psychology Bulletin, 16,* 118–132.

Aronson, E. (1997). *The jigsaw classroom.* New York: Longman.

Aronson, E. (1999). *The social animal* (8th ed.). New York: Worth/Freeman.

Aronson, E., Wilson, T. D., & Akert, R. M. (1999). *Social psychology* (3rd ed.). New York: Longman.

Arterberry, M. E., Yonas, A., & Bensen, A. S. (1989). Self-produced locomotion and development of responsiveness to textural gradients. *Developmental Psychology, 25,* 976–982.

Asarnow, R. F., Nuechterlein, K. H., Fogelson, D., Subotnik, K. L., Payne, D. A., Russell, A. T., et al. (2001). Schizophrenia and schizophrenia-spectrum personality disorders in the first-degree relatives of children with schizophrenia: The UCLA family study. *Archives of General Psychiatry, 58,* 581–588.

Asch, S. E. (1951). Effects of group pressure upon the modification and distortion of judgments. In H. Guetzkow (Ed.), *Groups, leadership, and men* (pp. 177–190). Pittsburgh, PA: Carnegie Press.

Asch, S. E. (1955). Opinions and social pressure. *Scientific American, 193,* 31–35.

Asch, S. E. (1956). Studies of independence and conformity: A minority of one against a unanimous majority. *Psychological Monographs, 70,* 1–70.

Ashcraft, M. H. (1989). *Human memory and cognition.* Glenview, IL: Scott, Foresman.

Ashe, P. C., Berry, M. D., & Boulton, A. A (2001). Schizophrenia, a neurodegenerative disorder with neurodevelopmental antecedents. *Progress in Neuro Psychopharmacology and Biological Psychiatry, 25,* 691–707.

Asher, S. R., & Hopmeyer, A. (2001). Loneliness in childhood. In G. Bear, K. Minke, & A. Thomas (Eds.), *Children's needs II: Psychological perspectives.* Silver Spring, MD: National Association of School Psychologists.

Ashmore, R. D., Deaux, K., McLaughlin-Volpe, T. (2004). An organizing framework for collective identity: Articulation and significance of multidimensionality. *Psychological Bulletin, 130,* 80–114.

Ashton, H. (1995). Protracted withdrawal from benzodiazepines: The post-withdrawal syndrome. *Psychiatric Annals, 25*(3), 174–179.

Ashton, M. C., Lee, K., & Goldberg, L. R. (2004). A hierarchical analysis of 1,710 English personality descriptive adjectives. *Journal of Personality and Social Psychology, 87,* 707–721.

Aspinwall, L. G., & Duran, R. E. F. (1999). Psychology applied to health. In A. M. Stec & D. A. Bernstein (Eds.), *Psychology: Fields of application* (pp. 17–38). Boston: Houghton Mifflin.

Aspinwall, L. G., & Taylor, S. E. (1992). Modeling cognition adaptation: A longitudinal investigation of the impact of individual differences and coping on college adjustment and performance. *Journal of Personality and Social Psychology, 63,* 989–1003.

Assefi, S. L., & Garry, M. (2003). Absolut® memory distortions: Alcohol placebos influence misinformation effect. *Psychological Science, 14,* 77–80.

Astin, J. A. (2004). Mind-body therapies for the management of pain. *Clinical Journal of Pain, 20,* 27–32.

Astin, J. A., Shapiro, S. L., Eisenberg, D. M., & Forys, K. L. (2003). Mind-body medicine: State of the science, implications for practice. *Journal of the American Board of Family Practice, 16,* 131–147.

Aston-Jones, G., Chiang, C., & Alexinsky, T. (1991). Discharge of noradrenergic locus coeruleus neurons in behaving rats and monkeys suggests a role in vigilance. *Progress in Brain Research, 88,* 501–520.

Atkinson, R. C., & Shiffrin, R. M. (1968). Human memory: A proposed system and its control processes. In K. Spence (Ed.), *The psychology of learning and motivation* (Vol. 2, pp. 89–195). New York: Academic Press.

August, G. J., Realmuto, G. M., Hektner, J. M., & Bloomquist, M. L. (2001). An integrated components preventive intervention for aggressive elementary school children: The early risers program. *Journal of Consulting and Clinical Psychology, 69,* 614–626.

Augustyn, T. (2001). *An evaluation of grizzly bear-human conflict in the Northwest Boreal Region of Alberta (1999–2000) and potential migration.* (Alberta Species at Risk Report, No. 10.) Alberta Fisheries and Wildlife Management Division.

Auld, D. S., & Robitaille, R. (2003). Glial cells and neurotransmission: An inclusive view of synaptic function. *Neuron, 40,* 389–400.

Auld, F., & Hyman, M. (1991). *Resolution of inner conflict: An introduction to psychoanalytic therapy.* Washington, DC: American Psychological Association.

Avaria, M., Mills, J. L., Kleinsteuber, K., Aros, S., Conley, M. R., Cox, C., et al. (2004). Peripheral nerve conduction abnormalities in children exposed to alcohol in utero. *Journal of Pediatrics, 144,* 338–343.

Aviezer, O., Sagi, A., Joels, T., & Ziv, Y. (1999). Emotional availability and attachment representations in kibbutz infants and their mothers. *Developmental Psychology, 35,* 811–821.

Avila, C. (2001). *Journal of Personality and Social Psychology, 80,* 311–324.

Ayache, D., Corre, A., Can Prooyen, S., & Elbaz, P. (2003). Surgical treatment of otosclerosis in elderly patients. *Otolaryngological Head and Neck Surgery, 129,* 674–677.

Ayllon, T. (1999). *How to use token economy and point systems* (2nd ed.). Austin, TX: Pro-Ed.

Ayllon, T., & Azrin, N. H. (1968). *The token economy: A motivational system for therapy and rehabilitation.* New York: Appleton-Century-Crofts.

Ayuso-Mateos, J. L., Vazquez-Barquero, J. L., Dowrick, C., Lehtinen, V., Dalgard, O. S., Casey, P., et al. (2001). Depressive disorders in Europe: Prevalence figures from the ODIN study. *British Journal of Psychiatry, 179,* 308–316.

Azar, B. (1996, November). Project explores landscape of midlife. *APA Monitor,* p. 26.

Azar, B. (2002). The "science of learning" moves mainstream. *Monitor on Psychology, 33,* 60–62.

Azorin, J.-M., Spiegel, R., Remington, G., Vanelle, J.-M., Pere, J.-J., Giguere, M., & Bourdeix, I. (2001). A double-blind comparative study of clozapine and risperidone in the management of severe chronic schizophrenia. *American Journal of Psychiatry, 158,* 1305–1313.

Baare, W. F. C., van Oel, C. J., Hushoff, H. E., Schnack, H. G., Durston, S., Sitskoorn, M. M., & Kahn, R. S. (2001). Volumes of brain structures in twins discordant for schizophrenia. *Archives of General Psychiatry, 58,* 33–40.

Baars, B. J. (2002). The conscious access hypothesis: Origins and recent evidence. *Trends in Cognitive Science, 6,* 47–52.

Babcock, Q., & Byrne, T. (2000). Student perceptions of methylphenidate abuse at a public liberal arts college. *Journal of American College Health, 49,* 143–145.

Babcock, R., & Salthouse, T. (1990). Effects of increased processing demands on age differences in working memory. *Psychology and Aging, 5,* 421–428.

Backman, L., & Nilsson, L. (1991). Effects of divided attention on free and cued recall of verbal events and action events. *Bulletin of the Psychonomic Society, 29,* 51–54.

Baddeley, A. (1982). *Your memory: A user's guide.* New York: Macmillan.

Baddeley, A. (1992). Working memory. *Science, 255,* 556–559.

Baddeley, A. (1998). *Human memory: Theory and practice.* Boston: Allyn & Bacon.

Baddeley, A. D. (2003). Working memory: Looking back and looking forward. *Nature Reviews Neuroscience, 4,* 829–839.

Baer, J. S., Sampson, P. D., Barr, H. M., Connor, P. D., & Streissguth, A. P. (2003) A 21–year longitudinal analysis of the effects of prenatal alcohol exposure on young adult drinking. *Archives of General Psychiatry, 60,* 377–385.

Bagley, C., & Tremblay, P. (1998). On the prevalence of homosexuality and bisexuality, in a random survey of 750 men aged 18–27. *Journal of Homosexuality, 36,* 1–18.

Bagwell, C. L., Newcomb, A. F., & Bukowski, W. M. (1998). Preadolescent friendship and peer rejection as predictors of adult adjustment. *Child Development, 69,* 140–153.

Bahrick, H. P., & Hall, L. K. (1991). Lifetime maintenance of high school mathematics content. *Journal of Experimental Psychology: General, 120,* 20–33.

Bahrick, H. P., Hall, L. K., & Berger, S. A. (1996). Accuracy and distortion in memory for high school grades. *Psychological Science, 7,* 265–271.

Bahrick, H. P., Hall, L. K., Noggin, J. P., & Bahrick, L. E. (1994). Fifty years of language maintenance and language dominance in bilingual Hispanic immigrants. *Journal of Experimental Psychology: General, 123,* 264–283.

Bailey, J. M., & Benishay, D. S. (1993). Familial aggregation of female sexual orientation. *American Journal of Psychiatry, 150,* 272–277.

Bailey, J. M., & Pillard, R. C. (1991). A genetic study of male sexual orientation. *Archives of General Psychiatry, 48,* 1086–1096.

Bailey, J. M., Dunne, M. P., & Martin, N. G. (2000). Genetic and environmental influences on sexual orientation and its correlates in an Australian twin sample. *Journal of Personality and Social Psychology, 78,* 524–536.

Bailey, K. P. (2002). Choosing between atypical antipsychotics: Weighing the risks and benefits. *Archives of Psychiatric Nursing, 16,* S2–S11A.

Baillargeon, R. (1992). A model of physical reasoning in infancy. In C. Rovee-Collier & L. P. Lipsett (Eds.), *Advances in infancy research.* Norwood, NJ: Ablex.

Baillargeon, R. (1994). How do infants learn about the physical world? *Current Directions in Psychological Science, 3,* 133–139.

Baillargeon, R. (1995). Physical reasoning in infancy. In M. S. Gazzaniga (Ed.), *The cognitive neurosciences* (pp. 181–204). Cambridge, MA: MIT Press.

Baillargeon, R. (2002). The acquisition of physical knowledge in infancy: A summary in eight lessons. In U. Goswami (Ed.), *Blackwell handbook of childhood cognitive development* (pp. 47–83). Malden, MA: Blackwell.

Baillargeon, R. (2004). Infants' physical world. *Current Directions in Psychological Science 13,* 89–94.

Baker, L. T., Vernon, P. A., & Ho, H. (1991). The genetic correlation between intelligence and speed of information processing. *Behavior Genetics, 21,* 351–367.

Baker, M. C. (2002). *The atoms of language: The mind's hidden rules of grammar.* New York: Basic Books.

Bakker, J., Honda, S., Harada, N., & Balthazart, J. (2003). The aromatase knockout (ArKO) mouse provides new evidence that estrogens are required for the development of the female brain. *Annals of the New York Academy of Science, 1007,* 251–262.

Balaban, M. T. (1995). Affective influences on startle in five-month-old infants: Reactions to facial expressions of emotion. *Child Development, 66*(1), 28–36.

Balat, O., Balat, A., Ugur, M. G., & Pence, S. (2003). The effect of smoking and caffeine on the fetus and placenta in pregnancy. *Clinical and Experimental Obstetrics and Gynecology, 30, 57–59.*

Balbin, E. G., Ironson, G. H., & Solomon, G. F. (1999). Stress and coping: The psychoneuroimmunology of HIV/AIDS. *Baillieres Best Practice and Research. Clinical Endocrinology and Metabolism, 13,* 615–633.

Baldessarini, R. J., & Tondo, L. (2000). Does lithium treatment still work? Evidence of stable responses over three decades. *Archives of General Psychiatry, 57,* 187–190.

Baldessarini, R. J., Tondo, L., Hennen, J., Viguera, A. C. (2002). Is lithium still worth using? An update of selected research. *Harvard Review of Psychiatry, 10, 59–75.*

Balfour, D. J. (2002). The neurobiology of tobacco dependence: A commentary. *Respiration, 69,* 7–11.

Ball, K., & Sekuler, R. (1992). Cues reduce direction uncertainty and enhance motion detection. *Perception and Psychophysics, 30,* 119–128.

Balldin, J., Berglund, M., Borg, S., Mansson, M., Bendtsen, P., Franck, J., et al. (2003). A 6-month controlled naltrexone study: Combined effect with cognitive behavioral therapy in outpatient treatment of alcohol dependence. *Alcohol Clinical and Experimental Research, 27,* 1142–1149.

Balleine, B., & Dickinson, A. (1994). Role of cholecystokinin in the motivational control of instrumental action in rats. *Behavioral Neuroscience, 108*(3), 590–605.

Ballou, M. (1995). Assertiveness training. In M. Ballou (Ed.), *Psychological interventions: A guide to strategies* (pp. 125–136). Westport, CT: Praeger.

Balon, R. (2004). Developments in treatment of anxiety disorders: Psychotherapy, pharmacotherapy, and psychosurgery. *Depression and Anxiety, 19*(2), 63–76.

Baltes, P. B. (1993). The aging mind: Potential and limits. *The Gerontologist, 33,* 580–594.

Baltes, P. B., Staudinger, U. M., Maercker, A., & Smith, J. (1995). People nominated as wise: A comparative study of wisdom-related knowledge. *Psychology and Aging, 10,* 155–166.

Banaji, M., Lemm, K. M., & Carpenter, S. J. (2001). The social unconscious. In A. Tesser & N. Schwarz (Eds.), *Blackwell handbook of social psychology: Intraindividual processes* (pp. 134–158). Oxford, UK: Blackwell.

Bancroft, J. (1994). Homosexual orientation: The search for a biological basis. *British Journal of Psychiatry, 164,* 437–440.

Bancroft, J. (1997). *Researching sexual behavior: Methodological issues.* Bloomington, IN: Indiana University Press.

Bandura, A. (1965). Influence of a model's reinforcement contingencies on the acquisition of imitative responses. *Journal of Personality and Social Psychology, 1,* 589–595.

Bandura, A. (1992). Self-efficacy mechanism in psychobiologic functioning. In R. Schwarzer (Ed.), *Self-efficacy: Thought control of action* (pp. 355–394). Washington, DC: Hemisphere.

Bandura, A. (1999). Social cognitive theory of personality. In L. Pervin & O. John (Eds.), *Handbook of personality: theory and research* (2nd ed., pp. 154–198). New York: Guilford.

Bandura, A., & Walters, R. H. (1963). *Social learning and personality development.* New York: Holt, Rinehart & Winston.

Bandura, A., Blanchard, E. B., & Ritter, B. (1969). The relative efficacy of desensitization and modeling approaches for inducing behavioral, affective, and attitudinal changes. *Journal of Personality and Social Psychology, 13,* 173–199.

Bandura, A., Ross, D., & Ross, S. A. (1963). Imitation of film-mediated aggressive models. *Journal of Abnormal and Social Psychology, 66,* 3–11.

Banich, M. T., & Heller, W. (1998). Evolving perspectives on lateralization of function. *Current Directions in Psychological Science, 7,* 1–2.

Banich, M. T., Stolar, N., Heller, W., & Goldman, R. B. (1992). A deficit in right-hemisphere performance after induction of a depressed mood. *Neuropsychiatry, Neuropsychology, and Behavioral Neurology, 5*(1), 20–27.

Banks, W. P., & Krajicek, D. (1991). Perception. *Annual Review of Psychology, 42,* 305–332.

Banta, B. D. (1997). Cooperation and competition in peaceful societies. *Psychological Bulletin, 121,* 299–320.

Bantick, S. J., Wise, R. G., Ploghaus, A., Clare, S., Smith, S. M., & Tracey, I. (2002). Imaging how attention modulates pain in humans using functional MRI. *Brain, 125,* 310–319.

Bar, M., & Biederman, I. (1998). Subliminal visual priming. *Psychological Science, 9,* 464–469.

Bara, B. G., Bucciarelli, M., & Johnson-Laird, P. N. (1995). Development of syllogistic reasoning. *American Journal of Psychology, 108,* 157–193.

Barber, J. P., Connolly, M. B., Crits-Christoph, P., Gladis, L., & Siqueland, L. (2000). Alliance predicts patients' outcome beyond in-treatment change in symptoms. *Journal of Consulting and Clinical Psychology, 68,* 1027–1032.

Barber, J. P., Crits-Christoph, P., & Paul, C. C. (1993). Advances in measures of psycho- dynamic formulations. *Journal of Consulting and Clinical Psychology, 61,* 574–585.

Barber, N. (1995). The evolutionary psychology of physical attractiveness: Sexual selection and human morphology. *Ethology and Sociobiology, 16,* 395–424.

Barclay, J. R., Bransford, J. D., Franks, J. J., McCarrell, N. S., & Nitsch, K. (1974). Comprehension and semantic flexibility. *Journal of Verbal Learning and Verbal Behavior, 13,* 471–481.

Bardo, M. T., Donohew, R. L., & Harrington, N. G. (1996). Psychobiology of novelty-seeking and drug-seeking behavior. *Behavioral Brain Research, 77*(1–2), 23–43.

Bareyre, F. M., Kerschensteiner, M., Raineteau, O., Mettenleiter, T. C., & Schwab, M. E. (2004). The injured spinal cord spontaneously forms a new intraspinal circuit in adult rats. *Nature Neuroscience, 7,* 269–277.

Bargh, J. A., & Ferguson, M. J. (2000). Beyond behaviorism: On the automaticity of higher mental processes. *Psychological Bulletin, 126,* 925–945.

Bargh, J. A., Chen, M., & Burrows, L. (1996). Automaticity of social behavior: Direct effects of trait construct and stereotype activation on action. *Journal of Personality and Social Psychology, 71,* 245–262.

Barker, L. M. (1997). *Learning and behavior: Biological, psychological, and sociocultural perspectives* (2nd ed.). Upper Saddle River, NJ: Prentice-Hall.

Barlow, D. H. (1988). *Anxiety and its disorders: The nature and treatment of panic and anxiety.* New York: Guilford.

Barlow, D. H., Gorman, J. M., Shear, M. K., & Woods, S. W. (2000). Cognitive-behavioral therapy, imipramine, or their combination for panic disorder: A randomized controlled trial. *Journal of the American Medical Association, 283,* 2529–2536.

Barlow, D. H., Raffa, S. D., & Cohen, E. M. (2002). Psychosocial treatments for panic disorders, phobias, and generalized anxiety disorder. In P. E. Nathan & J. M. Gorman (Eds.), *A guide to treatments that work* (2nd ed., pp. 301–335). London: Oxford University Press.

Barnett, J. E., & Scheetz, K. (2003). Technological advances and telehealth: Ethics, law, and the practice of psychotherapy. *Psychotherapy: Theory, Research, Practice, and Training, 40,* 86–93.

Barnett, W. S. (1998). Long-term cognitive and academic effects of early childhood education of children in poverty. *Preventive Medicine: An International Devoted Practice & Theory, 27,* 204–207.

Barnier, A. J., & McConkey, K. M. (1998). Posthypnotic responding away from the hypnotic setting. *Psychological Science, 9,* 256–262.

Baron, R. A., & Byrne, D. (1994). *Social psychology: Understanding human interaction* (7th ed.). Boston: Allyn & Bacon.

Baron, R. S., Kerr, N. L., & Miller, N. (1992). *Group process, group decision, group action.* Pacific Grove, CA: Brooks/Cole.

Barrett, L. F. (1995). Valence focus and arousal focus: Individual differences in the structure of affective experience. *Journal of Personality and Social Psychology, 69,* 153–166.

Barrett, L. F., Gross, J., Christensen, T. C., & Benvenuto, M. (2001). Knowing what you're feeling and knowing what to do about it: Mapping the relation between emotion differentiation and emotion regulation. *Cognition and Emotion, 15,* 713–724.

Barrett, L. F., Lane, R. D., Sechrest, L., & Schwartz, G. E. (2000). Sex differences in emotional awareness. *Personality and Social Psychology Bulletin, 26,* 1027–1035.

Barrett, L. F., Quigley, K. S., Bliss-Moreau, E., & Aronson, K. R. (2004). Interoceptive sensitivity and self-reports of emotional experience. *Journal of Personality and Social Psychology, 87,* 684–697.

Barrett, S. P., Gross, S. R., Garand, I., & Pihl, R. O. (2005). Patterns of simultaneous polysubstance use in Canadian rave attendees. *Substance Use and Misuse, 40, 1525–1537.*

Barrick, M. R., & Mount, M. K. (1991). The Big Five personality dimensions and job performance: A meta-analysis. *Personnel Psychology, 44,* 1–26.

Barron, F., & Harrington, D. M. (1981). Creativity, intelligence, and personality. *Annual Review of Psychology, 52,* 439–476.

Barron, K. E., & Harackiewicz, J. M. (2001). Achievement goals and optimal motivation: Testing multiple goal models. *Journal of Personality and Social Psychology, 80,* 706–722.

Barrowclough, C., King, P., Colville, J., Russell, E., Burns, A., & Tarrier, N. (2001). A randomized trial of the effectiveness of cognitive-behavioral therapy and supportive counseling for anxiety symptoms in older adults. *Journal of Consulting and Clinical Psychology, 69,* 756–762.

Barsalou, L. W. (1991). Deriving categories to achieve goals. In G. H. Bower (Ed.), *The psychology of learning and motivation* (pp. 1–64). New York: Academic Press.

Barsalou, L. W. (1993). Flexibility, structure, and linguistic vagary in concepts: Manifestations of a compositional system of perceptual symbols. In A. F. Collins, S. E. Gathercole, M. A. Conway, & P. E. Morris (Eds.), *Theories of memory* (pp. 29–102). Hillsdale, NJ: Erlbaum.

Barsky, A. J., Wool, C., Barnett, M. C., & Cleary, P. D. (1994). Histories of childhood trauma in adult hypochondriacal patients. *American Journal of Psychiatry, 151,* 397–401.

Bartlett, J. A. (2002). Addressing the challenges of adherence. *Journal of Acquired Immune Deficiency Syndrome, 29* (Suppl. 1), S2–S10.

Barton, J. J., Cherkasova, M., & O'Connor M. (2001). Covert recognition in acquired and developmental prosopagnosia. *Neurology, 57,* 1161–1168.

Bartoshuk, L. M. (1991). Taste, smell, and pleasure. In R. C. Bollef (Ed.), *The hedonics of taste* (pp. 15–28). Hillsdale, NJ: Erlbaum.

Bartoshuk, L. M. (2000). Comparing sensory experiences across individuals: Recent psychophysical advances illuminate genetic variation in taste perception. *Chemical Senses, 25,* 447–460.

Bartoshuk, L. M., & Wolfe, J. M. (1990). Conditioned taste aversion in humans: Are there olfactory versions? *Chemical Senses, 15,* 551.

Bashore, T. R., & Ridderinkhof, K. R. (2002). Older age, traumatic brain injury, and cognitive slowing: Some convergent and divergent findings. *Psychological Bulletin, 128,* 151–198.

Basoglu, M., Livanou, M., & Salcioglu, E. (2003). A single session with an earthquake simulator for traumatic stress in earthquake survivors. *American Journal of Psychiatry, 160,* 788–790.

Bass, E., & Davis, L. (1994). *The courage to heal* (3rd ed.). New York: Harper Perennial Library.

Bassett, A. S., Chow, E. W. C., O'Neill, S., & Brzustowicz, L. M. (2001). Genetic insights into the neurodevelopmental hypothesis of schizophrenia. *Schizophrenia Bulletin, 27,* 417–430.

Bates, E. (1993, March). *Nature, nurture, and language development.* Paper presented at the biennial meeting of the Society for Research in Child Development, New Orleans.

Batson, C. D. (1998). Altruism and prosocial behavior. In D. Gilbert, S. T. Fiske, & G. Lindzey (Eds.), *Handbook of social psychology* (Vol. 2, 4th ed., pp. 282–316). Boston: McGraw-Hill.

Batson, C. D., & Thompson, E. R. (2001). Why don't moral people act morally?: Motivational considerations. *Current Directions in Psychological Science, 10,* 54–57.

Batson, C. D., Sager, K., Garst, E., & Kang, M. (1997). Is empathy-induced helping due to self-other merging? *Journal of Personality and Social Psychology, 73,* 495–509.

Battaglia, G., Yeh, S. Y., & De Souza, E. B. (1988). MDMA-induced neurotoxicity: Parameters of degeneration and recovery of brain serotonin neurons. *Pharmacology, Biochemistry and Behavior, 29,* 269–274.

Baucom, D. H., Shoham, V., Mueser, K. T., Daiuto, A. D., & Stickle, T. R. (1998). Empirically supported couple and family interventions for marital distress and adult mental health problems. *Journal of Consulting and Clinical Psychology, 66,* 53–88.

Bauer, R. M. (1984). Autonomic recognition of names and faces in prosopagnosia: A neuropsychological application of the Guilty Knowledge Test. *Neuropsychologia, 22,* 457–469.

Baum, A., Gatchel, R. J., & Krantz, D. S. (1997). *Introduction to health psychology* (3rd ed.). New York: McGraw-Hill.

Baumeister, R. F. (2000). Gender differences in erotic plasticity: The female sex drive as socially flexible and responsive. *Psychological Bulletin, 126,* 347–374.

Baumeister, R. F., & Leary, M. R. (1995). The need to belong: Desire for interpersonal attachments as a fundamental human motivation. *Psychological Bulletin, 117*(3), 497–529.

Baumeister, R. F., Campbell, J. D., Krueger, J. I., & Vohs, K. D. (2003). Does high self-esteem cause better performance, interpersonal success, happiness, or healthier lifestyles? *Psychological Science in the Public Interest, 4,* 1–44.

Baumrind, D. (1971). Current patterns of parental authority. *Developmental Psychology Monographs, 4*(1, part 2).

Baumrind, D. (1986). *Familial antecedents of social competence in middle childhood.* Unpublished monograph, Institute of Human Development, University of California, Berkeley.

Baumrind, D., Larzelere, R. E., & Cowan, P. A. (2002). Ordinary physical punishment: Is it harmful? Comment on Gershoff. *Psychological Bulletin, 128,* 580–589.

Bazzano, L. A., He, J., Ogden, L. G., Loria, C. M., & Whelton, P. K. (2003). Dietary fiber intake and reduced risk of coronary heart disease in US men and women. *Archives of Internal Medicine, 163,* 1897–1904.

BBC (2005). Christmas Thief steals 'nun bun' Retrieved March 23, 2006, from http://news.bbc.co.uk/go/pr/fr/-/2/hi/americas/4562170.stm

BC Partners for Mental Health and Addictions (2002). Children, youth and mental disorders. [Electronic version]. Available: http://www.heretohelp.bc.ca/publications/factsheets/child_youth_mentaldisorders.shtml

BC Partners for Mental Health and Addictions Information (2003). Economic costs of mental disorders and addictions. [On-line]. Available: http://www.heretohelp.bc.ca/publications/factsheets/economiccosts.shtml

BC Partners for Mental Health and Addictions Information (2006). Suicide: Follow the warning signs. [On-line]. Available: http://72.14.207.104/search?q=cache:PRuJVtftbrUJ:www.heretohelp.bc.ca/publications/factsheets/suicide.pdf+suicide:+follow+the+warning+signs&hl=en&gl=ca&ct=clnk&cd=1

Beardslee, W. R., Gladstone, T. R. G., Wright, E. J., & Cooper, A. B. (2003). A family-based approach to the prevention of depressive symptoms in children at risk: Evidence of parental and child change. *Pediatrics, 112,* 119–131.

Beardsley, P. M., Sokoloff, P., Balster, R. L., & Schwartz, J. C. (2001). The D3R partial agonist, BP 897, attenuates the discriminative stimulus effects of cocaine and D-amphetamine and is not self-administered. *Behavioral Pharmacology, 12,* 1–11.

Bearman, P. S., & Moody, J. (2004). Suicide and friendships among American adolescents. *American Journal of Public Health, 94,* 89–95.

Beauchamp, G. K., Katahira, K., Yamazaki, K., Mennella, J. A., Bard, J., & Boyse, E. A. (1995). Evidence suggesting that the odortypes of pregnant women are a compound of maternal and fetal odortypes. *Proceedings of the National Academy of Sciences of the United States of America, 92,* 2617–2621.

Beauchamp-Turner, D. L., & Levinson, D. M. (1992). Effects of meditation on stress, health, and affect. *Medical Psychotherapy: An International Journal, 5,* 123–131.

Beaulieu, D. (2003). *Eye movement integration therapy: The comprehensive clinical guide.* Williston, VT: Crown House.

Beaumont, M., Batejat, D., Pierard, C., Coste, O., Doireau, P., Van Beers, P., et al. (2001). Slow release caffeine and prolonged (64-h) continuous wakefulness: effects on vigilance and cognitive performance. *Journal of Sleep Research, 10*(4), 265.

Beaumont, M., Batejat, D., Pierard, C., Van Beers, P., Denis, J. B., Coste, O., et al. (2004). Caffeine or melatonin effects on sleep and sleepiness after rapid eastward transmeridian travel. *Journal of Applied Physiology, 96,* 50–58.

Beaumont, S. L. & Zukanovic, R. (2005). Identity development in men and its relation to psychosocial distress and self-worth. *Canadian Journal of Behavioural Science, 37,* 70–81.

Bechara, A., Damasio, H., Tranel, D., & Damasio, A. R. (1997). Deciding advantageously before knowing the advantageous strategy. *Science, 275,* 1293–1295.

Beck, A. T. (1967). *Depression: Clinical, experimental and theoretical aspects.* New York: Harper & Row.

Beck, A. T. (1976). *Cognitive therapy and the emotional disorders.* New York: International Universities Press.

Beck, A. T. (1995). Cognitive therapy: A 30-year retrospective. In S. O. Lilienfeld (Ed.), *Seeing both sides: Classic controversies in abnormal psychology* (pp. 303–311). Pacific Grove, CA: Brooks/Cole. (Original work published 1991)

Beck, A. T. (2002). Cognitive models of depression. In R. L. Leahy & E. T. Dowd (Eds.), *Clinical advances in cognitive psychotherapy: Theory and Application* (pp. 29–61). New York: Springer.

Beck, A. T., & Emery, G. (1985). *Anxiety disorders and phobias: A cognitive perspective.* New York: Basic Books.

Beck, A. T., Brown, G., Berchick, R. J., Stewart, B. L., & Steer, R. A. (1990). Relationship between hopelessness and ultimate suicide: A replication with psychiatric outpatients. *American Journal of Psychiatry, 147,* 190–195.

Beck, A. T., Sokol, L., Clark, D., Berchick, R., & Wright, F. (1992). A crossover study of focused cognitive therapy for panic disorder. *American Journal of Psychiatry, 149,* 778–783.

Beck, J. S., & Beck, A. T. (1995). *Cognitive therapy: Basics and beyond.* New York: Guilford.

Becker, J. A. (1994). "Sneak-shoes," "sworders" and "nose-beards": A case study of lexical innovation. *First Language, 14,* 195–211.

Bedard, J., & Chi, M. T. H. (1992). Expertise. *Current Directions in Psychological Science, 1,* 135–139.

Beels, C. C. (2002). Notes for a cultural history of family therapy. *Family Process, 41,* 67–82.

Begley, S. (1997, September 29). Hope for "snow babies." *Newsweek,* pp. 62–63.

Behnke, S. (2003). *Hierarchical neural network for image interpretation.* New York: Springer.

Belin, P., Zatorre, R. J., & Ahad, P. (2002). Human temporal-lobe response to vocal sounds. *Brain Research and Cognitive Brain Research, 13,* 17–26.

Bella, S. D., & Peretz, I. (2003). Congenital amusia interferes with the ability to synchronize with music. *Annals of the New York Academy of Science, 999,* 166–169.

Belli, R. F., & Loftus, E. F. (1996). The pliability of autobiographical memory: Misinformation and the false memory problem. In D. C. Rubin (Ed.), *Remembering our past: Studies in autobiographical memory* (pp. 157–179). New York: Cambridge University Press.

Belmont, J. M., & Butterfield, E. C. (1971). Learning strategies as determinants of memory deficiencies. *Cognitive Psychology, 2,* 411–420.

Belsky, J., & Kelly, J. (1994). *The transition to parenthood.* New York: Dell.

Belsky, J., Spritz, B., & Crnic, K. (1996). Infant attachment security and affective-cognitive information processing at age 3. *Psychological Science, 7,* 111–114.

Bem, D. J. (1996). Exotic becomes erotic: A developmental theory of sexual orientation. *Psychological Review, 103,* 320–335.

Ben-Ari, A., & Gil, S. (2002). Traditional support systems: Are they sufficient in a culturally diverse academic environment? *British Journal of Social Work, 32,* 629–638.

Benecke, M. (1999). Spontaneous human combustion: Thoughts of a forensic biologist. *Skeptical Inquirer, 22,* 47–51.

Benedetti, F., & Amanzio, M. (1997). The neurobiology of placebo analgesia: From endogenous opioids to cholecystokinin. *Progress in Neurobiology, 52,* 109–125.

Benedetti, F., Arduino, C., & Amanzio, M. (1999). Somatotopic activation of opioid systems by target-directed expectations of analgesia. *Journal of Neuroscience, 19,* 3639–3648.

Benenson, J. F., & Christakos, A. (2003). The greater fragility of females' versus males' closest same-sex friendships. *Child Development, 74,* 1123–1129.

Benight, C. C., Swift, E., Sanger, J., Smith, A., & Zeppelin, D. (1999). Coping self-efficacy as a mediator of distress following a natural disaster. *Journal of Applied Social Psychology, 29,* 2443–2464.

Benjamin, K., Wilson, S. G., & Mogil, J. S. (1999). *Journal of Pharmacology & Experimental Therapeutics, 289,* 1370–1375.

Benjamin, L. T., Jr. (2000). The psychology laboratory at the turn of the 20th century. *American Psychologist, 55,* 318–321.

Benjamin, L. T., Jr., & Baker, D. B. (2004). *From séance to science: A history of the profession of psychology in America.* Belmont, CA: Thomson Wadsworth.

Bennet, W. M. (1994). Marijuana has no medicinal value. *Hospital Practice, 29*(4), 26–27.

Bennett, H. L., Giannini, J. A., & Davis, H. S. (1985). Nonverbal response to intraoperational conversation. *British Journal of Anaesthesia, 57,* 174–179.

Bennett, K. K., & Elliott, M. (2002). Explanatory style and health: Mechanisms linking pessimism to illness. *Journal of Applied Social Psychology, 32,* 1508–1526.

Ben-Shakhar, G., & Furedy, J. J. (1990). *Theories and applications in the detection of deception: A psychophysiological and international perspective.* New York: Springer-Verlag.

Ben-Shakhar, G., Bar-Hillel, M., & Kremnitzer, M. (2002). Trial by polygraph: Reconsidering the use of the guilty knowledge technique in court. *Law & Human Behavior, 26,* 527–541.

Benson, E. (2003a). Intelligence across cultures. *Monitor on Psychology, 34*(2), 56–58.

Benson, E. (2003b). Sex: The science of sexual arousal. *Monitor on Psychology, 34,* 50.

Benson, H. (1975). *The relaxation response.* New York: Morrow.

Ben-Zur, H. (2002b). Coping, affect and aging: The roles of mastery and self-esteem. *Personality & Individual Differences, 32*(2), 357–372.

Berenbaum, S. A., & Resnick, S. M. (1997). Early androgen effects on aggression in children and adults with congenital adrenal hyperplasia. *Psychoneuroendocrinology, 22,* 505–515.

Berg, E. P., Engel, B. A., & Forrest, J. C. (1998). Pork carcass composition derived from a neural network model of electromagnetic scans. *Journal of Animal Science, 76,* 18–22.

Berger, A., Henderson, M., Nadoolman, W., Duffy, V., Cooper, D., Saberski, L., & Bartoshuk, L. (1995). Oral capsaicin provides temporary relief for oral mucositis pain secondary to chemotherapy/radiation therapy. *Journal of Pain and Symptom Management, 10,* 243–248.

Berger, R., & Hannah, M. T. (Eds.). (1999). *Preventative approaches in couples therapy.* Bristol, PA: Brunner/Mazel.

Berger, S. E., & Adolph, K. E. (2003). Infants use handrails as tools in a locomotor task. *Developmental Psychology, 39,* 594–605.

Bergin, A. E. (1971). The evaluation of therapeutic outcomes. In A. E. Bergin & S. L. Garfield (Eds.), *Handbook of psychotherapy and behavior change: An empirical analysis* (pp. 217–270). New York: Wiley.

Berkowitz, L. (1999). Evil is more than banal: Situationism and the concept of evil. *Personality and Social Psychology Review, 3,* 246–253.

Berliner, D. L., Monti-Bloch, L., Jennings-White, C., & Diaz-Sanchez, V. (1996). The functionality of the human vomeronasal organ (VNO): Evidence for steriod receptors. *Journal of Steriod Biochemical Molecular Biology, 58,* 259–265.

Berman, R. F. (1991). Electrical brain stimulation used to study mechanisms and models of memory. L. Martinez & R. P. Kesner (Eds.), *Learning and memory: A biological view* (2nd ed.). San Diego: Academic Press.

Bermond, B., Fasotti, L., Nieuwenhuyse, B., & Schuerman, J. (1991). Spinal cord lesions, peripheral feedback and intensities of emotional feelings. *Cognition and Emotions, 5,* 201–220.

Bernard, L. L. (1924) *Instinct.* New York: Holt, Rinehart & Winston.

Bernat, J. A., Calhoun, K. S., Adams, H. E., & Zeichner, A. (2001). Homophobia and physical aggression toward homosexual and heterosexual individuals. *Journal of Abnormal Psychology, 110,* 179–187.

Berns, G. S., McClure, S. M., Pagnoni, G., & Montague, P. R. (2001). Predictability modulates human brain response to reward. *Journal of Neuroscience, 21,* 2793–2798.

Bernstein, D. A. (1970). The modification of smoking behavior: A search for effective variables. *Behaviour Research and Therapy, 8,* 133–146.

Bernstein, D. A., Borkovec, T. D., & Hazlett-Stevens, H. (2000). *Progressive relaxation training: A manual for the helping professions* (2nd ed.) New York: Praeger.

Bernstein, D. M., & Roberts, B. (1995). Assessing dreams through self-report questionnaires: Relation with past research and personality. *Dreaming: Journal of the Association for the Study of Dreams, 5,* 13–27.

Bernstein, I. L. (1978). Learned taste aversions in children receiving chemotherapy. *Science, 200,* 1302–1303.

Berridge, C. W., & Waterhouse, B. D. (2003). The locus coeruleus-noradrenergic system: Modulation of behavioral state and state-dependent cognitive processes. *Brain Research and Brain Research Reviews, 42,* 33–84.

Berridge, K. C. (1999). Pleasure, pain, desire and dread: Biopsychological components and relations. In D. Kahneman, E. Diener, & N. Schwarz (Eds.), *Understanding the quality of life: Scientific perspectives on enjoyment and suffering.* New York: Russell Sage Foundation.

Berry, J. W. (1993). Ethnic identity in plural societies. In Bernal, M.E., & Knight, G. P. (Eds.), *Ethnic identity: Formation and transmission among Hispanics and other minorities,* pp. 271–296. Albany, NY: State University of New York Press.

Berry, J. W., & Bennett, J. A. (1992). Cree conceptions of cognitive competence. *International Journal of Psychology, 27,* 73–88.

Berscheid, E., & Reis, H. T. (1998). Attraction and close relationships. In D. Gilbert, S. T. Fiske, & G. Lindzey (Eds.), *Handbook of social psychology* (Vol. 2, 4th ed., pp. 193–281). Boston: McGraw-Hill.

Bersoff, D. M. (1999). Why good people sometimes do bad things: Motivated reasoning and unethical behavior. *Personality and Social Psychology Bulletin, 25,* 28–39.

Berson, D. M., Dunn, F. A., & Takao, M. (2002). Phototransduction by retinal ganglion cells that set the circadian clock. *Science, 295,* 1070–1073.

Berthoud, H. R., & Neuhuber, W. L. (2000). Functional and chemical anatomy of the afferent vagal system. *Autonomic Neuroscience, 85,* 1–17.

Besner, D. & Stolz, J. (1999). What kind of attention modulates the stroop effect? *Psychonomic Bulletin and Review, 6(1),* 99–104.

Besson, M., Faita, F., Peretz, I., Bonnel, A.-M., & Requin, J. (1998). Singing in the brain: Independence of lyrics and tunes. *Psychological Science, 9,* 494–498.

Best, J. B. (1999). *Cognitive psychology* (5th ed.) Belmont, CA: Brooks/Cole.

Bettman, J. R., Johnson, E. J., & Payne, J. W. (1990). A componential analysis of cognitive effort in choice. *Organizational Behavior and Human Decision Processes, 45,* 111–139.

Beuckmann, C. T., & Yanagisawa, M. (2002). Orexins: From neuropeptide to energy homeostasis and sleep/wake regulation. *Journal of Molecular Medicine, 80,* 329–342.

Beutler, L. E. (2000). David and Goliath: When empirical and clinical standards of practice meet. *American Psychologist, 55,* 997–1007.

Beutler, L. E. (2002). The dodo bird is extinct. *Clinical Psychology: Science and Practice, 9,* 30–34.

Bevan, S., & Geppetti, P. (1994). Protons: small stimulants of capsaicin-sensitive sensory nerves. *Trends in Neuroscience, 17,* 509–512.

Bevins, R. A. (2001). Novelty seeking and reward: Implications for the study of high-risk behaviors. *Current Directions in Psychological Science, 10,* 189–193.

Beyerstein, B. L. (1999). Pseudoscience and the brain: Tuners and tonics for aspiring superhumans. In S. Della Sala (Ed.), *Mind myths: Exploring popular assumptions about the mind and brain* (pp. 59–82). Chichester, UK: Wiley.

Bhagat, R. S., Kedia, B. L., Harveston, P. D., & Triandis, H. C. (2002). Cultural variations in the cross-border transfer of organizational knowledge: An integrative framework. *Academy of Management Review, 27,* 204–221.

Bhatt, R. S., & Bertin, E. (2001). Pictorial cues and three-dimensional information processing in early infancy. *Journal of Experimental Child Psychology, 80,* 315–332.

Bhopal, R., Vettini, A., Hunt, S., Wiebe, S., Hanna, L., & Amos, A. (2004). Review of prevalence data in, and evaluation of methods for cross cultural adaptation of, UK surveys on tobacco and alcohol in ethnic minority groups. *British Medical Journal, 328,* 76.

Bhutta, A. T., Cleves, M. A., Casey, P. H., Cradock, M. M., & Anand, K. J. S. (2002). Cognitive and behavioral outcomes of school-aged children who were born preterm. *JAMA, 288,* 728–737.

Bialystok, E. (2005). Consequences of bilingualism for cognitive development. In J. F. Kroll and A.M.B. de Groot (Eds.). *Handbook of bilingualism: Psycholinguistic approaches* (pp. 417–432). New York: Oxford University Press.

Bickis, M., Kelly, I. W., & Byrnes, G. (1995). Crisis calls and temporal and lunar variables: A comprehensive study. *Journal of Psychology, 129,* 701–711.

Biederman, I. (1987). Recognition by components. *Psychological Review, 94,* 115–147.

Bierhaus, A., Wolf, J., Andrassy, M., Rohleder, N., Humpert, P. M., Petrov, D., et al. (2003). A mechanism converting psychosocial stress into mononuclear cell activation. *Proceedings of the National Academy of Sciences, 100,* 1920–1925.

Bierut, L. J., Heath, A. C., Bucholz, K. K., Dinwiddie, S. H., Madden, P. A., Statham, D. J., et al. (1999). Major depressive disorder in a community-based twin sample: Are there different genetic and environmental contributions for men and women? *Archives of General Psychiatry, 56,* 557–563.

Bigelow, A., MacLean, J., Wood, C., & Smith, J. (1990). Infants' responses to child and adult strangers: An investigation of height and facial configuration variables. *Infant Behavior and Development, 13,* 21–32.

Biklen, D. (1990). Communication unbound: Autism and praxis. *Harvard Educational Review, 60,* 290–314.

Billing, J., & Sherman, P. W. (1998). Antimicrobial functions of spices: Why some like it hot. *Quarterly Review of Biology, 73,* 3–49.

Binson, D., Michaels, S., Stall, R., Coates, T. J., Gagnon, J. H., & Catania, J. A. (1995). Prevalence and social distribution of men who have sex with men: United States and its urban centers. *Journal of Sex Research, 32*(3), 245–254.

Binzen, C. A., Swan, P. D., & Manore, M. M. (2001). Postexercise oxygen consumption and substrate use after resistance exercise in women. *Medicine and Science in Sports and Exercise, 33,* 932–938.

Birnbaum, S. G., Yuan, P. X., Wang, M., Vijayraghavan, S., Bloom, A. K., Davis, D. J., Gobeske, K. T., Sweatt, J. D., Manji, H. K., & Arnsten, A. F. T. (2004). Protein kinase C overactivity impairs prefrontal cortical regulation of working memory. *Science, 306,* 882–884.

Bishop, D. (1997). *Uncommon understanding.* Hove: Psychology Press.

Bjil, R. V., de Graaf, R., Hiripi, E., Kessler, R. C., Kohn, R., Offord, D. R., et al. (2003). The prevalence of treated and untreated mental disorders in five countries. *Health Affairs, 22,* 122–133.

Bjork, R. A. (1979). An information-processing analysis of college teaching. *Educational Psychologist, 14,* 15–23.

Bjork, R. A. (1999). Assessing our own competence: Heuristics and illusions. In D. Gopher & A. Koriat (Eds.), *Attention and performance XVII. Cognitive regulation of performance: Interaction of theory and application* (pp. 435–459). Cambridge: MIT Press.

Bjork, R. A. (2000). Independence in scientific publishing: Reaffirming the principle. *American Psychologist, 55,* 981–984.

Bjorklund, D. F., & Green, B. L. (1992). The adaptive nature of cognitive immaturity. *American Psychologist, 47,* 46–54.

Black, J. E., & Greenough, W. T. (1991). Developmental approaches to the memory process. In J. L. Martinez & R. P. Kesner (Eds.), *Learning and memory: A biological view* (2nd ed.). San Diego: Academic Press.

Blackwood, D. H. R., Visscher, P. M., & Muir, W. J. (2001). Genetic studies of bipolar affective disorder in large families. *British Journal of Psychiatry, 178* (Suppl. 14), 134–136.

Blackwood, N. J., Howard, R. H., Bentall, R. P., & Murray, R. M. (2001). Cognitive neuropsychiatric models of persecutory delusions. *American Journal of Psychiatry, 158,* 527–539.

Blagrove, M. (1996). Problems with the cognitive psychological modeling of dreaming. *Journal of Mind and Behavior, 17,* 99–134.

Blake, J., & de Boysson-Bardies, B. (1992). Patterns in babbling: A cross-linguistic study. *Journal of Child Language, 19,* 51–74.

Blake, R. (1998). What can be "perceived" in the absence of visual awareness? *Current Directions in Psychological Science, 6,* 157–162.

Blake, R., Sobel, K. V., & James, T. W. (2004). Neural synergy between vision and touch. *Psychological Science, 15,* 397–402.

Blakemore, S. J., Wolpert, D., & Frith, C. (2000). Why can't you tickle yourself? *Neuroreport, 11,* R-11–R-16.

Blakeslee, S. (2001, August 28). Therapies push injured brains and spinal cords into new paths. *New York Times.* Retrieved July 28, 2003, from http://www.nytimes.com/2001./08/28/health/anatomy/28REHA.html

Blakeslee, S. (2002, September 22). Exercising toward repair of the spinal cord. *The New York Times,* p. 36.

Blascovich, J., Spencer, S. J., Quinn, D., & Steele, C. (2001). African Americans and high blood pressure: The role of stereotype threat. *Psychological Science, 12,* 225–229.

Blass, T. (1991). Understanding behavior in the Milgram obedience experiment: The role of personality, situations, and their interactions. *Journal of Personality and Social Psychology, 60,* 398–413.

Blass, T. (1999). The Milgram paradigm after 35 years: Some things we now know about obedience to authority. *Journal of Applied Social Psychology, 29,* 955–978.

Blass, T. (2004). *The man who shocked the world: The life and legacy of Stanley Milgram.* New York: Basic Books.

Blass, T., & Schmitt, C. (2001). The nature of perceived authority in the Milgram paradigm: Two replications. *Current Psychology: Developmental, Learning, Personality, Social, 20,* 115–121.

Blatchford, P., Burke, J., Farquhar, C., & Plewis, I. (1989). Teacher expectations in infant school: Associations with attainment and progress, curriculum coverage and classroom interaction. *British Journal of Educational Psychology, 59,* 19–30.

Blatt, S. J., & Maroudas, C. (1992). Convergence of psychoanalytic and cognitive behavioral theories of depression. *Psychoanalytic Psychology, 9,* 157–190.

Blehar, M., & Rosenthal, N. (1989). Seasonal affective disorders and phototherapy. *Archives of General Psychiatry, 46,* 469–474.

Bleil, M. E., McCaffery, J. M., Muldoon, M. F., Sutton-Tyrrell, K., & Manuck, S. B. (2004). Anger-related personality traits and carotid artery atherosclerosis in untreated hypertensive men. *Psychosomatic Medicine, 66,* 633–639.

Block, A. R., Gatchel, R. J., Deardorff, W. W., & Guyer, R. D. (2003). *The psychology of spine surgery.* Washington, DC: APA Books.

Block, J. (2001). Millennial contrarianism: The Five-Factor approach to personality description 5 years later. *Journal of Research in Personality, 35,* 98–107.

Block, J. A. (1971). *Lives through time.* Berkeley: Bancroft Books.

Block, R. I., & Ghoneim, M. M. (1993). Effects of chronic marijuana use on human cognition. *Psychopharmacology, 110*(1–2), 219–228.

Blood, A. J., & Zatorre, R. J. (2001). Intensely pleasurable responses to music correlate with activity in brain regions implicated in reward and emotion. *Proceedings of the National Academy of Science, 98,* 11818–11823.

Bloom, L. (1995). *The transition from infancy to language: Acquiring the power of expression.* New York: Cambridge University Press.

Blow, A. J., & Timm, T. M. (2002). Promoting community through family therapy: Helping clients develop a network of significant social relationships. *Journal of Systematic Therapies, 21,* 67–89.

Blum, R. W., Beuhring, T., & Rinehart, P. M. (2000). *Protecting teens: Beyond race, income and family structure.* Minneapolis, MN: Center for Adolescent Health, University of Minnesota.

Blumberg, H. P., Leung, H.-C., Skudlarski, P., Lacadie, C. M., Fredericks, C. A., Harris, B. C., et al. (2003). A functional magnetic resonance imaging study of bipolar disorder: State- and trait-related dysfunction in ventral prefrontal cortices. *Archives of General Psychiatry, 60,* 601–609.

Blumberg, M. S., & Lucas, D. E. (1994). Dual mechanisms of twitching during sleep in neonatal rats. *Behavioral Neuroscience, 108*(6), 1196–1202.

Blume, E. S. (1998). *Secret survivors: Uncovering incest and its aftereffects in women.* New York: Ballantine.

Blumenthal, J. A., Babyak, M., Wei., J., O'Conner, C., Waugh, R., Eisenstein, E., et al. (2002). Usefulness of psychosocial treatment of mental stress-induced myocardial ischemia in men. *American Journal of Cardiology, 89,* 164–168.

Blundell, J. E., & Cooling, J. (2000). Routes to obesity: Phenotypes, food choices, and activity. *British Journal of Nutrition, 83,* S33–S38.

Bock, B. C., Marcus, B. H., & Pinto, B. M. (2001). Maintenance of physical activity following an individualized motivationally tailored intervention. *Annals of Behavioral Medicine, 23,* 79–87.

Bodian, S. (1999). *Meditation for dummies.* Indianapolis: IDG Books Worldwide.

Boehning, D., & Snyder, S. H. (2003). Novel neural modulators. *Annual Review of Neuroscience, 26,* 105–131.

Bogaert, A. F. (2003). Number of older brothers and social orientation: New tests and the attraction/behavior distinction in two national probability samples. *Journal of Personality and Social Psychology, 84,* 644–652.

Bogartz, R. S., Shinskey, J. L., & Speaker, C. J. (1997). Interpreting infant looking: The event set × event set design. *Developmental Psychology, 33,* 408–422.

Bogen, J. E. (1995). On the neurophysiology of consciousness: I. An overview. *Consciousness and Cognition, 4,* 52–62.

Bohner, G., & Schwarz, N. (2001). Attitudes persuasion and behavior. In A. Tesser & N. Schwarz (Eds.), *Blackwell handbook of social psychology: Intraindividual processes* (pp. 413–435). Oxford, UK: Blackwell.

Bolger, K. E., & Patterson, C. J. (2001). Developmental pathways from child maltreatment to peer rejection. *Child Development, 72,* 549–568.

Bolla, K. I., Brown, K., Eldreth, D., Tate, K. & Cadet, J. L. (2002). Dose-related neurocognitive effects of marijuana use. *Neurology, 59,* 1337–1343.

Bolles, R. C. (1975). *Theory of motivation* (2nd ed.). New York: Harper & Row.

Bonanno, G. A. (2004). Loss, trauma, and human resilience: Have we underestimated the human capacity to thrive after extremely aversive events? *American Psychologist, 59,* 20–28.

Bonci, A., Bernardi, G., Grillner, P., & Mercuri, N. B. (2003). The dopamine-containing neuron: Maestro or simple musician in the orchestra of addiction? *Trends in Pharmacological Science, 24,* 172–177.

Bond, G., Aiken, L., & Somerville, S. (1992). The Health Beliefs Model and adolescents with insulin-dependent diabetes mellitus. *Health Psychology, 11,* 190–198.

Bonk, V. A., France, C. R., & Taylor, B. K. (2001). Distraction reduces self-reported physiological reactions to blood donation in novice donors with a blunting coping style. *Journal of Psychosomatic Medicine, 63,* 447–452.

Bonwell, C. C., & Eison, J. A. (1991). *Active learning: Creating excitement in the classroom.* Washington, DC: George Washington University.

Boone, E.M. & Leadbeater, B.J. (2006). Game on: Diminishing risks for depressive symptoms in early adolescence through positive involvement in team sports. *Journal of Research on Adolescence, 16,* 79–90.

Booth, C. B., Clarke-Stewart, K. A., Vandell, D. L., McCartney, K., & Owen, M. T. (2002). Child-care usage and mother-infant "quality time." *Journal of Marriage and the Family, 64,* 16–26.

Booth, P. B., & Lindaman, S. (2000). Theraplay for enhancing attachment in adopted children. In H. G. Kaduson & C. Schaefer (Eds.), *Short-term play therapy for children.* New York: Guilford.

Borg, M. B., Jr. (2002). The Avalon Garden men's association: A community health psychology case study. *Journal of Health Psychology, 7,* 345–357.

Borkenau, P., Mauer, N., Riemann, R., Spinath, F. M., & Angleitner, A. (2004). Thin slices of behavior as cues of personality and intelligence. *Journal of Personality and Social Psychology, 86,* 599–614.

Borkenau, P., Riemann, R., Angleitner, A., & Spinath, F. M. (2001). Genetic and environmental influences on observed personality; Evidence from the German Observational Study of Adult Twins. *Journal of Personality and Social Psychology, 80,* 655–668.

Borkman, T. J. (1997). A selected look at self-help groups in the U.S. *Health and Social Care in the Community, 5,* 357–364.

Borkovec, T. C., & Costello, E. (1993). Efficacy of applied relaxation and cognitive behavioral therapy in the treatment of generalized anxiety disorder. *Journal of Consulting and Clinical Psychology, 61,* 611–619.

Borkowski, J. G., Weyhing, R. S., & Turner, L. A. (1986). Attributional retraining and the teaching of strategies. *Exceptional Children, 53,* 130–137.

Borman, W. C., Hanson, M. A., & Hedge, J. W. (1997). Personnel selection. *Annual Review of Psychology, 48,* 299–337.

Borsboom, D., Mellenbergh, G. J., & van Heerden, J. (2004). The concept of validity. *Psychological Review, 111,* 1061–1071.

Bosma, H., Marmot, M. G., Hemingway, H., Nicholson, A. C., Brunner, E., & Stansfeld, S. A. (1997). Low job control and risk of coronary heart disease in Whitehall II (prospective cohort) study. *British Medical Journal, 314,* 558–565.

Bosompra, K., Ashikaga, T., Worden, J. K., & Flynn, B. S. (2001). Is more optimism associated with better health? Findings from a population-based survey. *International Quarterly of Community Health Education, 20,* 29–58.

Boss, P. (1999). *Ambiguous loss: Learning to live with unresolved grief.* Cambridge, MA: Harvard University Press.

Botwinick, J. (1961). Husband and father-in-law: A reversible figure. *American Journal of Psychology, 74,* 312–313.

Botwinick, J. (1966). Cautiousness in advanced age. *Journal of Gerontology, 21,* 347–353.

Botwinick, J. (1977). Intellectual abilities. In J. E. Birren & K. W. Schaie (Eds.), *Handbook of the psychology of aging.* New York: Van Nostrand Reinhold.

Bouchard, T. J., Jr., & Pedersen, N. (1999). Twins reared apart: Nature's double experiment. In M. C. LaBuda & E. L. Grigorenko (Eds.), *On the way to individuality: Current methodological issues in behavioral genetics* (pp. 71–93). Hauppauge, NY: Nova Science.

Bourassa, M., & Vaugeois, P. (2001). Effects of marijuana use on divergent thinking. *Creativity Research Journal, 13,* 411–416.

Bouret, S. G., Draper, S. J., & Simerly, R. B. (2004). Trophic action of leptin on hypothalamic neurons that regulate feeding. *Science, 304,* 108–110.

Bouton, M. E. (2000). A learning theory perspective on lapse, relapse, and the maintenance of behavior change. *Health Psychology, 19,* 57–63.

Bouton, M. E. (2002). Context, ambiguity, and unlearning: Sources of relapse after behavioral extinction. *Biological Psychiatry, 52,* 976–986.

Bouton, M. E., Mineka, S., & Barlow, D. (2001). A modern learning theory perspective on the etiology of panic disorder. *Psychological Review, 107,* 4–32.

Bovasso, G. B., Eaton, W. W., & Armenian, H. K. (1999). The long-term outcomes of mental health treatment in a population-based study. *Journal of Consulting and Clinical Psychology, 67,* 529–538.

Bowden, C. L. (2000). Efficacy of lithium in mania and maintenance therapy of bipolar disorder. *Journal of Clinical Psychiatry, 61,* 35–40.

Bowden, C. L. (2003a). Acute and maintenance treatment with mood stabilizers. *International Journal of Neuropsychopharmacology,* 6(3), 269–275.

Bowden, C. L. (2003b). Valproate. *Bipolar Disorders, 5*(3), 189–202.

Bower, G. H. (1975). Cognitive psychology: An introduction. In W. K. Estes (Ed.), *Handbook of learning and cognitive processes* (Vol. 1, pp. 25–80). Hillsdale, NJ: Erlbaum.

Bower, J. E., Kemeny, M. E., Taylor, S. E., & Fahey, J. L. (1999). Cognitive processing, discovery of meaning, CD4 decline, and AIDS-related mortality among bereaved HIV- seropositive men. *Journal of Consulting and Clinical Psychology, 66,* 979–986.

Bower, J. M., & Parsons, L. M. (2003). Rethinking the "lesser brain". *Scientific American, 289,* 50–57.

Bowerman, M. (1996). The origins of children's spatial semantic categories: Cognitive versus linguistic determinants. In J. J. Gumperz & S. C. Levinson (Eds.), *Rethinking linguistic relativity: Studies in the social and cultural foundations of language* (No. 17, pp. 145–176). Cambridge: Cambridge University Press.

Bowlby, J. (1973). *Attachment and loss: Vol. 2. Separation.* New York: Basic Books.

Bowlby, J. (1980). *Loss: Sadness and depression.* New York: Basic Books.

Bowman, E. S., & Nurnberger, J. I. (1993). Genetics of psychiatry diagnosis and treatment. In D. L. Dummer (Ed.), *Current psychiatric therapy* (pp. 46–56). Philadelphia: Saunders.

Boyce, W., Doherty, M., Fortin, C., & Mackinnon, D. (2003). *Canadian youth, sexual health and HIV/AIDS study: Factors influencing knowledge, attitudes and behaviours.* Toronto, ON: Council of Ministers of Education.

Boyle, S. H., Williams, R. B., Mark, D. B., Brummett, B. H., Siegler, I. C., Helms, M. J., & Barefoot, J. C. (2004).Hostility as a predictor of survival in patients with coronary artery disease. *Psychosomatic Medicine, 66,* 629–632.

Bozarth, M. A., & Wise, R. A. (1984). Anatomically distinct opiate receptor fields mediate reward and physical dependence. *Science, 224,* 516–518.

Brach, J. S., FitzGerald, S., Newman, A. B., Kelsey, S., Kuller, L., VanSwearingen, J. M., & Kriska, A. M. (2003). Physical activity and functional status in community-dwelling older women. *Archives of Internal Medicine, 163,* 2565–2571.

Bracken, B. A., & McCallum, R. S. (1998). *Universal Nonverbal Intelligence Test (UNIT).* Boston: Riverside.

Bracken, P., & Thomas, P. (2001). Postpsychiatry: A new direction for mental health. *British Journal of Psychiatry, 322,* 724–727.

Bradley, M.T., Cullen, M.C., & Carle, S.B. (1993). Control question tests by police and laboratory polygraph operators on a mock crime and real event. Report No. DoDPI93-R.0012. Department of Defense Polygraph Institute, Ft. McClellan, AL 36205.

Brainerd, C. J., & Reyna, V. F. (1998). When things that were never experienced are easier to "remember" than things that were. *Psychological Science, 9,* 484–489.

Brainerd, C. J., Reyna, V. F., Wright, R., & Mojardin, A. H. (2003). Recollection rejection: False memory editing in children and adults. *Psychological Review, 110,* 762–784.

Brandimonte, M. A., Hitch, G. J., & Bishop, D. V. M. (1992). Influence of short-term memory codes on visual image processing: Evidence from image transformation tasks. *Journal of Experimental Psychology: Learning, Memory, and Cognition, 18,* 157–165.

Brandtstadter, J., & Renner, G. (1990). Tenacious goal pursuit and flexible goal adjustment: Explication and age-related analysis of assimilative and accommodative strategies of coping. *Psychology and Aging, 5,* 58–67.

Bransford, J. D., & Stein, B. S. (1993). *The ideal problem solver* (2nd ed.). New York: Freeman.

Bransford, J. D., Brown, A. L., & Cocking, R. R. (Eds.). (1999). *How people learn: Brain, mind, experience, and school.* Washington, DC: National Academy Press.

Branson, R., Potoczna, N., Kral, J. G., Lentes, K.-U., Hoehe, M. R., & Horber, F. F. (2003). Binge eating as a major phenotype of melanocortin 4 receptor gene mutations. *The New England Journal of Medicine, 348,* 1096–1103.

Braun, A. E., Balkin, T. J., & Wesensten, N. J. (1998). Dissociated pattern of activity in visual cortices and their projections during human rapid eye movement sleep. *Science, 279,* 91–95.

Bray, G. A., & Tartaglia, L. A. (2000). Medicinal strategies in the treatment of obesity. *Nature, 404,* 672–677.

Bredt, D. S., & Nicoll, R. A. (2003). AMPA receptor trafficking at excitatory synapses. *Neuron, 40,* 361–379.

Breggin, P. R. (1997). *Brain-disabling treatments in psychiatry: Drugs, electroshock, and the role of the FDA.* New York: Springer.

Brehm, S. (1992). *Intimate relationships.* New York: McGraw-Hill.

Brehm, S., Kassin, S., & Fein, S. (2005). *Social psychology* (6th ed.). Boston, MA: Houghton-Mifflin.

Breiter, H. C., Aharon, I., Kahneman, D., Dale, A., & Shizgal, P. (2001). Functional imaging of neural responses to expectancy and experience of monetary gains and losses. *Neuron, 30,* 619–639.

Brelsford, J. W. (1993). Physics education in a virtual environment. In *Proceedings of the 37th Annual Meeting of the Human Factors and Ergonomics Society.* Santa Monica, CA: Human Factors.

Bremner, J. D., Shobe, K. K., & Kihlstrom, J. F. (2000). False memories in women with self-reported childhood sexual abuse. *Psychological Science, 11,* 333–337.

Bremner, J. D., Vythilingam, M., Vermetten, E., Southwick, S. M., McGlashan, T., Nazeer, A., et al. (2003). MRI and PET study of deficits in hippocampal structure and function in women with childhood sexual abuse and posttraumatic stress disorder. *American Journal of Psychiatry, 160,* 924–932.

Bremner, J. D., Vythilingam, M., Vermetten, E., Vaccarino, V., & Charney, D. S. (2004). Deficits in hippocampal and anterior cingulate functioning during verbal declarative memory encoding in midlife major depression. *American Journal of Psychiatry, 161,* 637–645.

Brenes, G. A., Rapp, S. R., Rejeski, W. J., & Miller, M. E. (2002). Do optimism and pessimism predict physical functioning? *Journal of Behavioral Medicine, 25,* 219–231.

Brennan, F. X. & Charnetski, C. J. (2000). Explanatory style and Immunoglobulin A (IgA). *Integrative Physiological & Behavioral Science, 35,* 251–255.

Brennan, P. A., & Mednick, S. A. (1994). Learning theory approach to the deterrence of criminal recidivism. *Journal of Abnormal Psychology, 103,* 430–440.

Brennen, T., Baguley, T., Bright, J., & Bruce, V. (1990). Resolving semantically induced tip-of-the-tongue states for proper nouns. *Memory & Cognition, 18,* 339–347.

Brenner, R. A., Trumble, A. C., Smith, G. S., Kessler, E. P., & Overpeck, M. D. (2001). Where children drown, United States, 1995. *Pediatrics, 108,* 85–89.

Brenner, R., Azbel, V., Madhusoodanan, S., & Pawlowska, M. (2000). Comparison of an extract of hypericum (LI 160) and sertraline in the treatment of depression: a double-blind, randomized pilot study. *Clinical Therapeutics, 22,* 411–419.

Breslin, P. A., & Beauchamp, G. K. (1997). Salt enhances flavour by suppressing bitterness. *Nature, 387,* 563.

Breteler, M. H., Hilberink, S. R., Zeeman, G., & Lammers, S. M. (2004). Compulsive smoking: The development of a Rasch homogeneous scale of nicotine dependence. *Addiction and Behavior, 29,* 199–205.

Breuer, J., & Freud, S. (1974). Studies on hysteria. In J. A. Strachey (Ed. & Trans.), *The Pelican Freud Library* (Vol. 3). Harmondsworth, England: Penguin. (Original work published 1895)

Brewer, M. B. (2001). The many faces of social identity: Implications for political psychology. *Political Psychology, 22,* 115–125.

Brewer, W. F. (1977). Memory for the pragmatic implications of sentences. *Memory & Cognition, 5,* 673–678.

Brinckerhoff, L. C., Shaw, S. F., & McGuire, J. M. (1993). *Promoting postsecondary education for students with learning disabilities.* Austin, TX: Pro-Ed.

Brislin, R. (1993). *Understanding culture's influence on behavior.* Fort Worth: Harcourt, Brace, Jovanovich.

British Medical Association. (2000). *Acupuncture: Efficacy, safety, and practice.* London: Harwood Academic.

Broad, W. J., & Revkin, A. C. (2003, February 6). Engineers list all the ideas, striking them one by one. *New York Times.* Retrieved December 13, 2004, from http:/www.khbo.be/~lodew/Engineers%20List%20All%20the%20Ideas,%20Striking%20The m %20One%20by%20One.htm

Broadbent, E., Petrie, K. J., Alley, P. G., & Booth, R. J. (2003). Psychological stress impairs early wound repair following surgery. *Psychosomatic Medicine, 65,* 865–869.

Brock, J. W., Farooqui, S. M., Ross, K. D., & Payne, S. (1994). Stress-related behavior and central norepinephrine concentrations in the REM sleep-deprived rat. *Physiology and Behavior, 55*(6), 997–1003.

Brock, T. C., Green, M. C., & Reich, D. A. (1998). New evidence of flaws in the Consumer Reports study of psychotherapy. *American Psychologist, 53,* 62–72.

Brody, N., & Ehrlichman, H. (1998). *Personality psychology: The science of individuality.* Upper Saddle River, NJ: Prentice-Hall.

Brondolo, E., Rieppi, R., Erickson, S. A., Bagiella, E., Shapiro, P. A., McKinley, P., & Sloan, R. P. (2003). Hostility, interpersonal interactions, and ambulatory blood pressure. *Psychosomatic Medicine, 65,* 1003–1011.

Brooks-Gunn, J., & Chase-Lansdale, P. L. (2002). Adolescent parenthood. In M. H. Bornstein (Ed.), *Handbook of parenting* (2nd ed). Mahwah, NJ: Erlbaum.

Brown, A. L., Campione, J. C., Webber, L. S., & McGilly, K. (1992). Interactive learning environments: A new look at assessment and instruction. In B. Gifford & M. C. O'Connor (Eds.), *Changing assessments: Alternative views of aptitude, achievement, and instruction* (pp. 121–212). Boston: Kluever.

Brown, A. S. (1991). A review of the tip-of-the-tongue experience. *Psychological Bulletin, 109,* 204–233.

Brown, A. S., & Nix, L. A. (1996). Age-related changes in the tip-of-the-tongue experience. *American Journal of Psychology, 109,* 79–91.

Brown, A. S., Begg, M. D., Gravenstein, S., Schaefer, C. A., Wyatt, R. J., Bresnahan, M., et al. (2004). Serologic evidence of prenatal influenza in the etiology of schizophrenia [Electronic version]. *Archives of General Psychiatry, 61,* 774–780.

Brown, G. K., Beck, A. T., Steer, R. A., & Grisham, J. R. (2000). Risk factors for suicide in psychiatric outpatients: A 20-year prospective study. *Journal of Consulting and Clinical Psychology, 68,* 371–377.

Brown, G. W., & Moran, P. M. (1997). Single mothers, poverty and depression. *Psychological Medicine, 27,* 21–33.

Brown, J. (1958). Some tests of the decay theory of immediate memory. *Quarterly Journal of Experimental Psychology, 10,* 12–21.

Brown, P. D., & O'Leary, K. D. (2000). Therapeutic alliance: Predicting continuance and success in group treatment for spouse abuse. *Journal of Consulting and Clinical Psychology, 68,* 340–345.

Brown, R. A. (1973). *First language.* Cambridge: Harvard University Press.

Brown, R., & Kulik, J. (1977). Flashbulb memories. *Cognition, 5,* 73–99.

Brown, S. L., Nesse, R. M., Vinokur, A. D., & Smith, D. M. (2003). Providing social support may be more beneficial than receiving it: Results from a prospective study of mortality. *Psychological Science, 14,* 320–327.

Broytman, O., & Malter, J. S. (2004). Anti-Abeta: The good, the bad, and the unforeseen. *Journal of Neuroscience Research, 75,* 301–306.

Bruce, H. M. (1969). Pheromones and behavior in mice. *Acta Neurologica Belgica, 69,* 529–538.

Bruce, T. J., Spiegel, D. A., & Hegel, M. T. (1999). Cognitive-behavioral therapy helps prevent relapse and recurrence of panic disorder following Alpazolam discontinuation: A long-term follow-up of the Peoria and Dartmouth studies. *Journal of Consulting and Clinical Psychology, 67,* 151–156.

Bruck, M., Cavanagh, P., & Ceci, S. J. (1991). Fortysomething: Recognizing faces at one's 25th reunion. *Memory and Cognition, 19,* 221–228.

Brüning, J. C., Gautam, D., Burks, D. J., Gillette, J., Schubert, M., Orban, P. C., et al. (2000). Role of brain insulin receptor in control of body weight and reproduction. *Science, 289,* 2122–2125.

Brunvald, J. H. (1989). *Curses! Broiled again! The hottest urban legends going.* New York: Norton.

Bruyer, R. (1991). Covert face recognition in prosopagnosia. *Brain and Cognition, 15,* 223–235.

Bryant, R. A., & McConkey, K. M. (1989). Hypnotic blindness: A behavioral and experiential analysis. *Journal of Abnormal Psychology, 98,* 71–77.

Buckner, R. L., & Wheeler, M. E. (in press). The cognitive neuroscience of remembering. *Nature Reviews Neuroscience.*

Budney, A. J., Hughes, J. R., Moore, B. A., & Novy, P. L. (2001). Marijuana abstinence effects in marijuana smokers maintained in their home environment. *Archives of General Psychiatry, 58,* 917–924.

Budney, A. J., Moore, B. A., Vandrey, R. G., & Hughes, J. R. (2003). The time course and significance of cannabis withdrawal. *Journal of Abnormal Psychology, 112,* 393–402.

Bugental, D. B., & Goodnow, J. J. (1998). Socialization processes. In W. Damon & N. Eisenberg (Eds.), *Handbook of child psychology: Vol. 3. Social, emotional, and personality development* (5th ed., pp. 389–462). New York: Wiley.

Bui, K.-V. T., Peplau, L. A., & Hill, C. T. (1996). Testing the Rusbult model of relationship commitment and stability in a 15-year study of heterosexual couples. *Personality and Social Psychology Bulletin, 22,* 1244–1257.

Buka, S. L., Shenassa, E. D., & Niaura, R. (2003). Elevated risk of tobacco dependence among offspring of mothers who smoked during pregnancy: A 30-year prospective study. *American Journal of Psychiatry, 160,* 1978–1984.

Bulik, C. M., Sullivan, P. F., Wade, T. D., & Kendler, K. S. (2000). Twin studies of eating disorders: A review. *International Journal of Eating Disorders, 27,* 1–20.

Bulik, C. M., Tozzi, F., Anderson, C., Mazzeo, S. E., Aggen, S., & Sullivan, P. F. (2003). The relation between eating disorders and components of perfectionism. *American Journal of Psychiatry, 160,* 366–368.

Bullough, V. L. (1995, August). Sex matters. *Scientific American,* pp. 105–106.

Burchard, R. E. (1992). Coca chewing and diet. *Current Anthropology, 33*(1), 1–24.

Burger, J. M., & Caldwell, D. F. (2003). The effects of monetary incentives and labeling on the foot-in-the-door effect: Evidence for a self-perception process. *Basic and Applied Social Psychology, 25,* 235–241.

Burger, J. M., & Cornelius, T. (2003). Raising the price of agreement: Public commitment and the lowball compliance procedure. *Journal of Applied Social Psychology, 33,* 923–934.

Burger, J. M., & Guadagno, R. E. (2003). Self-concept clarity and the foot-in-the-door procedure. *Basic and Applied Social Psychology, 25,* 79–86.

Burke, H. B., Hoang, A., Iglehart, J. D., & Marks, J. R. (1998). Predicting response to adjuvant and radiation therapy in patients with early-stage breast carcinoma. *Cancer, 82,* 874–877.

Burleson, B. R., Albrecht, T. L., & Sarason, I. G. (Eds.). (1994). *Communication of social support: Messages, interactions, relationships, and community.* Thousand Oaks, CA: Sage.

Burleson, M. H., Gregory, W. L., & Trevarthen, W. R. (1995). Heterosexual activity: Relationship with ovarian function. *Psychoneuroendocrinology, 20*(4), 405–421.

Burnstein, E., & Branigan, C. (2001). Evolutionary analyses in social-psychology. In A. Tesser & N. Schwarz (Eds.), *Blackwell handbook of social psychology: Intraindividual processes* (pp. 3–21). Oxford, UK: Blackwell.

Burr, D. C., Morrone, C., & Fiorentini, A. (1996). Spatial and temporal properties of infant colour vision. In F. Vital-Durand, J. Atkinson, & O. J. Braddick (Eds.), *Infant vision* (pp. 63–77). Oxford: Oxford University Press.

Burris, C. T., Branscombe, N. R., & Klar, Y. (1997). Maladjustment implications of self and group gender-role discrepancies: An ordered-discrepancy model. *European Journal of Social Psychology, 27,* 75–95.

Burton, A. M., Wilson, S., Cowan, M., & Bruce, V. (1999). Face recognition in poor-quality video: Evidence from security surveillance. *Psychological Science, 10,* 243–248.

Bushman, B. J., & Anderson, C. A. (2001). Media violence and the American public: Scientific facts versus media misinformation. *American Psychologist, 56,* 477–489.

Bushman, B. J., & Huesmann, L. R. (2000). Effects of televised violence on aggression. In D. Singer & J. Singer (Eds.), *Handbook of children and the media* (pp. 223–254). Thousand Oaks, CA: Sage.

Buss, D. M. (1999). *Evolutionary psychology: The new science of the mind.* Boston: Allyn & Bacon.

Buss, D. M. (2003). *The evolution of desire: Strategies of human mating.* New York: Basic Books.

Buss, D. M. (2004). *Evolutionary psychology: The new science of the mind* (2nd ed.). Boston: Allyn & Bacon.

Buss, D. M., & Schmitt, D. P. (1993). Sexual strategies theory: An evolutionary perspective on human mating. *Psychological Review, 100,* 204–232.

Bussière, P., Cartwright, F., & Knighton, T. (2004). *Measuring up: Canadian Results of the OECD PISA Study: The Performance of Canada's Youth in Mathematics, Reading, Science and Problem Solving 2003 First Findings for Canadians Aged 15.* Ottawa: Statistics Canada, 2004.

Bustillo, J. R., Lauriello, J., Horan, W. P., & Keith, S. J. (2001) The psychosocial treatment of schizophrenia: An update. *American Journal of Psychiatry, 158,* 163–175.

Buston, P. M., & Emlen, S. T. (2003). Cognitive processes underlying human mate choice: The relationship between self-perception and mate preference in Western society. Proceedings of the National Academy of Sciences, 100, 8805–8810.

Butler, R. (1998). Information seeking and achievement motivation in middle childhood and adolescence: The role of conceptions of ability. *Developmental Psychology, 35,* 146–163.

Butterweck, V. (2003). Mechanism of action of St. John's Wort in depression: What is known? *CNS Drugs, 17*(8), 539–562.

Buunk, B. P., Zurriaga, R., Gonzalez-Roma, V., & Subirats, M. (2003). Engaging in upward and downward comparisons as a determinant of relative deprivation at work: A longitudinal study. *Journal of Vocational Behavior, 62,* 370–388.

Buunk, B. P., & Ybema, J. F. (2003). Feeling bad, but satisfied: The effects of upward and downward comparison upon mood and marital satisfaction. *British Journal of Social Psychology, 42,* 613–628.

Buxhoeveden, D. P., Switala, A. E., Roy, E., Litaker, M., & Casanova, M. F. (2001). Morphological differences between minicolumns in human and nonhuman primate cortex. *American Journal of Physical Anthropology, 115,* 361–371.

Byrne, D., & Nelson, D. (1965). Attraction as a linear function of proportion of positive reinforcements. *Journal of Personality and Social Psychology, 1,* 659–663.

Cabanac, M., & Morrissette, J. (1992). Acute, but not chronic, exercise lowers the body weight set-point in male rats. *Physiology and Behavior, 52*(6) 1173–1177.

Cabot, P. J. (2001). Immune-derived opioids and peripheral antinociception. *Clinical and Experimental Pharmacology and Physiology, 28,* 230–232.

Cabral, G. A., & Dove Pettit, D. A. (1998). Drugs and immunity: Cannabinoids and their role in decreased resistance to infectious disease. *Journal of Neuroimmunology, 83,* 116–123.

Cacioppo, J. T. (2002). Social neuroscience: Understanding the pieces fosters understanding the whole and vice versa. *American Psychologist, 57,* 819–831.

Cacioppo, J. T., Berntson, G. G., & Petty, R. E. (1997). *Persuasion. Encyclopedia of human biology* (Vol. 6, pp. 679–690). San Diego: Academic Press.

Cacioppo, J. T., Berntson, G. G., Sheridan, J. F., & McClintock, M. K. (2000). Multilevel integrative analyses of human behavior: Social neuroscience and the complementing nature of social and biological approaches. *Psychological Bulletin, 126,* 829–843.

Cacioppo, J. T., Crites, S. L., & Gardner, W. L. (1996). Attitudes to the right: Evaluative processing is associated with lateralized late positive event-related brain potentials. *Personality and Social Psychology Bulletin, 22,* 1205–1219.

Cacioppo, J. T., Gardner, W. L., Berntson, G. G. (1999). The affect system has parallel and integrative processing components: Form follows function. *Journal of Personality and Social Psychology, 76,* 839–855.

Cacioppo, J. T., Malarkey, W. B., Kiecolt-Glaser, J. K., Uchino, B. N., Sgoutas-Emch, S. A., Sheridan, J. F., et al. (1995). Heterogeneity in neuroendocrine and immune responses to brief psychological stressors as a function of autonomic cardiac activation. *Psychosomatic Medicine, 57,* 154–164.

Cacioppo, J. T., Petty, R. E., & Crites, S. L. (1993). Attitude change. In V. S. Ramachandran (Ed.), *Encyclopedia of human behavior* (pp. 261–270). San Diego: Academic Press.

Cacioppo, J. T., Poehlmann, K. M., Kiecolt-Glaser, J. K., Malarkey, W. B., Burleson, M. H., Berntson, G. G., & Glaser, R. (1998). Cellular immune responses to acute stress in female caregivers of dementia patients and matched controls. *Health Psychology, 17,* 182–189.

Cahill, L., & McGaugh, J. L. (1998). Mechanisms of emotional arousal and lasting declarative memory. *Trends in Neuroscience, 21,* 294–299.

Cahill, S. P., Carrigan, M. H., & Evans, I. M. (1998). The relationship between behavior theory and behavior therapy: Challenges and promises. In J. J. Plaud & G. H. Eifert (Eds.), *From behavior theory to behavior therapy* (pp. 294–319). Boston: Allyn & Bacon.

Cain, D. J., & Seeman, J. (Eds.). (2002). *Humanistic psychotherapies: Handbook of research and practice.* Washington, DC: APA Books.

Callen, D. J. A., Black, S. E., Gao, F., Caldwell, C. B., & Szalai, J. P. (2001). Beyond the hippocampus: MRI volumetry confirms widespread limbic atrophy in AD. *Neurology, 57,* 1669–1674.

Calvert, G. A., Bullmore, E. T., Brammer, M. J., Campbell, R., Williams, S. C., McGuire, P. K., et al. (1997). Activation of auditory cortex during silent lipreading. *Science, 276*(5312), 593–596.

Cameron, H. A., Tanapat, P., & Gould, E. (1998). Adrenal steroids and N-methyl-D-aspartate receptor activation regulate neurogenesis in the dentate gyrus of adult rats through a common pathway. *Neuroscience, 82,* 349–354.

Campbell, F. A., Pungello, E. P., Miller-Johnson, S., Burchinal, M., & Ramey, C. T. (2001). The development of cognitive and academic abilities: Growth curves from an early childhood educational experiment. *Developmental Psychology, 37,* 231–242.

Campbell, F. A., Tramer, M. R., Carroll, D., Reynolds, D. J., Moore, R. A., & McQuay, H. J. (2001). Are cannabinoids an effective and safe treatment option in the management of pain? A qualitative systematic review. *British Medical Journal, 323,* 13–16.

Campbell, P., Laurence, J-R., Nadon, R. (1988). Hypnosis, surgery and the social-psychological position. *British Journal of Experimental & Clinical Hypnosis, 5,* 143–149.

Campbell, R. S., & Pennebaker, J. W. (2003). The secret life of pronouns: Flexibility in writing style and physical health. *Psychological Science, 14,* 60–65.

Campbell, S. B. (1986). Developmental issues. In R. Gittelman (Ed.), *Anxiety disorders of childhood* (pp. 24–57). New York: Guilford.

Campbell, S. S., & Murphy, P. J. (1998). Extraocular circadian phototransduction in humans. *Science, 279,* 396–399.

Campione, J. C., Brown, A. L., & Ferrara, R. A. (1982). Mental retardation and intelligence. In R. J. Sternberg (Ed.), *Handbook of human intelligence* (pp. 392–490). Cambridge: Cambridge University Press.

Campos, J. J., Frankel, C. B., & Camras, L. (2004). On the nature of emotion regulation. *Child Development, 75,* 377–394.

Canadian Association of University Teachers (2001, May). Academic freedom in jeopardy at Toronto. [On-line]. Available: http://www.caut.ca/en/bulletin/issues/2001_may/default.asp.

Canadian Foundation for the Study of Infant Deaths. (2004). *Information about Sudden Infant Death Syndrome* [Electronic version]. Available: http://sidscanada.org/faq.htm.

Canadian Heirloom Series, Volume VI. Retrieved March 23, 2006, from http://collections.ic.gc.ca/heirloom_series/volume4/330–333.htm

Canadian Intellectual Property Office. (2004). Success stories: Canada's V-chip is now the international standard for controlling TV violence. Retrieved March 23, 2006, from http://strategis.ic.gc.ca/sc_mrksv/cipo/toolkit/ss_02-e.html

Canadian Medical Association. (1994). Canadian study of health and aging: study methods and prevalence of dementia. *Canadian Medical Association Journal, 150* (6), 899–913.

Canadian Mental Health Association (2006). Suicide statistics. [Electronic version]. Available: http://www.ontario.cmha.ca/content/about_mental_illness/suicide.asp?cID=3965

Canadian Press, (2004) Top court upholds spanking laws. Retrieved March 23, 2006, from http://www.fathers.ca/the_supreme_court_of_canada1.htm

Canadian Psychological Association, (1998). Convictions based solely on recovered memories. Retrieved March 23, 2006, from http://www.cpa.ca/cpasite/showPage.asp?id=1007&fr=

Canadian Sleep Society (2004). *Insomnia* [Electronic version]. Available: http://www.css.to/sleep/insomnia/pdf.

Canavero, S. Bonicalzi, V., De Lucchi, R., Davini, O., Podio, V., & Bisi, G (1998). Abolition of neurogenic pain by focal cortical ischemia. *Clinical Journal of Pain, 14,* 268–269.

Candia, V., Weinbruch, C., Elbert, T., Rockstroh, B., & Ray, W. (2003). Effective behavioral treatment of focal hand dystonia in musicians alters somatosensory cortical organization. *Proceedings of the National Academy of Sciences, 100,* 7942–7946.

Canli, T., Zhao, Z., Desmond, J. E., Kang, E., Gross, J., & Gabrieli, J. D. (2001). An fMRI study of personality influences on brain reactivity to emotional stimuli. *Behavioral Neuroscience, 115,* 33–42.

Cann, A., & Ross, D. A. (1989). Olfactory stimuli as context cues in human memory. *American Journal of Psychology, 102,* 91–102.

Cannon, T. D., Mednick, S. A., Parnas, J., Schulsinger, F., Praestholm, J., & Vestergaard, A. (1993). Developmental brain abnormalities in the offspring of schizophrenic mothers. *Archives of General Psychiatry, 50, 551–564.*

Cannon, T. D., van Erp, T. G. M., Rosso, I. M., Huttunen, M., Lonnqvist, J., Pirkola, T., et al. (2002). Fetal hypoxia and structural brain abnormalities in schizophrenic patients, their siblings, and controls. *Archives of General Psychiatry, 59,* 35–41.

Cannon, T. D., Zorrilla, L. E., Shtasel, D., Gur, R. E., Gur, R. C., Marco, E. J., Moberg, P., & Price, A. (1994). Neuropsychological functioning in siblings discordant for schizophrenia and healthy volunteers. *Archives of General Psychiatry, 51,* 651–661.

Cannon, W. B., & Washburn, A. L. (1912). An explanation of hunger. *American Journal of Physiology, 29,* 444–454.

Cao, Y., Vikingstad, E. M., Huttenlocher, P. R., Towle, V. L., & Levin, D. N. (1994). Functional magnetic resonance studies of the reorganization of the human head sensorimotor area after unilateral brain injury in the perinatal period. *Proceedings of the National Academy of Sciences of the United States of America, 91,* 9612–9616.

Capron, C., & Duyme, M. (1989). Assessment of effects of socio-economic status on IQ in a full cross-fostering study. *Nature, 340, 552–553.*

Capron, C., & Duyme, M. (1996). Effect of socioeconomic status of biological and adoptive parents on WISC-R subtest scores of their French adopted children. *Intelligence, 22,* 259–276.

Caragata, W. (1995, August 14). The price of fame. *Maclean's, 108,* p.16. [Electronic version] Retrieved from http://proquest.umi.com/pqdweb?index=0&did=6758420&SrchMode=1&sid=1&Fmt=3&VInst=PROD&VType=PQD&RQT=309&VName=PQD&TS=1149166935&clientId=10774

Caramazza, A., & Hillis, A. E. (1991). Lexical organization of nouns and verbs in the brain. *Nature, 349,* 788–790.

Cardemil, E. V., Reivich, K. J., & Seligman, M. E. P. (2002). The prevention of depressive symptoms in low-income minority middle school students [Electronic version]. *Prevention and Treatment, 5.*

Cardinal, R. N., Pennicott, D. R., Sugathapala, C. L., Robbins, T. W., & Everitt, B. J. (2001, May 24). Impulsive choice induced in rats by lesions of the nucleus accumbens core. *Science.* Retrieved August 18, 2003, from www.sciencemag.org

Cardinali, D. P., Bortman, G. P., Liotta, G., Perez Lloret, S., Albornoz, L.E., Cutrera, R.A., et al. (2002). A multifactorial approach employing melatonin to accelerate resynchronization of sleep-wake cycle after a 12 time-zone westerly transmeridian flight in elite soccer athletes. *Journal of Pineal Research, 32,* 41–46.

Cardon, L. R., & Fulker, D. W. (1993). Genetics of specific cognitive abilities. In R. Plomin, & G. McClearn (Eds.), *Nature, nurture, and psychology* (pp. 99–120). Washington, DC: American Psychological Association.

Cardon, L. R., Fulker, D. W., DeFries, J. C., & Plomin, R. (1992). Multivariate genetic analysis of specific cognitive abilities in the Colorado Adoption Project at age 7. *Intelligence, 16,* 383–400.

Carey, M. P., Carey, K. B., Maisto, S. A., Gordon, C. M., Schroeder, K. E. E., & Vanable, P. A. (2004). Reducing HIV-risk behavior among adults receiving outpatient psychiatric treatment: Results from a randomized controlled trial. *Journal of Consulting and Clinical Psychology, 72,* 252–268.

Carli, L. L., Ganley, R., & Pierce-Otay, A. (1991). Similarity and satisfaction in romantic relationships. *Personality and Social Psychology Bulletin, 17,* 419–426.

Carlson, E. A., Sroufe, L. A., & Egeland, B. (2004). The construction of experience: A longitudinal study of representation and behavior. *Child Development, 75,* 66–83.

Carlson, L. E. & Garland, S. N. (2005). Impact of mindfulness-based stress reduction (MBSR) on sleep, mood, stress and fatigue symptoms in cancer outpatients. *International Journal of Behavioral Medicine, 12,* 278–285.

Carlson, N. R. (1998). *Physiology of behavior* (6th ed.). Boston: Allyn & Bacon.

Carlson, N. R. (2001). *Physiology of behavior* (7th ed.). Boston: Allyn & Bacon.

Carlsson, K., Petrovic, P., Skare, S., Petersson, K. M., & Ingvar, M. (2000). Tickling expectations: Neural processing in anticipation of a sensory stimulus. *Journal of Cognitive Neuroscience, 12,* 691–703.

Carmichael, L. L., Hogan, H. P., & Walter, A. A. (1932). An experimental study of the effect of language on the reproduction of visually perceived form. *Journal of Experimental Psychology, 15,* 73–86.

Carney, R. M., McMahon, P., Freedland, K. E., Becker, L., Krantz, D. S., Proschan, M. A., et al. (1998). Reproducibility of mental stress-induced myocardial ischemia in the psychophysiological investigations of myocardial ischemia (PIMI). *Psychosomatic Medicine, 60,* 64–70.

Carney, S., Cowen, P., & Geddes, P. (2003). Efficacy and safety of electroconvulsive therapy in depressive disorders: A systematic review and meta-analysis. *Lancet, 361*(9360), 799–808.

Carraher, T. N., Carraher, D., & Schliemann, A. D. (1985). Mathematics in the streets and in the schools. *British Journal of Developmental Psychology, 3,* 21–29.

Carrasco, M., & McElree, B. (2001). Covert attention accelerates the rate of visual information processing. *Proceedings of the National Academy of Science, 98, 5363–5367.*

Carrigan, M. H., & Levis, D. J. (1999). The contributions of eye movements to the efficacy of brief exposure treatment for reducing fear of public speaking. *Journal of Anxiety Disorders, 13,* 101–118.

Carrillo, E., & Lopez, A. (Eds.). (2001). *The Latino psychiatric patient: Assessment and treatment.* Washington, DC: American Psychiatric Press.

Carroll, J. B. (1993). *Human cognitive abilities: A survey of factor-analytic studies.* New York: Cambridge University Press.

Carstensen, L. (1997, August). *Psychology and the aging revolution: Changes in social needs and social goals across the lifespan.* Paper presented at the annual convention of the American Psychological Association.

Carter, M. M., & Barlow, D. H. (1995). Learned alarms: The origins of panic. In W. T. O'Donohue & L. Krasner (Eds.), *Theories of behavior therapy: Exploring behavior change* (pp. 209–228). Washington, DC: American Psychological Association.

Cartwright, R. D. (1978). *A primer on sleep and dreaming.* Reading, MA: Addison-Wesley.

Cartwright, R. D. (1993). Who needs their dreams? The usefulness of dreams in psychotherapy. *Journal of the American Academy of Psychoanalysis, 21*(4), 539–547.

Carver, C. S., & Antoni, M. H. (2004). Finding benefit in breast cancer during the year after diagnosis predicts better adjustment 5 to 8 years after diagnosis. *Health Psychology, 23, 595–598.*

Carver, C. S., & Scheier, M. F. (2002). The hopeful optimist. *Psychological Inquiry, 13,* 288–290.

Carver, C. S., & Scheier, M. F. (2004). *Perspectives on personality* (5th ed.). Boston, MA: Allyn & Bacon.

Casacalenda, N., Perry, J. C., & Looper, K. (2002). Remission in major depressive disorder: A comparison of pharmacotherapy, psychotherapy, and control conditions. *American Journal of Psychiatry, 159,* 1354–1360.

Casagrande, M., Violani, C., Lucidi, F., Buttinelli, E., & Bertini, M. (1996). Variations in sleep mentation as a function of time of night. *International Journal of Neuroscience, 85,* 19–30.

Casbon, T. S., Curtin, J. J., Lang, A. R., & Patrick, C. J. (2003). Deleterious effects of alcohol intoxication: Diminished cognitive control and its behavioral consequences. *Journal of Abnormal Psychology, 112,* 476–487.

Case, L., & Smith, T. B. (2000). Ethnic representation in a sample of the literature of applied psychology. *Journal of Consulting and Clinical Psychology, 68,* 1107–1110.

Caseley-Rondi, G., Merikle, P.M., & Bowers, K.S. (1994). Unconscious cognition in the context of general anesthesia. *Consciousness and Cognition: An International Journal, 3,* 166–195.

Casey, S. M. (1993). *Set phasers on stun and other true tales of design, technology, and human error.* Santa Barbara, CA: Aegean.

Caspi, A. (1998). Personality development across the life course. In W. Damon & N. Eisenberg (Eds.), *Handbook of child psychology: Vol. 3. Social, emotional, and personality development* (5th ed., pp. 311–388). New York: Wiley.

Caspi, A. (2000). The child is the father of man: Personality continuities from childhood to adulthood. *Journal of Personality and Social Psychology, 78,* 158–172.

Caspi, A., & Roberts, B. (1999). Personality continuity and change. In L. Pervin & O. John (Eds.), *Handbook of personality: Theory and research* (2nd ed., pp. 300–326). New York: Guilford.

Caspi, A., & Silva, P. A. (1995). Temperamental qualities at age 3 predict personality traits in young adulthood: Longitudinal evidence from a birth cohort. *Child Development, 66,* 468–498.

Caspi, A., Begg, D., Dickson, N., Harrington, H., Langley, J., Moffitt, T. E., & Silva, P. A. (1997). Personality differences predict health-risk behaviors in young adulthood: Evidence from a longitudinal study. *Journal of Personality and Social Psychology, 73,* 1052–1063.

Caspi, A., Harrington, H., Milne, B., Amell, J. W., Theodore, R. F., & Moffitt, T. E. (2003). The human personality shows stability from age 3 to age 26. *Journal of Personality, 71,* 495–513.

Caspi, A., Henry, B., McGee, R. O., Moffitt, T. E., & Silva, P. A. (1995). Temperamental origins of child and adolescent behavior problems: From age 3 to Age 15. *Child Development, 66,* 55–68.

Caspi, A., McClay, J., Moffitt, T. E., Mill, J., Martin, J., Craig, I. W., et al. (2002). Role of genotype in the cycle of violence in maltreated children. *Science, 297,* 851–854.

Caspi, A., Sugden, K., Moffitt, T. E., Taylor, A., Craig, I.W., Harrington, H., et al. (2003). Influence of life stress on depression: Moderation by a polymorphism in the 5-HTT gene. *Science, 301,* 386–389.

Cassel, E., & Bernstein, D. A. (2001). *Criminal behavior.* Boston: Allyn & Bacon.

Castillo, R. (Ed.). (1997). *Meanings of madness.* Stamford, CT: Wadsworth.

Castro, L., & Toro, M. A. (2004). The evolution of culture: From primate social learning to human culture. *Proceedings of the National Academy of Sciences, 101,* 10235–10240.

Caterina, M. J., Schumacher, M. A., Tominaga, M., Rosen, T. A., Levine, J. D., & Julius, D. (1997). The capsaicin receptor: A heat-activated ion channel in the pain pathway. *Nature, 389,* 816–824.

Cattell, R. B. (1963). Theory of fluid and crystallized intelligence: A critical experiment. *Journal of Educational Psychology, 54,* 1–22.

Cattell, R. B., Eber, H. W., & Tatsuoka, M. (1970). *Handbook for the sixteen personality factor questionnaire (16PF).* Champaign, IL: Institute for Personality Testing.

Cavaiola, A. A., & Desordi, E. G. (2000). Locus of control in drinking driving offenders and nonoffenders. *Alcoholism Treatment Quarterly, 18,* 63–73.

Cavallaro, S., D'Agata, V., Manickam, P., Dufour, F., & Alkon, D.L. (2002). Memory-specific temporal profiles of gene expression in the hippocampus. *Proceedings of the National Academy of Sciences, 99,* 16279–16284

CBC News. (2005). Indepth: Retirement. Available: http://www.cbc.ca/printablestory.jsp.

CBC Unlocked. (2005). Toronto nursing home death toll up to 6. [Electronic version]. Available: http://www.cbcunlocked.com/artman/publish/article_584.shtml.

CBC. (2005). Lafleur's poor memory frustrates Gomery. March 9, 2005. Retrieved May 23, 2006, from http://www.cbc.ca/montreal/story/qc-lafleur20050309.html

CCAC. (1993). Guide to the care and use of experimental animals, Vol. 1.

Ceci, S. J., & Liker, J. K. (1986). A day at the races: A study of IQ, expertise and cognitive complexity. *Journal of Experimental Psychology: General, 115, 255–266*

Ceci, S. J., Huffman, M. L. C., Smith, E., & Loftus, E. F. (1994). Repeatedly thinking about a non-event: Source misattributions among preschoolers. *Consciousness and Cognition, 3,* 388–407

Centers for Disease Control and Prevention. (1999a). *Chronic diseases and their risk factors.* Washington, DC: U.S. Government Printing Office

Centers for Disease Control and Prevention. (1999b). *Suicide deaths and rates per 100,000.* Retrieved December 7, 2004, from http://www.cdc.gov/ncipc/data/us9794/suic.htm

Centers for Disease Control and Prevention. (2001). Deaths: Preliminary data for 2000. *National Vital Statistics Reports, 49,* 1–40

Centers for Disease Control and Prevention. (2002b). *A glance at the HIV epidemic.* Retrieved December 13, 2004, from http://www.cdc.gov/nchstp/od/news/At-a-Glance.pdf

Centers for Disease Control and Prevention. (2002c). *National Center for Health Statistics faststats, A to Z: Suicide.*

Centerwall, L. (1990). Controlled TV viewing and suicide in countries: Young adult suicide and exposure to television. *Social Psychiatry and Social Epidemiology, 25,* 149–153

Centonze, D., Picconi, B., Baunez, C., Borrelli, E., Pisani, A., Bernardi, G., & Calabresi, P. (2002). Cocaine and amphetamine depress striatal GABAergic synaptic transmission through D2 dopamine receptors. *Neuropsychopharmacology, 26,* 164–175.

Centre for Addictions Research of British Columbia (2004). *Canadian Addictions Survey.* [Electronic version]. Available: http://www.carbc.uvic.ca/links.htm

Cerf, C., & Navasky, V. (1998). *The experts speak: The definitive compendium of authoritative misinformation.* New York: Villard

Cervone, D., & Shoda, Y. (1999). *The coherence of personality: social cognitive bases of consistency, variability, and organization.* New York: Guilford

Chaiken, A. L., Sigler, E., & Derlega, V. J. (1974). Nonverbal mediators of teacher expectancy effects. *Journal of Personality and Social Psychology, 30,* 144–149

Chamberlin, J. (2000). Easing children's psychological distress in the emergency room. *Monitor on Psychology, 31,* 40–42.

Chambers, C.T., Hardial, J., Craig, K.D., Court, C., & Montgomery, C. (2005). Faces scales for the measurement of postoperative pain intensity in children following minor surgery. *The Clinical Journal of Pain, 21,* 277–285.

Chambless, D. L. (1990). Spacing of exposure sessions in the treatment of agoraphobia and simple phobia. *Behavior Therapy, 21,* 217–229.

Chambless, D. L., & Hollon, S. D. (1998). Defining empirically supported therapies. *Journal of Consulting and Clinical Psychology, 66,* 7–18.

Chambless, D. L., & Ollendick, T. H. (2001). Empirically supported psychological treatments. *Annual Review of Psychology, 52,* 685–716.

Champion, V., & Huster, G. (1995). Effect of interventions on stage of mammography adoption. *Journal of Behavioral Medicine, 18,* 159–188.

Chance, P. (1988, April). Knock wood. *Psychology Today.*

Chang, E. F., & Merzenich, M. M. (2003). Environmental noise retards auditory cortical development. *Science, 300,* 498–502.

Chapman, S., & Morrell, S. (2000). Barking mad? Another lunatic hypothesis bites the dust. *British Medical Journal, 321,* 1561–1563.

Charles, S. T., Mather, M., & Carstensen, L. L. (2003). Aging and emotional memory: The forgettable nature of negative images for older adults. *Journal of Experimental Psychology: General, 132,* 310–324.

Charleton, T., Gunter, B., & Coles, D. (1998). Broadcast television as a cause of aggression? Recent findings from a naturalistic study. *Emotional and Behavioral Difficulties, 3,* 5–13.

Charness, N. (1987). Component processes in bridge bidding and novel problem solving tasks. *Canadian Journal of Psychology, 41,* 223–243.

Charness, N. (2000). Can acquired knowledge compensate for age-related declines in cognitive efficiency? In S. H. Qualls & N. Abeles, (Eds.), *Psychology and the aging revolution: How we adapt to longer life* (pp. 99–117). Washington, DC: American Psychological Association.

Chase, T. N. (1998). The significance of continuous dopaminergic stimulation in the treatment of Parkinson's disease. *Drugs, 55* (Suppl. 1), 1–9.

Chastain, G., & Thurber, S. (1989). The SQ3R study technique enhances comprehension of an introductory psychology textbook. *Reading Improvement, 26,* 94–96.

Cheesman, J., & Merikle, P.M. (1981). Priming with and without awareness. *Perception and Psychophysics, 36, 387–395.*

Chen, M., & Bargh, J. A. (1997). Nonconscious behavioral confirmation processes: The self-fulfilling consequences of automatic stereotype activation. *Journal of Experimental Social Psychology, 33,* 541–560.

Chen, R., Cohen, L. G., & Hallett, M. (2002). Nervous system reorganization following injury. *Neuroscience, 111,* 761–773.

Chen, Z., & Siegler, R. S. (2000). Intellectual development in childhood. In R. J. Sternberg (Ed.), *Handbook of intelligence* (pp. 92–116). New York: Cambridge University Press.

Cheng, Y., Kawachi, I., Coakley, E. H., Schwartz, J., & Colditz, G. (2000). Association between psychosocial work characteristics and health functioning in American women: Prospective study. *British Medical Journal, 320,* 1432–1436.

Cherkin, D. C., Eisenberg, D., Sherman, K. J., Barlow, W., Kaptchuk, T. J., Street, J., & Deyo, R. A. (2001). Randomized trial comparing traditional Chinese medical acupuncture, therapeutic massage, and self-care education for chronic low back pain. *Archives of Internal Medicine, 161,* 1081–1088.

Chi, M. T., Feltovitch, P. J., & Glaser, R. (1981). Representation of physics knowledge by novices and experts. *Cognitive Science, 5,* 121–152.

Chidley, J. (1996). Toxic TV: Is TV violence contributing to aggression in kids? Maclean's, June 17. Retrieved March 23, 2006, from www.media-awareness.ca

Chien, W. W., & Banerjee, L. (2002). Caught between cultures: The young Asian American in therapy. In E. Davis-Russell (Ed.), *California School of Professional Psychology handbook of multicultural education, research, intervention, and training* (pp. 210–220). San Francisco: Jossey-Bass.

Chiles, J. A., Lambert, M. J., & Hatch, A. L. (1999). The impact of psychological interventions on medical cost offset: A meta-analytic review. *Clinical Psychology: Science and Practice, 6,* 204–220.

Chivers, M. L., Rieger, G., Latty, E., & Bailey, J. M. (2004). A sex difference in the specificity of sexual arousal. *Psychological Science, 15,* 736–744.

Cho, Z. H., Chung, S. C., Jones, J. P., Park, J. B., Park, H. J., Lee, H. J., et al. (1998). New findings of the correlation between acupoints and corresponding brain cortices using functional MRI. *Proceedings of the National Academy of Sciences, 95,* 2670–2673.

Cho, Z. H., Wong, E. K., & Fallon, J. D. (2001). *Neuroacupuncture*. Los Angeles: Q-puncture, Inc.

Chodosh, J., Reuben, D. B., Albert, M. S., & Seeman, T. E. (2002). Predicting cognitive impairment in high-functioning community-dwelling older persons: MacArthur studies of successful aging. *Journal of the American Geriatrics Society, 50*(6), 1051–1060.

Choi, J., & Silverman, I. (2003). Processes underlying sex differences in route-learning strategies in children and adolescents. *Personality and Individual Differences, 34,* 1153–1166.

Choi, Y. H., Jang, D. P., Ku, J. H., Shin, M. B., Kim, S. I. (2001). Short-term treatment of acrophobia with virtual reality therapy (VRT): A case report. *CyberPsychology and Behavior, 4,* 349–354.

Chomsky, N. (1965). *Aspects of the theory of syntax*. Cambridge, MA: MIT Press.

Chomsky, N. (1986). *Knowledge of language: Its nature, origin, and use*. New York: Praeger.

Choo, K. L., & Guilleminault, C. (1998). Narcolepsy and idiopathic hypersomnolence. *Clinical Chest Medicine, 19*(1), 169–181.

Chorney, M. L., Chorney, K., Sense, N., Owen, M. J., Daniels, J., McGuffin, P., et al. (1998). A quantitative trait locus (QTL) associated with cognitive ability in children. *Psychological Science, 9,* 159–166.

Chouinard, G. (2004). Issues in the clinical use of benzodiazepines: Potency, withdrawal, and rebound. *Journal of Clinical Psychiatry, 65*(Suppl. 5), 7–21.

Christensen, A., Atkins, D. C., Berns, S., Wheeler, J., Baucom, D. H., & Simpson, L. E. (2004). Traditional versus integrative behavioral couple therapy for significantly and chronically distressed married couples. *Journal of Consulting and Clinical Psychology, 72,* 176–191.

Christensen, H., Griffiths, K. M., & Jorm, A. F. (2004). Delivering interventions for depression by using the Internet: Randomized controlled trial. *British Medical Journal, 328,* 265.

Christensen, K. A., Stephens, M. A. P., & Townsend, A. L. (1998). Mastery in women's multiple roles and well-being: Adult daughters providing care to impaired parents. *Health Psychology, 17,* 163–171.

Chugani, H. T., & Phelps, M. E. (1986). Maturational changes in cerebral function in infants determined by 18FDG positron emission tomography. *Science, 231,* 840–843.

Cialdini, R. B. (1993). *Influence: Science and practice* (3rd ed.). New York: HarperCollins.

Cialdini, R. B. (1995). Principles and techniques of social influence. In A. Tesser (Ed.), *Advanced social psychology* (pp. 257–282). New York: McGraw-Hill.

Cialdini, R. B. (2001). *Influence: Science and practice* (4th ed.). Boston: Allyn & Bacon.

Cialdini, R. B., & Goldstein, N. J. (2004). Social influence: Compliance and conformity. *Annual Review of Psychology, 55,* 591–621.

Cialdini, R. B., & Trost, M. (1998). Social influence: Social norms, conformity, and compliance. In D. Gilbert, S. T. Fiske, & G. Lindzey (Eds.), *Handbook of social psychology* (Vol. 2, 4th ed., pp. 151–192). Boston: McGraw-Hill.

Cialdini, R. B., Wosinska, W. B., Barrett, D. W., Butner, J., & Gornik-Durose, M. (2001). The differential impact of two social influence principles on individualists and collectivists in Poland and the United States. In W. Wosinska, R. B. Cialdini, D.W. Barrett, & J. Reykowski (Eds.), *The practice of social influence in multiple cultures: Applied social research* (pp. 33–50). Mahwah, NJ: Erlbaum.

Ciapparelli, A., Dell'Osso, L., Tundo, A., Pini, S., Chiavacci, M. C., Di Sacco, I., & Cassano, G. B. (2001). Electroconvulsive therapy in medication-nonresponsive patients with mixed mania and bipolar depression. *Journal of Clinical Psychiatry, 62,* 552–555.

Ciccocioppo, R., Martin-Fardon, R., & Weiss, F. (2004). Stimuli associated with a single cocaine experience elicit long-lasting cocaine-seeking. *Nature Neuroscience, 7,* 495–496.

Ciccocioppo, R., Sanna, P. P., & Weiss, F. (2001). Cocaine-predictive stimulus induces drug-seeking behavior and neural activation in limbic brain regions after multiple months of abstinence: Reversal by D1 antagonists. *Proceedings of the National Academy of Sciences, 98,* 1976–1981.

City of Toronto (2005). Statement by Dr. David McKeown, Medical Officer of Health, Announcement re respiratory outbreak at Seven Oaks Nursing Home. [Electronic version]. Available: http://wx.toronto.ca/inter/it/newsrel.nsf/0/63b4e996664a64d185257 09200753944?OpenDocument

Clancy, S. A., McNally, R. J., Schacter, D. L., Lenzenweger, M. F., & Pitman, R. K. (2002). Memory distortion in people reporting abduction by aliens. *Journal of Abnormal Psychology, 111,* 455–461.

Clancy, S. A., Schacter, D. L., McNally, R. J., & Pittman, R. K. (2000). False recognition in women reporting recovered memories of sexual abuse. *Psychological Science, 11,* 26–31.

Clapham, K., & Abramson, E. E. (1985). Aversive conditioning of junk food consumption: A multiple baseline study. *Addictive Behaviors, 10,* 437–440.

Clark, D. M., Ehlers, A., McManus, F., Hackmann, A., Fennell, M., Campbell, H., et al. (2003). Cognitive therapy versus fluoxetine in generalized social phobia: A randomized placebo-controlled trial. *Journal of Consulting and Clinical Psychology, 71,* 1058–1067.

Clark, D. M., Salkovskis, P. M., Ost, L.-G., Breitholtz, E., Koehler, K. A., Westling, B. E., Jeavons, A., & Gelder, M. (1997). Misinterpretation of body sensations in panic disorder. *Journal of Consulting and Clinical Psychology, 65,* 203–213.

Clark, E. V. (1983). Meanings and concepts. In P. H. Mussen, J. H. Flavell, & E. M. Markman (Eds.), *Handbook of child psychology: Vol. 3. Cognitive development* (4th ed., pp. 787–840). New York: Wiley.

Clark, E. V. (1993). *The lexicon in acquisition*. Cambridge: Cambridge University Press.

Clark, F., Azen, S. P., Carlson, M., Mandel, D., LaBree, L., Hay, J., Zemke, R., Jackson, J., & Lipson, L. (2001). Embedding health-promoting changes into the daily lives of independent-living older adults: Long-term follow-up of occupational therapy intervention. *Journal of Gerontology: Psychological Sciences, 56B,* 60.

Clark, M. S., & Pataki, S. P. (1995). Interpersonal processes influencing attraction and relationships. In A. Tesser (Ed.), *Advanced social psychology* (pp. 283–332). New York: McGraw-Hill.

Clarke-Stewart, A., & Brentano, C. (2005).*'Til divorce do us part*. New Haven, CT: Yale Press.

Clarke-Stewart, K. A. (1989). Infant day care: Maligned or malignant? *American Psychologist, 44,* 266–273.

Clarke-Stewart, K. A., & Fein, G. G. (1983). Early childhood programs. In P. H. Mussen (Ed.), *Handbook of child psychology: Vol. 2. Infancy and developmental psychobiology* (pp. 917–1000). New York: Wiley.

Clausen, J., Sersen, E., & Lidsky, A. (1974). Variability of sleep measures in normal subjects. *Psychophysiology, 11,* 509–516.

Clay, R. (1996, December). Some elders thrive on working into late life. *APA Monitor,* p. 35.

Clay, R. A. (2001). Training that's more than bilingual. *Monitor on Psychology, 32,* 70–72.

Clay, R. A. (2002b). Psychotherapy *is* cost-effective. *Monitor on Psychology, 31,* Retrieved December 13, 2004 from http://www.apa.org/monitor/jan00/pr2.html

Clendenen, V. I., Herman, C. P., & Polivy, J. (1995). Social facilitation of eating among friends and strangers. *Appetite, 23,* 1–13.

Clifton, R. K., Rochat, P., Litovsky, R., & Perris, E. (1991). Object representation guides infants' reaching in the dark. *Journal of Experimental Psychology: Human Perception and Performance, 17,* 323–329.

Clower, C. E., & Bothwell, R. K. (2001). An exploratory study of the relationship between the Big Five and inmate recidivism. *Journal of Research in Personality, 35,* 231–237.

Cnattingius, S., Signorello, L. B., Anneren, G., Clausson, B., Ekbom, A., Ljunger, E., et al. (2000). Caffeine intake and the risk of first-trimester spontaneous abortion. *New England Journal of Medicine, 343,* 1839–1845.

Cobos, P., Sánchez, M., Pérez, N., & Vila, J. (2004). Effects of spinal cord injuries on the subjective component of emotions. *Cognition and Emotion, 18,* 281–287.

Cohen, C. E. (1981). Person categories and social perception: Testing some boundaries of the processing effects of prior knowledge. *Journal of Personality and Social Psychology, 40,* 441–452.

Cohen, J., & Servan-Schreiber, D. (1992). Context, cortex, and dopamine: A connectionist approach to behavior and biology in schizophrenia. *Psychological Review, 99,* 45–77.

Cohen, N. J., & Corkin, S. (1981). The amnesic patient H. M.: Learning and retention of a cognitive skill. *Neuroscience Abstracts, 7,* 235.

Cohen, P., Kasen, S., Chen, H., Hartmark, C., & Gordon, K. (2003). Variations in patterns of developmental transitions in the emerging adulthood period. *Developmental Psychology, 39,* 657–669.

Cohen, S., & Herbert, T. B. (1996). Health psychology: Psychological factors and physical disease from the perspective of human psychoneuroimmunology. *Annual Review of Psychology, 47,* 113–142.

Cohen, S., Doyle, W. J., Skoner, D. P., Gwaltney, J. M., Jr., & Newsom, J. T. (1995). State and trait negative affect as predictors of objective and subjective symptoms of respiratory viral infections. *Journal of Personality and Social Psychology, 68,* 159–169.

Cohen-Corey, S. (2002). The developing synapse: Construction and modulation of synaptic structures and circuits. *Science, 298,* 770–776.

Colak, A., Soy, O., Uzun, H., Aslan, O., Barut, S., Belce, A., et al. (2003). Neuroprotective effects of GYKI 52466 on experimental spinal cord injury in rats. *Journal of Neurosurgery, 98,* 275–281.

Colby, A., Kohlberg, L., Gibbs, J., & Lieberman, M. (1983). A longitudinal study of moral judgment. *Monographs of the Society for Research in Child Development, 48* (1, Serial No. 200).

Colcombe, S., & Kramer, A. F. (2003). Fitness effects on the cognitive function of older adults: A meta-analytic study. *Psychological Science, 14,* 125–130.

Cole, K. N., Mills, P. E., Dale, P. S., & Jenkins, J. R. (1991). Effects of preschool integration for children with disabilities. *Exceptional Children, 58,* 36–45.

Cole, R. A., & Jakimik, J. (1978). Understanding speech: How words are heard. In G. Underwood (Ed.), *Strategies of information processing* (pp. 67–116). London: Academic Press.

Coles, M. (1989). Modern mind-brain reading: Psychophysiology, physiology & cognition. *Psychophysiology, 26,* 251–269.

Collacott, E. A., Zimmerman, J. T., White, D. W., & Rindone, J. P. (2000). Bipolar permanent magnets for the treatment of chronic low back pain: A pilot study. *Journal of the American Medical Association, 283,* 1322–1325.

Collins, A. M., & Loftus, E. F. (1975). A spreading activation theory of semantic processing. *Psychological Review, 82,* 407–428.

Coltrane, S. (2001). Research on household labor: Modeling and measuring the social embeddedness of routine family work. In R. M. Milardo (Ed), *Understanding families into the new millennium: A decade in review.* Minneapolis, MN: National Council on Family Relations.

Colwill, R. M. (1994). Associative representations of instrumental contingencies. *Psychology of Learning and Motivation, 31,* 1–72.

Committee to Review the Scientific Evidence on the Polygraph. (2003). *The polygraph and lie detection.* Washington, DC: National Academies Press.

Compagnone, N. A., & Mellon, S. H. (2000). Neurosteroids: Biosynthesis and function of these novel neuromodulators. *Frontiers of Neuroendocrinology, 21,* 1–56.

Compas, B. E., Haaga, D. A. F., Keefe, F. J., Leitenberg, H., & Williams, D. A. (1998). Sampling of empirically supported psychological treatments from health psychology: Smoking, chronic pain, cancer, and bulimia nervosa. *Journal of Consulting and Clinical Psychology, 66,* 89–112.

Condon, J. W., & Crano, W. D. (1988). Inferred evaluation and the relationship between attitude similarity and interpersonal attraction. *Journal of Personality and Social Psychology, 54,* 789–797.

Conger, R. D., Cui, M., Bryant, C. M., & Elder, G. H. (2000). Competence in early adult romantic relationships: A developmental perspective on family influences. *Journal of Personality and Social Psychology, 79*(2), 224–237.

Conklin, H. M., & Iacono, W. G. (2002). Schizophrenia: A neurodevelopmental perspective. *Current Directions in Psychological Science, 11,* 33–37.

Conley, R. R., & Mahmoud, R. (2001). A randomized double-blind study of risperidone and olanzapine in the treatment of schizophrenia or schizoaffective disorder. *American Journal of Psychiatry, 158,* 765–774.

Connolly, M. B., Crits-Cristoph, P., & Barber, J. P. (2000). Transference patterns in the therapeutic relationship in supportive-expressive psychotherapy for depression. *Psychotherapy Research, 10*(3), 356–372.

Connor, L. T., Balota, D. A., & Neely, J. H. (1992). On the relation between feeling of knowing and lexical decision: Persistent subthreshold activation of topic familiarity? *Journal of Experimental Psychology: Learning, Memory, and Cognition, 18,* 544–554.

Consedine, N. S., & Magai, C. (2003) Attachment and emotion experience in later life: The view from emotions theory. *Attachment and Human Development, 5,* 165–187.

Consumer Reports. (1995, November). Mental health: Does therapy help? *Consumer Reports,* pp. 734–739.

Contrada, R. J., Ashmore, R. D., Gary, M. L., Coups, E., Egeth, J. D., Sewell, A., et al. (2000). Ethnicity-related sources of stress and their effects on well-being. *Current Directions in Psychological Science, 9,* 136–139.

Cook, M. & Mineka, S. (1990). Selective associations in the observational conditioning of fear in rhesus monkeys. *Journal of Experimental Psychology: Animal Behavior Processes, 16,* 372–389.

Cookson, J., & Duffett, R. (1998). Fluoxetine: Therapeutic and undesirable effects. *Hospital Medicine, 59,* 622–626.

Cooper, A. (2004). *The inmates are running the asylum: Why high tech products drive us crazy and how to restore the sanity* (2nd ed.). New York: Pearson.

Cooper, H. (1979). Pygmalion grows up: A model for teacher expectation communication and performance influence. *Review of Educational Research, 49,* 389–410.

Cooper, M. L., Russell, M., Skinner, J. B., Frone, M. R., & Mudar, P. (1992). Stress and alcohol use: The moderating effects of gender, coping, and alcohol expectancies. *Journal of Abnormal Psychology, 101,* 139–152.

Coovert, M. D., & Reeder, G. D. (1990). Negativity effects in impression formation: The role of unit formation and schematic expectations. *Journal of Experimental Social Psychology, 26,* 49–62.

Corbetta, M., Miezin, F. M., Dobmeyer, S., Shulman, G. L., & Petersen, S. E. (1991). Selective and divided attention during visual discriminations of shape, color, and speed: Functional anatomy by positron emission tomography. *Journal of Neuroscience, 11,* 2383–2402.

Coren, S. (1999). Psychology applied to animal training. In A. Stec & D. Bernstein (Eds.), *Psychology: Fields of application.* Boston: Houghton Mifflin.

Cork, R. C., Kihlstrom, J. F., & Hameroff, S. R. (1992). Explicit and implicit memory dissociated by anesthetic technique. *Society for Neuroscience Abstracts, 22,* 523.

Corkin, S. (2002). What's new with the amnesic patient H. M.? *Nature Reviews Neuroscience, 3,* 153–160.

Cormier, R. (2006, May 25). Doctor felt helpless to stop officer's mentally ill killer. *The Windsor Star.* [On-line]. Available: http://www.fpinfomart.ca/doc/doc_display.php?delta=10&cnd=y&key=ar|wistp3|94307|200605250097|5384972|1

Cornblatt, B., & Erlenmeyer-Kimling, L. E. (1985). Global attentional deviance in children at risk for schizophrenia: Specificity and predictive validity. *Journal of Abnormal Psychology, 94,* 470–486.

Cornelius, R. R. (1996). *The science of emotion.* Upper Saddle River, NJ: Prentice-Hall.

Corno, L., Cronbach, L. J., Kupermintz, H., Lohman, D. F., Mandinach, E. B., Porteus, A. W., & Talbert, J. E. (2002). *Remaking the concept of aptitude: Extending the legacy of Richard E. Snow.* Hillsdale, NJ: Erlbaum.

Cornoldi, C., DeBeni, R., & Baldi, A. P. (1989). Generation and retrieval of general, specific, and autobiographic images representing concrete nouns. *Acta Psychologica, 72,* 25–39.

Corr, P. J. (2002). J. A. Gray's reinforcement sensitivity theory: Tests of the joint subsystems hypothesis of anxiety and impulsivity. *Personality and Individual Differences, 33,* 511–532.

Correll, C. U., Leucht, S., & Kane, J. M. (2004). Lower risk for tardive dyskinesia associated with second-generation antipsychotics: A systematic review of 1-year studies. *American Journal of Psychiatry, 161,* 414–425.

Correll, J., Park, B., Judd, C. M., & Wittenbrink, B. (2002). The police officer's dilemma: Using ethnicity to disambiguate potentially threatening individuals. *Journal of Personality and Social Psychology, 83,* 1314–1329.

Corsini, R. J., & Wedding, D. (2001). *Current psychotherapies* (6th ed.). Itasca, IL: Peacock.

Coryell, W., Scheftner, W., Keller, M., Endicott, J., Maser, J., & Klerman, G. (1993). The enduring consequences of mania and depression. *American Journal of Psychiatry, 150,* 720–727.

Cosmides, L., & Tooby, J. (2004). *What is evolutionary psychology? Explaining the new science of the mind.* New Haven, CT: Yale University Press.

Costa, P. (2001, June). *New insights on personality and leadership provided by the five-factor model.* Paper presented at Annual Convention of American Psychological Society, Toronto, Canada.

Costa, P. T., & McCrae, R. R. (2002). Looking backwards: Changes in mean levels of personality traits from 80 to 12. In D. Cervone, & W. Mischel (Eds.), *Advances in personality science* (pp. 196–217). New York: Guilford Press.

Costa, P. T., Jr., & McCrae, R. (1992). *Revised NEO Personality Inventory: NEO PI and NEO Five-Factor Inventory (NEO FFI: Professional Manual).* Odessa, FL: Psychological Assessment Resources.

Costa, P. T., Jr., & McCrae, R. R. (1995). Primary traits of Eysenck's P-E-N system: Three- and five-factor solutions. *Journal of Personality and Social Psychology, 69,* 308–317.

Costermans, J., Lories, G., & Ansay, C. (1992). Confidence level and feeling of knowing in question answering: The weight of inferential processes. *Journal of Experimental Psychology: Learning, Memory, and Cognition 18,* 142–150.

Cote, J. K., & Pepler, C. (2002). A randomized trial of a cognitive coping intervention for acutely ill HIV-positive men. *Nursing Research, 51,* 237–244.

Cotter, D., Mackay, D, Landau, S. Kerwin, R., & Everall, I. (2001). Reduced glial cell density and neuronal size in the anterior cingulate cortex in major depressive disorder. *Archives of General Psychiatry, 58,* 545–553.

Courneya, K. S. (1995). Understanding readiness for regular physical activity in older individuals: An application of the theory of planned behavior. *Health Psychology, 14,* 80–87.

Court TV. Crime Library. (2005). Missing Persons: Courtney Struble. Retrieved January 12, 2007, from ttp://www.crimelibrary.com/missing children/courtney_struble.html

Courtney, C., Farrell, D., Gray, R., Hills, R., Lynch, L., Sellwood, E., et al. (2004). Long-term donepezil treatment in 565 patients with Alzheimer's disease (AD2000): Randomised double-blind trial. *Lancet, 363,* 2105–2115.

Cowan, D. T., Allan, L. G., Libretto, S. E., & Griffiths, P. (2001). Opiod drugs: A comparative survey of therapeutic and "street" use. *Pain, 2,* 193–203.

Cowan, N. (1988). Evolving concepts of memory storage, selective attention, and their mutual constraints within the human information-processing system. *Psychological Bulletin, 104,* 163–191.

Cox, M. J., & Paley, B. (2003). Understanding families as systems. *Current Directions in Psychological Science, 12,* 193–196.

CPA. (2000). Canadian code of ethics for psychologists, 3rd ed.

Craig, A. D. (2002). How do you feel? Interoception: the sense of the physiological condition of the body. *Nature Reviews: Neuroscience, 3,* 655–666.

Craig, A. D., & Bushnell, M. C. (1994). The thermal grill illusion: Unmasking the burn of cold pain. *Science, 265,* 252–254.

Craig, A. D., Bushnell, M. C., Zhang, E.T., & Blomqvist, A. (1994). A thalamic nucleus specific for pain and temperature sensation. *Nature, 372,* 770–773.

Craik, F. I. M., & Lockhart, R. S. (1972). Levels of processing: A framework for memory research. *Journal of Verbal Learning and Verbal Behavior, 11,* 671–684.

Craik, F. I. M., & Rabinowitz, J. C. (1984). Age differences in the acquisition and use of verbal information. In H. Bouma & D. G. Bouwhuis (Eds.), *Attention and performance* (Vol. 10, pp. 471–499). Hillsdale, NJ: Erlbaum.

Craik, F. I. M., & Tulving, E. (1975). Depth of processing and the recognition of words in episodic memory. *Journal of Experimental Psychology: General, 104,* 268–294.

Craik, F. I. M., Moroz, T. M., Moscovitch, M., Stuss, D. T., Winocur, G., Tulving, E., & Kapur, S. (1999). In search of the self: A positron emission topography study. *Psychological Science, 10,* 26–34.

Cramer, E. P. (1999). Hate crime laws and sexual orientation. *Journal of Sociology & Social Welfare, 26,* 5–24.

Cramer, K. M., & Perreault, L. A. (2006). Effects of predictability, actual controllability, and awareness of choice on perceptions of control. *Current Research in Social Psychology, 11,* 111–126.

Cramer, K. M., Nickels, J. B., & Gural, D. M. (1997). Uncertainty of outcomes, prediction of failure, and lack of control as factors explaining perceived helplessness. *Journal of Social Behaviour and Personality, 12,* 611–630.

Crandall, C. S., Preisler, J. J., & Aussprung, J. (1992). Measuring life event stress in the lives of college students: The Undergraduate Stress Questionnaire (USQ). *Journal of Behavioral Medicine, 15,* 627–662.

Crano, W. D., & Chen, X. (1998). The leniency contract and persistence of majority and minority influence. *Journal of Personality and Social Psychology, 74,* 1437–1450.

Craske, M. G. (1999). *Anxiety disorders: Psychological approaches to theory and treatment.* Boulder, CO: Westview Press.

Crawford, H. J., Brown, A. M., & Moon, C. E. (1993). Sustained attentional and disattentional abilities: Differences between low and highly hypnotizable persons. *Journal of Abnormal Psychology, 102*(4), 534–543.

Crawford, T. N., Cohen, P., & Brooks, J. S. (2001). Dramatic-erratic personality disorder symptoms: II. Developmental pathways from early adolescence to adulthood. *Journal of Personality Disorders, 15,* 336–350.

Creem, S. H., & Proffitt, D. R. (2001). Defining the cortical visual systems: "What," "where," and "how." *Acta Psychologia, 107,* 43–68.

Crick, F., & Koch, C. (1998). Consciousness and neuroscience. *Cerebral Cortex, 8,* 97–107.

Crick, N. (1997, June). Abused children have more conflicts with friends. *APA Monitor,* p. 32.

Crick, N. R., Casas, J. F., & Mosher, M. (1997). Relational and overt aggression in preschool. *Developmental Psychology, 33,* 579–588.

Crick, N. R., Werner, N. E., Casas, J. F., O'Brien, K. M., Nelson, D. A., Grotpeter, J. K., et al. (1999). Childhood aggression and gender: A new look at an old problem. In D. Bernstein (Ed.), *Nebraska Symposium on Motivation* (Vol. 44, pp. 75–141). Lincoln: University of Nebraska Press.

Cristobal, R. (2003). The psychoanalytic process in the light of attachment theory. In M. Cortina & M. Marrone (Eds.), *Attachment theory and the psychoanalytic process* (pp. 335–355). London: Whurr.

Critchley, E. M. (1991). Speech and the right hemisphere. *Behavioural Neurology, 4*(3), 143–151.

Crocker, J., & Park, L. E. (2004). The costly pursuit of self-esteem. *Psychological Bulletin, 130,* 392–414.

Crocker, J., & Wolfe, T. (2001). Contingencies of self-worth. *Psychological Review, 108,* 593–623.

Croen, L. A., Grether, J. K., & Selvin, S. (2001). The epidemiology of mental retardation of unknown cause. *Pediatrics, 107,* 86.

Croft, H., Settle, E., Jr., Houser, T., Batey, S. R., Donahue, R. M., & Ascher, J. A. (1999). A placebo-controlled comparison of the antidepressant efficacy and effects on sexual functioning of sustained-release bupropion and sertraline. *Clinical Therapeutics, 21,* 643–658.

Crombag, H. S., & Robinson, T. E. (2004). Drugs, environment, brain, and behavior. *Current Directions in Psychological Science, 13,* 107–111.

Cronbach, L. J. (1990). *Essentials of psychological testing* (5th ed.). New York: Harper & Row.

Cronbach, L. J. (1996). Acceleration among the Terman males: Correlates in midlife and after. In C. P. Benbow & D. J. Lubinski (Eds.), *Intellectual talent: Psychometric and social issues* (pp. 179–191). Baltimore: Johns-Hopkins University Press.

Cross, I. (2003). Music as a biocultural phenomenon. *Annals of the New York Academy of Sciences, 999,* 106–111.

Cross, S. E., & Madson, L. (1997). Models of the self: Self-construals and gender. *Psychological Bulletin, 122,* 5–37.

Cross, S. E., & Markus, H. R. (1999). The cultural constitution of personality. In L. Pervin & O. John (Eds.), *Handbook of personality research* (2nd ed., pp. 378–398). New York: Guilford.

Cross-National Collaborative Group. (1992). The changing rate of major depression: Cross-national comparisons. *Journal of the American Medical Association, 268,* 3098–3105.

Crowley, K., Callahan, M. A., Tenenbaum, H. R., & Allen, E. (2001). Parents explain more often to boys than to girls during shared scientific thinking. *Psychological Science, 12,* 258–261.

Crowther, J. H., Sanftner, J., Bonifazi, D. Z., & Shepherd, K. L. (2001). The role of daily hassles in binge eating. *International Journal of Eating Disorders, 29,* 449–454.

Cruz, A., & Green, B. G. (2000). Thermal stimulation of taste. *Nature, 403,* 889–892.

Cryan, J. F., O'Leary, O. F., Jin, S. H., Friedland, J. C., Ouyang, M., Hirsch, B. R., et al. (2004). Norepinephrine-deficient mice lack responses to antidepressant drugs, including selective serotonin reuptake inhibitors. *Proceedings of the National Academy of Science, 101,* 8186–8191.

Csernansky, J. G., Schindler, M. K., Splinter, N. R., Wang, L., Gado, M., Selemon, L. D., et al. (2004). Abnormalities of thalamic volume and shape in schizophrenia. *American Journal of Psychiatry, 161,* 896–902.

Culbertson, F. M. (1997). Depression and gender. An international review. *American Psychologist, 52,* 25–31.

Cumsille, P. E., Sayer, A. G., & Graham, J. W. (2000). Perceived exposure to peer and adult drinking as predictors of growth in positive alcohol expectancies during adolescence. *Journal of Consulting and Clinical Psychology, 68,* 531–536.

Curcio, C. A., Sloan, D. R., Jr., Packer, O., Hendrickson, A. E., & Kalina, R. E. (1987). Distribution of cones in human and monkey retina: Individual variability and radial asymmetry. *Science, 236,* 579–582.

Curran, H. V., & Monaghan, L. (2001). In and out of the K-hole: A comparison of the acute and residual effects of ketamine in frequent and infrequent ketamine users. *Addiction, 96,* 749–760.

Curtis, T., Miller, B. C., & Berry, E. H. (2000). Changes in reports and incidence of child abuse following natural disasters. *Child Abuse & Neglect, 24,* 1151–1162.

Cusack, K., & Spates, C. R. (1999). The cognitive dismantling of eye movement desensitization and reprocessing (EMDR) treatment of posttraumatic stress disorder (PTSD). *Journal of Anxiety Disorders, 13,* 87–99.

Czeisler, C. A., Duffy, J. F., Shanahan, T. L., Brown, E. N., Mitchell, J. F., Rimmer, D. W., et al. (1999). Stability, precision, and near 24-hour period of the human circadian pacemaker. *Science, 284,* 2177–2181.

D'Agostino, R. B., Sr., Grundy, S., Sullivan, L. M., & Wilson, P. (2001). Validation of the Framingham coronary heart disease prediction scores: Results of a multiple ethnic groups investigation. *Journal of the American Medical Association, 286,* 180–187.

D'Aliesio, R., & Leeder, J. (2004, March 6). Slain mountie laid to rest: Two thousand officers and 75 police dogs attend funeral for Cpl. Jim Galloway. [Electronic version]. *The Edmonton Journal.*

D'Esposito, M. (Ed.). (2003). *Neurological foundations of cognitive neuroscience.* Cambridge, MA: MIT Press.

D'Esposito, M., Detre, J. A., Alsop, D. C., & Shin, R. K. (1995). The neural basis of the central executive system of working memory. *Nature, 378,* 279–281.

d'Ydewalle, G., & Rosselle, H. (1978). Text expectations in text learning. In M. M. Gruneberg, P. E. Morris, & R. N. Sykes (Eds.), *Practical aspects of memory.* Orlando, FL: Academic Press.

Dadds, M. R., Spence, S. H., Holland, D. E., Barrett, P. M., & Laurens, K. R. (1997). Prevention and early intervention for anxiety disorders: A controlled trial. *Journal of Consulting and Clinical Psychology, 65,* 627–635.

Daglish, M. R., & Nutt, D. J. (2003). Brain imaging studies in human addicts. *European Neuropsychopharmacology, 13,* 453–458.

Dale, P. S. (1976). *Language and the development of structure and function.* New York: Holt, Rinehart & Winston.

Daley, K. C. (2004). Update on sudden infant death syndrome. *Current Opinion in Pediatrics, 16,* 227–232.

Dallman, M. F., Pecoraro, N., Akana, S. F., La Fleur, S. E., Gomez, F., Houshyar, H., et al. (2003). Chronic stress and obesity: A new view of "comfort food." *Proceedings of the National Academies of Science, 100,* 11696–11701.

Dalman, C., & Allebeck, P. (2002). Parental age and schizophrenia: Further support for an association. *American Journal of Psychiatry, 159,* 1591–1592.

Daly, J. J., Prudic, J., Devanand, D. P., Nobler, M. S., Mitchell, S., Lisanby, S. H., et al. (2001). ECT in bipolar and unipolar depression: Differences in speed of response. *Bipolar Disorders, 3,* 95–104.

Damasio, A. R. (1994). *Descartes' error.* New York: Putnam.

Damasio, A. R., Grabowski, T. J., Bechara, A., Damasio, H., Ponto, L. L. B., Parvizi, J., & Hichwa, R. D. (2000). Subcortical and cortical brain activity during the feeling of self-generated emotions. *Nature Neuroscience, 3,* 1049–1056.

Damon, W., & Hart, D. (1982). The development of self-understanding from infancy through adolescence. *Child Development, 53,* 841–864.

Darchia, N., Campbell, I. G., & Feinberg, I. (2003). Rapid eye movement density is reduced in the normal elderly. *Sleep, 26,* 973–977.

Dark, V. J., & Benbow, C. P. (1993). Cognitive differences among the gifted: A review and new data. In D. K. Detterman (Ed.), *Current topics in human intelligence* (Vol. 3, pp. 85–120). Norwood, NJ: Ablex.

Darkes, J., & Goldman, M. S. (1993). Expectancy challenge and drinking reduction. *Journal of Clinical and Consulting Psychology, 61,* 344–353.

Darwin, C. E. (1965). *The expression of emotions in man and animals.* Chicago: University of Chicago Press. (Original work published 1872)

Das, J. P. (2002). A better look at intelligence. *Current Directions in Psychological Science, 11,* 28–33.

Dasgupta, A. M., Juza, D. M., White, G. M., & Maloney, J. F. (1995). Memory and hypnosis: A comparative analysis of guided memory, cognitive interview, and hypnotic hypermnesia. *Imagination, Cognition, and Personality, 14*(2), 117–130.

Davanloo, H. (1999). Intensive short-term dynamic psychotherapy-central dynamic sequence: Phase of challenge. *International Journal of Short-Term Dynamic Psychotherapy, 13,* 237–262.

David, B., & Turner, J. C. (2001). Majority and minority influence: A single process self-categorization analysis. In C. de Dreu & N. K. De Vries (Eds.), *Group consensus and minority influence: Implications for innovation.* Oxford: Blackwell.

Davidson, J. K., & Moore, N. B. (1994). Guilt and lack of orgasm during sexual intercourse: Myth versus reality in college women. *Journal of Sex Education and Therapy, 20*(3), 153–174.

Davidson, J. M., Camargo, C. A., & Smith, E. R. (1979). Effects of androgen on sexual behavior in hypogonadal men. *Journal of Clinical Endocrinological Metabolism, 48,* 955–958.

Davidson, J. R. T., Rothbaum, B. O., van der Kolk, B. A., Sikes, C. R., & Farfel, G. M. (2001). Multicenter, double-blind comparison of sertraline and placebo in the treatment of posttraumatic stress disorder. *Archives of General Psychiatry, 58,* 485–492.

Davidson, J. R., Foa, E. B., Huppert, J. D., Keefe, F. J., Franklin, M. E., Compton, J. S., et al. (2004). Fluoxetine, comprehensive cognitive behavioral therapy, and placebo in generalized social phobia. *Archives of General Psychiatry, 61,* 1005–1013.

Davidson, K., Hall, P., & MacGregor, M. (1996). Gender differences in the relation between interview-derived hostility scores and resting blood pressure. *Journal of Behavioral Medicine, 19,* 185–201.

Davidson, P. R., & Parker, K. C. (2001). Eye movement desensitization and reprocessing (EMDR): A meta-analysis. *Journal of Consulting and Clinical Psychology, 69,* 305–316.

Davidson, R. J. (2000). Affective style, psychopathology, and resilience: Brain mechanisms and plasticity. *American Psychologist, 55,* 1196–1214.

Davidson, R. J., Kabat-Zinn, J., Schumacher, J., Rosenkranz, M., Muller, D., Santorelli, S. F., et al. (2003). Alterations in brain and immune function produced by mindfulness meditation. *Psychosomatic Medicine, 65,* 564–570.

Davidson, R. J., Pizzagalli, D., Nitschke, J. B., & Putnam, K. (2002). Depression: Perspectives from affective neuroscience. *Annual Review of Psychology, 53,* 545–574.

Davidson, R. J., Shackman, A. J., & Maxwell, J. S. (2004). Asymmetries in face and brain related to emotion. *Trends in Cognitive Science, 8,* 389–391.

Davies, C. (1999, April 21). Junior doctor is cleared in baby overdose death. *London Daily Telegraph,* p. 2.

Davies, R. J., & Stradling, J. R. (2000). The efficacy of nasal continuous positive airway pressure in the treatment of obstructive sleep apnea syndrome is proven. *American Journal of Respiratory Critical Care Medicine, 161,* 1775–1776.

Davis, J. A., & Smith, T. W. (1990). *General social surveys, 1972–1990: Cumulative codebook.* Chicago: National Opinion Research Center.

Davis, J. L., & Rusbult, C. (2001). Attitude alignment in close relationships. *Journal of Personality and Social Psychology, 81,* 65–84.

Davis, J. M., Chen, N., & Glick, I. D. (2003). A meta-analysis of the efficacy of second-generation antipsychotics. *Archives of General Psychiatry, 60,* 553–564.

Davis, K. D., Taylor, S. J., Crawley, A. P., Wood, M. L., & Mikulis, D. J. (1997). Functional MRI of pain- and attention-related activations in the human cingulate cortex. *Journal of Neurophysiology, 77,* 3370–3380.

Davis, K. L., Kahn, R. S., Ko, G., & Davidson, M. (1991). Dopamine in schizophrenia: A review and reconceptualization. *American Journal of Psychiatry, 148,* 1474–1486.

Davis, K. L., Stewart, D. G., Friedman, J. I., Buchsbaum, M., Harvey, P. D., Hof, P. R., et al. (2003). White matter changes in schizophrenia: Evidence for myelin-related dysfunction. *Archives of General Psychiatry, 60,* 443–456.

Davis, M. H., Luce, C., & Kraus, S. J. (1994). The heritability of characteristics associated with dispositional empathy. *Journal of Personality, 60,* 369–391.

Davis, M., Falls, W. A., Campeau, S., & Kim, M. (1993). Fear-potentiated startle: A neural and pharmacological analysis. *Behavioural Brain Research, 58*(1–2), 175–198.

Davis, R. A., & Moore, C. C. (1935). Methods of measuring retention. *Journal of General Psychology, 12,* 144–155.

Davison, G. C., & Neale, J. M. (1990). *Abnormal psychology* (5th ed.). New York: Wiley.

Dawda, D. (2000). Assessing emotional intelligence: Reliability and validity of the Bar On Emotional Quotient Inventory (EQ-i) in university students. *Personality and Individual Differences, 28,* 797–812.

Dawe, L. A., Platt, J. R., & Welsh, E. (1998). Spectral-motion aftereffects and the tritone paradox among Canadian subjects. *Perception and Psychophysics, 60,* 209–220.

Dawes, R. M. (1994). *House of cards: Psychology and psychotherapy built on myth.* New York: Free Press.

Dawes, R. M. (1998). Behavioral decision making and judgment. In D. Gilbert, S. T. Fiske, & G. Lindzey (Eds.), *Handbook of social psychology* (Vol. 1, 4th ed., pp. 497–549). Boston: McGraw-Hill.

Dawkins, K., & Potter, W. (1991). Gender differences in pharmacokinetics and pharmacodynamics of psychotropics: Focus on women. *Psychopharmacology Bulletin, 27,* 417–426.

Dawson, M., Schell, A. M., & Fillion, D. L. (2000). The electodermal system. In J. Cacioppo, L. Tassinary, & G. Bernston (Eds.), *Handbook of psychophysiology* (2nd ed., pp. 200–222). New York: Cambridge University Press.

Dawson-Basoa, M., & Gintzler, A. R. (1997). Involvement of spinal cord delta opiate receptors in the antinociception of gestation and its hormonal simulation. *Brain Research, 757,* 37–42.

Day, A. L., & Jreige, S. (2002). Examining Type A behavior pattern to explain the relationship between job stressors and psychosocial outcomes. *Journal of Occupational Health Psychology, 7,* 109–120.

de Araujo, I. E., Rolls, E. T., Kringelbach, M. L., McGlone, F., & Phillips, N. (2003). Taste-olfactory convergence, and the representation of the pleasantness of flavour, in the human brain. *European Journal of Neuroscience, 18,* 2059–2068.

De Benedittis, G., Lornenzetti, A., & Pieri, A. (1990). The role of stressful life events in the onset of chronic primary headache. *Pain, 40,* 65–75.

de Castro, J. M., & Goldstein, S. J. (1995). Eating attitudes and behaviors pre- and postpubertal females: Clues to the etiology of eating disorders. *Physiology and Behavior, 58*(1), 15–23.

de Charms, R., Levy, J., & Wertheimer, M. (1954). A note on attempted evaluations of psychotherapy. *Journal of Clinical Psychology, 10,* 233–235.

de Gelder, B., Frissen, I., Barton, J., & Hadjikhani, N. (2003). A modulatory role for facial expressions in prosopagnosia. *Proceedings of the National Academies of Science, 100,* 13105–13110.

De Houwer, A. (1995). Bilingual language acquisition. In P. Fletcher & B. MacWhinney (Eds.), *The handbook of child language* (pp. 219–250). Cambridge, MA: Blackwell.

de Lacoste-Utamsing, C., & Holloway, R. L. (1982). Sexual dimorphism in the human corpus callosum. *Science, 216,* 1431–1432.

De Nil, L. F., Kroll, R. M., & Houle, S. (2001). Functional neuroimaging of cerebellar activation during single word reading and verb generation in stuttering and nonstuttering adults. *Neuroscience Letters, 302,* 77–80.

de Quervain, D. J., Fischbacher, U., Treyer, V., Schellhammer, M., Schnyder, U., Buck, A., & Fehr, E. (2004). The neural basis of altruistic punishment. *Science, 305,* 1254–1258.

De Rios, M. D. (1992). Power and hallucinogenic states of consciousness among the Moche: An ancient Peruvian society. In C. A. Ward (Ed.), *Altered states of consciousness and mental health: A cross-cultural perspective.* Newbury Park, CA: Sage.

DeAngelis, T. (2001). APA has lead role in revising classification system. *Monitor on Psychology, 32,* 54–56.

Deardorff, J. (2004, March 7). Revving up the brain. *Chicago Tribune,* p. Q1.

Deary, I. J., & Caryl, P. G. (1993). Intelligence, EEG and evoked potentials. In P. A. Vernon (Ed.), *Biological approaches to the study of human intelligence* (pp. 259–315). Norwood, NJ: Ablex.

Deary, I. J., Whiteman, M. C., Starr, J. M., Whalley, L. J., & Fox., H. C. (2004). The impact of childhood intelligence on later life: Following up the Scottish mental surveys of 1932 and 1947. *Journal of Personality and Social Psychology, 86,* 130–147.

Deaux, K., & LaFrance, M. (1998). Gender. In D. Gilbert, S. T. Fiske, & G. Lindzey (Eds.), *Handbook of social psychology* (Vol. 1, 4th ed., pp. 778–828). Boston: McGraw-Hill.

DeBeurs, E., van Balkom, A. J. L. M., Lange, A., Koele, P., & van Dyck, R. (1995). Treatment of panic disorder with agoraphobia: Comparison of fluvoxamine, placebo, and psychological panic management combined with exposure and of exposure in vivo alone. *American Journal of Psychiatry, 152*(5), 683–691.

Deci, E. L., Koestner, R., & Ryan, R. M. (2001). A meta-analytic review of experiments examining the effects of extrinsic rewards on intrinsic motivation. *Psychological Bulletin, 125,* 627–668.

DeLisi, L. E., Maurizio, A., Yost, M., Papparozzi, C. F., Fulchino, C., Katz, C. L., et al. (2003). A survey of New Yorkers after the Sept. 11, 2001, terrorist attacks. *American Journal of Psychiatry, 160,* 780–783.

Delmolino, L. M., & Romanczyk, R. G. (1995). Facilitated communication: A critical review. *The Behavior Therapist 18,* 27–30.

Demaray, M. K., & Malecki, C. K. (2002). Critical levels of perceived social support associated with student adjustment. *School Psychology Quarterly, 17,* 213–241.

Dement, W. (1960). The effect of dream deprivation. *Science, 131,* 1705–1707.

Dement, W., & Kleitman, N. (1957). Cyclic variations in EEG during sleep and their relation to eye movements, body motility and dreaming. *Electroencephalography and Clinical Neurophysiology, 9,* 673–690.

Demo, D. H., Allen, K. R., & Fine, M. A. (Eds.). (2000). *Handbook of family diversity.* New York: Oxford University Press.

Denton, G. (1980). The influence of visual pattern on perceived speed. *Perception, 9,* 393–402.

Denton, K., & Krebs, D. (1990). From the scene to the crime: The effect of alcohol and social context on moral judgment. *Journal of Personality and Social Psychology, 59,* 242–248.

DePrince, A. P., & Freyd, J. J. (2004). Forgetting trauma stimuli. *Psychological Science, 15,* 488–492.

Derogowski, J. B. (1989). Real space and represented space: Cross-cultural perspectives. *Behavior and Brain Sciences, 12,* 51–73.

Derrington, A. M., & Webb, B. S. (2004). Visual system: How is the retina wired up to the cortex? *Current Biology, 14,* R14–15.

DeRubeis, R. J., & Crits-Christoph, P. (1998). Empirically supported individual and group psychological treatments for adult mental disorders. *Journal of Consulting and Clinical Psychology, 66,* 37–52.

DeRubeis, R. J., Gelfand, L. A., Tang, T. Z., & Simons, A. D. (1999). Medications versus cognitive behavior therapy for severely depressed outpatients: Mega-analysis of four randomized comparisons. *American Journal of Psychiatry, 156,* 1007–1013.

DeSchepper, B., & Treisman, A. (1996). Visual memory for novel shapes: Implicit coding without attention. *Journal of Experimental Psychology: Learning, Memory and Cognition 22,* 27–47.

Deutsch, M., & Gerard, H. B. (1955). A study of normative and informative social influences on individual judgments. *Journal of Abnormal and Social Psychology, 51,* 629–636.

Devine, P. G. (1989). Stereotypes and prejudice: Their automatic and controlled components. *Journal of Personality and Social Psychology, 56,* 5–18.

Devine, P. G., Plant, E. A., & Buswell, B. N. (2000). Breaking the prejudice habit: Progress and obstacles. In S. Oskamp (Ed.), *Reducing prejudice and discrimination* (pp. 175–190). Hillsdale, NJ: Erlbaum.

Devlin, J. T., Jamison, H. L., Matthews, P. M., & Gonnerman, L. M. (2004). Morphology and the internal structure of words. *Proceedings of the National Academy of Sciences, 101,* 14687–14688.

DeVries, R. (1969). Constancy of generic identity in the years three to six. *Monographs of the Society for Research in Child Development, 34* (3, Serial No. 127).

DeWitt, L. A., & Samuel, A. G. (1990). The role of knowledge-based function in music perception. *Journal of Experimental Psychology: General, 119,* 123–144.

Dhurandhar, N. V., Israel, B. A., Kolesar, J. M., Mayhew, G. F., Cook, M. E., & Atkinson, R. L. (2000). Increased adiposity in animals due to a human virus. *International Journal of Obesity, 24,* 989–996.

Diakidoy, I. N., & Spanoudis, G. (2002). Domain specificity in creativity testing: A comparison of performance on a general divergent-thinking test and a parallel, content-specific test. *Journal of Creative Behavior, 36,* 41–61.

Diamond, L. M. (2004). Emerging perspectives on distinctions between romantic love and sexual desire. *Current Directions in Psychological Science, 13,* 116–119.

Dickinson, A. (2001). Causal learning: Association versus computation. *Current Directions in Psychological Science, 10,* 127–132.

DiClemente, R. J., Wingood, G. M., Harrington, K. F., Lang, D. L., Davies, S. L., Hook, E. W., III, et al. (2004). Efficacy of an HIV prevention intervention for African American adolescent girls: A randomized controlled trial. *Journal of the American Medical Association, 292,* 171–179.

Didier, A., Carleton, A., Bjaalie, J. G., Vincent, J. D., Ottersen, O. P., Storm-Mathisen, J., & Lledo, P. M. (2001). A dendrodendritic reciprocal synapse provides a recurrent excitatory connection in the olfactory bulb. *Proceedings of the National Academy of Science, 98,* 6441–6446.

Diener, E. (2000). Subjective well-being: The science of happiness and a proposal for a national index. *American Psychologist, 55,* 34–43.

Diener, E. (2003). What is positive about positive psychology: The curmudgeon and Pollyanna. *Psychological Inquiry, 14,* 115–120.

Diener, E., & Biswas-Diener, R. (2002). Will money increase subjective well-being? *Social Indicators Research, 57,* 119–169.

Diener, E., & Diener, C. (1995). Most people are happy. *Psychological Science, 7,* 181–185.

Diener, E., & Seligman, M. E. P. (2004). Beyond money: Towards an economy of well-being. *Psychological Science in the Public Interest, 5,* 1–31.

Dinan, T. G. (2002). Lithium in bipolar mood disorder. *British Medical Journal, 324,* 989–990.

Dion, K. (2003). Prejudice, racism and discrimination. In T. Millon & M. Lerner (Eds.) *Handbook of psychology: Volume 5: Personality and social psychology* (pp. 507–536). Hoboken, NJ: Wiley.

Dittmann, M. (2003). Psychology's first prescribers. *Monitor on Psychology, 34,* 36–39.

Ditton, P. M. (1999). *Mental health and treatment of inmates and probationers* (Special Report NCJ 174463). Washington, DC: U.S. Department of Justice.

Dixon, M. J., Smilek, D., & Merikle, P. M. (2004). Not all synaesthetes are created equal: Projector versus associator synaesthetes. *Cognitive, Affective, & Behavioral Neuroscience, 4*(3), 335–343.

Dixon, M., Brunet, A., & Laurence, J.-R. (1990). Hypnotizability and automaticity: Toward a parallel distributed processing model of hypnotic responding. *Journal of Abnormal Psychology, 99,* 336–343.

Dixon, R.A. (2003). Themes in the aging of intelligence: Robust decline with intriguing possibilities. In R.J. Sternberg, J. Lautrey, & T. Lubart (Eds.), *Models of intelligence for the new millennium.* Washington, DC: American Psychological Association.

Dixon, R.A., & de Frais, C.M. (2004). The Victoria Longitudinal Study: From characterizing cognitive aging to illustrating changes in memory compensation. *Aging Neuropsychology, and Cognition, 11,* 346–376.

Dobrovitsky, V., Pimentel, P., Duarte, A., Froestl, W., Stellar, J. R., & Trzcinska, M. (2002). CGP 44532, a GABAB receptor agonist, is hedonically neutral and reduces cocaine-induced enhancement of reward. *Neuropharmacology, 42,* 626–632.

Dobrzecka, C., Szwejkowska, G., & Konorski, J. (1966). Qualitative versus directional cues in two forms of differentiation. *Science, 153,* 87–89.

Dobson, K. S. (Ed.). (2003). *Handbook of cognitive-behavioral therapies* (2nd ed.). New York: Guilford.

Dodson, C., & Reisberg, D. (1991). Indirect testing of eyewitness memory: The (non)effect of misinformation. *Bulletin of the Psychonomic Society, 29,* 333–336.

Dohrenwend, B. P., Raphael, K. G., Schwartz, S., Stueve, A., & Skodol, A. (1993). The structured event probe and narrative rating method for measuring stressful life events. In L. Goldenberger & S. Breznitz (Eds.), *Handbook of stress: Theoretical and clinical aspects* (2nd ed.). New York: The Free Press.

Dolan, M., & Park, I. (2002). The neuropsychology of antisocial personaity disorder. *Psychological Medicine, 32,* 417–427.

Dollinger, S. J. (2000). Locus of control and incidental learning: An application to college students. *College Student Journal, 34,* 537–540.

Domhoff, G. W. (1996). *Finding meaning in dreams: A quantitative approach.* New York: Plenum.

Domhoff, G. W. (2001). A new neurocognitive theory of dreams. *Dreaming: Journal of the Association for the Study of Dreams, 11,* 13–33.

Donegan, N. H., & Thompson, R. F. (1991). The search for the engram. In J. L. Martinez & R. P. Kesner (Eds.), *Learning and memory: A biological view* (2nd ed.). San Diego: Academic Press.

Donnerstein, E., Slaby, R. G., & Eron, L. D. (1995). The mass media and youth aggression. In L. Eron, J. Gentry, & P. Schlegel (Eds.), *Reason to hope: A psychosocial perspective on violence and youth* (pp. 219–250). Washington, DC: American Psychological Association.

Dorion, J.P. & Nicki, R.M. (2001). Epidemiology of gambling on Prince Edward Island: A Canadian microcosm? *Canadian Journal of Psychiatry, 46,* 413–417.

Dougall, A. L., Craig, K. J., & Baum, A. S. (1999). Assessment of characteristics of intrusive thoughts and their impact on distress among victims of traumatic events. *Psychosomatic Medicine, 61,* 38–48.

Dougherty, D. D., Baer, L., Cosgrove, G. R., Cassem, E. H., Price, B. H., Nierenberg, A. A., et al. (2002). Prospective long-term follow-up of 44 patients who received cingulotomy for treatment-refractory obsessive-compulsive disorder. *American Journal of Psychiatry, 159,* 269–275.

Dovidio, J. F., & Gaertner, S. L. (1998). On the nature of contemporary prejudice: The causes, consequences, and challenges of aversive racism. In J. L. Eberhardt & S. T. Fiske (Eds.), *Confronting racism: The problem and the response* (pp. 3–32). Thousand Oaks, CA: Sage.

Dovidio, J. F., & Gaertner, S. L. (2000). Aversive racism and selection decisions: 1989 and 1999. *Psychological Science, 11,* 319–323.

Dovidio, J. F., & Penner, L. A. (2001). Helping and altruism. In G. Fletcher & M. Clark (Eds.), *Blackwell handbook of social psychology: Interpersonal processes* (pp. 162–195). Boston: Blackwell.

Dovidio, J. F., Gaertner, S. L., & Kawakami, K. (2003). Intergroup contact: The past, present, and the future. *Group Processes and Intergroup Relations, 6,* 5–20.

Dovidio, J. F., Kawakami, K., & Beach, K. R. (2001). Implicit and explicit attitudes: Examination of the relationship between measures of intergroup bias. In R. Brown & S. Gaertner (Eds.), *Blackwell handbook of social psychology: Vol. 4. Intergroup relations* (pp. 175–197). Oxford, England: Blackwell.

Dovidio, J. F., Kawakami, K., & Gaertner, S. L. (2000). Reducing contemporary prejudice: Combating explicit and implicit bias at the individual and intergroup level. In S. Oskamp (Ed.), *Reducing prejudice and discrimination* (pp. 137–163). Hillsdale, NJ: Erlbaum.

Dovidio, J. F., Piliavin, J. A., Gaertner, S. L., Schroeder, D. A., & Clark, R. D., III. (1991). The arousal: cost-reward model and the process of intervention: A review of the evidence. In M. Clark (Ed.), *Review of personality and social psychology: Vol. 12. Prosocial behavior* (pp. 86–118). Newbury Park, CA: Sage.

Dovidio, J. F., Smith, J. K., Donnella, A. G., & Gaertner, S. L. (1997). Racial attitudes and the death penalty. *Journal of Applied Social Psychology, 27,* 1468–1487.

Downey-Lamb, M. M., & Woodruff-Pak, D. S. (1999). Early detection of cognitive deficits using eyeblink classical conditioning. *Alzheimer's Reports, 2,* 37–44.

Downing, J. E., & Miyan, J. A. (2000). Neural immunoregulation: Emerging roles for nerves in immune homeostasis and disease. *Immunology Today, 21,* 281–289.

Dowson, D. I., Lewith, G. T., & Machin, D. (1985). The effects of acupuncture versus placebo in the treatment of headache. *Pain, 21,* 35–42.

Draganski, B., Gaser, C., Busch, V., Schuierer, G., Bogdahn, U., & May, A. (2004). Neuroplasticity: Changes in grey matter induced by training. *Nature, 427,* 311–312.

Drayna, D., Manichaikul, A., de Lange, M., Snieder, H., & Spector, T. (2001). Genetic correlates of musical pitch recognition in humans. *Science, 291,* 1969–1972.

Dresner, R., & Grolnick, W. S. (1996). Constructions of early parenting, intimacy and autonomy in young women. *Journal of Social and Personal Relationships, 13,* 25–40.

Dreyfus, H. L., & Dreyfus, S. E. (1988). Making a mind versus modeling the brain: Intelligence back at a branchpoint. In S. R. Graubard (Ed.), *The artificial intelligence debate.* Cambridge: MIT Press.

Driscoll, M., & Gerstbrein, B. (2003). Dying for a cause: Invertebrate genetics takes on human neurodegeneration. *Nature Reviews Genetics, 4,* 181–194.

Druckman, D., & Bjork, R. A. (1994). *Learning, remembering, believing: Enhancing human performance.* Washington, DC: National Academy Press.

Drummond, S. P., Brown, G. G., Gillin, J. C., Stricker, J. L., Wong, E. C., & Buxton, R. B. (2000). Altered brain response to verbal learning following sleep deprivation. *Nature, 403,* 655–657.

Druss, B. G., Rosenheck, R. A., & Sledge, W. H. (2000). Health and disability costs of depressive illness in a major U.S. Corporation. *American Journal of Psychiatry, 157,* 1274–1278.

DuBois, D. L., Felner, R. D., Brand, S., Adan, A. M., & Evans, E. G. (1992). A prospective study of life stress, social support, and adaptation in early adolescence. *Child Development, 63,* 542–557.

DuBreuil, S. C., Garry, M., & Loftus, E. F. (1998). Tales from the crib: Memories of infancy. In S. J. Lynn, & K. M. McConkey (Eds.), *Truth in memory* (pp. 137–160). New York: Guilford.

Duckitt, J. H. (1994). *The social psychology of prejudice.* Westport, CT: Praeger.

Dudai, Y. (2004). The neurobiology of consolidations, or, how stable is the engram? *Annual Review of Psychology, 55,* 51–86.

Duffy, V. B., Fast, K., Cohen Z., Chodos, E., and Bartoshuk, L. M. (1999). Genetic taste status associates with fat food acceptance and body mass index in adults. *Chemical Senses, 24,* 545–546.

Dujovne, V., & Houston, B. (1991). Hostility-related variables and plasma lipid levels. *Journal of Behavioral Medicine, 14,* 555–564.

Duke, C. R., & Carlson, L. (1994). Applying implicit memory measures: Word fragment completion in advertising tests. *Journal of Current Issues and Research in Advertising, 15,* 1–14.

Dumont, F., & Corsini, R. J. (2000). *Six therapists and one client.* New York: Springer.

Duncan, B. L. (2002). The legacy of Saul Rosenwieg: The profundity of the dodo bird. *Journal of Psychotherapy Integration, 12*(1), 32–57.

Duncan, G. J., Brooks-Gunn, J., & Klebanov, P. K. (1994). Economic deprivation and early childhood development. *Child Development, 65,* 296–318.

Duncan, J., & Owen, A. M. (2000). Common regions of the human frontal lobe recruited by diverse cognitive demands. *Trends in Neurosciences, 23,* 475–483.

Dunn, J., & Hughes, C. (2001). "I got some swords and you're dead!": Violent fantasy, antisocial behavior, friendship, and moral sensibility in young children. *Child Development, 72,* 491–505.

Dunn, J., Brown, H., Slomkowski, C., Tesla, C., & Youngblade, L. (1991). Young children's understanding of other people's feelings and beliefs: Individual differences and their antecedents. *Child Development, 62,* 1352–1366.

Dunne, E., & Fitzpatrick, A. C. (1999). The views of professionals on the role of self-help groups in the mental health area. *Irish Journal of Psychological Medicine, 16,* 84–89.

Dutton, D. G., & Aron, A. P. (1974). Some evidence for heightened sexual attraction under conditions of high anxiety. *Journal of Personality and Social Psychology, 30,* 510–517.

Düzel, E., Vargha-Khamdem, F., Heinze, H. J., & Mishkin, M. (2001). Brain activity evidence for recognition without recollection after early hippocampal damage. *Proceedings of the National Academy of Science, 98,* 8101–8106.

Dweck, C. S. (1998). The development of early self-conceptions: Their relevance for motivational processes. In J. Heckhausen & C. S. Dweck (Eds.), *Motivation and self-regulation across the life span.* New York: Cambridge University Press.

Dyche, L., & Zayas, L. H. (2001). Cross-cultural empathy and training the contemporary psychotherapist. *Clinical Social Work Journal, 29,* 245–258.

Eagly, A. H. (1987). *Sex differences in social behavior: A social-role interpretation.* Hillsdale, NJ: Erlbaum.

Eagly, A. H. (1996). Differences between women and men: Their magnitude, practical importance, and political meaning. *American Psychologist, 51,* 158–159.

Eagly, A. H., & Chaiken, S. (1998). Attitude structure and function. In D. Gilbert, S. T. Fiske, & G. Lindzey (Eds.), *Handbook of social psychology* (Vol. 1, 4th ed., pp. 269–322). Boston: McGraw-Hill.

Eagly, A. H., & Wood, W. (1999). The orgins of sex diffrences in human behavior: Evolved dispositions versus social roles. *American Psychologist, 54,* 408–423.

East, P. L., & Jacobson, L. J. (2001). The younger siblings of teenage mothers: A follow-up of their pregnancy risk. *Developmental Psychology, 37,* 254–264.

Easterbrook, M.A., Kisilevsky, B.S., Muir, D.W., & Laplante, D.P. (1999). Newborns discriminate schematic faces from scrambled faces. *Canadian Journal of Experimental Psychology, 53,* 231–241.

Eaton, M. J., & Dembo, M. H. (1997). Differences in the motivational beliefs of Asian American and non-Asian students. *Journal of Educational Psychology, 89,* 433–440.

Ebert, S. A., Tucker, D. C., & Roth, D. L. (2002). Psychological resistance factors as predictors of general health status and physical symptom reporting. *Psychology Health & Medicine, 7,* 363–375.

Eberts, R., & MacMillan, A. C. (1985). Misperception of small cars. In R. Eberts & C. Eberts (Eds.), *Trends in ergonomics/human factors* (Vol. 2, pp. 30–39). Amsterdam: Elsevier.

Echeburua, E., de Corral, P., Garcia Bajos, E., & Borda, M. (1993). Interactions between self-exposure and alprazolam in the treatment of agoraphobia without current panic: An exploratory study. *Behavioural and Cognitive Psychotherapy, 21,* 219–238.

Edinger, J. D., Wohlgemuth, W. K., Radtke, R. A., Marsh, G. R., & Quillian, R. E. (2001). Cognitive behavioral therapy for treatment of chronic primary insomnia. *American Medical Association, 285,* 1856–1864.

Edwards, A. E., & Acker, L. E. (1972). A demonstration of the long-term retention of a conditioned GSR. *Psychosomatic Science, 26,* 27–28.

Edwards, G. (1987). The alcohol dependence syndrome: A concept as stimulus to enquiry. *British Journal of Addiction, 81,* 171–183.

Egbert, L. D., Battit, G. E., Welch, C. E., & Bartlett, M. K. (1964). Reduction of post-operative pain by encouragement and instruction of patients: A study of doctor-patient rapport. *New England Journal of Medicine, 270,* 825–827.

Egeland, J. A., Gerhard, D. S., Pauls, D. L., Sussex, J. N., Kidd, K. K., Allen, C. R., et al. (1987). Bipolar affective disorders linked to DNA markers on chromosome 11. *Nature, 325,* 783–787.

Ehlers, A. (1995). A 1-year prospective study of panic attacks: Clinical course and factors associated with maintenance. *Journal of Abnormal Psychology, 104,* 164–172.

Ehrensaft, M. K., Cohen, P., Brown, J., Smailes, E., Chen, H., & Johnson, J. G. (2003). Intergenerational transmission of partner violence: A 20-year prospective study. *Journal of Consulting and Clinical Psychology, 71,* 741–753.

Ehrlichman, H., & Halpern, J. N. (1988). Affect and memory: Effects of pleasant and unpleasant odors on retrieval of happy and unhappy memories. *Journal of Personality and Social Psychology, 55,* 769–779.

Eich, E. (1989). Theoretical issues in state dependent memory. In H. L. Roediger & F. I. M. Craik (Eds.), *Varieties of memory and consciousness.* Hillsdale, NJ: Erlbaum.

Eich, E., & Macaulay, D. (2000). Are real moods required to reveal mood-congruent and mood-dependent memory? *Psychological Science, 11,* 244–248.

Eich, E., & Metcalfe, J. (1989). Mood dependent memory for internal versus external events. *Experimental Psychology: Learning, Memory, and Cognition, 15,* 443–455.

Eich, J. E., Weingartner, H., Stillman, R. C., & Gillin, J. C. (1975). State dependent accessibility of retrieval cues in the retention of a categorized list. *Journal of Verbal Learning and Verbal Behavior, 14,* 408–417.

Eichorn, D. H., Clausen, J. A., Haan, N., Honzik, M. P., & Mussen, P. H. (1981). *Present and past in middle life.* New York: Academic Press.

Einhorn, H., & Hogarth, R. (1982). Prediction, diagnosis and causal thinking in forecasting. *Journal of Forecasting, 1,* 23–36.

Eisenberg, N. (1997, June). Consistent parenting helps children regulate emotions. *APA Monitor,* p. 17.

Eisenberg, N. (1998). Introduction. In W. Damon & N. Eisenberg (Eds.), *Handbook of child psychology: Vol. 3. Social, emotional, and personality development* (5th ed., pp. 1–24). New York: Wiley.

Eisenberg, N., & Fabes, R. A. (1998). Prosocial development. In W. Damon & N. Eisenberg (Eds.), *Handbook of child psychology: Vol. 3. Social, emotional, and personality development* (5th ed., pp. 701–778). New York: Wiley.

Eisenberg, N., Fabes, R. A., & Murphy, B. C. (1995). Relations of shyness and low sociability to regulation and emotionality. *Journal of Personality and Social Psychology, 68,* 505–518.

Eisenberg, N., Guthrie, I. K., Cumberland, A., Murphy, B. C., Shepard, S. A., Zhou, Q., et al. (2002). Prosocial development in early adulthood: A longitudinal study. *Journal of Personality and Social Psychology, 82,* 993–1006.

Eisenberg, N., Spinrad, T. L., Fabes, R. A., Reiser, M., Cumberland, A., Shepard, S. A., et al. (2004). The relations of effortful control and impulsivity to children's resiliency and adjustment. *Child Development, 75,* 25–46.

Eisenberger, R., & Rhoades, L. (2001). Incremental effects of reward on creativity. *Journal of Personality and Social Psychology, 81,* 728–741.

Eisenberger, R., & Shanock, L. (2003). Rewards, intrinsic motivation, and creativity: A case study of conceptual and methodological isolation. *Creativity Research Journal, 15,* 121–130.

Ekman, P. (1993). Facial expression and emotion. *American Psychologist, 48,* 384–392.

Ekman, P. (1994). Strong evidence for universals in facial expressions: A reply to Russell's mistaken critique. *Psychological Bulletin, 115*(2), 268–287.

Ekman, P., & Davidson, R. J. (1993). Voluntary smiling changes regional brain activity. *Psychological Science, 4*(5), 342–345.

Ekman, P., Friesen, W. V., & Ellsworth, P. (1972). *Emotion in the human face: Guidelines for research and a review of findings.* New York: Pergamon Press.

Ekman, P., Levenson, R. W., & Friesen, W. V. (1983). Autonomic nervous system activity distinguishes among emotions. *Science, 221,* 1208–1210.

El Yacoubi, M., Bouali, S., Popa, D., Naudon, L., Leroux-Nicollet, I., Hamon, M., et al. (2003). Behavioral, neurochemical, and electrophysiological characterization of a genetic mouse model of depression. *Proceedings of the National Academy of Sciences, 100,* 6227–6232.

Elashoff, J. D. (1979). Box scores are for baseball. *Brain and Behavioral Sciences, 3,* 392.

Eliot, A. J., Chirkov, V. I., Kim, Y., & Shelldon, K. M. (2001). A cross-cultural analysis of avoidance (relative to approach) personal goals. *Psychological Science, 12,* 505–510.

Elkin, I. (1994). The NIMH treatment of depression collaborative research program: Where we began and where we are. In A. E. Bergin & S. L. Garfield (Eds.), *Handbook of psychotherapy and behavior change* (pp. 114–139). New York: Wiley.

Elkin, I. (1999). A major dilemma in psychotherapy outcome research: Disentangling therapists from therapies. *Clinical Psychology: Science and Practice, 6,* 10–32.

Elliot, A. J., & Devine, P. G. (1994). On the motivational nature of cognitive dissonance: Dissonance as psychological discomfort. *Journal of Personality and Social Psychology, 67,* 382–394.

Elliott, C. L., & Greene, R. L. (1992). Clinical depression and implicit memory. *Journal of Abnormal Psychology, 101,* 572–574.

Elliott, R., Rubinsztein, J. S., Sahakian, B. J., & Dolan, R. J. (2002). The neural basis of mood-congruent processing biases in depression. *Archives of General Psychiatry, 59,* 597–604.

Elliott, R., Watson, J. C., & Goldman, R. N. (2004a). Empty chair work for unfinished interpersonal issues. In R. Elliott & J. Watson (Eds.), *Learning emotion-focused therapy: The process-experiential approach to change* (pp. 243–265). Washington, DC: American Psychological Association.

Elliott, R., Watson, J. C., & Goldman, R. N. (2004b). Two-chair work for conflict splits. In R. Elliott & J. Watson (Eds.), *Learning emotion-focused therapy: The process-experiential approach to change* (pp. 219–241). Washington, DC: American Psychological Association. Ellis, A. (1962). *Reason and emotion in psychotherapy.* New York: Lyle Stuart.

Ellis, A. (1962). *Reason and emotion in psychotherapy.* New York: Lyle Stuart.

Ellis, A. (1993). Reflections on rational-emotive therapy. *Journal of Consulting and Clinical Psychology, 61,* 199–201.

Ellis, A. (1995). Rational emotive behavior therapy. In R. J. Corsini & D. Wedding (Eds.), *Current psychotherapies* (5th ed., pp. 162–196). Itasca, IL: Peacock.

Ellis, A. (1997). Using rational emotive behavior therapy techniques to cope with disability. *Professional Psychology: Research and Practice, 28,* 17–22.

Ellis, A. (2004a). Why I (really) became a therapist. *Journal of Rational-Emotive and Cognitive Behavior Therapy, 22*(2), 73–77.

Ellis, A. (2004b). Why rational emotive behavior therapy is the most comprehensive and effective form of behavior therapy. *Journal of Rational-Emotive and Cognitive Behavior Therapy, 22*(2), 85–92.

Ellis, A. L., & Mitchell, R. W. (2000). Sexual orientation. In L. T. Szuchman & F. Muscarella (Eds.), *Psychological perspectives on human sexuality* (pp. 196–231). New York: Wiley.

Ellis, N. R. (1991). Automatic and effortful processes in memory for spatial location. *Bulletin of the Psychonomic Society, 29,* 28–30.

Elovainio, M., Kivimäki, M., & Vahtera, J. (2002). Organizational justice: Evidence on a new psychosocial predictor of health. *American Journal of Public Health, 92,* 105–108.

Emery, D. (2004). *Sucking on a penny will fool a breathalyzer test: An urban legend.* Retrieved December 13, 2004, from http://urbanlegends.about.com/library/bl_breathalyzer_penny.htm

Emery, G. (2004). Voice of Reason: Predictions for 2004 Revisited. *Skeptical Inquirer.* Retrieved March 23, 2006, from www.csicop.org/specialarticles/predictions-2004.html

Ende, G., Braus, D. F., Walter, S., Weber-Fahr, W., & Henn, F. A. (2000). The hippocampus in patients treated with electroconvulsive therapy. *Archives of General Psychiatry, 57,* 937–943.

Engebretson, T. O., & Stoney, C. M. (1995). Anger expression and lipid concentrations. *International Journal of Behavioral Medicine, 2,* 281–298.

Engel, A. K., Konig, P., Kreiter, A. K., Schillen, T. B., & Singer, W. (1992). Temporal coding in the visual cortex: New vistas on integration in the nervous system. *Trends in Neuroscience, 15,* 218–226.

Engel, S., Zhang, X., & Wandell, B. (1997). Colour tuning in human visual cortex measured with functional magnetic resonance imaging. *Nature, 388,* 68–71.

Engeland, H. V. (1993). Pharmacotherapy and behaviour therapy: Competition or cooperation? *Acta Paedopsychiatrica International Journal of Child and Adolescent Psychiatry, 56*(2), 123–127.

Engen, T., Gilmore, M. M., & Mair, R. G. (1991). Odor memory. In T. V. Getchell et al. (Eds.), *Taste and smell in health and disease.* New York: Raven Press.

Engle, R. W., & Oransky, N. (1999). The evolution from short-term to working memory: Multi-store to dynamic models of temporary storage. In R. Sternberg (Ed.), *The nature of human cognition* (pp. 514–555). Cambridge: MIT Press.

Engler, B. (2003). *Personality theories: An introduction* (6th ed.). Boston: Houghton Mifflin.

Enns, M.W & Reiss, J. P. (2006). Electroconvulsive therapy [Electronic version]. *Canadian Psychiatric Association – Position Paper.* Available: http://www.cpa-apc.org/Publications/Position_Papers/Therapy.asp

Enoch, M. A.(2003). Pharmacogenomics of alcohol response and addiction. *American Journal of Pharmacogenomics, 3,* 217–232.

Enright, R. D., Lapsley, D. K., & Levy, V. M., Jr. (1983). Moral education strategies. In M. Pressley & J. R. Levin (Eds.), *Cognitive strategy research: Educational application.* New York: Springer-Verlag.

Epping-Jordan, M. P., Watkins, S. S., Koob, G. F., & Markou, A. (1998). Dramatic decreases in brain reward function during nicotine withdrawal. *Nature, 393,* 76–79.

Epstein, L. H., Valoski, A., Wing., R. R., & McCurley, J. (1994). Ten-year outcomes of behavioral family-based treatment for childhood obesity. *Health Psychology, 13,* 373–383.

Erdberg, P. (1990). Rorschach assessment. In G. Goldstein & M. Hersen (Eds.), *Psychological assessment* (2nd ed.). New York: Pergamon Press.

Erdelyi, M. H. (1985). *Psychoanalysis: Freud's cognitive psychology.* San Francisco: Freeman.

Ericsson, K. A., & Simon, H. A. (1994). *Protocol analysis: Verbal reports as data* (Rev. ed.). Cambridge, MA: MIT Press.

Ericsson, K. A., & Staszewski, J. (1989). Skilled memory and expertise: Mechanisms of exceptional performance. In D. Klahr & K. Kotovsky (Eds.), *Complex information processing: The impact of Herbert A. Simon.* Hillsdale, NJ: Erlbaum.

Erikson, E. H. (1968). *Identity: Youth and crisis.* New York: Norton.

Eriksson, P. S., Perfilieva, E., Bjork-Eriksson, T., Alborn, A. M., Nordborg, C., Peterson, D. A., & Gage, F. H. (1998). Neurogenesis in the adult human hippocampus. *Nature Medicine, 4,* 1313–1317.

Eron, L. D., Huesmann, L. R., Lefkowitz, M. M., & Walder, L. O. (1996). Does television violence cause aggression? In D. F. Greenberg (Ed.), *Criminal careers: Vol. 2. The international library of criminology, criminal justice and penology* (pp. 311–321). Aldershot, UK: Dartmouth.

Essock, E. A., Sinai, M. J., McCarley J. S., Krebs, W. K., & DeFord, J. K. (1999). Perceptual ability with real-world nighttime scenes: Image-intensified, infrared, and fused-color imagery *Human Factors, 41,* 438–452.

Esterson, A. (2001). The mythologizing of psychoanalytic history: Deception and self-deception in Freud's account of the seduction theory episode. *History of Psychiatry, 12,* 329–352.

Evans, G. W., Wells, N. M., Chan, H.-Y. E., & Saltzman, H. (2000). Housing quality and mental health. *Journal of Consulting and Clinical Psychology, 68,* 526–530.

Evans, J. St. B. T., Handley, S. J., Harper, C. N. J., & Johnson-Laird, P. N. (1999). Reasoning about necessity and possibility: A test of the mental model theory of deduction. *Journal of Experimental Psychology: Learning, Memory, and Cognition, 25,* 1495–1513.

Evans, R. B. (2003). Georg von Bekesy: Visualization of hearing. *American Psychologist, 58,* 742–746.

Everaerd, W., & Laan, E. (1994). Cognitive aspects of sexual functioning and dysfunctioning. *Sexual and Marital Therapy, 9,* 225–230.

Everett, S. A., Warren, C. W., Santelli, J. S., Kann, L., Collins, J. L., & Kolbe, L. J. (2000). Use of birth control pills, condoms, and withdrawal among U.S. high school students. *Journal of Adolescent Health, 27,* 112–118.

Exner, J. E., Jr., & Ona, N. (1995). *RIAP-3: Rorschach Interpretation Assistance Program—version 3.* Odessa, FL: Psychological Assessment Resources.

Exton, M. S., von Auer, A. K., Buske-Kirschbaum, A., Stockhorst, U., Gobel, U., & Schedlowski, M. (2000). Pavlovian conditioning of immune function: animal investigation and the challenge of human application. *Behavior and Brain Research, 110,* 129–141.

Eysenck, H. J. (1952). The effects of psychotherapy: An evaluation. *Journal of Consulting Psychology, 16,* 319–324.

Eysenck, H. J. (1961). The effects of psychotherapy. In H. J. Eysenck (Ed.), *Handbook of abnormal psychology.* New York: Basic Books.

Eysenck, H. J. (1966). *The effects of psychotherapy.* New York: International Science Press.

Eysenck, H. J. (1978). An exercise in mega-silliness. *American Psychologist, 33,* 517.

Eysenck, H. J. (1986). What is intelligence? In R. J. Sternberg & D. K. Detterman (Eds.), *What is intelligence? Contemporary viewpoints on its nature and definition.* Norwood, NJ: Ablex.

Eysenck, H. J. (1987). Speed of information processing, reaction time, and the theory of intelligence. In P. A. Vernon (Ed.), *Speed of information-processing and intelligence* (pp. 21–67). Norwood, NJ: Ablex.

Eysenck, H. J. (1990a). Biological dimensions of personality. In L. A. Pervin (Ed.), *Handbook of personality: Theory and research* (pp. 244–276). New York: Guilford.

Eysenck, H. J. (1990b). Genetic and environmental contributions to individual differences: The three major dimensions of personality. *Journal of Personality, 58,* 245–261.

Eysenck, H. J. (1994). A biological theory of intelligence. In D. K. Detterman (Ed.), *Current topics in human intelligence* (Vol. 4). Norwood, NJ: Ablex.

Eysenck, M. W., & Keane, M. T. (1995). *Cognitive psychology: A student's handbook* (3rd ed.). Hillsdale, NJ: Erlbaum.

Fabes, R. A., Martin, C. L., & Hanish, L. D. (2003). Young children's qualities in same-, other-, and mixed-sex peer groups. *Child Development, 74,* 921–932.

Fabes, R. A., Shepard, S. A., Guthrie, I. K., & Martin, C. L. (1997). Roles of temperamental arousal and gender-segregated play in young children's social adjustment. *Developmental Psychology, 33,* 693–702.

Faedda, G., Tondo, L., Teicher, M., Baldessarini, R., Gelbard, H., & Floris, G. (1993). Seasonal mood disorders: Patterns of seasonal recurrence in mania and depression. *Archives of General Psychiatry, 50,* 17–23.

Fagan, J. F. (2000). A theory of intelligence as processing. *Psychology, Public Policy, and Law, 26,* 168–179.

Fagot, B. I. (1995). Psychosocial and cognitive determinants of early gender-role development. *Annual Review of Sex Research, 6,* 1–31.

Fagot, B. I. (1997). Attachment, parenting, and peer interactions of toddler children. *Developmental Psychology, 33,* 489–499.

Fagot, B. I., & Gauvain, M. (1997). Mother-child problem solving: Continuity through the early childhood years. *Developmental Psychology, 33,* 480–488.

Fahsing, I. A., Ask, K., & Granhag, P. A. (2004). The man behind the mask: Accuracy and predictors of eyewitness offender descriptions. *Journal of Applied Psychology, 89,* 722–729.

Fairweather, G. W., & Fergus, E. O. (1993). *Empowering the mentally ill.* Austin: Fairweather.

Farah, M. J. (2000). *The cognitive neuroscience of vision.* Malden, MA: Blackwell.

Farah, M. J., Illes, J., Cook-Deegan, R., Gardner, H., Kandel, E., King, P., et al. (2004). Science and society: Neurocognitive enhancement: What can we do and what should we do? *Nature Reviews Neuroscience, 5,* 421–425.

Farberman, R. (1999, February). As managed care grows, public unhappiness rises. *APA Monitor,* p. 14.

Farley, F (1986). The big T in personality. *Psychology Today, 20,* 44–52.

Farooqi, I. S., & O'Rahilly, S. (2004). Monogenic human obesity syndromes. *Recent Progress in Hormone Research, 59,* 409–424.

Farooqi, I. S., Jebb, S. A., Langmack, G., Lawrence, E., Cheetham, C. H., Prentice, A. M., et al. (1999). Effects of recombinant leptin therapy in a child with congenital leptin deficiency. *New England Journal of Medicine, 341,* 879–884.

Farooqi, I. S., Keogh, J. M., Kamath, S., Jones, S., Gibson, W. T., Trussel, R., et al. (2001). Metabolism: Partial leptin deficiency and human adiposity. *Nature, 414,* 34–35.

Farroni, T., Csibra, G., Simion, F., & Johnson, M. H. (2002). Eye contact detection in humans from birth. *Proceedings of the National Academy of Science, 99,* 9602–9605.

Fassler, D. G., & Dumas, L. S. (1997). *Help me, I'm sad: Recognizing, treating, and preventing childhood depression.* New York: Viking Press.

Faulkner, M. (2001). The onset and alleviation of learned helplessness in older hospitalized people. *Aging & Mental Health, 5,* 379–386.

Faust, J., Olson, R., & Rodriguez, H. (1991). Same-day surgery preparation: Reduction of pediatric patient arousal and distress through participant modeling. *Journal of Consulting and Clinical Psychology, 59,* 475–478.

Faymonville, M. E., Laureys, S., Degueldre, C., DelFiore, G., Luxen, A., Franck, G., et al. (2000). Neural mechanisms of antinociceptive effects of hypnosis. *Anesthesiology, 92,* 1257–1267.

Feder, B. J. (2004, May 31). Technology strains to find menace in the crowd. *The New York Times,* p. C1.

Feinberg, L., & Campbell, I. G. (1993). Total sleep deprivation in the rat transiently abolishes the delta amplitude response to darkness: Implications for the mechanism of the "negative delta rebound." *Journal of Neurophysiology, 70*(6) 2695–2699.

Feingold, A., & Mazzella, R. (1998). Gender differences in body image are increasing. *Psychological Science, 9,* 190–195.

Feldman, D. C., & Turnley, W. H. (2004). Contingent employment in academic careers: Relative deprivation among adjunct faculty. *Journal of Vocational Behavior, 64,* 284–307.

Feldman, R. P., & Goodrich, J. T. (2001). Psychosurgery: A historical overview. *Neurosurgery, 48,* 647–657.

Felten, D. L., Cohen, N., Ader, R., Felten, S. Y., Carlson, S. L., & Roszman, T. L. (1991). Central neural circuits involved in neural-immune interactions. In R. Ader (Ed.), *Psychoneuroimmunology* (2nd ed.). New York: Academic Press.

Felten, S. Y., Madden, K. S., Bellinger, D. L., Kruszewska, B., Moynihan, J. A., & Felten, D. L. (1998). The role of the sympathetic nervous system in the modulation of immune responses. *Advances in Pharmacology, 42,* 583–587.

Feltham, C. (2000). What are counselling and psychotherapy? In C. Feltham and I. Horton (Eds.), *Handbook of counselling and psychotherapy.* London: Sage.

Feng, R., Wang, H., Wang, J., Shrom, D., Zeng, X., & Tsien, J. Z. (2004). Forebrain degeneration and ventricle enlargement caused by double knockout of Alzheimer's presenilin-1 and presenilin-2. *Proceedings of the National Academy of Sciences, 101,* 8162–8167.

Feng-Chen, K. C., & Wolpaw, J. R. (1996). Operant conditioning of H-reflex changes synaptic terminals on primate motoneurons. *Proceedings of the National Academy of Science USA, 93,* 9206–9211.

Fenn, K. M., Nusbaum, H. C., & Margoliash, D. (2003). Consolidation during sleep of perceptual learning of spoken language. *Nature, 425,* 614–616.

Fenson, L., Dale, P. S., Reznick, J. S., & Bates, E. (1994). Variability in early communicative development. *Monographs of the Society for Research in Child Development, 59,* 173.

Fenton, W. S., & McGlashan, T. H. (1991). Natural history of schizophrenia subtypes: 1. Longitudinal study of paranoid, hebephrenic, and undifferentiated schizophrenia. *Archives of General Psychiatry, 48,* 969–977.

Fenton, W. S., & McGlashan, T. H. (1994). Antecedent, symptoms progression, and long-term outcome of the deficit syndrome in schizophrenia. *American Journal of Psychiatry, 151,* 351–356.

Ferguson, C. J. (2002). Media violence: Miscast causality. *American Psychologist, 57,* 446–447.

Fergusson, D. M., & Horwood, L. J. (1997). Early onset cannabis use and psychosocial adjustment in young adults. *Addiction, 92,* 279–296.

Fergusson, D., Glass, K. C., Waring, D., & Shapiro, S. (2004). Turning a blind eye: The success of blinding reported in a random sample of randomised, placebo controlled trials. *British Medical Journal, 328,* 432.

Fernández-Dols, J.-M. & Ruiz-Belda, M.-A. (1995). Are smiles a sign of happiness?: Gold medal winners at the Olympic Games. *Journal of Personality and Social Psychology, 69,* 1113–1119.

Ferraro, R., Lillioja, S., Fontvieille, A. M., Rising, R., Bogardus, C., & Ravussin, E. (1992). Lower sedentary metabolic rate in women compared with men. *Journal of Clinical Investigation, 90,* 780–784.

Festinger, L. (1954). A theory of social comparison processes. *Human Relations, 7,* 117–140.

Festinger, L. (1957). *A theory of cognitive dissonance.* Evanston, IL: Row, Petersen.

Festinger, L., & Carlsmith, J. M. (1959). Cognitive consequences of forced compliance. *Journal of Abnormal and Social Psychology, 58,* 203–210.

Field, A. E., Coakley, E. H., Must, A., Spadano, J. L., Laird, N., Dietz, W. H., Rimm, E., & Colditz, G. A. (2001). Impact of overweight on the risk of developing common chronic diseases during a 10-year period. *Archives of Internal Medicine, 161,* 1581–1586.

Field, T., Henteleff, T., Hernandez-Reif, M., Martinez, E., Mavunda, K., Kuhn, C., & Schangerg, S. (1998). Children with asthma have improved pulmonary functions after massage therapy. *Journal of Pediatrics, 132,* 854–858.

Field, T., Hernandez-Reif, M., Seligman, S., Krasnegor, J., Sunshine, W., Rivas-Chacon, R., et al. (1997). Juvenile rheumatoid arthritis: Benefits from massage therapy. *Journal of Pediatric Psychology, 22,* 607–617.

Field, T., Ironson, G., Scafidi, F., Nawrocki, T., Gonclaves, A., Burman, I., et al. (1996). Massage therapy reduces anxiety and enhances EEG pattern of alertness and math computations. *International Journal of Neuroscience, 86,* 197–205.

Fielder, W. R, Cohen, R. D., & Feeney, S. (1971). An attempt to replicate the teacher expectancy effect. *Psychological Reports, 29,* 1223–1228.

Fink, M. (1999). *Electroshock: Restoring the mind.* New York: Oxford University Press.

Finkel, D., Reynolds, C. A., McArle, J. J., Gatz, M., & Pedersen, N. L. (2003). Latent growth curve analyses of accelerating decline in cognitive abilities in late adulthood. *Developmental Psychology, 39,* 535–550.

Finn-Stevenson, M. & Zigler, E. (1999). *School of 21st century: Linking child care and education.* Boulder, CO: Westview Press.

Firestein, S. (2001). How the olfactory system makes sense of scents. *Nature, 413,* 211–218.

First, M. B., Pincus, H. A., Levine, J. B., Williams, J. B. W., Ustun, B., & Peele, R. (2004). Clinical utility as a criterion for revising psychiatric diagnoses. *American Journal of Psychiatry, 161,* 946–954.

Fischer, K. W., & Bidell, T. (1991). Constraining nativist inferences about cognitive capacities. In S. Carey & R. Gelman (Eds.), *The epigenesis of mind: Essays on biology and cognition* (pp. 199–235). Hillsdale, NJ: Erlbaum.

Fischer, K. W., & Hencke, R. W. (1996). Infants' construction of actions in context: Piaget's contribution to research on early development. *Psychological Science, 7,* 204–209.

Fischer, M. E., Vitek, M. E., Hedeker, D., Henderson, W. G., Jacobsen, S. J., & Goldberg, J. (2004). A twin study of erectile dysfunction. *Archives of Internal Medicine, 164,* 165–168.

Fischer, P. J., & Breakey, W. R. (1991). The epidemiology of alcohol, drug, and mental disorders among homeless persons. *American Psychologist, 46,* 1115–1128.

Fischer, S., Hallschmid, M., Elsner, A. L., & Born, J. (2002). Sleep forms memory for finger skills. *Proceedings of the National Academy of Sciences, 99,* 11987–11991.

Fish, T. A. (2005). *Survey of knowledge and attitudes of military personnel concerning post-traumatic stress disorder (PTSD) at a large Canadian Forces army Base.* Contractor's Report for the Director, Human Resources and Evaluation, Department of National Defence.

Fisher, C. B., & Fried, A. L. (2003). Internet-mediated psychological services and the American Psychological Association ethics code. *Psychotherapy: Theory, Research, Practice, and Training, 40,* 103–111.

Fisher, C. D. (2000). Mood and emotion while working: Missing pieces of job satisfaction? *Journal of Organizational Behavior, 21,* 185–202.

Fisher, W. A., Fisher, J. D., & Rye, B. J. (1995). Understanding and promoting AIDS-preventive behavior: Insights from the theory of reasoned action. *Health Psychology, 14,* 255–264.

Fiske, A. P., Kitayama, S., Markus, H. R., & Nisbett, R. E. (1998). The cultural matrix of social psychology. In D. T. Gilbert, S. T. Fiske, & G. Lindzey (Eds.), *Handbook of social psychology* (Vol. 2, 4th ed., pp. 915–981). Boston: McGraw-Hill.

Fiske, S. T. (1995). Social cognition. In A. Tesser (Ed.), *Advanced social psychology* (pp. 149–194). New York: McGraw-Hill.

Fiske, S. T. (1998). Stereotyping, prejudice, and discrimination. In D. Gilbert, S. T. Fiske, & G. Lindzey (Eds.), *Handbook of social psychology* (Vol.2, 4th ed., pp. 357–414). Boston: McGraw-Hill.

Fiske, S. T. (2000). Interdependence and the reduction of prejudice. In S. Oskamp (Ed.), *Reducing prejudice and discrimination* (pp. 115–135). Mahwah, NJ: Erlbaum.

Fitzgerald, P. B., Brown, T. L., & Daskalakis, Z. J. (2002). The application of transcranial magnetic stimulation in psychiatry and neurosciences research. *Acta Psychiatrica Scandinavia, 105,* 324–340.

Fitzgerald, P. B., Brown, T. L., Marston, N. A. U., de Castella, A., & Kulkarni, J. (2003). Transcranial magnetic stimulation in the treatment of depression. *Archives of General Psychiatry, 60,* 1002–1008.

Fitzgerald, T. E., Tennen, H., Afflect, G. S., & Pransky, G. (1993). The relative importance of dispositional optimism and control appraisals in quality of life after coronary artery bypass surgery. *Journal of Behavioral Medicine, 16,* 25–43.

Fitzpatrick, D. C., Olsen, J. F., & Suga, N. (1998). Connections among functional areas in the mustached bat auditory cortex. *Journal of Comparative Neurology, 391,* 366–396.

Fitzsimons, G. J., & Shiv, B. (2001). Nonconscious and contaminative effects of hypothetical questions on subsequent decision making. *Journal of Consumer Research, 28,* 224–238.

Fitzsimons, G. J., & Williams, P. (2000). Asking questions can change choice behavior: Does it do so automatically or effortfully? *Journal of Experimental Psychology: Applied, 6,* 195–206.

Flavell, J. E., Azrin, N., Baumeister, A., Carr, E., Dorsey, M., Forehand, R., et al. (1982). The treatment of self-injurious behavior. *Behavior Therapy, 13,* 529–554.

Flegal, K. M., Carroll, M. D., Ogden, C. L., & Johnson, C. L. (2002). Prevalence and trends in obesity among US adults, 1999–2000. *Journal of the American Medical Association, 288,* 1723–1727.

Flett, G. L., Blankstein, K. R., Hicken, D. J., & Watson, M. S. (1995). Social support and help-seeking in daily hassles versus major life events stress. *Journal of Applied Social Psychology, 25,* 49–58.

Flett, G. L., Hewitt, P. L., Blankstein, K. R., & Mosher, S. W. (1995). Perfectionism, life events, and depressive symptoms: A test of a diathesis-stress model. *Current Psychology: Developmental, Learning, Personality, Social, 14,* 112–137.

Flor, H. (2002). The modification of cortical reorganization and chronic pain by sensory feedback. *Applied Psychophysiological Biofeedback, 27,* 215–227.

Flor, H., Birbaumer, N., Herman, C., Ziegler, S., & Patrick, C. J. (2002). Aversive Pavlovian conditioning in psychopaths: Peripheral and central correlates. *Psychophysiology, 39,* 505–518.

Floyd, J. A. (2002). Sleep and aging. *Nursing Clinics of North America, 37,* 719–731.

Flynn, J. T. (1999). Searching for justice: The discovery of IQ gains over time. *American Psychologist, 54,* 5–20.

Foa, E. B., & Kozak, M. J. (1995). DSM-IV field trial: Obsessive-compulsive disorder. *American Journal of Psychiatry, 152,* 90–96.

Foa, E. B., Dancu, C. V., Hembree, E. A., Jaycox, L. H., Meadows, E. A., & Street, G. P. (1999). A comparison of exposure therapy, stress-inoculation training, and their combination for reducing posttraumatic stress disorder in female assault victims. *Journal of Consulting and Clinical Psychology, 67,* 194–200.

Foa, E. B., Franklin, M. E., Perry, K. J., & Herbert, J. D. (1996). Cognitive biases in generalized social phobia. *Journal of Abnormal Psychology, 105,* 433–439.

Folk, C. L., Remington, R. W., & Wright, J. H. (1994). The structure of attentional control: Contingent attentional capture by apparent motion, abrupt onset, and color. *Journal of Experimental Psychology: Human Perception and Performance, 20,* 317–329.

Folkman, S., & Lazarus, R. (1988). *Manual for the ways of coping questionnaire.* Palo Alto, CA: Consulting Psychologists Press.

Folkman, S., & Moskowitz, J. T. (2000). Stress, positive emotion, and coping. *Current Directions in Psychological Science, 9,* 115–118.

Folkman, S., Lazarus, R., Dunkel-Shetteer, DeLongis, A., & Gruen, R. (1986). Dynamics of a stressful encounter: Cognitive appraisal, coping, and encounter outcomes. *Journal of Personality and Social Psychology, 50,* 992–1003.

Foote, S. L., Bloom, F. E., & Aston-Jones, G. (1983). Nucleus locus coeruleus: New evidence of anatomical and physiological specificity. *Physiology Review, 63,* 844–914.

Forbes, D., Phelps, A., & McHugh, T. (2001). Treatment of combat-related nightmares using imagery rehearsal: A pilot study. *Journal of Traumatic Stress, 14,* 433–442.

Forbes, S., Bui, S., Robinson, B. R., Hochgeschwender, U., & Brennan, M. B. (2001). Integrated control of appetite and fat metabolism by the leptin-proopiommelanocortin pathway. *Proceedings of the National Academy of Science, 98,* 4233–4237.

Fosse, R., Stickgold, R., & Hobson, J. A. (2001). Brain-mind states: Reciprocal variation in thoughts and hallucinations. *Psychological Science, 12,* 30–36.

Foster, M. D. (2000). Positive and negative responses to personal discrimination: Does coping make a difference? *Journal of Social Psychology, 140,* 93–106.

Foster, M. D., & Dion, K. L. (2003). Dispositional hardiness and women's well-being relating to gender discrimination: The role of minimization. *Psychology of Women Quarterly, 27,* 197–208.

Foster, M. D., & Dion, K. L. (2004). The role of hardiness in moderating the relationship between global/specific attributions and actions against discrimination. *Sex Roles, 51,* 161–169

Foulke, E. (1991). Braille. In M. A. Heller & W. Shiff (Eds.), *The psychology of touch.* Hillsdale, NJ: Erlbaum.

Fountain, J. W. (2000, November 28). Exorcists and exorcisms proliferate across U.S. *The New York Times.*

Fowler, G. A. (2004, March 4). Calling all jewel thieves. *The Wall Street Journal,* p. B1.

Fox, A. S., & Olster, D. H. (2000). Effects of intracerebroventricular leptin administration on feeding and sexual behaviors in lean and obese female zucker rats. *Hormones and Behavior, 37,* 377–387.

Fox, N. (1997, June). Consistent parenting helps children regulate emotions. *APA Monitor,* p. 17.

Fox, P., Bain, P. G., Glickman, S., Carroll, C., & Zajicek, J. (2004). The effect of cannabis on tremor in patients with multiple sclerosis. *Neurology, 62,* 1105–1109.

Foxhall, K. (2000a). How will the rules on telehealth be written? *Monitor on Psychology, 31,* 38.

Fozard, J., Wolf, E., Bell, B., Farland, R., & Podolsky, S. (1977). Visual perception and communication. In J. Birren & K. Schaie (Eds.), *Handbook of the psychology of aging.* New York: Van Nostrand Reinhold.

Francis, H. W., & Niparko, J. K. (2003). Cochlear implantation update. *Pediatric Clinics of North America, 50,* 341–361.

Frank, D. A., Augustyn, M., Knight, W. G., Pell, T., & Zuckerman, B. (2001). Growth, development, and behavior in early childhood following prenatal cocaine exposure: A systematic review. *Journal of the American Medical Association, 285,* 1613–1625.

Frank, J. D., & Frank, J. B. (1991). *Persuasion and healing: A comparative study of psychotherapy* (3rd ed.). Baltimore, MD: Johns Hopkins University Press.

Frankenberg, W. K., & Dodds, J. B. (1967). The Denver developmental screening test. *Journal of Pediatrics, 71,* 181–191.

Fredrickson, B. L., & Joiner, T. (2002). Positive emotions trigger upward spirals toward emotional well-being. *Psychological Science, 13,* 172–175.

Freed, C. R., Greene, P. E., Breeze, R. E., Tsai, W. Y., DuMouchel, W., Kao, R., et al. (2001). Transplantation of embryonic dopamine neurons for severe Parkinson's disease. *New England Journal of Medicine, 344,* 710–719.

Freedman, J. L. (1992). Television violence and aggression: What psychologists should tell the public. In P. Suedfeld & P. E. Tetlock (Eds.), *Psychology and social policy.* New York: Hemisphere.

Freedman, J. L. (2002). *Media violence and its effect on aggression: Assessing the scientific evidence.* Toronto, ON: University of Toronto Press.

Freedman, J. L., & Fraser, S. C. (1966). Compliance without pressure: The foot-in-the-door technique. *Journal of Personality and Social Psychology, 4,* 195–202.

Freedman, R. (2003). Schizophrenia. *New England Journal of Medicine, 349,* 1738–1749.

Freedman, V. A., Aykan, H., & Martin, L. G. (2001). Aggregate changes in severe cognitive impairment among older Americans: 1993 and 1998. *Journal of Gerontology, 56B,* S100–S111.

Freeman, M. P., Freeman, S. A., & McElroy, S. L. (2002). The comorbidity of bipolar and anxiety disorders: Prevalence, psychobiology, and treatment issues. *Journal of Affective Disorders, 68,* 1–23.

Freeman, W., & Watts, J. W. (1942). *Psychosurgery.* Springfield, IL: Charles C. Thomas.

Fremgen, A., & Fay, D. (1980). Overextensions in production and comprehension: A methodological clarification. *Journal of Child Language, 7,* 205–211.

Freres, D. R., Gillham, J. E., Reivich, K., & Shatte, A. J. (2002). Preventing depressive symptoms in middle school students: The Penn Resiliency Program. *International Journal of Emergency Mental Health, 4,* 31–40.

Freud, A. (1946). *The ego and the mechanisms of defense.* New York: International Universities Press.

Frey, C. F., & Detterman, D. K. (2004). Scholastic assessment or g? *Psychological Science, 15*, 373–378.

Frey, P. L., & Gaertner, S. L. (1986). Helping and the avoidance of inappropriate interracial behavior: A strategy that perpetuates a nonprejudiced self-image. *Journal of Personality and Social Psychology, 50*, 1083–1090.

Fride, E., & Mechoulam, R. (1993). Pharmacological activity of the cannabinoid receptor agonist, anandamide, a brain constituent. *European Journal of Pharmacology, 231*, 313–314.

Fridlund, A., Sabini, J. P., Hedlund, L. E., Schaut, J. A., Shenker, J. I., & Knauer, M. J. (1990). Audience effects on solitary faces during imagery: Displaying to the people in your head. *Journal of Nonverbal Behavior, 14*(2), 113–137.

Fried, P. A., Watkinson, B., & Gray, R. (1992). A follow-up study of attentional behavior in 6-year-old children exposed prenatally to marijuana, cigarettes, and alcohol. *Neurotoxicity and Teratology, 14*(5), 299–311.

Fried, P.A., Watkinson, B., & Gray, R. (2003). Differential effects on cognitive functioning in 13- to 16-year olds prenatally exposed to cigarettes and marihuana. *Neurotoxiology and Teratology, 25*, 427–436.

Friedman, A., Kerkman, D., Brown, N.R., Stea, D., & Cappello (in press). Cross-cultural similarity and differences in North America. *Psychonomic Bulletin and Review.*

Friedman, E., Clark, D., & Gershon, S. (1992). Stress, anxiety, and depression: Review of biological, diagnostic, and nosologic issues. *Journal of Anxiety Disorders, 6*, 337–363.

Friedman, H. S., & Schustack, M. W. (2003). *Personality: Classic theories and modern research.* Boston: Allyn & Bacon.

Friedman, H. S., Tucker, J. S., Schwartz, J. E., Martin, L. R., Tomlinson-Keasey, C., Wingard, D. L., & Criqui, M. H. (1995a). Childhood conscientiousness and longevity: Health behaviors and cause of death. *Journal of Personality and Social Psychology, 68*, 696–703.

Friedman, H. S., Tucker, J. S., Schwartz, J. E., Tomlinson-Keasey, C., Martin, L. R., Wingard, D. L., & Criqui, M. H. (1995b). Psychosocial and behavioral predictors of longevity: The aging and death of the "Termites." *American Psychologist, 50*, 69–78.

Friedman, M. A., & Brownell, K. D. (1995). Psychological correlates of obesity: Moving to the next research generation. *Psychological Bulletin, 117*(1), 3–20.

Friedman, M., & Rosenman, R. H. (1974). *Type A behavior and your heart.* New York: Knopf.

Friedman, M., Ibrahim, H., Lee, G., & Joseph, N. J. (2003). Combined uvulopalatopharyngoplasty and radiofrequency tongue base reduction for treatment of obstructive sleep apnea/hypopnea syndrome. *Otolaryngological Head and Neck Surgery, 129*, 611–621.

Friendly, M., Beach, J. & Turiano, M. (2002). *Early childhood education and care in Canada 2001.* Toronto, ON: Childcare Resource and Research Unit, University of Toronto.

Fritzler, B. K., Hecker, J. E., & Losee, M. C. (1997). Self-directed treatment with minimal therapist contact: Preliminary findings for obsessive-compulsive disorder. *Behaviour Research and Therapy, 35*, 627–631.

Frodl, T., Meisenzahl, E. M., Zill, P., Baghai, T., Rujescu, D., Leinsinger, G., et al. (2004). Reduced hippocampal volumes associated with the long variant of the serotonin transporter polymorphism in major depression. *Archives of General Psychiatry, 61*, 177–183.

Fulbright, R. K., Troche, C. J., Skudlarski, P., Gore, J. C., & Wexler, B. E. (2001). Functional MR imaging of regional brain activation associated with the affective experience of pain. *American Journal of Roentgenology, 177*, 1205–1210.

Fuligni, A. J., & Pedersen, S. (2002). Family obligation and the transition to young adulthood. *Developmental Psychology, 38*(5), 856–868.

Fullerton, C. S., Ursano, R. J., & Wang, L. (2004). Acute stress disorder, posttraumatic stress disorder, and depression in disaster or rescue workers. *American Journal of Psychiatry, 161*, 1370–1376.

Funder, D. (2001a). Personality. *Annual Review of Psychology, 52*, 197–222.

Funder, D. (2001b). *The personality puzzle* (2nd ed.). New York: Norton.

Furey, M. L., Pietrini, P., & Haxby, J. V. (2000). Cholinergic enhancement and increased selectivity of perceptual processing during working memory. *Science, 290*, 2315–2319.

Furnham, A. (2001). Personality and individual differences in the workplace: Person-organization-outcome fit. In R. Hogan & B. Roberts (Eds.), *Personality psychology in the workplace* (pp. 223–251). Washington, DC: American Psychological Association.

Furstenberg, F. F., Brooks-Gunn, J., & Chase-Lansdale, L. (1989). Teenaged pregnancy and childbearing. *American Psychologist, 44*, 313–320.

Gaba, D. M., & Howard, S. K. (2002). Fatigue among clinicians and the safety of patients. *New England Journal of Medicine. 347*, 1249–1255.

Gabbard, G. O. (2000). *Psychodymanic psychiatry in clinical practice* (3rd ed.). Washington, DC: American Psychiatric Press, Inc.

Gabrieli, J. D. E., Fleischman, D. A., Keane, M. M., Reminger, S. L., & Morrell, F. (1995). Double dissociation between memory systems underlying explicit and implicit memory in the human brain. *Psychological Science, 6*, 76–82.

Gaertner, S. L., & Dovidio, J. F. (1986). The aversive form of racism. In J. F. Dovidio & S. L. Gaertner (Eds.), *Prejudice, discrimination, and racism* (pp. 61–89). Orlando, FL: Academic Press.

Gais, S., & Born, J. (2004). Low acetylcholine during slow-wave sleep is critical for declarative memory consolidation. *Proceedings of the National Academy of Sciences, 101*, 2140–2144.

Galatzer-Levy, R. M., Bachrach, H., Skolnikoff, A., & Waldron, S., Jr. (2000). *Does psychoanalysis work?* New Haven, CT: Yale University Press.

Galea, S., Ahern, J., Resnick H., Kilpatrick D., Bucuvalas M., Gold, J., & Vlahov, D. (2002a). Psychological sequelae of the September 11 terrorist attacks in New York City. *New England Journal of Medicine, 346*, 982–987.

Galea, S., Resnick, H., Ahern, J., Gold, J., Bucuvalas, M., Kilpatrick, D., et al. (2002b). Posttraumatic stress disorder in Manhattan, New York City, after the September 11th terrorist attacks. *Journal of Urban Health, 79*, 340–353.

Galef, B. G., & Wright, T. J. (1995). Groups of naive rats learn to select nutritionally adequate foods faster than do isolated rats. *Animal Behaviour 49*(2), 403–409.

Gallagher, M. (1998, January 26). Day careless. *National Review*, pp. 37–41.

Galotti, K. M. (1999). *Cognitive psychology in and out of the laboratory* (2nd ed.). Belmont, CA: Brooks/Cole.

Gan, T. J., Jiao, K. R., Zenn, M., & Georgiade, G. (2004). A randomized controlled comparison of electro-acupoint stimulation or ondansetron versus placebo for the prevention of postoperative nausea and vomiting. *Anesthesia and Analgesia, 99*, 1070–1075.

Ganchrow, J. R., Steiner, J. E., & Daher, M. (1983). Neonatal facial expressions in response to different qualities and intensities of gustatory stimuli. *Infant Behavior and Development, 6*, 189–200.

Gangestad, S. W., & Thornhill, R. (1997). Human sexual selection and developmental stability. In J. A. Simpson & D. T. Kenrick (Eds.), *Evolutionary social psychology* (pp. 169–195). Mahwah, NJ: Erlbaum.

Garber, J., Keiley, M. K., & Martin, N. C. (2002). Developmental trajectories of adolescents' depressive symptoms: Predictors of change. *Journal of Consulting and Clinical Psychology, 70*, 9–95.

Garcia, J., & Koelling, R. A. (1966). Relation of cue to consequences in avoidance learning. *Psychonomic Science, 4*, 123–124.

Garcia, S. M., Weaver, K., Moskowitz, G. B., & Darley, J. M. (2002). Crowded minds: The implicit bystander effect. *Journal of Personality and Social Psychology, 83*, 843–853.

Gardner, H. (1993). *Multiple intelligences: The theory in practice.* New York: Basic Books.

Gardner, H. (1999). Are there additional intelligences? The case for naturalist, spiritual, and existential intelligences. In J. Kane (Ed.), *Education, information and transformation: Essays on learning and thinking* (pp. 111–131). Englewood Cliffs, NJ: Prentice Hall.

Gardner, H. (2002). *Learning from extraordinary minds.* Mahwah, NJ: Erlbaum.

Gardner, R. A., & Gardner, B. T. (1978). Comparative psychology and language acquisition. *Annals of the New York Academy of Science, 309*, 37–76.

Gardner, R., Heward, W. L., & Grossi, T. A. (1994). Effects of response cards on student participation and academic achievement: A systematic replication with inner-city students during whole-class science instruction. *Journal of Applied Behavior Analysis, 27*, 63–71.

Garfield, S. L. (1998). Some comments on empirically supported treatments. *Journal of Consulting and Clinical Psychology, 66*, 121–125.

Garland, A. F., & Zigler, E. (1993). Adolescent suicide prevention: Current research and social policy implications. *American Psychologist, 48*, 169–182.

Garlick, D. (2002). Understanding the nature of general intelligence: The role of individual differences in neural plasticity as an explanatory mechanism. *Psychological Review, 109*, 116–136.

Garlick, D. (2003). Integrating brain science research with intelligence research. *Current Directions in Psychological Science, 12*, 185–188.

Garris, P. A., Kilpatrick, M., Bunin, M. A., Michael, D., Walker, Q. D., & Wightman, R. M. (1999). Dissociation of dopamine release in the nucleus accumbens from intracranial self-stimulation. *Nature, 398*, 67–69.

Garry, M., & Loftus, E. (1994). Pseudomemories without hypnosis. *International Journal of Clinical and Experimental Hypnosis, 42*(4), 363–373.

Gaster, B., & Holroyd, J. (2000). St. John's wort for depression: A systematic review. *Archives of Internal Medicine, 160*, 152–156.

Gates, G. A., & Miyamoto, R. T. (2003). Cochlear implants. *The New England Journal of Medicine, 349*, 421–423.

Gatewood, R. D., & Feild, H. S. (2001). *Human resource selection* (5th ed.). Fort Worth, TX: Harcourt.

Gathercole, S. E., Pickering, S. J., Ambridge, B., & Wearing, H. (2004). The structure of working memory from 4 to 15 years of age. *Developmental Psychology, 40*, 177–190.

Gauvain, M. (2001). *The social context of cognitive development.* New York: Guilford.

Gawande, A. (1998a, March 30). No mistake. *New Yorker.*

Gawande, A. (1998b, September 21). The pain perplex. *New Yorker.*

Gazzaniga, M. S., & LeDoux, J. E. (1978). *The integrated mind.* New York: Plenum.

Ge, X., Conger, R., & Elder, G. H. (2001) Pubertal transition, stressful life events, and the emergence of gender differences in adolescent depressive symptoms. *Developmental Psychology, 37,* 404–417.

Geary, D. C. (1999). Evolution and developmental sex differences. *Current Directions in Psychological Science, 8,* 115–120.

Geary, D. C. (2000). Evolution and proximate expression of human paternal investment. *Psychological Bulletin, 126,* 55–77.

Geddes, J. R., Burgess, S., Hawton, K., Jamison, K., & Goodwin, G. M. (2004). Long-term lithium therapy for bipolar disorder: Systematic review and meta-analysis of randomized controlled trials. *American Journal of Psychiatry, 161,* 217–222.

Geen, R. G. (1991). Social motivation. *Annual Review of Psychology, 42,* 377–399.

Geen, R. G. (1998a). Aggression and antisocial behavior. In D. Gilbert, S. T. Fiske, & G. Lindzey (Eds.), *Handbook of social psychology* (4th ed., Vol. 2, pp. 317–356). Boston: McGraw-Hill.

Gegenfurtner, K. R., & Kiper, D. C. (2003). Color vision. *Annual Review of Neuroscience, 26,* 181–206.

Gellhorn, E., & Loofbourrow, G. N. (1963). *Emotions and emotional disorders.* New York: Harper & Row.

Gelman, R., & Baillargeon, R. (1983). A review of some Piagetian concepts. In P. H. Mussen (Ed.), *Handbook of child psychology* (Vol. 3, pp. 167–230). New York: Wiley.

George, M. S. (2003). Stimulating the brain. *Scientific American, 289,* 66–73.

George, M. S., Anton, R. F., Bloomer, C., Teneback, C., Drobes, D. J., Lorberbaum, J. P., et al. (2001). Activation of prefrontal cortex and anterior thalamus in alcoholic subjects on exposure to alcohol-specific cues. *Archives of General Psychiatry, 58,* 345–352.

George, W. H., & Marlatt, G. A. (1986). The effects of alcohol and anger on interest in violence, erotica, and deviance. *Journal of Abnormal Psychology, 95,* 150–158.

Gerbner, G., Morgan, M., & Signorielli, N. (1994). *Television violence profile No. 16: The turning point.* Philadelphia: Annenberg School for Communication.

Gerin, W., Milner, D., Chawla, S., Pickering, T. G. (1995). Social support as a moderator of cardiovascular reactivity in women: A test of the direct effects and buffering hypotheses. *Psychosomatic Medicine, 57,* 16–22.

Gerschman, J. A., Reade, P. C., & Burrows, G. D. (1980). Hypnosis and dentistry. In G. D. Burrows & L. Dennerstein (Eds.), *Handbook of hypnosis and psychosomatic medicine.* Amsterdam: Elsevier.

Gershoff, E. T. (2002). Corporal punishment by parents and associated child behaviors and experiences: A meta-analytic and theoretical review. *Psychological Bulletin, 128,* 539–579.

Gershon, A. A., Dannon, P. N., & Grunhaus, L. (2003). Transcranial magnetic stimulation in the treatment of depression. *American Journal of Psychiatry, 160,* 835–845.

Gershon, J., Anderson, P., Graap, K., Zimand, E., Hodges, L., & Rothbaum, B. O. (2002). Virtual reality exposure therapy in the treatment of anxiety disorders. *The Scientific Review of Mental Health Practice, 1.* Retrieved October 12, 2002 from http://www.scientificmentalhealth.org/SRMHP/current.html

Geschwind, N. (1979). Specializations of the human brain. *Scientific American, 241,* 180–199.

Gfeller, J. D. (1994). Hypnotizability enhancement: Clinical implications of empirical findings. *American Journal of Clinical Hypnosis, 37*(2), 107–116.

Gianakos, I. (2002). Predictors of coping with work stress: The influences of sex, gender role, social desirability, and locus of control. *Sex Roles, 46,* 149–158.

Gibb, B. E., Alloy, L. B., Abramson, L. Y., Beevers, C. G., & Miller, I. W. (2004). Cognitive vulnerability to depression: A taxometric analysis. *Journal of Abnormal Psychology, 113,* 81–89.

Gibson, E. J., & Walk, R. D. (1960). The visual cliff. *Scientific American, 202,* 64–71.

Gibson, J. J. (1979). *The ecological approach to visual perception.* Boston: Houghton Mifflin.

Gigerenzer, G., Todd, P. M., & ABC Research Group. (2000). *Simple heuristics that make us smart.* New York: Oxford University Press.

Gilbert, C. D. (1992). Horizontal integration and cortical dynamics. *Neuron, 9,* 1–13.

Gilbert, D. T. (1998). Ordinary personology. In D. Gilbert, S. T. Fiske, & G. Lindzey (Eds.), *Handbook of social psychology* (Vol.2, 4th ed., pp. 89–150). Boston: McGraw-Hill.

Gilbert, D. T., & Malone, P. S. (1995). The correspondence bias. *Psychological Bulletin, 117,* 21–38.

Gilbert, D. T., & Wilson, T. D. (1998). Miswanting: Some problems in the forecasting of future affective states. In J. P. Forgas (Ed.), *Feeling and thinking: The role of affect in social cognition* (pp. 178–197). New York: Cambridge University Press.

Gilbert, R. M. (1984). Caffeine consumption. In G. A. Spiller (Ed.), *The methylxanthine beverages and foods: Chemistry, consumption, and health effects* (pp. 185–213). New York: Liss.

Gilbert, S. (1997, August 20). Two spanking studies indicate parents should be cautious. *New York Times Magazine.*

Gilbertson, M. W., Shenton, M. E., Ciszewski, A., Kasai, K., Lasko, N. B., Orr, S. P., & Pitman, R. K. (2002). Smaller hippocampal volume predicts pathologic vulnerability to psychological trauma. *Nature Neuroscience, 5,* 1242–1247.

Gilboa-Schechtman, E., & Foa, E. B. (2001). Patterns of recovery from trauma: The use of intraindividual analysis. *Journal of Abnormal Psychology, 110,* 392–400.

Giles, T. R. (1990). Bias against behavior therapy in outcome reviews: Who speaks for the patient? *The Behavior Therapist, 13,* 86–90.

Gillette, M. U. (1986). The suprachiasmatic nuclei: Circadian phase-shifts induced at the time of hypothalamic slice preparation are preserved in vitro. *Brain Research, 379,* 176–181.

Gillham, J. E. (Ed). (2000). *The science of optimism and hope: Research essays in honor of Martin E. P. Seligman.* Philadelphia: Templeton Foundation Press.

Gilligan, C. (1982). *In a different voice: Psychological theory and women's development.* Cambridge, MA: Harvard University Press.

Gilligan, C. (1993). Adolescent development reconsidered. In A. Garrod (Ed.), *Approaches to moral development: New research and emerging themes.* New York: Teachers College Press.

Gilliland, F. D., Li, Y.-F., & Peters, J. M. (2001). Effects of maternal smoking during pregnancy and environmental tobacco smoke on asthma and wheezing in children. *American Journal of Respiratory and Critical Care Medicine, 163,* 429–436.

Gillis, C. (2004). Illicit trade in oxycontin plagues Atlantic provinces. *Maclean's magazine.* [Electronic version]. Available: http://www.macleans.ca/topstories/canada/article.jsp?content=20040524_81278_81278

Gilmore, M. M., & Murphy, C. (1989). Aging is associated with increased Weber ratios for caffeine, but not for sucrose. *Perception and Psychophysics, 46,* 555–559.

Gilovich, T. (1997). Some systematic biases of everyday judgment. *Skeptical Inquirer, 21,* 31–35.

Giosan, C., Glovsky, V., & Haslam, N. (2001). The lay conception of "mental disorder": A cross-cultural study. *Transcultural Psychiatry, 38,* 317–332.

Givens, B. (1995). Low doses of ethanol impair spatial working memory and reduce hippocampal theta activity. *Alcoholism Clinical and Experimental Research, 19*(3), 763–767.

Gladue, B. A. (1994). The biopsychology of sexual orientation. *Current Directions in Psychological Science, 3*(5), 150–154.

Glantz, K., Rizzo, A., & Graap, K. (2003). Virtual reality for psychotherapy: Current reality and future possibilities. *Psychotherapy: Theory, Research, Practice, and Training, 40,* 55–67.

Glanz, J. (1997). Sharpening the senses with neural "noise." *Science, 277,* 1759.

Glanzer, M., & Cunitz, A. (1966). Two storage mechanisms in free recall. *Journal of Verbal Learning and Verbal Behavior, 5,* 351–360.

Gleaves, D. H., May, M. C., & Cardena, E. (2001). An examination of the diagnostic validity of dissociative identity disorder. *Clinical Psychology Review, 21,* 577–608.

Gleitman, L., & Landau, B. (1994). *The acquisition of the lexicon.* Cambridge: MIT Press.

Glenmullen, J. (2000). *Prozac backlash: Overcoming the dangers of Prozac, Zoloft, Paxil, and other antidepressants with safe, effective alternatives.* New York: Simon & Schuster.

Gleuckauf, R., & Quittner, A. (1992). Assertiveness training for disabled adults in wheelchairs: Self-report, role-play, and activity pattern outcomes. *Journal of Consulting and Clinical Psychology, 60,* 419–425.

Glick, P. T., & Fiske, S. (2001). Ambivalent sexism. In M. Zanna (Ed.), *Advances in experimental social psychology* (Vol. 33, pp. 115–188). New York: Academic Press.

Glover, J. A., Krug, D., Dietzer, M., George, B. W., & Hannon, M. (1990). "Advance" advance organizers. *Bulletin of the Psychonomic Society, 28,* 4–6.

Goenjian, A. K., Molina, L., Steinberg, A. M., Fairbanks, L. A., Alvarez, M. L., Goenjian, H. A., & Pynoos, R. S. (2001). Posttraumatic stress and depressive reactions among Nicaraguan adolescents after hurricane Mitch. *American Journal of Psychiatry, 158,* 788–794.

Gogtay, N., Giedd, J. N., Lusk, L., Hayashi, K. M., Greenstein, D., Vaituzis, A. C., Nugent, T. F., III, et al. (2004). Dynamic mapping of human cortical development during childhood through early adulthood. *Proceedings of the National Academy of Sciences, 101,* 8174–8179.

Gold, A. (1998). Letter to the Minister of Justice and Attorney General for Canada. Justice Building 239 Wellington Street Ottawa, Ontario, K1A 0H8. March 25. Retrieved March 23, 2006, from http://www.religioustolerance.org/rmtgold.htm

Gold, M. S. (1994). The epidemiology, attitudes, and pharmacology of LSD use in the 1990s. *Psychiatric Annals, 24*(3), 124–126.

Gold, P. E., Cahill, L., & Wenk, G. L. (2003). The lowdown on Ginkgo biloba. *Scientific American, 288,* 86–91.

Goldberg, J. F., Harrow, M., & Grossman, L. S. (1995). Course and outcome in bipolar affective disorder: A longitudinal follow-up study. *American Journal of Psychiatry, 152,* 379–384.

Goldblum, N. (2001). *The brain-shaped mind: A neural-network view: What the brain can tell us about the mind.* Cambridge: Cambridge University Press.

Goldenberg, I., & Goldenberg, H. (1995). Family therapy. In R. J. Corsini & D. Wedding (Eds.), *Current psychotherapies* (5th ed.). Itasca, IL: Peacock.

Goldfried, M. R., & Davison, G. C. (1994). *Clinical behavior therapy.* New York: Wiley.

Golding, N. L., Staff, N. P., & Spruston, N. (2002). Dendritic spikes as a mechanism for cooperative long-term potentiation. *Nature, 418,* 326–331.

Goldman, M. S., Darkes, J., & Del Boca, F. K. (1999). Expectancy meditation of biopsychosocial risk for alcohol use and alcoholism. In I. Kirsch (Ed.), *How expectancies shape experience* (pp. 233–262). Washington, DC: American Psychological Association.

Goldman, M. S., Del Boca, F. K., & Darkes, J. (1999). Alcohol expectancy theory: The application of cognitive neuroscience. In K. Leonard & H. Blane (Eds.), *Psychological theories of drinking and alcoholism* (2nd ed., pp. 203–246). New York: Guilford.

Goldman-Rakic, P. S. (1994). Specification of higher cortical functions. In S. H. Bromay & J. Grafman (Eds.), *Atypical cognitive deficits in developmental disorders.* Hillsdale, NJ: Erlbaum.

Goldstein, A. J., de Beurs, E., Chambless, D. L., & Wilson, K. A. (2000). EMDR for panic disorder with agoraphobia: Comparison with waiting list and credible attention-placebo control conditions. *Journal of Consulting and Clinical Psychology, 68,* 947–956.

Goldstein, E. B. (1999). *Sensation and perception* (5th ed.). Pacific Grove, CA: Brooks/Cole.

Goldstein, E. B. (2001). *Sensation and perception.* (6th ed.). Belmont, CA: Wadsworth.

Goldstein, I., & Rosen, R. C. (Eds.). (2002). Guest editors' introduction: Female sexuality and sexual dysfunction. *Archives of Sexual Behavior, 31,* 391.

Goldstein, M. H., King, A. P., & West, M. J. (2003). Social interaction shapes babbling: Testing parallels between birdsong and speech. *Proceedings of the National Academy of Sciences, 100,* 8030–8035.

Goldstein, R. Z., & Volkow, N. D. (2002). Drug addiction and its underlying neurobiological basis: Neuroimaging evidence for the involvement of the frontal cortex. *American Journal of Psychiatry, 159,* 1642–1652.

Goleman, D. (1995). *Emotional intelligence.* New York: Bantam Books.

Golomb, J., Kluger, A., De Leon, M. J., Ferris, S. H., Mittelman, M., Cohen, J., & George, A. E. (1996). Hippocampal formation size predicts declining memory performance in normal aging. *Neurology, 47,* 810–813.

Gone, J. (2004). Mental health services for Native Americans in the 21st century United States. *Professional Psychology: Theory and Practice, 35,* 10–18.

Gonzalez, J. S., Penedo, F. J., Antoni, M. H., Duran, R. E., McPherson-Baker, S., Ironson, G., et al. (2004). Social support, positive states of mind, and HIV treatment adherence in men and women living with HIV/AIDS. *Health Psychology, 23,* 413–418.

Goodale, M. A. & Milner, M. A. (2004). *Sight unseen: An exploration of conscious and unconscious vision.* Oxford: Oxford University Press, 140.

Goode, K. T., Haley, W. E., Roth, D. L., & Ford, G. L. (1998). Predicting longitudinal changes in caregiver physical and mental health: A stress process model. *Health Psychology, 17,* 190–198.

Goodenough, F. L. (1932). Expression of the emotions in a blind-deaf child. *Journal of Abnormal and Social Psychology, 27,* 328–333.

Goodman, G. S., Ghetti, S., Quas, J. A., Edelstein, R. S., Alexander, K. W., Redlich, A. D., et al. (2003). A prospective study of memory for child sexual abuse: New findings relevant to the repressed-memory controversy. *Psychological Science, 14,* 113–118.

Goodman, J. S., & Wood, R. E. (2004). Feedback specificity, learning opportunities, and learning. *Journal of Applied Psychology, 89,* 809–821.

Goodwin, F. K., & Jamison, K. R. (Eds.). (1990). *Manic-depressive illness.* New York: Oxford University Press.

Goodwin, F. K., Fireman, B., Simon, G. E., Hunkeler, E. M., Lee, J., & Revicki, D. (2003). Suicide risk in bipolar disorder during treatment with lithium and divalproex. *Journal of the American Medical Association, 290,* 1467–1473.

Goodwin, G. M., Bowden, C. L., & Calabrese, J. R. (2004). A pooled analysis of 2 placebo-controlled 18-month trials of lamotrigine and lithium maintenance in bipolar I disorder. *Journal of Clinical Psychiatry, 65*(3), 432–441.

Gooren, L. J., & Kruijver, F. P. (2002). Androgens and male behavior. *Molecular and Cellular Endocrinology, 198,* 31–40.

Gopnik, M., & Crago, M. B. (1991). Familial aggregation of developmental language disorder. *Cognition, 39,* 1–50.

Gordon, P. (2004, October 15). Numerical cognition without words: Evidence from Amazonia. *Science, 306,* 496–499.

Gorman, J. M. (2002). Treatment of generalized anxiety disorder. *Journal of Clinical Psychiatry, 63,* 17–23.

Gorman, J. M. (2003). Treating generalized anxiety disorder. *Journal of Clinical Psychiatry, 64* (Suppl. 2), 24–29.

Gosling, S. D. (2001). From mice to men: What can we learn about personality from animal research? *Psychological Bulletin, 127,* 45–86.

Gosling, S. D., Kwan, V. S. Y., & John, O. P. (2003). A dog's got personality: A cross-species comparative approach to personality judgments in dogs and humans. *Journal of Personality and Social Psychology, 85,* 1161–1169.

Gosling, S. D., Vazire, S., Srivastava, S., & John, O. P. (2004). Should we trust web-based studies? A comparative analysis of six preconceptions about Internet questionnaires. *American Psychologist, 59,* 93–104.

Goss Lucas, S., & Bernstein, D. A. (2005). *Teaching psychology: A step by step guide.* Mahwah, NJ: Erlbaum.

Gosselin, A., deGuise, J., & Paquette, G. (1997). Violence on Canadian television and some of its cognitive effects. *Canadian Journal of Communications, 22*(2). [Electronic version]. Retrieved March 26th, 2006, from http://www.cjconline.ca/viewarticle.php?id=415&layout=html

Gotlib, I. H., & Hammen, C. L. (1992). *Psychological aspects of depression: Toward cognitive interpersonal integration.* Chichester, England: Wiley.

Gotlib, I. H., Krasnoperova, E., Yue, D. N., & Joorman, J. (2004). Attentional biases for negative interpersonal stimuli in clinical depression. *Journal of Abnormal Psychology, 113,* 127–135.

Gottesman, I. I. (1991). *Schizophrenia genesis: The origins of madness.* New York: Freeman.

Gottfredson, L. S (1997). Why *g* matters: The complexity of everyday life. *Intelligence, 24,* 79–132.

Gottfredson, L. S. (2003). Dissecting practical intelligence theory: Its claims and evidence. *Intelligence, 31,* 343–397.

Gottfredson, L. S. (2004). Intelligence: Is it the epidemiologists' elusive "fundamental cause" of social class inequalities in health? *Journal of Personality and Social Psychology, 86,* 174–199.

Gottfredson, L. S., & Deary, I. J. (2004). Intelligence predicts health and longevity, but why? *Current Directions in Psychological Science, 13,* 1–4.

Gottfried, A. (1997, June). Parents' role is critical to children's learning. *APA Monitor,* p. 24.

Gottfried, J. A., & Dolan, R. J. (2003). The nose smells what the eye sees: Crossmodal visual facilitation of human olfactory perception. *Neuron, 39,* 375–386.

Götz, J., Streffer, J. R., David, D., Schild, A., Hoerndli, F., Pennanen, L., et al. (2004). Transgenic animal models of Alzheimer's disease and related disorders: Histopathology, behavior and therapy. *Molecular Psychiatry, 9,* 664–683.

Gould, E., Beylin, A., Tanapat, P., Reeves, A., & Schors, T. J. (1999). Learning enhances adult neurogenesis in the hippocampal formation. *Nature Neuroscience, 2,* 260–265.

Gould, R. A., Otto, M. W., Pollack, M. H., & Yap, L. (1997). Cognitive behavioral and pharmacological treatment of generalized anxiety disorder: A preliminary meta-analysis. *Behavior Therapy, 28,* 285–305.

Government of Canada. (2003). The reconviction rate of federal offenders 2003–02. Retrieved March 23 2006, from http://ww2.psepc-sppcc.gc.ca/publications/corrections/200302_e.asp

Grant, H., & Dweck, C. S. (2003). Clarifying achievement goals and their impact. *Journal of Personality and Social Psychology, 85,* 541–553.

Grant, J. E., & Kim, S. W. (2002). *Stop me because I can't stop myself: Taking control of impulsive behavior.* New York: McGraw-Hill.

Grassi, L., Rasconi, G., Pedriali, A., Corridoni, A., & Bevilacqua, M. (2000). Social support and psychological distress in primary care attenders. *Psychotherapy and Psychosomatics, 69,* 95–100.

Graves, L., Pack, A., & Abel, T. (2001). Sleep and memory: A molecular perspective. *Trends in Neurosciences, 24,* 237–243.

Gray, J. A. (1991). Neural systems, emotions, and personality. In J. Madden IV (Ed.), *Neurobiology of learning, emotion, and affect* (pp. 272–306). New York: Raven Press.

Gray, J. R., Chabris, C. F., & Braver, T. S. (2003). Neural mechanisms of general fluid intelligence. *Nature Neuroscience, 6,* 316–322.

Gray, J. E. & O'Reilly, R. L. (2005). Canadian compulsory community treatment laws: Recent reforms. *International Journal of Law and Psychiatry, 28,* 13–22.

Gray, N. S., MacCulloch, M. J., Smith, J., Morris, M., & Snowden, R. J. (2003). Forensic psychology: Violence viewed by psychopathic murderers. *Nature, 423,* 497.

Gray-Little, B., & Hafdahl, A. R. (2000). Factors influencing racial comparisons of self-esteem: A quantitative review. *Psychological Bulletin, 126,* 26–54.

Graziano, M. S. A., Alisharan, S. E., Hu, X., & Gross, C. G. (2002). The clothing effect: Tactile neurons in the precentral gyrus do not respond to the touch of the familiar primate chair. *Proceedings of the New York Academy of Sciences, 99,* 11930–11933.

Graziano, M. S., Taylor, C. S., & Moore, T. (2002). Complex movements evoked by microstimulation of precentral cortex. *Neuron, 34,* 841–851.

Green, A. I., & Patel, J. K. (1996) The new pharmacology of schizophrenia. *Harvard Mental Health Letter, 13*(6), 5–7.

Green, C. S., & Bavelier, D. (2003). Action video game modifies visual selective attention. *Nature, 423,* 534–537.

Green, J. T., & Woodruff-Pak, D. S. (2000). Eyeblink classical conditioning: Hippocampal formation is for neutral stimulus associations as cerebellum is for association response. *Psychological Bulletin, 126,* 138–158.

Green, R. A., Cross, A. J., & Goodwin, G. M. (1995). Review of the pharmacology and clinical pharmacology of 3,4-methylenedioxymethamphetamine (MDMA or "ecstacy"). *Psychopharmacology, 119,* 247–260.

Greenberg, J., Pyszczynski, T., & Solomon, S. (2003). A perilous leap from Becker's theorizing to empirical science: Terror management and research. In D. Leichty (Ed.), *Death and denial: Interdisciplinary essays: The legacy of Ernest Becker.* New York: Praeger.

Greenberg, L. S., & Malcolm, W. (2002). Resolving unfinished business: Relating process to outcome. *Journal of Consulting and Clinical Psychology, 70*(2), 406–416.

Greenberg, M. T., Lengua, L. J., Coie, J. D., Pinderhughes, E. E., Bierman, K., Dodge, K. A., et al. (1999). Predicting developmental outcomes at school entry using a multiple-risk model: Four American communities. *Developmental Psychology, 35,* 403–417.

Greenblatt, D., Harmatz, J., & Shader, R. I. (1993). Plasma alprazolam concentrations: Relation to efficacy and side effects in the treatment of panic disorder. *Archives of General Psychiatry, 50,* 715–732.

Greene, E., & Loftus, E. F. (1998). Psycholegal research on jury damage awards. *Current Directions in Psychological Science, 7,* 50–54.

Greenfield, P. M. (1994). Video games as cultural artifacts. *Journal of Applied Developmental Psychology, 15,* 3–12.

Greenough, W. T. (1997, November). We can't focus just on ages 0 to 3. *APA Monitor,* p. 3.

Greenough, W. T., Black, J. E., & Wallace, C. S. (1987). Experience and brain development. *Child Development, 58,* 539–559.

Greenwald, A. G., & Banaji, M. R. (1995). Implicit social cognition: Attitudes, self-esteem, and stereotypes. *Psychological Review, 102,* 4–27.

Greenwald, A. G., Draine, S. C., & Abrams, R. L. (1996). Three cognitive markers of unconscious semantic activation. *Science, 273,* 1699–1702.

Greenwald, A. G., Klinger, M. R., & Schuh, E. S. (1995). Activation by marginally perceptible ("subliminal") stimuli: Dissociation of unconscious from conscious cognition. *Experimental Psychology: General, 124*(1), 22–42.

Greer, A. E., & Buss, D. M. (1994). Tactics for promoting sexual encounters. *Journal of Sex Research, 31*(3), 185–201.

Gregg, V., Gibbs, J. C., & Basinger, K. S. (1994). Patterns of developmental delay in moral judgment by male and female delinquents. *Merrill-Palmer Quarterly, 40,* 538–553.

Griesler, P. C., Kandel, D. B., & Davies, M. (1998). Maternal smoking in pregnancy, child behavior problems, and adolescent smoking. *Journal of Research on Adolescence, 8,* 159–185.

Griffitt, W. B., & Guay, P. (1969). "Object" evaluation and conditioned affect. *Journal of Experimental Research in Personality, 4,* 1–8.

Grigorenko, E. L. (2002). In search of the genetic engram of personality. In D. Cervone & W. Mischel (Eds.), *Advances in personality science* (pp. 29–82). New York: The Guilford Press.

Grinspoon, L. (1999). The future of medical marijuana. *Forsch Komplementarmed, 6,* 40–43.

Grinspoon, L., Bakalar, J. B., Zimmer, L., & Morgan, J. P. (1997). Marijuana addiction. *Science, 277,* 749, 750–752.

Grinspoon, S., Thomas, E., Pitts, S., Gross, E., Mickley, D., Killer, K., et al. (2000). Prevalence and predictive factors for regional osteopenia in women with anorexia nervosa. *Annals of Internal Medicine, 133,* 790–794.

Grob, C., & Dobkin-de-Rios, M. (1992). Adolescent drug use in cross-cultural perspective. *Journal of Drug Issues, 22*(1), 121–138.

Groopman, J. (2000, January 24). Second opinion. *The New Yorker,* pp. 40–49.

Gross, J. J. (2001). Emotion regulation in adulthood: Timing is everything. *Current Directions in Psychological Science, 10,* 214–219.

Grosz, H. I., & Zimmerman, J. (1970). A second detailed case study of functional blindness: Further demonstration of the contribution of objective psychological data. *Behavior Therapy 1,* 115–123.

Grotevant, H. D. (1998). Adolescent development in family contexts. In W. Damon & N. Eisenberg (Eds.), *Handbook of child psychology: Vol. 3. Social, emotional, and personality development* (5th ed., pp. 1097–1150). New York: Wiley.

Grunberg, N. E. (1994). Overview: Biological processes relevant to drugs of dependence. *Addiction, 89*(11), 1443–1446.

Grusec, J. E., & Goodnow, J. J. (1994). Impact of parental discipline methods on the child's internalization of values. *Developmental Psychology, 30,* 4–19.

Grusec, J. E., Davidov, M., & Lundell, L. (2002). Prosocial and helping behavior. In P. K. Smith & C. H. Hart (Eds.), *Blackwell handbook of childhood social development* (pp. 457–474). Malden, MA: Blackwell.

Guadagno, R. E., Asher, T., Demaine, L. J., & Cialdini, R. B. (2001). When saying yes leads to saying no: Preference for consistency and the reverse foot-in-the-door effect. *Personality and Social Psychology Bulletin, 27,* 859–867.

Guerin, D. W., Gottfried, A. W., & Thomas, C. W. (1997). Difficult temperament and behaviour problems: A longitudinal study from 1.5 to 12 years. *International Journal of Behavioral Development, 21,* 71–90.

Guerlain, S. (1993). Factors influencing the cooperative problem-solving of people and computers. *Proceedings of the Human Factors and Ergonomics Society 37th Annual Meeting* (pp. 387–391). Santa Monica, CA: Human Factors Society.

Guerlain, S. (1995). Using the critiquing approach to cope with brittle expert systems. *Proceedings of the Human Factors and Ergonomics Society 39th Annual Meeting, I* (pp. 233–237). Santa Monica, CA: Human Factors Society.

Guevara, M. A., Lorenzo, I., Ramos, J., & Corsi-Cabrera, M. (1995). Inter- and intrahemispheric EEG correlation during sleep and wakefulness. *Sleep, 18*(4), 257–265.

Guilford, J. P. (1959). Traits of creativity. In H. H. Anderson (Ed.), *Creativity and its cultivation* (pp. 142–161). New York: Harper & Row.

Guilford, J. P., & Hoepfner, R. (1971). *The analysis of intelligence.* New York: McGraw-Hill.

Gunnoe, M. L., & Mariner, C. L. (1997). Toward a developmental-contextual model of the effects of parental spanking on children's aggressoin. *Archives of Pediatrics and Adolescent Medicine, 151,* 768–775.

Gupta, M. A., & Gupta, A. K. (2002, May 13). Use of eye movement desensitization and reprocessing (EMDR) in the treatment of dermatologic disorders. *Journal of Cutaneous Medicine and Surgery: Incorporating Medical and Surgical Dermatology, 6–5,* 415–421.

Gupta, R. K., & Moller, H.-J. (2003). St. John's wort: An option for the primary care treatment of depressive patients? *European Archives of Psychiatry and Clinical Neuroscience, 253*(3), 140–148.

Gupta, V. K., & Reiter, E. R. (2004). Current treatment practices in obstructive sleep apnea and snoring. *American Journal of Otolaryngology, 25,* 18–25.

Gur, R. C., Mozley, L. H., Mozley, P. D., Resnick, S. M., Karp, J. S., Alavi, A., et al. (1995). Sex differences in regional cerebral glucose metabolism during a resting state. *Science, 267,* 528–531.

Gur, R. C., Skolnic, B. E., & Gur, R. E. (1994). Effects of emotional discrimination tasks on cerebral blood flow: Regional activation and its relation to performance. *Brain and Cognition, 25*(2), 271–286.

Gur, R. E., Cowell, P. E., Latshaw, A., Turetsky, B. I., Grossman, R. I., Arnold, S. E., et al. (2000). Reduced dorsal and orbital prefrontal gray matter volumes in schizophrenia. *Archives of General Psychiatry, 57,* 761–768.

Gura, T. (1999). Leptin not impressive in clinical trial. *Science, 286,* 881–882.

Gurman, A. S., & Jacobson, N. S. (2002). *Clinical handbook of couple therapy* (3rd ed.). New York: Guilford Press.

Gustafsson, J. E., & Undheim, J. O. (1996). Individual differences in cognitive functions. In D. C. Berliner & R. C. Calfee (Eds.), *Handbook of educational psychology* (pp. 186–242). New York: Simon & Schuster Macmillan.

Gustavino, C., Katz, B.F.G., Polack, J.D., Levitin, D.J. & Dubois, D. (2005). Ecological validity of soundscape reproduction. *Acta Acustica United With Acustica, 91,* 333–341.

Guyer, B., Freedman, M. A., Strobino, D. M., & Sondik, E. J. (2000). Annual summary of vital statistics: Trends in the health of Americans during the 20th century. *Pediatrics, 106,* 1307–1317.

Ha, H., Tan, E. C., Fukunaga, H., & Aochi, O. (1981). Naloxone reversal of acupuncture analgesia in the monkey. *Experimental Neurology, 73,* 298–303.

Haaga, D. A. (2000). Introduction to the special section on stepped care models in psychotherapy. *Journal of Consulting and Clinical Psychology, 68,* 547–548.

Haber, R. N. (1979). Twenty years of haunting eidetic imagery: Where's the ghost? *The Behavioral and Brain Sciences, 2,* 583–629.

Haberlandt, K. (1999). *Human memory: Exploration and application.* Boston: Allyn & Bacon.

Haberstroh, J. (1995). *Ice cube sex: The truth about subliminal advertising.* South Bend, IN: Cross Cultural Publications/Crossroads.

Hacking, I. (1995). *Rewriting the soul: Multiple personality and the sciences of memory.* Princeton, NJ: Princeton University Press.

Hackman, J. R. (1998). Why don't teams work? In R. S. Tindale, J. Edwards, & E. J. Posavac (Eds.), *Applications of theory and research on groups to social issues.* New York: Plenum.

Haddock, G., & Zanna, M. P. (1998b). Authoritarianism, values, and the favorability and structure of antigay attitudes. In G. Herek (Ed.), *Stigma and sexual orientation: Understanding prejudice against lesbians, gay men, and bisexuals. Psychological perspectives on lesbian and gay issues.* Thousand Oaks, CA: Sage.

Hadjikhani, N., & de Gelder, B. (2003). Seeing fearful body expressions activates the fusiform cortex and amygdale. *Current Biology, 13,* 2201–2205.

Haefner, H., & Maurer, K. (2000). The early course of schizophrenia: New concepts for early intervention. In G. Andrews & S. Henderson (Eds.), *Unmet need in psychiatry: Problems, resources, responses* (p. 218–232). New York: Cambridge University Press.

Hagen, E. P. (1980). *Identification of the gifted.* New York: Teachers College Press.

Hagen, M. A. (2001). Damaged goods?: What, if anything, does science tell us about the long-term effects of childhood sexual abuse? *Skeptical Inquirer, 25,* 54–59.

Hahdahl, K., Iversen, P. M., & Jonsen, B. H. (1993). Laterality for facial expressions: Does the sex of the subject interact with the sex of the stimulus face? *Cortex, 29*(2), 325–331.

Hahn, C.-S., & DiPietro, J. A. (2001). In vitro fertilization and the family: Quality of parenting, family functioning, and child psychosocial adjustment. *Developmental Psychology, 37,* 37–48.

Haier, R. J., White, N. S., & Alkire, M. T. (2003). Individual differences in general intelligence correlate with brain function during nonreasoning tasks. *Intelligence, 31,* 429–441.

Haldeman, D. C. (1994). The practice and ethics of sexual orientation-conversion therapy. *Consulting and Clinical Psychology, 62*(2), 221–227.

Halford, G. S., Maybery, M. R., O'Hare, A. W., & Grant, P. (1994). The development of memory and processing capacity. *Child Development, 65,* 1338–1356.

Hall, C. S., Lindzey, G., & Campbell, J. P. (1998). *Theories of personality* (4th ed.). New York: Wiley.

Hall, G. C. N. (2001). Psychotherapy research with ethnic minorities: Empirical, ethical, and conceptual issues. *Journal of Consulting and Clinical Psychology, 69,* 502–510.

Hall, J. A. (1984). *Nonverbal sex differences.* Baltimore, MD: Johns-Hopkins University Press.

Hall, L. K., & Bahrick, H. P. (1998). The validity of metacognitive predictions of widespread learning and long-term retention. In G. Mazzoni & T. Nelson (Eds.), *Metacognition and cognitive neuropsychology: Monitoring and control processes* (pp. 23–36). Mahwah, NJ: Erlbaum.

Hall, P., & Davidson, K. (1996). The misperception of aggression in behaviorally hostile men. *Cognitive Therapy and Research, 20,* 377–389.

Hall, W., & Degenhardt, L. (2003). Medical marijuana initiatives: Are they justified? How successful are they likely to be? *CNS Drugs, 17,* 689–697.

Halligan, P. W., & David, A. S. (Eds.). (1999). *Conversion hysteria: Towards a cognitive neuropsychological account.* Hove, UK: Psychology Press.

Halloran, M. J., & Kashima, E. S. (2004). Social identity and worldview validation: The effects of ingroup identity primes and mortality salience on value endorsement. *Personality and Social Psychology Bulletin, 30,* 915–925.

Halpern, D. F. (1997). Sex differences in intelligence. *American Psychologist, 52,* 1091–1102.

Hamann, S., Herman, R. A., Nolan, C. L., & Wallen, K. (2004). Men and women differ in amygdala response to sexual stimuli. *Nature Neuroscience, 7,* 411–416.

Hamarat, E., Thompson, D., Steele, D., Matheny, K., & Simons, C. (2002). Age differences in coping resources and satisfaction with life among middle-aged, young-old, and oldest-old adults. *Journal of Genetic Psychology, 163*(3), 360–367.

Hamilton, C. E. (2000). Continuity and discontinuity of attachment from infancy through adolescence. *Child Development, 71,* 690–694.

Hamilton, D. L., & Sherman, J. (1994). Social stereotypes. In R. S. Wyer & T. K. Srull (Eds.), *Handbook of social cognition* (2nd ed.).

Hamilton, W. D. (1964). The evolution of social behavior: Parts I and II. *Journal of Theoretical Biology 7,* 1–52.

Hamm, A. O., Vaitl, D., & Lang, P. J. (1989). Fear conditioning, meaning, and belongingness: A selective association analysis. *Journal of Abnormal Psychology, 98,* 395–406.

Hammer, E. (1968). Projective drawings. In A. I. Rabin (Ed.), *Projective techniques in personality assessment.* New York: Springer.

Hammerness, P., Basch, E., & Ulbricht, C. (2003). St. John's wort: A systematic review of adverse effects and drug interactions for the consultation psychiatrist. *Journal of Consultation Liaison Psychiatry, 44*(4), 271–282.

Hampel, H., Teipel, S. J., Fuchsberger, T., Andreasen, N., Wiltfang, J., Otto, M., et al. (2004). Value of CSF-amyloid 1–42 and tau as predictors of Alzheimer's disease in patients with mild cognitive impairment. *Molecular Biology, 9,* 705–710.

Haney, M., Ward, A. S., Comer, S. D., Foltin, R. W., & Fischman, M. W. (1999). Abstinence symptoms following smoked marijuana in humans. *Psychopharmacology, 141,* 395–404.

Hankin, B. L., & Abramson, L. Y. (2001). Development of gender differences in depression: An elaborated cognitive vulnerability-transactional stress theory. *Psychological Bulletin, 127,* 773–796.

Hannesonn, D., (2002). Characterization of kindling's effects on spatial cognition: Implications for the mechanisms of kindling-induced mnemonic dysfunction. *Dissertation Abstracts International: Section B: The Sciences and Engineering, 62*(11-B), 5422.

Hannigan, S. L., & Reinitz, M. T. (2001). A demonstration and comparison of two types of inference-based memory errors. *Journal of Experimental Psychology: Learning, Memory, and Cognition, 27,* 931–940.

Hanson, G., & Venturelli, P. J. (1995). *Drugs and society* (4th ed.). Boston: Jones & Bartlett.

Hanson, S. J., & Burr, D. J. (1990). What connectionist models learn: Learning and representations in connectionist networks. *Behavioral and Brain Sciences, 13,* 471–518.

Happe, F. G. E., Winner, E., & Brownell, H. (1998). The getting of wisdom: Theory of mind in old age. *Developmental Psychology, 34,* 358–362.

Harasty, J., Double, K. L., Halliday, G. M., Kril, J. J., & McRitchie, D. A. (1997). Language-associated cortical regions are proportionally larger in the female brain. *Archives of Neurology, 54,* 171–176.

Harbluk, J. L. & Noy, I.Y. (2002). *The impact of cognitive distraction on driver visual behaviour and vehicle control.* Ottawa: Transport Canada.

Hardimann, P. T., Dufresne, R., & Mestre, J. (1989). The relation between problem categorization and problem solving among experts and novices. *Memory & Cognition, 17,* 627–638.

Hardy, C.L., Bukowski, W.M., & Sippola, L.K. (2002). Stability and change in peer relationships during the transition to middle-level school. *Journal of Early Adolescence, 22,* 117–142.

Hare, R. D. (1993). *Without conscience: The disturbing world of the psychopaths among us.* New York: Pocket Books.

Harlow, H. F. (1949). The formation of learning sets. *Psychological Review, 56,* 51–65.

Harmen, S. M., Metter, E.J., Tobin, J.D., Pearson, J., & Blackman, M.R., (2001). Longitudinal effects of aging on serum total and free testosterone levels in healthy men. *Journal of Clinical Endocrinology and Metabolism, 86:2,* 724–31.

Harmon-Jones, E., Brehm, J. W., Greenberg, J., Simon, L., & Nelson, D. E. (1996). Evidence that the production of negative consequences is not necessary to produce cognitive dissonance. *Journal of Personality and Social Psychology, 72,* 515–525.

Harper, D. G., Stopa, E. G., McKee, A. C., Satlin, A., Harlan, P. C., Goldstein, R., & Volicer, L. (2001). Differential circadian rhythm disturbances in men with Alzheimer disease and frontotemporal degeneration. *Archives of General Psychiatry, 58,* 353–360.

Harris, C. V., & Goetsch, V. L. (1990). Multi-component flooding treatment of adolescent phobia. In E. L. Feindler & G. R. Kalfus (Eds.), *Adolescent behavior therapy handbook* (Vol. 22). New York: Springer.

Harris, D. A. (1999). Brian's law [Electronic version]. Available: http://www.lawyers.ca/dharris/articles/brianslaw.htm

Harris, D. A. (1999). *Susan Nelles case* [Electronic version]. Available: http://www.lawyers.ca/dharris/articles/susannellescase.htm.

Harris, G. C., & Aston-Jones, G. (1995). Involvement of D2 dopamine receptors in the nucleus acumbens in opiate withdrawal syndrome. *Nature, 371,* 155–157.

Harris, J. R. (1995). Where is the child's environment? A group socialization theory of development. *Psychological Review, 102,* 458–489.

Harris, J. R. (2000). Context-specific learning, personality, and birth order. *Current Directions in Psychological Science, 9,* 174–177.

Hart, A. J., Whalen, P. J., Shin, L. M., McInerney, S. C., Fischer, H., & Rauch, S. L. (2000). Differential response in the human amygdala to racial outgroup vs. ingroup face stimuli. *Neuroreport, 11,* 2351–2355.

Hart, C. L., Taylor, M. D., Smith, G. D., Whalley, L. J., Starr, J. M., Hole, D. J., et al. (2003). Childhood IQ, social class, deprivation, and their relationships with mortality and morbidity risk in later life: Prospective observational study linking the Scottish mental survey of 1932 and the midspan studies. *Psychosomatic Medicine, 65,* 877–883.

Harter, S. (1998). The development of self representations. In W. Damon & N. Eisenberg (Eds.), *Handbook of child psychology: Vol. 3. Social, emotional, and personality development* (5th ed., pp. 553–618). New York: Wiley.

Hartmann, H. (1958). *Ego psychology and the problem of adaptation.* New York: International Universities Press.

Hartup, W. W., & Stevens, N. (1997). Friendships and adaptation in the life course. *Psychological Bulletin, 121,* 355–370.

Harvard Mental Health Letter. (2001). New treatments for cocaine addiction. *Harvard Mental Health Letter, 17,* 6–7.

Hatcher, D., Brown, T., & Gariglietti, K. P. (2001). Critical thinking and rational emotive behavior therapy. *Inquiry: Critical Thinking Across the Disciplines, 20,* 6–18.

Hatfield, J., Job, R. F. S., Hede, A. J., Carter, N. L., Peploe, P., Taylor, R., & Morrell, S. (2002). Human response to environmental noise: The role of perceived control. *International Journal of Behavioral Medicine, 9,* 341–359.

Hathaway, W. (2002, December 22). Henry M: The day one man's memory died. *Hartford Courant.*

Hattori, M., Fujiyama A., Taylor, T. D., Watanabe, H., Yada, T., Park, H. S., et al. (2000). The DNA sequence of human chromosome 21. *Nature, 405,* 311–319.

Haugen, J. E. (2001). Electronic noses in food analysis. *Advances in Experimental Medicine and Biology, 488,* 43–57.

Hawkes, C. (2003). Olfaction in neurodegenerative disorders. *Movement Disorders, 18,* 364–372.

Hawkins, E. H., Cummins, L. H., & Marlatt, G. A. (2004). Preventing substance abuse in American Indian and Alaska Native youth: Promising strategies for healthier communities. *Psychological Bulletin, 130,* 304–323.

Hawkins, H. L., Kramer, A. R., & Capaldi, D. (1993). Aging, exercise, and attention. *Psychology and Aging, 7,* 643–653.

Haxby, J. V., Gobbini, M. I., Furey, M. L., Ishai, A., Schouten, J. L., & Pietrini, P. (2001). Distributed and overlapping representations of faces and objects in ventral temporal cortex. *Science, 293,* 2425–2430.

Hayes, A. M., & Harris, M. S. (2000). The development of an integrative therapy for depression. In S. L. Johnson & A. M. Hayes (Eds.), *Stress, coping, and depression* (pp. 291–306). Mahwah, NJ: Erlbaum.

Hayley, S., Merali, Z., & Anisman, H. (2003). Stress and cytokine-elicited neuroendocrine and neurotransmitter sensitization: Implications for depressive illness. *International Journal on the Biology of Stress, 6,* 19–32.

Hays, P. A. (1995). Multicultural applications of cognitive-behavior therapy. *Professional Psychology: Research and Practice, 26,* 309–315.

Hays, W. L. (1981). *Statistics* (3rd ed). New York: Holt, Rinehart & Winston.

He, L. F. (1987). Involvement of endogenous opioid peptides in acupuncture analgesia. *Pain, 31,* 99–121.

Health Canada. (1995). *Horizons three young Canadians' alcohol and other drug use: Increasing our understanding.* D. Hewitt, G. Vinje, & P. MacNeil (Eds.). [Electronic version]. Available: http://www.hc-sc.gc.ca/ahc-asc/pubs/drugs-drogues/1996_horizons/index_e.html

Health Canada. (1998). *The Aboriginal Head Start on Reserve program* [Electronic version]. Available: http://www.hc-sc.gc.ca/ahc-asc/media/nr-cp/1998/1998_71bk1_e.html

Health Canada. (2003). Important drug warning [Electronic version]. Available: http://www.hc-sc.gc.ca/dhp-mps/medeff/advisories-avis/prof/2003/paxil_hpc-cps_e.html.

Health Canada. (2004). 2002 Canadian sexually transmitted infections (STI) surveillance report: Pre-lease. Ottawa, ON: Population and Public Health Branch, Health Canada.

Health Canada. (2004). Important drug warning [Electronic version]. Available: http://www.hc-sc.gc.ca/dhp-mps/medeff/advisories-avis/prof/2004/prozac_hpc-cps_e.html.

Heart and Stroke Foundation of Canada (2002). Smoking statistics [Electronic version]. Available: http://ww2.heartandstroke.ca/Page.asp?PageID=33&ArticleID=1076&Src=news&From=SubCategory

Health Canada. (2005). Smoking and your body. [Electronic version]. Available: http://www.hc-sc.gc.ca/hl-vs/tobac-tabac/body-corps/index_e.html

Heatherton, T. F., Macrae, C. N., & Kelley, W. M. (2004). What the social brain sciences can tell us about the self. *Current Directions in Psychological Science, 13,* 190–193.

Hebb, D. O. (1949). *The organization of behavior.* New York: Wiley.

Hebb, D. O. (1955). Drives and the C. N. S. (conceptual nervous system). *Psychological Review, 62,* 243–254.

Hecker, J. E., & Thorpe, G. L. (1992). *Agoraphobia and panic: A guide to psychological treatment.* Boston: Allyn & Bacon.

Hecker, J. E., Losee, M. C., Fritzler, B. K., & Fink, C. M. (1996). Self-directed versus therapist-directed cognitive behavioral treatment for panic disorder. *Journal of Anxiety Disorders, 10,* 253–265.

Heckman, T. G., Anderson, E. S., Sikkema, K. J., Kochman, A., Kalichman, S., & Anderson, T. (2004). Emotional distress in nonmetropolitan persons living with HIV disease enrolled in a telephone-delivered, coping improvement group intervention. *Health Psychology, 23,* 94–100.

Hedley, A. A., Ogden, C. L., Johnson, C. L., Carroll, M. D., Curtin, L. R., & Flegal, K. M. (2004). Prevalence of overweight and obesity among US children, adolescents, and adults, 1999–2002. *Journal of the American Medical Association, 291,* 2847–2850.

Heekeren, H. R., Marrett, S., Bandettini, P. A., & Ungerleider, L. G. (2004). A general mechanism for perceptual decision-making in the human brain. *Nature, 431,* 859–862.

Hegarty, J. D., Baldessarini, R. J., Tohen, M., Waternaux, C., & Oepen, G. (1994). One hundred years of schizophrenia: A meta-analysis of the outcome literature. *American Journal of Psychiatry, 151,* 1409–1416.

Heiby, E. M., DeLeon, P. H., & Anderson, T. (2004). A debate on prescription privileges for psychologists. *Professional Psychology: Research and Practice, 35,* 336–344.

Heider, E. (1972). Universals of color naming and memory. *Journal of Experimental Psychology, 93,* 10–20.

Heilman, K. M., & Valenstein, E. (Eds.). (2003). *Clinical neuropsychology* (4th ed.). New York: Oxford University Press.

Heim, C., Newport, J., Heit, S., Graham, Y. P., Wilcox, M., Bonsall, R., et al. (2000). Pituitary-adrenal and autonomic responses to stress in women after sexual and physical abuse in childhood. *Journal of the American Medical Association, 284,* 592–597.

Heiman, J. R. (2002). Sexual dysfunction: Overview of prevalence, etiological factors, and treatments. *Journal of Sex Research, 39,* 73–78.

Heine, S. J. (2003). Self-enhancement in Japan? A reply to Brown & Kobayashi. *Asian Journal of Social Psychology, 6,* 75–84.

Heine, S. J., & Lehman, D. R. (1997). Culture, dissonance, and self-affirmation. *Personality and Social Psychology Bulletin, 23,* 389–400.

Heine, S. J., Harihara, M., & Niiya, Y. (2002). Terror management in Japan. *Asian Journal of Social Psychology, 5,* 187–196.

Hejmadi, A., Davidson, R. J., & Rozin, P. (2000). Exploring Hindu Indian emotion expressions: Evidence for accurate recognition by Americans and Indians. *Psychological Science, 11,* 183–187.

Helgesen, S. (1998). *Everyday revolutionaries: Working women and the transformation of American life.* New York: Doubleday.

Helmchen, C., Lindig, M., Petersen, D., & Tronnier, V. (2002). Disappearance of central thalamic pain syndrome after contralateral parietal lobe lesion: Implications for therapeutic brain stimulation. *Pain, 98,* 325–330.

Helmers, K. F., & Krantz, D. S. (1996). Defensive hostility, gender and cardiovascular levels and responses to stress. *Annals of Behavioral Medicine, 18,* 246–254.

Helmers, K. F., Krantz, D. S., Merz, C. N. B., Klein, J., Kop, W. J., Gottdiener, J. S., & Rozanski, A. (1995). Defensive hostility: Relationship to multiple markers of cardiac ischemia in patients with coronary disease. *Health Psychology, 14,* 202–209.

Helms, J. E. (1992). Why is there no study of cultural equivalence in standardized cognitive ability testing? *American Psychologist, 47,* 1083–1101.

Helms, J. E. (1997). The triple quandary of race, culture, and social class in standardized cognitive ability testing. In D. P. Flanagan, J. L. Genshaft, & P. L. Harrison (Eds.), *Contemporary intellectual assessment: Theories, tests, and issues.* New York: Guilford Press.

Helson, R., & Moane, G. (1987). Personality change in women from college to midlife. *Journal of Personality and Social Psychology, 53,* 176–186.

Helzer, J. E., Canino, G. J., Yeh, E., Bland, R. C., Lee, C. K., Hwu, H., & Newman, S. (1990). Alcoholism—North America and Asia: A comparison of population surveys with the diagnostic interview schedule. *Archives of General Psychiatry, 47,* 313–319.

Henderson, B., & Bernard, A. (Eds.). (1998). *Rotten reviews and rejections.* Wainscott, NY: Pushcart Press.

Hendrick, B. (2003, May 8). Exam day rituals help students feel lucky. *Naples Daily News.*

Hendrick, C., & Hendrick, S. S. (2003). Romantic love: Measuring cupid's arrow. In S. J. Lopez & C. R. Snyder (Eds.), *Positive psychological assessment: A handbook of models and measures* (pp. 235–249). Washington, DC: American Psychological Association.

Henig, R. (2004, April 4). The quest to forget. *The New York Times,* p. 32.

Henkel, L. A. (2004). Erroneous memories arising from repeated attempts to remember. *Journal of Memory and Language, 50,* 26–46.

Henry, W. P. (1998). Science, politics, and the politics of science: The use and misuse of empirically validated treatment research. *Psychotherapy Research, 8,* 126–140.

Hense, R. L., Penner, L. A., & Nelson, D. L. (1995). Implicit memory for age stereotypes. *Social Cognition, 13,* 399–416.

Herbert, J. D., Lilienfeld, S. O., Lohr, J. M., Montgomery, R. W., O'Donohue, W. T., Rosen, G. M., & Tolin, D. F. (2000). Science and pseudoscience in the development of eye movement desensitization and reprocessing: Implications for clinical psychology. *Clinical Psychology Review, 20,* 945–971.

Hergenhahn, B. R., & Olson, M. (1997). *An introduction to theories of learning* (5th ed.). Upper Saddle River, NJ: Prentice-Hall.

Hergenhahn, B. R., Olson, M. H., & Cramer, K. M. (2003). *An introduction to theories of personality* (Canadian edition). Toronto, ON: Prentice Hall.

Herman, C. P., Roth, D. A., & Polivy, J. (2003). Effects of the presence of others on food intake: A normative interpretation. *Psychological Bulletin, 129,* 873–886.

Herman, L. M., Richards, D. G., & Wolz, J. P. (1984). Comprehension of sentences by bottlenosed dolphins. *Cognition, 16,* 129–219.

Herpertz, S. C., Werth, U., Lukas, G., Qunaibi, M., Schuerkens, A., Kunert, H.-J., et al. (2001). Emotion in criminal offenders with psychopathy and borderline personality disorder. *Archives of General Psychiatry, 58,* 737–745.

Herrenkohl, T., Hill, K., Chung, I.-J., Guo, J., Abbott, R. D., & Hawkins, D. J. (2004). Protective factors against serious violent behavior in adolescence: A prospective study of violent children. *Social Work Research, 27*(3), 179–191.

Herrmann, D. J., & Searleman, A. (1992). Memory improvement and memory theory in historical perspective. In D. Herrmann, H. Weingartner, A. Searlman, & C. McEvoy (Eds.), *Memory improvement: Implications for memory theory.* New York: Springer-Verlag.

Herrnstein, R. J., & Murray, C. (1994). *The bell curve: Intelligence and class structure in American Life.* New York: Free Press.

Hertenstein, M. J., & Campos, J. J. (2004). The retention effects of an adult's emotional displays on infant behavior. *Child Development, 75,* 585–613.

Herz, R. S., & Cahill, E. D. (1997). Differential use of sensory information in sexual behavior as a function of gender. *Human Nature, 8,* 275–286.

Herzog, D. B. (1982). Bulimia: The secretive syndrome. *Psychosomatics, 22,* 481–487.

Herzog, D. B., Dorer, D. J., Keel, P. K., Selwyn, S. E., Ekeblad, E. R., Flores, A. T., et al. (1999). Recovery and relapse in anorexia and bulimia nervosa: A 7.5-year follow-up study. *Journal of the American Academy of Child and Adolescent Psychiatry, 38,* 829–837.

Herzog, D. B., Greenwood, D. N., Dorer, D. J., Flores, A. T., Ekeblad, E. R., Richards, A., et al. (2000). Mortality in eating disorders: A descriptive study. *International Journal of Eating Disorders, 28,* 20–26.

Hespos, S. J., & Baillargeon, R. (2001). Infants' knowledge about occlusion and containment events: A surprising discrepancy. *Psychological Science, 12,* 141–147.

Hespos, S. J., & Spelke, E. S. (2004). Conceptual precursors to language. *Nature, 430,* 453–456.

Hess, R. D., Chih-Mei, C., & McDevitt, T. M. (1987). Cultural variations in family beliefs about children's performance in mathematics: Comparisons among People's Republic of China, Chinese-American, and Caucasian-American families. *Journal of Educational Psychology, 79,* 179–188.

Hesse, J., Mogelvang, B., & Simonsen, H. (1994). Acupuncture versus metropolol in migraine prophylaxis: A randomized trial of trigger point inactivation. *Journal of Internal Medicine, 235,* 451–456.

Hetherington, E. M., & Clingempeel, W. G. (1992). Coping with marital transitions. *Monographs of the Society for Research in Child Development, 57* (2–3, Serial No. 227).

Hetherington, E. M., & Stanley-Hagan, M. (2002). Parenting in divorced, single-parent, and stepfamilies. In M. H. Bornstein (Ed.), *Handbook of parenting* (2nd ed.). Mahwah, NJ: Erlbaum.

Hettema, J. M., Neale, M. C., & Kendler, K. S. (2001). A review and meta-analysis of the genetic epidemiology of anxiety disorders. *American Journal of Psychiatry, 158,* 1568–1578.

Heuer, H., Kleinsorge, T., Klein, W., & Kohlisch, O. (2004). Total sleep deprivation increases the costs of shifting between simple cognitive tasks. *Acta Psychologica (Amsterdam), 117,* 29–64.

Heward, W. L. (1997). Four validated instructional strategies. *Behavior and Social Issues, 7,* 43–51.

Hewstone, M. (2003). Intergroup contact: Panacea for prejudice? *Psychologist, 16,* 352–355.

Heymsfield, S. B., Greenberg, A. S., Fujioa, K., Dixon, R. M., Kushner, R., Hunt, T., et al. (1999). Recombinant leptin for weight loss in obese and lean adults. *Journal of the American Medical Association, 282,* 1568–1575.

Heywood, C. A., & Kentridge, R. W. (2003). Achromatopsia, color vision, and cortex. *Neurology Clinics, 21,* 483–500.

Hickok, G., Bellugi, U., & Klima, E. S. (1996). The neurobiology of sign language and its implications for the neural basis of language. *Nature, 381,* 699–702.

Hicks, R. A., Fernandez, C., & Pelligrini, R. J. (2001). The changing pattern of sleep habits of university students: An update. *Perceptual and Motor Skills, 93,* 648.

Highley, J. R., Walker, M. A., Crow, T. J., Esiri, M. M., & Harrison, P. J. (2003). Low medial and lateral right pulvinar volumes in schizophrenia: A postmortem study. *American Journal of Psychiatry, 160,* 1177–1179.

Hildebrandt, M. G., Steyerberg, E. W., Stage, K. B., Passchier, J., Kragh-Soerensen, P., and the Danish University Antidepressant Group. (2003). Are gender differences important for the clinical effects of antidepressants? *American Journal of Psychiatry, 160,* 1643–1650.

Hilgard, E. R. (1965). *Hypnotic susceptibility.* New York: Harcourt, Brace & World.

Hilgard, E. R. (1977). *Divided consciousness: Multiple controls in human thought and action.* New York: Wiley.

Hilgard, E. R. (1979). *Personality and hypnosis: A study of imaginative involvement.* Chicago: University of Chicago Press.

Hilgard, E. R. (1982). Hypnotic susceptibility and implications for measurement. *International Journal of Clinical and Experimental Hypnosis, 30,* 394–403.

Hilgard, E. R. (1992). Divided consciousness and dissociation. *Consciousness and Cognition, 1,* 16–31.

Hilgard, E. R., & Marquis, D. G. (1936). Conditioned eyelid responses in monkeys, with a comparison of dog, monkey, and man. *Psychological Monographs, 47,* 186–198.

Hilgard, E. R., Morgan, A. H., & MacDonald, H. (1975). Pain and dissociation in the cold pressor test: A study of "hidden reports" through automatic key-pressing and automatic talking. *Journal of Abnormal Psychology, 84,* 280–289.

Hill, B. (1968). *Gates of horn and ivory.* New York: Taplinger.

Hill, D. L., & Mistretta, C. M. (1990). Developmental neurobiology of salt taste sensation. *Trends in Neuroscience, 13,* 188–195.

Hill, D. L., & Przekop, P. R., Jr. (1988). Influences of dietary sodium on functional taste receptor development: A sensitive period. *Science, 241,* 1826–1828.

Hill, J. O., & Peters, J. C. (1998). Environmental contributions to the obesity epidemic. *Science, 280,* 1371–1374.

Hill, T., Lewicki, P., Czyzewska, M., & Boss, A. (1989). Self-perpetuating biases in person perception. *Journal of Personality and Social Psychology, 57,* 373–386.

Hilliard, R. B., Henry, W. P., & Strupp, H. H. (2000). An interpersonal model of psychotherapy: Linking patient and therapist developmental history, therapeutic process, and types of outcome. *Journal of Consulting and Clinical Psychology, 68,* 125–133.

Hilton, D. (2002). Thinking about causality: Pragmatic, social and scientific rationality. In P. E. Carruthers, S. Stich, & M. Siegal (Eds.), *The cognitive basis of science* (pp. 211–231). New York: Cambridge University Press.

Hinshaw, S. P., Zupan, B. A., Simmel, C., Nigg, J. T., & Melnick, S. (1997). Peer status in boys with and without attention-deficit hyperactivity disorder: Predictions from overt and covert antisocial behavior, social isolation, and authoritative parenting beliefs. *Child Development, 68,* 880–896.

Hinton, D., Um, K., & Ba, P. (2001). Kyol goeu ('wind overload') Part I: A cultural syndrome of orthostatic panic among Khmer refugees. *Transcultural Psychiatry, 38,* 403–432.

Hinton, J. (1967). *Dying.* Harmondsworth, England: Penguin.

Hiroto, D. S. (1974). Locus of control and learned helplessness. *Journal of Experimental Psychology, 102,* 187–193.

Hirschfeld, R. M. A., & Vornik, L. A. (2004). Newer antidepressants: Review of efficacy and safety of escitalopram and duloxetine. *Journal of Clinical Psychiatry, 65* (Suppl. 4), 46–52.

Hirschfeld, R. M., Allen, M. H., McEvoy, J. P., Keck, P. E., Jr, & Russell, J. M. (1999). Safety and tolerability of oral loading divalproex sodium in acutely manic bipolar patients. *Journal of Clinical Psychiatry, 60,* 815–818.

Hirsch-Pasek, K., Treiman, R., & Schneiderman, M. (1984). Brown and Hanlon revisited: Mothers' sensitivity to ungrammatical forms. *Journal of Child Language, 11,* 81–88.

Ho, B.-C., Andreasen, N. C., Nopoulos, P., Arndt, S., Magnotta, V., & Flaum M. (2003). Progressive structural brain abnormalities and their relationship to clinical outcome: A longitudinal magnetic resonance imaging study early in schizophrenia. *Archives of General Psychiatry, 60,* 585–594.

Ho, D. Y., & Chiu, C. (1998). Component ideas of individual, collectivism, and social organization. In U. Kim, C. Kagitcibasi, & H. C. Triandis (Eds.), *Individualism and collectivism: Theory, method, and applications.* Thousand Oaks, CA: Sage.

Ho, Y.-C., Cheung, M., & Chan, A. S. (2003). Music training improves verbal but not visual memory: Cross-sectional and longitudinal explorations in children. *Neuropsychology, 17,* 439–450.

Hobson, J. (1997). Dreaming as delirium: A mental status analysis of our nightly madness. *Seminar in Neurology, 17,* 121–128.

Hobson, J. A., & Stickgold, R. (1994). Dreaming: A neurocognitive approach. *Consciousness and Cognition, 3,* 1–15.

Hobson, J. A., Pace-Schott, E. F., Stickgold, R., & Kahn, D. (1998). To dream or not to dream? Relevant data from new neuroimaging and electrophysical studies. *Current Opinions in Neurobiology, 8,* 239–244.

Hochhalter, A., Sweeney, W., Bakke, B. L., Holub, R. J., & Overmier, J. B. (2001). Improving face recognition in alcohol dementia. *Clinical Gerontologist, 22,* 3–18.

Hoffert, M. J. (1992). The neurophysiology of pain. In G. M. Aronoff (Ed.), *Evaluation and treatment of chronic pain.* Baltimore: Williams & Wilkins.

Hoffman, H. G., Granhag, P. A., See, S. T. K., & Loftus, E. F. (2001). Social influences on reality-monitoring decisions. *Memory and Cognition, 29,* 394–404.

Hoffman, R. E., Hawkins, K. A., Gueorguieva, R., Boutros, N. N., Rachid, F., Carroll, K., & Krystal, J. H. (2003). Transcranial magnetic stimulation of left temporoparietal cortex and medication-resistant auditory hallucinations. *Archives of General Psychiatry, 60,* 49–56.

Hogan, R. J., & Ones, D. (1997). Conscientiousness and integrity at work. In R. Hogan, J. Johnson, & S. Briggs (Eds.), *Handbook of personality psychology* (pp. 849–873). San Diego: Academic Press.

Hogarth, R. M., & Einhorn, H. J. (1992). Order effects in belief updating: The belief adjustment model. *Cognitive Psychology, 24,* 1–55.

Hoge, C. W., Castro, C.A., Messer, S.C., McGurk, D., Cotting, D.I., & Koffman, R.L. (2004). Combat duty in Iraq and Afganistan, Mental health problems, and barriers to care. *The New England Journal of Medicine,* 351, 13–22.

Hoglinger, G. U., Widmer, H. R., Spenger, C., Meyer, M., Seiler, R. W., Oertel, W. H., & Sautter, J. (2001). Influence of time in culture and BDNF pretreatment on survival and function of grafted embryonic rat ventral mesencephalon in the 6 OHDA rat model of Parkinson's disease. *Experimental Neurology, 167,* 148–157.

Hohman, A. A., & Shear, M. K. (2002). Community-based intervention research: Coping with the "noise" of real life in study design. *American Journal of Psychiatry, 159,* 201–207.

Holahan, C. K. (1994). Women's goal orientations across the life cycle: Findings from the Terman Study of the Gifted. In B. F. Turner & L. E. Troll (Eds.), *Women growing older* (pp. 35–67). Thousand Oaks, CA: Sage.

Holden, C. (1996). Small refugees suffer the effects of early neglect. *Science, 274,* 1076–1077.

Hollis, K. A. (1997). Contemporary research on Pavlovian conditioning: A "new" functional analysis. *American Psychologist, 52,* 956–964.

Hollon, S. D., Thase, M. E., & Markowitz, J. C. (2002). Treatment and prevention of depression. *Psychological Science in the Public Interest, 3,* 39–77.

Holman, B. R. (1994). Biological effects of central nervous system stimulants. *Addiction, 89*(11), 1435–1441.

Holmes, D. S. (1991). *Abnormal psychology.* New York: HarperCollins.

Holmes, T. H., & Rahe, R. H. (1967). The Social Readjustment Rating Scale. *Journal of Psychosomatic Research, 11,* 213–218.

Holtzheimer, P. E., III, Russo, J., & Claypoole, K. H. (2004). Shorter duration of depressive episode may predict response to repetitive transcranial magnetic stimulation. *Depression and Anxiety, 19*(1), 24–30.

Holway, A. H., & Boring, E. G. (1941). Determinants of apparent visual size with distance variant. *American Journal of Psychology, 54,* 21–37.

Hong, Y., Morris, M. W., Chiu, C., & Benet-Martinez, V. (2000). Multicultural minds: A dynamic constructivist approach to culture and cognition. *American Psychologist, 55,* 709–720.

Honts, C. R., & Quick, B. D. (1995). The polygraph in 1996: Progress in science and the law. *North Dakota Law Review, 71,* 997–1020.

Hood, M. Y., Moore, L. L., Sundarajan-Ramamurti, A., Singer, M., Cupples, L. A., & Ellison, R. C. (2000). Parental eating attitudes and the development of obesity in children: The Framingham children's study. *International Journal of Obesity, 24,* 1319–1325.

Hooley, J. M. (2004). Do psychiatric patients do better clinically if they live with certain kinds of families? *Current Directions in Psychological Science, 13,* 202–205.

Hopper, K., & Wanderling, J. (2000) Revisiting the developed versus developing country distinction in course and outcome in schizophrenia: Results from ISoS, the WHO Collaborative Followup Project. *Schizophrenia Bulletin, 26,* 835–846.

Horgan, J. (1996, December). Why Freud isn't dead. *Scientific American,* pp. 106–111.

Horn, J. L. (1982). The theory of fluid and crystallized intelligence in relation to concepts of cognitive psychology and aging in adulthood. In F. I. M. Craik & S. Trehub (Eds.), *Aging and cognitive processes* (pp. 201–238). New York: Plenum.

Horne, J. A. (1988). *Why we sleep: The functions of sleep in humans.* Oxford: Oxford University Press.

Horner, P. J. & Gage, F. H. (2002). Regeneration in the adult and aging brain. *Archives of Neurology, 59,* 1717–1720.

Horney, K. (1937). *Neurotic personality of our times.* New York: Norton.

Horowitz, L. M., Rosenberg, S. E., & Bartholomew, K. (1993). Interpersonal problems, attachment styles, and outcome in brief dynamic psychotherapy. *Journal of Consulting and Clinical Psychology, 61,* 549–560.

Horwitz, A. V., Widom, C. S., McLaughlin, J., & White, H. R. (2001). The impact of childhood abuse and neglect on adult mental health: A prospective study. *Journal of Health and Social Behavior, 42,* 184–201.

Horwitz, P., & Christie, M. A. (2000). Computer-based manipulatives for teaching scientific reasoning: An example. In M. J. Jacobson & R. B. Kozuma (Eds.), *Innovations in science and mathematics education: Advanced designs for technologies of learning* (pp. 163–191). Mahwah, NJ: Erlbaum.

Hötting, K., & Röder, B. (2004). Hearing cheats touch, but less in congenitally blind than in sighted individuals. *Psychological Science, 15,* 60–64.

Houlihan, M., Fraser, I., & Welling, L. (2005, July). *Face perception and event-related potentials.* Presentation at the joint meeting of Canadian Society for Brain Behavior and Cognitive Science and Experimental Psychology Society, Montreal.

Houlihan, M. E., Pritchard, W. S., & Robinson, J. H. (2001). Effects of smoking/nicotine on performance and event-related potentials during a short-term memory scanning task. *Psychopharmacology, 156,* 388–396.

Houpt, T. R. (1994). Gastric pressure in pigs during eating and drinking. *Physiology and Behavior, 56*(2), 311–317.

House, J. S., Landis, K. R., & Umberson, D. (1988). Structures and processes of social support. *Annual Review of Sociology, 14,* 293–318.

Houston, B., & Vavac, C. (1991). Cynical hostility: Developmental factors, psychosocial correlates and health behaviors. *Health Psychology, 10,* 9–17.

Howard, D. V. (1983). *Cognitive psychology.* New York: Macmillan.

Howarth, E., & Weissman, M. M. (2000). The epidemiology and cross-national presentation of obsessive-compulsive disorder. *Psychiatric Clinics of North America, 23,* 493–507.

Howe, M. J. A., Davidson, J. W., & Sloboda, J. A. (1998). Innate talent: Reality or myth? *Behavioral and Brain Sciences, 21,* 399–442.

Hoyle, R. H. (1993). Interpersonal attraction in the absence of explicit attitudinal information. *Social Cognition, 11,* 309–320.

Hoyle, R. H., Harris, M. J., & Judd, C. M. (2002). *Research methods in social relations.* Belmont, CA: Wadsworth.

Hoyt, M. F. (1995). Brief psychotherapies. In A. S. Gurman & S. B. Messer (Eds.), *Essential psychotherapies: Theory and practice* (pp. 441–487). New York: Guilford.

Hrobjartsson, A., & Gotzsche, P. C. (2001). Is the placebo powerless?: An analysis of clinical trials comparing placebo with no treatment. *The New England Journal of Medicine, 344,* 1594–1602.

Hser, Y. I., Hoffman, V., Grella, C. E., & Anglin, M. D. (2001). A 33-year follow-up of narcotics addicts. *Archives of General Psychiatry, 58,* 503–508.

Hu, F. B., Stampfer, M. J., Manson, J. E., Grodstein, F., Colditz, G. A., Speizer, F. E., Willett, W. C. (2000). Trends in the incidence of coronary heart disease and changes in diet and lifestyle in women. *New England Journal of Medicine, 343,* 530–537.

Hu, S., Patatucci, A. M. L., Patterson, C., Li, L., Fulker, D. W., Cherny, S. S., et al. (1995). Linkage between sexual orientation and chromosome Xq28 in males but not females. *Nature Genetics, 11,* 248–256.

Hua, J. Y., & Smith, S. J. (2004). Neural activity and the dynamics of central nervous system development. *Nature Neuroscience, 7,* 327–332.

Hubble, M. A., Duncan, B. L., & Miller, S. D. (Eds.). (1999). *The heart and soul of change: What works in psychotherapy.* Washington, DC: American Psychological Association.

Hubel, D. H. (1988). Eye, Brain, and Vision. *Scientific American Library Series, No 22.* W H Freeman & Co (Sd). Retrieved March 23, 2006, from http://neuro.med.harvard.edu/site/dh/bcontex.htm

Hubel, D. H., & Wiesel, T. N. (1979). Brain mechanisms of vision. *Scientific American, 241,* 150–162.

Hudson, W. (1960). Pictorial depth in perception in subcultural groups in Africa. *Journal of Social Psychology, 52,* 183–208.

Hudspeth, A. J. (1997). How hearing happens. *Neuron, 19,* 947–950.

Huesmann, L. R. (1995). *Screen violence and real violence: Understanding the link.* Auckland, NZ: Media Aware.

Huesmann, L. R. (1998). The role of social information processing and cognitive schema in the acquisition and maintenance of habitual aggressive behavior. In R. G. Geen & E. Donnerstein (Eds.), *Human aggression.* San Diego: Academic Press.

Huesmann, L. R., & Eron, L. D. (1986). *Television and the aggressive child: A cross-national comparison.* Hillsdale, NJ: Erlbaum.

Huesmann, L. R., Moise, J., Podolski, C., & Eron, L. (1997, April). *Longitudinal relations between early exposure to television violence and young adult aggression: 1977–1992.* Paper presented at the annual meeting of the Society for Research in Child Development, Washington, DC.

Huesmann, L. R., Moise-Titus, J., Podolski, C., & Eron, L. D. (2003). Longitudinal relations between children's exposure to TV violence and their aggressive and violent behavior in young adulthood: 1977–1992. *Developmental Psychology, 39,* 201–221.

Huestis, M. A., Gorelick, D. A., Heishman, S. J., Preston, K. L., Nelson, R. A., Moolchan, E. T., & Frank, R. A. (2001). Blockade of effects of smoked marijuana by the CB1-selective cannabinoid receptor antagonist SR141716. *Archives of General Psychiatry, 58,* 322–328.

Hughes, J. R., Higgins, S. T., & Bickel, W. K. (1994). Nicotine withdrawal versus other drug withdrawal syndromes: Similarities and dissimilarities. *Addiction, 89*(11), 1461–1470.

Huizink, A. C., Mulder, E. J. H., & Buitelaar, J. K. (2004). Prenatal stress and risk for psychopathology. *Psychological Bulletin, 130,* 115–142.

Hull, C. L. (1943). *Principles of behavior.* New York: Appleton-Century-Crofts.

Hull, C. L. (1951). *Essentials of behavior.* New Haven, CT: Yale University Press.

Hunsley, J., & Rumstein-McKean, O. (1999). Improving psychotherapeutic services via randomized trials, treatment manuals, and component analysis designs. *Journal of Clinical Psychology, 55,* 1507–1517.

Hunsley, J., Lee, C. M., & Wood, J. M. (2003). Controversial and questionable assessment techniques. In S. O. Lilienfeld & S. J. Lynn (Eds.), *Science and pseudoscience in clinical psychology* (pp. 39–76). New York: Guilford Press.

Hunt, C. B. (1980). Intelligence as an information processing concept. *British Journal of Psychology, 71,* 449–474.

Hunt, E. (1983). On the nature of intelligence. *Science, 219,* 141–146.

Hunt, M. (1982). *The universe within.* New York: Simon & Schuster.

Hunt, R., & Rouse, W. B. (1981). Problem solving skills of maintenance trainees in diagnosing faults in simulated power plants. *Human Factors, 23,* 317–328.

Hunter, R. H. (1995). Benefits of competency-based treatment programs. *American Psychologist, 50,* 509–513.

Hurt, H., Brodsky, N. L., Betancourt, L., & Braitman, L. E. (1995). Cocaine-exposed children: Follow-up through 30 months. *Journal of Developmental and Behavioral Pediatrics, 16*(1), 29–35.

Huston, A. C., & Wright, J. C. (1989). The forms of television and the child viewer. In G. Comstock (Ed.), *Public communication and behavior* (Vol. 2, pp. 103–159). San Diego: Academic Press.

Huttenlocher, P. R. (1990). Morphometric study of human cerebral cortex development. *Neuropsychologia, 28,* 517–527.

Hyde, J. S. (1986). Gender differences in aggression. In J. S. Hyde & M. C. Linn (Eds.), *The psychology of gender: Advances through meta-analysis.* Baltimore: Johns Hopkins University Press.

Hyde, J. S., & Durik, A. M. (2000). Gender differences in erotic plasticity–Evolutionary or sociocultural forces? Comment on Baumeister (2000). *Psychological Bulletin, 126,* 375–379.

Hyde, K. L., & Peretz, I. (2004). Brains that are out of tune but in time. *Psychological Science, 15,* 356–360.

Hygge, S., Evans, G.W., & Bullinger, M. (2002). A prospective study of some effects of aircraft noise on cognitive performance in schoolchildren. *Psychological Science, 13,* 469–474.

Hyman, I. A. (1995). Corporal punishment, psychological maltreatment, violence, and punitiveness in America: Research, advocacy, and public policy. *Applied and Preventative Psychology, 4,* 113–130.

Hyman, I. E., & Pentland, J. (1996). The role of mental imagery in the creation of false childhood memories. *Journal of Memory and Language, 35,* 101–117.

Hyman, I. E., Jr. (2000). The memory wars. In U. Neisser & I. E. Hyman Jr. (Eds.), *Memory observed* (2nd ed., pp. 374–379). New York: Worth.

Hyman, S. E. (2003). Diagnosing disorders. *Scientific American, 289,* 96–103.

Hypericum Depression Trial Study Group. (2002). Effect of *Hypericum perforatum* (St. John's wort) in major depressive disorder: A randomized, controlled trial. *Journal of the American Medical Association, 287,* 1807–1814.

Igalens, J., & Roussel, P. (1999). A study of the relationships between compensation package, work motivation, and job satisfaction. *Journal of Organizational Behavior, 20,* 1003–1025.

Iijima, M., Arisaka, O., Minamoto, F., & Arai, Y. (2001). Sex differences in children's free drawings: A study on girls with congenital adrenal hyperplasia. *Hormones and Behavior, 40,* 99–104.

Ilgen, D. R., & Pulakos, E. D. (Eds.). (1999). *The changing nature of performance: Implications for staffing, motivation, and development.* San Francisco, CA: Jossey-Bass.

Inciardi, J. A., Surratt, H. L., & Saum, C. A. (1997). *Cocaine-exposed infants: Social, legal, and public health issues.* Thousand Oaks, CA: Sage.

Indovina, I., & Sanes, J. N. (2001). On somatotopic representation centers for finger movements in human primary motor cortex and supplementary motor area. *Neuroimage, 13,* 1027–1034.

Ingram, R. E., Miranda, J., & Segal, Z. V. (1998). *Cognitive vulnerability to depression.* New York: Guilford.

Inoue-Nakamura, N., & Matsuzawa, T. (1997). Development of stone tool use by wild chimpanzees (Pan troglodytes). *Journal of Comparative Psychology, 111,* 159–173.

Interactive Advertising Bureau of Canada. (2006). Canadian Online Advertising Grows Dramatically in 2004, 2005 [Electronic version]. Available: http://www.iabcanada.com/newsletters/050908.shtml

International Human Genome Sequencing Consortium. (2001). Initial sequencing and analysis of the human genome. *Nature, 409,* 860–921.

Internet Hockey Database (2006). Alexandre Daigle's profile [Electronic version]. Available: http://www.hockeydb.com/ihdb/stats/pdisplay.php3?pid=00001230.

Inzlicht, M., & Ben-Zeev, T. (2000). A threatening intellectual environment: Why females are susceptible to experiencing problem-solving deficits in the presence of males. *Psychological Science, 11,* 365–371.

Irnich D., Behrens, N., Molzen, H., Konig, A., Gleditsch, J., Krauss, M., et al. (2001). Randomised trial of acupuncture compared with conventional massage and "sham" laser acupuncture for treatment of chronic neck pain. *British Medical Journal, 322,* 1574–1578.

Ironson, G., Freund, B., Strauss, J. L., & Williams J. (2002). Comparison of two treatments for traumatic stress: A community-based study of EMDR and prolonged exposure. *Journal of Clinical Psychology, 58,* 113–128.

Irwin, M., Daniels, M., Smith, T., Bloom, E., & Weiner, H. (1987). Impaired natural killer cell activity during bereavement. *Brain, Behavior, and Immunity, 1,* 98–104.

Iwahashi, K., Matsuo, Y., Suwaki, H., Nakamura, K., & Ichikawa, Y. (1995). CYP2E1 and ALDH2 genotypes and alcohol dependence in Japanese. *Alcoholism Clinical and Experimental Research, 19*(3), 564–566.

Iwamura, Y., Iriki, A., & Tanaka, M. (1994). Bilateral hand representation in the postcentral somatosensory cortex. *Nature, 369,* 554–556.

Izard, C. (1993). Organizational and motivational functions of discrete emotions. In M. Lewis and J. M. Haviland (Eds.), *Handbook of emotions.* New York: Guilford.

Izard, C., Fine, S., Schultz, D. Mostow, A., Ackerman, B., & Youngstrom, E. (2001). Emotion knowledge as a predictor of social behavior and academic competence in children at risk. *Psychological Science, 12,* 18–23.

Jack, C. R. Jr., Petersen, R. C., Xu, Y. C., O'Brien, P. C., Smith, G. E., Ivnik, R. J., et al. (1999). Prediction of AD with MRI-based hippocampal volume in mild cognitive impairment. *Neurology, 52,* 1397–1403.

Jackson, B., Sellers, R. M., & Peterson, C. (2002). Pessimistic explanatory style moderates the effect of stress on physical illness. *Personality & Individual Differences, 32,* 567–573.

Jackson, D.N. (1977). *Jackson vocational interest survey.* London, ON: Research Psychologists Press.

Jackson, J. W. (2002). The relationship between group identity and intergroup prejudice is moderated by sociostructural variation. *Journal of Applied Social Psychology, 32,* 908–933.

Jackson, L.M., Pratt, M.W., Hunsberger, B., & Pancer, S.M. (2005). Optimism as a mediator of the relation between perceived parental authoritativeness and adjustment among adolescents: Finding in the sunny side of the street. *Social Development, 14,* 273–304.

Statistics Canada. (2004). Health reports: Use of cannabis and other illicit drugs. [Electronic verson]. Available: http://www.statcan.ca/Daily/English/040721/d040721a.htm

Jacob, S., & McClintock, M. K. (2000). Psychological state and mood effects of steroidal chemosignals in women and men. *Hormones and Behavior, 37,* 57–78.

Jacob, S., Kinnunen, L. H., Metz, J., Cooper, M., & McClintock, M. K. (2001). Sustained human chemosignal unconsciously alters brain function. *Neuroreport, 12,* 2391–2394.

Jacobi, C., Hayward, C., de Zwaan, M., Kraemer, H. C., & Agras, W. S. (2004). Coming to terms with risk factors for eating disorders: Application of risk terminology and suggestions for a general taxonomy. *Psychological Bulletin, 130,* 19–65.

Jacobs, G. D., Pace-Schott, E. F., Stickgold, R., & Otto, M. W. (2004). Cognitive behavior therapy and pharmacotherapy for insomnia: A randomized controlled trial and direct comparison. *Archives of Internal Medicine, 164,* 1888–1896.

Jacobson, E. (1938). *Progressive relaxation.* Chicago: University of Chicago Press.

Jacobson, N. S., Christensen, A., Prince, S. E., Cordova, J., & Eldridge, K. (2000). Integrative behavioral couples therapy: An acceptance-based, promising new treatment for couple discord. *Journal of Consulting and Clinical Psychology, 68,* 351–355.

Jacoby, L. L., Marriott, M. J., & Collins, J. G. (1990). The specifics of memory and cognition. In T. K. Srull & R. S. Wyer (Eds.), *Advances in social cognition: Vol. 3. Content and process specificity in the effects of prior experiences.* Hillsdale, NJ: Erlbaum.

Jaffee, S. R., Caspi, A., Moffitt, T. E., & Taylor, A. (2004). Physical maltreatment to antisocial child: Evidence of an environmentally mediated process. *Journal of Abnormal Psychology, 113,* 44–55.

Jaffee, S., & Hyde, J. S. (2000). Gender differences in moral orientation: A meta-analysis. *Psychological Bulletin, 126,* 703–726.

Jahnke, J. C., & Nowaczyk, R. H. (1998). *Cognition.* Upper Saddle River, NJ: Prentice-Hall.

James, J. E. (2004). Critical review of dietary caffeine and blood pressure: A relationship that should be taken more seriously. *Psychosomatic Medicine, 66,* 63–71.

James, W. (1884). Some omissions of introspective psychology. *Mind, 9,* 1–26.

James, W. (1890). *Principles of psychology.* New York: Holt.

James, W. (1892). *Psychology: Briefer course.* New York: Holt.

Jancke, L., & Kaufmann, N. (1994). Facial EMG responses to odors in solitude and with an audience. *Chemical Senses, 19*(2), 99–111.

Jang, K. L., Livesley, W. J., & Vernon, P. A. (1996). Heritability of the Big Five personality dimensions and their facets: A twin study. *Journal of Personality,* 64, 577–591.

Janik, V. M. (2000). Whistle matching in wild bottlenose dolphins. *Science, 289,* 1355–1357.

Janno, S., Holi, M., Tuisku, K., & Wahlbeck, K. (2004). Prevalence of neuroleptic-induced movement disorders in chronic schizophrenia patients. *American Journal of Psychiatry, 161,* 160–163.

Janowiak, J. J., & Hackman, R. (1994). Meditation and college students' self-actualization and rated stress. *Psychological Reports, 75*(2), 1007–1010.

Janowitz, H. D. (1967). Role of gastrointestinal tract in the regulation of food intake. In C. F. Code (Ed.), *Handbook of physiology: Alimentary canal 1.* Washington, DC: American Physiological Society.

Janszky, J., Szucs, A., Halasz, P., Borbely, C., Hollo, A., Barsi, P., & Mirnics, Z. (2002). Orgasmic aura originates from the right hemisphere. *Neurology, 58,* 302–304.

Jason, L. A., Witter, E., & Torres-Harding, S. (2003). Chronic fatigue syndrome, coping, optimism and social support. *Journal of Mental Health, 12,* 109–118.

Je, J., Vupputuri, S., Allen, K., Prerost, M. R., Hughes, J., Whelton, P. K. (1999). Passive smoking and the risk of coronary heart disease—A meta-analysis of epidemiological studies. *New England Journal of Medicine, 340,* 920–926.

Jefferis, B. M. J. H., Power, C., & Hertzman, C. (2002). Birth weight, childhood socioeconomic environment, and cognitive development in the 1958 British birth cohort study [Electronic version]. *British Medical Journal, 325,* 305.

Jenkins, G. D., Jr., Mitra, A., Gupta, N., & Shaw, J. D. (1998). Are financial incentives related to performance? A meta-analytic review of empirical research. *Journal of Applied Psychology, 83,* 777–787.

Jenkins, J. G., & Dallenbach, K. M. (1924). Oblivescence during sleep and waking. *American Journal of Psychology, 35,* 605–612.

Jenkins, M. R., & Culbertson, J. L. (1996). Prenatal exposure to alcohol. In R. L. Adams, O. A. Parsons, J. L. Culbertson, & S. J. Nixon (Eds.), *Neuropsychology for clinical practice: Etiology, assessment, and treatment of common neurological disorders* (pp. 409–452). Washington, DC: American Psychological Association.

Jenner, P. (2001). Parkinson's disease, pesticides and mitochondrial dysfunction. *Trends in Neuroscience, 24,* 245–246.

Jennings, J. R., Monk, T. H., & van der Molen, M. W. (2003). Sleep deprivation influences some but not all processes of supervisory attention. *Psychological Science, 14,* 473–479.

Jensen, A. R. (1993). Why is reaction time correlated with psychometric g? *Current Directions in Psychological Science, 2,* 53–55.

Jensen, A. R. (1998). *The g factor: The science of mental ability.* Westport, CT: Praeger.

Jensen, M., & Karoly, P. (1991). Control beliefs, coping efforts, and adjustment to chronic pain. *Journal of Consulting and Clinical Psychology, 59,* 431–438.

Jeon, Y., & Polich, J. (2003). Meta-analysis of P300 and schizophrenia: Patients, paradigms, and practical implications. *Psychophysiology, 40,* 684–701.

Jevtovic-Todorovic, V., Wozniak, D. F., Benshoff, N. D., & Olney, J. W. (2001). A comparative evaluation of the neurotoxic properties of ketamine and nitrous oxide. *Brain Research, 895,* 264–267.

Johansen, J. P., Fields, H. L., & Manning, B. H. (2001). The affective component of pain in rodents: Direct evidence for a contribution of the anterior cingulate cortex. *Proceedings of the National Academy of Sciences, 98,* 8077–8082.

John, O., & Srivastava, S. (1999). The big five taxonomy: History, measurement, and theoretical perspectives. In L. Pervin & O. John (Eds.), *Handbook of personality: Theory and research* (2nd ed., pp. 102–138). New York: Guilford.

Johnson, D. R., Westermeyer, J., Kattar, K., & Thuras, P. (2002). Daily charting of posttraumatic stress symptoms: A pilot study. *Journal of Nervous & Mental Disease, 190,* 683–692.

Johnson, J. G., Cohen, P., Dohrenwend, B. P., Link, B. G., & Brook, J. S. (1999). A longitudinal investigation of social causation and social selection processes involved in the association between socioeconomic status and psychiatric disorders. *Journal of Abnormal Psychology, 108,* 490–499.

Johnson, J. G., Cohen, P., Smailes, E. M., Kasen, S., & Brook, J. S. (2002). Television viewing and aggressive behavior during adolescence and adulthood. *Science, 295,* 2468–2471.

Johnson, J. M., & Endler, N. S. (2002). Coping with human immunodeficiency virus: Do optimists fare better? *Current Psychology: Developmental, Learning, Personality, Social, 21,* 3–16.

Johnson, J. S., & Newport, E. L. (1989). Critical period effects in second language learning. *Cognitive Psychology, 21,* 60–99.

Johnson, J., & Vickers, Z. (1993). Effects of flavor and macronutrient composition of food servings on liking, hunger and subsequent intake. *Appetite, 21*(1), 25–39.

Johnson, L. E., & Thorpe, G. L. (1994). Review of psychotherapy and counseling with minorities: A cognitive approach to individual differences, by Manuel Ramirez. *Behavioural and Cognitive Psychotherapy, 22,* 185–187.

Johnson, M. A., Dziurawiec, S., Ellis, H., & Morton, J. (1991). Newborns' preferential tracking of face-like stimuli and its subsequent decline. *Cognition, 4,* 1–19.

Johnson, M. K., & Raye, C. L. (1998). False memories and confabulation. *Trends in Cognitive Sciences, 2,* 137–145.

Johnson, S. P. (2004). Development of perceptual completion in infancy. *Psychological Science, 15,* 769–775.

Johnson, S. P., Amso, D., & Slemmer, J. A. (2003). Development of object concepts in infancy: Evidence for early learning in an eye-tracking paradigm. *Proceedings of the National Academy of Sciences, 100,* 10568–10573.

Johnson, W. R., & Neal, D. (1998). Basic skills and the black-white earnings gap. In C. Jencks & M. Phillips (Eds.), *The black-white test score gap* (pp. 480–497). Washington, DC: Brookings Institute Press.

Johnson-Laird, P. N. (1983). *Mental models: Toward a cognitive science of language, inference, and consciousness.* Cambridge: Harvard University Press.

Jonas, E., Schimel, J., Greenberg, J., & Pyszczynski, T. (2002). The Scrooge effect: Evidence that mortality salience increases prosocial attitudes and behavior. *Personality and Social Psychology Bulletin, 28,* 1342–1353.

Jones, G. V. (1990). Misremembering a common object: When left is not right. *Memory & Cognition, 18,* 174–182.

Jones, J. T., Pelham, B. W., Carvallo, M., & Mirenberg, M. C. (2004). How do I love thee? Let me count the Js: Implicit egotism and interpersonal attraction. *Journal of Personality and Social Psychology, 87,* 665–683.

Jones, L. V., & Appelbaum, M. I. (1989). Psychometric methods. *Annual Review of Psychology, 40,* 23–44.

Jones, M. A., Botsko, M., & Gorman, B. S. (2003) Predictors of psychotherapeutic benefit of lesbian, gay, and bisexual clients: The effects of sexual orientation matching and other factors. *Psychotherapy: Theory, Research, Practice, Training, 40,* 289–301.

Jones, W. H. S. (Ed. & Trans.). (1923). *Hippocrates* (Vol. 1). London: William Heinemann.

Josephson, W. & Proulx, J. (2000). Healthy relationships project: results from year three. *Healthy Relationships Violence Prevention Website.* Retrieved March 23, 2006, from http://www.m4c.ns.ca

Josephson, W. L. (1987). Television violence and children's aggression: Testing the priming, social script, and disinhibition predictions. *Journal of Personality and Social Psychology, 53,* 882–890.

Josephson, W. L. (1995). Television violence: A review of the effects on children of different ages. Report to the Department of Canadian Heritage. Retrieved March 23, 2006, from http://www.cfc-efc.ca/docs/mnet/00001068.htm

Joy, J. E., Watson, S. J., Jr., & Benson, J. A., Jr. (1999). *Marijuana and medicine: Assessing the science base.* Washington, DC: National Academy Press.

Judd, F. K., Jackson, H. J., Komiti, A., Murray, G., Hodgins, G., Fraser, C. (2002). High prevalence disorders in urban and rural communities. *Australian and New Zealand Journal of Psychiatry, 36,* 104–113.

Judgments of the Supreme Court of Canada (1995). A. (L.L.) v. B. (A.), 4 S.C.R. 536 [Electronic version]. Available: http://scc.lexum.umontreal.ca/en/1995/1995rcs4– 536/1995rcs4–536.html

Judgments of the Supreme Court of Canada (2003). Starson v. Swayze, 1 S.C.R. 722, 2003 SCC 32 [Electronic version]. Available: http://scc.lexum.umontreal.ca/en/2003/2003scc32/2003scc32.html

Julien, R. M. (2001). *A primer of drug action* (9th ed.). New York: Freeman.

Jung, C. G. (1933). *Psychological types.* New York: Harcourt, Brace and World.

Juraska, J. M. (1998). Neural plasticity and the development of sex differences. *Annual Review of Sex Research, 9,* 20–38.

Jusczyk, P. W., Smith, L. B., & Murphy, C. (1981). The perceptual classification of speech. *Perception and Psychophysics, 1,* 10–23.

Jussim, L. (1989). Teacher expectations: Self-fulfilling prophecies, perceptual biases, and accuracy. *Journal of Personality and Social Psychology, 57,* 469–480.

Jussim, L., & Eccles, J. S. (1992). Teacher expectations: II. Construction and reflection of student achievement. *Journal of Personality and Social Psychology, 63,* 947–961.

Just, M. A., Carpenter, P. A., Keller, T. A., Emery, L., Zajac, H., & Thulborn, K. R. (2001). Interdependence of nonoverlapping cortical systems in dual cognitive tasks. *Neuroimage, 14,* 417–426.

Just, N., & Alloy, L. B. (1997). The response styles theory of depression: Tests and an extension of the theory. *Journal of Abnormal Psychology, 106,* 221–229.

Kadotani, H., Kadotani, T., Young, T., Peppard, P. E., Finn, L., Colrain, I. M., et al. (2001). Association between apolipoprotein E epsilon4 and sleep-disordered breathing in adults. *Journal of the American Medical Association, 285,* 2888–2890.

Kahn, D. A. (1995). New strategies in bipolar disorder: Part II. Treatment. *Journal of Practical Psychiatry and Behavioral Health, 3,* 148–157.

Kahn, E., & Rachman, A. W. (2000). Carl Rogers and Heinz Kohut: A historical perspective. *Psychoanalytic Psychology, 17,* 294–312.

Kahneman, D., & Tversky, A. (1984). Choices, values, and frames. *American Psychologist, 29,* 341–356.

Kajiya, K., Inaki, K., Tanaka, M., Haga, T., Kataoka, H., & Touhara, K. (2001). Molecular bases of odor discrimination: Reconstitution of olfactory receptors that recognize overlapping sets of odorants. *Journal of Neuroscience, 21,* 6018–6025.

Kales, A., & Kales, J. (1973). Recent advances in the diagnosis and treatment of sleep disorders. In G. Usdin (Ed.), *Sleep research and clinical practice.* New York: Brunner/Mazel.

Kalish, H. I. (1981). *From behavioral science to behavior modification.* New York: McGraw-Hill.

Kallgren, C. A., Reno, R. R., & Cialdini, R. B. (2000). A focus theory of normative conduct: When norms do and do not affect behavior. *Personality and Social Psychology Bulletin, 26,* 1002–1012.

Kamarck, T. W., Annunziato, B., Amateau, L. M. (1995). Affiliation moderates the effects of social threat on stress-related cardiovascular responses: Boundary conditions for a laboratory model of social support. *Psychosomatic Medicine, 57,* 183–194.

Kamphuis, J. H., & Emmelkamp, P. M. (2001). Traumatic distress among support-seeking female victims of stalking. *American Journal of Psychiatry, 158,* 795–798.

Kanaya, T., Scullin, M. H., & Ceci, S. J. (2003). The Flynn effect and U.S. policies. *American Psychologist, 58,* 778–790.

Kanazawa, S. (2004). General intelligence as a domain-specific adaptation. *Psychological Review, 111,* 512–523.

Kane, J. M. (1989). Current status of neuroleptic therapy. *Journal of Clinical Psychiatry, 50,* 322–328.

Kane, J. M., Eerdekens, M., Lindenmayer, J.-P., Keith, S. J., Lesem, M., & Karcher, K. (2003). Long-acting injectable risperidone: Efficacy and safety of the first long-acting atypical antipsychotic. *American Journal of Psychiatry, 160,* 1125–1132.

Kanki, B. J., & Foushee, H. C. (1990). Crew factors in the aerospace workplace. In S. Oskamp & S. Spacepan (Eds.), *People's reactions to technology* (pp. 18–31). Newbury Park, CA: Sage.

Kanner, B. (1995). *Are you normal?* New York: St. Martin's Press.

Kaplan, M. F., & Miller, C. E. (1987). Group decision making and normative vs. informational influence: Effects of type of issue and assigned decision rule. *Journal of Personality and Social Psychology, 53,* 306–313.

Kaptchuk, T. J. (2001). Methodological issues in trials of acupuncture. *Journal of the American Medical Association, 285,* 1015–1016.

Kapur, N. (1999). Syndromes of retrograde amnesia: A conceptual and empirical synthesis. *Psychological Bulletin, 125,* 800–825.

Kapur, S. (2003). Psychosis as a state of aberrant salience: A framework linking biology, phenomenology, and pharmacology in schizophrenia. *American Journal of Psychiatry, 160,* 13–23.

Kapur, S., & Mann, J. J. (1993). Antidepressant action and the neurobiologic effects of ECT: Human studies. In C. E. Coffey (Ed.), *The clinical science of electroconvulsive therapy.* Washington, DC: American Psychiatric Press.

Kapur, S., Sridhar, N., & Remington, G. (2004). The newer antipsychotics: Underlying mechanisms and the new clinical realities. *Current Opinion in Psychiatry, 17*(2), 115–121.

Kapur, S., Tulving, E., Cabeza, R. and McIntosh, A.R. (1996). The neural correlates of intentional learning of verbal materials: A PET study in humans. Cogntive *Brain Research, 4(4), 243–249.*

Karau, S. J., & Williams, K. D. (1997). The effects of group cohesiveness on social loafing and social compensation. *Group Dynamics, 1,* 156–168.

Kardes, F. R. (1999). Psychology applied to consumer behavior. In A. M. Stec & D. A. Bernstein (Eds.), *Psychology: Fields of application* (pp. 82–97). Boston: Houghton Mifflin.

Kareken, D. A., Mosnik, D. M., Doty, R. L., Dzemidzic, M., & Hutchins, G. D. (2003). Functional anatomy of human odor sensation, discrimination, and identification in health and aging. *Neuropsychology, 17,* 482–495.

Karni, A., Meyer, G., Adams, M., Turner, R., & Ungerleider, L. G. (1994). The acquisition and retention of a motor skill: A functional MRI study of long-term motor cortex plasticity. *Abstracts of the Society for Neuroscience, 20,* 1291.

Karon, B. P., & Widener, A. J. (1997). Repressed memories and World War II: Lest we forget. *Professional Psychology: Research and Practice, 28*(4), 338–340.

Karp, D. A. (1991). A decade of reminders: Changing age consciousness between fifty and sixty years old. In B. B. Hess & E. W. Markson (Eds.), *Growing old in America* (pp. 67–92). New Brunswick, NJ: Transaction.

Kasagi, F., Akahoshi, M., & Shimaoki, K. (1995). Relation between cold pressor test and development of hypertension based on 28-year follow-up. *Hypertension, 25,* 71–76.

Kass, S. (1999). Frequent testing means better grades, studies find. *APA Monitor, 30,* 10.

Kassin, S. M., Rigby, S., & Castillo, S. R. (1991). The accuracy-confidence correlation in eyewitness testimony: Limits and extensions of the retrospective self-awareness effect. *Journal of Personality and Social Psychology, 61,* 698–707.

Kastenbaum, R., Kastenbaum, B. K., & Morris, J. (1989). *Strengths and preferences of the terminally ill: Data from the National Hospice Demonstration Study.*

Katkin, E. S., Wiens, S., & Öhman, A. (2001). Nonconscious fear conditioning, visceral perception, and the development of gut feelings. *Psychological Science, 12,* 366–370.

Kato, S., Wakasa, Y., & Yamagita, T. (1987). Relationship between minimum reinforcing doses and injection speed in cocaine and pentobarbital self-administration in crab-eating monkeys. *Pharmacology, Biochemistry, and Behavior, 28,* 407–410.

Katz, A. N., & Fodor, J. A. (1963). The structure of a semantic theory. *Language, 39,* 170–210.

Katz, S. E., & Landis, C. (1935). Psychologic and physiologic phenomena during a prolonged vigil. *Archives of Neurology and Psychiatry, 34,* 307–317.

Katzell, R. A., & Thompson, D. E. (1990). Work motivation: Theory and practice. *American Psychologist, 45,* 144–153.

Kauffman, N. A., Herman, C. P., & Polivy, J. (1995). Hunger-induced finickiness in humans. *Appetite, 24,* 203–218.

Kawakami, K., Dion, K. L., & Dovidio, J. F. (1998). Racial prejudice and stereotype activation. *Personality and Social Psychology Bulletin, 24,* 407–416.

Kawakami, K., Dovidio, J. F., Moll, J., Hermsen, S., & Russin, A. (2000). Just say no (to stereotyping): Effects of training in the negation of stereotypic associations on stereotype activation. *Journal of Personality and Social Psychology, 78,* 871–888.

Kawamura, N., Kim, Y., & Asukai, N. (2001). Suppression of cellular immunity in men with a past history of posttraumatic stress disorder. *American Journal of Psychiatry, 158,* 484–486.

Kaye, J. A., Swihart, T., Howieson, D., Dame, A., Moore, M. M., Karnos, T., et al. (1997). Volume loss of the hippocampus and temporal lobe in healthy elderly persons destined to develop dementia. *Neurology, 48,* 1297–1304.

Kaye, W. H., Klump, K. L., Frank, G. K., & Strober, M. (2000). Anorexia and bulimia nervosa. *Annual Review of Medicine, 51,* 299–313.

Kazarian, S. S., & Evans, D. R. (Eds.). (2001). *Handbook of cultural health psychology.* New York: Academic Press.

Kazdin, A. E. (1994a). *Behavior modification in applied settings* (5th ed.). Pacific Grove, CA: Brooks/Cole.

Kazdin, A. E. (1994b). Methodology, design, and evaluation in psychotherapy research. In A. E. Bergin & S. L. Garfield (Eds.), *Handbook of psychotherapy and behavior change* (4th ed., pp. 19–71). New York: Wiley.

Kazdin, A. E., & Weisz, J. R. (1998). Identifying and developing empirically supported child and adolescent treatments. *Journal of Consulting and Clinical Psychology, 66,* 19–36.

Keating, D. P. (1990). Adolescent thinking. In S. S. Feldman & G. R. Elliott (Eds.), *At the threshold: The developing adolescent* (pp. 4–89). Cambridge, MA: Harvard University Press.

Kee, M., Hill, S. M., & Weist, M. D. (1999). School-based behavior management of cursing, hitting, and spitting in a girl with profound retardation. *Education and Treatment of Children, 22,* 171–178.

Keefe, F. J., & France, C. R. (1999). Pain: Biopsychosocial mechanisms and management. *Current Directions in Psychological Science, 8,* 137–141.

Keel, P. K., & Klump, K. L. (2003). Are eating disorders culture-bound syndromes?: Implications for conceptualizing their etiology. *Psychological Bulletin, 129,* 749–769.

Keesey, R. E., & Powley, T. L. (1986). The regulation of body weight. *Annual Review of Psychology, 37,* 109–133.

Kehoe, E. J., & Macrae, M. (1998). Classical conditioning. In W. O'Donohue (Ed.), *Learning and behavior therapy* (pp. 36–58). Boston: Allyn & Bacon.

Keinan, G., Friedland, N., & Ben-Porath, Y. (1987). Decision making under stress: Scanning of alternatives under physical threat. *Acta Psychologica, 64,* 219–228.

Keller, A., & Vosshall, L. B. (2004). A psychophysical test of the vibration theory of olfaction. *Nature Neuroscience, 7,* 337–338.

Keller, A., Ford, L. H., & Meacham, J. A. (1978). Dimensions of self-concept in preschool children. *Developmental Psychology, 14,* 483–489.

Keller, M. B., McCullough, J. P., Klein, D. N., Arnow, B., Dunner, D. L., Gelenberg, A. J., et al. (2000). A comparison of nefazodone, the cognitive behavioral-analysis system of psychotherapy, and their combination for the treatment of chronic depression. *New England Journal of Medicine, 342,* 1462–1470.

Kelley, A. E., & Berridge, K. C. (2002). The neuroscience of natural rewards: Relevance to addictive drugs. *Journal of Neuroscience, 22,* 3306–3311.

Kelley, K. W. (1985). Immunological consequences of changing environmental stimuli. In G. P. Moberg (Ed.), *Animal stress.* Bethesda, MD: American Physiological Society.

Kelley, W. M., Miezen, F. M., McDermott, K. B., Buckner, R. L., Raichle, M. E., Cohen, N. J., et al. (1998). Hemispheric asymmetry for verbal and nonverbal memory encoding in human dorsal frontal cortex. *Neuron, 20,* 927–936.

Kellman, P. J., & Banks, M. S. (1998). Infant visual perception. In W. Damon, D. Kuhn, & R. Siegler (Eds.), *Handbook of child psychology: Vol. 2. Cognition, language and perception* (5th ed., pp. 103–146). New York: Wiley.

Kellum, K. K., Carr, J. E., & Dozier, C. L. (2001). Response-card instruction and student learning in a college classroom. *Teaching of Psychology, 28,* 101–104.

Kelly, G. A. (1980). A psychology of the optimal man. In A. W. Landfield & L. M. Leitner (Eds.), *Personal construct psychology: Psychotherapy and personality.* New York: Wiley.

Kelly, J. F. (2003). Self-help for substance-use disorders: History, effectiveness, knowledge gaps and research opportunities. *Clinical Psychology Review, 23*(5), 639–663.

Kelly, J. B. & Caspary, D. M. (2005). Pharmacology of the inferior colliculus. In J. A. Winer and C. E. Schreiner (Eds.) *The Inferior Colliculus.* New York: Springer-Verlag. (Chapter 9) 248–281.

Kelly, M., Dunbar, S., Gray, J.E., & O'Reilly, R.L. (2002). Treatment delays for involuntary psychiatric patients associated with reviews of treatment capacity. *Canadian Journal of Psychiatry, 47,* 181–185.

Kelly, T. H., Foltin, R. W., Emurian, C. S., & Fischman, M. W. (1990). Multidimensional behavioral effects of marijuana. *Progress in Neuro-Psychopharmacology and Biological Psychiatry, 14,* 885–902.

Kelsoe, J. R., Spence, M. A., Loetscher, E., Foguet, M., Sadovnick, A. D., Remick, R. A., et al. (2001). A genome survey indicates a possible susceptibility locus for bipolar disorder on chromosome 22. *Proceedings of the National Academy of Science, 98,* 585–590.

Keltner, D., & Buswell, B. N. (1996). Evidence for the distinctiveness of embarrassment, shame, and guilt: A study of recalled antecedents and facial expressions of emotion. *Cognition and Emotion, 10,* 117–125.

Kemeny, M. E. (2003). The psychobiology of stress. *Current Directions in Psychological Science, 12,* 124–129.

Kemper, S., Greiner, L. H., Marquis, J. G., Prenovost, K., & Mitzner, T. L. (2001). Language decline across the life span: Findings from the Nun Study. *Psychology and Aging, 16,* 227–239.

Kempermann, G., Gast, D., & Gage, F. H. (2002). Neuroplasticity in old age: Sustained fivefold induction of hippocampal neurogenesis by long-term environmental enrichment. *Annals of Neurology, 52,* 135–143.

Kendall, P. C. (1999). Clinical significance. *Journal of Consulting and Clinical Psychology, 67,* 283–284.

Kendall, P. C., & Chambless, D. L. (Eds.). (1998). Special section: Empirically supported psychological therapies. *Journal of Consulting and Clinical Psychology, 66,* 3–167.

Kendall, P. C., & Sheldrick, R. C. (2000). Normative data for normative comparisons *Journal of Consulting and Clinical Psychology, 68,* 767–773.

Kendler, K. S. (2001). Twin studies of psychiatric illness: An update. *Archives of General Psychiatry, 58,* 1005–1014.

Kendler, K. S., & Diehl, N. S. (1993). The genetics of schizophrenia: A current genetic-epidemiologic perspective. *Schizophrenia Bulletin, 19,* 87–112.

Kendler, K. S., Gardner, C. O., & Prescott, C. A. (2002). Toward a comprehensive developmental model for major depression in women. *American Journal of Psychiatry, 159,* 1133–1145.

Kendler, K. S., Hettema, J. M., Butera, F., Gardner, C. O., & Prescott, C. A. (2003). Life event dimensions of loss, humiliation, entrapment, and danger in the prediction of onsets of major depression and generalized anxiety. *Archives of General Psychiatry, 60,* 789–796.

Kendler, K. S., Jacobson, K. C., Myers, J., & Prescott, C. A. (2002). Sex differences in genetic and environmental risk factors for irrational fears and phobias. *Psychological Medicine, 32,* 209–217.

Kendler, K. S., Kessler, R. C., Walters, E. E., MacLean, C., Neale, M. C., Heath, A. C., & Eaves, L. J. (1995). Stressful life events, genetic liability, and onset of an episode of major depression in women. *American Journal of Psychiatry, 152,* 833–842.

Kendler, K. S., Kuhn, J., & Prescott, C. A. (2004). The interrelationship of neuroticism, sex, and stressful life events in the prediction of episodes of major depression. *American Journal of Psychiatry, 161,* 631–636.

Kendler, K. S., Meyers, J., Prescott, C. A., & Neale, M. C. (2001). The genetic epidemiology of irrational fears and phobias in men. *Archives of General Psychiatry, 58,* 257–265.

Kendler, K. S., Neale, M. C., Kessler, R. C., Heath, A. C., & Eaves, L. J. (1992). Major depression and generalized anxiety disorder: Same genes, (partly) different environments? *Archives of General Psychiatry, 49,* 716–722.

Kendler, K. S., Thornton, L. M., & Gardner, C. O. (2000). Stressful life events and previous episodes in the etiology of major depression in women: An evaluation of the "kindling" hypothesis. *American Journal of Psychiatry, 157,* 1243–1251.

Kendler, K. S., Thornton, L. M., & Gardner, C. O. (2001). Genetic risk, number of previous depressive episodes, and stressful life events in predicting onset of major depression. *American Journal of Psychiatry, 158,* 582–586.

Kendler, K. S., Thornton, L. M., & Prescott, C. A. (2001). Gender differences in the rates of exposure to stressful life events and sensitivity to their depressogenic effects. *American Journal of Psychiatry, 158,* 587–593.

Kendler, K. S., Thornton, L. M., Gilman, S. E., & Kessler, R. C. (2000). Sexual orientation in a U.S. national sample of twin and nontwin sibling pairs. *American Journal of Psychiatry, 157,* 1843–1846.

Kenrick, D. T. (1994). Evolutionary social psychology: From sexual selection to social cognition. In M. Zanna (Ed.), *Advances in experimental social psychology* (Vol. 26, pp. 75–122). San Diego: Academic Press.

Kenrick, D. T., & Trost, M. R. (1997). Evolutionary approaches to relationships. In S. Duck (Ed.), *Handbook of personal relationships: Theory, research, and interventions* (2nd ed., pp. 151–177) Chichester, England: Wiley.

Kenrick, D. T., Keefe, R. C., Bryan, A. Barr, A., & Brown, S. (1995). Age preferences and mate choice among homosexuals and heterosexuals: A case for modular psychological mechanisms. *Journal of Personality and Social Psychology, 69,* 1166–1172.

Kenrick, D. T., Neuberg, S. L., & Cialdini, R. B. (2002). *Social psychology: Unraveling the mystery* (2nd ed.). Boston: Allyn & Bacon.

Kensinger, E. A., & Corkin, S. (2004). Two routes to emotional memory: Distinct neural processes for valence and arousal. *Proceedings of the National Academy of Sciences, 101,* 3310–3315.

Kent, S., Rodriguez, F., Kelley, K. W., & Dantzer, R. (1994). Reduction in food and water intake induced by microinjection of interleukin-1b in the ventromedial hypothalamus of the rat. *Physiology and Behavior, 56*(5), 1031–1036.

Kepner, J. (2001). Touch in Gestalt body process psychotherapy: Purpose, practice, and ethics. *Gestalt Review, 5,* 97–114.

Kerr, D. P., Walsh, D. M., & Baxter, D. (2003). Acupuncture in the management of chronic low back pain: A blinded randomized controlled trial. *Clinical Journal of Pain, 19*(6), 364–370.

Kerr, N. L., & Tindale, R. S. (2004). Group performance and decision making. *Annual Review of Psychology, 55,* 623–655.

Kessler, R. C. (1997). The effects of stressful life events on depression. *Annual Review of Psychology, 48,* 191–214.

Kessler, R. C., Berglund, P., Demler, O., Jin, R., Koretz, D., Merikangas, K.R., et al. (2003). The epidemiology of major depressive disorder: Results from the national comorbidity survey replication (NCS-R). *Journal of the American Medical Association, 289,* 3095–3105.

Kessler, R. C., McGonagle, K. A., Zhao, S., Nelson, C. B., Hughes, M., Eshleman, S., et al. (1994). Lifetime and 12-month prevalence of DSM-III-R psychiatric disorders in the United States. *Archives of General Psychiatry, 51,* 8–19.

Kety, S. S., Wender, P. H., Jacobsen, B., Ingraham, L. J., Jansson, L., Faber, B., & Kinney, D. K. (1994). Mental illness in the biological and adoptive relatives of schizophrenic adoptees. *Archives of General Psychiatry, 51,* 442–455.

Khan, J., Wei, J. S., Ringner, M., Saal, L. H., Ladanyi, M., Westermann, F., et al. (2001). Classification and diagnostic prediction of cancers using gene expression profiling and artificial neural networks. *Nature Medicine, 7,* 673–679.

Kiecolt-Glaser, J. K., & Glaser, R. (1992). Psychoneuroimmunology: Can psychological interventions modulate immunity? *Journal of Consulting and Clinical Psychology, 60,* 569–575.

Kiecolt-Glaser, J. K., & Glaser, R. (2001). Stress and immunity: Age enhances the risks. *Current Directions in Psychological Science, 10,* 18–21.

Kiecolt-Glaser, J. K., & Newton, T. L. (2001). Marriage and health: His and hers. *Psychological Bulletin, 127,* 472–503.

Kiecolt-Glaser, J. K., McGuire, L., Robles, T. F., & Glaser, R. (2002). Psychoneuroimmunology: Psychological influences on immune function and health. *Journal of Consulting & Clinical Psychology, 70,* 537–547.

Kiecolt-Glaser, J. K., Page, G. G., Marucha, P. T., MacCallum, R. C., & Glaser, R. (1998). Psychological influences on surgical recovery: Perspectives from psychoneuroimmunology. *American Psychologist, 11,* 1209–1218.

Kiecolt-Glaser, J. K., Preacher, K. J., MacCallum, R. C., Atkinson, C., Malarkey, W. B., & Glaser, R. (2003). Chronic stress and age-related increases in the proinflammatory cytokine IL-6. *Proceedings of the National Academy of Sciences, 100,* 9090–9095.

Kieffer, K. M., Schinka, J. A., & Curtiss, G. (2004). Person-environment congruence and personality domains in the prediction of job performance and work quality. *Journal of Counseling Psychology, 51,* 168–177.

Kieseppä, T., Partonen, T., Haukka, J., Kaprio, J., & Lönnqvist, J. (2004). High concordance of bipolar I disorder in a nationwide sample of twins. *American Journal of Psychiatry, 161,* 1814–1821.

Kiesler, D. J. (1996). *Contemporary interpersonal theory and research.* New York: Wiley.

Kiewra, K. A. (1989). A review of note-taking: The encoding storage paradigm and beyond. *Educational Psychology Review, 1,* 147–172.

Kihlstrom, J. F. (1999). The psychological unconscious. In L. Pervin & O. John (Eds.), *Handbook of personality* (pp. 424–442). New York: Guilford.

Kilgard, M. P., & Merzenich, M. M. (1998). Cortical map reorganization enabled by nucleus basalis activity. *Science, 279,* 1714–1718.

Kilgour, A. R., & Lederman, S. J. (2002). Face recognition by hand. *Perception and Psychophysics, 64,* 339–352.

Kilts, C. D., Schweitzer, J. B., Quinn, C. K., Gross, R. E., Faber, T. L., Muhammad, F., et al. (2001). Neural activity related to drug craving in cocaine addiction. *Archives of General Psychiatry, 58,* 334–341.

Kimble, G. A. (2000). Behaviorism and unity in psychology. *Current Directions in Psychological Science, 9,* 208–212.

Kimchi, R. (2003). Relative dominance of holistic and component properties in the perceptual organization of visual objects. In M. A. Peterson & G. Rhodes (Eds.), *Perception of faces, objects, and scenes* (pp. 235–268). New York: Oxford University Press.

Kimura, D. (2004). Human sex differences in cognition: fact, not predicament. *Sexualities, Evolution & Gender, 6,* 45–53.

King, J., & Pribram, K. H. (Eds.). (1995). *The scale of conscious experience: Is the brain too important to be left to specialists to study?* Mahwah, NJ: Erlbaum.

Kingdom, F. A. (2003). Color brings relief to human vision. *Nature Neuroscience, 6,* 641–644.

Kinney, H. C., Korein, J., Panigrahy, A., Dikkes, P., & Goode, R. (1994). Neuropathological findings in the brain of Karen Ann Quinlan: The role of the thalamus in the persistent vegetative state. *New England Journal of Medicine, 330* (21), 1469–1475.

Kinsey, A. C., Pomeroy, W. B., & Martin, C. E. (1948). *Sexual behavior in the human male.* Philadelphia: Saunders.

Kinsey, A. C., Pomeroy, W. B., Martin, C. E., & Gebhard, P. H. (1953). *Sexual behavior in the human female.* Philadelphia: Saunders.

Kircher, J. C., Horowitz, S. W., & Raskin, D. C. (1988). Meta-analysis of mock crime studies of the control question polygraph technique. *Law and Human Behavior, 12,* 79–90.

Kirchler, E., & Zani, B. (1995). Why don't they stay home? Prejudice against ethnic minorities in Italy. *Journal of Community and Applied Social Psychology, 5,* 59–65.

Kirkpatrick, B., Buchanan, R. W., Ross, D. E., & Carpenter, W. T., Jr. (2001). A separate disease within the syndrome of schizophrenia. *Archives of General Psychiatry, 58,* 165–171.

Kirmayer, L. J., Fletcher, C. M., Boothroyd, L. J. (1997). Inuit attitudes toward deviant behavior: A vignette study. *Journal of Nervous and Mental Disease, 185,* 78–86.

Kirsch, I. (1994a). Clinical hypnosis as a nondeceptive placebo: Empirically derived techniques. *American Journal of Clinical Hypnosis, 37*(2), 95–106.

Kirsch, I. (1994b). Defining hypnosis for the public. *Contemporary Hypnosis, 11*(3), 142–143.

Kirsch, I., & Braffman, W. (2001). Imaginative suggestibility and hypnotizability. *Psychological Science, 10,* 57–61.

Kirsch, I., & Lynn, S. J. (1995). The altered state of hypnosis: Changes in theoretical landscape. *The American Psychologist, 50,* 846–858.

Kirsch, I., Moore, T. J., Scoboria, A., & Nicholls, S. S. (2002). The emperor's new drugs: An analysis of antidepressant medication data submitted to the U.S. Food and Drug Administration [Electronic version]. *Prevention and Treatment, 5,* np.

Kishioka, S., Miyamoto, Y., Fukunaga, Y., Nishida, S., & Yamamoto, H. (1994). Effects of a mixture of peptidase inhibitors (Amastatin, Captopril and Phosphoramidon) on met enkephalin, betaa mixture of peptidase inhibitors (Amastatin, Captopril and Phosphoramidon) on met enkephalin, beta-endorphin, dynorphin (1–13) and electroacupun. *Japanese Journal of Pharmacology, 66,* 337–345.

Kisilevsky, B. S., Hains, S. M. J., Lee, K., Xie, X., Huang, H., Ye, H. H., et al. (2003). Effects of experience on fetal voice recognition. *Psychological Science, 14,* 220–224.

Kitamura, C., & Burnham, D. (2003). Pitch and communicative intent in mother's speech: Adjustments for age and sex in the first year. *Infancy, 4,* 85–110.

Kitayama, S., & Markus, H. R (1992, May). *Construal of self as cultural frame: Implications for internationalizing psychology.* Paper presented to the Symposium on Internationalization and Higher Education, Ann Arbor.

Kitayama, S., & Uchida, Y. (2003). Explicit self-criticism and implicit self-regard: Evaluating self and friend in two cultures. *Journal of Experimental Social Psychology, 39,* 476–482.

Kitayama, S., Snibbe, A. C., Markus, H. R., & Suzuki, T. (2004). Is there any "free" choice?: Self and dissonance in two cultures. *Psychological Science, 15,* 527–533.

Kjaer, T. W., Bertelsen, C., Piccini, P., Brooks, D., Alving, J., & Lou, H. C. (2002). Increased dopamine tone during meditation-induced change of consciousness. *Cognitive Brain Research, 13,* 255–259.

Kjellberg, A., Landstrom, U., Tesarz, M., Soderberg, L., & Akerlund, E. (1996). The effects of nonphysical noise characteristics, ongoing task and noise sensitivity on annoyance and distraction due to noise at work. *Journal of Environmental Psychology, 16,* 123–136.

Klahr, D., & Simon, H. (1999). Studies of scientific discovery: Complementary approaches and convergent findings. *Psychological Bulletin, 125,* 524–543.

Klaus, M. H., & Kennell, J. H. (1976). *Maternal infant bonding: The impact of early separation or loss on family development.* St. Louis: Mosby.

Klausner, H. A., & Lewandowski, C. (2002). Infrequent causes of stroke. *Emergency Medicine Clinics of North America, 20,* 657–670.

Kleber, H. D. (2003). Pharmacologic treatments for heroin and cocaine dependence. *American Journal of Addiction, 12* (Suppl. 2), S5–S18.

Kleemola, P., Jousilahti, P., Pietinen, P., Vartiainen, E., & Tuomilehto, J. (2000). Coffee consumption and the risk of coronary heart disease and death. *Archives of Internal Medicine, 160,* 3393–3400.

Klein, D. C., & Seligman, M. E. P. (1976). Reversal of performance deficits and perceptual deficits in learned helplessness and depression. *Journal of Abnormal Psychology, 85,* 11–26.

Klein, D. N. (1993). False suffocation alarms, spontaneous panics, and related conditions: An integrative hypothesis. *Archives of General Psychiatry, 50,* 306–316.

Klein, D., Lewinsohn, P. M., Seeley, J. R., & Rohde, P. (2001). A family study of major depressive disorder in a community sample of adolescents. *Archives of General Psychiatry, 58,* 13–20.

Klein, M. (1960). *The psychoanalysis of children.* New York: Grove Press.

Klein, P. D. (1998). A response to Howard Gardner: Falsifiability, empirical evidence, and pedagogical usefulness in educational psychologies. *Canadian Journal of Education, 23,* 103–112.

Klein, R. (1999). Donald O. Hebb. In R. A. Wilson and F. C. Keil (Eds.), *MIT Encyclopedia of the Cognitive Sciences* (pp. 366–367). Cambridge, MA: The MIT Press.

Kleinknecht, R. A. (1991). *Mastering anxiety: The nature and treatment of anxious conditions.* New York: Plenum.

Kleinknecht, R. A. (1994). Acquisition of blood, injury, and needle fears and phobias. *Behaviour Research and Therapy, 32,* 817–823.

Kleinknecht, R. A. (2000). Social phobia. In M. Hersen & M. K. Biaggio (Eds.), *Effective brief therapies: A clinician's guide.* New York: Academic Press.

Kleinman, A. (1991, April). *Culture and* DSM-IV: *Recommendations for the introduction and for the overall structure.* Paper presented at the National Institute of Mental Health-sponsored Conference on Culture and Diagnosis, Pittsburgh, PA.

Kleinman, A. (2004). Culture and depression. *New England Journal of Medicine, 351,* 951–953.

Klepp, K.-I., Kelder, S. H., & Perry, C. L. (1995). Alcohol and marijuana use among adolescents: Long-term outcomes of the class of 1989 study. *Annals of Behavioral Medicine, 17,* 19–24.

Kline, R. B. (2004). *Beyond significance testing: Reforming data analysis methods in behavioral research.* Washington, DC: APA.

Kline, S., & Groninger, L. D. (1991). The imagery bizarreness effect as a function of sentence complexity and presentation time. *Bulletin of the Psychonomic Society, 29,* 25–27.

Kling, K. C., Hyde, J. S., Showers, C. J., & Buswell, B. N. (1999). Gender differences in self-esteem: A meta-analysis. *Psychological Bulletin, 125,* 470–500.

Klintsova, A. Y., & Greenough, W. T. (1999). Synaptic plasticity in cortical systems. *Current Opinion in Neurobiology, 9,* 203–208.

Klohnen, E., & Bera, S. (1998). Behavioral and experiential patterns of avoidantly and securely attached women across adulthood: A 31-year longitudinal perspective. *Journal of Personality and Social Psychology, 74,* 211–223.

Klosko, J. S., Barlow, D. H., Tassinari, R., & Cerny, J. A. (1990). A comparison of alprazolam and behavior therapy in treatment of panic disorder. *Journal of Consulting and Clinical Psychology, 58,* 77–84.

Kluger, A. N., & DeNisi, A. (1998). Feedback interventions: Toward the understanding of a double-edged sword. *Current Directions in Psychological Science, 7,* 67–72.

Klunk, W. E., Engler, H., Nordberg, A., Wang, Y., Blomqvist, G., Holt, D. P., et al. (2004). Imaging brain amyloid in Alzheimer's disease with Pittsburgh Compound-B. *Annals of Neurology, 55,* 306–319.

Knecht, S., Floel, A., Drager, B., Breitenstein, C., Sommer, J., Henningsen, H., et al. (2002). Degree of language lateralization determines susceptibility to unilateral brain lesions. *Nature Neuroscience, 5,* 695–699.

Knobe, J., & Malle, B. F. (2002). Self and other in the explanation of behavior: 30 years later. *Psychologica Belgica, 42,* 113–130.

Knox, S., Burkard, A. W., Johnson, A. J., Suzuki, L. A., & Ponterotto, J. G. (2003). African American and European American therapists' experiences of addressing race in cross-racial psychotherapy dyads. *Journal of Counseling Psychology, 50,* 466–481.

Koch, C., & Davis, J. L. (Eds.). (1994). *Large-scale neuronal theories of the brain.* Cambridge: MIT Press.

Koelega, H. S. (1993). Stimulant drugs and vigilance performance: A review. *Psychopharmacology, 111*(1), 1–16.

Koenigsberg, H. W. (1994). The combination of psychotherapy and pharmacotherapy in the treatment of borderline patients. *Journal of Psychotherapy Practice and Research, 3*(2), 93–107.

Koepp, M. J., Gunn, R. N., Lawrence, A. D., Cunningham, V. J., Dagher, A., Jones, T., et al. (1998). Evidence for striatal dopamine release during a video game. *Nature, 393,* 266–268.

Koh, P. O., Undie, A. S., Kabbani, N., Levenson, R., Goldman-Rakic, P. S., & Lidow, M. S. (2002). Up-regulation of neuronal calcium sensor-1 (NCS-1) in the prefrontal cortex of schizophrenic and bipolar patients. *Proceedings of the National Academies of Science, 100,* 313–317.

Kohlberg, L., & Gilligan, C. (1971). The adolescent as a philosopher: The discovery of the self in a postconventional world. *Daedalus, 100,* 1051–1086.

Köhler, W. (1924). *The mentality of apes.* New York: Harcourt Brace.

Köhler, W. (1976). *The mentality of apes* (E. Winter, Trans.). Oxford, UK: Liveright.

Kohn, P. M., & MacDonald, J. E. (1992a). Hassles, anxiety, and negative well-being. *Anxiety, Stress & Coping: An International Journal, 5,* 151–163.

Kohn, P. M., & Macdonald, J. E. (1992b). The survey of recent life experiences: A decontaminated hassles scale for adults. *Journal of Behavioral Medicine, 15,* 221–236.

Kok, M. R., & Boon, M. E. (1996). Consequences of neural network technology for cervical screening: increase in diagnostic consistency and positive scores. *Cancer, 78,* 112–117.

Kolata, G. (2003, April 22). Hormone studies: What went wrong? *The New York Times.*

Kolb, B., Gibb, R., & Robinson, T. E. (2003). Brain plasticity and behavior. *Current Directions in Psychological Science, 12,* 1–5.

Komatsu, S.-I., & Naito, M. (1992). Repetition priming with Japanese Kana scripts in word-fragment completion. *Memory & Cognition, 20,* 160–170.

Konkol, R. J., Murphey, L. J., Ferriero, D. M., Dempsey, D. A., & Olsen, G. D. (1994). Cocaine metabolites in the neonate: Potential for toxicity. *Journal of Child Neurology, 9*(3), 242–248.

Konradi, C., Eaton, M., MacDonald, M. L., Walsh, J., Benes, F. M. & Heckers, S. (2004). Molecular evidence for mitochondrial dysfunction in bipolar disorder. *Archives of General Psychiatry, 61,* 300–308.

Koob, G. F., & Bloom, F. E. (1988). Cellular and molecular mechanisms of drug dependence. *Science, 242,* 715–723.

Kopelowicz, A., Liberman, R. P., & Zarate, R. (2002). Psychosocial treatments for schizophrenia. In P. E. Nathan & J. M. Gorman (Eds.), *A guide to treatments that work* (2nd ed., pp. 201–228). London: Oxford University Press.

Koppenaal, L., & Glanzer, M. (1990). An examination of the continuous distractor task and the "long-term recency effect." *Memory & Cognition, 18,* 183–195.

Koran, L. M., Hackett, E., Rubin, A., Wolkow, R., Robinson, D. (2002). Efficacy of sertraline in the long-term treatment of obsessive-compulsive disorder. *American Journal of Psychiatry, 159,* 88–95.

Kordower, J. H., Emborg, M. E., Bloch, J., Ma, S. Y., Chu, Y., Leventhal, L., et al. (2000). Neurodegeneration prevented by lentiviral vector delivery of GDNF in primate models of Parkinson's disease. *Science, 290,* 767–773.

Korner, J., & Leibel, R. L. (2003). To eat or not to eat—How the gut talks to the brain. *The New England Journal of Medicine, 349,* 926–928.

Korochkin, L. I. (2000). New approaches in developmental genetics and gene therapy: Xenotransplantation of Drosophila embryonic nerve cells into the brain of vertebrate animals. *Genetika, 36,* 1436–1442.

Korotkov, D., Gilmour, I. Charboneau, D., & Berry, P., (2001). *Using the ABC model as a basis for the assessment and treatment of problematic sexual behaviour: A conceptualization.* ONTABA Conference, Toronto ON, November 8.

Korteling, J. (1991). Effects of skill integration and perceptual competition on age-related differences in dual-task performance. *Human Factors, 33,* 35–44.

Koshizuka, S., Okada, S., Okawa, A., Koda, M., Murasawa, M., Hashimoto, M., et al. (2004). Transplanted hematopoietic stem cells from bone marrow differentiate into neural lineage cells and promote functional recovery after spinal cord injury in mice. *Journal of Neuropathology and Experimental Neurology, 63,* 64–72.

Kosslyn, S. M. (1988). Aspects of a cognitive neuroscience of mental imagery. *Science, 240,* 1621–1626.

Kosslyn, S. M. (1994). *Image and mind.* Cambridge: Harvard University Press.

Kotani, N., Hashimoto, H., Sato, Y., Sessler, D. I., Yoshioka, H., Kitayama, M., et al. (2001). Preoperative intradermal acupuncture reduces postoperative pain, nausea and vomiting, analgesic requirement, and sympathoadrenal responses. *Anesthesiology, 95,* 349–356.

Kouri, E. M., Pope, H. G., & Lukas, S. E. (1999). Changes in aggressive behavior during withdrawal from long-term marijuana use. *Psychopharmacology, 143,* 302–308.

Kouyoumdjian, H. (2004). Influence of unannounced quizzes and cumulative exams on attendance and study behavior. *Teaching of Psychology, 31,* 110–111.

Kozak, M. J., Liebowitz, M. R., & Foa, E. B. (2000). Cognitive behavior therapy and pharmacotherapy for obsessive-compulsive disorder: The NIMH-sponsored collaborative study. In W. K. Goodman, M. V. Rudorfer, & J. D. Maser (Eds.), *Obsessive-compulsive disorder: Contemporary issues in treatment* (pp. 501–530). Mahwah, NJ: Erlbaum.

Kozel, F. A., Padgett, T. M., & George, M. S. (2004). A replication study of the neural correlates of deception. *Behavioral Neuroscience, 118,* 852–856.

Krahn, L. E. (2003). Sleep disorders. *Seminars in Neurology, 23*(3), 307–314.

Krakauer, J. (1997). *Into thin air.* New York: Villard.

Krakow, B., Hollifield, M., Johnston, L., Koss, M., Schrader, R., Warner, T. D., et al. (2001). Imagery rehearsal therapy for chronic nightmares in sexual assault survivors with posttraumatic stress disorder: a randomized controlled trial. *Journal of the American Medical Association, 286,* 537–545.

Kramer, A. F., & Willis, S. (2002). Enhancing the cognitive vitality of older adults. *Current Directions in Psychological Science, 11,* 173–177.

Kramer, A. F., Larish, J., Weber, T., & Bardell, L. (1999). Training for executive control: Task coordination strategies and aging. In D. Gopher & A. Koriat (Eds.), *Attention and Performance XVII.* Cambridge: MIT Press.

Krantz, D. S., & McCeney, M. K. (2002). Effects of psychological and social factors on organic disease: A critical assessment of research on coronary heart disease. *Annual Review of Psychology, 53,* 341–369.

Krantz, D., & Durel, L. (1983). Psychobiological substrates of the Type A behavior pattern. *Health Psychology, 2,* 393–411.

Krantz, D., Contrada, R., Hill, D., & Friedler, E. (1988). Environmental stress and biobehavioral antecedents of coronary heart disease. *Journal of Consulting and Clinical Psychology, 56,* 333–341.

Kraus, W. E., Houmard, J. A., Duscha, B. D., Knetzger, K. J., Wharton, M. B., McCartney, J. S., et al. (2002). Effects of the amount and intensity of exercise on plasma lipoproteins. *The New England Journal of Medicine, 347,* 1483–1492.

Krause, N., & Shaw, B. A. (2000). Role-specific feelings of control and mortality. *Psychology and Aging, 15,* 617–626.

Kraut, R., Olson, J., Banaji, M., Bruckman, A., Cohen, J., & Couper, M. (2004). Psychological research online: Report of board of scientific affairs' advisory group on the conduct of research on the Internet. *American Psychologist, 59,* 105–117.

Krauzlis, R. J. (2002). Reaching for answers. *Neuron, 34,* 673–674.

Krebs, R. L. (1967). *Some relations between moral judgment, attention, and resistance to temptation.* Unpublished doctoral dissertation, University of Chicago, Chicago, IL.

Kring, A. M., & Gordon, A. H. (1998). Sex differences in emotion: Expression, experience, and physiology. *Journal of Personality & Social Psychology, 74,* 686–703.

Kristof, N. D. (1997, August 17). Where children rule. *New York Times Magazine.*

Kronfol, Z., & Remick, D. G. (2000). Cytokines and the brain: Implications for clinical psychiatry. *American Journal of Psychiatry, 157,* 683–694.

Krosnick, J. A., Betz, A. L., Jussim, L. J., & Lynn, A. R. (1992). Subliminal conditioning of attitude. *Personality and Social Psychology Bulletin, 18,* 152–162.

Krueger, J. (2001). Null hypothesis significance testing. *American Psychologist, 56,* 16–26.

Krueger, R. (2000). Phenotypic, genetic, and nonshared environment parallels the structure of personality: A view from the multidimensional personality questionnaire. *Journal of Personality and Social Psychology, 79,* 1057–1067.

Krueger, R. F., Markon, K. E., & Bouchard, T. J., Jr. (2003). The extended genotype: The heritability of personality accounts for the heritability of recalled family environments in twins reared apart. *Journal of Personality, 71,* 809–833.

Kruger, D. J. (2003). Evolution and altruism: Combining psychological mediators with naturally selected tendencies. *Evolution and Human Behavior, 24,* 118–125.

Kryger, M. H., Roth, T., & Dement, W. C. (2000). *Principles and practice of sleep medicine* (3rd ed.). Philadelphia: Saunders.

Kübler-Ross, E. (1975). *Death: The final stage of growth.* Englewood Cliffs, NJ: Prentice-Hall.

Kuhs, H., & Tolle, R. (1991). Sleep deprivation therapy. *Biological Psychiatry, 29,* 1129–1148.

Kujala, T., Karma, K., Ceponiene, R., Belitz, S., Turkkila, P., Tervaniemi, M., & Naatanen, R. (2001). Plastic neural changes and reading improvement caused by audiovisual training in reading-impaired children. *Proceedings of the National Academy of Science, 98,* 10509–10514.

Kuncel, N. R., Hezlett, S. A., & Ones, D. S. (2001). A comprehensive meta-analysis of the predictive validity of the Graduate Records Examinations: Implications for graduate student selection and performance. *Psychological Bulletin, 127,* 162–181.

Kuncel, N. R., Hezlett, S. A., & Ones, D. S. (2004). Academic performance, career potential, creativity, and job performance: Can one construct predict them all? *Journal of Personality and Social Psychology, 86,* 148–161.

Kurzban, R., Tooby, J., & Cosmides, L. (2001). Can race be erased? Coalitional computation and social categorization. *Proceedings of the National Academy of Science, 98,* 15387–15392.

Kushner, M. G., Thuras, P., Kaminski, J., Anderson, N., Neumeyer, B., & Mackenzie, T. (2000). Expectancies for alcohol to affect tension and anxiety as a function of time. *Addictive Behaviors, 25,* 93–98.

Kvorning, N., Holmberg, C., Grennert, L., Aberg, A., & Akeson, J. (2004). Acupuncture relieves pelvic and low-back pain in late pregnancy. *Acta Obstetrics and Gynecology Scandinavia, 83,* 246–250.

Kwan, M., Greenleaf, W. J., Mann, J., Crapo, L., & Davidson, J. M. (1983). The nature of androgen action on male sexuality: A combined laboratory-self-report study on hypogonadal men. *Journal of Clinical Endocrinology and Metabolism, 57,* 557–562.

Kwate, N. O. A. (2001). Intelligence or misorientation? *Journal of Black Psychology, 27,* 221–238.

Kyllonen, P. C., & Christal, R. E. (1990). Reasoning ability is (little more than) working-memory capacity?! *Intelligence, 14,* 389–433.

Kyrios, M., Sanavio, E., Bhar, S., & Liguori, L. (2001). Associations between obsessive-compulsive phenomena, affect, and beliefs: Cross-cultural comparisons of Australian and Italian data. *Behavioural and Cognitive Psychotherapy, 29,* 409–422.

Laan, E., Everaerd, W., Van Aanhold, M. T., & Rebel, M. (1993). Performance demand and sexual arousal in woman. *Behavior Research and Therapy, 31,* 25–36.

LaBar, K. S., Gatenby, J. C., Gore, J. C., LeDoux, J. E., & Phelps, E. A. (1998). Human amygdala activation during conditioned fear acquisition and extinction: A mixed-trial fMRI study. *Neuron, 20,* 937–945.

Laboratory of Comparative Human Cognition. (1982). Culture and intelligence. In R. J. Sternberg (Ed.), *Handbook of intelligence* (pp. 642–722). New York: Cambridge University Press.

Labouvie-Vief, G. (1982). Discontinuities in development from childhood. In T. M. Field, A. Huston, H. C. Quay, L. Troll, & G. E. Finley (Eds.), *Review of human development.* New York: Wiley.

Lacayo, A. (1995). Neurologic and psychiatric complications of cocaine abuse. *Neuropsychiatry, Neuropsychology, and Behavioral Neurology, 8*(1), 53–60.

Ladd, G. (2005). *Peer relationships and social competence of children and youth.* New Haven, CT: Yale University Press.

Ladd, G. W., & Troop-Gordon, W. (2003). The role of chronic peer difficulties in the development of children's psychological adjustment problems. *Child Development, 74,* 1344–1367.

Laeng, B., Svartdal, F., & Oelmann, H. (2004). Does color synesthesia pose a paradox for early-selection theories of attention? *Psychological Science, 15,* 277–281.

Laforge, R. G., Greene, G. W., & Prochaska, J. O. (1994). Psychosocial factors influencing low fruit and vegetable consumption. *Journal of Behavioral Medicine, 17,* 361–388.

LaFrance, M., Hecht, M. A., & Paluck, E. L. (2003). The contingent smile: A meta-analysis of sex differences in smiling. *Psychological Bulletin, 129,* 305–334.

Lafrance, M. N., & Stoppard, J. M. (In press). Constructing a non-depressed self: Women's accounts of recovery from depression. Feminism & Psychology.

Lahey, B. B., Loeber, R., Hart, E. L., Frick, P. J., & Applegate, B. (1995). Four-year longitudinal study of conduct disorder in boys: Patterns and predictors of persistence. *Journal of Abnormal Psychology, 104,* 83–93.

Lai, C. S. L., Fisher, S. E., Hurst, J. A., Vargha-Khadem, F., & Monaco, A. P. (2001). A forkhead-domain gene is mutated in severe speech and language disorder. *Nature, 413,* 519–523.

Lakdawalla, D. N., Bhattacharya, J., & Goldman, D. P. (2004). Are the young becoming more disabled? *Health Affairs, 23,* 168–176.

Lalumière, M. L., Blanchard, R., & Zucker, K. J. (2000). Sexual orientation and handedness in men and women: A meta-analysis. *Psychological Bulletin, 126,* 575–592.

Lam, C. M. (2001). Adolescent development in the context of Canadian-Chinese immigrant families. *Dissertation Abstracts International, 62,* 2239.

Lam, D. H., Watkins, E. R., Hayward, P., Bright, J., Wright, K., Kerr, N., Parr-Davis, G., & Sham, P. (2003). A randomized controlled study of cognitive therapy for relapse prevention for bipolar affective disorder: outcome of the first year. *Archives of General Psychiatry, 60,* 145–152.

Lam, T. H., Ho, S. Y., Hedley, A. J., Mak, K. H., & Peto, R. (2001). Mortality and smoking in Hong Kong: case-control study of all adult deaths in 1998. *British Medical Journal, 323,* 361.

Lamar, J. (2000). Suicides in Japan reach a record high. *British Medical Journal, 321,* 528.

Lamb, M. E. (1998). Assessments of children's credibility in forensic contexts. *Current Directions in Psychological Science, 7,* 43–46.

Lamb, M. E. (Ed.). (1997). *The role of the father in child development* (3rd ed.). New York: Wiley.

Lambert, M. J., & Barley, D. E. (2001). Research summary on the therapeutic relationship and psychotherapy outcome. *Psychotherapy, 38,* 357–361.

Lambert, M. J., & Bergin, A. E. (1994). The effectiveness of psychotherapy. In A. E. Bergin & S. L. Garfield (Eds.), *Handbook of psychotherapy and behavior change* (4th ed.). New York: Wiley.

Lambert, M. J., & Hill, C. E. (1994). Assessing psychotherapy outcomes and processes. In A. E. Bergin & S. L. Garfield (Eds.), *Handbook of psychotherapy and behavior change* (4th ed.). New York: Wiley.

Lambert, N. M. (1999). Developmental trajectories in psychology: Applications to education and training. *American Psychologist, 54,* 991–1002.

Lamme, V., Zipser, K., & Spekreijse, H. (1998). Figure-ground activity in primary visual cortex is suppressed by anesthesia. *Proceedings of the National Academies of Science, 95,* 3263–3268.

Landrigan, C. P., Rothschild, J. M., Cronin, J. W., Kaushal, R., Burdick, E., Katz, J. T., Lilly, C. M., Stone, P. H., Lockley, S. W., Bates, D. W., & Czeisler, C. A. (2004). Effect of reducing interns' work hours on serious medical errors in intensive care units. *New England Journal of Medicine, 351,* 1838–1848.

Landsdale, M., & Laming, D. (1995). Evaluating the fragmentation hypothesis: The analysis of errors in cued recall. *Acta Psychologica, 88,* 33–77.

Lang, A. R., Goeckner, D. J., Adesso, V. J., & Marlatt, G. A. (1975). Effects of alcohol on aggression in male social drinkers. *Journal of Abnormal Psychology, 84,* 508–518.

Lang, P. J. (1995). The emotion probe: Studies of motivation and attention. *American Psychologist, 50*(5), 372–385.

Lang, P. J., & Melamed, B. G. (1969). Avoidance conditioning therapy of an infant with chronic ruminative vomiting. *Journal of Abnormal Psychology, 74,* 1–8.

Langenberg, P., Ballesteros, M., Feldman, R., Damron, D., Anliker, J., Havas, S. (2000). Psychosocial factors and intervention-associated changes in those factors as correlates of change in fruit and vegetable consumption in the Maryland WIC 5 a day promotion program. *Annals of Behavioral Medicine, 22,* 307–315.

Langlois, J. H., Kalakanis, L., Rubenstein, A. J., Larson, A., Hallam, M., & Smoot, M. (2000). Maxims or myths of beauty: A meta-analytic and theoretical review. *Psychological Bulletin, 126,* 390–423.

Langlois, M. W., Cramer, K. M., & Mohagen, R. G. (2002). Delineating the unique effects of predictability, controllability, and choice in perceptions of control. *Current Research in Social Psychology, 7,* 163–181.

Langreth, R. (2002, February 4). Viagra for the brain. *Forbes,* 46–52.

Lansky, D., & Wilson, G. T. (1981). Alcohol, expectations and sexual arousal in males: An information processing analysis. *Journal of Abnormal Psychology, 89,* 528–538.

Lapointe, L. (1990). *Aphasia and related neurogenic language disorders.* New York: Thieme Medical.

Larsen, R. J., & Buss, D. (2005). *Personality psychology* (2nd ed.). New York: McGraw-Hill.

Larsen, R. J., & Buss, D. M. (2002). *Personality psychology.* New York: McGraw-Hill.

Larson, G. E., & Saccuzzo, D. P. (1989). Cognitive correlates of general intelligence: Toward a process theory of g. *Intelligence, 13,* 5–32.

Larson, J. R., Jr., Christensen, C., Franz, T. M., & Abbott, A. S. (1998). Diagnosing groups: The pooling, management, and impact of shared and unshared case information in team-based medical decision making. *Journal of Personality and Social Psychology, 75,* 93–108.

Larson, M. C., Gunnar, M. R., & Hertsgaard, L. (1991). The effects of morning naps, car trips, and maternal separation on adrenocortical activity in human infants. *Child Development, 62,* 362–372.

Larson, R. W., & Verma, S. (1999). How children and adolescents spend time across the world: Work, play, and developmental opportunities. *Psychological Bulletin, 125,* 701–736.

Larzelere, R. E. (1996). A review of the outcomes of parental use of nonabusive or customary physical punishment. *Pediatrics, 98,* 824–828.

Lashley, K. S. (1950). In search of the engram. *Society of Experimental Biology, Symposium 4,* 454–482.

Latané, B. (1981). The psychology of social impact. *American Psychologist, 36,* 343–356.

Latkin, C. A., Sherman, S., & Knowlton, A. (2003). HIV prevention among drug users: Outcome of a network-oriented peer outreach intervention. *Health Psychology, 22,* 332–339.

Lau, I. Y.-M., Lee, S., & Chiu, C. (2004). Language, cognition, and reality: Constructing shared meanings through communication. In M. Schaller & C. S. Crandall (Eds.), *The psychological foundations of culture* (pp. 77–97). Mahwah, NJ: Erlbaum.

Laughlin, P. L. (1999). Collective induction: Twelve postulates. *Organizational Behavior and Human Decision Processes, 80,* 50–69.

Law, D. J., Pellegrino, J. W., & Hunt, E. B. (1993). Comparing the tortoise and the hare: Gender differences and experience in dynamic spatial reasoning tasks. *Psychological Science, 4,* 35–40.

Lawford, B. R., Young, R. M., Rowell, J. A., Qualichefski, J., Fletcher, B. H., Syndulko, et al. (1995). Bromocriptine in the treatment of alcoholics with the D2 dopamine receptor A1 allele. *Nature Medicine, 1*(4), 337–341.

Lawless, H. T., & Engen, T. (1977). Associations to odors: Interference, memories and verbal learning. *Journal of Experimental Psychology, 3,* 52–59.

Lawrie, S. M., Whalley, H. C., Abukmeil, S. S., Kestelman, J., Donnelly, L., Miller, P., et al. (2001). Brain structure, genetic liability, and psychotic symptoms in subjects at high risk of developing schizophrenia. *Biological Psychiatry, 49,* 811–823.

Lazarus, A. A. (1971). *Behavior therapy and beyond.* New York: McGraw-Hill.

Lazarus, R. S. (1999). *Stress and emotion: A new synthesis.* New York: Springer.

Lazarus, R. S., & Folkman, S. (1984). *Stress, appraisal, and coping.* New York: Springer-Verlag.

Lazarus, R. S., Opton, E. M., Nomikos, M. S., & Rankin, M. O. (1965). The principle of short-circuiting of threat: Further evidence. *Journal of Personality, 33,* 622–635.

Le, B., & Agnew, C. R. (2003). Commitment and its theorized determinants: A meta-analysis of the investment model. *Personal Relationships, 10,* 37–57.

Lea, M., Spears, R., & de Groot, D. (2001). Knowing me, knowing you: Anonymity effects on social identity processes within groups. *Personality and Social Psychology Bulletin, 27,* 526–537.

Leaper, C., Anderson, K. J., & Sanders, P. (1998). Moderators of gender effects on parents' talk to their children: A meta-analysis. *Developmental Psychology, 34,* 3–27.

Learning Disabilities Association of Canada (2002). *Official definition of learning disabilities* [Electronic version]. Available: http://www.ldac-taac.ca/Defined/defined_ new-e.asp

Leary, M. R. (2004). The function of self-esteem in terror management theory and sociometer theory: Comment on Pyszczynski et al. (2004). *Psychological Bulletin, 130,* 478–482.

Leboe, J. P., Leboe, L.C., & Milliken, B. (2003). Another look at the effect of a surprising intervening event on negative priming. *Canadian Journal of Experimental Psychology, 57(2),* 115

Lecrubier, Y., Clerc, G., Didi, R., & Kieser, M. (2002). Efficacy of St. John's wort extract WS 5570 in major depression: A double-blind, placebo-controlled trial. *American Journal of Psychiatry, 159,* 1361 1366.

LeDoux, J. E. (1995). Emotion: Clues from the brain. *Annual Review of Psychology, 46,* 209–235.

LeDoux, J. E. (1996). *The emotional brain.* New York: Simon & Schuster.

Lee, K., Williams, L. M., Breakspear, M., & Gordon, E. (2003). Synchronous Gamma activity: A review and contribution to an integrative neuroscience model of schizophrenia. *Brain Research Reviews, 41,* 57–78.

Lee, M. (1981). Fifty goals in thirty-nine games. CBC News, December 31. Retrieved March 23, 2006, from http://archives.cbc.ca/IDC-1-41-1093-6056/sports/gretzky/clip6

Lee, R. M., & Yoo, H. C. (2004). Structure and measurement of ethnic identity for Asian American college students. *Journal of Counseling Psychology, 51,* 263–269.

Lee, S., Colditz, G., Berkman, L., & Kawachi, I. (2003). Caregiving to children and grandchildren and risk of coronary heart disease in women. *American Journal of Public Health, 93,* 1939–1944.

Lee, T. M. C., Liu, H.-L., Tan, L.-H., Chan, C. C. H., Mahankali, S., Feng, C.-M., et al. (2002). Lie detection by functional magnetic resonance imaging. *Human Brain Mapping, 15,* 157–164.

Lee, V. E., Brooks-Gunn, J., & Schnur, E. (1988). Does Head Start work? A 1-year follow-up comparison of disadvantaged children attending Head Start, no preschool, and other preschool programs. *Developmental Psychology, 24,* 210–222.

Leeb, R. T., & Rejskind, F. G. (2004). Here's looking at you kid! A longitudinal study of perceived gender differences in mutual gaze behavior in young infants. *Sex Roles, 50*(1–2), 1–5.

Lehman, D. R., Chiu, C., & Schaller, M. (2004). Psychology and culture. *Annual Review of Psychology, 55,* 689–714.

Lehman, H. E. (1967). Schizophrenia: IV. Clinical features. In A. M. Freedman, H. I. Kaplan, & H. S. Kaplan (Eds.), *Comprehensive textbook of psychiatry.* Baltimore: Williams & Wilkins.

Leibel, R. L., Rosenbaum, M., & Hirsch, J. (1995). Changes in energy expenditure resulting from altered body weight. *New England Journal of Medicine, 332*(10), 621–628.

Leibowitz, H. W., Brislin, R., Perlmutter, L., & Hennessy, R. (1969). Ponzo perspective illusion as a manifestation of space perception. *Science, 166,* 1174–1176.

Leigh, B. C., & Stacy, A. W. (2004). Alcohol expectancies and drinking in different age groups. *Addiction, 99,* 215–227.

Leiner, H. C., Leiner, A. L., & Dow, R. S. (1993). Cognitive and language functions of the human cerebellum. *Trends in Neuroscience, 16,* 444–447.

Leippe, M. R., Manion, A. P., & Romanczyk, A. (1992). Eyewitness persuasion: How and how well do fact finders judge the accuracy of adults' and children's memory reports? *Journal of Personality and Social Psychology, 63,* 181–197.

Leitch, A. (1978). Penfield, Wilder. *A Princeton Companion.* Princeton, NJ: Princeton University Press.

Lemly, B. (2000, February). Isn't she lovely? *Discover,* 43–49.

Lemmer, B., Kern, R. I., Nold, G., & Lohrer, H. (2002). Jet lag in athletes after eastward and westward time-zone transition. *Chronobiology International, 19,* 743–764.

Lenneberg, E. H. (1967). *Biological foundations of language.* New York: Wiley.

Leonard, B. E. (1992). *Fundamentals of psychopharmacology.* New York: Wiley.

Leonhardt, D. (2000, May 24). Makes sense to test for common sense. Yes? No? *New York Times.*

Leopold, D. (2002). Distortion of olfactory perception: Diagnosis and treatment. *Chemical Senses, 27,* 611–615.

Lepore, L., & Brown, R. (1997). Category and stereotype activation: Is prejudice inevitable? *Journal of Personality and Social Psychology, 72,* 275–287.

Lepore, S. J. (1995a). Cynicism, social support, and cardiovascular reactivity. *Health Psychology, 14,* 210–216.

Lepore, S. J. (1995b). Measurement of chronic stressors. In S. Cohen, R. C. Kessler, & L. U. Gordon (Eds.), *Measuring stress: A guide for health and social scientists.* New York: Oxford University Press.

Lepore, S. J., Evans, G., & Schneider, M. (1991). Dynamic role of social support in the link between chronic stress and psychological distress. *Journal of Personality and Social Psychology, 61,* 899–909.

Lerner, J. S., Gonzalez, R. M., Small, D. A., & Fischhoff, B. (2003). Effects of fear and anger on perceived risks of terrorism: A national field experiment. *Psychological Science, 14,* 144–150.

Lettvin, J. Y., Maturana, H. R., McCulloch, W. S., & Pitts, W. H. (1959). What the frog's eye tells the frog's brain. *Proceedings of the Institute of Radio Engineers, 47,* 1940–1951.

LeVay, S. (1991). A difference in hypothalamic structure between heterosexual and homosexual men. *Science, 253,* 1034–1037.

Levenson, H. (2003). Time-limited dynamic psychotherapy: An integrationist perspective. Journal of Psychotherapy Integration, 13, 300–333.

Levenson, H., & Strupp, H. H. (1997). Cyclical maladaptive patterns: Case formulation in time-limited dynamic psychotherapy. In T. D. Eells (Ed.), *Handbook of psychotherapy case formulation* (pp. 84–115). New York: Guilford.

Levenson, R. W., Ekman, P., & Friesen, W. V. (1990). Voluntary facial action generates emotion-specific autonomic nervous system activity. *Psychophysiology, 27*(4), 363–384.

Levenson, R. W., Ekman, P., Heider, K., & Friesen, W. V. (1992). Emotion and autonomic nervous system activity in the Minangkabau of West Sumatra. *Journal of Personality and Social Psychology, 62*(6), 972–988.

Levenston, G. K., Patrick, C. J., Bradley, M. M., & Lang, P. J. (2000). The psychopath as observer: Emotion and attention in picture processing. *Journal of Abnormal Psychology, 109,* 373–385.

Levine, R., Sato, S., Hashimoto, T., & Verna, J. (1995). Love and marriage in eleven cultures. *Journal of Cross-Cultural Psychology, 26,* 554–571.

Levine, S. (1999, February 1). In a loud and noisy world, baby boomers pay the consequences. *International Herald Tribune.*

Levinson, D. J., Darrow, C. N., Klein, E. B., Levinson, M. H., & McKee, B. (1978). *The seasons of a man's life.* New York: Knopf.

Levinson, S. C. (1996). Language and space. *Annual Review of Anthropology, 25,* 353–382.

Levinthal, C. F. (1996). *Drugs, behavior, and modern society.* Boston: Allyn & Bacon.

Levy, B. R., Slade, M. D., Kunkel, S. R., & Kasl, S. V. (2002). Longevity increased by positive self-perceptions of aging. *Journal of Personality & Social Psychology, 83*(2), 261–270.

Levy, G. D., Taylor, M. G., & Gelman, S. A. (1995). Traditional and evaluative aspects of flexibility in gender roles, social conventions, moral rules, and physical laws. *Child Development, 66,* 515–531.

Levy-Shiff, R. (1994). Individual and contextual correlates of marital change across the transition to parenthood. *Developmental Psychology, 30,* 591–601.

Lewicki, P. (1992). Nonconscious acquisition of information. *American Psychologist, 47,* 796–801.

Lewinsohn, P. M., & Rosenbaum, M. (1987). Recall of parental behavior by acute depressives, remitted depressives, and nondepressives. *Journal of Personality and Social Psychology, 52,* 611–619.

Lewinsohn, P. M., Joiner, T. E., & Rohde, P. (2001). Evaluation of cognitive diathesis-stress models in predicting Major Depressive Disorder in adolescents. *Journal of Abnormal Psychology, 110,* 203–215.

Lewis, C. E., Jacobs Jr., D. R., McCreath, H., Kiefe, C. I., Schreiner, P. J., Smith, D. E., & Williams, O. D. (2000). Weight gain continues in the 1990s: 10-year trends in weight and overweight from the CARDIA study. *American Journal of Epidemiology, 151,* 1172–1181.

Ley, R. (1994) The "suffocation alarm" theory of panic attacks: A critical commentary. *Journal of Behavior Therapy and Experimental Psychiatry, 25,* 269–273.

Li, L. C., & Kim, B. S. K. (2004). Effects of counseling style and client adherence to Asian cultural values on counseling process with Asian American college students. *Journal of Counseling Psychology, 51,* 158–167.

Li, S. C., Lindenberger, U., Hommel, B., Aschersleben, G., Prinz, W., & Baltes, P. B. (2004). Transformations in the couplings among intellectual abilities and constituent cognitive processes across the life span. *Psychological Science, 15,* 155–163.

Li, S., Cullen, W., Anwyl, R., & Rowan, M. J. (2003). Dopamine-dependent facilitation of LTP induction in hippocampal CA1 by exposure to spatial novelty. *Nature Neuroscience, 6,* 526–531.

Li, W., Piëch, V., & Gilbert, C. D. (2004). Perceptual learning and top-down influences in primary visual cortex. *Nature Neuroscience, 7,* 651–657.

Liben, L. (1978). Perspective-taking skills in young children: Seeing the world through rose-colored glasses. *Developmental Psychology, 14,* 87–92.

Liberman, R. P., Wallace, C. J., Blackwell, G., Kopelowicz, A., Vaccaro, J. V., & Mintz, J. (1998). Skills training versus psychosocial occupational therapy for persons with persistent schizophrenia. *American Journal of Psychiatry, 155,* 1087–1091.

Lichtman, A. H., Dimen, K. R., & Martin, B. R. (1995). Systemic or intrahippocampal cannabinoid administration impairs spatial memory in rats. *Psychopharmacology, 119,* 282–290.

Lickey, M., & Gordon, B. (1991). *Medicine and mental illness: The use of drugs in psychiatry.* San Francisco: Freeman.

Lieberman, A., & Pawl, J. (1988). Clinical applications of attachment theory. In J. Bellsky & T. Nezworski (Eds.), *Clinical applications of attachment.* Hillsdale, NJ: Erlbaum.

Lieberman, J. A., Tollefson, G., Tohen, M., Green, A. I., Gur, R. E., Kahn, R., et al. (2003). Comparative efficacy and safety of atypical and conventional antipsychotic drugs in first-episode psychosis: A randomized, double-blind trial of olanzapine versus haloperidol. *The American Journal of Psychiatry, 160,* 1396–1404.

Lieberman, M. A. (1996). Perspective on adult life crises. In V. L. Bengtson (Ed.), *Adulthood and aging: Research on continuities and discontinuities* (pp. 146–168). New York: Springer.

Lieberman, M. A., & Tobin, S. (1983). *The experience of old age.* New York: Basic Books.

Lieberman, P. (1991). *Uniquely human.* Cambridge: Harvard University Press.

Liepert, J., Bauder, H., Miltner, W. H. R., Taub, E., & Weiller, C. (2000). Treatment-induced cortical reorganization after stroke in humans. *Stroke, 31,* 1210.

Light, K. C., Girdler, S. S., Sherwood, A., Bragdon, E. E., Brownley, K. A., West, S. G., & Hinderliter, A. L. (1999). High stress responsivity predicts later blood pressure only in combination with positive family history and high life stress. *Hypertension, 33,* 1458–1464.

Light, L. L. (1991). Memory and aging: Four hypotheses in search of data. *Annual Review of Psychology, 42,* 333–376.

Lilienfeld, S. O., & Marino, L. (1999). Essentialism revisited: Evolutionary theory and the concept of mental disorder. *Journal of Abnormal Psychology, 108,* 400–411.

Lilienfeld, S. O., Lynn, S. J., Kirsch, I., Chaves, J. F., Sarbin, T. R., Ganaway, G. K., & Powell, R. A. (1999). Dissociative identity disorder and the sociocognitive model: Recalling the lessons of the past. *Psychological Bulletin, 125,* 507–523.

Lilienfeld, S. O., Wood, J., & Garb, H. N. (2000). The scientific status of projective tests. *Psychological Science in the Public Interest, 1,* 27–66.

Lillywhite, A. R., Wilson, S. J., & Nutt, D. J. (1994). Successful treatment of night terrors and somnambulism with paroxetine. *British Journal of Psychiatry, 16,* 551–554.

Lim, B.-C., & Ployhart, R. E. (2004). Transformational leadership: Relations to the five-factor model and team performance in typical and maximum contexts. *Journal of Applied Psychology, 89,* 610–621.

Lin, K.-M. & Poland, R. E. (1995). Ethnicity, culture, and psychopharmacology. In F. E. Bloom & D. J. Kupfer (Eds.), *Psychopharmacology: The fourth generation of progress.* New York: Raven Press.

Lin, S., Thomas, T. C., Storlien, L. H., & Huang, X. F. (2000). Development of high fat diet-induced obesity and leptin resistance in C57Bl/6J mice. *International Journal of Obesity Related Metabolic Disorders, 24,* 639–646.

Lindsay, D. S., Hagen, L., Read, J. D., Wade, K., & Gary, M. (2004). True photographs and false memories. *Psychological Science, 15,* 149–154.

Lindvall, O., & Hagell, P. (2001). Cell therapy and transplantation in Parkinson's disease. *Clinical Chemistry and Laboratory Medicine, 39,* 356–361.

Linn, R. L., & Gronlund, N. E. (2000). *Measurement and assessment in teaching* (8th ed.). Upper Saddle River, NJ: Merrill/Prentice-Hall.

Lippa, R. A. (2003). Are 2D:4D finger-length ratios related to sexual orientation?: Yes for men, no for women. *Journal of Personality and Social Psychology, 85,* 179–188.

Lira, A., Zhou, M., Castanon, N., Ansorge, M. S., Gordon, J. A., Francis, J. H., et al. (2003). Altered depression-related behaviors and functional changes in the dorsal raphe nucleus of serotonin transporter-deficient mice. *Biological Psychiatry, 54,* 960–971.

Lisanby, S. H. (2002). Update on magnetic seizure therapy: A novel form of convulsive therapy. *Journal of ECT, 18*(4), 182–188.

Lisanby, S. H. (Ed.). (2004). *Brain stimulation in psychiatric treatment.* Washington, DC: American Psychiatric Association.

Lisanby, S. H., Luber, B., Schlaepfer, T. E., & Sackeim, H. A. (2003). Safety and feasibility of magnetic seizure therapy (MST) in major depression: Randomized within-subject comparison with electroconvulsive therapy. *Neuropsychopharmacology, 28*(10), 1852–1865.

Liu, S., Prince, M., Blizard, B., & Mann, A. (2002). The prevalence of psychiatric morbidity and its associated factors in general health care in Taiwan. *Psychological Medicine, 32,* 629–637.

Liu, Y., Gao, J.-H., Liu, H.-L., & Fox, P. (2000). The temporal response of the brain after eating revealed by functional MRI. *Nature, 405,* 1058–1062.

Lively, W. M. (2001). Syncope and neurologic deficits in a track athlete: A case report. *Medicine and Science in Sports and Exercise, 33,* 345–347.

Livingstone, M. S., & Hubel, D. H. (1987). Psychological evidence for separate channels for the perception of form, color, movement and depth. *Journal of Neuroscience, 7,* 3416–3468.

Lochman, J. E., & Wells, K.,C. (2004). The coping power program for preadolescent aggressive boys and their parents: Outcome effects at 1-year follow-up. *Journal of Consulting and Clinical Psychology, 72,* 571–578.

Locke, E. A. (2000). Motivation, cognition, and action: An analysis of studies of task goals and knowledge. *Applied Psychology: An International Review, 49,* 408–429.

Locke, E. A., & Latham G. P. (1990). *A theory of goal setting & task performance.* Englewood Cliffs, NJ: Prentice Hall.

Locke, E. A., & Latham, G. P. (2002). Building a practically useful theory of goal setting and task motivation: A 35-year odyssey. *American Psychologist, 57,* 705–717.

Lockhart, R. S., & Craik, F. I. M. (1990). Levels of processing: A retrospective commentary on a framework for memory research. *Canadian Journal of Psychology, 44,* 87–112.

Locurto, C. (1991a). Beyond IQ in preschool programs? *Intelligence, 15,* 295–312.

Locurto, C. (1991b). Hands on the elephant: IQ, preschool programs, and the rhetoric of inoculation—a reply to commentaries. *Intelligence, 15,* 335–349.

Loeber, R. T., Cintron, C. M. B., & Yurgelun-Todd, D. A. (2001). Morphometry of individual cerebellar lobules in schizophrenia. *American Journal of Psychiatry, 158,* 952–954.

Loehlin, J. C. (1989). Partitioning environmental and genetic contributions to behavioral development. *American Psychologist, 44,* 1285–1292.

Loehlin, J. C. (1992). *Genes and environment in personality development.* Newbury Park, CA: Sage.

Loehlin, J. C., Neiderhiser, J. M., & Reiss, D. (2003). The behavior genetics of personality and the NEAD study. *Journal of Research in Personality, 37,* 373–387.

Loewenstein, G. (1994). The psychology of curiosity: A review and reinterpretation. *Psychological Bulletin, 116*(1), 75–98.

Loftus, E. F. (1992). When a lie becomes memory's truth: Memory distortion after exposure to misinformation. *Psychological Science, 3,* 121–123.

Loftus, E. F. (1997a). Memory for a past that never was. *Current Directions in Psychological Science, 6,* 60–65.

Loftus, E. F. (1997b). Repressed memory accusations: Devastated families and devastated patients. *Applied Cognitive Psychology, 11,* 25–30.

Loftus, E. F. (1998). The price of bad memories. *Skeptical Inquirer, 22,* 23–24.

Loftus, E. F. (2003, January). *Illusions of memory.* Presentation at the 25th Annual National Institute on the Teaching of Psychology, St. Petersburg Beach, Florida.

Loftus, E. F. (2004). Memories of things unseen. *Current Directions in Psychological Science, 13,* 145–147.

Loftus, E. F., & Guyer, M. (2002). Who abused Jane Doe? The hazards of the single case history (Part 1). *Skeptical Inquirer, 26,* 24–32.

Loftus, E. F., & Ketcham, K. (1991). *Witness for the defense.* New York: St. Martin's Press.

Loftus, E. F., & Ketcham, K. (1994). *The myth of repressed memory: False memories and allegations of sexual abuse.* New York: St. Martin's Press.

Loftus, E. F., & Palmer, J. C. (1974). Reconstruction of automobile destruction: An example of the interaction between language and memory. *Journal of Verbal Learning and Verbal Behavior, 13,* 585–589.

Logue, A. W. (1985). Conditioned food aversion in humans. *Annals of the New York Academy of Sciences, 104,* 331–340.

Lohman, D. F. (1989). Human intelligence: An introduction to advances in theory and research. *Review of Educational Research, 59,* 333–373.

Lohman, D. F. (2000). Complex information processing and intelligence. In R. J. Sternberg (Ed.), *Handbook of human intelligence* (2nd ed., pp. 285–340). Cambridge, MA: Cambridge University Press.

Lohman, D. F. (2004). Aptitude for college: The importance of reasoning tests for minority admissions. In R. Zwick (Ed.), *Rethinking the SAT: The future of standardized testing in college admissions.* New York: RoutledgeFalmer.

Lohman, D. F. (in press). The role of nonverbal ability tests in the identification of academically gifted students: An aptitude perspective. *Gifted Child Quarterly.* Retrieved December 13, 2004, from http://faculty.education.uiowa.edu/dlohman/pdf/Role_of_ Nonverbal_Ability.pdf

Lohman, D. F., & Hagen, E. (2001a). *Cognitive abilities test (Form 6).* Itasca, IL: Riverside.

Lohman, D. F., & Hagen, E. (2001b). *Cognitive abilities test (Form 6): Interpretive guide for teachers and counselors.* Itasca, IL: Riverside.

Lohr, J. M., Hooke, W., Gist, R., & Tolin, D. F. (2003) Novel and controversial treatments for trauma-related stress disorders. In S. O. Lilienfeld, S. J. Lynn, & J. M. Lohr (Eds.), *Science and pseudoscience in clinical psychology* (pp. 243–272). New York: Guilford Press.

LoLordo, V. M. (2001). Learned helplessness and depression. In M. E. Carroll & J. B. Overmier (Eds.), *Animal research and human health: Advancing human welfare through behavioral science* (pp. 63–77). Washington, DC: American Psychological Association.

London Daily Telegraph. (1998, September 19). "'Cat' that turned out to be a clock." *London Daily Telegraph.*

Longo, N., Klempay, S., & Bitterman, M. E. (1964). Classical appetitive conditioning in the pigeon. *Psychonomic Science, 1,* 19–20.

Lonn, S., Ahlbom, A., Hall, P., & Feychting, M. (2004). Mobile phone use and the risk of acoustic neuroma. *Epidemiology, 15,* 653–659.

Lopes, L. L. (1982). Procedural debiasing (Tech. Rep. WHIPP 15). Madison: University of Wisconsin, Human Information Processing Program.

Lord, C. G. (1997). *Social psychology.* Fort Worth: Harcourt, Brace.

Lorist, M. M., & Tops, M. (2003). Caffeine, fatigue, and cognition. *Brain and Cognition, 53,* 82–94.

Losh, S. C., Tavani, C. M., Njoroge, R., Wilke, R., & McAuley, M. (2003). What does education really do? Educational dimensions and pseudoscience support in the American general public, 1979–2001. *Skeptical Inquirer, 27,* 30–35.

Löw, K., Crestani, F., Keist, R., Benke, D., Brunig, I., Benson, J. A., et al. (2000). Molecular and neuronal substrate for the selective attenuation of anxiety. *Science, 290,* 131–134.

Lubinski, D. (2004). Introduction to the special section on cognitive abilities: 100 years after Spearman's (1904) "'General intelligence,' objectively determined and measured." *Journal of Personality and Social Psychology, 86,* 96–111.

Lubinski, D., & Benbow, C. P. (1995). An opportunity for empiricism [Review of the book *Multiple intelligences: The theory in practice*]. *Contemporary Psychology, 40,* 935–938.

Lubinski, D., Benbow, C. P., Shea, D. L., Eftekhari-Sanjani, H., & Halverson, M. B. J. (2001). Men and women at promise for scientific achievement: Similarity not dissimilarity. *Psychological Science, 12,* 309–317.

Luborsky, L. (1997). The core conflictual relationship theme: A basic case formulation method. In T. D. Eells (Ed.), *Handbook of psychotherapy case formulation* (pp. 58–83). New York: Guilford.

Luborsky, L., & Crits-Christoph, P. (1998). *Understanding transference: The Core Conflictual Relationship Theme Method* (2nd ed.). Washington, DC: American Psychological Association.

Luborsky, L., Rosenthal, R., & Diguer, L. (2003). Are some psychotherapies much more effective than others? *Journal of Applied Psychoanalytic Studies, 5*(4), 455–460.

Luborsky, L., Rosenthal, R., Diguer, L., Andrusyna, T. P., Berman, J. S., Levitt, J. T., et al. (2002). The dodo bird verdict is alive and well–mostly. *Clinical Psychology: Science and Practice, 9,* 2–12.

Luborsky, L., Singer, B., & Luborsky, L. (1975). Comparative studies of psychotherapies: Is it true that everyone has won and all must have prizes? *Archives of General Psychiatry, 32,* 995–1008.

Lucas, R. E., Clark, A. E., Georgellis, Y., & Diener, E. (2004). Unemployment alters the set point for life satisfaction. *Psychological Science, 15,* 8–13.

Lucas, R. E., Diener, E., & Larsen, R. J. (2003). Measuring positive emotions. In S. J. Lopez & C. R. Snyder (Eds.), *Positive psychological assessment: A handbook of models and measures.* Washington, DC: American Psychological Association.

Luchins, A. S. (1942). Mechanization in problem solving: The effect of Einstellung. *Psychological Monographs, 54* (6, Whole No. 248).

Lue, T. F. (2000). Drug therapy: Erectile dysfunction. *New England Journal of Medicine, 342,* 1802–1813.

Lundqvist, D., Esteves, F., & Öhman, A. (1999). The face of wrath: Critical features for conveying facial threat. *Cognition and Emotion, 13,* 691–711.

Lundström, J. N., Boyle, J. A., & Jones-Gotman, M. (2006). Sit up and smell the roses better: Olfactory sensitivity to phenyl ethyl alcohol is dependent on body position. *Chemical Senses, 0,* 251.

Luntz, B. K., & Widom, C. S. (1994). Antisocial personality disorder in abused and neglected children grown up. *American Journal of Psychiatry, 151,* 670–674.

Luo, Q., Perry, C., Peng, D., Jin, Z., Xu, D., Ding, G., & Xu, S. (2003). The neural substrate of analogical reasoning: An fMRI study. *Cognitive Brain Research, 17,* 527–534.

Luria, Z. (1992, February). *Gender differences in children's play patterns.* Paper presented at University of Southern California, Los Angeles.

Lustig, C., & Hasher, L. (2001). Implicit memory is not immune to interference. *Psychological Bulletin, 127,* 615–628.

Lustig, R. H., Sen, S., Soberman, J. E., & Velasquez-Mieyer, P. A. (2004). Obesity, leptin resistance, and the effects of insulin reduction. *International Journal of Obesity, 28,* 1344–1348.

Lutz, D. J., & Sternberg, R. J. (1999). Cognitive development. In M. H. Bornstein & M. E. Lamb (Eds.), *Developmental psychology: An advanced textbook* (4th ed.) Mahwah, NJ: Erlbaum.

Lykken, D. T. (1998). *A tremor in the blood: Uses and abuses of the lie detector.* Cambridge, MA: Perseus Publishing.

Lykken, D. T. (1999). *Happiness: What studies on twins show us about nature, nurture, and the happiness set point.* New York: Golden Books.

Lynam, D. R. (1996). The early identification of chronic offenders: Who is the fledgling psychopath? *Psychological Bulletin, 120,* 209–234.

Lynn, S. J., & Rhue, J. W. (1986). The fantasy-prone person: Hypnosis, imagination, and creativity. *Journal of Personality and Social Psychology, 51,* 404–408.

Lynn, S. J., Lilienfeld, S. O., & Lohr, J. M. (Eds.). (2003). *Science and pseudoscience in clinical psychology.* New York: Guilford Press.

Lynn, S. J., Loftus, E. F., Lilienfeld, S. O., & Lock, T. (2003). Memory recovery techniques in psychotherapy: Problems and pitfalls. *Skeptical Inquirer, 27*(4), 40–46.

Lynn, S. J., Myers, B., & Malinoski, P. (1997). Hypnosis, pseudomemories, and clinical guidelines: A sociocognitive perspective. In J. D. Read & D. S. Lindsay (Eds.), *Recollections of trauma: Scientific evidence and clinical practice. NATO ASI series: Series A: Life sciences* (Vol. 291, pp. 305–336). New York: Plenum Press.

Lynn, S. J., Vanderhoff, H., Shindler, K., & Stafford, J. (2002). Defining hypnosis as a trance vs. cooperation: Hypnotic inductions, suggestibility, and performance standards. *American Journal of Clinical Hypnosis, 44,* 231–240.

Lynskey, M. T., Heath, A. C., Bucholz, K. K., Slutske, W. S., Madden, P. A. F., Nelson, E. C., et al. (2003). Escalation of drug use in early-onset cannabis users vs. co-twin controls. *Journal of the American Medical Association, 289,* 427–433.

Lyons, D., & McLoughlin, D. M. (2001). Clinical review: Psychiatry. *British Medical Journal, 323,* 1228–1231.

Lyons, T. (2002, September 28). Debate rages over safety of ECT, or shock therapy, used on elderly. *Canadian Press* [Electronic version]. Available: http://www.ect.org/news/debaterages.html

Lyubomirsky, S. (2001). Why are some people happier than others?: The role of cognitive and motivational processes in well-being. *American Psychologist, 56,* 239–249.

Lyubomirsky, S., & Nolen-Hoeksema, S. (1995). Effects of self-focused rumination on negative thinking and interpersonal problem solving. *Journal of Personality and Social Psychology, 69,* 176–190.

Ma, S. H., & Teasdale, J. D. (2004). Mindfulness-based cognitive therapy for depression: Replication and exploration of differential relapse prevention effects. *Journal of Consulting and Clinical Psychology, 72,* 1–40.

MacAndrew, C., & Edgerton, R. B. (1969). *Drunken comportment.* Chicago: Aldine.

MacArthur Foundation. (1999). *Research network on successful midlife development.* Vero Beach, FL: The John D. and Catherine T. MacArthur Foundation. Retrieved December 13, 2004, from http://midmac.med.harvard.edu/

MacDonald, M., & Bernstein, D. A. (1974). Treatment of a spider phobia with in vivo and imaginal desensitization. *Journal of Behavior Therapy and Experimental Psychiatry, 5,* 47–52.

Mace, W. M. (1977). James J. Gibson's strategy for perceiving: Ask not what's inside your head, but what your head's inside of. In R. Shaw & J. Bransford (Eds.), *Perceiving, acting, and knowing* (pp. 43–66). Hillsdale, NJ: Erlbaum.

MacEvoy, S. P., & Paradiso, M. A. (2001). Lightness constancy in primary visual cortex. *Proceedings of the National Academy of Science, 98,* 8827–8831.

Mack, A. (2003). Inattentional blindness: Looking without seeing. *Current Directions in Psychological Science, 12,* 180–184.

Mack, A., & Rock, I. (1998). *Inattentional blindness.* Cambridge, MA: MIT Press.

Mackay, H. C., Barkham, M., Rees, A., & Stiles, W. B. (2003). Appraisal of published reviews of research on psychotherapy and counseling with adults 1990–1998. *Journal of Consulting and Clinical Psychology, 71,* 652–656.

Mackie, D. M., Hamilton, D. L., Susskind, S. J., & Rosselli, F. (1996). Social psychological foundations of prejudice. In C. N. Macrae, C. Stangor, & M. Hewstone (Eds.), *Stereotypes and stereotyping* (pp. 41–78). New York: Guilford.

Mackintosh, N. J., & Bennett, E. S. (2003). The fractionation of working memory maps onto different components of intelligence. *Intelligence, 31,* 519–531.

MacLatchy, H.A. & Stewart, S.H. (2001). The context-specific positive alcohol outcome expectancies of university women. *Addictive Behaviours, 26,* 31–49.

MacLean, K. (2003). The impact of institutionalization on child development. *Development and Psychopathology, 15,* 853–884.

MacMillan, H. L., Fleming, J. E., Steiner, D. L., Lin, E., Boyle, M. H., Jamieson, E., et al. (2001). Childhood abuse and lifetime psychopathology in a community sample. *American Journal of Psychiatry, 158,* 1878–1883.

MacQueen, G. M., Campbell, S., McEwen, B. S., Macdonald, K., Amano, S., Joffe, R. T., et al. (2003). Course of illness, hippocampal function, and hippocampal volume in major depression. *Proceedings of the National Academies of Science, 100,* 1387–1392.

Maddi, S. R., & Khoshaba, D. M. (2005). *Resilence at work.* New York: American Management Association.

Maddux, J. E., & Gosselin, J. T. (2003). Self-efficacy. In M. R. Leary & J. P. Tangney (Eds.), *Handbook of self and identity* (pp. 218–238). New York: Guilford Press.

Madon, S., Guyll, M., Spoth, R. L., Cross, S. E., & Hilbert, S. J. (2003). The self-fulfilling influence of mother expectations on children's underage drinking. *Journal of Personality and Social Psychology, 84,* 1188–1205.

Madon, S., Smith, A., Jussim, L., Russell, D. W., Eccles, J., Palumbo, P., & Walkiewicz, M. (2001). Am I as you see me or do you see me as I am? Self-fulfilling prophecies and self-verification. *Personality and Social Psychology Bulletin, 27,* 1214–1224.

Maess, B., Koelsch, S., Gunter, T. C., & Friederici, A. D. (2001). Musical syntax is processed in Broca's area: An MEG study. *Nature Neuroscience, 4,* 540–545.

Maestripieri, D. (2004). Developmental and evolutionary aspects of female attraction to babies [Electronic version]. *Psychological Science Agenda, 18*(1).

Magee, J. C., & Johnston, D. (1997). A synaptically controlled, associative signal for Hebbian plasticity in hippocampal neurons. *Science, 275,* 209–213.

Mahesh Yogi, M. (1994). *Science of being and art of living.* New York: NAL/Dutton.

Mahler, H. I. M., & Kulik, J. A. (2002). Effects of a videotape information intervention for spouses on spouse distress and patient recovery from surgery. *Health Psychology, 21,* 427–437.

Maier, S. F., & Watkins, L. R. (2000). The immune system as a sensory system: Implications for psychology. *Current Directions in Psychological Science, 9,* 98–102.

Maier, W., Gansicke, M., Gater, R., Reziki, M., Tiemens, B. & Urzua, F. (1999). Gender differences in the prevalence of depression: A survey in primary care. *Journal of Affective Disorders, 53,* 241–252.

Main, M. (1996). Introduction to the special section on attachment and psychopathology: Vol. 2. Overview of the field of attachment. *Journal of Consulting and Clinical Psychology, 64,* 237–243.

Maiter, S. (2004). Considering context and culture in child protection services to ethnically diverse families: An example from research with parents from the Indian subcontinent (South Asians). *Journal of Social Work Research and Evaluation, 5,* 63–80.

Mak, A. (2006), Recovered memories of child sexual abuse: A father's story. Retrieved March 23, 2006, from http://www.injusticebusters.com/04/Mak_Adriaan.shtml

Malarkey, W. B., Kiecolt-Glaser, J. K., Pearl, D., & Glaser, R. (1994). Hostile behavior during marital conflict alters pituitary and adrenal hormones. *Psychosomatic Medicine, 56,* 41–51.

Malaspina, D., Goetz, R. R., Friedman, J. H., Kaufmann, C. A., Faraone, S. V., Tsuang, M., et al. (2001). Traumatic brain injury and schizophrenia in members of schizophrenia and bipolar disorder pedigrees. *American Journal of Psychiatry, 158,* 440–446.

Malberg, J. E., Eisch, A. J., Nestler, E. J., & Duman, R. S. (2000). Chronic antidepressant treatment increases neurogenesis in adult rat hippocampus. *Journal of Neuroscience, 20,* 9104–9110.

Malenka, R. C. (1995). LTP and LTD: Dynamic and interactive processes of synaptic plasticity. *The Neuroscientist, 1,* 35–42.

Malenka, R. C., & Nicoll, R. A. (1999). Long-term potentiation—a decade of progress? *Science, 285,* 1870–1874.

Malgrange, B., Rigo, J. M., Van de Water, T. R., Staecker, H., Moonen, G., & Lefebvre, P. P. (1999). Growth factor therapy to the damaged inner ear: Clinical prospects. *International Journal of Pediatric Otorhinolaryngology, 49* (Suppl. 1), S19–S25.

Malinski, M. K., Sesso, H. D., Lopez-Jimenez, F., Buring, J. E., & Gaziano, J. M. (2004). Alcohol consumption and cardiovascular disease mortality in hypertensive men. *Archives of Internal Medicine, 164,* 623–628.

Malleret, G., Haditsch, U., Genoux, D., Jones, M. W., Bliss, T. V. P., Vanhoose, A. M., et al. (2001). Inducible and reversible enhancement of learning, memory, and long-term potentiation by genetic inhibition of calcineurin. *Cell, 104,* 675–686.

Maltby, N., Kirsch, I., & Mayers, M. (2002). Virtual reality exposure therapy for the treatment of fear of flying: A controlled investigation. *Journal of Consulting and Clinical Psychology, 70*(5), 1112–1118.

Mandelid, L. J. (2003). Dodofugl-dommen og psykoterapeuters credo. [The Dodo-bird verdict and the beliefs of psychotherapists]. *Tidsskrift for Norsk Psykologforening, 40*(4), 307–312.

Maner, J. K., Luce, C. L., Neuberg, S. L., Cialdini, R. B., Brown, S., & Sagarin, B. J. (2002). The effects of perspective taking on motivations for helping: Still no evidence for altruism. *Personality and Social Psychology Bulletin, 28,* 1601–1610.

Manji, H. K., Bowden, C. L., & Belmaker, R. H. (Eds.). (2000). *Bipolar medications: Mechanisms of action.* Washington, DC: American Psychiatric Press.

Mannuzza, M., Schneider, F. R., Chapman, T. F., Liebowitz, M. R., Klein, D. F., & Fyer, A. J. (1995). Generalized social phobia. *Archives of General Psychiatry, 52,* 230–237.

Mansfield, P. K., Voda, A., & Koch, P. B. (1995). Predictors of sexual response changes in heterosexual midlife women. *Health Values, 19*(1), 10–20.

Manson, J. E., Skerrett, P. J., Greenland, P., & VanItallie, T. B. (2004). The escalating pandemics of obesity and sedentary lifestyle: A call to action for clinicians. *Archives of Internal Medicine, 164,* 249–258.

Mantell, E. O., Ortiz, S. O., & Planthara, P. M. (2004). What price prescribing? A commentary on the effect of prescription authority on psychological practice. *Professional Psychology: Research and Practice, 35,* 164–169.

Maquet, P. (2001). The role of sleep in learning and memory. *Science, 294,* 1048–1052.

March, J., Silva, S., Petrycki, S., Curry, J., Wells, K., Fairbank, J., et al. (2004). Fluoxetine, cognitive-behavioral therapy, and their combination for adolescents with depression: Treatment for Adolescents with Depression Study (TADS) randomized controlled trial. *Journal of the American Medical Association, 292,* 807–820.

Marcia, J. E. (2002). Adolescence, identity, and the Bernardone family. *Identity, 2,* 199–209.

Marcotte, D. E., & Wilcox-Goek, V. (2001). Estimating the employment and earnings costs of mental illness: Recent developments in the United States. *Social Science and Medicine, 53,* 21–27.

Marcus, G. F. (1996). Why do children say "breaked"? *Current Directions in Psychological Science, 5,* 81–85.

Marenco, S., & Weinberger, D. R. (2000). The neurodevelopmental hypothesis of schizophrenia: Following a trail of evidence from cradle to grave. *Developmental Psychopathology, 12,* 501–527.

Margetic, S., Gazzola, C., Pegg, G. G., & Hill, R. A. (2002). Leptin: A review of its peripheral actions and interactions. *Obesity, 26,* 1407–1433.

Markman, E. M. (1994). Constraints children place on word meanings. In P. Bloom (Ed.), *Language acquisition: Core readings* (pp. 154–173). Cambridge, MA: MIT Press.

Marks, I. M. (2002). Reduction of fear: Towards a unifying theory. *Psicoterapia Cognitiva e Comportamentale, 8*(1), 63–66.

Markus, H. R., & Kitayama, S. (1991). Culture and the self: Implications for cognition, emotion, and motivation. *Psychological Review, 98,* 224–253.

Markus, H. R., & Kitayama, S. (1997). Culture and the self: Implications for cognition, emotion, and motivation. In L. A. Peplau & S. Taylor (Eds.), *Sociocultural perspectives in social psychology* (pp. 157–216). Upper Saddle River, NJ: Prentice-Hall.

Marleau, J. D. & Webanck, T. (1997). Parricide and violent crimes: A Canadian study. *Adolescence, 32–126,* 357.

Marmar, C. R. (1990). Psychotherapy process research: Progress, dilemmas, and future directions. *Journal of Consulting and Clinical Psychology, 58,* 265–272.

Marrack, P., Kappler, J., & Kotzin, B. L. (2001). Autoimmune disease: Why and where it occurs. *Nature Medicine, 7,* 899–905.

Marsh, A. A., Elfenbein, H. A., & Ambady, N. (2003). Nonverbal "accents": Cultural differences in facial expressions of emotion. *Psychological Science, 14,* 373–377.

Marshall, J., & Oberwinkler, J. (1999). The colourful world of the mantis shrimp. *Nature, 401,* 873–874.

Martin, C. L., & Fabes, R. A. (2001). The stability and consequences of young children's same-sex peer interactions. *Developmental Psychology, 37,* 431–446.

Martin, C. L., & Ruble, D. (2004). Children's search for gender cues. *Current Directions in Psychological Science, 13,* 67–70.

Martin, D. J., Garske, J. P., & Davis, M. K. (2000). Relation of the therapeutic alliance with outcome and other variables: A meta-analytic review. *Journal of Consulting & Clinical Psychology, 68,* 438–450.

Martin, G. L., & Pear, J. (2002). *Behavior modification: What it is and how to do it* (7th ed.). Upper Saddle River, NJ: Prentice-Hall.

Martin, R. A. (2001). Humor, laughter, and physical health: Methodological issues and research findings. *Psychological Bulletin, 127,* 504–519.

Martin, R. C., Sawrie, S. M., Knowlton, R. C., Bilir, E., Gilliam, F. G., Faught, E., et al. (2001). Bilateral hippocampal atrophy: Consequences to verbal memory following temporal lobectomy. *Neurology, 57,* 597–604.

Martin, R., Gran, B., Zhao, Y., Markovic-Plese, S., Bielekova, B., Marques, A., et al. (2001). Molecular mimicry and antigen-specific t cell responses in multiple sclerosis and chronic cns lyme disease. *Journal of Autoimmunity, 16,* 187–192.

Martindale, C. (1981). *Cognition and consciousness.* Homewood, IL: Dorsey Press.

Martindale, C. (1991). *Cognitive psychology: A neural-network approach.* Pacific Grove, CA: Brooks/Cole.

Martinez, C. R., & Forgatch, M. S. (2001). Preventing problems with boys' noncompliance: Effects of a parent training intervention for divorcing mothers. *Journal of Consulting and Clinical Psychology, 69,* 416–428.

Martinez, M. (2000). *Education as the cultivation of intelligence.* Mahwah, NJ: Erlbaum.

Martino, G., & Marks, L. E. (2001). Synesthesia: Strong and weak. *Current Directions in Psychological Science, 10,* 61–65.

Marzuk, P. M., Tardiff, K., Leon, A. C., Hirsch, C. S., Stajic, M., Portera, L., et al. (1995). Fatal injuries after cocaine use as a leading cause of death among young adults in New York City. *New England Journal of Medicine, 332*(26), 1753–1757.

Masand, P., Popli, A. P., & Welburg, J. B. (1995). Sleepwalking. *American Family Physician, 51*(3), 649–653.

Maslach, C. (2003). Job burnout: New directions in research and intervention. *Current Directions in Psychological Science, 12,* 189–192.

Maslach, C., & Goldberg, J. (1998). Prevention of burnout: New perspectives. *Applied and Preventive Psychology, 7,* 63–74.

Masland, R. H. (2001). Neuronal diversity in the retina. *Current Opinion in Neurobiology, 11,* 431–436.

Maslow, A. H. (1943). A theory of human motivation. *Psychological Review, 50,* 370–396.

Maslow, A. H. (1954). *Motivation and personality.* New York: Harper.

Maslow, A. H. (1971). *The farther reaches of human nature.* New York: McGraw-Hill.

Massaro, D. W., & Cowan, N. (1993). Information processing models: Microscopes of the mind. *Annual Review of Psychology, 44,* 383–425.

Massaro, D. W., & Stork, D. G. (1998). Speech recognition and sensory integration. *American Scientist, 86,* 236–244.

Masson, M. E. J., & MacLeod, C. M. (1992). Reenacting the route to interpretation: Enhanced perceptual identification without prior perception. *Journal of Experimental Psychology: General, 121,* 145–176.

Masters, W. H., & Johnson, V. E. (1966). *Human sexual response.* Boston: Little, Brown & Co.

Mathalon, D. H., Sullivan, E. V., Lim, K. O., & Pfefferbaum, A. (2001). Progressive brain volume changes and the clinical course of schizophrenia in men: A longitudinal magnetic resonance imaging study. *Archives of General Psychiatry, 58,* 148–157.

Mather, M., Canli, T., English, T., Whitfield, S., Wais, P., Ochsner, K., et al. (2004). Emotionally valenced stimuli in older and younger adults. *Psychological Science, 15,* 259–263.

Matlin, M. W. (1998). *Cognition* (4th ed.). Fort Worth, TX: Harcourt Brace.

Matson, J., Sevin, J., Fridley, D., & Love, S. (1990). Increasing spontaneous language in autistic children. *Journal of Applied Behavior Analysis, 23,* 227–223.

Matsuda, K. T., Cho, M. C., Lin, K. M., Smith, M. W., Young, A. S., & Adams, J. A. (1996). Clozapine dosage, serum levels, efficacy, and side-effect profiles: a comparison of Korean-American and Caucasian patients. *Psychopharmacology Bulletin, 32,* 253–257.

Matsumoto, D. (2000) *Culture and psychology: People around the world.* Belmont, CA: Wadsworth.

Matsumoto, D., & Ekman, P. (1989). American-Japanese cultural differences in intensity ratings of facial expressions of emotion. *Motivation and Emotion, 13,* 143–157.

Mattanah, J. F., Hancock, G. R., & Brand, B. L. (2004). Parental attachment, separation-individuation, and college student adjustment: A structural equation analysis of mediational effects. *Journal of Counseling Psychology, 51,* 213–225.

Matte, T. D., Bresnahan, M., Begg, M., & Susser, E. (2001). Influence of variation in birthweight within normal range and within sibships on IQ at 7 years: Cohort study. *British Medical Journal, 323,* 310–314.

Matthies, E., Hoeger, R., & Guski, R. (2000). Living on polluted soil: Determinants of stress symptoms. *Environment and Behavior, 32,* 270–286.

Mattingly, J. B., Rich, A. N., Yelland, G., & Bradshaw, J. L. (2001). Unconscious priming eliminates automatic binding of colour and alphanumeric form in synaesthesia. *Nature, 410,* 580–582.

Maupin, H. E., & Fisher, J. R. (1989). The effects of superior female performance and sex-role orientation in gender conformity. *Canadian Journal of Behavioral Science, 21,* 55–69.

Maurer, D. & Lewis, T.L. (2001). Visual acuity: The role of visual input in inducing postnatal change. *Clinical Neuroscience Research, 1,* 239–247.

Maxwell, J. P. (2003). The imprint of childhood physical and emotional abuse: A case study on the use of EMDR to address anxiety and a lack of self-esteem. *Journal of Family Violence, 18,* 281–293.

Mayberry, R. I., & Lock, E. (2003). Age constraints on first versus second language acquisition. *Brain and Language, 87,* 369–384.

Mayberry, R. I., Lock, E., Kazmi, H. (2002). Linguistic ability and early language exposure. *Nature, 417,* 38.

Mayer, D. J., & Price, D. D. (1982). A physiological and psychological analysis of pain: A potential model of motivation. In D. W. Pfaff (Ed.), *The physiological mechanisms of motivation.* New York: Springer-Verlag.

Mayer, F. S., & Sutton, K. (1996). *Personality: An integrative approach.* Upper Saddle River, NJ: Prentice-Hall.

Mayer, R. E. (1992). *Thinking, problem solving, and cognition* (2nd ed.). New York: Freeman.

Mayes, L., Cicchetti, D., Acharyya, S., & Zhang, H. (2003). Developmental trajectories of cocaine-and-other-drug-exposed and non-cocaine-exposed children. *Journal of Developmental Behavioral Pediatrics, 24,* 323–335.

Mazoyer, B., Tzouri-Mazoyer, N., Mazard, A., Denis, M., & Mellet, E. (2002). Neural basis of image and language interactions. *International Journal of Psychology, 37,* 204–208.

Mazzoni, G. A., & Loftus, E. F. (1996). When dreams become reality. *Consciousness and Cognition, 5,* 442–462.

Mazzoni, G., & Memon, A. (2003). Imagination can create false autobiographical memories. *Psychological Science, 14,* 186–188.

McAdams, D. P. (1997). A conceptual history of personality psychology. In R. Hogan, J. Johnson, & S. Briggs (Eds.), *Handbook of personality psychology* (pp. 4–40). San Diego: Academic Press.

McAuley, E. (1992). The role of efficacy cognitions in the prediction of exercise behavior in middle-aged adults. *Journal of Behavioral Medicine, 15,* 65–88.

McAuley, E., Kramer, A. F., & Colcombe, S. J. (2004). Cardiovascular fitness and neurocognitive function in older adults: A brief review. *Brain, Behavior, and Immunity, 18,* 214–220.

McCall, W. V., Dunn, A., & Rosenquist, P. B. (2004). Quality of life and function after electroconvulsive therapy. *British Journal of Psychiatry, 185,* 405–409.

McCarthy, H. D., Ellis, S. M., & Cole, T. J. (2003). Central overweight and obesity in British youth aged 11–16 years: Cross sectional surveys of waist circumference. *British Medical Journal, 326,* 624.

McCarty, M. F. (1995). Optimizing exercise for fat loss. *Medical Hypotheses, 44*(5), 325–330.

McClelland, D. C. (1958). Risk-taking in children with high and low need for achievement. In J. W. Atkinson (Ed.), *Motives in fantasy, action, and society* (pp. 306–321). Princeton, NJ: Van Nostrand.

McClelland, D. C. (1985). *Human motivation.* Glenview, IL: Scott, Foresman.

McCloskey, D. I. (1978). Kinesthetic sensibility. *Physiological Reviews, 58,* 763.

McCloskey, M. (1983). Naïve theories of motion. In D. Gentner & K. Stevens (Eds.), *Mental models* (pp. 299–324). Northvale, NJ: Erlbaum.

McClure, E. B. (2000). A meta-analytic review of sex differences in facial expression processing and their development in infants, children, and adolescents. *Psychological Bulletin, 126,* 424–453.

McCrady, B. S., Epstein, E. E., & Kahler, C. W. (2004). Alcoholics anonymous and relapse prevention as maintenance strategies after conjoint behavioral alcohol treatment for men: 18-month outcomes. *Journal of Consulting and Clinical Psychology, 72,* 870–878.

McCrae, R. R., & Costa, P. T., Jr. (2004). A contemplated revision of the NEO Five-Factor Inventory. *Personality and Individual Differences, 36,* 587–596.

McCrae, R. R., Costa, P. T., Jr., Martin, T. A., Oryol, V. E., Rukavishnikov, A. A., et al. (2004). Consensual validation of personality traits across cultures. *Journal of Research in Personality, 38,* 179–201.

McDaniel, M. A., Maier, S. F., & Einstein, G. O. (2002). "Brain-Specific" nutrients: A memory cure? *Psychological Science in the Public Interest, 3,* 12–38.

McDermott, K. B. (2002). Explicit and implicit memory. In V. S. Ramachandran (Ed.), *Encyclopedia of the human brain* (Vol. 2, pp. 773–781). New York: Academic Press.

McDermott, K. B., & Roediger, H. L. (1998). Attempting to avoid illusory memories: Robust false recognition of associates persists under conditions of explicit warnings and immediate testing. *Journal of Memory and Language, 39,* 508–520.

McDonald, J. J., Teder-Salejarvi, W. A., & Hillyard, S. A. (2000). Involuntary orienting to sound improves visual perception. *Nature, 407,* 906–908.

McDonald, R., & Siegel, S. (2004). The potential role of drug onset cues in drug dependence and withdrawal: Reply to Bardo (2004), Bossert & Shaham (2004), Bouton (2004), and Stewart (2004). *Experimental and Clinical Psychopharmacology, 12,* 23–26.

McDougall, I. (2002). Magic tool or dangerous quackery? Once-popular 'recovered memory' therapy has left many victims struggling in its controversial wake. *Toronto Sun, June 23, 2002*

McDougall, S. J. P., de Bruijn, O., & Curry, M. B. (2000). Exploring the effects of icon characteristics on user performance: The role of icon concreteness, complexity, and distinctiveness. *Journal of Experimental Psychology: Applied, 6,* 291–306.

McElroy, S. L., Zarate, C. A., & Cookson, J. (2004). A 52-week, open-label continuation study of lamotrigine in the treatment of bipolar depression. *Journal of Clinical Psychiatry, 65*(2), 204–210.

McEwen, B. S. (1998). Protective and damaging effects of stress mediators. *New England Journal of Medicine, 338,* 171–179.

McEwen, B. S., & Seeman, T. (1999). Protective and damaging effects of mediators of stress: Elaborating and testing concepts of allostasis and allostatic load. *Annals of the New York Academy of Sciences, 896,* 30–47.

McGaugh, J. L. (2003). *Memory and emotion.* New York: Columbia University Press.

McGehee, D. S., Heath, M. J. S., Gelber, S., Devay, P., & Role, L. W. (1995). Nicotine enhancement of fast excitatory synaptic transmissions in CNS by presynaptic receptors. *Science, 269,* 1692–1696.

McGill (2005). Press release: Dr. Brenda Milner: Elected to the American Academy of Arts and Sciences. Found on December 29, 2006, at: http://mni.mcgill.ca/announce/AmericanAcademy2005Milner_eng.htm.

McGlashan, T. H., & Hoffman, R. E. (2000). Schizophrenia as a disorder of reduced synaptic connectivity. *Archives of General Psychiatry, 57,* 637–648.

McGlone, J. (1980). Sex differences in human brain asymmetry: A critical survey. *The Behavioral and Brain Sciences, 3,* 215–263.

McGlynn, F. D., Moore, P. M., Lawyer, S., & Karg, R. (1999). Relaxation training inhibits fear and arousal during in vivo exposure to phobia-cue stimuli. *Journal of Behavior Therapy and Experimental Psychiatry, 30,* 155–168.

McGorry, P. D., Yung, A. R., Phillips, L. J., Yuen, H. P., Francey, S., Cosgrave, E. M., et al. (2002). Randomized controlled trial of interventions designed to reduce the risk of progression to first-episode psychosis in a clinical sample with subthreshold symptoms. *Archives of General Psychiatry, 59,* 921–928.

McGue, M. (1992). When assessing twin concordance, use the probandwise not the pairwise rate. *Schizophrenia Bulletin, 18,* 171–176.

McGuffin, P., Rijsdijk, F., Andrew, M., Sham, P., Katz, R., & Cardno, A. (2003). The heritability of bipolar affective disorder and the genetic relationship to unipolar depression. *Archives of General Psychiatry, 60,* 497–502.

McIntyre, L., Walsh, G., & Connor, S.K. (2001). *a follow-up study of child hunger in Canada* (Cat. No.: MP32–28/01-1-2E). Ottawa, ON: Applied Research, Branch Strategic Policy, Development of Human Resources.

McKim, M.K., Cramer, K.M., Stuart, B., & O'Connor, D.L. (1999). Infant care decisions and attachment security: The Canadian 'transition to child care' study. *Canadian Journal of Behavioural Science, 31, (2),* 92–106.

McLeod, J. D., Kessler, R. C., & Landis, K. R. (1992). Speed of recovery from major depressive episodes in a community sample of married men and women. *Journal of Abnormal Psychology, 101,* 277–286.

McLeod, P., & Dienes, Z. (1996). Do fielders know where to go to catch the ball or only how to get there? *Journal of Experimental Psychology: Human Perception and Performance, 22,* 531–543.

McLeod, P., Reed, N., & Dienes, Z. (2003). Psychophysics: How fielders arrive in time to catch the ball. *Nature, 426,* 244–245.

McLoyd, V. C. (1998). Socioeconomic disadvantage and child development. *American Psychologist, 53,* 185–204.

McMillan, E. (2005). Why you shouldn't take Lenny Briscoe's lie-detector test. *Skeptics Canada.* Retrieved March 23, 2006, from http://www.skeptics.ca/articles/eric-polygraph.html

McNally, R. J. (2003). Recovering memories of trauma: A view from the laboratory. *Current Directions in Psychological Science, 12,* 32–35.

McNally, R. J., Clancy, S. A., & Schacter, D. L. (2001). Directed forgetting of trauma cues in adults reporting repressed or recovered memories of childhood sexual abuse. *Journal of Abnormal Psychology, 110,* 151–156.

McNally, R. J., Clancy, S. A., Schacter, D. L., & Pittman, R. K. (2000a). Cognitive processing of trauma cues in adults reporting repressed, recovered, or continuous memories of childhood sexual abuse. *Journal of Abnormal Psychology, 109,* 355–359.

McNally, R. J., Clancy, S. A., Schacter, D. L., & Pittman, R. K. (2000b). Personality profiles, dissociation, and absorption in women reporting repressed, recovered, or continuous memories of childhood sexual abuse. *Journal of Consulting and Clinical Psychology, 68,* 1033–1037.

McNeil, J. E., & Warrington, E. K. (1993). Prosopagnosia: A face-specific disorder. *Quarterly Journal of Experimental Psychology: Human Experimental Psychology, 46A*(1), 1–10.

McPhail, T. L., & Penner, L. A. (1995, August). *Can similarity moderate the effects of aversive racism?* Paper presented at the 103rd annual meeting of the American Psychological Association, New York.

McQuaid, J. R., Granholm, E., McClure, F. S., Roepke, S., Pedrelli, P., Patterson, T. L., et al. (2000). Development of an integrated cognitive behavioral and social skills training intervention for older patients with schizophrenia. *Journal of Psychotherapy Practice and Research, 9,* 149–156.

McQuaid, J. R., Monroe, S. M., Roberts, J. E., Kupfer, D. J., & Frank, E. (2000). A comparison of two life stress assessment approaches: Prospective prediction of treatment outcome in recurrent depression. *Journal of Abnormal Psychology, 109,* 787–791.

McTigue, K. M., Harris, R., Hemphill, B., Lux, L., Sutton, S., Bunton, A. J., & Lohr, K. N. (2003). Screening and interventions for obesity in adults: Summary of the evidence for the U.S. Preventive Services Task Force. *Annals of Internal Medicine, 139,* 933–949.

Media Awareness Network. (2006). Government and industries response to media violence. Retrieved March 23, 2006, from http://www.media-awareness.ca/english/issues/violence/govt_industry_responses.cfm?RenderForPrint=1

Medin, D. L., & Bazerman, M. H. (1999). Broadening behavioral decision research: Multiple levels of cognitive processing. *Psychonomic Bulletin & Review, 6,* 533–546.

Medin, D. L., Ross, B. H., & Markman, A. B. (2001). *Cognitive psychology* (3rd ed.). Fort Worth, TX: Harcourt.

Meeus, W. H., & Raaijmakers, Q. A. W. (1995). Obedience in modern society. *Journal of Social Issues, 51,* 155–176.

Mehle, T. (1982). Hypothesis generation in an automobile malfunction inference task. *Acta Psychologica, 52,* 87–116.

Mehta, M. A., Goodyer, I. M., & Sahakian, B. J. (2004). Methylphenidate improves working memory and set-shifting in AD/HD: Relationships to baseline memory capacity. *Journal of Child Psychology and Psychiatry, 45,* 293–305.

Meichenbaum, D. (1977). *Cognitive behavior modification: An integrative approach.* New York: Plenum.

Meichenbaum, D. H. (1995). Cognitive-behavioral therapy in historical perspective. In B. Bongar & L. E. Beutler (Eds.), *Comprehensive textbook of psychotherapy: Theory and practice* (pp. 140–158). New York: Oxford University Press.

Mel, B. (1997). SEEMORE: Combining color, shape, and texture histogramming in a neurally inspired approach to object recognitiion. *Neural Computation, 8,* 777–804.

Melchior, C. L. (1990). Conditioned tolerance provides protection against ethanol lethality. *Pharmacology, Biochemistry and Behavior, 37,* 205–206.

Meltzer, H. Y. (1997). Treatment-resistant schizophrenia: The role of clozapine. *Current Medical Research Opinion, 14,* 1–20.

Melzack, R., & Wall, P. D. (1965). Pain mechanisms: A new theory. *Science, 150,* 971–979.

Memon, A., Vrij, A., & Bull, R. (2004). *Psychology and law: Truthfulness, accuracy and credibility* (2nd ed.). New York: Wiley.

Menaker, M., & Vogelbaum, M. A. (1993). Mutant circadian period as a marker of suprachiasmatic nucleus function. *Journal of Biological Rhythms, 8,* 93–98.

Meng, C. F., Wang, D., Ngeow, J., Lao, L., Peterson, M., & Paget, S. (2003). Acupuncture for chronic low back pain in older patients: A randomized, controlled trial. *Rheumatology (Oxford), 42,* 1508–1517.

Menini, A., Picco, C., & Firestein, S. (1995, February 2). Quantal-like current fluctuations induced by odorants in olfactory receptor cell. *Nature, 373,* 435–437.

Menkes, M. S., Matthews, K. A., Krantz, D. S., Lundberg, V., Mead, L. A., Qaqish, B., et al. (1989). Cardiovascular reactivity to the cold pressor as a predictor of hypertension. *Hypertension, 14,* 524–530.

Mennella, J. A., & Beauchamp, G. K. (1996). The human infant's response to vanilla flavors in mother's milk and formula. *Infant Behavior and Development, 19,* 13–19.

Menon, G. J., Rahman, I., Menon, S. J., & Dutton, G. N. (2003). Complex visual hallucinations in the visually impaired: The Charles Bonnet syndrome. *Survey Ophthalmology, 48,* 58–72.

Mercer, C. H., Fenton, K. A., Johnson, A. M., Wellings, K., Macdowall, W., McManus, et al. (2003). Sexual function problems and help seeking behaviour in Britain: National probability sample survey. *British Medical Journal, 327,* 426–427.

Merckelbach, H., Devilly, G. J., & Rassin, E. (2002). Alters in dissociative identity disorder: Metaphors or genuine entities? *Clinical Psychology Review, 22,* 481–497.

Mesquita, B., & Frijda, N. H. (1992). Cultural variations in emotions: A review. *Psychological Bulletin, 112,* 179–204.

Messer, S. B., & Kaplan, A. H. (2004). Outcomes and factors related to efficacy of brief psychodynamic therapy. In D. P. Charman (Ed.), *Core processes in brief psychodynamic psychotherapy: Advancing effective practice* (pp. 103–118).

Messer, S. B., & Wampold, B. E. (2002). Let's face facts: Common factors are more potent than specific therapy ingredients. *Clinical Psychology: Science and Practice, 9,* 21–25.

Messick, S. (1982). Test validity and the ethics of assessment. *Diagnostica, 28*(1), 1–25.

Messick, S. (1989). Validity. In R. Linn (Ed.), *Educational measurement* (3rd ed., pp. 13–103). New York: American Council on Education/Macmillan.

Messick, S. (2000). Consequences of test interpretation and use: The fusion of validity and values in psychological assessment. In R. D. Goffin & E. Helmes (Eds.), *Problems and solutions in human assessment: Honoring Douglas N. Jackson at seventy* (pp. 3–20). New York: Kluwer Academic/Plenum.

Messinger, A., Squire, L. R., Zola, S. M., & Albright, T. D. (2001). Neuronal representations of stimulus associations develop in the temporal lobe during learning. *Proceedings of the National Academy of Science, 98,* 12239–12244.

Messinger, D. S., Bauer, C. R., Das, A., Seifer, R., Lester, B. M., Lagasse, L. L., et al. (2004). The maternal lifestyle study: Cognitive, motor, and behavioral outcomes of cocaine-exposed and opiate-exposed infants through three years of age. *Pediatrics, 113,* 1677–1685.

Metzinger, T. (Ed.). (2000). *Neural correlates of consciousness: Empirical and conceptual questions.* Cambridge: MIT Press.

Meyer, B. H. F. L., Ehrhardt, A. A., Rosen, L. R., & Gruen, R. S. (1995). Prenatal estrogens and the development of homosexual orientation. *Developmental Psychology, 31*(1), 12–21.

Meyer, G. J., Finn, S. E., Eyde, L. D., Kay, G. G., Moreland, K. L., Dies, R. R., et al. (2001). Psychological testing and psychological assessment: A review of evidence and issues. *American Psychologist, 56,* 128 165.

Meyer, J. D., & Salovey, P. (1997). What is emotional intelligence? In P. Salovey & D. Sluyter (Eds.), *Emotional development and emotional intelligence* (pp. 3–31). New York: Basic Books.

Meyer, R. G. (1975). A behavioral treatment of sleepwalking associated with test anxiety. *Behavior Therapy and Experimental Psychiatry, 6,* 167–168.

Mezey, E., Key, S., Vogelsang, G., Szalayova, I., Lange, G. D., & Crain, B. (2003). Transplanted bone marrow generates new neurons in human brains. *Proceedings of the National Academy of Sciences, 100,* 1364–1369.

Mezulis, A. H., Abramson, L. Y., Hyde, J. S., & Hankin, B. L. (2004). Is there a universal positivity bias in attributions? A meta-analytic review of individual, developmental, and cultural differences in the self-serving attributional bias. *Psychological Bulletin, 130,* 711–747.

Mezzacappa, E. S., Katkin, E. S., & Palmer, S. N. (1999). Epinephrine, arousal and emotion: A new look at two-factor theory. *Cognition and Emotion, 13,* 181–199.

Michaud, D. S., Giovannucci, E., Willett, W. C., Colditz, G. A., Stampfer, M. J., & Fuchs, C. S. (2001). Physical activity, obesity, height, and the risk of pancreatic cancer. *Journal of the American Medical Association, 286,* 921–929.

Middlebrooks, J. C., Clock, A. E., Xu, L., & Green, D. M. (1994, May 6). A panoramic code for sound location by cortical neurons. *Science, 264,* 842–844.

Mieda, M., Willie, J. T., Hara, J., Sinton, C. M., Sakurai, T., & Yanagisawa, M. (2004). Orexin peptides prevent cataplexy and improve wakefulness in an orexin neuron-ablated model of narcolepsy in mice. *Proceedings of the National Academy of Sciences, 101,* 4649–4654.

Miklowitz, D. J., & Alloy, L. B. (1999). Psychosocial factors in the course and treatment of bipolar disorder: Introduction to the special section. *Journal of Abnormal Psychology, 108,* 555–557.

Milberger, S., Biederman, J., Faraone, S. V., & Chen, L. (1997). Further evidence of an association between attention-deficit/hyperactivity disorder and cigarette smoking: Findings from a high-risk sample of siblings. *American Journal on Addictions, 6,* 205–217.

Milgram, S. (1963). Behavioral study of obedience. *Journal of Abnormal and Social Psychology, 67,* 371–378.

Milgram, S. (1965). Some conditions of obedience and disobedience to authority. *Human Relations, 18,* 57–76.

Milgram, S. (1974). *Obedience to authority.* New York: Harper & Row.

Milgram, S. (1977, October). Subject reaction: The neglected factor in the ethics of experimentation. *Hastings Center Report* (pp. 19–23).

Miller, C. L., Miceli, P. J., Whitman, T. L., & Borkowski, J. G. (1996). Cognitive readiness to parent and intellectual-emotional development in children of adolescent mothers. *Developmental Psychology, 32,* 533–541.

Miller, E. K., & Cohen, J. D. (2001). An integrative theory of prefrontal cortex function. *Annual Review of Neuroscience, 24,* 167–202.

Miller, G. (1956). The magical number seven, plus or minus two: Some limits on our capacity to process information. *Psychological Review, 63,* 81–97.

Miller, G. (2003). Spying on the brain, one neuron at a time. *Science, 300,* 78.

Miller, G. A. (1991). *The science of words.* New York: Scientific American Library.

Miller, J. (2001). The cultural grounding of social psychological theory. In A. Tesser & N. Schwarz (Eds.), *Blackwell handbook of social psychology: Intraindividual processes* (pp. 22–43). Oxford, UK: Blackwell.

Miller, J. D., Lynam, D., Zimmerman, R. S., Logan, T. K., Leukefeld, C., & Clayton, R. (2004). The utility of the Five Factor Model in understanding risky sexual behavior. *Personality and Individual Differences, 36,* 1611–1626.

Miller, J. G. (1994). Cultural diversity in the morality of caring: Individually oriented versus duty-based interpersonal moral codes. *Cross-cultural Research, 28,* 3–39.

Miller, J. G. (2002). Bringing culture to basic psychological theory—Beyond individualism and collectivism: Comment on Oyserman et al. *Psychological Bulletin, 128,* 97–109.

Miller, J. G., & Bersoff, D. M. (1994). Cultural influences on the moral status of reciprocity and the discounting of endogenous motivation. *Personality and Social Psychology Bulletin, 20,* 592–607.

Miller, K. F., Smith, C. M., Zhu, J., & Zhang, H. (1995). Preschool origins of cross-national differences in mathematical competence: The role of number-naming systems. *Psychological Science, 6,* 56–60.

Miller, L. C., Putcha-Bhagavatula, A., & Pedersen, W. C. (2002). Men's and women's mating preferences: Distinct evolutionary mechanisms? *Current Directions in Psychological Science, 11,* 88–93.

Miller, L. K. (1999). The savant syndrome: Intellectual impairment and exceptional skill. *Psychological Bulletin, 125,* 31–46.

Miller, L. T., & Vernon, P. A. (1992). The general factor in short-term memory, intelligence, and reaction time. *Intelligence, 16,* 5–29.

Miller, L. T., & Vernon, P. A. (1997). Developmental changes in speed of information processing in young children. *Developmental Psychology, 33,* 549–554.

Miller, M. G., & Teates, J. F. (1985). Acquisition of dietary self-selection in rats with normal and impaired oral sensation. *Physiology and Behavior, 34*(3), 401–408.

Miller, N. E. (1959). Liberalization of basic S-R concepts: Extensions to conflict behavior, motivation, and social learning. In S. Koch (Ed.), *Psychology: A study of science* (Vol. 2, pp. 196–292). New York: McGraw-Hill.

Millon, T., & Davis, R. D. (1996). *Disorders of personality.* DSM-IV *and beyond* (2nd ed.). New York: Wiley.

Milner, B. (1965). Visually-guided maze learning in man: Effects of bilateral hippocampal, bilateral frontal, and unilateral cerebral lesions. *Neuropsychologia, 3,* 317–338.

Milner, B. (1966). Amnesia following operation on temporal lobes. In C. W. M. Whitty & O. L. Zangwill (Eds.), *Amnesia.* London: Butterworth.

Milner, B. (2005). The medial temporal-lobe amnesic syndrome. *Psychiatric Clinics of North America, 28(3),* 599–611.

Milner, B., & Penfield, W. (1955). The effect of hippocampal lesions on recent memory. *Transactions of the American Neurological Association,* 80, 42–48.

Miltenberger, R. G. (2003). *Behavior modification: Principles and procedures* (3rd ed.). Pacific Grove, CA: Wadsworth.

Ming, E. E., Adler, G. K., Kessler, R. C., Fogg, L. F., Matthews, K. A., Herd, J. A., & Rose, R. M. (2004). Cardiovascular reactivity to work stress predicts subsequent onset of hypertension: The air traffic controller health change study. *Psychosomatic Medicine, 66.* 459–465.

Minuchin, S., & Fishman, H. (1981). *Family therapy techniques.* Cambridge: Harvard University Press.

Miotto, K., Darakjian, J., Basch, J., Murray, S., Zogg, J., & Rawson, R. (2001). Gamma-hydroxybutyric acid: Patterns of use, effects and withdrawal. *American Journal on Addictions, 10,* 232–241.

Miranda, J., & Green, B. L. (1999). The need for mental health services research focusing on poor young women. *Journal of Mental Health Policy and Economics, 2,* 73–89.

Mischel, W. (2002). *Introduction to personality* (7th ed.). Fort Worth, Texas: Harcourt Brace.

Mischel, W. (2004). Toward an integrative science of the person. *Annual Review of Psychology, 55,* 1–22.

Mischel, W., & Shoda, Y. (1999). Integrating dispositions and processing dynamics. In L. Pervin & O. John (Eds.), *Handbook of personality: Theory and research* (2nd ed., pp. 197–218). New York: Guilford.

Mischel, W., Shoda, Y., & Mendoza-Denton, R. (2002). Situation-behavior profiles as a locus of consistency in personality. *Current Directions in Psychological Science, 11,* 50–54.

Mischel, W., Shoda, Y., & Smith, R. (2004). *Introduction to personality: Toward an integration* (7th ed.) New York: Wiley.

Mitchell, D. B. (1991). Implicit memory, explicit theories. *Contemporary Psychology, 36,* 1060–1061.

Mitchell, J. P., Heatherton, T. F., & Macrae, C. N. (2002). Distinct neural systems subserve person and object knowledge. *Proceedings of the National Academy of Sciences, 99,* 15238–15243.

Mitchell, K. J., & Zaragoza, M. S. (1996). Repeated exposure to suggestion and false memory: The role of contextual variability. *Journal of Memory and Learning, 35,* 246–260.

Miura, I. T., Okomoto, Y., Kim, C. C., Steere, M., & Fayol, M. (1993). First graders' cognitive representation of number and understanding of place value. *Journal of Educational Psychology, 81,* 109–114.

Moen, P., Erickson, W. A., Agarwal, M., Fields, V., & Todd, L. (2000). *The Cornell Retirement and Well-Being Study. Final Report.* Ithaca, NY: Cornell University.

Moffitt, T. E. (2002). Teen-aged mothers in contemporary Britain. *Journal of Child Psychology & Psychiatry & Allied Disciplines, 43,* 727–742.

Mogenson, G. J. (1976). Neural mechanisms of hunger: Current status and future prospects. In D. Novin, W. Wyrwicka, & G. Bray (Eds.), *Hunger: Basic mechanisms and clinical applications.* New York: Raven.

Mohr, C., Rohrenbach, C. M., Landis, T., & Regard, M. (2001). Associations to smell are more pleasant than to sound. *Journal of Clinical and Experimental Neuropsychology, 23,* 484–489.

Mokdad, A. H., Ford, E. S., Bowman, B. A., Dietz, W. H., Vinicor, F., Bales, V. S., et al. (2003). Prevalence of obesity, diabetes, and obesity-related health risk factors, 2001. *Journal of the American Medical Association, 289,* 76–79.

Molden, D. C., & Dweck, C. S. (2000). Meaning and motivation. In C. Sansone & J. M. Harackiewicz (Eds.), *Intrinsic and extrinsic motivation: The search for optimal motivation and performance.* San Diego, CA: Academic Press.

Moldin, S. O., & Gottesman, I. I. (1997). At issue: Genes, experience, and chance in schizophrenia—positioning for the 21st century. *Schizophrenia Bulletin, 23,* 547–561.

Molsa, P. K., Marttila, R. J., & Rinne, U. K. (1995). Long-term survival and predictors of mortality in Alzheimer's disease and multi-infarct dementia. *Acta Neurologica Scandinavica, 91,* 159–164.

Monane, M., Leichter, D., & Lewis, O. (1984). Physical abuse in psychiatrically hospitalized children and adolescents. *Journal of the American Academy of Child and Adolescent Psychiatry, 23,* 653–658.

Mondor, T. & Finely, A. (2003). The perceived urgency of auditory warning alarms used in the hospital operating room is inappropriate. *Canadian Journal of Anesthesia 50,* 221–228.

Moniz, E (1948). How I came to perform prefrontal leucotomy. *Proceedings of the first international congress of psychosurgery* (pp. 7–18). Lisbon: Edicoes Atica.

Monroe, S. M., Rohde, P., Seeley, J. R., & Lewinsohn, P. M. (1999). Life events and depression in adolescence: Relationship loss as a prospective risk factor for first onset of major depressive disorder. *Journal of Abnormal Psychology, 108,* 606–614.

Monroe, S. M., Thase, M., & Simons, A. (1992). Social factors and the psychobiology of depression: Relations between life stress and rapid eye movement sleep latency. *Journal of Abnormal Psychology, 101,* 528–537.

Monsebraaten, L. (2006, April). Why child care matters [Electronic version]. *The Toronto Star.* Available: http://www.thestar.com/NASApp/cs/ContentServer?pagename=thestar/Layout/Article_Type1&c=Article&pubid=968163964505&cid=1144058495576&call_page=TS_NationalReport&call_pageid=1012319932217&call_pagepath=News/NationalReport

Monteith, M. J., Sherman, J. W., & Devine, P. G. (1998). Suppression as a stereotype control strategy. *Personality & Social Psychology Review, 2,* 63–82.

Monteith, M. J., Zuwerink, J. R., & Devine, P. G. (1994). Prejudice and prejudice reduction: Classic challenges and contemporary approaches. In P. G. Devine, D. L. Hamilton, & T. M. Ostrom (Eds.), *Social cognition: Impact on social psychology* (pp. 324–346). San Diego, CA: Academic Press.

Montmayeur, J. P., Liberles, S. D., Matsunami, H., & Buck, L. B. (2001). A candidate taste receptor gene near a sweet taste locus. *Nature Neuroscience, 4,* 492–498.

Montoya, I. D., Gorelick, D. A., Preston, K. L., Schroeder, J. R., Umbricht, A., Cheskin, L. J., et al. (2004). Randomized trial of buprenorphine for treatment of concurrent opiate and cocaine dependence. *Clinical and Pharmacological Therapeutics, 75,* 34–48.

Mookadam, F., & Arthur, H. M. (2004). Social support and its relationship to morbidity and mortality after acute myocardial infarction: Systematic overview. *Archives of Internal Medicine, 164,* 1514–1518.

Moon, Y. (2003). Don't blame the computer: When self-disclosure moderates the self-serving bias. *Journal of Consumer Psychology, 13,* 125–137.

Moore, D. (2005). Are parents too paranoid about letting their kids have Halloween fun? *Canadian Press.* Published Sunday, October 30.

Moore, J. W., Tingstom, D. H., Doggett, R. A., & Carlyon, W. D. (2001). Restructuring an existing token economy in a psychiatric facility for children. *Child & Family Behavior Therapy, 23,* 53–60.

Moore, R. Y. (1997). Circadian rhythms: Basic neurobiology and clinical applications. *Annual Review of Medicine, 48,* 253–266.

Moos, R., Schaefer, J., Andrassy, J., & Moos, B. (2001). Outpatient mental health care, self-help groups, and patients' one-year treatment outcomes. *Journal of Clinical Psychology, 57,* 273–287.

Moradi, B., & Hasan, N. T. (2004). Arab American persons' reported experiences of discrimination and mental health: The mediating role of personal control. *Journal of Counseling Psychology, 51,* 418–428.

Moran, A. (1996). *The psychology of concentration in sports performance: A cognitive analysis.* Hove, England: Psychology Press.

Moran, C. C. (2002). Humor as a moderator of compassion fatigue. In C. R. Figley (Ed.), *Treating compassion fatigue* (pp. 139–154). New York: Brunner-Routledge.

Moran, D. R. (2000, June). *Is active learning for me?* Poster presented at APS Preconvention Teaching Institute, Denver.

Moran, G., Pederson, D.R., & Krupka, A. (2005). Maternal unresolved attachment status impedes the effectiveness of interventions with adolescent mothers. *Infant Mental Health Journal, 26,* 231–249.

Moran, P. W. (2000). The adaptive practice of psychotherapy in the managed care era. *Psychiatric Clinics of North America, 23,* 383–402.

Moreland, R. L., & Beach, S. R. (1992). Exposure effects in the classroom: The development of affinity among students. *Journal of Experimental Social Psychology, 28,* 255–276.

Morgan, C. D., & Murray, H. A. (1935). A method for investigating fantasy: The Thematic Apperception Test. *Archives of Neurology and Psychiatry, 34,* 289–306.

Morgan, D., Diamond, D. M., Gottschall, P. E., Ugen, K. E., Dickey, C., Hardy, J., et al. (2000). A beta peptide vaccination prevents memory loss in an animal model of Alzheimer's disease. *Nature, 408,* 982–985.

Morganstern, J., Labouvie, E., McCrady, B. S., Kahler, C. W., & Frey, R. M. (1997). Affiliation with Alcoholics Anonymous after treatment: A study of its therapeutic effects and mechanism of action. *Journal of Consulting and Clinical Psychology, 65,* 768–777.

Morris, C. D., Bransford, J. D., & Franks, J. J. (1977). Levels of processing versus transfer appropriate processing. *Journal of Verbal Learning and Verbal Behavior, 16,* 519–533.

Morris, J. S., DeGelder, B., Weiskrantz, L., & Dolan, R. J. (2001). Differential extrageniculostriate and amygdala responses to presentation of emotional faces in a cortically blind field. *Brain, 124,* 1241–1252.

Morris, J. S., Ohman, A., & Dolan, R. J. (1998). Conscious and unconscious emotional learning in the human amygdala. *Nature, 393,* 467–470.

Morris, L. (2000, December 5). Hold the anaesthetic. I'll hypnotise myself instead. *Daily Mail,* p. 25.

Morris, P. H., Gale, A., & Duffy, K. (2002). Can judges agree on the personality of horses? *Personality and Individual Differences, 33,* 67–81.

Morrison, B., & Fraser, I. H. (2005). Hook and release angling, a car accident and the power of suggestion with witnesses. *Advocates' Quarterly, 30* (2), 239–250.

Morrison, K. H., Bradley, R., & Westen, D. (2003). The external validity of controlled clinical trials of psychotherapy for depression and anxiety: A naturalistic study. *Psychology and Psychotherapy: Theory, Research & Practice, 76*(2), 109–132.

Morrongiello, B. A., & Hogg, K. (2004). Mothers' reactions to children misbehaving in ways that can lead to injury: Implications for gender differences in children's risk taking and injuries. *Sex Roles, 50*(1–2), 103–118.

Morrongiello, B.A. & Fenwick, K.D. (1991). Infants' coordination of auditory and visual depth information. *Journal of Experimental Child Psychology, 52,* 277–296.

Mortimer, J. A., Snowdon, D. A., & Markesbery, W. R. (2003). Head circumference, education, and risk of dementia: Findings from the nun study. *Journal of Clinical and Experimental Neuropsychology, 25,* 671–679.

Mortimer, R. G., Goldsteen, K., Armstrong, R. W., & Macrina, D. (1988). *Effects of enforcement, incentives, and publicity on seat belt use in Illinois.* University of Illinois, Dept. of Health & Safety Studies, Final Report to Illinois Dept. of Transportation (Safety Research Report 88–11).

Moscovici, S. (1985). Social influence and conformity. In G. Lindzey & E. Aronson (Eds.), *The handbook of social psychology* (Vol. 2, 3rd ed.). New York: Random House.

Moss, E., Bureau, J.-F., Cyr, C., Mongeau, C., & St.-Laurent, D. (2004). Correlates of attachment at age 3: Construct validity of the preschool attachment classification system. *Developmental Psychology, 40,* 323–334.

Most, S. B., Simons, D. J., Scholl, B. J., Jimenez, R., Clifford, E., & Chabris, C. F. (2001). How not to be seen: The contribution of similarity and selective ignoring to sustained inattentional blindness. *Psychological Science, 12,* 9–17.

Mostert, M. P. (2001). Facilitated communication since 1995: A review of published studies. *Journal of Autism and Developmental Disorders, 31,* 287–313.

Muchinsky, P. (1993). *Psychology applied to work* (4th ed.). Pacific Grove, CA: Brooks/Cole.

Muir, J. L. (1997). Acetylcholine, aging, and Alzheimer's disease. *Pharmacological and Biochemical Behavior, 56*(4), 687–696.

Mullen, B. (1986). Atrocity as a function of lynch mob composition: A self-attention perspective. *Personality and Social Psychology Bulletin, 12,* 187–197.

Mulligan, D.E., Dobson, M.W. and McCracken, J. (2004). A simulation for learning strategy and perceptual skill in hockey. Proceedings of the Seventh IASTED International Conference: Computers and Advanced Technology in Education, Kauai, Hawaii, USA.

Mumford, M. D., Connelly, M. S., Helton, W. B., Strange, J. M., & Osburn, H. K. (2001). On the construct validity of integrity tests: Individual and situational factors as predictors of test performance. *International Journal of Selection and Assessment, 9,* 240–257.

Mumme, D. L., & Fernald, A. (2003). The infant as onlooker: Learning from emotional reactions observed in a television scenario. *Child Development, 74,* 221–237.

Munte, T. F., Altenmuller, E., & Jancke, L. (2002). The musician's brain as a model of neuroplasticity. *Nature Reviews Neuroscience, 3,* 473–478.

Murphy, K. R., Cronin, B. E., & Tam, A. P. (2003). Controversy and consensus regarding the use of cognitive ability testing in organizations. *Journal of Applied Psychology, 88,* 660–671.

Murray, B. (2000). Learning from real life. *APA Monitor, 31,* 72–73.

Murray, E. A., & Mishkin, M. (1985). Amygdalectomy impairs crossmodal association in monkeys. *Science, 228,* 604–606.

Murray, H. A. (1938). *Explorations in personality.* New York: Oxford University Press.

Mussweiler, T. (2003). "Everything is relative": Comparison processes in social judgment: The 2002 Jaspars Lecture. *European Journal of Social Psychology, 33,* 719–733.

Myers, B. J. (1987). Mother-infant bonding as a critical period. In M. H. Bornstein (Ed.), *Sensitive periods in development: Interdisciplinary perspectives.* Hillsdale, NJ: Erlbaum.

Myers, D. G. (2000). The funds, friends, and faith of happy people. *American Psychologist, 55,* 56–57.

Myers, M. G., Reeves, R. A., Oh, P. I., & Joyner, C. D. (1996). Overtreatment of hypertension in the community? *American Journal of Hypertension, 9,* 419–425.

Myers, P. I., & Hammill, D. D. (1990). *Learning disabilities: Basic concepts, assessment practices, and instructional strategies.* Austin, TX: Pro-Ed.

Nabeshima, T., & Yamada, K. (2000). Neurotrophic factor strategies for the treatment of Alzheimer disease. *Alzheimer Disease & Associated Disorders, 14* (Suppl. 1), S39–46.

Nadeau, C. (2000). The Case of David Milgaard. Retrieved March 23, 2006, from http://ace.acadiau.ca/soci/agt/soc

Nader, K., Bechara, A., & Van der Kooy, D. (1997). Neurobiological constraints on behavioral models of motivation. *Annual Review of Psychology, 48,* 85–114.

Naëgelé, B., Thouvard, V., Pépin, J.-L., Lévy, P., Bonnet, C., Perret, J. E., et al. (1995). Deficits of cognitive functions in patients with sleep apnea syndrome. *Sleep, 18*(1), 43–52.

Nairne, J. S. (2003). Sensory and working memory. In A. F. P. Healy, R. W. Proctor, & I. B. Weiner (Eds.), *Handbook of psychology: Vol. 4. Experimental psychology* (pp. 423–444). New York: Wiley.

Naito, M., & Miura, H. (2001). Japanese children's numerical competencies: Age- and schooling-related influences on the development of number concepts and addition skills. *Developmental Psychology, 37,* 217–230.

Najavits, L. M., Ghinassi, F., Van Horn, A., Weiss, R. D., Siqueland, L., Frank, A., et al. (2004). Therapist satisfaction with four manual-based treatments on a national multisite trial: An exploratory study. *Psychotherapy: Theory, Research, Practice, Training, 41,* 26–37.

Nakamura, J., & Csikszentmihalyi, M. (2001). Catalytic creativity. *American Psychologist, 56,* 337–341.

Nakano, K., & Kitamura, T. (2001). The relation of the anger subcomponent of Type A behavior to psychological symptoms in Japanese and foreign students. *Japanese Psychological Research, 43,* 50–54.

Nakayama, K. (1994). James J. Gibson: An appreciation. *Psychological Review, 101,* 329–335.

Nash, I. S., Mosca, L., Blumenthal, R. S., Davidson, M. H., Smith, S. C., Jr., & Pasternak, R. C. (2003). Contemporary awareness and understanding of cholesterol as a risk factor: Results of an American Heart Association national survey. *Archives of Internal Medicine, 163,* 1597–1600.

Nathan, P. E., Stuart, S. P., & Dolan, S. L. (2000). Research on psychotherapy efficacy and effectiveness: Between Scylla and Charybdis? *Psychological Bulletin, 126,* 964–981.

National Institutes of Health Consensus Conference. (1998). Acupuncture. *Journal of the American Medical Association, 280,* 1518–1524.

National Institutes of Health. (2001). *Eating disorders: Facts about eating disorders and the search for solutions* (NIH Publication No. 01–4901). Washington, DC: U.S. Department of Health and Human Services.

National Task Force on the Prevention and Treatment of Obesity. (2000). Dieting and the development of eating disorders in overweight and obese adults. *Archives of Internal Medicine, 160,* 2581–2589.

Naumann, A., & Daum, I. (2003). Narcolepsy: Pathophysiology and neuropsychological changes. *Behavioral Neurology, 14,* 89–98.

Navarrete-Palacios, E., Hudson, R., Reyes-Guerrero, G., & Guevara-Guzman, R. (2003). Lower olfactory threshold during the ovulatory phase of the menstrual cycle. *Biological Psychology, 63,* 269–279.

Needham, A., & Baillargeon, R. (1999). Effects of prior experience on 4.5 month-old infants' object segregation. *Infant Behavior & Development, 21,* 1–24.

Neher, A. (1991). Maslow's theory of motivation: A critique. *Journal of Humanistic Psychology, 31,* 89–112.

Nehra, A., & Kulaksizoglu, H. (2002). Combination therapy for erectile dysfunction: Where we are and what's in the future. *Current Urology Reports, 3,* 467–470.

Neisser, U. (1967). *Cognitive psychology.* New York: Appelton-Century-Crofts.

Neisser, U. (1998). *The rising curve: Long-term gains in I.Q. and related measures.* Washington, DC: American Psychological Association.

Neisser, U. (2000). Memorists. In U. Neisser & I. E. Hyman Jr. (Eds.), *Memory observed* (2nd ed., pp. 475–478). New York: Worth.

Neisser, U., Boodoo, G., Bouchard, T. J., Boykin, A. W., Brody, N., Ceci, S. J., et al. (1996). Intelligence: Knowns and unknowns. *American Psychologist, 51,* 77–101.

Neitz, M., & Neitz, J. (1995, February 17). Numbers and ratios of visual pigment genes for normal red-green color vision. *Science, 267,* 1013–1016.

Nelson, C. A. (1997). The neurobiological basis of early memory development. In N. Cowan (Ed.), *The development of memory in childhood: Studies in developmental psychology* (pp. 41–82). Hove, England: Psychology Press/Erlbaum/Taylor & Francis.

Nelson, D. L. (1999). Implicit memory. In D. E. Morris & M. Gruneberg (Eds.), *Theoretical aspects of memory.* London: Routledge.

Nelson, D. L., McKinney, V. M., & Bennett, D. J. (1999). Conscious and automatic uses of memory in cued recall and recognition. In B. H. Challis & B. M. Velichkovsky (Eds.), *Stratification in cognition and consciousness* (p. 173–202). Amsterdam: John Benjamins.

Nelson, D. L., McKinney, V. M., Gee, N. R., & Janczura, G. A. (1998). Interpreting the influence of implicitly activated memories on recall and recognition. *Psychological Review, 105,* 299–324.

Nelson, K. (1986). Event knowledge and cognitive development. In K. Nelson (Ed.), *Event knowledge: Structure and function in development* (pp. 1–19). Hillsdale, NJ: Erlbaum.

Nelson, K. (1993). The psychological and social origins of autobiographical memory. *Psychological Science, 4,* 7–14.

Nemeroff, C. B. (1998). Psychopharmacology of affective disorders in the 21st century. *Biological Psychiatry, 44,* 517–525.

Nemeroff, C. B., Heim, C. M., Thase, M. E., Klein, D. N., Rush, A. J., Schatzberg, A. F., et al. (2003). Differential responses to psychotherapy versus pharmacotherapy in patients with chronic forms of major depression and childhood trauma. *Proceedings of the National Academy of Science, 100,* 14293–14296.

Nesca, M. & Koulack, D. (1994). Recognition memory, sleep, and circadian rhythms. *Canadian Journal of Experimental Psychology, 48,* 359–379.

Nestler, E. J. (2001). Molecular basis of long-term plasticity underlying addiction. *National Review of Neuroscience, 2,* 119–128.

Neugarten, B. L. (1977). Personality and aging. In J. E. Birren & K. W. Schaie (Eds.), *Handbook of the psychology of aging.* New York: Van Nostrand Reinhold.

Neumann, C. S., Grimes, K., Walker, E. F., & Baum, K. (1995). Developmental pathways to schizophrenia: Behavioral subtypes. *Journal of Abnormal Psychology, 104,* 558–566.

Neumeister, A., Bain, E., Nugent, A. C., Carson, R. E., Bonne, O., Luckenbaugh, D. A., et al. (2004). Reduced serotonin type 1A receptor binding in panic disorder. *Journal of Neuroscience, 24,* 589–591.

Neuwelt, E. A. (2004). Mechanisms of disease: The blood-brain barrier. *Neurosurgery, 54,* 131–140.

Neville, H. J., Bavelier, D., Corina, D., Rauschecker, J., Karni, A., Lalwani, A., et al. (1998). Cerebral organization for language in deaf and hearing subjects: Biological constraints and effects of experience. *Proceedings of the National Academy of Science USA, 95,* 922–929.

Newberg, A., Alavi, A., Baime, M., Pourdehnad, M., Santanna, J., & d'Aquili, E. (2001). The measurement of regional cerebral blood flow during the complex cognitive task of meditation: A preliminary SPECT study. *Psychiatry Research, 106,* 113–122.

Newell, A., & Simon, H. A. (1972). *Human problem solving.* Englewood Cliffs, NJ: Prentice-Hall.

Newman, E. A. (2003). New roles for astrocytes: Regulation of synaptic transmission. *Trends in Neuroscience, 26,* 536–542.

Newman, J. P., Wolff, W. T., & Hearst, E. (1980). The feature positive effect in adult human subjects. *Journal of Experimental Psychology: Human Learning and Memory, 6,* 630–650.

Newsome, J. T. (1999). Another side to caregiving: Negative reactions to being helped. *Current Directions in Psychological Science, 8,* 183–187.

Newsome, J. T., & Schulz, R. (1998). Caregiving from the recipient's perspective: Negative reactions to being helped. *Health Psychology, 17,* 172–181.

Neziroglu, F., McKay, D., & Yaryura-Tobias, J. A. (2000). Overlapping and distinctive features of hypochondriasis and obsessive-compulsive disorder. *Journal of Anxiety Disorders, 14,* 603–614.

Ng, B.-Y. (2000). Phenomenology of trance states seen at a psychiatric hospital in Singapore: A cross-cultural perspective. *Transcultural Psychiatry, 37,* 560–579.

Niaura, R., Bock, B., Lloyd, E. E., Brown, R., Lipsitt, L. P., & Buka, S. (2001). Maternal transmission of nicotine dependence: Psychiatric, neurocognitive and prenatal factors. *American Journal on Addictions, 10,* 16–29.

Nicassio, P. M., Meyerowitz, B. E., & Kerns, R. D. (2004). The future of health psychology interventions. *Health Psychology, 23,* 132–137.

NICHD Early Child Care Research Network. (2003). Does amount of time spent in child care predict socioemotional adjustment during the transition to kindergarten? *Child Development,* 74, 976–1005.

NICHD Early Child Care Research Network. (2005). *Child care and child development: Results from the NICHD Study of Early Child Care and Youth Development.* New York: Guilford.

Nichols, R. (1978). Twin studies of ability, personality, and interests. *Homo, 29,* 158–173.

Nicholson, I. R., & Neufeld, R. W. J. (1993). Classification of the schizophrenias according to symptomatology: A two factor model. *Journal of Abnormal Psychology, 102,* 259–270.

Nickell, J. (1997, January/February). Sleuthing a psychic sleuth. *Skeptical Inquirer, 21,* 18–19.

Nickell, J. (2001). Exorcism! Driving out the nonsense. *Skeptical Inquirer, 25,* 20–24.

Nickels, J. B., Cramer, K. M., & Gural, D. M. (1992). Toward unconfounding prediction and control: Predictionless control made possible. *Canadian Journal of Behavioural Sciences, 24,* 156–170

Nickerson, C., Schwarz, N., Diener, E., & Kahneman, D. (2003). Zeroing in on the dark side of the American dream: A closer look at the negative consequences of the goal for financial success. *Psychological Science, 14,* 531–536.

Niederhoffer, K. G., & Pennebaker, J. W. (2002). Sharing one's story: On the benefits of writing or talking about emotional experience. In C. R. Snyder & S. J. Lopez (Eds.), *Handbook of positive psychology* (pp. 573–583). London: Oxford University Press.

Niemela, M., & Saarinen, J. (2000). Visual search for grouped versus ungrouped icons in a computer interface. *Human Factors, 42,* 630–635.

Nienhuys, J. W. (2001). Spontaneous human combustion: Requiem for Phyllis. *Skeptical Inquirer, 25,* 28–34.

Nietzel, M. T., Bernstein, D. A., Kramer, G, & Milich, R. (2003). *Introduction to clinical psychology* (6th ed.). Englewood Cliffs, NJ: Prentice-Hall.

Nietzel, M. T., Speltz, M. L., McCauley, E. A., & Bernstein, D. A. (1998). *Abnormal psychology.* Boston: Allyn & Bacon.

Nijhawan, R. (1997). Visual decomposition of colour through motion extrapolation. *Nature, 386,* 66–69.

Nijstad, B. A., Stroebe, W., & Lodewijkx, H. F. M. (2003). Production blocking and idea generation: Does blocking interfere with cognitive processes? *Journal of Experimental Social Psychology, 39,* 531–548.

Nikki (2004). Psychic to the stars: Psychic clairvoyant readings. Retrieved March 23, 2006, from http://www.psychicnikki.com/predictions.html

Nilsson, G. (1996, November). Some forms of memory improve as people age. *APA Monitor,* p. 27.

Nilsson, T. (2005). Ensuring colour legibility. AIC Colour 05–10th Congress of the International Colour Assocation, 749–752.

Nisbett, R. E., & Masuda, T. (2003). Culture and point of view. *Proceedings of the National Academy of Sciences, 100,* 11163–11170.

Nishimura, T., Mikami, A., Suzuki, J., & Matsuzawa, T. (2003). Descent of the larynx in chimpanzee infants. *Proceedings of the National Academy of Science, 100,* 6930–6933.

Niznikiewicz, M. A., O'Donnell, B. F., Nestor, P. G., Smith, L., Law, S., Karapelou, M., et al. (1997). ERP assessment of visual and auditory language processing in schizophrenia. *Journal of Abnormal Psychology, 106,* 85–94.

Noble, H. B. (2000, January 25). Outgrowth of new field of tissue engineering. *New York Times.*

Nobler, M. S., Oquendo, M. A., Kegeles, L. S., Malone, K. M., Campbell, C., Sackeim, H. A., & Mann, J. J. (2001). Decreased Regional Brain Metabolism After ETC. *American Journal of Psychiatry, 158,* 305–308.

Nolan, R. P., Spanos, N. P., Hayward, A. A., & Scott, H. A. (1995). The efficacy of hypnotic and nonhypnotic response-based imagery for self-managing recurrent headache. *Imagination, Cognition, and Personality, 14*(3), 183–201.

Noland, V. J., Liller, K. D., McDermott, R. J., Coulter, M. L., & Seraphine, A. E. (2004). Is adolescent sibling violence a precursor to college dating violence? *American Journal of Health Behavior, 28,* 13–22.

Nolen-Hoeksema, S. (1990). *Sex differences in depression.* Stanford, CA: Stanford University Press.

Nolen-Hoeksema, S. (2001). Gender differences in depression. *Current Directions in Psychological Science, 10,* 173–176.

Nolen-Hoeksema, S., Larson, J., & Grayson, C. (1999). Explaining gender differences in depression. *Journal of Personality and Social Psychology, 77,* 1061–1072.

Nolen-Hoeksma, S., Morrow, J., & Fredrickson, N. (1993). Response styles and the duration of episodes of depressed mood. *Journal of Abnormal Psychology, 102,* 20–28.

Noll, R. B. (1994). Hypnotherapy for warts in children and adolescents. *Journal of Developmental and Behavioral Pediatrics, 15*(3), 170–173.

Norcross, J. C. (2002). *Psychotherapy relationships that work: Therapist contributions and responsiveness to patients.* London: Oxford University Press.

Norcross, J. C., Hedges, M., & Prochaska, J. O. (2002). The face of 2010: A Delphi poll on the future of psychotherapy. *Professional Psychology: Research and practice, 33,* 316–322.

Norcross, J. C., Santrock, J. W., Campbell, L. F., Smith, T. P., Sommer, R., & Zuckerman, E. L. (2000). *Authoritative guide to self-help resources in mental health.* New York: Guilford.

Northcut, T. B., & Heller, N. R. (Eds.). (1999). *Enhancing psychodynamic therapy with cognitive-behavioral techniques.* Northvale, NJ: Aronson.

Nosek, B. A., Banaji, M., & Greenwald, A. G. (2002). Harvesting implicit group attitudes and beliefs from a demonstration web site. *Group Dynamics: Theory, Research, and Practice, 6,* 101–115.

Nourkova, V. V., Bernstein, D. M., & Loftus, E. F. (2004) Biography becomes autobiography: Distorting the subjective past. *American Journal of Psychology, 117,* 65–80.

Nowak, M. A., Komarova, N. L., & Niyogi, P. (2001). Evolution of universal grammar. *Science, 291,* 114–118.

Nowinski, J. (1999). Self-help groups for addictions. In B. S. McCrady & E. E. Epstein (Eds.), *Addictions: A comprehensive guidebook* (pp. 328–347). New York: Oxford University Press.

Nugent, F. (1994). *An introduction to the profession of counseling.* Columbus, OH: Merrill.

Nunn, J. A., Gregory, L. J., Brammer, M., Williams, S. C., Parslow, D. M., Morgan, M. J., et al. (2002). Functional magnetic resonance imaging of synesthesia: Activation of V4/V8 by spoken words. *Nature Neuroscience, 5,* 371–375.

Nurnberger, J. (1993). Genotyping status report for affective disorder. *Psychiatric Genetics, 3,* 207–214.

Nyberg, L., Persson, L., Hebib, R., Tulving, E. Cabeza, R., Houle, S. Persson, J. & McIntosh, A.R. (2000). Large scale neurocognitive networks underlying episodic memory. *Journal of Cognitive Neuroscience, 12* (1), 163–173.

O'Conner-Von, S. (2000). Preparing children for surgery: An integrative research review. *Association of Perioperative Registered Nurses Journal, 71,* 334.

O'Donohue, W., Fisher, J. E., & Hayes, S. C. (Eds.). (2003). *Cognitive behavior therapy: Applying empirically supported techniques in your practice.* New York: Wiley.

O'Farrell, T. J. (1995). Marital and family therapy. In R. K. Hester & W. R. Miller (Eds.), *Handbook of alcoholism treatment approaches* (2nd ed., pp. 195–220). Boston: Allyn & Bacon.

O'Leary, D. S., Block, R. I., Koeppel, J. A., Flaum, M., Schulz, S. K., Andreason, N. C., et al. (2002). Effects of smoking marijuana on brain perfusion and cognition. *Neuropsychopharmacology, 26,* 802–816.

Ochsner, K. N., & Lieberman, M. D. (2001). The emergence of social cognitive neuroscience. *American Psychologist, 56,* 717–734.

Oden, M. H. (1968). The fulfillment of promise: 40-year follow-up of the Terman gifted group. *Genetic Psychology Monographs, 17,* 3–93.

Oellerich, T. (2000). Rind, Tromovitch, and Bauserman: Politically incorrect—scientifically correct. *Sexuality and Culture 4,* 67–81.

Oettingen, G., Pak, H., & Schnetter, K. (2001). Self-regulation of goal setting: Turning free fantasies about the future into binding goals. *Journal of Personality and Social Psychology, 80,* 736–753.

Oh, S. (2000). Rave fever. *Maclean's, April.*

Öhman, A., & Mineka, S. (2001). Fears, phobias, and preparedness: Toward an evolved module of fear and fear learning. *Psychological Review, 108,* 483–522.

Öhman, A., & Mineka, S. (2003). The malicious serpent: Snakes as a prototypical stimulus for an evolved module of fear. *Current Directions in Psychological Science, 12,* 5–9.

Öhman, A., & Soares, J. F. (1994). "Unconscious anxiety": Phobic responses to masked stimuli. *Journal of Abnormal Psychology, 103*(2), 231–240.

Öhman, A., Dimberg, U., & Öst, L. G. (1985). Animal and social phobias: A laboratory model. In S. Reiss & R. R. Bootzin (Eds.), *Theoretical issues in behavior therapy.* Orlando, FL: Academic Press.

Ohring, R., Graber, J. A., & Brooks-Gunn, J. (2002). Girls' recurrent and concurrent body dissatisfaction: Correlates and consequences over 8 years. *International Journal of Eating Disorders, 31*(4), 404–415.

Oishi, S., Diener, E., Lucas, R. E., & Suh, E. M. (1999). Cross-cultural variations in predictors of life-satisfaction: Perspectives from needs and values. *Personality and Social Psychology Bulletin, 25,* 980–990.

Olds, E.S., & Punambolam, R. J. (2002). The decay and interruption of interactions between search mechanisms. *Vision Research, 42(6),* 747–760.

Olds, J. (1973). Commentary on positive reinforcement produced by electrical stimulation of septal areas and other regions of rat brain. In E. S. Valenstein (Ed.), *Brain stimulation and motivation: Research and commentary.* Glenview, IL: Scott, Foresman.

Olds, J., & Milner, P. (1954). Positive reinforcement produced by electrical stimulation of septal areas and other regions of the rat brain. *Journal of Comparative and Physiological Psychology, 47,* 419–427.

Olfson, M., Marcus, S. C., Druss, B., Elinson, L., Tanielian, T., & Pincus, H. A. (2002). National trends in the outpatient treatment of depression. *Journal of the American Medical Association, 287,* 203–209.

Olfson, M., Mechanic, D., Hansell, S., Boyer, C. A., & Walkup, J. (1999). Prediction of homelessness within three months of discharge among inpatients with schizophrenia. *Psychiatric Services, 50,* 667–673.

Oliner, S. P., & Oliner, P. M. (1988). *The altruistic personality: Rescuers of Jews in Nazi Europe.* New York: Free Press.

Olio, K. A. (1994). Truth in memory. *American Psychologist, 49,* 442–443.

Olivares, R., Michalland, S., & Aboitiz, F. (2000). Cross-species and intraspecies morphometric analysis of the corpus callosum. *Brain and Behavior and Evolution, 55,* 37–43.

Olson, J. M., & Hafer, C. L. (2001). The psychology of legitimacy: Emerging perspectives on ideology, justice, and intergroup relations. In John T. Jost and B. Major (Eds). *The psychology of legitimacy: Emerging perspectives on ideology, justice, and intergroup relations.* (pp. 157–175). New York: Cambridge University Press.

Olson, L. (1997). Regeneration in the adult central nervous system. *Nature Medicine, 3,* 1329–1335.

Olson, M. A., & Fazio, R. H. (2001). Implicit attitude formation through classical conditioning. *Psychological Science, 12,* 413–417.

Onaivi, E. S., Leonard, C. M., Ishiguro, H., Zhang, P. W., Lin, Z., Akinshola, B. E., & Uhl, G. R. (2002). Endocannabinoids and cannabinoid receptor genetics. *Progress in Neurobiology, 66,* 307–344.

Ones, D. S., Viswesvaran, C., & Schmidt, F. L. (2003). Personality and absenteeism: A meta-analysis of integrity tests. *European Journal of Personality, 17,* S19–S38.

Ones, D., & Viswesvaran, C. (2001). Personality at work: Criterion focused occupational personality scales used in personnel selection. In R. Hogan & B. Roberts (Eds.), *Personality psychology in the workplace* (pp. 63–92). Washington, DC: American Psychological Association.

Ontario Ministry of Health and Long-Term Care (2001). Mental health amendments: Questions and answers [Electronic version]. Available: http://www.health.gov.on.ca/english/public/pub/mental/faq.html.

Operario, D., & Fiske, S. T. (2001). Stereotypes: Processes, structures, content, and context. In R. Brown & S. Gaertner (Eds.), *Blackwell handbook in social psychology: Intergroup processes* (pp. 22–44). Oxford, UK: Blackwell.

Oppel, S. (2000, March 5). Managing ABCs like a CEO. *St. Petersburg Times,* 1A, 12–13A.

Oquendo, M. A., & Mann, J. J. (2000). The biology of impulsivity and suicidality. *Psychiatric Clinics of North America, 23,* 11–25.

Oquendo, M. A., Ellis, S. P., Greenwald, S., Malone, K. M., Weissman, M. M., & Mann, J. J. (2001). Ethnic and sex differences in suicide rates relative to major depression in the United States. *American Journal of Psychiatry, 158,* 1652–1658.

Orne, M. T., & Evans, F. J. (1965). Social control in the psychological experiment: Antisocial behavior and hypnosis. *Journal of Personality and Social Psychology, 1,* 189–200.

Orpana, H., & Lemyre, L. (2004). Explaining the social gradient in health in Canada: Using the National Population Health Survey to examine the role of stressors. *International Journal of Behavioral Medicine, 11,* 143–151.

Osherson, D., Perani, D., Cappa, S., Schnur, T., Grassi, F., & Fazio, F. (1998). Distinct brain loci in deductive versus probabilistic reasoning. *Neuropsychologia, 36,* 369–376.

Oskamp, S., & Schultz, P. W. (1998). *Applied social psychology* (2nd ed.). Upper Saddle River, NJ: Prentice-Hall.

Öst, L.-G. (1978). Behavioral treatment of thunder and lightning phobia. *Behavior Research and Therapy, 16,* 197–207.

Öst, L.-G. (1992). Blood and injection phobia: Background and cognitive, physiological and behavioral variables. *Journal of Abnormal Psychology, 101,* 68–74.

Öst, L.-G., Hellström, K., & Kåver, A. (1992). One- versus five-session exposure in the treatment of needle phobia. *Behavior Therapy, 23,* 263–282.

Öst, L.-G., Salkovskis, P. M., & Hellström, K. (1991). One-session therapist-directed exposure vs. self-exposure in the treatment of spider phobia. *Behavior Therapy, 22,* 407–422.

Öst, L.-G., Svensson, L., Hellström, K., & Lindwall, R. (2001). One-session treatment of specific phobias in youths: A randomized clinical trial. *Journal of Consulting and Clinical Psychology, 69,* 814–824.

Otsuka, R., Watanabe, H., Hirata, K., Tokai, K., Muro, T., Yoshiyama, M., et al. (2001). Acute effects of passive smoking on the coronary circulation in healthy young adults. *Journal of the American Medical Association, 286,* 436–441.

Otten, L. J., Henson, R. N., & Rugg, M. D. (2002). State-related and item-related neural correlates of successful memory encoding. *Nature Neuroscience, 5,* 1339–1344.

Otto, M. W., Pollack, M. H., Gould, R. A., Worthington, J. J., III, McArdle, E. T., Rosenbaum, J. F., & Heimberg, R. G. (2000). A comparison of the efficacy of clonazepam and cognitive-behavioral group therapy for the treatment of social phobia. *Journal of Anxiety Disorders, 14,* 345–358.

Ottosson, H., Ekselius, L., Grann, M., & Kullgren, G. (2002). Cross-system concordance of personality disorder diagnoses of *DSM-IV* and Diagnostic Criteria for Research of ICD-10. *Journal of Personality Disorders, 16,* 283–292.

Ouimette, P. C., Finney, J. W., & Moos, R. H. (1997). Twelve-step and cognitive-behavioral treatment for substance abuse: A comparison of treatment effectiveness. *Journal of Consulting and Clinical Psychology, 65,* 230–240.

Overmier, J. B. (2002). On learned helplessness. *Integrative Physiological & Behavioral Science, 37,* 4–8.

Overton, D. A. (1984). State dependent learning and drug discriminations. In L. L. Iverson, S. D. Iverson, & S. H. Snyder (Eds.), *Handbook of psychopharmacology* (Vol. 18). New York: Plenum.

Overton, P. G., Richards, C. D., Berry, M. S. & Clark, D. (1999). Long-term potentiation at excitatory amino acid synapses on midbrain dopamine neurons. *Neuroreport, 10,* 221–226.

Oyserman, D., Coon, H. M., & Kemmelmeier, M. (2002). Rethinking individualism and collectivism: Evaluation of theoretical assumptions and meta-analyses. *Psychological Bulletin, 128,* 3–72.

Ozer, D. J. (1999). Four principles of personality assessment. In L. Pervin & O. John (Eds.), *Handbook of personality: Theory and research* (2nd ed., pp. 671–689). New York: Guilford.

Özgen, E. (2004). Language, learning, and color perception. *Current Directions in Psychological Science, 13,* 95–98.

Özgen, E., & Davies, I. R. L. (2002). Acquisition of categorical color perception: A perceptual learning approach to the linguistic relativity hypothesis. *Journal of Experimental Psychology: General, 131,* 477–493.

Pachankis, J. E., & Goldfried, M. R. (2004). Clinical issues in working with lesbian, gay, and bisexual clients. *Psychotherapy: Theory, Research, Practice, Training, 41,* 227–246.

Paik, H., & Comstock, G. (1994). The effects of television violence on antisocial behavior: A meta-analysis. *Communication Research, 21,* 516–546.

Paivio, A. (1986). *Mental representations: A dual coding approach.* New York: Oxford University Press.

Paivio, S. C., & Greenberg, L. S. (1995). Resolving "unfinished business": Efficacy of experiential therapy using empty-chair dialogue. *Journal of Consulting and Clinical Psychology, 63,* 419–425.

Pajares, F. (2004). Albert Bandura: Biographical sketch. Retrieved month day, year, from http://www.emory.edu/EDUCATION/mfp/bandurabio.html

Palkovitz, R., Copes, M. A., & Woolfolk, T. N. (2001). It's like . . . you discover a new sense of being: Involved fathering as an evoker of adult development. *Men & Masculinities, 4*(1), 49–69.

Palmer, F. H., & Anderson, L. W. (1979). Long-term gains from early intervention: Findings from longitudinal studies. In E. Zigler & J. Valentine (Eds.), *Project Head Start: A legacy of the war on poverty.* New York: Free Press.

Palmer, S. E. (1999). *Vision science: Photons to phenomenology.* Cambridge, MA: MIT Press.

Palmeri, T. J., Blake, R., Marois, R., Flanery, M. A., & Whetsell, W. Jr. (2002). The perceptual reality of synesthetic colors. *Proceedings of the National Academy of Sciences, 99,* 4127–4131.

Palmisano, M., & Herrmann, D. (1991). The facilitation of memory performance. *Bulletin of the Psychonomic Society, 29,* 557–559.

Paloski, W. H. (1998). Vestibulospinal adaptation to microgravity. *Otolaryngol Head and Neck Surgery, 118,* S39–S44.

Paltry, A.L. & Pelletier, L.G. (2001). Extraterrestrial beliefs and experiences: An application of the theory of reasoned action. *The Journal of School Psychology, 14,* 199–217.

Paoletti, M. G. (1995). Biodiversity, traditional landscapes and agroecosystem management. *Landscape and Urban Planning, 31*(1–3), 117–128.

Pape, H. C., Munsch, T., & Budde, T. (2004). Novel vistas of calcium-mediated signalling in the thalamus. *Pflugers Archives, 448,* 131–138.

Parish, C. L., Finkelstein, D. I., Tripanichkul, W., Satoskar, A. R., Drago, J., & Horne, M. K. (2002). The role of interleukin-1, interleukin-6, and glia in inducing growth of neuronal terminal arbors in mice. *Journal of Neuroscience, 22,* 8034–8041.

Park, D. C. (2001, August). *The aging mind.* Paper presented at the annual convention of the American Psychological Association, San Francisco.

Park, J., White, A. R., & Ernst, E. (2001). New sham method in auricular acupuncture. *Archives of Internal Medicine, 161,* 894.

Park, Y. M., Matsumoto, K., Jin Seo, Y., Kang, M. J., & Nagashima, H. (2002). Effects of age and gender on sleep habits and sleep trouble for aged people. *Biological Rhythm Research, 33,* 39–51.

Parke, R. D. (2002). Fathers and families. In M. H. Bornstein (Ed.), *Handbook of parenting* (2nd ed., pp. 27–63). Mahwah, NJ: Erlbaum.

Parker, G., Gladstone, G., & Chee, K. T. (2001). Depression in the planet's largest ethnic group: The Chinese. *American Journal of Psychiatry, 158,* 857–864.

Parker, J. G., Saxon, J. L., Asher, S. R., & Kovacs, D. M. (2001). Dimensions of children's friendship adjustment: Implications for understanding loneliness. In K. J. Rotenberg & S. Hymel (Eds.), *Loneliness in childhood and adolescence.* New York: Cambridge University Press.

Parker, J.R. (2003). Object recognition and location in a practical context, Procter and Gamble 2003 Analytical Symposium, Cincinnati, Ohio, September 10.

Parker, L.A. (2003). Taste avoidance and taste aversion: Evidence for two different processes. *Learning and Behavior, 31,* 165–172

Parkin, A. J., & Walter, B. M. (1991). Aging, short-term memory, and frontal dysfunction. *Psychobiology, 19,* 175–179.

Parnas, J., Cannon, T., Jacobsen, B., Schulsinger, H., Schulsinger, F., & Mednick, S. (1993). Lifetime *DSM-III-R* diagnostic outcomes in the offspring of schizophrenic mothers. *Archives of General Psychiatry, 50,* 707–714.

Pascalis, O., de Haan, M., & Nelson, C. A. (2002). Is face processing species specific during the first year of life? *Science, 296,* 1321–1323.

Pascual-Leone, A. (2001). The brain that plays music and is changed by it. *Annals of the New York Academy of Science, 930,* 315–329.

Pascual-Leone, A., & Torres, F. (1993). Plasticity of the sensorimotor cortex representation of the reading finger in Braille readers. *Brain, 116,* 39–52.

Patel, A. D., & Balaban, E. (2001). Human pitch perception is reflected in the timing of stimulus-related cortical activity. *Nature Neuroscience, 4,* 839–844.

Patel, S. R., White, D. P., Malhotra, A., Stanchina, M. L., & Ayas, N. T. (2003). Continuous positive airway pressure therapy for treating sleepiness in a diverse population with obstructive sleep apnea: Results of a meta-analysis. *Archives of Internal Medicine, 163,* 565–571.

Patrick, C. J., Bradley, M. M. & Lang, P. J. (1993). Emotion in the criminal psychopath: Startle reflex modulation. *Journal of Abnormal Psychology, 102,* 82–92.

Patrick, C. J., Cuthbert, B. N., & Lang, P. J. (1994). Emotion in the criminal psychopath: Fear imaging processing. *Journal of Abnormal Psychology, 103,* 523–534.

Patterson, C. J. (2002). Lesbian and gay parenthood. In M. H. Bornstein (Ed.), *Handbook of parenting* (2nd ed., pp. 255–274). Mahwah, NJ: Erlbaum.

Pattie, F. A. (1935). A report of attempts to produce uniocular blindness by hypnotic suggestion. *British Journal of Medical Psychiatry, 15,* 230–241.

Patton, G. C., Coffey, C., Carlin, J. B., Degenhardt, L., Lynskey, M., & Hall, W. (2002). Cannabis use and mental health in young people: Cohort study. *British Medical Journal, 325,* 1195–1198.

Patton, G. C., McMorris, B. J., Toumbourou, J. W., Hemphill, S. A., Donath, S., & Catalano, R. F. (2004). Puberty and the onset of substance use and abuse [Electronic version]. *Pediatrics, 114*(3), e300–6.

Pauk, W. (2002). *How to study in college.* Boston: Houghton Mifflin.

Pauk, W., & Fiore, J. P. (2000). *Succeed in college!* Boston: Houghton Mifflin.

Paul, G. L. (1969). Behavior modification research: Design and tactics. In C. M. Franks (Ed.), *Behavior therapy: Appraisal and status* (pp. 29–62). New York: McGraw-Hill.

Paul, G. L. (2000). Milieu therapy. In A. E. Kazdin (Ed.), *The encyclopedia of psychology.* Washington, DC: American Psychological Association.

Paul, G. L., & Lentz, R. J. (1977). *Psychosocial treatment of chronic mental patients: Milieu versus social learning programs.* Cambridge: Harvard University Press.

Paul, G. L., Stuve, P., & Cross, J. V. (1997). Real-world inpatient programs: Shedding some light—A critique. *Applied and Preventive Psychology, 6,* 193–204.

Paulhus, D. L., Fridhandler, B., & Hayes, S. (1997). Psychological defense: Contemporary theory and research. In R. Hogan, J. Johnson, & S. Briggs (Eds.), *Handbook of personality psychology* (pp. 544–588). San Diego: Academic Press.

Paulhus, D. L., Trapnell, P., & Chen, D. (1999). Birth order effects on personality and achievement within families. *Psychological Science, 10,* 482–488.

Pauls, D. L., Alsobrook, J. P., II, Goodman, W., Rasmussen, S., & Leckman, J. F. (1995). A family study of obsessive-compulsive disorder. *American Journal of Psychiatry, 152,* 76–84.

Paus, T., Zijdenbos, A., Worsley, K., Collins, D. L., Blumenthal, J., Giedd, J. N., et al. (1999). Structural maturation of neural pathways in children and adolescents: In vivo study. *Science, 283,* 1908–1911.

Payne, J. W., Bettman, J. R., & Johnson, E. J. (1992). Behavioral decision research: A constructive processing perspective. *Behavioral decision research: A constructive processing perspective, 43,* 87–131.

Pear, J., & Martin, G. L. (2002). *Behavior modification: What it is and how to do it* (7th ed.). Englewood Cliffs, NJ: Prentice Hall.

Pearce, M. J., Jones, S. M., Schwab-Stone, M. E., & Ruchkin, V. (2003). The protective effects of religiousness and parent involvement on the development of conduct problems among youth exposed to violence. *Child Development, 74,* 1682–1696.

Peck, J. W. (1978). Rats defend different body weights depending on palatability and accessibility of their food. *Journal of Comparative and Physiological Psychology, 92,* 555–570.

Pedersen, P. B., & Draguns, J. G. (2002). *Counseling across cultures.* Thousand Oaks, CA: Sage.

Peigneux, P., Laureys, S., Delbeuck, X., & Maquet, P. (2001). Sleeping brain, learning brain: The role of sleep for memory systems. *Neuroreport, 12,* A111–A124.

Penedo, F. J., & Dahn, J. (2004). Psychoneuroimmunology and aging. In M. Irwin & K. Vedhara (Eds.), *Psychoneuroimmunology.* New York: Kluwer.

Penfield, W. & Mathieson, G. (1974). Memory: Autopsy findings and comments on the role of hippocampus in experimental recall. *Archives of Neurology, 31(3),* 145–154.

Penfield, W., & Rasmussen, T. (1968). *The cerebral cortex of man: A clinical study of localization of function.* New York: Hafner.

Pennebaker, J. W. (1995). *Emotion, disclosure, and health.* Washington, DC: American Psychological Association.

Pennebaker, J. W. (2002). *Emotion, disclosure, and health.* Washington, DC: American Psychological Association.

Pennebaker, J. W., & O'Heeron, R. C. (1984). Confiding in others and illness rate among spouses of suicide and accidental death victims. *Journal of Abnormal Psychology, 93,* 473–476.

Pennebaker, J. W., Colder, M., & Sharp, L. K. (1990). Accelerating the coping process. *Journal of Personality and Social Psychology, 58,* 528–537.

Pennebaker, J. W., Kiecolt-Glaser, J. K., & Glaser, R. (1988). Disclosure of traumas and immune function: Health implications for psychotherapy. *Journal of Consulting and Clinical Psychology, 56,* 239–245.

Penner, L. A. (2002). Dispositional and organizational influences on sustained volunteerism: An interactionist perspective. *Journal of Social Issues, 58,* 447–467.

Penner, L. A., & Craiger, J. P. (1992). The weakest link: The performance of individual group members. In R. W. Swezey & E. Salas (Eds.), *Teams: Their training and performance* (pp. 57–74). Norwood, NJ: Ablex.

Penner, L. A., & Finkelstein, M. A. (1998). Dispositional and structural determinants of volunteerism. *Journal of Personality and Social Psychology, 74,* 525–537.

Penner, L. A., Brannick, M., Connell, P., & Webb, S. (in press). The effects of the September 11 attacks on volunteering: An archival analysis. *Journal of Applied Social Psychology.*

Penner, L. A., Dovidio, J. F., Schroeder, D. A., & Piliavin, J. A. (in press). Altruism and prosocial behavior. *Annual Review of Psychology.*

Penner, L. A., Dovidio, J., & Albrecht, T. L. (2001). Helping victims of loss and trauma: A social psychological perspective. In J. Harvey & E. Miller (Eds.), *Loss and trauma: General and close relationship perspectives* (pp. 62–85). Philadelphia: Brunner Routledge.

Penner, L. A., Fritzsche, B. A., Craiger, J. P., & Friefeld, T. R. (1995). Measuring the prosocial personality. In J. Butcher & C. D. Spielberger (Eds.), *Advances in personality assessment* (Vol. 10, pp. 147–163). Hillsdale, NJ: Erlbaum.

Penninx, B. W., Beekman, A. T., Honig, A., Deeg, D. J., Schoevers, R. A., van Eijk, J. T., & van Tilburg, W. (2001). Depression and cardiac mortality: Results from a community-based longitudinal study. *Archives of General Psychiatry, 58,* 221–227.

Peplau, L. A. (2003). Human sexuality: How do men and women differ? *Current Directions in Psychological Science, 12,* 37–40.

Peppard, P. E., Young, T., Palta, M., Dempsey, J., & Skatrud, J. (2000). Longitudinal study of moderate weight change and sleep-disordered breathing. *Journal of the American Medical Association, 284,* 3015–3021.

Perlis, M. L., Sharpe, M., Smith, M. T., Greenblatt, D., & Giles, D. (2001). Behavioral treatment of insomnia: Treatment outcomes and the relevance of medical and psychiatric morbidity. *Journal of Behavioral Medicine, 24,* 281–296.

Perls, F. S. (1969). *Ego, hunger and aggression: The beginning of Gestalt therapy.* New York: Random House.

Perls, F. S., Hefferline, R. F., & Goodman, P. (1951). *Gestalt therapy.* New York: Julian Press.

Peroutka, S. J., Newman, H., & Harris, H. (1988). The subjective effects of 3,4-methylenedioxymethamphetamine in recreational users. *Neuropharmacology, 1*(4), 273–277.

Persons, J. B., & Silberschatz, G. (1998). Are results of randomized controlled trials useful to psychotherapists? *Journal of Consulting and Clinical Psychology, 66,* 126–135.

Persons, J. B., Davidson, J., & Tompkins, M. A. (2001). *Essential components of cognitive-behavior therapy for depression.* Washington, DC: American Psychological Association.

Pervin, L. A. (1996). *The science of personality.* New York: Wiley.

Pervin, L. A., & John, O. P. (2001). *Personality: Theory and research* (8th ed.). Oxford, England: Wiley.

Peterson, A. C. (1987, September). Those gangly years. *Psychology Today,* pp. 28–34.

Peterson, C. (1995, April). *The preschool child witness: Errors in accounts of traumatic injury.* Paper presented at the biennial meeting of the Society for Research in Child Development, Indianapolis.

Peterson, C., & Seligman, M. E. P. (1984). Causal explanations as a risk factor for depression: Theory and evidence. *Psychological Review, 91,* 347–374.

Peterson, C., Maier, S. F., & Seligman, M. E. (1993). *Learned helplessness: A theory for the age of personal control.* New York: Oxford University Press.

Peterson, C., Seligman, M. E. P., Yurko, K. H., Martin, L. R., & Friedman, H. S. (1998). Catastrophizing and untimely death. *Psychological Science, 9,* 127–130.

Peterson, D. R. (2003). Unintended consequences: Ventures and misadventures in the education of professional psychologists. *American Psychologist, 58,* 791–800.

Peterson, L. R., & Peterson, M. J. (1959). Short-term retention of individual verbal items. *Journal of Experimental Psychology, 58,* 193–198.

Peterson, M. A., & Rhodes, G. (2003). *Perception of faces, objects, and scenes.* New York: Oxford University Press.

Petitto, L.A. & Marentette, P.F. (1991). Babbling in the manual mode: Evidence for the ontogeny of language. *Science, 251,* 1493–1496.

Petrie, K. J., Booth, R. J., Pennebaker, J. W. (1998). The immunological effects of thought suppression. *Journal of Personality and Social Psychology, 75,* 1264–1272.

Petrie, K. J., Booth, R. J., Pennebaker, J. W., & Davison, K. P. (1995). Disclosure of trauma and immune response to a Hepatitis B vaccination program. *Journal of Consulting and Clinical Psychology, 63,* 787–792.

Petrill, S. A., Lipton, P. A., Hewitt, J. K., Plomin, R., Cherny, S. S., Corley, R., & DeFries, J. C. (2004). Genetic and environmental contributions to general cognitive ability through the first 16 years of life. *Developmental Psychology, 40,* 805–812.

Petrill, S. A., Plomin, R., Berg, S., Johansson, B., Pederson, N. L., Ahern, F., & McClearn, G. E. (1998). The genetic and environmental relationship between general and specific cognitive abilities in twins age 80 and older. *Psychological Science, 9,* 183–189.

Petrocelli, J. V. (2002). Effectiveness of group cognitive-behavioral therapy for general symptomatology: A meta-analysis. *Journal of Specialists in Group Work, 27,* 92–115.

Petrovic, P., Kalso, E., Petersson, K. M., & Ingvar, M. (2002). Placebo and opioid analgesia: Imaging a shared neuronal network. *Science, 295,* 1737–1740.

Pettigrew, T. F. (1979). The ultimate attribution error: Extending Allport's cognitive analysis of prejudice. *Personality and Social Psychology Bulletin, 5,* 461–476.

Pettigrew, T. F., & Tropp, L. R. (2000). Does intergroup contact reduce prejudice? Recent meta-analytic findings. In S. Oskamp (Ed.), *Reducing prejudice and discrimination* (pp. 93–114). Mahwah, NJ: Erlbaum.

Pettit, D. L., Shao, Z, & Yakel, J. L. (2001). Beta-amyloid(1–42) peptide directly modulates nicotinic receptors in the rat hippocampal slice. *Journal of Neuroscience, 21,* RC120.

Pettit, G. S., & Dodge, K. A. (2003). Violent children: Bridging development, intervention, and public policy. *Developmental Psychology, 39,* 187–188.

Petty, R. E., & Wegener, D. T. (1998). Attitude change: Multiple roles for persuasion variables. In D. Gilbert, S. T. Fiske, & G. Lindzey (Eds.), *Handbook of social psychology* (Vol.1, 4th ed., pp. 323–390). Boston: McGraw-Hill.

Petty, R., Cacioppo, J., & Goldman, R. (1981). Personal involvement as a determinant of argument-based persuasion. *Journal of Personality and Social Psychology, 41,* 847–855.

Pham, L. B., Taylor, S. E., & Seeman, T. E. (2001) Effects of environmental predictability and personal mastery on self-regulatory and physiological processes. *Personality & Social Psychology Bulletin, 27,* 611–620.

Phelan, J. C., Link, B. G., Stueve, A., & Pescosolido, B. A. (2000). Public conceptions of mental illness in 1950 and 1996: What is mental illness and is it to be feared? *Journal of Health and Social Behavior, 41,* 188–207.

Phelps, E. A., O'Connor, K. J., Cunningham, W. A., Funayama, E. S., Gatenby, J. C., Gore, J. C., & Banaji, M. R. (2000). Performance on indirect measures of race evaluation predicts amygdala activation. *Journal of Cognitive Neuroscience, 12,* 729–738.

Phelps, M. E., & Mazziotta, J. C. (1985). Positron emission tomography: Human brain function and biochemistry. *Science, 228,* 799–809.

Phillips, N. A. (2000). Female sexual dysfunction: Evaluation and treatment. *American Family Physician, 62,* 127–136, 141–142.

Phinney, J. S., Ferguson, D. L., & Tate, J. D. (1997). Intergroup attitudes among ethnic minority adolescents: A causal model. *Child Development, 68,* 955–969.

Phipps, M. G., Blume, J. D., & DeMonner, S. M. (2002). Young maternal age associated with increased risk of postneonatal death. *Obstetrics and Gynecology, 100,* 481–486.

Piaget, J. (1952). *The origins of intelligence in children.* New York: International Universities Press.

Pickering, A. D., & Gray, J. A. (1999). The neuroscience of personality. In L. Pervin & O. John (Eds.), *Handbook of personality: Theory and research* (2nd ed., pp. 277–299). New York: Guilford.

Pickler, N. (2002, November 19). *NTSB cites fatigue, sleep apnea in fatal train wreck.* Associated Press. Retrieved August 25, 2003, from http://newsobserver.com/24hour/nation/v-print/story/626769p-4807167c.html.

Pike, K. M., Walsh, B. T., Vitousek, K., Wilson, G. T., & Bauer, J. (2003). Cognitive behavior therapy in the posthospitalization treatment of anorexia nervosa. *American Journal of Psychiatry, 160,* 2046–2049.

Piliavin, J. A., Dovidio, J. F., Gaertner, S. L., & Clark, R. D., III. (1981). *Emergency intervention.* New York: Academic Press.

Pillard, R. C., & Bailey, J. M. (1998). Human sexual orientation has a heritable component. *Human Biology, 70,* 347–365.

Pillemer, K., & Suitor, J. J. (2002). Explaining mothers' ambivalence towards their adult children. *Journal of Marriage and Family, 64,* 602–613.

Pilling, S., Bebbington, P., Kuipers, E., Garety, P., Geddes, J., Orbach, G., & Morgan, C. (2002). Psychological treatments in schizophrenia: I. Meta-analysis of family intervention and cognitive behavior therapy. *Psychological Medicine, 32,* 763–782.

Pincus, T., & Morley, S. (2001). Cognitive-processing bias in chronic pain: A review and integration. *Psychological Bulletin, 127,* 599–617.

Pinel, J. P. J. (1993). *Biopsychology.* Boston: Allyn & Bacon.

Pinker, S. (1994). *The language instinct: How the mind creates language.* New York: Morrow.

Pitman, R. K., Shin, L. M., & Rauch, S. L. (2001). Investigating the pathogenesis of posttraumatic stress disorder with neuroimaging. *Journal of Clinical Psychiatry, 62,* 47–54.

Pitschel-Walz, G., & Leutch, S., Bauml, J., Kissling, W., & Engel, R. R. (2001) The effect of family interventions on relapse and rehospitalization in schizophrenia: A meta-analysis. *Schizophrenia Bulletin, 27,* 73–92.

Platania, J., & Moran, G. P. (2001). Social facilitation as a function of mere presence of others. *Journal of Social Psychology, 141,* 190–197.

Plomin, R. (1994). *Genetics and experience: The developmental interplay between nature and nurture.* Newbury Park, CA: Sage.

Plomin, R. (2002). Individual differences research in a postgenomic era. *Personality and Individual Differences, 33,* 909–920.

Plomin, R., & Caspi, A. (1999). Behavioral genetics and personality. In L. Pervin & O. John (Eds.), *Handbook of personality research* (2nd ed.). New York: Guilford.

Plomin, R., & Crabbe, J. C. (2000). DNA *Psychological Bulletin, 126,* 806–828.

Plomin, R., & McGuffin, P. (2003). Psychopathology in the postgenomic era. *Annual Review of Psychology, 54,* 205–228.

Plomin, R., & Spinath, F. M. (2004). Intelligence: Genetics, genes, and genomics. *Journal of Personality and Social Psychology, 86,* 112–129.

Plomin, R., Corley, R., Caspi, A., Fulker, D. W., & DeFries, J. C. (1998). Adoption results for self-reported personality: Not much nature or nurture? *Journal of Personality and Social Psychology, 75,* 211–218.

Plomin, R., DeFries, J. C., Craig, I. W., & McGuffin, P. (2002). *Behavioral genetics in the postgenomic era.* Washington, DC: American Psychological Association.

Plomin, R., DeFries, J. C., McClearn, G. E., & McGuffin, P. (2001). *Behavioral genetics* (4th ed.). New York: Worth.

Ploner, M., Gross, J., Timmermann, L., & Schnitzler, A. (2002). Cortical representation of first and second pain sensation in humans. *Proceedings of the National Academy of Sciences, 99,* 12444–12448.

Plous, S. (1996). Attitudes toward the use of animals in psychological research and education: Results from a national survey of psychologists. *American Psychologist, 51,* 1167–1180.

Plutchik, R., & Conte, H. R. (Eds.). (1997). *Circumplex models of personality and emotions.* Washington, DC: American Psychological Association.

Poczwardowski, A., & Conroy, D. E. (2002). Coping responses to failure and success among elite athletes and performing artists. *Journal of Applied Sport Psychology, 14,* 313–329.

Pol, H. E. H., Schnack, H. G., Bertens, M. G. B. C., van Haren, N. E. M., van der Tweel, I., Staal, W. G., et al. (2002). Volume changes in gray matter in patients with schizophrenia. *American Journal of Psychiatry, 159,* 244–250.

Poldrack, R. A., & Wagner, A. D. (2004). What can neuroimaging tell us about the mind? *Current Directions in Psychological Science, 13,* 177–181.

Polivy, J., & Herman, C. P. (2002). If at first you don't succeed: False hopes of self-change. *American Psychologist, 57,* 677–689.

Pollack, I. (1953). The assimilation of sequentially coded information. *American Journal of Psychology, 66,* 421–435.

Polusny, M. A., & Follette, V. M. (1995). Long-term correlates of child sexual abuse: Theory and review of the empirical literature. *Applied and Preventive Psychology, 4,* 143–166.

Polusny, M. A., & Follette, V. M. (1996). Remembering childhood abuse: A national survey of psychologists' clinical practices, beliefs, and personal experiences. *Professional Psychology: Research and Practice, 27,* 41–52.

Pomerantz, E. M., Altermatt, E. R., & Saxon, J. L. (2002). Making the grade but feeling distressed: Gender differences in academic performance and internal distress. *Journal of Educational Psychology, 94,* 396–404.

Pomerantz, J. R., & Kubovy, M. (1986). Theoretical approaches to perceptual organization. In K. R. Boff, L. Kaufman, & J. P. Thomas (Eds.), *Handbook of perception and human performance* (pp. 36-1-36-46) New York: Wiley.

Poole, D. A., Lindsay, D. S., Memon, A., & Bull, R. (1995). Psychotherapy and the recovery of memories of childhood sexual abuse: U.S. and British practitioners' opinions, practices, and experiences. *Journal of Consulting and Clinical Psychology, 63,* 426–437.

Pope, H. G., Gruber, A. J., Hudson, J. I., Huestis, M. A., Yurgelun-Todd, D. (2001). Neuropsychological performance in long-term cannabis users. *Archives of General Psychiatry, 58,* 909–915.

Pope, H. G., Jr., Hudson, J. I., Bodkin, J. A., & Oliva, P. (1998). Questionable validity of "dissociative amnesia" in trauma victims: Evidence from prospective studies. *British Journal of Psychiatry, 172,* 210–215.

Pope, K. S. (1998). Pseudoscience, cross-examination, and scientific evidence in the recovered memory controversy. *Psychology, Public Policy, and Law, 4,* 1160–1181.

Pope-Davis, D. B., Reynolds, A. L., Dings, J. G., & Nielson, D. (1995). Examining multicultural counseling competencies of graduate students in psychology. *Professional Psychology: Research and Practice, 26,* 322–329.

Porges, S. W., Doussard, R. J. A., & Maita, A. K. (1995). Vagal tone and the physiological regulation of emotion. *Monographs of the Society for Research on Child Development, 59*(2–3), 167–186, 250–283.

Port, C. L., Engdahl, B., & Frazier, P. (2001). A longitudinal and retrospective study of PTSD among older prisoners of war. *American Journal of Psychiatry, 158,* 1474–1479.

Porte, H. S., & Hobson, J. A. (1996). Physical motion in dreams: One measure of three theories. *Journal of Abnormal Psychology, 105,* 329–335.

Porter, R. H. (1991). Human reproduction and the mother-infant relationship. In T. V. Getchell et al. (Eds.), *Taste and smell in health and disease.* New York: Raven Press.

Porter, R. H., Cernich, J. M., & McLaughlin, F. J. (1983). Maternal recognition of neonates through olfactory cues. *Physiology and Behavior, 30,* 151–154.

Porter, R. H., Makin, J. W., Davis, L. B., & Christensen, K. M. (1992). Breast-fed infants respond to olfactory cues from their own mother and unfamiliar lactating females. *Infant Behavior and Development, 15,* 85–93.

Porter, S., Birt, A. R., Yuille, J. C., & Lehman, D. R. (2000). Negotiating false memories: Interviewer and rememberer characteristics relate to memory distortion. *Psychological Science, 11,* 507–510.

Porter, S., Yuille, J. C., & Lehman, D. R. (1999). The nature of real, implanted, and fabricated memories for emotional childhood events: Implications for the recovered memory debate. *Law & Human Behavior, 23,* 517–537.

Posener, J. A., DeBattista, C., Williams, G. H., Kraemer, H. C., Kalehzan, B. M., & Schatzberg, A. F. (2000). 24-hour monitoring of cortisol and corticotropin secretion in psychotic and nonpsychotic major depression. *Archives of General Psychiatry, 57,* 755–760.

Posner, M. I. (1978). *Chronometric explorations of the mind.* Hillsdale, NJ: Erlbaum.

Posner, M. I., & DiGirolamo, G. J (2001). Cognitive neuroscience: Origins and promise. *Psychological Bulletin, 126,* 873–889.

Posner, M. I., & Peterson, S. E. (1990). The attention system of the human brain. *Annual Review of Neurosciences, 13,* 24–42.

Posner, M. I., & Raichle, M. E. (1994). *Images of mind.* New York: Scientific American Books.

Potkin, S. G., Saha, A. R., Kujawa, M. J., Carson, W. H., Ali, M., Stock, E., et al. (2003). Aripiprazole, an antipsychotic with a novel mechanism of action, and risperidone vs placebo in patients with schizophrenia and schizoaffective disorder. *Archives of General Psychiatry, 60,* 681–690.

Potter, P. T., & Zautra, A. J. (1997). Stressful life events' effects on rheumatoid arthritis disease activity. *Journal of Consulting and Clinical Psychology, 65,* 319–323.

Potter, W. Z., & Rudorfer, M. V. (1993). Electroconvulsive therapy, a modern medical procedure. *New England Journal of Medicine, 328,* 882–883.

Pousset, F. (1994). Cytokines as mediators in the central nervous system. *Biomedical Pharmacotherapy, 48,* 425–431.

Povinelli, D. J., & Bering, J. M. (2002). The mentality of apes revisited. *Current Directions in Psychological Science, 11,* 115–119.

Powch, I. G., & Houston, B. K. (1996). Hostility, anger-in, and cardiovascular activity in White women. *Health Psychology, 15,* 200–208.

Powell, L. H., Shahabi, L., & Thoresen, C. E. (2003). Religion and spirituality: Linkages to physical health. *American Psychologist, 58,* 36–52.

Powers, D. E. (2004). Validity of the Graduate Records Examination (GRE) General test scores for admission to colleges of veterinary medicine. *Journal of Applied Psychology, 89,* 208–219.

Powley, T. L., & Keesey, R. E. (1970). Relationship of body weight to the lateral hypothalamic feeding syndrome. *Journal of Comparative & Physiological Psychology, 70,* 25–36.

Poyares, D., Guilleminault, C., Ohayon, M. M., & Tufik, S. (2004). Chronic benzodiazepine usage and withdrawal in insomnia patients. *Journal of Psychiatric Research, 38,* 327–334.

Pratkanis, A. R. (1992). The cargo-cult science of subliminal persuasion. *Skeptical Inquirer, 16,* 260–273.

Pratkanis, A. R., & Aronson, E. (1991). *Age of propaganda: The everyday use and abuse of persuasion.* New York: Freeman.

Pratkanis, A. R., Eskenazi, J., & Greenwald, A. G. (1994). What you expect is what you believe (but not necessarily what you get): A test of the effectiveness of self-help audiotapes. *Basic and Applied Social Psychology, 15,* 251–276.

Preciado, J. (1994). The empirical basis of behavior therapy applications with Hispanics. *Behavior Therapist, 17, 63–65.*

Preece, J., Sharp, H., Benyon, D., Holland, S., & Carey, T. (1994). *Human-computer interaction.* Reading, MA: Addison-Wesley.

Premack, D. (1965). Reinforcement theory. In D. Levine (Ed.), *Nebraska symposium on motivation* (Vol. 13, pp. 123–180). Lincoln: University of Nebraska Press.

Premack, D. (1971). Language in chimpanzees? *Science, 172,* 808–822.

Premack, D., & Premack, A. J. (1983). *The mind of an ape.* New York: Norton.

Prentice, D. A., & Miller, D. T. (2002). The emergence of homegrown stereotypes. *American Psychologist, 57,* 352–359.

Prescott, J. W. (1996). The origins of human love and violence. *Pre- and Peri-Natal Psychology Journal, 10,* 143–188.

Preston, E. (2002). Detecting deception. *APS Observer,* 15, 19, 49.

Prinzmetal, W. (1992). The word superiority effect does not require a T-scope. *Perception and Psychophysics, 51,* 473–484.

Prior, M. (1999). Resilience and coping: The role of individual temperament. In E. Frydenberg (Ed.), *Learning to cope: Developing as a person in complex societies.* New York: Oxford University Press.

Prochaska, J. O. (1994). Strong and weak principles for progressing from precontemplation to action on the basis of twelve problem behaviors. *Health Psychology, 13,* 47–51.

Prochaska, J. O., & DiClemente, C. C. (1992). Stages of change in the modification of problem behaviors. In M. Hersen, R. M. Eisler, & P. M. Miller (Eds.), *Progress in behavior modification.* Sycamore, IL: Sycamore Press.

Prochaska, J. O., DiClemente, C., & Norcross, J. (1992). In search of how people change: Application to addictive behaviors. *American Psychologist, 47,* 1102–1114.

Prochaska, J. O., Velicer, W. F., Rossi, J. S., Goldstein, M. G., Marcus, B. H., Rakowski, W., et al. (1994). Stages of change and decisional balance for 12 problem behaviors. *Health Psychology, 13,* 39–46.

Proctor, R., & Van Zandt, T. (1994). *Human factors in simple and complex systems.* Boston: Allyn & Bacon.

Pryor, T. (1995). Diagnostic criteria for eating disorders: *DSM-IV* revisions. *Psychiatric Annals, 25*(1), 40–45.

Psychosocial Paediatrics Committee. (2003). Impact of media use on children and youth. *Paediatrics and Child Health, 8(5),* 301–306.

Public Health Agency of Canada (2002). *Genetic and biological factors* [Electronic version]. Available: http://www.phac-aspc.gc.ca/dca-dea/publications/healthy_dev_partb_8_e.html

Public Health Agency of Canada (2002a). Mental illnesses in Canada: An Overview [Electronic version]. Available: http://www.phac-aspc.gc.ca/publicat/miic-mmac/chap_1_e.html

Public Health Agency of Canada (2002b). Anxiety Disorders [Electronic version]. Available: http://www.phac-aspc.gc.ca/publicat/miic-mmac/chap_4_e.html

Public Health Agency of Canada (2002c). Personality Disorders [Electronic version]. Available: http://72.14.207.104/search?q=cache:-g9RNyi24pIJ:www.phac-aspc.gc.ca/publicat/miic-mmac/chap_5_e.html+statistics+Canada+antisocial+personality+disorder&hl=en&gl=ca&ct=clnk&cd=1

Public Health Agency of Canada (2003). Anxiety disorders: Future directions for research and treatment [Electronic version]. Available: http://www.phac-aspc.gc.ca/mh-sm/mentalhealth/pubs/anxiety/appendices.htm

Public Health Agency of Canada (2004). Program overview [Electronic version]. Available: http://www.phac-aspc.gc.ca/dca-dea/programs-mes/ahs_overview_e.html

Public Health Agency of Canada (2005). Youth and Violence [Electronic version]. Available: http://www.phac-aspc.gc.ca/ncfv-cnivf/familyviolence/html/nfntsyjviolence_e.html.

Public Health Agency of Canada. (2004). Early childhood education and care as a determinant of health [Electronic version]. Available: http://www.phac-aspc.gc.ca/ph-sp/phdd/overview_implications/07_ecec.html

Puca, A. A., Daly, M. J., Brewster, S. J., Matis, T. C., Barrett, J., Shea-Drinkwater, M., et al. (2001). A genome-wide scan for linkage to human exceptional longevity identifies a locus on chromosome 4. *Proceedings of the National Academy of Sciences, 10,* 1073.

Pugh, K. R., Mencl, W. E., Shaywitz, B. A., Shaywitz, S. E., Fulbright, R. K., Constable, R. T., et al. (2000). The angular gyrus in developmental dyslexia: Task-specific differences in functional connectivity within posterior cortex. *Psychological Science, 11,* 51–56.

Purcell, D. G., & Stewart, A. L. (1991). The object-detection effect: Configuration enhances perception. *Perception and Psychophysics, 50,* 215–224.

Purves, D., Williams, M., Nundy, S., & Lotto, R. B. (2004). Perceiving the intensity of light. *Psychological Review, 111,* 142–158.

Pyszczynski, T., Greenberg, J., Solomon, S., Arndt, J., & Schimel, J. (2004). Why do people need self-esteem? A theoretical and empirical review. *Psychological Bulletin, 130,* 435–468.

Quinn, G. E., Shin, C. H., Maguire, M. G., & Stone, R. A. (1999). Myopia and ambient lighting at night. *Nature, 399,* 113–114.

Quintana, S. M. (1998). Children's developmental understanding of ethnicity and race. *Applied and Preventive Psychology, 7,* 27–45.

Quintana, S. M., & Bernal, M. E. (1995). Ethnic minority training in counseling psychology: Comparisons with clinical psychology and proposed standards. *The Counseling Psychologist, 23*(1), 102–121.

Quitkin, F. M., Petkkova, E., McGrath, P. J., Taylor, B., Beasley, C., Stewart, J., et al. (2003). When should a trial of fluoxetine for major depression be declared failed? *American Journal of Psychiatry, 160,* 734–740.

Quitkin, F. M., Rabkin, J. G., Gerald, J., Davis, J. M., & Klein, D. F. (2000). Validity of clinical trials of antidepressants. *American Journal of Psychiatry, 157,* 327–337.

Rabbitt, P. (1977). Changes in problem solving ability in old age. In J. E. Birren & K. W. Schaie (Eds.), *Handbook of the psychology of aging.* New York: Van Nostrand Reinhold.

Rabinowitz, J., De Smedt, G., Harvey, P. D., & Davidson, M. (2002). Relationship between premorbid functioning and symptom severity as assessed at first episode of psychosis. *American Journal of Psychiatry, 159,* 2021–2026.

Rabinowitz, J., Lichtenberg, P., Kaplan, Z., Mark, M., Nahon, D., & Davidson, M. (2001). Rehospitalization rates of chronically ill schizophrenic patients discharged on a regimen of risperidone, olanzapine, or conventional antipsychotics. *American Journal of Psychiatry, 158,* 266–269.

Racenstein, J. M., Harrow, M., Reed, R., Martin, E., Herbener, E., & Penn, D. L. (2002). The relationship between positive symptoms and instrumental work functioning in schizophrenai: A 10-year follow-up study. *Schizophrenia Research, 56,* 95–103.

Rachlin, H. (2000). *The science of self-control.* Cambridge: Harvard University Press.

Rachman, S. J. (1990). *Fear and courage* (2nd ed.). San Francisco: Freeman.

Rada, J. B., & Rogers, R. W. (1973). *Obedience to authority: Presence of authority and command strength.* Paper presented at the annual convention of the Southeastern Psychological Association.

Radvansky, G. A. (1999). Aging, memory, and comprehension. *Current Directions in Psychological Science, 8,* 49–53.

Raguram, R., & Bhide, A. (1985). Patterns of phobic neurosis: A retrospective study. *British Journal of Psychiatry, 147,* 557–560.

Raine, A., Brennan, P., & Mednick, S. (1994). Birth complications combined with early maternal rejection at age 1 year predispose to violent crime at age 18 years. *Archives of General Psychiatry, 51,* 984–988.

Raine, A., Lencz, T., Bihrle, S., LaCasse, L., & Colletti, P. (2000). Reduced prefrontal gray matter volume and reduced autonomic activity in antisocial personality disorder. *Archives of General Psychiatry, 57,* 119–127.

Raine, A., Mellingen, K., Liu, J., Venables, P., & Mednick, S. A. (2003). Effects of environmental enrichment at ages 3–5 years on schizotypal personality and antisocial behavior at ages 17 and 23 years. *American Journal of Psychiatry, 160,* 1627–1635.

Rainville, P. (2002). Brain mechanisms of pain affect and pain modulation. *Current Opinion in Neurobiology, 12,* 195–204.

Rainville, P., Duncan, G. H., Price, D. D., Carrier, B., & Bushnell, M. C. (1997). Pain affect encoded in human anterior cingulate but not somatosensory cortex. *Science, 277,* 968–971.

Rakic, P. (2002). Neurogenesis in adult primate neocortex: An evaluation of the evidence. *Nature Reviews Neuroscience, 3,* 65–71.

Rakowski, W., Ehrich, B., Dube, C., Pearlman, D. N., Goldstein, M. G., Peterson, K. K., et al. (1996). Screening mammography and constructs from the transtheoretical model: Associations using two definitions of the stages-of-adoption. *Annals of Behavioral Medicine, 18,* 91–100.

Ramachandran, V. S. (1988, August). Perceiving shape from shading. *Scientific American,* pp. 76–83.

Ramachandran, V. S., & Hubbard, E. M. (2001). Psychophysical investigations into the neural basis of synaesthesia. *Proceedings of the Royal Society, 268,* 979–983.

Ramachandran, V. S., & Rogers-Ramachandran, D. (2000). Phantom limbs and neural plasticity. *Archives of Neurology, 57,* 317–320.

Ramey, C. T. (1992). High-risk children and IQ: Altering intergenerational patterns. *Intelligence, 16,* 239–256.

Ramey, C. T., & Ramey, S. L. (1998). Early intervention and early experience. *American Psychologist, 53,* 109–121.

Ramey, S. L. (1999). Head Start and preschool education: Toward continued improvement. *American Psychologist, 54,* 344–346.

Ramirez, S. Z., Wassef, A., Paniagua, F. A., & Linskey, A. O. (1996). Mental health providers' perceptions of cultural variables in evaluating ethnically diverse clients. *Professional Psychology: Research and Practice, 27,* 284–288.

Rapee, R., Brown, T., Antony, M., & Barlow, D. (1992). Response to hyperventilation and inhalation of 5.5% carbon dioxide-enriched air across *DSM-III* anxiety disorders. *Journal of Abnormal Psychology, 101,* 538–552.

Rapp, S. R., Brenes, G., & Marsh, A. P. (2002). Memory enhancement training for older adults with mild cognitive impairment: A preliminary study. *Aging & Mental Health, 6*(1), 5–11.

Rasch, V. (2003). Cigarette, alcohol, and caffeine consumption: Risk factors for spontaneous abortion. *Acta Obstetric Gynecology Scandivia, 82,* 182–188.

Raschka, L. B. (1984). Sleep and violence. *Canadian Journal of Psychiatry, 29,* 132–134.

Raskin, D. C. (1986). The polygraph in 1986: Scientific, professional and legal issues surrounding applications and acceptance of polygraph evidence. *Utah Law Review, 1,* 29–74.

Raskin, N. J., & Rogers, C. R. (1995). Person-centered therapy. In J. J. Corsini & D. Wedding (Eds.), *Current psychotherapies* (5th ed., pp. 128–161). Itasca, IL: Peacock.

Raskin, N. J., & Rogers, C. R. (2001). Person-centered therapy. In R. J. Corsini & D. Wedding (Eds.), *Current psychotherapies* (6th ed.) Itasca, IL: Peacock.

Rasmussen, K. G. (2003). Clinical applications of recent research on electroconvulsive therapy. *Bulletin of the Menninger Clinic, 67*(1), 18–31.

Ratcliff, R., & McKoon, G. (1989). Memory models, text processing, and cue-dependent retrieval. In H. L. Roediger & F. I. M. Craik (Eds.), *Varieties of memory and consciousness.* Hillsdale, NJ: Erlbaum.

Ratner, C. (1994). The unconscious: A perspective from sociohistorical psychology. *Journal of Mind and Behavior, 15*(4), 323–342.

Rattenborg, N., Lima, S. L., & Amlaner, C. J. (1999). Half-awake to the risk of predation. *Nature, 397,* 397–398.

Raudenbush, B., & Meyer, B. (2002). Effect of nasal dilators on pleasantness, intensity and sampling behaviors of foods in the oral cavity. *Rhinology, 39,* 80–83.

Rauschecker, J. P., & Shannon, R. V. (2002). Sending sound to the brain. *Science, 295,* 1025–1029.

Rauscher, F. H., Shaw, G. L., Levine, L. J., Wright, E. L., Dennis, W. R., & Newcomb, R. L. (1997). Music training causes long-term enhancement of preschool children's spatial-temporal reasoning. *Neurological Research, 19,* 2–8.

Ray, O. (2004). How the mind hurts and heals the body. *American Psychologist, 59,* 29–40.

Raynor, H. A., & Epstein, L. H. (2001). Dietary variety, energy regulation, and obesity. *Psychological Bulletin, 127,* 325–341.

Razali, S. M., Aminah, K., & Umeed, A. (2002). Religious-cultural psychotherapy in the management of anxiety patients. *Transcultural Psychiatry, 39,* 130–136.

Reber, A. S. (1992). The cognitive unconscious: An evolutionary perspective. *Consciousness and Cognition: An International Journal, 1*(2), 93–133.

Redd, M., & de Castro, J. M. (1992). Social facilitation of eating: Effects of social instruction on food intake. *Physiology and Behavior, 52,* 749–754.

Redd, W. H. (1984). Psychological intervention to control cancer chemotherapy side effects. *Postgraduate Medicine, 75,* 105–113.

Reder, L. M., & Ritter, F. E. (1992). What determines initial feeling of knowing? Familiarity with question terms, not the answer. *Journal of Experimental Psychology: Learning, Memory, and Cognition, 18,* 435–451.

Reed, G. M., Kemeny, M. E., Taylor, S. E., Wang, H.-Y. J., & Visscher, B. R. (1994). "Realistic acceptance" as a predictor of decreased survival time in gay men with AIDS. *Health Psychology, 13,* 299–307.

Reed, R. R. (2004). After the holy grail: Establishing a molecular basis for mammalian olfaction. *Cell, 116,* 329–336.

Reed, S. K. (2000). *Cognition* (5th ed.). Belmont, CA: Wadsworth.

Reed, S. K. (2004). *Cognition: Theory and applications* (6th ed.). Belmont, CA: Wadsworth/Thompson Learning.

Reedy, M. N. (1983). Personality and aging. In D. S. Woodruff & J. E. Birren (Eds.), *Aging: Scientific perspectives and social issues* (2nd ed.). Monterey, CA: Brooks/Cole.

Reeve, J. M. (1996). *Understanding motivation and emotion.* New York: Harcourt, Brace, Jovanovich.

Reeves, R. A., Baker, G. A., Boyd, J. G., & Cialdini, R. B. (1991). The door-in-the-face technique: Reciprocal concessions vs. self-presentational explanations. *Journal of Social Behavior and Personality, 6,* 545–558.

Reger, M. A., Welsh, R. K., Watson, G. S., Cholerton, B., Baker, L. D., & Craft, S. (2004). The relationship between neuropsychological functioning and driving ability in dementia: A meta-analysis. *Neuropsychology, 18,* 85–93.

Regier, D. A., Narrow, W., Rae, D., Manderschied, R., Locke, B., & Goodwin, F. (1993). The de facto U.S. mental and addictive disorders service system: Epidemiologic catchment area prospective 1-year prevalence rates of disorders and services. *Archives of General Psychiatry, 50,* 85–94.

Reich, D. A. (2004). What you expect is not always what you get: The roles of extremity, optimism, and pessimism in the behavioral confirmation process. *Journal of Experimental Social Psychology, 40,* 199–215.

Reingold, E. M., Charness, N., Pomplun, M., & Stampe, D. M. (2001). Visual span in expert chess players: Evidence from eye movements. *Psychological Science, 12,* 48–55.

Reisenzein, R. (1983). The Schachter theory of emotion: Two decades later. *Psychological Bulletin, 94,* 239–264.

Reiss, A. J., & Roth, J. A. (1993). *Understanding and preventing violence.* Washington, DC: National Academy Press.

Reiss, D., & Marino, L. (2001). Mirror self-recognition in the bottlenose dolphin: A case of cognitive convergence. *Proceedings of the National Academy of Science, 98,* 5937–5942.

Reiss, D., Neiderhiser, J. M., Hetherington, E. M., & Plomin, R. (2000). *The relationship code: Deciphering genetic and social influences on adolescent development.* Cambridge, MA: Harvard University Press.

Reitman, D., & Drabman, R. S. (1999). Multifaceted uses of a simple timeout record in the treatment of a noncompliant 8-year-old boy. *Education and Treatment of Children, 22,* 136–145.

Rendall, D., Cheney, D. L., & Seyfarth, R. M. (2000). Proximate factors mediating "contact" calls in adult female baboons (*Papio cynocephalus ursinus*) and their infants. *Journal of Comparative Psychology, 114,* 36–46.

Reneman, L., Lavalaye, J., Schmand, B., de Wolff, F. A., van den Brink, W., den Heeten, G. J., & Booij, J. (2001). Cortical serotonin transporter density and verbal memory in individuals who stopped using 3,4-methylenedioxymethamphetamine (MDMA or "ecstasy"). *Archives of General Psychiatry, 58,* 901–906.

Reno, R. R., Cialdini, R. B., & Kallgren, C. A. (1993). The transsituational influence of social norms. *Journal of Personality and Social Psychology, 64,* 104–112.

Rensink, R. A. (2004). Visual sensing without seeing. *Psychological Science, 15,* 27–32.

Rentz, D. M., Huh, T. J., Faust, R. R., Budson, A. E., Scinto, L. F. M., Sperling, R. A., & Daffner, K. R. (2004). Use of IQ-adjusted norms to predict progressive cognitive decline in highly intelligent older individuals. *Neuropsychology, 18,* 38–49.

Rescorla, L. A. (1981). Category development in early language. *Journal of Child Language, 8,* 225–238.

Rescorla, R. A. (1968). Probability of shock in the presence and absence of CS in fear conditioning. *Journal of Comparative and Physiological Psychology, 66,* 1–5.

Rescorla, R. A., & Wagner, A. R. (1972). A theory of Pavlovian conditioning: Variations in the effectiveness of reinforcement and nonreinforcement. In A. H. Black & W. F. Prokasy (Eds.), *Classical conditioning II.* New York: Appleton Century Crofts.

Reynolds, C. F., III, Frank, E., Perel, J. M., Imber, S. D., Cornes, C., Miller, M. D., et al. (1999). Nortriptyline and interpersonal psychotherapy as maintenance therapies for recurrent major depression: A randomized controlled trial in patients older than 59 years. *Journal of the American Medical Association, 281,* 39–45.

Reynolds, D. V. (1969). Surgery in the rat during electrical analgesia induced by focal brain stimulation. *Science, 164,* 444–445.

Reynolds, J. S., & Perrin, N. A. (2004). Mismatches in social support and psychosocial adjustment to breast cancer. *Health Psychology, 23,* 425–430.

Rhodes, G., Halberstadt, J., & Brajkovich, G. (2001). Generalization of mere exposure effects to averaged composite faces. *Social Cognition, 19,* 57–70.

Ricaurte, G. A., Yuan, J., Hatzidimitriou, G., Cord, B. J., & McCann, U. D. (2002). Severe dopaminergic neurotoxicity in primates after a common recreational dose regimen of MDMA ("ecstasy"). *Science, 297,* 2260–2263.

Ricciardelli, L. A., & McCabe, M. P. (2004). A biopsychosocial model of disordered eating and the pursuit of muscularity in adolescent boys. *Psychological Bulletin, 130,* 179–205.

Riccio, D. C., Millin, P. M., & Gisquet-Verrier, P. (2003). Retrograde amnesia: Forgetting back. *Current Directions in Psychological Science, 12,* 41–44.

Rice, G., Anderson, C., Risch, H., & Ebers, G. (1999). Male homosexuality: Absence of linkage to microsatellite markers at Xq28. *Science, 284,* 665–667.

Rice, M. E. (1997). Violent offender research and implications for the criminal justice system. *American Psychologist, 52,* 414–423.

Richards, J. M., & Gross, J. J. (2000). Emotion regulation and memory: The cognitive costs of keeping one's cool. *Journal of Personality and Social Psychology, 79,* 410–424.

Richards, J. M., Beal, W. E., Seagal, J. D., & Pennebaker, J. W. (2000). Effects of disclosure of traumatic events on illness behavior among psychiatric prison inmates. *Journal of Abnormal Psychology, 109,* 156–160.

Richards, K. C., Anderson, W. M., Chesson, A. L. Jr., & Nagel, C. L. (2002). Sleep-related breathing disorders in patients who are critically ill. *Journal of Cardiovascular Nursing, 17,* 42–55.

Richards, M., Shipley, B., Fuhrer, R., & Wadsworth, M. E. J. (2004). Cognitive ability in childhood and cognitive decline in mid-life: Longitudinal birth cohort study. *British Medical Journal, 328,* 552.

Richards, P. S., & Bergin, A. E. (Eds.). (2000). *Handbook of psychotherapy and religious diversity* (pp. 105–129). Washington, DC: American Psychological Association Press.

Richards, T. L., Corina, D., Serafini, S., Steury, K., Echelard, D. R., Dager, S. R., et al. (2000). Effects of a phonologically driven treatment for dyslexia on lactate levels measured by proton MR spectroscopic imaging. *American Journal of Neuroradiology, 21,* 916–922.

Richardson, P. H., & Vincent, C. A. (1986). Acupuncture for the treatment of pain: A review of evaluative research. *Pain, 24,* 15–40.

Richardson-Klavehn, A., & Bjork, R. A. (1988). Measures of memory. *Annual Review of Psychology, 39,* 475–543.

Rickels, K., & Rynn, M. (2002). Pharmocotherapy of generalized anxiety disorder. *Journal of Clinical Psychiatry, 63* (Suppl. 14), 9–16.

Rickels, K., Schweizer, E., Weiss, S., & Zavodnick, S. (1993) Maintenance drug treatment of panic disorder: II. Short- and long-term outcome after drug taper. *Archives of General Psychiatry, 50,* 61–68.

Rickels, K., Zaninelli, R., McCafferty, J., Bellew, K., Iyengar, M., & Sheehan, D. (2003). Paroxetine treatment of generalized anxiety disorder: A double-blind, placebo-controlled study. *American Journal of Psychiatry, 160,* 749–756.

Ridley, M. (2000). *Genome: The autobiography of a species in 23 chapters.* New York: HarperCollins.

Riegel, K. F. (1975). Toward a dialectical theory of development. *Human Development, 18,* 50–64.

Riemsma, R. P., Pattenden, J., Bridle, C., Sowden, A. J., Mather, L., Watt, I. S., & Walker, A. (2003). Systematic review of the effectiveness of stage based interventions to promote smoking cessation. *British Medical Journal, 326,* 1175–1177.

Riggio, R. E. (1989). *Introduction to industrial/organizational psychology.* Glenview, IL: Scott, Foresman.

Rihmer, Z. (2001). Can better recognition and treatment of depression reduce suicide rates? A brief review. *European Psychiatry, 16,* 406–409.

Rind, B., & Tromovitch, P. (1997). A meta-analytic review of findings from national samples on psychological correlates of child sexual abuse. *Journal of Sex Research, 34,* 237–255.

Rind, B., Tromovitch, P., & Bauserman, R. (1998). A meta-analytic examination of assumed properties of child sexual abuse using college samples. *Psychological Bulletin, 124,* 22–53.

Rioult-Pedotti, M.-S., Friedman, D., & Donoghue, J. P. (2000). Learning-induced LTP in neocortex. *Science, 290,* 533–536.

Ripple, C. H., Gilliam, W. S., Chanana, N., & Zigler, E. (1999). Will fifty cooks spoil the broth? The debate over entrusting Head Start to the states. *American Psychologist, 54,* 327–343.

Ro, T., Shelton, D., Lee, O. L., & Chang, E. (2004). Extrageniculate mediation of unconscious vision in transcranial magnetic stimulation-induced blindsight. *Proceedings of the National Academy of Sciences, 101,* 9933–9935.

Robbins, J. (2000, July 4). Virtual reality finds a real place as a medical aid. *New York Times.*

Robbins, T. W., & Everitt, B. J. (1999). Interaction of the dopaminergic system with mechanisms of associative learning and cognition: Implications for drug abuse. *Psychological Science, 10,* 199–202.

Roberts, B. W., & Delvecchio, W. F. (2000). The rank-order consistency of traits from childhood to old-age: A quantitative review of longitudinal studies. *Psychological Bulletin, 126,* 3–25.

Roberts, B. W., Caspi, A., & Moffitt, T. E. (2001). The kids are alright: Growth and stability in personality development from adolescence to adulthood. *Journal of Personality & Social Psychology, 81*(4), 670–683.

Roberts, B. W., Helson, R., & Klohnen, E. C. (2002). Personality development and growth in women across 30 years: Three perspectives. *Journal of Personality, 70,* 79–102.

Roberts, K.P. (2002). Children's ability to distinguish between memories from multiple sources: Implications for the quality and accuracy of eyewitness statements. *Developmental Review, 22,* 403–435.

Roberts, M. C. (2002). The process and product of the Felix decree review of empirically supported treatments: Prospects for change. *Clinical Psychology: Science and Practice, 9,* 217–219.

Robertson, I. (2005) Potty-mouth man can't fool science. *Toronto Sun.* Wednesday, March 30.

Robertson, I. H., & Murre, J. M. J. (1999). Rehabilitation of brain damage: Brain plasticity and principles of guided recovery. *Psychological Bulletin, 125,* 544–575.

Robertson, J., & Robertson, J. (1971). Young children in brief separation: A fresh look. *Psychoanalytic Study of the Child, 26,* 264–315.

Robins, R. W., Gosling, S., & Craik, K. H. (2000). Trends in psychology: An empirical issue. *American Psychologist, 55,* 277–278.

Robins, R. W., John, O. P., & Caspi, A. (1998). The typological approach to studying personality. In R. B. Cairns & L. R. Bergman (Eds.), *Methods and models for studying the individual* (pp. 135–160). Thousand Oaks, CA: Sage.

Robinson, N. M., Zigler, E., & Gallagher, J. J. (2000). Two tails of the normal curve: Similarities and differences in the study of mental retardation and giftedness. *American Psychologist, 55,* 1413–1424.

Robinson, T. N., Wilde, M. L., Navracruz, L. C., Haydel, K. F., & Varady, A. (2001). Effects of reducing children's television and video game use on aggressive behavior: A randomized controlled trial. *Archives of Pediatrics and Adolescent Medicine, 155,* 17–23.

Robles, T. F., & Kiecolt-Glaser, J. K. (2003). The physiology of marriage: Pathways to health. *Physiology and Behavior, 79,* 409–416.

Rock, I. (1983). *The logic of perception.* Cambridge, MA: MIT Press. Rock, I., & Gutman, D. (1981). The effect of inattention on form perception. *Journal of Experimental Psychology: Human Perception and Performance, 7,* 275–285.

Rodgers, J. (2000). Cognitive performance amongst recreational users of "ecstasy." *Psychopharmacology, 151,* 19–24.

Rodrigo, M. F., & Ato, M. (2002). Testing the group polarization hypothesis by using logit models. *European Journal of Social Psychology, 32,* 3–18.

Rodriguez de Fonseca, F., Carrera, M. R. A., Navarro, M., Koob, G. F., & Weiss, F. (1997). Activation of corticotropin-releasing factor in the limbic system during cannabinoid withdrawal. *Science, 276,* 2050–2054.

Rodriguez, I., Greer, C. A., Mok, M. Y., & Mombaerts, P. (2000). A putative pheromone receptor gene expressed in human olfactory mucosa. *Nature Genetics, 26,* 18–19.

Roediger, H. L., & Gallo, D. A. (2001). Levels of processing: Some unanswered questions. In M. Naveh-Benjamin, M. Moscovitch, & H.L. Roediger (Eds.), *Perspectives on human memory and cognitive aging: Essays in honour of Fergus Craik* (pp. 28–47). New York: Psychology Press.

Roediger, H. L., & McDermott, K. B. (1992). Depression and implicit memory: A commentary. *Journal of Abnormal Psychology, 101,* 587–591.

Roediger, H. L., & McDermott, K. B. (2000). Tricks of memory. *Current Directions in Psychological Science, 9,* 123–127.

Roediger, H. L., III, Jacoby, D., & McDermott, K. B. (1996). Misinformation effects in recall: Creating false memories through repeated retrieval. *Journal of Memory and Learning, 35,* 300–318.

Roediger, H. L., III. (1990). Implicit memory: Retention without remembering. *American Psychologist, 45,* 1043–1056.

Roediger, H. L., Marsh, E. J., & Lee, C. J. (2002). Varieties of memory. In H. Pashler (Ed.), *Stevens' handbook of experimental psychology* (Vol. 2, pp. 1–41). New York: Wiley.

Roehrich, L., & Goldman, M. S. (1995). Implicit priming of alcohol expectancy memory processes and subsequent drinking behavior. *Experimental and Clincial Psychopharmocology, 3,* 402–410.

Roffwarg, H. P., Muzio, J. N., & Dement, W. C. (1966). Ontogenetic development of the human sleep-dream cycle. *Science, 152,* 604–619.

Rogers, A. A., Aldrich, M. S., & Lin, A. (2001). A comparison of three different sleep schedules for reducing daytime sleepiness in narcolepsy. *Journal of Sleep and Sleep Disorders Research, 24,* 385–391.

Rogers, C. R. (1951). *Client-centered therapy.* Boston: Houghton Mifflin.

Rogers, C. R. (1961). *On becoming a person.* Boston: Houghton Mifflin.

Rogers, C. R. (1970). *Carl Rogers on encounter groups.* New York: Harper & Row.

Rogers, C. R. (1980) *A way of being.* Boston: Houghton Mifflin.

Rogers, J., Madamba, S. G., Staunton, D. A., & Siggins, G. R. (1986). Ethanol increases single unit activity in the inferior olivary nucleus. *Brain Research, 385,* 253–262.

Rogoff, B., & Waddell, K. J. (1982). Memory for information organized in a scene by children from two cultures. *Child Development, 53,* 1224–1228.

Rohan, M. J., & Zanna, M. P. (1996). Value transmission in families. In C. Seligman, J. M. Olson, & M. P. Zanna (Eds.), *The psychology of values: The Ontario symposium* (Vol. 8, pp. 253–276). Mahwah, NJ: Erlbaum.

Rohan, M., Parow, A., Stoll, A. L., Demopulos, C., Friedman, S., Dager, S., et al. (2004). Low-field magnetic stimulation in bipolar depression using an MRI-based stimulator. *American Journal of Psychiatry, 161,* 93–98.

Roid, G. H. (2003). *Stanford-Binet Intelligence Scale* (5th ed.). Itasca, IL: Riverside.

Roisman, G. I., Masten, A. S, Coatsworth, J. D., & Tellegen, A. (2004). Salient and emerging developmental tasks in the transition to adulthood. *Child Development, 75,* 123–133.

Rolls, E. T. (1997). Taste and olfactory processing in the brain and its relation to the control of eating. *Critical Review of Neurobiology, 11,* 263–287.

Rome, E. S., Ammerman, S., Rosen, D. S., Keller, R. J., Lock, J., Mammel, K. A., et al. (2003). Children and adolescents with eating disorders: The state of the art. *Pediatrics, 111,* e98–e108.

Romeder, J.M. (1990). *The self-help way: Mutual aid and health.* Ottawa: Canadian Council on Social Development.

Romeo, R. D., Richardson, H. N., & Sisk, C. L. (2002). Puberty and the maturation of the male brain and sexual behavior: Recasting a behavioral potential. *Neuroscience and Biobehavioral Review, 26,* 381–391.

Romer, D., Jamieson, K. H., & deCoteau, N. J. (1998). The treatment of persons of color in local television news: Ethnic blame discourse or realistic group conflict? *Communication Research, 25,* 286–305.

Rosch, E. (1975). Cognitive representations of semantic categories. *Journal of Experimental Psychology: General, 104,* 192–223.

Rosch, E., Mervis, C. B., Gray, W. D., Johnson, D. M., & Boyes-Braem, P. (1976). Basic objects in natural categories. *Cognitive Psychology, 8,* 382–439.

Rosellini, L. (1998, April 13). When to spank. *U.S. News and World Report,* pp. 52–58.

Rosen, B. C., & D'Andrade, R. (1959). The psychosocial origins of achievement motivation. *Sociometry, 22,* 188–218.

Rosen, D., Stukenberg, K. W., & Saeks, S. (2001). The group-as-a-whole-object relations model of group psychotherapy. *Bulletin of the Menninger Clinic, 65,* 471–488.

Rosen, G. M. (1999). Treatment fidelity and research on eye movement desensitization and reprocessing (EMDR). *Journal of Anxiety Disorders, 13,* 173–184.

Rosen, R. (1991). *The healthy company.* Los Angeles: Tarcher.

Rosenbach, M. L., Hermann, R. C., & Dorwart, R. A. (1997). Use of electroconvulsive therapy in the Medicare population between 1987 and 1992. *Psychiatric Services, 48,* 1537–1542.

Rosenbaum, M., & Bennett, B. (1986). Homicide and depression. *American Journal of Psychiatry, 143,* 367–370.

Rosenberg, H. J., Rosenberg, S. D., Ernstoff, M. S., Wolford, G. L., Amdur, R. J., Elshamy, M. R., et al. (2002). Expressive disclosure and health outcomes in a prostate cancer population. *International Journal of Psychiatry in Medicine, 32,* 37–53.

Rosenfarb, I. S., Goldstein, M. J., Mintz, J., & Nuechterlein, K. H. (1995). Expressed emotion and subclinical psychopathology observable within the transactions between schizophrenic patients and their family members. *Journal of Abnormal Psychology, 104,* 259–267.

Rosenfarb, I. S., Nuechterlein, K. H., Goldstein, M. J., & Subotnik, K. L. (2000). Neurocognitive vulnerability, interpersonal criticism, and the emergence of unusual thinking by schizophrenic patients during family transactions. *Archives of General Psychiatry, 57,* 1174–1179.

Rosenfeld, J. P. (1995). Alternative views of Bashore and Rapp's (1993) alternatives to traditional polygraphy: A critique. *Psychological Bulletin, 117*(1), 159–166.

Rosenkranz, M. A., Jackson, D. C., Dalton, K. M., Dolski, I., Ryff, C. D., Singer, B. H., et al. (2003). Affective style and in vivo immune response: Neurobehavioral mechanisms. *Proceedings of the National Academy of Sciences, 100,* 11148–11152.

Rosenstock, I. M. (1974). Historical origins of the health belief model. *Health Education Monographs, 2,* 328–335.

Rosenthal, R. R. (1966). *Experimenter effects in behavioral research.* New York: Appleton-Century-Crofts.

Rosenthal, R. R., & Jacobson, L. (1968). *Pygmalion in the classroom.* New York: Holt, Rinehart & Winston.

Rosenzweig, M. R., & Bennett, E. L. (1996). Psychobiology of plasticity: Effects of training and experience on brain and behavior. *Behavioural Brain Research, 78,* 57–65.

Ross, C. A. (1997). *Dissociative identity disorder: Diagnosis, clinical features, and treatment of multiple personality.* New York: Wiley.

Ross, C. A., Anderson, G., Fleisher, W. P., & Norton, G. R. (1991). The frequency of multiple personality disorder among psychiatric inpatients. *American Journal of Psychiatry, 148,* 1717–1720.

Ross, S. I., & Jackson, J. M. (1991). Teachers' expectations for Black males' and Black females' academic achievement. *Personality and Social Psychology Bulletin, 17,* 78–82.

Ross, S. M., & Ross, L. E. (1971). Comparison of trace and delay classical eyelid conditioning as a function of interstimulus interval. *Journal of Experimental Psychology, 91,* 165–167.

Roth, H. L., Lora, A. N., & Heilman, K. M. (2002). Effects of monocular viewing and eye dominance on spatial attention. *Brain, 125,* 2023–2035.

Roth, M. D., Arora, A., Barsky, S. H., Kleerup, E. C., Simmons, M., & Tashkin, D. P. (1998). Airway inflammation in young marijuana and tobacco smokers. *American Journal of Respiratory Critical Care Medicine, 157,* 928–937.

Rothbart, M. K., & Bates, J. E. (1998). Temperament. In W. Damon & N. Eisenberg (Eds.), *Handbook of child psychology: Vol. 3. Social, emotional, and personality development* (5th ed., pp. 105–176). New York: Wiley.

Rothbart, M. K., & Derryberry, D. (2002). Temperament in children. In C. von Hofsten & L. Baeckman (Eds.), *Psychology at the turn of the millennium: Vol. 2. Social, developmental, and clinical perspectives* (pp. 17–35). Florence, KY: Taylor & Frances/Routledge.

Rothbart, M. K., Ahadi, S. A., & Evans, D. E. (2000). Temperament and personality: Origins and outcomes. *Journal of Personality and Social Psychology, 78,* 122–135.

Rothbaum, B. O., Hodges, L. F., Alarcon, R., Ready, D., Shahar, F., Graap, K., et al. (1999). Virtual reality exposure therapy for PTSD Vietnam veterans: A case study. *Journal of Traumatic Stress, 12,* 263–271.

Rothbaum, B. O., Hodges, L. F., Kooper, R., & Opdyke, D. (1995). Effectiveness of computer-generated virtual reality graded exposure in the treatment of acrophobia. *American Journal of Psychiatry, 152,* 626–628.

Rothbaum, B. O., Hodges, L., Anderson, P. L., Price, L., & Smith, S. (2002). Twelve-month follow-up of virtual reality and standard exposure therapies for fear of flying. *Journal of Consulting and Clinical Psychology, 70,* 428–432.

Rothbaum, B. O., Hodges, L., Smith, S., Lee, J. H., & Price, L. (2000). A controlled study of virtual reality exposure therapy for the fear of flying. *Journal of Consulting and Clinical Psychology, 68,* 1020–1026.

Rothbaum, F., Pott, M., Azuma, H., Miyake, K., & Weisz, J. (2000). The development of close relationships in Japan and the United States: Paths of symbiotic harmony and generative tension. *Child Development, 71,* 1121–1142.

Rottenstreich, Y., & Tversky, A. (1997). Unpacking, repacking, and anchoring: Advances in support theory. *Psychological Review, 104,* 406–415.

Rotter, J. B. (1982). *The development and application of social learning theory.* New York: Praeger.

Rotton, J. (1990). Individuals under stress. In C. E. Kimble (Ed.), *Social psychology: Living with people.* New York: Brown.

Rotton, J., & Kelly, I. W. (1985). Much ado about the full moon: A meta-analysis of lunar-lunacy research. *Psychological Bulletin, 97,* 286–306.

Rounsaville, B. J., & Carroll, K. M. (2002). Commentary on dodo bird revisited: Why aren't we dodos yet? *Clinical Psychology: Science & Practice, 9*(1), 17–20.

Rovee-Collier, C. (1999). The development of infant memory. *Current Directions in Psychological Science, 8,* 80–85.

Rowe, D. C. (1997). Genetics, temperament, and personality. In R. Hogan, J. Johnson, & S. Briggs (Eds.), *Handbook of personality psychology* (pp. 367–386). San Diego: Academic Press.

Roy, D. K., & Pentland, A. P. (2002). Learning words from sights and sounds: A computational model. *Cognitive Science, 26,* 113–146.

Rozin, P. (1982). "Taste-smell confusions" and the duality of the olfactory sense. *Perception and Psychophysics, 31,* 397–401.

Rozin, P. (1996). Sociocultural influences on human food selection. In E. D. Capaldi (Ed.), *Why we eat what we eat: The psychology of eating* (pp. 233–263). Washington DC: American Psychological Association.

Rozin, P., Dow, S., Moscovitch, M., & Rajaram, S. (1998). The role of memory for recent eating experiences in onset and cessation of meals. Evidence from the amnesic syndrome. *Psychological Science, 9,* 392–396.

Rubin, B. M. (1998, February 8). When he's retiring and she isn't. *Chicago Tribune,* Sect. 1, pp. 1ff.

Rubin, E. (1915). *Synsoplevede figure.* Copenhagen: Gyldendalske.

Rubin, K. H., Bukowski, W., & Parker, J. G. (1998). Peer interactions, relationships, and groups. In W. Damon & N. Eisenberg (Eds.), *Handbook of child psychology: Vol. 3. Social, emotional, and personality development* (5th ed., pp. 619–700). New York: Wiley.

Rubinstein, S., & Caballero, B. (2000). Is Miss America an undernourished role model? *Journal of the American Medical Association, 283,* 1569.

Ruble, D. N., & Martin, C. L. (1998). Gender development. In W. Damon & N. Eisenberg (Eds.), *Handbook of child psychology: Vol. 3. Social, emotional, and personality development* (5th ed., pp. 933–1016). New York: Wiley.

Rudman, L. A., Greenwald, A. G., Mellott, D. S., & Schwartz, J. L. K. (1999). Measuring the automatic components of prejudice: Flexibility and generality of the Implicit Association Test. *Social Cognition, 17,* 437–465.

Rudolph, K. D., Lambert, S. F., Clark, A. G., & Kurlakowsky, K. D. (2001). Negotiating the transition to middle school: The role of self-regulatory processes. *Child Development, 72,* 929–946.

Rudorfer, M. V., Henry, M. E., & Sackheim, H. A. (1997). Electroconvulsive therapy. In A. Tasman, J. Kay, & J. A. Lieberman (Eds.), *Psychiatry* (pp. 1535–1556). Philadelphia: Saunders.

Rueck, C., Andreewitch, S., & Flyckt, K. (2003). Capsulotomy for refractory anxiety disorders: Longer-term follow-up of 26 patients. *American Journal of Psychiatry, 160*(3), 513–521.

Rueckert, L., Baboorian, D., Stavropoulos, K., & Yasutake, C. (1999). Individual differences in callosal efficiency: Correlation with attention. *Brain and Cognition, 41,* 390–410.

Ruff, C. C., Knauff, M., Fangmeier, T., & Spreer, J. (2003). Reasoning and working memory: Common and distinct neuronal processes. *Neuropsychologia, 41,* 1241–1253.

Ruffman, T., Perner, J., Naito, M., Parkin, L., & Clements, W. A. (1998). Older (but not younger) siblings facilitate false belief understanding. *Developmental Psychology, 34,* 161–174.

Rugg, M. D., & Coles, M. G. H. (Eds.). (1995). *Electrophysiology of mind.* New York: Oxford University Press.

Ruiz, P., Varner, R. V., Small, D. R, & Johnson, B. A. (1999). Ethnic differences in the neuroleptic treatment of schizophrenia. *Psychiatric Quarterly, 70,* 163–172.

Rumbaugh, D. M. (Ed.). (1977). *Language learning by a chimpanzee: The Lana project.* New York: Academic Press.

Rumelhart, D. E., & McClelland, J. L. (1986). *Parallel distributed processing: Explorations in the microstructure of cognition: Vol. 1. Foundations.* Cambridge, MA: Bradford.

Rumelhart, D. E., & Todd, P. M. (1992). Learning and connectionist representations. In D. E. Meyer & S. Kornblum (Eds.), *Attention and performance XIV: Synergies in experimental psychology, artificial intelligence, and cognitive neuroscience* (pp. 3–30). Cambridge: MIT Press.

Runyon, M., & Kenny, M. C. (2002). Relationship of attributional style, depression, and posttrauma distress among children who suffered physical or sexual abuse. *Child Maltreatment, 7,* 254–264.

Rusbult, C. E., & Van Lange, P. A. M. (2003). Interdependence, interaction and relationships. *Annual Review of Psychology, 54,* 351–375.

Ruscio, J. (2001). Administering quizzes at random to increase students' reading. *Teaching of Psychology, 28,* 204–206.

Rushton, J. P. (1990). Creativity, intelligence, and psychoticism. *Personality and Individual Differences, 11,* 1291–1298.

Ruskin, P. E., Silver-Aylaian, M., Kling, M. A., Reed, S. A., Bradham, D. D., Hebel, J. R., et al. (2004). Treatment outcomes in depression: Comparison of remote treatment through telepsychiatry to in-person treatment. *American Journal of Psychiatry, 161,* 1471–1476.

Russell, J. A. (1991). Culture and the categorization of emotions. *Psychological Bulletin, 110,* 426–450.

Russell, J. A. (1994). Is there universal recognition of emotion from facial expression? A review of the cross-cultural studies. *Psychological Bulletin, 155*(2), 102–141.

Russell, J. A. (1995). Facial expressions of emotion: What lies beyond minimal universality? *Psychological Bulletin, 118,* 379–391.

Rutter, M. (2003). Commentary: Causal processes leading to antisocial behavior. *Developmental Psychology, 39,* 372–378.

Rutter, M. L. (1997). Nature-nurture integration. The example of antisocial behavior. *American Psychologist, 52,* 390–398.

Rutter, M., O'Connor, T. G., & ERA Study Team. (2004). Are there biological programming effects for psychological development? Findings from a study of Romanian adoptees. *Developmental Psychology, 40,* 81–94.

Rutter, M., Pickles, A., Murray, R., & Eaves, L. (2001). Testing hypotheses on specific environmental causal effects on behavior. *Psychological Bulletin, 127,* 291–324.

Ryan, A. M. (2001). The peer group as a context for the development of young adolescent motivation and achievement. *Child Development, 72,* 1135–1150.

Ryan, R. H., & Geiselman, R. E. (1991). Effects of biased information on the relationship between eyewitness confidence and accuracy. *Bulletin of the Psychonomic Society, 29,* 7–9.

Rymer, R. (1993). *Genie: A scientific tragedy.* New York: HarperCollins.

Rynders, J., & Horrobin, J. (1980). Educational provisions for young children with Down's syndrome. In J. Gottlieb (Ed.), *Educating mentally retarded persons in the mainstream* (pp. 109–147). Baltimore: University Park Press.

Saarni, C., Mummer, D. L., & Campos, J. J. (1998). Emotional development: Action, communication, and understanding. In W. Damon & N. Eisenberg (Eds.), *Handbook of child psychology: Vol. 3. Social, emotional, and personality development* (5th ed., pp. 237–310). New York: Wiley.

Sabini, J., Siepmann, M., & Stein, J. (2001). The really fundamental attribution error in social psychological research. *Psychological Inquiry, 12,* 1–5.

Sachs, J. (1967). Recognition memory for syntactic and semantic aspects of connected discourse. *Perception and Psychophysics, 2,* 437–442.

Sackeim, H. A. (1985, June). The case for ECT. *Psychology Today,* pp. 36–40.

Sackeim, H. A. (1994). Central issues regarding the mechanisms of action of electroconvulsive therapy: Directions for future research. *Psychopharmacology Bulletin, 30,* 281–308.

Sackeim, H. A., Haskett, R. F., Mulsant, B. H., Thase, M. E., Mann, J. J., Pettinati, H. M., et al. (2001). Continuation pharmacotherapy in the prevention of relapse following electroconvulsive therapy: A randomized controlled trial. *Journal of the American Medical Association, 285,* 1299–1307.

Sackeim, H. A., Prudic, J., Devanand, D. P., Nobler, M. S., Lisanby, S. H., Peyser, S., et al. (2000). A prospective, randomized, double-blind comparison of bilateral and right unilateral electroconvulsive therapy at different stimulus intensities. *Archives of General Psychiatry, 57,* 425–434.

Sacks, O. (1992, July 27). The landscape of his dreams. *New Yorker.*

Sacks, O. (2002, October 7). The case of Anna H. *New Yorker,* pp. 62–73.

Saffran, J. R., Senghas, A., & Trueswell, J. C. (2001). The acquisition of language by children. *Proceedings of the National Academy of Science, 98,* 12874–12875.

Safren, S. A., Gershuny, B. S., Marzol, P., Otto, M. W., & Pollack, M. H. (2002). History of childhood abuse in panic disorder, social phobia, and generalized anxiety disorder. *Journal of Nervous and Mental Disease, 190,* 453–456.

Saini, S., Barr, H., & Bessant, C. (2001). Sniffing out disease using the artificial nose. *Biologist (London), 48,* 229–233.

Sakairi, Y. (1992). Studies on meditation using questionnaires. *Japanese Psychological Review, 35*(1), 94–112.

Saklofske, D.H., Tulsky, D.S., Wilkins, C., & Weiss, L.G. (2003). Canadian WISC-III directional base rates of score discrepancies by ability level. *Canadian Journal of Behavioural Science, 35,* 210–218.

Salin-Pascual, R., Gerashchenko, D., Greco, M., Blanco-Centurion, C., & Shiromani, P. J. (2001). Hypothalamic regulation of sleep. *Neuropsychopharmacology, 25* (Suppl. 5), S21.

Salloum, I. M., Cornelius, J. R., Thase, M. E., Daley, D. C., Kirisci, L., & Spotts, C. (1998). Naltrexone utility in depressed alcoholics. *Psychopharmacological Bulletin, 34,* 111–115.

Salovey, P., & Sluyter, D. J. (Eds.). (1997). *Emotional development and emotional intelligence: Educational implications.* New York: Basic Books.

Salthouse, T. A. (1990). Working memory as a processing resource in cognitive aging. *Developmental Review, 10,* 101–124.

Salthouse, T. A. (1996). The processing-speed theory of adult age differences in cognition. *Psychological Review, 103,* 403–428.

Salthouse, T. A. (2000). Aging and measures of processing speed. *Biological Psychology, 54,* 35–54.

Salthouse, T. A., & Prill, K. A. (1987). Inferences about age impairments in inferential reasoning. *Psychology and Aging, 2,* 43–51.

Salvi, R. J., Chen, L., Trautwein, P., Powers, N., & Shero, M. (1998). Hair cell regeneration and recovery of function in the avian auditory system. *Scandinavian Audiology Supplement, 48,* 7–14.

Salzer, M. S., Rappaport, J., & Segre, L. (1999). Professional appraisal of professionally led and self-help groups. *American Journal of Ortho-Psychiatry, 69,* 536–540.

Salzman, C. (2003). New uses for lithium and anticonvulsants. *Harvard Review of Psychiatry, 11*(5), 230–244.

Sammons, M. T., & Schmidt, N. B. (2001). *Combined treatments for mental disorders: A guide to psychological and pharmacological interventions.* Washington, DC: American Psychological Association.

Sammons, M. T., Paige, R. U., & Levant, R. F. (Eds.). (2003). *Prescriptive authority for psychologists: A history and guide.* Washington, DC: APA Books.

Samuel, A. G. (2001). Knowing a word affects the fundamental perception of the sounds within it. *Psychological Science, 12,* 348–351.

Sanai, N., Tramontin, A. D., Quinones-Hinojosa, A., Barbaro, N. M., Gupta, N., Kunwar, S., et al. (2004). Unique astrocyte ribbon in adult human brain contains neural stem cells but lacks chain migration. *Nature, 427,* 740–744.

Sanchez-Ramos, J., Song, S., Cardozo-Pelaez, F., Hazzi, C., Stedeford, T., Willing, A., et al. (2000). Adult bone-marrow stromal cells differentiate into neural cells in vitro. *Experimental Neurology, 164,* 247–256.

Sanders Thompson, V. L., Bazile, A., & Akbar, M. (2004). African Americans' perceptions of psychotherapy and psychotherapists. *Professional Psychology: Research and Practice, 35,* 19–26.

Sanders, M. R., & Dadds, M. R. (1993). *Behavioral family intervention.* Boston: Allyn & Bacon.

Sanders, M. R., Markie-Dadds, C., Tully, L. A., & Bor, W. (2000). The triple p—positive parenting program: A comparison of enhanced, standard, and self-directed behavioral family intervention for parents of children with early onset conduct problems. *Journal of Consulting and Clinical Psychology, 68,* 624–640.

Sanderson, W. C., Rapee, R. M., & Barlow, D. H. (1989). The influence of an illusion of control on panic attacks induced via inhalation of 5.5% carbon dioxide-enriched air. *Archives of General Psychiatry, 46,* 157–162.

Saper, C. B., Chou, T. C., & Scammell, T. E. (2001). The sleep switch: Hypothalamic control of sleep and wakefulness. *Trends in Neurosciences, 24,* 726–731.

Sarason, B. R., Sarason, I. G., & Gurung, R. A. R. (1997). Close personal relationships and health outcomes: A key to the role of social support. In S. Duck (Ed.), *Handbook of personal relationships* (pp. 547–573). New York: Wiley.

Sarason, I. G. (1984). Stress, anxiety, and cognitive interference: Reactions to tests. *Journal of Personality and Social Psychology, 46*(4), 929–938.

Sarason, I. G., Johnson, J., & Siegel, J. (1978). Assessing impact of life changes: Development of the life experiences survey. *Journal of Clinical and Consulting Psychology, 46,* 932–946.

Sarason, I. G., Sarason, B. R., Keefe, D. E., Hayes, B. E., & Shearin, E. N. (1986). Cognitive interference: Situational determinants and traitlike characteristics. *Journal of Personality and Social Psychology, 51,* 215–226.

Sasaki, Y., Jadjikhani, N., Fischl, B., Liu, A. K., Marret, S., Dale, A. M., & Tootell, R. B. H. (2001). Local and global attention are mapped retinotopically in human occipital cortex. *Proceedings of the National Academy of Sciences, 98,* 2077.

Sato, T. (1997). Seasonal affective disorder and phototherapy: A critical review. *Professional Psychology: Research and Practice, 28,* 164–169.

Satterfield, J. M., Folkman, S., & Acree, M. (2002). Explanatory style predicts depressive symptoms following AIDS-related bereavement. *Cognitive Therapy and Research, 26,* 393–403.

Sattler, D. N., Kaiser, C. F., & Hittner, J. B. (2000). Disaster preparedness: Relationships among prior experience, personal characteristics, and distress. *Journal of Applied Social Psychology, 30,* 1396–1420.

Saufley, W. H., Otaka, S. R., & Bavaresco, J. L. (1985). Context effects: Classroom tests and context independence. *Memory & Cognition, 13,* 522–528.

Saura, C. A., Choi, S. Y., Beglopoulos, V., Malkani, S., Zhang, D., Rao, B. S., et al. (2004). Loss of presenilin function causes impairments of memory and synaptic plasticity followed by age-dependent neurodegeneration. *Neuron, 42,* 23–36.

Savage-Rumbaugh, E. S. (1990). Language acquisition in a non-human species: Implications for the innateness debate. *Developmental Psychology, 23,* 599–620.

Savage-Rumbaugh, E. S., Murphy, J., Sevcik, R. A., Brakke, K. E., Williams, S. L., & Rumbaugh, D. M. (1993). Language comprehension in age and child. *Monographs of the Society for Research in Child Development, 58*(3–4).

Savage-Rumbaugh, E. S., Pate, J. L., Lawson, J., Smith, S. T., & Rosenbaum, S. (1983). Can a chimpanzee make a statement? *Journal of Experimental Psychology: General, 112,* 469–487.

Savage-Rumbaugh, S., & Brakke, K. E. (1996). Animal language: Methodological and interpretive issues. In M. Bekoff & D. Jamieson (Eds.), *Readings in animal cognition* (pp. 269–288). Cambridge: MIT Press.

Savage-Rumbaugh, S., Shanker, S. G., & Taylor, T. J. (2001). *Apes, language and the human mind.* New York: Oxford University Press.

Savastano, H. I., & Miller, R. R. (1998). Time as content in Pavlovian conditioning. *Behavioural Processes, 44,* 147–162.

Saveliev, S. V., Lebedev, V. V., Evgeniev, M. B., & Korochkin, L. I. (1997). Chimeric brain: Theoretical and clinical aspects. *International Journal of Developmental Biology, 41,* 801–808.

Savelkoul, M., Post, M. W. M., de Witte, L. P., & van den Borne, H. B. (2000). Social support, coping, and subjective well-being in patients with rheumatic diseases. *Patient Education and Counseling, 39,* 205–218.

Savic, I., Berglund, H., Gulyas, B., & Roland, P. (2001). Smelling of odorous sex hormone-like compounds causes sex-differentiated hypothalamic activations in humans. *Neuron, 31,* 661–668.

Savin-Williams, R. C., & Demo, D. H. (1984). Developmental change and stability in adolescent self-concept. *Developmental Psychology, 20,* 1100–1110.

Saxe, L., & Ben-Shakhar, G. (1999). Admissibility of polygraph tests: The application of scientific standards post-Daubert. *Psychology, Public Policy, and Law, 5,* 203–223.

Sayers, J. (1991). *Mother of psychoanalysis.* New York: Norton.

Scarr, S. (1997). The development of individual differences in intelligence and personality. In H. W. Reese & M. D. Franzen (Eds.), *Biological and neuropsychological mechanisms: Life-span developmental psychology* (pp. 1–22). Hillsdale, NJ: Erlbaum.

Scarr, S. (1998). How do families affect intelligence? Social environmental and behavior genetic prediction. In J. J. McArdle & R. W. Woodcock (Eds.), *Human cognitive abilities in theory and practice* (pp. 113–136). Mahwah, NJ: Erlbaum.

Scarr, S., & Carter-Saltzman, L. (1982). Genetics and intelligence. In R. Sternberg (Ed.), *Handbook of human intelligence* (pp. 792–896). Cambridge, UK: Cambridge University Press.

Schachter, S., & Singer, J. (1962). Cognitive, social and physiological determinants of emotional state. *Psychological Review, 69,* 379–399.

Schacter, D. L. (1999). The seven sins of memory: Insights from psychology and cognitive neuroscience. *American Psychologist, 54,* 182–203.

Schacter, D. L., Chiu, C.-Y. P., & Ochsner, K. N. (1993). Implicit memory: A selective review. *Annual Review of Neuroscience, 16,* 159–182.

Schacter, D. L., Church, B., & Treadwell, J. (1994). Implicit memory in amnesic patients: Evidence for spared auditory priming. *Psychological Science, 5,* 20–25.

Schacter, D. L., Cooper, L. A., Delaney, S. M., Peterson, M. A., & Tharan, M. (1991). Implicit memory for possible and impossible objects: Constraints on the construction of structural descriptions. *Journal of Experimental Psychology: Learning, Memory, and Cognition, 17,* 3–19.

Schaefer, J., Sykes, R., Rowley, R., & Baek, S. (1988, November). *Slow country music and drinking.* Paper presented at the 87th annual meeting of the American Anthropological Association, Phoenix, AZ.

Schaeffer, C. M., Petras, H., Ialongo, N., Poduska, J., & Kellam, S. (2003). Modeling growth in boys' aggressive behavior across elementary school: Links to later criminal involvement, conduct disorder, and antisocial personality disorder. *Developmental Psychology, 39,* 1020–1035.

Schafer, J., & Brown, S. A. (1991). Marijuana and cocaine effect expectancies and drug use patterns. *Journal of Consulting and Clinical Psychology, 59,* 558–565.

Schaffer, C. E., Davidson, R. J., & Saron, C. (1983). Frontal and parietal EEG asymmetry in depressed and non-depressed subjects. *Biological Psychiatry, 18,* 753–762.

Schaie, K. W. (1993). The Seattle longitudinal study of adult intelligence. *Current Directions in Psychological Science, 2*(6), 171–175.

Schaie, K. W. (1996). Intellectual development in adulthood. In J. E. Birren, K. Schaie, R. P. Abeles, M. Gatz, & T. A. Salthouse (Eds.), *Handbook of the psychology of aging* (4th ed., pp. 266–286). San Diego: Academic Press.

Scharf, M., Mayseless, O., & Kivenson-Baron, I. (2004). Adolescents' attachment representations and developmental tasks in emerging adulthood. *Developmental Psychology, 40,* 430–444.

Scharff, J. S., & Scharff, D. E. (1998). *Object relations individual psychotherapy.* Northvale, NJ: Aronson.

Schaubroeck, J., Jones, J. R., & Xie, J. J. (2001). Individual differences in utilizing control to cope with job demands: Effects on susceptibility to infectious disease. *Journal of Applied Psychology, 86,* 265–278.

Scheerer, M., Rothmann, R., & Goldstein, K. (1945). A case of "idiot savant": An experimental study of personality organization. *Psychology Monograph, 58*(4), 1–63.

Scheier, M. F., Matthews, K. A., Owens, J. F., Magovern, G. J., Lefebvre, R. C., Abbott, R. A., et al. (1989). Dispositional optimism and recovery from coronary artery bypass surgery: The beneficial effects on physical and psychological well-being. *Journal of Personality and Social Psychology, 57,* 1024–1040.

Schiff, M., Duyme, M., Dumaret, A., Stewart, J., Tomkiewicz, S., & Feingold, J. (1978). Intellectual status of working class children adopted early into upper-middle class families. *Science, 200,* 1503–1504.

Schiffman, S. S., Graham, B. G., Sattely-Miller, E. A., & Warwick, Z. (1999). Orosensory perception of dietary fat. *Current Directions in Psychological Science, 7,* 137–143.

Schildkraut, J. J., & Mooney, J. J. (2004). Toward a rapidly acting antidepressant: The normetanephrine and extraneuronal monoamine transporter (Uptake 2) hypothesis. *American Journal of Psychiatry, 161,* 909–911.

Schiller, P. H. (1996). On the specificity of neurons and visual areas. *Behavior and Brain Research, 76,* 21–35.

Schmidt, N. B., Lerew, D. R., & Jackson, R. J. (1999). Prospective evaluation of anxiety sensitivity in the pathogenesis of panic: Replication and extension. *Journal of Abnormal Psychology, 108,* 532–537.

Schmidt, N. B., Storey, J., Greenberg, B. D., Santiago, H. T., Li, Q., & Murphy, D. L. (2000). Evaluating gene × psychological risk factor effects in the pathogenesis of anxiety: A new model approach. *Journal of Abnormal Psychology, 109,* 308–320.

Schmidt, R. A., & Bjork, R. A. (1992, July). New conceptualizations of practice: Common principles in three paradigms suggest new concepts for training. *Psychological Science, 3*(4), 207–217.

Schmolck, H., Buffalo, E. A., & Squire, L. R. (2000). Memory distortions over time: Recollections of the O. J. Simpson trial verdict after 15 and 32 months. *Psychological Science, 11,* 39–47.

Schnabel, T. (1987). Evaluation of the safety and side effects of antianxiety agents. *American Journal of Medicine, 82* (Suppl. 5A), 7–13.

Schnapf, J. L., Kraft, T. W., & Baylor, D. A. (1987). Spectral sensitivity of human cone photoreceptors. *Nature, 325,* 439–441.

Schneider, B. H., Atkinson, L., & Tardif, C. (2001). Child-parent attachment and children's peer relations: A quantitative review. *Developmental Psychology, 37,* 86–100.

Schneider, T. R., Ring, C., & Katkin, E. S. (1998). A test of the validity of the method of constant stimuli as an index of heartbeat detection. *Psychophysiology, 35,* 86–89.

Schneider, W., & Bjorklund, D. F. (1998). Memory. In W. Damon, D. Kuhn, & R. Siegler (Eds.), *Handbook of child psychology: Vol. 2. Cognition, language and perception* (5th ed., pp. 467–521). New York: Wiley.

Schneiderman, B. (1992). *Designing the user interface* (2nd ed.) Reading, MA: Addison-Wesley.

Schneiderman, N., Antoni, M. H., Saab, P. G., & Ironson,G. (2001). Health psychology: Psychosocial and biobehavioral aspects of chronic disease management. *Annual Review of Psychology, 52, 555–580.*

Schneidman, E. S. (1987). A psychological approach to suicide. In G. VandenBos & B. K. Bryant (Eds.), *Cataclysms, crises, and catastrophes: Psychology in action. The master lectures* (Vol. 6, pp. 147–183). Washington, DC: American Psychological Association.

Schnurr, P. P., Ford, J. D., Friedman, M. J., Green, B. L., Dain, B. J., & Sengupta, A. (2000). Predictors and outcomes of posttraumatic stress disorder in World War II veterans exposed to mustard gas. *Journal of Consulting and Clinical Psychology, 68,* 258–268.

Schroeder, D. A. (1995). An introduction to social dilemmas. In D. Schroeder (Ed.), *Social dilemmas: Perspectives on individuals and groups* (pp. 1–13). Westport, CT: Praeger.

Schroeder, D. A., Penner, L. A., Dovidio, J. F., & Piliavin, J. A. (1995). *The psychology of helping and altruism: Problems and puzzles.* New York: McGraw-Hill.

Schultheiss, O. C., & Rohde, W. (2002). Implicit power motivation predicts men's testosterone changes and implicit learning in a contest situation. *Hormones and Behavior, 41,* 195–202.

Schultz, D. P., & Schultz, S. E. (1998). *Psychology and work today* (7th ed.). Upper Saddle River, NJ: Prentice-Hall.

Schultz, D. P., & Schultz, S. E. (2001). *Theories of personality.* Pacific Grove, CA: Brooks Cole.

Schultz, D., & Schultz, S. (2002). *Psychology and work today.* Upper Saddle River, NJ: Prentice-Hall.

Schulz, R. (1978). *The psychology of death, dying, and bereavement.* Reading, MA: Addison-Wesley.

Schulz, R., Beach, S. R., Lind, B., Martire, L. M., Zdaniuk, B., Hirsch, C., et al. (2001). Involvement in caregiving and adjustment to death of a spouse: Findings from the caregiver health effects study. *Journal of the American Medical Association, 285,* 3123–3129.

Schulz-Hardt, S., Frey, D., Luthgens, C., & Moscovici, S. (2000). Biased information search in group decision making. *Journal of Personality and Social Psychology, 78,* 665–669.

Schwab, M. E. (2004). Nogo and axon regeneration. *Current Opinion in Neurobiology, 14,* 118–124.

Schwartz, B., & Reisberg, D. (1991). *Learning and memory.* New York: Norton.

Schwartz, B., & Robbins, S. J. (1995). *Psychology of learning and behavior* (4th ed.). New York: Norton.

Schwartz, C. E., Wright, C. I., Shin, L. M., Kagan, J., & Rauch, S. L. (2003). Inhibited and uninhibited infants "grow up": Adult amygdalar response to novelty. *Science, 300,* 1952–1953.

Schwartz, J. (2004, September 5). Always on the job, employees pay with health. *The New York Times,* p. 1.

Schwartz, M. W., Woods, S. C., Porte Jr., D., Seeley, R. J., & Baskin, D. G. (2000). Central nervous system control of food intake. *Nature, 404,* 661–671.

Schwarz, N., & Bohner, G. (2001). The construction of attitudes. In A. Tesser & N. Schwarz (Eds.), *Blackwell handbook of social psychology: Intraindividual processes* (pp. 436–457). Oxford, UK: Blackwell.

Schwarz, N., & Scheuring, B. (1992). Frequency reports of psychosomatic symptoms: What respondents learn from response alternatives. *Zeutschrift fur Klinische Psychologie, 22,* 197–208.

Schwarzer, R. (2001). Social-cognitive factors in changing health-related behaviors. *Current Directions in Psychological Science, 10,* 47–51.

Schweinhart, L. J., & Weikart, D. P. (1991). Response to "Beyond IQ in preschool programs?" *Intelligence, 15,* 313–315.

Schwender, D., Klasing, D., Daunderer, M., Maddler, C., Poppel, E., & Peter, K. (1995). Awareness during general anesthetic: Definition, incidence, clinical relevance, causes, avoidance, and medicolegal aspects. *Anaesthetist, 44,* 743–754.

Schwenk, K. (1994, March 18). Why snakes have forked tongues. *Science, 263,* 1573–1577.

Science. (2001). Endel Tulving. Retrieved March 23, 2006, from http://www.science.ca/scientists/scientistprofile.php?pID=20

Scrivener, L. (1980) Marathon of Hope story. *The Toronto Star.* Retrieved March 23, 2006, from http://www.terryfoxrun.org/english/marathon/default.asp?s=1

Sears, R. (1977). Sources of satisfaction of the Terman gifted men. *American Psychologist, 32,* 119–128.

Secord, D., & Peevers, B. (1974). The development and attribution of person concepts. In T. Mischel (Ed.), *Understanding other persons.* Oxford: Blackwell.

Seegert, C. R. (2003). Token economies and incentive programs: Behavioral improvement in mental health inmates housed in state prisons. *Behavior Therapist, 26*(1), 208, 210–211.

Seeman, M. V. (2004). Gender differences in the prescribing of antipsychotic drugs. *American Journal of Psychiatry, 161,* 1324–1333.

Seeman, T., & Chen, X. (2002). Risk and protective factors for physical functioning in older adults with and without chronic conditions: MacArthur studies of successful aging. *Journals of Gerontology: Series B. Psychological Sciences & Social Sciences, 57*(3), S135–S144.

Segal, L., & Suri, J. F. (1999). Psychology applied to product design. In A. M. Stec & D. A. Bernstein (Eds.), *Psychology: Fields of application.* Boston: Houghton Mifflin.

Segal, Z. V., Gemar, M., & Williams, S. (2000). Differential cognitive response to a mood challenge following successful cognitive therapy or pharmacotherapy for unipolar depression. *Journal of Abnormal Psychology, 108,* 3–10.

Segal, Z. V., Williams, M. G., & Teasdale, J. D. (2001) *Mindfulness-based cognitive therapy for depression: A new approach to preventing relapse.* New York: Guilford Press.

Segerstrom, S. C., Taylor, S. E., Kemeny, M. E., & Fahey, J. L. (1998). Optimism is associated with mood, coping, and immune change in response to stress. *Journal of Personality and Social Psychology, 74,* 1646–1655.

Seiger, A., Nordberg, A., Vonholst, H., Backman, L., Ebendal, T., Alafuzoff, I., et al. (1993). Intracranial infusion of purified nerve growth factor to an Alzheimer patient: The 1st attempt of a possible future treatment strategy. *Behavioral Brain Research, 57,* 255–261.

Sejnowski, T. J., & Destexhe, A. (2000). Why do we sleep? *Brain Research, 886,* 208–223.

Sejnowski, T. J., Chattarji, S., & Stanton, P. K. (1990). Homosynaptic long-term depression in hippocampus and neocortex. *Seminars in the Neurosciences, 2, 355–363.*

Sekuler, R., & Blake, R. (1994). *Perception* (3rd ed.). New York: McGraw-Hill.

Selemon, L. D., Mrzljak, J., Kleinman, J. E., Herman, M. M., & Goldman-Rakic, P. S. (2003). Regional specificity in the neuropathologic substrates of schizophrenia: A morphometric analysis of Broca's area 44 and area 9. *Archives of General Psychiatry, 60,* 69–77.

Seligman, M. E. P. (1975). *Helplessness: On depression, development, and death.* San Francisco: Freeman.

Seligman, M. E. P. (1991). *Learned optimism.* New York: Knopf.

Seligman, M. E. P. (1995). The effectiveness of psychotherapy: The *Consumer Reports* study. *American Psychologist, 50,* 965–974.

Seligman, M. E. P. (2002). *Authentic happiness: Using the new positive psychology to realize your potential for lasting fulfillment.* New York: Free Press.

Seligman, M. E. P., & Csikszentmihalyi, M. (2000). Positive psychology: An introduction. *American Psychologist, 55,* 5–14.

Seligman, M. E. P., & Schulman, P. (1986). Explanatory style as a predictor of productivity and quitting among life insurance agents. *Journal of Personality and Social Psychology, 50,* 832–838.

Seligman, M. E. P., Castellon, C., Cacciola, J., Shulman, P., Luborsky, L., Ollove, M., & Downing, R. (1988). Explanatory style change during cognitive therapy for unipolar depression. *Journal of Abnormal Psychology, 97,* 13–18.

Sell, R. L., Wells, J. A., & Wypij, D. (1995). The prevalence of homosexual behavior and attraction in the United States, the United Kingdom, and France: Results of national population-based samples. *Archives of Sexual Behavior, 24*(3), 235–248.

Selye, H. (1956). *The stress of life.* New York: McGraw-Hill.

Selye, H. (1976). *The stress of life* (2nd ed.). New York: McGraw-Hill.

Semmler, C., Brewer, N., & Wells, G. L. (2004). Effects of postidentification feedback on eyewitness identification and nonidentification confidence. *Journal of Applied Psychology, 89,* 334–346.

Semple, M. N., & Scott, B. H. (2003). Cortical mechanisms in hearing. *Current Opinion in Neurobiology, 13,* 167–173.

Senghas, A., & Coppola, M. (2001). Children creating language: How Nicaraguan sign language acquired a spatial grammar. *Psychological Science, 12,* 323–328.

Serpell, R. (1994). The cultural construction of intelligence. In W. J. Lonner & R. S. Malpass (Eds.), *Psychology and culture.* Boston: Allyn & Bacon.

Serpell, R. (2000). Intelligence and culture. In R. J. Sternberg (Ed.), *Handbook of intelligence* (pp. 549–577). New York: Cambridge University Press.

Servan-Schreiber, E., & Anderson, J. R. (1990). Learning artificial grammars with competitive chunking. *Journal of Experimental Psychology: Learning, Memory, and Cognition, 16,* 592–608.

Sevcik, R. A., & Savage-Rumbaugh, E. S. (1994). Language comprehension and use by great apes. *Language and Communication, 14,* 37–58.

Seybold, K. S., & Hill, P. C. (2001). The role of religion and spirituality in mental and physical health. *Current Directions in Psychological Science, 10,* 21–24.

Shadish, W. R., Cook, T. D., & Campbell, D. T. (2002). *Experimental and quasi-experimental designs for generalized causal inference.* Boston: Houghton Mifflin.

Shadish, W. R., Matt, G. E., Navarro, A. M., & Phillips, G. (2000). The effects of psychological therapies under clinically representative conditions: A meta-analysis. *Psychological Bulletin, 126,* 512–529.

Shaffer, D. R. (1973). *Social and personality development* (Box 4–2). Pacific Grove, CA: Brooks/Cole.

Shafritz, K. M., Gore, J. C., & Marois, R. (2002). The role of the parietal cortex in visual feature binding. *Proceedings of the National Academy of Sciences, 99,* 10917–10922.

Shah, J. (2003). Automatic for the people: How representations of significant others implicitly affect goal pursuit. *Journal of Personality and Social Psychology, 84,* 661–681.

Shalev, A. Y., Bonne, M., & Eth, S. (1996). Treatment of posttraumatic stress disorder: A review. *Psychosomatic Medicine, 58,* 165–182.

Shalev, A. Y., Peri, T., Brandes, D., Freedman, S., Orr, S. P., & Pitman, R. K. (2000). Auditory startle response in trauma survivors with posttraumatic stress disorder: A prospective study. *American Journal of Psychiatry, 157,* 255–261.

Shams, L., Kamitani, Y., & Shimojo, S. (2000). Illusions: What you see is what you hear. *Nature, 408,* 788.

Shand, M. A. (1982). Sign-based short-term memory coding of American Sign Language and printed English words by congenitally deaf signers. *Cognitive Psychology, 14,* 1–12.

Shapiro, A. F., Gottman, J. M., & Carrere, S. (2000). The baby and the marriage: Identifying factors that buffer against decline in marital satisfaction after the first baby arrives. *Journal of Family Psychology, 14,* 59–70.

Shapiro, D. H., & Walsh, R. N. (Eds.). (1984). *Meditation: Classical and contemporary perspectives.* New York: Aldine.

Shapiro, F. (1989a). Eye movement desensitization: A new treatment for post-traumatic stress disorder. *Journal of Behavior Therapy and Experimental Psychiatry, 20,* 211–217.

Shapiro, F. (1989b). Efficacy of the eye movement desensitization procedure in the treatment of traumatic memories. *Journal of Traumatic Stress, 2,* 199–223.

Shapiro, F. (1995). *Eye movement desensitization and reprocessing: Basic principles, protocols, and procedures.* New York: Guilford.

Shapiro, F. (2001). *Eye movement desensitization and reprocessing: Basic principles, protocols, and procedures* (2nd ed.). New York, NY: Guilford Press.

Shapiro, F. (Ed.). (2002). *EMDR as an integrative psychotherapy approach: Experts of diverse orientations explore the paradigm prism.* Washington, DC: APA.

Shapiro, F., & Maxfield, L. (2002). Eye movement desensitization and reprocessing (EMDR): Information processing in the treatment of trauma. *Journal of Clinical Psychology, 58,* 933–936.

Shaw, B. A., Krause, N., Chatters, L. M., Connell, C. M., & Ingersoll-Dayton, B. (2004). Emotional support from parents early in life, aging, and health. *Psychology and Aging, 19,* 4–12.

Shaw, C.A., & McEachren, J.C. (2001). Is there a general theory of neuroplasticity (p. 497). In C. Shaw & J. McEachren (Eds.). *Toward a Theory of Neruoplasticity.* New York: Psychology Press.

Shaw, J. S., III. (1996). Increases in eyewitness confidence resulting from persistent questioning. *Journal of Experimental Psychology: Applied, 2,* 126–146.

Shaw, S. F., Cullen, J. P., McGuire, J. M., & Brinckerhoff, L. C. (1995). Operationalizing a definition of learning disabilities. *Journal of Learning Disabilities, 28,* 586–597.

Shaywitz, B. A., Shaywitz, S. E., Pugh, K. R., Constable, R. T., Skudlarski, P., Fulbright, R. K., et al. (1995). Sex differences in the functional organization of the brain for language. *Nature, 373,* 607–609.

Shea, M. T., Stout, R., Gunderson, J., Morey, L. C., Grilo, C. M., McGlashan, T., et al. (2002). Short-term diagnostic stability of schizotypal, borderline, avoidant, and obsessive-compulsive personality disorders. *American Journal of Psychiatry, 159,* 2036–2041.

Sheehy, R., & Horan, J. J. (2004). Effects of stress inoculation training for 1st-year law students. *International Journal of Stress Management, 11*(1), 41–55.

Sheldon, K. M., & Kasser, T. (2001). Getting older, getting better? Personal striving and psychological maturity across the life span. *Developmental Psychology, 37,* 491–501.

Sheldon, K. M., & King, L (2001). Why positive psychology is necessary. *American Psychologist, 56,* 216–217.

Shepard, R. N., & Metzler, J. (1971). Mental rotation of three-dimensional objects. *Science, 171,* 701–703.

Shepherd, C., Kohut, J. J., & Sweet, R. (1989). *News of the weird.* New York: New American Library.

Shepperd, J. A. (1993). Productivity loss in performance groups: A motivation analysis. *Psychological Bulletin, 113,* 67–81.

Sher, K. J., Wood, M. D., Wood, P. K., & Raskin, G. (1996). Alcohol outcome expectancies and alcohol use: A latent variable cross-lagged panel study. *Journal of Abnormal Psychology, 105,* 561–574.

Shera, C. A., Guinan, J. J., & Oxenham, A. J. (2002). Revised estimates of human cochlear tuning from otoacoustic and behavioral measurements. *Proceedings of the National Academy of Sciences, 99*(5), 3318–3323.

Shergill, S. S., Brammer, M. J., Williams, S. C., Murray, R. M., & McGuire, P. K. (2000). Mapping auditory hallucinations in schizophrenia using functional magnetic resonance imaging. *Archives of General Psychiatry, 57,* 1033–1038.

Sherif, M. (1937). An experimental approach to the study of attitudes. *Sociometry, 1,* 90–98.

Sherman, J. W., & Klein, S. B. (1994). Development and representation of personality impressions. *Journal of Personality and Social Psychology, 67,* 972–983.

Sherman, S. J. (1980). On the self-erasing nature of errors of prediction. *Journal of Personality and Social Psychology, 39,* 211–221.

Sherwin, B. B., & Gelfand, M. M. (1987). The role of androgen in the maintenance of sexual functioning in oophorectomized women. *Psychosomatic Medicine, 49,* 397–409.

Shiffman, S., Engberg, J. B., Paty, J. A., & Perz, W. G. (1997). A day at a time: Predicting smoking lapse from daily urge. *Journal of Abnormal Psychology, 106,* 104–116.

Shiller, R. J. (2001). *Irrational exuberance.* Princeton, NJ: Princeton University Press.

Shimamura, A. P., Berry, J. M., Mangels, J. A., Rusting, C. L., & Jurica, P. J. (1995). Memory and cognitive abilities in university professors: Evidence for successful aging. *Psychological Science, 6,* 271–277.

Shiner, R. L., Masten, A. S., & Roberts, J. M. (2003). Childhood personality foreshadows adult personality and life outcomes two decades later. *Journal of Personality, 71,* 1145–1170.

Shinohara, T., Bredberg, G., Ulfendahl, M., Pyykkö, I., Olivius, N. P., Kaksonen, R., et al. (2002). Neurotrophic factor intervention restores auditory function in deafened animals. *Proceedings of the National Academy of Sciences, 99,* 1657–1660.

Shiraev, E., & Levy, D. (2004). *Cross-cultural psychology: Critical thinking and contemporary applications* (2nd ed.). Boston: Allyn & Bacon.

Shiwach, R. S., Reid, W. H., & Carmody, T. J. (2001). An analysis of reported deaths following electroconvulsive therapy in Texas, 1993–1998. *Psychiatric Services, 52,* 1095–1097.

Shoda, Y., & LeeTiernan, S. (2002). What remains invariant? Finding order within a person's thoughts, feelings, and behavior across situations. In D. Cervone & W. Mischel (Eds.), *Advances in personality science* (pp. 241–270). New York: Guilford Press.

Shoptaw, S., Yang, X., Rotheram-Fuller, E. J., Hsieh, Y. C., Kintaudi, P. C., Charuvastra, V. C., & Ling. W. (2003). Randomized placebo-controlled trial of baclofen for cocaine dependence: Preliminary effects for individuals with chronic patterns of cocaine use. *Journal of Clinical Psychiatry, 64,* 1440–1448.

Shore, B. M., & Delcourt, M.A.B. (1996). Effective curricular and program practices in gifted education and their interface with general education. *Journal for the Education of the Gifted, 20,* 138–154.

Shore, B. M., & Irving, J. A. (2005). Inquiry as a pedagogical link between expertise and giftedness: The High Ability and Inquiry Research Group at McGill University. *Gifted and Talented International, 20,* 37–40.

Shreeve, J. (1993, June). Touching the phantom. *Discover,* pp. 35–42.

Shweder, R. A., Much, N. C., Mahapatra, M., & Park, L. (1994). The "big three" of morality (autonomy, community, and divinity), and the "big three" explanations of suffering, as well. In A. Brandt & P. Rozin (Eds.), *Morality and health.* Stanford, CA: Stanford University Press.

Siebert, S. E., & Kraimer, M. L. (2001). The five-factor model of personality and career success. *Journal of Vocational Behavior, 58,* 1–21.

Siegal, M. (1997). *Knowing children: Experiments in conversation and cognition* (2nd ed.). Hove, UK: Psychology Press/Erlbaum/Taylor & Francis.

Siegel, J. M. (2004). Hypocretin (orexin): Role in normal behavior and neuropathology. *Annual Review of Psychology, 55,* 125–148.

Siegel, J. M., & Rogawski, M. A. (1988). A function for REM sleep: Regulation of noradrenergic receptor sensitivity. *Brain Research Review, 13,* 213–233.

Siegel, S., Hirson, R. E., Krank, M. D., & McCully, J. (1982). Heroin "overdose" death: The contribution of drug associated environmental cues. *Science, 216,* 430–437.

Siegler, R. S. (1994). Cognitive variability: A key to understanding cognitive development. *Current Directions in Psychological Science, 3,* 1–4.

Sigmundsson, T., Suckling, J., Maier, M., Bullmore, E., Greenwood, K., Ron, M., et al. (2001). Structural abnormalities in frontal, temporal, and limbic regions and interconnecting white matter tracts in schizophrenic patients with prominent negative symptoms. *American Journal of Psychiatry, 158,* 234–243.

Sikes, C. K., & Sikes, V. N. (2003). A look at EMDR: Technique, research, and use with college students. *Journal of College Student Psychotherapy, 18,* 65–76.

Silber, M. H. (2001). Sleep disorders. *Neurology Clinics, 19,* 173–186.

Silbersweig, D. A., Stern, E., Frith, C., Cahill, C., Holmes, A., Grootoonk, S., et al. (1995). A functional neuroanatomy of hallucinations in schizophrenia. *Nature, 378,* 176–179.

Silverman, K., Evans, A. M., Strain, E. C., & Griffiths, R. R. (1992). Withdrawal syndrome after the double-blind cessation of caffeine consumption. *New England Journal of Medicine, 327,* 1109–1114.

Silverman, K., Svikis, D., Robles, E., Stitzer, M. L., & Bigelow, G. E. (2001). A Reinforcement-Based Therapeutic Workplace for the Treatment of Drug Abuse: Six-Month Abstinence Outcomes. *Experimental and Clinical Psychopharmacology, 9,* 14–23.

Silverstein, L. B. (1996). Evolutionary psychology and the search for sex differences. *American Psychologist, 51,* 160–161.

Silverthorne, C. (2001) Leadership effectiveness and personality: A cross cultural evaluation. *Personality & Individual Differences, 30,* 303–309.

Silvotti, L., Montanu, G., & Tirindelli, R. (2003). How mammals detect pheromones. *Journal of Endocrinological Investigation, 26,* 49–53.

Simeon, D., Greenberg, J., Knutelska, M., Schmeidler, J., & Hollander, E. (2003). Peritraumatic reactions associated with the World Trade Center disaster. *The American Journal of Psychiatry, 160,* 1702–1705.

Simion, F., Cassia, V. M., Turati, C., & Valenza, E. (2003). Non-specific perceptual biases at the origins of face processing. In O. Pascalis & A. Slater (Eds.), *The development of face processing in infancy and early childhood* (pp. 13–25). Hauppauge, NY: Nova Science.

Simon, D.J. & Resink, R.A. (2005). Change Blindness, Past, Present and Future. *Trends in Cognitive Psychology, 9(1),* 16–20.

Simons, D. J., & Chabris, C. F. (1999). Gorillas in our midst: Sustained inattentional blindness for dynamic events. *Perception, 28,* 1059–1074.

Simons, D. J., & Levin, D. T. (1997). Failure to detect changes to attended objects. *Investigative Ophthalmology and Visual Science, 38,* S747.

Simons, J. S., & Spiers, H. J. (2003). Prefrontal and medial temporal lobe interactions in long-term memory. *Nature Reviews Neuroscience, 4,* 637–648.

Simonton, D. K. (1999). Creativity and genius. In L. Pervin & O. John (Eds.), *Handbook of personality research* (2nd ed., pp. 629–652). New York: Guilford.

Simonton, D. K. (2002). In C. R. Snyder & J. Shane (Eds.), *Handbook of positive psychology* (pp. 189–201). London: Oxford University Press.

Simpson, J. A., & Kenrick, D. T. (1997). *Evolutionary social psychology.* Mahwah, NJ: Erlbaum.

Simpson, J. A., & Rholes, W. S. (2000). Caregiving, attachment theory, and the connection theoretical orientation. *Psychological Inquiry, 11,* 114–117.

Simpson, S., Hurtley, S. M., & Marx, J. (2000). Immune cell networks. *Science, 290,* 79.

Sinclair, R. C., Hoffman, C., Mark, M. M., Martin, L. L., & Pickering, T. L. (1994). Construct accessibility and the misattribution of arousal. *Psychological Science, 5*(1), 15–19.

Singer, L. T., Arendt, R., Minnes, S., Farkas, K., Salvator, A., Kirchner, L., & Kliegman, R. (2002). Cognitive and motor outcomes of cocaine-exposed infants. *Journal of the American Medical Association, 287*(15), 1952–1960.

Sinha, P., & Poggio, T. (1996). I think I know that face. *Nature, 384,* 404.

Sinha, R., & Parsons, O. A. (1996). Multivariate response patterning of fear and anger. *Cognition and Emotion, 10,* 173–198.

Sirvio, J. (1999). Strategies that support declining cholinergic neurotransmission in Alzheimer's disease patients. *Gerontology, 45,* 3–14.

Skinner, B. F. (1938). *The behavior of organisms.* New York: Appleton.

Skinner, B. F. (1961). *Cumulative record* (3rd ed.). Englewood Cliffs, NJ: Prentice-Hall.

Skre, I., Onstad, S., Toregersen, S., Lyngren, S., & Kringlin, E. (2000). The heritability of common phobic fear: A twin study of a clinical sample. *Journal of Anxiety Disorders, 14,* 549–562.

Slamecka, N. J., & McElree, B. (1983). Normal forgetting of verbal lists as a function of their degree of learning. *Journal of Experimental Psychology: Learning, Memory, and Cognition, 9,* 384–397.

Slater, A., Mattock, A., Brown, E., & Bremmer, J. G. (1991). Form perception at birth. *Journal of Experimental Child Psychology, 51,* 395–406.

Slentz, C. A., Duscha, B. D., Johnson, J. L., Ketchum, K., Aiken, L. B., Samsa, G. P., et al. (2004). Effects of the amount of exercise on body weight, body composition, and measures of central obesity: STRRIDE—A randomized controlled study. *Archives of Internal Medicine, 164,* 31–39.

Slife, B. D., & Reber, J. S. (2001). Eclecticism in psychotherapy: Is it really the best substitute for traditional theories? In B. D. Slife, R. N. Williams, & S. H. Barlow (Eds.), *Critical issues in psychotherapy* (pp. 213–234). Thousand Oaks, CA: Sage.

Sloan, D. M., Strauss, M. E., & Wisner, K. L. (2001). Diminished response to pleasant stimuli by depressed women. *Journal of Abnormal Psychology, 110,* 488–493.

Slomkowski, C., & Dunn, J. (1996). Young children's understanding of other people's beliefs and feelings and their connected communication with friends. *Developmental Psychology, 32,* 442–447.

Slotnick, S. D., & Schacter, D. L. (2004). A sensory signature that distinguishes true from fales memories. *Nature Neuroscience, 7,* 664–672.

Slutske, W., Eisen, S., Xian, H., True, W., Lyons, M. J., Goldberg, J., et al. (2001). A twin study of the association between pathological gambling and antisocial personality disorder. *Journal of Abnormal Psychology, 110,* 297–308.

Small, B. J., & Bäckman, L. (1999). Time to death and cognitive performance. *Current Directions in Psychological Science, 8,* 168–172.

Small, D. M., Gregory, M. D., Mak, Y. E., Mesulam, M. M., & Parrish, T. (2003). Dissociation of neural representation of intensity and valuation in human gustation. *Neuron, 39,* 701–711.

Small, J.A. and Perry, J. (2005). Do you remember? How caregivers question their spouses who have Alzheimer's disease and the impact on communication. *Journal of Speech, Language, and Hearing Research, 48–1,* 125–136.

Small, S. A., Tsai, W. Y., DeLaPaz, R., Mayeux, R., & Stern, Y. (2002). Imaging hippocampal function across the human life span: Is memory decline normal or not? *Annals of Neurology, 51,* 290–295.

Smeets, G., de Jong, P. J., & Mayer, B. (2000). If you suffer from a headache, then you have a brain tumor: Domain-specific reasoning 'bias' and hypochondriasis. *Behaviour Research and Therapy, 38,* 763–776.

Smith, A. M., Malo, S. A., Laskowski, E. R., Sabick, M., Cooney, W. P., III, Finnie, S. B., et al. (2000). A multidisciplinary study of the 'yips' phenomenon in golf: An exploratory analysis. *Sports Medicine, 30,* 423–437.

Smith, D. (2003a). Angry thoughts, at-risk hearts. *Monitor on Psychology, 34,* 46.

Smith, E. (1998). Mental representation and memory. In D. Gilbert, S. T. Fiske, & G. Lindzey (Eds.), *Handbook of social psychology* (4th ed., Vol. 1, pp. 391–445). Boston: McGraw-Hill.

Smith, E. E. (2000). Neural bases of human working memory. *Currents Directions in Psychological Science, 9,* 45–49.

Smith, E. E., Geva, A., Jonides, J., Miller, A., Reuter-Lorenz, P., & Koeppe, R. A. (2001). The neural basis of task-switching in working memory: Effects of performance and aging. *Proceedings of the National Academy of Sciences, 98,* 2095–2100.

Smith, E., & Mackie, D. (2000). *Social psychology* (2nd ed.). Philadelphia: Taylor & Francis.

Smith, E., & Quellar, S. (2001). Mental representations. In A. Tesser & N. Schwarz (Eds.), *Blackwell handbook of social psychology: Intraindividual processes* (pp. 499–517). Oxford, UK: Blackwell.

Smith, J. (1993). *Understanding stress and coping.* New York: Macmillan.

Smith, J., & Baltes, P. B. (1990). A study of wisdom-related knowledge: Age/cohort differences in responses to life-planning problems. *Developmental Psychology, 26,* 494–505.

Smith, K. M., Larive, L. L., & Romananelli, F. (2002). Club drugs: Methylenedioxymethamphetamine, flunitrazepam, ketamine hydrochloride, and gamma-hydroxybutyrate. *American Journal of Health Systems Pharmacology, 59,* 1067–1076.

Smith, L. B., & Sera, M. D. (1992). A developmental analysis of the polar structure of dimensions. *Cognitive Psychology, 24,* 99–142.

Smith, M. (1988). Recall of spatial location by the amnesic patient HM. Special issue: Single case studies in amnesia—Theoretical advances. *Brain and Cognition, 7,* 178–183.

Smith, M. L., Glass, G. V., & Miller, T. I. (1980). *The benefits of psychotherapy.* Baltimore: Johns Hopkins University Press.

Smith, N. T. (2002). A review of the published literature into cannabis withdrawal symptoms in human users. *Addiction, 97,* 621–632.

Smith, P. B., & Bond, M. H. (1999). *Social psychology across cultures: Analysis and perspectives* (2nd ed.). Boston: Allyn & Bacon.

Smith, P. K., & Drew, L. M. (2002). Grandparenthood. In M. H. Bornstein (Ed.), *Handbook of parenting* (2nd ed.). Mahwah, NJ: Erlbaum.

Smith, S. M., Glenberg, A. M., & Bjork, R. A. (1978). Environmental context and human memory. *Memory & Cognition, 6,* 342–355.

Smith, S. M., Vela, E., & Williamson, J. E. (1988). Shallow input processing does not induce environmental context-dependent recognition. *Bulletin of the Psychonomic Society, 26,* 537–540.

Smith, S. S., O'Hara, B. F., Persico, A. M., Gorelick, D. A., Newlin, D. B., Vlahov, D., et al. (1992). Genetic vulnerability to drug abuse: The D2 dopamine receptor Taq i B1 restriction fragment length polymorphism appears more frequently in polysubstance abusers. *Archives of General Psychiatry, 49,* 723–727.

Smith, S., & Donnerstein, E. (1998). Harmful effects of exposure to media violence: Learning of aggression, emotional desensitization, and fear. In R. Geen & E. Donnerstein (Eds.), *Human aggression: Theories, research, and implications for policy.* New York: Academic Press.

Smith, T. W., & Ruiz, J. M. (2002). Psychosocial influences on the development and course of coronary heart disease: Current status and implications for research and practice. *Journal of Consulting & Clinical Psychology, 70,* 548–568.

Smith, T. W., & Suls, J. (2004). Introduction to the special section on the future of health psychology. *Health Psychology, 23,* 115–118.

Smith, T. W., Orleans, C. T., & Jenkins, C. D. (2004). Prevention and health promotion: Decades of progress, new challenges, and an emerging agenda. *Health Psychology, 23,* 126–131.

Smith, V. L. (1991). Prototypes in the courtroom: Lay representations of legal concepts. *Journal of Personality and Social Psychology, 44,* 787–797.

Snarey, J. (1987). A question of morality. *Psychological Bulletin, 97,* 202–232.

Snellingen, T., Evans, J. R., Ravilla, T., & Foster, A. (2002). Surgical interventions for age-related cataract. *Cochrane Database System Review, 2,* CD001323.

Snodgrass, S. R. (1994). Cocaine babies: A result of multiple teratogenic influences. *Journal of Child Neurology,* 9(3), 227–233.

Snow, R. E. (1995). Pygmalion and intelligence? *Current Directions in Psychological Science, 4,* 169–171.

Snyder, A. W., & Mitchell, D. J. (1999). Is integer arithmetic fundamental to mental processing?: The mind's secret arithmetic. *Proceedings of the Royal Society of London, 266,* 587–592.

Snyder, M., & Haugen, J. A. (1995). Why does behavioral confirmation occur? A functional perspective on the role of the target. *Personality and Social Psychology Bulletin, 21,* 963–974.

Soetens, E., Casaer, S., D'Hooge, R., & Hueting, J. E. (1995). Effect of amphetamine on long-term retention of verbal material. *Psychopharmacology, 119,* 155–162.

Sokoloff, L. (1981). Localization of functional activity in the central nervous system by measurement of glucose utilization with radioactive deoxyglucose. *Journal of Cerebral Blood Flow and Metabolism, 1,* 7–36.

Sokolowska, M., Siegel, S., & Kim, J. A. (2002). Intraadministration associations: Conditional hyperalgesia elicited by morphine onset cues. *Journal of Experimental Psychology: Animal Behavior Processes, 28,* 309–20.

Solomon, A. (1998, January 12). Anatomy of melancholy. *New Yorker,* pp. 46–61.

Solomon, P. R., Adams, F., Silver, A., Zimmer, J., & DeVeaux, R. (2002). Ginkgo for memory enhancement: a randomized controlled trial. *Journal of the American Medical Association, 288,* 835–840.

Solomon, R. L. (1980). The opponent-process theory of acquired motivation: The costs of pleasure and the benefits of pain. *American Psychologist, 35,* 691–712.

Solomon, R. L., Kamin, L. J., & Wynne, L. C. (1953). Traumatic avoidance learning: The outcomes of several extinction procedures with dogs. *Journal of Abnormal and Social Psychology, 48,* 291–302.

Solowij, N., Stephens, R. S., Roffman, R. A., Babor, T., Kadden, R., Miller, M., et al. (2002). Cognitive functioning of long-term heavy cannabis users seeking treatment. *Journal of American Medical Association, 287,* 1123–1131.

Sommer, R. (1999). Applying environmental psychology. In D. A. Bernstein & A. M. Stec (Eds.), *The psychology of everyday life.* Boston: Houghton Mifflin.

Sones, B., & Sones, R. (2003). Love and lie detectors. Retrieved March 23, 2006, from http://www.signonsandiego.com/news/features/strange/20030416-9999-strange138.html

Sora, I., Hall, F. S., Andrews, A. M., Itokawa, M., Li, X. F., Wei, H. B., et al. (2001). Molecular mechanisms of cocaine reward: combined dopamine and serotonin transporter knockouts eliminate cocaine place preference. *Proceedings of the National Academy of Science, 98,* 5300–5305.

Sørensen, H. J., Mortensen, E. L., Reinisch, J. M., & Mednick, S. A. (2003). Do hypertension and diuretic treatment in pregnancy increase the risk of schizophrenia in offspring? *American Journal of Psychiatry, 160,* 464–468.

Sorof, J. M., Lai, D., Turner, J., Poffenbarger, T., & Portman, R. J. (2004). Overweight, ethnicity, and the prevalence of hypertension in school-aged children. *Pediatrics, 113,* 475–482.

Sorrentino, R. M., & Roney, C. J. R. (2000). *The uncertain mind: Individual differences in facing the unknown.* Philadelphia: Psychology Press.

Sowdon, J. (2001). Is depression more prevalent in old age? *Australian & New Zealand Journal of Psychiatry, 35,* 782–787.

Sowell, E. R., Peterson, B. S., Thompson, P. M., Welcome, S. E., Henkenius, A. L., & Toga, A. W. (2003). Mapping cortical change across the human life span. *Nature Neuroscience, 6,* 309–315.

Spangler, G., Fremmer-Bombik, E., & Grossman, K. (1996). Social and individual determinants of infant attachment security and disorganization. *Infant Mental Health Journal, 17,* 127–139.

Spanier, C., Frank, E., McEachran, A. B., Grochocinski, V. J., & Kupfer, D. J. (1996). The prophylaxis of depressive episodes in recurrent depression following discontinuation of drug therapy: Integrating psychological and biological factors. *Psychological Medicine, 26,* 461–475.

Spanos, N. P. (1994). Multiple identity enactments and multiple personality disorder: A sociocognitive perspective. *Psychological Bulletin, 116,* 143–165.

Spanos, N. P. (1996). *Multiple identities and false memories: A sociocognitive perspective.* Washington, DC: American Psychological Association.

Spanos, N. P., Burnley, M. C. E., & Cross, P. A. (1993). Response expectancies and interpretations as determinants of hypnotic responding. *Journal of Personality and Social Psychology, 65*(6), 1237–1242.

Sparkes, S., Grant, V. L., & Lett, B. T. (2003). Role of conditioned taste aversion in the development of activity anorexia. *Appetite,* 41, 161–165.

Spearman, C. E. (1904). General intelligence objectively determined and measured. *American Journal of Psychology, 15,* 201–293.

Spearman, C. E. (1927). *The abilities of man.* New York: Macmillan.

Spears, R., Postmes, T., Lea, M., & Watt, S. E. (2001). A SIDE view of social influence. In J. P. Forgas & K. D. Williams (Eds.), *Social influence: Direct and indirect processes. The Sydney symposium of social psychology* (pp. 331–350). Philadelphia, PA: Psychology Press.

Speckhard, A. (2002). Voices from the inside: Psychological responses to toxic disasters. In J. M. Havenaar & J. G. Cwikel (Eds.), *Toxic turmoil: Psychological and societal consequences of ecological disasters* (pp. 217–236). New York: Plenum.

Specter, M. (2004, February 2). Miracle in a bottle. *New Yorker,* 64–75.

Spector, P. E. (2002). Employee control and occupational stress. *Current Directions in Psychological Science, 11,* 133–136.

Spector, P. E. (2003). *Industrial & organizational psychology: Research and practice* (3rd ed.). New York: Wiley.

Spelke, E. S., Breinlinger, K., Macomber, J., & Jacobson, K. (1992). Origins of knowledge. *Psychological Review, 99,* 605–632.

Spence, C., & Read, L. (2003). Speech shadowing while driving: On the difficulty of splitting attention between eye and ear. *Psychological Science, 14,* 251–256.

Spence, S. H., Donovan, C., Brechman-Toussaint, M. (2000). The treatment of childhood social phobia: The effectiveness of a social skills training-based, cognitive-behavioral intervention, with and without parental involvement. *Journal of Child Psychology and Psychiatry and Allied Disciplines, 41,* 713–726.

Spencer, S., Steele, C. M., & Quinn, D. (1997). *Under suspicion on inability: Stereotype threats and women's math performance.* Unpublished manuscript.

Sperry, R. W. (1968). Hemisphere deconnection and unity in conscious awareness. *American Psychologist, 23,* 723–733.

Sperry, R. W. (1974). Lateral specialization in the surgically separated hemispheres. In F. O. Schmitt & F. G. Wordon (Eds.), *The neurosciences third study program.* Cambridge: MIT Press.

Spiegel, D. (Ed.). (1994). *Dissociation: Culture, mind, and body.* Washington, DC: American Psychiatric Press.

Spiegel, D. A., & Bruce, T. J. (1997). Benzodiazepines and exposure-based cognitive behavior therapies for panic disorder: Conclusions from combined treatment trials. *American Journal of Psychiatry, 151,* 876–881.

Spinath, F. M., Harlaar, N., Ronald, A., & Plomin, R. (2004). Substantial genetic influence on mild mental impairment in early childhood. *American Journal of Mental Retardation, 109,* 34–43.

Spira, J. L. (2001). Study design casts doubt on value of St. John's wort in treating depression. *British Medical Journal, 322,* 493.

Spitz, H. H. (1991). Commentary on Locurto's "Beyond IQ in preschool programs?" *Intelligence, 15,* 327–333.

Spitz, H. H. (1997). *Nonconscious movements: From mystical messages to facilitated communication.* Hillsdale, NJ: Erlbaum.

Spitzer, R. L., Gibbon, M., Skodol, A. E., & Williams, J. B. W., & First, M. B. (Eds.). (1994). *DSM-IV casebook: A learning companion to the Diagnostic and Statistical Manual of Mental Disorders, fourth edition.* Washington, DC: American Psychiatric Association.

Spitzer, R., First, M., Williams, J., Kendler, K., Pincus, A., & Tucker, G. (1992). Now is the time to retire the term "Organic Mental Disorders." *American Journal of Psychiatry, 149,* 240–244.

Sprecher, S., Hatfield, E., Anthony, C., & Potapova, E. (1994). Token resistance to sexual intercourse and consent to unwanted sexual intercourse: College students' dating experiences in three countries. *Journal of Sex Research, 31*(2), 125–132.

Springer, K., & Belk, A. (1994). The role of physical contact and association in early contamination sensitivity. *Developmental Psychology, 30*(6), 864–868.

Springer, S. P., & Deutsch, G. (1989). *Left brain, right brain.* San Francisco: Freeman.

Squire, L. (1987). *Memory and brain.* New York: Oxford University Press.

Squire, L. R. (1986). Mechanisms of memory. *Science, 232,* 1612–1619.

Squire, L. R. (1992). Memory and the hippocampus: A synthesis from findings with rats, monkeys, and humans. *Psychological Review, 99,* 195–231.

Squire, L. R., & McKee, R. (1992). The influence of prior events on cognitive judgments in amnesia. *Journal of Experimental Psychology: Learning, Memory, and Cognition, 18,* 106–115.

Squire, L. R., Amara, D. G., & Press, G. A. (1992). Magnetic resonance imaging of the hippocampal formation and mamillary nuclei distinguish medial temporal lobe and diencephalic amnesia. *Journal of Neuroscience, 10,* 3106–3117.

Srinivas, K. (1993). Perceptual specificity in nonverbal priming. *Journal of Experimental Psychology: Learning, Memory, and Cognition 19,* 582–602.

Srivastava, A., Locke, E. A., & Bartol, K. M. (2001). Money and subjective well-being: It's not the money, it's the motives. *Journal of Personality and Social Psychology, 80,* 959–971.

Srivastava, S., John, O. P., Gosling, S. D., & Potter, J. (2003). Development of personality in early and middle adulthood: Set like plaster or persistent change? *Journal of Personality and Social Psychology, 84,* 1041–1053.

St. Clair, M. (1999). *Object relations and self-psychology: An introduction.* Pacific Grove, CA: Brooks/Cole.

St. John, W. (2003, September 28). In U.S. funeral industry, triple-wide isn't a trailer. *The New York Times,* p. 1.

Stacey, J., & Biblarz, T. J. (2001). (How) Does the sexual orientation of parents matter? *American Sociological Review, 66,* 159–183.

Staddon, J. E. R., & Ettinger, R. H. (1989). *Learning: An introduction to the principles of adaptive behavior.* San Diego: Harcourt Brace Jovanovich.

Stahl, S. M. (2002). Selective actions on sleep or anxiety by exploiting GABA-A/benzodiazepine receptor subtypes. *Journal of Clinical Psychiatry, 63,* 179–180.

Standing, L., Conezio, J., & Haber, R. N. (1970). Perception and memory for pictures: Single-trial learning of 2500 visual stimuli. *Psychonomic Science, 19,* 73–74.

Stankov, L. (1989). Attentional resources and intelligence: A disappearing link. *Personality and Individual Differences, 10,* 957–968.

Stanley, B. G., Willett, V. L., Donias, H. W., & Ha-Lyen, H. (1993). The lateral hypothalamus: A primary site mediating excitatory aminoacid-elicited eating. *Brain Research, 63*(1–2), 41–49.

Stansfeld, S. A., & Marmot, M .G. (Eds.). (2002). *Stress and the heart: Psychosocial pathways to coronary heart disease.* London: BMJ Books.

Stanton-Hicks, M., & Salamon, J. (1997). Stimulation of the central and peripheral nervous system for the control of pain. *Journal of Clinical Neurophysiology, 14,* 46–62.

Stapleton, S. (2001, February 19). Miles to go before I sleep: America is becoming a culture of sleeplessness. *Amednews.* Retrieved December 7, 2004, from http://www.ama-assn.org/sci-pubs/amnews/pick_01/hlsa0219.htm

Stasser, G. (1991). Pooling of unshared information during group discussion. In S. Worchel, W. Wood, & J. Simpson (Eds.), *Group processes and productivity.* Beverly Hills, CA: Sage.

Stasser, G., Stewart, D., & Wittenbaum, G. M. (1995). Expert roles and information exchange during discussion: The importance of knowing who knows what. *Journal of Experimental Social Psychology, 31,* 244–265.

Statistics Canada. (2002). 2001 census: Marital status, common-law status, families, dwellings and households [Electronic version]. Available: http://www.statcan.ca/Daily/English/021022/d021022a.htm

Statistics Canada. (2003). Health Indicators [Electronic version]. Available: http://www.statcan.ca/english/freepub/82-221-XIE/01103/toc.htm

Statistics Canada. (2004). Divorces [Electronic version]. Available: http://www.statcan.ca/Daily/English/040504/d040504a.htm

Statistics Canada. (2004). Panic Disorder and Coping. *Supplement to Health Reports, 15,* 33–63 [Electronic version]. Available: http://www.statcan.ca/english/freepub/82–003-SIE/2004000/panic.htm

Statistics Canada. (2005a). Provincial drop-out rates – Trends and consequences [Electronic version]. Available: http://www.statcan.ca/english/freepub/81–004-XIE/2005004/drop.htm

Statistics Canada. (2005b). Population by sex and age group [Electronic version]. Available: http://www40.statcan.ca/l01/cst01/demo10a.htm

Statistics Canada. (2006). Canadian tobacco use monitoring saurvey. [Electronic version]. Available: http://www.statcan.ca/cgi-bin/imdb/p2SV.pl?Function=getSurvey&SDDS=4440&lang=en&db=IMDB&dbg=f&adm=8&dis=2

Statistics Canada data, 1991, CANSIM II.

Statistics Canada. (2001). Television Viewing. The Daily. Retrieved March 23, 2006, from http://www.statcan.ca/Daily/English/010125/d010125a.htm

Statistics Canada. (2003). Television Viewing. The Daily. Retrieved March 23, 2006, from http://www.statcan.ca/Daily/English/050331/d050331b.htm

Staudt, M., Grodd, W., Niemann, G., Wildgruber, D., Erb, M., & Krageloh-Mann, I. (2001). Early left periventricular brain lesions induce right hemispheric organization of speech. *Neurology 2001, 57,* 122–125.

Steele, C. M. (1997). A threat in the air: How stereotypes shape intellectual identity and performance. *American Psychologist, 52,* 613–629.

Steele, C. M., & Aronson, J. (2000). Stereotype threat and the intellectual test performance of African Americans. In C. Stangor (Ed.), *Stereotypes and prejudice: Essential readings* (pp. 369–389). Philadelphia: Psychology Press/Taylor & Francis.

Steele, T. D., McCann, U. D., & Ricaurte, G. A. (1994). 3,4-methylenedioxymethamphetamine (MDMA, ecstacy): Pharmacology and toxicology in animals and humans. *Addiction, 89*(5), 539–551.

Steffen, P. R., McNeilly, M., Anderson, N., & Sherwood, A. (2003). Effects of perceived racism and anger inhibition on ambulatory blood pressure in African Americans. *Psychosomatic Medicine, 65,* 746–750.

Steiger, H., Young, S. N., Ng Ying Kin, N. M. K., Koerner, N., Israel, M., Lageix, P., & Paris, J. (2001). Implications of impulsive and affective symptoms for serotonin function in bulimia nervosa. *Psychological Medicine, 31,* 85–95.

Stein, D. J., Versiani, M., Hair, T., & Kumar, R. (2002). Efficacy of paroxetine for relapse prevention in social anxiety disorder: A 24-week study. *Archives of General Psychiatry, 59,* 1111–1118.

Stein, D. M., & Lambert, M. J. (1995). Graduate training in psychotherapy: Are therapy outcomes enhanced? *Journal of Consulting and Clinical Psychology, 63,* 182–196.

Stein, K. D., Goldman, M. S., & Del Boca, F. K. (2000). The influence of alcohol expectancy priming and mood manipulation on subsequent alcohol consumption. *Journal of Abnormal Psychology, 109,* 106–115.

Stein, M. A. (1993, November 30). Spacewalking repair team to work on Hubble flaws; shower head inspires a device to improve focusing ability. *Los Angeles Times,* A1, A5.

Stein, M. B., Chavira, D. A., & Jang, K. L. (2001). Bringing up bashful baby: Developmental pathways to social phobia. *Psychiatric Clinics of North America, 24,* 661–675.

Steinberg, L. (1990). Autonomy, conflict, and harmony in the family relationship. In S. S. Feldman & G. R. Elliott (Eds.), *At the threshold: The developing adolescent* (pp. 255–276). Cambridge, MA: Harvard University Press.

Steinberg, L., Lamborn, S. D., Darling, N., Mounts, N. S., & Dornbusch, S. M. (1994). Over-time changes in adjustment and competence among adolescents from authoritative, authoritarian, indulgent, and neglectful families. *Child Development, 65,* 754–770.

Steinbrook, R. (2004a). The AIDS epidemic in 2004. *New England Journal of Medicine, 351,* 115–117.

Steindler, D. A. & Pincus, D. W. (2002). Stem cells and neuropoiesis in the adult human brain. *Lancet, 359,* 1047–1054.

Steiner, J. M., & Fahrenberg, J. (2000). Authoritarianism and social status of former members of the Waffen-SS and SS and of the Wehrmacht: An extension and reanalysis of the study published in 1970. *Koelner Zeitschrift fuer Soziologie und Sozialpsychologie, 52,* 329–348.

Stepanski, E. J., & Perlis, M. L. (2000). Behavioral sleep medicine. An emerging subspecialty in health psychology and sleep medicine. *Journal of Psychosomatic Research, 49,* 343–347.

Stephan, K. E., Marshall, J. C., Friston, K. J., Rowe, J. B., Ritzl, A., Zilles, K., & Fink, G. R. (2003). Lateralized cognitive processes and lateralized task control in the human brain. *Science, 301,* 384–386.

Stephens, R. S., Roffman, R. A., & Simpson, E. E. (1994). Treating adult marijuana dependence: A test of the relapse prevention model. *Journal of Consulting and Clinical Psychology, 62*(1), 92–99.

Steriade, M., & McCarley, R. W. (1990). *Brainstem control of wakefulness and sleep.* New York: Plenum.

Stern, K., & McClintock, M. K. (1998). Regulation of ovulation by human pheromones. *Nature, 392,* 177–179.

Sternberg, E. M. (2001). Neuroendocrine regulation of autoimmune/inflammatory disease. *Journal of Endocrinology, 169,* 429–435.

Sternberg, R. J. (1985). *Beyond IQ: A triarchic theory of human intelligence.* Cambridge, England: Cambridge University Press.

Sternberg, R. J. (1988a). Triangulating love. In R. J. Sternberg & M. L. Barnes (Eds.), *The psychology of love* (pp. 500–520). New Haven: Yale University Press.

Sternberg, R. J. (1988b). *The triarchic mind.* New York: Cambridge Press.

Sternberg, R. J. (1989). Domain generality versus domain specificity: The life and impending death of a false dichotomy. *Merrill-Palmer Quarterly, 35,* 115–130.

Sternberg, R. J. (1996). *Successful intelligence.* New York: Simon & Schuster.

Sternberg, R. J. (1997a). Construct validation of a triangular love scale. *European Journal of Social Psychology, 27,* 313–335.

Sternberg, R. J. (1999). Ability and expertise: It's time to replace the current model of intelligence. *American Educator Spring 1999,* pp. 10–51.

Sternberg, R. J. (2001). What is the common thread of creativity?: Its dialectical relation to intelligence and wisdom. *American Psychologist, 56,* 360–362.

Sternberg, R. J. (2004). Culture and intelligence. *American Psychologist, 59,* 325–338.

Sternberg, R. J. (Ed.). (2000). *Handbook of human intelligence* (2nd ed.). Cambridge, MA: Cambridge University Press.

Sternberg, R. J., & Dess, N. K. (2001). Creativity for the new millennium. *American Psychologist, 56,* 332.

Sternberg, R. J., & Grigorenko, E. L. (Eds.). (2004a). *Creativity: From potential to realization.* Washington, DC: APA Books.

Sternberg, R. J., & Kaufman, J. C. (1998). Human abilities. *Annual Review of Psychology, 49,* 479–502.

Sternberg, R. J., & Lubart, T. I. (1992). Buy low and sell high: An investment approach to creativity. *Current Directions in Psychological Science, 1*(1), 1–5.

Sternberg, R. J., & O'Hara, L. A. (1999). Creativity and intelligence. In R. J. Sternberg, et al. (Eds.), *Handbook of creativity* (pp. 251–272). New York: Cambridge University Press.

Sternberg, R. J., & Williams, W. M. (1997). Does the graduate record examination predict meaningful success of graduate training of psychologists? A Case Study. *American Psychologist, 52,* 630–641.

Sternberg, R. J., Hojjat, M., & Barnes, M. L. (2001). Empirical tests of aspects of a theory of love as a story. *European Journal of Personality, 15,* 199–218.

Sternberg, R. J., Lautrey, J., & Lubart, T. I. (2003). Where are we in the field of intelligence, how did we get here, and where are we going? In R. J. Sternberg, J. Lautrey, et al. (Eds.), *Models of intelligence: International perspectives* (pp. 3–25). Washington, DC: American Psychological Association.

Sternberg, R. J., Wagner, R. K., Williams, W. M., & Horvath, J. A. (1995). Testing common sense. *American Psychologist, 50,* 912–927.

Stevens, A. (1996). *Private myths: Dreams and dreaming.* Cambridge, MA: Harvard University Press.

Stevens, D. G. (1995, July 29). New Doppler radar off to stormy start. *Chicago Tribune.*

Stevens, J. C., & Hooper, J. E. (1982). How skin and object temperature influence touch sensation. *Perception and Psychophysics, 32,* 282–285.

Stevens, R. (1999, April 21). Personal communication.

Stevenson, H. (1992). *A long way from being number one: What we can learn from East Asia.* Washington, DC: Federation of Behavior, Psychological and Cognitive Sciences.

Stevenson, R. J., & Boakes, R. A. (2003). A mnemonic theory of odor perception. *Psychological Review, 110,* 340–364.

Stewart, L., & Walsh, V. (2002). Congenital amusia: All the songs sound the same. *Current Biology, 12,* R420–421.

Stewart, R. E., DeSimone, J. A., & Hill, D. L. (1997). New perspectives in a gustatory physiology: Transduction, development, and plasticity. *American Journal of Physiology, 272,* C1–C26.

Stewart, R., & Przyborski, S. (2002). Non-neural adult stem cells: Tools for brain repair? *Bioessays, 24,* 708–713.

Stewart, W. F., Ricci, J. A., Chee, E., Hahn, S. R., & Morganstein, D. (2003). Cost of lost productive work time among US workers with depression. *Journal of the American Medical Association, 289,* 3135–3144.

Stewart-Williams, S. (2004). The placebo puzzle: Putting together the pieces. *Health Psychology, 23,* 198–206.

Stewart-Williams, S., & Podd, J. (2004). The placebo effect: Dissolving the expectancy versus conditioning debate. *Psychological Bulletin, 130,* 324–340.

Stice, E., & Fairburn, C. G. (2003). Dietary and dietary-depressive subtypes of bulimia nervosa show differential symptom presentation, social impairment, comorbidity, and course of illness. *Journal of Consulting and Clinical Psychology, 71,* 1090–1094.

Stice, E., & Shaw, H. (2004). Eating disorder prevention programs: A meta-analytic review. *Psychological Bulletin, 130,* 206–227.

Stickgold, R., Malia, A., Maguire, D., Roddenberry, D., & O'Connor, M. (2000). Replaying the game: Hypnagogic images in normals and amnesics. *Science, 290,* 350–353.

Stickgold, R., Rittenhouse, C. D., & Hobson, J. A. (1994). Dream splicing: A new technique for assessing thematic coherence in subjective reports of mental activity. *Consciousness and Cognition, 3*(1), 114–128.

Stillman, J. A. (2002). Gustation: Intersensory experience par excellence. *Perception, 31,* 1491–1500.

Stillwell, M. E. (2002). Drug-facilitated sexual assault involving gamma-hydroxybutyric acid. *Journal of Forensic Science, 47,* 1133–1134.

Stipek, D. J., & Ryan, R. H. (1997). Economically disadvantaged preschoolers: Ready to learn but further to go. *Developmental Psychology, 33,* 711–723.

Stoff, D. M., Breiling, J., & Maser, J. D. (Eds.). (1997). *Handbook of antisocial behavior.* New York: Wiley.

Stone, A., & Valentine, T. (2003). Perspectives on prosopagnosia and models of face recognition. *Cortex, 39,* 31–40.

Stone, J. (2003). Self-consistency for low self-esteem in dissonance processes: The role of self-standards. *Personality and Social Psychology Bulletin, 29,* 846–858.

Stone, J., & Cooper, J. (2001). A self-standards model of cognitive dissonance. *Journal of Experimental Social Psychology, 37,* 228–243.

Stone, L. D., & Pennebaker, J. W. (2002). Trauma in real time: Talking and avoiding online conversations about the death of Princess Diana. *Basic and Applied Social Psychology, 24,* 173–183.

Stoney, C. M., & Finney, M. L. (2000). Social support and stress: Influences on lipid reactivity. *International Journal of Behavioral Medicine, 7,* 111–126.

Stoney, C. M., & Hughes, J. W. (1999). Lipid reactivity among men with a parental history of myocardial infarction. *Psychophysiology, 36,* 484–490.

Stoney, C. M., Bausserman, L., Niaura, R., Marcus, B., & Flynn, M. (1999). Lipid reactivity to stress: II. Biological and behavioral influences. *Health Psychology, 18,* 251–261.

Stoney, C. M., Niaura, R., Bausserman, L., & Matacin, M. (1999). Lipid reactivity to stress: Comparison of chronic and acute stress responses in middle-aged airline pilots. *Health Psychology, 18,* 241–250.

Strain, E. C., Mumford, G. K., Silverman, K., & Griffiths, R. R. (1994). Caffeine dependence syndrome: Evidence from case histories and experimental evaluations. *Journal of the American Medical Association, 272*(13), 1043–1048.

Strathearn, L., Gray, P. H., O'Callaghan, M. J., & Wood, D. O. (2001). Childhood neglect and cognitive development in extremely low birth weight infants: A prospective study. *Pediatrics, 108,* 142–151.

Strayer, D. L., & Johnston, W. A. (2001). Driven to distraction: Dual-task studies of simulated driving and conversing on a cellular phone. *Psychological Science, 12,* 462–466.

Strayer, D. L., Drews, F. A., & Crouch, D. J. (2003). Fatal distraction? A comparison of the cell-phone driver and the drunk driver. In D. V. McGehee, J. D. Lee, & M. Rizzo (Eds.) *Driving Assessment 2003: International symposium on human factors in driver assessment, training, and vehicle design* (pp. 25–30). Iowa City, IA: University of Iowa Public Policy Center.

Strayer, D. L., Drews, F. A., & Johnston, W. A. (2003). Cell phone-induced failures of visual attention during simulated driving. *Journal of Experimental Psychology: Applied, 9,* 23–32.

Strayer, D. L., Drews, F. A., Crouch, D. J., & Johnston, W. A. (2004). Why do cell phone conversations interfere with driving? In W. R. Walker & D. Herrmann (Eds.), *Cognitive technology: Transforming thought and society.* Jefferson, NC: McFarland.

Streissguth, A. P., Barr, H. M., Bookstein, F. L., Sampson, P. D., & Olson, H. C. (1999). The long-term neurocognitive consequences of prenatal alcohol exposure: A 14-year study. *Psychological Science, 10,* 186–190.

Strickland, T., Ranganath, V., Lin, K.-M., Poland, R., Mendoza, R., & Smith, M. (1991). Psychopharmacologic considerations in the treatment of Black American populations. *Psychopharmacology Bulletin, 27,* 441–448.

Strohmetz, D. B., Rind, B., Fisher, R., & Lynn, M. (2002). Sweetening the till: The use of candy to increase restaurant tipping. *Journal of Applied Social Psychology, 32,* 300–309.

Stromberg, C. D., Haggarty, D. J., Leibenluft, R. F., McMillian, M. H., Mishkin, B., et al. (1988). *The psychologist's legal handbook.* Washington, DC: Council for the National Register of Health Service Providers in Psychology.

Stroop, J. R. (1935). Studies of interference in serial verbal reactions. *Journal of Experimental Psychology, 18,* 643–662.

Strupp, H. H., & Hadley, S. W. (1979). Specific versus non-specific factors in psychotherapy. *Archives of General Psychiatry, 36,* 1125–1136.

Stuart, G. J., & Hausser, M. (2001). Dendritic coincidence detection of EPSPs and action potentials. *Nature Neuroscience, 4,* 63–71.

Student Life Education Company Inc. (2005) *Be a zero hero: a presenter's guide to ending impaired driving.* Toronto, ON. www.studentlifeeducation.com/downloads/materials_catalogue.doc

Sturm, R. (2003). Increases in clinically severe obesity in the United States, 1986–2000. *Archives of Internal Medicine, 163,* 2146–2148.

Sturm, R., & Wells, K. B. (2001). Does obesity contribute as much to morbidity as poverty or smoking? *Public Health, 115,* 229–235.

Subrahmanyam, K., & Greenfield, P. M. (1994). Effect of video game practice on spatial skills in girls and boys. *Journal of Applied Developmental Psychology, 15,* 13–32.

Suddath, R. L., Christison, G. W., Torrey, E. F., Casanova, M. F., & Weinberger, D. R. (1990). Anatomical abnormalities in the brains of monopsychotic twins discordant for schizophrenia. *New England Journal of Medicine, 322,* 789–794.

Sue, D. (1992). *Asian and Caucasian subjects' preference for different counseling styles.* Unpublished manuscript, Western Washington University.

Sue, D. W., Bingham, R. P., Porché-Burke, L., & Vasquez, M. (1999). The diversification of psychology: A multicultural revolution. *American Psychologist, 54,* 1061–1069.

Sue, S., & Okazaki, S. (1990). Asian-American educational achievements: A phenomenon in search of an explanation. *American Psychologist, 45,* 913–920.

Sue, S., Zane, N., & Young, K. (1994). Research on psychotherapy with culturally diverse populations. In A. E. Bergin & S. L. Garfield (Eds.), *Handbook of psychotherapy and behavior change.* New York: Wiley.

Suedfeld, P., & Tetlock, P. (2001). Individual differences in information processing. In A. Tesser & N. Schwarz (Eds.), *Blackwell handbook of social psychology: Intraindividual processes* (pp. 284–304). Oxford, England: Blackwell.

Sufka, K. J. & Price, D. D. (2002). Gate control theory reconsidered. *Brain and Mind, 3,* 277–290.

Suh, E., Diener, E., & Fujita, F. (1996). Events and subjective well-being: Only recent events matter. *Journal of Personality and Social Psychology, 70,* 1091–1102.

Suinn, R. M. (2001). The terrible twos: Anger and anxiety. *American Psychologist, 56,* 27–36.

Sullivan, H. S. (1954). *The psychiatric interview.* New York: Norton.

Sullivan, P. F. (1995). Mortality in anorexia nervosa. *American Journal of Psychiatry, 152,* 1073–1074.

Sullivan, P. F., Kendler, K. S., & Neale, M. C. (2003). Schizophrenia as a complex trait: Evidence from a meta-analysis of twin studies. *Archives of General Psychiatry, 60,* 1187–1192.

Suls, J., & Rothman, A. (2004). Evolution of the biopsychosocial model: Prospects and challenges for health psychology. *Health Psychology, 23,* 119–125.

Suls, J., & Wan, C. K. (1993). The relationship between trait hostility and cardiovascular reactivity: A quantitative review and analysis. *Psychophysiology, 30,* 1–12.

Sundberg, N., & Sue, D. (1989). Research and research hypotheses about effectiveness in intercultural counseling. In P. Pederson, J. Draguns, W. Lonner, & J. Trimble (Eds.), *Counseling across cultures* (3rd ed.). Honolulu: University of Hawaii Press.

Suomi, S. (1999). Attachment in rhesus monkeys. In J. Cassidy & P. Shaver (Eds.), *Handbook of attachment* (pp. 181–197). New York: Guilford.

Super, C. M., & Super, D. E. (2001). *Opportunities in psychology careers.* Chicago: VGM Career Books.

Süss, H. M., Oberauer, K., Wittmann, W. W., Wilhelm, O., & Schulze, R. (2002). Working memory explains reasoning ability—and a little bit more. *Intelligence, 30,* 261–288.

Suzdak, P. D., Glowa, J. R., Crawley, J. N., Schwartz, R. D., Skolnick, P., & Paul, S. M. (1986). A selective imidazobenzodiazepine antagonist of ethanol in the rat. *Science, 234,* 1243–1247.

Svartberg, M., Stiles, T. C., & Seltzer, M. H. (2004). Randomized, controlled trial of the effectiveness of short-term dynamic psychotherapy and cognitive therapy for cluster C personality disorders. *American Journal of Psychiatry, 161,* 810–817.

Swaab, D. F., & Hofman, M. A. (1995). Sexual differentiation of the human hypothalamus in relation to gender and sexual orientation. *Trends in Neuroscience, 18*(6) 264–270.

Swaab, D. F., Chung, W. C., Kruijver, F. P., Hofman, M. A., & Ishunina, T. A. (2001). Structural and functional sex differences in the human hypothalamus. *Hormones and Behavior, 40,* 93–98.

Swan, G. E., & Carmelli, D. (1996). Curiosity and mortality in aging adults: A 5-year follow-up of the Western Collaborative Group Study. *Psychology and Aging, 11,* 449–453.

Swarte, N. B., van der Lee, M. L., van der Bom, J. G., van den Bout, J., & Heintz, A. P. M. (2003). Effects of euthanasia on the bereaved family and friends: A cross sectional study. *British Medical Journal, 327,* 189.

Sweller, J., & Gee, W. (1978). Einstellung: The sequence effect and hypothesis theory. *Journal of Experimental Psychology: Human Learning and Memory, 4,* 513–526.

Swets, J. A. (1992). The science of choosing the right decision threshold in high-stakes diagnostics. *American Psychologist, 47,* 522–532.

Swets, J. A. (1996). *Signal detection theory and ROC analysis in psychology and diagnostics.* New Jersey: Erlbaum.

Swets, J. A., Dawes, R. M., & Monahan, J. (2000). Psychological science can improve diagnostic decisions. *Psychological Science in the Public Interest, 1,* 1–26.

Swindle, R., Jr., Heller, K., Pescosolido, B., & Kikuzawa, S. (2000). Responses to nervous breakdowns in America over a 40-year period: Mental health policy implications. *American Psychologist, 55,* 740–749.

Swithers, S. E., & Hall, W. G. (1994). Does oral experience terminate ingestion? *Appetite, 23*(2), 113–138.

Symons, D. (1979). *The evolution of human sexuality.* Oxford, UK: Oxford University Press.

Symons, D. (1995). Beauty is in the adaptations of the beholder: The evolutionary psychology of human female sexual attractiveness. In P. R. Abramson & S. D. Pinkerton (Eds.), *Sexual nature, sexual culture* (pp. 80–118). Chicago: University of Chicago Press.

Szymanski, K., Garczynski, J., & Harkins, S. (2000). The contribution of the potential for evaluation to coaction effects. *Group Processes and Intergroup Relations, 3,* 269–283.

Tabbarah, M., Crimmins, E. M., & Seeman, T. E. (2002). The relationship between cognitive and physical performance: MacArthur studies of successful aging. *Journals of Gerontology: Series A: Biological Sciences and Medical Sciences, 57,* 228–235.

Tagliabue, J. (1999, January 28). Devil gets his due, but Catholic church updates exorcism rites. *International Herald Tribune,* p. 6.

Takayama, Y., Sugishita, M., Kido, T., Ogawa, M., & Akiguchi, I. (1993). A case of foreign accent syndrome without aphasia caused by a lesion of the left precentral gyrus. *Neurology, 43,* 1361–1363.

Takeuchi, A. H., & Hulse, S. H. (1993). Absolute pitch. *Psychological Bulletin, 113,* 345–361.

Tanaka, H., Taira, K., Arakawa, M., Toguti, H., Urasaki, C., Yamamoto, Y., et al. (2001). Effects of short nap and exercise on elderly people having difficulty sleeping. *Psychiatry and Clinical Neurosciences, 55,* 173–174.

Tanaka, J. W. & Curran, T. (2001). A neural basis for expert object recognition. *Psychological Science*, 12, 43–47.

Tanaka, J.W., Curran, T., & Sheinberg, D.L. (2005). The training and transfer of real-world perceptual expertise. *Psychological Science, 16,* 145–151.

Tanaka-Matsumi, J., & Higginbotham, H. N. (1994). Clinical application of behavior therapy across ethnic and cultural boundaries. *Behavior Therapist, 17,* 123–126.

Tanda, G., Pontieri, F. E., & Di Chiara, G. (1997). Cannabinoid and heroin activation of mesolimbic dopamine transmission by a common mu1 opioid receptor mechanism. *Science, 276,* 2048–2050.

Tan-Laxa, M. A., Sison-Switala, C., Rintelman, W., & Ostrea, E. M. (2004). Abnormal auditory brainstem response among infants with prenatal cocaine exposure. *Pediatrics, 113,* 357–360.

Tannen, D. (1994). *Gender and discourse.* New York: Oxford University Press.

Tanner, J. M. (1978). *Foetus into man: Physical growth from conception to maturity.* London: Open Books.

Tansley, B. W and Moggridge, T.P. (2001). Image photometry applied to measuring visual displays. Proceedings of SPIE Vol. 4295 Flat Panel Display Technology and Display Metrology II, 4295B–26.

Tarabar, A. F., & Nelson, L. S. (2004). The gamma-hydroxybutyrate withdrawal syndrome. *Toxicological Reviews, 23,* 45–49.

Tardiff, C.Y. & Geva, E. (2006). The link between acculturation disparity and conflict among Chinese Canadian immigrant mother-adolescent dyads. *Journal of Cross-Cultural Psychology, 37,* 191–211.

Tarr, S. J., & Pyfer, J. L. (1996). Physical and motor development of neonates/infants prenatally exposed to drugs in utero: A meta-analysis. *Adapted Physical Activity Quarterly, 13,* 269–287.

Task Force on Promotion and Dissemination of Psychological Procedures. (1995). Training in and dissemination of empirically validated psychological treatments: Report and recommendations. *Clinical Psychologist, 48,* 3–23.

Tasker, F., & Golombok, S. (1995). Adults raised as children in lesbian families. *American Journal of Orthopsychiatry, 65*(2), 203–215.

Tassi, P., & Muzet, A. (2001). Defining states of consciousness. *Neuroscience and Biobehavioral Reviews, 25,* 175–191.

Taubenfeld, S. M., Milekic, M. H., Monti, B., & Alberini, C. M. (2001). The consolidation of new but not reactivated memory requires hippocampal C/EBPb. *Nature Neuroscience, 4,* 813–818.

Tavris, C. (2002). The high cost of skepticism. *Skeptical Inquirer, 26*(4), 41–44.

Tavris, C. (2003). Mind games: Psychological warfare between therapists and scientists. *The Chronicle of Higher Education, 49,* B7–B9.

Tavris, C. (2004, January 3). *From Dora to Jane Doe: The use and abuse of case studies.* Paper presented at the 26th Annual National Institute on the Teaching of Psychology, St. Petersburg, Florida.

Taylor, H. A., & Tversky, B. (1992). Spatial mental models derived from survey and route descriptions. *Journal of Memory and Language, 31,* 261–292.

Taylor, J. G. (2002). Paying attention to consciousness. *Trends in Cognitive Science, 6,* 206–210.

Taylor, S. (2003). Outcome predictors for three PTSD treatments: Exposure therapy, EMDR, and relaxation training. *Journal of Cognitive Psychotherapy, 17,* 149–161.

Taylor, S. E. (1995). *Health psychology* (3rd ed.). New York: McGraw-Hill.

Taylor, S. E. (1999). *Health psychology* (4th ed.). New York: McGraw-Hill.

Taylor, S. E. (2002). *Health psychology* (5th ed.). New York: McGraw-Hill.

Taylor, S. E., & Aspinwall, L. G. (1996). Mediating processes in psychosocial stress: Appraisal, coping, resistance, and vulnerability. In H. B. Kaplan (Ed.), *Psychosocial stress: Perspectives on structure, theory, life course, and methods* (pp. 71–110). New York: Academic Press.

Taylor, S. E., Dickerson, S. S., & Klein, L. C. (2002). Toward a biology of social support. In C. R. Snyder & S. L. Lopez (Eds.), *Handbook of positive psychology* (pp. 556–569). London: Oxford University Press.

Taylor, S. E., Kemeny, M. E., Reed, G. M., Bower, J. E., & Gruenewald, T. L. (2000a). Psychological resources, positive illusions, and health. *American Psychologist, 55,* 99–109.

Taylor, S. E., Klein, L. C., Lewis, B. P., Gruenewald, T. L., Gurung, R. A. R., & Updegraff, J. A. (2000b). Biobehavioral responses to stress in females: Tend-and-befriend, not fight-or-flight. *Psychological Review, 107,* 411–429.

Taylor, S., Peplau, A. & Sears, R. (2000). *Social psychology* (10th ed.) Upper Saddle, NJ: Prentice-Hall.

Taylor, S., Peplau, A., & Sears, D. (2003). *Social psychology* (11th ed.). Upper Saddle River, NJ: Prentice-Hall.

Tecott, L. H., Sun, L. M., Akana, S. F., Strack, A. M., Lowenstein, D. H., Dallman, M. F., & Julius, D. (1995). Eating disorder and epilepsy in mice lacking 5-HT2C serotonin receptors. *Nature, 374,* 542–546.

Teigen, K. H. (1994). Yerkes-Dodson: A law for all seasons. *Theory and Psychology, 4*(4), 525–547.

Tellegen, A., Lykken, D. T., Bouchard, T. J., Wilcox, K. J., Segal, N. L., & Rich, S. (1988). Personality similarity in twins reared apart and together. *Journal of Personality and Social Psychology, 54,* 1031–1039.

Tenenbaum, H. R., & Leaper, C. (2003). Parent-child conversations about science: The socializations of gender inequities? *Developmental Psychology, 39,* 34–47.

Teng, Y. D., Lavik, E. B., Qu, X., Park, K. I., Ourednik, J., Zurakowski, D., et al. (2002). Functional recovery following traumatic spinal cord injury mediated by a unique polymer scaffold seeded with neural stem cells. *Proceedings of the National Academy of Science, 99,* 3024–3029.

Tepper, B. J., & Ullrich, N. V. (2002). Influence of genetic taste sensitivity to 6-n-propylthiouracil (PROP), dietary restraint and disinhibition on body mass index in middle-aged women. *Physiology and Behavior, 75,* 305–312.

Ter Riet, G., Kleijnen, J., & Knipschild, P. (1990). Acupuncture and chronic pain: A criteria-based meta-analysis. *Journal of Clinical Epidemiology, 43,* 1191–1199.

Terman, J. S., Terman, M., Lo, E. S., & Cooper, T. B. (2001). Circadian time of morning light administration and therapeutic response in winter depression. *Archives of General Psychiatry, 58,* 69–75.

Terman, L. M., & Oden, M. H. (1947). *The gifted child grows up: Vol. 4. Genetic studies of genius.* Stanford, CA: Stanford University Press.

Terman, L. M., & Oden, M. H. (1959). *The gifted group at midlife.* Stanford, CA: Stanford University Press.

Terrace, H. S., Petitto, L. A., Sanders, D. L., & Bever, J. G. (1979). Can an ape create a sentence? *Science, 206,* 891–902.

Tesser, A. (2001). Self-esteem: The frequency of temporal-self and social comparisons in people's personal appraisals. In A. Tesser & N. Schwarz (Eds.), *Blackwell handbook of social psychology: Intraindividual processes* (pp. 479–498). Oxford, UK: Blackwell.

Thaker, G. K., & Carpenter, W. T., Jr. (2001). Advances in schizophrenia. *Nature Medicine, 7,* 667–671.

Thaler, E. R., Kennedy, D. W., & Hanson, C.W. (2001). Medical applications of electronic nose technology: Review of current status. *American Journal of Rhinology, 15,* 291–295.

Thanos, P. K., Volkow, N. D., Freimuth, P., Umegaki, H., Ikari, H., Roth, G., et al. (2001). Overexpression of dopamine D2 receptors reduces alcohol self-administration. *Journal of Neurochemistry, 78,* 1094–1103.

Thase, M. E. (2002). Antidepressant effects: The suit may be small, but the fabric is real. *Prevention & Treatment, 5,* Article 32. Retrieved December 13, 2004, from http://www.journals.apa.org/prevention/volume5/pre0050032c.html

The Department of Justice Canada, FPT Heads of Prosecutions Committee Working Group. *Report on the Prevention of Miscarriages of Justice.* Retrieved March 23, 2006, from http://www.canada.justice.gc.ca/en/dept/pub/hop/index.html

Theeuwes, J., Godijn, R., & Pratt, J. (2004). A new estimation of the duration of attentional dwell time. *Psychonomic Bulletin and Review, 11,* 60–64.

Theofilopoulos, S., Goggi, J., Riaz, S. S., Jauniaux, E., Stern, G. M., & Bradford, H. F. (2001). Parallel induction of the formation of dopamine and its metabolites with induction of tyrosine hydroxylase expression in foetal rat and human cerebral cortical cells by brain-derived neurotrophic factor and glial-cell derived neurotrophic factor. *Brain Research: Developmental Brain Research, 127,* 111–122.

Thom, A., Sartory, G., & Jöhren, P. (2000). Comparison between one-session psychological treatment and benzodiazepine in dental phobia. *Journal of Consulting and Clinical Psychology, 68,* 378–387.

Thomas, A., & Chess, S. (1977). *Temperament and development.* New York: Brunner/Mazel.

Thomas, E. L., & Robinson, H. A. (1972). *Improving reading in every class: A sourcebook for teachers.* Boston: Allyn & Bacon.

Thommasen, H.V., Baggaley, E., Thommasen, C., & Zhang, W. (2005). Prevalence of depression and prescriptions for antidepressants, Bella Coola Valley, 2001. *Canadian Journal of Psychiatry, 50,* 346–352.

Thompson, D. S., & Pollack, B. G. (2001, August 26). Psychotropic metabolism: Gender-related issues. *Psychiatric Times, 14.* Available: http://www.mhsource.com/pt/p010147.html

Thompson, J. K. (1996). Introduction: Assessment and treatment of binge eating disorder. In J. K. Thompson (Ed.), *Body image, eating disorders, and obesity* (pp. 1–22). Washington, DC: American Psychological Association.

Thompson, J. K., & Stice, E. (2001). Thin-ideal internalization: Mounting evidence for a new risk factor for body-image disturbance and eating pathology. *Current Directions in Psychological Science, 10,* 181–183.

Thompson, P. M., Giedd, J. N., Woods, R. P., Macdonald, D., Evans, A. C., & Toga, A. W. (2000). Growth patterns in the developing brain detected by using continuum mechanical tensor maps. *Nature, 404,* 190–193.

Thompson, P. M., Hayashi, K. M., Simon, S. L., Geaga, J. A., Hong, M. S., Sui, Y., et al. (2004). Structural abnormalities in the brains of human subjects who use methamphetamine. *Journal of Neuroscience, 24,* 6028–6036.

Thompson, R. A. (1998). Early sociopersonality development. In W. Damon & N. Eisenberg (Eds.), *Handbook of child psychology: Vol. 3. Social, emotional, and personality development* (5th ed., pp. 25–104). New York: Wiley.

Thompson, S. C., Sobolow-Shubin, A., Galbraith, M. E., Schwankovksy, L., & Cruzen, D. (1993). Maintaining perceptions of control: Finding perceived control in low control circumstances. *Journal of Personality and Social Psychology, 64,* 293–304.

Thompson, W. G. (1995). Coffee: Brew or bane. *American Journal of the Medical Sciences, 308*(1), 49–57.

Thomson, C. P. (1982). Memory for unique personal events: The roommate study. *Memory & Cognition, 10,* 324–332.

Thoreson, C. J., Bradley, J. C., Bliese, P. D., & Thoreson, J. D. (2004). The big five personality traits and individual job performance growth trajectories in maintenance and transitional job stages. *Journal of Applied Psychology, 89,* 835–853.

Thorndike, E. L. (1898). Animal intelligence: An experienced study of the associative process in animals. *Psychological Monographs, 2* (Whole No. 8).

Thorndike, E. L. (1905). *The elements of psychology.* New York: Seiler.

Thorndike, R. L. (1968). [Review of the book *Pygmalion in the classroom*]. *American Educational Research Journal, 5,* 708–711.

Thorndike, R. L., & Hagen, E. P. (1996). *Form 5 CogAT interpretive guide of school administrators: All levels.* Chicago: Riverside.

Thorndike, R. M. & Dinnel, D. L. (2001). *Basic statistics for the behavioral sciences.* Upper Saddle River, NJ: Prentice-Hall.

Thorngren, J. M., & Kleist, D. M. (2002). Multiple family group therapy: An inter-personal/postmodern approach. *Family Journal–Counseling and Therapy for Couples and Families, 10,* 167–176.

Tian, H.-G., Nan, Y., Hu, G., Dong, Q.-N., Yang, X.-L., Pietinen, P., & Nissinen, A. (1995). Dietary survey in a Chinese population. *European Journal of Clinical Nutrition, 49,* 27–32.

Tiihonen, J., Kuikka, J., Bergstrom, K., Hakola, P., Karhu, J., Ryynänen, O.-P., & Föhr, J. (1995). Altered striatal dopamine re-uptake site densities in habitually violent and non-violent alcoholics. *Nature Medicine, 1(7),* 654–657.

Timberlake, W. (1980). A molar equilibrium theory of learned performance. In G. H. Bower (Ed.), *The psychology of learning and motivation* (Vol. 14, pp. 1–58). San Diego: Academic Press.

Timberlake, W., & Farmer-Dougan, V. A. (1991). Reinforcement in applied settings: Figuring out ahead of time what will work. *Psychological Bulletin, 110*(3), 379–391.

Tinbergen, N. (1989). *The study of instinct.* Oxford, UK: Clarendon.

Tindale, R. S., & Kameda, T. (2000). "Social sharedness" as a unifying theme for information processing in groups. *Group Processes and Intergroup Relations, 3,* 123–140.

Todorov, C., Freeston, M. H., & Borgeat, F. (2000). On the pharmacotherapy of obsessive-compulsive disorder: Is a consensus possible? *Canadian Journal of Psychiatry, 45,* 257–262.

Toh, K. L., Jones, C. R., He, Y., Eide, E. J., Hinz, W. A., Virshup, D. M., et al. (2001). An hPer2 phosphorylation site mutation in familial advanced sleep phase syndrome. *Science, 291,* 1040–1043.

Tolman, E. C., & Honzik, C. H. (1930). Introduction and removal of reward and maze performance in rats. *University of California Publication in Psychology, 4,* 257–265.

Tomasello, M. (2000). Culture and cognitive development. Current Directions in Psychological Science, 9, 37–40.

Tomes, H. (1999, April). The need for cultural competence. *APA Monitor,* p. 31.

Toni, N., Buchs, P. A., Nikonenko, I., Bron, C. R., & Muller, D. (1999). LTP promotes formation of multiple spine synapses between a single axon terminal and a dendrite. *Nature, 402,* 421–425.

Torasdotter, M., Metsis, M., Henriksson, B. G., Winblad, B., & Mohammed, A. H. (1998). Environmental enrichment results in higher levels of nerve growth factor mRNA in the rat visual cortex and hippocampus. *Behavior and Brain Research, 93,* 83–90.

Toronto Police Service, 2003. Toronto Murder Statistics for 1998–2003. [Electronic version]. Available: http://www.torontopolice.on.ca/homicide/statistics.php.

Torrens, D., Thompson, V.A., & Cramer, K.M. (1999). Individual differences and the belief bias effect: Mental models, logical necessity, and abstract reasoning. *Thinking and Reasoning, 5, 1–28.*

Townsend, J. M., Kline, J., & Wasserman, T. H. (1995). Low-investment copulation: Sex differences in motivational and emotional reactions. *Ethology and Sociobiology, 16*(1), 25–51.

Trabasso, T. R., & Bower, G. H. (1968). *Attention in learning.* New York: Wiley.

Transport Canada (2003). *Canadian motor vehicle traffic collision statistics.* [Electronic version]. Available: http://www.tc.gc.ca/roadsafety/tp/tp3322/2003/menu.htm

Transport Canada, (2003). What you should know about cell phones and driving: http://www.tc.gc.ca/mediaroom/infosheets/info-cellphones.htm

Treboux, D., Crowell, J. A., & Waters, E. (2004). When "new" meets "old": Configurations of adult attachment representations and their implications for marital functioning. *Developmental Psychology, 40,* 295–314.

Treiber, F. A., Musante, L., Kapuku, G., Davis, C., Litaker, M., & Davis, H. (2001). Cardiovascular (CV) responsivity and recovery to acute stress and future CV functioning in youth with family histories of CV disease: A 4-year longitudinal study. *International Journal of Psychophysiology, 41,* 65–74.

Treisman, A. (1988). Features and objects: The 14th Bartlett memorial lecture. *Quarterly Journal of Experimental Psychology, 40,* 201–237.

Treisman, A. (1999). Feature binding, attention, and object perception. In G. W. Humphreys, J. Duncan., & A. Treisman (Eds.), *Attention, space, and action* (pp. 91–111). New York: Oxford University Press.

Tremblay, A., & Bueman, B. (1995). Exercise-training, macronutrient balance and body weight control. *International Journal of Obesity, 19*(2), 79–86.

Tremblay, R. E., Pagani-Kurtz, L., Mâsse, L., Vitaro, F., & Pihl, R. O. (1995). A bimodal preventive intervention for disruptive kindergarten boys: Its impact through mid-adolescence. *Journal of Consulting and Clinical Psychology, 63,* 560–568.

Tremblay, R. E., Pihl, R. O., Vitaro, F., & Dobkin, P. (1994). Predicting early onset of male antisocial behavior from preschool behavior. *Archives of General Psychiatry, 51,* 732–739.

Triandis, H. C. (1998). Vertical and horizontal individualism and collectivism: Theory and research implications for international management. In J. L. C. Cheng, R. B. Peterson, et al. (Eds.), *Advances in international comparative management* (Vol. 12, pp. 7–35). Stamford, CT: JAI Press.

Triandis, H. C., & Trafimow, D. (2001). Cross-national prevalence of collectivism. In C. Sedikides & M. B. Brewer (Eds.), *Individual self, relational self, collective self* (pp. 259–276). New York: Psychology Press.

Tri-council (2005). *Ethical conduct for research involving humans.* Public Works and Government Services Canada.

Trillin, A. S. (2001, January 29). Betting your life. *New Yorker,* pp. 38–41.

Tronick, E. Z. (1989). Emotions and emotional communication in infants. *American Psychologist, 44,* 112–119.

Troop, L. R., & Wright, S. (2001). In group identification as the inclusion of ingroup in the self. *Personality and Social Psychology Bulletin, 27,* 585–600.

Trope, Y., Cohen, O., & Alfieri, T. (1991). Behavior identification as a mediator of dispositional inference. *Journal of Personality and Social Psychology, 61,* 873–883.

Trower, P. (1995). Adult social skills: State of the art and future directions. In W. O'Donohue & L. Krasner (Eds.), *Handbook of psychological skills training: Clinical techniques and applications* (pp. 54–80). Boston: Allyn & Bacon.

Trujillo, C. M. (1986). A comparative evaluation of classroom interactions between professors and minority and non-minority college students. *American Educational Research Journal, 23,* 629–642.

Trujillo, K. A., & Akil, H. (1991). Inhibition of morphine tolerance and dependence by the NMDA receptor antagonist MK-801. *Science, 251,* 85–87.

Trull, T. J., & Sher, K. J. (1994). Relationship between the five-factor model of personality and Axis I disorders in a nonclinical sample. *Journal of Personality and Social Psychology, 103,* 350–360.

Trunzo, J. J., & Pinto, B. M. (2003). Social support as a mediator of optimisim and distress in breast cancer survivors. *Journal of Consulting and Clinical Psychology, 71,* 805–811.

Truscott, D. & Crook, K. (2004). *Ethics for the practice of psychology in Canada.* Edmonton, AB: University of Alberta Press.

Tseng, W., Kan-Ming, M., Li-Shuen, L., Guo-Qian, C., Li-Wah, O., & Hong-Bo, Z. (1992). Koro epidemics in Guangdong China. *Journal of Nervous and Mental Disease, 180,* 117–123.

Tsuang, M. T., Stone, W. S., & Faraone, S. V. (2000). Toward reformulating the diagnosis of schizophrenia. *American Journal of Psychiatry, 157,* 1041–1950.

Tucker, C. M., & Herman, K. C. (2002). Using culturally sensitive theories and research to meet the academic needs of low-income African American children. *American Psychologist, 57,* 762–773.

Tuckman, B. W. (2003). The effect of learning and motivation strategies training on college students' achievement. *Journal of College Student Development, 4,* 430–437.

Tuller, D. (2004, January 27). Britain poised to approve medicine derived from marijuana. *The New York Times,* p. F5.

Tulving, E. (1983). *Elements of episodic memory.* New York: Oxford University Press.

Tulving, E. (1993). Self-knowledge of an amnesic individual is represented abstractly. In T. K. Srull & R. S. Wyer (Eds.), *The mental representation of trait and autobiographical knowledge about the self: Advances in social cognition* (Vol. 5). Hillsdale, NJ: Erlbaum.

Tulving, E. (2000). Introduction to memory. In M. S. Gazzaniga (Ed.), *The new cognitive neurosciences* (pp. 727–732). Cambridge, MA: MIT Press.

Tulving, E. (2002). Episodic memory: From mind to brain. *Annual Review of Psychology, 53,* 1–25.

Tulving, E., & Psotka, J. (1971). Retroactive inhibition in free recall: Inaccessibility of information available in the memory store. *Journal of Experimental Psychology, 87,* 1–8.

Tulving, E., & Schacter, D. L. (1990). Priming and human memory systems. *Science, 247,* 301–306.

Tulving, E., Hayman, C. A. G., & Macdonald, C. A. (1991). Long-lasting perceptual priming and semantic learning in amnesia: A case experiment. *Journal of Experimental Psychology: Learning, Memory, and Cognition, 17,* 595–617.

Tulving, E., Schacter, D. L., & Stark, H. (1982). Priming effects in word-fragment completion are independent of recognition memory. *Journal of Experimental Psychology: Learning, Memory, and Cognition, 8,* 336–342.

Tuomilehto, J., Lindstrom, J., Eriksson, J. G., Valle, T. T., Hamalainen, H., Ilanne-Parikka, P., et al. (2001). Prevention of type 2 diabetes mellitus by changes in lifestyle among subjects with impaired glucose tolerance. *New England Journal of Medicine, 344,* 1343–1350.

Turati, C. (2004). Why faces are not special to newborns: An alternative account of the face preference. *Current Directions in Psychological Science, 13,* 5–8.

Turiel, E. (1998). The development of morality. In W. Damon & N. Eisenberg (Eds.), *Handbook of child psychology: Vol. 3. Social, emotional, and personality development* (5th ed., pp. 863–932). New York: Wiley.

Turkheimer, E., & Waldron M. (2000). Nonshared environment: A theoretical, methodological, and quantitative review. *Psychological Bulletin, 126,* 78–108.

Turkheimer, E., Haley, A., Waldron, M., D'Onofrio, B., & Gottesman, I. I. (2003). Socioeconomic status modifies heritability of IQ in young children. *Psychological Science, 14,* 623–628.

Turkington, C. (1987). Special talents. *Psychology Today,* pp. 42–46.

Turkkan, J. S. (1989). Classical conditioning: The new hegemony. *Behavioral & Brain Sciences, 12,* 121–179.

Turner, B. G., Beidel, D. C., Hughes, S., & Turner, M. W. (1993). Test anxiety in African-American school children. *School Psychology Quarterly, 8,* 140–152.

Turner, D. C., Robbins, T. W., Clark, L., Aron, A. R., Dowson, J., & Sahakian, B. J. (2003). Cognitive enhancing effects of modafinil in healthy volunteers. *Psychopharmacology (Berlin), 165,* 260–269.

Turner, J. C. (1991). *Social influence.* Pacific Grove, CA: Brooks/Cole.

Turner, R. J., & Lloyd, D. A. (2004). Stress burden and the lifetime incidence of psychiatric disorder in young adults: Racial and ethnic contrasts. *Archives of General Psychiatry, 61,* 481–488.

Turner, S. M., DeMers, S. T., Fox, H. R., & Reed, G. M. (2001). APA's guidelines for test user qualifications: An executive summary. *American Psychologist, 56,* 1099–1113.

Turtle, J., Lindsay, R. C. L., & Wells, G. L. (2003). Best practice recommendations for eyewitness evidence procedures: New ideas for the oldest way to solve a case. *Canadian Journal of Police and Security Services, 1,* 5–18.

Tuszynski, M. H., & Blesch, A. (2004). Nerve growth factor: From animal models of cholinergic neuronal degeneration to gene therapy in Alzheimer's disease. *Progress in Brain Research, 146,* 441–449.

Tversky, A. (1972). Elimination by aspects: A theory of choice. *Psychological Review, 79,* 281–299.

Tversky, A., & Kahneman, D. (1974). Judgment under uncertainty: Heuristics and biases. *Science, 185,* 1124–1131.

Tversky, A., & Kahneman, D. (1981). The framing of decisions and the psychology of choice. *Science, 211,* 453–458.

Tversky, A., & Kahneman, D. (1991). Loss aversion in riskless choice: A reference dependent model. *Quarterly Journal of Economics, 106,* 1039–1061.

Tversky, A., & Kahneman, D. (1993). Probabilistic reasoning. In A. Goldman (Ed.), *Readings in philosophy and cognitive science* (pp. 43–68). Cambridge: MIT Press.

Tversky, B., & Tuchin, M. (1989). A reconciliation of the evidence on eyewitness testimony: Comments on McCloskey and Zaragoza. *Journal of Experimental Psychology: General, 118,* 86–91.

Tyler, R. S., Dunn, C. C., Witt, S. A., & Preece, J. P. (2003). Update on bilateral cochlear implantation. *Current Opinion in Otolaryngological Head and Neck Surgery, 11,* 388–393.

U. S. Bureau of Labor Statistics. (2004). *American Time Use Survey.* Washington, DC: U.S. Department of Labor.

U. S. Department of Health and Human Services. (2001a). *Alzheimer's disease fact sheet.* Washington, DC: U.S. Public Health Service (NIH Publication No. 01–3431).

U. S. Surgeon General. (1999). *Mental health: A report of the surgeon general.* Rockville, MD: U.S. Department of Health and Human Services.

Uchida, Y., Kitayama, S., Mesquita, B., & Reyes, J. A. (2001, June). *Interpersonal sources of happiness: The relative significance in Japan, the Philippines, and the United States.* Paper presented at Annual Convention of American Psychological Society, Toronto, Canada.

Uchino, B. N., Cacioppo, J. T. & Kiecolt-Glaser, J. K. (1996). The relationship between social support and physiological process: A review with emphasis on underlying mechanisms and implications for health. *Psychological Bulletin, 119,* 488–531.

Uchino, B. N., Uno, D., & Holt-Lunstad, J. (1999). Social support, physiological processes, and health. *Current Directions in Psychological Science, 8,* 145–148.

Uhl, G. R., Sora, I., & Wang, Z. (1999). The mu opiate receptor as a candidate gene for pain: polymorphisms, variations in expression, nociception, and opiate responses. *Proceedings of the National Academy of Sciences, 96,* 7752–7755.

Ulett, G. A. (2003). Acupuncture, magic, and make-believe. *The Skeptical Inquirer, 27*(2), 47–50.

Ullian, E. M., Sapperstein, S. K., Christopherson, K. S., & Barres, B. A. (2001). Control of synapse number by glia. *Science, 291,* 657–661.

Ullmann, L. P., & Krasner, L. (1965). *Case studies in behavior modification.* New York: Holt, Rinehart & Winston.

Ungless, M. A., Whistler, J. L., Malenka, R. C., & Bonci, A. (2001). Single cocaine exposure in vivo induces long-term potentiation in dopamine neurons. *Nature, 411,* 583–587.

Urban, N. N. (2002). Lateral inhibition in the olfactory bulb and in olfaction. *Physiology and Behavior, 77,* 607–612.

Urry, H. L., Nitschke, J. B., Dolski, I., Jackson, D. C., Dalton, K. M., Mueller, C. J., et al. (2004). Making a life worth living: Neural correlates of well-being. *Psychological Science, 15,* 367–372.

Valencia-Flores, M., Castano, V. A., Campos, R. M., Rosenthal, L., Resendiz, M., Vergara, P., et al. (1998). The siesta culture concept is not supported by the sleep habits of urban Mexican students. *Journal of Sleep Research, 7,* 21–29.

Valenstein, E. S. (Ed.). (1980). *The psychosurgery debate.* San Francisco: Freeman.

Valenza, E., Simion, F., Assia, V. M., & Umilta, C. (1996). Face preference at birth. *Journal of Experimental Psychology: Human Perception and Performance, 22,* 892–903.

Van Ameringen, M. A., Lane, R. M., Walker, J. R., Bowen, R. C., Chokka, P. R., Goldner, E. M., et al. (2001). Sertraline treatment of generalized social phobia: A 20-week, double-blind, placebo-controlled study. *American Journal of Psychiatry, 158,* 275–281.

Van Bezooijen, R., Otto, S. A., & Heenan, T. A (1983). Recognition of vocal expression of emotion: A three-nation study to identify universal characteristics. *Journal of Cross-Cultural Psychology, 14,* 387–406.

Van der Lely, H. K. J. (1994). Canonical linking rules: Forward versus reverse linking in normally developing and specifically language-impaired children. *Cognition, 51,* 29–72.

Van Essen, D. C., Anderson, C. H., & Felleman, D. J. (1992). Information processing in the primate visual system: An integrated systems perspective. *Science, 255,* 419–423.

van IJzendoorn, M. H. (1995). Adult attachment representations, parental responsiveness, and infant attachment: A meta-analysis on the predictive validity of the Adult Attachment Interview. *Psychological Bulletin, 117,* 387–403.

Van Lange, P. A. M., & Sedikides, C. (1998). Being more honest but not necessarily more intelligent than others: Generality and explanations for the Muhammad Ali effect. *European Journal of Social Psychology, 28,* 675–680.

van Praag, H., Christie, B. R., Sejnowski, T. J., & Gage, F. H. (1999). Running enhances neurogenesis, learning, and long-term potentiation in mice. *Proceedings of the National Academy of Sciences, 96,* 13427–13431.

Van Sickel, A. D. (1992). Clinical hypnosis in the practice of anesthesia. *Nurse Anesthesiologist, 3,* 67–74.

Van Tol, H., Caren, M., Guan, H.-C., Ohara, K., Bunzow, J., Civelli, O., et al. (1992). Multiple dopamine D4 receptor variants in the human population. *Nature, 358,* 149–152.

Van Wel, F., ter Bogt, T., & Raaijmakers, Q. (2002). Changes in the parental bond and the well-being of adolescents and young adults. *Adolescence, 37*(146), 317–333.

VandeCreek, L., Janus, M.-D., Pennebaker, J. W., & Binau, B. (2002). Praying about difficult experiences as self-disclosure to God. *International Journal for the Psychology of Religion,* 12, 29–39.

Vanman, E. J., Saltz, J. L., Nathan, L. R., & Warren, J. A. (2004). Racial discrimination by low-prejudiced whites. *Psychological Science, 15,* 711–714.

Vattano, F. (2000). *The mind: Video teaching modules* (2nd ed.). Fort Collins, CO: Colorado State University and Annenberg/CPB.

Vecera, S. P., Vogel, E. K., & Woodman, G. F. (2002). Lower region: A new cue for figure-ground assignment. *Journal of Experimental Psychology: General, 131,* 194–205.

Velicer, C. M, Heckbert, S. R., Lampe, J. W., Potter, J. D., Robertson, C. A., & Taplin, S. H. (2004). Antibiotic use in relation to the risk of breast cancer. *Journal of the American Medical Association, 291,* 827–835.

Velligan, D. I., Bow-Thomas, C. C., Huntzinger, C., Ritch, J., Ledbetter, N., Prihoda, T. J., & Miller, A. L. (2000). Randomized controlled trial of the use of compensatory strategies to enhance adaptive functioning in outpatients with schizophrenia. *American Journal of Psychiatry, 157,* 1317–1328.

Venter, J. C., et al. (2001). The sequence of the human genome. *Science, 291,* 1304–1351.

Verger, P., Dab, W., Lamping, D. L., Loze, J.-Y., Deschaseaux-Voinet, C., Abenhaim, A., & Rouillon, F. (2004). The psychological impact of terrorism: An epidemiologic study of posttraumatic stress disorder and associated factors in victims of the 1995–1996 bombings in France. *American Journal of Psychiatry, 161,* 1384—1389.

Verghese, J., Lipton, R. B., Katz, M. J., Hall, C. B., Derby, C. A., Kuslansky, G., et al. (2003). Leisure activities and the risk of dementia in the elderly. *New England Journal of Medicine, 348,* 2508–2516.

Vernet, M. E., Robin, O., & Dittmar, A. (1995). The ohmic perturbation duration, an original temporal index to quantify electrodermal responses. *Behavioural Brain Research, 67*(1), 103–107.

Vickers, A. J., Rees, R. W., Zollman, C. E., McCarney, R., Smith, C. M., Ellis, N., Fisher, P., & Van Haselen, R. (2004). Acupuncture for chronic headache in primary care: Large, pragmatic randomised trial. *British Medical Journal, 328,* 744.

Viglione, D. J., & Rivera, B. (2003). Assessing personality and psychopathology with projective methods. In J. R. Graham & J. A. Naglieri (Eds.), *Handbook of psychology: Vol. 10. Assessment psychology* (pp. 531–552). New York: Wiley.

Vincent, C. A., & Richardson, P. H. (1986). The evaluation of therapeutic acupuncture: Concepts and methods. *Pain, 24,* 1–13.

Visser, P. S., Krosnick, J. A., & Lavrakas, P. J. (2000). Survey research. In H. T. Reis & C. Judd (Eds.), *Handbook of research methods in social and personality psychology* (pp. 223–252) Cambridge, UK: Cambridge University Press.

Viswesvaran, C., & Ones, D. S. (2000). Measurement error in "Big Five factors" personality assessment: Reliability generalization across studies and measures. *Educational and Psychological Measurement, 60,* 224–235.

Vitaliano, P. P., Zhang, J. M., & Scanlan, J. M. (2003). Is caregiving hazardous to one's physical health? A meta-analysis. *Psychological Bulletin, 129,* 946–972.

Vocisano, C., Klein, D. N., Arnow, B., Rivera, C., Blalock, J. A., Rothbaum, B., Vivian, D., et al. (2004). Therapist variables that predict symptom change in psychotherapy with chronically depressed outpatients. *Psychotherapy: Theory, Research, Practice, Training, 41,* 255–265.

Vogel, E. K., & Machizawa, M. G. (2004). Neural activity predicts individual differences in visual working memory capacity. *Nature, 428,* 748–751.

Vokey, J. R. (2002). Subliminal messages. In J. R. Vokey & S. W. Allen (Eds.), *Psychological sketches* (6th ed., pp. 223–246). Lethbridge, Alberta, Canada: Psyence Ink.

Vokey, J. R., & Read, J. D. (1985). Subliminal messages: Between the devil and the media. *American Psychologist, 40,* 1231–1239.

Volavka, J., Czobor, P., Sheitman, B., Lindenmayer, J. P., Citrome, L., McEvoy, J. P., et al. (2002). Clozapine, olanzapine, risperidone, and haloperidol in the treatment of patients with chronic schizophrenia and schizoaffective disorder. *American Journal of Psychiatry, 159,* 255–262.

Volkow, N. D., Chang, L., Wang, G. J., Fowler, J. S., Franceschi, D., Sedler, M. J., et al. (2001). Higher cortical and lower subcortical metabolism in detoxified methamphetamine abusers. *American Journal of Psychiatry, 158,* 383–389.

Volpicelli, J. R., Ulm, R. R., Altenor, A., & Seligman, M. E. P. (1983). Learned mastery in the rat. *Learning and Motivation, 14,* 204–222.

Volz, H. P., & Laux, P. (2000). Potential treatment for subthreshold and mild depression: A comparison of St. John's wort extracts and fluoxetine. *Comprehensive Psychiatry, 41,* 133–137.

Volz, J. (2000). Successful aging. The second 50. *APA Monitor,* 31, 24–28.

von Bekesy, G. (1960). *Experiments in hearing.* New York: McGraw-Hill.

Von Wright, J. M., Anderson, K., & Stenman, U. (1975). Generalization of conditioned GSRs in dichotic listening. In P. M. A. Rabbitt & S. Dornic (Eds.), *Attention and performance V.* New York: Academic Press.

Voracek, M., & Fisher, M. L. (2002). Shapely centrefolds? Temporal change in body measures: trend analysis. *British Medical Journal, 325,* 1447–1448.

Vorel, S. R., Liu, X., Hayes, R. J., Spector, J. A., & Gardner, E. L. (2001). Relapse to cocaine-seeking after hippocampal theta burst stimulation. *Science, 292,* 1175–1178.

Vyse, S. A. (2000). *Believing in magic: The psychology of superstition* (2nd ed.) New York: Oxford University Press.

Wachtel, S. R., ElSohly, M. A., Ross, S. A., Ambre, J., & de Wit, H. (2002). Comparison of the subjective effects of Delta-sup-9-tetrahydrocannabinol and marijuana in humans. *Psychopharmacology, 161,* 331–339.

Wadden, T. A., Berkowitz, R. I., Sarwer, D. B., Prus-Wisniewski, R., & Steinberg, C. (2001). Benefits of lifestyle modification in the pharmacologic treatment of obesity: A randomized trial. *Archives of Internal Medicine, 161,* 218–227.

Wade, C. (1988, April). *Thinking critically about critical thinking in psychology.* Paper presented at the annual meeting of the Western Psychological Association, San Francisco, CA.

Wade, T., Martin, N. G., & Tiggemann, M. (1998). Genetic and environmental factors for the weight and shape concerns characteristic of bulimia nervosa. *Psychological Medicine, 28,* 761–771.

Wade, W. A., Treat, T. A., & Stuart, G. L. (1998). Transporting an empirically supported treatment for panic disorder to a service clinic setting: A benchmarking strategy. *Journal of Consulting and Clinical Psychology, 66,* 231–239.

Wadsworth, S. J., Olson, R. K., Pennington, B. F., & DeFries, J. C. (2000). Differential genetic etiology of reading disability as a function of IQ. *Journal of Learning Disabilities, 33,* 192–200.

Waelti, P., Dickinson, A., & Schultz, W. (2001). Dopamine responses comply with basic assumptions of formal learning theory. *Nature, 412,* 43–48.

Wager, T. D., Rilling, J. K., Smith, E. E., Sokolik, A., Casey, K. L., Davidson, R. J., et al. (2004). Placebo-induced changes in fMRI in the anticipation and experience of pain. *Science, 303,* 1162–1167.

Wagner, A. D. (1999). Working memory contributions to human learning and remembering. *Neuron, 22,* 19–22.

Wagner, K. D., Ambrosini, P., Rynn, M., Wohlberg, C., Yang, R., Greenbaum, M.S., et al. (2003). Efficacy of sertraline in the treatment of children and adolescents with major depressive disorder: Two randomized controlled trials. *Journal of the American Medical Association, 290,* 1033–1041.

Wagner, U., Gais, S., & Born, J. (2001). Emotional memory formation is enhanced across sleep intervals with high amounts of rapid eye movement sleep. *Learning and Memory, 8,* 112–119.

Wagner, U., Gais, S., Haider, H., Verleger, R., & Born, J. (2004). Sleep inspires insight. *Nature, 427,* 352–355.

Wahlsten, D. (1997). Leilani Muir versus the philosopher king: Eugenics on trial in Alberta. *Genetica, 99,* 185–198.

Wakefield, J. C. (1999). Evolutionary versus prototype analyses of the concept of disorder. *Journal of Abnormal Psychology, 108,* 374–399.

Walbeck, K., Forsen, T., Osmond, C., Barker, D. J., & Ericksson, J. G. (2001). Association of schizophrenia with low maternal body mass index, small size at birth, and thinness during childhood. *Archives of General Psychiatry, 58,* 48–52.

Walberg, H. J. (1987). Studies show curricula efficiency can be attained. *NASSP Bulletin, 71,* 15–21.

Waldrop, M. M. (1987). The working of working memory. *Science, 237,* 1564–1567.

Walker, E. F., & Diforio, D. (1998). Schizophrenia: A neural diathesis-stress model. *Psychological Review, 104,* 667–685.

Walker, L. (1991). The feminization of psychology. *Psychology of Women Newsletter of Division, 35,* 1, 4.

Walker, L. J. (1989). A longitudinal study of moral reasoning. *Child Development, 60,* 157–166.

Walker, L. J. (1995). Sexism in Kohlberg's moral psychology? In W. M. Kurtines & J. L. Gewirtz (Eds.), *Moral development: An introduction* (pp. 83–107). Boston: Allyn & Bacon.

Walker, L.J., Gustafson, P., & Hennig, K.H. (2001). The consolidation/transition model in moral reasoning development. *Developmental Psychology, 37,* 187–197.

Walkup, J. T., Labellarte, M. J., Riddle, M. A., Pine, D. S., Greenhill, L., Klein, R., et al. (2001). Fluvoxamine for the treatment of anxiety disorders in children and adolescents. *The New England Journal of Medicine, 344,* 1279–1285.

Wallace, R. K., & Benson, H. (1972). The physiology of meditation. *Scientific American, 226,* 84–90.

Wallen, K., & Lovejoy, J. (1993). Sexual behavior: Endocrine function and therapy. In J. Shulkin (Ed.), *Hormonal pathways to mind and brain.* New York: Academic Press.

Wallerstein, R. S. (2002). The growth and transformation of American ego psychology. *Journal of the American Psychoanalytic Association, 50,* 135–169.

Wallis, G., & Bülthoff, H. H. (2001). Effects of temporal association on recognition memory. *Proceedings of the National Academy of Sciences, 98*(8), 4800–4804.

Wallis, J. D., Anderson, K. C., & Miller, E. K. (2001). Single neurons in prefrontal cortex encode abstract rules. *Nature, 411,* 953–956.

Wallman, J., Gottlieb, M. D., Rajaram, V., & Fugate-Wentzek, L. A. (1987). Local retinal regions control local eye growth and myopia. *Science, 237,* 73–76.

Walton, G. E., Bower, N. J. A., & Bower, T. G. R. (1992). Recognition of familiar faces by newborns. *Infant Behavior and Development, 15,* 265–269.

Wampold, B. E., Lichtenberg, J. W., & Waehler, C. A. (2002). Principles of empirically supported interventions in counseling psychology. *Counseling Psychologist, 30,* 197–217.

Wanek, J. E., Sackett, P. R., & Ones, D. S. (2003). Towards an understanding of integrity test similarities and differences: An item-level analysis of seven tests. *Personnel Psychology, 56,* 873–894.

Wang, C., Collet, J. P., & Lau, J. (2004). The effect of Tai Chi on health outcomes in patients with chronic conditions: A systematic review. *Archives of Internal Medicine, 164,* 493–501.

Wang, X., Merzenich, M. M., Sameshima, K., & Jenkins, W. M. (1995). Remodelling of hand representation in adult cortex determined by timing of tactile stimulation. *Nature, 378,* 71–75.

Warburton, D. M. (1995). Effects of caffeine on cognition and mood without caffeine abstinence. *Psychopharmacology, 119,* 66–70.

Ward, C. (1994). Culture and altered states of consciousness. In W. J. Lonner & R. S. Malpass (Eds.), *Psychology and culture.* Boston: Allyn & Bacon.

Warrington, E. K., & Weiskrantz, L. (1970). The amnesic syndrome: Consolidation of retrieval? *Nature, 228,* 626–630.

Watanabe, K., & Shimojo, S. (2001). When sound affects vision: Effects of auditory grouping on visual motion perception. *Psychological Science, 12,* 109–116.

Watanabe, S., Sakamoto, J., & Wakita, M. (1995). Pigeons' discrimination of paintings by Monet and Picasso. *Journal of Experimental Analysis of Behavior, 63,* 165–174.

Watanabe, T., Náñez, J. E., & Sasaki, Y. (2001). Perceptual learning without perception. *Nature, 413,* 844–848.

Waterman, A. S. (1982). Identity development from adolescence to adulthood: An extension of theory and a review of research. *Developmental Psychology, 18,* 341–358.

Waters, E., Merrick, S., Treboux, D., Crowell, J., & Albersheim, L. (2000). Attachment security in infancy and early adulthood: A twenty-year longitudinal study. *Child Development, 71,* 684–689.

Watkins, L. R., & Maier, S. F. (2003). When good pain turns bad. *Current Directions in Psychological Science, 12,* 232–235.

Watson, J. B. (1913). Psychology as the behaviorist views it. *Psychological Review, 20,* 158–177.

Watson, J. B. (1919). *Psychology from the standpoint of a behaviorist.* Philadelphia: Lippincott.

Watson, J. B. (1925). *Behaviorism.* London: Kegan Paul, Trench, Trubner.

Watt, N. F., & Saiz, C. (1991). Longitudinal studies of premorbid development of adult schizophrenics. In E. F. Walker (Ed.), *Schizophrenia: A life-course in developmental perspective* (pp. 157–192). San Diego, CA: Academic Press.

Wearden, A. J., Tarrier, N., Barrowclough, C., Zastowny, T. R., & Rahill, A. A. (2000). A review of expressed emotion research in health care. *Clinical Psychology Review, 20,* 633–666.

Wechsler, D. (1939). *The measurement of adult intelligence.* Baltimore: Williams & Wilkins.

Wechsler, D. (1949). *The Wechsler Intelligence Scale for Children.* New York: Psychological Corporation.

Wechsler, D. (2003). *Wechsler Intelligence Scale for Children* (4th ed.). San Antonio, TX: Psychological Corporation.

Weekes, J. R., Lynn, S. J., Green, J. P., & Brentar, J. T. (1992). Pseudomemory in hypnotized and task-motivated subjects. *Journal of Abnormal Psychology, 101,* 356–360.

Wegner, D. M., Fuller, V. A. & Sparrow, B. (2003) Clever hands: Uncontrolled intelligence in facilitated communication. *Journal of Personality and Social Psychology, 85,* 5–19.

Wegner, D. M., Wenzlaff, R. M., & Kozak, M. (2004). Dream rebound: The return of suppressed thoughts in dreams. *Psychological Science, 15,* 232–236.

Weiler, B. L., & Widom, C. S. (1996). Psychopathy and violent behavior in abused and neglected young adults. *Criminal Behaviour and Mental Health, 6,* 253–271.

Weinberg, J., & Levine, S. (1980). Psychobiology of coping in animals: The effects of predictability. In S. Levine & H. Ursin (Eds.), *Coping and health.* New York: Plenum.

Weinberg, R. A. (1989). Intelligence and IQ: Landmark issues and great debates. *American Psychologist, 44,* 98–104.

Weinberg, R. A., Scarr, S., & Waldman, I. D. (1992). The Minnesota transracial adoption study: A follow-up of IQ test performance at adolescence. *Intelligence, 16,* 117–135.

Weiner, B. (1980). *Human motivation.* New York: Holt, Rinehart & Winston.

Weiner, B. (1993). On sin versus sickness: A theory of perceived responsibility and social motivation. *American Psychologist, 48*(9), 957–965.

Weinfield, N. S., Sroufe, L. A., & Egeland, B. (2000). Attachment from infancy to early adulthood in a high-risk sample: continuity, discontinuity, and their correlates. *Child Development, 71,* 695–702.

Weinraub, M., Horvath, D. L., & Gringlas, M. B. (2002). Single parenthood. In M. H. Bornstein (Ed.), *Handbook of parenting: Vol. 3. Being and becoming a parent* (2nd ed., pp. 109–140). Mahwah, NJ: Erlbaum.

Weinstein, D. (1999, July 24). Who are you? *Sunday Telegraph Magazine,* pp. 24–26.

Weiskrantz, L. (2004). Roots of blindsight. *Progress in Brain Research, 144,* 229–241.

Weiss, B., & Weisz, J. R. (1995). Relative effectiveness of behavioral versus nonbehavioral child psychotherapy. *Journal of Consulting and Clinical Psychology, 63,* 317–320.

Weiss, F., Ciccocioppo, R., Parsons, L. H., Katner, S., Liu, X., Zorrilla, E. P., et al. (2001). Compulsive drug-seeking behavior and relapse: Neuro-adaptation, stress, and conditioning factors. *Annals of the New York Academy of Science, 937,* 1–26.

Weissberg, R. P., Kumpfer, K. L., & Seligman, M. E. P. (2003). Prevention that works for children and youth. *American Psychologist, 58,* 425–432.

Weissman, M. M., Bland, R., Joyce, P. R., Newman, S., Wells, J. E., & Wittchen, H. U. (1993). Sex differences in rates of depression: Cross-national perspectives. *Journal of Affective Disorders, 29,* 77–84.

Weissman, M. M., Markowitz, J. C., & Klerman, G. L. (2000). *Comprehensive guide to interpersonal psychotherapy.* New York: Basic Books.

Weisstein, N., & Harris, C. S. (1974). Visual detection of line segments: An object superiority effect. *Science, 186,* 752–755.

Weisz, J. R., & Jensen, P. S. (1999). Efficacy and effectiveness of psychotherapy and pharmacotherapy with children and adolescents. *Mental Health Services Research, 1,* 125–157.

Weisz, J. R., Weiss, B., Han, S. S., Granger, D. A., & Morton, T. (1995). Effects of psychotherapy with children and adolescents revisited: A meta-analysis of treatment outcome studies. *Psychological Bulletin, 117,* 450–468.

Wells, G. L., & Bradfield, A. L. (1999). Distortions in eyewitness' recollections: Can the postidentification-feedback effect be moderated? *Psychological Science, 10,* 138–144.

Wells, G. L., & Olson, E. A. (2003). Eyewitness testimony. *Annual Review of Psychology, 54,* 277–295.

Wells, G. L., Olson, E. A., & Charman, S. D. (2002). The confidence of eyewitnesses in their identifications from lineups. *Current Directions in Psychological Science, 11,* 151–154.

Weltzin, T. E., Bulik, C. M., McConaha, C. W., & Kaye, W. H. (1995). Laxative withdrawal and anxiety in bulimia nervosa. *International Journal of Eating Disorders, 17*(2), 141–146.

Werker, J. F. & Tees, R.C. (1999). Influences on infant speech processing: Toward a new synthesis. *Annual Review of Psychology, 50,* 509–535.

Werner, E. (2003, January 28). Police: Sons kill mom, dismember her after seeing it done on "The Sopranos." *Naples Daily News.*

Wertheimer, M. (1987). *A brief history of psychology* (3rd ed.). New York: Holt, Rinehart & Winston.

Wesensten, N. J., Belenky, G., Kautz, M. A., Thorne, D. R., Reichardt, R. M., & Balkin, T. J. (2002). Maintaining alertness and performance during sleep deprivation: Modafinil versus caffeine. *Psychopharmacology (Berlin), 159,* 238–247.

Westen, D. (1998). The scientific legacy of Sigmund Freud: Toward a psychodynamically informed psychological science. *Psychological Bulletin, 124,* 333–371.

Westen, D., & Gabbard, G. O. (1999). Psychoanalytic approaches to personality. In L. Pervin & O. John (Eds), *Handbook of personality: Theory and research* (2nd ed., pp. 57–101). New York: Guilford.

Westen, D., & Morrison, K. (2001). A multidimensional meta-analysis of treatments for depression, panic, and generalized anxiety disorder: An empirical examination of the status of empirically supported therapies. *Journal of Consulting and Clinical Psychology, 69,* 875–899.

Westmaas, J. L., & Silver, R. C. (2001). The role of attachment in responses to victims of life crises. *Journal of Personality and Social Psychology, 80,* 425–438.

Weston, C., & Went, F. (1999). Speaking up for yourself: Description and evaluation of an assertiveness training program for people with learning disabilities. *Mental Handicap, 27,* 110–115.

Weuve, J., Kang, J. H., Manson, J. E., Breteler, M. M. B., Ware, J. H., & Grodstein, F. (2004). Physical activity, including walking, and cognitive function in older women. *Journal of the American Medical Association, 292,* 1454–1461.

Whalen, P. J. (1998). Fear, vigilance, and ambiguity: Initial neuroimaging studies of the human amygdala. *Current Directions in Psychological Science, 7,* 177–188.

Whalley, L. J., Starr, J. M., Athawes, R., Hunter, D., Pattie, A., & Deary, I. J (2000). Childhood mental ability and dementia. *Neurology, 55,* 1455–1459.

Wharton, C. M., Grafman, J., Flitman, S. S., Hansen, E. K., Brauner, J., Marks, A., & Honda, M. (2000). Toward neuroanatomical models of analogy: A positron emission tomography study of analogical mapping. *Cognitive Psychology, 40,* 173–197.

Wheeler, S. C., & Petty, R. E. (2001). The effects of stereotype activation on behavior: A review of possible mechanisms. *Psychological Bulletin, 127,* 797–826.

Whimbey, A. (1976). *Intelligence can be taught.* New York: Bantam.

Whincup, P. H., Gilg, J. A., Emberson, J. R., Jarvis, M. J., Feyerabend, C., Bryant, A., et al. (2004). Passive smoking and risk of coronary heart disease and stroke: Prospective study with cotinine measurement. *British Medical Journal, 329,* 200–205.

Whisman, M. A. (1999). Marital dissatisfaction and psychiatric disorders: Results from a national comorbidity study. *Journal of Abnormal Psychology, 108,* 701–706.

Whitam, F. L., Diamond, M., & Martin, J. (1993). Homosexual orientation in twins: A report on 61 pairs and three triplet sets. *Archives of Sexual Behavior, 22*(3), 187–206.

Whitbourne, S. K., Zuschlag, M. K., Elliot, L. B., & Waterman, A. D. (1992). Psychosocial development in adulthood: A 22-year sequential study. *Journal of Personality and Social Psychology, 63,* 260–271.

White, D. E., & Glick, J. (1978). *Competence and the context of performance.* Paper presented at the meeting of the Jean Piaget Society, Philadelphia.

White, F. J. (1998). Nicotine addiction and the lure of reward. *Nature Medicine, 4,* 659–660.

White, P., Lewith, G., Hopwood, V., & Prescott, P. (2003). The placebo needle: Is it a valid and convincing placebo for use in acupuncture trials? A randomised, single-blind, cross-over pilot trial. *Pain, 106,* 401–409.

Whitman, T. L., Borkowski, J. G., Keogh, D. A., & Week, K. (2001). *Interwoven lives: Adolescent mothers and their children.* Mahwah, NJ: Lawrence Erlbaum.

Whitney, P. (2001). Schemas, frames, and scripts in cognitive psychology. In N. J. Smelser & P. B. Baltes (Eds.), *International encyclopedia of the social and behavioral sciences.* The Netherlands: Elsevier.

Whittlesea, B.W.A. & Leboe, J.P. (2000). The heuristic basis of remembering and classification: Fluency, generation, and resemblance. *Journal of Experimental Psychology: General, 129, 84–106.*

Whorf, B. L. (1956). *Language, thought, and reality.* Cambridge/New York: MIT Press/Wiley.

Wible, C. G., Anderson, J., Shenton, M. E., Kricun, A., Hirayasu, Y., Tanaka, S., et al. (2001). Prefrontal cortex, negative symptoms, and schizophrenia: An MRI study. *Psychiatry Research, 108, 65–78.*

Wickens, C. D. (1992). *Engineering psychology and human performance* (2nd ed.) New York: HarperCollins.

Wickens, C. D. (2002). Situation awareness and workload in aviation. *Current Directions in Psychological Science, 11,* 128–133.

Wickens, C. D., & Carswell, C. M. (1997). Information processing. In G. Salvendy (Ed.), *Handbook of human factors and ergonomics* (2nd ed., pp. 89–122). New York: Wiley Interscience.

Wickens, C. D., Gordon, S. E., & Liu, Y. (1998). *An introduction to human factors engineering.* New York: Longman.

Wickens, C. D., Stokes, A., Barnett, B., & Hyman, F. (1992). The effects of stress on pilot judgment in a MIDIS simulator. In O. Svenson & J. Maule (Eds.), *Time pressure and stress in human judgment and decision making* (pp. 271–292). New York: Plenum.

Wickham, D. (2001, September 3). Castration often fails to halt offenders. *USA Today.*

Widiger, T. A. (1997). The construct of mental disorder. *Clinical Psychology: Science and Practice, 4,* 262–266.

Widom, C. S. (1989) The cycle of violence. *Science, 244,* 160–166.

Widom, C. S. (2000). Childhood victimization: Early adversity, later psychopathology. *National Insitute of Justice Journal, 19,* 2–9.

Wiedenfeld, S., O'Leary, A., Bandura, A., Brown, S., Levine, S., & Raska, K. (1990). Impact of perceived self-efficacy in coping with stressors on components of the immune system. *Journal of Personality and Social Psychology, 59,* 1082–1094.

Wiens, S., Mezzacappa, E. S., & Katkin, E. S. (2000). Heartbeat detection and the experience of emotions. *Cognition & Emotion, 14,* 417–427.

Wiertelak, E. P., Maier, S. F., & Watkins, L. R. (1992). Cholecystokinin antianalgesia: Safety cues abolish morphine analgesia. *Science, 256,* 830–833.

Wigfield, A., & Eccles, J. S. (2000). Expectancy-value theory of achievement motivation. *Contemporary Educational Psychology, 25,* 68–81.

Wilcoxon, H. C., Dragoin, W. B., & Kral, P. A. (1971). Illness-induced aversions in rat and quail: Relative salience of visual and gustatory cues. *Science, 171,* 826–828.

Willams, R. B. (2001). Hostility and heart disease: Williams et al. (1980). *Advances in Mind-Body Medicine, 17, 52–55.*

Williams, G. V., & Goldman-Rakic, P. S. (1995). Modulation of memory fields by dopamine D1 receptors in prefrontal cortex. *Nature, 376, 572–575.*

Williams, J. E., & Best, D. L. (1990). *Measuring stereotypes: A multination study* (Rev. ed.). Newbury Park, CA: Sage.

Williams, K. D., & Sommer, K. L. (1997). Social ostracism by coworkers: Does rejection lead to loafing or compensation? *Personality and Social Psychology Bulletin, 23,* 693–706.

Williams, L. M. (1994). What does it mean to forget child sexual abuse? A reply to Loftus, Garry, and Feldman (1994). *Journal of Consulting and Clinical Psychology, 62,* 1182–1186.

Williams, T. J., Pepitone, M. E., Christensen, S. E., Cooke, B. M., Huberman, A. D., Breedlove, N. J., et al. (2000). Finger-length ratios and sexual orientation. *Nature, 404,* 455–456.

Willis, S. L., & Schaie, K. W. (1999). Intellectual functioning in midlife. In S. L. Willis & J. D. Reid (Eds.), *Life in the middle: Psychological and social development in middle age* (pp. 233–247). San Diego, CA: Academic Press.

Willis, W. D., Jr. (1988). Dorsal horn neurophysiology of pain. *Annals of the New York Academy of Science, 531,* 76–89.

Wills, T. A., Sandy, J. M., Yaeger, A., & Shinar, O. (2001). Family risk factors and adolescent substance use: Moderation effects oft temperament dimension. *Developmental Psychology, 37,* 283–297.

Wilson, A. E., & Ross, M. (2000). The frequency of temporal-self and social comparisons in people's personal appraisals. *Journal of Personality and Social Psychology, 78,* 928–942.

Wilson, G. T. (1985). Limitations of meta-analysis in the evaluation of the effects of psychological therapy. *Clinical Psychology Review, 5,* 35–47.

Wilson, G. T. (1995). Behavior therapy. In R. J. Corsini & D. Wedding (Eds.), *Current psychotherapies* (5th ed., pp. 197–228). Itasca, IL: Peacock.

Wilson, G. T. (1997). Dissemination of cognitive behavioral treatments: Commentary. *Behavior Therapy, 28,* 473–475.

Wilson, G. T., Loeb, K. L., Walsh, B. T., Labouvie, E., Petkova, E., Liu, X., & Waternaux, C. (1999). Psychological versus pharmacological treatments of bulimia nervosa: Predictors and processes of change. *Journal of Consulting and Clinical Psychology, 67,* 451–459.

Wilson, G. T., Nathan, P. E., O'Leary, K. D., & Clark, L. A. (1996). *Abnormal psychology.* Boston: Allyn & Bacon.

Winemiller, M. H., Billow, R. G., Laskowski, E. R., & Harmsen, W. S. (2003). Effect of magnetic vs sham-magnetic insoles on plantar heel pain: A randomized controlled trial. *Journal of the American Medical Association, 290,* 1474–1478.

Winer, G. A., Cottrell, J. E., Gregg, V., Fournier, J. S., & Bica, L. A. (2002). Fundamentally misunderstanding visual perception: Adults' belief in visual emissions. *American Psychologist, 57,* 417–424.

Winkielman, P., & Berridge, K. C. (2004). Unconscious emotion. *Current Directions in Psychological Science, 13,* 120–123.

Winkielman, P., Bernston, G. G., & Cacioppo, J. T. (2001). The psychophysiological perspective on the social mind. In A. Tesser & N. Schwarz (Eds.), *Blackwell handbook of social psychology: Intraindividual processes* (pp. 89–109). Oxford, UK: Blackwell.

Winner, E. (2000). Giftedness: Current theory and research. *Current Directions in Psychological Science, 9,* 153–156.

Winson, J. (1990, November). The meaning of dreams. *Scientific American,* pp. 86–96.

Winter, D. G. (1996). *Personality: Analysis and interpretation of lives.* New York: McGraw-Hill.

Wise, R. A., & Rompre, P. P. (1989). Brain dopamine and reward. *Annual Review of Psychology, 40,* 191–225.

Wiseman, R., West, D., & Stemman, R. (1996, January/February). Psychic crime detectives: A new test for measuring their successes and failures. *Skeptical Inquirer, 21,* 38–58.

Witkiewitz, K., & Marlatt, G. A. (2004). Relapse prevention for alcohol and drug problems: That was Zen, this is Tao. *American Psychologist, 59,* 224–235.

Witt, S. D. (1997). Parental influence on children's socialization to gender roles. *Adolescence, 32,* 253–259.

Wittchen, H. U., & Hoyer, J. (2001). Generalized anxiety disorder: Nature and course. *Journal of Clinical Psychiatry, 62,* 15–19.

Wittchen, H. U., Zhao, S., Kessler, R. C., & Eaton, W. W. (1994). *DSM-III-R:* Generalized anxiety disorder in the national comorbidity survey. *Archives of General Psychiatry, 51,* 355–364.

Wittgenstein, L. (1953). *Philosophical investigations.* New York: Macmillan.

Wixted, J. T. (2004). The psychology and neuroscience of forgetting. *Annual Review of Psychology, 55,* 235–269.

Woelk, H. (2000). Comparison of St. John's wort and imipramine for treating depression: Randomised controlled trial. *British Medical Journal, 321,* 536–539.

Wohl, J. (1995). Traditional individual psychotherapy and ethnic minorities. In J. F. Aponte, R. Y. Rivers, & J. Wohl (Eds.), *Psychological interventions and cultural diversity* (pp. 74–91). Boston: Allyn & Bacon.

Wohlfarth, T., Storosum, J. G., Elferink, A. J. A., van Zweiten, B. J., Fouwels, A., & van den Brink, W. (2004). Response to tricyclic antidepressants: Independent of gender? *American Journal of Psychiatry, 161,* 370–372.

Wolf, H., Angleitner, A., Spinath, F., Reimann, R., & Strelau, J. (2004). Genetic and environmental influences on the EPQ-RS scales: A twin study using self- and peer-reports. *Personality and Individual Differences. 37,* 579–590.

Wolfe, J. M. (1998). What can 1 million trials tell us about visual search? *Psychological Science, 9,* 33–39.

Wolfe, J. M., Alvarez, G. A., & Horowitz, T. S. (2000). Attention is fast but volition is slow. *Nature, 406,* 691.

Wolman, C., van den Broek, P., & Lorch, R. F. (1997). Effects of causal structure and delayed story recall by children with mild mental retardation, children with learning disabilities, and children without disabilities. *Journal of Special Education.*

Wolpe, J. (1958). *Psychotherapy by reciprocal inhibition.* Stanford, CA: Stanford University Press.

Wolpe, J., & Plaud, J. J. (1997). Pavlov's contributions to behavior therapy: The obvious and the not so obvious. *American Psychologist, 52,* 966–972.

Wong, B. Y. L. (1986). Metacognition and special education: A review of a view. *Journal of Special Education, 20,* 9–29.

Wong, C. G., Gibson, K. M., & Snead, O. C. (2004). From the street to the brain: Neurobiology of the recreational drug gamma-hydroxybutyric acid. *Trends in Pharmacological Science, 25,* 29–34.

Wong, S. E., Martinez-Diaz, J. A., Massel, H. K., Edelstein, B. A., Wiegand, W., Bowen, L., & Liberman, R. P (1993). Conversational skills training with schizophrenic inpatients: A study of generalization across settings and conversants. *Behavior Therapy, 24,* 285–304.

Wood, W. (2000). Attitude change: Persuasion and social influence. *Annual Review of Psychology, 51,* 539–570.

Wood, W., & Eagly, A. H. (2002). A cross-cultural analysis of the behavior of women and men: Implications for the origins of sex differences. *Psychological Bulletin, 128,* 699–727.

Wood, W., Wong, F. Y., & Chachere, G. (1991). Effects of media violence on viewers' aggression in unconstrained social interaction. *Psychological Bulletin, 109,* 371–383.

Woodcock, R. W., McGrew, K. S., & Mather, N. (2001). *Woodcock-Johnson III Tests of Cognitive Abilities.* Itasca, IL: Riverside.

Woodhead, M. (1988). When psychology informs public policy: The case of early childhood intervention. *American Psychologist, 43,* 443–454.

Woodworth, R. S., & Schlosberg, H. (1954). *Experimental psychology.* New York: Holt.

Woolfolk-Hoy, A. (1999). Psychology applied to education. In A. Stec & D. Bernstein (Eds.), *Psychology: Fields of application* (pp. 61–81). Boston: Houghton Mifflin.

Woolley, J. D. (1997). Thinking about fantasy: Are children fundamentally different thinkers and believers from adults? *Child Development, 68,* 991–1011.

Worchel, S., Cooper, J., Goethals, G. R., & Olson, J. (2000). *Social psychology.* Belmont, CA: Wadsworth.

World Health Organization Mental Health Survey Consortium. (2004). Prevalence, severity, and unmet need for treatment of mental disorders in the World Health Organization World Mental Health Surveys. *Journal of the American Medical Association, 291,* 2581–2590.

World Health Organization. (2002a). *Nutrition: Controlling the global obesity epidemic.* Retrieved December 13, 2004, from http:www.who.int/nut/obs.htm

World Health Organization. (2002b). *WHO collaborative project on psychological problems in general health care.* Retrieved August 27, 2003, from http://www.who.int/msa/mnh/ems/primacare/ppghc/ppghc.htm

World Health Organization. (2003). *AIDS epidemic update.* Geneva, Switzerland: WHO.

Wren, C. S. (1998, September 22). For crack babies, a future less bleak. *New York Times.* Retrieved December 13, 2004, from http://query.nytimes.com/gst/abstract.html?res=F40715FA3B540C718EDDA00894D0494D81

Wren, C. S. (1999, February 24). U.N. drug board urges research on marijuana as medicine. *New York Times.* Retrieved December 13, 2004, from http://query.nytimes.com/gst/abstract.html?res=F10A13F83A590C778EDDAB0894D1494D81

Wright, B. A., & Fitzgerald, M. B. (2001). Different patterns of human discrimination learning for two interaural cues to sound location. *Proceedings of the National Academy of Science, 98,* 12307–12312.

Wright, B. A., & Zecker, S. G. (2004). Learning problems, delayed development, and puberty. *Proceedings of the National Academy of Sciences, 101,* 9942–9946.

Wright, E. F., Voyer, D., Wright, R. D., & Roney, C. (1995). Supporting audiences and performance under pressure: The home-ice disadvantage in hockey championships. *Journal of Sport Behavior, 18,* 21–28.

Wurtman, R. J., & Wurtman, J. J. (1995). Brain serotonin, carbohydrate-craving, obesity and depression. *Obesity Research, 3* (Suppl. 4), 477S–480S.

Wyer, R. S., Jr. (2004). The cognitive organization and use of general knowledge. In J. T. Jost & M. R. Banaji (Eds.), *Perspectivism in social psychology: The yin and yang of scientific progress* (pp. 97–112). Washington, DC: American Psychological Association.

Yaffe, K., Barnes, D., Nevitt, M., Lui, L.-Y., & Covinsky, K. (2001). A prospective study of physical activity and cognitive decline in elderly women. *Archives of Internal Medicine, 161,* 1703–1708.

Yakimovich, D., & Saltz, E. (1971). Helping behavior: The cry for help. *Psychonomic Science, 23,* 427–428.

Yalom, I. D. (1995). Stimulus-driven attentional capture. *Current Directions in Psychological Science, 2,* 156–161.

Yamaguchi, S., Isejima, H., Matsuo, T., Okura, R., Yagita, K., Kobayashi, M., & Okamura, H. (2003). Synchronization of cellular clocks in the suprachiasmatic nucleus. *Science, 302,* 1408–1412.

Yang, C.-M. & Spielman, A. J. (2001). The effect of delayed weekend sleep pattern on sleep and morning functioning. *Psychology and Health, 16,* 715–725.

Yantis, S. (1993). Stimulus-driven attentional capture. *Current Directions in Psychological Science, 2,* 156–161.

Yela, C., & Sangrador, J. L. (2001). Perception of physical attractiveness throughout loving relationships. *Current Research in Social Psychology, 6,* 57–75.

Yesavage, J. A., Leirer, V. O., Denari, M., & Hollister, L. E. (1985). Carry-over effects of marijuana intoxication on aircraft pilot performance: A preliminary report. *American Journal of Psychiatry, 142,* 1325–1329.

Yesavage, J. A., Mumenthaler, M. S., Taylor, J. L., Friedman, L., O'Hara, R., Sheikh, J., et al. (2002). Donepezil and flight simulator performance: Effects on retention of complex skills. *Neurology, 59,* 123–125.

Yonas, A., Arterberry, M. E., & Granrud, C. D. (1987). Space perception in infancy. In R. Vasta (Ed.), *Annals of child development* (Vol. 4, pp. 1–34). Greenwich, CT: JAI Press.

Yonkers, K., Kando, J., Cole, J., & Blumenthal, S. (1992). Gender differences in pharmacokinetics and pharmacodynamics of psychotropic medication. *American Journal of Psychiatry, 149,* 587–595.

York, J. L., & Welte, J. W. (1994). Gender comparisons of alcohol consumption in alcoholic and nonalcoholic populations. *Journal of Studies on Alcohol, 55*(6), 743–750.

Yoshimasu, K., Washio, M., Tokunaga, S., Tanaka, K., Liu, Y., Kodama, H., et al. (2002). Relation between Type A behavior pattern and the extent of coronary atherosclerosis in Japanese women. *International Journal of Behavioral Medicine, 9,* 77–93.

Young, M. (1971). Age and sex differences in problem solving. *Journal of Gerontology, 26,* 331–336.

Young, T. J. (1993). Parricide rates and criminal street violence in the United States: Is there a correlation? *Adolescence, 28,* 171–172.

Young, T., Skatrud, J., & Peppard, P. E. (2004). Risk factors for obstructive sleep apnea in adults. *Journal of the American Medical Association, 291,* 2013–2016.

Youniss, J., & Yates, M. (1997). *Community service and social responsibility in youth.* Chicago: University of Chicago Press.

Younkin, S. G. (2001). Amyloid beta vaccination: reduced plaques and improved cognition. *Nature Medicine, 7,* 18–19.

Yukl, G. A., Latham, G. P., & Purcell, E. D. (1976). The effectiveness of performance incentives under continuous and variable ratio schedules of reinforcement. *Personnel Psychology, 29,* 221–232.

Zadnik, K. (2001). Association between night lights and myopia: True blue or a red herring? *Archives of Ophthalmology, 119,* 146.

Zahn-Waxler, C., Friedman, R. J., Cole, P. M., Mizuta, I., & Hiruma, N. (1996). Japanese and United States preschool children's responses to conflict and distress. *Child Development, 67,* 2462–2477.

Zahn-Waxler, C., Radke-Yarrow, M., Wagner, E., & Chapman, M. (1992). Development of concern for others. *Developmental Psychology, 28,* 1038–1047.

Zajonc, R. B. (1965). Social facilitation. *Science, 149,* 269–274.

Zajonc, R. B. (1998). Emotions. In D. Gilbert, S. T. Fiske, & G. Lindzey (Eds.), *Handbook of social psychology* (Vol. 1, 4th ed., pp. 591–634). Boston: McGraw-Hill.

Zajonc, R. B. (2001). Mere exposure: A gateway to the subliminal. *Current Directions in Psychological Science, 10,* 224–228.

Zakzanis, K. K., & Young, D. A. (2001). Memory impairment in abstinent MDMA ("Ecstasy") users: A longitudinal investigation. *Neurology, 56,* 966–969.

Zammit, S., Allebeck, P., Andreasson, S., Lundberg, I., & Lewis, G. (2002). Self reported cannabis use as a risk factor for schizophrenia in Swedish conscripts of 1969: Historical cohort study. *British Medical Journal, 325,* 1199.

Zammit, S., Allebeck, P., Dalman, C., Lundberg, I., Hemmingson,T., Owen, M. J., & Lewis, G. (2003). Paternal age and risk for schizophrenia. *British Journal of Psychiatry, 183,* 405–408.

Zaragoza, M. S., Payment, K. E., Ackil, J. K., Drivdahl, S. B., & Beck, M. (2001). Interviewing witnesses: Forced confabulation and confirmatory feedback increase false memories. *Psychological Science, 12,* 473–477.

Zarbatany, L., Hartmann, D. P., & Rankin, D. B. (1990). The psychological functions of preadolescent peer activities. *Child Development, 61,* 1067–1080.

Zarbatany, L., McDougall, P., & Hymel, S. (2000) Gender-differentiated experience in the peer culture: Links to intimacy in preadolescence. *Social Development, 9,* 62–79.

Zatorre, R. J. (2003a). Absolute pitch: A model for understanding the influence of genes and development on neural and cognitive function. *Nature Neuroscience, 6,* 692–695.

Zatorre, R. J. (2003b). Music and the brain. *Annals of the New York Academy of Sciences, 999,* 4–14.

Zeki, S. (1992). The visual image in mind and brain. *Scientific American, 267,* 68–76.

Zelenski, J. M., & Larsen, R. J. (1999). Susceptibility to affect: A comparison of three taxonomies. *Journal of Personality, 67,* 761–791.

Zeman, A. (2001). Consciousness. *Brain, 124,* 1263–1289.

Zernike, K. (2000, October 3). Colleges shift emphasis on drinking. *New York Times.*

Zhang, G., & Simon, H. A. (1985). STM capacity for Chinese words and idioms: Chunking and acoustical loop hypothesis. *Memory & Cognition, 13,* 193–201.

Zhang, Y., Hoon, M. A., Chandrashekar, J., Mueller, K. L., Cook, B., Wu, D., et al. (2003). Coding of sweet, bitter, and umami tastes: Different receptor cells sharing similar signaling pathways. *Cell, 112,* 293–301.

Zhao, M., Momma, S., Delfani, K., Carlen, M., Cassidy, R. M., Johansson, C. B., et al. (2003). Evidence for neurogenesis in the adult mammalian substantia nigra. *Proceedings of the National Academy of Sciences, 100,* 7925–7930.

Zhou, L., Yang, W., Liao, S., & Zou, H. (2000). A comparative study of event-related potentials between simulated crime condition and criminal field visiting condition in lie detection. *Chinese Journal of Clinical Psychology, 8,* 86–88.

Zhou, Q., Eisenberg, N., Wang, Y., & Reiser, M. (2004). Chinese children's effortful control and dispositional anger/frustration relations to parenting styles and children's social functioning. *Developmental Psychology, 40,* 352–366.

Zigler, E. F., & Muenchow, S. (1992). *Head Start: The inside story of America's most successful educational experiment.* New York: Basic Books.

Zigler, E., & Seitz, V. (1982). Social policy and intelligence. In R. J. Sternberg (Ed.), *Handbook of human intelligence* (pp. 586–641). Cambridge, UK: Cambridge University Press.

Zigler, E., Taussig, C., & Black, K. (1992). Early childhood intervention: A promising preventive for juvenile delinquency. *American Psychologist, 47,* 997–1006.

Zillmann, D. (1984). *Connections between sexuality and aggression.* Hillsdale, NJ: Erlbaum.

Zimbardo, P. G. (1973). The psychological power and pathology of imprisonment. In E. Aronson & R. Helmreich (Eds.), *Social psychology.* New York: Van Nostrand.

Zimbardo, P. G. (2004). Does psychology make a significant difference in our lives? *American Psychologist, 59,* 339–351.

Zimmerman, B. J., & Schunk, D. H. (2003). Albert Bandura: The scholar and his contributions to educational psychology. In B. J. Zimmerman (Ed,), *Educational psychology: A century of contributions* (pp. 431–457). Mahwah, NJ: Erlbaum.

Zimmerman, M., McDermut, W., & Mattia, J. I. (2000). Frequency of anxiety disorders in psychiatric outpatients with major depressive disorder. *American Journal of Psychiatry, 157,* 1337–1340.

Zimmerman, M., Reischl, T., Seidman, E., Rappaport, J., Toro, P., & Salem, D. (1991). Expansion strategies of a mutual help organization. *American Journal of Community Psychology, 19,* 251–279.

Zinbarg, R. E., & Barlow, D. H. (1996). Structure of anxiety and the anxiety disorders: A hierarchical model. *Journal of Abnormal Psychology, 105,* 181–193.

Zinbarg, R. E., & Mineka, S. (1991). Animal models of psychopathology: II. Simple phobia. *The Behavior Therapist, 14,* 61–65.

Zoellner, L. A., Foa, E. B., Brigidi, B. D., & Przeworski, A. (2000). Are trauma victims susceptible to "false memories"? *Journal of Abnormal Psychology, 109,* 517–524.

Zornberg, G. L., & Pope, H. G., Jr. (1993). Treatment of depression in bipolar disorder: New directions for research. *Journal of Clinical Psychopharmacology, 13,* 397–408.

Zorumski, C., & Isenberg, K. (1991). Insights into the structure and function of GABA-benzodiazepine receptors: Ion channels and psychiatry. *American Journal of Psychiatry, 148,* 162–173.

Zou, Z., Horowitz, L. F., Montmayeur, J.-P., Snapper, S., & Buck, L. B. (2001). Genetic tracing reveals a stereotyped sensory map in the olfactory cortex. *Nature, 414,* 173–179.

Zucker, A. N., Ostrove, J. M., & Stewart, A. J. (2002). College-educated women's personality development in adulthood: Perceptions and age differences. *Psychology & Aging, 17*(2), 236–244.

Zuckerman, M. (1979). *Sensation seeking: Beyond the optimal level of arousal.* Hillsdale, NJ: Erlbaum.

Zuckerman, M. (1984). Sensation seeking: A comparative approach to a human approach. *Behavioral and Brain Sciences, 7,* 413–471.

Zuckerman, M. (1996). "Conceptual clarification" or confusion in "The study of sensation seeking" by J. S. H. Jackson and M. Maraun. *Personality and Individual Differences, 21,* 111–114.

Zuckerman, M. (1998). Psychobiological theories of personality. In D. F. Barone, M. Hersen, & V. B. Hasselt (Eds.), *Advanced personality* (pp. 123–154). New York: Plenum.

Zuckerman, M. (2004). The shaping of personality: Genes, environments, and chance encounters. *Journal of Personality Assessment, 82,* 11–22.

Zuercher-White, E. (1997). *Treating panic disorder and agoraphobia: A step-by-step clinical guide.* Oakland, CA: New Harbinger.

Zuger, A. (1998, July 28). A fistful of aggression is found among women. *New York Times,* pp. B8, B12.

Zurada, J. M. (1995). *Introduction to artificial neural systems.* Boston: PWS.

CREDITS

PHOTOGRAPHS

Chapter 1: p. 1: Digital Vision/RF/Getty Images. **p. 3:** CP/Montreal Star. **p. 5:** Photograph courtesy of www.baddesigns.com. **p. 6:** © Tom Stewart/Corbis. **p. 7 (top):** Lucidio Studio Inc./Corbis. **p. 7 (bottom):** © Charles Gupton/Corbis. **p. 12 (top):** Alinari Archives/Corbis. **p. 12 (bottom):** Archivio Iconografico, S.A./Corbis. **p. 13:** Psychology Archives—The University of Akron. **p. 14:** HUP-SF Psychological Lab pf, courtesy of the Harvard University Archives. **p. 17:** Courtesy of Wellesley College Archives, photo by Partridge. **p. 18:** Michael Newman/PhotoEdit. **p. 19:** Photodisc. **p. 20 (top):** © Bob Daemmrich/The Image Works. **p. 20 (bottom):** © Richard T. Nowitz/Corbis. **p. 24:** © Francis Dean/The Image Works. **p. 26:** Images.com/Corbis.

Chapter 2: p. 30: Photodisc. **p. 31:** Mason Morfitt/Getty Images. **p. 34 (top):** Eric Bean/Getty Images. **p. 34 (bottom):** David Young-Wolff/PhotoEdit. **p. 35:** Everett Collection. **p. 36:** AP Images/CO, Kevin Frazer. **p. 39:** Gabe Palmer/Corbis. **p. 42 (top):** AP/Wide World Photos. **p. 42 (bottom):** Photodisc. **p. 43:** CP/COC/Mike Ridgewood. **p. 45:** CP/Johantha Hayword. **p. 47:** Bettmann/Corbis. **p. 50:** Bob Daemmrich/Stock, Boston, LLC. **p. 53:** Robin Nelson/PhotoEdit. **p. 54:** A. Ramey/PhotoEdit.

Chapter 3: p. 57: John Allison/Peter Arnold/Alamy. **p. 63:** Micrograph produced by John E. Heuser of Washington University School of Medicine. **p. 66:** CP/Chuck Stoody. **p. 68:** Don Fawcett/Photo Researchers, Inc. **p. 70:** CP/Montreal Star. **p. 71:** Canadian Press wirephoto. **p. 72:** Levin et al.(1989). "The brain: Integrated three-dimensional display of MR and PET Images." *Radiology*, 172:783–789. **p. 73:** From "New findings of the correlation between acupoints and corresponding brain cortices using functional MRI," by Cho et al, Proceedings of the National Academy of Sciences, Vol.95, March 1998, page 2671. **p. 74:** CP/Ted-Rhodes. **p. 76:** Courtesy of Brenda Milner. **p. 77:** © Dr. D. Dickson/Peter Arnold, Inc. **p. 78:** Klunk et al, "Imaging brain amyloid in Alzheimer's disease with Pittsburgh Compound-B," *Annals of Neurology* 2004; 55: 306–319. Reprinted with permission of John Wiley & Sons, Inc. **p. 83 (top):** The Cleveland FES Center at the Cleveland VA Medical Center and Case Western University. **p. 83 (bottom):** Bob Daemmrich/Stock, Boston, LLC. **p. 85:** © Dan McCoy/Rainbow. **p. 98:** © Tom Brakefield/Corbis. **p. 100:** Terry Wild Studio.

Chapter 4: p. 104: RF/image 100/Corbis. **p. 108:** RF/Perry Mastrovito/Corbis. **p. 110:** Photo provided by NCT Group, Inc., Stamford, CT. **p. 113:** "Scanning electron micrographs," by Robert Preston and Joseph E. Hawkins, Kresge Hearing Research Institute, University of Michigan. **p. 114:** Jazz Sign/Lebrecht/The Image Works. **p. 115:** David Young-Wolff/PhotoEdit. **p. 120:** Courtesy of Dr. Frank Schaeffel. **p. 121:** Omikron/Photo Researchers, Inc. **p. 125:** Bettmann/Corbis. **p. 128:** Fritz Goro/Getty Images. **p. 133:** © Gary Braasch. **p. 135:** Omikron/Photo Researchers, Inc. **p. 136:** L.M. Bartoshuk and V.B. Duffy. **p. 140:** Alain Evrard/Photo Researchers, Inc. **p. 141:** J.D.Sloane/Index Stock Imagery. **p. 142:** © Reuters/Corbis. **p. 143:** © Bob Daemmrich/The Image Works. **p. 144:** Chris Cole/Getty Images.

Chapter 5: p. 150: Chris Cole/Getty Images. **p. 153:** Stephen R. Swinburne/Stock, Boston, LLC. **p. 157:** Rick Gayle Studio/Corbis. **p. 159:** Farrell Grehan/Photo Researchers, Inc. **p. 163:** © Frank Whitney/Rainbow. **p. 166 (top):** AP/Wide World Photos. **p. 166 (bottom):** Donald Weber/Getty Images. **p. 167 (top):** Ira Kirschenbaum/Stock, Boston, LLC. **p. 167 (bottom):** RF/Photo Bliss/Alamy. **p. 169:** Courtesy George Eastman House. **p. 170:** Phillip Kent/www.anamorphosis.com. **p. 175:** CP/Kingston-Whig – Standard – Ian MacAlpine. **p. 176:** © Esbin-Anderson/The Image Works. **p. 179:** Mark Richards/PhotoEdit. **p. 184:** Courtesy Ron Rensink, University of British Columbia. **p. 186:** © Larry Mulvehill/Rainbow. **p. 187:** Photodisc.

Chapter 6: p. 190: Eyewire. **p. 193:** Jean Heguy/First Light/Getty Images. **p. 198 (top):** CP/Adrian Brown. **p. 198 (bottom):** © Steven Needham/Envision. **p. 200:** DeWitt Jones/Corbis. **p. 202 (left):** Archives of the History of American Psychology—The University of Akron. **p. 202 (right):** Nina Leen/Getty Images. **p. 205:** Frank Lotz Miller/Black Star. **p. 206:** © Bob Daemmrich/The Image Works. **p. 207:** Rick Smolan/Stock, Boston, LLC. **p. 208:** Courtesy of the Lincoln Electric Company. **p. 210:** CP/Mike Ridewood. **p. 212:** Lang and Melamed, 1969. **p. 214:** Lawrence Migdale/Stock, Boston, LLC. **p. 215:** CP/Larry MacDougal. **p. 219:** *The Mentality of Apes* by W. Kohler, 1976, courtesy of Routledge. **p. 220:** Jon Brennels/Time and Life Pictures/Getty Images. **p. 220:** Paul Chesley/Getty Images. **p. 221:** Albert Bandura, Stanford University. **p. 225:** Charles Gupton/Stock, Boston, LLC. **p. 226:** M. Ferguson/PhotoEdit. **p. 227 (top):** CP/Hamilton Spectator/Ron Albertson. **p. 227 (bottom):** Rhoda Sidney/Stock, Boston, LLC.

Chapter 7: p. 231: Gary S. Chapman/Getty Images. **p. 234:** Mary Kate Denny/Getty Images. **p. 235:** © Jeff Greenberg/The Image Works. **p. 239:** Frank Siteman/Stock, Boston, LLC. **p. 243:** AP/Wide World Photos. **p. 245:** Photo by Susan Schwartzenberg, © Franco Magnani. **p. 247:** Bob Daemmrich/PhotoEdit. **p. 251:** Todd Warshae/Getty Images. **p. 255:** AP/Wide World Photos. **p. 258:** Paul Conklin. **p. 261:** Courtesy of Professor Dominique Muller. **p. 264:** Paul Gilham/Getty Images. **p. 266:** © Robert Burke Photography.

Chapter 8: p. 270: Eyewire. **p. 273:** Vincent Besnault/Getty Images. **p. 274:** CP/Steve White. **p. 275:** CP/Kevin Frayer. **p. 276:** From *Cognitive Psychology and its Implications* by John R. Anderson ©2000, 1995, 1985, 1980, by Worth Publishers and W.H. Freeman and Company. **p. 277 (left):** NASA. **p. 277 (right):** Joe Sohm/Stock, Boston, LLC. **p. 278:** Courtesy of Rick Tobias. **p. 284:** Jason Homa/Getty Images. **p. 285:** AFP/Getty Images. **p. 287:** CP/Robert Taylor. **p. 289:** Wharton et al, "Toward neuroanatomical models of analogy: A positron tomography study of analogical mapping." *Cognitive Psychology*, Vol. 40, No. 3, May 1 2000. **p. 295:** CP/Ian Jackson. **p. 302:** © Eastcott/Momatiuk/The Image Works. **p. 304:** © Joe McNally/Corbis Sygma. **p. 307:** © Jeff Greenberg/Rainbow. **p. 310:** Ronald H. Cohn/The Gorilla Foundation/koko.org.

Chapter 9: p. 315: Royalty Free/Photodisc/Getty Images. **p. 316:** © David Welling/Animals Animals. **p. 324:** Will & Deni McIntyre/Photo Researchers, Inc. **p. 327:** © Bob Daemmrich/The Image Works. **p. 328:** David Young-Wolff/PhotoEdit. **p. 329:** Reuters/Corbis. **p. 330:** Patrick Ward/Stock, Boston, LLC. **p. 334:** David Parker/Photo Researchers, Inc. **p. 335:** Grant Mason/Manni Mason's Pictures. **p. 336:** CP/Winnepeg Free Press/Phil Hossack. **p. 340:** Photo by Jules Asher at NIMH. **p. 341:** Kenneth Murray/Photo Researchers, Inc. **p. 343:** PACHA/Corbis. **p. 344:** © Larry Mulvehill/The Image Works. **p. 345:** © 1994 Joel Gordon. **p. 346:** Don MacKinnon/Getty Images.

Chapter 10: p. 351: Steve Prezant/Corbis. **p. 356:** Copyright © 2004 by The Riverside Publishing Company. All rights reserved. Photograph reproduced with permission of the publisher. **p. 360:** Paul Darrow/Corbis. **p. 366:** CP/Hamilton Spectator/Cathie Coward. **p. 371:** Charles Gupton/Corbis. **p. 374:** Hulton Deutsch/Corbis. **p. 376:** © Skjold/The Image Works. **p. 380:** CP/Jean Baptiste Benavent. **p. 381:** Edison National Historic Site.

Chapter 11: p. 384: Bob Daemmrich/PhotoEdit. **p. 385:** CP Photo. **p. 386:** Fabrina Griffin/AFP/Getty Images. **p. 388:** Dwight Kuhn. **p. 389:** CP/Ryan Remiorz. **p. 390:** © Okoniewski/The Image Works. **p. 395:** Richard Howard. **p. 397:** Jamie Marshall-Tribaleye Images. **p. 398:** CP/Aaron Harris. **p. 403:** Mary Kate Denny/PhotoEdit. **p. 406:** Jorge Uzon/Corbis. **p. 408:** AP Images/Matt Dunham. **p. 410:** Reprinted with permission of the publisher from Henry. A. Murray, *Thematic Apperception Test,* Cambridge, Mass.: Harvard University Press, Copyright © 1943 by the President and

Fellows of Harvard College. © 1971. **p. 413:** David Joel/Getty Images. **p. 416:** © Kathy McLaughtlin/The Image Works. **p. 418:** Filippo Monteforte/Getty Images. **p. 424:** Bob Daemmrich/The Image Works. **p. 428 (left):** Eastcott/Momatiuk/Woodfin Camp. **p. 428 (middle):** Rick Smolan/Stock, Boston, LLC. **p. 428 (right):** Jonathan Blair/Woodfin Camp.

Chapter 12: p. 433: CP/Toronto Sun/Veronica Henn. **p. 436:** © Les Stone/Corbis Sygma. **p. 437:** Bettmann/Corbis. **p. 438:** Lennart Nilsson/Albert Bonniers Forlag AB, *Behold Man*, Little Brown and Company. **p. 440:** Charles A. Nelson, Ph.D., Institute of Child Development, University of Minnesota. **p. 441:** Petit Format/J. DaCunha/Photo Researchers, Inc. **p. 444:** ©George S. Zimbel 2004. **p. 445:** Courtesy of Carolyn Rovee-Collier. **p. 448:** © Pedrick/The Image Works. **p. 453:** © Jose Polleross/The Image Works. **p. 454:** © Jim Craigmyle/Corbis. **p. 456:** Martin Rogers/Stock, Boston, LLC. **p. 457:** Michael Newman/PhotoEdit. **p. 459:** © B. Mahoney/The Image Works. **p. 463:** David Grossman/Photo Researchers, Inc. **p. 465:** Jeff Greenberg/Photo Researchers, Inc. **p. 466:** AP/Wide World Photos. **p. 470:** CP/Ryan Remiorz. **p. 476:** Steve Liss/Getty Images. **p. 479:** Michael Newman/PhotoEdit. **p. 480:** CP/Frank Gunn.

Chatper 13: p. 485: Eyebyte/Alamy. **p. 487:** Lori Adamski Peek/Getty Images. **p. 489 (top):** Smiley N. Pool/Corbis. **p. 489 (middle):** Bill Alkofer/Corbis/Sygma. **p. 489 (bottom):** AP Images/Phil Cole. **p. 490:** Marcel Mahlerbe/The Image Works. **p. 494:** AP/Wide World Photos. **p. 495:** Photofest. **p. 496:** CP/Ryan Remiorz. **p. 497:** AP Images/PA. **p. 500:** © Lauren Greenfield/Corbis Sygma. **p. 506:** Boehringer Ingelheim, International GmbH/photo Lennart Nilsson, *The Incredible Machine*, National Geographic Society. **p. 507:** Bruce Ayres/Getty Images. **p. 508:** © Esbin-Anderson/The Image Works. **p. 513:** © Gustavo Gilabert/Corbis.

Chapter 14: p. 518: Nano Calvo/VW/The Image Works. **p. 520:** Mary Evans Picture Library. **p. 523:** Bob Daemmrich/Stock, Boston, LLC. **p. 524:** © Bettmann/Corbis. **p. 527:** John Neubauer/PhotoEdit. **p. 530:** Robert Caputo/Aurora. **p. 532:** Bruce Plotkin/Getty Images. **p. 534:** CP/Jonathan Hayward. **p. 538:** © Michael Childers/Corbis Sygma. **p. 539:** AP Images/ Canadian Press/Aaron Harris. **p. 541:** Steve Kagan/Getty Images. **p. 543:** AP/Wide World Photos. **p. 548:** Charlotte Miller.

Chapter 15: p. 552: Erich Lessing/Art Resource. **p. 555:** CP/National Archives of Canada. **p. 556 (top):** Bill Bachmann/PhotoEdit. **p. 556 (bottom):** © J.L. Dugas/Corbis Sygma. **p. 557:** © Corbis. **p. 564 (top):** CP/Calgary Sun/Carlos Amar. **p. 564 (bottom):** Reuters/Corbis. **p. 565:** Mitchell Gerber/Corbis. **p. 568 (top):** Photodisc. **p. 568 (bottom):** Dr. Susan Mineka. **p. 571:** Photofest. **p. 574:** CP/Fred Chartrand. **p. 575 (top):** Anthony Redpath/Corbis. **p. 575 (bottom):** Laura Farr/ZUMA/Corbis. **p. 577:** © Dan McCoy/Rainbow. **p. 581 (top):** Dr. Silbersweig/E. Stern/Cornell Medical Center. **p. 581 (bottom):** Grunnitus/Photo Researchers, Inc. **p. 584:** National Institute of Mental Health. **p. 587:** Hillsboro County Sheriff, Tampa, Florida.

Chapter 16: p. 592: Simon Maras/Corbis. **p. 594:** Stock Montage. **p. 595:** © Hank Morgan/Rainbow. **p. 596:** Edmund Engelman. **p. 597:** M. Grecco/Stock, Boston, LLC. **p. 599:** Michael Rougier/Getty Images. **p. 601:** Zigy Kaluzny/Getty Images. **p. 602:** Georgia Tech Photo by Gary Meek. **p. 606:** Udo Kroener/Alamy. **p. 608:** Institute for Rational-Emotive Therapy. **p. 610:** James Wilson/Woodfin Camp. **p. 619:** Spencer Grant/PhotoEdit. **p. 621:** CP/Edmonton Sun/Robert Taylor. **p. 622:** The Medical History Museum of the University of Zurich. **p. 623:** Will & Deni McIntyre/Photo Researchers, Inc. **p. 625:** Mario Tama/Getty Images.

Chapter 17: p. 635: Ben Rice/Photonica/Getty Images. **p. 637:** AP/Wide World Photos. **p. 639:** Reuters/Corbis. **p. 640:** Banana Stock/Alamy. **p. 642 (top):** Michael Newman/PhotoEdit. **p. 642 (bottom):** © Tom McCarthy/ Rainbow. **p. 644:** Peter Ginter. **p. 645:** © Bob Daemmrich/The Image Works. **p. 647:** David Woo/Stock, Boston, LLC. **p. 653:** Joshua Correll. **p. 654:** Bonnie Kamin/PhotoEdit. **p. 655:** Robert Brenner/PhotoEdit. **p. 658:** Michelle Bridwell/PhotoEdit. **p. 660:** © D.P.A./The Image Works. **p. 662:** AP/ Wide World Photos. **p. 663:** Reynolds/The Image Works. **p. 664:** Reuters/Corbis. **p. 665 (top):** Jeff Palmer/AFP/Getty Images. **p. 665 (bottom):** L'osservatore Romano - Vatican Pool/Getty Images. **p. 669:** David Young-Wolff/PhotoEdit. **p. 670:** From the film *Obedience* © 1965 by Stanley Milgram and distributed by Penn State Media Sales.**p. 672 (top):** John Chiasson/Getty Images. **p. 672 (bottom):** AP Images/Canadian Press/Jacques Boissinot. **p. 673:** © Mark Ludak/The Image Works. **p. 675:** © Ellen Senisi/The ImageWorks. **p. 676:** Benali/Getty Images. **p. 679:** Mark C. Burnett/Photo Researchers, Inc.

TEXT CREDITS

Figure 1.2, p. 4: From *Developmental Psychology: Theory, Research and Applications,* 1st edition by Shaffer. © 1985. Reprinted with permission of Wadsworth, a division of Thomson Learning: www.thomsonrights.com. Fax 800 730-2215. **Figure 1.3, p. 5:** From *American Journal of Psychology*. Copyright 1961 by the Board of Trustees of the University of Illinois. Used with permission of the University of Illinois Press. **Table 1.2, p. 11:** From P. Rozin, S. Dow, M. Moscovitch, and S. Rajaram, "The role of memory for recent eating experiences in onset and cessation of meals. Evidence from the amnesic syndrome," *Psychological Science* 9, 1998, pp. 392–396. Reprinted by permission of Blackwell Publishing, www.blackwell-synergy.com.

Figure 3.12, p. 73: Source: Cho, Z. H., Chung, S. C., Jones, J.P., Park, J.B., Park, H. J., Lee, H. J., Wong, E. K., & Min, B. I. (1998). "New findings of the correlation between acupoints and corresponding brain cortices using functional MRI" *Proceedings of the National Academy of Science USA*, 95, 5, pp. 2670–2673. Copyright l998 National Academy of Sciences, U.S.A. **Figure 3.18, p. 81:** From *The Cerebral Cortex of Man*, by Wilder Penfield and Theodore Rasmussen, Macmillan, © 1950, Macmillan Publishing Company. Reprinted by permission of The Gale Group. **Figure 3.19, p. 84:** From Hubel, D., "Eye, Brain, and Vision," *American Scientific Library*, 1988, pp. 138–139. Reprinted by permission of the illustrator, Carol Donner, S.A. **Figure 3.22, p. 90:** Reprinted by permission of the publisher from *The Postnatal Development of the Human Cerebral Cortex*, Vol. I-VIII by Jesse LeRoy Conel, Cambridge, Mass: Harvard University Press, Copyright © 1939, 1975 by the President and Fellows of Harvard College.

Table 4.1, p. 111: *Fundamentals of Sensation and Perception* by M. W. Levine and J. M. Shefner, Addision Wesley, 1981. Reprinted by permission of the author. **Figure 4.6, p. 115:** G.L. Rasmussen and W.F. Windle, *Neural Mechanisms of the Auditory and Vestibular Systems*, 1960. Courtesy of Charles C. Thomas, Publisher, Springfield, Illinois. **Figure 4.12, p. 123** From *Sensation and Perception*, Fourth Edition by Stanley Coren, Lawrence M. Ward, and James T. Enns, p. 275; Copyright © 1994. Reprinted with permission of John Wiley & Sons, Inc. **Figure 4.22, p. 132:** Ramachandran, V.S. & Hubbard, E.M. (2001), "Psychophysical Investigations into the Neural Basis of Synaesthesia," from *Proceeding of the Royal Society of London B Biological Sciences*, 268, 979–983 (figure #3).

Figure 5.14, p. 172: From *Sensation and Perception*, Fourth Edition by Stanley Coren, Lawrence M. Ward, and James T. Enns, p. 393; Copyright © 1994. Reprinted with permission of John Wiley & Sons, Inc. **Figure 5.16, p. 174:** From Beiderman, I., *Matching Image Edges To Object Memory*, from the *Proceedings of the IEEE First International Conference on Computer Vision*, pp. 364–392, 1987 IEEE. Copyright © 1997 IEEE. **Figure 5.18, p. 175:** From *Sensation and Perception*, Fourth Edition by Stanley Coren, Lawrence M. Ward, and James T. Enns, p. 393; Copyright © 1994. Reprinted with permission of John Wiley & Sons, Inc. **Figure 5.20, p. 176:** Reprinted with permission from Weisstein & Harris, *Science*, 1974, 186, 725–755. Copyright 1974 AAAS. **Figure 5.22, p. 177:** Romelhart, D.E., and McClelland, J.L. (1986) *Parallel Distributing Processing*, Volume 1: Foundations. Cambridge, MA: MIT Press. Copyright © 1986 by the Massachusetts Institute of Technology. Reprinted by permission. **Figure 5.23, p. 178:** Johnson, M.A., Dziurawiec, S., Ellis, H., and Morton, J.

(1991). "Newborns' Preferential Tracking of Face-Like Stimuli and Its Subsequent Decline." *Cognition*, 4, 1–19. Reprinted by permission of Elsevier Science Publishing.

Figure 6.7, p. 204: From *The Psychology of Learning and Memory* by Douglas L. Hintzman. © 1978 by W.H. Freeman and Company. Used with permission. **Figure 6.9, p. 209:** Adapted from, "Teaching Machines," by B.F. Skinner. Copyright © 1961 by Scientific American, Inc. All rights reserved. Reprinted with permission.

Figure 7.2, p. 235: From Tulving, Schacter & Stark, "Priming Effects in Word-Fragment Completion are Independent of Recognition Memory," *Journal of Experimental Psychology: Learning, Memory, and Cognition*, Vol. 8, p. 339. Copyright © 1982 by the American Psychological Association. Adapted with permission. **Figure 7.5, p. 239:** Reprinted from "Contextual Prerequisites for Understanding: Some Investigations of Comprehension and Recall," by Bransford and Johnson, *Journal of Verbal Learning and Verbal Behavior*, Vol. 61, pp. 717–726, Copyright 1972, with permission from Elsevier. **Figure 7.6, p. 242:** *Cognitive Psychology: Memory, Language and Thought* by Howard, Darlene, V., © 1967. Reprinted by permission of Prentice-Hall, Inc., Upper Saddle River, NJ. **Figure 7.11, p. 250:** From *Cognitive Psychology, A Neural-Network Approach* 1st edition by Martindale. © 1991. Reprinted with permission of Wadsworth, a division of Thomson Learning: www.thomsonrights.com. Fax 800 730-2215. **Figure 7.17, p. 257:** From Tulving and Psotka, "Retroactive Inhibition in Free Recall: Inaccesibility of Information Available in the Memory Store," *Journal of Experimental Psychology*, Vol. 87, p. 4. Copyright © 1971 by the American Psychological Association. Adapted with permission.

Figure 8.6, p. 279: Paul Whitney, *Psychology of Language*. Copyright © 1998 by Houghton Mifflin Company. Reprinted with permission. **Figure 8.8, p. 280:** Reprinted with permission from "Mental Rotation of Three-Dimensional Objects," R. Shepard et al., *Science*, Vol. 171, #3972, pp. 701–703, 19 February 1971. Copyright 1971 AAAS. **Figure 8.9, p. 283:** From Paul Whitney, *The Psychology of Language*, Figure 3.4. Copyright 2004 by Houghton Mifflin Company. Used by permission. **Figure 8.10, p. 288:** Reprinted from *Cognitive Psychology Journal*, Vol. 40, pg. 179, "Comparing Stimulus Patterns," by C.M. Wharton et al., (2000) *Toward Neuroanatomical Models of Analogy: A Positron Emission Tomagraphy Study of Analogical Mapping*, Copyright 2000, with permission from Elsevier.

Figure 9.3, p. 319: From John A Bargh, Mark Chen, and Lara Burrows, "Automaticity of Social Behavior: Direct Effects of Trait Construction and Stereotype Activation on Action," *Journal of Personality and Social Psychology*, Vol. 71, No. 2, p. 235, figure 1. Copyright © 1996 by the American Psychological Association. Reprinted with permission. **Figure 9.2, p. 319:** From D.L. Schacter, L.A. Cooper, S.M. Delancy, M.A. Peterson, and M. Tharan's article, "Implicit Memory for Possible and Impossible Objects: Contrainst on the Construction of Structural Descriptions," from *Journal of Experimental Psychology: Learning Memory and Cognition*, Vol. 17, p. 4. Copyright © 1991 by the American Psychological Association. Adapted with permission. **Figure 9.5, p. 324:** From James Horne, *Why We Sleep: The Functions of Sleep in Humans and Other Mammals*. Copyright © 1989. By permission of Oxford University Press. For more information, go to www.oup.com **Figure 9.6, p. 325:** Adapted from Cartwright, *A Primer of Sleep and Dreaming*, Reading Mass. Addison-Wesley, 1978. Reprinted by permission. **Figure 9.7, p. 326:** Reprinted with permission from "Ontogenetic Development of the Human Sleep Dream Cycle," Roffwarg et al., *Science*, Vol. 152, pg. 606, 29 April 1966 (revised 1969). Copyright 1966 AAAS. **Figure 9.9, p. 334:** From Ernest R. Hilgard, *Hypnotic Age Susceptibility*. Copyright © 1965. Reprinted by permission of the Estate of Ernest R. Hilgard. **Figure 9.10, p. 335:** Pattie, F.A. (1935). "A Report at Attempts to Produce Unocular Blindness by Hypnotic Suggestion." *British Journal of Medical Psychiatry*, 15, 230–241. Reprinted by permission. **Figure 9.12, p. 340:** From Laurie Roehrich and Mark S. Goldman, "Implicit Priming of Alcohol Expectancy Memory Processes and Subsequent Drinking Behavior," *Experimental and Clinical Psychopharmacology*, Vol. 3, No. 4, pp. 402–410, figure 1, pg. 406. Copyright © 1995 by the American Psychological Association. Reprinted with permission.

Figure 10.1, p. 355: Simulated items similar to those in the Wechsler Intelligence Scales for Adults and Children. Copyright 1949, 1955, 1974, 1981, 1991, and 1997 by Harcourt Assessment, Inc. Reproduced with permission. All rights reserved. "Wechsler" is a trademark of Harcourt Assessment, Inc., registered in the United States of America and/or other jurisdictions. **Figure 10.3, p. 362:** From Steele, C.M., "A Threat in the Air: How Stereotypes SHape Intellectual Indentity and Performance," *American Psychologist*, June 1997, Vol. 652, No. 6, p. 620. Copyright © 1997 by the American Psychological Association. Reprinted with permission. **Figure 10.4, p. 363:** Reprinted with permission of the publisher and author from "Familial Studies of Intelligence: A Review," by T. Bouchard et al., *Science*, Vol. 212, #4498, pp. 1055–9, 29 May 1981. Copyright 1981 AAAS.

Figure 11.2, p. 389: From Douglast T. Kenrick, Richard C. Keefe, Angela Bryan, Alicia Barr, and Stephanie Brown, "Age Preference and Mate Choice Among Homosexuals and Heterosexuals: A Case for Modular Psychological Machanisms," *Journal of Personality and Social Psychology*, Vol. 69, No. 6, p. 1169. Copyright © 1995 by the American Psychological Association. Adapted with permission. **Figure 11.5, p. 394:** "The Hypothalamus and Hunger," from M.W. Schwartz, S.C. Woods, D. Porte, Jr., R.J. Seeley, and D.G. Baskin, "Central Nervous System Control of Food Intake," *Nature 404*, pp. 661–671. **Figure 11.6, p. 403:** Adapted from W.H. Masters and V.E. Johnson. *Human Sexual Response*, p. 5 (Boston: Little, Brown and Company, 1966). **Figure 11.12, p. 423:** Figure 3 from "Voluntary Facial Action Generates Emotion-Specific Autonomic Nervous System Activity," by R.W. Levenson, P. Ekman, and W.V. Friesen, *Psychophysiology*, 1990, 24, 363–384. Copyright © 1990 the Society for Psychophysiological Research. Reprinted with permission of the author and the publisher from Levenson, Ekman, and Friesen, 1990. **Figure 11.13, p. 429:** From Aronoff, J., Barclau, A.M., and Stevenson, L.A., "The Recognition of Threatening Facial Stimuli," *Journal of Personality and Social Psychology*, Vol. 54, p. 651. Copyright © 1988 by the American Psychological Association. Adapted with permission.

Figure 12.3, p. 446: Baillargeon, R. (1992). "A model of physical reasoning in infancy." In C. Rovee-Collier & L.P. Lipsitt (eds.), *Advances in infancy research*. Norwood, N.J.: Ablex Publishing Corp., pp. 305–371. Reprinted by permission. **Figure 12.6, p. 475:** From S.-C. Li, U. Lindenberger, B. Hommel, G. Aschersleben, W. Prinz, and P.B. Baltes, "Transformations in the couplings among intellectual abilities and constituent cognitive processes across the life span," *Psychological Science 15*, 2004, pp. 155–163 Reprinted by permission of Blackwell Publishing, www.blackwell-synergy.com.

Figure 13.2, p. 492: "The General Adaptation Syndrome" from *Stress Without Distress* by Hans Selye, M.D. Copyright © 1974 by Hans Selye, M.D. Reprinted by permission of HarperCollins Publishers Inc. **Figure 13.4, p. 498:** Adapted from Lazarus, Opton, Nornikos, and Rankin, *Journal of Personality*, 33.4. Copyright © 1965 Duke University Press. Reprinted with permission. **Figure 13.5, p. 514:** From Prochaska, W., DiClemente, C., and Norcross, J., "In Search of How People Change: Application to Addictive Behaviors," *American Psychologist*, Vol. 47, pp. 1102–1114. Copyright © 1992 by the American Psychological Association. Adapted with permission.

Figure 14.1, p. 521: Adapted from *Personality: Strategies and Issues*, by Robert M. Liebert and Michael D. Spiegler. Copyright © 1990 by Wadsworth, Inc. Reprinted by permission of Brooks/Cole Publishing Company, Pacific Grove, CA 93950. **Figure 14.3, p. 531:** Eysenck, H.J., Rachman, S., "The Causes and Cures of Neurosis: An Introduction to Modern Behavior Therapy Based on Learning Theory and the Principle of Conditioning." 1965. Edits. Reprinted with permission. **Figure 14.4, p. 537:** Reprinted from *Journal of Behavior Therapy and Experimental Psychiatry*, Vol. 13, A. Bandura, "The Assessment and Predictive Generality of Self-Percepts of Efficacy," pp. 195–199. Copyright 1982, with permission from

Elsevier. **Table 14.3, p. 547:** Reproduced by special permission of the publisher, Psychological Assessment Resources, Inc., Odessa, FL 33556. From the *NEO Personality Inventory* by Paul Costa and Robert McCrae. Copyright © 1978, 1985, 1989, 1991 by PAR, Inc. **Figure 14.6, p. 548:** Emmanuel F. Hammer, PhD, "Projective Drawings," in Rabin, ed. *Projective Techniques in Personality Assessment*, pp. 375–376. Copyright © 1968 by Springer Publishing Company, Inc., New York. Used by permission.

Figure 15.4, p. 585: From J. Zubin and B. Spring, "A New View of Schizophrenia," *Journal of Abnormal Psychology*, 86, p. 110. Copyright © 1977 by the American Psychological Association. Adapted with permission.

Figure 16.2, p. 605: Source: After Matson, J., Sevin, J., Fridley, and Love, S. (1990). "Increasing Spontaneous Language in Autistic Children," *Journal of Applied Behavior Analysis*, 23, pp. 227–233. **Figure 16.4, p. 615:** From G.R. Patterson, "Intervention for Boys with Conduct Problems: Multiple Settins, Treatments, and Criteria," *Journal of Consulting and Clinical Psychology*, Vol. 42, p. 476. Copyright © 1974 by the American Psychological Association. Adapted with permission.

Figure 17.5, p. 650: L. Festinger and J.M. Carlsmith, "Cognitive Consequences of Forced Compliance," *Journal of Abnormal and Social Psychology*, 58, 203–210. APA. **Figure 17.7, p. 658:** From C. Byrne and D. Nelson, "Attraction as a Linear Function of Proportion of Positive Reinforcements," *Journal of Personality and Social Psychology*, Vol. I, p. 661. Copyright © 1965 by the American Psychological Association. Adapted with permission. **Figure 17.9, p. 660:** From "Triangulating Love," in R.J. Sternberg & M.L. Barnes, *The Psychology of Love,* pp. 500, 520. Reprinted by permission of the publisher, Yale University Press. **Figure 17.10, p. 662:** From R.R. Reno, R.B. Cialdini, and C.A. Kallgren, "The Transsituational Influence of Social Norms," from *Journal of Personality and Social Psychology*, Vol. 64, p. 106. Copyright © 1993 by the American Psychological Association. Adapted with permission. **Figure 17.13, p. 671:** Courtesy of Alexandra Milgram. From S. Milgram, "Behavioral Study of Obedience," *Journal of Abnormal and Social Psychology*, 67, 371–378. Copyright © 1963 by the American Psychological Association. Adapted by permission of the publisher and literary executor.

Figure 1, p. A2: From *Time Magazine*, January 17, 1994. © 1994 Time Inc. Reprinted by permission.

Name Index

Subject Index/Glossary